Columbia Companion
to
Twentieth-Century
Philosophies

To my granddaughters,

Irene and Nancy,

and to 'their' world without me.

Columbia Companion to Twentieth-Century Philosophies

Edited by Constantin V. Boundas

Columbia University Press   New York

Columbia University Press
Publishers Since 1893
New York

First published in the United Kingdom by
Edinburgh University Press Ltd 2007

Library of Congress Cataloging-in-Publication Data

A complete CIP record is available from the Library of Congress

ISBN 978-0-231-14202-1 (cloth : alk. paper)

c 10 9 8 7 6 5 4 3 2 1

Contents

Twentieth-Century Continental Philosophy

Non-Western Philosophies in the Twentieth Century

Preface

Accepting the responsibility of putting together a companion volume for the twentieth-century philosophies was both humbling and exhilarating. Humbling, because, whatever decision one makes for the organization, scope, and purpose of such a work, one must first embark on a daring journey of surveying, identifying, connecting, and distinguishing vast bodies of knowledge, opinions, polemics, problems, putative solutions, interpretations and framings. Faced with such a daunting task, one soon reaches the conclusion that the only way to bring the volume to its completion will be to stretch to the very limits of one's knowledge and that, no matter how many precautions one takes, the frame, the connections and identifications, as well as the silences and omissions in it, will be broadcasting the editor's shortcomings to one and all. But compiling this volume was also an exhilarating endeavor. Once the limits of one's knowledge have been accepted, and the interpretive work of the imposed frame has been welcomed as the indispensable gift of reading, even the compilation of a companion volume emerges as a kind of doing philosophy – rather than merely registering what is available to the eye of the surveyor. Moreover, the humility imposed by the immensity of the task stresses the need for a truly collaborative venture that multiplies the interpretive frames and displaces the limits of one's own knowledge towards the strengths of one's collaborators – a multiplication and a displacement that are both reassuring and unsettling.

The present *Columbia Companion to Twentieth-Century Philosophies* addresses readers who have some acquaintance with the philosophical preoccupations of the twentieth century and who seek to increase and render more coherent their understanding of these preoccupations, with the assistance of men and women whose research and writing are more advanced than their own. Graduate students in the humanities, and members of the educated public belong here. But the present companion volume is also addressed to professionals who will appreciate the texts that offer overviews of certain areas of philosophical investigations while avoiding the standard encyclopedic synopses by inspecting their chosen subject through a more personal lens – albeit with a few important exceptions. Given the centrality that the issues surrounding sense, mind, language, and values have acquired in the analytic philosophical tradition of the twentieth century, the authors of the chapters on logical positivism, philosophy of mind, philosophy of language, and ethics were encouraged to opt for something approximating an encyclopedic presentation. Reading these four chapters would give a fairly accurate picture of the ambitions and agendas of the analytic philosophical tradition. As for the other chapters of the section, by allowing themselves a more personal entry point, authors are capable of enlivening particular segments of the encyclopedic agendas and, perhaps, of offering the reader the tools necessary for turning an encyclopedic registry into a narrative, with well-defined principal and subordinate clauses. A similar distribution of tasks runs through the section on the twentieth-century Continental philosophy, where the chapters on the Hegelian legacy, hermeneutics, Marxisms, and political philosophy constitute the encyclopedic registry, whereas the chapters on phenomenology, life, and Continental aesthetics (for example) stand for the more focused points of entry.

This volume is composed of three parts: a section that highlights the multi-dimensional work of twentieth-century philosophers identified with the analytic tradition; a section that presents and discusses the work of those who, during the century, identified themselves with the continental European tradition; and a third section, comprised of non-Western philosophical insights (Indian, Chinese, Japanese and African), Idealism, pragmatism and process philosophy, which are not the exclusive property of the analytic tradition, were housed nevertheless in the section of the analytic tradition, because most of their spokesmen, after the early part of the century, were analytically trained, and because the authors of the relevant chapters for the present volume have had an analytic training as well.

Sections one and two (analytic and continental philosophies, respectively) combine chapters on the main philosophical agendas of each tradition (logical positivism, ordinary language philosophy, naturalism, phenomenology, hermeneutics, structuralism, and so on) with chapters on the many philosophies of (mind, language, logic, mathematics, science, religion, and so on) the proliferation of which turns out to be a mark of the twentieth century. Each chapter was assigned to a philosopher whose research and writing has already demonstrated a degree of excellence. No chapter can claim exhaustive coverage of its subject matter, either in terms of who said and did what or in terms of what was said or done. Each contributor was encouraged to show his or her point of view in the included texts, so that the volume can be read profitably by everyone, including specialists seeking new perspectives.

I wrote the General Introduction to the work, and then the two shorter introductions to the analytic and Continental sections, with two goals in mind: to create a frame for the polyvocity of the philosophical claims advanced during the twentieth century – a frame that could facilitate the reader's quest for family resemblances; and to question the usefulness of the conviction that there are two rival ways of doing philosophy – the analytic and the Continental. For my frame, I made use of Habermas's neo-Kantian triad of cognitive interests. The reader may remember that, in his critique of the logical positivist refusal to account for the presence of (foundational) regulative interests of reason, Habermas insisted that technical, hermeneutic, and ludic interests are the regulative/constitutive, *sine qua non* conditions for the sense and truth of claims made by natural scientists, scientists of the human mind and its products, and by those responsible for artistic production and consumption. I do not claim in my introduction that the Habermasian frame for the organization of the philosophers' twentieth-century travels is the *only* one – or even the best one – for this purpose; other framings are certainly possible. But this frame helped me in my effort to come up with one philosophical narrative for the entire century, that could maintain similarities (wherever they existed) and differences (wherever the act of forcing divergent positions into the same model would border on dishonesty). For example, on the side of similarities, the Habermasian frame allowed me to see the entire analytic philosophical tradition as an important chapter in the Continental hermeneutic tradition, and allows me, perhaps, to co-ordinate the dominant tendencies of the two in terms of the logic of confirmation and the logic of discovery, respectively. From the side of differences, the same frame helped me understand the positivist passion for verification as a species of the rational interest for technical control, and to distinguish it from another species of technical control – the one embodied in the phenomenologist's quest for the noematic nucleus of sense, en route to grasping the things themselves. At any rate, the General Introduction reflects my own perspective on the philosophies of the twentieth century; many of my readers may disagree with the way I shuffled the cards, and, if this encourages them to try their own interpretive framings, I will consider my efforts well spent.

The reader may also be puzzled by my decision to retain the distribution of the contributing philosophers' input into analytic and Continental (sections one and two of the work), coming after the rather strong claims of my introductions concerning the unhelpful nature of these designations. I would suggest some caution at this point. My introductions do not suggest that that there is no distinction to be made; they suggest that the distinction should not be hardened into a difference between two natural kinds. Surely, cultural, social, educational, and economic differences do enter into the articulation of two different styles of doing philosophy during that century – including, perhaps, the perception of what is and what is not scientific, given earlier (long before the twentieth century) decisions regarding means to overcome the skepticism precipitated by the collapse of religious and politico-social verities. To organize the available material while discounting the designations that formed these philosophers' self-consciousness struck me as an unwarranted erasure of the pre-philosophical doxic realm that often functioned as the *a priori* of twentieth-century philosophy. This is not to say, of course, that, with a different conception and scope of a companion volume in mind, a collective work that would do away with the designations I retained may not be the next winning step in the chronicling of the philosophical achievements of the twentieth century.

Mindful of the selective nature of each included chapter, some overlapping in the offering of the different agendas was allowed, in the hope that the combination of different concentrations and foci might come to approximate the sort of completeness that no individual chapter could possibly claim for itself. Even so, readers are bound to discover omissions, silences, and absences in the present *Companion* that they may decide not to forgive. I beg them only to remember that it was not the saturation of the field with information to which our contributions aspired but rather the capturing of the creative philosophical intensity, felt in the various agendas and fields.

I should not conclude this preface without thanking Jackie Jones, Carol MacDonald and Nicola Wood of Edinburgh University Press for the encouragement and guidance they gave me during the long gestation of the present work; or without acknowledging the huge intellectual debt that I owe to all those who contributed to this volume. The successful orchestration of a collective work depends, for the most part, on the quality of the contributions submitted – and the contributions to this volume have all been excellent. Whatever failures the reader may discover should be attributed to me – the general editor – and to the limits of my horizons that shaped the final framing. The twentieth century has been, from a philosophical point of view, a giant among centuries, and having begun to survey it for the sake of this volume fills me with a profound sense of humility. The success of the present volume will be, I think, guaranteed, should it inspire those who savor the texts we include, and help them fulfill the only promise that a companion text could make – to send its readers to the original works of those who left their mark on the century.

General Introduction

Constantin V. Boundas

Philosophy looked poised to enter the twentieth century confident in its future. The leading professional journals of the year 1900 display, thematically and stylistically, a healthy pluralism, a critical attitude, tempered by an acute awareness of differences, the will to subject differences to rational scrutiny, and a commendable spirit of collegiality and internationalism. This spirit is also evident in the impressive gathering of philosophers for the World Philosophy Congress that takes place between the 1st and the 5th of August of 1900, at the Lycée Louis-le-Grand, in Paris, under the presidency of Emile Boutroux, and with the capable assistance of Xavier Léon, Louis Couturat and Henri Halévy. The participants in the Congress meet in four groups (logic, scientific philosophy and philosophy of science; history of philosophy; metaphysics and general philosophy; and ethics and social issues); and count among their numbers scholars of the caliber of Henri Bergson, Moritz Cantor, Louis Couturat, Paul Painlevé, Giuseppe Peano, Henri Poincaré, Bertrand Russell, Ernst Schroeder, and Paul Tannery.

Signs of the national differences in philosophical themes and styles, which break out later in the century, are already visible. France's preoccupation with the post-Kantian, critical investigation of the sciences – the philosophical thread that will give us later in the century Gaston Bachelard, Georges Canguilhem and Michel Foucault – is well attested. At the World Congress, for example, Boutroux celebrates with these words the 'newly re-discovered' association of philosophy and the sciences (which, according to him, after Schelling and Hegel had gone their separate ways):

> Without identifying themselves with the scientists, philosophers are in the process of searching now for a human truth, instead of an individual satisfaction. They must therefore, like the scientists, move towards a collective work in order to benefit from the division of research and make their efforts converge. There is no philosophical truth unless all the elements that can come together are understood and agreed upon so that one is able to see a harmony and a unity springing forth. (Lalande 1900: 483)

And J. J. Gourd, of the University of Geneva, speaks in the same spirit of the progress of philosophy 'towards science and in science.' This progress, he points out, is visible in the fact that contemporary philosophy opts for reflected rather than spontaneous knowledge; searches for the necessary and the universal; looks for demonstrative concepts; shuns authority; systematizes its field according to the spirit and procedure of the sciences; and sees the questions of yesteryear turned to solutions and new premises. And in an anticipation of French philosophical positions still to come, Gourd concludes that this progress presupposes that we get rid of the alleged identity of the object of science with reality itself. Progress presupposes a steady march from empiricism to rationalism to a 'phenomenist idealism' (Lalande 1900: 494).

Similar signs are clearly present in the philosophical journals of the time. Thus, *Revue de Métaphysique et de Morale* (in its eighth year in 1900), under the influence of its founder, the 'critical idealist' Leon Brunschvicg, devotes an entire volume to essays discussing logic, number, mathematics, geometry, science (deductive and experimental), the notion of the continuum, finality without intelligence, and problems of perception. Early century volumes of this journal display an enviable awareness of what philosophers are thinking and publishing outside France, and offer detailed discussions of essays and books having been published elsewhere. The 1900 volume, for example, features Louis Couturat with three essays, one of which is on Whitehead; and Henri Poincaré, with a response to Russell's principles of geometry. The same philosophico-scientific agenda is, albeit with different premises and ambitions, further promoted by essays authored by the positivists Edouard Le Roy and Joseph Wilbois. The only exception to this 'philosophers-look-at-science' issue is Brunschvicg's paper on 'La vie réligieuse' and a paper by Albert Leclerc, 'Le même enseignement moral convient-il aux deux sexes?' – bound to amuse and provoke today's readers with claims about the different rational and affective structures of the two genders that call for different moral educational strategies. *Revue Philosophique de la France et de l'Etranger*, in its 49th and 50th volumes in the year 1900, shows less dedication to the neo-Kantian critical epistemology and philosophy of science, but does not fail to publish eleven out of its twenty-six essays on subjects ranging from the '*acuité stéréoscopique*' to 'biological sociology.' *Revue de Philosophie*, in the first year of its life at the dawn of the century, seems less focused: it publishes essays on the history of philosophy, aesthetics, ethics, and epistemology, but without failing to include an essay on crystallography, another on neurons, and a third – this one authored by Pierre Duhem – on an exhaustive analysis of the notion of the '*mixte*' throughout the ages.

Across the channel, *Mind. A Quarterly Review of Psychology and Philosophy*, edited at the time by George Frederick Stout, is engaged in sorting out the strengths and the weaknesses of British Hegelianism, giving ample space to F. H. Bradley, J. E. McTaggart, and their critics. But the British pragmatist, Ferdinand Canning Scott Schiller, is also present, and so is Ferdinand Tönnies, Henry Sidgwick (whose death is also announced in the 1900 issue), an essay on pragmatism by W. Caldwell and another on vitalism by C. S. Myers. Here, the sign of things to come carries the signature of George Eduard Moore for the essay, 'Necessity.' (Bertrand Russell will have to wait until the next year, 1901, to be included in *Mind*, with two essays – 'On the Notion of Order' and 'Is Position in Time and Space Absolute or Relative?' As the title of the journal clearly shows – but also its contents – the differentiation of psychology from philosophy had not yet reached the status of a dogma. A commendable awareness of what goes on beyond the shores of the British Isles is also displayed in *Mind*'s reception and list of an impressive array of non-English language philosophy journals and books, and in the critical discussion of their contents. (German philosophy journals will disappear from *Mind's* entries during the First World War, and this seems to coincide with a loss of the global curiosity of the early century).

Patterns of actual and future philosophical tendencies are less clear among American contributors to the journals of the day. *The Philosophical Review*, Volume IX, edited by J. G. Schurman and J. E. Creighton of the Sage School of Philosophy at Cornell University, hosts essays in the history of philosophy, psychology and associationism, metaphysics and ethics. John Dewey and G. H. Mead are both present; and besides an essay by F. Paulhan surveying contemporary French philosophy (a practice that was to be maintained for a number of years to come), the journal has the good sense to reward its readers with summaries of many articles appearing in philosophy journals in France, Germany, and the United Kingdom.

Germany seems to be more inclined to maintain a solid interest in the history of philosophy along with the philological and hermeneutic dexterity that such an interest presupposes and nurtures. Thus, *Philosophisches Jahrbuch*, Volume 13, contains essays on Plato, Augustine, Tertullian, Hilarius of Poitiers, Bonaventura, and Descartes. On the other hand, it does not shy away from essays on the psychology of children and animals, causality and teleology, and the concept of the beautiful. The Italian journals in circulation at the time appear to be equally eclectic and historico-philosophically oriented.

Neither the World Congress nor the philosophy journals of the early century, however, are preparing us for what the century is really to become – a century of crises, responses to those crises, innovations, and retrenchments. To be sure, philosophical concepts and methods have always been so many responses to urgently felt questions, but never before the twentieth century have philosophical questions been linked with so many crises – real or phantasized – marking the space between the symptoms of potentially fatal diseases of culture and intellect *and* the emerging hope that health may be just around the corner. Crises certainly have existed before, but the twentieth century has the distinction of having diagnosed itself as being in a critical condition many more times, by many more cultural physicians, and with many more fatal symptoms than in any other period – including the crisis-prone Hellenistic times.

It is not hard to come up with a list of these crises: first, global crises like the crisis in the idea of (Western) science shaking the foundations of (European) humanity; the crisis in centuries-old assumptions concerning meaningful language; the crisis in foundationalism; the crisis precipitated by forgetting the ontological difference; crises in legitimation; the 'death of Man' crisis; the crisis in representation; the crisis in grand meta-narratives. And then, from a more regional point of view, albeit no less seriously, the century witnesses also the crisis in the status of values and in the meaning of the terms used to designate them; crises in the old image of thought; crises in the foundations of mathematics and logic; crisis in the empiricist dogmas; crisis in metaphysics and ontology; crisis in non-gendered and non-raced philosophies, and so on. The century is indeed punctuated with crises but is equally crisscrossed by reductive retrenchments – retrenchments that intensify the efforts to overcome crises. Descartes's gesture of 'suspension' is multiplied and repeated many times – first, as the reduction to consciousness (Husserl and descriptive phenomenology) and, later on, as

the reduction of consciouness (in positivist/neo-positivist agendas and in manifestations of French structuralism and poststructuralism).

In what follows, I visit some of these crises, the reductions that they precipitated,
and the remedies they proposed for the restoration of the patient's health. To help me,
I choose the neo-Kantian frame of the early Jürgen Habermas, with its three
interrelated cognitive interests – the technical, the hermeneutic, and the emancipatory
– for what this frame offers me in deciding on the sites to visit, and on the order
according to which they can be visited. Some of the prominent philosophers of the
century would reject my choice outright because of its dependence on a narrative that
they oppose. I need not defend my frame here; nor do I wish to do so. I am only using it
in order to give the bewildering diversity of the philosophical concerns and pronouncements of the century some kind of order. I claim no privileged status for my
choice; different choices may prove themselves far more helpful.

Technical Scientific Interest: Crises and Resolutions

Phenomenology

1900 is the year of the publication of the first volume of Edmund Husserl's *Logical
Investigations*, and, therefore, arguably the year that phenomenology comes into its
own. Although the crisis theme must wait until 1936 (Husserl 1936) to become the
motivation behind the phenomenological dream of philosophy as rigorous science,
the hindsight that will read it backwards into the early writings of Husserl is not
without merit. Some readers may find it strange that I choose to discuss Husserlian
phenomenology under the heading, 'technical scientific interest.' I will concede
gladly that hermeneutic and even emancipatory interests do not fail to motivate
and sustain the agenda of the descriptive phenomenologist in the attempt to retrieve
the things themselves. Nevertheless, the hyperbolic demands for apodicticity and
adequate evidence that punctuate the search for the springs of sense chisel out an
Idea of scientificity whose overarching cognitive interest cannot but be oriented
towards organization, mastery, and control. Derrida's decision to render the 'intentionality' of the phenomenologist as '*vouloir dire*' reflects, I think, beautifully this
orientation.

If, as Husserl thought, the crisis in the foundations of Western (European) humanity
is the outcome of the wrong epistēmē (the Galilean mathematization of the world)
hiding from view the source of all sense – whether this is consciousness or intersubjectivity or the Lifeworld – a rigorous transcendental philosophy must return to
this source and make a complete inventory of its sense-giving processes, including
those of the incriminated epistēmē. Such a repetition would require a moment of
purification – the epochē – a reduction of the given to consciousness or to the
Lifeworld. A strictly descriptive account of the phenomena disclosed after the
reduction (phenomenological intuition) and an imaginative variation of the profiles
of these phenomena (eidetic intuition) should then be able to reveal with apodicticity
or with adequate evidence, the static and genetic accomplishments of the transcendental field. Consequently, for Husserl, the way out of the crisis he diagnosed is the

repetition of the source and the articulation of a 'new' epistemic program, that of transcendental phenomenology. The latter promises to ground the new epistēmē as well as the regional epistēmēs, which, before the advent of phenomenology, were suspended in thin air. This grounding has as its central objective the repudiation of the perspectivism, relativism, and incommensurability that plague psychological, historicist, and naturalist accounts of sense, and the firm establishment of the conclusion that the world is one and ordered.

Logical Positivism

It is not customary to think of the logical positivists in the context of a crisis that had to be overcome. Theirs was a program for the unification of sciences, the purification of the epistemic field from false pretenders, and for the firm establishment of cognitive sense. This program was motivated by an optimistic vision of how much science can achieve, as long as it is truly science. But a program in order to be philosophical – instead of an aleatory road sign merely recording the vacuous claim that 'philosophy is what philosophers do' – must be an answer to questions made urgent by the fact that they subsist in a context threatening to muffle them – and to muffle them to our own detriment. The questions of the logical positivists were about the 'given' and about the best tools that could become available for the protection of the given against false pretenders and their sneaky ways of usurping it: paradox mongerers, victims of perceptual illusions, speakers of metaphorical and equivocal language, or subjects of emotive distortions, esthetic reveling, and cognitive nonsense. In this sense, logical positivism can be read as a destructive and constructive program at once – critical of those whose carelessness or deliberate scheming keeps postponing the enlightened promise of cognitive and social progress through clear thinking, *and* solicitous of those with the right determination to seek truth through univocity and verifiability.

At its best, the logical positivist platform included four desiderata: the distinction between analytic and synthetic; the demonstration that mathematics can be reduced to logic and that the consistency and completeness of logic can be established; the formulation of a verification/falsification criterion of cognitive sense as a necessary condition for any statement to have truth values; and the adoption of this criterion by all fields of investigation having scientific aspirations. But, despite sustained and clever efforts, the failure of the logical positivist program has been resounding. The analytic/synthetic distinction, in any rigorous formulation of it, was shown to be unattainable; the consistency and completeness of axiomatic systems came under damaging fire; the verifiability/falsifiability criterion of cognitive sense was denounced for either proving more or for proving less than it was meant to do in the interest of science; its adoption, therefore, was given up for being restrictive of scientific inquiry itself.

Apart from the criticisms that those laboring in the positivist field found themselves compelled to formulate, the critique of those who never shared in the positivist enlightenment were equally damaging. The agenda of phenomenology, in its preoccupation with the sense-bestowing acts of transcendental subjectivity, was light years away from the protocol statements of the positivists, which were supposed to record the here and now of perceptual 'objects' for the sake of a verifiable construction of cognitive meaning. Hermeneutics, on the other hand, before Heidegger, Gadamer, and Ricoeur, had accepted Dilthey's legitimation of the *Geistenwischenschaften*, his methodological dualism (sciences of Nature/sciences of the Spirit), and the resulting immunization of the sciences of the Spirit against the temptation to buy into the methods and procedures of the natural sciences, under the penalty of being found cognitively meaningless if they did not. With Heidegger, Gadamer, and Ricoeur, hermeneutics outgrew the legacy of methodological dualism, and asked the sciences of Nature themselves to become attentive to the sense and direction of their protocols and procedures, thematizing as it were the workings of interpretive rationality in the field of scientific theory formation. Finally, the neo-Kantian frame of early Habermas (*Knowledge and Human Interests*) added a decisive blow to the multifaceted critique of logical positivism. Having inherited the mantle of the Critical Theory of Society, Habermas intervened in the *PositivismusStreit* of the 1960s and 1970s, arguing that rationality should not be limited to the (very legitimate) Interest in controlling nature (whether internal to human beings or external to them). In a way reminiscent of Dilthey, Habermas safeguarded the legitimacy of the natural scientific method, but also limited it to the domain constituted by the imperatives of explanation and control. He then went on to argue that the rational Interest in understanding and communication legitimates the persistence of hermeneutic dialogue in the domain of human psychology, history, and culture – provided that (a jab at Heidegger and Gadamer) this hermeneutic dialogue is not expected to deliver more than it is able to do, that is, provided that a *Verstehen* philosophy does not pretend to be, on its own, a philosophy of emancipation. Emancipation, that is, liberation from oppressive sedimentations of psychic distortions and from ideological distortions of social structures and institutions, requires the skillful mobilization and interplay of explanation and understanding, being informed by an image of mental and cultural health, and authenticated in the processes of self-integration, self-understanding, and self-creation.

Faced with all this opposition, the original agenda of the logical positivists had to be withdrawn, but retreat here did not amount to the obliteration of the theoretical desiderata that gave strength to the movement. The vision of a unified science and the lure of a materialist ontology with which logical positivism came to be identified had a long history of their own, and were able to survive many a challenge. By the early 1950s, progressively sophisticated research in artificial intelligence (AI) had succeeded in empowering what came to be known as 'eliminative materialism' – arguably the most promising scion of materialism and unified science. The vision behind eliminative materialism is reflected in what the Churchlands hope the new ways of configuring the functions of the brain will offer to philosophical reflection: 'The brain is a kind of computer, though most of its properties remain to be discovered . . . The brain does compute functions, functions of great complexity but not in the classical fashion . . . Brains are computers in a radically different style' (Churchland and Churchland 1998: 61).

The Churchlands acknowledge that this radically different style 'may require revision of the very intuitions that now seem so secure'; but they hasten to add that such revisions are commonplace in the history of science. When it comes to questions about the degree of similarity between brains and machines and the relevant (causal) factors that permit us to infer conscious intelligence, they concede that there is room for disagreement over relevance, but they also counter the arguments of their critics by exploiting the present dearth of knowledge about cognition and semantics, in a way that strengthens the hope for the success of their cause and challenges the pessimism of the nay-sayers. The dearth of knowledge does nothing to dampen the enthusiasm of the eliminative materialists of the last quarter of the century or to slow down the movement from hope to self-congratulation. Their conviction is summed up as follows:

> By the late '60s, every good materialist expected that epistemological theory would one day make explanatory contact, perhaps even a reductive contact, with a proper theory of brain function . . . The time has arrived. Experimental neuroscience has revealed enough of the brain's microphysical organization, and mathematical analysis and computer simulation have revealed enough of its functional significance, that we can now address epistemological issues directly. Indeed, we are in a position to reconstruct, in neurocomputational terms, issues in the philosophy of science specifically. (Churchland and Churchland 1998: 257)

'The only real question,' Paul Churchland adds, 'is how large the doctrinal and ontological gap will turn out to be, between the triumphant new framework [eliminative materialism] and its poorly informed historical predecessor [folk psychology]' (Churchland and Churchland 1998: 273).

Hermeneutic Interest: Language as a Philosophical Problem

The division of philosophers in the twentieth century into the analytic and continental schools often prevents us from seeing that, for both camps, the investigation of language as a philosophical problem (perhaps, as *the* philosophical problem) is central to their philosophical self-understanding. Their access to language as a philosophical issue does not, at first glance, yield a unified front, but, on closer scrutiny, similarities are not hard to find. We may well think that it is rather pointless to speak of similarities when language is being discussed as 'the house of Being,' by Heidegger; 'on holiday and in use' by Wittgenstein and Austin; as 'an instrument of communication' by Habermas; 'an instrument of control, made to be believed and obeyed' by Deleuze and Guattari; 'a system of differential values' by the structuralists; 'the site of traces and deferrals' by Derrida; 'the space of interpellation by the Other' in Levinas's texts; or as 'a picture of states of affairs' and the assemblage of 'language games' by Wittgenstein. However, similarities (or better, resonances) do exist among the questions and problems that ushered in all these characterizations of language, despite their prima facie incongruity.

The 'Analytic' Agenda

The 'linguistic turn' that gave the 'analytic tradition,' in the twentieth century, a raison d'être (sometimes, the only one), was motivated by four – often intermeshing – considerations: 1. To arrive at a sufficiently purified, reconstructed, and unambiguous (artificial) language, which, unlike everyday language, would be able to express, and minister to, the exactness of the sciences of nature and the analyticity of logic and mathematics; 2. To mine the wealth of ordinary language and to explore its resources in order to check the excesses and prevent the misleading philosophical conundrums which arise whenever 'language is on holiday'; 3. To assist in the conceptual analytic task of philosophers by dissipating the fog that is endemic in the 'surface grammar' of our natural languages; and, therefore, 4. To enable a more successful communication and offer therapy for the illusions suffered as the result of our allowing the vagaries of ordinary language to beguile us.

It is, therefore, fair to say that the 'regulative ideas' spearheading the linguistic turn of the analytic tradition have sometimes helped articulate a variant of hermeneutic rationality and sometimes a variant of reductivism and reconstruction. They have supported (and were also supported by) the conviction that philosophy is essentially a critical rather than a constructive activity, and they carved out a domain of investigation that, unlike the domain of the linguist, was fully philosophical. The objective of analysis was never the linguistic sign per se; rather, its objective was the concept or the conceptual schema that linguistic signs strive to convey. In this sense, the linguistic turn of the analytic tradition was really a turn towards conceptual analysis. Anthony Quinton's classification of the varieties of conceptual analysis pursued by twentieth-century Austro-Anglo-American philosophers offer the right context for the four different preoccupations with language that I have just suggested:

> First, a conservative, even quietist, line could be taken to the effect that our existing conceptual apparatus is perfectly all right as it is and that the conflicts and perplexities that confront us from time to time arise from our incompetent handling of it. On this view the task of philosophy is the local and piecemeal clarification of our existing conceptual equipment and not its reform or replacement as a whole . . . Another point of view, at the opposite extreme, is the kind of conceptual libertarianism which Carnap seems sometimes to support. It holds that there is nothing to prevent your choosing any consistent conceptual scheme you like, except perhaps its complexity or unfamiliarity. Finally . . . it could be held that conceptual systems . . . are subject to the pragmatic test of trial and error. (Quinton 1966: 147–8)

When, for example, G. E. Moore focuses on a complex concept or a complex proposition, carves out its constituents, and shows the way in which they fit together, he is following the linguistic turn according to the second and third tendencies that I listed, and pursues conceptual analysis in accordance with Quinton's first option. When Russell expresses doubts about our intuitive linguistic correctness, substitutes for it the search for canonical forms, hidden in the casual grammar and syntax of ordinary language, and promotes this substitution as the correct philosophical method, he is proceeding according to my first tendency. When Carnap and the logical positivist school take a concept in ordinary use and redefine it in order to make it more useful to science, analytic skills are put to the service of my first tendency of the linguistic turn again, but along the lines of Quinton's second option. Finally, when it comes to analysis as therapy, it is possible to discern two variants: an iconoclastic one towards the philosophical tradition, *and* one of immunization against conceptual confusion, paradox mongering, category mistakes, and plain nonsense. Speaking of the iconoclastic tendencies of linguistic analysis, Strawson had this to say:

> The reasons why the thing was exciting were really two. On the one hand, in the face of this refined examination of actual linguistic practice, a lot of traditional philosophical theorizing began to look extraordinarily crude . . . and it was of course extremely exhilarating to see these huge and imposing edifices of thought just crumbling away . . . to the tune of this fairly modest sort of piping. (Magee 1971: 116)

As for the tendency of immunization, Wittgenstein's *Tractatus* is a good candidate, as it states that the only reason philosophical problems persist is that we misunderstand the logic of our language. To excavate the real structure of language behind the apparent is to give ourselves the mirror-image of the structure of the world. All the possible choices that the actual world may make are already reflected in language (Magee 1971: 35). It is worth noting here that Wittgenstein's proposed therapy was richer than the run-of-the-mill reductionism of the logical positivists. In arguing for the homology between the form of representation of language and the form of reality, Wittgenstein was determined to safeguard the thinkable and the sayable against falling prey to nebulosity and nonsense; but he was equally determined to protect what cannot be said (beyond the linguistic form of representation) from being defiled in spurious and senseless utterances. One may think that Wittgenstein, in letting go the agenda of the *Tractatus* and with his later preference for the irreducible variety of discourse – the 'language games' and the 'forms of life' of the *Logical Investigations* – counted exactness and precision in language among the philosopher's illusions. And yet, the curative function of linguistic philosophy was not abandoned. Description could still remove philosophical perplexities, and misunderstandings of language were still conceived as an essential, preliminary step to achieving philosophical understanding (Pears 1971: 44). Despite important differences between them, this conclusion resonates with J. L. Austin's position for whom the investigation of ordinary uses of the expressions of a natural language did have a positive value: The revelation of an unnecessary entanglement in a pseudo-problem, and also the possible discovery of a genuine problem or a suggestion for its solution.

The 'Continental' Agenda

In the last fifty years of the century, the re-appropriation of the linguistic structuralism of Ferdinand de Saussure allowed the diacritic sign (the sign whose value is strictly determined by its place in a system of relations of signs) to support powerful investigations into linguistic, literary, mythic, visual, cinematic, and anthropological codes. Structuralism rivaled (and was rivaled by) post-Heideggerian hermeneutics, for which linguistic, literary, mythic, and other documents were so many expressive acts that intentionally constitute the real. In the same period, a Nietzsche-inspired genealogy of discursive practices, centering around the work of Michel Foucault, was set to work to analyze the formations and deformations of knowledges and disciplines, of the subject, of disciplinarity and governmentality, and to expose the intricate relations between power and the will to truth. Grammatology and decon-struction, in the writings of Derrida, discovered in the play of difference and repetition of the diacritic sign the law of textuality, and brought it to bear upon questions of justice and legality, hospitality and the gift, temporality and messianic thought without messiahs. Contrary to a misapprehension that lasted for a long time, none of these developments intended to build a 'prison house' for language. The investigation into the manner in which language operates was not pursued for its own sake, but for the sake of a broader understanding of how non-linguistic structures, sedimentations and forces were arranged inside meaningful wholes.

On the other hand, at the center of phenomenological investigations, during the twentieth century, one finds the linguistic sign as the expression of an agent's intentions. The agenda of a return to the things themselves was grounded upon this. But, despite the care with which Husserl attempted to chisel it out and to prevent it from running away in an endless series of unintended signifiers and signifieds, the expressive sign did not survive the critique of intersubjectivity and temporality that the philosophies of difference mounted against it. Jacques Derrida convincingly showed that the sign's expressive function could not be disentangled from its indicative function and, therefore, that the hoped for containment of the slippage of meaning could not be seriously maintained, given the inevitable slide from the expressive to the indexical sign. The sign-index lent itself to two different appro-priations: the hermeneutic attempt to discover the generative mechanism and the dynamism responsible for the sign's seriatim proliferation; and the structuralist strategy of containing this proliferation in an identity of the sign guaranteed by the sign's diacritic relation to all the other signs/members of series that were capable of being circumscribed.

This is in a nutshell the story of the continental European interest in language from the beginning of the century until the 1970s. The transparency of the expressive sign, due to its location and function in the heart of subjectivity receded, first, because of the opacity, polyvocity, and distanciation of the hermeneutic sign-index (alias, symbol); and then again later because of the sign-differential value, the identity of which was established with a set of axioms laid out initially by the Swiss linguist, Ferdinand de Saussure.

The story, perhaps, would gain in depth, if we picked up its guiding thread at the site where post-Heideggerean hermeneutics and Derridean grammatology began to offer themselves as alternative approaches to language and textuality. Hermeneutics understood writing as the inscription of a discourse in a state of alienation, and made the overcoming of this alienation the reason for its existence. As a discourse of assistance, hermeneutics raised *belonging* and *hearing* into structural features of discourse. To read is to hear the text, to actualize a virtual discourse – rather than mastering its meaning. If the language of appropriation must be used (and herme-neutics did not really avoid this use), the absolving gloss is always at hand: to appropriate is to mark a victory over alienation, to make the *a-topon* familiar, to let the living waters of *anamnesis* revitalize a land that forgetting had left parched.[1]

Grammatology (later evolving into deconstruction), on the other hand, made the issue of the production of discourse and of the text essential: from its point of view, the text is a stage, and writing, a *mise en scène*; *mimesis*, as a result, loses its pertinence in an endless play of hide and seek. Texts are no longer homely spaces; they are fishnets and labyrinths in which one could become caught and lost for ever. If the author is still invoked, it is not for the sake of the famous hermeneutic simultaneity, but rather for the sake of a temporality that is specific to the world of texts. As for the referent, it is not only bracketed for the sake of a world where the simultaneity of the *is* and the *is not* prevails, but it loses its pertinence altogether: one can always find a referent, but what one actually finds is going to be another text.

Emancipatory Interest: Crisis in the grand Narratives

The expression 'grand narrative' comes from Jean-François Lyotard's *The Postmodern Condition*. It refers to the discursive strategies with the help of which modernity legitimated the pursuit of knowledge, by linking knowledge to emancipation and progress. In its French incarnation, the grand narrative proposed that the pursuit and accessibility of knowledge is a necessary condition for the making of free citizens. In its German version, the modernist narrative oscillated between the Kantian co-ordination of distinct language games (descriptive, prescriptive, and ludic) for the sake of the ethical life, on one hand, and the Hegelian Idea becoming conscious of itself, on the other.

Jürgen Habermas, in the 1960s, did speculate that the inability of modern states to generate and sustain myths and ideologies of self-legitimation was a more credible reason for the impending crises and collapse of these states than the economic worsening cycles and crashes predicted by Marx (Habermas 1975). In the 1970s and 1980s, Habermas again searched for ethico-dialogical procedures that would, in the absence of commitment to the old grand narratives, be capable of sustaining substantive rationality and rational consensus among citizens.[2] It was to these speculations and arguments that Jean-François Lyotard was responding in the 1970s, with the claim that the grand Western narratives had already delegitimized themselves, and that consensus (the will to consensus) was nothing but the nostalgia for the modernist strategies, which were responsible for the crisis in the first place. The fact is, Lyotard argued, that our postmodern times no longer believe in grand narratives – they do not believe in the link that previous centuries strove to establish between knowledge and emancipation. There is no longer a valuing of knowledge for its ability to build characters and to make free citizens. Knowledge has become a force of production, and is being translated, processed, stored, and delivered in ways unfriendly to the old narratives. Spearheaded by unheard-of technological advances, today's epistēmē delivers the goods, legitimating itself through 'performativity.' Technology 'proves the proof' and the need for experts mounts – except that the experts are no longer called upon to facilitate the emancipation of citizens; they are called upon to fill posts in the system where the cultivation of imagination is promoted for the sake of re-arranging data (Lyotard 1984: 44–7). The Frankfurt School had already called this syndrome the triumph of instrumental reason at the expense of substantive rationality.

Rather than searching for a new narrative for the legitimation of knowledge (the way that Habermas did), Lyotard advocated assent to the prevailing incredulity, without nostalgia for what has been lost. Nevertheless, in order to prevent a performativity-driven closing of horizons, the atrophy and elimination of alternatives, and the ensuing injustice against the plural, Lyotard appealed to what he took to be the modern scientific paradigm – open to experimentation, the plural, and the unexpected, and encouraging, so he thought, the paralogic and the paradoxic. In the Kantian narrative, 'categories' constitute and legitimate epistēmē; but it is thanks to 'regulative Ideas' that epistēmē is made into an infinite task for human reason. By offering horizons for repetition, directionality and mobile totalizations, Ideas prevent the ultimate closure of horizons. To the extent that performativity is threatening because it tends to put regulative Ideas out of play and to establish the terrorism of consensus, the way out of the crisis experienced by the grand narratives, from Lyotard's point of view, passes through dissent – not through grand stories, but rather by means of *petit récits* – the more, the merrier. The circulation of such stories may facilitate and sustain agonistic relations among citizens as well as the vision of a plural justice without consensus (Lyotard 1984: 60–7).

Jean-François Lyotard's proposed alternative to the grand narratives, *sui generis* that it may be because of its dependence on, and alliance with, a late twentieth-century trend towards a philosophy of difference and multiplicity, is not unique to him. The early century disparagement of (neo-) Hegelianism in Britain; the dismemberment of the Kantian corpus into so many *natures mortes* to be used either as practice targets or as laboratories for the darts and the scalpels of conceptual and linguistic analysts; the disdain of the logical positivists for everything that is neither analytic nor empirically verifiable; the general retreat away from the synthetic a priori that used to hold the grand narratives together; Popper's Procrustean strategy demanding that everything be formulated into well-formed conjectures and be subjected to repeated refutations; the anti-foundationalist wave of the second half of the century fueled by Rorty's neo-pragmatist agenda; the culpabilisation by Heidegger of the grand narratives for their complicity in the obliteration of the ontological difference between Being and beings; the Levinasian denunciation of ontology and the welcoming of the Other by an Ethics-turned-into-*prima-philosophia*; the Foucauldian vivisection of all knowledge claims and the discovery of their dependence upon power games; the Deleuzean substitution of the 'interesting' and the 'remarkable' for the 'true' and the 'false' of yesteryear – through all this, the best and liveliest philosophies of the century conspired in a loud proclamation of the demise of the old narratives, even in the rare moments that they could be found paying lip service to them.

The dissipation of conceptual fog

Analytic philosophy during the first half of the century had no need for long and involved arguments to persuade its devotees that they did not believe in grand narratives any longer; no need for soothing stories to induce the acceptance of existing alternatives. Analysis was the alternative, and the laborers in the field were not inclined to mourn the passing of an era that they were busy dismantling. A selection of programmatic declarations made at the time makes the point eloquently.

[The great metaphysicians of the past] set many examples of philosophizing which we are often scolded . . . for refusing to follow: We, it is said, shirk giving concrete guidance; we do not preach; we are untheological; we are excessively microscopic; we neglect political problems; our moral philosophy is too thin; and in general, we stick too closely to the grindstone and go too little out in the woods. . . . The time is not yet ripe for new global syntheses. (Gilbert Ryle, in Pears, 1957: 164)

Or again, this time Quinton:

[W]e first remark and with some confidence, that there cannot be a moral philosophy which will tell us what in particular we are to do. All philosophy has to do is to 'understand what is,' and moral philosophy has to understand morals which exist, not to make them or give directions for making them. (Quinton 1966: 157)

And again:

Another traditional department of academic philosophy that has suffered some neglect in recent years is the philosophical study of politics. . . . I should not want to see it resurrected in its old form, with genuine philosophical problems and discussions inextricably embedded in a mass of alien matter, mixed up with history, theoretical political science, recommendations of policies, the comparative study of institutions and so on. . . . It seems to me, then, that the work that is already being done, and which will, one hopes, increase on problems of a conceptual or methodological order arising in law, history and the social sciences provides some answer to the charge that our preoccupations are trivial, academic or unreal. (Quinton 1966: 161, 162)

Here, 'the death of God' hardly generates a yawn; it seems to belong to yesterday's news.

Only timidly, and around the mid-century point, some analytic philosophers thought it necessary to solicit the adoption of grand narratives for their own positions. John Rawls is an example, in his quest for justice as fairness, and its decision-making procedure taking place behind a 'veil of ignorance' (Rawls 1971). In Rawls's thought-experiment, self-interested individuals, in need of justice, come together to regulate the future of their society – to pick principles of justice. If a 'veil of ignorance' could prevent these parties from a wholesale pursuit of self-interest, their choices would be fair to all: not knowing their identities or the situations they could find themselves in, after their decision is taken, choosing a set of fair principles for all would strike them as the more acceptable outcome for everyone involved. Rawls, in reviving the old social contract tradition, provides it with the aura of the *grand récit* sustaining the Kantian imperative, and renders what is rational for all to choose in fair circumstances, obligatory.

Despite a very different agenda, Charles Taylor also, in the second half of the century, reached a similar conclusion (Taylor 1992). He argues that the choice of our ethical and political principles presuppose that we recognize ourselves, our identities, our moral judgements, our language and our communities as occurring in a system that transcends our subjective desires. We share, he says, a historically created common sense which is prior to, and decisive over convergent or divergent 'opinions.' Implicit in this claim is the *Sittlichkeit* of German idealism and the assumption of an affective common sense without which it would be impossible to judge the morality of an act.

The survival of the grand narratives can also be witnessed in the work of Jürgen Habermas. Situated within the tradition of Critical Theory, his discourse ethics, to the extent that it attempts to disclose the procedures capable of grounding understanding and truth, appears initially unencumbered by grand narratives. After all, not every foundationalism builds on *grand récits*. But, on closer inspection, the kind of relation that it attempts to establish between truth and emancipation through consensus provides us, not only with a foundation, but with one that has its place within the (incomplete) emancipatory tale of the Enlightenment. For Habermas, the competence of a native speaker extends beyond the mastery of an abstract system of linguistic rules. Participation in normal discourse requires, in addition to this system, communicative competence grounded on a universal pragmatics. Utterances are integrated into a form of intersubjectivity of mutual understanding, presupposing a tacit consensus about what it means to communicate. Communicative competence, therefore, relates to an ideal speech situation that constitutes the transcendental/empirical ground of dialogic understanding and of uncoerced, agreed upon truth (Habermas 1970).

Despite such efforts, the appeal of grand narratives was indeed waning. The anti-foundationalist wave of the 1970s and 1980s, strengthened by the neo-pragmatist agenda of Richard Rorty, threw its weight behind the search for new expressions of the emancipatory interest in a post-*grand récits* period (Rorty 1991a; and 1991b: 164–76). Denouncing the Kantian heritage and its undying preoccupation with the loss of religion that gave the grand narratives an aura of legitimacy, Rorty's anti-foundationalism boldly refused to couch its agenda in terms of 'emancipation': without the presumption of a human nature, he argued, there was nothing to emancipate, and the place of the old narratives of emancipation should be taken over by narratives of solidarity, cosmopolitanism, and historical progress. Putting solidarity (with 'our' community) and liberal democracy ahead of philosophy, and communication ahead of truth, neo-pragmatism promoted the quest for new, contingent vocabularies capable of getting us what we need. And what we need – we can hear at this point the echo of John Stuart Mill's distinction between the public and the private spheres – is the eradication (or, at least, the minimization) of cruelty, and the imagination and freedom to create and assert ourselves. The transhistorical foundations proposed by the old narratives are, in this context, replaced by a local and temporary 'we,' sharing practices that need no justification apart from their being shared, and being content to call 'true' whatever turns out to be the result of free and open encounters. Borrowing the vision from Peirce, Rorty declares this liberal democratic community to be constituted by competing hypotheses, which are allowed to grow together 'until the harvest' comes. Pluralism and tolerance, therefore, are the basic tenets of such a community, that Rorty calls 'a society of ironists' whose members entertain a healthy doubt about vocabulary, and do not think that their vocabulary is any closer to reality than other vocabularies.

Nevertheless, a community of ironists exists only in the tension between commitment and the recognition of the contingency of this commitment. The relativism threatened by the frank admission that there are no neutral standpoints, that vocabularies are always justified post facto, and that moral principles are 'reminders of' institutions (rather than their justification) is accompanied by the belief that the vocabulary of the liberal ironist citizen delivers the goods that 'we' want (diminution of cruelty, self-creation and assertion, pluralism, and tolerance); that it is foolish 'to scratch where it does not itch'; and that the ethos of the liberal ironist guarantees the ability to revise vocabularies and to learn from her mistakes.

Emancipation after the Grand Narratives

Be that as it may, it is clear that the debate about the *grand récits* and their subsequent atrophy did not cause the disappearance of the emancipatory interest from the agendas of the philosophers of the century. The legacies of Marx and Freud, with or without support from grand narratives, kept the fires of emancipation burning. As soon as a narrow, economist-determinist reading of Marx came to face seriously the exigencies of revolutionary transformation (*praxis*), philosophers had to take into consideration issues of subjectivity, consciousness-formation, and alienation. It is one thing to demonstrate that the devaluation of the human world is intensified with the increase in value of the world of things; or to show the objective structures of human alienation in a capitalist economy (alienation of labor's product, of the process of labor, and of the producers from each other); but it is quite another to account for the voluntary servitude that causes producers and consumers to like their chains. For the emancipatory interest to be rekindled, those who labored in the Marxist field found it necessary to develop theories of ideological obscurantism and to hold this obscurantism responsible for misunderstanding things and people in situations of distorted communication. These discussions started with an optimistic faith in liberation from the *camera obscura* upside down effect, and from the Babel of pseudo-communication, through a resolute stepping into the clearing of objective reality. But then, with Habermas, we came to witness the replacement of 'objective reality' by that which can be agreed upon in free and uncoerced dialogue, informed by communicative competence. Or again, with Louis Althusser, a radical epistemological break separated ideology from knowledge (ideology and science) and swept away all temptations to see science as the 'sublation' of the pre-scientific and ideological. The scientific object is no longer the truth *of* the ideological, Althusser argued. It is the truth *for* the ideological – its unmasking and demystification. Ideology is not 'false consciousness'; it is a particular social reality specific to social practices, one that interpellates individuals and constructs subjects. What Althusser called 'theory' – the science of all practices, including the ideological – was meant to be the arbiter of an enlightened emancipation. It was not long after that that the century found it necessary to pronounce the notion of ideology useless – a conclusion that was reached as soon as the notion of human nature (whether in chains or whether slated for liberation) lost its credibility and support.

It is worth remembering that the interest in emancipation found, throughout the century, one more resourceful site of support in the theory and practice of Freudian psychoanalysis. Philosophical interest in psychoanalysis generated two streams of research and writing: one of them focused on the status of psychoanalytic theory, and got busy over its ability (or lack thereof) to formulate testable hypotheses, and to submit its concepts to operational verifiability. The same stream focused also on the implications that psychoanalysis carries for traditional philosophical questions concerning ethics and free will. As for the other stream, it was the one that recognized in psychoanalytic theory the potential for a powerful critique of culture, and strove to contextualize some of its findings and hypotheses, preventing them from claiming any kind of ontological finality.

Although analytic philosophers tended to be clustered in greater numbers in the first stream, the epistemological and philosophico-scientific preoccupations that their work in this area exhibited were not exclusively their own. Paul Ricoeur's impressive hermeneutic work on Freud (*Freud and Philosophy: An Essay on Interpretation*, 1970), Habermas's critical-theoretical choice of psychoanalysis (*Knowledge and Human Interests*, 1971) and his writings on systematically distorted communication and communicative competence (1970) – they all testify to the vivid continental European interest in the status of the theory. The same vivid interest in the status of psychoanalysis was demonstrated in the archeological investigations of Michel Foucault, in the reconstructive reading of Freud by Jacques Lacan, the grammatological and deconstructive preoccupations of Jacques Derrida and his followers, the anti-Oedipal and schizoanalytic project of Gilles Deleuze and Félix Guattari, and the ambivalent stance of feminist philosophers toward Freud, Lacan and psychoanalysis.

At any rate, analytically inclined philosophers have been mostly skeptical – if not negative – about the possibility of forming 'predictively confirmed psychoanalytic hypotheses,' as opposed to proposed explanations that *seem* to make sense of phenomena. As a result, they also have tended to be cautious in general about calls to recruit psychoanalysis for the critique of culture. I think, however, that it would be more accurate to speak of ambivalence here – an ambivalence that can be found among analysts as much as it can be found among continentals. Certainly, there has been no unanimity among those who reflected on Freudian psychoanalysis as a cultural critique. It is true that Jürgen Habermas presented psychoanalysis as a paradigm discipline for the demonstration of how best to think of the emancipatory interest in a cognitive way; that Herbert Marcuse (*Eros and Civilization*, 1955), after some emendations of Freud's text, tried to bring together Freudianism and Marxism in what seemed for a while to be a potent social and cultural critique; that Jacques Lacan took it upon himself to rewrite Freudian theory in a new key – the key of the 'fall' of the *infans* from the bliss of the absorption in the pre-Oedipal mother and its recovery by the realm of the symbolic (language and culture). But it is also true that Jean-Paul Sartre (*Being and Nothingness*, 1942) concluded that the unconscious motives and drives, so central to Freud's theory, threaten human freedom, and that he went on to substitute his own theory of bad faith for the Freudian unconscious. Gilles Deleuze and Félix Guattari (*Anti-Oedipus: Capitalism and Schizophrenia*, 1980) saw in the Freudian Oedipus the truth of capitalism, the matrix of double binds that precipitate the clinical entities of paranoia and schizophrenia, and substituted for Freudo-Lacanian psychoanalysis their own brand of schizoanalysis. Among the feminists,

Simone de Beauvoir (*The Second Sex*, 1949), Kate Millett (*Sexual Politics*, 1970), Shulamith Firestone (*The Dialectic of Sex*, 1970), Ti-Grace Atkinson, and Luce Irigaray, to name only a few, expressed strong reservations about Freud's emancipatory potential. Others, beginning in the late 1970s, condemned Freudian psychoanalysis as a rationalization of women's oppression, but welcomed it as a priceless description of the time-bound social and cultural processes that result in the domestication of women. Gayle Rubin ('The Traffic of Women', 1975), Juliet Mitchell (*Psychoanalysis and Feminism*, 1974), and Nancy Chodorow (*The Reproduction of Mothering*, 1978) belong to this group. Perhaps, among the members of this group we could also count Hélène Cixous and Julia Kristeva, whose qualified appropriation of Freud takes place within the psychoanalytic culture recreated by Jacques Lacan, and in the context of discourse analyses that unmask the prevailing use of language for the sake of patriarchal oppression.

Be that as it may, between the 1960s and the 1980s, on the European continent – especially in France – a combination of strong denunciations of the usual theoretical expressions of the emancipatory interest and of new and aggressive attempts towards a reformulation of it became almost canonical and they deserve to be mentioned here.

Foucault's resistance

With Foucault, the threat to freedom no longer comes from performativity-driven system imperatives, rendering politically irrelevant the versatility of citizens, in their capacity to be the players of diverse language games. Rather, the threat comes from the effects of the will to truth, the ethical complicity of individuals in their becoming-subject, and the ongoing subtle play of power and resistance. Foucault called 'archeological' his analyses of the discourse of the human sciences responsible for the formation of changing *epistē*mēs; and 'genealogical,' the investigation of the dynamic relationships between power/resistance, themselves responsible for subject-formation and subjection. Archeology uncovers the historical *a priori* of a society at a given time – an *a priori* that represents the limits of what is visible and sayable at that time, thereby enabling things to be seen, said, and to be presumed true. In folding the forces of the outside ('internalizing' them would be a variant expression here, if it were not for Foucault's desire to avoid the language of interiority) – in making themselves the sites of the sayable, the visible, and the affective of a given period, individuals subject themselves to outside forces and make themselves capable of thinking, willing, and acting in recognizably similar ways: they give themselves a style. For Foucault, therefore, the subject is the after-effect of a folding – the outcome of an ethical *askesis* that gives rise to a subject, which is ipso facto subjected. Loosening up the constraints of the subjectivation process that, through counter-memory, thinking otherwise, testing the limits of subjectivity and experimenting with alternative subject-formations are now the guiding principles of a post-*grand récits* emancipatory interest: permanent resistance takes over the entire domain of Foucauldean politics.

The politics of aporias

The destiny of the post-grand récits interest in emancipation, in Derrida's 'deconstruction,' is inextricably linked to an effort to redefine what is involved in the political space as such. Rather than striving to clarify the essentially contested concepts of the political, and to fix their identity, deconstruction insists on their irreducibly aporematic structure and makes the *aporia* the essence of the political decision. An *aporia* is the result of a concept being related to another concept by means of chiastic slippages, and of the ensuing exchange and incorporation in a concept of determinations and predicates which normally belong to its counterpart. For example, for gifts to be possible – without entering the circuit of exchange that would destroy their 'identity' as gifts – they must escape entanglement in calculations, duty or moral considerations: the donor should not intend the gift and the donee should not be indebted by it. But then, to the extent that it is impossible, in the last analysis, according to Derrida, to prevent gifts from ever entering the logic of exchange, but equally impossible to dispense with gift-giving, an *aporia* is generated, whereby the conditions that render the pure gift impossible must also be the conditions of the gift's possibility. Faced with *aporias*, rather than thinking reductively, Derrida invites us to push against the limit, in the direction of an *à-venir* that can never be thought as anyone's future. Aporematic concepts function as the guardians of Derrida's emancipatory interest, as the latter permeates the domain of the political: hospitality, for example, being understood as neither assimilation of the *xenos* nor as the total appropriation of my space by the other; justice, as the undeconstructible preoccupation with the singular, which cannot escape the contamination of the generality of the law; the demand of democracy that equality and singularity be reconciled; the *aporia* generated by the relationship between nation-state and its immigrants; and so forth. The irreducibility of these *aporias* leads Derrida to the conclusion that the emancipatory interest inscribed in democracy carries already always a promise and an endless process of perfectibility.

At this point, the suspicion towards institutions, the resistance to the *proprium* and to essences, and the choice of the Derridean deconstructionist to be already always on the margins, usher in the quest for a community of singularities – a community without community – 'the community of those that have nothing in common.' Jean-Luc Nancy and Giorgio Agamben are among those who, with help from Blanchot, towards the end of the century, took it upon themselves to think about a community able to survive the Rousseauesque lament for a lost intimacy. In the absence of a common substance, they argued, the emancipatory interest will be borne by 'singularities' that share in (*partagent*) the exposure of their finitude/mortality. The community promised by this vision can no longer be the result of work – labor or planning. The minimum of 'communication' required for its arrival is best approached through limitation: 'I no longer hear in it what the other wants to say to me, but I hear that the other speaks and that there is an essential archi-articulation of voices which constitutes the being-in-common' (Nancy 1991: 76).

Nomadism

A rearticulation of the emancipatory interest also runs through Deleuze and Guattari's work. Their contribution to the discussion is best understood, as François Zourabichvili argued, by taking into account the simultaneous presence in their texts of two attitudes – subversion and perversion (Zourabichvili 1998). Their subversive tendencies tend to cluster around the concepts minority/majority and nomad/sedentary, developed in *A Thousand Plateaus* (1987), in an attempt to rally together those in a position to stand against the state's capturing forces. It was in this context that Deleuze and Guattari issued an appeal to minor, transformative forces (of life, politics, thought, artistic creation) and to their capacity to escape the sedentarism and stratification that are dear to majorities. Nomads, having portable roots, were granted the ability to reterritorialize upon the line and the trajectory of their own deterritorialization.

In the nomadology that emerges from Deleuze and Guattari's writings, one can still hear the echo of the Marxist reading of the state as the 'capturing apparatus' in the hands of the ruling class, being maintained for the sake of that class's interests. The sedentaries (alias the majority or the majoritarians) are the state or the state-apparatus or, rather, the state-form; the nomads (alias the multitudes or masses or minorities) are those whose investments of desire do not coincide with the interests of the state – but with a difference: in Deleuze and Guattari's post-Marxist context, the nomads do not want to become the state or to take over the state apparatus – not even temporarily; rather, they strive to dismantle it or to flee from it. When all is said and done, the nomad is the one who tries to prevent the social sedimentation of desire from blocking the connective process of the production of desire. Nomadic lines of flight are lines of subversion and transformation of the well-organized and smoothly-functioning in-stitutions of the sedentaries.

But there is another side to Deleuze and Guattari's posture towards the political – a posture that Zourabichvili again qualified as 'perverse' (Zourabichvili 1998: 357). Politics is a posture, a matter of perception, the result of a conversion that allows the development of a mechanics of resistance to the present. With respect to Deleuze and Guattari's subversive tendencies, the emancipatory interest manifests itself in the question 'how best to flee,' without being deprived of weapons or of the artifices that will be needed on the line of deterritorialization. The question of the best means available for fleeing, in turn, leads to Deleuze and Guattari's 'perversion.' The true bearer of the emancipatory interest is not the sadist, Zourabichvili argues following Deleuze, for the latter, steeped in the language of the law, and contesting the fiction of the deduction of the law from an alleged principle of the good, chooses to *subvert* the old law ironically by maintaining its form, while, at the same time, replacing its content with precepts deduced from a 'principle of evil.' Rather, the true bearer of the emancipatory interest is, according to Deleuze and Guattari, the masochist, for he chooses to *pervert* the law by submitting to it humorously in order to savor the pleasures that the law prohibits and punishes.

Despite all the reservations that Deleuze and Guattari harbor against actual democracies, their option for the becoming-democratic, inscribed in the politics of a universal brotherhood *à venir*, is unmistakable. In the Deleuzean story, the people (to whom the political theorist appeals) is missing; 'a new people and a new earth *à venir*' gives Deleuze and Guattari's political posture 'a purposefulness without purpose' – provided, that is, that the clarion for a new people and a new earth is not intercepted as a teleological anticipation with messianic aspirations. Deleuze and Guattari did not designate or name the people to come or the new earth; they did say, though, that the new 'race' exists only as an oppressed race, and it suffers only in the name of the oppression. They did claim that race is always inferior and minoritarian, and that 'race' is not defined by its purity, but rather by the impurity conferred upon it by a system of domination.

Gender, Race and Ethnicity

Nowhere else have the modernist grand narratives been subjected to more rigorous critique than in the texts of feminists and post-colonial writers. And nowhere else, perhaps, have calls for the reconfiguration of the interest in emancipation been louder and more persistent. Linda Alcoff correctly pointed out that a lot of this is due to the realization of the fact that modernism rests on a paradox: it asks for gender, racial, ethnic, and other group identities to be considered irrelevant to the distribution of social and political rights, while, at the same time, it insists on the naturalization and the acceptability of all these differences (Alcoff and Mendieta 2003: 6). The tensions generated by this paradox, according to Alcoff, inspired, in the twentieth century, two alternative strategies: either to deconstruct group identities in order to emphasize their irrelevance to the struggle for social justice or to create a new social and political framework that would encourage the pursuit of justice in the face of unassimilated differences.

In the 1940s, Simone de Beauvoir offered a philosophical voice to intuitions and political struggles that pre-dated her own work. Without using what later on became a canonical disjunction, she drove a wedge between gender and sex: she proclaimed that one is not born a woman, but that one becomes a woman, thanks to the ubiquity of a man-made myth – the myth of womanhood – which attributes to femininity the irreconcilable predicates of virgin and whore. Gender, she argued, is mainly a social fabrication that benefits those in power. Man and woman are not natural terms; they are socially overcoded. The myth, responsible for the enslavement of women, has prevented half the human race from assuming the position of the subject, in humanity's struggle for recognition in freedom.

Later on, after de Beauvoir's manifesto, feminists chose to challenge the Kantian universalistic presuppositions, especially those made in the context of ethics and moral philosophy – presuppositions, resting, as they argued, on a 'sexual contract' that favours men. Carol Gilligan's *In a Different Voice: Psychoanalytical Theory and Women's Development* (1982) is one of the most effective examples of this challenge. The universalistic presuppositions of the dominant scientific methodology also came under fire for their uncritical assumptions regarding the alleged neutrality, disembodied status, and autonomy of the theorist and the scientist. In Jacqueline Donovan's words, the twentieth century witnessed the restoration of 'emotion, sympathy, empathy, and compassion to the philosophical debate, revalidating them as relevant ethical and epistemological sources for ethical behavior.'[3] Moreover, feminism in the twentieth century promotes with considerable success the disentanglement of political philosophy from the rights of autonomous individuals and the abstractions of an alleged equality of opportunity, in favor of men and women whose identities, rights and duties are organized in contexts of power differentials.

It is important to recall here that with the advent of poststructuralism and of the philosophies of different political agendas predicated on an emancipatory interest, which proposes the reversal of the existing polarity of genders, or even champions equality between genders, races and ethnicities, were deemed to be regressive. Instead, emancipation was assumed to require the transformation of all binary oppositions into multiplicities. Luce Irigaray's new ways of thinking the feminine; her quest for a new imaginary and a new symbolic by women and for women; her reference to women in the metonymy of the 'two lips, without suture'; and her advocacy of sexuate rights and female jouissance would have re-introduced gender dualism, if it were not for the fact that Irigaray's overall strategy showed decisively that woman is not self-identical (Irigaray 1985a): woman is the sex that is not one. This is why the demand that different rights be codified and legislated for each sex is not made for the sake of equality or fair power redistribution; it is rather advanced for the sake of challenging the structure itself – the structure that necessitates inequalities and the abstract discourse of equality.[4] The same consideration motivated the demand for a new, sexuate speech and writing, and the denunciation of the illusion that speech is (or should be) gender-blind. Whether conceived as the mimicking of the dominant patriarchal discourse or whether anticipated as a new, disruptive, tactile, and fluid style, the proposed *parler femme* (speaking [as] woman) was meant to challenge the dominant discursive mechanisms in view of the commitment to the plural and the multiple.[5] The objective was to find words that would not only name but keep the other alive through allusive means, that is, through strategies of 'brushing against' or 'touching' the other.

In the course of their attempts to articulate their theoretical standpoints and to co-ordinate their political and strategic programs, feminists during the twentieth century did not strike a univocal posture towards Freud. Some of them denounced his 'masculinist' biases; others, without being blind to his biases, discovered in Freud's psychoanalytic theory (and in Lacan's re-articulation of it) tools and analyses capable of displacing the hegemony of patriarchal discourse and practice. They credited Freud for having shown that the subject is always a subject-in-process/in trial; and for having shown the way for translating the ethics of psychoanalysis into political engagement. French feminists (Julia Kristeva, for example [*Pouvoirs de l'horreur* (1980); *Les nouvelles maladies de l'âme* (1993)]), having to contend with Lacan's rereading of Freud, accepted a lot from him – including, in some cases, his symbolic; but they also moved beyond Lacan, towards the pre-Oedipal processes associated with the maternal function as expressed in the work of Melanie Klein (Chodorow 1989: Chap. 6). As a result, love took, for them, precedence over the Lacanian mirror stage, as they strove to articulate an ethic between love and transgression, offering alternatives to the juridical models that presuppose autonomous subjects and the force of law.

The century was not bereft of champions of strong identity agendas. The slogans, 'As a woman I want to be free,' 'Black is beautiful,' 'Serbia to the Serbs' cannot be understood only as expressions of regressive attitudes or of reactive passions. What they seem to propose for theoretical reflection is that 'it is not at all clear that the future would be better off without the rich differences of life-interpretations that are developed via the social identities based on ethnicity, gender, sexuality, and other such group categories' (Alcoff and Mendieta 2003: 2). But even without trying to devine the future and the role that difference and hybridity should be allowed to play in it, a few voices kept insisting that power, instead of opposing the 'carnavalesque,' was in fact strengthened by the 'hybrid appropriation of subaltern attributes.' Some writers even argued for a 'strong agenda for group identity,' on the grounds that 'the racial, [gender] and/or ethnic life-world provides the resources and nurturing required for the development, even, of individual talent and accomplishment such that distinctive contributions can be made to human civilization.' But the fact remains that even this stronger program sought a middle point between the essentialist and the skeptical arguments surrounding the epistemic status of identities. This middle point was articulated during the last third of the century with the help of what came to be known as 'standpoint epistemology' (Code 1988). The general idea here is this: although the view from nowhere is impossible, relativism can still be avoided if one's 'constructed' identity is allowed to co-exist with a realist epistemic status, which assigns to one's perspective a multi-dimensional life world. A standpoint may reveal facts that are not available to those who do not occupy the same standpoint, explaining thereby why the marginalized and oppressed may often have an epistemic privilege; it would also permit the differentiation and assessment of spurious and legitimate identities. Along these lines, towards the end of the century, philosophers focused on 'mobile subjectivities' and 'coalition politics' (Young 1990: Chap. 6). In the words of Kathy Robinson, '[L]etting difference be is not the outcome of "the fuzzy ambiguity of pluralism" but an active attention to multiplicity; not the claim that all claims are equally valid, but the call to attend to all calls to order with a sympathetic ear for what does not or will not fit.'[6] Iris Marion Young called the politics underlying such claims, the politics of 'unassimilated otherness' (Young 1990).

Here, my story about the philosophical life of the twentieth century must come to an end. In the concluding years of the century, the prophecy of philosophy's death – either as a result of its 'realization' (Feuerbach) or through the successful training of the fly to find its way out of the bottle (Wittgenstein) – was still unfulfilled. Upwards of 700 philosophy journals were in circulation world-wide. The mass production of philosophers by an ever-increasing number of universities and colleges throughout the world; the 'publish or perish' imperative that those competing for the posts of the 'public professor' had to internalize; the scholastic zeal of competing philosophical agendas; the 'greening' of philosophy made possible by the interface of the political and the philosophical; and, last but not least, the availability of talent in abundance, conspired in keeping philosophy alive and well. Journals, with a few notable exceptions, were accepting writings for publication that represented, in terms of method, style, and content, the colors of the agenda belonging to each one of them (rival colors need not apply). But the plethora of periodical publications of all stripes guaranteed that all deserving (and sometimes non-deserving) submissions were able to see the light of day. It is this glut that makes it difficult to discern distinct national philosophical tendencies and trends, despite the fact that the distribution and concentration of similarly-minded, in style and content, professionals in different institutions were responsible for the creation of pockets of rival 'institutional power.' Such rival institutional power continued to feed the exclusive disjunctions between Oxford or Warwick, Paris I or Paris VIII, Yale or SUNY at Stonybrook, Waterloo or Guelph.

In a quick survey of the philosophy journals in circulation during the last year of the century, one is struck by the presence of two tendencies, situated at opposite poles and being intolerant of one another, as well by the existence of a growing in-between space, populated by representatives of different agendas where philosophy was done without the need to demarcate and to trumpet rival domains. I want to conclude this introduction with a few words on the two tendencies and on the promise held by the in-between space.

The end of the century is marked, on one hand, by an inward-looking and strong, in some circles, tendency to cultivate philosophical gardens, walled in and perfectly protected against the intrusion of the Lifeworld. Philosophy is what philosophers do, and what they do best in this case is debating, with increasing sophistication and argumentative dexterity, the credentials of an epistemic certainty far stronger than anything warranted by our need to make sense of the world and to navigate successfully in it. Philosophy is at its best, this tendency alleged, when it emulates and reproduces the ontological parsimony of the natural scientist, in the (made-to-look) new, but decisively post-Cartesian effort to reduce the mental to the physical, to exorcise vagueness and metaphoricity, and to be vigilant against any threatening contamination of its genre by modes of writing that come to it from different quarters (with the exception perhaps of the natural scientific). The 1999 volume of the British journal, *Mind*, is one of the best mirrors of all that: essays on disquotationalism, necessity, non-supervenient relations, Tarski, vagueness, counterfactuals, self-deception, logical constants, mentioning and quoting, and phenomenal consciousness make up the volume. There is nothing trivial about these essays – my point is not this; my point is that their authors seem to have forgotten the sequence of problems and questions of which their essays are distant echoes – indeed to have made it a point of honor to forget this genealogy and to take pride in their ability to contribute their penny's-worth to a discussion without antecedents (but with guaranteed consequences). I call this tendency the 'immaculate conception' of philosophical issues and concepts.

The opposite pole, at the end of the century, was occupied by those who seemed capable of creating philosophical concepts only after indulging in the most catachresic mingling of genres possible (the more, the merrier), the hybridization of discourse, and the flight away from any vestiges of representational 'canons' – to the point of a total blurring of whatever diagram could possibly have supported sense. Here, a chain of atopical fragments is reinforced by the circulation of dechronologized segments – the mixture being calculated to revitalize the satiated palate of the tourist-reader. I call this tendency 'conception through promiscuous couplings.' What I find reprehensible in it is that it attempts to join together the *askesis* of the copula (Deleuze's vision of writing as stuttering) and the *jouissance* of promiscuous copulation, in full disregard of the law of the inverse relation between pleasure and desire. Manifestations of this tendency abound among the epigoni of deconstruction, Deleuzo-Guattarian rhizomatics, Lacanian psychoanalysis, and Cultural Studies, who, without the style, the intensity, or even the passion of their prototypes, multiply *aporias*, fake the stuttering, and raise the volume of the lament for an unredeemed desire, as they keep on publishing in order not to perish. It seems to me that the opposition between immaculate conceivers and non-discriminating fornicators had come, by the end of the century, to replace the division between analysts and continentals by transforming the 'microscopic' and 'micrologic' tendencies of the former and the paratactic and synthesizing tendencies of the latter into the sterility of hyper-specialization or the prattle of the effete.

Mercifully, the end of the century left philosophy with an in-between space, populated with less flamboyant, yet hard-working and reliable laborers. A wide range of journal publications testifies to the reliability of these laborers and to the variety of the issues and topics that they were choosing to handle. The four issues of the 1999 volume of the *Revue Philosophique de la France et de l' Étranger* (in its 189th year of publication) dedicated their pages to fine essays on Machiavelli, post-Kantian critique, cognitivism, and the notion of the whole, respectively. The 1999 volume of the *Revue de Métaphysique et de Morale* saw three issues given to Condillac, the baroque, and pre-Kantian critique, and a fourth to a variety of themes, ranging from Franz Rosenzweig's critique of the philosophies of the spirit to Husserl's passive syntheses. The *Revue Internationale de Philosophie*, in its 53rd year of publication in 1999, devoted its four issues to American pragmatism, Hannah Arendt, neuroscience, and to Hegel's critique of Kant. A variety of philosophers (Parmenides, Plato, Aristotle, Averroes, Malebranche, Spinoza, Pascal) and issues (soul, natural philosophy, subjectivity, the vacuum, Jansenism) were present in the *Archiv für Geschichte der Philosophie*, in its 81st year of publication in 1999. Not to be outdone, the *Zeitschrift für Philosophische Forshung* (in its 67th year in 1999) sported fine essays on the history of philosophy but also on systematic philosophy on questions of creativity, happiness, determinism, consequentialism, ideal grammar, and on the philosophies of the Stoics, Rousseau, Kant, Hegel, and George H. Mead. A survey of Italian and Spanish philosophy journals exhibits a similar interest in the history of philosophy, coupled with a sober judgement brought to bear on the choice and the manner of addressing issues of current concern. The *Rivista di Filosofia*, for instance, in its 90th year in 1999, published essays on biology and ethics, on Donald Davidson, logical empiricism, Karl Löwith, Russell, Robert Brandom, time and mental causality, and the 'Annales' group. The *Annuario Filosofico*, in its 32nd year in 1999, displayed essays on utilitarian justice and the paralogisms of liberalism, the Cartesian idea of philosophy, the Aristotelian roots of humanism, Aristotelian friendship, and on Spinoza on religion. On the North American side of the Atlantic, the *Philosophical Review* finished the century showcasing the historico-philosophical continuity of the concerns of its contributors: 'The Cartesian Circle,' 'Leibniz on Freedom and Necessity,' 'Kant on Self-Consciousness,' 'Leibniz on God's Knowledge on Counterfactuals,' 'Locke's Resemblance Theses' are five out of the eleven essays included in its 1999 volume that mark the showcase of philosophical sobriety and substance, in the space between the *glossolalia* of promiscuous writing and the *natures mortes* of the immaculate conception. With a different philosophical agenda, *Philosophy Today* displayed a similar sobriety. Its 43rd volume of 1999 included essays on Husserl, Merleau-Ponty, de Beauvoir, Heidegger, Ricoeur, Foucault, Deleuze and Guattari, Levinas, Kierkegaard and Derrida, language, sexual difference, embodiment, death, and repetition.

It is with those who, at the end of the century, walked the royal middle road that my sympathies lie. I never entertained the idea of an imminent death for philosophy. But even if news about philosophy's death are always already premature, its health and vigor cannot be taken for granted. It seems to me that its health and vigor very much depend on the maintenance and the expansion of what I called the space in between. After all, those who conceive immaculately as much as those who conceive in unholy alliances share one thing – the demise of philosophy – although they differ radically on who comes after philosophy. The former place their bets on the scientist; the latter, on the sophist.

Notes

1. For this paragraph and the next, I draw on the work of Jean Greisch, *Herméneutique et grammatologie* (Paris: CNRS, 1977).
2. See Jürgen Habermas (1981), *The Theory of Communicative Action, Volume 1. Reason and the Radicalization of Society*, trans. Thomas McCarthy, Boston: Beacon Press; Jürgen Habermas (1990), 'Discourse Ethics: Notes on a Program of Philosophical Justification,' in Seyla Benhabib and Fred Dallmayr (eds), *The Communicative Ethics Controversy*, Cambridge: MIT Press, pp. 60–110.
3. See Professor Donovan's chapter, 'Analytic Feminist Philosophy' in this volume.
4. See Luce Irigaray 1991, 1991a, 2001.
5. See Luce Irigaray 1985b; 1991c; 1991d; 1991e; and Hélène Cixous 1986.
6. Kathy Robinson, 'The Man Question', quoted by Professor Donovan in 'Analytic Feminist Philosophy' in this volume.

References

Alcoff, L. M. and E. Mendieta (eds) (2003), 'Introduction: Identities: Modern and Post-modern,' in *Identities. Race, Class, Gender, and Nationality*, London: Blackwell.

Chodorow, N. (1989), *Feminism and Psychoanalytic Theory*, New Haven, Yale University Press.

Churchland, P. M. and P. S. Churchland (1998), 'Could a Machine Think?' in P. M. Churchland and P. S. Churchland (eds) (1998), *On the Contrary. Critical Essays, 1987–1997*, Cambridge: MIT Press, pp. 47–63.

Churchland, P. M. (1998). 'A Deeper Unity: Some Feyerabendian Themes in Neurocomputational Form,' in P. M. Churchland and P. S. Churchland (eds) (1998), *On the Contrary. Critical Essays, 1987–1997*, Cambridge: MIT Press, pp. 257–79.

Cixous, H. (1986), *The Newly Born Woman*, trans. B. Wing, Minneapolis: University of Minnesota Press.

Code, L. (1988), *What Can She Know: Feminist Theory and the Construction of Knowledge*, Ithaca: Cornell University Press.

Greisch, J. (1977), *Herméneutique et grammatologie*, Paris: CNRS.

Habermas, J. (1970), 'Towards a Theory of Communicative Competence', *Inquiry* 13 (1970): 360–75.

Habermas, J. (1971), *Knowledge and Human Interests*, trans. J. J. Shapiro, Boston: Beacon Press.

Habermas, J. (1975), *Legitimation Crisis*, trans. T. McCarthy, Boston: Beacon Press.

Habermas, J. (1981), *The Theory of Communicative Action, Volume 1. Reason and the Radicalization of Society*, trans. Thomas McCarthy, Boston: Beacon Press.

Habermas, J. (1990), 'Discourse Ethics: Notes on a Program of Philosophical Justification,' in S. Benhabib and F. Dallmayr (eds), *The Communicative Ethics Controversy*, Cambridge: MIT Press, pp. 60–110.

Husserl, E. (1936), 'Die Krisis der europäischen Wissenschaften und die transcendentale Phänomenologie. Eine Einleitung in die phänomenologische Philosophie,' *Philosophia* 1.

Irigaray, L. (1985a), *This Sex Which Is Not One*, trans. C. Porter with C. Burke, Ithaca: Cornell University Press.

Irigaray, L. (1985b), *Parler n'est jamais neutre*, Paris: Minuit.

Irigaray, L. (1991a), 'The Necessity for Sexuate Rights,' in M. Whitford (ed.), *The Irigaray Reader*, Oxford: Blackwell, pp. 198–203.

Irigaray, L. (1991b), 'How to Define Sexuate Rights?' in M. Whitford (ed.), *The Irigaray Reader*, Oxford: Blackwell, pp. 204–12.

Irigaray, L. (1991c), 'The Power of Discourse and the Subordination of the Feminine,' in M. Whitford (ed.), *The Irigaray Reader*, Oxford: Blackwell, pp. 118–32.

Irigaray, L. (1991d), 'Questions,' in M. Whitford (ed.), *The Irigaray Reader*, Oxford: Blackwell, pp. 133–9.

Irigaray, L. (1991e), 'The Three Genres,' in M. Whitford (ed.), *The Irigaray Reader*, Oxford: Blackwell, pp. 140–53.

Irigaray, L. (2001), 'The Representation of Women,' in Irigaray (2001), *Democracy Begins Between Two*, trans. Kirsten Anderson, New York: Routledge, pp. 174–84.

Lalande, A. (1900), 'Le Congrés International de Philosophie' *Revue Philosophique de la France et de l' Etranger*, 50: 481–508. (See also the entire address of M. E. Boutroux in *Revue de Metaphysique et de Monde* (1900) 8: 503–11.)

Lyotard, J.-F. (1984), *The Postmodern Condition: A Report on Knowledge*, trans. G. Bennington and B. Massumi, Minneapolis: University of Minnesota Press.

Magee, B. (ed.) (1971), *Modern British Philosophy*, London: Secker and Warburg.

Nancy, J.-L. (1991), *The Inoperative Community*, Minneapolis: University of Minnesota Press.

Outlaw, L. T. (1996), *On Race and Philosophy*, New York: Routledge.

Pears, D. F. (1957), *The Nature of Metaphysics*, London: Macmillan.

Quinton, A. (1966), 'Final Discussion,' in D. F. Pears (1996), *The Nature of Metaphysics*, London: Macmillan, pp. 142–63.

Rawls, J. (1971), *A Theory of Justice*, Cambridge: Harvard University Press.

Ricoeur, P. (1970), Freud and Philosophy, trans D. Savage, New Haven: Yale Univesity Press.

Rorty, R. (1991a), *Relativism and Truth. Philosophical Papers, Volume 1*, Cambridge: Cambridge University Press.

Rorty, R. (1991b), 'Habermas and Lyotard on Postmodernity,' in R. Rorty (1991), *Essays on Heidegger and Others. Philosophical Papers, Volume 2*, Cambridge: Cambridge University Press, pp. 164–76.

Taylor, C. (1992), *Sources of the Self: The Making of Modern Identity*, Cambridge, MA: Harvard University Press.

Young, I. M. (1990). *Justice and the Politics of Difference*, Princeton: Princeton University Press.

Zourabichvili, F. (1998), 'Deleuze et le possible', in E. Alliez (ed.) (1998), *Gilles Deleuze: Une vie philosopique*, Paris and La Pléssis-Robinson: Institut Synthélabo, pp. 335–57.

Twentieth-Century
Analytic Philosophy

How to recognize Analytic Philosophy

Constantin V. Boundas

The distinction between analytic and continental European philosophies is nowadays yawning – which does not mean that there have not been, until the very end of the twentieth century (or that they are not now) philosophers passionately defending it. It has become a liability for those who wish to maintain the philosophical identities that this exclusive disjunction proposes because what they maintain is demonstrably false. No one has come up with a list of necessary and sufficient objective criteria for grouping philosophers according to the disjuncts. Claims that it is possible to concoct such a list depended on ignorance of the fact that, whatever else the 'continental' philosopher is doing, she is also doing (conceptual) analysis; and that, whatever else the 'analytic' philosopher is doing, she is doing it in the context of an ongoing European philosophical tradition that knows no borders, because, as Husserl put it, 'Europe' is not a place on the map but rather an Idea expressing a preference for *logos* and *antilogos*, instead of *polemos*. Maintaining the distinction has become a liability to the extent that it prevents philosophers from realizing that the work that they are doing and the results that they are reaching are often being anticipated, tested, verified, or falsified in the 'laboratories' of the philosophical tribe that they consider alien to their own.

This does not mean that there is no division to be reckoned with. The entire twentieth century witnessed 'continentals' sometimes expressing strong preference for reading comics if the alternative were reading 'analytic' philosophy; and 'analysts' often hurling at the 'continentals' accusations of paradox mongering, vagueness, and deliberate (if not criminal) stirring up of fog, resulting in the blindness that Bishop Berkeley had already denounced. Division there has been, but no philosophically respectable distinction. It seems to me that we need to be reminded again that not every division reflects a genuine philosophical distinction. I think that the twentieth century for a long time maintained a division having grounded it on a pre-philosophical *doxa* mistaken for *epistēmē*. Evidently, the hold that *doxa* may have on people – including philosophers – can be very strong, stronger even than the hold of knowledge, because it reflects pre-philosophical context and assumptions, without which the work of the philosopher – or any kind of work – is not possible.

It is, therefore, reflection on *doxa* that is likely to yield a list of criteria capable of answering the question, 'how do we recognize "analytic" philosophers?' – provided that we keep in mind that *doxa* never yields an exhaustive set of necessary and sufficient conditions for the identification of anything. If, as I am inclined to maintain, the identity 'analytic philosopher' (no less than the identity of the 'continental philosopher') is doxic, the line of demarcation between the two camps will have more to do with extra-philosophical and pre-philosophical factors than those who toe the rival lines would like to admit. When all is said and done, I agree with Alan Montefiore's advice to the effect that 'any really adequate explanation of the differences between analytic and continental must be extremely complex; one no doubt would have to trace it out by reference to cultural factors, social factors, political factors – perhaps economic factors – and the inter-relationships of all these factors with each other' (Magee 1971a: 203). But I am more inclined than he seems to be to hold the power/knowledge nexus (the way that Michel Foucault accounted for it) responsible for the apparent coherence of the *doxa* in question.

Now, if it is granted to me that a pre-philosophical or extra-philosophical *doxa* is the key to the fuzzy identity that was paraded during the twentieth century under the name 'analytic philosophy,' I think that the eleven criteria that I list below offer an adequate sketch and plausible enough collective profile for those who did philosophy 'analytically.'

1. Philosophy, *index sui*. Geoffrey Warnock expresses this criterion by means of the following contrast:

> Philosophers in Continental Europe have traditionally been looked to for what one might call comment on the human predicament – taking moral standpoints, and very often political standpoints . . . Whereas both Austin and Moore regarded philosophy very much as an academic discipline, a subject with its own problems and its own standards, capable of proceeding quite independently of what was going on in the world at large. (Magee 1971b: 98)

What Warnock says about Austin and Moore applies to the majority of analytic luminaries – with the exception, perhaps of Russell, a few early logical positivists, and some of those who, after the 1950s, made political philosophy the center of their research and writing. It is worth noticing that Warnock's contrast between continental and analytic philosophies rests on a restricted notion of the 'world at large' – a world that, according to Warnock, was unapologetically bracketed by the champions of 'analytic' philosophy. If the 'world at large' comes to include – as it should – breakthroughs in physics and mathematics; if it comes to include the conflict of the grand ideologies that striated the space of the twentieth century; the political upheavals and the unequal distribution of labor and wealth; and the *Umwelten* of those who spoke in the name of philosophy, at the time – then any talk of bracketing the wider world betrays a shocking naivety. This naivety can be maintained only through a pre-philosophical belief-system that isolates the philosopher – bearer of opinions and speaker of conviction – from the philosopher/pope, who formulates dogma only as he speaks *ex cathedra*, from a standpoint that lies outside the 'world at large.'

2. Kantian heritage. The self-image that the Austro–Anglo–American analytic philosophy of the century projects testifies to the influence of the Kantian critique:

philosophy is essentially a critical – as opposed to constructive – activity. For example, Strawson's descriptive metaphysics (the attempt to uncover the general structure of our conceptual scheme) as opposed to any revisionary metaphysics belongs here (Strawson 1990). The same can be said for the two phases of Wittgenstein's philosophy, despite their striking dissimilarities: the drawing of linguistic boundaries – as in the early period – around all factual discourse; or – as in the late period – the drawing of internal boundaries between different areas of discourse are repetitions of the Kantian critical gesture – that of circumscribing the space of all rational discourse (Magee 1971c: 45–6). Similarly, the genealogy of preventing the factual, the ethical, and the aesthetic genres of discourse from running into one another can be traced back to Kant, without recourse this time to the Kantian doctrine of the faculties and the constructions of *sensus communis*. It is, finally, in the context of the Kantian heritage that Wittgenstein's *Tractatus* protects through silence the unthinkable, after clearly designating what is thinkable and sayable.

3. Iconoclasm. Here is Gilbert Ryle:

[The big metaphysicians of the past] set many examples of philosophizing which we are often scolded . . . .for refusing to follow: We, it is said, shirk giving concrete guidance; we do not preach; we are untheological; we are excessively microscopic; we neglect political problems; our moral philosophy is too thin; and in general, we stick too closely to the grindstone and go too little out in the woods. (Pears 1966: 164)

The possible ambiguity of the clause 'it is said' in the quoted passage is laid to rest by Ryle himself in a less qualified statement of the same text: 'So while we ought to realize how untheological our interests have recently become, we need not, I think, feel professionally apologetic about it' (Pears 1966: 160).

Lest it be thought that Ryle does not speak for the entire analytic tradition, here is Peter Strawson:

The reasons why the thing was exciting were really two. On the one hand, in the face of this refined examination of actual linguistic practice, a lot of traditional philosophical theorizing began to look extraordinarily crude . . . and it was of course extremely exhilarating to see these huge and imposing edifices of thought just crumbling away . . . to the tune of this fairly modest sort of piping. (Magee 1971d: 116)

4. The linguistic turn. The piety that characterized the continental, hermeneutic turn towards language in the twentieth century never became the motivation for the linguistic turn of the 'analytic' tendency. None of the grand claims of the continentals in the name of language 'interpellating' us to 'the house of being' was made by analytically inclined philosophers; in fact, such claims were dismissed as plain nonsense. Nor do we find among analysts the (opposite) obsessive fear of the continentals of being caught (for ever) inside linguistic and textual fishnets. That

the conceptual schema itself might or might not function as a prison house became the subject matter of considerable and never-ending disputation. The objective of the analytic investigation was never the linguistic sign per se; rather, the objective was the concept or the conceptual schema that linguistic signs convey. Anthony Quinton's classification of the varieties of conceptual analysis pursued by twentieth-century Austro-Anglo-American philosophers amplifies this point, as it shows the ambitions and the limits of the analytic preoccupation with language, and the modalities of analysis which sustained it:

> First, a conservative, even quietist, line could be taken to the effect that our existing conceptual apparatus is perfectly all right as it is and that the conflicts and perplexities that confront us from time to time arise from our incompetent handling of it. On this view the task of philosophy is the local and piecemeal clarification of our existing conceptual equipment and not its reform or replacement as a whole . . . Another point of view, at the opposite extreme, is the kind of conceptual libertarianism which Carnap seems sometimes to support. It holds that there is nothing to prevent your choosing any consistent conceptual scheme you like, except perhaps its complexity or unfamiliarity. Finally . . . it could be held that conceptual systems . . . are subject to the pragmatic test of trial and error. (Pears 1966: 148)

5. The 'what is x ?' question. 'Analysis' in the early part of the century did not shun the Platonic line of questioning, 'what is x ?' On the contrary, if the meaning of the analysandum, 'x,' could be captured in the analysans, 'a, b, and c,' an important part of the philosopher's task was thought to have been accomplished. Whether the analysans captured the ordinary use of the term/concept in question or whether it proposed how the term/concept should be used, the analysis intended was of single linguistic/ conceptual units – and not of longer syntagms of discourse. Only later on, when use became the key to meaning, the dogma of analyticity came under fire, and speech act theory began to thematize questions of contextual relevance and of the pragmatics of discourse – only then the Platonic question, without ever disappearing altogether, lost its earlier prestige and its hold upon the philosophers of the century.

6. Theory anxiety. Bernard Williams wrote in 'The Spell of Linguistic Philosophy' that one of the basic limitations of linguistic philosophy was the underestimation of the importance and irreducibility of theory (Magee 1978: 144). An inflated opinion regarding clarity and literal-mindedness has often been the result or the indispensable companion of this underestimation. In my opinion, many of the strategies and tactics of analytic philosophy can be traced back to this anxiety: the sharp distinction between the logic of discovery and the logic of proof that sustained, among others, Karl Popper's programme of falsifiability, and created so many unnecessary misunder- standings between British analysis and continental hermeneutics; the skepticism or even the rude dismissals by philosophers, inside educational institutions, of disciplines like sociology, psychology, psychoanalysis, political studies, critical theory or cultural studies; or the frequent inability to handle wholesale critique of institutions and social arrangements that required as their springboards counterfactual or utopian premises.

7. The doubting Thomas syndrome. Twentieth-century analytic philosophy never stopped asking the question which runs through British empiricism, 'what grounds do you have for your claim to knowledge?' And the most frequently entertained assumption was that all our empirical knowledge rests upon reports of direct experience. During the moments when the question of reference (to direct experience) receded behind the question of meaning, it was the parallel question 'what does it really mean to say so and so?' that led to the search for the real form of the fact recorded – the fact disguised behind systematically misleading expressions. It was on this soil that analysis was declared to be the proper method of philosophy – analysis of the forms of propositions in quest for 'the true underlying form and syntax of valid knowledge claims' (Magee, 1971e: 26). To disclose the pre-philosophical, doxic element at work here, it is enough to remember that the distinction between meaningful and meaningless expressions was really a distinction between *cognitively* meaningful and cognitively meaningless expressions – the latter being perfectly capable of conveying other, non-cognitive meanings. But then the distinction was really between expressions that could be proven either true or false and expressions that could not be proven either true or false. The pre-philosophical *doxa* behind this biconditional (meaningfulness iff epistemically warrantable as either true or false) was not expected to explain why indeed philosophy should be identified with a certain version of epistemology – at least not before the relaxation of the epistemological vise and the euphoria of pluralism that one finds, for example, in Wittgenstein's *Philosophical Investigations*.

8. Historical amnesia. Among the continentals, one often encounters the view that doing philosophy and creating philosophical concepts involves, as if it were for the first time, the entire history of philosophy, repeats it, and breathes new life into it. In fact, the continentals have often claimed that the history of philosophy is to the philosopher what the laboratory is to the scientist. Very few, if any, analytically trained philosophers can be found, in the twentieth century, making programmatic declarations of this nature. It is not as if they were unaware of the history of their discipline. Rather their awareness was of two kinds: either they confronted this history as a reservoir of cases of philosophy on holiday; or they chose from among its themes and issues those that helped them sharpen their analytic tools and bring about, with their help, a clearer formulation of the old problem and a more persuasive resolution of it. In the process, the specificity of the old problem, the antecedents and the consequents that tied it to its context and made it the problem that is was, were forgotten, as if the identity of the problem remained unaffected by its diachrony and only the solutions differed from each other, according to different degrees of plausibility. At its best, this approach resulted in the substitution of a *long durée* history by the short sequences and the short memory involved in the philosophical exchanges of the senior common room and the pages of leading periodical publications. At its worst, an amnesia of the historical dimension leaves one with the impression that a veritable war was declared against philosophy's past.

9. Micrology. Ryle's characterization of analytic philosophy as 'microscopic' names what, throughout the century, was analysis's strength and weakness: by meticulously circumscribing the problem that she was willing to discuss, by resisting the temptation to trace as many as possible of its relations with associated problems, by (artificially) isolating and putting it under the microscope, the analytic philosopher was often able to achieve refined analyses of enviable clarity, coherence, and persuasion. The diacritic nature of the philosophical problem subjected to analysis was not considered seriously – its being what it was not made to depend on the system of relations within which it was found. Analysis confronted problems and concepts as if they were substances. Assuming an aloof posture towards 'synthetic' philosophical endeavours or by postponing them *ad calendas* ('The time is not yet ripe for new global syntheses') (Pears 1966: 156), analysis was micrologic, syncopatic, episodic, and eclectic. Nevertheless, in moments when a synthetic vision was permitted to take hold, the preferred modality of discourse turned hypotactic – not paratactic: the 'if-then' connective triumphed over the conjunctive, 'and . . . and . . . and.' And it is a pity that, faithful to its occlusion of the genetic and the historical, analysis worked with a spatial and horizontal 'if . . . then,' rather than with a temporal and vertical one.

10. Mistaking ideologies for cognitive errors and nonsense. There is no doubt that the logical positivists (or at least, a number among them) wielded the verifiability criterion of meaning in order to distinguish epistemically respectable claims from the ideological rubbish that was piling up between the two World Wars. The falsifiability imperative of Karl Popper was also, even more explicitly, targeting these same threats. One could even think of the voices rising in favor of 'the dissipation of conceptual fog' as so many attempts to exorcise the cruel irresponsibility of the ideological. But what strikes us, *post facto*, in all that is the misplaced, 'rationalist' optimism that ideologies can fritter away if only we can uncover their feet of clay. The ignorance hidden behind this optimism as to how ideologies function and are maintained is patent. One could say that here the unexamined, pre-philosophical opinion about ideology masquerades as potent rationalist intervention.

11. The rhetoric of analysis. To the extent that philosophical analysis took itself to be a 'movement' with a method and perhaps a program of its own, one should not be surprised to hear that analysis had a rhetoric of its own. 'Rhetoric,' as I use the term here, is a style of thinking, talking, gesturing, and writing which by having been adopted by the members of a group gives its users an identity of their own. This style is not contingently related to the content of the group's beliefs; it does not behave according to the form/matter distinction, where form is imposed upon something neutral and unrelated to it. In 'rhetoric,' the style reflects the ideational, ethical, aesthetic, and political forces of the pre-philosophical system of beliefs captured in the philosophical content of the proposition or the argument under question. The style is not necessarily conveyed through language. The time is ripe for someone to undertake in earnest the research and documentation of the analytic style; the results will be precious. Here, I offer only three examples.

● The search for the counter-example, more often found among the formalists of the 'analytic' philosophy, the discovery of which would force one to withhold, without any further ado, the verdict of soundness from a chain of valid logical connections and inferences. The counter-example was to the logician what the falsifiabilty process was to the epistemologist.

- The distant (non-engaged and non-engaging) look or the expression of perplexity overlaid with a touch of irony, attempting to make the 'unwashed' realize how unfathomably unhelpful their contribution to the discussion was.
- The expression of satisfaction with one's discursive dexterity built into the blood-curdling adverb, 'surely,' that often prefaced the 'clincher' in an argumentative riposte; the humility-inducing discovery and unveiling of a 'howler' (much more devastating in the case that it was open to the accusation of a 'logical howler'); and the intolerance towards syntactically creative languages, dismissed as 'convoluted,' often justifying the riposte of the 'unwashed,' built into the witticism, *'je ne comprends pas; donc, vous êtes idiots.'*

References

Magee, B (ed.) (1971a), 'Conversation with Alan Montefiore,' in *Modern British Philosophy*, London: Secker and Warburg, pp. 202–17.

Magee, B (ed.) (1971b), 'Conversation with Geoffrey Warnock: The Philosophies of Moore and Austin,' in *Modern British Philosophy*, London: Secker and Warburg, pp. 83–99.

Magee, B (ed.) (1971c), 'Conversation with David Pears: The Two Philosophies of Wittgenstein,' in *Modern British Philosophy*, London: Secker and Warburg, pp. 31–47.

Magee, B (ed.) (1971d), 'Conversation with Peter Strawson,' in *Modern British Philosophy*, London: Secker and Warburg, pp. 115–30.

Magee, B (ed.) (1971e), 'Conversation with Stuart Hampshire. The Philosophy of Russell: I,' in *Modern British Philosophy*, London: Secker and Warburg, pp. 17–30.

Magee, B. (1978), 'Dialogue with Bernard Williams: The Spell of Linguistic Philosophy,' in *Men of Ideas: Some Creators of Contemporary Philosophy*, London: BBC, pp. 139–49.

Pears, D. F. (ed.) (1966), 'Final Discussion,' in *The Nature of Metaphysics*, London: Macmillan, pp. 142–64.

Strawson, P. [1959] (1990), *Individuals: An Essay in Descriptive Metaphysics*, London: Routledge.

Kant and the Analytic Tradition

Robert Hanna

Introduction

The influence of the eighteenth-century Critical Philosophy of Immanuel Kant (1724–1804) on the analytic tradition is both originative and protean.[1] Analytic philosophy historically emerged from an extended theoretical struggle with Kant's Critical metaphysical doctrine of *transcendental idealism*. But even more than that, the very idea of analysis can be made theoretically intelligible only in relation to Kant's basic Critical philosophical aims, methods, and theses. Quite ironically, however, precisely to the extent that the analytic tradition finally pulled itself free from its Kantian roots and became an independent philosophical enterprise closely associated with the methods, epistemology, and metaphysics of the natural sciences, it also rejected three assumptions that make philosophical analysis itself possible: (1) the analytic-synthetic distinction, (2) the *a priori-a posteriori* distinction, and (3) the necessary equivalence of apriority and necessity. So by the end of the twentieth century, the analytic tradition had effectively cut the ground out from under itself philosophically, if by no means institutionally. Or to put the same point more pointedly: the analytic tradition committed cognitive suicide by rejecting the very ideas of analyticity and analysis. This in turn strongly suggests that only by fully coming to terms with its Kantian foundations can the analytic tradition revivify itself in the twenty-first century.

A sketch of Kant's Critical Philosophy

Not surprisingly, Kant's Critical Philosophy is to be found primarily in his three *Critiques*: the *Critique of Pure Reason* (1781/87), the *Critique of Practical Reason* (1788), and the *Critique of the Power of Judgement* (1790). But the Critical Philosophy is not exhausted by the *Critiques*. Kant's *Prolegomena to Any Future Metaphysics* (1783), *Metaphysical Foundations of Natural Science* (1786), and *Jäsche Logic* (1800) all complement and supplement the first *Critique*; his *Grounding for the Metaphysics of Morals* (1785), *Religion within the Boundaries of Mere Reason* (1793), and *Metaphysics of Morals* (1797), similarly complement and supplement the second *Critique*; and his *Anthropology from a Pragmatic Point of View* (1798) and the unfinished and post-humously published *Transition from the Metaphysical Foundations of Natural Science to*

Physics (also known as the *Opus postumum*) together make up his final Critical reflections on human nature and physical nature.

But what *is* the Critical Philosophy? In a word, *it's all about us*. Less telegraphically put, the Critical Philosophy is a comprehensive theory of human nature, carried out by means of detailed analyses of human 'cognition,' human volition or 'the power of choice,' and human 'reason.' Cognition, volition, and reason are all 'faculties,' which in turn are innate, spontaneous mental 'capacities' or 'powers.' The innateness of a mental capacity means that the capacity is intrinsic to the mind, and not the acquired result of experiences, habituation, or learning. Correspondingly, the spontaneity of a mental capacity implies that the acts or operations of the capacity are:

1. causally and temporally unprecedented, in that (a) those specific sorts of act or operation have never actually happened before, and (b) antecedent events do not provide fully sufficient conditions for the existence or effects of those acts or operations,
2. underdetermined by external sensory informational inputs, even though they may have been triggered by those very inputs,
3. creative in the sense of being recursively constructive, or able to generate infinitely complex outputs from finite resources, and also
4. self-guiding.

Cognition is a faculty for the conscious mental representation of objects. Volition, or the power of choice, is a faculty for causing actions by means of conscious desires. And reason is a faculty for cognizing or choosing according to 'principles,' which are necessary and strictly normative rules of the human mind or human action, and constitute either theoretical laws or practical laws. Theoretical reason is cognizing that is aimed at *the truth of judgements*, according to necessary and strictly normative rules of logic and in particular according to the Law of Non-Contradiction, which says that only those propositions that are not both true and false can be true. Practical reason by contrast is choosing that is aimed at either *the instrumental good of actions* or *the non-instrumental good of actions*, and the latter according to strictly normative rules of morality and in particular according to the unconditional universal non-instrumental moral law or Categorical Imperative, which says that only those chosen acts whose act-intentions, when generalized to every possible rational agent and to every possible context of intentional action, are internally consistent and also coherent with the general aims of rational agents as such, can be morally good.

What makes the Critical Philosophy a specifically *critical* philosophy, however, is Kant's striking and substantive thesis – which amounts to a mitigated form of rationalism – to the effect that the human faculty of reason, whether theoretical or practical, is intrinsically constrained by the brute fact of human finitude, or our *animality*. More precisely, this is to say that our capacity of reason is intrinsically constrained by the special contingent conditions of all human animal embodiment: the faculties of 'sensibility,' and 'desire' or 'drive.' In what ways constrained? The answer is that human sensibility strictly limits our theoretical reason to the cognition of sensory appearances or phenomena, and that human desire or drive strictly limits our practical reason to choices that are bound up with our psychophysical and psychosocial well-being or 'happiness.' So rational creatures like us are nevertheless *essentially human*, and indeed *all-too-human*: 'out of the crooked timber of humanity, nothing straight can ever be made' (*IUH* 8: 23).

By sharp contrast, the theoretical reason of a divine cognizer, or 'intellectual intuition' (*CPR* B72), is conceivable by us; and such a being would know 'things-in-themselves' or objective 'noumena' – that is, supersensible Really Real objects whose essences are constituted by mind-independent intrinsic non-relational proper-ties – directly and infallibly by thinking alone. Similarly, the practical reason of a divine agent or 'holy will,' which is a *subjective* noumenon, is also conceivable by us; and such a being would do the right thing directly and infallibly by intending alone. Kant thinks that we cannot help being able to conceive such beings, and that an essential part of our rational intellectual and moral make-up is the fact that we are finite embodied minds who burden ourselves with invidious comparative thoughts about these non-finite, non-embodied minds. We crave a transcendent or superhuman justification for our finite embodied thoughts and actions. So for Kant, to be human is not only *to be* finite and embodied, and also *to know* that we are finite and embodied, but most importantly of all, *to wish that we weren't.*

On the theoretical side of the rational human condition, this inherent anthropo-centric limitation specifically means that human cognition is sharply constrained by three special conditions of sensibility: two formal conditions, namely the necessary *a priori* representations of space and time (*CPR* A38–9/B55–6*)*; and one material condition, namely affection, or the triggering of cognitive processes by the direct givenness of something existing outside the human cognitive faculty (*CPR* A19/B33). The basic consequence of these constraints is *transcendental idealism*. Transcendental idealism, as the name obviously suggests, is the conjunction of two sub-theses: (1) *the transcendentalism thesis* and (2) *the idealism thesis*.

The transcendentalism thesis says that the representational contents of cognition are strictly determined in their underlying forms or structures by a set of primitive or underived, universal, innate, spontaneous a priori human cognitive capacities, also known as 'cognitive faculties.' These cognitive faculties include (a) the 'sensibility,' or the capacity for spatial and temporal representation via sensory 'intuition' (*CPR* A22/B36); (b) the 'understanding,' or the capacity for conceptualization or 'thinking' (*CPR* A51/B75); (c) the power of 'imagination,' which on the one hand comprehends the specific powers of 'memory' (*A* 7: 182–5), 'imaging,' and 'schematizing' (*CPR* A137–42/B176–81), but also on the other hand includes the synthesizing or mental-processing power of the mind more generally (*CPR* A78/B103); (d) 'self-conscious-ness' (*CPR* B132) or the capacity for 'apperception,' which is the ground of unity for all conceptualizing and judging (*CPR* B406); and finally (e) reason, which as we have already seen is the capacity for logical inference and practical decision-making. The whole system of cognitive capacities is constrained in its operations by both 'pure general logic,' the topic-neutral or ontically uncommitted, *a priori*, universal, and categorically normative science of the laws of thought, and also by 'transcendental logic,' which is pure general logic that is semantically and modally restricted by an explicit ontic commitment to the proper objects of human cognition.

The idealism thesis says that the proper objects of human cognition are nothing but objects of our sensory experience – appearances or phenomena – and not things-in-themselves or noumena, owing to the fact that space and time are nothing but subjective *a priori* forms of our sensory intuition (Kant calls this 'the ideality of space and time'), together with the assumption that space and time are intrinsic relational properties of every object in space and time (*CPR* A19–49/B33–73, A369) (*P* 4: 293). Appearances, in turn, are token-identical with the intersubjectively communicable contents of sensory or experiential representations. Correspondingly, the essential forms or structures of the appearances are type-identical with the representational forms or structures that are generated by our universal *a priori* innate spontaneous human mental capacities: 'objects must conform to our cognition' (*CPR* Bxvi), and 'the object (as an object of the senses) conforms to the constitution of our faculty of intuition' (*CPR* Bxvii).

This leads directly to a new Kantian conception of rational knowledge as a reflective awareness of just those formal elements of representational content that express the spontaneous transcendental activity of the subject in synthesizing that content: 'reason has insight only into what it itself produces according to its own design' (*CPR* Bxiii). So Kantian rational insight is a special form of self-knowledge. More specifically, Kantian rational insight includes elements of conceptual 'decomposition,' of pure 'formal intuition,' and also of the 'figurative synthesis' or 'transcendental synthesis of the imagination' or '*synthesis speciosa*' (*CPR* A5/B9, B151, B160 n.). At the same time however, it is crucial to recognize Kant's fallibilistic thesis to the effect that rational insight yields at best only a subjective sufficiency of belief or 'conviction,' but not, in and of itself, objective 'certainty' (*CPR* A820–2/B848–0). The world must independently contribute a 'given' element, the manifold of sensory content, in order for knowledge to be possible. So for Kant rational knowledge is *mitigated* rational knowledge, that is, rational knowledge under *anthropocentric constraints*.

Putting transcendentalism and idealism together, we then have the complex conjunctive Kantian metaphysical thesis of transcendental idealism:

> Human beings can cognize and know only either sensory appearances or the forms or structures of those appearances – such that sensory appearances are token-identical with the contents of our objective sensory cognitions, and such that the essential forms and structures of the appearances are type-identical with the representational forms or structures generated by our own cognitive faculties, especially the intuitional representations of space and time – and therefore we can neither cognize, nor scientifically know,[2] nor even meaningfully assert or deny, anything about things-in-themselves. (*CPR* A369, B310–11)

But what is the *point* of transcendental idealism? Kant's immensely brilliant answer, worked out in rich (and occasionally stupefying) detail in the *Critique of Pure Reason*, is that transcendental idealism alone adequately explains how synthetic *a priori* propositions – that is, non-logically necessary, experience-independent truths – are semantically possible or objectively valid, and also how human freedom of the will is both logically and metaphysically possible. His two-part thought in a nutshell is this:

1. *the synthetic apriority thesis*, which says that all and only empirically meaningful synthetic a priori propositions express one or more of the transcendental conditions for the possibility of our human experience of objective appearances, and
2. *the transcendental freedom thesis*, which says that the synthetic *a priori* proposition (call it '*F*') which says that human noumenal (a.k.a. 'transcendental') freedom of the will exists, *cannot be scientifically known to be true*, yet (a) *F* is logically consistent with the true synthetic *a priori* proposition (call it '*G*') which says that the total mechanical system of inert macrophysical material bodies in phenomenal nature – bodies that are in fact constituted by fundamental attractive and repulsive forces under natural laws – have deterministic temporally antecedent nomologically sufficient causes, (b) the actual truth of *G* underdetermines the truth value of *F*, and (c) both the metaphysical possibility and the actual truth of *F* are presuppositions of human morality.

This shows us that the ultimate upshot of Kant's metaphysics is thoroughly anthropocentric and practical. Otherwise put, Kant fully rejects scientific or reductive naturalism, the view that science – more precisely, exact science, or mathematics-plus-physics – is, as Wilfrid Sellars most aptly put it, 'the measure of all things' (Sellars 1963a: 173). On the contrary, for Kant scientific reductionism leads directly to epistemic and moral skepticism (*CPR* Bxxix). Moreover, by a fundamental explanatory inversion or 'Copernican Revolution,' for Kant exact science is grounded on the transcendental metaphysics of rational human nature (Hanna 2006b). But it gets even better than this. In order to allow for the possibility of human freedom, he also holds that we must sharply *limit* the epistemic and metaphysical scope of exact science: 'I have therefore found it necessary to deny *scientific knowing* (*Wissen*) in order to make room for [moral] *faith* (*Glauben*)' (*CPR* Bxxx). Indeed, practical reason has both explanatory and ontological *priority* over theoretical reason (*CPrR* 5: 120–1). So, perhaps surprisingly, the key to Kant's metaphysics is his ethics.

The Neo-Kantian Link

By the end of the twentieth century, analytic philosophy comfortably dominated both the European and Anglo-American philosophical scenes (Soames 2003). But at the beginning of the century things were very different: the dominant philosophy was neo-Kantianism, and analytic philosophers were Young Turks. Neo-Kantianism was a German philosophical movement that ran its course from roughly 1870 to roughly 1945. It consisted in the close study and passionate promulgation of Kant's Critical Philosophy *plus* some editorial changes and critical updates, whereby certain troublesome concepts and doctrines (that is, things-in-themselves and their metaphysical status) were omitted or finessed, and whereby certain themes (that is, Kant's psychology, his idealism, or his philosophy of the exact sciences) were specially emphasized and further developed. The neo-Kantians' famous unifying slogan, 'Back to Kant!,' was the motto of Otto Liebmann's *Kant und die Epigonen* (1865). Other leading neo-Kantians included Alois Riehl, Hermann Cohen, Paul Natorp, Heinrich Rickert, and Ernst Cassirer.

Neo-Kantianism carried over into the early twentieth century in three significantly different versions: (1) a *science-oriented* neo-Kantianism (mainly centered in Marburg) that was fuelled by contemporary developments in the exact sciences, together with classical empiricism in the tradition of David Hume and J. S. Mill; (2) a *psychologistic* neo-Kantianism (mainly centered in Göttingen) that reacted against science-oriented neo-Kantianism and fused with the emerging science of empirical psychology; and (3) an *idealistic* neo-Kantianism (mainly centered in Heidelberg) that merged with elements of the Hegelian tradition. Psychologistic neo-Kantianism led to *phenomenology*. Idealistic neo-Kantianism led to *British Hegelianism*. And science-oriented neo-Kantianism led to *logical positivism*.

In this way, the mediating link between the Critical Philosophy and the analytic tradition is neo-Kantianism. Analytic philosophy emerged in the period from the *fin de siècle* to the mid-1930s by means of, on the one hand, a sharp reaction against neo-Kantianism and British Hegelianism, which pulled it in the direction of Platonism and radical realism, and on the other hand, the anti-metaphysical impetus provided by logical positivism, which, rather confusingly, also pulled analytic philosophy simultaneously in the opposite direction of conventionalism and anti-realism. This inner conflict in the foundations of analytic philosophy between Platonism and realism on one side, and conventionalism and anti-realism on the other, later worked itself out in the historical-philosophical careers of the paired concepts of *the analytic proposition* (a necessary *a priori* truth by virtue of logical laws and logical definitions – or perhaps 'meanings' – alone) and *analysis* (the process of knowing an analytic proposition). There will be more to say about these important notions below. The crucial point at the moment is that they make sense only in relation to a neo-Kantian and thereby Kantian backdrop. Without Kant's Critical Philosophy, *there would have been no such thing as analytic philosophy*.

What is Analytic Philosophy?

The analytic tradition is based on two core ideas: (1) that all necessary truth is logical truth, which is the same as analytic *a priori* truth, and that there are no non-logical or non-analytic necessary truths (the thesis of *modal monism*), and (2) that all *a priori* knowledge is knowledge of analytic truths and follows directly from the cognitive process of (2.1) decomposing analytic propositions into conceptual or metaphysical simples which are mind-independently real yet immediately and infallibly apprehended with self-evidence, and then (2.2) rigorously logically reconstructing those propositions by formal deduction from (a) general logical laws and (b) premises that express non-logical definitional knowledge in terms of the simple constituents (the thesis of *a priori knowledge as decompositional analysis*).

Both core ideas are explicitly anti-Kantian. For Kant holds (1*) that there are two irreducibly different kinds of necessary *a priori* truth, namely (a) logically or analytically necessary *a priori* truths, and (b) non-logically or synthetically necessary *a priori* truths (the thesis of *modal dualism*), and (2*) that *a priori* knowledge can be directed to either analytically or synthetically necessary *a priori* truths, but in either case, as we have seen already, this knowledge stems essentially from a reflective awareness of just those formal elements of representational content that express the spontaneous transcendental activity of the subject in cognitively synthesizing or mentally processing that content (the thesis of *a priori knowledge as self-knowledge*).

So what is analytic philosophy? The simple answer is: analytic philosophy is what Gottlob Frege, G. E. Moore, Bertrand Russell, and Rudolf Carnap did for a living after they rejected Kant. The subtler answer (because it includes the major contribution of Ludwig Wittgenstein) is that it is *the rise and fall of the concept of analyticity*.

Frege was undoubtedly the founding grandfather of analytic philosophy, by virtue of his bold and brilliant attempt to reduce arithmetic systematically to pure logic, whose theorems are all analytic (Frege 1879, 1953, 1964)[3] and thereby demonstrate (1) that Kant was miserably mistaken in holding that all arithmetic truth and knowledge is synthetic a priori, and (2) that arithmetic proof is a fully rigorous and scientific enterprise. This is the beginning of the project of *logicism*, which Russell, Wittgenstein, and Carnap all pursued in the first three decades of the twentieth century. Logicism provides the first half of modal monism. The second half of modal monism is provided by the rejection of the very idea of a synthetic *a priori* proposition. This was the unique contribution of Wittgenstein and Carnap, via the Vienna Circle and logical positivism, in the third and fourth decades of the twentieth century. Frege himself held, like Kant, that geometry is synthetic *a priori* (Frege 1953, 1971).

Kant, Moore, and the Nature of Judgement

In view of Frege's partial Kantianism, Moore was in fact the founding father of philosophical analysis. Paradoxically, however, Moore invented analysis not so much by writing about it, as instead by *living it*, that is, by virtue of his passionately and relentlessly deploying the method of decompositional analysis in his early philosophical writings (Langford 1952; Moore 1903, 1922), and by the powerful influence of his charismatic philosophical personality on Russell and Wittgenstein (Levy 1980).

Moore began his philosophical career as a neo-Kantian, and wrote his fellowship dissertation on Kant for Trinity College Cambridge under the direction of the neo-Kantian philosophical psychologist James Ward (Ward 1911), who had previously been Moore's undergraduate supervisor and mentor at Trinity. Ward himself had been equally influenced by Kant and by Franz Brentano, whose *Psychology from an Empirical Standpoint* (1874) had influentially resuscitated the Scholastic notion of intentionality, or the object-directedness of mind, and also controversially asserted that intentionality is the essence of all mental phenomena. Now according to Brentano, every act of intentionality – every mental phenomenon – has an intentional object or 'immanent objectivity.' Intentional objects in turn have the ontological property of 'inexistence' or *existence-in*, which means that their being necessarily depends on the being of the act of intentionality itself. So for Brentano the act of intentionality literally *contains* its intentional objects as intrinsic contents. Consequently, an intentional object cannot also exist outside the mind, as a thing-in-itself. It is therefore equivalent to what Kant called an 'appearance' (Brentano 1973: 81). One fundamental implication of Brentano's view is *logical psychologism*, which is the explanatory reduction of the necessary, *a priori*, and universal subject-matter of logic to the contingent, *a posteriori*, and relativized subject-matter of empirical psychology (Hanna 2006a: Chap. 1).

Like other young philosophers with minds of their own, Moore vigorously rejected the teachings of his teacher. Moore's specific act of rebellion against his Brentanian and Kantian mentor Ward was to develop a sharply anti-psychologistic, anti-idealistic, and radically realistic critique of Kant's theory of judgement. This critique was later published in his remarkable papers 'The Nature of Judgement' [1899] (1993b) and 'The Refutation of Idealism' [1903] (1993c). In the same year as 'Refutation,' Moore also published a brilliant, ground-breaking, and radically realistic (and in fact, moral intuitionist) extension of Kant's ethics in his *Principia Ethica*.

Moore's ostensible target in 'The Nature of Judgement' is the neo-Hegelian F. H. Bradley's theory of judgement in his *Principles of Logic* (1883). But the real target is Kant (Hanna 2001: 55–6). Moore's basic objection is that Bradley's – read: Kant's – theory of judgement involves a fundamental psychologistic confusion between two senses of the 'content' of a cognition: (1) content as that which literally belongs to the phenomenally conscious mental act of cognizing (the psychologically immanent content, or intentional act-content); and (2) content as that at which the mental act is directed, or 'about' (the psychologically transcendent content, or objective intentional content). The communicable meaning and truth-or-falsity of the judgement belong strictly to objective intentional content. According to Moore, the Bradley-Kant theory of judgement assimilates the objective intentional content of the judgement (that is, the proposition) to the act-content of judging. This is what, in the Preface to *Principia Ethica*, Moore glosses as 'the fundamental contradiction of modern Epistemology – the contradiction involved in both distinguishing and identifying the *object* and the *act* of Thought, 'truth' itself and its supposed *criterion*' (Moore 1903: xx).

Given this 'contradiction,' the communicable meaning and the truth-or-falsity of cognition are both reduced to the point of view of a single phenomenally conscious subject. The unpalatable consequences are that meaning becomes unshareably private (semantic solipsism) and that truth turns into mere personal belief (cognitive relativism).

For Moore himself, by contrast, judgements are essentially truth-bearing or falsity-bearing connections of mind-independent Platonic universals called 'concepts.' So concepts are decidedly not, as they were for Kant, simple or complex unities of mental content under the analytic and synthetic unities of self-consciousness. Nor do Moorean concepts and judgements relate to objects in the world, as concepts and judgements alike had for Kant, via directly referential, singular, existential, non-conceptual sensory mental representations, or intuitions. On the contrary and in explicit rejection of Kant's theory of judgement, for Moore complex concepts and judgements alike are mind-independent logically unified semantic complexes built up out of simple concepts grasped by direct Platonic insight. But not only that: according to Moore the world itself is nothing but a nexus of simple or complex concepts insofar as they enter into true propositions. No wonder then that – as Moore's fellow Cambridge Apostle and philosophical sparring partner, the logician and economist

John Meynard Keynes, later wrily reported – Moore once had a nightmare in which he could not distinguish propositions from tables (Keynes 1949: 94).

Moore's 'Refutation of Idealism' and his corresponding Aristotelian Society paper, 'Kant's Idealism' (1904), are even more explicitly anti-Kantian. Here Moore ingeniously doubly assimilates Kant's transcendental idealism to Brentano and to Berkeley by interpreting Kantian appearances as sensory intentional objects that 'in-exist' or are nothing but immanent contents of phenomenal consciousness. This of course completely overlooks Kant's crucial distinction between inner sense and outer sense, not to mention his equally crucial doctrine of empirical realism (*CPR* A370–2), and his Refutation of Idealism (*CPR* B274–9). And, regrettably, it also led to another hundred years of phenomenalistic interpretations of Kant's theory of appearances.

By vivid contrast to Kant's supposed phenomenalism, however, Moore's radical realism is the thesis that every object exists as the external relatum of the intentionality of a sheer transparent subjective consciousness. But this implies, in an odd reversal of Brentano's doctrine of mental phenomena – whereby intentional objects reduce to 'immanent objectivities' – that all intentional contents are now external intentional objects, and that therefore there will be as many mind-independently real objects as there are fine-grained differences between intentional contents. Moore therefore uses the transparency of consciousness to escape Brentano's Box of narrowly ideal phenomenal content, only to lose himself in a Platonic Looking-Glass world of unrestrictedly many real intentional objects, one for every possible act of thought – presumably even including the impossible ones that the White Queen boasted of having before breakfast (Carroll 1988). Brentano's student, the radical phenomenological ontologist Alexius Meinong, had gone through precisely the same looking-glass (Meinong 1960). Russell's great task as an analytic philosopher was to bring them all back alive.

Kant, Russell, and Logicism

Russell, like Moore, began his philosophical career as a psychologistic neo-Kantian, in an early treatise on the nature of geometry, *An Essay on the Foundations of Geometry* (1897), that was also based on *his* Trinity fellowship dissertation. The basic point of the *Essay* was to determine what could be preserved of Kant's Euclid-oriented theories of space and geometry after the discovery and development of non-Euclidean geometries. Russell had been supervised by Ward too, and by the mathematician and logician A. N. Whitehead. At the same time there was also a significant Hegelian element in Russell's early thought, inspired by his close study of Bradley's *Logic* and discussions with another Trinity man and fellow Apostle, the imposingly-named Scottish Hegelian metaphysician John McTaggart Ellis McTaggart. Despite being a close friend of Russell's, Moore wrote a sternly critical review of the *Essay* that accused Russell of committing the 'Kantian fallacy' of grounding *a priori* modal claims on psychological facts (Moore 1899). Moore's criticism seems to have almost instantly liberated Russell from his neo-Kantian and Hegelian beliefs. This, combined with the close study of Meinong's writings, led him to a radically realistic Moorean see-through epistemology and a correspondingly rich Looking-

Glass ontology of concrete and abstract real individuals, although he very prudently stopped well short of accepting the existence or subsistence of Meinongian impossibilia (Russell 1993: 169–70).

In any case, powered up by strong shots of Moore and Meinong, Russell's titanically brilliant, restless, and obsessive intellect (see Monk 1996: part I) was now focused exclusively on the logical foundations of mathematics, and deeply engaged with the works of George Boole, Frege, and the Italian logician Guiseppe Peano. By 1903 Russell had produced the massive *Principles of Mathematics*, and then by 1910, in collaboration with Whitehead, the even more massive *Principia Mathematica*. Above all, however, on the collective basis of his intellectual encounters with Kant, Bradley, Boole, Frege, Peano, Whitehead, Moore, and Meinong, he developed a fundamental conception of *pure or symbolic logic*. Pure or symbolic logic as Russell understood it, is the non-psychological universal necessary and *a priori* science of deductive consequence, expressed in a bivalent propositional and polyadic predicate calculus with identity as well as quantification over an infinity of individuals, properties, and various kinds of functions. Pure or symbolic logic in this heavy-duty sense has direct metaphysical implications. But most importantly for our purposes here, Russell's logic expresses the direct avoidance of Kant's appeal to intuition in the constitution of mathematical propositions and reasoning:

> [T]he Kantian view . . . asserted that mathematical reasoning is not strictly formal, but always uses intuitions, *i.e.* the *a priori* knowledge of space and time. Thanks to the progress of Symbolic Logic, especially as treated by Professor Peano, this part of the Kantian philosophy is now capable of a final and irrevocable refutation. (Russell 1996: 4)

The result of all these influences, together with Russell's maniacally creative intellectual drive in the period from 1900 to 1913, was a seminal conception of philosophical analysis based on a radically Platonistic, atomistic, and logicistic realism, according to which (1) not merely arithmetic but all of mathematics including geometry reduces to pure or symbolic logic, (2) propositions literally contain the simple concrete particulars (instantaneous sense data) and simple abstract universals (properties or relations) that populate the mind-independently real world (Russell 1981), and (3) both the simple concrete particulars and abstract universals are known directly and individually by cognitive acts of self-evident and infallible acquaintance (Russell 1995). In autobiographical retrospect, Russell explicitly identified his conception of analysis with his complete rejection of Kant's metaphysics: 'Ever since I abandoned the philosophy of Kant . . . I have sought solutions of philosophical problems by means of analysis; and I remain firmly persuaded . . . that only by analysing is progress possible' (Russell 1959: 14–15).

Kant, Wittgenstein, and the *Tractatus*

But that tells only *part* of the story about Russellian analysis. In fact Russell's program of philosophical analysis had fundamentally collapsed by 1914, mainly as the result of Russell's tumultuous personal and philosophical encounters with the young Wittgenstein:

> [Wittgenstein] had a kind of purity which I have never known equalled except by G. E. Moore. . . . He used to come to see me every evening at midnight, and pace up and down my room like a wild beast for three hours in agitated silence. Once I said to him: 'Are you thinking about logic or about your sins?' 'Both,' he replied, and continued his pacing. I did not like to suggest that it was time for bed, as it seemed probable both to him and me that on leaving me he would commit suicide. (Russell 1975: 330)

From 1912 onwards Wittgenstein was ostensibly Russell's research student, working with him on the philosophy of logic and the logical foundations of mathematics, and supposedly becoming Russell's philosophical successor. But the student, who was as personally difficult as he was philosophically brilliant, soon very helpfully pointed out to his teacher the irreversible philosophical errors in his work-in-progress *Theory of Knowledge*. This criticism changed Russell's philosophical life, and he abandoned *Theory of Knowledge* shortly thereafter:

> I wrote a lot of stuff about Theory of Knowledge, which Wittgenstein criticised with the greatest severity[.] His criticism . . . was an event of first-rate importance in my life, and affected everything I have done since. I saw he was right, and I saw that I could not hope ever again to do fundamental work in philosophy. My impulse was shattered, like a wave dashed to pieces against a breakwater. . . . I *had* to produce lectures for America, but I took a metaphysical subject although I was and am convinced that all fundamental work in philosophy is logical. My reason was that Wittgenstein persuaded me that what wanted doing in logic was too difficult for me. So there was really no vital satisfaction of my philosophical impulse in that work, and philosophy lost its hold on me. That was due to Wittgenstein more than to the war. (Russell 1975: 282)

Despite being shattered to pieces against a breakwater, nevertheless in typical Russellian fashion he promptly sat down and wrote *Our Knowledge of the External World* (1914) for his Lowell Lectures at Harvard. And leaving aside Russell's self-dramatizing, the simple facts of the matter are (1) that Wittgenstein had seriously challenged four fundamental elements of Russell's seminal conception of analysis, and (2) that Russell had no effective reply to Wittgenstein's challenges.

   Recall that Russell's notion of analysis in the period from 1900 to 1913 is logicistic, Platonistic, radically realistic, and grounded epistemically on a series of self-evident infallible acquaintances with the simple concrete or abstract constituents of propositions. One problem with this notion is that Russell never provides an adequate explanation of how a human mind in real time and space can be directly related to causally inert non-spatiotemporal universals (the problem of *non-empirical knowledge*). Another problem is how propositions construed as ordered complexes of individuals, properties, and relations, along with logical connectives or constants such as *all*, *some*, *and*, *or*, *not*, and *if-then*, can ever be formally or materially unified into coherent, semantically unambiguous truth-bearers (the problem of *the unity of the proposition*). A third problem is that the notion of a direct self-evident infallible acquaintance with logical constants, as if they were regular objects alongside real individuals, properties, and relations, seems absurd (the problem of *the nature of the logical constant*). And a fourth and final problem is that Russell never adequately clarifies the nature or status of logical necessity, and in particular whether logical truths are analytic *a priori*, synthetic *a priori*, or something else (the problem of *the nature of necessity*). To be sure, all four problems had already been handled by Kant by means of his transcendental idealism: non-empirical knowledge is based on transcendental reflection or self-knowledge; the unity of the proposition is based on the transcendental unity of apperception; logical constants are nothing but pure concepts of the understanding; and logical necessity is irreducibly analytic necessity, not synthetic necessity. But it was precisely the Kantian approach that Russell was completely rejecting. So these possible solutions to his problems were already ruled out, and he was thereby driven into a theoretical cul de sac.

Russell and Wittgenstein were personally divided by World War I. Russell very bravely professed pacifism in a nation hell-bent on smashing the Germans, and was imprisoned by the British government and lost his Trinity fellowship – a bellicose and by now philosophically alienated McTaggart working hard to bring this about – for his troubles. Wittgenstein went back to Austria and very bravely fought on the German side, and was imprisoned by the Allies in Italy after the German surrender for *his* troubles. Back in England, however, by the end of the Great War Russell had completely capitulated to Wittgenstein's conception of philosophical analysis. He officially recorded this conversion in his long essay, 'The Philosophy of Logical Atomism':

> The following is the text of a course of eight lectures delivered in Gordon Square London, in the first months of 1918, which are very largely concerned with explaining certain ideas which I learned from my friend and former pupil, Ludwig Wittgenstein. I have had no opportunity of knowing his views since August, 1914, and I do not even know whether he is alive or dead. (Russell 1956: 177)

Those 'certain ideas' which Russell learned from Wittgenstein were elaborately worked out in a stunningly unorthodox masterpiece written from 1913 to 18 and published in 1921, the *Tractatus Logico-Philosophicus*. More precisely, Wittgenstein's 'logico-philosophical treatise' offers a radically new conception of philosophical analysis, according to which:

1. not only mathematics but also metaphysics reduces to the propositions of logic (including both the truth-functional tautologies and the logico–philosophical truths of the *Tractatus* itself) together with factual propositions;
2. factual propositions and facts alike reduce to logically-structured complexes of ontologically neutral 'objects,' which can variously play the structural roles of both particulars and universals (including both properties and relations);

3. factual propositions are nothing but linguistic facts that 'picture' other facts according to one-to-one isomorphic correspondence relations;

4. all non-factual propositions are either (a) 'senseless' truth-functional tautologies expressing nothing but the formal meanings and deductive implications of the logical constants, (b) the logico-philosophical propositions of the *Tractatus* itself, or (c) 'nonsensical' pseudo-propositions that violate logico-syntactic rules and logico-semantic categories, especially including all the synthetic a priori claims of traditional metaphysics;

5. the logical constants do not represent facts or refer to objects of any sort (prop. 4.0312) but instead merely 'display' the *a priori* logical 'scaffolding of the world' (prop. 6.124), which is also 'the limits of my language' (prop. 5.6), and can only be 'shown' or non-propositionally indicated, *not* 'said' or propositionally described;

6. the logical form of the world is therefore 'transcendental' (prop. 6.13); and finally

7. the logical form of the world reduces to the language-using metaphysical subject or ego, who is not in any way part of the world but in fact solipsistically identical to the world itself.

Wittgenstein's radically new 'transcendental' conception of analysis is thus also radically ontologically ascetic, since ultimately everything logically reduces to one simple thing: the language-using metaphysical subject or ego. Indeed, it is by means of theses (5) and (6) that Wittgenstein directly expresses the surprising and often-overlooked but quite indisputable fact that the *Tractatus* is every bit as much a neo-Kantian idealistic metaphysical treatise directly inspired by Arthur Schopenhauer's *World as Will and Representation* (1819/1844/1859),[4] and thereby mediately inspired by Kant's first *Critique*,[5] as it is a logico-philosophical treatise inspired by Frege's *Begriffsschrift* and Russell's and Whitehead's *Principia*. In short, the *Tractatus* is fundamentally an essay in *transcendental logic*:

> The limit of language is shown by its being impossible to describe the fact which corresponds to (is the translation of) a sentence, without simply repeating the sentence. (This has to do with the Kantian solution of the problem of philosophy.) (Wittgenstein 1980: 10e)

The *Tractatus* ends with the strangely moving proposition, '*Wovon man nicht sprechen kann, darüber muss mann schweigen*': 'Whereof one cannot speak, thereof one must be silent' (prop. 7). What on earth does this mean? One possible interpretation, now known as the 'resolute' reading, is that proposition 7 is saying that the *Tractatus* itself (except for the Preface and proposition 7) is literally nonsense (see, for example, Diamond 1991). But against a Schopenhauerian and Kantian backdrop, this extreme and implausible reading can be smoothly avoided, because proposition 7 is then instead saying this:

1. that traditional metaphysics has been destroyed by the philosophical logic of the *Tractatus* just as Kant's first *Critique* had destroyed traditional metaphysics;

2. that the logico-philosophical propositions of the *Tractatus* itself *would have* counted as literally nonsensical because they are neither factual propositions nor truth-functional logical truths, *were it not for* the much deeper fact
3. that these Tractarian propositions are *self-manifesting transcendental truths in the Kantian sense* about the nature of logic, and thus have the basic function of constituting a logical stairway or 'ladder' between the factual natural sciences and ethics; and finally
4. that ethics consists exclusively in mystical feeling and noncognitive volitions (props 6.4–6.522), not propositional thoughts.

So, at the end of the *Tractatus*, Wittgenstein logically transcends scientific knowledge in order to reach the ethical standpoint. And this is precisely why he told the journal editor Ludwig von Ficker in 1919 that 'the book's point is an ethical one' (Brockhaus 1991: 296). As we have already seen, Kant makes essentially the same profound philosophical move in the B edition Preface to the first *Critique*: 'I had to deny scientific knowing (*Wissen*) in order to make room for [moral] faith (*Glauben*)' (*CPR* Bxxx).

Kant, Carnap, and Logical Positivism

Wittgenstein conformed his actions to his written words, and gave up philosophy for roughly ten years after the publication of the *Tractatus*. During Wittgenstein's 'silent decade' – equally but oppositely, Kant's own silent decade had immediately *preceded* the publication of the first *Critique* – Carnap was discovering his own voice. Falling into what will by now no doubt seem like a familiar pattern, and indeed very like Russell, Carnap started his philosophical career as a neo-Kantian philosopher of the foundations of geometry:

> I studied Kant's philosophy with Bruno Baum in Jena. In his seminar, the *Critique of Pure Reason* was discussed in detail for an entire year. I was strongly impressed by Kant's conception that the geometrical structure of space is determined by our forms of intuition. The after-effects of this influence were still noticeable in the chapter on the space of intuition in my dissertation, *Der Raum* [published in 1922]. . . . Knowledge of intuitive space I regarded at the time, under the influence of Kant and the neo-Kantians, especially Natorp and Cassirer, as based on 'pure intuition,' and independent of contingent experience. (Carnap 1963: 4, 12)

Carnap's progress away from Kant's metaphysics also followed the familiar dual pattern of (1) treating post-Kantian developments in the exact sciences as refutations of basic Kantian theses, and (2) replacing transcendental idealism with philosophical logic. By the end of the 1920s and into the early parts of the 1930s, Carnap had been heavily influenced by the Theory of Relativity and by the close study of Frege's writings, along with Russell's and Whitehead's *Principia*, Russell's *Our Knowledge of the External World*, and above all the *Tractatus*. Carnap's intellectual ferment was expressed in two important books, *The Logical Structure of the World* (1928), and *The Logical Syntax of Language* (1934).

The Logical Structure of the World played a crucial variation on Russell's Platonistic conception of philosophical analysis by turning it into *constructive empiricism*, which can be glossed as follows:

The natural world as a whole is the object of analysis. But the simples out of which the world is logically constructed are not Really Real mind-independent substances but instead nothing but subjective streams of experience and a single fundamental relation, *the recollection of similarity*.

Correspondingly, *Logical Syntax* converts Wittgenstein's transcendental conception of analysis into *logico-linguistic conventionalism*, which can be glossed this way:

There is no One True Logic, just as there is no One True Natural Language, but instead there are as many distinct logical languages as there are formal symbolic calculi constructed on the models of the *Begriffsschrift* and *Principia*, plus distinct axiom-systems, or distinct sets of logical constants, or distinct notions of logical consequence; and the choice of precisely which logical language is to be adopted as the basis of the exact sciences is purely a pragmatic matter (whether voluntaristic or social) having nothing to do with logic itself.

The overall result is that Kant's 'transcendental turn' from the apparent world to a set of *a priori* world-structures that are imposed on phenomenal appearances by our innate spontaneous cognitive capacities, is replaced by Carnap with a 'linguistic turn' from the apparent world to a set of *a priori* world-structures that are imposed on those phenomenal appearances by the syntax and semantics of our logical and natural languages. Needless to say, however, even *after* the linguistic turn, the gambit of imposing *a priori* logico-linguistic structures on phenomenal appearances remains basically a neo-Kantian and thereby Kantian move. Indeed, the very same Carnapian fusion of pure logic and epistemological neo-Kantianism is vividly evident in C. I. Lewis's *Mind and the World Order* (1929) and Nelson Goodman's *The Structure of Appearance* (1951/1966).

In any case, Carnap's *Logical Structure* and *Logical Syntax*, together with the basic writings of Frege, Russell, and Wittgenstein, and also Moritz Schlick's *General Theory of Knowledge* (1925), became the philosophical basis of the Vienna Circle, which flourished throughout most of the 1930s, until the coming-to-power of the Nazis in Germany caused the diaspora of its core membership to England and the USA. The political leanings of the inner circle of the Circle were radical socialist, universalist, egalitarian, and communist. So staying in Austro-Germany would have most certainly meant their cultural and intellectual deaths, and probably their actual deaths too.

The Circle philosophically professed logical positivism or logical empiricism, which is essentially the fusion of Carnap's constructive empiricism and logical convention-alism, plus the explicit rejection of Kant's notion of the synthetic *a priori*. According to Carnap, synthetic *a priori* propositions are meaningless because they violate rules of the logical syntax of language (Carnap 1959). And according to Schlick, the official founder and leader of the Circle, synthetic *a priori* propositions are meaningless because they are neither tautological logical truths (analytic truths) nor verifiable factual empirical truths, and analyticity and verifiability exhaust the possible sources of cognitive significance (Schlick 1949). The Carnap-Schlick attack on the synthetic *a priori*, plus constructive empiricism, plus logico-linguistic conventionalism, plus the general semantic thesis that all and only meaningful propositions are either analytic logical truths or else verifiable empirical factual propositions (the Verifiability Principle or VP), were all crisply formulated and beautifully written up for English-speaking philosophers in A. J. Ayer's *Language, Truth, and Logic* (1936).

It is, however, a notorious and serious problem for Ayer in particular, and for the Vienna Circle more generally, that the VP itself is neither an analytic proposition nor a factual proposition. Looked at with a wide lens, the problem of the logico-semantic status of the VP is merely a special case of Wittgenstein's earlier worry about the logico-semantic status of his Tractarian logico-philosophical propositions. A standard 'solution' to the special worry is to say that the VP is a *meta-linguistic* or *meta-logical* proposition: the VP is nothing but a further bit of language and logic that also happens to be about language and logic. But unfortunately that in turn only invokes an even more general and intractable worry about the logico-semantic status of meta-languages and meta-logics: *the logocentric predicament*.[6] The obvious way out of these problems would be to return to Kantian modal dualism and say that the VP is non-logically necessary or synthetic *a priori*. But of course this violates the official positivist ban on the synthetic *a priori*.

Kant, Quine, and the Analytic-Synthetic Distinction

Although the official or institutional acceptance of the basic tenets of logical positivism by the leading Anglo-American philosophy departments did not fully occur until the end of the 1950s, by 1945 all that actually remained of Kant's metaphysical legacy for philosophers in the analytic tradition were (1) the analytic-synthetic distinction, and (2) the general notion of the *a priori*, including the idea that apriority and necessity entail each other. It is to be particularly noted that both doctrines are intrinsic parts of the original foundations of analytic philosophy.

Yet these doctrines were to be repeatedly attacked from 1950 onwards until the end of the century by Carnap's protégé and greatest critic, W. V. O. Quine. In fact, Quine's 'Two Dogmas of Empiricism' (1951) effectively destroyed logical empiricism or positivism and the philosophical basis of the analytic tradition along with it. So the analytic tradition quietly committed cognitive suicide by undermining its own Kantian foundations. After reflecting on this striking fact, it will perhaps seem to be a very puzzling thing that the *institution* of analytic philosophy has been able to get along so well since 1950 without any philosophical foundations. A possible solution to this puzzle will be proposed later.

The two dogmas of logical empiricism attacked by Quine are (1) the thesis that there is a sharp and significant distinction between analytic and synthetic truths, and (2) the thesis of 'reductionism,' which says that every empirically meaningful proposition has a unique translation into a determinate set of logically independent atomic propositions in a sense-datum language. Now any proposition that expresses the unique translation of an empirically meaningful proposition into a determinate set of logically independent propositions in a sense-datum language is itself going to be an analytic proposition. So if (1) goes down, then (2) also goes down. Therefore the crucial dogma is the analytic-synthetic distinction.

Quine's argument against the analytic-synthetic distinction in 'Two Dogmas' is famously crisp and proceeds like the basic steps of a dance. He starts by defining analyticity as the truth of a statement by virtue of meanings alone, independently of fact. Then he discards *intensional* meanings – that is, meanings that (a) are essentially descriptive in character, (b) are underdetermined by reference, (c) uniquely determine cross-possible-worlds extensions of terms, and (d) directly entail the modal concepts of necessity and possibility – on the grounds that intensions are nothing but 'obscure intermediary entities' unhelpfully inserted between words and their Fregean reference or *Bedeutung*. Then he distinguishes between two types of analytic truth: (a) the truths of classical bivalent first-order predicate logic with identity, and (b) analytic statements that are not truths of class (a), but that can be systematically translated into truths of class (a) by systematically replacing synonyms with synonyms. Then he accepts the analytic truths of class (a) as provisionally unproblematic, and focuses on the analytic truths of class (b). Then he considers, case by case, three attempts to give a clear and determinate account of synonymy: definition, interchangeability, and semantic rules. Then he shows that each attempt ends in circularity by employing various notions that presuppose or entail the unreduced concept of intensional identity, and rejects them all. And then finally he concludes that without the provision of a non-circular account of synonymy, 'a boundary between analytic and synthetic statements simply has not been found. That there is such a distinction to be drawn at all is an unempirical dogma, a metaphysical article of faith' (Quine 1961: 37).

This argument changed the face of twentieth-century philosophy: yet it is a *very* bad argument. The many problems with it can be sorted into two sorts: (1) those having to do with whether his argument actually applies to *Kant's* analytic-synthetic distinction, and (b) those having to do with the soundness of his argument against the logical positivists' analytic-synthetic distinction.

1. Quine's argument clearly does not apply to Kant's analytic-synthetic distinction, for two reasons. First, Quine says that a statement is analytic if and only if it is true by virtue of meanings independently of fact. But for Kant, this gloss would also hold true of synthetic *a priori* propositions, because (a) 'meanings' for him include both concepts and *intuitions*, (b) synthetic apriority is defined in terms of a proposition's semantic dependence on pure intuitions, and (c) Quine presupposes without argument that there are no such things as synthetic *a priori* propositions. Kant would therefore reject the 'if' part of Quine's definition of analyticity. Second, according to Kant, a proposition is analytic if and only if it is necessarily true by virtue of intrinsic structural semantic relations between conceptual intensions. Since Quine will not countenance intrinsically structured intensions as meanings, this implies that Kant would also reject the 'only if' part of Quine's definition of analyticity. Indeed, since Quine rejects all semantic appeals to intensions from the outset, his attack on analyticity simply cannot apply to Kant's theory.

2. Furthermore Quine's argument is clearly unsound, for four reasons. First, since

he explicitly *accepts* analytic propositions of class (a), it is false to say that no sharp boundary can be found between analytic and synthetic statements. For there *is* by Quine's own reckoning a sharp boundary between analytic truths of class (a) and all other truths. Second, as J. J. Katz points out, even if we focus exclusively on analytic truths of class (b), those based on synonymy, the argument against the intelligibility of such truths is based entirely on an argument by cases, and Quine never gives an argument to show that his set of cases is exhaustive (Katz 1986: 28–32). Third, as H. P. Grice and P. F. Strawson argue, even if we grant that Quine has shown that *every possible* attempt to define analyticity in terms of synonymy for cases of class (b) ends in circularity with respect to the notion of intensional identity, he still has not shown that an explanation of analyticity in terms of a circular network of irreducibly intensional notions is a philosophically *bad* thing: philosophical analysis can be a semantically *non-reductive* and *holistic* enterprise (Grice and Strawson 1956). Fourth and perhaps most damningly of all, Quine's arguments for the rejection of intensions are both insufficient and self-stultifying, because he himself covertly presupposes intensions in order to explain the analytic truths of class (a) (Hanna 2001: 175–80, and Strawson 1957).

So Quine's attack on the analytic-synthetic distinction does not actually apply to Kant, and is based on an unsound argument to boot. Still, the attack almost universally convinced analytic philosophers. For example, in a forty-year survey article on the philosophy of language and mind published in the *Philosophical Review* in 1992, Tyler Burge asserted that 'no clear reasonable support has been devised for a distinction between truths that depend for their truth on meaning alone and truths that depend for their truth on their meaning together with (perhaps necessary) features of their subject-matter' (Burge 1992: 9–10). This seems astounding when it is recalled that to reject the analytic-synthetic distinction is to undermine the foundations of philosophical analysis itself. Fortunately there was at least one prominent analytic philosopher after 1945 who was willing to challenge Quine's apostasy: P. F. Strawson.

Kant, Strawson, and Transcendental Arguments

At this point there is an important twist in the plot of our historical narrative: Strawson, the primary *defender* of philosophical analysis after Quine, was also a *Kantian* philosopher. But as we shall see, Strawson's highly influential version of Kantian philosophy nevertheless leaves twenty-first century Kantians with a fundamental leftover problem to solve.

Strawson initially worked in philosophical logic, was strongly influenced by the *Critique of Pure Reason*, and also wrote an important treatise in transcendental metaphysics. Trained at Oxford before World War II by neo-Kantians and British Hegelians, and – along with his Oxford contemporaries J. L. Austin, Ayer, Michael Dummett, Grice, and Gilbert Ryle – heavily influenced by the logico-linguistic tradition stemming from Frege, Russell, and Wittgenstein, Strawson was arguably the most important British philosopher from 1945 to the end of the century.

We have already seen that along with Grice, Strawson defended the analytic-synthetic distinction against Quine by developing a non-reductive and holistic conception of philosophical analysis (Strawson 1992). This in turn is intimately connected with Strawson's vigorous defense of irreducible conceptual intensionality in both logic and semantics, in *Introduction to Logical Theory* (1952), *Logico-Linguistic Papers* (1971), and *Subject and Predicate in Logic and Grammar* (1974). Here it is obvious that Strawson's line of thinking runs strongly parallel to Kant's theory of judgement, analyticity, and logic, which is also explicitly based on irreducible conceptual intensionality.

Irreducible conceptual intensionality is also a basic theme of Strawson's immensely influential book on Kant, *The Bounds of Sense* (1966). *Bounds* not only made it respectable for analytic philosophers to write books on topics in the history of philosophy; it also developed a highly original and still controversial interpretation of the first *Critique* that is at once semantically-oriented (Strawson treats Kant as a verificationist), anti-psychologistic (he rejects Kant's transcendental psychology), and anti-idealistic (he accuses Kant of Berkeleyanism).

The crucial move in *Bounds*, however, is to connect Kant's seminal idea of a 'transcendental deduction' or 'transcendental proof' (*CPR* A84–92/B116–24, B274–9, A734–8/B762–6) directly with the logico-semantic concept of a *presupposition* that Strawson had developed in *Introduction to Logical Theory*. The result is the more-or-less Kantian notion of a *transcendental argument*. Now a presupposition can be contextually defined as follows: A proposition Q presupposes a proposition P if and only if the truth of P is a necessary condition of the truth of Q and also a necessary condition of the falsity of Q. Thus P is a necessary condition of the meaningfulness and truth-valuedness of Q. So what then is a transcendental argument? In its general form it looks like this:

1. Assume either the truth or the falsity of the proposition Q, where Q is a contingent claim about the world of human experience.
2. Show that the proposition P is a (or the) presupposition of Q, where P is a claim that is necessarily true and *a priori* if it is true at all.
3. Derive the truth, and thus also the necessity and apriority, of P.

A transcendental argument is also an *anti-skeptical* argument when P states the logical denial of some skeptical thesis such as the Cartesian dream-skeptic's 'Possibly nothing exists outside my own phenomenally conscious states' (which is what Kant calls the thesis of 'problematic idealism' at *CPR* B274) and Q states a proposition that the skeptic herself also rationally accepts, such as 'I am conscious of my existence as determined in time' (*CPR* B275).

Strawson made essential use of transcendental arguments in his ground-breaking book *Individuals: An Essay in Descriptive Metaphysics* (Strawson 1959: 40). Kant of course held that *his* transcendental deductions and proofs entailed transcendental psychology, transcendental idealism, and the synthetic apriority of P. Nevertheless Strawson ultimately rejects transcendental idealism and modal dualism alike in favour of a thoroughly anti-psychologistic, non-reductive, holistic, analytical realism about individual universals, individual material objects, and individual persons (Strawson 1992).

But there is a serious worry about Strawson's key notion of a transcendental argument. It is arguable that step (2) will never work unless semantic verificationism is true, and further that verificationism is true only if transcendental idealism is true and *P* is synthetic *a priori* (Stroud 1968, and 1984: Chap. 4). If this criticism is correct, then either verificationism and transcendental idealism are true and *P* is synthetic *a priori*, or else transcendental arguments are invalid. Alternatively, if this criticism is not correct, then it must be shown how step (2) can still work without verificationism, transcendental idealism, or the synthetic *a priori*. This is an unsolved problem that all Kantian philosophers after Strawson must face up to.

Kant, Scientific Naturalism, and the *A Priori*

In *The Rise of Scientific Philosophy* (1951), the logical positivist and Vienna Circle inner-circle member Hans Reichenbach sketched an influential and widely-accepted history of the progress of modern philosophy that culminates with analytic philosophy, and ties it directly to the progress of the exact sciences. The basic idea is that philosophy is legitimate precisely to the extent that (1) it is analysis, and (2) it works on fundamental problems arising from mathematics and physics. This is an important historical thesis, not only because it resuscitates Locke's seventeenth-century conception of philosophy as an 'underlabourer' for the flagship sciences of the Scientific Revolution, but also and indeed primarily because it is directly connected with the thesis of scientific or reductive naturalism.

As we saw above, scientific or reductive naturalism asserts, in Sellars's excellent phrase, that 'science is the measure of all things' (Sellars 1963b: 173). More generally, scientific naturalism includes four basic theses:

1. *anti-supernaturalism*, or the rejection of any sort of explanatory appeal to non-physical, non-spatiotemporal entities or causal powers;
2. *scientism*, or the dogmatic thesis that the exact sciences are the paradigms of reasoning and rationality, both as regards their methodology and their content;
3. *physicalist metaphysics*, or the thesis that all the facts are reducible to fundamental physical facts; and
4. *radical empiricist epistemology*, or the thesis that all knowledge is *a posteriori*.[7]

Now each of the theses of scientific naturalism is flagrantly anti-Kantian, in that it is the direct contradictory of some basic Kantian doctrine. Thus thesis (1) directly contradicts Kant's theory of transcendental freedom. Thesis (2) directly contradicts Kant's doctrine that logic and ethics are the paradigms of theoretical and practical reasoning. Thesis (3) directly contradicts Kant's transcendental idealism. And thesis (4) directly contradicts Kant's theory of the *a priori*.

Quine was the leading scientific naturalist (Quine 1969; Fogelin 1997). But his confident assertion of scientific or reductive naturalism would not, perhaps, have convinced most mainstream analytic philosophers of its truth, without the additional support of the highly influential doctrine of *scientific essentialism* that was developed by Saul Kripke and Hilary Putnam in the 1970s (see Note 7 above). According to scientific essentialism:

1. natural kinds like gold and water have microphysical essences;
2. these essences are either known or are at least in principle knowable by contemporary natural science;
3. propositions stating these essences, such as 'Water is H_2O,' are necessarily true because statements of identity are necessarily true if true at all; and
4. essentialist necessary truths about natural kinds are knowable only *a posteriori*.

Unlike Quine, scientific essentialists are both scientific realists and also strong proponents of the idea that modal logic is the analytic philosopher's fundamental analytical tool. So exact science and modal logic are *really deep*. If scientific essentialism is correct, then not all necessary truths are *a priori* (and possibly even *all* necessary truths are *a posteriori*), and the very last substantive Kantian metaphysical and epistemological thesis in the analytic tradition goes the way of all flesh too.

We now have in place the means to offer a possible solution to the historico-philosophical puzzle described earlier. This puzzle was: how has analytic philosophy managed to get on so well institutionally since 1950 despite the fact that its Kantian foundations were undermined by Quine's attack on the analytic-synthetic distinction? And the possible solution I am proposing is: despite its foundational crisis, the analytic tradition has flourished since the middle of the twentieth century by affirming scientific naturalism, and by latching itself for dear life onto the high speed train of the exact sciences.

Kant and the Fate of Analysis

But is this high-speed train actually heading straight for a big smash-up? In 1947, Wittgenstein had precisely that thought:

> The truly apocalyptic view of the world is that things do not repeat themselves. It isn't absurd, that is, to believe that the age of science and technology is the beginning of the end for humanity; the idea of great progress is a delusion, along with the idea that the truth will ultimately be known; that there is nothing good or desirable about scientific knowledge and that mankind, in seeking it, is falling into a trap. It is by no means obvious that this is not how things are. (Wittgenstein 1980: 56e)

Let us suppose that Wittgstenstein is correct, and that analytic philosophy – as someone wittily wrote about the history of the nineteenth century – began with *Great Expectations* but ended with *Lost Illusions*. Nevertheless a positive moral can still be extracted from this otherwise downbeat story. Analytic philosophy *could* revivify itself in the twenty-first century by critically recovering its Kantian foundations, and by rethinking and rebuilding its own foundations in the light of this critical recovery.

What I mean is this. Analytic philosophers *could* directly engage with Kant's two revolutionary ideas (1) that natural science is ultimately all about the intrinsic structures and causal functions of a directly humanly perceivable macrophysical empirical reality, not about microphysical noumena and their humanly unobservable non-relational essences (let us call this Kant's *manifest realism*), and (2) that the exact sciences presuppose and are inherently constrained by rational human nature, and all theoretical reasoning including pure logic and mathematics is categorically normative at its basis, because practical rationality is explanatorily and ontologically prior to theoretical rationality (let us call this *the priority of practical reason over theoretical reason*). In these ways, it seems at least possible that the seemingly unbridgeable explanatory and ontological gaps that opened up in mid- and late-twentieth-century philosophy between the basic subject matters of post-Quinean analysis (the impersonal, unobservable, valueless, and amoral noumenal micro-world described by mathematical physics) and ordinary human experience (the common sense world of first-person experience, macrophysical objects, human values, and moral normativity) could ultimately close themselves up and become a single integrated set of facts about rational human animals and their macrophysical directly observable world. If so, this would in effect merge and reconcile the two otherwise seemingly incommensurable and unreconcileable fundamental conceptions of human beings and their world that – in another burst of inspired phraseology – Sellars evocatively called 'the scientific image' and 'the manifest image' (Sellars 1963b).

Kant dealt with essentially the same clash of fundamental philosophical images under the rubrics of *nature* and *freedom* (Hanna 2006b). And in that way, the possibility of integrating those images returns us full-circle to Kant's notion of philosophy as a self-critical *rational anthropology* (*JL* 9: 25–6). So it appears that the analytic philosophy has this fate, that either it will eventually achieve genuine autonomy as a form of rational anthropology in the Kantian sense, or else it will inwardly perish and become no more than a sub-department of the exact sciences. But the choice is entirely up to us.

Notes

1. For convenience, I cite Kant's works infratextually in parentheses. The citations normally include both an abbreviation of the English title and the corresponding volume and page numbers in the standard 'Akademie' edition of Kant's works: *Kants gesammelte Schriften*, edited by the Königlich Preussischen (now Deutschen) Akademie der Wissenschaften (Berlin: G. Reimer [now de Gruyter], 1902–). For references to the first *Critique*, however, I follow the common practice of giving page numbers from the A (1781) and B (1787) German editions only. I generally use the standard English translations, but have occasionally modified them where appropriate. Here is a list of the abbreviations and English translations of the works I cited or consulted in preparing this chapter:

     A Anthropology from a Pragmatic Point of View, trans. M. Gregor, The Hague: Martinus Nijhoff, 1974.

     CPJ Critique of the Power of Judgement, trans. P. Guyer and E. Matthews, Cambridge: Cambridge University Press, 2000.

     CPR Critique of Pure Reason, trans. P. Guyer and A. Wood, Cambridge: Cambridge University Press, 1997.

     CPrR Critique of Practical Reason, trans. L. W. Beck, Indianapolis: Bobbs-Merrill, 1956.

     GMM Grounding for the Metaphysics of Morals, trans. J. Ellington, Indianapolis: Hackett, 1981.

IUH 'Idea of a Universal History of Mankind from a Cosmopolitan Point of View,' in
Kant on History, trans. L. W. Beck, New York: Bobbs-Merrill, 1963, pp. 11–26.

JL 'The Jäsche Logic,' in *Immanuel Kant: Lectures on Logic*, trans. J. M. Young,
Cambridge: Cambridge University Press, 1992. pp. 519–640.

MFNS Metaphysical Foundations of Natural Science, trans. J. Ellington, Indianapolis:
Bobbs-Merrill, 1970.

MM Metaphysics of Morals, trans. M. Gregor, Cambridge: Cambridge University Press,
1996.

OP Opus postumum, trans. E. Förster and M. Rosen, Cambridge: Cambridge University
Press, 1993.

P Prolegomena to Any Future Metaphysics, trans. J. Ellington, Indianapolis: Hackett,
1977.

PC Immanuel Kant: Philosophical Correspondence, 1759–99, trans. A. Zweig, Chicago:
University of Chicago Press, 1967.

Rel Religion within the Boundaries of Mere Reason, trans. A. Wood and G. Di Giovanni,
Cambridge: Cambridge University Press, 1998.

2. Kant distinguishes carefully between (1) 'cognition' (*Erkenntnis*), or the conscious mental representation of objects (*CPR* A320/B376), which does *not* strictly imply either belief, truth, or justification (*CPR* A58–9/B83), and (2) 'scientific knowing' (*Wissen*), which *does* strictly imply belief, truth, and justification (*CPR* A820–31/B848–59). From this simple terminological point, however, it follows that to the considerable extent that the first *Critique* is all about the nature, scope, and limits of human *Erkenntnis*, then it is fundamentally a treatise in cognitive semantics, and *not* fundamentally a treatise in epistemology. See Hanna 2001, esp. pp. 18 and 30.

3. According to Frege in the *Foundations of Arithmetic*, a proposition is analytic if and only if it is provable either from a general law of logic alone, or from general laws of logic plus 'logical definitions.' One problem with this account is that unless general laws of logic are provable from themselves, they do not strictly speaking count as analytic. Another and more serious problem is that the precise semantic and epistemic status of logical definitions was never adequately clarified or settled by Frege; see Benacerraf 1981. But the most serious problem is that Frege's set theory contains an apparently insoluble contradiction discovered by Russell in 1901, as a direct consequence of the unrestricted set-formation axiom in Frege's *Basic Laws of Arithmetic*: *Russell's Paradox*, which says that the set of all sets not members of themselves is a member of itself if and only if it is not a member of itself.

4. Wittgenstein told G. H. Von Wright that 'he had read Schopenhauer's *Die Welt als Wille und Vorstellung* in his youth and that his first philosophy was Schopenhauerian episte-mological idealism' (Von Wright, 'Biographical Sketch of Wittgenstein,' p. 6). This is also fully explicit in Wittgenstein's *Notebooks 1914–1916*. See also Brockhaus 1991.

5. Wittgenstein read the *Critique of Pure Reason* in 1919 while interned as a POW at Como in Italy. See Monk 1990: 158.

6. The logocentric predicament says that logic is *epistemically circular*, in the sense that any attempt to explain or justify logic must presuppose and use some or all of the very logical principles and concepts that it aims to explain or justify. See Hanna 2006a, Chap. 3; and Ricketts 1985.

7. There are two ways of holding the thesis that all knowledge is *a posteriori*. One way asserts the existence of necessary *a posteriori* truths, and this is the doctrine of *scientific essentialism*, as defended in the 1970s by Saul Kripke and Hilary Putnam. See: Kripke 1993 and 1980; Putnam 1975a, 1975b and 1975c; Soames 2003, Vol. 2, Chaps. 14–17; and Hanna 1998. The

other way asserts that all truths are contingent and *a posteriori*, and this is the doctrine of *modal scepticism*, as defended by Quine in 'Two Dogmas of Empiricism' and *Word and Object*, especially Chaps. 2 and 6.

References

(For citations from the works of Kant, see the Notes.)

Ayer, A.J. [1963] (1952), *Language, Truth, and Logic*, New York: Dover.

Benacerraf, P. (1981), 'Frege: The Last Logicist,' in P. French (ed.) (1981), *Midwest Studies of Philosophy: The Foundations of Analytic Philosophy*, Minneapolis: University of Minneapolis Press, pp. 17–35.

Bradley, F. H. (1883), *Principles of Logic*, London: G. E. Stechert.

Brentano, F. (1973), *Psychology from an Empirical Standpoint*, trans. A. C. Rancurello et al., London: Routledge and Kegan Paul.

Brockhaus, R. (1991), *Pulling Up the Ladder: The Metaphysical Roots of Wittgenstein's Tractatus Logico-Philosophicus*, La Salle: Open Court.

Burge, T. (1992), 'Philosophy of Language and Mind: 1950–1990,' *Philosophical Review* 101: 3–51.

Carnap, R. (1937), *The Logical Syntax of Language*, London: Kegan, Paul, Trench, Trubner.

Carnap, R. (1959), 'The Elimination of Metaphysics through Logical Analysis of Language,' in A. J. Ayer (ed.) (1959), *Logical Positivism*, New York: Free Press, pp. 60–81.

Carnap, R. (1963), 'Intellectual Autobiography,' in P. Schilpp (ed.) (1963), *The Philosophy of Rudolf Carnap*, La Salle: Open Court, pp. 3–84.

Carnap, R. (1967), *The Logical Structure of the World*, trans. R. George, Berkeley: University of California Press.

Carroll, L. (1980), *Through the Looking Glass*, New York: Dial.

Diamond, C. (1991), *The Realistic Spirit: Wittgenstein, Philosophy, and the Mind*, Cambridge: MIT Press.

Fogelin, R. (1997), 'Quine's Limited Naturalism,' *Journal of Philosophy* 94: 543–63.

Frege, G. (1964), *Basic Laws of Arithmetic*, trans. M. Furth, Berkeley: University of California Press.

Frege, G. (1879), *Begriffschrift*, Halle: a/S.

Frege, G. (1953), *Foundations of Arithmetic*, trans. J.L. Austin, 2nd edn, Evanston: Northwestern University Press.

Frege, G. (1971), 'On the Foundations of Geometry,' in G. Frege (1971), *On the Foundations of Geometry and Formal Theories of Arithmetic*, trans. E.-H. Kluge, New Haven: Yale University Press, pp. 22–37; 49–112.

Goodman, N. (1966), *The Structure of Appearance*, 2nd edn, Indianopolis: Bobbs-Merrill.

Grice, H. P. and P.F. Strawson (1956), 'In Defense of a Dogma,' *Philosophical Review* 65: 141–58.

Hanna, R. (1998), 'A Kantian Critique of Scientific Essentialism,' *Philosophy and Phenomenological Research* 58: 497–528.

Hanna, R. (2001), *Kant and the Foundations of Analytic Philosophy*, Oxford: Clarendon/Oxford University Press.

Hanna, R. (2006a), *Rationality and Logic*, Cambridge: MIT Press.

Hanna, R. (2006b), *Kant, Science, and Human Nature*, Oxford: Oxford University Press.

Katz, J. (1986), *Cogitations*, New York: Oxford University Press.

Keynes, J. M. (1949), 'My Early Beliefs,' in J. M. Keynes (1949), *Two Memoirs*, London: R. Hart-Davis, pp. 78–103.

Kripke, S. (1993), 'Identity and Necessity,' in A.W. Moore (ed.) (1993), *Meaning and Reference*, Oxford: Oxford University Press, pp. 162–91.

Kripke, S. (1980), *Naming and Necessity*, 2nd edn, Cambridge: Harvard University Press.

Langford, C. H. (1952), 'The Notion of Analysis in Moore's Philosophy,' in P. Schilpp (ed.) (1952), *The Philosophy of G. E. Moore*, 2nd edn, New York: Tudor, pp. 321–42.

Liebmann, O. (1865), *Kant und die Epigonen*, Canstatt: Emil Geiger.

Levy, P. (1980), *Moore: G. E. Moore and the Cambridge Apostles*, New York: Holt, Rinehart and Winston.

Lewis, C. I. (1956), *Mind and the World Order*, New York: Dover.

Meinong, A. (1960), 'The Theory of Objects,' in R. M. Chisholm (ed. and trans.) (1960), *Realism and the Background of Phenomenology*, Glencoe: Free Press, pp. 76–117.

Monk, R. (1996), *Bertrand Russell*, London: Jonathan Cape.

Monk, R. (1990), *Ludwig Wittgenstein: The Duty of Genius*, London: Jonathan Cape.

Moore, G. E. (1899), 'Review of Russell's *Essay on the Foundations of Geometry*,' *Mind* 8: 397–405.

Moore, G. E. (1903), *Principia Ethica*, Cambridge: Cambridge University Press.

Moore, G. E. (1904), 'Kant's Idealism,' *Proceedings of the Aristotelian Society* 4: 127–40.

Moore, G. E. (1922), *Philosophical Studies*, London: Kegan Paul, Trench, Trubner.

Moore, G. E. (1952), 'Analysis,' in D. Schilpp (ed.) (1952), *The Philosophy of G. E. Moore*, 2nd, edn, New York: Tudor, pp. 660–7.

Moore, G. E. (1993a), *G. E. Moore: Selected Writings*, London: Routledge.

Moore, G. E. [1899] (1993b), 'The Nature of Judgement,' in G. E. Moore (1993), *G. E. Moore: Selected Writings*, London: Routledge, pp. 1–19.

Moore, G. E. [1903] (1993c), 'The Refutation of Idealism,' in G. E. Moore (1993), *G. E. Moore: Selected Writings*, London: Routledge, pp. 23–44.

Putnam, H. (1975a), 'Explanation and Reference,' in H. Putnam (1975), *Mind, Language, and Reality: Philosophical Papers, Volume 2*, Cambridge: Cambridge University Press, pp. 196–214.

Putnam, H. (1975b), 'Is Semantics Possible?,' in Putnam (1975), *Mind, Language, and Reality: Philosophical Papers, Volume 2*, Cambridge: Cambridge University Press, pp. 139–52.

Putnam, H. (1975c), 'The Meaning of "Meaning",' in H. Putnam (1975), *Mind, Language, and Reality: Philosophical Papers, Volume 2*, Cambridge: Cambridge University Press, pp. 215–71.

Quine, W. V. O. (1960), *Word and Object*, Cambridge: MIT Press.

Quine, W. V. O. (1961), 'Two Dogmas of Empiricism,' in W. V. O. Quine (1961), *From a Logical Point of View*, 2nd edn, New York: Harper and Row, pp. 20–46.

Quine, W. V. O. (1969), 'Epistemology Naturalized,' in W. V. O. Quine (1969), *Ontological Relativity*, New York: Columbia, pp. 69–90.

Reichenbach, H. (1951), *The Rise of Scientific Philosophy*, Berkeley: University of California Press.

Ricketts, T. (1985), 'Frege, the *Tractatus*, and the Logocentric Predicament,' *Philosophers' Annual* 8: 247–59.

Russell, B. (1897), *An Essay on the Foundations of Geometry*, Cambridge: Cambridge University Press.

Russell, B. (1914), *Our Knowledge of the External World*, London: Allen and Unwin.

Russell, B. (1956), 'The Philosophy of Logical Atomism,' in B. Russell (1956), *Logic and Knowledge*, London: Unwin Hyman, pp. 177–281.

Russell, B. (1959), *My Philosophical Development*, London: Allen and Unwin.

Russell, B. (1975), *Autobiography*, London: Unwin.

Russell, B. (1981), 'Knowledge by Acquaintance and Knowledge by Description,' in B. Russell (1981), *Mysticism and Logic*, Totowa: Barnes and Noble, pp. 152–67.

Russell, B. (1992), *Theory of Knowledge: The 1913 Manuscript*, London: Routledge.

Russell, B. (1993), *Introduction to Mathematical Philosophy*, London: Routledge.

Russell, B. (1995), *The Problems of Philosophy*, Indianapolis: Hackett.

Russell, B. (1996), *Principles of Mathematics*, 2nd edn, New York: W. W. Norton.

Schilpp, P. (ed.), (1952), *The Philosophy of G. E. Moore*, 2nd edn, New York: Tudor.

Schlick, M. (1949), 'Is There a Factual A Priori?,' in H. Feigl and W. Sellars (eds) (1949), *Readings in Philosophical Analysis*, New York: Appleton-Century-Crofts, pp. 277–85.

Schlick, M. (1985), *General Theory of Knowledge*, trans. A Blumberg. La Salle: Open Court.

Schopenhauer, A. (1969), *World as Will and Representation*, trans. E. F. J. Payne, 2 vols, New York: Open Court.

Sellars, W. (1963a), 'Empiricism and the Philosophy of Mind,' in W. Sellars, *Science, Perception and Reality*, New York: Humanities Press, pp. 127–96.

Sellars, W. (1963b), 'Philosophy and the Scientific Image of Man,' in W. Sellars (1963), *Science, Perception and Reality*, New York: Humanities Press, pp. 1–40.

Soames, S., (2003), *Philosophical Analysis in the Twentieth Century*, 2 vols, Princeton: Princeton University Press.

Strawson, P. (1952), *Introduction to Logical Theory*, London: Methuen.

Strawson, P. (1957), 'Propositions, Concepts, and Logical Truths,' *Philosophical Quarterly* 7: 15–25.

Strawson, P. (1959), *Individuals: An Essay in Descriptive Metaphysics*, London: Methuen.

Strawson, P. (1966), *The Bounds of Sense*, London: Methuen.

Strawson, P. (1971), *Logico-Linguistic Papers*, London: Methuen.

Strawson, P. (1974), *Subject and Predicate in Logic and Grammar*, London: Methuen.

Strawson, P. (1992), *Analysis and Metaphysics*, New York: Oxford University Press.

Stroud, B. (1968), 'Transcendental Arguments,' *Journal of Philosophy* 65: 241–56.

Stroud, B. (1984), *The Significance of Philosophical Skepticism*, Oxford: Oxford University Press.

Ward, J., (1911), 'Psychology,' in *Encyclopedia Britannica*, 11th edn, 29 vols, New York: Encyclopedia Britannica Co., vol. xxii, 547–604.

Whitehead, A. N. and B. Russell (1962), *Principia Mathematica*, Cambridge: Cambridge University Press.

Wittgenstein, L. (1980), *Culture and Value*, trans. P Winch, Chicago: University of Chicago Press.

Wittgenstein, L. (1981), *Tractatus Logico-Philosophicus*, trans. C. K. Ogden, London: Routledge and Kegan Paul.

Metaphysical and Moral Idealism

Leslie Armour

The metaphysical and moral idealism that dominated philosophy in Britain and North America in the last decades of the nineteenth-century reached its zenith in the early years of the twentieth-century. It then faced serious challenges, but it also received support from unexpected sources – first from physicists like Sir James Jeans and Sir Arthur Eddington and then from Kurt Gödel, thought by many to be the most original logician and mathematician of the century. Idealism's proponents continued to struggle, but at the end of the century the movement was showing signs of returning to its roots in reflection on the inter-relations of language and experience, as they were first expressed by James Frederick Ferrier (1854). John Haldane (1991) says, '[T]he ideas [Ferrier] expresses are suggestive of the sort of linguistic analytical "phenomenology" associated with Wittgenstein and Husserl.' This chapter traces the story of that idealism. A companion chapter by Nicholas Rescher deals with some interesting and more recent varieties of epistemological idealism.

The movement had its nineteenth-century roots in a critique of the Scottish philosophy of common sense and later of British empiricism and of the moral utilitarians, Jeremy Bentham and John Stuart Mill. It responded with a metaphysics of unity, an appeal to experience structured by reason, a morality based on self-realisation within a community, and a politics of responsibility that led on to the welfare state. It gained considerable momentum from the historical and scientific critiques of Christian revelation. F. H. Bradley abhorred the evangelical Anglicanism of his clergyman father; Bernard Bosanquet hoped to see the churches turned into museums; and J. M. E. McTaggart was an avowed atheist. But the idealist world view insisted that spirit was more real than matter. And ultimately it drew strength from the insistence of thinkers like John Polkinghorne (1998, 2004) on the religious significance of a Platonic realism in mathematics.

With rare exceptions, the creators of moral and metaphysical idealism sought to re-establish notions of community and responsibility that had been threatened by the social changes of the industrial revolution and to provide an insight into reality that would include but see beyond the scientific world picture. Idealism's immediate background was a revulsion at a Victorian society that amassed great wealth based on a rapidly growing scientific understanding applied to technology; and an empire having left the poor in a smoky poverty comforted by gin and beer. Ferrier began the movement in Scotland, but it was Thomas Hill Green who revelled in being a direct descendent of Oliver Cromwell who gave it its momentum. The urge to restore the lost hopes of the English revolution of 1640 and the democratic thrust of the American revolution of 1776 was in many writers not far from the surface.

Behind this was a mounting ambivalence about science. Science was transforming the world in a way that could ameliorate many social and personal problems, but it also separated people from their spiritual roots and their contact with whatever was more than human. The idealist philosophers hoped to re-open that contact without denigrating science.

As a movement that tried to reconcile conflicting patterns of ideas and promote tolerance while preserving a central sense of human dignity, the movement built on the tradition of the Cambridge Platonists of the late seventeenth century – especially Ralph Cudworth – and the Berkeleyan idealism in the eighteenth century. The movement was often called 'Hegelian' and Hegel's notion of unity developing out of opposites was central, but it was a humanised Hegel mixed with the English tradition of tolerance that carried the day. Many idealists believed in progress, but some had doubts. The preface to F. H. Bradley's *Appearance and Reality* (1897) tells us that 'the world is the best of all possible worlds and everything in it is a necessary evil.' Bradley lived on until 1924 insisting, equally, that 'in a world where all is rotten it is a man's work to cry "stinking fish"'.

As the twentieth century opened, the dominant thrust was hopeful. Josiah Royce (1901) adapted the mathematical infinity of Georg Cantor to support the notion of a genuine community of free human beings and, although J. M. E. McTaggart's politics were conservative,[1] his notion that, beneath the surface turmoil of experience, there was a timeless reality in which love prevailed expressed an Edwardian sense that, at bottom, everything was fine (McTaggart 1927). The personalist movement launched by Borden Parker Bowne (1908) in Boston and sustained in Methodist colleges across the United States, was brought to fruition by Ralph Tyler Flewelling (1926, 1952) at the University of Southern California, who harnessed Methodist enthusiasm to reason. Bernard Bosanquet's argument (1923) that the unity of knowledge would reveal an Absolute implied by scientific investigation sustained those who hoped that religion based on emotion might be replaced by a world view that would finally reveal the place of humanity in reality.

The ethic of self-realisation that went with this was based on metaphysics. The human being can, through knowledge, share in the infinity of the underlying reality and, as we expand our knowledge, we see that we are bound together as expressions of this infinity and we each have a duty to help the others achieve the understanding that will bring our potentialities to life. Within this framework could be found a variety of views. The American personalists took a strong view of individuality, though they did not deny collective responsibility. McTaggart found all reality in individual centres of experience, while Josiah Royce developed a philosophy centered on community. F. H. Bradley suggested that individuals did not have an ultimate reality and Royce was accused by his California-based contemporary George Holmes Howison (1902, and Buckham and Stratton 1934) of being in danger of losing the individual in the Absolute. World War I dampened hope, but idealists responded to the challenge. The last important work of Josiah Royce was *War and Insurance* (1914), an ingenious attempt to create a new world order in which war and the arms industry would become unprofitable.[2] John Watson's influential *The State in Peace and War* (1919) sought a model for an international order.

Changing views of logic and knowledge played important roles in the decline of idealism. Hegel's philosophy was based on a logic of concepts, not of propositions, and was a descendent of a logic of ideas which had been made use of by supposed empiricists like Locke as much as by rationalists like Descartes. But the logics of Russell and Frege – logics based on the structure of propositions – came to dominate the field. They were powerful tools for analysing arguments and made it appear that all necessary truths based on reason were logical tautologies, powerless to give us insight into reality. Idealists were aware of this. In 1903 Josiah Royce said, 'I think it probable that at least some of God's people will in the near future be saved in part by Symbolic Logic' (Clendenning 1985). He knew logic might prove to be the Achilles' heel of idealism (Royce 1951).

And, indeed, 'idealist logic' remains a subject of controversy. Despite important skirmishes into patterns of reasoning by Brand Blanshard and later by R. G. Collingwood, idealist logicians did not emerge to confront the new opponents in a very effective way. There have been more recent attempts to fill this gap (Armour 1971; Harris 1987; Allard 2005), but the work is no doubt incomplete. The fact that there may be concepts which are necessary for talking sense about the world leaves open the possibility of a logic which metaphysicians can use – a possibility explored in Leslie Armour's *The Rational and the Real* (1961).

Another major problem was that in the 1920s there was a calamitous loss of the major figures. Bosanquet, Bradley, and McTaggart died in three successive years: Bosanquet in 1923, Bradley in 1924, and McTaggart in 1925. John and Edward Caird, Josiah Royce, and George Holmes Howison died before or during World War I. J. H. Muirhead, chiefly a historian (and above all the chronicler of the history of English idealism) was almost 70, and J. A. Smith, one of the most promising of the next generation – though his work was largely left unpublished in the archives at Magdalen College Oxford – was over 60 when Bradley died. H. H. Joachim, still in his mid-fifties at the time, was described by T. S. Eliot (1988) as 'the best philosopher here [at Oxford],' but his great book on truth (Joachim 1939) made little impact. In Canada, John Watson was to live on another fifteen years, and John Macdonald was to go on much longer, but Watson's main work was completed, and Macdonald was isolated in Alberta (Armour and Trott 1981). James Edward Creighton, another Canadian idealist, who became the first president of the American Philosophical Association, died, like Bradley, in 1924.

Perhaps the most important cause of the idealists' problems was the notion that science provided the only route to knowledge of reality. In any case, idealism was widely thought to entail that the world depended on mind – ours, the Absolute's or God's – and science was thought to show that this was not so not least because we now know that mind itself is a latecomer on the evolutionary scene. Idealist scientists like Sir James Jeans and Sir Arthur Eddington argued that science supported them, and Bernard Bosanquet struggled to show that science was not threatened by idealism. Popularly, the subjective idealism of Bishop Berkeley (still strongly defended by A. A.

Luce in 1954) was not distinguished from the objective idealism of Hegel, for mind was seen as unfolding in the rational order of nature.

The principal players and movements

Oxford idealism was preoccupied always with unity. Some of the concern was practical. If politics was to be informed by learning, the dons had to reach out across class lines. The growing split between science and religion – Matthew Arnold's 'ignorant armies [that] clash by night'[3] – divided the university. Hegel's thought was seen as a source of unity, but his dialectical logic and dense prose had limited appeal for English ears accustomed to common sense and plain speaking.

Bradley's original argument was simple enough: to show the unity of the world you need only show that all attempts to divide things fail. They all involve relations, and relation is, said Bradley, a concept 'infected' with contradiction. If A and B are related, either the relation is a new term between A and B or it is just a property of A or B. In the first case more relations will be needed ad infinitum, and one will never get a connection; in the latter the terms are not related. Without exception, however, the idealists of the nineteenth century and early twentieth century questioned the intelligibility of Bradley's implied unity. McTaggart asked what one could say about a seamless and perfect unity. Indeed, as the twentieth century got under way, Bradley (1935) himself had doubts. He developed more sophisticated accounts of relations but in replying to a review he gave James Ward, a Cambridge idealist, hints of another metaphysic. He said the Absolute:

> realised perfectly in no one part of the universe . . . still is realised in every part, and it seems manifest in a scale of degrees, the higher of which comprehends the lower . . . The system of metaphysics . . . which I have not tried to write, would aim at arranging the facts of the world on this principle, the same principle which outside philosophy is unconsciously used to judge of higher and lower. (Bradley 1935: 232–9)

Bradley even called for a new religion based on a positive metaphysics.

Bradley's original argument led to what might be called 'reductive absolute idealism' – the position that all distinctions are mere appearances. The 'other metaphysics' was like Bernard Bosanquet's philosophy a constructive absolute idealism. Bosanquet's argument was that our serious knowledge forms systems. Science involves a continuous explanation which involves the universe without any gaps, history is a continuous story and societies are organic unities in which all the individuals find their individuality in their relation to others. The logic of such systems involves a world in which the parts are understood through the systems to which they belong.

McTaggart rejected the implied logic of both systems, and turned to pluralism. He insisted that the world must contain distinct individuals if only because each of us is a perceiver who sees the world from a distinct perspective. He thought, like his pupil Bertrand Russell, that we can talk sense about the world only by naming things and distinguishing them from other things by assigning each some items from our list of properties.

Josiah Royce sought a way out of these quarrels – a solution which would enable us to talk about the unity of the Absolute without losing the ability to discern and talk about discrete individuals. His earliest philosophical writings stressed unity – the very possibility of error, he argued, implies that truth is all-inclusive. But such a truth seems beyond knowledge and somehow stultifying if all genuine truth already exists. Royce began with the idea of knowledge as reflection. To know something is to reflect on it. But this seems to create an infinite regress. In the 'Supplementary Essay' to his Gifford Lectures (1901), Royce says that a universe, however unified, that includes self reflection generates an infinite series. To think about an object is to reflect, but reflection adds something new. If the world is a system and if infinity is essential to it, we must explain how infinity can be accommodated in any possible world.

Royce drew on Georg Cantor and Richard Dedekind and would have welcomed what Jules Richard and Kurt Gödel later had to say. Gödel, indeed, emerged as the most determined spokesman for a kind of mathematical Platonism which amounted to mathematical idealism. But before Gödel, Royce conceded that in several senses the infinite is not totalisable: it is an incompletable series because it consists of reality and our reflections on it. When we try to describe it we must reflect on those reflections – and so on ad infinitum. Its properties include the exhibition of Cantor's transfinite numbers, the integers and the larger set of the numbers which represent the points on the real line. These are more than a dense set. Between any two there is another number. But these do not exhaust the line. Some of the numbers – those which interested Dedekind most of all – are 'irrational,' that is, they are numbers which cannot be expressed as fractions. Such numbers have endless descriptions. The universe exceeds the possibilities of rational computability in just the way that Richard and Gödel would later suggest. Neither Royce nor Gödel would have said that the universe is anything but 'objectively there' or that it is itself irrational, only that the truth about it exceeds rational demonstration and cannot be summed to a final total. The universe is infinite in the central Cusanist-Cartesian sense: it exceeds all possible categories. In order to prove that the universe could be fitted into any set of categories, we would have to have a completeness proof for some system – at least, say, that of elementary arithmetic.

Dedekind had suggested, however, that there is some way of summing things short of counting them in an ordinary sense. This can produce what he called a 'cut.' One can divide numbers (however many there are) into two groups, those greater than x and those equal to or smaller than x. By using sophisticated techniques for making such 'cuts,' we can locate everything in sets. The sets can be manipulated by Boolean algebra and other devices. In short, we can find a property which runs through each system and touches every member without actually having to count all the members. Royce found a way of doing this for infinite totalities of things other than numbers. He starts with the simple map, one which contains itself. There is not only an infinite series, there is an infinite series of series. If the map is called N, there will be a series of maps, $N1$ which begins with the first representation, $N2$ which begins with the second representation and so forth. Each named series marks out an infinity of entities without counting them. We can refer to the whole series by a single name.

The basis of Royce's calculation is a simple analogy with the map. Suppose that there exists an infinity of real beings each of which (or whom) is a knowing agent. They must stand in some relation to one another; they must have some order in order to exist. Royce thinks that the mind of God is like the first map, the agents are like God in many respects – perhaps most – except that they hold subordinate places in the order. An infinity of entities can be ordered in this way by some orienting property. Such a plan touches everything by means of orienting things to some end without having to count them. The elements in this cosmic linkage are persons and Royce says that 'personality is an essentially ethical category.' But personal moral properties have a certain independence and all the conscious beings can be ordered in terms of them by divine providence. Later, Gödel, too, concluded that he could prove the existence of a being much like Royce's God (Sobel 1997: 241–52; Wang 1996).

Royce's later philosophy was influenced by a debate in Berkeley with John Watson and George Holmes Howison in 1895 and 1896. Royce struggled to accommodate individuals and to conceive the Absolute in a way that did not render individuality unimportant, but neither of his opponents found the changes altogether satisfactory. Watson, a Scot whose working life was spent at Queen's University in Canada, left his later comments on Royce in notes now in the archives in Kingston, Ontario.[4] Watson says:

> Shortly, Royce's Absolute comes to this: The Absolute has experience of the total reality or world. The Absolute thinks a Possible Reality which is wider than the total reality or world; the Absolute attends to or wills the total reality or world excluding all possible reality except this totality; in so willing the Absolute finds satisfaction in love.[5]

All this amounts, in Watson's view, to the picture of a tyrant God. Indeed Royce does say what Watson objects to most strongly:

> In this sense, then it is not I who win salvation, but God who works in me. The higher Self is originally not myself at all . . . This spirit is essentially from God . . . [It] is precisely so much of a man as is not his own but God's. (Royce 1901: 251)

Watson's conviction was essentially that selves cannot be arranged in an ultimate moral hierarchy. Each is infinitely valuable and an end in itself. Any God must therefore be understood as a community of moral equals. In the Christian incarnation God becomes one of us.

To Howison, too, the central argument with Royce was over moral theory. Howison believed that the moral order required every moral agent, no one is dispensable, but Royce said that the moral order 'did not require him [any particular agent] once . . . hence it may not need him 10 minutes along.'[6] So Howison said Royce's God is in these terms a moral monster for whom persons exist only as elements in the 'divine plan.' Howison always takes the Kantian position that morality depends on the notion that each rational agent is an end in himself or herself. Howison insists:

I might say in general that, whereas Berkeley's is a theological or theocentric idealism, and Kant's an anthropocentric one so far as it rests on theoretical reason or knowledge, but a theo-anthropocentric one, based on the *moral* world of mutually dutiful beings, so far as it concerns the world of ultimate or transcendent realities, mine is centred in the total 'City of God', the whole circuit of minds, God being included among them. I might therefore describe it as a socio-centric idealism . . . The experiences of the [totality] of minds constitutes the City of God. (Howison 1902)

Royce was not the last of the Absolute idealists. In the last quarter of the twentieth century, Timothy Sprigge (1983) returned to the questions that preoccupied the nineteenth-century idealists, though he has often given them a new twist. In the companion article in this volume Nicholas Rescher notes that Sprigge's work not only has resonances of Berkeley but goes back beyond him to Spinoza. One might add that Sprigge has affinities to both Royce and Bosanquet. Sprigge is a panpsychist and insists that mind is the inner essence of a reality which appears, nonetheless, to be physical in its apparent structure. Sprigge insists that something must lie behind the immediacies of phenomenal experience, for the immediately given does not seem coherent and self-sustaining. He says that to suppose a non-psychical nature is to suppose that something very unlike what we experience (and having evidently no tendency which follows from its accepted descriptions to produce anything like what we experience) nonetheless exists and does produce our experiences. The properties which one would have to assign to physical objects so as to make them independent of mind would have to be qualities which did not appear in experience or in thought and therefore would be basically unknown and unknowable. Sprigge's world 'consists of innumerable centres of experience each of which is the "in itself" of some physically ultimate particle or event.'

In the United States the personalists became the dominant idealist group, though Brand Blanshard, who had studied at Oxford in Bradley's time, continued to develop the theories of knowledge of the older idealists. He insisted, however, (Blanshard 1939) that he was a 'rationalist' rather than an idealist. The inter-war leaders of the personalist movement, Edgar Sheffield Brightman and Ralph Tyler Flewelling, the founding editor of *The Personalist*, were philosophers of religion and culture. Brightman, who began his career as a biblical scholar, had his personal faith shaken by the death of his young wife. He analysed (1930, 1940) the problem of God and evil and concluded that no God could eliminate evil because all systems, by reason of their logical ordering properties, excluded a 'dysteleological surd.' Bruce Marshall's novel *The Month of the Falling Leaves* (1963) chronicles the adventures of a young man who writes a thesis on the dysteleological surd and finds that it is a best seller in Poland. Several Methodist institutions, including Boston University, Ohio Wesleyan, and the University of Southern California cemented the association of personal idealism with denominational religion, creating almost the only case of a close association of a school of American philosophy with a religious denomination other than the traditional alliance between Catholics and Thomists.

Flewelling (1934) said he was 'more or less in sympathy' with Royce, Bosanquet and with Bosanquet's younger disciple Alfred Hoernlé who taught at Harvard and in South Africa. But his philosophy stresses the independence of particular selves. Like McTaggart, he saw the Absolute as logically empty, but his philosophy, unlike McTaggart's, is rooted in temporal experience. His philosophy entails a more traditional idea of the divine 'Intelligence' though, like Watson and Howison, he sees God as expressed through a community and his moral theories are close to theirs. The return to experience was carried on by William Ernest Hocking (1912, 1940) at Harvard. He tried to rescue elements in the Hegelian dialectic and to find a 'dialectic of experience.' Peter Bertocci (1952, 1970) continued the personalist tradition.

Idealism, Religion, and Science

The idealist metaphysics that descended from Hegel was replete with quasi-theological notions. The Absolute (despite Bradley's warnings and Bosanquet's doubts about religion) was widely taken as a kind of God. It had been explicitly tied to a reformed Christianity by John Caird and to evolutionary thought by Edward Caird. Caird's pupil John Watson carried such notions to North America where he proclaimed God to be community. The unfolding of the Absolute in history was thought to be a kind of theodicy: the evil in the world was a stage, a necessary unfolding on the way to a utopia or the perfected community imagined by Howison – a community which might well substitute for heaven. To non-idealists, this suggested that moral and metaphysical idealism was either at odds with science, an alternative world scheme, or, at best, a kind of allegory, a way of telling the story of science which only seemed to be more human and more closely tied to traditional Christian values. William Temple (1934) who became the Archbishop of Canterbury had been an Oxford don and developed an idealism that in many ways resembled Bosanquet's but denied that Christianity had been surpassed. As Absolutism gave way among many groups of idealist philosophers to pluralism and personalism, the picture changed. But there was no doubt that the American personalists with their Methodist connections were taken to be defending at least the remnants of mainline Protestant Christianity.

In fact, however, virtually none of the philosophers was openly critical of science (John Elof Boodin was an exception) and nearly all idealist philosophers wanted to build on science, not to supplant it. But they did believe that the world described by science was part of a larger whole and that reason might give us a glimpse of some properties of that whole. They looked for support of their views in elements of science. Bosanquet (1923) talked about relativity theory and its tendency to undermine the traditional subject-object dichotomy though not to undermine claims to objective knowledge; but though Bosanquet admired Samuel Alexander's (1920) *Space, Time, and Deity* he had doubts about attempts to use notions of evolution and cosmological development to justify metaphysics.[7] Bosanquet's vision of a unified understanding of science was developed by Errol Harris, who studied at Oxford and was directly influenced by the earlier Oxford tradition. The main thrust of Bosanquet's views on science re-emerged nearly two decades later in Harris's work (1954).

Sir Arthur Eddington's writings (1920, 1928, 1929, 1939) viewed physics as a grounding for metaphysics. Science, he thought, had disposed of the notion that the world consists of material particles in absolute space. Observers proved important in quantum theory (in a different way than they had in Einstein's relativity theories), and the disposal of absolute space seemed to tell against materialism and some kinds of mind-matter dualism. Eddington, no subjectivist, was a mathematical idealist who saw reality as an expression of an intelligence that thought in equations and made them the ultimate reality. Sir James Jeans said:

> The final truth about a phenomenon resides in the mathematical description of it . . . The making of models or pictures to explain mathematical formulae, and the phenomena they describe is not a step towards, but a step away from reality; it is like making graven images of a spirit. (Jeans 1930: 176–7)

This universe of 'pure thought,' he conceded, poses problems about time. He warned his readers, though, to be cautious of such generalizations.

Viscount Haldane (1921) was a little more cautious. In a long correspondence with Gustavus Watts Cunningham (1916–24) he explored the relation of the mind to reality as he saw it emerging in contemporary science. His claim, shared by Watts Cunningham, is that our knowledge shapes our consciousness of the world in a way which makes the two inseparable.

The most important mathematical idealist turned out to be Kurt Gödel who believed that the ultimate reality consists of mathematical entities (Gödel 1986, Yourgrau 1991, Wang 1996). He could not accept that mathematics is simply a set of rules which we create arbitrarily for, after all, we have no alternatives to the objects described in number theory. He saw his 'incompleteness' theorem (which suggests that we know more than we can prove) not as showing that there is anything arbitrary about our mathematical knowledge but as showing that mathematics outruns the merely human mind. His ideas are directly related to those that appear in the late works of Josiah Royce. Though Gödel never mentioned Royce, he did mention the Yale philosopher Wilmon Henry Sheldon (1954) and Brand Blanshard. Royce, however, drew on Georg Cantor and used arguments like those of Richard whose theories were clearly a precursor to Gödel's. Gödel believed that he could prove the existence of God and saw the material objects that appear in physical theories as 'postulates' of a physics that lacks the purity of mathematical truth.

John Elof Boodin criticised science but tried hard to integrate his philosophy with the cosmologies of his time. A hand-written note (1921) exposes the pith of his position more clearly than his main books (1925, 1934). In the note he argues that science has so far proved itself good at analysis and at charting the dispersion of energy and the running-down of systems, but its only explanation for the apparent 'upward movement' of evolution is 'chance.' He says chance cannot be a sufficient explanation.

Susan Stebbing (1937) thought Jeans and Eddington strayed beyond their field of competence. They misused language. She used a train of thought which can also be found in G. E. Moore's defence of common sense and Ludwig Wittgenstein's *On Certainty*. Philosophers who maintain that time is unreal or that material objects are not (ultimately) 'real,' are casting doubts, she thought, on our common sense ideas of elephants, trains, and stars. But these concepts seem to work quite well. Their inadequacy is not noticed by scientific investigators who talk about the objects in their laboratories and the automobiles on the street in quite ordinary ways. Do idealist philosophers have additional knowledge or are they using words in an unusual way? Ms Stebbing thought they did not have additional knowledge.

Jeans and Eddington would have said she misunderstood them. Eddington used to tell his audiences that the table in front of him really consisted of things described by physics and consisted mostly of empty space, but he did not mean that the ordinary concepts had no use, only that their underlying reality was expressed by physical equations.

In addition to his critiques of science, Boodin wanted to claim that philosophy had knowledge of its own. Boodin's idealism recalls Plato and the Cambridge Platonists (he frequently cited Henry More) and associates God with the source of the multiplicity of forms which descend from the original unity of things. Boodin's philosophy resembles Whitehead's but while it is often philosophically more sophisticated it offers a challenge to the claims of science to describe reality adequately. Whitehead's (1929) Platonic eternal objects remained in the background but came to the foreground in Boodin's writings. But in his passion for community and individual self-realisation he was close to the personalists, especially Flewelling whom he knew well when they both lived in Los Angeles.

Idealism, History, and Hegel

All these thinkers – the Platonists whose philosophy came from mathematics and physics as much as the Hegelians whose metaphysics drew on more traditional argument from reason and experience – remained within the central tradition of moral and metaphysical idealism. R. G. Collingwood, too, began by trying to reconstruct the English idealist tradition in a way that drew heavily on Hegel, but he soon followed H. Wildon Carr (1924) and others who drew on Benedetto Croce. Hegel had made the unfolding of the Absolute Idea in time his central and continuing theme, but for Collingwood 'philosophy as history' came to have a different meaning. In his first major work (1924) he searched for the ways in which all the bits of human knowledge might fit together. But where Bosanquet had seen all knowledge as forming a seamless whole, Collingwood saw science, history and philosophy as forming an ascending hierarchy of forms. These forms represent structures of the human mind, and philosophy is about 'the self-recognition of mind in its own mirror.' Mind's knowledge of itself is the map of all the intelligible objects. Like Vico, Collingwood thought we can understand history because we make it and in so doing we learn about the nature of intelligible objects and begin to trace the map. Collingwood's God is always the universal foundation for intelligibility and not a distant spirit. In Collingwood's later works, especially the *Essay on Metaphysics* (1940), the historical and social workings of the mind are central. The limits of the human imagination – in the Coleridgean sense – are expressed at any historical moment by a set of absolute presuppositions which colour the ways in which the world is seen.

Collingwood and J. A. Smith were close and some of Collingwood's changing views came from Smith, who carefully delineated his own association with Croce and others

(Muirhead and Lewis 1965). Smith's Hibbert Lectures (1914–16) spelled out many of his interests. Collingwood's theory of truth and related logic of question and answer attracted attention (Armour 1969), and William Dray (1998) developed Collingwood's philosophy of history.

Though Collingwood had travelled a long way from Hegel, Hegelianism was in the background and more directly it was alive and well in the thought of G. R. G. Mure, who was just three years younger than Collingwood (though he lived on until 1979, thirty-seven years after Collingwood's death). Mure is best remembered for his study of Hegel (1950). But his *Retreat from Truth* (1958) outlines another strategy for dealing with the difficulties confronted by Collingwood: 'Hegel's solution was to contend that to recognise a limit is already to have surpassed it.' In confronting conceptual limits, we come to see the nature of what lies on the other side. Thus we might imagine a series of studies which examined religion, history, science, and language, and try to show how the limits expose relations with the others. Oxford idealism was entering its darkest days as Mure wrote but Mure said (1978) that H. H. Joachim struck him as a better philosopher than Bradley and Bosanquet.

Science and Mathematical Idealism

As the century ended, then, traditional notions of idealism continued to have life. There is a tendency of mathematical physics and logic to sustain forms of mathematical idealism, following the work of Gödel. And the philosophical role of a Platonic mathematical realism in the philosophy of religion appears in the work of John Polkinghorne (1998, 2004) and others. One may think that idealism's future developments are likely to lie in the analysis of logical and mathematical realism and in the analysis of the various forms of discourse. As John Haldane (1991) suggested, idealism has returned to its roots in the thought of James Frederick Ferrier (1854). A different combination of scientific interpretation and philosophical analysis has produced John Leslie's study (2001). Leslie argues that reality consists of infinite minds which may be presided over by something like Leibniz's God but may consist of many minds each of which has its own claim to divinity. The theory is a cross between Spinoza and McTaggart with strong Malebranchiste undertones.

The picture of the world that emerges from our sciences is nonetheless that of a world of entities which have an objective existence. But science has importantly developed in ways that Eddington, Jeans, and Gödel foresaw. The things presented to our senses are relative to our experiences of them but behind them are logical structures. These entities exist whether we think and speak about them or not, but they do not have univocal descriptions. To be known they have to be interpreted in ways that lead us past our subjective experiences, and there is always more than one interpretation. The interpretations are like the meanings of words. There is nothing to be known about a word except its syntactical properties and its meanings. So there is nothing to be known about the world except its interpretations and the logical properties of the entities open to interpretation, along with what can be known of the interpreters and their activities. The world is more like a book to be read – and a book that *is being read* – than it is like a collection of bits of matter (Armour 1992). But the world we live in seems also to demand moral discourse, and the horrors of the twentieth century convinced most people that though we might doubt that we know what is right, we certainly know that some things are evil. And this knowledge is as objective as any other.

The place for idealism, then, may well be in finding a way of describing the world so that we can relate all these modes of discourse. It does seem likely that the solution is that the world, as our science suggests, consists of entities that need to be read, that there is a way of orienting ourselves that gives sense to religion, and that the world exhibits objective intelligence in ways that make it possible for there to be objective moral knowledge.

Notes

1. He was by no means conservative in everything. He was a strong supporter of higher education for women and an early advocate of the rights of homosexuals, but was a determined patriot in World War I and generally a supporter of conservative politics.
2. Royce's plan was that countries would insure against war. Their premiums would be increased by actions that made war more likely. Taking part in an arms race might be one and adopting bellicose policies another.
3. Arnold's 'On Dover Beach' had its roots in a sermon by John Henry Newman that reflected the nineteenth-century struggles in Oxford.
4. Most of this material is in Box 6 of the collection 1064.1; some is in Box 10 of 1064. Much of it is part of a large body of material rescued from a chicken coop in the early 1990s.
5. Archive 1064 Box 10, File 1, p. 26 (pages are un-numbered).
6. Howison Archives, Bancroft Library, the University of California, Berkeley. The letter is undated but the archivists ascribe it to 1886.
7. The special Theory of Relativity made time relative to the observer. Later the general theory made it possible to think of a universal time determined by the motion of material particles. But Gödel (1949, 261–5) showed that for some rotational universes it is not possible to sum the motions of the particles. Objectivity depends on a shared mathematics and the way one thinks of 'subject and object' depends on the view one takes of the relativity problems.

References

Alexander, S. (1920), *Space, Time and Deity*, 2 vols, London: Macmillan.
Allard, J. W. (2005), *The Logical Foundations of Bradley's Metaphysics: Judgement, Inference, and Truth*, Cambridge: Cambridge University Press.
Armour, L. (1961), *The Rational and the Real*, The Hague: Martinus Nijhoff.
Armour, L. (1969), *The Concept of Truth*, Assen: Vangorcum; and New York: Humanities Press.
Armour, L. (1971), *Logic and Reality*, Assen: Vangorcum; and New York: Humanities Press.
Armour, L. (1992), *Being and Idea*, Hildesheim: Georg Olms.
Armour, L., and E. Trott (1981), *The Faces of Reason: Philosophy and Culture in English Canada, 1850–1950*, Waterloo: Wilfrid Laurier University Press.
Bertocci, P. A. (1952), *An Introduction to Philosophy of Religion*, New York: Prentice-Hall.
Bertocci, P. A. (1970), *The Person God Is*, London: Allen & Unwin; and New York: Humanities Press.

Blanshard, B. (1939), *The Nature of Thought*, London: Allen and Unwin.

Bogumil, G. (1994), *Bibliography of American Personalism*, Lublin: Oficyna Wydawnicza, Czas.

Bogumil, G. (1995), *American Personalism*, Lublin: Oficyna Wydawnicza, Czas.

Boodin, J. E. (1921), 'Notes on Science and Life,' appended to a typescript of an Aristotelian Society Paper read at 21 Gower Street, London, 7 March 1921, Boodin Archive, University of California at Los Angeles.

Boodin, J. E. (1925), *Cosmic Evolution*, New York: Macmillan.

Boodin, J. E. (1934), *God: A Cosmic Philosophy of Religion*, New York: Macmillan.

Boodin, J. E. (1939), *The Social Mind*, New York: Macmillan.

Bosanquet, B. (1889), *The Philosophical Theory of the State*, London: Macmillan.

Bosanquet, B. (1920), *Implication and Linear Inference*, London: Macmillan.

Bosanquet, B. (1923), *The Meeting of Extremes in Contemporary Philosophy*, London: Macmillan.

Bosanquet, B. (1934), *A History of Aesthetics*, London: Allen and Unwin.

Bowne, B. P. (1908), *Personalism*, Boston: Houghton Mifflin.

Bradley, F. H. (1893), *Appearance and Reality*, London: Swan Sonnenschein, 2nd edn 1897, Oxford: Clarendon Press.

Bradley, F. H. (1935), *Collected Essays*, 2 vols, Oxford: Clarendon Press.

Brightman, E. S. (1930), *The Problem of God*, New York: Abingdon.

Brightman, E. S. (1940), *A Philosophy of Religion*, New York: Prentice-Hall.

Buckham, J. W., and G. M. Stratton (1934), *George Holmes Howison: Philosopher and Teacher; a Selection from his Writings, with a Biographical Sketch*, Berkeley: University of California Press.

Carr, H. W. (1924), *The Scientific Approach to Philosophy; Selected Essays and Reviews*, London: Macmillan.

Clendenning, J. (1985), *The Life and Thought of Josiah Royce*, Madison: The University of Wisconsin Press.

Collingwood, R. G. (1924), *Speculum Mentis*, Oxford: Clarendon Press.

Collingwood, R. G. (1938a), *An Autobiography*, Oxford: Clarendon Press.

Collingwood, R. G. (1938b), *The Principles of Art*, Oxford: Oxford University Press.

Collingwood, R. G. (1940), *An Essay on Metaphysics*, Oxford: Clarendon Press.

Collingwood, R. G. [1942] (1998, ed. D. Boucher), *The New Leviathan*, Oxford: Clarendon Press.

Collingwood, R. G. (1946), *The Idea of History*, Oxford: Oxford University Press.

Cunningham, G. W. (1916–24), Correspondence with Richard Burdon Haldane (Viscount), Watts Cunningham Archives, Cornell University, Ithaca.

Cunningham, G. W. (1933), *The Idealistic Argument in Recent British and American Philosophy*, New York: Century.

Dray, W. (1998), *History as Reenactment*, Oxford: Oxford University Press.

Eddington, A. S. (1920), *Space, Time and Gravitation*, Cambridge: Cambridge University Press.

Eddington, A. S. (1928), *The Nature of the Physical World*, Cambridge: Cambridge University Press.

Eddington, A. S. (1929), *Science and the Unseen World*, New York: Macmillan.

Eddington, A. S. (1939), *The Philosophy of the Physical Sciences*, Cambridge: Cambridge University Press.

Eliot, T. S. (1988), *Letters, Volume 1*, ed. Valerie Eliot, London: Faber and Faber.

Ewing, A. C. (1933), *Idealism: A Critical Survey*, London: Methuen.

Ewing, A. C. (1957), *The Idealist Tradition from Berkeley to Blanshard*, Glencoe: Free Press.

Ferrier, J. F. (1854), *Institutes of Metaphysics*, Edinburgh: W. Blackwood.

Flewelling, R. T. (1926), *Creative Personality*, New York: Macmillan.

Flewelling, R. T. (1934), Letter of 5 March, 1934 to Norbert Oldgeering, University of Southern California Archives.

Flewelling, R. T. (1952), *The Person or the Significance of Man*, Los Angeles: Ward Ritchie Press.

Goldstein, R. (2005), *Incompleteness, the Proof and Paradox of Kurt Gödel*, New York: Norton.

Gödel. K. (1949), 'A Remark about the Relationship between Relativity Theory and Idealistic Philosophy' in P. A. Schilpp (ed.), *Albert Einstein Philosopher-Scientist*, La Salle: Open Court, pp. 555–62.

Gödel, K. (1986), 'Some . . . Theorems on the Foundations of Mathematics and their Philosophical Implications,' in S. Feferman, J. Dawson, S. Kleene, G. Moore, J. van Heijenoort (eds), *Collected Works, Volume 3*, New York: Oxford University Press, pp. 304–22.

Haldane, E., and J. Haldane [1899] (1991), *James Frederick Ferrier*, Edinburgh: Oliphant Anderson & Ferrier; reprinted Bristol: Thoemmes Press, with an introduction by John Haldane.

Haldane, R. B. (1921), *The Reign of Relativity*, London: John Murray.

Harris, E. (1954), *Nature, Mind, and Modern Science*, London: Allen and Unwin.

Harris, E. (1987), *Formal, Transcendental and Dialectical Thinking*, Albany: State University of New York Press.

Hocking, W. E. (1912), *The Meaning of God in Human Experience*, New Haven: Yale University Press.

Hocking, W. E. (1940), *Living Religions and a World Faith*, New York: Macmillan.

Hoernlé, R. F. A. (1920), *Studies in Contemporary Metaphysics*, New York: Harcourt Brace.

Hoernlé, R. F. A. (1927), *Idealism as a Philosophy*, New York: Harcourt Brace.

Hoernlé, R. F. A. (1939), *South African Native Policy and the Liberal Spirit*, Capetown: University of Capetown Press.

Howison, G. H. (1902), Letter of 25 February, 1902, Bancroft Library, University of California, Berkeley.

Jeans, J. [1930] (1937), *The Mysterious Universe*, Harmondsworth: Pelican Books.

Joachim, H. H. (1939), *The Nature of Truth*, London: Oxford University Press.

Leslie, J. (2001), *Infinite Minds, A Philosophical Cosmology*, Oxford: Clarendon Press.

Lewis, H. D. (ed.) [1956] (2004), *Contemporary British Philosophy*, London: Routledge.

Luce, A. A. (1954), *Sense without Matter*, Edinburgh: Nelson.

Marshall, B. (1963), *The Month of the Falling Leaves*, London: Constable.

McTaggart, J. M. E. [1921] (1927), *The Nature of Existence*, 2 vols, Cambridge: Cambridge University Press.

Metz, R. (1938), *A Hundred Years of British Philosophy*, London: Allen and Unwin.

Muirhead, J. H. (1931), *The Platonic Tradition in Anglo-Saxon Philosophy*, London: Allen and Unwin.

Mure, G. R. G. (1950), *A Study of Hegel's Logic*, Oxford: Clarendon Press.

Mure, G. R. G. (1958), *Retreat from Truth*, Oxford: Blackwell.

Mure, G. R. G. (1978), *Idealist Epilogue*, Oxford: Clarendon Press.

Paton, H. J. (1955), *The Modern Predicament: A Study in the Philosophy of Religion* [Gifford lectures delivered in the University of St Andrews, 1950–1], London: Allen and Unwin.

Polkinghorne, J. (1998), *Belief in God in an Age of Science*, New Haven: Yale University Press.

Polkinghorne, J. (2004), *Science and the Trinity: The Christian Encounter with Reality*, London: SPCK.

Royce, J. [1899] (1901), *The World and the Individual*, 2 vols, New York: Macmillan.

Royce, J. (1914), *War and Insurance*, New York: Macmillan.

Royce, J. (1951), *Royce's Logical Essays*, ed. Daniel S. Robinson, Dubuque: William C. Brown.

Sheldon, W. H. (1954), *God & Polarity, a Synthesis of Philosophies*, New Haven: Yale University Press.

Smith, J. A. (1914–16), *The Hibbert Lectures*. The second series of these unpublished essays is in the archives of Magdalen College, Oxford (Magdalen Mss. 1026 I-3). There are notes by R. G. Collingwood in the Bodleian Library, Modern Manuscripts.

Sobel, G. H. (1997), 'Gödel's Ontological Proof,' in J. J. Thompson (ed.), *On Being and Saying, Essays for Richard Cartwright*, Cambridge: MIT Press, pp. 241–61.

Sprigge, T. (1983), *The Vindication of Absolute Idealism*, Edinburgh: Edinburgh University Press.

Stebbing, L. S. (1937), *Philosophy and the Physicists*, London: Methuen.

Temple, W. (1934), *Nature, Man and God*, London: Macmillan.

Wang, H. (1988), *Reflections on Kurt Gödel*, Cambridge: MIT Press.

Wang, H. (1996), *A Logical Journey from Gödel to Philosophy*, Cambridge: MIT Press.

Watson, J. (1897), *Christianity and Idealism*, with an Introductory Essay by George Holmes Howison, New York: Macmillan.

Watson, J. (1919), *The State in Peace and War*, Glasgow: Maclehose.

Whitehead, A. N. (1929), *Process and Reality*, New York: Macmillan; and Cambridge: Cambridge University Press, revd edn 1978, David Ray Griffin and Donald W. Sherburne (eds), New York: Free Press (Macmillan).

Yourgrau, P. (1991), *The Disappearance of Time: Kurt Gödel and the Idealistic Tradition in Philosophy*, Cambridge: Cambridge University Press.

Anglo-American Neo-Idealism

Nicholas Rescher

Historically, idealists have emphasized and indeed often prioritized the role of our human mind-guided modus operandi over that of nature-at-large as basis for the philosophical understanding of ourselves and our place in the world's scheme of things. Idealism has many versions. To begin with, there is the *causal* idealism that looks to the productive role of mind or spirit in the constituting of nature.[1] Then, too, there is the *axiological* idealism that assigns a formative role to values.[2] There is also the *absolute* idealism which, despite Hegelian kinship, found its root inspection – at least among English-speaking philosophers – in Bishop Berkeley's combination of anti-materialism with a spiritualism of sorts. Such a position was represented in England by Bradley and Bosanquet and in the USA by Josiah Royce, Ernest Hocking and Wilbur Marshall Urban. But none of these three idealisms found widespread favor in the Anglo-American orbit in their original version. Instead, a quite different approach came to the fore – one that was based on the way in which we humans operate with concepts and the language in which they are incorporated.

This Anglo-American neo-idealism is grounded in nineteenth-century German post-Hegelian idealism. Hegel's own teaching was an ontologically based view of the operation of spirit and mind upon the historical stage of cosmic developments. Its defining motto was that the real is rational. But the German school of idealism that followed him returned to the standpoint of the earliest philosophers of pre-Socrates Greece who bifurcated the realm of nature (of *phusis*) and that of human contrivance (of *nomos*). And in shifting to an epistemological rather than ontological perspective, the founders of this approach insisted upon maintaining a fundamental distinction between the natural and the human sciences, especially in stressing the following points.

1. The natural sciences are *ahistorical* in their concerns. Carbon atoms behave always and everywhere as carbon atoms must. But the human sciences are inescapably historical: everything that is of human contrivance has it origin and its end in a context of historical developments.
2. The natural sciences are *value-free*, material nature has no place for judgements or worth. But human affairs are invariably value-invoking and human actions are guided by judgements of desirability and values.
3. Explanation and understanding in natural sciences proceeds with reference to

laws of nature. But in the human sciences explanation and understanding proceeds with reference to *social norms*: customs, habits, conventions, practices, and so on. Thus while the orientation of natural science is causal, that of the human science is hermeneutic.

4. Accordingly, the natural sciences are based upon outward-geared *observation* and their correlation and statistics. But the human sciences always involve an element of intuition – of empathy or sympathy or analogy to how things stand in relation to our own inward-geared *personal human experience*.

This in essence was the standpoint of the historically oriented German post-Hegelian idealists – of such thinkers as Wilhelm Dilthey (1833–1911), Wilhelm Windelband (1848–1915) and Heinrich Rickert (1863–1936).

The first of these – Dilthey – was also the most influential.[3] He elaborately defended the view that the human 'sciences' are so geared to cultural phenomena that their effective pursuit calls for an experientially internalized understanding. Only on the basis of lived experience can we achieve the empathetic understanding required for the explanation of human affairs. People are cognitively guided agents who function on the basis of meanings, intentions, values, purposes all of which need to be grasped 'from within' if one is to achieve an adequate understanding of human affairs.

In Germany itself, the 'human sciences' tradition was taken over and absorbed into a school of 'hermeneutically' oriented thinkers who effectively attenuated the link to 'science' and, taking textual studies in classical scholarship and religious exegesis as the guiding model for humane studies, saw textual interpretation rather than scientific explanation as the paradigm for the study of human phenomena. In the twentieth century, Martin Heidegger (1889–1976) and Hans Gadamer (1900–2001) became principal figures in this school of thought. But while this hermeneutic tradition ultimately came to exert considerable influence on the Anglo-American philosophical orbit in the late twentieth century, the development of Anglo-American neo-Idealism had also other sources of inspiration.

In some ways, this philosophical tendency is a phoenix-like revival of earlier approaches. In Britain Idealism entered the twentieth century through the Oxford neo-Hegelian movement of F. H. Bradley and Bernard Bosanquet, but the reaction against this from the Cambridge philosophers Bertrand Russell and G. E. Moore effectively put paid to this tendency. In the USA the initially influential Idealism of Royce and Hocking at Harvard was torpedoed by their colleagues Edwin Holt, William Pepperell Montague, Ralph Barton Perry and their allies at Chicago and elsewhere. The 1912 collective on *The New Realism* contributed to the influences in the USA which proved fatal to American flirtations with absolute Idealism there. Moreover, throughout the Anglo-American realm,[4] G. E. Moore's 'Refutation of Idealism,' published in his 1922 *Philosophical Studies*, exerted a great influence. Moore's classic essay evoked a widely ignored response in W. T. Stace's 1934 'Refutation of Realism' which argued with Berkeleyian inspiration that there could be no valid inference from the subjective principle impressions to anything objective above and beyond them. And so, during the inter-war era only a handful of philosophers – pre-eminently A. C. Ewing in Britain and Brand Blanshard in the USA – continued to uphold Idealist theses and theories. By the end of the second third of the twentieth century the standard line of Anglo-American philosophy was to characterize idea Idealism as anti-realism and to see this as caught in the dilemma between a virtually unintelligible obscurantism on the one hand and a flat out denial of the cognitive authority of science on the other. (The earlier work of Hilary Putnam exhibits this tendency.[5])

An early augury of changes to come were Nicholas Rescher's lectures on 'Conceptual Idealism' delivered in the School of Litterae Humaniores at the University of Oxford in the Trinity Term of 1970, subsequently published in a book of that title issued by Basil Blackwell in Oxford in 1973. Rescher had been a student of Stace's in the late 1940s, but his main influences were the British neo-Hegelians of the generation of 1880 and their German precursors. He argued that while positivists and materialists want to explain human phenomena by means characteristic for the exploration of inert nature, idealists hold that a proper understanding of the 'material' realm ultimately requires reference to characteristically human proceedings. Human actions – including our cognitive commitments and belief-acceptability determinations – must be explained in sui generis terms involving norms and values. And this even goes for our adequacy determinations regarding the explanation of processes and events existing in the realm of nature. The very concepts we use here are based on our understanding of human phenomena.

His strongly pragmatic sympathies led Rescher to acknowledge the special claims of the natural sciences to an objective validity betokened by the effectiveness in matters of prediction and control over nature. But nevertheless from a conceptual standpoint the thought instrumentalities they employ are in significant measure modeled on our human self understanding with respect to our cognitive modus operandi. Here at the hermeneutic level it is the conceptual rather than causal standpoint that is paramount. And Rescher integrated this conceptualistic approach with a revisiting of various key themes of traditional idealism, pre-eminently including cognitive systematization and the coherence theory of truth, as well as dialectics and its role in cognitive evolution.[6]

Although Rescher made the tactical mistake of defending Idealism by that name (a step that doubtless impeded the response to his views), he nevertheless proved to be right in thinking that if Idealistic ideas and doctrines were once again going to gain acceptance this would have to occur on the basis of restating the issues and reformulating the doctrines of Idealism in the idiom of the analytic mode of philosophizing that Idealism's arch-enemies, Russell and Moore, had inaugurated. Only by infiltrating Idealist ideas and views into the doctrinal and methodological position of its prime opponents could the doctrine be made accessible in the climate of thought prevailing in Anglo-American philosophy in the final third of the twentieth century.

This circumstance is also illustrated by the interesting segment of latter-day Idealism that is represented by the work of Joseph Margolis.[7] For Margolis, it is we humans and our works that stand at the center of the philosophical stage. And he echoes Dilthey's insistence on a definitive difference in conceptualization and approach between the natural and the human sciences when viewed internally from the angle of their own claims and aspirations. For viewed objectively, so Margolis urges, both are simply artifacts, though instrumentatively produced by humans in a changing historical context with a view to understanding and explanation. Natural science, too, is simply another human production in no way privileged over the rest. Thus for Margolis – unlike many of his more natural-science minded contemporaries – it is ultimately the human sciences that stand at the forefront and in this regard he drew heavily on the continental tradition of philosophy.

The idealistically oriented thinkers of the late twentieth century all in one way or another took up Dilthey's hermeneutic approach and insisted that human phenomena – our understanding of nature included – must be understood in fundamentally anthropocentric terms, be they cognitive (reasons, explanations), evaluative (values, aims, purposes), or social (norms, rules, conventions). However, they reinstituted this position by deriving ideas and inspirations from various sectors of important work in twentieth-century analytic philosophy – Carnap and C. I. Lewis for Rescher, Wittgenstein and Kripke on rule following for McDowell and, in the case of Brandom, David Lewis on convention, as well as John Dewey on social practices.

John McDowell's *Mind and World*, based on his 1991 John Locke lectures at Oxford, was a key part of this movement (McDowell 1996). As McDowell sees it the Cartesian separation of mind from matter is profoundly wrong because much of our thought operates in such a way as to be inseparable from their objects and would be unthinkable in the absence of their objects. But clearly this co-ordination can also be seen in reverse to mean that various objects of our cognition are irremediably mind-dependent and will not be as they are in the absence of mind. And of course just this is the salient doctrine of Idealism.

At the center of McDowell's thought is the post-Cartesian problem of integrating thought and physical nature. His project is to insert us – viewed as rational agents functioning in the world on the basis of beliefs and desires and deploying norms and values in shaping them (conceptualizing beings functioning in what Wilfred Sellars called 'the space of reasons') – into the natural world as science considers it, albeit as something of a separate and differential island. But though this island is distanced from the merely physical reality of inert matter, there is nevertheless a cognitive causeway that connects the two. In effect, McDowell seeks to achieve this connection by returning to Kant's distinction between spontaneity and receptivity and effectively co-ordinating these via the insight that 'the world' as we deal with it is an intellectual construction, so that by the time we confront it it is too late to ask how it can be that thought can be in touch with the world.

McDowell seeks for a middle ground of a mitigated naturalism 'that makes room for meaning' between the 'bald naturalism' of a scientism that leaves 'nature disenchanted' with regard to human interests on the one hand and on the other a 'rampant Platonism' committed to a nature-detached domain of norms, values, and reasons. As he sees it, human reason stands in the foreground for understanding pretty much anything that concerns ourselves. We understand and explain human affairs with reference to their position in the 'space of reasons.' Reaching back to earlier episodes in philosophical history, McDowell's position drew inspiration not only from Ludwig Wittgenstein's later ideas regarding the conventions that govern our communicative discourse about things but also from Immanuel Kant's distinction between the causality of reason and the causality of nature.

Robert Brandom's (Brandom 1994) position is in some ways akin to McDowell's but approaches the issues from a very different angle. With him, it is the social practices that underline our use of language in communication and their validation that stand in the foreground. As Brandom sees it, many of the objectively descriptive features of things must be understood in terms of our socially conditioned practical interactions with them. What appear as objectively descriptive features of things are in fact dispositional through the linguistically mediated responses they invoke in us. Accordingly what seems on first view to involve questions about reality turn out on closer inspection to come down to issues regarding our use of concepts in characterizing reality and thus to reflect what is – at bottom – a social practice of sorts with respect to of the linguistic domestication of concepts.

Brandom thus integrates Fregean concerns for the mechanisms by which language comes into contact with the extra-linguistic world with deliberations regarding conventionality as articulated by his teacher David Lewis. And, reaching back even further, Brandom brings into the foreground a conception of social practice as expounded by John Dewey, orienting it towards the inferential practices that govern our mechanisms of linguistic communication. Clearly insofar as our attempts to depict and explain this world we live in involve ideas geared to convention we return once more to the salient idealistic view that our grasp of nature is definitively mediated and in mentalistic terms of reference in a way that is not just mind-produced but mind-patterned. What thus links all of these diverse latter-day Idealists together in orientation is their insistence upon the salience in philosophical understanding of factors characteristic of the human sphere: reasons, rules, customs, conventions, symbols, norms, values, priorities, and the like.

What we have here is thus a revisiting from the vantage point of the analytic mode of twentieth-century philosophy the nineteenth-century Idealism of Dilthey and his congeners with their emphasis on two different modes of understanding and explanation – the one linked to sciences of nature and the other to the 'sciences' oriented to the works of human kind – with the key to philosophical understanding seen to lie not in the ideas and paradigms geared to the understanding of inert nature but to the products and processes of human artifice. Here the definitive resources of the cognitive processes of homo sapiens – rationality, convention, evaluation, conceptualization, symbolization, and communication – and the correlation of human praxis in relation to norms, conventions, principles, and so on are the principal instruments of philosophical inquiry. For all of these latter day Idealists alike abandon scientific reductionism and the positivism characteristic of philosophy in the first half of the twentieth century to seek the pivotal instrumentalities of philosophical understanding in the sphere of human artifice rather than nature.

Although on the issue of a *causal* reductionism the thinkers of this group may differ, nevertheless on the issue of *conceptual* reductionism they agree in being drastically opposed. They all insist on the hermeneutic autonomy of the human domain – that the principal phenomena of the human sciences can only be grasped via principles characteristic of this domain and absent elsewhere. And within this domain they see the concept-machinery of everyday life as paramount – the ideas at work in our ordinary thought and discourse have a primacy and privileged position in the matters of understanding and explanation here and cannot be supplemented by technical innovations. With human affairs, understanding and explanation have to proceed from within the setting of ordinary human thought experiences, and the generalization for externalized observation – however useful in some respects – is not the basis for adequate understanding. Here this latter-day neo-Idealism reflects the nineteenth-century influence of Dilthey rather than that of the British neo-Hegelians.

And so, while no particular credit or credence will accrue to any Anglo-American philosopher who adopts the self-description of neo-Diltheyian — seeing that a majority of her colleagues have never even heard of Wilhelm Dilthey – nevertheless this in effect is what most of the contemporary neo-Idealists are.

Most but not all. For now and again there emerges a thinker of Idealist tendency who looks to entirely different sources of inspection. One instance of this in the line of thought at issue in the neo-Idealism of this sort is anti-realism which finds expression in John Foster's self-avowedly idiosyncratic but nevertheless provocative 1982 book on *The Case for Idealism*. His approach is substantially detached from the sort of position we are here considering, given the fact that its sole historical reference point is the ontological Idealism of Bishop Berkeley.

Yet another one of these unusual flowers in the garden of contemporary Idealism is Timothy Sprigge. His 1983 book, *The Validation of Absolute Idealism*, not only has resonances of Berkeley but goes back beyond him to Spinoza. As Sprigge sees it, natural reality is concurrently both mental and physical in its make-up. He ingeniously defends a dual-aspect pan-psychism of sorts, accordingly to which the universe is mental in its inner essence and physical only in its overt structure.

Notes

1. In the twentieth century, this sort of position was principally espoused in France, in the work of Henri Bergson and Teilhard de Chardin.
2. Initiated by Plato in antiquity and reaffirmed by Leibniz, this position has in recent years been eloquently advocated by the Canadian philosopher John Leslie. See Leslie 1979 and 1996.
3. For the voluminous Dilthey literature see Hermann 1969.
4. On these developments see Kuklick 1977.
5. See Putnam 1975. Putnam condemns the neo-positivist theory of science popular in the 1930–60 era as 'based on an idealist or ideal-tendency world view . . . that does not correspond to reality.'
6. See Rescher 1973a, 1973b, 1977, 1979, 1989, 1991, 2003.
7. His substantial trilogy entitled *The Persistence of Reality* was published in Oxford by Basil Blackwell in the late 1980s although part of the material had already appeared in various publications over the preceding decade.

References

Brandom, R. (1994), *Making it Explicit: Reasoning, Representing and Discursive Commitment*, Cambridge: Harvard University Press.
Foster, J. (1982), *The Case for Idealism*, London: Routledge and Kegan Paul.

Hermann, J. (1969), *Bibliographie Wilhelm Dilthey: Wueller und Literatur*, Berlin and Basel: Weinheim.

Kuklick, B. (1977), *The Rise of American Philosophy*, New Haven: Yale University Press.

Leslie, J. (1979), *Value and Existence*, Oxford: Clarendon Press.

Leslie, J. (1996), *Universes*, London: Routledge.

McDowell, J. [1994] (1996), *Mind and World*, Cambridge: Harvard University Press.

Putnam, H. (1975), 'Mind and Reality,' in H. Putnam (1975), *Philosophical Papers, Volume 2*, Cambridge: Cambridge University Press, pp. 272–90.

Rescher, N. (1973a), *The Coherence Theory of Truth*, Oxford: Clarendon Press.

Rescher, N. (1973b), *Conceptual Idealism*, Oxford: Basil Blackwell.

Rescher, N. (1977), *Dialectics*, Albany: State University of New York Press.

Rescher, N. (1979), *Cognitive Systematization*, Oxford: Basil Blackwell.

Rescher, N. (1989), *A Useful Inheritance*, Savage: Rowman and Littlefield.

Rescher, N. (1991), *Human Knowledge in Idealistic Perspective*, Princeton: Princeton University Press.

Rescher, N. (2003), *Cognitive Idealization*, Cambridge: Cambridge Scholars Press.

Sprigge, T. L. S. (1983), *The Validation of Absolute Idealism*, Edinburgh: Edinburgh University Press.

Ordinary Language Philosophy

Kelly Dean Jolley

Ludwig Wittgenstein revered the work of Gottlob Frege and kept tabs on the location of obscure works of Frege in the Cambridge library. J. L. Austin translated Frege's *Foundations of Arithmetic* into English and made it a part of the philosophy curriculum at Oxford. I mention these facts because the tradition of Ordinary Language Philosophy (OLP) began with Frege. Frege's three essays in his *Logical Investigations*, along with his 'On Concept and Object,' were the first essays of OLP. Beginning the story of OLP with Frege helps to bring certain features in the tradition rightly to the front: in particular, it underscores OLP's insistent self-description as logic and its steadfast anti-psychologism. When these features are emphasized, OLP's metaphilosophical preoccupation becomes easier to understand, as does its relationships to phenomenology and to analytic philosophy. And works like Wittgenstein's *Tractatus* can be seen as belonging to the tradition, not just in virtue of isolated remarks like 5.5563: 'All propositions of our colloquial language are actually, just as they are, logically completely in order,' but in virtue of their overall shapes and aims.

In what follows I concentrate on Ludwig Wittgenstein and J. L. Austin and as a result many philosophers who are OLPers or whose work stands in significant relations to OLP are here ignored: John Cook-Wilson, H. A. Prichard, John Wisdom, P. F. Strawson, Elizabeth Anscombe, Peter Geach, O. K. Bouwsma, Zeno Vendler, Paul Ziff, Norman Malcolm, Virgil Aldrich, Frank Ebersole, John McDowell, Charles Travis, et al. My hope is that what I say about Wittgenstein and Austin will suggest how to see patterns of sameness and difference among these others. OLP is still alive and well, even if it no longer is called OLP.

Ordinary Language Philosophy As Logic

Like most identifiable traditions in philosophy, OLP may be seen as organized around a slogan: 'Logic is internal to thinking and talking.' The slogan is understood differently by different OLPers, but its centrality to one's work marks out a philosopher as an OLPer. Consider Frege's distinction between concepts and objects. Frege sees clearly, particularly in his 'On Concept and Object,' that his distinction distinguishes uses of words. Words are a concept-phrase or an object-phrase only in use. Benno Kerry, the critic Frege responds to in 'On Concept and Object,' denies that the distinction distinguishes uses of words. For Kerry, the words, 'the concept,' in the set of words, 'the concept "horse,"' determines the set of words as a concept-phrase: 'The concept "horse" is a concept easily attained' is a proposition about a concept. The use of the words is irrelevant to the determination; the words determine themselves. Frege's disagreement with Kerry can be highlighted by applying Frege's Context Principle: *never ask for the meaning of a word in isolation, but only in the context of a proposition*. For Frege, words can be a concept-phrase only in the context of a proposition; for Kerry, words can be a concept-phrase in isolation from a proposition.[1]

A chasm exists between these views. On the Frege view, if the logical roles of words are determined by use, logical form is determined by use. Logical form cannot be taken in, as it were, by eye or ear. Words as such do not determine logical form. Whether words should be symbolized in *Begriffschrift* with a blank spot (as a concept-phrase) or without (as an object-phrase) is not determined unless the words are employed; unemployed words are unsymbolizable. On the Kerry view, logical form is determined apart from use. Words as such determine their logical form. Features of words do the determining. The features determine the way that the words should be symbolized in *Begriffschrift*. And the features can be called upon when there is a question about whether the words have been correctly or incorrectly used. Central to the Kerry view is the idea that language use does not as such involve logic. Language is used; and then logic comes upon the scene; and then logic judges whether the use is correct or incorrect: here the used words, there the logic that judges them. Kerry takes the words, 'the concept "horse,"' to determine their own logical form – they have the form of a concept-phrase, they carry a blank spot with them. But (Kerry thinks) they can still be the subject of a sentence – an object-phrase. And so Frege's claim that the distinction between concept and object is absolute has been falsified, for Kerry has just relativized the distinction: 'The concept "horse" is a concept easily acquired.' But for Frege the absoluteness of the distinction involves there being no such distinction in isolation from a proposition – from use. Kerry's taking the words, 'the concept "horse,"' to determine their own logical form confuses instead of relativizes the distinction. No words in use are simultaneously a concept-phrase and an object-phrase.

OLPers, particularly Wittgenstein and Austin, deeply internalized Frege's lesson about concepts and objects. But they did not just deeply internalize the lesson – they also widely extended it. Both Wittgenstein and Austin recognized many more distinctions of the concept/object sort than Frege did.

Wittgenstein saw logical – he called them *grammatical* – distinctions as of the concept/object sort. For example, the early remarks of *Philosophical Investigations* are redolent of that sort of distinction. Wittgenstein comments there that the different uses of words, the different kinds of words, are *absolutely* unlike (Wittgenstein 1958: 1 and 10; my emphasis). Wittgenstein's 'absolutely' is the successor to Frege's 'absolutely.' Austin usually saw grammatical distinctions as of the concept/object sort, too. In 'A Plea for Excuses,' (1961), for example, Austin rediscovered the adverb for philosophy by discovering the absolute unlikeness of the adverb to other kinds of words. Many of Austin's Thirteen Rules and Lessons in 'Plea' are, rightly understood, Fregean rules and lessons. Austin's justly celebrated distinction between accidents and mistakes is a distinction between the differently shaped blank-spots each word carries with it in

Austin's stories. Austin's stories contribute to logic. They are, we might say, little logic parables. So, too, although in different ways, are Wittgenstein's fictitious natural histories and language-games.[2]

Wittgenstein and Austin differed in the way that they went on from Frege and I do not want to eliminate their differences. It is a fact that, although Austin usually saw grammatical distinctions as of the concept/object sort, his position occasionally changed.

Note the contrast-term Wittgenstein favours for the term 'use': 'on holiday' or 'idle' (Wittgenstein 1958: 38, 132). When he uses one of these contrast-terms, Wittgenstein is giving notice of the non-use of words and of the troubles it causes. Although he may seem occasionally to contrast 'use' with 'abuse,' his point is typically that some word which is unused appears to be used. So when Wittgenstein asks his reader to consider how a word is used in the language-game that is its original home (Wittgenstein 1958: 116), his point is not that there the word is used correctly, but rather that there the word is really used. Ordinary language provides the standard of use, not the standard of correct use. By refusing to use 'abuse,' Wittgenstein insists on the internality of logic to used language – to thinking and talking. He does not think that language can be used illogically. For him, no use of words is a possible but logically impermissible use of words. That is why ordinary language is all right – because ordinary language is used language – we do talk and think in it – and not because it is correctly used language.

Austin sometimes contrasts 'use' with 'abuse;' he is sometimes distinguishing the correct from the incorrect use of words: one can't abuse ordinary language without paying for it (Austin 1961). The use/abuse distinction and its concomitants creep into Austin in numerous places, for example, in Lesson Twelve in 'Plea': *Trailing Clouds of Etymology* (Austin 1961: 149–51). As happens there, sometimes for Austin the etymology and formation of words, as well as their history, contribute to determining the logical form of the words and do so in a way that is independent of the use of the words in particular circumstances of thinking or talking. This allows Austin to rate the circumstantial use of the words as correct or incorrect. It is at such times that Austin dreams of 'a revised and enlarged *Grammar*,' or of 'a true and comprehensive *science of language*' (Austin 1961: 180); he sometimes believes he has discovered features of words that allow the words to determine their own logical form independently of their use in particular circumstances. Although restyled, there is a little Kerry in Austin.

When Austin takes to task Wittgenstein for overblown talk about the infinite uses of language, the difference between Austin and Wittgenstein is starkest (Austin 1961: 221). Austin insists that, given enough time, the uses of language can, like the species of beetles, be listed. But instead of rebuking Wittgenstein, Austin's insistence shows that he does not quite mean by 'use' what Wittgenstein means by it. Given what Wittgenstein means by 'use,' talk of infinite uses is not overblown. Wittgenstein takes a word to have a use if we give it a use.

Given what Austin means by 'use,' his treating ordinary language as the First Word – as 'embodying the inherited experiences and acumen of many generations of men' (Austin 1961: 133) – is unsurprising. It is also unsurprising that Wittgenstein does not treat ordinary language as the First Word. Noting this helps to explain interesting differences in their critical lexicons and in their critical styles.

Despite their differences, the influence of Frege on Wittgenstein and Austin allows their work sensibly to be understood as logic. This use of 'logic' is a projection of the term, no doubt; but I think that seeing the path of the projection from Frege onwards shows it to be a tolerable projection.

A commonplace contrast with OLP has been Ideal Language Philosophy. My earlier mentions of the *Tractatus* and of *Begriffschrift* were meant as a shots-across-the-bow of this commonplace contrast. ILP and OLP do contrast, but not in the commonplace way. Consider again the two ways of understanding language and logic I have been contrasting. The Frege way reckons their (internal) relationship to rule out illogical uses of language; the Kerry way reckons their (external) relationship to rule in illogical uses of language. Most ILPers go the Kerry way; but so, too, do some OLPers (Austin sometimes). Deciding whether a philosopher takes the Frege or the Kerry way is not indicated by whether the philosopher's writings are formally or informally dressed. The presence of formalisms in Wittgenstein does not mean he sometimes takes the Kerry way; the non-presence of formalisms in Austin does not mean that he always takes the Frege way. A surer indicator of ways taken is the presence of the Theory of Types or of some *simulacrum*. As I noted, Austin sometimes does think that a word can be grammatically Typified in isolation from its current use. Wittgenstein does not think a word can be Typified in that way. Wittgenstein's parting shot toward Types comes late in *Philosophical Investigations* – 'When a sentence is called senseless, it is not as it were its sense that is senseless' (Wittgenstein 1958: 500).

Ordinary Language Philosophy's Anti-Psychologism

Frege comments in *Foundations* that failing to observe the Context Principle almost always results in taking meanings to be mental pictures or acts of the individual mind. So to take meanings is to psychologize them. The corruption of *Philosophical Investigations* 43 that eventually became the brief battle hymn of OLP – 'Don't ask for the meaning, ask for the use' – is, first and foremost, a Context Principle mnemonic. Asking for the use instead of the meaning is a way of resisting the urge to go spelunking in the inner, hunting mental pictures or acts of mind.

One unfortunate effect of OLP's steadfast anti-psychologism was the difficulty that critics, as well as OLPers themselves, had in distinguishing anti-psychologism from behaviorism. A case is Gilbert Ryle. In his *Concept of Mind* (1949), he wars against (Cartesian) psychologism. But among the civilian casualties (wounded, not dead) was psychology itself, the reality of the inner. Other OLPers were clearer about the difference, and clearer about the potential for confusion: consider Wittgenstein (1958: 300–8); and Austin's review of *Concept of Mind* (Austin 1970). Wittgenstein recognizes that attacking psychologism is not and should not devolve into attacking psychology. Much like Kant in the Refutation of Idealism, Wittgenstein is not targeting the inner, but rather a certain conception of the inner – a conception of the inner as a realm of self-standing and self-announcing items.

The steadfast anti-psychologism of OLP has often been missed – not only because it has been mistaken for pro-behaviorism, but also because so much of what OLPers routinely appeal to or involve in their work seems to be itself broadly psychological.

OLPers routinely appeal to what we say, to what we call things, to what we do with them, to their placement in our lives and our placement in saying them. Such appeals may themselves seem psychologistic. But they are not. For the OLPer, such appeals are required in order to do the logic of OLP. The details of our uses of language, the props and scenery among which we stage our talkings and thinkings, the addresses of our addresses – all enter into the fixing of logical form. This seems strange only on the denial of the internality of logic to used language. Whether or not 'I do' is performative ('. . . take you to be my husband') or constative ('. . . know that $2 + 2 = 4$') is not fixed by the words themselves, but rather by the particular circumstances in which they are spoken – by the question that prompts them, by who asks it (and where he is standing), by who answers it (and where she is standing), by the scene of the question and answer, and so on.

OLP as Phenomenology

Austin flirted with the idea of describing his philosophy as Linguistic Phenomenology (Austin 1961: 130). He ended the flirtation not because the description was wrong, but because it was too much of a mouthful. (Austin shied away from anything that suggested that his style of being a philosopher was that of a specialist in the sui generis.)

Like phenomenology, OLP is defined by its relationship to logic and to psychologism. Both OLP and phenomenology treat psychologism as a confusion, a radical vice, and not as a competing theory. This is a decisive treatment; it defines a kind of logician, a certain understanding of logic. Again, it is to treat logic as internal to thinking and talking. When logic is treated this way, the psychologizer cannot be seen as proffering an alternative view of logic, but rather as missing the phenomena of logic altogether; the psychologizer is looking in the wrong place. This requires that the anti-psychologizer reconceptualize his critical task. The task is reorienting the psychologizer instead of falsifying his psychologism. Good phenomenological descriptions, like Austin's stories or Wittgenstein's natural histories, serve precisely the task of reorienting.

One interesting but little remarked upon similarity between OLP and phenomenology is, to use Kant's terminology, the focus of each on spontaneity, specifically on synthesis. Phenomenology criticized Kant for failing to appreciate, or fully to appreciate, the synthetic character even of analytic judgement. Kant and the Kantians too often treated analytic judgement as if it made itself – as if it were unlike synthetic judgements in not involving spontaneity. But for the phenomenologist, as well as for Wittgenstein, analytic judgement or grammatical remarks involved spontaneity. The way in which spontaneity is involved for each is different, and it leads to different things, but the similarity remains.

For the phenomenologists, the spontaneity of analytic judgement meant that phenomenology had proper work to do even at the level of the analytic judgement; it meant that the fastness of logic itself could be breached by crafty phenomenologists. Intentionality is present even in analytic judgement. Since it is, the phenomenology of logic has the task of elucidating the consciousness that constitutes the ideal formations of logic. In less formidable terms, this means that there is a critical task facing the phenomenologist of logic even when he reaches analytic judgement. The task is that of limning the sense and limits of spontaneous cognitive life as those are present in analytic judging, and (so) in all judging.

Some of the positivists misunderstood the spontaneity of the analytic, and tried to account for it as (the result of) convention. Wittgenstein used the term 'conventional' when talking about the spontaneity of grammatical remarks, but he meant something quite different by it from what the positivists meant. It is not just that Wittgenstein's notion of convention goes deeper than that of the positivists, but that it goes deeper in another place. For Wittgenstein, one of the crucial lessons that philosophy has to teach is how deep conventionality, spontaneity, goes in human life. Philosophy for Wittgenstein brings home the spontaneity of human nature itself. Human lives are as reticulate with spontaneity as is human language. Wittgenstein sometimes investigates spontaneity by talking about the 'arbitrariness' of language or of rules of grammar. He is constantly concerned to show that the rules of grammar are the rules of sense in lives in which there is language. The arbitrariness of the rules does not attenuate them as rules. In fact, the arbitrariness, the spontaneity, is crucial to their being the rules of sense in lives in which there is language. Language is the house of Being – so says Heidegger; well, in this case, the house is a home for us because its rules are our rules – the rules we follow, the rules we give.

Wittgenstein and the phenomenologists understand spontaneity as bound up with responsibility. But neither thinks of the responsibility of spontaneity as responsibility to something, but rather as responsibility for something. Human spontaneity should be responsible for itself, for the sense humans make in their lives with language, and human spontaneity *is* (generally) responsible for itself. But that responsibility is not guaranteed and it can be found to be limited in disorienting ways and at alarming moments. As Austin and others have noted, sometimes words fail us. And that means that sometimes we fail ourselves. But we can (must) typically count on our words, just as we can (must) typically count on ourselves.

OLP and Analytic Philosophy

Analytic philosophy is a system of streams from Fregean headwaters. Each stream carries with it Frege's anti-psychologism and his profound concern with logic, although how, and how much of, each of these is carried varies among the streams. OLP is one of these streams. As in the other streams, a process rightly called analysis was often performed by OLPers. But the analyses of OLP tend to be of a different sort from the analyses in other streams of analytic philosophy: OLP-analyses tend not to be performed as an anodyne for vagueness in ordinary language. Instead, they tend to be performed as an anodyne for imperspicuity in ordinary language: the analyses substitute one form of expression for another, where the sense of each is exactly the same, but the second renders perspicuous the logical form or the grammar of the first. The analyses, in other words, perform much the same function as the translation of ordinary language into a *Begriffschrift*. (Such 'translations' or analyses cannot be anodynous for vagueness, since, to the extent that the ordinary language statement is vague, it will either resist 'translation' or analysis, or it will retain its vagueness through 'translation' or analysis.) The *analysans* does not outrank the *analysandum* in definiteness of sense; the *analysandum* outranks the *analysans* only in that its apparent logical form – its surface grammar – and its real logical form – depth grammar – are separated by less distance. Austin's stories, Wittgenstein's fictitious natural histories and descriptions of language-games – each of these serves a similar purpose, that of making perspicuous the sense we make.

The OLP-stream of analytic philosophy differs from other streams most importantly in its characterizing problematic. The characterizing problematic of most streams of analytic philosophy is Skepticism's argument with Dogmatism. But the characterizing problematic of OLP is Indifferentism's argument with Criticism.[3] OLP's chief critical concern is the disagreement of the understanding with itself. Such disagreement can seem irresolvable – and, if it does, it leads to condemning the understanding as such and to condemning its exercises. This condemning can look like skepticism, but it is not any straightforward skepticism, for example, Cartesian skepticism. The condemning goes deeper than Cartesian skepticism, condemning even Cartesian skepticism itself. (The condemning is of the reality of discourse itself – of thinking and talking.) OLP responds critically to this condemning. It strives to bring the understanding back into agreement with itself; it strives to true the understanding's relationship with itself.

Metaphilosophy and Therapy

Metaphilosophy preoccupied OLP. The most solemn pieties of OLP were methodological pieties. OLP typically understood itself as teaching a method instead of as advocating conclusions. Ryle's radical distinction between *knowing-how* and *knowing-that* is embodied in the self-understanding of OLP.

The most notorious piece of methodological instruction given by OLPers was to compare philosophy to therapy. Few, if any, OLPers thought that philosophy was therapy, of course. (And some, like Austin, never seriously made the comparison at all.) But many did think the comparison was enlightening.[4] To see why, attend to Wittgenstein's handling of the comparison. As I described above, Wittgenstein insists on the contrast between used and idle words. One reason he insists on the contrast is that the contrasts are not self-intimating: I may intend to use a word, believe I am using a word, and still, for all that, I may fail to use the word. Use-illusions are possible.

Use-illusions are insensitive to the conventional modes of philosophical responsiveness. Counterexamples do not affect them, since, when a use-illusion occurs, the illuded person is not (yet) advancing a claim. And, since no claim is (yet) advanced, an appeal to intuition has nothing to rebut. The illuded person will not have given an argument open to standard criticisms, since there is no argument (yet) given. Nothing (yet) follows from anything else; nothing (yet) is true or false. And yet the illuded person is in a state that is philosophically significant, even while that state eludes conventional modes of philosophical responsiveness. It was to draw attention to the existence of such states, and to highlight the difficulty of philosophical responsiveness to them, that OLPers compared their philosophical work to therapy. The illuded person needs to be disillusioned – but how? The use-illusion is not a state self-intimating as such, but it is nonetheless an intimate matter. To disillusion the person requires something quite different from showing that a claim staked fails in universality or that an argument made is invalid or unsound. It is not that the illuded person believes or accepts something that stands at a distance from the person (say, in a Third Realm) and that is itself wrong – false. The illuded person is wrong. And not wrong metonymically – as when we say the person is wrong because the Third Realm item the person is related to is itself wrong. No; the illuded person is wrong personally.

For the wrongness to become personal in this way requires not only a shift in how we think about what is philosophically significant, but also in how to respond to this sort of significance. Since the illuded person is personally wrong, the illuded person must play a more active role in being righted than if the person were metonymically wrong. (That the illuded person actively participates in this mode of responsiveness is an important check on the mode. The check helps keep the response from collapsing into purely political or merely personal criticism.) Righting the wrong often requires finding the particular words that allow the illuded person to see the illusion for what it is – the particular words that allow the illuded person to escape from the fly-bottle and that reveal the fly-bottle as a fly-bottle.

Method in philosophy has the Anti-Augustinian property: when someone asks us about philosophical method, we think we know what it is; when no one asks, particularly when we are rapt in a philosophical problem, we do not know what it is. OLP coped with this property by keeping its treatment of problems cheek-by-jowl with its methodological instructions.

The importance of coping with this property is manifested, for instance, by Wittgenstein's posting his methodological remarks at the dialectical center of both the *Tractatus* and *Philosophical Investigations*, and by (what Ryle once called) the governessy accents of *Philosophical Investigations*. Ryle and Austin shared this accent with Wittgenstein: the accent marks the span of Austin's work, and it crops up routinely in Ryle's. The accent signals OLP's longing for philosophical governance – the longing for philosophy to manage itself and to be both independent and profitable. (This longing anchors OLP's response to Indifferentism.) The metaphilosophical preoccupation of OLP should not be depicted as a forsaking of the noonday hard digging of philosophizing for a twilight reclining chat. What a philosopher says about philosophizing is no more to be taken at face-value than anything (else) a philosopher says when philosophizing: metaphilosophy is philosophy. For OLPers, the metaphilosophical and methodological claims a philosopher makes are fully intelligible, if they are, only in relation to the rest of the philosopher's work. Failure to grasp this has led to wildly irrelevant responses to the work of OLPers. Over and over again, OLPers are criticized as if their metaphilosophical and methodological claims were meant to withstand judgement outside of relation to the rest of the OLPer's work. As a result, OLPers have been dismissed as slogan-mongers – and mongers of bad slogans, at that. But, as a matter of fact, the critic is slogan-mongering by attempting to judge the claims outside of relation to the rest of the work.

OLP understands philosophy to lengthen, to deepen and to heighten the process of understanding. And 'understanding,' as I am insisting here and above, is the key term in OLP, the term that plays the role in its terminological economy that 'knowledge' does in the economies of many other philosophical traditions. OLP's characteristic movements occur at the level of the distinction between sense and nonsense, not at the level of the distinction between truth and falsity. Understanding waxes; knowledge wanes. (Of course, knowledge does not wane as such – only in its importance in OLP.) OLP insists on the Romance in philosophy's Enlightenment.

G. E. Moore and OLP

Moore was a philosophical giant. But to count G. E. Moore an OLPer is to miscount; he was not an OLPer. Of course Moore in his work did again and again do the sorts of things that OLPers often do: Moore insisted on reminding himself and his reader of what words mean; he granted to the plain man a complicated kind of jurisdiction in philosophy; he toiled in the mazeways of skepticism; he unabashedly deployed arguments *ad hominem* (although not *ad personam*) against his interlocutors. But in all this Moore pointed the way to OLP without being on the way himself.

What kept Moore from being an OLPer was his view of philosophical questions themselves. Now of course Moore insists that we often ask a philosophical question without knowing quite what question our interrogatory words express. But Moore does not ever seriously doubt that there is a philosophical question that the words express. We can rightly say that Moore doubted the clarity of the questions that philosophers asked, and we can rightly say that he often doubted whether philosophers really believed the answers they gave to the questions; but we cannot rightly say that he doubted whether there were philosophical questions to be asked and answers to be given to them. That Moore took this view of philosophical questions is shown by his deep unease with his own answers to them. Moore, I think, believed his answers; but he also did not believe his answers. ('I believe; help thou my unbelief.') His deep unease was the result of the mismatch between his understanding of the questions and the believability of his answers to them: given his view of the questions, the very believability of his answers to them made the answers hard to believe. Moore, much like John the Baptist, helped to usher in the New Law while living under the Old.

Notes

1. I am idealizing Frege here. The historical Frege's self-understanding is closer to Kerry, and so his position in 'On Concept and Object' is doctrinally more complicated than I am presenting it to be, and diagnostically less complicated. Frege's closeness to Kerry makes it unclear whether Wittgenstein's or Austin's use of 'use' (described below) is the more historically Fregean; I judge each to have equal claim to the title. For more on Frege and Kerry, see my 'Frege at Therapy' in Stocker 2004.
2. Parables often illustrate the use, the grammar, of some word or phrase. For example, in Jesus's famous Parable of the Good Samaritan, the parable illustrates the use of 'neighbour,' revealing it to have a different grammar in the religious life from what the lawyer whose question prompts the parable understands it to have.

3. Indifferentism becomes a player on the stage of philosophy in a crucial paragraph of the First Preface to the *Critique of Pure Reason* (Aix-x).
4. The trick the OLPers need to turn is that of managing to see philosophy as like therapy without thereby seeing it as a species of therapy. Morris Lazerowitz is a good example of an OLPer who compared the two and who was not always able to turn the trick.

References

Aldrich, V. 'Illocutionary Space,' *Philosophy and Phenomenological Research* 32 (1) (Sept.), pp. 15–28.

Anscombe, G. E. M. (2000), *Intention*, Cambridge: Harvard University Press.

Austin, J. L. (1961), *Philosophical Papers*, Oxford: Oxford University Press.

Austin, J. L. (1962a), *How To Do Things With Words*, Oxford: Oxford University Press.

Austin, J. L. (1962b), *Sense and Sensibilia*, Oxford: Oxford University Press.

Austin, J. L. (1970), 'Intelligent Behavior,' in O. Wood, and G. Pitcher (eds) (1970), *Ryle*, Garden City, New York: Doubleday and Co. Inc.

Bell, D. (1979), *Frege's Theory of Judgment*, Oxford: Oxford University Press.

Chappell, V. C. (ed.) (1964), *Ordinary Language: Essays in Philosophical Method*, Englewood Cliffs: Prentice Hall, Inc.

Clarke, T. (1972) 'The Legacy of Skepticism,' *The Journal of Philosophy* 69 (20) (Nov.), pp. 754–69.

Bouwsma, O. K. (1965), *Philosophical Essays*, Lincoln: University of Nebraska Press.

Cavell, S. (1969), *Must We Mean What We Say?*, New York: Charles Scribner's Sons.

Cavell, S. (1979), *The Claim of Reason*, Oxford: Oxford University Press.

Diamond, C. (1991), *Realism and the Realistic Spirit*, Cambridge: MIT Press.

Ebersole, F. (1967), *Things We Know: Fourteen Essays on Problems of Knowledge*, Eugene: University of Oregon Press.

Frege, G. (1996), 'On Concept and Object,' in P. Geach and M. Black (eds) (1996), *Translation from the Philosophical Writings of Gottlob Frege*, Oxford: Blackwell, pp. 42–55.

Frege, G. (1968), *Foundations of Arithmetic*, trans. J. L. Austin, Oxford: Basil Blackwell.

Frege, G. (1977), *Logical Investigations*, trans. P. Geach, and R. Stoothoff, New Haven: Yale University Press.

Frege, G. (1977), *Translations from the Philosophical Writings of Gottlob Frege*, trans. P. Geach, and M. Black, Oxford: Basil Blackwell.

Geach, P. (1957), *Mental Acts*, London: Routledge and Kegan Paul.

Jolley, K. (2004), 'Frege at Therapy,' in B. Stocker (ed.) (2004), *Post-Analytic Tractatus*, Burlington: Ashgate Publishing Company, pp. 85–97.

Kant, I. (1961), *Critique of Pure Reason*, trans. N. Kemp Smith, London: Macmillan.

Lazerowitz, M. (1968), *Philosophy and Illusion*, London: Allen and Unwin.

Lazerowitz, M. (1964), *Studies in Metaphilosophy*, London: Routledge and Kegan Paul.

McDowell, J. (1994), *Mind and World*, Cambridge: Harvard University Press.

Malcolm, N. (1959), *Dreaming*, London: Routledge and Kegan Paul.

Moore, G. E. (1962), *Philosophical Papers*, New York: Collier Books.

Palmer, A. (1988), *Concept and Object*, London: Routledge.

Rorty, R. (ed.) (1967), *The Linguistic Turn*, Chicago: University of Chicago Press.

Ryle, G. (1971), *Collected Papers*, Oxford: Oxford University Press.

Ryle, G. (1954), *Dilemmas*, London: Cambridge University Press.

Ryle, G. (1949), *The Concept of Mind*, London: Hutchinson's University Library.

Sellars, W. (1978), 'Descartes and Berkeley: Some Reflections on the Theory of Ideas,' in P. Machemer, and R. Turnbull (eds) (1978), *Studies in Perception*, Columbus: Ohio State University Press, pp. 259–311.

Stroll, A. (1988), *Surfaces*, Minneapolis: University of Minnesota Press.

Travis, C. (1989), *The Uses of Sense*, Oxford: Oxford University Press.

Vendler, Z. (1967), *Linguistics in Philosophy*, Ithaca: Cornell University Press.

Vendler, Z. (1972), *Res Cogitans*, Ithaca: Cornell University Press.

Wisdom, J. (1966), 'The Metamorphosis of Metaphysics,' in J. N. Findlay (ed.), *Studies in Philosophy*, Oxford: Oxford University Press.

Wisdom, J. (1952), *Other Minds*, Oxford: Basil Blackwell.

Wisdom, J. (1970), *Paradox and Discovery*, Berkeley: University of California Press.

Wisdom, J. (1964), *Philosophy and Psycho-Analysis*, Oxford: Basil Blackwell.

Wittgenstein, L (1958), *Philosophical Investigations*, trans. G. E. M. Anscombe, New York: Macmillan.

Ziff, P. (1960), *Semantic Analysis*, Ithaca: Cornell University Press.

Logical Positivism and the Vienna Circle

Bernard Hodgson

The philosophical movement of logical positivism originated in the early 1920s with a group of philosophers and scientists who gathered around Moritz Schlick when he became professor of Philosophy at the University of Vienna – hence, the alternative designation of the Vienna Circle. Among the leading philosophers, besides Schlick, were Rudolph Carnap, Otto Neurath, Herbert Feigl, and Friedrich Waismann. Allied with the Vienna group were philosophers from the Berlin school of which Hans Reichenbach, Richard von Mises and Carl Hempel were prominent members. The group was later joined in the early 1930s by a philosopher who became its leading exponent to the English speaking world – Alfred Ayer. The most significant initial stimulus for the thoughts of the members of the Vienna Circle was found in their sympathetic response to the early work of Ludwig Wittgenstein, in particular, his *Tractatus Logico-Philosophicus*. More generally, the work of the Vienna Circle can be understood as giving systematic articulation to nothing less than the dominant 'positivist' or 'naturalist' orientation of the prevailing scientific world-view of the twentieth century. However, it should be emphasized that positivist thought patterns are no transient fashion, but have deep and classic roots – in particular, that of traditional empiricism, especially as set forth by David Hume. In fact, participants within the Vienna Circle preferred to have their philosophical position characterized as that of logical empiricism. A brief reminder, then, of the principles of empiricist epistemology will provide an instructive preamble to an examination of the basic tenets of logical positivism.

Historical Background

It is a commonplace that British empiricists argued their viewpoint against that of Continental rationalists. But both of their epistemologies intended an absolute or incorrigible *foundation* or grounding for legitimate knowledge claims. Moreover, both of these groundings were of an *atomistic*, *reductionist* sort. For instance, in rationalism, as articulated by Descartes, the rules of reliable inquiry exhibited two phases, that of analysis and synthesis. In analysis, by pure reasoning, we resolve a complex proposition into the simple ideas of which it is comprised; these simple ideas are taken to *represent* or correspond to the exact essence or 'simple nature' of different types of reality – for example, matter as infinitely mutable spatial extension. Although sensory experience, such as observing a piece of wax change its properties as it burns, plays an 'occasioning' or 'stimulus' role for the analysis of pure reason, such simple ideas of simple natures are identified by analysis as innate or inborn within the mind. Moreover, insofar as these ideas are clearly and distinctly apprehended by direct intellectual inspection, their truth is inherently evident. In synthesis, on the basis of the propositions expressed by simple ideas, we deduce or 'derive back' what is true in the original complex propositions and, thereby, construct our knowledge of a more complex reality – for instance, the basic laws of motion of physical objects.

In classical empiricism the *structure* of reliable inquiry resembles that just adumbrated. For example, Hume follows Descartes in considering that most beliefs express complex ideas and that the legitimation of belief begins by resolving complex ideas into the simple ideas out of which they are compounded. However, for empiricists, there are no innate simple ideas which the mind finds within itself on the occasion of experience. Nor do legitimate simple ideas correspond to the abstract essences of things as apprehended by intellectual intuition, but to the basic *sense-impressions* encountered in our external sensation of the physical world or the introspection of the 'operations of our minds.' For classical empiricists, then, genuine knowledge was a construction upon elemental units or atoms of human *sensory experience*. And the algorithm of later empiricists for discrediting certain beliefs as knowledge remained essentially that of Hume: belief systems express complex ideas. Break down the complex ideas into the simple ideas of which they are comprised. If some of the atomic elements of certain beliefs cannot be matched with corresponding elements of our sensory experience, then there is something illegitimate about the original system of beliefs. Having failed to conform to adequate 'empirical control,' the system's claim to knowledge is, at least to some degree, ill-founded.

Radical Empiricism

Logical positivism follows the lead of classical empiricism in dismissing claims to knowledge that transcend the limits of sense-experience. And although there was some internal controversy within the Vienna Circle on the issue, the preferred ultimate grounding for our beliefs was in atomistic units of experience, or 'sense data.' However, the modus operandi of logical positivism can best be described as a *radicalisation* of the perspective of classical empiricism. Although it had been Hume's own stated objective to introduce the 'experimental method' patterned after Newtonian science into the study of traditional philosophical problems, positivists sharpened and ramified Hume's objective. Their aim in this regard was twofold. First, philosophical doctrines were themselves to be assessed by the criteria of scientific reasoning. Philosophy could not assume for itself any unique form of cognitive judgement or insight in order to resist the application of scientific epistemology to its own knowledge claims. It was in this especially positivist sense that logical positivists endorsed Kant's interest to 'set philosophy upon the sure path of science.' Secondly, it was the explicit goal of logical positivism to assist in the *unification of science* by means of a severe 'physicalism'. Ideally, all the propositions of science would be expressed in the language of physics as a semantic preliminary to deducing the fundamental laws of all the special sciences, *including* the human sciences, from the laws of physics.

Clearly, in the light of such aims, logical positivism understood physical science as the model or exemplar of all bona fide knowledge – insofar as any beliefs are rational at all, they are to be justified by the methods of the physical sciences. In this one may locate the positivism of logical positivism; the modifier 'logical' is to be found in the practice of positivists of applying the new techniques of mathematical logic to their scrutiny of the syntactic structure and semantic content of the propositions put forth in different belief systems. In the enactment of such scientific epistemology lay the most definitive radicalisation of the principles of traditional empiricism. According to logical positivists, the illegitimate character of proposed beliefs lies not only in claiming to have knowledge that overrides the limits of sense-experience, but in attempting to say what cannot be even meaningfully said, in breaking the rules of intelligible discourse. Indeed, the preclusion of authentic knowledge for any belief system follows upon the transgression of such rules. Let us see how in examining the core of the logical positivists' analysis of language.

Basically, positivists classified linguistic utterances according to three basic types. As the labeling of these types varied among different positivists, we shall follow that of Ayer (Ayer 1946: Chaps 1 and 4). In the first category are to be found 'analytic statements,' for example: 'All vixens are female foxes.' Any such proposition is true *ex vi terminorum*, that is, by the meaning of its constituent terms. Once we are apprised of the definition of the subject term 'vixen,' we can ascertain that the meaning of the predicate term 'female fox' can be 'analyzed out' of the meaning of the subject term. Logical positivists concede that the truth of analytic statements can be known *a priori* or independently of experience, and that they can be known as necessary, certain truths, but emphasize that such knowledge is of a 'trivial' sort: by social convention we have simply decided to define our terms in certain ways. Accordingly, analytic statements are construed as empty 'tautologies' which supply no information about the 'world,' about extra-linguistic reality: whether or not there are any vixens in existence, the definition of 'vixen' would not be impugned. The second classification is comprised of 'synthetic statements,' for example, 'All unsupported bodies fall with constant acceleration.' In contrast to analytic statements, synthetic statements are known only *a posteriori*, that is, on the basis of observation or sense-experience. Such statements are only contingently, not necessarily true: they could have been false if the properties and relations of objects in the world, including law-like relations, had been different. Hence, unlike analytic statements, their denials are not self-contradictory: although one would be affirming an inconsistency of the logical form A is not A, in asserting that vixens are not female foxes, one would only be asserting that A is not B in saying that unsupported bodies do not fall with a constant acceleration. Synthetic statements clearly do make a truth-claim about the world beyond words, about the character of extra-linguistic reality, although positivists stress that such statements are only empirical *hypotheses* whose truth can only be known with probability, never certainty, as it is always possible for the course of future experience to falsify such statements – such, for instance, was the fate of 'The earth is flat.'

It is a cardinal doctrine of logical positivism that the preceding two categories are mutually exclusive and jointly exhaustive of the domain of cognitively meaningful statements, of those statements which have an identifiable truth value, whether true or false. Most critically, against Kant's view, positivists insist that there are no synthetic *a priori* statements. Consider, for instance, Kant's understanding that mathematical propositions *are* of such a kind, that is, that a statement such as '$2 + 3 = 5$' can be known independently of experience even though it does inform us of the quantitative or spatial structure of extra-linguistic reality. On the contrary, according to positivists, on proper analysis, the meaning content of the numerical concepts of '$2 + 3 = 5$' would reduce to '$1 + 1 + 1 + 1 + 1 = 1 + 1 + 1 + 1 + 1$', an instance of the tautologous logical principle of identity, that $A = A$.

We have observed that positivists continue the empiricist tradition in arguing that if a statement is not an analytic tautology but intends to inform us about the world, then its truth or falsehood is determined by sense-experience – in technical language, all such statements are of a synthetic *a posteriori* kind. But such a consideration provides the positivist with the basis for an empiricist criterion of cognitive significance whose purpose is to demarcate sense from nonsense, or intelligible, meaningful propositions from nonsensical utterances. These grounds are formulated in the celebrated/notorious Verifiability Principle of Meaning for synthetic statements – again, those making knowledge claims about extra-linguistic reality rather than merely explicating the meaning of terms. Ayer puts the principle as a slogan: 'The meaning of a proposition is its method of verification' (Ayer 1946: 13). More precisely, the entire meaning of a (synthetic) proposition is to be identified with the sense-experiences which would verify its truth and those which would exhibit its falsehood. Therefore, and this is the absolutely critical point, if there are *no* observations or experiences relevant to determining the truth or falsehood of some sentence, then the sentence would not be a genuine statement at all, but merely a 'pseudo-statement' which, although it resembled the grammatical form of authentic statements, could be seen, upon analysis, to be a meaningless utterance that lacked a truth-value.

Two qualifications are in order: First, sometimes the verification of a meaningful synthetic proposition will not be a practical possibility, as with a current assertion that there is organic life on Europa, one of the moons of Jupiter. However, such a statement remains a cognitively meaningful one as long as we can conceive what sorts of observation would verify/falsify the statement if we could undertake them. Secondly, the most fundamental statements of physical science itself are in the logical form of laws or universal generalizations. As such statements refer to an infinite number of potential instantiations of them, we must accept that our verification of such statements by means of observed instances will necessarily remain only a partial, never a completely conclusive verification.

In the light of the above considerations, positivists may be thought to consider the third category of linguistic 'statements' as constituting what might be called a 'mutant' class. This class consists in *metaphysical assertions*, that is, experientially unverifiable sentences, which are, therefore, cognitively meaningless utterances that are neither true nor false. The immense and dramatic significance of logical positivism for twentieth century culture lay in the *application* of the verifiability principle to specify the *kinds* of assertions that were to be placed in the third category as meaningless metaphysical nonsense, without cognitive significance. In the first instance, and not surprisingly, positivists used the verifiability principle in an attempt to *eliminate* most of the foremost principles of traditional metaphysics (Carnap 1959b). Consider, for instance, the familiar debate between realist and idealist philosophers concerning the 'ontological status' of external physical objects. Do, as realists would contend, such objects exist independently of the perceptions of minds, or only, as subjective idealists would claim, as ideas in the minds of some perceivers? According to positivists, both idealist and realist principles fail the empirical test of the verifiability principle as it is not possible for sense-experience to determine the truth or falsity of either thesis; hence, both theses are cognitively meaningless and, *a fortiori*, there is no intelligible way to adjudicate the original dispute. A similar assessment would await the traditional metaphysical argument between monists who affirm: 'All reality is comprised of one substance,' and pluralists who counter with: 'There are many real substances.' Both sentences are empirically undecidable and, therefore, neither true nor false.

Of course, with the exception of a certain range of metaphysically oriented philosophers, there was no great outcry among the educated public to the positivists' dismissal of classical metaphysical doctrines. Indeed, many welcomed what was taken to be a scientifically well-founded excision of metaphysical babble, however histori-cally prestigious. On the other hand, positivists also deployed the verifiability principle as a logical club to wield against some of the most prized realms of human belief; in particular, ethical and religious assertions were classified as cognitively meaningless, as nonsensical metaphysical utterances. And it is in this context that logical positivist doctrines were frequently received with vehement indignation within the general culture, with some critics maintaining that the views of positivism were those of the anti-Christ, with advocates of positivism being charged, with Socrates, as corrupters of youth, and so on. What, in particular, then, did positivists say concerning the logical analysis of religious and ethical assertions?

At one level of analysis, the positivist interpretation of religious sentences is quite straightforward. If a theologian, working within the classical Judeo-Christian tradition, were to say: 'God is infinitely powerful,' his judgement would be predicating a supra-empirical property of a transcendent entity which judgement could not, in principle, be verified or refuted within the finite limits of human sense-experience and would be, therefore, literally meaningless. But consider if such a theologian were to seek to adjust his religious theses to the finite scope of human experience by affirming an analogical sentence such as 'God loves us as a father loves his children.' In the light of such semantic modesty, a characteristic positivist response is to remind the theologian of the basic logical principle of double negation, that the meaning of any proposition, p, is logically equivalent to the denial of its negation (p iff not not p). It follows from this principle that if there is nothing which an assertion denies, then there is nothing which it asserts either. Hence, if any statement is to be classified as cognitively meaningful, someone who affirms such a statement must be able to specify what conceivable experiences would count *against* the truth-claim of the statement (Flew 1955: 96–9, from which the preceding example is derived). In the attribution of properties to human beings that does not typically pose a conundrum: for instance, if I say that John loves his children as a father would, I would accept that the meaningfulness of this affirmation would render it liable to falsification if John did nothing to relieve the suffering of his child if he became gravely ill. On the other hand, positivists charge, theologians typically would not deem the persistent misery of the child, even after his biological father pleaded for God's intercession through prayer, as empirical evidence against divine love, but rather, say, a test of the father's faith. In fact, positivists continue, it is customary for theologians and fellow believers not to countenance *any* possible experience as confuting the ascription of positive attributes to God; accordingly, for positivists, all such religious utterances are without cognitive significance. As Ayer succinctly summarizes the positivist conclusion: '[A]ll utterances about the nature of God are nonsensical' (Ayer 1952: 115).

When we turn to moral judgements such as 'Everyone ought to keep his promises' or 'Stealing is wrong,' one might have expected that they would have fared better than religious assertions in escaping the censure of the verifiability principle. For only a minority of philosophers and laymen would intend such judgements to make an assertion about some supra-empirical world of moral values. On the contrary, many would agree with 'naturalist' interpretations such as that of classical utilitarians in which the rightness of an action is determined by its aggregated consequences for social happiness, and such a criterion is deliberately put forth as an experientially verifiable one. However, in a radically revisionary interpretation of the meaning of moral judgements, logical positivists analysed them as primarily *expressing* or 'giving vent' to feelings of approval/disapproval to certain actions, motives, character traits, and so on, in an attempt to excite similar emotions in others (Carnap 1935: Chap.1; Reichenbach 1951: Chap 17; Ayer 1952: Chap. vi; Stevenson 1945). But since moral judgements are merely expressions of feeling, they are, as Ayer bluntly claimed, as unverifiable for the same reason as cries of pain are unverifiable (Ayer 1952: 108–9). Consequently, moral judgements also become understood as cognitively meaningless sentences that are neither true nor false. *A fortiori*, there can be no scientific or rational justification for moral judgments per se, and thus, there is no such thing as genuine moral knowledge. The only 'why question' that can be significantly asked is one seeking a *causal explanation*, rather than a rational justification, for the espousal of moral principles. And the answer to this meaningful question belongs to the empirical sciences, not to an autonomous ethics – for instance, to a sociological investigation of the moral education or 'social conditioning' which is causally responsible for the formation of an agent's ethical feelings.

Unity of Science

One might characterize the positivist aim to construct a unified science with the comment that a dramatic but less drastic destiny was in store for the statements of the special sciences than with the elimination of religious and moral statements from the domain of meaningful discourse. Rather, as anticipated above, the statements of the special sciences were to be *reduced* to those of physics (Carnap 1981b and 1959a; Hempel 1949; Neurath 1959). The fundamental direction of the reduction would be from sociology to psychology to biology to chemistry to physics. The initial reduction in this schema avowed a thesis of methodological individualism–that all true statements concerning social systems can be deduced from statements concerning the properties of individuals and their relations to other individuals. Although such a thesis was contentious enough, the problematic core of the reductionist program lay in the next stratagem – that all the propositions of psychology involving the 'intentional meaning' of the states of mind of human subjects could be translated into propositions concerning the physical events of either the external bodily behavior or internal neural states of these subjects. For it was only the description of such physical events that could provide the empirical confirmation or refutation of psychological statements, and, hence, capture their meaning. As Hempel tersely concluded: '[T]he statements of psychology are consequently physicalist statements. Psychology is an integral part of physics' (Hempel 1949: 378). The prospects for translating psychological statements into physicalist counterparts would turn on the adequacy of the translation of psychological terms into physical ones. Originally, the favored method for such translation followed Carnap in construing a psychological term as dispositional in character and providing a chain of reduction sentences for the term, each one of which provided a partial determination of the criteria of application of a mentalistic predicate on the basis of observation, in particular, for the satisfaction of particular test conditions (Carnap 1936: secs 8–10). For example, consider the central psychological predicate of micro-economic theory: the 'preference' of a consumer for one commodity-bundle, say A, over another, B. An empirical interpretation of such 'preference' by means of a reduction sentence might run roughly as follows: 'If any consumer S is not subject to external constraint, such as government rationing, and is directly presented with A and B, then S prefers A to B if and only if S purchases A but not B.'

Whatever the technicalities of the empirical interpretation of 'mentalistic' predicates, it is imperative for our purposes to observe that there is a deeply significant constraint on the experiential test conditions and responses for the ascription of such predicates to subjects: such conditions and responses must be 'objective' in the sense that they must be intersubjectively accessible. This is necessary in order that the original psychological statements be verifiable by *public* observation, not by the introspective reports of the intractably private experiences of individual persons. Only then would the empirical tests of psychological statements be amenable to the requirement of repeatability by informed inquirers exhibited by the experimental procedures of the mature sciences. In general, the meaning of any synthetic statement is established by the conditions of its verification and such verification is inescapably public verification. It was precisely here, however, that the philosophical worm turned with respect to the general coherence of logical positivism. Let me explain.

Problems for Positivism

We have noted the specific manner in which logical positivism provided a 'linguistic turn' to the basic doctrines of classical empiricism. However, German positivism did not seek to divest itself of its heritage in British empiricism in concentrating on the conditions of meaningful discourse. The rational constraint on legitimate knowledge claims was still to be found in the 'empirical control' of such claims, that is to say, in the content of veridical experience. But then if the linguistic turn was to deliver the epistemic goods promised, there had to be a clear, logically compelling link between certain canonical elements of meaningful language and certain canonical elements of human experience. But the problems facing leading positivists in identifying, explaining, and arguing this connection were profound and, in the final analysis, self-defeating.

The most intractable conundrum was one which deeply challenged any empiricist epistemology, either classical or contemporary. The exact, general instrument for an empiricist justification of beliefs would have to be provided by a reliable procedure for *comparing* either Humean simple ideas with simple sense-impressions or positivist basic statements with elementary experiences. Such a procedure would be eminently appropriate if the impressions or experiences were of such a transparently infallible sort that they transferred a recognizably certain or 'self-certifying' character to the simple ideas or basic statements representing them, such that the ideas or statements could constitute an incontestably adequate 'foundation' for knowledge. This empiricist project was certainly an heroic one, but it ran aground for certain fundamental, and related, philosophical reasons.

In the context of logical positivism, the foundering centered on the interpretation and defense of 'protocol sentences.' To use a pivotal positivist distinction: in the formal mode of speech, such statements are just those basic statements of empirical control mentioned above; as Carnap characterized them: 'statements needing no justification and serving as a foundation for all the true remaining statements of science'; in the material mode of speech, such statements were taken to 'refer to the given, and describe directly given experience or phenomena, that is, the simplest states of which knowledge can be had' (Carnap 1981a: 153). But it is in just the attempt reasonably to *connect* the formal and material modes of protocol statements that the members of the Vienna Circle fell out among themselves revealing an irreparable incoherence among the internal principles of logical positivism.

In the first instance, in reporting the 'sensory data' of immediate experience, protocol statements would be recording the states of mind of particular subjects, as experiences are undergone and only undergone by individual subjects. However, if such statements were to serve their intended purpose of supplying the 'primitive' descriptions that could publicly verify the particular and law-like statements of science, on pain of a dead-ended solipsism, they could not be phrased in a subject's private language, but only in a public language the meanings of whose terms could be intersubjectively communicated and understood by practitioners within a scientific community. As outlined above, the protocols of verification were to be expressed in a physicalist language locating and describing objects by publicly accessible spatio-temporal predicates. None of the foremost positivists wished to challenge the publicity requirement on the meaning of practicable protocols, but the requirement provided an initial indication that the manner in which all meaningful propositions were to be grounded in the immediately given experience of individuals was a problematic one. Indeed, in turning to the content of the immediately given in experience itself, we can see that this problem encountered an insurmountable difficulty.

Put baldly, the problem can be, and was, formulated in the question: 'Is the given a myth?' More precisely, is there a uniquely identifiable immediate experience that can successfully play the epistemic role demanded of it, that is, that can adjudicate the truth-claims of all meaningful synthetic statements? In effect, what logical positivists were reaching for, in the steps of their classical empiricist forbears, was a *language-exit* rule for any belief system, for any 'language game,' in order to ascertain whether the game actually does make experiential contact with reality. But there is no such experiential exit from language in the first place. The favored candidate for such an exit was through the use of demonstratives, gesture, ostension – a linguistic pointing to the real beyond language and its conceptualization. For example, in looking at my pen I might say: 'That blue here now.' But pointing does not make its point. In order adequately to refer, the intended referent must be discriminated from irrelevant background factors and this can be effected only through the conceptual mediation of language. Only thus can I successfully refer, for instance, to the color blue of my pen, but not its cylindrical shape. In fact, critics of positivistic empiricism, including American pragmatists such as Nelson Goodman and W. V. O. Quine who were significantly influenced by logical positivists, challenged the very existence of any conceptually or linguistically unmediated given in perceptual experience. Under the threat of solipsism, we may grant that there are 'mind-independent' sensory stimuli, but any experience they provoke is mediated by symbol systems informed by conceptual schemata. As Goodman commented: 'That we know what we see is no truer than we see what we know' (Goodman 1972a: 142). Or consider Quine's inimitable characterization of the protocol language as: 'a fancifully fancyless medium of unvarnished news' (Quine 1960: 2). In more literal terms, as any recognizable content to experience will unavoidably be linguistically conceptualized, in comparing the sense of protocol statements to the 'raw data' of experiential content to ascertain whether the sense does or does not correspond to the content, we simply have no way, in principle, of identifying the second term of the comparison. *For linguistic constructions can only be compared with other linguistic constructions.* Put another way, even if it were accessible, unvarnished news would provide no usable truth-conditions for protocol statements. Consequently, the logic of the situation faced by positivists was one of an epistemic dilemma: if the content of the immediately given in experience is identified by being articulated or described, then it will be so in the form of a propositional judgement; but then it will be at best a tentative, probable empirical hypothesis among others, and cannot provide the incorrigible foundation for all such hypotheses. If the content of the immediately given cannot be put into propositional form – if it is ineffable – then it cannot deliver a rational constraint on any empirical proposition, let alone provide the ultimate, decisive grounding for such propositions. One can only infer propositional contents from other propositional contents. (See Williams 1977: 30–1 for his version of the dilemma.)

To be fair, the most prominent logical positivists clearly recognized the preceding dilemma. However, they quarreled among themselves in response to it, and their various responses only exacerbated the predicament exposed in the dilemma. Carnap took refuge behind the distinction between the formal and material mode of speech, arguing that we should restrict our epistemological investigations to the formal mode of the relation between self-certifying protocol statements and the less certain scientific statements from which the former were derived, insisting that only metaphysical confusion arose from attempting, in the material mode, to determine the kind of reality described by protocol statements (Carnap 1981a: 159). Unfortunately, Carnap's philosophical posture in such a reply revealed a dubious evasiveness insofar as he himself affirmed a primary referential element to the meaning of protocol statements, and such statements at least intended a reference to extralinguistic reality, however problematic to identify. Neurath, on the other hand, moved furthest among the logical positivists in an 'idealist' direction in de-emphasizing the epistemic significance of protocol statements, let alone the contact such statements permitted with an extralinguistic world through direct sensory experience (Neurath 1981). Rather, Neurath emphasized that all statements, including those protocols in which an individual scientist reports his observations, are subject to interpretation by others, and, consequently, are themselves liable to empirical refutation. Accordingly, Neurath contended that what counts as an epistemically more basic statement within a scientific theory is only a matter for a decision by convention for the scientists working with such a theory. In fact, given such considerations, Neurath opted for a coherence theory of truth wherein truth consists in the agreement or consistency of the statements of a scientific theory with each other, rather than the correspondence of such statements with 'mind-independent' facts. Schlick, however, continued this internal dialectic of the Vienna Circle in appraising such a coherence theory as an 'astounding error,' as countenancing arbitrary fairy tales as true as long as they are consistent with each other (Schlick 1959: 215). In striking contrast to Neurath, and leaping where Carnap feared to tread, Schlick re-entrenched a fundamental thesis of classical empiricism by insisting that if our scientific knowledge is to make contact with reality, then there must be an ultimate origin for such knowledge in first personal encounters with immediate experience; legitimate scientific statements must be compared with such experiential evidence, not just with each other. In this respect, Schlick would agree with C. I. Lewis that, 'If there be no datum given to the human mind, then knowledge must be contentless and arbitrary; there would be nothing for it to be true to' (Lewis 1956: 38–9). Nevertheless, Schlick did seem to recognize the force of the second conditional of the dilemma presented above, but responded by boldly embracing its horn. Appreciating that the very expression of protocol statements would require that they themselves be construed as corrigible hypotheses unsuitable to serve as an incorrigible logical foundation for other hypotheses, Schlick argued that we should understand the decisive experiential confirmation of any meaningful synthetic statement to be provided by a category of admittedly inexpressible 'observation statements' (Schlick 1959: sect. vii; and 1981, sects. 8 and 9). Although such 'statements' lose their meaning as soon as they are written down, nevertheless, they furnish the single and unshakeable point of contact between knowledge and reality in the 'feeling of finality' of the *actual act* of confirming hypotheses. Even though Schlick has been severely criticized for the obscurity of his explanation of such observation statements, his insistence that only they capture the real purport of the entire system of scientific statements, namely, 'a means of finding one's way among the facts' (Schlick 1959: 226), points to a more plausible pragmatist rendering of the positivist verifiability principle that will be explained below.

Before doing so, another fundamental conundrum confronted by logical positivism needs to be elucidated, in particular, its response to the issue of the 'ontological status' of the theoretical constructs of science. We find that it is common for the theoretical hypotheses of mature science to include apparent reference to imperceptible or unobservable entities – for instance, electrons, neutrons, bosons, and all the other particles in the 'particular zoo' of micro-physics. But would it be reasonable to be 'ontologically committed' to the actual existence of such unobservable entities? Frankly, a coherent answer to this question was deeply embarrassing for logical positivists. On the one hand, with respect to working consistently with the verifiability principle of meaning, it would appear that a forthrightly negative answer should be given: surely there would be as negligible a way of directly confirming or refuting the assertion of the literal existence of an imperceptible 'physical' entity by perceptual experience as there would be the existence of a trans-empirical God. And some positivists, notably Schlick, agreed with such a position in espousing a doctrine of *instrumentalism* wherein 'unobservables' are construed as 'convenient fictions,' or 'logical constructs' for facilitating inferences, especially predictions, about the ob-servable things which literally do exist (Schlick [*Gesammelte*] 1938: 67–9). On the other hand, such a hard-headed empiricist perspective ran up against the self-understanding of theory-construction of the very physical scientists for whom positivist philosophers were pleased to serve as underlaborers. For a countervailing thesis of 'realism' bespeaks the consensus of most practicing physical scientists in affirming the actual existence of the imperceptible particles posited by theoretical physics. From such an ontological perspective, the description of the motions of unobservable entities at the micro-physical level is postulated in order to provide a coherent understanding of – to 'make sense' of – regularities in observable phenomena at the macro-level. For instance, if gases really *are* comprised of imperceptible molecules whose velocity is increased when gases are heated, then it is understandable that the pressure on the sides of a closed container in which a gas is contained would increase with the heating of the gas, since its molecules would impact on such sides with greater momentum. Moreover, as Hempel himself came to acknowledge, the statements reporting the experiential evidence with which practicing scientists actually do test their theoretical hypotheses are themselves 'theory-laden': such test statements include irreducible reference to unobservable, theoretical constructs. Hempel draws our attention, for example, to the fact that descriptions of observable phenomena can be used in an empirical confirmation of the relativistic theory of the deflection of light rays only if 'conjoined with a considerable body of astronomical and optical theory' (Hempel 1965a: 112). Such a feature of the actual procedures of empirical verification in scientific inquiry led Hempel to conclude that the appropriate site of empirical testability and, hence, cognitive significance, is not that of individual statements assessed in isolation but rather that of whole theoretical systems used in the conceptualization and explanation of observable phenomena (Hempel 1965b: 213 and sect. 4).

The Pragmatist Shift

The actionist and holistic interpretations of empirical testability set forth by, respec-tively, Schlick and Hempel, move in the direction of a certain pragmatist development of positivist principles. Indeed, this has been the most significant evolution of logical positivism since the middle of the twentieth century. And it is Carnap, especially in his classic paper, 'Empiricism, Semantics, and Ontology,' who provides the most emphatic example of this development. In this work, Carnap concentrates on the fundamental question of the relation between language and reality in distinguishing between two types of ontological question, the first legitimate, the second a bogus pseudo-question. In the first place, we may ask an acceptable *internal* question which, however, has only a trivial answer following upon the adoption of an overall linguistic framework by a particular community in order to interpret, explain, and predict sensory appearances. For instance, within the theoretical framework of contemporary science, we choose to deploy variables that take unobservable entities (for example, electrons, positrons) as values, and a general term or higher order predicate that designates the class of such entities – for example, this object is an unobservable entity. But then the internal ontological question, 'Are there unobservable entities?' has a trivial affirmative answer: it follows analytically from the linguistic forms used in the framework or system of discourse. Secondly, we may pose an illegitimate *external* question about the system of entities taken as a whole, such as: 'Are there really unobservable entities? What is the 'ontological status' of such entities? Do they have reality?' In dealing with such questions Carnap continues his positivism but with a pragmatic twist: such traditional philosophical questions remain classified as cognitively meaningless so that affirmative or negative answers to the questions are pseudo-statements. However, a significant question can be asked about the linguistic framework in practical, pragmatic terms. Will the decision to adopt the framework, and the ontology defined by it, be efficacious in predicting and navigating our sense-experiences? (Carnap 1972: 36). And there is no *a priori* answer to this question. The proof of its usefulness will be found in its use to realize the aim for which it was adopted. It is not obvious, however, that such a 'pragmatic shift' does not remove from logical positivism the very epistemic equipment which was used to serve its own primary objective – the demarcation of scientific sense from metaphysical nonsense, of cognitively meaningful statements from the meaningless ones which masquerade under the grammatical form of the former. In effect, a pragmatist re-orientation of logical positivism threatens to be self-defeating at increasing levels of vulnerability.

Consider first the challenge, orchestrated especially by Quine (1972), to the fundamental positivist distinction between analytic and synthetic statements. Within a pragmatist orientation human belief systems are no longer understood as abstracted propositional structures but as evolving social practices. Moreover, a holistic perspective is taken on the pragmatics of the belief system: It is not primarily *individual* concepts or propositions that are to be understood as instruments for managing our experiences in pursuit of our aims. Rather the entire conceptual system or linguistic framework employed by a particular communal culture or sub-culture is to be so understood. But, given this holistic perspective, the interpretation of the epistemic properties of the individual statements of a system of beliefs changes considerably from a traditional empiricist one. In effect, the necessity, contingency, certitude, corrigibility, analytic, synthetic, and so on, features of our assertions become a *function of our practical attitude towards them*, with the consequence that there are no longer any absolute, hard-fast dichotomies between analytic/synthetic, certain/dubitable, self-certifying/corrigible, and so on, categorizations of individual statements. Basically, if we decide that it would be efficacious in the general pursuit of our ends by means of our overall conceptual system to take certain statements as unshakeable in the face of experience, and others as corrigible, then we may, if we are interested in epistemic categories, call the former analytic, necessary, certain; and the latter synthetic, contingent, dubitable. But the confrontation of these attitudes with future experience may lead us to alter the relative practical entrenchment of any particular statement and, hence, to reclassify its epistemic status. In upshot, as Quine explains, no statement, or the belief it expresses, is immune to revision in the light of experience, but nor is any statement precluded from being retained no matter what experience we undergo (Quine 1972: 65).

Of course, a positivist pragmatist might grant Quine's discrediting of the analytic/synthetic distinction yet insist that the primary intent of the empirical testability constraint on meaning remain: unless a system of statements, in whatever domain, makes a practical difference to coping with the demands of our experience, the system is without cognitive significance. However, it is just here that the logical positivist evolution into a pragmatist perspective leaves it liable to forfeiting its original privileging of natural scientific knowledge over traditional 'metaphysical' belief systems, including those of religion and ethics. And it is of the first order of importance to observe that Quine's pragmatic empiricism is similarly vulnerable.

We may begin to recognize such a major consequence in realizing that Carnap's pragmatic criterion for the rationality of choosing language forms or conceptual schemes, that is: 'Are our experiences such that the use of the linguistic forms in question will be expedient and fruitful?' (Carnap 1972: 36), is a hopelessly vague criterion, as is Quine's criterion requiring that a conceptual scheme be an efficacious 'device for working a manageable structure into the flux of experience' (Quine 1972: 67). For the critical question, even though it is conveniently seldom asked, is: '*What counts as experience?*'. And the answer, implicit in the writings of both pragmatic positivists such as Carnap and pragmatic empiricists such as Quine, indicates that such pragmatism is that of wolves in sheep's clothing. More specifically, the understanding of *empirical content* in both varieties of pragmatism bespeaks what might be called a certain 'perceptualism' or 'sensationism' – namely, experience is circumscribed by its grounding in sense-perception, by our dealings with external sensory stimuli; or, in terms of Kant's empiricist commitments, objects are given for empirical knowledge only in sensible or spatio-temporal intuition. It is revealing that no argument is provided for this basic assumption (or better presumption) by Carnap or Quine, even though consequences of the utmost significance follow from it. Most importantly, for our purposes, it is instructive to observe that the posture of conceptual tolerance and theoretical pluralism, deliberately advertised in the pragmatism of both Carnap and Quine, is seriously misleading, as the tolerance actually delivered continues to move in a tight circle. Hence, Quine, in an apparently generous open-mindedness, places gods and sub-atomic particles on the same epistemological footing: they are both introduced as 'cultural posits' to facilitate our navigation of experience; however, as experience is bounded by sensationism, Quine has every confidence in favouring electrons over gods, on the pragmatic grounds of the 'higher degree which they expedite our dealings with *sense*-experience' (Quine 1972: 67; my emphasis). A similar conservatism in liberalist disguise informs the pragmatist turn in the logical positivism of Neurath, Schlick, Hempel, and Carnap. Essentially, such a pragmatic stance would urge tolerance of the introduction of any type of entity cum language form as long as such an introduction moved within the compass of natural scientific theory-construction and control. But such a constraint is seen as innocuous enough since Quine and our logical positivists are at one in viewing our cultural heritage as evolving quite admirably into our scientific heritage in any case.

Needless to say, there has been substantive critical response to such scientistic pragmatism and its perceptualist interpretation of the content of human experience. The central figure, within classical pragmatism itself, was William James, followed in more recent philosophy, arguably, by the 'later' Wittgenstein, and explicitly, by such philosophers as Richard Rorty (Wittgenstein 1969; Rorty 1991). James's perspective, furthermore, remains a fundamental challenge to the scientism of subsequent positivists and pragmatists and is, therefore, worth reviewing. In effect, one can interpret James as charging positivistically conservative empiricists with inconsistency in a fundamental presupposition of empiricist epistemology, in particular with hypocrisy in their prized *fallibilism* – that no factual belief is immune to revision. For, on fallibilist grounds, there is simply no right to an incorrigible belief that our experience does not range beyond sensory bounds. James deepens his challenge, furthermore, with his famous/infamous corollary of the will to believe: unless we will to believe in the existence of certain kinds of entities, we will not have the experiences pertaining to such entities which provides evidence for their existence (James 1969a: secs ix and x). As James explains, belief is often 'father to fact.' Not surprisingly, with this corollary, James's own positivist critics thought all hell breaks loose, or more ominously, all heaven breaks loose. And James did not disappoint them. For his first candidate as object of the right for a will to believe was God, proposing that unless our 'passional nature' moved us to believe in the existence of God, we might lack the internal religious experience of the presence of a superhuman consciousness who was concerned with providing for our well-being. No doubt, a case might be made here that James' own radicalization of empiricism was no more than a recipe for wishful thinking on the part of individuals. But it is the purport of later radical pragmatists writing in the spirit of James that a similar case cannot be made against non-scientific *communal* belief systems expressed in the symbol systems or conceptual schemes of particular historical cultures or sub-cultures. The basic consideration here is that a pragmatic positivism is hoist by its own petard. For the same pragmatic-empiricist criterion for the reflective appraisal of a language form or conceptual framework for science can be rationally re-applied to a non-scientific belief system – namely, that the conceptual scheme as a whole is an effective, fruitful one for the end of 'working a manageable structure into the flux of experience' (Quine 1972: 67). It is just that this end need not be realized solely in the explanation, prediction and control of sensory stimuli. But then there may be more things in heaven and earth than ever dreamt by logical positivists, even those who have donned pragmatist garments on scientistic bodies. Of course, there may not be, but such a momentous conclusion cannot simply be assumed, without argument, by perceptualist dogma. Rather, tough-minded positivists also need to give due consideration to the equally tough-minded perspective of James when he concludes:

> Humbug is humbug, even though it bear the scientific name, and the total expression of human experience, as I view it objectively, invincibly urges me beyond the narrow 'scientific' bounds. Assuredly, the real world is of a different temperament – more intricately built than physical science allows. (James 1999: 564)

The last sentence from the James's quotation prompts a critical insight into a cognate problem for logical positivists in their 'emotivist' analysis of the meaning of moral judgements outlined above. Without joining issue on the vexed question as to whether a description of intentional action and its motives can, in principle, be 'reduced to' or 'translated into' the language of physical science, it is evident that a naively simplified physicalist conception of ethical motivation undermines a credible positivist understanding of moral discourse. Let me elucidate this comment. Admittedly, in claiming that moral judgements are 'pure expressions of feeling,' or imperatives rooted in such feelings, logical positivists correctly emphasize the essential *practicality* of such judgements. Since it is a primary function of moral discourse to guide our conduct, to answer such questions as 'what shall I do?', then to say that something is good, or ought to be done, must provide a reason for seeking a certain kind of end or performing a particular kind of action. And it has been a fundamental tenet of the British empiricism within which positivists take their philosophical bearing that the cognitive states of propositional belief have no tendency to move anyone to action; only our 'passions' or affective states (desires, inclinations, attitudes, and so on) are capable of motivating us to seek or avoid the end praised or condemned. However, logical positivists, following Hume, contend that such motivating states are not in themselves states concerning which judgements of truth or falsity can be meaningfully predicated: in Hume's terms, affective states are concrete, integral units of immediate experience, 'original existences' that lack the 'representational' dimension of bona fide truth claims such that they could correspond or fail to correspond with what is 'in reality' the case (Hume 1888: 415). Hence, since positivists interpret moral judgements as essentially expressions of such affects or emotions, they are classified as neither true nor false. However, it seems to me that Spinoza had a significantly more penetrating insight on this issue. As he comments: 'A true knowledge of good and evil cannot restrain any emotion in so far as that knowledge is true, but only in so far as it is considered an emotion' (Spinoza 1992: Part IV, Prop. XIV).

An important implication of Spinoza's point in the preceding quotation might be put in the following way. Even if the internal emotive character of moral judgements did render them neither true nor false, the Humean/positivist inference to their non-rationality begs the critical question until compelling reasons are offered for believing what is 'true or false' exhausts the meaning of what is 'reasonable or unreasonable.' But the belief in such a limitation to practical reason is a profoundly wrongheaded one. We may concede that some subsets of the entire class of affective states are not the sort of things which are accessible to rational (or irrational) assessment. Bodily sensations and momentary impulses are cases in point. Generally speaking, although such mental events are among the 'moving forces' of human behavior, they are too episodic and passive to be among those affects concerning which stable rational plans can be deliberately devised. However, in contrast to 'merely' physical or lower level systems, the system of elements comprising the human agent, due to the inclusion of a cognitive consciousness, is not dumb to the origin of his emotions and desires, but can become aware of, can learn to identify the cause (or effects) of his motivating states. Most importantly, to the extent to which the human subject acquires such reflexive knowledge, that is, self-knowledge, he acquires the capacity for rationally controlling his desires, for criticizing and modifying his given passions. In this way, he is able to refashion the motivating states he happens to have and redirect them towards more inherently satisfying ends. Hence, in moving away from an inordinately sensory model of motivation adopted by logical positivists, with its overly 'passive' concept of the subject as a receiver of motivating stimuli, we are in a position to see reason or reflective consciousness, as, *pace* Hume, an 'active' power vis-à-vis the passions which move us to action. But then, through the medium of such rational appraisal, we are provided with an epistemic basis for establishing, against positivist disclaimers, the cognitively meaningful status of moral discourse, *independently* of the question of its truth or falsity.

The Legacy of Logical Positivism

Given that the above critical perspectives on logical positivism are directed towards such fundamental theses of its philosophy, it might be understandably questioned whether any substantive positive legacy can be salvaged for the Vienna Circle. I believe the answer is significantly affirmative but we need to be precisely selective in identifying its meritorious impact. And such a legacy is more narrowly focused than prominent logical positivists had intended.

Broadly speaking, we have seen that logical positivists developed a severely empiricist epistemology in order to dismiss belief systems that did not imitate the method of scientific inquiry in providing meaningful discourse. In this 'research program' positivists can be seen as exponents of a radically *deflationary* philosophy, as the 'great debunkers' of the rationality of some of the most cherished categories of human belief – especially in the so-called 'spiritual' realm of the assertion of religious and moral principles. However, with respect to moral judgements, we have observed that their inherent 'rationality conditions' are more suitably located in the reasonableness of an agent's motivations to espouse the judgements than in the experiential truth conditions for the judgements per se; and with respect to religious utterances, logical positivists have pre-emptively assumed that the content of human experience does not range beyond sensory constraints in concluding that there are no empirical truth-conditions for such utterances.

However, a good deal of the philosophical work of logical positivism was directed toward the 'in-house' analysis of the epistemology of empirical science itself. And it is here that I think a lasting positivist legacy is to be more exactly located. Note that even this more circumscribed commendation did not go without a major challenge in twentieth-century philosophy of science. Most significantly, mid-century inquiry into scientific epistemology parted company with atemporal positivist accounts of the 'logical structure' and empirical testability of particular scientific theories by taking a decidedly *historicist* turn. For example, in the monumentally influential work of Thomas Kuhn, the validation of a theoretical system in a basic domain of science was to be understood in the manner in which a revolutionary new system replaced a dominant predecessor – for instance, the way in which relativistic mechanics took the place of absolute Newtonian mechanics (Kuhn 1970: Chap. 9) And on some historicist readings of theory-choice in the actual development of natural science, the episte-mological findings were dramatically different from central epistemological views of logical positivists. For most positivists were committed to an objective, cumulative interpretation of the history of theory-choice in a particular domain of science wherein successor theories corresponded more closely, and more comprehensively, to the truth about a theory-neutral world than the theories they replaced. However, on, for instance, Kuhn's reading of the same history, we must accept a thesis of the *incommensurability* of a historically dominant scientific theory or 'paradigm' and its previously sovereign predecessor: Given the 'meaning variance' of basic physical concepts such as 'space' and 'mass' in shifting from one paradigm to its successor, the manner in which the experiential evidence is conceptualized will be internal to each paradigm. Consequently, there will be no trans-historical empirical truth-conditions with which to compare objectively the cumulative truth or 'cognitive content' of a paradigm and its successor: any empirical verification or falsification will necessarily be limited to an internal experiential test of a single paradigm.

The 'incommensurability' objection offers a serious challenge to positivist claims that an operationally effective 'decision-procedure' can be found in experiential verification for the most significant statements in the corpus of scientific knowledge – that is, theoretical hypotheses. Such an objection finds a non-historical cousin in the thesis of the 'underdetermination of theory by data' (Quine 1960: Chap. 1, Sect. 5). Even for a particular historical period, two competing theories may be both consistent with the observable data in the relevant domain of inquiry. In resisting the 'epistemic relativism' of such incommensurability and indeterminacy, logical positivism exhibits C. I. Lewis's characterization of traditional epistemology as reflecting the 'historical shadow of Euclidean geometry' (Lewis 1956: 241), which shadow, in its strongest version, implies a *singularity* in legitimate scientific theory-construction – that is to say, only *one* scientific theory would provide a warranted explanation/prediction of a particular empirical phenomenon. However, such Euclidean severity on the part of logical positivism is not essential in order for its philosophy to serve what I take to be its truly permanent and significant contribution to our intellectual culture. A recourse to Charles Saunders Peirce's notion of 'secondness' will help to explain this contribution.

Suppose, then, we are engaged in the traditional quest to understand reality by devising certain 'conceptual systems' or 'theoretical structures' to organize and interpret the observable phenomena of the physical or human world. As Peirce explained, one of the three basic categories of being, the apprehension of which is essential to our knowledge of reality, is that of 'secondness' (Peirce 1966a; 1966b).

Indeed, secondness is the index of *reality itself* in the form primarily of an experience of resistance, of reaction to one of our actions as, to use Peirce's telling example, when a blindfold person suddenly runs up against a post (Peirce 1966a: 151). Such an encounter with secondness, then, is the mark of the 'brute existence' of something beyond any knower's ego. But it is just such pre-eminent recognition of and respect for the inescapable resistance or experiential obduracy of actual reality that remains the permanently valuable lesson of the general perspective of logical positivism – indeed of the empiricist tradition within which it moves. At the heart of this lesson is positivism's incontrovertible insight into the limits of 'voluntarism' in our attempt to know our world. And such a lesson continues to have especially imperative force in the face of the sometimes excessively voluntarist character of 'social constructivist' accounts of scientific knowledge that became prevalent in the latter half of the twentieth century.

In order to elucidate this lesson we might return to our previous example of the theoretical explanation of the observation that the pressure on the sides of a closed container regularly increases with an increase in the temperature of the enclosed gas. We have noted that the theoretical explanation of this phenomenon is by means of a 'higher level' law concerning the increase in momentum of the molecular particles constituting the gas. Granted our theoretical law includes reference to imperceptible entities; nevertheless, insofar as the law is true, logical positivists are united with classical empiricists and pragmatists in insisting that its truth will exhibit a 'difference that makes a difference.' More particularly, the implications of the law will have 'practical bearings' in terms of specific predictions of future experiences following upon actions undertaken – in our example, there will be an increase in observable measurable pressure on the sides of the container upon the deliberate raising of the temperature of the gas. Admittedly recent philosophical inquiry has moved some positivists to concede epistemic indeterminacy: there is no *a priori* guarantee that, even in the long run, only one scientific theory will be true of certain kinds of events. Nature is not necessarily conceptually monogamous. For example, there could very well be distinct theoretical frameworks whose conception and use succeeds in predicting and controlling the experience of expanding gases. In this sense, theories are more like maps than mirrors.

However, not any theory-construction goes. As Peirce's notion of secondness reminds us, insofar as the theoretical structures we use to interpret the phenomenal world are inadequate, this domain will 'resist our will' to navigate it conceptually: experiential evidence can still *select against* those theories the application of which will lead us to act upon the world in ineffective ways. Believing otherwise we shall be traveling conceptually blindfold and shall no doubt run up against the brute existence of a mind-independent reality that proves repellent to our conceptual control. For instance, arguably, at sufficiently low frequencies, black body radiation can be successfully explained or predicted by means of either a particulate or undulate theoretical framework, but *not* one of caloric fluid. But it is precisely here that we remain most profoundly in debt to the philosophical legacy of logical positivism. Yes, the conceptual schemes we construct are freely willed. But if such willing becomes arbitrary in that it remains indifferent to the constraint of empirical test, then our conceptual structures will fail us in our efforts to understand and deal with reality by means of the structures. Only by remaining open to the testimony of shared experience can the siren song of the arbitrary will be reliably withstood. And it is to just such integrity that we are called by the Vienna Circle.

References

The following consists only of the location of sources referenced in the text. For a more extended list of primary and secondary sources concerning logical positivism, the reader is referred to the ample bibliographies in the Ayer, Feigl and Sellars, and Hanfling anthologies listed below – especially that of Ayer. Dates in square brackets refer to original dates of publication if there is also reference to a later location.

Ayer, A. J. (ed.) [1946] (1952), *Language, Truth, and Logic*, 2nd edn, New York: Dover.

Ayer, A. J. (ed.) (1959), *Logical Positivism*, New York: Macmillan.

Carnap, R. (1935), *Philosophy and Logical Syntax*, London: Kegan Paul.

Carnap, R. (1936, 1937), 'Testability and Meaning,' *Philosophy of Science* 3: 419–71; and 4: 2–40.

Carnap, R. [1931] (1959a), 'Psychology in Physical Language,' in A. J. Ayer (ed.) (1959), *Logical Positivism*, New York: Macmillan, pp. 165–98.

Carnap, R. [1932] (1959b), 'The Elimination of Metaphysics through Logical Analysis of Language,' in A. J. Ayer (ed.) (1959), *Logical Positivism*, New York: Macmillan, pp. 60–81.

Carnap, R. [1950] (1972), 'Empiricism, Semantics, and Ontology,' in H. Morick (ed.) (1972), *Challenges to Empiricism*, Belmont: Wadsworth, pp. 28–46.

Carnap, R. [1932] (1981a), 'Protocol Statements and the Formal Mode of Speech,' in O. Hanfling (ed.) (1981), *Essential Readings in Logical Positivism*, Oxford: Basil Blackwell, pp. 150–60.

Carnap, R. [1938] (1981b), 'Logical Foundations of the Unity of Science,' in O. Hanfling (ed.) (1981), *Essential Readings in Logical Positivism*, Oxford: Basil Blackwell, pp. 112–29.

Feigl, H. and W. Sellars (eds) (1949), *Readings in Philosophical Analysis*, New York: Appleton-Century-Crofts.

Flew, A. (1955), 'Theology and Falsification,' in A. Flew, and A. MacIntyre (eds), *New Essays in Philosophical Theology*, London: SCM Press, sect. A, pp. 96–9.

Flew, A., and A. MacIntyre (eds) (1955), *New Essays in Philosophical Theology*, London: SCM Press.

Goodman, N. (1972a), 'Review of E. H. Gombrich, *Art and Illusion*,' in N. Goodman (1972), *Problems and Projects*, Indianapolis: Bobbs-Merrill, pp. 141–6.

Goodman, N. (1972b), *Problems and Projects*, Indianapolis: Bobbs-Merrill.

Hanfling, O. (ed.) (1981), *Essential Readings in Logical Positivism*, Oxford: Basil Blackwell.

Hempel, C. G. [1935] (1949), 'The Logical Analysis of Psychology,' in H. Feigl and W. Sellars (eds) (1949), *Readings in Philosophical Analysis*, New York: Appleton-Century-Crofts, pp. 373–84.

Hempel, C. G. (1965a), 'Empiricist Criteria of Cognitive Significance: Problems and Changes,' in C. G. Hempel (1965), *Aspects of Scientific Explanation*, New York: The Free Press, pp. 101–22

Hempel, C. G. (1965b), *Aspects of Scientific Explanation*, New York: The Free Press.

Hume, D. [1739–40] (1888), *A Treatise of Human Nature*, ed. L. A. Selby-Briggs, Oxford: Oxford University Press.

James, W. [1897] (1969a), 'The Will to Believe,' in W. James, *Essays in Pragmatism*, A. Castell (ed.), New York: Hafner, pp. 88–109.

James, W. (1969b), *Essays in Pragmatism*, ed. A. Castell, New York: Hafner.

James, W. [1902] (1999), *The Varieties of Religious Experience*, New York: Modern Library.

Kuhn, T. S. (1970), *The Structure of Scientific Revolutions*, 2nd edn, Chicago: University of Chicago Press.

Lewis, C. I. [1929] (1956), *Mind and the World Order*, New York: Dover.

Morick, H. (ed.) (1972), *Challenges to Empiricism*, Belmont: Wadsworth.

Neurath, O. [1931–2] (1959), 'Sociology and Physicalism,' in A. J. Ayer (ed.) (1959), *Logical Positivism*, New York: Macmillan, pp. 282–317

Neurath, O. [1932–3] (1981), 'Protocol Sentences,' in O. Hanfling (ed.) (1981), *Essential Readings in Logical Positivism*, Oxford: Basil Blackwell, pp. 160–8.

Peirce, C. S. [1891] (1966a), 'The Architecture of Theories,' in C. S. Peirce (1966), *Selected Writings*, ed. P. P. Wiener, New York, pp. 142–59.

Peirce, C. S. [1903–11] (1966b), 'Letters to Lady Welby,' in C. S. Peirce (1966), *Selected Writings*, ed. P. P. Wiener, New York: Dover, pp. 380–432.

Quine, W. V. O. [1951] (1972), 'Two Dogmas of Empiricism' in H. Morick (ed.) (1972), *Challenges to Empiricism*, Belmont: Wordsworth, pp. 46–70

Quine, W. V. O. (1960), *Word and Object*, Cambridge: MIT Press.

Reichenbach, H. (1951), *The Rise of Scientific Philosophy*, Berkeley: University of California Press.

Rorty, R. (1991), *Objectivity, Relativism, and Truth*, Cambridge: Cambridge University Press.

Schlick, M. [1934] (1959), 'The Foundation of Knowledge,' in A. J. Ayer (ed.) (1959), *Logical Positivism*, New York: Macmillan, pp. 209–27.

Schlick, M. [1938] (1981), 'Structure and Content,' in O. Hanfling (ed.) (1981), *Essential Readings in Logical Positivism*, Oxford: Basil Blacwell, pp. 131–49

Schlick, M. (1938), *Gesammelte Aufsatze*, Vienna: Gerold & Co.

Spinoza, B. [1677] (1992), *Ethics* in B. Spinoza (1992), *Ethics, Treatise on the Emendation of the Intellect, and Selected Letters*, ed. S. Feldman, trans. S. Shirley, Indianapolis: Hackett.

Stevenson, C. L. (1945), *Ethics and Language*, New Haven: Yale University Press.

Williams, M. (1977), *Groundless Belief: An Essay on the Possibility of Epistemology*, Oxford: Basil Blackwell.

Wittgenstein, L. (1969), *On Certainty* ed. G. E. M. Anscombe and G. H. von Wright, trans. by D. Paul and G. E. M. Anscombe, Oxford: Blackwell.

Naturalism

Peter Loptson

The idea of naturalism as a comprehensive philosophical stance is one that is widely regarded as clear, reasonably stable in intension, and tolerably well understood, whether one is an advocate or an opponent of that stance. The approximate idea is one according to which the world is a unitary causally interconnected system, without 'gods' or systemic 'purposes,' and best understood, or only rationally intelligible, by scientific means. Yet it proves quite challenging to give the idea detail and precision, with a result that won't be bland and uncontroversial, at least for most philosophers, or with a result that won't be obviously absurd.

Those challenges have in fact led some contemporary philosophers to conclude that, in spite of appearances – long-standing historical usage, and continued avowals and self-ascriptions by philosophers major and minor – the concept of naturalism is not actually coherent or intelligible. Stephen Stich, for example, says:

> [I]t is my contention that there is *no* defensible naturalistic criterion [that is, a criterion to identify a claim as naturalistic], just as there is no defensible criterion of empirical meaningfulness . . . [if naturalists] can be provoked into proposing and criticizing criteria with the same energy that the positivists displayed, it's my bet that . . . naturalism will ultimately suffer the same fate as positivism did: It will die the death of a thousand failures. (Stich 1996: 197)

And Bas van Fraassen tells us: 'To identify what naturalism is, apart from something praiseworthy, I have found nigh-impossible . . . Most likely it can not be identified with any factual thesis at all' (Van Fraassen 1996: 172) Barry Stroud, for his part, says:

> 'Naturalism' seems rather like 'World Peace.' Almost everyone swears allegiance to it, and is willing to march under its banner. But disputes can still break out about what is appropriate or acceptable to do in the name of that slogan. And like world peace, once you start specifying concretely exactly what it involves and how to achieve it, it becomes increasingly difficult to reach a consistent and exclusive 'naturalism'. (Stroud 1996: 43ff.)

These expressions of conceptual pessimism are, of course, themselves parts of the naturalist saga in twentieth-century philosophy. To discover whether that pessimism is justified it will be appropriate to do a certain amount of conceptual geography, a good deal of it necessarily historical.

An initial challenge is posed by what is (to be) meant by 'nature.' Apart from characterizing the latter in a positive way, with content, there are immediately posed questions of contrast and potential exclusion. What is not-nature evidently should include 'super-nature' – the supernatural. The latter presumably includes God; and, one would think, gods, goblins, and spirits of every sort, and also the occult, and the paranormal. Yet, for some, the occult and the paranormal are just parts of nature that physics hasn't yet got around to, hasn't yet expanded its theoretical posits and instruments of detection to encompass, though no doubt eventually it will. And for Thomists, and perhaps certain Whiteheadians, nature, at least in a sense, includes God: the principles of nature involve God, as creator (or 'co-creator'). Nature involves and includes God in still a different way for Spinoza, who is in fact frequently numbered as a prominent naturalist in the history of philosophy, and was consciously hailed as a conceptual ancestor and iconic figure by the early twentieth-century American philosophers who appropriated the term 'naturalist' for themselves. With God (apart from Spinoza's God) goes, standardly, systemic purpose for the world; nature as conceived by naturalism is usually understood as excluding large-scale or systemic teleology. Yet of course Thomistic 'naturalism' centrally involves systemic teleology, as will Whiteheadian process 'naturalism.'

It is possible to be too ecumenical; and it is not unreasonable to seek to demarcate a historical movement of thought appropriately called 'naturalism,' with a founding expression in antiquity, and a continued presence in philosophy ever since; any philosophical position that includes a God or overall purposes for the world or its non-living parts will be, by definition, not a part of that movement. This is not to claim that there are not quite significant differences among different historical phases and manifestations of the naturalism intended. At any rate, the ancient atomist philosophers, perhaps most notably Democritus, may be regarded as the founders of naturalism in the sense meant in this chapter. Democritean naturalism affirmed the unity of the world, the absence of guiding purposes or minds for it, and its operating as a closed system of deterministic causal laws. It also affirmed what we may call a 'micro-determination' thesis according to which everything in and of the world in some way reduces to and is explainable by simplest units – those units being physical or material in character. Democritean naturalism evidently had gods – just not guiding or creating ones. The world – nature – as Democritus conceived it, is an entirely physical system of material particles (and larger objects they form), and empty space; it is also infinite, in time and space, and without goal or purpose.

It seems reasonable to suggest that, even if minor or lesser gods can somehow or other appear in a naturalist system, as they do in Democritus's, naturalism in our sense is god-excluding in a way that is at least reasonably intuitive, and straightforward. (Interpretations of Spinoza differ. For some, his 'God' really just is nature, and Spinoza is an atheist, as Hume claimed he was. For others, Spinoza's God is a god in a not merely nominal sense; in which case Spinoza will lose entitlement to membership in the naturalist club, just as will Whitehead and his followers.) Likewise, large-scale purposes are reasonably, intuitively, and straightforwardly at odds with the fundamental naturalist idea as understood here, even if a variety of facets of small-scale teleology in nature may pose complications. So Aristotelian or other schools of thought for which there may be purposes or meanings for the world and major significant unintelligent parts of it (like species of living things) are automatically non-naturalist.

These are the (relatively) easy exclusions that are possible (and necessary) for making up the naturalist idea. Another, not conceptually or philosophically as easy, is posed by the abstract. Can a naturalist (in our sense) be a Platonic (or some other sort of) realist with respect to numbers, triangles, other mathematical objects or items; or properties, propositions, and further intensional things? This matter seems in fact difficult and not to have an obvious answer. Yet it is nonetheless in one clear and special sense a question whose answer is obvious and straightforward. We will want it to turn out that physics, in its instantiations and developments at least since Galileo, will count, paradigmatically in fact, as naturalist. And physics, since Galileo, essentially involves mathematics and apparently also other putatively intensional concepts and territories (properties, for example). It may be that projects of nominalist philosophers of physics have been able, or will be able, to show that, and how, physics and other natural sciences do not (need to) imply or include the reality of abstract entities. This is a matter of detail whose content and outcome is not of concern at this initial stage of seeking to frame the naturalist idea. I signal my own view that the problem of the abstract has not gone away, is not trivial or easily dismissible, and is at least apparently in a certain tension with some of the features of, or motivations to, naturalism. But at the same time there is no doubt that there should be available to naturalism whatever treatment of that problem may finally be held to be most satisfactory for physics and the philosophy of physics. In that respect at least the abstract and the intensional are not conceptual complexities, or perplexities, for naturalism.

Still more complex, in different ways, is the mental. Must a naturalist be a materialist (of one sort or other) in respect of mind? Democritus was, as were his ancient atomist successors, the Epicureans. The issue is not, of course, just whether there are immaterial thinking substances, and whether supposing that there are is compatible with naturalism (in our sense). It is whether there is a real and irreducible segment and category of the world that is not physical, in any respect that physics at least so far knows (theoretically) of, and that is comprised of *thinkings*, acts, states, or processes of consciousness, with or without immaterial subjects of those thinkings.

The most useful way to approach this matter is I think to avail oneself of a (pre-Kantian) notion of phenomena, and realities they correspond to in one way or other and with one degree or other of accuracy of fit. (Since some naturalist positions are anti-metaphysical realist, we will want to allow a possibly very anodyne sense of 'corresponding realities.') Naturalism will not dispute that there are mental (psychological) phenomena. (In the same sense of the term, naturalism will also affirm that there are what may be called abstract 'phenomena,' and that there are no such things as divine, supernatural, or meaning-of-the-world phenomena.) Different naturalist theories and research programs will advance and defend different accounts of the realities that correspond to, or underlie mental phenomena. We need not insist that in order to qualify as naturalist, every such account must be materialist.

Still, we find from well before the early modern period a regularly appearing idea that there is a nature part of the world and a part made up of free agents, and their conscious and volitional states and actions – where nature and agents are seen as obviously contrasting. Plato's Socrates complains of Anaxagoras's book about mind that it turned out only to discuss physical aspects of the world – that mind was missing from it. And Aquinas, in his *Summa Theologiae*, says, casually and straightforwardly, as a view he imagines an atheist opponent will affirm: 'All natural things can be reduced to one principle, which is nature; and all voluntary things can be reduced to one principle, which is human reason, or will' (Pegis 1997: 21–2).

I want at this stage to indicate that the naturalist, in all historical periods, certainly supposes that there is something which presents itself to the inquiring observer as thinkings and sensings, and indeed that the naturalist is characteristically eager that his or her theories will give a good and proper account of such matters. And also to indicate that there is a prima facie presumption in non-naturalist camps that thinkings, sensings, and (free) acts are precisely what a study of Nature will not be investigating, or if it tries to, not investigating completely or successfully.

An area corollary (or apparently corollary) to the mental is what twentieth-century philosophy has called the 'indexical' or 'egocentric' or perspectival. If I am Loptson, and I am warm, is that a different fact from the fact that Loptson is warm; and, if different, irreducibly so, with ontological implications? If it is now 2007, is the fact that it is now known that smoking is harmful the same as the fact that this is known in 2007? And so on. The issue here is whether there are irreducible or essential indexical facts, facts that are so from observers' perspectives. Focused concern with this domain has been peculiar to the twentieth century. It would seem that a pure naturalism would deny the reality of irreducible perspectival facts.

There are other problem areas and questions facing what naturalism is conceptually. One very important one, which naturalism from Democritus to the present has regularly confronted, and tried to deal with in quite different ways, is what to say about the normative or evaluative. Historically, the major focus under this heading has been upon the ethical. What account will naturalism have of good and bad, justice, and the morally obligatory and impermissible? In more recent years naturalism has sought to (or it has been asked to) contend with additional matters of normativity posed by reason and knowledge. What account will naturalism have of what it is for a belief (or an inference) to be rational, or to be justified? In both cases (the ethical and the sphere of rational agency), and for the normative generally, critics argue that naturalism cannot plausibly or successfully meet what is required. The question arises as to whether naturalism as such is a position silent about or eliminative of the normative, or whether there can be (in some suitable sense) naturalistic normativity.

Pure naturalism, in our sense, seems only to be found, before the seventeenth century, among the ancient atomists. The ancient Stoics were materialists and determinists (and evidently also, whether or not consistently and successfully, nominalists); but they seem as well to have believed in a world-purpose, and possibly also a world-soul. None of the other ancient schools assigned to the physical universe and its causal structure a guide or model of the real. Aristotle was to be hailed by some of the early twentieth-century American naturalists as an iconic prototype figure. And there is an important sense in which this view has some justification. Aristotle does have, consistently, the attitude of the empirical observer and inquirer, and the target of his investigations is a single, unitary world (with the diversities that inquiry will disclose). Even Aristotelian theism does not altogether quash this identification. Aristotle's God is a (pre-modern) physicist's god, postulated to explain (features of) the world, and importantly part of – and, apart from his explanatory role, really rather a minor part of – the whole system of the world. Aristotle fails nonetheless as a naturalist primarily because of the pervasive presence of teleology in his system, including for non-living things; and also because of his acceptance of too many brute facts. He does think that observation warrants so supposing. But the naturalist commitment is to a unitary system of the world that should actively be expected to involve components that are not apparent, and that underlie and unite appearance into larger systemic coherencies.

After the ancients, philosophy was wholly dominated by theistic conceptions, fully and integrally until the time of Bacon and Galileo, and at least nominally until the eighteenth century. Even Hobbes, despite the charges of his many enemies, and despite his own claims that such conceptions as immaterial substance are meaningless, affirms the soundness of a first cause argument for God, and the truth of the Christian religion. Newton famously includes, in the general scholium to the *Principia*, his own case for theism; his locating that case within the framework and content of the system of nature that he had assembled constitutes that system as teleologically and super-naturally grounded and historically consolidates the natural theology worldview so prominent during the Enlightenment.

Full philosophical naturalism appears in the eighteenth century with Hume, and the French *philosophes*, including thinkers like La Mettrie, not directly connected to the authors of the *Encyclopédie*. The *OED* assigns a date of 1750 for the earliest explicit use of the term *naturalism* in English in approximately our philosophical sense. Soon after, a 1757 letter of Warburton, one of Hume's bitterest philosophical enemies, refers to Hume's work as aimed 'to establish *naturalism*, a species of atheism, instead of religion.' (Warburton's definition is essentially identical to Alvin Plantinga's, more than 120 years later.) Irreligion aside, Humean naturalism introduces a new compli-cating dimension of the naturalist idea, which is still present in twentieth-century naturalism. Humean naturalism involves, at its centre and foundation, the idea of states of consciousness (impressions, and the ideas which are their typically paler copies, in Hume's vocabulary). For Hume these states are found in other animals as well as humans. This conception just continues what we find in Hobbes (and Locke). But Hume, following Locke, is agnostic or indifferent with respect to the fundamental ontological character of these states. They are to be taken to be real, indeed, given, regardless of whether they are actually material or physical states, and whatever relation they may have to the latter. Indeed, Hume explicitly sees impressions as lacking physical or spatial locations, which would appear to imply some sort of ontological dualism; or else a proto-positivism, which will insist that serious or scientific inquiry must confine itself to phenomena (in the pre-Kantian sense noted earlier), and eschew as idle speculation, if not actually meaningless, what may underlie phenomena and their nature. At any rate, the phenomena that natural and naturalistic investigation is to explore include states of sensing, imagining, believing, emoting, reasoning, feeling, and sundry other psychological states (and kinds of states).

Enlightenment naturalistic social science and philosophy very quickly met with fundamental challenges, and those challenges continued into the nineteenth and twentieth centuries to define the central ground of contestation between naturalism and primary (philosophical) anti-naturalism. That challenge was initially mounted by Kant. Central to the philosophy of the *Critique of Pure Reason* is the idea that free rational agency cannot be understood or analyzed as a part of nature – even where nature is allowed to include states of consciousness, impressions and their ilk. Free rational agents (for Kant), and their doings (and perhaps some of the products of those doings, including culture, art, law, morality, and philosophy itself) transcend nature.

Ever since 1781, when the (first edition of the) *Critique of Pure Reason* appeared, philosophy has been dominated by the quarrel between naturalism and 'transcendentalism' (or agent anomalism). For many thinkers and movements of thought, one or the other of these two paradigms has been so dominant as to eclipse the other. Nonetheless, each has continued to be a primary and apparently fixed part of the philosophical terrain. John McDowell, a leading contemporary agent anomalist, has in fact claimed that awareness of the irreducible rivalry of the two paradigms is what constitutes and defines modernity.

In spite of the continuing influence of Kant, empirical research into human nature, conceived as part of animal nature, continued and advanced throughout the nineteenth century. Newton's general scholium notwithstanding, the physics that was his legacy was, in both its theoretical formulations and practical implementations, thoroughly naturalistic. The chemistry that Priestley, Laplace, and others added to Newtonian mechanics, in Laplace's phrase, had no need of a theistic hypothesis or of teleology. Darwin's all-important revolution in biology represents a comprehensive naturalisation of the study of living things, as does the development later in the nineteenth century by Wundt and his colleagues of a thoroughgoing experimental psychology. Comte added the terms 'positivism,' 'sociology,' and 'altruism' to the vocabularies of philosophy and science, with the intention to contribute to a naturalised scientific study of physical, psychological, and social phenomena.

Despite these developments, part of the Kantian legacy that no branch or tradition in philosophy has escaped was a sharp separation of philosophy and empirical inquiry. The twentieth century in philosophy dawns in fact with the internalization of this separation – most markedly in Great Britain and German Europe. The British innovators and 'rebels' (against Idealism) spoke for common-sense realism and logico-semantical analysis; the Austrians for phenomenology. But both involved a worldview that honoured empirical science, keeping it nevertheless on the periphery: there is what philosophers do and then there is what scientists do; and these are very different things. It is reasonable to see these developments as due to the influence of Kant; pre-Kantian philosophical 'research' was seamlessly continuous with the sciences.

A largely neglected part of the extraordinarily creative role of Bertrand Russell in philosophy in the first half of the twentieth century is his articulation of a genuinely naturalistic philosophy. Virtually alone, and with only a few imitators or successors in his country, Russell conceived of philosophy as in need of understanding and incorporating the theoretical findings and broad vision of the sciences – physics, primarily, which was in the process of undergoing dramatic revolutionary transformations – but also new developments in social science – especially psychology (specifically, at different periods in his work, psychoanalysis, and behaviorism). Russell's influence was almost entirely outside his country – in the United States and (between the two World Wars) Austria and Germany. The Germanic revolt against Idealism took the form of phenomenology and of a realism akin to that of G. E. Moore, but the idea of 'scientific philosophy' also took root quickly, manifesting itself in the formation and the work of the Vienna Circle and of similar groupings of philosophers and scientists beyond Vienna.

Naturalist philosophy has taken both metaphysical-realist and anti-metaphysical form. This ambivalence about metaphysics – the project of producing a comprehensive theory of reality – is clearly identifiable in Hume, the foundational naturalist in the modern period: Hume sometimes applauds and seeks to contribute to metaphysics, and sometimes would like to consign it to the flames as a tissue of sophistry and illusion. Russell was unambiguously pro-metaphysics, as was Quine, whose respective pieces 'What There Is' (1956) and 'On What There Is' (1961) are important creative contributions to metaphysics and to naturalist philosophy. In German Europe, on the other hand, those drawn to 'scientific philosophy' saw in it only sophistry and illusion. This was primarily due to what they regarded as the errors and obfuscations of German post-Kantian idealist metaphysics, responsible, as they thought, for the cultural and intellectual rot in the German world and the devastation of World War I. As a result, the German scientific philosophers adopted Comtean positivism as their model, reconceiving it in the guise of 'logical positivism.' Inquiry was to be limited to phenomena, and theory, necessarily only of or for phenomena, conceived as marking 'the bounds of sense.' German naturalist empiricism has a decidedly Kantian coloration, despite the Vienna Circle's repudiations of Kant and the official espousing of Hume, Russell, and the author of the *Tractatus Logico-Philosophicus* as models.

The most important of the central European scientific philosophers were Rudolf Carnap and Hans Reichenbach, with Karl Popper and Alfred Tarski also very significant. Other influential figures were Carl Hempel, Moritz Schlick, Herbert Feigl, Friedrich Waismann and Otto Neurath. Most of them – not Schlick, who was murdered by one of his students in 1936 – became émigré intellectuals, the majority of them settling in and hugely enriching the philosophical culture of the United States. Their presence increased the already considerable significance of naturalist philosophy in America. In its initial stages, professions of naturalism in the United States had not been unambiguous. This is particularly evident in the case of one of the earliest of the American self-styled naturalists, George Santayana. In some contexts, Santayana seems to subscribe explicitly to the naturalist creed. In others, his naturalism seems to be a version of an atheist metaphysical realism – that is, the position that there are no deities, but there is an objective world that is independent of minds or observers. This stance, of course, is compatible with Aristotelian teleology and with the Kantian transcendental position. (It is noteworthy that Santayana explicitly identified Hegel as a naturalist and that he (like Comte) had an aesthetic and valuational attraction to

Roman Catholicism.) What is missing from Santayana is a *programmatic* component of typical naturalism, that is, the idea that naturalist philosophy must be committed to the analysis and reduction of apparently not naturalist phenomena in scientific terms, and actual attempts to implement this commitment in particular cases.

A giant of earlier twentieth-century American philosophy, John Dewey, is also a self-described naturalist. Dewey called his philosophical position empirical naturalism, or (sometimes and more aptly) naturalistic empiricism. Dewey is, of course, one of the central thinkers of the pragmatist tradition, focusing on the active life of the experimenting social creatures that we are. Exploring the relations of naturalism and pragmatism – the latter being the distinctively American contribution to philosophy (though it has roots in the ancient sophist school) is not an easy thing to do because pragmatism is so protean a philosophical tradition. Developed originally by Peirce and James, continued by Dewey, and now revived, in new mode, by Rorty, and others, pragmatism flirts with common sense (metaphysical) realism, anti-metaphysics, moral realism, conventionalism, naturalism, transcendentalism, and is both the friend of science and the foe of 'scientism.'

Two other prominent developments in American philosophy command the attention of the historian of naturalism in twentieth-century philosophy. The first is the appearance of the so-called 'new realist' school (its members include E. B. Holt, W. T. Marvin, W. P. Montague, R. B. Perry, W. B. Pitkin, and E. G. Spaulding); its successor is the 'critical realist' school (whose most prominent member is R. W. Sellars). The Introduction to *The New Realism* (1912) affirms a strong relationship between philosophy, as it ought to be practiced, and science:

Consciousness, life, infinity, and continuity are genuine and identical topics of investigation, whether they happen to be alluded to by psychologists, biologists, logicians, and mathematicians, or by philosophers. And it is reasonable to hope that the difference of training and aptitude between the special scientist and the philosopher should yield a summation of light, rather than misunderstanding and confusion. (Marvin 1912: 37)

Nevertheless, the new realists rejected naturalism as an instance of what they call 'particularism.' It was Sellars who continued to emphasize the proximity of science and critical realism – in his case with naturalist commitments.

One other major presence of American naturalism can be found in the seminal work of Willard Van Orman Quine. While chary of the labels 'scientistic' and 'positivist,' Quine 'admit(ted) naturalism, and even glor(ied) in it.' (Hahn and Schilpp 1986: p. 430). It has been said that naturalism in the second half of the twentieth century just is the philosophy of Quine; and opposition to naturalism, opposition to Quine's philosophy. Quine's distinctively naturalist contributions include his systematic and career-long attempts to eliminate the 'intensional' from serious theorizing, preeminently in his rejection of the analytic/synthetic distinction. Critics regularly misunderstood this rejection, often taking it to be less radical than it was – as though it were (merely) a body of complaints about the fact that analyses of analyticity (and of cognate concepts) had not been as rigorous, sharp-boundaried, and non-circular as they needed to be. In fact, Quine was continuing the programs of logical empiricism, with a goal of replacing 'meanings' with behaviorist and physicalist analogues. Not surprisingly, opposition to the intensional was accompanied by opposition to the intentional – the mental – as a theoretically respectable, and distinctive, category of science.

Quine also famously developed naturalized epistemology. It seems clear that his goal was not to offer new analyses of what it is to be a rational agent, or to have a justified belief; but rather to propose a re-alignment of epistemology as limited to study of patterns of behavior (including linguistic behavior and neurological responses) of humans in their cognitive (big-brain-deploying) interactions with the world. (Alvin Goldman's reliabilist theory of justification, according to which a justified belief is a belief produced by means that over long periods of time have tended to give beliefs corresponding to fact, is a contribution to what is essentially this Quinean naturalist agenda.) Quine endorsed the idea of applying Darwinian natural selection to issues and problems of epistemology. At least part of what has led to forms of radical skepticism, from the ancient Pyrrhonians down to Descartes, Hume, and Russell – revolving around the question of how the isolated individual human organism is able to reach beyond its 'interiority' and to achieve genuine contact and alignment with the world, resulting in factual claims – can now be answered. For the naturalizing epistemologist, humans have been naturally selected to tend to have true beliefs and, once this has become a propensity and a skill, it leads to novel and not obviously utilitarian applications, bringing about bodies of knowledge like scientific psychology, history, and mathematical physics.

Naturalized epistemology has not, of course, gone without critical objections. Yet, it seems that some responses do miss the point: the goal of 'scientific philosophy' is not necessarily to preserve everything philosophers have thought to be valid research projects and endeavors of theory. In its most modest moments, naturalistic philosophy of a Quinean stripe asks that it not be assumed, without examination, that rational agency and irreducible normativity are theoretically sound notions. Other critics have disputed whether there are any compelling reasons to believe that natural selection would favor tendencies toward the formation of true beliefs rather than merely empirically adequate, or approximately true, ones. In fact, though, evolutionary analysis is replete with functions that meet a need of inclusive fitness; it would seem to make excellent Darwinian sense that a large-brained creature might plausibly, over time, refine empirical adequacy, or approximate truth, in the direction of truth itself, even if the former belief were just as good from the evolutionary standpoint as the latter.

Another movement in recent philosophy is 'supervenience naturalism.' The idea of supervenience – it has roots also in the earlier concept of emergence – seems to have developed principally out of the increasing sophistications and conundra of materialism in the philosophy of mind. Only some materialists have rejected altogether mental concepts as unscientific (and, for some, involving something like Rylean category mistakes if the attempt is made to unite those concepts with the physical). Quineans and eliminative materialists notwithstanding, most philosophers in the later twentieth century have wanted to affirm both the reality and the theoretical – indeed, scientific – respectability, of the mental. Differences naturally exist in the details: some, for example, reaffirm a category that many had thought dead and buried – the notion of sense data – that is, inner subjective object-like entities, immediately experienced in some experiences; the popular current term (for the experience or its object) is 'qualia.' Less contestable has been the notion of the mental state, event, episode, or process itself – whatever its object or objects may be. Thinkings and sensings are held, except by the more severe and exacting of 'scientific philosophers,' to be items whose reality and (much of whose) nature are confirmed by daily observation and experience. There is virtual unanimity that these items, at least the individual cases ('tokens') of them, insofar as they are identifiable as states of human beings (or other animals) are in fact neural or some other physical states or processes in the brain of the human or (other) animal. Even where there is agreement that (at least some relatively 'atomic') mental state tokens are in fact neural states, there is plenty of disagreement thereafter. Davidson's position – 'anomalous monism' – affirms token-token identity, but rejects type-type identity, as well as any possible discovery of psycho–physical laws. This position is really anti-naturalist, despite the fact that it conceives the world in terms of entirely physical realities. Less problematically naturalist will be some varieties of epiphenomenalism – a position in the philosophy of mind which seems never to go away, however regularly it is repudiated. Epiphenomenalism is formally ontologically dualist; as argued earlier, the spirit of Democritean naturalism allows for non-materialist options. What is key to naturalism is the idea of a single unitary world, with a single set of nomological principles underscoring that unity. (As Hume had put it, '[N]atural and moral evidence link together, and form only one chain of argument . . . they are of the same nature, and derived from the same principles.') It would seem that such a set might include dualist laws or principles – most plausibly and unobjectionably, perhaps, if they were epiphenomenalist ones.

Supervenience is the idea that a physical state of the world, subject to the same physical laws, 'fixes' or determines states, events, or processes held to be 'supervenient' upon them – such states, events and processes including (individual) mental or psychological ones. The idea is often put with reference to possible worlds, either as the claim that no two possible worlds with the same physical contents and laws can be such that the one has a given psychological state and the other does not, or (more weakly) as the claim that a designated psychological state which is in fact found in a world with a specified physical content and body of physical laws is never found in a world with the same physical laws but diverse physical content.

From the naturalist point of view, supervenience may seem to be a way of having your cake and eating it too. Every phenomenon that, at some time or other, has been problematic for naturalizing theory, but asserted to be real by some philosophers, can be 'saved' and secured, if we agree to say that it supervenes on some physical configuration or other, in a suitably lawlike way. The cost of such an agreement would seem to be minimal. For example, a particularly prominent case of putative supervenience is provided by ethics. A number of recent philosophers have revived naturalism in ethics, in a significantly novel way. Perhaps there are no possible worlds where suitable configurations of pleasure-and-pain states, themselves understood purely physicalistically, have (or lack) good, evil, or justice.

In fact, a revived naturalizing ethics seems importantly at odds with the historic naturalistic conception we have discerned in and since Democritus. Naturalism, as we understand the notion, regards the world as in an important sense a cold and impersonal place; in this world, persons, thoughts, and possibly even free choices exist, but never (objective) rights and wrongs. Indeed, the issue dividing Hume and Kant – the issue of whether free rational agency transcends what the investigation of the natural world can accommodate – loses all conceptual focus if a project of naturalizing ethics, either in the old-fashioned way or in its new guises, can have real or coherent content.

A recent volume of Sir Peter Strawson's discusses 'social naturalism.' The latter turns out to be the later philosophy of Wittgenstein. It would be difficult to find a twentieth-century philosopher more opposed to the central tenets of naturalism than Wittgenstein. Wittgenstein's affinities are with Aristotle and with pragmatism (both of which, to be sure, have been claimed as having naturalist congeniality). Aristotle, pragmatism, and Wittgenstein, all claim that some parts of life, and what we know, and do, are not understandable by systematic theory, still less natural science; which seems quite fundamentally at variance with naturalism.

With respect to the future, we may anticipate continued expansion of naturalist philosophical endeavors in cognitive science and materialist philosophy of mind. The opposing agent-anomalist position remains also alive and well, and interestingly, creatively exemplified in the work of Brandom, McDowell, and others. Viewed with detachment, it is striking how entrenched the two positions are, how long this has been the case, how research-active each is, and how astonishingly confident each is that the other is mistaken, and that history is on its side. (One of the papers in a recent critical anthology on naturalism is called, revealingly, 'Farewell to Philosophical Naturalism.' There are *many* other articles and books in similar vein; and many other confident, triumphalist pieces of writing on the other side of this divide.) For those who aspire to or value progress in philosophy, this may be a depressing reflection, but there seems every reason to expect that energetic variations on this polarity will be found as actively at play at the end of the current century as at its beginning.

References

Brandom, Robert (1994), *Making it Explicit*, Cambridge, MA: Harvard University Press.
De Caro, Mario, and David Macarthur (eds) (2004), *Naturalism in Question*, Cambridge, MA: Harvard University Press.
Dennett, Daniel C. (1996), *Kings of Minds*, New York: Basic Books.
Dretske, Fred (1995), *Naturalizing the Mind*, Cambridge, MA: MIT Press.
Hahn, L. E., and P. A. Schilpp (eds) (1986), *The Philosophy of W. V. O. Quine*, La Salle: Open Court.
Holt, E. B., W. T. Marvin, W. P. Montague, R. B. Perry, W. B. Pitkin, E. G. Spaulding (1912), *The New Realism*, New York: Macmillan.
Hume, D. (1999), *An Enquiry Concerning Human Understanding*, Oxford: Oxford University Press.
Marvin, W. et al. (1912), *The New Realism*, New York: Macmillan.
McDowell, John (1998), *Mind, Value, and Reality*, Cambridge, MA: Harvard University Press.

Millikan, R. G. (1984), *Language, Thought, and Other Biological Categories: A New Foundation for Realism*, Cambridge: MIT Press.

Pegis, A. C. (ed. and trans.) (1997), *The Basic Writings of Saint Thomas Aquinas*, vol. 1, Indianapolis: Hackett.

Quine, W. V. O. (1961), *From a Logical Point of View*, 2nd edn, New York and Evanston: Harper and Row.

Quine, W. V. O. (1969), *Ontological Relativity and Other Essays*, Columbia University Press: New York.

Reichenbach, H. (1951), *The Rise of Scientific Philosophy*, Berkeley and Los Angeles: University of California Press.

Russell, B. (1948), *Human Knowledge: Its Scope and Limits*, New York: Simon and Schuster.

Russell, B. (1956), *Logic and Knowledge*, London: George Allen and Unwin.

Sellars, W. (1991), *Science, Perception and Reality*, Atascadero: Ridgeview.

Stich, S. (1996), *Deconstructing the Mind*, Oxford: Oxford University Press.

Strawson, P. F. (1985), *Skepticism and Naturalism: Some Varieties*, New York: Columbia University Press.

Stroud, B. (1996), 'The Charm of Naturalism,' *Proceedings and Addresses of the American Philosophical Association* 70 (2) (Nov.): 43–4.

Van Fraassen, B. (1996), 'Science, Materialism, and False Consciousness,' in J. Kvanvig (ed.) (1996), *Warrant in Contemporary Epistemology*, Lanham: Rowman and Littlefield.

Pragmatism

Nicholas Rescher

Pragmatism as a philosophical doctrine traces back to the Academic skeptics in classical antiquity. Denying the possibility of achieving authentic knowledge (*epistēmē*) regarding the real truth, they taught that we must make do with *plausible information* (*to pithanon*) adequate to the needs of practice. However, pragmatism as a determinate philosophical doctrine descends from the work of Charles Sanders Peirce. For him, pragmatism was primarily a theory of meaning, with the meaning of any concept that has application in the real world inhering in the relations that link experiential conditions of application with observable results. But by the 'practical consequences' of the acceptance of an idea or a contention, Peirce meant the consequences for *experimental* practice – 'experimental effects' or 'observational results' – so that for him the meaning of a proposition is determined by the essentially positivist criterion of its experiential consequences in strictly *observational* terms. And, moving beyond this, Peirce also taught that pragmatic effectiveness constitutes a quality control monitor of human cognition – though here again the practice issue is that of *scientific* praxis and the standard of efficacy pivoting on the issue of specifically *predictive* success. Peirce developed his pragmatism in opposition to Idealism, seeing that the test of applicative success can lead mere theorizing to stub its toe on the hard rock of reality. But his successors softened up the doctrine, until with some present-day 'pragmatists' the efficacy of ideas consists in their mere *adoption* by the community rather than – as with Peirce – in the success that the community may (or may not!) encounter as it puts those ideas into practice.

Although Peirce developed pragmatism into a substantial philosophical theory, it was William James who put it on the intellectual map in his enormously influential *Pragmatism: A New Name for Some Old Ways of Thinking* (1907). However, James changed (and – as Peirce himself saw it – ruined) Peircean pragmatism. For where Peirce saw in pragmatism a road to impersonal and objective standards, James gave it a personalized and subjectivized twist. With James, it was the personal (and potentially idiosyncratic) idea of efficacy and success held by particular people that provided the pragmatic crux, and not an abstracted community of ideally rational agents. For him, pragmatic efficacy and applicative success did not relate to an impersonalized community of scientists but to a diversified plurality of flesh and blood individuals. For James, truth is accordingly what reality impels and compels human individuals to believe; it is a matter of 'what pays by way of belief' in the course of human activity within the circumambient environment and its acquisition is an invention rather than a revelation. With James, the tenability of a thesis is determined in terms of its experiential consequences in a far wider than merely *observational* sense – a sense that embraces the affective sector as well.

Pragmatism has had a mixed reception in Europe. In Italy, Giovanni Papini and Giovanni Vailati espoused the doctrine and turned it into a party platform for Italian philosophers of science. In Britain, F. C. S. Schiller was an enthusiastic follower of William James, while F. P. Ramsey and A. J. Ayer endorsed pivotal aspects of Peirce's thought. Among continental participants, Rudolf Carnap also put pragmatic ideas to work on issues of logic and philosophy of language and Hans Reichenbach reinforced Peirce's statistical and probabilistic approach to the methodology and prolification of induction. However, the reception of pragmatism by other philosophers was by no means universally favorable. F. H. Bradley objected to the subordination of cognition to practice because of what he saw as the inherent incompleteness of all merely practical interests. G. E. Moore criticized William James's identification of true beliefs with useful ones – among other reasons because utility is changeable over time. Bertrand Russell objected that beliefs can be useful but yet plainly false. And various continental philosophers have disapprovingly seen in pragmatism's concern for practical efficacy – 'for success' and 'paying off' – the expression of characteristically American social attitudes: crass materialism and naive populism. Pragmatism was thus looked down upon as a quintessentially American philosophy – a philosophical expression of the American go-getter spirit with its success-oriented ideology.

However, Americans have had no monopoly on practice-oriented philosophizing. Karl Marx's ideas regarding the role of practice and its relation to theory have had a vast subsequent influence (some of it upon otherwise emphatically non-Marxist thinkers such as Max Scheler). Important recent developments of praxis-oriented philosophy within a Marx-inspired frame of reference are represented by Tadeusz Kotarbinski in Poland and Jürgen Habermas in Germany. Kotarbinski has endeavored to put the theory of *praxis* on a systematic basis within a special discipline he designates as *praxiology*. Habermas has pursued the concept of *praxis* deeply into the domain of the sociological implications of technology.

Still, be this as it may, pragmatism has found its most favorable reception in the USA, and has never since Peirce's day lacked dedicated advocates there, however variant their approach. At Harvard in the next generation after James, C. I. Lewis was concerned to apply pragmatism to the validation of logical systems. He focused upon (and in his own work sought to develop) the idea of alternative systems of logic among which one must draw on guides of pragmatic scientificity and utility. And for all his differences with Lewis, W. V. O. Quine continued this thinker's emphasis on the pragmatic dimension of choice among alternative theoretical systems. Richard Rorty has endeavored to renovate John Dewey's rejection of abstract logical and conceptual rigidities in favor of the flexibilities of expediency in practice. In a cognate spirit Joseph Margolis has re-emphasized pragmatism's anti-absolutism based on the transiencies of historical change. And Nicholas Rescher's 'methodological pragmatism' has sought to return pragmatism to its Peircian roots by giving the doctrine a specifically methodological turn, seeing that anything methodological – a tool, procedure, instrumentality, program or policy of action, and so on – is best validated in terms of its ability to achieve the purposes at issue, its success at accomplishing its appropriate task. Since cognitive methods must be pivotal here, it follows that even the factual domain can be viewed in such a light that practical reason becomes basic to the theoretical.

One overarching and ironic fact pervades the divergent development of pragmatism, namely that the doctrine can be seen either as a validation of objectively cogent standards or as a subverter of them. There is a pragmatism of the right, a Peircian or objective pragmatism of 'what works *impersonally*' – though proving efficient and effective for the realization of some appropriate purpose in an altogether person-indifferent way ('successful prediction,' 'control over nature,' 'efficacy in need fulfillment.') And there is a pragmatism of the left, a Jamesian or subjective pragmatism of 'what works for *X*' in proving efficient and effective for the realization of a particular person's (or group's) wishes and desires. The objective pragmatists stand in the tradition of Peirce and include F. P. Ramsey, C. I. Lewis, Rudolf Carnap; the subjective pragmatists stand in the tradition of William James and include F. C. S. Schiller and Richard Rorty. (John Dewey straddles the fence by going to a social inter-personalism that stops short of impersonalism.) Looking at James, Peirce saw subjective pragmatism as a corruption and degradation of the pragmatic enterprise since its approach is not a venture in validating objective standards but in *deconstructing* them to dissolve standards as such into the variegated vagaries of idiosyncratic positions and individual inclinations. And this is how objective pragmatists view the matter down to the present day – this writer included.

It is instructive to review the historical situation more closely.

Charles Sanders Peirce (1839–1914)

In the hands of this founding father, pragmatism had two principal components; one regarding meaning and one as regarding truth. Peirce's meaning pragmatism encompasses a pragmatic view of the meaning of concepts and ideas. The crux, so Peirce maintained, lay in the 'pragmatic maxim':

> To ascertain the meaning of an intellectual conception one should consider what practical consequences might conceivably result from the truth of that conception; and the sum of these consequences will constitute the entire meaning of the conception. (Peirce 1934; V: sec. 5.412)[1]

Meaning, in sum is, as meaning does. As Peirce put it in his classic essay on 'How to Make our Ideas Clear' (1878): '[T]here is no distinction of meaning so fine as to consist in anything but a possible difference of practice' (Peirce 1934, V: 401–9). Peirce insisted that the prime function of our beliefs regarding the world is to commit us to rules for action – to furnish guidance to our behavior about what to think, say and do; above all, to canalize our expectations in matters of observation and experiment in scientific contexts.

And much the same sort of story here told with respect to meaning holds also with respect to truth. Those theses are true whose implementation in practice 'work out' by way of yielding success in matters of prediction and application. For Peirce the best route to this distinction is the scientific method whose rivals – evidence ignoring tenacity, pious adherence to authority, *a priori* speculation, and the like – simply cannot compare with it in point of producing trustworthy results (Peirce 1934, V: secs 538–47). True factual beliefs, ipso facto, are those that achieve efficacy through guiding our expectations, beliefs, and actions in satisfying ways – where specifically cognitive satisfactions are at issue. And they must achieve this on a systemic basis.

As Peirce saw it, truth in scientific matters consists in those contentions that are 'fated to be ultimately agreed to by all who investigate [scientifically]' (Peirce 1934, V: sec. 5.407). It is what the community of rational inquirers is destined to arrive at in the end – the ultimate consensus of informed opinion among investigators committed to the principles of science. To his mind, it is not mere inquiring as such but *properly conducted* inquiring that must eventually get at the truth of things. As Pierce saw it, it is the scientific method – not the scientific doctrine of the day – that is crucial for rational inquiry. And he rejected an ideology of the look-to-science-for-all-the-answers sort for the same reason that he rejected dogmatism of any sort, because it is itself ultimately unscientific.

William James (1842–1910)

William James adopted an approach to pragmatism that was distinctly different from that of Peirce. For, as he saw it, pragmatism's characteristic tactic is to construe truth in terms of a potentially diversified utility in whose light there is nothing fixed or monolithic about truth:

> *The* Truth: what a perfect idol of the rationalistic mind! I read in an old letter – from a gifted friend who died too young – these words: 'In everything, in science, art, morals, and religion, there *must* be one system that is right and *every* other wrong.' How characteristic of the enthusiasm of a certain stage of young! At twenty-one we rise to such a challenge and expect to find the system. It never occurs to most of us even later that the question 'What is *the* Truth?' is no real question (being irrelevant to all conditions) and that the whole notion of *the* truth is an abstraction from the fact of truths in the plural. (James 1907: 115)

On this basis, James held that 'the true' is only the expedient in our way of thinking, just as the right is only the expedient in our way of behaving' (James 1907: 106). He sought to replace 'the truth' with a diversified plurality of truths.

For James, pragmatism seeks to reject the construction of 'high-fallutin' philosophical conceptions like truth, beauty, and justice, and to put work-a-day utility, serviceability, efficiency, and effectiveness in their place. And pragmatic 'success' is seen as a matter of getting things done in the setting of our everyday life affairs. As James put it, '[I]deas become true just insofar as they help us to get into satisfactory relation with other parts of our experience' (James 1907: 34),[2] where those 'other parts' reach beyond the range of theorizing, of inquiry and question-resolution. Turning away from matters of rational inquiry as such, James rejected the idea that there is a 'pure,' disinterestedly neutral and wholly impersonal realm of meaningful cognition. To his mind, concepts like 'knowledge,' 'truth,' 'meaning,' and the like are to serve the interests not just of rational inquiry but of life in general. James accordingly construed pragmatic success not in terms of specifically epistemic efficiency in scientific matters of prediction and control but rather in terms of psychological satisfactions. After all, 'Truth for us is simply a collective name for verification-processes . . . Truth is *made*, just as health, wealth, and strength are made, in the course of experience' (James 1907: 104). And at times James came perilously close to a 'wishful thinking' view of truth that conflated the narrower *evidential* reasons for the substance of a belief with the broader *prudential* reasons why its adoption could prove advantageous. And so while Peirce construed those pragmatically pivotal 'practical consequences' as being consequences that are observationally and experimentally determinable in a uniform way by any community of scientific investigators, James took them to relate to the bearing of beliefs on the affective condition of individuals.

James thus construed pragmatism very differently from Peirce, not as a doctrine that provides a fixed standard of adequacy, but as an invitation to pluralism – to a relativistic diversity of views that allows not only for differences among individuals but even differences within individuals as an embodiment of many selves with natural inclinations operating in diverse circumstances. Peirce's pragmatism was indeed success oriented – but the success it envisioned was that of the communally impersonal objectives of science. But with James it became a matter of serving the personal needs of differently constituted human individuals in their varying subjective reactions to objective conditions. And so with James, reality lies substantially in the eyes of the beholder: 'Each thinker, however, has dominant habits of attention; and these practically elect from among the various [thought] worlds someone to be for him the world of ultimate realities' (James 1983: 923). Walt Whitman's 'I am multitudes' was an idea that appealed to James. While 'inconsistencies' may worry some of his readers, they did not faze William James himself. It was not for nothing that he saw the idea of an objective and fixed truth as a specter that must give way to expediency.

John Dewey (1859–1952)

With John Dewey a yet different approach to pragmatism emerged – one that was not grounded in science (à la Peirce) or in personalistic psychology (à la James), but in social ethics. For Dewey regarded the scope of practicable intellectual effort as confined to determinations of utility for us humans as beings coexisting in organized societies.

As Dewey saw it, ideas and beliefs are nothing but artificial thought-instruments, mere conveyers of man-made meanings, shaped by social processes and procedures. Dewey joins with the other pragmatists in emphasizing the primacy of experience and experiment over the indications of speculation and over the urgings of experience-abstractive theorizing. For him, theoretical logic is a direly insufficient basis of knowledge because 'such logic only abstracts some aspect of the existing course of events in order to reduplicate it as a petrified eternal principle by which to explain the very change of which it is the [static] formalization' (Dewey 1909: 90; 88). Truth is not a matter of logically static fixity; instead, it is that which gets endorsed and accepted by the community. Its sole validation is the sanction of social approbation and custom, and when those 'truths' no longer satisfy social needs others are found to replace them. Truth resides in agreement: social consensus does not merely *evidentiate* truth, but is its *creator*.[3]

In this way, Dewey turned pragmatism into a more decidedly social direction. To be sure, Peirce too had looked to a community; but this was only the abstraction of an idealized long-run community of scientific inquirers. Dewey's community, however, was the concrete society as it actually functions about us here and now. His enterprise was the improvement of that society, specifically its movement in the direction of a more perfect democracy. As he saw it, only in a healthy democracy will personal development achieve its best prospects and only enlightened individuals will operate a thriving democracy. Accordingly, Dewey regarded education – the training of an intelligent electorate – as a key requisite for a viable society. The natural Darwinism of cultural selection militates alike for social, cultural, and individual progress. Dewey viewed the human condition in terms of an ongoing process of communally beneficial self-development.

John Dewey, like Peirce before him, saw inquiry as a self-corrective process whose procedures and norms must be evaluated and revised in the light of subsequent experience. But Dewey regarded this reworking as a social and communal process proceeding in the light of values that are not (as with Peirce) connected specifically to science (that is, prediction and experimental control), but rather values that are more broadly rooted in the psychic disposition of ordinary people at large – the moral and aesthetic dimension now being specifically included. Peirce's pragmatism is scientifically elitist, James's is psychologically personalistic, Dewey's is democratically populist. To be sure, Dewey here envisioned a community that sensibly acknowledges the findings of science. But this proved no problem for him because he saw the good society, the *rational* society, as more or less automatically geared to a commitment to scientific endeavors and principles. For all his rejection of metaphysics the nineteenth-century vision of socio-cultural progressiveness was deep rooted in Dewey's mind.

C. I. Lewis (1883–1964)

C. I. Lewis and Rudolf Carnap were pragmatists of a stripe rather different from their predecessors. For in their hands, pragmatism came to focus not on issues of effectiveness in factual inquiry – let alone on satisfactions in the conduct of life – but rather on the acceptability of claims in formal systems of logic or mathematics. Not the experiential knowledge of everyday life or of natural science but the abstract truths of the formal sciences were the subject of their pragmatism. With Lewis, the fundamental fact that pragmatism had to address was the proliferation of different mathematical systems (different geometries, for example) and of different logical systems (such as classical, modal, and many-valued logic). As Lewis saw it, this meant that there is no one single right system among competitive rivals. For when pragmatic utility is our guide, here the question is not which system is correct but which system is optimal for the purposes at hand.

The framework of Lewis's reflections was already well formed before his 1929 magnum opus *Mind and the World Order* (1956 reprint; also Lewis 1923), in which he proposed to project pragmatism into the domain of logic. A logical system, so he maintained, is a purely formal structure – abstract and detached from sensory experience so that impersonal facts are irrelevant to its contents. Accordingly, contentions of the format 'the thesis T obtains in the formalized logical system L' will be true analytically. But this of course pivots the issue of T's actual acceptability upon that of L. And here Lewis took a pragmatic line, holding that we have to appraise the acceptability of entire systems on the pragmatic grounds of their efficacy with respect to the range of correlative purposes. As Lewis saw it, considerations of the format 'The particular logical system L is the appropriate instrumentability with respect to a certain range of application' (for example, 'Intuitionistic logic is the proper instrument for developing arithmetic') provide the pivot on which the acceptability of the theses at issue in such systems depends. Only on the basis of experience – by trying and seeing – can one validate such judgements. Pragmatic success is once again our standard, but now the experiential data at issue are not sensory facts but cognitive facts about abstract relationships – not success in accommodating observations but success in meeting the needs of efficient reasoning. And it is thus formal (inferential) rather than physical (experiential) practice that is at issue.

Lewis extended this line of thought from a pragmatic validation of the *a priori* propositions of logic and mathematics to articulate also a neo-Kantian pragmatic account of the conceptual categories that afford the terms of reference for our thought about the world. He held that while it is indeed necessary to use *a priori* categories for the descriptive and explanatory characterization of experience, nevertheless these categories are not absolute and fixed but variable and capable of alteration or replacement in the light of our experience regarding what is useful and effective for these purposes. The categories are thus *a priori* with respect to any particular inquiry or group thereof – but *not* with respect to our inquiries-in-general. On this basis, Lewis contended, the pragmatic approach represents the proper way to assess both the acceptability of logical and mathematical systems and that of the fundamental presuppositions and principles of empirical inquiry. And so, in refusing to follow James and Dewey into an enlarged pragmatism of success with lived experiences at large, Lewis returned to the Peircean idea of a strictly epistemic pragmatism geared to efficacy with respect to our specifically cognitive operations.

Rudolf Carnap (1891–1970)

In focusing on logico-mathematical issues Lewis was followed by Rudolf Carnap, who explicitly acknowledged this indebtedness.[4] Carnap maintained that the appropriateness (acceptability) of a formal system – say, classical vs. intuitionistic mathematics – lies in how effectively we can operate with the system at issue in the relevant functional context (calculation or mathematical demonstration, for example). Applicative utility is once again the key consideration here.

In much the same spirit as that of Lewis, Carnap maintained that two sorts of issues arise in communicative contexts: *system-external* questions about the existence of the entities that are supposedly available as objects of discussion, and *system-internal* questions about the substantive features that are being attributed to such objects. Internal issues have factual answers that can be substantiated through the rules and procedures of the given language-framework; external issues relate to the initial choice of that framework itself. As Carnap saw it, those external issues relating to the adoption of a particular linguistic framework are subject to his so-called Principle of Tolerance: 'We have in every respect complete liberty with regard to the forms of language. Everyone, that is, is free to choose the rules of his language, and thereby his logic, in any way he wishes' (Carnap 1937: XV). Or at least this is so insofar as considerations of theoretical general principles go, for such a decision is not actually a 'cognitive' or 'factual' but rather is a *practical* decision that can (and should) be motivated by functional consideration of purposive efficacy such as simplicity, efficiency, and fruitfulness. To this extent, then, Carnap moved in the direction of pragmatism. But then he came to a sticking point.

For while Carnap saw the choice among alternative frameworks as subject to constraints of rationality and was prepared to accept the finding of one framework's being more efficient and effective than another relative to certain purposes, he was unwilling to move from classing choices in the spectrum better/worse to classing them as correct/incorrect – and not even in the contextualized mode of 'correct for *this* particular application.' For Carnap, applicative efficacy was not evidence of appropriateness but was the decisive factor in its own right. By thus totally disassociating the issues of utility and correctness, Carnap emptied pragmatic considerations of any evidential bearing upon matters in science or everyday life. Thus, for him, the superior utility of (for example) a framework of discussion based on the centrality of substantial things would not – even if established – support a claim that things/substances exist, and would not authorize truth-attribution for any claims to reality here (Carnap 1937: sec. 17).

Accordingly, Carnap remained a strict conventionalist: he did not operate a pragmatic epistemology but set the epistemic and the pragmatic dimensions into a diametrically opposed contrast with one another. Carnap's pragmatism only warrants choice in matters of procedure and never provides for the substantiation of factual contentions, which, on his approach, one can never maintain as true but only as more or less probable. Pragmatic considerations here became a substitute rather than a basis for claims to matters of truth or existential fact. With Carnap a pragmatically oriented probability is all-predominant and matters of truth are consigned to oblivion.

W. V. O. Quine (1908–2002)

Quine's pragmatism took a line that was, in a way, even more radical than Carnap's. For with Quine the cognitive status of human language-formulated cognition as a whole – rather than that of some particular system or concept-framework – becomes the pivot upon which pragmatic considerations are to be hinged. To his mind, the issue of validation is uncompromisingly holistic.

Rejecting Carnap's probabilism Quine returned to the earlier evolution-influenced standpoint of Dewey. And he followed Dewey in his commitment to a pragmatic approach to language as an instrumentality of human communicative practice. As he himself put it:

Philosophically I am bound to Dewey by the rationalism that dominated his last three decades. With Dewey I hold that knowledge, mind, and meaning are part of the same world that they have to do with and that they are to be studied in the same empirical spirit that actuates natural science. There is no place for *a priori* philosophy. (Quine 1969: 26)

Like Dewey before him, Quine rejected the idea of a somehow absolute foundation for knowledge. For him, the authorizing basis of any such theory must lie in its broader role in our cognition, and specifically in its contribution to our scientific view of the world's modus operandi, recognizing the impracticability of claiming any absolutistic correspondence between a concept framework and the independent reality it purportedly depicts.

Quine is first and foremost a 'naturalist' in regarding science as a court of final appeal. As he sees it, natural science constitutes an inquiry into reality which, while fallible and corrigible, is not answerable to any supra-scientific tribunal, and needs no further justification. Observation and the hypothetico-deductive method provide for all that we need within science and all that we need for validating our claims about science as well (Quine 1981: 72). And to this scientific naturalism Quine adds a Peirce-reminiscent touch of evolutionism in that for him scientific realism – the position that, as best as we can possibly tell it, things really are as science depicts them to be – is simply part and parcel of our evolutionary imprinted cognitive endowment: 'The very notion of an object at all, concrete or abstract, is a human contribution, a feature of our inherited approaches for organizing the amorphous matter of neural input' (Quine 1992: 6). But of course *how* we configure that 'notion of an object' depends on the substantive state of things in the science of the day – a variable situation that turns on the comparative success of competing scientific theories. And so a decidedly pragmatic perspective – one that encompasses explanatory utility, fallibility, success in prediction and control, and the like – enters into Quine's thought via his commitment to the primacy of scientific method. Thus for Quine, as for C. I. Lewis, our fundamental categories of thought, while indeed *a priori* in the local context of our particular investigations, are based *a posteriori* in the wider setting of our experience-guided inquiry-at-large, and can always be challenged and changed under the pressure of enlarged experience.[5]

Hilary Putnam (b. 1926)

Hilary Putnam embodies the continuity of Harvard's pragmatist tradition (Putnam 1995). As Putnam sees it, pragmatism's salient idea is something that he (together with Wittgenstein, Rorty, and philosophical modernists generally) is prepared to endorse – namely that is makes no sense to try to get at 'the actual truth' of things if this is taken to involve anything like the Kantian contrast between 'how things are in themselves' and 'how things appear to us humans.' Putnam has it that if *this* is what is at stake in the philosophical quest for truth, then the whole project must be abandoned because the very idea of such a deeper truth is nonsense upon stilts (to use Jeremy Bentham's vivid expression), seeing that it is truth from our human point of view that is the only thing that could possibly be of concern for us. All this is decidedly reminiscent of Putnam's philosophical hero, William James.

Moreover, Putnam's approach to pragmatism also returns to the wider perspective of James, Mead, and Dewey rather than to the narrower focus on logic, language, and mathematics favored by C. I. Lewis and Carnap. He construes pragmatism as insisting upon the decisive role for normative appraisal of the quality of life as its livers experience it. And so for Putnam, as for James and Dewey, pragmatism advances philosophy's project of enlightenment as an organon for criticism of accepted ideas of all sorts on the basis of practical considerations.

Putnam is highly effective at presenting Jamesian views in the contemporary idioms of philosophical discussion. He is outstanding among contemporary expositors in his ability to describe James's thought in a way that at once renders it relevant to issues of contemporary debate and to highlight its philosophical creativity. Consider an example. In expounding his formula that truth is a matter of expediency – of success in application – James is shockingly indecisive as to what exactly constitutes this sort of success – is it evidential adequacy, predictive efficacy, psychological congeniality, contextual fit and coherence, or what? To the frustration of his adherents and to the vexation of his interpreters, James will sometimes take the one line and sometimes the other. But here Putnam offers an ingenious resolution. A sensible pragmatism, he suggests, would not see this vacillation as a matter of inconsistency. It would, rather, exploit the idea that what is at issue is not an indecisive disjunction but a complex conjunction, and that true success 'is a matter of satisfying these [multiple] desiderata simultaneously,' so that the issue becomes 'a matter of trade-offs rather than final rules' (Putnam 1995: 10).

To his credit, Putnam seeks to free pragmatism from the anarchic relativism of the postmoderns. He writes:

> From the earliest of Peirce's Pragmatist writings, Pragmatism has been character-ized by antiscepticism . . . [even while conceding] that there are no metaphysical guarantees to be had that even our most firmly held beliefs will never need revision. That one can be both fallibilistic *and* antisceptical is perhaps *the* basic insight in American Pragmatism. (Putnam 1996: 10)

But while Putnam is emphatic in his desire *that* our cognitive theorizing should move away from skepticism to objectivistic realism under the aegis of a pragmatism of the life-enhancing sort that he favors, he is by no means as clear and detailed as one might wish on the questions of just *how* it will manage to do so.

Nicholas Rescher (1928–)

Rescher's methodological pragmatism has it that while base-level issues about thought and action are to be resolved in terms of *standards*, those standards themselves are to be evaluated in terms of their efficacy and efficiency with respect to the teleology of the domain in question. To be sure, this matter of goal realization calls for different modes of implementation depending on the domain at issue. In the case of formal sciences like logic and mathematics, the superiority of one method over another may become manifest through purely theoretical considerations of problem-solving effectiveness in theoretical matters. Here we need never leave our armchairs. But with other enterprises – inquiry in the natural sciences, for example, or the management of political and public affairs – there is no substitute for experiencing the results of our actual efforts 'out in the field,' so to speak. And – obviously – we have no inquiry-independent way of telling what this truth is so as to compare the products of our inquiries with it. Any attempt to appraise the adequacy of our theorizing on its own, purely theoretical terms is thus ultimately futile. And this indicates the need for a belief-independent control of the correctness of our theorizing, some theory-external reality principle to serve as a standard of adequacy. And just here is where pragmatism can come to the rescue by bringing methodology into the foreground.

On this basis Rescher proposes to have pragmatism revert to its scientific roots in Peirce's thought. To be sure, historical experience indicates there are various alternative approaches to determining 'how things work in the world.' The examples of such occult cognitive frameworks as those of numerology (with its benign ratios), astrology (with its astral influences), and black magic (with its mystic forces) indicate that alternative explanatory frameworks exist, and that these can have very diverse degrees of merit. Now in the Western, Faustian intellectual tradition, the ultimate arbiter of rationality is represented by a very basic concept of knowledge-wed-to-practice, and the ultimate validation of our beliefs lies in the combination of theoretical and practical *success*, with 'practice' construed in its pragmatic and affective sense. Here the governing standards of scientific rationality are implicit in the description-transcending goals of *explanation*, *prediction*, and pre-eminently *control* over nature. (And thus the crucial factor is not, for example, sentimental 'at-oneness with nature' – think of the magician vs. the mystic vs. the sage as cultural ideals.) It is the issue of whether or not our thought-guided actions actually achieve their intended goals that provides for a theory-external check on the adequacy of our theorizing.

Such a pragmatic approach to science does not take an instrumentalistic stance that abandons the pursuit of truth and sees the practical issues of prediction and control as the sole goals of the enterprise. Rather, it sees praxis as paramount because there just is no prospect of any more direct alternative, any immediate comparison of these claims with the science-independent 'real-truth' of things. The capacity of our cognitive tools to meet their *theoretical* goals can be monitored *obliquely*, by appraising their realization of our *practical* goals. The practical and *purposive* aspects of cognition thus comes to the fore. The governing quality controls of our mechanisms of inquiry – its methods, concepts, and so on, that furnish the whole machinery by which we build up our world-picture (knowledge, *epistēmē*, science) – emerge as fundamentally pragmatic. We are led to the recognition that here effective *praxis* is the ultimate quality-control arbiter of acceptable *theoria*: that we must monitor the adequacy of our scientific knowledge by way of assessing the efficacy of its applications in guiding our expectations and actions in matters of prediction and control.

And at this point Rescher brings rational selection upon the scene. For in a community of rational agents, there is bound to be a parallelism between applicative efficacy and substantive justification. This circumstance has far-reaching ramifications, since pragmatism here becomes conjoined to evolutionism. And control is a pivotal factor. To be sure, if a bounteous nature satisfied our every whim spontaneously, without effort and striving on our part, the situation would be very different. For then the beliefs which guide and canalize our activities would generally not come into play – they would remain inoperative on the sidelines, never being 'put to the test.' There would then be no need for active (and thought-guided) intervention in 'the natural course of things' within an unco-operative (at best indifferent, at worst hostile) environment. But *as things stand* we are constantly called upon to establish varying degrees of 'control over nature' to satisfy even our most basic needs (to say nothing of our virtually limitless wants).

The developmental perspective and the pragmatic approach thus join together into a seamless whole. A continuous thread links together the entire tradition of realistic pragmatism in its conviction that the ongoing work of an enduring community of rationally competent inquirers will be self-monitoring – that mistakes will be detected and reduced in the course of time. The guiding conviction is that the community will, over the course of time, learn how to improve its procedures of inquiry through the processes of inquiry itself, so that rational inquiry is in this sense self-monitoring and self-corrective. And here we cannot reasonably look on nature as a friendly collaborator in our human efforts, systematically shielding us against the consequences of our follies and crowning our cognitive endeavors with a wholly undeserved success that ensues for reasons wholly independent of any actual adequacy vis-à-vis the intended range of purpose.

And so, Rescher reaffirms Peirce's grounding insight. Our cognitive methods are able to earn credit as giving a trustworthy picture of the world precisely because they evolve under the casual pressure of that world. In sum, science stands forth as superior in its claims to providing an appropriate inquiry method on grounds that are essentially pragmatic. And this pragmatic superiority of science as a resource in matters of effective description, explanation, prediction, and control both manifests and serves to explain its emergence in cognitive evolution by rational selection.

Richard Rorty (b. 1931)

Richard Rorty's 'pragmatism' is decidedly postmodern in its tendency to subjectivistic relativism. For as Rorty sees it, questions of truth and validity should not concern the philosopher at all: pragmatism insists 'that one can be a philosopher precisely by being anti-Philosophical' (Rorty 1982: xiii). And despite his avowed attachment to Dewey (whom he deems one of the twentieth century's three most important philosophers, along with Martin Heidegger and Ludwig Wittgenstein), the threads of pragmatic thought that Rorty weaves together into his own so-called 'neopragmatism' are substantially nihilistic in tenor and tendency. For Rorty in effect pictures pragmatism as an essentially negative and deconstructionist position. According to him, pragmatism 'says that truth is not the sort of thing one should expect to have a philosophically interesting theory about' (Rorty 1982: xiii). The pragmatist accordingly advocates the 'post-Philosophical culture [of] the philosopher who has abandoned pretensions to [traditionalistic] Philosophy' (Rorty 1982: xl). Such a pragmatism abandons any idea of rational quality-control on the processes of inquirers and question-resolving deliberations. As Rorty himself puts it:

> Let me sum up by offering a . . . characterization of pragmatism: it is the doctrine that there are no constraints on inquiry save conversational ones – no wholesale constraints derived from the nature of the objects, or of the mind, or of language, but only those retail constraints provided by the remarks of our fellow inquirers . . . The pragmatist tells us that it is useless to hope that objects will constrain us to believe the truth about them, if only they are approached with an unclouded mental eye, or a rigorous method, or a perspicuous language . . . The only sense in which we are constrained to truth is that . . . we can make no sense of the notion that the view which can survive all objections might be false. But objections – conversational constraints – cannot be anticipated. There is no method for knowing *when* one has reached the truth, or when one is closer to it than before. (Rorty 1982: 165–6)

It is curious, however, to see how readily a doctrine that rejects 'wholesale constraints' is willing to offer wholesale generalizations. For Rorty has it that 'truth, on this view I am advocating, is the normal result of normal discourse' (Rorty 1978) while ignoring that discourse, normal or otherwise, takes us no further – even at best and most – than to what its participants happen to *purport* to be true. For to say that there are no rational constraints on the products in inquiry apart from those imposed by the conventions and practices of the inquirers is giving them unrealistically inflated credit. The community may agree by convention what words like 'cat' and 'mat' – or 'just' and 'unjust' – mean and what the accepted criteria for relating such terms to one another are to be. But once these matters of convention are settled, the issue of whether a cat is actually on the mat or whether self-serving deceit is unjust hinges on other matters – matters that relate to the world's realities. To think that the former is the whole story whereas the latter is a negotiable irrelevancy is to take a stance that is, to put it mildly, problematic.

Rorty writes:

> If we give up this hope [for getting at the truth of things in contexts of inquiry regarding nature's ways] we shall lose what Nietzsche called 'metaphysical comfort,' but we may gain a renewed sense of community. Our identification with our community . . . our intellectual heritage – is heightened when we see this community as *ours* rather than *nature's*, *shaped* rather than *found*, one among many which men have made. In the end, the pragmatists tell us, what matters is our loyalty to other human beings clinging together in the dark, not our hope of getting things right. James, in arguing . . . that 'the trail of the human serpent is over all' was reminding us that our glory is our participation in fallible and transitory human projects, not in our obedience to personal nonhuman constraints. (Rorty 1982: 166)

When William James wrote that 'Human arbitrariness has done away with the divine necessity of scientific logic' (James 1907: 57), he half regretted this supposed fact. But Rorty rejoices in it. For him, the desirable stance is that of the 'ironists' – those 'never quite able to take themselves seriously' because of a recognition of the limited and imperfect nature of their own cognitive positions. For Peirce's fallibilism notwithstanding, commitment to doing the very best that we can manage in the circumstances makes good rational sense. Rorty's dismissive 'ironism' embraces the insouciant indifference of the standpoint that 'a hundred years hence it all won't matter anyhow.' One recent defender of his position declares that 'To many contemporary pragmatists, Rorty's disinterest in the practical consequences of intellectual discourse – his valuing of a discourse that makes no difference – disqualifies his membership [in the pragmatic movement]' (Langsdorf and Smith 1995: 7). There is much to be said for this.

Notes

1. Note that Peirce here says, 'from the truth of that conception,' that is, from that conception's actually being true – and not 'from *believing* the truth of that conception.' This difference is one point that separates him from William James.
2. A first approximation to a plausibly acceptable reformulation would make certain crucial additions, namely: ideas *generally come to be recognized as* true just insofar as they are seen to stand in a harmonious relationship with other parts of our *cognitive* experience. What such a recasting does is to make explicit the epistemic aspect of the situation, recognizing that truth as such is something rather different from its recognition as such.
3. The later Dewey backed away from this position. Thus in his reply to Arthur Murphy in *The Philosophy of John Dewey* (1951, ed. by Paul Schilpp, La Salle: Open Court) Dewey endorses the stronger classical doctrine. Discussing his earlier theories that 'Scientific conceptions are not a revelation of prior and independent reality' in *The Quest for Certainty* (1929, New York: Minton Balch, p. 165), Dewey now indicates that the negative emphasis belongs on 'revelation' and *not* on 'prior and independent reality' (pp. 560–5).
4. See Carnap's statement in E. A. Schilpp (ed.) [(1963), *The Philosophy of Rudolf Carnap*, La Salle: Open Court, p. 861]. This work contains a comprehensive bibliography of Carnap's writings.
5. See Lewis 1923. Quine acknowledges Lewis's influence in *Perspectives in Quine* (Barrett and Gibson 1990: 292). For a fuller account of Quine's pragmatism see McHenry 1995.

References

Barrett, R. B., and R. F. Gibson (eds) (1990), *Perspectives in Quine*, Oxford: Basil Blackwell.

Carnap, R. (1937), *The Logical Syntax of Language*, London: Routledge and Kegan Paul.

Dingler, H. (1930), 'Zum Problem des Regressus in infinitum,' in F. J. von Rinlelen (ed.) (1930), *Philosophia Perennis, Volume 2*, Regensburg: J. Habbel, pp. 571–86.

James, W. (1897), *The Will to Believe and Other Essays in Popular Philosophy*, New York and London.

James, W. (1907), *Pragmatism: A New Name for Some Old Ways of Thinking*, New York: Longmans, Green.

Lewis, C. I. (1923), 'A Pragmatic Conception of the A Priori,' *The Journal of Philosophy* 20: 169–77.

Lewis, C. I. (1929), *Mind and the World Order*, New York and Chicago: C. Scribner's Sons.

Lewis, C. I. (1962), *An Analysis of Knowledge and Valuation*, La Salle: Open Court.

Margolis, J. (2003), *The Unraveling of Scientism: American Philosophy at the End of the Twentieth Century*, Ithaca: Cornell University Press.

McHenry, L. B. (1995), 'Quine's Pragmatic Ontology,' *Journal of Speculative Philosophy* 9: 147–58.

Peirce, C. S. (1931–58), *Collected Papers*, ed. C. Hartshorne, P. Weiss, and A. Burks, 8 vols, Cambridge: Harvard University Press.

Putnam, H. (1996), *Pragmatism: An Open Question*, Oxford: Basil Blackwell.

Quine, W. V. O. (1969), *Ontological Relativity and Other Essays*, New York: Columbia University Press.

Quine, W. V. O. (1981), *Theories and Things*, Cambridge: Harvard University Press.

Quine, W. V. O. (1992), 'Structure and Nature', *The Journal of Philosophy* 89 (1992): 5–9.

Rescher, N. (1973), The *Primacy of Practice*, Oxford: Basil Blackwell.

Rescher, N. (1977), *Methodological Pragmatism*, Oxford: Basil Blackwell.

Rescher, N. (1999), *Realistic Pragmatism*, Albany: State University of New York Press.

Rescher, N. (2001), *Cognitive Pragmatism*, Pittsburgh: University of Pittsburgh Press.

Rorty, R. (1982), *Consequences of Pragmatism* Minneapolis: University of Minnesota Press.

The Promise of Process Philosophy

Nicholas Rescher

1. Historical Background

In recent years, 'process philosophy' has virtually become a code-word for the doctrines of Alfred North Whitehead and his followers. But of course, this cannot really be what process philosophy is ultimately about: if there indeed is a 'philosophy' of process, it must pivot not on a *thinker* but on a *theory*. What is at issue must, in the end, be a philosophical position that has a life of its own, apart from any particular exposition or expositor.

Whitehead himself fixed on 'process' as a central category of his philosophy because he viewed time and change as definitively central and salient metaphysical issues. Invoking the name of Bergson, he adopted 'Nature is a process' as a leading principle, and saw temporality, historicity, change, and passage as fundamental facts to be reckoned within our understanding of the world (Whitehead 1920: Chap. 3). This view was underpinned by Whitehead's appreciation of Leibnizian *appetition* – the striving through which all things endeavor to bring new features to realization (Whitehead 1929: 47, 124). And at the back of this lay the Heraclitean doctrine that 'all things flow,' and the rejection of a Parmenidean/atomistic view that nature consists in the changeable interrelations among stable, unchanging units of existence (Whitehead 1929: 318, 471).

As Whitehead himself thus emphasized, process philosophy does not represent a somehow personal position but reflects a major tendency or line of thought that traces back through the history of philosophy to the days of the pre-Socratics. Its leading exponents were Heraclitus, Leibniz, Bergson, Peirce, and William James – and it ultimately moved on to include Whitehead and his school (Charles Hartshorne, Paul Weiss), but also such other philosophers as Samuel Alexander, and C. Lloyd Morgan.

As is often the case in philosophy, the position at issue is best understood in terms of what it opposes.

From the time of Aristotle, Western metaphysics has had a marked bias in favour of *things*. Aristotle's insistence on the metaphysical centrality of ostensively indicatable objects (with *tode ti* as a pointable-at *this*) had an enduring and far-reaching impact. In fact, it does not stretch matters unduly to say that the Aristotelian view of the primacy of substance and its ramifications (see *Metaphysics* IV, 2; 10003b6–11) – with its focus on mid-size physical objects of the order of a rock, a tree, a cat, or a human being – has proved to be decisive for much of Western philosophy.

However, another variant line of thought was also current from the earliest times onward. After all, the concentration on perduring physical *things* as existents in nature slights the equally good claims of another ontological category, namely processes, events, occurrences – items better indicated by verbs than nouns. Clearly, storms and heat-waves are every bit as real as dogs and oranges. Even on the surface of it, verbs have as good a claim to reality as nouns. For process theorists, *becoming* is no less important than *being* – rather the reverse. The phenomenology of change is stressed precisely because the difference between a museum and the real world of an ever-changing nature is to be seen as crucial to our understanding of reality.

Moreover, processes are not in general a matter of the doings of things. The fire's heat causes the water to boil. But it is clearly not a *thing*. To be sure, some events and processes relate to the doings or undergoings of things (the collapse of the bridge) or of people (Smith's learning a poem). And other events and processes relate to the co-ordinated doings of things (an eclipse of the sun) or of people (a traffic jam). But many events and processes are patently subjectless in that they do not consist of the doings of one or more personal or impersonal agents (a frost, for example, or a magnetic field). What is at work in these self-subsistent or subjectless processes are not 'agents' but 'forces.' And these can be diffusely located (the Hubble expansion of the universe) or lack any real location at all (the Big Bang).

The progenitor of this rival metaphysical tradition was Heraclitus. For him, reality is not a constellation of things at all, but one of processes. The fundamental 'stuff' of the world is not material substance but volatile flux, namely 'fire,' and all things are versions thereof (*puros tropai*). Process is fundamental: the river is not an *object*, but a continuing flow; the sun is not a *thing*, but an enduring fire. Everything is a matter of process, of activity, of change (*panta rhei*). Not stable things but fundamental forces and the varied and fluctuating activities they manifest constitute the world. We must at all costs avoid the fallacy of materializing nature.

The principal standard bearer of this line of thought into the domain of modern philosophy was Leibniz, who maintained that all of the 'things' that figure in our experience (animals alone grudgingly excepted) are mere phenomena and not really 'substances' at all. The world in fact consists of clusters of processes he call *monads* (units) which are 'centers of force' or bundles of activity. For Leibniz, processes rather than things furnish the basic materials of ontology.

Against this historical background, it seems sensible to understand 'process philosophy' as a doctrine committed or at any rate inclined to certain basic propositions:

1. that time and change are among the principal categories of metaphysical understanding,
2. that process is a principal category of ontological description,
3. that process are more fundamental, or at any rate not less fundamental than things for the purposes of ontological theory,
4. that several if not all of the major elements of the ontological repertoire (God, nature-as-a whole, persons, material substances) are best understood in process terms,

5. that contingency, emergence, novelty, and creativity are among the fundamental categories of metaphysical understanding.

A process philosopher, then, is someone for whom temporality, activity, and change – of alteration, striving, passage, and novelty-emergence – are the cardinal factors for our understanding of the real. Ultimately it is a question of priority – of viewing the time-bound aspects of the real as constituting its most characteristic and significant features. For the process philosopher, process has priority over product – both ontologically and epistemically.

This process-oriented approach is thus historically too pervasive and systematically too significant to be restricted in its reference to one particular philosopher and his school. Indeed, one cardinal task for the partisans of process at this particular juncture of philosophical history is to prevent the idea of 'process philosophy' from being marginalized through a limitation of its bearing to the work and influence of any one single individual or group.

2. Process Ontology

To be sure, one way of downgrading processes is not to question their reality, but rather their significance. On this perspective, it is conceded that nature is indeed replete with many and varied activities and processes, but insisted that they are simply the doings of substantial agents and thereby secondary and derivative. Every verb must have a subject and every event or occurrence is a matter of the agency of things. Denying the ontological autonomy of processes, this process-reducibility doctrine insists all there is in the world are things and their properties and actions. This position reasserts the orthodoxy that maintains the ontological substance-bias of Western philosophy.

The fly in its ointment is that the world is full of processes that do not represent the action of things (save on a rather naive and obsolescent atomist/materialistic model of nature). While processes *can* be the doings of things the idea that they *must* be so is nothing but an unhelpful prejudice. When water freezes or evaporates, it is not a 'thing' (or collection thereof) that is active in producing this result. The 'freshening' of the wind, the forming of waves in the water, the pounding of the surf, the erosion of the shore-line are all processes that are not really the machinations of identifiable 'things.' Consider such a process as 'a fluctuation in the earth's magnetic field' or 'a weakening of the sun's gravitational field.' Clearly such processes will make an impact on things (magnetic needles, for example). But by no stretch of the imagination are these processes themselves the doings/activities of things/substances. There is not a *thing*, 'a magnetic field' or 'a gravitational field' that *does* something or *performs* certain actions – nor does the worth or sum *project* such a field. Where is the thing that is being active when we have a fall in barometric pressure? For the process philosopher, the classical principle *operari sequitur esse* is reversed: his motto is *esse sequitur operari*, since being follows from operation because what there is in the final analysis is the product of processes. As process philosophers see it, processes are basic and things derivative, because it takes a mental process (of separation) to extract 'things' from the blooming buzzing confusion of the world's physical processes. Traditional metaphysics sees processes (such as the rod's snapping under the strain when bent sufficiently) as the manifestation of dispositions (fragility) which must themselves be rooted in the stable properties of things. Process metaphysics involves an inversion of this perspective. It takes the line that the categorical properties of things are simply stable clusters of process-engendering dispositions.

But is the domain of process-dispositions really free from the need for a rooting in the categorical properties of things? Is the dispositional realm autonomous – that is, can dispositions be self-activating? After all, dispositions are matters of if-then. If this is all we have, can we then *ever* move to the categorical sphere? The answer is affirmative. We can do this provided we have *nested* dispositions. If all we had were dispositions of the form 'When and where p, there q' then, of course, we would need a categorical input (namely p) to have a categorical output. But with nested dispositions of the form 'When and where (when and where p, there q), there r' we can in fact get a categorical output from hypothetical inputs. Where dispositions are sufficiently complex (that is, nested), a transition from the dispositional to the categorical sector is possible. Mere dispositions can combine to engender categorical actualities. And so processes (rod-snappings) can occur in the framework of a process ontology that has no recourse to processual substances with categorical properties that ground underwrite the dispositions (such as rod-fragility) that processes actualize.

Thus we must not forget that even on the basis of an ontology of substance and property, dispositional properties are *epistemologically* fundamental. Without them, a thing is inert, undetectable, disconnected from the world's causal commerce, and inherently unknowable. Our only epistemic access to the absolute properties of things is through inferential triangulation from their dispositional properties – or better from the processes through which these manifest themselves. Accordingly, a substance ontologist cannot get by without processes. If his things are totally inert – if they *do* nothing – they are pointless and can neither act nor become known. For without processes there is no access to dispositions and without dispositional properties, substances lie outside our cognitive reach. We can only observe what things *do* – via their discernible effects – what they *are*, over and above this, is a matter of theory project on this basis. And here process ontology cuts the Gordian knot. In its sight, things simply *are* what they *do*.

Processes can conceivably make do without things. (As the example of 'it is getting colder' shows, there can be 'subjectless' processes; processes which – to all appearances – are not like sneezing or dissolving encompassed in the activities of things.) But, no workable substance ontology can operate without a heavy reliance on processes. A substance, after all, is determined (individuated) as such by its properties, and there are just two major types here, namely the dispositional and the absolute (nondispositional, categorical). But the dispositional ones are crucial – at any rate from an epistemic point of view. For all that we can ever observe about a substance is what it does – what sorts of impacts (changes, effects) it produces in interaction with others – that is, what sorts of processes it engenders. The absolute (nondispositional) properties that we attribute to things are always the product of a theory-bound conjecture – features imputed to things to provide a causal explanation for their impacts upon others. As Leibniz insisted, a substance is primarily a center of force, a bundle of dispositions to exert impacts of various sorts upon the others. Substances can come upon the stage of consideration only through the mediation of processes.

A process ontology thus greatly simplifies matters. Instead of a two-tier reality that combines things with their inevitable co-ordinated processes, it settles for a one-tier ontology of process alone. It sees things not just as the *products* of processes (as one cannot avoid doing) but also as the *manifestations* of processes – as complex bundles of co-ordinated processes. It replaces the troublesome ontological dualism of *thing* and *activity* with an internally complex monism of activities of varying, potentially compounded sorts. If simplicity is an advantage, process ontology has a lot to offer.

3. Process and 'the Problem of Universals'

Let us now turn from particulars to universals. Recourse to process is also a helpful device for dealing with the classical problem of universals. We are surrounded on all sides by instances of types of items more easily conceived of as processes than as substantial things – not only physical items like a magnetic field or an *aurora borealis*, but also conceptual artifacts like words or letters of the alphabet, let alone songs, plays, or poems.

By their very nature as such, processes have patterns and periodicities that render them in-principle repeatable. After all, to say that an item has a *structure* of some sort is to attribute to it something that other items can in principle also have.[1] But, of course, structure, though repeatable ('abstractable'), is itself not an abstraction – it is something that a concrete item concretely exhibits. Abstraction does not *create* structure, but presupposes it.

Classically, there are three rival theories of 'universals' which see them, respectively, as:

1. *made by minds* (nominalism): imputed to things by minds in virtue of their (the mind's) operation,
2. *found (by minds) in things* (Platonic realism): perceived by minds pre-existing aspects of things,
3. *generated in mind-thing interaction* (conceptualism).

Now a substance ontology, which is bound to see universals as simply being the properties of things (Aristotelian secondary substances), encounters serious difficulties here. For on its basis one is driven inexorably towards Platonism. We want universals to be objective, but can only secure this status for them on the basis of a Platonic realism. And when we look more closely at the sorts of things at issue – letters of the alphabet, say, or poems – this doesn't really seem to be such an attractive option.

But with process universals – conceived of as multiply instantiable processual structures – there are fewer difficulties. Processes are inherently universal and repeatable; to be a process is to be a process of a certain sort, a certain specifiable make-up. What concretizes processes is simply their spatiotemporal emplacement, their positioning in the framework of reality. And so, a process as such is by its very nature a concrete universal – any actual process is *at once* concrete and universal. There is, presumably, little or no problem about process types because these can be accounted for in terms of a commonality of structure.

In particular, colors, say, or numbers, or poems, lend themselves naturally to a process account. Take phenomenal colors, for example. A *mental* process such as perceiving or imagining a certain shade of red is simply a way of perceiving redly or imagining redly (in a certain particular way). A universal – shade of phenomenal red, for example – ceases to be a mysterious *object* of some sort and becomes a specifiable feature of familiar processes (perceivings, imaginings). How distinct minds can perceive the same universal is now no more mysterious than how distinct autos can share the same speed. Otherwise mysterious-seeming universals such as odors or fears are simply shared structural features of mental processes. Universals are pulled down from the Platonic realm to become structural features of the ways in which we concretely conduct the business of thinking. Recourse to a process approach is once again a useful problem-solving device.

4. Process Philosophy of Nature

Let us now turn from matters of ontology to issues in the process philosophy of nature.

A classical atomism whose ontology consists only of atoms and the void is the ultimate contrary to a process philosophy. A physics of fields and forces that operate on their own, without an embedding in things, is the quintessence of a process philosophy of nature. But wherein lies the appeal of such a view?

A substance-ontologist is committed to seeing the physical world (nature) as a collection of *things* and *objects*. And on this basis, he immediately faces the problem of accounting for *laws* that co-ordinate the behavior of things. (How do all hydrogen atoms learn how to behave like hydrogen atoms?) But by seeing the world as a matrix of processes – by viewing nature as the substantiation of a family of operative principles (taken in their all-inclusive systemic totality) – we secure straightaway a coherent conceptualization of nature in a way that removes such difficulties. For the idea of law is inherent in the very concept of a process. And we can *understand* the world's processes – precisely because we ourselves are a party to them, seeing that we ourselves, in our own make-up and being, participate in the operation of nature.

A process approach thus simplifies greatly the problem of securing a coherent view of nature. Modern physics teaches us that at the level of the very small there are no ongoing *things* (substances, objects) at all in nature – no particulars with a continuing descriptive identity of their own – there are only patterns of process that exhibit stabilities. (The orbit-jump of an 'electron' is not the mysterious transit of a well-defined physical object at all.) Only those stability-waves of continuous process provide for any sort of continuity of existence. The development of stable 'things' begins at the sub-sub-microscopic level with a buzzing proliferation of 'events' that have little if any fixed nature in themselves but only exist in reciprocal interaction with each other, and which have no stable characteristics in and of themselves, but only come to exhibit spatiotemporally stable aspects at the level of statistical aggregates.

It was, in a way, unfortunate for them that the founding fathers of process philosophy did not witness the rise of the quantum theory. The classical conception of an atom was predicated on the principle that 'by definition, atoms cannot be cut up or broken into smaller parts,' so that 'atom-splitting' was a contradiction in terms. The demise of classical atomism brought on by the dematerialization of physical matter brings much aid and comfort to a process-oriented metaphysics. Matter in the small, as contemporary physics concerns it, is not a Rutherfordian planetary system of particle-like objects, but a collection of fluctuating processes organized into stable structures (insofar as there is indeed stability at all) by statistical regularities – that is, by regularities of comportment at the level of aggregate phenomena. Twentieth-century physics has thus turned the tables on classical atomism. Instead of very small *things* (atoms) combining to produce standard processes (windstorms and such), modern physics envisions very small processes (quantum phenomena) combining to produce standard things (ordinary macro-objects) as a result of their modus operandi.

The quantum view of reality demolished the most substance-oriented of all ontologies – classical atomism. For it holds that, at the micro-level, what was usually deemed a physical *thing*, a stably perduring object, is itself no more than a statistical pattern – a stability wave in a surging sea of process. Those so-called enduring 'things' come about through the compilation of stabilities in statistical fluctuations – much like gusts of wind. Processes are not the machinations of stable things; things are the stability-patterns of variable processes. All such perspective of modern physics at the level of fundamentals dovetail smoothly into the traditional process approach.

Neither the logic of object and predicate nor even the grammar of subject and verb prevail in the language of nature, but the language of differential equations, the language of process. In this regard as in so many others, Leibniz had insight far beyond his time. Important though logic and language are (and he stresses that they are *very* important), it is the mathematical language of process – of transformation functions and differential equations – that is of the greatest help in depicting the world's physical realities. (This is something of which Whitehead, himself a first-rate mathematician, was keenly aware.)

5. Process Psychology: Difficulties of the Self

Next, let us briefly consider the utility of the process approach in philosophical psychology.

The self or ego has always been a stumbling-block for Western philosophy because of its resistance to accommodation within its favored framework of substance-ontology. The idea that 'the self' is a *thing* (substance), and that whatever takes place in 'my mind' and 'my thoughts' is a matter of the activity of a thing of a certain sort (a 'mind'-substance) is no more than a rather blatant sort of fiction – a somewhat desperate effort to apply the thing paradigm to a range of phenomena that it just doesn't fit.

It feels uncomfortable to conceptualize *people* (persons) as *things* (substances) – oneself above all – because we resist flat-out identification with our bodies. Aristotle already bears witness to this difficulty of accommodating the self or soul into a substance metaphysic. It is, he tells us, the 'substantial form,' the *entelechy* of the body.

But this accommodation strategy raises more problems than it solves, because the self or soul is so profoundly unlike the other sorts of entelechy-examples that Aristotle is able to provide.

People instinctively dislike being described in thing-classificatory terms. As Sartre indicates, a wrong-doer may be prepared to say 'I did this or that act' (Sartre 1956) but will resist saying 'I am a thief,' 'I am a murderer.' Such object-property attributions indicate a fixed nature that we naturally see as repugnant to ourselves. People generally incline to see themselves and their doings in processual terms as sources of teleological, agency-purposive activities geared to the satisfaction of needs and wants as they appear in the circumstances of the moment. In application to ourselves, at any rate, static thing-classifiers are naturally distasteful to us.

If we are committed to conceiving of a *person* within the framework of a classical thing-metaphysic, then we are going to be impelled inexorably towards the materialist view that the definitive facet of a person is his body and its doings. For of everything that appertains to us, it is clearly our *body* that is most readily assimilated to the substance paradigm. Think here of David Hume's ventures into self-apprehension:

> From what (experiential) impression could this idea (of *self*) be derived? This question is impossible to answer without a manifest contradiction and absurdity; and yet it is a question which must necessarily be answered, if we would have the idea of self pass for clear and intelligible . . . For my part, when I enter most intimately into what I call *myself*, I always stumble on some particular perception or other, of heat or cold, light or shade, love or hatred, pain or pleasure. I never can catch *myself* at any time without a perception, and never can observe anything but the perception.[2]

Here Hume is perfectly right. Any such quest for *observational* confrontation with a personal core substance, a self or ego that constitutes the particular person that one is, is destined to end in failure. The only 'things' about ourselves we can get hold of *observationally* are the body and its activities.

However, from the angle of a process metaphysic the situation has a rather different look. We have difficulties apprehending what we *are* but little difficulty experiencing what we *do*. Our bodily and mental activities lie open to experiential apprehension. There is no problem with experiential access to the processes and patterns of process that characterize us personally – our doings and undergoings, either individually or patterned into talents, skills, capabilities, traits, dispositions, habits, inclinations, and tendencies to action and inaction are, after all, what characteristically define a person as the individual he is. What makes my experience mine is not some peculiar qualitative character that it exhibits as the property of an object, but simply its forming part of the overall ongoing process that defines and constitutes my life.

Once we conceptualize the core 'self' of a person as a unified manifold of actual and potential process – of action and capacities, tendencies, and dispositions to action (both physical and psychical) – then we have a concept of personhood that renders the self or ego experientially accessible, seeing that experiencing itself simply *consists* of such processes. On a process-oriented approach, the self or ego (the constituting core of a person as such, that is, as the particular person he is) is simply a megaprocess – a *structured system of processes*, a cohesive and (relatively) stable center of agency. The unity of person is a unity of experience – the integrative coalescence of all of our diverse micro-experience as part of one unified macro-process. (It is the same sort of unity of process that links each minute's level into a single overall journey.) The crux of this approach is the shift in orientation from substance to process – from a unity of hardware, of physical machinery, to a unity of software, of programming or mode of functioning.

Miguel de Unamuno claims that Descartes got it backwards – that instead of *cogito, ergo sum res cogitans* it should be: *sum res cogitans, ergo cogito* (de Unamuno 1982: 52). But this is not so. Descartes's reversal of Scholasticism's traditional substantialist perspective is perfectly in order, based on the sound idea that activity comes first ('*Im Anfang war die Tat*,' as Goethe said) – that what we do defines what we are. The fundamentality of psychic process for the constitution of a self was put on the agenda of modern philosophy by Descartes.

Leibniz went even further in generalizing the view that agency defines the agent. Along Cartesian lines he saw the unity of the self as a unity of process, taking its individuality to consist in a unified characteristic mode of acting (of perceiving the world). But in this regard the self was, for Leibniz, paradigmatic for substance in general. In effect, Leibniz's monadology took the Cartesian process approach to the personal self and *universalized* it to encompass substance in general. A substance, like a self, is just as much a 'thing' as a center of action.

The salient advantage of this process-geared view of the self as an internally complex process of 'leading a life (of a certain sort)' – with its natural division into a varied manifold of constituent sub-processes – is that it does away with the need for a mysterious and experientially inaccessible unifying substantial *object* (on the lines of Kant's 'transcendental ego') to constitute a self out of the variety of its experiences. The unity of self comes to be seen as a unity of process – of one large megaprocess that encompasses many smaller ones in its make-up. Such an approach wholly rejects the thing-ontologists' view of a person as an *entity* existing separately from its actions, activities, and experiences. We arrive at a view of mind that dispenses with the Cartesian 'ghost in the machine' and looks to the unity of mind as a unity of functioning – of *operation* rather than *operator*. A 'self' is viewed not as a *thing* but as an integrated process.

On this basis, the Humean complaint – 'One experiences feeling this and doing that, but one never experiences *oneself*' – is much like the complaint of the person who says 'I see him picking up that brick, and mixing that batch of mortar, and troweling that brick into place, but I never see him building a wall.' Even as 'building the wall' just exactly *is* the complex process that is *composed* of those various activities, so – from the process point of view – our self just *is* the complex process *composed* of those various physical and psychic experiences and actions in their systemic interrelationship.

The process-based approach in philosophical psychology doubtless has difficulties of its own. But they pale into insignificance compared to those of the traditional substantival approach.

6. Process Theology

Let us now move on to another theme, process theology.[3] The neo–Platonic sympathies of the Church Fathers impelled the theology of the Western monotheistic religions to the orthodox philosophical stance that to see God as existent we must conceive of him as a being, a *substance* of some (presumably very nonstandard) sort. And to the pleasure of philosophers and the vexation of theologians, this has opened up a host of theoretical difficulties. For example: (1) On the classical conception of the matter, a substance must always originate from substances. Q: Whence God? A: From himself; He is *causa sui*; (2) Substances standardly have contingent properties. Q: Does God? A: No; He is in all respects (self) necessitated; (3) Substances standardly have spatiotemporal emplacement. Q: Does God? A: No; He, unlike standard substances, exists altogether outside place and time. And so on. No sooner has Western theology made God a substance in order to satisfy its ontological predilections than it has to break all the rules for substances, and take away with one hand what it seemed to give us with the other.

But in conceptualizing God in terms of a *process* that is at work in and beyond the world, we overcome many such difficulties at one blow. For it now becomes far easier to understand how God can be and be operative. To be sure, conceiving of God in process terms invokes recourse to various processes of a very special kind. But extraordinary (or even supra-natural) *processes* pose far fewer difficulties than extraordinary (or let alone supra-natural) *substances*. After all, many sorts of processes, are in their own way, unique – or, at any rate, very radically different from all others. It is not all that hard to see that processes like the creation of a world or the inauguration of its nomic structure are by their very nature bound to be unusual. But in the world of processes, that is not all that strange.

Moreover there is now little difficulty in conceiving God as a *person*. For once we have an account of personhood in process terms as a systemic complex of characteristic activities, it is no longer all that strange to see God in these terms as well. If we processify the human person, then we can more readily conceive of the divine person in process terms as well. God can now be conceptualized as a complex system of characterized processes that creates and sustains the world and endows it with law, beauty (harmony and order), value and meaning.

The process approach accordingly affords a framework for conceiving of God in a way that not only removes many of the difficulties inherent in the thing-oriented, substantial approach of traditional metaphysics, but also makes it vastly easier to provide a philosophical rationale for the leading conceptions of Judeo-Christian religiosity.

7. The Agenda For Process Philosophy

As these deliberations indicate, the process approach has many assets. But it has some significant liabilities as well. For it is by no means unfair to the historical situation to say that process philosophy at present remains no more than a glint in the mind's eye of certain philosophers. A thoroughly worked-out, fully-fledged development of this line of approach simply does not yet exist as an accomplished fact. All that we really have so far are suggestions, sketches, and expressions of confidence. The work of actually developing the process doctrine to the point where it can be compared with other major philosophical projects like materialism or absolute idealism still remains to be done. Many writers have hinted at a process philosophy, but nobody has yet really developed one – not even Whitehead, though he has perhaps gone further in this direction than anyone else.

Take just one example of the utility of the process approach. What is it that makes '*this* typing of AND' and '*that* typing of AND' two instances of the same process? Obviously it is not the sameness of the product – otherwise indistinguishable ANDs can in principle be produced in very different ways by very different processes. Rather, structural identity of operation is the crux: the two concrete processes invoked are simply two different spatiotemporal instances of the same generic procedure – that is, that exactly the same recipe is followed in either case. But how such structures are to be characterized in general is far from clear. Clearly the theory of process individuation and reidentification needs to be carefully developed. And this issue is complicated because some ordinary language processes are in fact collected together as such not through processual sameness but merely a sameness of product. Take Aristotle's example of 'building a house.' Clearly, housebuilding is not really a single sort of process at all but a family of processes linked only by a similarity of product. This sort of complexity needs to be taken into proper account.

Moreover, we require a more detailed theoretical analysis of the inter-relationships of processes. It is clear, for example, that two such relationships are fundamental:

1. the process/subprocess relation that makes one process into a subsidiary component or constituent of another, and
2. the concrete-process/process-type relationship that renders two given concrete processes instances of a common type – presumably under the aegis of a principle of commonality of structure.

The character and connection between these modes of process relationship is something that very much needs to be clarified.

A good deal of work thus remains. To develop an adequate groundwork for process philosophy we need:

1. an analysis of the conception of process in its various manifestations and an explanation of which of its features have primary importance for metaphysical purposes,
2. a survey of the major sorts of processes that bear importantly in metaphysical issues,
3. a clear scheme for distinguishing the salient features of diverse processes: life vs inert, conscious vs unconscious,
4. a classifying taxonomy of processes of various sorts,
5. a reasoned schema for distinguishing and characterizing natural processes in a hierarchical format (proto-physical, physical, chemical, biological, social) suitably distinguishing each level from and yet relating it to the next,

6. provision of a cogently developed line of argument for the primacy of process,
7. an integrated and co-ordinated presentation of the scientific and philosophical ideas relating to processes,
8. a thorough-going examination of the nature of such process-oriented conceptions as emergence, novelty, innovation, and creativity.

We do not really as yet have any of these in fully developed form. And even if we did so, this would only be the starting point. To provide an adequate account of process philosophy we need cogent and integrated series of well-developed expositions and arguments to articulate and substantiate the central theses of this position. A great deal of work accordingly remains to be done before process philosophy becomes anything like a well-defined philosophical doctrine.

The fact is that we simply do not have a developed process philosophy in hand. Perhaps, as Andrew J. Reck has noted, '[T]he unfinished and never-to-be-finished quality of (processual) flux has seduced many adherents to the metaphysics of process among systematic theory-building' (Reck 1975: 59). Be this as it may, the fact remains that at this stage of the historical dialectic, process philosophy is not so much a developed *doctrine* as a projected *program*. At this stage, process philosophy is not an accomplished fact; it is no more than a promising, hopefully developable project of research. True to itself, process philosophy is not a finished product but an ongoing project of inquiry.[4]

Notes

1. The events that constitute a process must be temporally co-ordinated. But they need not be casually connected. The king's morning toilette is a process. He arises, and then washes, and then brushes his teeth, and so on. The unifying linkage of this complex process is 'and then.' But there is no connection. (He does not brush his teeth *because* he has washed.) Such examples show that specifically *causal* processes constitute only a particular sort of process.
2. Hume 1888, Bk II, Pt IV, sect. 6, 'Of Personal Identity'. In the Appendix, Hume further elaborates: 'When I turn my reflection on *myself*, I never can perceive this *self* without some one or more perceptions; nor can I ever perceive anything but the perceptions. It is the composition of these, therefore, which forms the SELF.'
3. For a useful anthology on the topic see Cousins 1971, which seeks to integrate the tradition of Whitehead with that of Teilhard de Chardin.
4. This draws upon a paper that initially appeared in R. W. Burch and H. J. Saatkamp, Jr (eds) (1992), *Frontiers in American Philosophy*, College Station: Texas A&M University Press and was reprinted in *Process Studies* 25 (1996): 55–71. I am indebted to Johanna Seibt and Devid Carey for constructive comments on a draft of this discussion.

References

Cousins, E. H. (1971), *Process Theology: Basic Writings*, New York: Newman Press.
de Unamuno, M. (1982), *Del sentimiento tragico de la vida*, ed. P. F. Garcia, Madrid: Espasa-Calpe.
Hume, D. [1739–40] (1888), *A Treatise of Human Nature*, ed. L. A. Selby-Briggs, Oxford: Oxford University Press.

Reck, A. J. (1975), 'Process Philosophy: A Categorical Analysis,' in R. C. Whittemore (ed.) (1975), *Studies in Process Philosophy II*, New Orleans: Springer, pp. 58–91.

Sartre, J.-P. (1956), 'Bad Faith,' in J.-P. Sartre (1956), *Being and Nothingness*, trans. H. Barnes, New York: Pocket Books, pp. 47–70.

Whitehead, A. N. (1920, *The Concept of Nature*, Cambridge: Cambridge University Press.

Whitehead, A. N. (1929), *Process and Reality*, Cambridge: Cambridge University Press.

Metaphysics

Douglas McDermid

1. Introduction: Prolegomena to Past Metaphysics

We begin in paradox: not with philosophy, but poetry; not with the twentieth century, but the nineteenth; and not with an argument, but with a rhyming couplet. The couplet comes from the Dedication to *Don Juan*, where Byron mocks Coleridge's addiction to obscure metaphysics with a quip both wry and wise: 'Explaining metaphysics to the nation – I wish he would explain his Explanation (Byron 1824: 15–16). Byron was no philosopher; but here his wish was sound and I will honour its spirit. Before attempting to explain recent Anglophone 'metaphysics to the nation,' then, I shall very briefly explain my Explanation.

Bust and Boom

Half a century ago, it would have been much easier to write an article on this then unfashionable subject and much more difficult to find anyone willing to read it. True, the first quarter of the twentieth century witnessed significant developments in metaphysics: the long twilight of Absolute Idealism; and the revolt, led by G. E. Moore and Bertrand Russell, against the speculative excesses of the Anglo-Hegelians. Yet by mid-century analytic metaphysicians were fast becoming an endangered species, preyed upon voraciously by two movements indebted in different ways to Wittgenstein. First, there was logical positivism, whose tough-minded partisans brusquely dismissed metaphysics as nonsense; second, there was linguistic philosophy, whose suave apostles dissolved old disputes by tracing them back to the abuse of ordinary language.

By the late 1950s, however, these two movements were either moribund (as in the case of orthodox positivism) or sliding slowly into decadence (as in the case of linguistic philosophy), and the once-disreputable field of metaphysics experienced a renaissance within Anglo-American circles. Beginning with P. F. Strawson (1959) and W. V. O. Quine (1960) (influenced, truth to tell, by linguistic philosophy and by logical positivism, respectively), this process of self-renewal continued from the 1960s to the end of the twentieth century, thanks in no small part to the work of Roderick Chisholm, Donald Davidson, Michael Dummett, Saul Kripke, and David Lewis.

The result is that metaphysics is now back in business – and doing a booming trade. This is very good news for metaphysicians, of course; but it is bad news for those entrusted with chronicling their progress. For the sheer amount of material creates a serious difficulty for the commentator: that of an *embarras de richesse*. There are too many giants and gods to name, too many crucial debates to recount and ponder, too much argumentation to unpack and assess. Given that we cannot say everything about anything, or something about everything, can we still say anything worth saying? I think we can.

The Explanation Explained

I elected to proceed through compromise. I have sought to steer clear of two extremes: on the one hand, the Scylla of an uninformative generality; on the other, the Charybdis of a vertiginous particularity. Instead of saying a worthless word or two apiece about a dozen major problems, or presenting a cliché-ridden philosophical genealogy of the 'And-Quine-begat-Davidson' variety, I have opted for greater depth and selectivity of focus. But in order to ensure that most of the century's major periods and figures are represented, it is essential that such depth and selectivity be coupled with a suitably broad range of examples. Argument and detail there thus must be; but let there be breadth and perspective as well. Let sweep and scope abound – but not if the price is vacuity.

Sensible of the ways these desiderata constrain each other, I have thought it best to structure my discussion around three fundamental questions:

Q1. What critiques of traditional metaphysics were advanced by Anglophone philosophers in the first half of the century?

Q2. Can twentieth-century analytic philosophers be justly accused of neglecting the traditional problems of metaphysics?

Q3. How has analytic philosophy's concern with language – the much ballyhooed 'linguistic turn' – influenced the way(s) metaphysics is actually done?

My plan of attack is simple: I address (Q1) in Section 2, (Q2) in Section 3, and (Q3) in Section 4. My answers to these queries contain many concrete examples; and it is my hope that the curious reader will go on to explore, in greater detail than I can possibly manage here, the authors and schools to which I allude.

2. The Critique of Metaphysics Continued

Ever since Kant's first *Critique*, sophisticated denials of the very possibility of metaphysics have become commonplace. In the first half of the twentieth century, philosophers composed many artful variations on this Kantian theme – though some of these variations were played in decidedly un-Kantian keys. Let us attend to this trend and its diverse manifestations in the English-speaking philosophical world.

First, we must bring into sharper focus the target – or rather targets – at which critics aimed their shafts. Here, then, are just a few prominent old-fashioned ideas about the pretensions, the presuppositions, and the proper sphere of metaphysics: (1) There is such a thing as truth in metaphysics; metaphysical claims are not meaningless, but may be evaluated for objective truth or falsity; (2) Metaphysical doctrines may be true, yet conflict with common sense or ordinary language (that is, with what the 'person in the street' would think or say); (3) Certain metaphysical problems are perennial; for the conceptual scheme needed to formulate them is not a historically conditioned cultural artifact, but reflects the necessary structures of reason itself; (4) Metaphysics is an autonomous *a priori* discipline independent of – and to be sharply distinguished from – all modes of empirical inquiry (for example, science, history, and so on); (5) Metaphysics is concerned with a special realm of being: a Reality lurking behind the second-rate realm of mere appearance kenned by vulgar common sense or its extension, science; (6) Metaphysical disputes are to be addressed by means of closely reasoned argument, not by invoking 'subjective' pragmatic or aesthetic criteria; and (7) General questions about reality as a whole – about its 'ultimate' nature or structure, say – can be meaningfully posed and answered.

Let us now direct our attention away from the targets and back towards the archer – and their arrows.

Against Traditional Metaphysics: Five Families of Critiques

In this subsection I describe five (ideal) types of critiques all influential prior to the rebirth of metaphysics in the late 1950s. In each case, I outline the views of some advocate(s) of the anti-metaphysical stance in question, and specify which of the claims listed above that stance seems primarily intended to combat.

Verificationism

Philosophers given to understanding the meaning of statements in terms of their method of verification (that is, what would count for or against them) have long looked askance at the grand and abstract claims made by metaphysicians. Here are three expressions of this basic idea:

1. **James**: According to William James (1907), there can be no difference (in theory) that makes no difference (in practice). This pragmatic, no-nonsense maxim brings speculative flights of fancy down to earth in two ways. First, disagreements between partisans of rival metaphysical positions can be dismissed as merely verbal – unless it can be shown that there is some concrete practical difference between them. Secondly, if there is some genuine practical difference between two competing theories, we may favor the one that 'works' best for us (that is, the one that best serves our interests) (see Theses 1, 4 and 6).

2. **Ayer**: According to logical positivists such as the young A. J. Ayer (1936), a sentence is meaningful only if it is either (a) analytic (true or false in virtue of the meaning of its terms); or (b) empirically verifiable (experience or observation is relevant to determining its truth-value). But – alas! – the claims of metaphysicians are both non-analytic and unverifiable. Accordingly, what metaphysicians say or write is neither true nor false; it is mere sound and fury, signifying nothing (Thesis 1).

3. **Carnap**: According to Rudolf Carnap (1951), the adoption of a certain ontological scheme is not a theoretical problem; so-called 'external questions' about the adequacy of such linguistic frameworks – that is, questions about whether the entities posited by a framework 'really' exist – are meaningless because undecidable. The issue is pragmatic: instead of asking whether a given framework is true, we should ask whether it is useful (how well it serves our purposes) (Theses 1 and 6).

Commonsensism

Some insisted that philosophical theses must cohere with our shared and entrenched view of things (for example, that there is an external world, that I exist, that there are minds other than my own, that time is real, and so on). Instinctively suspicious of what Strawson (1959) called 'revisionary' (as opposed to 'descriptive') metaphysics (Strawon 1959: 9–11) this commonsensical outlook found a redoubtable champion in G. E. Moore:

4. **Moore**: According to Moore (1925), metaphysical theories should be rejected when they run counter to common sense – as, in fact, they often have done. For instance, when a philosopher (such as J. M. E. McTaggart (1908)) boldly affirms the unreality of time, he must be in the wrong; if time is unreal, then it is never the case that one thing happens before another – and that, Moore (1911) intimates, is absurd. Philosophy's proper task is not to question or attack propositions belonging to the 'Common Sense view of the world', but to give an analysis of their meaning (Thesis 2).

Linguistic Philosophy

Next, some alleged that the formulation of many a metaphysical problem is vitiated by a misunderstanding of ordinary language – that is, (roughly) of the way non-philosophers employ certain words (for instance, 'mind,' 'knowledge,' 'real,' 'simple,' and so on). Here are three examples:

5. **Ryle**: According to Gilbert Ryle (1949), the mind–body problem assumes that Jones' mind belongs to the same category as Jones's body (that is, it assumes that minds are things, but different sorts of things than bodies). Yet this, Ryle argues, is a 'category mistake': misled by surface grammar, we conclude that facts about our mental life belong to a logical type to which they do not belong. Since the mind-body problem is spurious, solutions to that problem – Cartesian dualism, materialism, and immaterialism – are as unnecessary as they are confused.

6. **Wittgenstein**: According to the later Wittgenstein, philosophers should 'bring words back from their metaphysical use to their everyday use' (Wittgenstein 1953: sect. 116). For instance, metaphysicians have sought to identify the 'building blocks' of reality (that is, the primary elements or simple constituent parts of which complex entities are composed). This quest for simples is quixotic, because acontextual talk of absolute simplicity is senseless; what counts as simple (or composite) is relative to an established scheme of description. Once we acknowledge this, we will no longer be tempted to use the word 'simple' in a special metaphysical sense (Theses 2 and 7).

7. **Austin**: According to J. L. Austin (1962), grandiose queries about 'the Nature of

Reality' ignore the fact that the word 'real' is 'substantive-hungry': we speak of 'a real F' to distinguish the genuine article from phonies, fakes, or imitations of F (as in 'That's a decoy, not a real duck'). Hence we cannot portentously ask 'What is Real?' (full stop) in the manner of old-fashioned metaphysicians. Since, moreover, the decoy exists no less than the duck, we can neither equate what is unreal with what is nonexistent, nor contrast what is real with a second-rate realm of Being, à la Plato.

Historicism

Inspired by the Hegelian dictum that philosophy is its own time held in thought, some philosophers have seen the problems of metaphysics as made, not found; as contingent human creations, as opposed to timeless and inevitable enigmas which reason must confront in order to stay true to itself. To appreciate how different morals can be drawn from such historicism, consider the cases of John Dewey and R. G. Collingwood:

8. **Dewey**: According to Dewey (1920), the traditional questions of metaphysics (and epistemology too, for that matter) should not be answered, because they rest on assumptions we needn't endorse. Since metaphysical and epistemological problems presuppose vocabularies and dichotomies that reflect contingent historical and cultural conditions, present-day philosophers should shun the bogus problems of Being and Knowledge and instead directly address 'the problems of men' (see Thesis 3).

9. **Collingwood**: According to Collingwood (1940), all the metaphysician can do is uncover 'absolute presuppositions,' that is, the most basic assumptions made by different people or cultures in their systematic thinking about the world. Because such presuppositions are not propositions (and hence neither true nor false), the metaphysician cannot prove or refute them; his task is rather to describe them. The metaphysician is, then, a special kind of historian (see Theses 3 and 4).

Naturalism

Eliding the distinction between philosophy and science, naturalists voiced skepticism about the idea that metaphysics is somehow a law unto itself. The pragmatist tradition can claim two prominent defenders of this line: Dewey and Quine.

10. **Dewey**: Metaphysicians from Plato to Bradley have assumed that philosophy can discover truths about a reality inaccessible to science; but this, Dewey (1925) opined, is an absurd and self-serving delusion. Philosophy has no distinctive method, and there is no special domain of objects or truths it can proudly call its own. Far from rivaling science, then, philosophy must be prepared to draw freely – and gratefully – on science's results. Metaphysics is no exception (see Theses 4 and 5).

11. **Quine**: According to Quine (1951, 1960), there is no such thing as 'first philosophy': no pure a priori super-discipline sitting condescendingly in judgement over science's labors and evolving conceptual schemes. Philosophy is continuous with science, not prior to it; and there is no realm of reality exclusively reserved for the metaphysician. What distinguishes the philosopher from the scientist is not the objects they study, but rather the breadth of the categories they employ (see Theses 4 and 5).

E Pluribus Unum?

Our critiques are a diverse lot, but such unruly diversity can be instructive. I make here three interrelated observations:

1. First, there is considerable disagreement about exactly what is wrong with metaphysics. (A glance at the theses challenged by each of 1–11 is sufficient to confirm this.) The doctors are agreed that the patient is ill; but they offer different diagnoses. Or – to return to the metaphor used earlier – many of our critics are aiming at different targets.
2. Second, not only do the targets differ; so do the perspectives of the archers, whose critiques are launched from a variety of philosophical standpoints or orientations. Most notably, there is a distinction between those critiques that are derived directly from some thesis about language or meaning (1–3, 5–7) and those that are not (4, 8–11).
3. Third, whereas some of our philosophers campaign for the abolition of metaphysics, other less radical souls yearn only for reform. Thus Ayer and his Positivist cohorts were unabashed abolitionists; James, Collingwood and Quine, reformers. Other figures are harder to place; Dewey, for instance, shows signs of wanting to have it both ways.

We can now appreciate both how and why old-fashioned metaphysics came under fire prior to the mid-1950s. However, we may inadvertently have left some with the impression that our philosophers have turned, with quasi-Oedipal fury, against the very philosophical tradition(s) that sired them. Is this indeed the case? To this question we now turn.

3. Past and Present: A Study in Continuity

It would be a crude blunder to suppose that analytic philosophers have cut themselves off from the past, or that they are committed *ex officio* to the perverse view that philosophy officially begins with Frege or the first number of *Mind*. Fortunately, no one even superficially acquainted with metaphysics in the analytic tradition will be tempted to accept this view of its leading practitioners, who have offered sophisticated treatments of many time-honored topics: the mind-body problem, personal identity, substance, essentialism, identity, change, causation, freedom and determinism, fatalism, the existence of God, monism versus pluralism, the nature of space and time, and universals (to name only a few).[1] There has, in short, been no lack of serious engagement with traditional issues. In order to shed light on the nature of this engagement, I propose to consider a case study: the problem of metaphysical realism, or whether the world is mind- or language-independent. So let us now look at what twentieth-century English-language philosophy has had to say about this classic conundrum.

From Idealism to Realism

Throughout the last quarter of the nineteenth century, English-language philosophy was dominated by various forms of imported Idealism, as a host of leading philosophers – T. H. Green, Bernard Bosanquet, F. H. Bradley, and J. M. E. McTaggart in England, and Josiah Royce in America – fell under the spell of post-Kantian thought. Hegel soon supplanted Hume as the philosopher of choice; the Humean bonfire was extinguished; and speculative metaphysics was graciously spared. With common sense fast becoming the new philosophical heresy, realism became anathema – as did the related conception of truth as correspondence between our judgements and a ready-made world unconditioned by thought or consciousness.

Less than a generation later, Idealism had lost much of its prestige; and a good deal of the credit (or blame) for this is commonly given to G. E. Moore. In hindsight, it has become tempting to read his 'Refutation of Idealism' (1903) as if its author were a pedantic incarnation of St. George, singlehandedly slaying the dragon of Idealism armed with nothing but a sharp distinction – namely, that between the act of awareness and its object. As fairy-tales go, however, this is poor stuff. For one thing, there were realists before Moore – just as there were brave men before Agamemnon. And instead of dying a dramatically quick and convenient death, Idealism lived on – albeit in a wary and enfeebled state – long after Moore's onslaught; its later doughty defenders included Michael Oakeshott (1933), Brand Blanshard (1939), and T. L. S. Sprigge (1983). Moreover, Idealism took its revenge: it influenced some of its most vociferous detractors. A case in point is the pragmatism of William James (1907) and F. C. S. Schiller (1907), whose critiques of various doctrines – the 'copy' theory of truth, the idea of an unconceptualized Given, the pre-Kantian conception of the mind as receptive and passive – owe much to the Idealist tradition they disparaged. Dewey's (1929) later polemics against what he dubbed 'the spectator theory of knowledge' are similarly informed by the writings of Kant, Hegel and their English-speaking epigoni.

From Realism To Phenomenalism – and Back Again

Although realism did not score an immediate or unequivocal triumph, it nevertheless became a philosophical force to be reckoned with. Growing increasingly confident and self-conscious, realists turned away from polemics against outsiders and began to focus on internecine disagreements, the most celebrated of which was the quarrel between the New Realists and the Critical Realists: New Realists such as Ralph Barton Perry (1912) and E. B. Holt (1912) enthusiastically advocated a revivified form of direct realism, whereas Critical Realists such as George Santayana (1920) and Arthur Lovejoy (1930) demurred.

But anti-realist reaction soon set in. Ironically, this backlash to the movement led by Moore came about partly because realist philosophers took up yet another of Moore's obsessions – namely, the nature of sense perception and its objects. Persuaded that sense-data were the direct objects of perception, tough-minded empiricists gravitated towards non-realist views, with Berkeleyan and Millian pedigrees: they maintained that physical objects were reducible to (or are Russellian 'logical constructions' out of) sense-data, and held that statements about physical objects could be translated without remainder into statements about (actual or possible) subjective experiences. This view – phenomenalism – gained support in many quarters, and it is not hard to see why. If one is a sense-data theorist committed to a verificationist theory of meaning, what else could statements about physical objects mean? Moreover, if physical objects are nothing over and above sets of sense-data, and if we have direct and incorrigible knowledge of our own sense-data, how could there be a general problem about our knowledge of the physical world? Phenomenalism thus shrank the chasm between mind and world to a mere crack, thereby endearing itself to those burdened with Cartesian epistemological anxieties.

Despite phenomenalism's promise, and the care and elegance with which A. J. Ayer (1936) and C. I. Lewis (1946) formulated it, the view eventually fell from favour. Some of the arguments against it – such as Roderick Chisholm's (1948) charge that statements about physical objects could not be translated into statements about sense-data – were aimed specifically at phenomenalism. Other criticisms, however, were directed against nonmetaphysical doctrines associated with classical phenomenalism; examples include Wittgenstein's (1953) argument against a logically private language, Ryle's (1949) case against sense-data, and Austin's (1962) critique of the argument from illusion, as well as his reservations about foundationalist theories of knowledge.

As phenomenalism and orthodox verificationism withered away, realism resurfaced in a variety of forms in the 1960s. Direct realist theories of perception were revived and rendered both rigorous and respectable, as in the early work of D. M. Armstrong (1961); moreover, even direct realism's detractors tended to remain within the realist fold (as in the representative realism defended by Frank Jackson (1977)). Tough-minded scientific realism of the sort advanced by J. J. C. Smart (1963) also met with a warm welcome, especially among those who embraced Quinean naturalism.

So realism was apparently back on top; but the balance of power was about to shift – yet again.

Contemporary Debate: Recent Critiques of Realism

In the last quarter of the twentieth century, opposition to metaphysical realism rose dramatically and assumed diverse guises: Michael Dummett's anti-realism, Hilary Putnam's 'internal' (or 'pragmatic') realism, Thomas Kuhn's constructivism, Nelson Goodman's irrealism, Richard Rorty's neo-pragmatism, and Donald Davidson's nuanced reflections on truth and objectivity. To give the flavor of the debate, here are ten objections to realism, along with noteworthy rejoinders:

The Comparison Argument
According to Goodman (1978), Richard Rorty (1979, 1982, 1989, 1991) and Putnam (1981, 1983, 1990), the Given of traditional empiricism is a pernicious myth: observation is theory-laden, and we cannot justify our beliefs by comparing them with something unconceptualized. Defending justification-by-comparison, William

Alston (1996) has claimed that the anti-realist's complaint that we can never get outside of language is ill-founded.

The New 'Master Argument'
Goodman (1978) has suggested that since nothing can be said about the world, apart from some frame of reference used to describe it (that is, some theory or language), the idea that there is a world independent of such frameworks is senseless. If David Stove (1991) and Israel Scheffler (1999) are right, this attempt to dress up Berkeley's infamous Master Argument in linguistic garb is no more attractive than the baroque original.

The Argument from Conceptual Relativity
Putnam (1987) maintains that metaphysical realists cannot accommodate the phenomenon of conceptual relativity: since objects exist relative to conceptual schemes; it is senseless to ask what exists absolutely, independent of the choice of a scheme. According to Ernest Sosa (1993b) and John Searle (1998), however, this is a nonsequitur: there is no incompatibility between the affirmation of realism and the relativity Putnam describes.

The Model-Theoretic Argument
According to metaphysical realism, a theory that is epistemically ideal (that is, that satisfies all operational and theoretical constraints) could nevertheless be false. Invoking the Lowenheim-Skolem theorem, Putnam (1983) has argued that this cannot be. Putnam's intricate argument has been the subject of detailed attacks by David Lewis (1984), Michael Devitt (1991), and Alston (1996), among others.

The Argument from Verificationist Semantics
According to Michael Dummett (1978), debates about realism are ultimately debates about meaning; and to deny that the meaning of a given class of sentences is given by verification-transcendent truth conditions – to deny, that is, that such sentences have determinate truth-values, independently of means of knowing them – is effectively to abandon realism about that class of sentences. But we *should* deny that statements about the world have verification-transcendent truth-conditions; otherwise, Dummett thinks, we will be hard pressed to explain how we learn languages or manifest linguistic competence. Realists such as Devitt (1991) and Alston (1996) claim Dummett misconceives the realism issue by semanticizing it, and they insist that his case for a verificationist theory of meaning fails.

The Argument from Facts
According to Davidson (1990, 1999), realists must pledge allegiance to a version of the correspondence theory of truth which affirms the existence of facts. Yet if Davidson's 'Slingshot Argument' (1969, 1990) is sound, there is at most only one fact to which all true sentences correspond, in which case the correspondence theory is drained bone-dry of content. Searle (1995) has countered by attacking the Slingshot Argument, whereas Sosa (1993a) has pleaded that realists need not be committed to facts.

The Argument from Massive Error
If the world is as independent of our epistemic capacities as realists think, then it seems the vast mass of our beliefs could be false; but since Putnam (1981) and Davidson (1986) have assured us that such massive error is unthinkable, the realist's ultra-objective world is a 'world well lost', to quote Rorty (1982). Realist reaction has ranged from Peter van Inwagen's (1988) attack on the characterization of realism underlying this argument, to Thomas Nagel's (1986) skepticism about any theory of mind or language which guarantees we must be mainly in the right about the way the world is.

The Argument from Truth-Making
Truth is a property of sentences; but there would be no sentences if there were no languages. Since languages are human creations, Rorty (1989) concludes that truth is not 'out there' waiting to be discovered. Searle (1998) alleges that arguments of this sort rest on a use-mention confusion: from the fact that the languages used to describe reality are social constructions, it does not follow that what such languages describe is a social construction (that is, that the world is language- or mind-dependent).

The Argument from The History of Science
Reflections on the history of science seem to undermine the case for scientific realism. The problem is neatly posed by Putnam (1978): since entities posited by past scientific theories have turned out not to exist, why suppose the posits of our current theories will not meet with the same fate? Sosa (1993b) notes that whatever damage arguments of this sort may do to the cause of scientific realism, they leave commonsense realism untouched; and Devitt (1991) has sought to show that they are not fatal to the former position either.

The Argument from Incommensurability
According to Kuhn (1970), there is no way to compare scientific paradigms: there is no neutral observational input untainted by theory, and terms employed in different theories may mean different things. Since scientists working in incommensurable paradigms toil in 'different worlds,' there is no knowable world utterly independent of theory. Kuhn's claims about incommensurability have been contested by many philosophers, including realists such as Gerald Vision (1988) and Devitt (1991).

Note that not all who oppose realism propound a positive rival doctrine. Rorty's (1991) Polonius-like recommendation is that we neither realists nor anti-realists be; both positions are answers to a question – 'What makes our sentences true?' – that makes sense only if we are in the grip of the representationalist picture of language his neo-pragmatism abjures. Davidson, too, has refused to characterize himself as an anti-realist – and his repudiation of epistemic theories of truth (1990) and his critique of the very idea of a conceptual scheme (1974) separate him from Goodman and Putnam.

A Quartet of Morals

We have travelled a long way quickly: from Bradley to Rorty, and from Moore to Searle. What morals does our century-spanning case study support? Four merit a quick mention:

1. The century-long concern with realism suggests that Anglophone metaphysicans are not at all indifferent to their discipline's history; on the contrary, they address traditional problems, and gleefully purloin the arguments of past masters (for example, Berkeley, Kant, Hegel, and so on).
2. It illustrates the central role that sophisticated argumentation (and plenty of it) has played in analytic metaphysics. Indeed, one of the most impressive features of the contemporary realism debate is the dialectical inventiveness of the participants.
3. The realism debate exemplifies a sense in which analytic metaphysics, despite its piecemeal character, nevertheless qualifies as systematic. Arguments advanced for and against realism stimulate, and have been stimulated by, debates in other areas of metaphysics and in areas of philosophy outside metaphysics: epistemology, the philosophy of language, philosophy of mind, and philosophy of science.
4. It reveals a leading tendency of analytic philosophy: its attempt to transform our understanding of a traditional and seemingly intractable problem by reformulating it in terms of language. This is part and parcel of the linguistic turn, whose influence on metaphysics is the theme of our next section.

4. From Language and Reality: Metaphysics and The Linguistic Turn

And so we turn at last to the third and final question on our agenda: in what ways has the linguistic turn affected the way(s) in which metaphysics is actually done? Lest this last query be misconstrued, let me stress that we are not concerned here with the ways in which analytic philosophy's preoccupation with language has led some to denounce or despise metaphysics; that is a topic we have already discussed. The present question asks us to reflect on how the concern with language has re-oriented or informed constructive theorizing in metaphysics.

Here is something like an answer, in the form of five examples. Most are relatively recent; indeed, all save the first are drawn from the last quarter-century. Other illustrations might equally well have been chosen – there is no lack of them – but given space limitations these will serve our purpose.

Logical Atomism: Russell and Wittgenstein

Russell's Theory of Descriptions (1905) applied the old appearance/reality contrast to language itself; for it encouraged us to distinguish a statement's superficial grammatical form from its underlying logical form, discoverable through philosophical analysis. Exploiting this idea in a systematic and rigorous fashion, the logical atomism of Russell (1918) and Wittgenstein (1921) claimed that philosophers could lay bare the structure of reality by understanding the structure of an ideal (or 'logically perfect') language which mirrors or reflects it. Thus the curious and intricate ontology of Wittgenstein's *Tractatus* (with its facts, states of affairs, and simple objects) ultimately rests on his Picture Theory of meaning, according to which propositions must have the same structure or form as what they depict or represent.

Davidson

Using the fiction of an omniscient interpreter, Donald Davidson (1977, 1986) argued that most of our beliefs are true. The root idea is that an interpreter is constrained by the Principle of Charity, and so must maximize agreement between himself and those he interprets. But if most of our beliefs agree with those of an interpreter whose beliefs are all true, then most of our beliefs must be true.

This point might seem purely epistemological; but Davidson stresses its implications for metaphysics. For if our worldview is fundamentally sound, then attending carefully to the broad structural features of our language (with the aid of a Tarski-inspired theory of truth) may yield truths about the structure of reality itself. This method is proffered, not as a substitute for careful argumentation, but as a way of clarifying and refocusing it – as when, for instance, a philosopher defends an ontology of events on the grounds that far too many of our ordinary beliefs (about change) would be false unless the existence of such entities is admitted.

Dummett

We have already had occasion to mention the views of Michael Dummett. But Dummett's work should also be discussed in the present connection, since his views on realism can be seen as part of a broader program: that of reformulating traditional metaphysical controversies as debates within the philosophy of language.

The philosophy of language is granted a kind of foundational status by Dummett; as he puts it, 'the theory of meaning underlies metaphysics' (Dummett 1978: xl). Accordingly, disputes about the existence of some entity or class of entities – mathematical objects, say, or the future, or the past – can be recast as disputes about the *meaning* of a certain class of statements – what Dummett calls 'the disputed class' (that is, mathematical statements, statements in the future tense, statements in the past tense, and so on). If this approach is sound, then a wide range of metaphysical problems can be fruitfully re-presented as turning on disagreements between realists and anti-realists in some domain – disagreements, that is, between those who hold that the statements of the disputed class in question have objective truth-values independent of our means of ascertaining them, and those who deny this.

Kripke

Saul Kripke's (1980) groundbreaking work in modal logic and the philosophy of language has had many important implications for metaphysics. Here, unfortunately, just one example must suffice.

According to Kripke, true identity statements which involve what he calls 'rigid designators' – that is, terms that refer to the same thing in every possible world – are necessarily true. Despite appearances, this scholastic-sounding doctrine is far from philosophically dull or trivial. For one thing, it suggests there are truths that are necessary, yet not knowable *a priori*. This means we must disentangle or decouple two distinctions philosophers have long run together: the metaphysical distinction between necessary and contingent truths and the epistemological distinction between the *a priori* and *a posteriori*. Moreover, Kripke uses this thesis about identity to motivate a rejection of the psycho–physical identity theory, according to which mental states (for example, pain) are identical with a certain physical state (for example, the stimulation of C-fibers). Having discarded this popular solution to the mind-body problem, Kripke avers that the problem itself is 'wide open and extremely confusing' (Kripke 1980: 155).

Lewis

Another influential contributor to recent debates about the metaphysics of modality is David Lewis (1973a, 1986). Undeterred by incredulous stares, Lewis maintains that (possible) worlds other than the actual one exist.

Many analytic philosophers have invoked possible worlds in some context or other – to explain the distinction between necessary and contingent truths, say, or to further our understanding of counterfactuals (as in Lewis's own (1973a)). For the rank and file, however, talk of possible worlds has been just that: mere talk, or a handy *façon de parler*. Not so for Lewis, whose preferred label for his position is modal realism (that is, realism about possible worlds). Modal realism affirms the existence of a plurality of worlds: since 'absolutely *every* way that a world could be is a way that some world *is*' (Lewis 1986: 3), there are possible worlds that are distinct from ours but equally real. True, we may (and do) call ours the actual world, but it must be borne in mind that 'actual' functions as an indexical (such as 'here'); to call a world actual is to say that it is where we find ourselves, not to say that it and it alone exists.

Morals and Caveats

It is clear from the foregoing that reflection on language and logic has stimulated twentieth-century Anglophone metaphysics in myriad ways. In some cases, such reflection has led philosophers to take a fresh look at old topics (as in the cases of Kripke on the mind-body problem, or Dummett on realism); in others, it has opened up new avenues of inquiry (as in the case of Lewis on possible worlds).

Nevertheless, it is easy to exaggerate the novelty of the linguistic turn. For this reason, I will offer two quick and bland caveats in the name of equilibrium. First, the inspiration behind the linguistic turn was not unprecedented: as Ian Hacking (1975) has reminded us, language has long mattered to philosophy – which is not, of course, to say that it has always mattered for the same reasons. Second, analytic philosophers are certainly not the only twentieth-century philosophers to whom language has mattered; their continental contemporaries pondered language at length as well and drew their own conclusions. But that, as they say, is another story.

5. The Infinite Museum

This completes our official tour of the Museum of Recent Metaphysical Curiosities. Like all such tours, ours has of necessity been highly compressed, selective and somewhat arbitrary. For that reason it will inevitably leave some tourists dissatisfied; they were rather hoping to take a gander at this or that famous exhibit, prominently featured in their glossy but well-thumbed Baedakers. Such querulous daytrippers must be sternly reminded that our museum is an immense labyrinth, and that our tour's purpose has been to supply them not with its floor plan but rather with an Ariadne's thread: a slender cord to keep them from going astray, if and when they wander alone through the winding passages of this maze – a maze that is always being simultaneously demolished and rebuilt. Crumbling but forever renovated, condemned yet expanding, our paradoxical museum is a fitting home for what Borges called 'las ilustres incertidumbres que son la metafisica.'[2]

Notes

1. Given space limitations and related constraints, I cannot discuss these problems without superficiality of truly criminal proportions. I regret this, and I urge those interested in these topics to consult the relevant entries in Kim and Sosa (1995), Craig (1998), or Audi (1999).
2. '[T]he renowned uncertainties of metaphysics,' a line from 'La Fama' ('Fame') (Borges 1999: 452–3).

References

Alston, W. (1996), *A Realist Conception of Truth*, Ithaca: Cornell University Press.
Armstrong, D. M. (1961), *Perception and the Physical World*, London: Routledge and Kegan Paul.
Audi, R. (ed.) (1999), *The Cambridge Dictionary of Philosophy*, 2nd edn, New York: Cambridge University Press.
Austin, J. L. (1962), *Sense and Sensibilia*, Oxford: Clarendon Press.
Ayer, A. J. (1936), *Language, Truth and Logic*, London: Victor Gollancz.
Blanshard, B. (1939), *The Nature of Thought*, 2 vols, London: Allen and Unwin.
Borges, J. L. (1999), *Selected Poems* (bilingual edn), New York: Penguin.
Byron, G. G., Lord [1824] (1973), *Don Juan*, Harmondsworth: Penguin.
Carnap, R. (1951), 'Empiricism, Semantics, and Ontology,' *Revue International de Philosophie* 4: 20–40.
Chisholm, R. M. (1948), 'The Problem of Empiricism,' *Journal of Philosophy* 45: 512–17.
Collingwood, R. G. (1940), *An Essay on Metaphysics*, Oxford: Clarendon Press.
Cook Wilson, J. (1926), *Statement and Inference, with Other Philosophical Papers*, ed. A. S. L. Farquharson, Oxford: Clarendon Press.
Craig, E. (ed.) (1998), *Routledge Encyclopaedia of Philosophy*, London: Routledge.
Davidson, D. (1969), 'True to the Facts,' in Davidson (1984), *Inquiries into Truth and Interpretation*, Oxford: Clarendon Press, pp. 27–54.
Davidson, D. (1974), 'On the Very Idea of a Conceptual Scheme,' in Davidson (1984), *Inquiries into Truth and Interpretation*, Oxford: Clarendon Press, pp. 183–98.

Davidson, D. (1977), 'The Method of Truth in Metaphysics,' in D. Davidson (1984), *Inquiries into Truth and Interpretation*, Oxford: Clarendon Press, pp. 199–214.

Davidson, D. (1984), *Inquiries into Truth and Interpretation*, Oxford: Clarendon Press.

Davidson, D. (1986), 'A Coherence Theory of Truth and Knowledge,' in E. Lepore (ed.), (1986), *Truth and Interpretation: Perspectives on the Philosophy of Donald Davidson*, Oxford: Basil Blackwell, pp. 307–19.

Davidson, D. (1990), 'The Structure and Content of Truth,' *Journal of Philosophy* 87: 279–328.

Davidson, D. (1999), 'Is Truth a Goal of Inquiry? Discussion with Rorty,' in U. M. Zeglen (ed.) (1999), *Donald Davidson: Truth, Meaning, and Knowledge*, London: Routledge, pp. 17–19.

Devitt, M. (1991), *Realism and Truth*, 2nd edn, Cambridge: Basil Blackwell.

Dewey, J. (1920), *Reconstruction in Philosophy*, New York: Holt.

Dewey, J. (1925), *Experience and Nature*, Chicago: Open Court.

Dewey, J. (1929), *The Quest for Certainty*, New York: Minton, Balch & Co.

Dummett, M. (1978), *Truth and Other Enigmas*, London: Duckworth.

Feldman, F. (1974), 'Kripke on the Identity Theory,' *Journal of Philosophy* 71: 665–76.

Gallois, A. (1974), 'Berkeley's Master Argument,' *Philosophical Review* 83: 55–69.

Goodman, N. (1978), *Ways of Worldmaking*, Indianapolis: Hackett.

Hacking, I. (1975), *Why does Language Matter to Philosophy?*, New York: Cambridge University Press.

Holt, E. B. (ed.) (1912), *The New Realism*, New York: Macmillan.

Jackson, F. (1977), *Perception: A Representative Theory*, Cambridge: Cambridge University Press.

James, W. (1907), *Pragmatism*, New York: Longmans, Green.

Kim, J., and E. Sosa (eds) (1995), *A Companion to Metaphysics*, Cambridge: Blackwell.

Kripke, S. (1980), *Naming and Necessity*, Cambridge: Harvard University Press.

Kuhn, T. (1970), *The Structure of Scientific Revolutions*, 2nd edn, Chicago: University of Chicago Press.

Lewis, C. I. (1946), *An Analysis of Knowledge and Valuation*, LaSalle: Open Court.

Lewis, D. (1973a), *Counterfactuals*, Cambridge: Harvard University Press.

Lewis, D. (1973b), 'Causation,' *Journal of Philosophy* 70: 556–67.

Lewis, D. (1984), 'Putnam's Paradox,' *Australasian Journal of Philosophy* 62: 221–36.

Lewis, D. (1986), *On the Plurality of Worlds*, Oxford: Blackwell.

Lovejoy, A. O. (1930), *The Revolt Against Dualism*, New York: Norton.

Lycan, W. (1974), 'Kripke and the Materialists,' *Journal of Philosophy* 71: 677–89.

McTaggart, J. M. E. (1908), 'The Unreality of Time,' *Mind* 68: 457–84.

Moore, G. E. (1903), 'The Refutation of Idealism,' *Mind* 12: 433–53.

Moore, G. E. [1911] (1953), *Some Main Problems of Philosophy*, London: Allen and Unwin.

Moore, G. E. [1925] (1959), 'A Defence of Common Sense,' in *Philosophical Papers*. London: Allen and Unwin, 32–59.

Nagel, T. (1986), *The View from Nowhere*, New York: Oxford University Press.

Oakeshott, M. (1933), *Experience and its Modes*, Cambridge: Cambridge University Press.

Perry, R. B. (1912), *Present Philosophical Tendencies*, New York: Longmans, Green.

Putnam, H. (1978), *Meaning and The Moral Sciences*, London: Routledge and Kegan Paul.

Putnam, H. (1981), *Reason, Truth and History*, Cambridge: Cambridge University Press.

Putnam, H. (1983) *Realism and Reason*, Cambridge: Cambridge University Press.

Putnam, H. (1987), *The Many Faces of Realism*, LaSalle: Open Court.

Putnam, H. (1990), *Realism with a Human Face*, Cambridge: Harvard University Press.

Putnam, Hilary (1999), *The Threefold Cord: Mind, Body and the World*, New York: Columbia University Press.

Quine, W. V. O. (1951), 'Two Dogmas of Empiricism,' in Quine (1953), *From a Logical Point of View*, Cambridge: Harvard University Press, pp. 20–46.

Quine, W. V. O. (1953), *From a Logical Point of View*, Cambridge: Harvard University Press.

Quine, W. V. O. (1960), *Word and Object*, Cambridge: MIT Press.

Rorty, R. (1979), *Philosophy and the Mirror of Nature*, Princeton: Princeton University Press.

Rorty, R. (1982), *Consequences of Pragmatism*. Minneapolis: University of Minnesota Press.

Rorty, R. (1989), *Contingency, Irony, and Solidarity*, Cambridge: Cambridge University Press.

Rorty, R. (1991), *Objectivity, Relativism and Truth*, Cambridge: Cambridge University Press.

Russell, B. (1905), 'On Denoting,' *Mind* 14: 479–93.

Russell, B. (1918), 'The Philosophy of Logical Atomism,' in R. Marsh (ed.) (1956), *Logic and Knowledge*, London: Allen and Unwin, pp. 175–281.

Ryle, G. (1949), *The Concept of Mind*, London: Hutchinson.

Santayana, G. (1920), 'Three Proofs of Realism,' in D. Drake (ed.) (1920), *Essays in Critical Realism*, London: Macmillan.

Scheffler, I. (1999), 'A Plea for Plurealism,' *Transactions of the C. S. Peirce Society* 35: 425–36.

Schiller, F. C. S. (1907), *Studies in Humanism*, London: Macmillan.

Searle, J. (1995), *The Construction of Social Reality*. New York: Basic Books.

Searle, J. (1998), *Mind, Language and Society: Philosophy in the Real World*, New York: Basic Books.

Smart, J. J. C. (1963), *Philosophy and Scientific Realism*, London: Routledge and Kegan Paul.

Sosa, E. (1993a), 'Epistemology, Realism, and Truth,' *Philosophical Perspectives* 7: 1–16.

Sosa, E. (1993b), 'Putnam's Pragmatic Realism,' *Journal of Philosophy* 90: 605–26.

Sprigge, T. L. S. (1983), *The Vindication of Absolute Idealism*, Edinburgh: Edinburgh University Press.

Stove, D. (1991), *The Plato Cult and Other Philosophical Follies*, Oxford: Basil Blackwell.

Strawson, P. F. (1959), *Individuals: An Essay in Descriptive Metaphysics*, London: Methuen.

Van Inwagen, P. (1988), 'On Always Being Wrong,' *Midwest Studies in Philosophy* 12: 95–111.

Vision, G. (1988), *Modern anti-realism and manufactured truth*, London: Routledge.

Wittgenstein, L. (1921), *Tractatus Logico-Philosophicus*, trans. D. F. Pears and B. F. McGuinness, London: Routledge.

Wittgenstein, L. (1953), *Philosophical Investigations*, trans. G. E. M. Anscombe, Oxford: Blackwell.

Epistemology

John Greco

Epistemology has been traditionally concerned with two major questions: what is knowledge? and what can we know? These questions about the nature and scope of knowledge quickly lead to others: assuming that knowledge is superior to mere opinion, what is it that distinguishes the two? What makes knowledge 'justified' or 'warranted'? A related question concerns the structure of knowledge: is knowledge like a pyramid, with a sure foundation supporting the remaining edifice? Or is knowledge more like a raft, with all parts of the structure tied together in relations of mutual support? More generally: what is the nature of the mind–world relation that constitutes knowing rather than merely believing? Given that knowledge involves a mind representing the world, how must mind and world be related for knowledge of the world to be possible?

These are the perennial questions of epistemology, going back at least as far as Plato's *Theaetetus*. These same questions dominated twentieth-century epistemology as well, but their treatment in that century was influenced by two distinctive themes. The first was that knowledge importantly depends on the nature of the knower and her relationship to her environment. Put differently, knowledge importantly depends on the sort of cognitive equipment that the knower possesses, and on whether there is a 'good fit' between that sort of equipment and the environment that the knower inhabits. The second theme involves a distinction between two projects of epistemology: 'the project of explanation' and 'the project of vindication.' The project of explanation is the focus of Plato's *Theaetetus*: it asks what knowledge is, and tries to explain the difference between knowing and not knowing. The project of vindication has also been prominent since the early days of epistemology, and is closely related to Pyrrhonian skepticism. This is the project of showing that we have knowledge, in general or in a particular domain. The first project is concerned to explain what knowledge is and how it is possible, whereas the second is concerned to establish that knowledge exists. Epistemology in the twentieth century clearly privileged the project of explanation over the project of vindication. Even further, there emerged a sense that the project of vindication is somehow flawed or misguided to begin with, and that the true task of epistemology is the project of explanation.

These different understandings of epistemology's project have no small influence on how epistemology is done. For example, the two understandings dramatically influence how epistemology approaches the problem of skepticism. If the project is vindication, it would seem that skepticism must be answered on its own terms – one must establish that we have knowledge, using only assumptions that the skeptic would allow. Anything less would be dialectically unsatisfactory, begging the very question at issue. If the project is explanation, however, then things change. Now the project is not to establish that we have knowledge, but to explain how knowledge is possible. In that case, it is perfectly appropriate to challenge assumptions behind the skeptic's arguments. In fact, it is now appropriate to assume that the skeptical conclusion is false.

An example will help to illustrate the point. Suppose that a skeptical argument proceeds as follows:

1. Knowledge of the world is possible only if sensory perception is a reliable way of forming true beliefs about the world.
2. But sensory perception is not very reliable – it leads us to make mistakes about the world all the time.

Therefore,

3. Knowledge of the world is impossible.

The obvious place to challenge this argument is premise 2. Even if sensory perception sometimes leads us astray, we want to insist that in general sensory perception is reliable and so premise 2 is false. But suppose we are trying to show that premise 2 is false, and in a way that does not beg the question against a skeptic who is making the argument. In that case it seems clear that we cannot succeed. For the only way we could know that premise 2 is false is by relying on our knowledge of the world – it is only by knowing the world that we know that sensory perception is (in general) reliable. But it is precisely knowledge of the world that is at issue in the argument, and so showing that premise 2 is false seems impossible.

But suppose that the project is explanation rather than vindication. In that case there is no worry about begging the question against the argument's conclusion. Since there is no worry about showing or establishing anything, there can be no worry about showing or establishing in a way that is dialectically inappropriate. Rather, the task now is to explain how knowledge is possible, and this means explaining where the argument has gone wrong. In other words, the project of explanation assumes that the skeptical conclusion is false, and tries to identify the premise of the argument that is making the mistake. Notice that the assumption in question is methodological rather than substantive. In other words, the assumption that knowledge is possible is internal to the project of explaining how knowledge is possible.

But one wants to insist: how do we know that knowledge is possible? That question has not been answered. True, but this is just to insist that the project of explanation is not the project of vindication. What is more, many twentieth-century epistemologists have argued that the project of vindication is misguided from the start. Boiled down to its bare bones, the project asks us to show that we have knowledge, but using only a restricted set of premises allowed by a skeptical opponent. But why is that project worthwhile? Why is it worthwhile, or even interesting, to establish that conclusion from a set of assumptions so restricted? (Sosa 1994; Greco 2002).

Even worse, it would seem that the idea of completing the task is a non-starter. For how can one show that one has knowledge in a domain without using premises from the domain in question? For example, consider skepticism about the world. On the one hand, the skeptic wants us to show that we have knowledge of the world. On the other hand, we are not allowed to use premises that are about the world, since knowledge about the world is what is at issue. Is completing this task possible? Once clearly stated, it seems obvious that it is not. But this says less about our epistemic condition than it does about the dialectical situation – *of course* it is impossible to show that sort of thing, using premises restricted in that sort of way.

Considerations such as these led many epistemologists to abandon the project of vindication altogether. The task became, rather, to investigate the facts about human cognition, and how that sort of cognition allows the sort of knowledge we assume that human beings typically have. From this point of view, empirical psychology and the cognitive sciences in general become directly relevant to epistemology's central questions. By contrast, *a priori* investigations seem less relevant, and to a large extent unmotivated (Quine 1969; Goldman 1986; Kornblith 1994).

The Structure of Knowledge: Foundationalism and Coherentism

Questions about the structure of knowledge were already being raised at the beginning of the century. The logical positivist Moritz Schlick defended a version of foundationalism, proposing that all empirical knowledge rests on a foundation of basic 'observation statements.' Observation statements were considered to be about sensory appearances (or 'sense data'), and in need of no justification beyond their grounding in immediately given experience. Schlick's contemporary, Otto Neurath, defended a version of coherentism. Neurath invoked the metaphor of a raft, in which all the parts of the structure are tied together in relationships of mutual support. There is no privileged foundation of knowledge, Neurath argued. Knowledge is constructed only by standing on one part of the structure while building or repairing another (Sosa 1980; Ayer 1982).

The debate between foundationalism and coherentism took center stage later in the century, in the writings of Wilfred Sellars and Roderick Chisholm. Sellars launched an influential attack against 'The Myth of the Given,' arguing that nothing could play the role of a foundation for knowledge. Sellars's argument took the form of the following dilemma. Suppose that the foundations of knowledge have the content of a judgement, such as Schlick's observation statements about sense data. In that case, the judgement must be in need of some further justification; it requires grounding in experience, for example, and so it is not itself a foundation. Alternatively, suppose that the foundations of knowledge do not themselves have the content of a judgement. Suppose, for example, that the sense data themselves are the foundations of knowledge, and that sense data have only phenomenal (rather than conceptual) content. In that case, the proposed foundations do not have the right sort of content to act as grounds for non-foundational knowledge. For how could something that lacks conceptual content act as evidence? How could it support (or imply, or make probable) anything? The conclusion, Sellars argued, is that nothing can play the role of a foundation for knowledge: nothing can both (1) ground further knowledge and (2) not itself be in need of further grounding. The structure of knowledge, many concluded, must be more like Neurath's raft (Sellars 1963; Williams 1977; Bonjour 1978).

Roderick Chisholm proposed foundationalist epistemic principles that seemed to many to escape Sellars's dilemma. According to Chisholm, some states of a person are self-presenting in the following sense: if S is in the state in question, then S is justified in believing that he is in that state. For example, if S is appeared to as if there is a white, round object, then S is justified in believing that he is appeared to as if there is a white, round object. In effect, Chisholm denied the second horn of Sellars's dilemma – that nothing lacking conceptual content can ground justification for something else. On the contrary, Chisholm argued, the fact that S is in some self-presenting state justifies S's belief that he is in that state.

Moreover, Chisholm argued, one may formulate epistemic principles for memory and perceptual beliefs. For example:

For any subject S, if S believes, without ground for doubt, that he is perceiving something to be F, then it is evident for S that he perceives something to be F. (Chisholm 1977: 78)

For any subject S, if S believes, without ground for doubt, that he remembers perceiving something to be F, then it is beyond reasonable doubt for S that he does remember perceiving something to be F. (Chisholm 1977: 81)

According to Chisholm, these principles specify necessary truths about epistemic justification. It is the nature of epistemic justification, he argued, that beliefs satisfying the specified conditions have the specified epistemic status. These principles were supposed by Chisholm to be universal as well as necessary. That is, they were supposed to apply to any cognitive being who satisfies their antecedent, independently of that being's particular make-up or environment.

Foundationalism and coherentism are historically tied to the project of vindication – both theories arise in response to Pyrrhonnian concerns about a regress of justification, and about the possibility of demonstrating that one has knowledge. However, both theories can be understood as part of the project of explanation as well. In this context, each tries to explain how justification and knowledge must be structured in order for knowledge to be possible. And if the task is to explain the structure of human knowledge, then foundationalism seems to have the advantage. This is because human beings are fitted with cognitive equipment that suggests a foundationalist structure. Put simply, not all human cognitive faculties are reasoning faculties. Sometimes our cognition involves reasoning; sometimes it works by inferring a conclusion from prior beliefs acting as premises for an inference. But not all human cognition works that way. Sometimes we form beliefs on the basis of sensory experience. Sometimes we remember things. Sometimes we reflect, and form beliefs about our own thinking on the basis of that reflection. All this suggests exactly what foundationalism claims; that while some knowledge is based on further reasons, some knowledge is foundational in the following sense: it is knowledge, but it is not based on further knowledge acting as its grounds or reasons.

Of course, not all noninferential cognition produces knowledge. At the very least, a cognitive faculty must reliably produce true beliefs to produce knowledge. The foundationalist insists that any number of our faculties do this, however. For example, perception and memory reliably produce true beliefs, at least in certain conditions, but neither perception nor memory involves inference. How do we know which of our cognitive faculties reliably produce true beliefs, and in which conditions? These are empirical questions, which can only be answered by empirical means. Again, once the project of vindication is put aside in favor of the project of explanation, empirical psychology and the cognitive sciences become relevant to the questions of epistemology.

The Analysis of Knowledge and the Gettier Problem

Recall that 'the project of explanation' is the project of explaining what knowledge is. Put another way: it is the project of explaining the difference between knowing and not knowing. One form this project can take is the attempt to state necessary, sufficient and informative conditions for knowledge. Note that conditions can be necessary and sufficient without being informative. Hence a philosopher might propose that knowledge is true belief that is not true by accident. But even if all and only knowledge is true belief that is not true by accident, we will not have an adequate analysis until we know what 'not true by accident' means. Note also that a proposed analysis can be more or less informative. An adequate analysis of knowledge must go some way toward an informative explanation of what knowledge is.

Before 1963 there was a good consensus among philosophers regarding the analysis of knowledge. Going back to an idea already in Plato, the rough consensus was that knowledge is true belief that is backed up by adequate justification. Hence Chisholm proposed the following account of knowledge:

S knows that P IFF
1. S accepts P,
2. S has adequate evidence for P, and
3. P is true.

A. J. Ayer defended a similar account:

S knows that P IFF
1. P is true,
2. S is sure that P is true, and
3. S has the right to be sure that P is true.

In 1963, Edmund Gettier published a short paper that destroyed this consensus (Gettier 1963). Gettier offered two examples intended to show that the conditions stated above are not sufficient for knowledge. Here is an example in the spirit of Gettier's originals.

Case 1: On the basis of excellent reasons, S believes that her co-worker Mr Nogot owns a Ford: Nogot testifies that he owns a Ford, and this is confirmed by S's own relevant observations. From this S infers that someone in her office owns a Ford. As it turns out, S's evidence is misleading and Nogot does not in fact own a Ford. However, another person in S's office, Mr Havit, does own a Ford, although S has no reason for believing this (Lehrer 1965).

The point of the example is that S's belief (that someone in her office owns a Ford) is both true and justified: S has good evidence that the belief is true, and on the basis of that evidence S has the right to be sure that it is true. Nevertheless, S does not know that someone in her office owns a Ford. What has gone wrong?

The moral that epistemologists drew from Gettier's examples is that 'subjective' justification is not sufficient for knowledge, even when joined to true belief. Notice that S's justification for her belief is 'subjective' in the following sense: From S's point of view, there is good reason for thinking that the belief is true. Put differently: given what S has to go on, it is appropriate for S to think that her belief is true. Gettier's examples show that this sort of justification, even together with true belief, is not sufficient for knowledge.

In the face of these considerations, three options present themselves. All three were pursued in the wake of Gettier's examples: (1) The conditions stated above are necessary for knowledge, but not sufficient. One must add a fourth condition to the three already stated; (2) The conditions stated above are formally adequate, but we must rethink our notion of justification. Justification is not merely subjective; (3) Justification is not relevant to knowledge. Rather, knowledge is true belief plus some condition other than justification.

An example of approach (1) is the 'indefeasibility' analysis of knowledge. The guiding idea is that knowledge is true justified belief, where S's justification is 'indefeasible' in something like the following sense: there is no true proposition Q such that adding Q to S's reasons for believing P would result in S's no longer being justified in believing P (for example, Klein 1971; Swain 1974). For example, in the Nogot example there are truths that S is unaware of, such that adding those truths to S's reasons would undermine or defeat any justification those reasons give S for believing P. Take, for example, the true proposition that Nogot does not own a Ford. Adding this to S's reasons for believing P (that someone in her office owns a Ford) would result in S's no longer being justified in believing P.

A danger for any such account is that the conditions for knowledge are made too strong, so that now not enough counts as knowledge. In particular, it seems that one can always imagine misleading truths such that, if those truths were added to S's reasons for believing P, then S's justification for believing P would be defeated. For example, take some proposition R that is extremely improbable but true. Then let Q be the proposition (R or not-P). Adding Q to S's reason for believing P will defeat S's justification for believing P, for nearly any P whatsoever. And in that case indefeasibility accounts are too strong – they result in almost no beliefs counting as knowledge.

An example of approach (2) is the 'reliabilist' account of knowledge and justification. The guiding idea behind this approach is that justification is not merely a matter of what is subjectively appropriate, or appropriate from *S*'s point of view. Rather, a belief is justified only if it is formed by reasoning processes (or other cognitive processes) that are in fact reliable. In other words, justification requires that *S*'s belief is formed in a way that is objectively adequate, and not merely subjectively appropriate (for example, Goldman 1976). Plausibly, this explains why *S*'s belief in the Nogot example is not justified: *S*'s belief was formed on the basis of misleading evidence, and that is not an objectively reliable way of forming one's beliefs.

Problems arise for this sort of account, however. Even if we agree that it rules correctly in the Nogot example, the account seems less promising in the face of examples such as the following.

Case 2: Walking down the road, *S* seems to see a sheep in the field and on this basis believes that there is a sheep in the field. However, due to an unusual trick of light, *S* has mistaken a dog for a sheep, and so what she sees is not a sheep at all. Nevertheless, unsuspected by *S*, there is a sheep in another part of the field (Chisholm 1977).

Here the reliabilist is faced with a dilemma. If eyesight need not be perfectly reliable to give rise to knowledge, then it would seem that the account incorrectly allows knowledge in Case 2. Suppose, then, that eyesight must be perfectly reliable to give rise to knowledge. In that case it seems that the account is too strong – many of our visual beliefs ought to count as knowledge, even if our eyesight is not perfectly reliable.

An example of approach (3) is the causal theory of knowledge. As with reliabilist theories, the guiding idea is that knowledge must be caused in the right sort of way. But here the idea is something like this: in cases of knowledge, *S*'s belief is caused by the fact that makes it true. For example, in a case of straightforward perceptual knowledge, *S* believes that there is a cat on the mat because there is a cat on the mat. The fact that there is a cat on the mat causes a perceptual process to take place, which in turn causes *S* to believe that there is a cat on the mat (Goldman 1967). This approach nicely handles both Cases 1 and 2. However, it clearly fails in regard to a third case.

Case 3: Unknown to Henry, the district he has just entered is full of papier-mâché facsimiles of barns. These facsimiles look from the road exactly like barns, but are really just façades, without back walls or interiors, quite incapable of being used as barns. They are so cleverly constructed that travelers invariably mistake them for barns. Having just entered the district, Henry has not encountered any facsimiles; the object he sees is a genuine barn. But if the object on that site were a facsimile, Henry would mistake it for a barn (Goldman 1976).

Clearly, *S* does not know that there is a barn in front of him, although his belief that there is a barn in front of him is caused by the fact that there is.

The above survey represents only a few of the many attempts to respond to the problem raised by Gettier's short paper. During the years between 1963 and 1983, over 100 papers were published on the Gettier problem. However, it is fair to say that epistemologists reached no consensus regarding how the problem ought to be solved (Shope 1983). By the end of the twentieth century, discussion of the Gettier problem considerably waned. This was not because the problem had been solved, but because discussion of it had opened interesting new avenues of research.

The Nature of Epistemic Justification: Internalism versus Externalism

When we claim that someone knows something we are making a value judgement – we are saying that there is something intellectually good or right about what (or how) the person believes. One central task of 'the project of explanation' is to investigate the sort of normativity that knowledge claims involve. In fact, we can rephrase one of the central issues of the Gettier literature in just these terms: what sort of normative status does knowledge require? What makes knowing more valuable than not knowing? In the latter part of the twentieth century, this question took on a life of its own. In other words, epistemologists began to focus on the nature of epistemic normativity as a question in its own right. The most prominent form that this new investigation took was the debate between internalism and externalism about epistemic justification.

It was suggested above that knowledge is a normative notion. There is something normatively better about knowledge, as opposed to mere opinion, or even mere true opinion. Notice, however, that we can make other sorts of intellectual evaluation as well. Even if some belief falls short of knowledge, we may nevertheless judge that it is justified, or rational, or reasonable, or responsible. In each such case, we are saying that there is something normatively better about the belief in question, as opposed to mere opinion, or even mere true opinion. Internalists claim that the epistemically normative status of a belief is entirely determined by factors that are relevantly 'internal' to the believer's perspective on things. That is, when a person S has some belief, whether that belief is justified (or rational, or reasonable, or responsible) for S is entirely a function of factors that are relevantly internal to S's perspective. By contrast, the 'externalist' in epistemology denies this. The externalist says that the epistemic status of a belief is not entirely determined by factors that are internal to the believer's perspective.

Several points are worthy of mention. First, internalism is a rather strong thesis, in the sense that it says that epistemic status is entirely a function of internal factors. By contrast, externalism in epistemology is a relatively weak thesis. Second, we have already noted that there is a variety of epistemic evaluations: we may judge that a belief is justified, or rational, or reasonable, or intellectually responsible, and these need not mean the same thing. It is possible, then, to be an internalist about some kinds of epistemic status and an externalist about others. Hence there is a variety of internalisms and a corresponding variety of externalisms. Third, we get different understandings of internalism (and externalism) depending on different ways that we understand 'internal to S's perspective.' The most common way to understand the phrase is as follows: some factor F is internal to S's perspective just in case S has some sort of privileged access to whether F obtains. For example, a factor F is internal to S's perspective if S can know by reflection alone whether F obtains (Ginet 1975; Chisholm 1977; Goldman 1980; Alston 1985, 1986).

Finally, it is apparent that some varieties of internalism are initially more plausible than others. Consider that we can evaluate both persons and their beliefs in two very different ways. Broadly speaking, we can make our evaluations either from an 'objective' point of view or from a 'subjective' point of view. From the objective point of view, we can ask whether there is a 'good fit' between the person's cognitive powers and the world. For example, we can ask whether the person has a sound understanding of the world around him, or whether he has a good memory, or accurate vision. Also from this point of view, we can ask whether a person's methods of investigation are 'reliable,' in the sense that they are likely to produce accurate results. On the other hand, there is a second broad category of epistemic evaluation. This sort does not concern whether a belief is objectively well formed, but whether it is subjectively well formed. It asks not about objective fitness, but about subjective appropriateness. It is clear that internalism is pretty much a nonstarter with respect to evaluations of the first category. Evaluations from an objective point of view involve factors such as accuracy, reliability, and appropriate causal relations to one's environment. And these are paradigmatically external factors. Therefore, internalism is best understood as a thesis about the second broad category of epistemic evaluation: it is a thesis about what factors determine subjective appropriateness.

Putting all this together, we arrive at the following understanding of internalism: whether a belief b is subjectively appropriate for a person S is entirely a matter of factors that are internal to S's perspective.

Suppose we use the term 'epistemic justification' to name the sort of subjective appropriateness (if any) that is required for knowledge. Early versions of internalism were about epistemic justification in this sense. Later in the twentieth century, some epistemologists defended internalist accounts of other kinds of subjective appropriateness. For example, it is plausible that rationality is an important normative property independent of knowledge, and that whether a belief is rational is entirely a matter of factors that are internal to S's perspective (Foley 1987, 1993).

One consideration commonly put forward in favour of internalism began with an assumption about the nature of epistemic justification. Namely, a belief b is epistemically justified for a person S just in case S's believing b is epistemically responsible. However, the argument continued, epistemic responsibility is entirely a matter of factors that are internal to S's perspective. Therefore, epistemic justification is entirely a matter of factors that are internal to S's perspective (Ginet 1975; Bonjour 1985). Externalists countered that responsibility is not just a matter of internal factors. For example, prior negligence is a factor determining present responsibility, even if that negligence is not now internal to S's perspective. An example illustrates the point.

Maria believes that Dean Martin is Italian. She believes this because she seems to remember clearly that it is so, and she presently has no reason for doubting her belief. But suppose also that Maria first came to this belief carelessly and irresponsibly (although she has now forgotten this). Many years ago, she formed her belief on the basis of testimony from her mother, who believes that all good singers are Italian. At the time Maria knew that her mother was an unreliable source in these matters, and she realized that it was not rational to accept her mother's testimony (Greco 1990).

The moral externalists draw from the example is that 'etiology matters' for epistemic responsibility. In other words, whether a belief counts as epistemically responsible depends, in part, on how the belief was formed. But etiology is an external factor, and so understanding epistemic justification in terms of epistemic responsibility does not motivate internalism about epistemic justification. In fact, it motivates externalism about epistemic justification.

A second consideration put forward in favor of internalism was that externalism makes an answer to skepticism too easy. Philosophical problems are supposed to be difficult. If the externalist has an easy answer to the problem of skepticism, then that is a good reason to think that externalism is false. At the very least, internalists argued, it is a good reason to think that externalists have changed the subject – that they are no longer talking about our traditional notions of justification and knowledge (Bonjour 1985; Fumerton 1995).

How does externalism make an answer to skepticism too easy? The idea is roughly as follows. According to the skeptic, one can know via sense perception only if we know that sense perception is reliable. Similarly, one can know by inductive reasoning only if one knows that inductive reasoning is reliable. This creates problems for internalists, because it is hard to see how one can have non-circular evidence for knowledge about the reliability of one's cognitive powers. There is no such problem for externalists however, since externalists can deny the initial assumption of the skeptical argument. That is, externalists can insist that our cognitive powers give rise to knowledge so long as they are reliable. There need be no requirement, on an externalist account, that one know that one's cognitive powers are reliable.

The present line of reasoning is that externalism makes the reply to skepticism too easy. In effect, the claim is that only internalism can give a satisfying reply to traditional skeptical concerns. On the contrary, externalists have responded, if one concede internalism then it is impossible to give a satisfying reply to traditional skeptical concerns. This response by externalists takes Hume's skeptical reasoning seriously. Like internalists, Hume believed that one's empirical evidence gives rise to knowledge only if one knows that one's evidence is reliable. For example, Hume thought one must know that sensory appearances are a reliable guide to reality. Likewise, he thought, one must know that observed cases are a reliable indication of unobserved cases. But there is no way to know such things, Hume argued, without reasoning in a circle. And so there is no way to know such things at all. The externalist's point is this: if one adopts an internalist account of epistemic justification, then Hume has all the premises he needs to mount his skeptical argument (Greco 1999, 2000).

The Nature of Epistemic Normativity: Virtues and Rules in Epistemology

We have seen that epistemology in the twentieth century became focused on the nature of epistemic normativity. One manifestation of this focus was the dispute between internalism and externalism about the nature of epistemic justification. A second was a new interest in 'virtue epistemology' (Sosa 1991; Zagzebski 1996).

The best way to understand virtue theory, both in ethics and in epistemology, is as a thesis about direction of analysis. In sum, virtue theories make the normative properties of persons most fundamental, and then understand other normative properties in terms of these. Consider that in ethics we can make several kinds of evaluation. Most importantly, we can ask:

1. Which actions are right (appropriate, required, permitted)?
2. What things are good (valuable)?
3. What makes a person good (virtuous, admirable)?
4. What makes a life worthwhile (desirable, enviable)? What sort of life constitutes human flourishing?

Different kinds of moral theory make different kinds of evaluation most fundamental. Thus consequentialist theories make evaluations in category (2) most fundamental. For example, hedonistic utilitarianism claims that only pleasure is essentially good. The normative properties of actions, persons and lives are then understood in relation to this fundamental value. Deontological theories in ethics change this direction of analysis, making the evaluations in category (1) fundamental. Virtue theories, by contrast, make the evaluations in (3) and (4) fundamental. A virtue theory begins by asking what makes persons virtuous and their lives worthwhile, and then understands what is right and what is good in relation to that.

Virtue theories in epistemology mirror the structure of virtue theories in ethics. They make the (epistemically) normative properties of persons fundamental, and understand other sorts of (epistemically) normative properties in terms of these. For example, a virtue theory tries to understand key normative notions such as justified belief, knowledge, and evidence in terms of the intellectual virtues.

Different versions of virtue theory emerge depending on how the intellectual virtues are understood. At the end of the twentieth century, two understandings of the virtues competed to address a broad range of epistemological problems and issues. The first way of understanding the intellectual virtues follows Aristotle in making a strong distinction between intellectual virtues and moral virtues. Whereas the moral virtues are acquired traits of character, such as courage and temperance, the intellectual virtues are broad cognitive abilities or powers. For example, Aristotle defined 'intuitive reason' as the ability to grasp first principles, and he defined 'science' as the ability to demonstrate further truths from these. Epistemologists in the twentieth century added to Aristotle's list of cognitive powers, by including accurate perception, reliable memory, and various kinds of good reasoning (Sosa 1991; Goldman 1992; Plantinga 1993; Greco 1999, 2000). The second way of understanding the intellectual virtues rejects Aristotle's way of distinguishing between intellectual virtues and moral virtues. On this second view, the intellectual virtues are also acquired character traits, such as intellectual courage and intellectual carefulness (Code 1987; Montmarquet 1993; Zagzebski 1996).

The resources of virtue theory were employed to address a broad range of problems and issues in epistemology. Some of these problems and issues were quite traditional, while others pushed the boundaries of the field, opening up new interests and new lines of research. Virtue theory made its contemporary début as a contribution to the debate between foundationalism and coherentism. Ernest Sosa argued that the sources of foundational knowledge could be understood as various noninferential cognitive powers. Coherence-seeking reason could also be understood as an intellectual virtue or power, but one that required other sources for its virtuous operation. Virtue theory has also been employed to address traditional problems about the nature of knowledge and about skepticism.

Recall what we referred to above as an uninformative analysis of knowledge: that knowledge is true belief that is not true by accident. This analysis is promising as far as it goes, but we need a better understanding of what 'not true by accident' means. A virtue approach suggests the following: S's belief is not true by accident, in the relevant sense, when S believes the truth as the result of intellectual virtue. In general, a success is not true by accident if it is the result of some agent's powers or abilities. If the archer is skilled, it is no accident that her arrow hits her target. If the painter is talented, it is no accident that his portrait resembles his subject. The current idea is that believing the truth is a kind of intellectual success. In cases of knowledge, this success is no accident in the sense that it is grounded in the knower's intellectual abilities (Sosa 1991; Zagzebski 1996; Lehrer 2000; Riggs 2002; Greco 2004).

One important version of skepticism concerns our ability to rule out alternatives to what we claim to know. Consider Descartes' belief that he is sitting by the fire. Presumably he has this belief because this is how things appear to him by perception. However, Descartes reasons, things could appear to him just as they do even if he were in fact not sitting by the fire, but was instead sleeping, or mad, or the victim of an evil deceiver. The point is not that these other things might well be true, or that they ought to be taken seriously as practical possibilities. Rather, it is that Descartes cannot rule these possibilities out. And if he cannot rule them out, then he cannot know that he is sitting by the fire. The problem is that Descartes's reasoning seems to generalize. In general, one cannot know anything about the world unless one can rule out various skeptical possibilities. But since one cannot rule these out, it follows that one cannot know anything about the world.

A virtue theory provides useful resources for addressing this line of argument. One assumption of the skeptical argument is that knowledge requires ruling out all possibilities, no matter how 'far out' or 'far off.' But suppose we are thinking of knowledge as true belief grounded in the knower's intellectual powers or abilities. In general, an ability is a disposition to achieve some success. For example, the ability to play tennis implies various dispositions in the tennis player – dispositions to return the ball successfully, to serve successfully, and so on. But abilities are tied to their bases and to their appropriate conditions: to say that someone has the ability to play tennis is not to say that she would retain that ability if she were blind. Neither is it to say that she would play successfully in any conditions whatsoever, no matter how inhospitable to playing tennis. Likewise, intellectual abilities such as perception and induction are tied to their bases and to their appropriate conditions. If that is right, then mere possibilities do not undermine one's intellectual abilities in normal conditions – no more than the mere possibility of hurricanes undermines one's ability to play tennis on a beautiful day, or the mere possibility of blindness undermines one's ability to play tennis while sighted (Greco 2000).

The new focus on epistemic normativity brought with it a focus on intellectual agency as well. Epistemologists at the end of the century turned their attention to such issues as the relations between intellect and will, the cognitive role of the emotions, the social dimensions of intellectual agency, and the relations between intellectual agency and luck. Epistemology also saw a new focus on the intellectual virtues themselves, and a renewed interest in long neglected intellectual goods such as wisdom and understanding.

Bibliography

Alston, W. (1985), 'Concepts of Epistemic Justification,' *Monist* 68: 57–89.

Alston, W. (1986), 'Internalism and Externalism in Epistemology,' *Philosophical Topics* 14: 179–221.

Austin, J. L. (1962), *Sense and Sensibilia*, Oxford: Oxford University Press.

Ayer, A. J. (1956), *The Problem of Knowledge*, London: Macmillan.

Ayer, A. J. (1982), *Philosophy in the Twentieth Century*, London: Random House.

Bonjour, L. (1978), 'Can Empirical Knowledge Have a Foundation?,' *American Philosophical Quarterly* 15: 1–13.

Bonjour, L. (1985), *The Structure of Empirical Knowledge*, Cambridge: Harvard University Press.

Chisholm, R. (1957), *Perceiving: A Philosophical Study*, Ithaca: Cornell University Press.

Chisholm, R. (1966), *The Theory of Knowledge*, Englewood Cliffs: Prentice Hall.

Chisholm, R. (1977), *The Theory of Knowledge*, 2nd edn, Englewood Cliffs: Prentice Hall.

Chisholm, R. (1982), *The Foundations of Knowing*, Minneapolis: University of Minneapolis Press.

Chisholm, R. (1989), *The Theory of Knowledge* 3rd edn, Englewood Cliffs: Prentice Hall.

Code, L. (1987), *Epistemic Responsibility*, Hanover: University of New England and Brown University Press.

Fogelin, R. (1994), *Pyrrhonian Reflections, Knowledge and Justification*, Oxford: Oxford University Press.

Foley, R. (1987), *The Theory of Epistemic Rationality*, Cambridge: Harvard University Press.

Foley, R. (1993), *Working without a Net: A Study in Egocentric Epistemology*, Oxford: Oxford University Press.

Fumerton, R. (1995), *Metaepistemology and Skepticism*, Lanham: Rowman and Littlefield.

Gettier, E. (1963), 'Is Justified True Belief Knowledge?,' *Analysis* 23: 121–3.

Ginet, C. (1975), *Knowledge, Perception and Memory*, Dordrecht: Reidel.

Goldman, A. (1967), 'A Causal Theory of Knowing,' *Journal of Philosophy* 64: 357–72.

Goldman, A. (1976), 'Discrimination and Perceptual Knowledge,' *Journal of Philosophy* 73: 771–91.

Goldman, A. (1980), 'The Internalist Conception of Justification,' *Midwest Studies in Philosophy* 5: 27–51.

Goldman, A. (1986), *Epistemology and Cognition*, Cambridge: Harvard University Press.

Goldman, A. (1992), 'Epistemic Folkways and Scientific Epistemology,' in A. Goldman (1992), *Liaisons: Philosophy Meets the Cognitive and Social World*, Cambridge: MIT Press, pp. 155–77.

Greco, J. (1990), 'Internalism and Epistemically Responsible Belief,' in *Synthese* 85: 245–77.

Greco, J. (1999), 'Agent Reliabilism,' in J. Tomberlin (ed.) (1999), *Philosophical Perspectives 13, Epistemology*, Atascadero: Ridgeview Press.

Greco, J. (2000), *Putting Sceptics in their Place: The Nature of Sceptical Arguments and their Role in Philosophical Inquiry*, Cambridge: Cambridge University Press.

Greco, J. (2002), 'How to Reid Moore,' *The Philosophical Quarterly* 52: 544–63.

Greco, J. (2004), 'Knowledge as Credit for True Belief', in M. DePaul, and L. Zagzebski (eds) (2004), *Intellectual Virtue: Perspectives from Ethics and Epistemology*, Oxford: Oxford University Press.

Klein, P. (1971), 'A Proposed Definition of Propositional Knowledge,' *Journal of Philosophy* 68: 471–82.

Kornblith, H. (ed.) (1994), *Naturalizing Epistemology*, Cambridge: MIT Press.

Kornblith, H. (2001), *Epistemology: Internalism and Externalism*, Malden: Blackwell.

Lehrer, K. (1965), 'Knowledge, Truth and Evidence,' *Analysis* 25: 168–75.

Lehrer, K. (2000), *Theory of Knowledge*, 2nd edn, Boulder: Westview Press.

Montmarquet, J. (1993), *Epistemic Virtue and Doxastic Responsibility*, Lanham: Rowman and Littlefield.

Moore, G. E. (1962), *Philosophical Papers*, New York: Collier Books.

Plantinga, A. (1993), *Warrant and Proper Function*, Oxford: Oxford University Press.

Quine, W. V. O. (1969), 'Epistemology Naturalized' in Quine, W. V. O. (1969), *Ontological Relativity and Other Essays*, New York: Columbia University Press, pp. 69–90.

Riggs, W. (2002), 'Reliability and the Value of Knowledge,' *Philosophy and Phenomenological Research* 64: 79–96.

Sellars, W. (1963), 'Empiricism and the Philosophy of Mind,' in W. Sellars (1963), *Science, Perception and Reality*, London: Routledge, pp. 127–96.

Shope, R. (1983), *The Analysis of Knowing*, Princeton: Princeton University Press.

Sosa, E. (1980), 'The Raft and the Pyramid: Coherence versus Foundations in the Theory of Knowledge,' in *Midwest Studies in Philosophy* 5:3–25. (Reprinted in Sosa 1991.)

Sosa, E. (1983), 'Nature Unmirrored, Epistemology Naturalized', *Synthèse* 55: 49–72. (Reprinted in Sosa 1991.)

Sosa, E. (1991), *Knowledge in Perspective*, Cambridge: Cambridge University Press.

Sosa, E. (1994), 'Philosophical Scepticism and Epistemic Circularity,' *Proceedings from the Aristotelian Society* 68 (Supp.): 263–90.

Stroud, B. (1994), 'Scepticism, "Externalism," and the Goal of Epistemology,' *Proceedings from the Aristotelian Society* 68 (Supp.): 291–307.

Swain, M. (1974), 'Epistemic Defeasibility,' *American Philosophical Quarterly* 11: 15–25.

Williams, M. (1977), *Groundless Belief*, Malden: Blackwell.

Zagzebski, L. (1996), *Virtues of the Mind*, Cambridge: Cambridge University Press.

Philosophy of Language: 1950–2000

Tyler Burge

The last half of the twentieth century in philosophy of language has seen, I hazard to say, some of the most intense and intellectually powerful discussions in any academic field during the period.[1] Yet the achievements in these areas have not been widely appreciated by the general intellectual public. This is partly because they are abstract and difficult. But it is also partly a reflection of the lamentably weak lines of communication between philosophy and the rest of culture, especially in America. In my view, this situation developed during the professionalization of philosophy in the positivist period. Indeed, positivism's harsh judgement of the cognitive value of most of nonscientific culture should probably be given much of the blame. Logical positivism casts a long shadow. Its overthrow in the early 1950s is the central event at the outset of the period that I shall discuss. Elements from this movement motivated and colored much that followed. Philosophy's challenge has been to maintain the movement's clarity and respect for argument, while loosening its restrictions on method and subject matter.

Logical positivism aimed to make philosophy scientific – to end the succession of philosophical systems that seemed to promise no analog of scientific progress. To support this aim, the movement presented an account of why philosophy had failed to be scientific and what its proper scope and limits are. This account rested on a theory of meaning coupled with a theory of knowledge. The theory of meaning was the most original proposal of the movement. It consisted of two main principles. One was that the meaning of a sentence is its method of verification or confirmation (*the verificationist principle*). The other was that statements of logic and mathematics, together with statements that spell out meaning relations, are *analytic* in the specific sense that they are *true purely in virtue of their meaning and provide no information about the world: they are vacuously or degenerately true*. It was typically claimed that analytic truth is truth in virtue of conventions or other activities whose products are not rationally legitimated.

The verificationist principle was supposed to explain why philosophy, particularly metaphysics, had failed. The idea was that since philosophy associates no method of verification with most of its claims, those claims are meaningless. To be meaningful and produce knowledge, philosophy was supposed to imitate science in associating its claims with methods of testing them for truth.

The logical positivists saw both principles about meaning as underwriting an empiricist theory of knowledge, a theory according to which all nonvacuous knowledge is justifiable only by reference to sense experience. Science was supposed successful only because it checks and justifies its claims by reference to sense experience. Logic and mathematics, the traditional sources of difficulty for empiricism, were counted useful but vacuous in that they are analytic. Thus, all cognitively meaningful, nonvacuous claims about the world were supposed to be justifiable only by methods of verification that lead ultimately to sense experience.

This empiricism varies but slightly from that of Hume. The attempt to explain the limits of philosophy by reference to scientific method is an adaptation of Kant's broadly similar attempt. What distinguished the movement most sharply from its philosophical predecessors was its radical theory of meaning, represented by the verificationist principle, and its dispassionate, communal approach to philosophical discussion practiced by its leading proponents – men like Carnap, Schlick, Neurath, Reichenbach, and Hempel. The theory of meaning gave philosophy a new focus and caught the attention of the intellectual public because of its radical implication that a lot that passed for serious intellectual discourse (outside philosophy as well as in it) was in fact 'meaningless.' The intellectual power, seriousness, and openness of the movement's leaders obtained for the movement a number of talented interlocutors.

Problems with the verificationist principle dogged the movement almost from the beginning. There was a difficulty with self-application. It is hard to cite a method of verification that is associated with the principle itself; and in the absence of such a method, the principle is 'cognitively meaningless' by its own account. Some proponents counted the principle analytic and, therefore, vacuously true. But this claim was difficult to make credible because the principle seemed so much more contentious than other purportedly analytic claims. Moreover, to admit that one's philosophy was cognitively vacuous was not to pay it much of a compliment. Among positivists, Carnap maintained the most sophisticated position on the issue. He recommended as a practical proposal, to be judged by its theoretical fruits, a linguistic framework within which the principle counted as analytic. He regarded the principle as a proposal for clarifying the informal meaning of 'meaning.' Given its allegedly practical cast, this position was not persuasive to those not already convinced. Moreover, it encountered problems with the notions of linguistic framework, analyticity, and the practical-theoretical distinction some of which I shall discuss (Carnap 1937, 1964a).

There was also a difficulty in stating what counts as an admissible method of confirmation. Various proposals about the structure of confirmation were found to be revivals of traditional philosophical pictures (such as phenomenalism) in disguise. The proposals lacked scientific status. More generally, most of the more precise formulations either included parts of metaphysics as meaningful or excluded parts of science as meaningless. This problem led to a number of reformulations of the verificationist principle. But frustration with this difficulty finally led Hempel in 1950 to agnosticism about the truth of any suitably powerful verificationist principle (Hempel 1950).

Quine's frontal attacks on both primary principles of logical positivism in the early 1950s marked the true end of the movement. His criticism of the verificationist principle aimed at the fundamental issue. Quine claimed that methods of confirmation in science could not be associated with single sentences, as the principle required. He held that sentences can be confirmed or disconfirmed only in relation to other sentences, in the context of theories. This general claim earned the loose title 'holism'. On this view, a method of confirmation cannot be uniquely associated with any one sentence as its meaning.[2] Holism, understood in this general sense, came to be buttressed by many examples from the practice of science. It has held the field in empirical domains ever since.

Quine also challenged the idea that the notion of analyticity had any application. The attack spilled over into a campaign against a variety of different notions associated with the specific notion of analyticity that I characterized. Since Quine himself often failed to distinguish among these notions, the attack on the original notion has been neglected in the controversy over the broader campaign.

Quine's primary and strongest point was that the claim that some sentences are vacuously true has no explanatory or cognitive advantage. He maintained that there is no ground for claiming that the relevant sentences are vacuously true, with no dependence on the way the world is, as opposed to true because of obvious and ubiquitous (in traditional terms, 'necessary') features of reality. Quine's strongest point is not that the notion of meaning is incoherent or requires some special explanation. It is that there is no good argument for characterizing the distinction between the supposed instances of analytic truths (including logical truths and truths of 'meaning analysis') and instances of other truths in terms of vacuous truth and subject matter independence (Quine 1966a and cf. 1966b).

Carnap defended the claim that logic is analytic by holding it to be a practical proposal that is itself analytic – to be judged by its fruits in explicating meanings (Schilp 1963: 917ff). This defense paralleled his defense of the verificationist principle against the objection concerning self-application. Quine held that Carnap's notion of a practical proposal could not be distinguished from that of a theoretical proposal, for theoretical proposals in science are judged 'pragmatically,' by their theoretical fruitfulness.

Quine also criticized other attempts to spell out the claim that logic is analytic, or vacuously true. As against the view that logic is true by convention, he pointed out that logic has an infinite number of theorems. One might imagine, for the sake of argument, that individual axioms were true by conventional stipulation. But deriving the consequences of these axioms requires that one already assume logic. The main principles of logic seem prior to any activity that might be regarded as a laying down of linguistic meaning.[3]

Many positivists sympathized with Frege's logicist program of defining mathematical terms in logical terms, and deriving mathematical theorems from logical axioms together with the definitions.[4] Unlike Frege, they saw the program as aiding the empiricist cause of counting mathematics vacuously true. Many problems already clouded this vision. But Quine added to them by indicating that the vacuity of definitions is at best a passing trait. He noted that when definitions are incorporated into theories, they become subject to theoretical criticism and revision, thus not vacuously true. This point was subsequently substantiated by consideration of numerous theoretical definitions in science and mathematics which had turned out to be false or theoretically inadequate (cf. Quine 1966a, 1951 and Putnam 1962).

By considering the practice of linguistic interpretation, Carnap tried to provide an empirical basis for distinguishing between meaning postulates and theoretical postulates (cf. Carnap 1964b). Carnap's proposals are historically important because they motivated Quine to initiate his project of producing a theory of 'radical translation' (discussed below). But quite apart from their great oversimplifications and their reliance on shaky psychological assumptions, Carnap's proposals are, I think, weak in that they never come to grips with the problem of defending analyticity. Although they may provide a start toward *some* distinction between meaning explications and ordinary theoretical postulates, they give no prima facie ground for distinguishing between nonvacuous and vacuous truth, or between true principles that are rationally legitimated and those that are not rationally legitimated. So they give no support to empiricist epistemology; the original motivation for invoking analyticity.

There was something more general than empiricism at stake in the dispute over analyticity. The positivists hoped 'first principles,' the boundaries of rational discussion, could be established as vacuously true and not subject to philosophical questions about legitimation. First principles included logic, but also other principles about the boundaries of rational discussion, such as the verificationist principle or the claim that certain truths are vacuously true and not subject to rational legitimation. If these principles were themselves analytic, they could be exempted from the traditional metaphysical and epistemological questions. Carnap maintained a principle of tolerance that allowed there to be different 'first principles' which could be 'adopted' for pragmatic reasons. But it was fundamental to his view, as well as the views of other less liberal positivists, that neither establishing nor changing a framework of such principles is subject to rational ('theoretical') considerations. Such changes were supposed to be 'prompted' or 'chosen' or were 'merely practically' motivated.

Quine's attack on analyticity calls this distinction into question. Indeed, what I regard as his fundamental criticisms of analyticity have never been satisfactorily answered: no clear reasonable support has been devised for a distinction between truths that depend for their truth on their meaning alone and truths that depend for their truth on their meaning together with (perhaps necessary) features of their subject matter. Similarly, neither Carnap nor anyone else has succeeded in distinguishing between nonrational grounds for adopting 'first principles' and grounds that traditionalists (as well as Quine) might count as rational but obvious (or even rational but disputable). Quine thought that the grounds were covertly empirical. Traditionalists would think that the grounds were rational but *a priori* and relevant to deep structural aspects of the world. In any case, the relevant notion of analyticity has lost its central place in philosophical discussion. Quine's attack, somewhat against his own proclivities, reopened a path to traditional metaphysical and epistemological questions about 'first principles' – a path to the traditional fundamental questions of philosophy. The positivists did not succeed in placing any questions – least of all those about their own two first principles – off limits from rational inquiry.

Quine argued against another notion called 'analyticity,' with no indication that it was distinct from the first. In this second sense, a statement is 'analytic' (henceforth '*analytic-2*') if it is derivable from logic together with definitions.[5] Analyticity-2 is by itself clearly of no use to empiricism or to attempts to end traditional philosophy, for it is completely neutral on the metaphysical and epistemological status of logical truth and definitions. The two notions were run together by many philosophers because of an assumption common since Kant, that logic and definitions are vacuously true. Frege and Russell (not to speak of Aristotle and Leibniz) preceded Quine in rejecting this assumption.[6]

Quine ran together the two notions of analyticity for a different reason. He thought that both were useless. His complaint against analyticity-2 was that it has no clear explanatory value, and that all attempts to explicate the relevant notion of definition utilize notions that are equally useless. The key notion in explaining definitions was synonymy or sameness of meaning. Expanding on points about definitions mentioned earlier, Quine maintained that there is no explanatorily useful distinction between ordinary theoretical postulates and statements that give the meaning of terms, or between attributions of changes of meaning and attributions of changes of belief. Thus Quine proposed a general skepticism about the use of the notion of meaning itself.

The criticisms of analyticity-2 were more widely disputed than those of analyticity. I think them far less successful. But because of Quine's skepticism about the very notion of meaning, the issue over whether a notion of meaning could be clarified replaced the question of whether analyticity could be defended as the focus of discussion. Partly because clarifying the notions of meaning and logic sufficed for defending analyticity-2, this latter notion tended to obscure analyticity in the debate.

Many philosophers maintained that Quine's demands for a clarifying explication of the distinction were misplaced. They held that a distinction could be grounded in a practice rather than a principle – that the existence of a practice of explaining meaning, or giving dictionary definitions, gave credence to there being some distinction between meaning explication, or synonymy, and ordinary theoretical postulates (Grice and Strawson 1956; Putnam 1985). Defenders of analyticity-2 commonly held that definitions or meaning explications could not turn out false. In this, I believe they were mistaken. But in their claims that there is a tenable distinction between explications of meaning and (other) theoretical postulates, defenders of analyticity-2 seem to me to be on stronger ground. Quine held, in effect, that a practice without a principle could not be justified. Moreover, he doubted that the distinctions that his opponents were pointing to need be explained by utilizing any notion of meaning (cf. for example Quine 1960: 67).

This dispute reflected a deeper division over ordinary practice. The division affected both linguistic and philosophical method. The positivist movement, influenced by Frege through Russell, Carnap, and Wittgenstein, had propagated the view that the study of linguistic meaning was the proper starting point for philosophy.[7] Language and meaning were supposed to elicit initial agreement better than other traditional starting points, such as the nature of concepts, or first metaphysical and epistemological principles. By the 1950s the linguistic turn had taken hold. It was filtered through two very different traditions.

One of these traditions derived from Frege's attempts to find a perfect language to express the structure of mathematics. This approach was taken up by the positivists, Russell, Wittgenstein, and eventually Quine. Frege's concern with mathematics was broadened by others to include all of science. The underlying idea was that though language was a reasonable focus for philosophy, it had to be understood in the light of reforms needed for scientific purposes.

The other tradition derived from G. E. Moore's insistence on the primacy of ordinary judgements and practices in dealing with philosophical problems. In Moore's ethical and epistemological writings, examples were given more weight than theory; and ordinary judgements were accorded priority over philosophical principles. Moore's emphases were taken up and applied to linguistic practice in Wittgenstein's highly original later work. In the late 1940s and the 1950s, before and after the publication of *Philosophical Investigations* (1953), concentration on the details and nuances of everyday linguistic practice became the watchword of 'ordinary-language philosophy.'[8] Proponents of this approach tended to assume that the wisdom of centuries was embedded in ordinary practices. Philosophical problems were seen to be either solvable or dissolvable by reference to ordinary practice.

Thus, both traditions took philosophy of language as the starting point for doing philosophy. In the 1950s both tended to be contemptuous of philosophy's past. But the tradition deriving from Frege took science, logic, or mathematics as the source of inspiration for linguistic and philosophical investigation, whereas the tradition deriving from Moore took ordinary practice as the touchstone for linguistic and philosophical judgement. The former tradition distrusted intuition and championed theory. The latter distrusted principles and championed examples.[9]

As approaches to understanding language and as starting points for doing philosophy, each tradition had its weaknesses. In both cases, impatience with standard philosophical problems led to attempts at quick fixes that in retrospect seem shallow. The ordinary-language tradition produced some brilliant linguistic observation. It provided new tools for dealing with philosophical problems, and a sensitivity to linguistic distinctions. But as philosophical method, it faced numerous difficulties, never adequately dealt with, in deriving philosophical conclusions from linguistic examples.[10] As a way of understanding language, the tradition tended to be anecdotal, and its legacy of specific contributions is rather thin. Only a few works made durable contributions to linguistic understanding. Austin produced a taxonomy of speech acts (acts like asserting, promising, commanding) that embedded them in a larger view of human action. The taxonomy became a starting point for much work on pragmatics. Some of Strawson's early work on the speech act of referring and on presupposition bore fruit.[11] The tradition's primary contribution to the philosophy of language, its focus on details of usage, yielded better results when it later allied itself with systematic theory.

Influenced by the spectacular development of logic since Frege, the logical-constructionist tradition aimed at clarifying philosophical problems by formulating them in a precise logical system. Where ordinary notions were indefinite or vague, they were to be replaced by more precise analogs. The pressure to state precise rules of inference uncovered a vast array of distinctions. Logic itself may be regarded as a clarification of ordinary logical concepts. Logical constructionism yielded some notable early successes in producing new logics – particularly in the analysis of necessity and of temporal notions (Carnap 1946; Marcus 1946; Prior 1957; Kripke

1963; Church 1951). As a philosophical method, however, it was limited by a tendency to assume that philosophical problems would disappear if they were replaced by logical problems or problems in constructing a scientific language. Many philosophical problems arise in nonscientific discourse and cannot be solved by laying down rules for the use of notions in a science. Even most of those problems closely related to the sciences are not solved merely by clarifying logical relations.

As an approach to understanding language, the tradition's method of replacement was calculated to ignore certain aspects of language use as detrimental to scientific purposes. Thus, vagueness, ambiguity, indexicality, singular reference, implicature, intentionality, and so on, were ignored (by one writer or another) because of preconceptions about well-behaved logical systems or about the needs of science.

Frege's influence on the logical-constructionist tradition has already been mentioned. One of the most important developments in the 1950s was the upsurge of interest in Frege's own work, particularly his essays in the philosophy of language. Frege's name had been kept alive by Russell, Carnap, and Wittgenstein in the early part of the century, and by Church, Carnap, and Quine in the 1940s and early 1950s. But what provoked widespread consideration of his work was the publication in 1952 of *Translations of the Philosophical Writings of Gottlob Frege*, edited and translated by Geach and Black. Belatedly, during the 1950s, Frege came to be widely recognized as the father of twentieth-century philosophy (Frege 1952).

The philosophy of language became a vibrant, semi-autonomous discipline in the 1960s and early 1970s. In fact, it was considered by many to be the new 'first philosophy.'[12] The subject came of age, in my judgement, out of four primary sources. One was Frege's great influence and example. Another was the combination of the strong points of ordinary-language philosophy and logical constructionism: logical theory was brought to bear on ordinary language, with the aim of understanding it rather than reforming it. A third was the need to interpret the failure of the positivists' verificationist principle. And a fourth was a revival of traditional issues about singular reference. These sources fed discussion of three main problem areas: issues associated with logical form, issues associated with meaning, and issues associated with reference. Frege's work was seminal in the discussion of all three problem areas. Each of the remaining three sources was primary for one of the three problem areas. I shall briefly mention some of Frege's contributions to the philosophy of language. Then I shall say something about the other sources of stimulation.

Frege made the first deep advance on the logic of Aristotle when in 1879 he stated the syntax and semantics for propositional calculus and first- and second-order quantificational logic. This work laid the foundation for one of the great intellectual developments of the century – that of mathematical logic. This advance gave philosophy a range of new problems and a new framework for discussing old ones. Influenced by Frege's work, as filtered through Russell and Wittgenstein, the development of formal semantics by Gödel, Tarski, Church, Carnap, and others in the 1930s and 1940s became the cornerstone for attempts in the 1960s and 1970s to provide an account of the truth conditions, logical form, and compositional structure of natural languages. Frege pioneered a method of finding logical form in natural languages by providing structures to account for actual inferences. His semantical explications of various linguistic constructions became both examples of how to theorize about language and contenders among competing accounts.

Frege also gave an argument for distinguishing between two semantical notions – sense and reference. The argument is so profound, despite its surface simplicity, that it has become a reference point for philosophical discussion of language and mind. He observed that a statement that 'Hesperus is Phosphorus' has a different cognitive value from a statement that 'Hesperus is Hesperus.' The one is potentially informative where the other is not. Since the referents of the component expressions of the two statements are the same, he located the difference in a difference in the sense, or cognitive value, expressed by the names 'Hesperus' and 'Phosphorus.' Theoretical development and explication of the notions of reference and sense as a result became fundamental problems for the philosophy of language.[13]

A second source of the flowering of the philosophy of language was a cross-pollination of the interests of ordinary-language philosophy with the methods of logical constructionism. Strawson and Quine made a start at unifying these traditions. Trained in an environment that took ordinary language seriously, Strawson did significant work in the 1950s and early 1960s on referring, truth value gaps, and presupposition. He attempted to broaden the scope of logic to deal with insights derived from the ordinary-language tradition (Strawson 1971).

Quine continued the logical-constructionist tradition. He aimed at providing a language adequate for the purposes of science. In *Word and Object*, a work of enormous influence, Quine argued that science could be formalized in first-order quantificational logic (without constant singular terms) together with set theory (see especially Chaps 3–6). In carrying out this argument, Quine discussed a wide variety of linguistic constructions and showed a remarkable sensitivity to inferential patterns associated with them. Even where he ended by dismissing a possible account as useless to science, he frequently made it attractive to others whose purposes were less reformist.

Quine's *Word and Object* also influenced philosophical method. His ontological preoccupations indicated to many how philosophy of language could provide a framework for discussing traditional issues in metaphysics. Quine had advocated the view that a theory was committed to the existence of some sort of entity just in case entities of that sort had to be regarded as values of bound variables in irreducibly basic assertions of the theory (Quine 1948, reprinted in Quine 1953). In *Word and Object*, Quine (intentionally) blurred the distinction between language and theory. He then made natural assumptions about what sentences were true, considered various ways of paraphrasing or reducing those sentences into others with more perspicuous logical forms, and finally used the logical forms as bases for discussing pros and cons of admitting the existence of various sorts of entities – properties, stuffs, events, propositions, sets, numbers, mental states, sensations, physical objects, and so on. Quine advocated a broadly materialist position that was tempered by a reluctant Platonism about sets. Quine's materialism was not new. But his defense of it in the context of a systematic investigation of language and logical form lent it new interest. Partly because of *Word and Object*, ontological issues became the dominant preoccupation of metaphysics, including the philosophy of mind, in the two decades that followed.

The approach to language through a study of logical form, illustrated in Frege's and Quine's work, was taken up and made prominent by Davidson. Davidson relinquished Quine's aim of reforming language and proposed a particular formal framework – that of giving a finitely axiomatized Tarskian truth theory – for displaying the logical form and 'meaning' of natural language sentences. The question of the sense in which Davidson's truth theories illuminate meaning is a complex and controversial one. But the contributions of his approach (and more generally of approaches that utilize classical logic) to studies of logical form are, I think, substantial and lasting.[14] Other philosophers proposed various types of intentional logic in the analysis of logical form.[15] Some of this work on logical form was conducted as applied logic. Some of it was directed to clarifying traditional philosophical investigations. Either way, much of it exemplifies high standards of creativity and argument.

The rise of generative linguistics coincided with the flowering of the philosophy of language (Chomsky 1957, 1965). In retrospect it is striking how little the two disciplines influenced one another in the 1960s. There were some significant exchanges about the sense in which one knows a language, about innate ideas, and about the proper subject matter of linguistics. There is no question that linguists were influenced by the methods of logic, and that philosophers were influenced by the notion of a level of language – then called 'deep structure' – that is not immediately evident to ordinary speakers. But Chomsky's early emphasis on the relative purity of syntax matched poorly with philosophers' preoccupation with semantic and pragmatic issues. As linguistics took a more systematic interest in semantics and pragmatics in the early to mid-1970s (largely in response to philosophy), however, the two subjects began to come together. Much of the earlier work by philosophers on logical form has since been assimilated and modified within linguistics. This development surely counts as one of the successes of philosophy, in its traditional role as midwife to the sciences.

A third source of stimulation for the philosophy of language was the need to assimilate the failure of the verificationist principle. This source led to intense discussion of the form and prospects of a 'theory of meaning.' The discussion is so complex that glossing over it without being misleading is impossible in a chapter such as this one. I shall mention just a few strands of the discussion.

I noted that Quine criticized the verificationist principle by claiming that methods of confirmation cannot be associated with individual sentences. Roughly speaking, Quine accepted the positivist assumption that meaning is, if anything, a method of confirmation. But in view of the holistic nature of confirmation – the inability to associate confirmation with particular, definite linguistic sentential units – and the seeming impossibility of giving a general account of how disconfirmatory experiences lead one to revise theory, he concluded that there could be no theory of meaning. Indeed, he thought that the very notion of meaning had no place in a true account of the world. Even many who doubted Quine's radical skepticism about the cognitive value of the notion of meaning found this holism about meaning persuasive, and to be a source of doubt about a general theory of meaning. Some philosophers, like Dummett, accepted verificationism and sought to limit the holism to scientific theory. He held that meaning in ordinary, non-scientific discourse was dependent on more atomistic criteria for applying terms. Others, like Putnam, rejected verificationism but accepted a version of holism because of the variety of considerations that enter into determining constancy of meaning through changes of belief. Still others thought that the holism was restricted by considerations from the theory of reference, which I will discuss below.

Quine extended his criticism of the notion of meaning into arguments for the indeterminacy of translation (Quine 1960, Chaps 1 and 2, and 1969). He held that in any case in which one translates a natural language, there will be many equally ideal overall translations of the language which are so different that one translates a given sentence *S* into a true sentence while another translates *S* into a false sentence. Quine provided two sorts of argument for this position. One began with the claim that physical theory is underdetermined by all possible evidential considerations – so that two equally good but incompatible physical theories could be ideally but equally well justified. He then attempted to show that translation would be indeterminate even when one of these physical theories was fixed. Quine concluded that since physical theory is the proper standard for objective reality, translation does not concern anything definite that is objectively real. Quine's other argument took up Carnap's attempt to show that attributions of meaning (and analyticity) have an empirical basis. He provided a detailed theory of the method of translation. In this theory he attempted to show that our evidence for translation is too sparse even to underwrite determinate translations for terms that are ostensibly about ordinary macrophysical objects, like 'rabbit.'

Quine's thesis about translation was of profound philosophical value in that it opened a new area of philosophical discussion. His second argument stimulated discussion of the evidence and methods for interpreting such linguistically basic phenomena as assent, the logical connectives, and observation terms. But his conclusion has not found wide support. The evidence Quine allows for translation in the second argument has been widely thought to be unduly restrictive. And the claim of the first argument (which informs the second as well) that the relevant sort of indeterminacy of translation relative to physical theory – that is, physics, chemistry, biology, behavioral psychology, but not cognitive psychology or linguistics – would be damning to the cognitive status of translation has seemed to many to be unconvincing (Chomsky 1969).

Davidson's proposal that a Tarskian theory of truth provides the form for a theory of meaning provoked intense debate in North America and England (Davidson 1967, reprinted in Davidson 1984: 17–42, cf. McDowell 1976). The most stable result of this proposal was the work on logical form that it occasioned. The idea that a theory of truth simply is a theory of meaning has been widely disputed. Tarski's theory depends on a translation from the language for which the theory of truth is given to the language in which the theory is given. Many thought that unless one provided a theory of this translation, one would not have provided a *theory* of meaning. Davidson made some plausible suggestions for liberalizing Quine's strictures on translation. But the main theoretical upshot of his proposal was the idea that meanings are truth conditions – requirements whose fulfillment would constitute the truth of a sentence or proposition. Such truth conditions were to be systematically and informatively displayed in a theory of truth. Even though his idea captures relatively little of what many philosophers wanted in a theory of meaning, it does develop one major strand, initiated by Frege, in the notion of meaning – the idea that meanings, in one sense, are truth conditions. And it provided a systematic way of displaying deep inferential relations among truth conditions. Davidson held that this was as much system as one could hope for in a 'theory' of meaning.

Influenced by mathematical intuitionism and by Wittgenstein, Dummett criticized the view that meaning should be understood in terms of truth conditions. He took proof rather than truth as a paradigm of linguistic 'use,' which he considered the basic notion in understanding meaning. He claimed that meaning could not 'transcend' the conditions under which linguistic understanding could be put to use and manifested. Sentences outside of science were associated with criteria of application, useful in communication (Dummett 1975, 1976: 67–137). Dummett used these ideas in discussing a wide variety of profound metaphysical issues, which are outside the scope of this essay. His approach to meaning, though rich and deeply provocative, has not been widely accepted, partly because of its 'antirealist' metaphysical associations, and partly because it has been seen by many as a recrudescence of verificationism. Understanding relations between confirmation, or use, and truth conditions remains, however, a complex and fundamental matter.

Concerned more with what makes expressions meaningful than with the structure of a language, Grice attempted to analyze linguistic meaning in terms of a special sort of communicative intention. He claimed that linguistic meaning is to be understood in terms of what a person means by an utterance. And this latter sort of meaning is to be understood in terms of the person's intending the utterance to produce some effect in an audience by means of the recognition of this intention. The linguistic meaning of the utterance is roughly the content of the intention (Grice 1957, 1968, 1969, all reprinted in Grice 1989; cf. Schiffer 1972). Thus, certain mental states were taken to be analytically basic to understanding language. Mental states do appear to predate language. But it is difficult to see how some of our more sophisticated thoughts would be possible without language, or independent of language for their individuation. This issue about the relation between mind and language is extremely complex, and in need of further exploration.

Grice contributed another idea to the understanding of meaning. He pointed out that it is not always easy to distinguish between the linguistic meaning of an utterance and various contextual suggestions that might be associated with the meaning of the utterance – what Grice called 'conversational implicatures.' Grice produced an impressive theory of implicature that has been developed by linguists and philosophers.[16]

The fourth source of stimulation to the philosophy of language was a major shift in the theory of reference. Frege had made some remarks that suggested that the reference of a proper name is fixed by definite descriptions that a speaker associates with the name. Thus the name 'Aristotle' would have as its referent whatever satisfied a definite description like 'the pupil of Plato and teacher of Alexander the Great.' (Frege did not try to eliminate names from the descriptions.) Russell purified and generalized this sort of view. He claimed that reference could rest either on acquaintance – an immediate, infallible, complete knowledge of an object – or on description. Russell came to think that acquaintance was associated only with the expressions 'I,' 'this' (as applied to a sense datum), and perhaps 'now.' All other instances of apparent singular reference, including reference with proper names and most demonstrative expressions, were based on description (cf. Frege 1984; Russell 1956).

This view of reference was questioned by Wittgenstein and in subsequent work by Searle and Strawson (Wittgenstein 1953; secs 79, 87; Searle 1958; Strawson 1959: Chap. 6). Searle and Strawson suggested that the reference of proper names was fixed by a cluster of descriptions associated with the name by a community of speakers. The effect of this suggestion was twofold. It loosened the relation between the reference of names and any one associated definite description. And it portrayed reference as dependent on more than descriptions in the mental repertoire of the speaker. Reference depended partly on the speaker's relations to others in the community.

These suggestions were radicalized in such a way as to produce a completely different picture of reference. In 1966 Donnellan pointed out that there is a use even of definite descriptions in which their meaning – the conditions laid down by the definite descriptions – does not fix the referent (or at any rate, a referent relevant to understanding the speaker). For example, a person can use the definite description 'the man drinking the martini' to refer to a woman across the room who is sipping a soft drink (Donnellan 1966; also Linsky 1963). Here the person picked out by the speaker seems partly independent of the description that the speaker associates with his act of reference.

The decisive further move was made in 1970 by Kripke and Donnellan, independently of one another. They produced a series of examples that indicated that the referents of proper names are in many cases not fixed by any set of descriptions the speaker associates with the name – or even by descriptions associated with the name by members of the speaker's community (Kripke 1980; Donnellan 1972). To use one of Kripke's examples, 'Jonah' might refer to a definite prophet, even though much of the descriptive material associated with the name is false, and even if not enough were known about the relevant historical figure to describe him in such a way as to distinguish him from all other historical figures. The speaker's whole community of contemporaries might be ignorant. Yet the name might still have a definite referent.

Implicit in the examples was a positive account of how the reference of names is fixed. The reference seemed to depend on relations between the speaker and his social and physical environments that are best understood not by investigating the speaker's mental repertoire but by inquiring into the chain of circumstances that led to the speaker's acquisition or present use of the name. These relations involve a mix of causal and intentional elements and include a person's reliance on others to fix a referent. Kripke sketched a picture according to which there was an initial dubbing or baptism, followed by a chain of uses of the name that are presumed by the users to maintain the referents of uses by those from whom they acquired the name. Such a chain of uses might maintain a referent even if descriptions associated with the name changed or became distorted. The conditions under which the chain maintains an initial referent, or changes to a new one, were subsequently found to be quite complicated (cf. Evans 1973; Devitt 1981). But the rough shape of the account has come to be widely accepted.

Kripke embedded his account of names in a theory of necessity. He counted names 'rigid designators' – expressions that maintained a certain constancy of reference through variation in the possible worlds by reference to which modal sentences might be evaluated. This theory revived a number of traditional questions about essence and necessity, which are outside the scope of this paper. In its enrichment of metaphysics as well as philosophy of language, however, Kripke's *Naming and Necessity* is a major landmark of the period.

Kripke and Putnam, independently, provided examples for thinking that natural kind terms are, like proper names, dependent for their referents not on a set of associated descriptions but on complex relations to the environment (Kripke 1980; Putnam 1975). Putnam also sketched an approach to understanding the meaning of natural kind terms that was based on accounting for the fact that we can successfully explain to someone in short order how to use many common nouns. He proposed that the 'meaning' of a term should be conceived as a combination of the referent of the term with what he called a 'stereotype'. The stereotype need not be complete enough to fix the referent by itself. It might even be untrue of the referent. Its role is to help another person in a given community to get on to the referent. This sketch has a number of problems. But it seems to me to be valuable in its attempt to explicate the success of dictionaries and other short, purpose-dependent explanations of meaning in our ordinary lives.

The main upshot of these papers on reference has been to portray reference as dependent on more than the beliefs, inferences, and discriminatory powers of the individual. Reference seems to depend on chains of acquisition and on the actual nature of the environment, not purely on the beliefs and discriminative abilities of the person doing the referring. This result suggests that reference cannot be reduced to psychological states of individuals, unless these states are themselves individuated partly in terms of the individual's relations to his community and/or physical environment.

Some philosophers have maintained that there is nothing more to the 'meaning' or semantical value of certain expressions – for example, proper names and demonstratives – than their referents. Such expressions are counted 'directly referential.' Others have held that such expressions express a Fregean sense that indicates a unique referent, but that is not easily paraphrased in language. Yet others maintain an intermediate view.[17]

The terms of this dispute are, in my opinion, often less clear than they might be. Many of the differences hinge on what is to be meant by 'meaning' or 'semantics.' Insofar as one sees these notions as applying to some communally common mastery of what is said – some idealized common denominator of understanding – then the direct reference views have substantial plausibility, at least as applied to some linguistic contexts. Insofar as one follows Frege in seeing these notions as applying to intentional cognitive content, something that individuals are expressing in thought in the use of these expressions, the direct reference views are inapplicable. Problems in this area, including several that survive clarification of the objectives of 'semantics,' remain a source of ferment.

Looking back over the last thirty years, I find the results on reference and some of those on logical form more substantial and durable than the results in the theory of meaning. The torrent of talk about a *theory* of meaning has even come to seem a bit naive. All the approaches to meaning seem to have some merit in bringing to light some aspect of the complex notion. The metadiscussion of what might be involved in a theory of meaning has been of genuine philosophical interest. But nothing that could be called a theory has elicited much agreement or shown many of the other sociological symptoms of systematic theoretical knowledge. It may be that the problem is too complex and simply needs more time. Or it may be that Quine (and implicitly Davidson) is right that a theory of meaning in anything like the accepted sense is not possible. Philosophers of language who have worked on meaning have usually wanted – and even presumed that they must have – a theory that reduces meaning to something more basic or scientifically 'respectable.' They have wanted a theory that explains what meaning is in other terms. But the notion may not be suitable to such explanation or reduction. It may be too multifaceted. There may be no general notion of meaning that will serve as *explanandum*. Various associated sub-notions may be more suitable. Or the notion(s) of meaning may be too basic – so that a theory *of* meaning may be less appropriate than theories that make use of various notions of meaning.

However this may be, it seems unlikely that cognitive psychology and linguistics – much less philosophy and ordinary discourse – will do without some conception(s) of meaning. Some notion of intentional content is needed to talk about propositional attitudes. And the linguistic practices of paraphrase and semantical explication are too regular to make it credible that they are without cognitive import. The idea that there is something cognitively suspect about the notion of meaning – an idea that has been made common by Quine's doubts during the last forty years – seems to me difficult to support. There are many such notions in ordinary life that do not enter into general laws of the sort found in the natural sciences. It would be absurd to suggest that all such notions are cognitively disreputable. Nevertheless, extreme care is required in the use of notions of meaning. Such notions will probably remain a topic of philosophical discussion for the foreseeable future.

Gradually but unmistakably, in the latter part of the 1970s, the philosophy of language lost its place as the dominant starting point for philosophical activity. No other area of philosophy assumed quite the status that the philosophy of language had had since the 1950s. But the degree of interest in relatively 'pure' philosophy of language has certainly diminished. Moreover, there has been a perceptible shift of ferment toward issues in the philosophy of mind.

Some reasons for this change are internal to the subject. The discussions of meaning by Quine and Grice showed that there is a systematic interplay between meaning and propositional attitudes, like belief and intention. Although most discussion of language made some reference to this relation, there had been little concentrated reflection on the propositional attitudes. Therefore, dialectical pressure built toward a shift to the philosophy of mind.

Another internal reason was that some of the most difficult and persistent specific problems within the philosophy of language – accounting for Frege's puzzle about Hesperus and Phosphorus in the light of the new theory of reference, accounting for the cognitive value of demonstratives, giving an account of the truth conditions and logical form of sentences about propositional attitudes, explicating *de re* belief – all pointed toward the philosophy of mind.

A broader internal reason is that the philosophy of language seemed to have exhausted some of its promise in illuminating traditional philosophical questions, the questions that drew most philosophers into the subject. The original hope – among the positivists and among postpositivist philosophers of language – was that by clarifying issues about language, philosophy would put itself on a firmer footing for understanding the larger traditional problems. There is no simple account of how much of this hope was fulfilled. The philosophy of language improved methods of argument and sensitivity to relevant distinctions. It opened up perspectives on traditional issues that are new and worthwhile. And at least as regards the theory of reference, it laid the groundwork for a very different conception of many traditional issues. But by the late 1970s or early 1980s philosophy of language no longer seemed the obvious propaedeutic for dealing with central philosophical problems.

As I have intimated, one ground for this shift was that many philosophers felt that philosophy of language had done its job – that the natural development of philosophical reasoning led into the philosophy of mind, or other adjacent areas. Another ground was that some of the discussions, particularly of the theory of meaning and of what 'semantics' should or should not do, seemed to be at impasses. There has been a paucity of important, large, new philosophical ideas in the subdiscipline for over a decade.

A further ground lay in the increasing specialization of the philosophy of language. One product of success was the development of a vocabulary and set of problems that had lives of their own – not directly dependent on issues in the rest of philosophy. Much of the work in the semantics of reference and on the (disputed) border between semantics and pragmatics seemed to gain in precision and systematic power by making idealizations that ruled many difficult philosophical problems out of court. This is sometimes the method of a successful science. But it reduces the motivation to study the philosophy of language for larger philosophical rewards.

An external reason for the shift was the rise of the computer paradigm in psychology, and the appearance of intellectually substantial findings in psychology that had apparent significance for philosophical problems.

The shift during the 1980s away from taking the philosophy of language as the dominant starting place for doing philosophy – a starting point with direct and widely-recognized relevance to most other areas of philosophy – did not, however, leave the field stagnant in the 1990s. Philosophy of language was no longer the closest thing to 'first philosophy.' (No other area clearly took its place, probably to the good.) But the field retained vigor, partly through the influx of young talent, partly because many issues that had been raised earlier continued to sustain interest and development.

In fact, most of the main issues developed in the 1990s were developments or revisitings of work done in the 1970s or earlier. The fruitful interaction with linguistics continued. Linguistics became more sophisticated in addressing problems that had been initiated within philosophy. Philosophers became more attuned to the use of methods and results in linguistics. Philosophy of language during the 1980s and 1990s took on the character of 'normal science.' Much of the best work involved the kind of specialization that marks maturing disciplines that have much in common with (and in some ways overlap) a maturing science – here, the science of linguistics. Nothing initiated in the field from the mid-1980s onward was comparable, in evident, broad philosophical applicability and significance, to the overturning of the analytic-synthetic distinction; the initial discussions of theories of logical form, truth-conditions, and context-dependence; Grice's work on implicature; or the revolution in the theory of reference. I will describe a sampling of discussions in the last years of the twentieth century. Inevitably, this survey leaves out many significant topics and much excellent work.

The closing of the gap between some philosophy of language and linguistics was closely allied with work that centered on contextual aspects of language and language use. Context was central in three loosely distinguishable areas of discussion: the theory of reference with singular expressions, the theory of anaphora, and theories of 'unspoken' elements in linguistic understanding. The three areas are closely associated. So the present categorization inevitably under-characterizes connections among them.

Work on the theory of singular reference centered both on the mechanisms of reference for proper names, demonstratives, and indexicals, and on the relation between reference and meaning or sense. Discussion of relations between 'directly referential' elements and descriptive or quantificational elements continued. I believe that discussion in this area is still hampered by insufficient attention to characterizing and distinguishing possible *explananda*. I think that what one takes linguistic items to 'express' and what 'express' is to mean invites deeper reflection. Correspondingly, there needs to be deeper reflection on what is to be meant by 'meaning' and 'sense,' and what relations there are between language and thought.[18]

The theory of anaphora and of contextual presuppositions gained serious impetus from work of Irena Heim and of Hans Kamp on discourse analysis. This work advances accounts that are more realistic than older accounts, of the way conversation pursues threads over discourses longer than individual sentences. It also yields much greater insight into the complex phenomena of pronominal cross-reference, presupposition, and quantification, which marked one of the initial entries of formal logic into the study of natural language (Heim 1988; Kamp 1984; Kamp and Reyle 1993; Neale 1992; Stalnaker 1999).

Theories of 'unspoken' elements in linguistic understanding bear on the distinction between semantics and pragmatics. Issues about restrictions on quantification, ellipses in discourse, and so on, elicited vigorous disputes about whether unspoken elements, especially those that bear on truth-conditions, should be regarded as present in the very logical form of the sentences, or rather in background extra-linguistic understanding of the speaker's intentions in the context. Since it seems to me that there cannot be a general bar against idiosyncratic assertive uses of language, where the language foregoes using syntactically definite sentences and relies heavily on context, I do not see how there can be a general bar against relying on nonlinguistic aspects of the context to fill out truth-conditions and an intended logical form. But the issue can be seen to center on sentences that are understood to be grammatical, yet perhaps not fully explicit.

The connections among the various areas of linguistics – syntax, truth-conditional semantics, pragmatics – seem to me sufficiently open to empirical determination that successful settling of the details of these matters is probably not in the immediate offing. The role of an individual's thought and intention, and the ability to determine what a person's thought and intention are independently of full linguistic utterance, will, I think, be central to any correct comprehensive account. Nevertheless, individual examples are of great philosophical interest. The connections among syntax, semantics, and pragmatics – and the very understanding of what tasks to give to pragmatics – remain an open and fruitful area of philosophical discussion.[19]

A further phenomenon that drew intense philosophical discussion in the 1990s was vagueness. Some of this work picked up from discussions that derived from the 1970s. A new impetus came from Timothy Williamson's book *Vagueness*. Williamson maintained that 'the proposition a vague sentence expresses in a borderline case is true or false, and we cannot know which.' He maintained that vague predicates have sharp boundaries and vagueness just is incurable inability to know what the predicate's boundaries are, because any true borderline judgement might have occurred – without the judge being any the wiser – if the predicate's meaning had differed just enough to have made the judgement false. This view was widely regarded as implausible. But it stimulated discussion and turned attention to epistemic issues that had been barely developed in previous work.[20]

A variety of semantical and logical positions were occupied by philosophers who wrote about vagueness. Some authors, along with Williamson, advocated classical logic as a means of capturing the truth-conditions and logical form of vague utterances (or sentences) in natural language. Others developed versions of the super-valuational approach. Yet others supported other truth-value-gap approaches, such as that of relying on the Kleene strong or weak truth-tables (Fine 1975; Kamp 1981; Soames 1999; Graff 2000).

What seems to me salutary about much of this work is that issues regarding the psychology and epistemology of language use – and the way words or concepts get their ranges of application – came to be integrated into more purely logical semantical approaches. In particular, several approaches explored the possibility that contextual shifts in attention or interest play a large role in where borders are taken to be. According to some of these approaches, the relevant shifts play a significant role in one's sense of there being, from a context-free point of view, an indeterminacy in the application ranges (extensions) of linguistic expressions.[21] It seems to me that, as with Williamson's proposal, some of these accounts of why we cannot know sharp boundaries for vague expressions or concepts are not very fully motivated and are implausible. But the invocation of a role for interest-dependence and context-dependence is valuable.

I believe that a neglected aspect of the problem is also idealization. The role of idealization in scientific and commonsense reasoning seems to me relevant to understanding conditions under which we formalize natural language. I believe that it plays a role in commitment to classical bivalence, even when we are formalizing natural language. Idealizations are responsive to considerations of context and background knowledge. Exploring this matter would, I think, enrich the context-dependent approaches.

Some work in philosophy of language in the period of the 1990s was of a more global kind – reminiscent of the large 'theories of meaning' that characterized the 1960s and 1970s. There was a spate of deflationary accounts of truth, reference, or meaning. The burden of these accounts is that one or more of these notions comes to less than traditional accounts assume, and that the relevant notions lack both explanatory value and philosophical interest. I do not find these accounts plausible, either in detail or in their overall thrust. Their presence provides, however, a challenge to uncritical use of these notions.[22]

Another global issue is worth mentioning. This is the nature of the relation between thought and language. In *Origins of Analytic Philosophy*, Michael Dummett claimed:

What distinguishes analytical philosophy, in its diverse manifestations, from other schools is the belief, first, that a philosophical account of thought can be attained through a philosophical account of language, and secondly, that a comprehensive account can only be so attained. (Dummett 1993: 4)

As a stipulation, this claim can, of course, be admitted. But as a characterization it is exceptionally narrow.

There is no question that one of Frege's great contributions to philosophy was his example of reflection on language, as a starting point for understanding thought and knowledge. This example, along with Frege's development and use of logic, is rightly seen as decisively influencing subsequent mainstream philosophy. Moreover, several prominent philosophers hold versions of the view that Dummett articulates: Carnap, Quine, Davidson, Dummett, and (if and only if the language of thought is included!) Fodor. But neither Frege nor Russell maintained that thought should be explained comprehensively and ultimately in terms of language. And many other philosophers who would be counted, by any ordinary reckoning, as analytical philosophers do not fit the characterization: Strawson, Grice, Donnellan, and Chisholm, from an older generation; Lewis, Evans, Peacocke, and Stalnaker, among my generation. Many other philosophers who clearly belong in the analytic tradition – Kripke, Kaplan, and Putnam, for example – do not, as far as I know, even take a definite position on Dummett's touchstone issue.

Looking forward, the philosophy of language will benefit from close attention to the relation between language and thought, as well as that between language and context. This attention is explicit in the interest in pragmatics, and in consideration of the role of use and understanding in determining linguistic meaning and interpretation. I believe that serious work on the relation between linguistic and perceptual reference, on language-learning, and on linguistic change will also require more reflection on the relations between language and thought.

Looking backward, although reflection on language lies at the historical roots of analytic philosophy, analytic philosophy is not a school or ideology. The name itself has lost any genuine descriptive value.[23] What holds together philosophers who talk to one another and who are called 'analytic philosophers' is a common history and an inheritance of tools, distinctions, and standards. In this history, which continues, language is an object of reflection in a way that befits its specialness in human experience.

Notes

1. This chapter is mostly composed of the first half of my 1992 article 'Philosophy of Language and Mind: 1950–1990.' It contains some additional material about the last ten years of the twentieth century. What follows is a historical overview of the philosophy of language pitched to nonspecialists. I have concentrated on English-speaking philosophy, which in these areas has been dominantly North American since the 1960s. The scope of the presentation has, of course, forced me to omit many topics that are of great importance. I will mention a few of these: intentional contexts, quantifying in, the concept of truth, the relation between theories of meaning and metaphysical issues like realism, the semantical and epistemic paradoxes, speech-act theory and other topics in pragmatics, and the subject matter of linguistics. I think that in some loose sense, however, I have caught some of what would be widely counted 'the mainstream' of philosophical discussion. I am grateful to Jay Atlas, Warren Goldfarb, and the editors of *The Philosophical Review* for good advice on the original article, and to Christopher Peacocke and Robert Stalnaker for pointers regarding the additional material.

2. Quine 1951; reprinted in Quine's *From a Logical Point of View* (pp. 20–46); cf. also Quine 1960, Chap. 1. Similar points were made by Hempel at about the same time (cf. Hempel 1965: 112–13, 117). But Quine's work had greater impact, perhaps because of his colorful and forceful exposition and because he attacked the analytic-synthetic distinction as well.

3. Quine 1966c – 'Truth By Convention'. The point goes back to Lewis Carroll.

4. Frege 1968, 1967. For an exposition of a positivist interpretation of the logicist program, see Hempel 1986.

5. Quine 1951. Quine says little about analyticity as opposed to analyticity-2 in 'Two Dogmas.' Since this article has unfortunately received vastly more attention than 'Carnap on Logical Truth,' and since much of the attack on analyticity-2 in 'Two Dogmas,' taken by itself, is not very persuasive, many philosophers are even now baffled about why Quine's criticism of 'analyticity' is important. I might note that there is a third conception of 'analyticity': roughly a truth is 'analytic' (in this note, '*analytic-3*') if it states a containment relation between concepts or meanings. This conception is not, I think, equivalent to either of the other two. It differs from analyticity-2 in that it need not (should not) count at least some logical truths as 'analytic-3'. It differs from analyticity in that it need not (should not) count analytic-3 truths vacuous, or independent for their truth of a subject matter. Locke thought of analyticity-3 to be equivalent to analyticity. Leibniz held analyticity-2 and analyticity-3 to be equivalent. Kant seems to have thought of all three conceptions as equivalent. In my view, analyticity-3 has not played an important role in the period I am discussing.

6. Frege saw logic as the discipline that applied to all subject matters, and held in particular that it was committed to the existence of an infinity of extensions (including numbers) and functions (1968 – e.g., sec. 14 and generally – or 1985). Russell's logicism is substantially similar to Frege's in holding logic to be about abstract entities that are structures in all domains of the world: 'Logic . . . is concerned with the real world just as truly as zoology though with its more abstract and general features' (Russell 1971: Chap. 16). Aristotle thought that definitions stated essences, and that logic uncovered fundamental structures in the world (cf. *Posterior Analytics* I 1–4; II 10, 19; *Metaphysics* IV 4). Leibniz thought that all knowledge of the world could be derived, at least by God, from logical principles by analysis of concepts (cf., for example, 'Primary Truths'; 'Discourse on Metaphysics,' sec. 8; and 'Monadology', sec. 31 (Leibniz 1989)). More broadly, the idea that, by understanding conceptual relations, one could gain deep and fundamental knowledge of the world is a characteristic tenet of rationalism.

7. For a remarkable collection of methodologically oriented articles from this period, see Rorty 1967.
8. Wittgenstein 1953. Austin 1961 are perhaps the outstanding examples of attempts to apply observations about ordinary linguistic use to traditional philosophical problems.
9. The most sophisticated and fascinating example of this dispute occurs in a famous exchange between Carnap and Strawson (cf. P. F. Strawson, 'Carnap's View on Constructed Systems versus Natural Languages in Analytic Philosophy' and Carnap's 'P. F. Strawson on Linguistic Naturalism', both in Schilp 1963: 503–18, 933–9. Cf., also, Stanley Cavell, 'Must We Mean What We Say?', in Cavell 1976).
10. The discussion of the paradigm-case argument marks, I think, the downfall of the method (cf. Watkins 1957, and Donnellan 1967).
11. Austin 1965; Strawson 1950, 1952. For more recent work in this tradition, see Searle, 'A Taxonomy of Illocutionary Acts' (1975) and 'Indirect Speech Acts' (1975), reprinted in his *Expression and Meaning* (1979: 1–29, 30–57); and Atlas 1989.
12. For a fine statement of this view, see Dummett 1967.
13. A systematic discussion of almost all of Frege's work in philosophy of language is in Dummett 1973, and 1981. Cf. also Burge 2005.
14. Davidson 1984, especially 'Truth and Meaning' (pp. 17–42), 'Theories of Meaning and Learnable Languages' (pp. 3–16), 'Quotation' (pp. 79–92), 'On Saying That' (pp. 93–108), and 1980, especially 'The Logical Form of Action Sentences' (pp. 105–21); Burge 1973, and 1974; Higginbotham 1983; Quine, 'Quantifiers and Propositional Attitudes', in *Ways of Paradox*; Kaplan, 'Quantifying In', in *Words and Objections* 1969; Soames 1985.
15. Stalnaker 1968; van Fraassen 1983; Lewis 1973; Church 1973a, 1973b; Montague 1974; Kit Fine 1975; Kaplan 1979; Barwise and Perry, *Situations and Attitudes* 1983.
16. Paul Grice, *Studies in the Way of Words*, Part 1, given as lectures in 1967, but influential, through his teaching, on Strawson's work as far back as the early 1950s.
17. The 'direct reference' view is at least suggested by Kripke. But its main proponent has been Kaplan (1989). Cf., also, various articles in Salmon, and Soames 1988. A neo-Fregean view is developed in McDowell 1977; in Evans 1982; and in Ackerman 1979. Two significantly different intermediate views may be found in John Searle 1983; and in Burge 1977, and 1983.
18. Examples of work on mechanisms of reference are: Davies 1982; Neale 1990; Braun 1996; King 1996 and 1999. An argument that names have some sort of linguistic meaning that makes names with the same referent linguistically different is presented in Heck 1995. I think that this argument is broadly on the right track.
19. Sperber and Wilson 1986; Bach 1994; Stanley and Szabo 2000 – cf. the symposium on the same issue including Bach, Stephen Neale, Stanley, and Szabo; Levinson 2000; Stanley 2000.
20. Williamson 1994; 1995; Schiffer 1999; Burgess 2001. Cf. the symposium among Williamson, Paul Horwich, and Stephen Schiffer in *Philosophy and Phenomenological Research* (1997) 57: 921–53.
21. Sainsbury 1990, published as pamphlet 1991, and reprinted in 1999; Tappenden 1993; Raffman 1994, as well as the last three works cited in the previous note.
22. Brandom 1994, and cf. the symposium with Brandom, John McDowell, Gideon Rosen, Richard Rorty, and Jay Rosenberg in *Philosophy and Phenomenological Research* (1997) 57: 153–204; Field 2001; Horwich 1999. For a complex discussion that makes some concessions to deflationary conceptions, see Wright 1992. For further, more fully non-deflationary views see Davidson 1990; Peacocke 1993.
23. On this point, see the Introduction to my *Truth, Thought, Reason*.

References

Ackerman, D. (1979), 'Proper Names, Propositional Attitudes and Non-Descriptive Con-
notations,' *Philosophical Studies* 35: 55–69.
Atlas, J. (1989), *Philosophy without Ambiguity*, Oxford: Oxford University Press.
Austin, J. L. [1946] (1961), 'Other Minds,' in J. L. Austin (1961), *Philosophical Papers*, Oxford:
Oxford University Press, pp. 76–116.
Austin, J. L. (1965), *How to Do Things with Words*, New York: Oxford University Press.
Bach, K. (1994), 'Conversational Implicature,' *Mind and Language* 9: 124–62.
Barwise, J., and J. Perry (1983), *Situations and Attitudes*, Cambridge: MIT Press.
Brandom, R. (1994), *Making it Explicit*, Cambridge: Harvard University Press.
Braun, D. (1996), 'Demonstratives and their Linguistic Meanings,' *Nous* 30: 145–73.
Burge, T. (1973), 'Reference and Proper Names,' *Journal of Philosophy* 70: 425–39.
Burge, T. (1974), 'Truth and Singular Terms,' *Nous* 8: 309–25.
Burge, T. (1977), 'Belief De Re,' *Journal of Philosophy* 74: 338–63.
Burge, T. (1983), 'Russell's Problem and Intentional Identity,' in J. Tomberlin (ed.) (1983),
Agent, Language, and the Structure of the World, Indianapolis: Hackett, pp. 79–110.
Burge, T. (1992), 'Philosophy of Language and Mind, 1950–1990,' *The Philosophical Review*
101: 3–51.
Burge, T. (2005), *Truth, Thought, Reason: Essays on Frege*, Oxford: Oxford University Press.
Burgess, J. (2001), 'Vagueness, Epistemicism and Response-Dependence,' *Australasian Journal
of Philosophy* 79: 507–24.
Carnap, R. (1937), *The Logical Syntax of Language*, London: Routledge and Kegan Paul.
Carnap, R. (1946), 'Modalities and Quantification,' *Journal of Symbolic Logic* 11: 33–64.
Carnap, R. (1964a), 'Empiricism, Semantics, and Ontology,' in R. Carnap (1964), *Meaning and
Necessity*, Chicago: Chicago University Press, Appendix A.
Carnap, R. (1964b), 'Meaning and Synonymy in Natural Languages,' in R. Carnap (1964),
Meaning and Necessity, Chicago: Chicago University Press, Appendix D.
Cavell, S. (1976), *Must We Mean What We Say?*, Cambridge: Cambridge University Press.
Chomsky, N. (1957), *Syntactic Structures*, The Hague: Mouton Co.
Chomsky, N. (1965), *Aspects of the Theory of Syntax*, Cambridge: MIT Press.
Chomsky, N. (1969), 'Quine's Empirical Assumptions,' in D. Davidson and J. Hintikka (eds)
(1969), *Words and Objections: Essays on the Work of W. V. Quine*, Dordrecht: Reidel, pp. 206–42.
Church, A. (1951), 'A Formulation of the Logic of Sense and Denotation,' in P. Henle, H.
Kallen, and S. Langer (eds) (1951), *Structure, Method, and Meaning: Essays in Honor of
Henry Sheffer*, New York: Liberal Arts, pp. 8–24.
Church, A. (1973a), 'Outline of a Revised Formulation of the Logic of Sense and Denotation,
Part I,' *Nous* 7: 24–33.
Church, A. (1973b), 'Outline of a Revised Formulation of the Logic of Sense and Denotation,
Part II,' *Nous* 8: 135–56.
Davidson, D. (1967), 'Truth and Meaning,' *Synthèse* 17: 304–23.
Davidson, D. (1980), *Essays on Actions and Events*, Oxford: Oxford University Press.
Davidson, D. (1984), *Inquiries into Truth and Interpretation*, Oxford: Oxford University Press.
Davidson, D. (1990), 'The Structure and Content of Truth,' *Journal of Philosophy* 87, 279–328.
Davies, M. (1982), 'Individuation and the Semantics of Demonstratives,' *Journal of Philo-
sophical Logic* 11: 287–310.
Devitt, M. (1981), *Designation*, New York: Columbia University Press.
Donnellan, K. S. (1966), 'Reference and Definite Descriptions,' *The Philosophical Review* 75:
281–304.

Donellan K. S. (1967), 'The Paradigm-Case Argument,' in P. Edwards (ed.) (1967), *The Encyclopedia of Philosophy*, New York: The Macmillan Company and the Free Press, vol. 5, pp. 39–44.

Donnellan, K. S. (1972), 'Proper Names and Identifying Descriptions,' in D. Davidson and G. Harman (eds) (1972), *Semantics of Natural Language*, Dordrecht: Reidel, pp. 356–79.

Dummett, M. (1967), 'Frege,' in P. Edwards, (ed.) (1967), *The Encyclopedia of Philosophy*, vol. 3, New York: The Macmillan Company, and the Free Press, pp. 225–37.

Dummett, M. (1973), *Frege: Philosophy of Language*, London: Duckworth.

Dummett, M. (1975), 'The Philosophical Basis of Intuitionistic Logic,' in S. Guttenplan (ed.) (1975), *Mind and Language*, Oxford: Oxford University Press, pp. 97–122.

Dummett, M. (1981), *The Interpretation of Frege's Philosophy*, Cambridge: Harvard University Press.

Dummett, M. (1993), *Origins of Analytical Philosophy*, Cambridge: Harvard University Press.

Evans, G. (1973), 'The Causal Theory of Names,' *Proceedings of the Aristotelian Society* 47 (suppl.): 187–208.

Evans, G. (1982), *The Varieties of Reference*, Oxford: Oxford University Press.

Evans, G., and J. McDowell (1976), *Truth and Meaning*, Oxford: Oxford University Press.

Field, H. (2001), *Truth and the Absence of Fact*, Oxford: Oxford University Press.

Fine, K. (1975), 'Vagueness, Truth, and Logic,' *Synthèse* 30: 265–300.

Frege, G. (1952), *Translations of the Philosophical Writings of Gottlob Frege*, ed. P. Geach, and M. Black, Oxford: Basil Blackwell.

Frege, G. (1967), *The Basic Laws of Arithmetic*, ed. M. Furth, Berkeley: University of California Press.

Frege, G. (1968), *The Foundations of Arithmetic*, trans. J. L. Austin, Evanston: Northwestern University Press.

Frege, G. (1985), 'Thoughts,' in B. McGuiness (ed.) (1985), *Collected Papers*, Oxford: Basil Blackwell, pp. 351–72.

Graff, D. (2000), 'Shifting Sands: An Interest-Relative Theory of Vagueness,' *Philosophical Topics* 28: 45–79.

Grice, H. P. (1957), 'Meaning,' *The Philosophical Review* 66: 377–88.

Grice, H. P. (1968), 'Utterer's Meaning, Sentence-Meaning, and Word-Meaning,' *Foundations of Language* 4: 225–42.

Grice, H. P. (1969), 'Utterer's Meaning and Intentions,' *The Philosophical Review* 78: 147–77.

Grice, H. P. (1989), *Studies in the Way of Words*, Cambridge: Harvard University Press.

Grice, H. P., and P. F. Strawson (1956), 'In Defense of a Dogma,' *The Philosophical Review* 65: 141–58.

Heck, R. (1995), 'A Sense of Communication,' *Mind* 104: 79–106.

Heim, I. (1988), *The Semantics of Definite and Indefinite Noun Phrases*, New York: Garland.

Hempel, C. [1945] (1986), 'On the Nature of Mathematical Truth,' in P. Benacerraf, and H. Putnam (1986), *The Philosophy of Mathematics*, Cambridge: Cambridge University Press, pp. 377–93.

Higginbotham, J. (1983), 'The Logical Form of Perceptual Reports,' *Journal of Philosophy* 80: 100–27.

Horwich, P. (1999), *Meaning*, Oxford: Oxford University Press.

Kamp. H. (1981), 'The Paradox of the Heap,' in U. Monnich (ed.) (1981), *Aspects of Philosophical Logic*, Dordrecht: Reidel, 225–77.

Kamp, H. (1984), 'A Theory of Truth and Semantical Representation,' in T. Janssen, and T. Stokhof (eds) (1984), *Truth, Interpretation, and Information*, Dordrecht: Foris, pp. 1–41.

Kamp, H., and U. Reyle (1983), *From Discourse to Logic*, Dordrecht: Kluwer.

Kaplan, D. (1969), 'Quantifying In,' in *Words and Objections: Essays on the Work of W. V. Quine*, ed. D. Davidson, and J. Hintikka, Dordrecht: Reidel.

Kaplan, D. (1979), 'On the Logic of Demonstratives,' in P. French (ed.) (1979), *Contemporary Perspectives in the Philosophy of Language*, Minneapolis: University of Minnesota Press, pp. 401–14.

Kaplan, D. (1989), 'Demonstratives,' in J. Almog, J. Perry, and H. Wettstein (eds) 1989), *Themes from Kaplan*, New York: Oxford University Press.

Keefe, R., and P. Smith (1999), *Vagueness: A Reader*, Cambridge: MIT Press.

King, J. (1996), 'Structured Propositions and Sentence Structure,' *Journal of Philosophical Logic* 25:495–521.

King, J. (1999), 'Are Complex "That" Phrases Devices of Direct Reference?' *Nous* 33: 155–82.

Kripke, S. (1963), 'Semantical Analysis of Modal Logic I,' *Zeitschrift fur Mathematische Logik* 9: 67–96.

Kripke, S. (1980), *Naming and Necessity*, Cambridge: Harvard University Press.

Leibniz, G. W. (1989), *Philosophical Essays*, trans. R. Ariew, and D. Garber, Indianapolis: Hackett.

Levinson, S. (2000), *Presumptive Meanings: The Theory of Generalized Conversational Implicatures*, Cambridge: MIT Press.

Lewis, D. (1973), *Counterfactuals*, Oxford: Basil Blackwell.

Linsky, L. (1963), 'Reference and Referents,' in C. Caton (ed.) (1963), *Philosophy and Ordinary Language*, Urbana: University of Illinois Press, pp. 74–89.

Marcus, R. B. (1946), 'A Functional Calculus of First-Order Based on Strict Implication,' *Journal of Symbolic Logic* 11: 1–16.

McDowell, J. (1976), 'Truth Conditions, Bivalence, and Verificationism,' in G. Evans, and J. McDowell (eds) (1976), *Truth and Meaning*, Oxford: Oxford University Press, pp. 42–66.

McDowell, J. (1977), 'On the Sense and Reference of a Proper Name,' *Mind* 86: 159–85.

Montague, R. (1974), *Formal Philosophy*, ed. R. Thomason, New Haven: Yale University Press.

Neale, S. (1990), *Descriptions*, Cambridge: MIT Press.

Neale, S. (1992), 'Descriptive Pronouns and Donkey Anaphora,' *Journal of Philosophy* 15: 53–63.

Peacocke, C. (1993), 'Truth and Proof,' in J. Haldane, and C. Wright (eds), *Reality, Representation, and Projection*, Oxford: Oxford University Press, pp. 165–90.

Prior, A. N. (1957), *Time and Modality*, Oxford: Oxford University Press.

Putnam, H. (1975), 'Is Semantics Possible?' in H. Putnam (1975), *Philosophical Papers*, vol. 2, Cambridge: Cambridge University Press, pp. 139–52.

Putnam, H. (1985), 'The Analytic and the Synthetic,' in H. Putnam (1975), *Philosophical Papers*, vol. 2, Cambridge: Cambridge University Press, pp. 33–69.

Quine, W. V. O. (1948), 'On What There Is,' *Review of Metaphysics* 2: 21–38.

Quine, W. V. O. (1951), 'Two Dogmas of Empiricism,' *The Philosophical Review* 60: 20–43.

Quine, W. V. O. (1953), *From a Logical Point of View*, Cambridge: Harvard University Press.

Quine, W. V. O. (1960), *Word and Object*, Cambridge: MIT Press.

Quine, W. V. O. (1966a), 'Carnap on Logical Truth,' in W. V. O. Quine (1966), *The Ways of Paradox*, New York: Random House, pp. 100–25.

Quine, W. V. O. (1966b), 'On Carnap's Views on Ontology,' in W. V. O. Quine (1966), *The Ways of Paradox*, New York: Random House, pp. 126–34.

Quine, W. V. O. (1966c), 'Truth by Convention,' in W. V. O. Quine (1966), *The Ways of Paradox*, New York: Random House, pp. 70–99.

Quine, W. V. O. (1969), *Ontological Relativity*, New York: Columbia University Press.

Raffman, D. (1994), 'Vagueness without Paradox,' *The Philosophical Review* 103: 41–74.

Rorty, R. (ed.) (1967), *The Linguistic Turn*, Chicago: University of Chicago Press.

Russell, B. (1956), 'The Philosophy of Logical Atomism,' in Robert C. Marsh (ed.) (1956), *Logic and Knowledge: Essays, 1901–1950*, London: Allen and Unwin, pp. 175–281.

Russell, B. [1919] (1971), *Introduction to Mathematical Philosophy*, New York: Simon and Schuster.

Sainsbury, R. M. (1990), 'Concepts without Boundaries,' King's College, London Department of Philosophy, inaugural lecture, delivered 6 Nov.

Sainsbury, R. M. (1995), 'Vagueness, Ignorance and Margin for Error,' *British Journal of Philosophy of Science* 46: 589–601.

Salmon, N., and S. Soames (eds) (1988), *Propositions and Attitudes*, Oxford University Press.

Schiffer, S. (1972), *Meaning*, Oxford: Oxford University Press.

Schiffer, S. (1999), 'The Epistemic Theory of Vagueness,' *Philosophical Perspectives* 13: 481–503.

Schilp, P. A. (ed.) (1963), *The Philosophy of Rudolf Carnap*, Peru: Open Court.

Searle, J. (1958), 'Proper Names,' *Mind* 67: 166–73.

Searle, J. (1979), *Expression and Meaning*, Cambridge: Cambridge University Press.

Searle, J. (1983), *Intentionality*, Cambridge: Cambridge University Press.

Soames, S. (1985), 'Lost Innocence,' *Linguistics and Philosophy* 8: 59–71.

Soames, S. (1999), *Understanding Truth*, New York: Oxford University Press.

Sperber, D., and D. Wilson (1986), *Relevance*, Cambridge: Harvard University Press.

Stalnaker, R. (1968), 'A Theory of Conditionals,' in N. Rescher (ed.) (1968), *Studies in Logical Theory. American Philosophical Quarterly* Monograph Series No. 2, Oxford: Basil Blackwell.

Stalnaker, R. (1999), 'On the Representation of Context,' in R. Stalnaker (1999), *Context and Content*, Oxford: Oxford University Press, pp. 97–113.

Stanley, J. (2000), 'Context and Logical Form,' *Linguistics and Philosophy* 23: 391–434.

Stanley, J., and Z. Szabo (2000), 'On Quantifier Domain Restriction,' *Mind and Language* 15: 219–261.

Strawson, P. F. (1950), 'On Referring,' *Mind* 59: 320–44.

Strawson, P. F. (1952), *Introduction to Logical Theory*, London: Methuen.

Strawson, P. F. (1959), *Individuals*, London: Routledge.

Strawson, P. F. (1971), *Logico-Linguistic Papers*, Bungay: Methuen & Co.

Tappenden, J. (1993), 'The Liar and Sorites Paradoxes: Toward a Unified Treatment,' *Journal of Philosophy* 90: 551–7.

van Fraassen, B. (1983), 'Presuppositions, Supervaluations, and Free Logic,' in G. Lambert (ed.) (1983), *The Logical Way of Doing Things*, New Haven: Yale University Press, pp. 69–72.

Watkins, J. W. N. (1957), 'Farewell to the Paradigm-Case Argument,' *Analysis* 18: 25–33.

Williamson, T. (1994), *Vagueness*, London: Routledge.

Wittgenstein, L. (1953), *Philosophical Investigations*, trans. G. E. M. Anscombe, New York: Macmillan.

Wright, C. (1992), *Truth and Objectivity*, Cambridge: Harvard University Press.

Philosophy of Mind: 1950–2000[1]

Tyler Burge

I want to outline some of the main developments in the philosophy of mind in the last half of the twentieth century. Behaviorism dominated psychology during approximately the same period that logical positivism dominated philosophy. The principles of behaviorism are less easily stated than those of logical positivism. It is perhaps better seen as a method that eschewed use of mentalistic vocabulary in favor of terms that made reference to dispositions to behavior. Both movements aimed at banishing nonscientific speculation, and forcing theory to hew as closely as possible to methods of confirmation. Both methodological doctrines came to be seen as restrictive, even on the practice of science.

Behaviorism had a run of influence within philosophy. It was a favored view of some of the later positivists. They made use of the verificationist principle to attempt to dissolve the mind–body problem and the problem of other minds, declaring these problems meaningless. And they appealed to behavioral analysis of mentalistic terms as a way of maintaining strict experimental control on mentalistic language. The simplistic picture of confirmation associated with the verificationist principle, a picture that ignored the role of auxiliary hypotheses, paralleled and abetted the behaviorist blindness to the role of background assumptions in mentalistic attributions. As we shall see, this blindness led to the collapse of behaviorism.

In postwar, postpositivistic philosophy, the early logical constructionists thought that behavioristic language was the most suitable way to 'reconstruct' mentalistic language in scientific terms. Ordinary-language philosophers purported to find behaviorist underpinnings for ordinary language. Behaviorism influenced positivistic construals of psychology, Quine's theory of the indeterminacy of translation, Ryle's work on the concept of mind, and Malcolm's explications of discourse about dreaming and sensations (Ryle 1949; Malcolm 1959; Quine 1960). These philosophers shared a tendency to think that theorizing in psychology or philosophy of mind should dispense with mentalistic vocabulary, or interpret it in nonmentalistic terms, as far as possible. They thought that such vocabulary should be largely replaced with talk about stimulations and about dispositions to behavior. Some philosophers thought that ordinary mentalistic terms could be defined or adequately explicated (for any cognitively respectable purpose) in these latter terms. Others thought that ordinary mentalistic terms were hopelessly unscientific or philosophically misleading, so no real explication was possible.

The demise of behaviorism in philosophy is less easily attributed to a few decisive events than is the fall of logical positivism. There was a series of influential criticisms of behaviorism beginning in the late 1950s and extending for a decade (Chisholm 1957, Chap. 11; Geach 1957, Chap. 1; Chomsky 1959, reprinted in Fodor and Katz 1964; Putnam 1975a; Fodor 1968). The main cause of the shift seemed, however, to be a gradually developed sense that behaviourist methods were unduly restrictive and theoretically unfruitful. A similar development was unfolding within psychology, linguistics, and computer science, with an array of nonbehaviorist articles in the late 1950s and early 1960s (in psychology: Miller 1956; Bruner et al. 1960; Sperling 1960; Neisser 1963; Posner 1963; Sternberg 1966; in linguistics: Chomsky 1957; in computer science: Newell et al. 1958).

The attempts to provide behavioristic *explications* of mentalistic terms fell prey to various instances of a single problem. The behavioristic explications succeeded only on the implicit assumption that the individual had certain background beliefs or wants. As a crude illustration, consider an explication of belief as a disposition to assert. Even ignoring the fact that 'assert' is not a behavioral notion, but presupposes assumptions about mind and meaning, the analysis could work only with the proviso that the subject wants to express his beliefs and knows what they are. Eliminating these mentalistic background assumptions proved an impossible task, given behaviorist methodological strictures. The problem, stated less methodologically, is that mental causes typically have their behavioral effects only because of their interactions with one another.

As behaviorism slipped from prominence in philosophy in the 1950s and early 1960s, it left two heirs, which gradually formed an uneasy alliance. One of these heirs was naturalism. The other was functionalism.

A doctrine I will call 'naturalism' (and sometimes called 'physicalism') emerged first as a distinctive point of view in the philosophy of mind in the early 1950s. This view maintains two tenets. One is that there are no mental states, properties, events, objects, sensations over and above ordinary physical entities, entities identifiable in the physical sciences or entities that common sense would regard as physical. The formulation's vague expression 'over and above' matches the doctrine's vagueness: the doctrine does not entail an identity theory in ontology. It does require some sort of materialism about the mind. Naturalism coupled this ontological position with an ideological or methodological demand. It demanded that mentalistic discourse be explained, or eliminated in favor of discourse that is 'acceptable,' or on some views already found, in the natural or physical sciences. Thus, we find repeated calls for 'explaining' rationality or intentionality. In its materialism, naturalism emphasized ontology in a way that behaviorism did not. Its ideological program, however, continued the behaviorist attempt to make psychology and philosophy of mind more scientific by limiting the supposed excesses of mentalism.

As I have noted, many of the later logical positivists were naturalists. But issues about mind tended to be submerged in the general positivist program. The mind–body problem began to receive direct attention from a naturalistic point of view in articles by Quine, Place, and Smart, in the 1950s (Quine 1952; Place 1956; Smart 1959). Place and Smart tried to identify mental states and events – primarily sensations and afterimages

– with physical states and events. Smart thought that one could identify types of sensations in a 'topic–neutral' way that would leave it open whether or not they were physical; he then predicted that each type of sensation would turn out to be a neural state of some kind. For example, he paraphrased 'I am having an afterimage of an orange' as 'I am in a state like the one I am in when I am seeing an orange.' He thought that this translation would overcome any conceptual obstacles to identifying mental states with physical states. It would sidestep, for example, issues about the qualitative properties of afterimages. Science was supposed to settle the mind-body problem empirically – in favor of what came to be known as *type-type identity theory*, or *central state materialism*.

During the mid- to late 1960s materialism became one of the few orthodoxies in American philosophy. It is difficult to say why this happened. No single argument obtained widespread acceptance. Perhaps the success in biochemistry during the 1950s in providing some sense of the chemical underpinnings of biological facts encouraged the expectation that eventually mental facts would receive a similar explication in neural terms. Moreover, there were some spectacular advances in animal neurophysiology during the period (Lettvin et al. 1959; Hubel, and Wiesel 1959, 1962). Perhaps the attempts of the positivists and behaviorists to make philosophy scientific had as a natural outgrowth the view that philosophical problems would eventually be solved by progress in the natural sciences – with the help of analytical clarification by philosophers. In any case, several philosophers in the 1960s defended either some form of the type-type identity theory or some form of eliminationism (the view that mentalistic talk and mental entities would eventually lose their place in our attempts to describe and explain the world).[2]

The most influential paper of this period was written several years before, in 1956: Sellars's 'Empiricism and the Philosophy of Mind.' The article is a grand attempt to portray mental episodes as explanatory posits that hold a place in our conceptual scheme by virtue of their explanatory usefulness (in Sellars 1963a). Sellars tried to undermine the view that knowledge of one's own mental events was intrinsically privileged or posed an obstacle to the empirical discovery that mental events are neural events. Although in my view the argumentation in this paper is not satisfyingly clear or convincing, the picture it paints of the status of mentalistic discourse is profoundly conceived.

Whereas materialism became widely accepted during the 1960s, issues surrounding naturalism's ideological demand remained intensely controversial. Putnam raised a serious objection to type-type identity theories of the sort that Smart had made popular. He suggested that it is implausible that a sensation like pain is identical with a single neural state in all the many organisms that feel pain, in view of their enormously varied physiologies. He also pointed out that it is even more implausible to think that any given type of thought – for example, a thought that thrice 3 is 9 or a thought that one's present situation is dangerous – is realized by the same physical state in every being that thinks it. Not only the probable existence of extraterrestrials, the variety of higher animals, and the possibility of thinking robots (a possibility most materialists were eager to defend), but the plasticity of the brain seemed to make the type-type identity theory untenable (Putnam 1975b; Block and Fodor 1972). Mental states seemed 'multirealizable.' Materialism maintained its dominance, but needed a new form. Putman's observation seemed to show that if mentalistic discourse was to be explicated in 'scientifically acceptable' terms, the terms would have to be more abstract than neural terms.

Responses to Putnam's observation led to a more specific materialist orthodoxy. The response proceeded on two fronts: ontological and ideological. Most materialists gave up the type-type identity theory in favor of an ontology that came to be known as the token identity theory. Although a mental state or event-kind was not identified with any one physical (neural) kind, each instance of a mental state and each particular mental event token was held to be identical with some instance of a physical state or with some physical event token. This claim allowed that the occurrence of a thought that thrice 3 is 9 could be identical with the occurrence of one sort of physical event in one person, whereas a different occurrence of the same kind of thought could be identical with the occurrence of a different sort of physical event in another person.

Although this ontological position is still widely maintained, no one argument for it has gained wide acceptance. The commonest consideration adduced in its favor is its supposed virtue in simplifying our understanding of mind-body causation. Davidson gave a profound but controversial *a priori* argument along these lines (Davidson 1970). He held, first, that there are causal relations between mental and physical events; second, that causal relations between events must be backed by laws of a complete, closed system of explanation ('backed' in the sense that the predicates of the laws must be true of the events that are causally related); third, that there are no psychophysical or purely mentalistic laws that form a complete, closed system of explanation. He concluded that since there can be no psychophysical or mentalistic laws that would provide the relevant backing for the causal relations between mental and physical events, there must be purely physical laws that back such relations. This is to say that physical predicates apply to mental events – that mental events are physical.

Davidson has not been ideally clear or constant in formulating and arguing for the third premise. But given the conception of 'complete, closed system' that he usually adverts to, this premise seems plausible. The second premise is more doubtful. I do not think it *a priori* true, or even clearly a heuristic principle of science or reason, that causal relations must be backed by any particular kind of law. I think that we learn the nature and scope of laws (and the variety of sorts of 'laws') that back causal relations through empirical investigation. It is not clear that psychophysical counter-factual generalizations – or nonstrict 'laws' – cannot alone 'back' psychophysical causal relations.

Most philosophers accepted the token identity theory as the simplest account that both reconciled materialism with multirealizability and raised no metaphysical issues about mind-body causation. Insofar as the view rests on the hope of finding empirical correlations between types that would inductively support token identities, however, it seems highly speculative. Some philosophers adopted an even more liberal materialism. They held, roughly, that although an instance of a mental event kind may not be an instance of a physical natural kind, they are always *constituted* of events that are instances of physical natural kinds.[3]

In any case, materialism in one form or another has widespread support among North American philosophers; largely on grounds of its supposed virtues in interpreting causation between mental and physical events. There is a vague sense abroad that alternatives amount to superstition. One common idea is that there is some intrinsic mystery in seeing mental events, imagined as nonphysical, as interacting with physical events. Descartes thought this too; and perhaps there was some plausibility to it, given his conceptions of mental and physical substance. But Cartesian conceptions of substance are not at issue nowadays, and the exact nature of the problem in its modern form needs clearer articulation than it is usually given.

A better-reasoned argument along these lines goes as follows. Macrophysical effects depend on prior macrophysical states or events according to approximately deterministic patterns described by physical laws. Mental causes often give rise to physical movements of human bodies. If such causation did not consist in physical processes, it would yield departures from the approximately deterministic patterns described by physical laws. It would interfere with, disrupt, alter, or otherwise 'make a difference' in the physical outcomes. But there is no reason to think that this occurs. Physical antecedent states seem to suffice for the physical effects. Appeal to mentalistic causation that does not consist in physical causation appears, on this reasoning, to invoke physically ungrounded causation that requires us to doubt the adequacy of current forms of physical explanation, even within the physical realm. Not surprisingly, such invocation is widely thought to be unattractive.

This reasoning – and other parallel arguments focusing on the effect of physical processes on mental states – has some force, perhaps enough to nourish materialism indefinitely. But I think that materialism merits more skepticism than it has received in North American philosophy during the last two decades. At any rate, the argument just outlined is not as forceful as it may appear.

Why should mental causes of physical effects interfere with the physical system if they do not *consist in* physical processes? Thinking that they must surely depends heavily on thinking of mental causes on a physical model – as providing an extra 'bump' or transfer of energy on the physical effect. In such a context, instances of 'overdetermination' – two causes having the same effect – must seem to be aberrations. But whether the physical model of mental causation is appropriate is part of what is at issue. Moreover, the sense in which mental causes must 'make a difference' if they do not consist in physical processes is in need of substantial clarification. There are many ways of specifying differences they do make that do not conflict with physical explanations.

It seems to me that we have substantial reason, just from considering mentalistic and physicalistic explanatory goals and practice – before ontology is even considered – to think that mentalistic and physicalistic accounts of causal processes will not interfere with one another. They appeal to common causes (in explaining the physiology and psychology of cognitive processes, for example) and common or at least constitutively related effects (in physiological and psychological explanations of an instance of a man's running to a store, for example). It seems to me perverse, independently of ontological considerations, to assume that these explanations might interfere with one another. They make too few assumptions about one another to allow such an assumption.

There are surely *some* systematic, even necessary, relations between mental events and underlying physical processes. It seems overwhelmingly plausible that mental events depend on physical events in some way or other. But constitution, identity, and physical composition are relations that have specific scientific uses in explaining relations between entities invoked in physical chemistry and biochemistry. These relations so far have no systematic use in nonmetaphysical, scientific theories bridging psychology and neurophysiology. They seem to me to be just one set of possibilities for accounting for relations between entities referred to in these very different explanatory enterprises. Where science does not make clear use of such relations, philosophy should postulate them with some diffidence.

The apparent fact that there are no gaps in physical chains of causation and that mental causes do not disrupt the physical system is perhaps ground for some sort of broad supervenience thesis – no changes in mental states without some sort of change in physical states. But the inference to materialism is, I think, a metaphysical speculation that has come, misleadingly, to seem a relatively obvious scientific-commonsensical bromide.

The issue of mind–body causation is extremely complex and subtle. In recent years, this issue has become an object of intense interest. Much of the discussion concerns 'epiphenomenalism' (cf. e.g. Kim 1984; Sosa 1984; Block 1990a). The causal picture that motivates materialism is so firmly entrenched that many philosophers have come to worry that mental 'aspects' of events really do not 'make a difference': Maybe mental 'aspects' or properties of physical events, in something like the manner of relations between phenotypal properties of parents and their offspring, ride inertly and parasitically on underlying causal relations characterized by the genetic properties of parents and offspring. I think that these worries can be answered, even within a materialist framework. But I think that the very existence of the worries is the main point of philosophical interest. The worry about epiphenomenalism is, in my view, a sign that materialist theories have done a poor job of accounting for the relation between mind–body causal interaction and mentalistic explanation. They have done little to account for the fact that virtually all our knowledge and understanding of the nature and existence of mental causation derives from mentalistic explanations, not from non-intentional functionalist or neurological accounts.[4]

We determine the nature of the causation, and the sort of laws or lawlike generalizations that accompany it, by scrutinizing actual explanations in psychology and ordinary discourse. If there turned out to be no clear sense in which mental events fell under predicates that are uncontroversially physical, then it would seem reasonable to count the mental events nonphysical. As far as I can see, there is no reason to be anything but relaxed in the face of this possibility. I see no powerful, clearly articulated reason for worrying about the existence of mind–body causation, or the gaplessness of chains of physical events, if this possibility were realized. What counts in supporting our belief in mind–body causation is the probity of mentalistic explanations. As long as they are informative and fruitful, we can assume that they are relating genuine events, whatever their metaphysical status.

Otherwise put: the theme in naturalism that deserves the status of orthodoxy is not its materialism and not its demand that mentalistic discourse be given some ideologically acceptable underpinning. It is its implicit insistence that one not countenance any form of explanation that will not stand the scrutiny of scientific and other well-established, pragmatically fruitful methods of communal check and testing. (More crudely, it is the opposition to miracles and to postulation of unverified interruptions in chains of causation among physical events.) But the relevant methods are to be drawn from reflection on what works in actual explanatory practice, not from metaphysical or ideological restrictions on these practices. These points are subject to various interpretations. But I think that taking them seriously motivates less confidence in materialist metaphysics than is common in North American philosophy.

I have been discussing ontological responses to Putnam's observation that various kinds of physical states could be, and are, associated with mental states of a given type. The ideological response to Putnam's observation was the development of a new paradigm for indicating how mental states could be given identifications in non-mentalistic terms. Philosophers looked not to neurophysiology but to computer programming as a source of inspiration. Identifying a mental state with some sort of abstract state of a computer appeared to avoid the problems of identifying mental kinds with neural kinds. And unlike the nonreductive forms of token–identity materialism, it promised means of explaining mentalistic notions in other terms, or at least of supplementing and illuminating mentalistic explanation. Most philosophers found the terms of this supplementation compatible with materialism. This new account came to be known as *functionalism*.[5]

The guiding intuition of functionalism was that what entirely determines what kind of state or event a mental state or event is, is its place in a causal or functional network in the mental life of the individual. The original stimulus to this view was a proposed analogy between the mind and a computer program. To specify such a program, one needed to specify possible inputs into the system, the operations that would pass the machine from one state to another, the states that the machine would pass through, and the output of the machine, given each possible input and given the states it was already in. The machine might be either deterministic or probabilistic. On most versions of functionalism, the internal states were to be specified purely in terms of their 'place' in the system of input and output – in terms of the possible dependency relations they bore to other states and ultimately to input and output. Input and output were to be specified in nonintentional, nonmentalistic terms. Types of mental states and events were supposed to be determined entirely by the relations of functional dependency within the whole system of input and output.

The notion of determination is subject to three main interpretations. One, the least ambitious and least reductive, claims only that each mental kind supervenes on a place in the functional system, in the sense that the individual would be in a different kind of mental state if and only if he were not in the functional state corresponding to that kind. The other two purport to say what mental kinds 'consist in.' One version ('analytic functionalism') claims that a functionalist specification of such relations explicates the meaning of mentalistic terms. Another ('scientific functionalism') makes the lesser claim that such a specification gives the true essence of mental kinds, in something like the way that molecular constitution gives the true essence of a natural kind like *water*. Both of these latter two versions claim that functionalist discourse provides the 'real explanatory power' latent in mentalistic explanation.[6]

Analytic and scientific functionalism are clearly liberalized heirs to behaviorism. They share with behaviorism the insistence on nonintentional specifications of input (stimulus) and output (response), and the belief that mentalistic explanation is somehow deficient and needs a nonmentalistic underpinning. They also expand on the behaviorist idea that mental states are individuated partly in terms of their relations. Whereas behaviorists focused largely on relations to behavior, functionalists included relations to other mental states, and relations to stimulating input into the system. This is an insight already present in Frege, who claimed that sense is inseparable from a network of inferential capacities.

It has been common to combine functionalism with token-identity materialism. Functionalism was supposed to provide insight into the nature of mental kinds, whereas token-identity materialism provided insight into the nature of mental particulars – into the instantiation of the mental kinds in particular individuals. The computer analogy seemed compelling to many: mentalistic discourse was a sort of gloss on an underlying network functional flow chart, which was ultimately realized in different physical ways in different machines or organisms. Thus neural descriptions were seen as lying at the bottom of a three-level hierarchy of descriptions of the same human subject.

The functionalist position – in its least reductionist garb – was given distinctive form by Fodor. Fodor maintained that the intentional content of propositional attitudes is irreducible via functionalist specifications. But he held that such content is expressed by inner mental representations that have syntactic properties, inner words and sentences that were presumed to be instantiated somehow in the brain. Fodor further claimed that mental representations have their causal roles in virtue of their formal or syntactic properties, and that the input and output of functionalist specifications should be seen as symbols (Fodor 1975, 1981; Field 1978). This picture brought the functionalist tradition into line with a fairly literal interpretation of the computer analogy: psychological explanation was modeled on *proofs* or other types of symbol manipulation by a digital computer. The causal aspects of psychological explanation were to be understood in terms of the physical relations among the particular neural states or events that instantiated the symbolic representations.

Something like this picture had been proposed by Sellars (Sellars 1963b; cf. Harman 1973). But Fodor presented his view as an interpretation of work in psycholinguistics and cognitive psychology. To many it gained plausibility because of its appeal to specific scientific practices. The picture and its relation to psychological theory are still very much in dispute.[7] Fodor's work drew attention from linguists, psychologists, and computer scientists. It also benefited from and helped further a significant shift in the degree to which the details of scientific practice were seen to be relevant to philosophical problems about mind.

Until the mid- to late 1970s most philosophy in this area was carried on in a relatively *a priori* analytic spirit. Even those philosophers, such as type-type identity theorists or skeptics about mental states, who purported to take science as a model for philosophy of mind had little to say about the theories of any science. They saw themselves as freeing philosophy from obstacles to scientific progress (whose direction was often predicted with considerable confidence). This was true not only of the philosophy of mind, but of much of the rest of philosophy – even much of the philosophy of natural science, with the exception of historical work in the tradition of Thomas Kuhn (Kuhn 1962). It is an interesting question why a shift to reflection on specific aspects of science occurred. A similar shift occurred in the philosophies of science and mathematics. Both disciplines undertook much more concentrated discussions of a wider variety of the details of scientific practice, beginning about twenty years ago.[8] Philosophizing about biology, a science that had not conformed to positivist conceptions of law and explanation, came to prominence in this period. Perhaps it took two decades for the criticisms of positivism to be digested sufficiently for a more open-minded consideration of the actual practice of the sciences to develop. In any case, interest in the details of psychology should be seen in the context of intellectual movements outside the scope of this essay.

The demise of behaviorism might similarly be viewed as requiring a period of assimilation before psychology could be considered a worthwhile object of philosophical reflection. Of course, there was a more positive side to the reconsideration of the practice of psychology. The computer paradigm was a natural object of interest. The continuing success of Chomsky's program in linguistics, coupled as it was with claims that it was a part of a psychology of the mind, made philosophers increasingly interested in mentalistic psychology. And an intellectually substantial cognitive and developmental psychology, and psycholinguistics, offered new forms to questions relevant to traditional philosophical issues: the role of intentional content in explanation, the mind-body problem, differences between language and thought, the innateness and universality of various conceptual and linguistic structures, the scope and limits of human rationality. How much the reflection on psychology will enrich and advance philosophical inquiry remains an open question. Quite a lot of the work in this area seems to me very unreflective. It is at best rare that scientific practice answers philosophical questions in a straightforward way. But philosophy has traditionally given and received aid in the rise of new sciences or new scientific paradigms.

Let us return to functionalism. Although functionalism has enjoyed substantial support – at least among specialists in the philosophy of mind – it has not lacked detractors. The analytic and scientific versions of functionalism have always been afflicted with a programmatic, unspecific character that has seemed to many to render them unilluminating as *accounts* of particular mental kinds.

There are more specific criticisms. Many philosophers find the application of any form of functionalism to sensations like pain or color implausible. For them, the causal relations of the sensations seem less fundamental to their character than their qualitative aspects.[9]

Searle mounted a controversial argument, similar to some of those directed against the applicability of functionalism to qualitative aspects of sensations, to show that functionalism could not account for any propositional attitudes. He postulated a room in which stations are manned by a person who does not understand Chinese, but who memorizes the Chinese words of given instructions. These stations are postulated to correspond to the stages of processing a language. The person is able to produce appropriate Chinese sentences as output, given any Chinese sentence as input. Searle claimed that although the system could be set up to meet the functionalist requirements for understanding Chinese, there is no understanding of Chinese in the room. Most opponents claim that the whole system can be credited with understanding Chinese. Searle finds this reply unconvincing.[10]

A more complex issue concerns the specific formulation of a functionalist account. Clearly, people can share meanings and many beliefs even though they maintain very different theories about the world. Maintaining different theories entails making different inferences, which correspond to different causal relations among the different sets of mental states associated with the theories. So not just any network of causal relations among mental states and events can be relevant to a functional account, on pain of counting no one as sharing any beliefs or meanings. One needs to find a network that is common to all the possible inference networks and theories in which any given belief (or meaning) might be embedded. But it is very difficult to imagine there being such common causal networks for each given belief (or meaning).[11]

Another approach to understanding intentional content and mental kinds developed out of the work on reference. That work showed that proper names and natural kind expressions could succeed in referring even though the speaker's knowledge of the referent was incomplete or defective. Reference depends not just on background descriptions that the speaker associates with the relevant words, but on contextual, not purely cognitive relations that the speaker bears to entities to which a term applies.

The work on reference is relevant to the meaning of terms and to the identity of concepts. For the meaning of a wide range of nonindexical terms and the nature of a wide range of concepts are dependent on the referent or range of application in the sense that if the referent were different, the meaning of the term, and the associated concept, would be different. (Here let us simply take concepts to be elements in the intentional contents of propositional attitudes, elements that have referential aspects.) For example, different meanings or concepts would be expressed by the word-forms 'chair' and 'arthritis' if the word-forms did not apply exactly to chairs and to instances of arthritis.

The points about reference can be extended to many such terms and concepts. An individual can think of a range of entities via such terms and concepts even though the thinker's knowledge of the entities is not complete enough to pick out that range of entities except through the employment of those terms and concepts. What the individual knows about the range of entities – and hence about those many meanings or concepts whose identities are not independent of their referential range of applications – need not provide a definition that distinguishes them from all other (possible) meanings or concepts. So the meanings of many terms – and the identities of many concepts – are what they are even though what the individual knows about the meaning or concept may be insufficient to determine it uniquely. Their identities are fixed by environmental factors that are not entirely captured in the explicatory or even discriminatory abilities of the individual, unless those discriminatory abilities include application of the concept itself. Since most propositional attitudes, like specific beliefs, are the kinds of mental kinds that they are because of the meanings, concepts, or intentional contents that are used to specify them, the identities of many mental kinds depend on environmental factors that are not entirely captured in the (nonintentionally specified) discriminatory abilities of the individual. I have just developed one motivation for what is called '*anti-individualism.*'

Anti-individualism is the view that not all of an individual's mental states and events can be type-individuated independently of the nature of the entities in the individual's environment. There is, on this view, a deep individuative relation between the individual's being in mental states of certain kinds and the nature of the individual's physical or social environments. Anti-individualism was supported not only through abstract considerations from the theory of reference, but also through specific thought experiments. For example, one can imagine two individuals who are, for all relevant purposes, identical in the intrinsic physical nature and history of their bodies (described in isolation of their environments). But the two individuals can be imagined to have interacted with different metals (one aluminum, one an aluminum look-alike) in their respective environments. The metals need resemble one another only to the level of detail that the two individuals have noticed. The individuals know about as much about the metals as most ordinary people do, but neither could tell the difference if given the other metal. In such a case, it seems that one individual has thoughts like *aluminum is a light metal*, whereas the other individual (lacking any access to aluminum, even through interlocutors) has analogous thoughts about the other metal. Similar thought experiments appear to show that a person's thoughts can be dependent on relations to a social environment as well as a purely physical one. Some environmental dependence or other can be shown for nearly all empirically applicable terms or concepts.[12]

The thought experiments made trouble for the standard forms of functionalism, which limited specifications or input and output to the surfaces of the individual. The thought experiments suggested that all an individual's internal functional transactions could remain constant, while his mental states (counterfactually) varied. Some philosophers proposed extending the functional network into the physical or social environments. Such a proposal reduces the reliance on the computer paradigm and requires a vastly more complex account. The main problems for it are those of accounting for (or specifying an illuminating supervenience base for) the notions of meaning, reference, and social dependence, in nonintentional terms. These are tasks commonly underestimated, in my view, because of the programmatic nature of the functionalist proposals.

Most philosophers seem to have accepted the thought experiments. But there remains disagreement about how they bear on mentalistic explanation, especially in psychology. Some have held that no notion of intentional content that is thus dependent for its individuation on matters external to the individual could serve in explaining the individual's behavior. Many of these philosophers have tried to fashion surrogate notions of content or of 'mental' states to serve explanatory purposes. Others have maintained that such positions are based on mistakes and that the ordinary notions of intentional content and mental state can and do play a role in ordinary explanation and explanation in psychology. The debate concerns the interpretation of actual psychological practice and the relation between psychological explanation and explanation in other sciences.[13]

In my view, however, the main interest of the thought experiments lies in their giving new forms to many old issues. The arguments for anti-individualism are new.

But the broad outline of the conclusion that they support is not. It is clearly maintained by Aristotle, Hegel, and Wittgenstein, and arguably present in Descartes and Kant.[14] Emergence of an old doctrine in a new form is a source of vitality in philosophy. Issues about self-knowledge, skepticism, *a priori* knowledge, personhood, the nature of meaning, the mind-body problem, are all deeply affected by considerations about necessary, individuative relations between an individual's mind and his environment. The line of development from the anti-descriptivist theories of reference to anti-individualist accounts of mind promises, I think, to enrich traditional philosophy.

In the last decade of the twentieth century, the relation between anti-individualism and other issues in philosophy came under intense scrutiny. I will discuss two areas of discussion that fall under this general heading. One is perception and perceptual thought. The other is self-knowledge. The decade was also marked by the emergence of widespread reflection on qualitative aspects of the mental, and on the nature of consciousness.

I begin with the two issues associated with anti-individualism. The first concerns questions about singular *de re* aspects of representation. I touch on two issues within this sub-area, both having to do with the nature of perceptual representation.

In *Languages of Art*, Goodman developed an account of the 'syntax' of pictorial representation that distinguishes it from propositional representation. Many have thought that Goodman's work points toward an account of non-propositional form for perceptual representation. Roughly, Goodman counted non-propositional representations – particularly drawings – as analog representations. Analog representations are analog if (for relevant purposes) dense. Representations are dense if between any two types there is a third. An associated idea is that in analog representations, every discernible difference in the representational medium makes a representational difference. There is much that is not right about Goodman's account, even for pictures. Still, many have thought that Goodman was on to an important distinction between perceptual and conceptual (propositional) representation, particularly regarding the second idea. Others pursued a similar path independently (Goodman 1968; Haugeland 1981; Dretske 1981; Evans 1982; Peacocke 1989, and 1992).

Making the distinction in a clear and psychologically relevant way resists simple stories. There is the following baseline point that functions as a challenge: seemingly any representational content can be mimicked by or converted into propositional form. What distinguishes (some particular form of) non-propositional, non-conceptual representational content? Since perception seems both to indicate particulars and to categorize them in certain ways, one has a prima facie analog of subject-predicate form implicit in perception. Some have claimed that one cannot make sense of representation that plays a role in epistemology unless one takes the representation to be propositional and thus capable of yielding reasons.[15]

I believe that the position that distinguishes perceptual from conceptual representational form is correct. I believe this largely on empirical grounds. There is no need to appeal to propositionally marked states to explain the representational capacities, principally perceptual capacities, of numerous animals. But perception and action in these animals *is* best explained in terms of representational states. The representational organization of vision, hearing, and touch does not seem to be propositional. In most

empirical work on these senses, no systematic attribution of propositional representations is made. Similarly, the representational organization of grasping or of eating does
not seem to be propositional. No reasonable, full account can carry out the inquiry
independently of empirical work in psychology. But the need for conceptual clarification in understanding the distinction seems to me to be deep and complex.

A related issue about perceptual representation concerns its semantics rather than
its form. The issue centers on the nature of the relation between the singular element
in perceptual belief and the particulars that the perceptual belief is about. Developing
the view in anti-individualism that representational states are (commonly) individuated in terms of their relations to the environment, some, following Evans, maintained that a perceptual state and a perceptual belief could not be the same type of state
or belief if it were a perception or belief about a different particular. Similarly, a given
type of perceptual state or belief that is about a given particular could not have been the
same if there had been an illusion of a particular instead of a genuine perceptual object
in the environment (cf. Evans 1982; McDowell 1986; Peacock 1992; McDowell 1994).
On the other hand, there is both commonsense and scientific ground for thinking that
the types of states that perceivers are in are the same as between veridical perceptions,
perceptions of indiscernible duplicates, and referential perceptual illusions (Searle
1983; Burge 1991). This issue raises important questions about the nature of
perceptual states and perceptual beliefs and about the nature of illusion.

A second large sub-area in the development of issues associated with anti-individualism bears on the nature of self-knowledge. Discussion centered on the question of
whether anti-individualism is compatible with some sort of authoritative or privileged
warrant for certain types of self-knowledge. Inevitably, this question forced reflection
on the nature of self-knowledge and its role in various human pursuits. The issue was
first raised in independent papers by Burge and Davidson. Each defended a type of
compatibilism about the relation between anti-individualist individuation of certain
mental states and a capacity to know nonempirically what those states are (Burge
1988a; Davidson 1987). This claim was resisted or qualified by a number of
philosophers.[16]

The bulk of the discussion came to center on the nature of self-knowledge – or
rather, the nature of various types of self-knowledge. Some philosophers maintained
that all self-knowledge is at least implicitly empirical. Some maintained that apparent
cases of privileged or authoritative self-knowledge are to be understood in an
expressivist or otherwise deflationary way. Others attempted to understand the
apparently special character of some knowledge of what one is thinking or what
one believes – without explaining that character away. What I regard as the most
interesting developments of this approach appealed to some constitutive role of self-
knowledge in having beliefs, in having a concept of belief, in being rational, or in being
a deliberative person. These matters are complex, and deserve, I think, further
development.[17]

I want to highlight one further area of intense discussion in the philosophy of mind
in the 1990s. This one is largely independent of issues about anti-individualism. The
area concerns the nature of qualitative experience, including the nature of consciousness. Consciousness and representationality, or aboutness, have long been regarded as

the two major marks of mind. An important question is whether one mark can be reduced to the other; and if not, what relative places the two marks have in our understanding of mind.

The discussion of these matters at the end of the twentieth century must be seen against the background of four important papers. I have already mentioned two of these: Block's 'Troubles with Functionalism' (1978), and Searle's 'Minds, Brains, and Programs' (1980). Each paper offers a forceful example that suggests that functionalist accounts of the representational aspects of mind fail to come to grips with qualitative aspects of experience. A third paper, Nagel's 'What is it Like to be a Bat?' (1974), offers a compelling way of thinking about qualitative aspects of experience, summarized in his phrase 'what it is like'. Finally, Jackson's 'Epiphenomenal Qualia' (1982), gives an argument against materialism that features the difficulty of accounting for phenomenal qualities in material terms. These papers set many cross-currents going. I will not be able to survey nearly all of them. I will concentrate on one strand of development—the relation between qualitative and representational aspects of mind.

Many of the original responses to these papers focused on defending either functionalism or materialism – the original targets of the papers. As interest in strict forms of functionalism waned, the debate over functionalism was largely replaced by a closely related, but slightly different debate. Some functionalists took the tack of *assuming* that some form of functionalism is true of representational states, and then arguing that qualitative phenomena are essentially and solely representational. Others argued to the same conclusion with no antecedent commitment to functionalism.

Harman's 'The Intrinsic Quality of Experience' (1990) claimed that qualitative aspects of experience are simply certain types of representational aspects of experience. Qualitative aspects of experience are the aspects that have to do with what it is like to have an experience, feeling, or sensation. Harman argued that putatively intrinsic aspects of experience, for example the felt quality of pain, had been conflated with intrinsic aspects of the 'intentional object' of an experience. Against the Jackson thought experiment he maintained that a person blind from birth fails to know what it is like to see something red because he or she does not have the full concept of red and so does not fully understand what it is for something to be red. Finally, Harman argued against invoking the inverted spectrum to show that representational constancy is compatible with qualitative difference. Harman's paper defended what came to be known as 'representationalism' – the view that qualitative aspects of experience are nothing other than representational aspects.

This paper was followed by – and in many cases it engendered – several further papers defending representationalist construals of qualitative mental phenomena (Dretske 1995, 1996; Tye 1995; Rey 1992). The position was opposed by other philosophers, who maintained that phenomenal qualities, or phenomenal qualitative aspects of experience, commonly have representational content and representational functions but are not to be reduced to them (Block 1990b, 1996; Loar 1997; McGinn 1991).

Most papers in this area, on both sides, give what seems to me too little attention to what is to be meant by 'representation.' Harman admitted that his notion of intentional object is crude. I think it vulnerable. I think that the notion will not convincingly support the first of Harman's three arguments. There is, however, a clearer conception of representation that provides a basis for much of the representationalist discussion. According to this conception 'x represents y' should be understood roughly as: 'appropriate types of which x is an instance are dependent in a lawful or lawlike way on appropriate types of which y is an instance, and this connection between x and y has functional value for the life of the organism that contains x.'[18] It is certainly plausible that on this conception of representation, qualitative color registrations are representational. It also follows from the view that feelings of pain and sensations like orgasms are representational. For example, a state of feeling pain is in a lawlike relation to instances of bodily damage or disorder, and this relation surely has a functional value in the life of the organism. So the state of feeling pain 'represents' the bodily damage or disorder. This result has been embraced and defended by some representationalists (Tye 1990).

I believe that this notion of representation is too broad. It deems the states of very simple creatures to be 'representational states.' For example, it counts as representational states the sensory states underlying thermotactic responses of protozoa. One can coherently talk this way. Some psychologists and physiologists do talk this way. This notion of representation is, however, not needed to explain such simple phenomena. It is a mere gloss on points that can be made in physiological, ecological, and functional terms. By contrast, a more intuitive, restrictive notion of representation does have prima facie explanatory force in the ethology of the perceptual and cognitive systems of less primitive animals and in the psychology of human beings. Dretske and others hope to reduce the more ordinary notion(s) of representation to the very broad one. I think that there is no ground for optimism about this project.[19] It is doubtful, moreover, that the simple notion is one that opponents of representationalism have been concerned with when they doubt that qualitative aspects of experience are 'representational.' I believe that a less inclusive, or more specific notion is needed to sort out issues between representationalists and their opponents.

Laying this issue aside, there remain difficulties for the representationalist position, even formulated with the broad notion of representation. One is that it produces unattractive results in cases like the feeling of pain. If an individual has a phantom limb, the position maintains that there is no pain – since there is no bodily damage that is functionally connected to the state of feeling pain; there is only a representation of pain that hallucinates the pain. This view has actually been embraced by proponents of representationalism. It seems to me clearly unacceptable.

A second difficulty is that despite the inclusiveness of the cited conception of representation, there still appear to be qualitative states that do not 'represent' in this inclusive sense. There seem to be qualitative aspects of experience that have no function in the life of the organism. They constitute dysfunction or noise. Blurriness in a visual experience is an example. These cases have been treated as misrepresentations or as representations of blurriness, but it is hard to see that they have any representational function at all. They make no contribution to reproductive fitness, and they seem to get in the way of proper functions. This result is incompatible with the representationalist program.

Harman's second argument seems to me to beg the question. It does, however, highlight interesting and difficult issues about the relation between qualitative aspects of perception and representational aspects. In the case of (say) visual perception it is certainly hard to separate out qualitative aspects from representational aspects. We identify most qualitative aspects of perception with terms that indicate what is normally represented when our consciousness is marked by those aspects. For example, although few philosophers still think that experience (by a normal-sighted person) of red is itself in any way red, we currently have no better, easily accessible, public way to characterize the qualitative aspect of the experience than in terms of its relation to red surfaces. This fact makes it hard to see how to describe, much less explain, the qualitative aspect of experience in a way that abstracts from its representational role. And this difficulty encourages representationalism.

Opponents of representationalism typically maintain that the qualitative aspects of perception play a role in determining the mode of presentation or the representational content of the perception, and are not to be explained in terms of this role. The idea is that at least some aspects of qualitative states are dependent on the nature of the neural substrate and not on the sorts of correlations with objects of representation that determine representational content. This view seems to me correct. But it will provide little explanatory illumination until relations between qualitative feels and neural underpinnings are better and more specifically understood.

Harman's third argument centers on the inverted spectrum. How to describe and evaluate this type of thought experiment remains difficult and disputed. I think that the case can be elaborated in various ways that make representationalism implausible. But the issues are very delicate and complex, and I will not try to review them here. There has been considerable, nuanced discussion of issues surrounding inverted spectra (Shoemaker 1982 and 1996 ('Intrasubjective/Intrasubjective'); Block 1990b).

One reason why the issue of representationalism has been of such interest is that it bears on the nature of consciousness. Qualitative or phenomenal states, as ordinarily felt, provide the most obvious instances of consciousness. Feelings involved in sensations like pains and tickles, phenomenal aspects of the experience of color or sound, the experience of warmth or of being touched, seem to be the paradigmatic center of consciousness. There are then issues about the relation between consciousness and representation that parallel those about the relation between qualitative aspects of experience and representation. In fact, positions on consciousness run the gamut from arguments that there is no such thing as qualitative aspects of experience, to functionalist reductionism, to simple representationalist views, to higher-order thought views, to claims that consciousness is irreducible, to claims that consciousness is both irreducible and a ground for dualist theories of mind.[20]

The variety of theories about consciousness, and the depth of disagreement among theorists, suggests that there may be differences at the intuitive level – differences about the *explanandum*. Block suggested fruitfully that there are at least two notions of consciousness. One has to do with phenomenal, felt, qualitative aspects of experience. Another has to do with accessibility to rational deliberation, or at least to reflection and use in verbal and other rational enterprises (Block 1995; cf. Burge 'Two Kinds of Consciousness,' in Block et al. 1998: 427–34). Whether or not this view is correct, it seems to me to have engendered greater awareness of the complexity and elusiveness of phenomena that have been discussed in philosophizing about consciousness.

Discussion of consciousness has opened up what had been a neglected, almost taboo subject in philosophy. This has been a good thing. On the other hand, it seems to me that progress toward genuine understanding has been at best mixed. The difficulty of the subject has not only provoked a number of wildly implausible theories; but has also encouraged what seems to me to be some backsliding in methodology and clarity of discussion in many presentations in this area. Metaphors, appeals to disputed and sketchily described introspection, unexplained terms, hastily and poorly explained technicalia, and grandiose programs have been more prominent than is good for a subject. These are early days. A certain amount of floundering is inevitable in initial work on a difficult topic. It may well be that a deeper scientific grip on relevant areas of neural, sensory, and cognitive psychology will be necessary before impressive progress emerges. It is well also to remember that many of the most fundamental aspects of our experience of the world – aspects that throw up some of the most basic and long-standing philosophical problems – have a way of remaining puzzling, despite progress in associated sciences. Consciousness may remain a case in point.

I want to close by summarizing some of the main changes in the philosophy of mind (and language) in the second half of the twentieth century. Three major, possibly durable contributions in this area during the period are the criticism of the positivist theory of meaning; the development of a vastly more sophisticated sense of logical form, as applied to natural language; and the fashioning of the nondescriptivist account of reference, with the extension of the line of thought associated with this account into the philosophy of mind. Different philosophers would, of course, provide different lists of achievements, given their own sense of what is true and important.

The dominant currents during the period are more easily agreed upon. The central event is the downfall of positivism and the re-opening for discussion of virtually all the traditional problems in philosophy. This event was accompanied by the rediscovery of Frege, the application of logical theory to language, and the rise of the philosophy of language both as a preliminary to reflection on other subjects, and as a more nearly autonomous discipline. The computer paradigm and complex outgrowths of the philosophy of language have brought the philosophy of mind to dominance in the last two decades.

Positivism left behind a strong orientation toward the methods of science. This orientation has fuelled the acceptance of materialism in the philosophy of mind and, somewhat belatedly, the development of areas of philosophy (philosophy of physics, mathematics, biology, psychology, linguistics, social science) that take the specifics of scientific theories and practices into account.

For all this, the main direction of philosophy during the period has been toward a broader-based, more eclectic, less ideological approach to philosophical problems – and a greater receptivity to interplay between modern philosophy and the history of philosophy. Philosophy of mind emerged as an area of intense ferment not simply as a product of interaction between philosophy and such disciplines as psychology and linguistics. That ferment also represents a greater interest in traditional questions, questions about what is morally and intellectually distinctive about being human. It is hard to overemphasize the degree to which leading North American philosophers have since the 1950s broadened their sympathies toward traditional questions that still help frame what it is to lead a reflective life. This broadening seems not to have seriously undermined the standards of rigor, clarity, and openness to communal check bequeathed by such figures as Frege, Russell, Carnap, Hempel, Gödel, Church, and Quine. Partly because of its close connection with the development of mathematical logic in this century, the standards of argument in philosophy have certainly been raised.

A corollary of this change, and of the personal example of the positivists in carrying on open, dispassionate discussion, has been the emergence of philosophical community. One of the glories of English-speaking philosophy in the last forty years has been the fruitful participation of many philosophers in the same discussions. Unlike much traditional philosophy and much philosophy in other parts of the world, English-speaking philosophy has been an open, public forum. The journals of the field bear witness to a sharing of philosophical concerns, vocabularies, and methods of dispute. We now take this sharing for granted. But in historical perspective, it is remarkable. Although I think that philosophy is not and never will be a science, it has taken on this much of the spirit of science. That is, to my mind, the more important achievement.

This overview has provided at best a blurred glimpse of the enormous complexity and variety of discussion in the philosophy of mind during the last five decades. It is deficient as a picture not only in its oversimplifications and limited scope, but also in its failure to convey the life and nature of the animal. Philosophy is not primarily a body of doctrine, a series of conclusions or systems or movements. Philosophy, both as product and as activity, lies in the detailed posing of questions, the clarification of meaning, the development and criticism of argument, the working out of ideas and points of view. It resides in the angles, nuances, styles, struggles, and revisions of individual authors. In an overview of this sort, almost all the real philosophy must be omitted. For those not initiated into these issues, the foregoing is an invitation. For those who are initiated, it is a reminder – a reminder of the grandeur, richness, and intellectual substance of our subject.

Notes

1. This chapter consists mostly of the second half of my article 'Philosophy of Language and Mind: 1950–1990.' I have added further material that concentrates on the last decade of the century. I present a historical overview pitched to nonspecialists. The scope of the article has, of course, led to omission of many important topics – for example, personal identity, action theory, the innateness of mental structures, knowledge of language, the nature of psychological explanation, the nature of concepts, many strands in the mind-body problem, and the legacy of Wittgenstein. I am grateful to Ned Block, Susan Carey, and the editors of *The Philosophical Review* for good advice.

2. The central state identity theory is defended in Armstrong 1968, and Lewis 1966. Eliminative materialism, which derives from Quine, is defended in Feyerabend 1963; Rorty 1965; and Dennett 1969. Many of these works, and several other significant ones, are collected in O'Connor 1969.

3. Hellman and Thompson 1977; Boyd 1980. Another source of reformulations of materialism has been the discussion of supervenience principles. Cf. Kim 1979. It is worth noting, however, that supervenience of the mental on the physical does not entail materialism.

4. The lack of attention to our source of knowledge of mental causation is one reason why there has recently been a small outpouring of worries among materialists that a form of epiphenomenalism – the view that mentalistic properties or descriptions are causally irrelevant – must be taken seriously.

5. Cf. Turing 1950. Turing's article provided an impetus and a vivid illustration of the computer paradigm, but it was itself an expression of behaviorism about the mind. The papers that inspired machine functionalism were Hilary Putnam's, 'Minds and Machines,' (1960), 'Robots: Machines or Artificially Created Life?' (1964), and 'The Mental Life of Some Machines' (1967), in *Philosophical Papers*, vol. 2 (1975: 362–85, 387–407, 408–28). Putnam states an explicitly functionalist view in 'The Nature of Mental States' (1967), but the idea is not far from the surface of his earlier papers. A type of functionalism less tied to computers was proposed in Lewis 1966, and Armstrong 1968.

6. The nonreductive version is the least common. It is expressed in the introduction of Jerry Fodor's *RePresentations*, but he maintains it neither very long before nor very long after. The analytic version may be found in Armstrong 1968; Lewis 1972; Shoemaker 2003. Putnam proposed the scientific version in 'The Nature of Mental States.' A view more instrumentalist than functionalist but which bears broad comparison appears in Dennett 1971.

7. For opposition from different angles to the computer analogy or to other aspects of the language-of-thought hypothesis, see Churchland 1979; Peacocke 1983; Stich 1983; Stalnaker 1984; Dennett 1987; Smolensky 1988.

8. The change in the philosophy of physics was foreshadowed by early articles of Hilary Putnam's – for example, 'An Examination of Grünbaum's Philosophy of Geometry' (1963), 'A Philosopher Looks at Quantum Mechanics' (1965), both in *Philosophical Papers*, vol. 1 (1975: 93–129, 130–58). But it caught on and received new impetus with the articles of John Earman – for example, 'Who's Afraid of Absolute Space?' (1970). For an overview of broadly analogous changes in the philosophy of mathematics, see Tymoczko 1985.

9. Criticism of this aspect of functionalism may be found in Block 1978, and 1980. An influential article with a different, but related, point is Thomas Nagel, 'What is It Like to Be a Bat?' (1974). Cf., also, Jackson 1982. The numerous defenses of functionalism on this score include: Sydney Shoemaker, 'Functionalism and Qualia,' and 'Absent Qualia are Impossible – a Reply to Block,' in *Identity, Cause and Mind* (2003: 184–205, 309–26); and David Lewis, 'Mad Pain and Martian Pain', in his *Philosophical Papers* 1983.

10. Searle 1980. Searle's argument is anticipated in Block 1978.

11. These problems have long been recognized. But as with some of the fundamental difficulties with positivism, such recognition does not always convince proponents of a program to give it up. For a summary of some of these problems, see Putnam 1988.

12. Burge 1982, 1986a, 1988a, 1989a, 'The Meaning of "Meaning"' in Putnam 1975 (vol. 2: 215–71). Putnam's argument, however, was not applied to intentional elements in mind or meaning. In fact, it contained remarks that are incompatible with anti-individualism about mental states. Much in his subsequent papers is, however, anti-individualistic. Cf. 'Computational Psychology and Interpretation Theory,' in Putnam 1983 (pp. 139–54), and Putnam 1988, Chap. 5. But ambivalences remain. Cf. Putnam 1988: 19–22.

13. For versions of the former approach, see White 1982; Stich; Fodor 1987; Loar. For defenses of anti-individualistic conceptions of psychology, see Dretske 1981; Burge 1986b, and 1989b; Baker 1987; and Stalnaker 1989.

14. Descartes's Demon hypothesis is paradigmatically individualistic. But Descartes thought that the hypothesis was incoherent. His causal argument for the existence of the physical

world (in Meditation 6) and his principle that the reality of ideas cannot exceed the reality of their objects are anti-individualistic in spirit. The question of whether Descartes was an individualist is very complex and entangled with his views about God. As regards Kant, the Refutation of Idealism (*Critique of Pure Reason*, B 274ff.) contains a fundamentally anti-individualistic strategy. But the overall question of how to interpret Kant with regard to anti-individualism is, again, very complex, since it is bound up with the interpretation of his transcendental idealism.

15. McDowell 1994. Cf. also the 1998 exchange between Peacocke and McDowell in *Philosophy and Phenomenological Research* 57: 1998.
16. Paul Boghossian 1989; Gallois 1996. For a collection of articles developing both sides of this issue, see P. Ludlow and Martin 1998.
17. Davidson 1984, reprinted in Davidson 2001 (pp. 3–14); Shoemaker 1994, reprinted in Shoemaker et al. 1996; Moran 1994; Burge 1995; Kobes 1996. A collection of articles that provides some indication of the range of this discussion is in Wright et al. 1998.
18. Dretske 1995, Chap. 1. A similar but somewhat different view can be found in Millikan 1984, and 1989.
19. Dretske relies partly on a view that in *mental* representation, there is learning. In the relevant sense of learning, all animals and all unicellular organisms, including amoebae, learn. No animal is confined to fixed hard-wired, purely reflexive behavior. So Dretske's line seems to me to do nothing to solve the problem.
20. Works representing these various positions, and intermediate ones, are as follows: Dennett 1988 and 1991; Dretske 1993 and 1995; Rosenthal 1986; Searle 1992; Levine 1993; Davies 1996; Siewart 1998; Chalmers 1996. For further discussion that hinges on more technical and methodological issues, see Block, and Stalnaker 1999; Chalmers, and Jackson 2001. A good anthology is *The Nature of Consciousness*, Block et al., 1998.

References

Armstrong, D. M. (1968), *A Materialist Theory of the Mind*, New York: Humanities Press.

Baker, L. R. (1987), *Saving Belief*, Princeton: Princeton University Press.

Block, N. (1978), 'Troubles with Functionalism,' in C. W. Savage (ed.) (1978), *Minnesota Studies in the Philosophy of Science*, vol. 9, Minneapolis: University of Minnesota Press, pp. 435–39.

Block, N. (1980), 'Are Absent Qualia Impossible?' *Philosophical Review* 89: 257–74.

Block, N. (1990a), 'Can the Mind Change the World?' in G. Boolos (ed.) (1990), *Meaning and Method: Essays in Honor of Hilary Putnam*, Cambridge: Cambridge University Press, pp. 137–70.

Block, N. (1990b), 'Inverted Earth,' *Philosophical Perspectives* 4: 51–79.

Block, N. (1995), 'On a Confusion about a Function of Consciousness,' *Behavioural and Brain Sciences* 18: 227–47.

Block, N. (1996), 'Mental Paint and Mental Latex,' in E. Villanueva (ed.) (1996), *Philosophical Issues 7: Perception*, Atascadero: Ridgeview, pp. 19–49.

Block, N., O. Flanagan, and G. Guzeldere (eds) (1998), *The Nature of Consciousness*, Cambridge: MIT Press.

Block, N., and J. Fodor (1972), 'What Psychological States Are Not,' *The Philosophical Review* 81: 159–81.

Block, N., and R. Stalnaker (1999), 'Conceptual Analysis, Dualism, and the Explanatory Gap,' *The Philosophical Review* 108: 1–46.

Boghossian, P. (1989), 'Content and Self-Knowledge,' *Philosophical Topics* 17: 5–26.

Boyd, R. (1980), 'Materialism without Reductionism: What Physicalism does not Entail,' in N. Block (ed.) (1980), *Readings in Philosophy of Psychology*, vol. 1, Cambridge University Press, pp. 67–106.

Burge, T. (1979), 'Individualism and the Mental,' *Midwest Studies* 4: 73–121.

Burge, T. (1982), 'Other Bodies,' in A. Woodfield (ed.) (1982), *Thought and Object: Essays on Intentionality*, London: Oxford University Press, pp. 97–120.

Burge, T. (1986a), 'Intellectual Norms and Foundations of Mind,' *Journal of Philosophy* 83: 697–720.

Burge, T. (1986b), 'Individualism and Psychology,' *The Philosophical Review* 95: 3–45.

Burge, T. (1988a), 'Cartesian Error and the Objectivity of Perception,' in D. D. Grimm, and R. H. Merrill (eds) (1988), *Contents of Thought*, Tucson: University of Arizona Press, pp. 62–98.

Burge, T. (1988b), 'Anti-Individualism and Self-Knowledge,' *Journal of Philosophy* 85: 649–63.

Burge, T. (1989a), 'Wherein is Language Social?' in A. George (ed.) (1989), *Reflections on Chomsky*, Oxford: Basil Blackwell, pp. 175–91.

Burge, T. (1989b), 'Causation and Individuation in Psychology,' *Pacific Philosophical Quarterly* 70: 303–22.

Burge, T. (1991), 'Vision and Intentional Content,' in E. Lepore and R. van Gulick (eds) (1991), *John Searle and his Critics*, Oxford: Blackwell, pp. 195–214.

Burge, T. (1992), 'Philosophy of Language and Mind: 1950–1990,' *The Philosophical Review* 101: 3–51.

Burge, T. (1995), 'Our Entitlement to Self-Knowledge,' *Proceedings of the Aristotelian Society*: 1–26.

Bruner, J., J. Goodnow, and G. Austin (1956), *A Study of Thinking*, New York: John Wiley.

Chalmers, D. (1996), *The Conscious Mind: In Search of a Fundamental Theory*, Oxford: Oxford University Press.

Chalmers, D., and F. Jackson (2001), 'Conceptual Analysis and Reductive Explanation,' *The Philosophical Review* 110: 315–61.

Chisholm, R. (1957), *Perceiving*, Ithaca: Cornell University Press.

Chomsky, N. (1957), *Syntactic Structures*, The Hague: Mouton.

Chomsky, N. (1959), review of *Verbal Behaviour* by B. F. Skinner, *Language* 35: 26–58.

Churchland, P. M. (1979), *Scientific Realism and the Plasticity of Mind*, Cambridge: Cambridge University Press.

Davidson, D. (1980), 'Mental Events,' in D. Davidson (1980), *Essays on Actions and Events*, Oxford: Oxford University Press, pp. 207–28.

Davidson, D. (1984), 'First Person Authority,' *Dialectica* 38: 101–10.

Davidson, D. (1987), 'Knowing One's Own Mind,' *Proceedings and Addresses of the American Philosophical Association*: 441–58.

Davidson, D. (2001), *Subjective, Intersubjective, Objective*, Oxford: Oxford University Press.

Davies, M. (1996), 'Externalism and Experience,' in A. Clark, J. Ezquerro, and J. M. Larrazabal (eds) (1996), *Philosophy and Cognitive Science: Categories, Consciousness, and Reasoning*, Dordrecht: Kluwer, pp. 1–33.

Dennett, D. (1969), *Content and Consciousness*, New York: Routledge and Kegan Paul.

Dennett, D. (1971), 'Intentional Systems,' *Journal of Philosophy* 68: 87–106.

Dennett, D. (1987), *The Intentional Stance*, Cambridge: MIT Press.

Dennett. D. (1988), 'Quining Qualia,' in A. Marcel, and E. Bisiach (eds) (1988), *Consciousness in Contemporary Science*, Oxford: Oxford University Press, pp. 42–77.

Dennett, D. (1991), *Consciousness Explained*, Boston: Little, Brown.

Dretske, F. (1981), *Knowledge and the Flow of Information*, Cambridge: MIT Press.

Dretske, F. (1993), 'Conscious Experience,' *Mind* 102: 263–83.

Dretske, F. (1995), *Naturalizing the Mind*, Cambridge: MIT Press.

Dretske, F. (1996), 'Phenomenal Externalism, or If Meanings Ain't in the Head, Where Are Qualia?', in E. Villanueva (ed.) (1996), *Philosophical Issues 7: Perception*, Atascadero: Ridgeview, pp. 143–58.

Earman, J. (1970), 'Who's Afraid of Absolute Space,' *Australasian Journal of Philosophy* 48: 287–319.

Evans, G. (1082), *The Varieties of Reference*, Oxford: Oxford University Press.

Feyerabend, P. (1963), 'Materialism and the Mind-Body Problem,' *Review of Metaphysics* 17: 49–66.

Field, H. (1978), 'Mental Representation,' *Erkenntnis* 13: 9–61.

Fodor, J. (1968), *Psychological Explanation*, New York: Random House.

Fodor, J. (1975), *The Language of Thought*, Cambridge: Harvard University Press.

Fodor, J. (1981), *RePresentations*, Cambridge: MIT Press.

Fodor, J. (1987), *Psychosemantics*, Cambridge: MIT Press.

Fodor, J., and J. Katz (eds) (1964), *The Structure of Language*, Englewood Cliffs: Prentice-Hall.

Gallois, A. (1996), *The World Without, the Mind Within*, Cambridge: Cambridge University Press.

Geach, P. (1957), *Mental Acts*, London: Routledge.

Goodman, N. (1968), *Languages of Art*, Indianapolis: Bobbs-Merrill.

Harman, G. (1973), *Thought*, Princeton: Princeton University Press.

Harman, G. (1990), 'The Intrinsic Quality of Experience,' in J. Tomberlin (ed.) (1990), *Philosophical Perspectives*, vol. 4, Atascadero: Ridgeview Publishing Co, pp. 31–52.

Haugeland J. (1981), 'Analog and Analog,' *Philosophical Topics 12: 213–26.*

Hellman, G., and F. W. Thompson (1977), 'Physicalist Materialism,' *Nous* 11: 309–45.

Hubel, D. H., and T. N. Wiesel (1959), 'Receptive Fields of Single Neurones in the Cat's Striate Cortex,' *Journal of Physiology* 148: 574–91.

Hubel, D. H., and T. N. Wiesel (1962), 'Receptive Fields, Binocular Interaction, and Functional Architecture in the Cat's Visual Cortex,' *Journal of Physiology* (London) 160: 106–54.

Jackson, F. (1982), 'Epiphenomenal Qualia,' *Philosophical Quarterly* 32: 125–36.

Kim, J. (1979), 'Causality, Identity, and Supervenience in the Mind-Body Problem,' *Midwest Studies in Philosophy* 4: 31–50.

Kim J. (1984), 'Epiphenomenal and Supervenient Causation,' *Midwest Studies* 9: 257–70.

Kobes, B. (1996), 'Mental Content and Hot Self-Knowledge,' *Philosophical Topics* 24: 71–99.

Kuhn, T. (1962), *The Structure of Scientific Revolutions*, Chicago: Chicago University Press.

Lettvin, J. Y. (1959), 'What the Frog's Eye Tells the Frog's Brain,' *Proc. Inst. Radio Engrs* 47.

Levine, J. (1993), 'On Leaving Out What It's Like,' in M. Davies, and G. Humphries (eds) (1993), *Consciousness*, Oxford: Blackwell.

Lewis, D. (1966), 'An Argument for the Identity Theory,' *Journal of Philosophy* 63: 17–25.

Lewis, D. (1972), 'Psychophysical and Theoretical Identification,' *Australasian Journal of Philosophy* 50: 249–58.

Lewis, D. (1983), 'Mad Pain and Martian Pain,' in D. Lewis (1983), *Philosophical Papers*. vol. 1, New York: Oxford University Press, pp. 122–32.

Loar, B. (1988), 'Social Content and Psychological Content,' in D. D. Grimm, and R. H. Merrill (eds) (1988), *Contents of Thought*, Tucson: University of Arizona Press, pp. 99–139.

Loar, B. (1997), 'Phenomenal States,' in N. Block, O. Flanagan, and G. Guzeldere (eds) (1997), *The Nature of Consciousness: Philosophical Debates*, Cambridge: MIT Press, pp. 597–616.

Ludlow, P., and N. Martin (eds) (1998), *Externalism and Self-Knowledge*, Stanford: CSLI Publications.

Malcolm, N. (1959), *Dreaming*, London: Routledge and Kegan Paul.

McDowell, J. (1986), 'Singular Thought and the Extent of Inner Space,' in J. McDowell, and P. Pettit (eds) (1986), *Subject, Thought, and Context*, Oxford: Oxford University Press, pp. 137–68.

McDowell, J. (1994), *Mind and World*, Cambridge: Harvard University Press.

McGinn, C. (1991), *The Problem of Consciousness*, Oxford: Blackwell.

Miller, G. (1956), 'The Magic Number 7 Plus or Minus 2: Some Limits on our Capacity for Processing Information,' *Psychological Review* 63: 81–97.

Miller, G., E. Galanter, and K. Pribram (1960), *Plans and the Structure of Behaviour*, New York: Holt, Rinehart and Winston.

Millikan, R. (1984), *Language, Thought, and Other Biological Categories*, Cambridge: MIT Press.

Millikan, R. (1989), 'Biosemantics,' *Journal of Philosophy* 86: 281–97.

Moran, R. (1994), 'Interpretation Theory and the First-Person,' *Philosophical Quarterly* 44: 154–73.

Nagel, T. (1974), 'What is it Like to be a Bat?' *Philosophical Review* 83: 435–50.

Neisser, U. (1963), 'The Multiplicity of Thought,' *British Journal of Psychology* 54: 1–14.

Newell, A., and J. C. Shaw (1958), 'Elements of a Theory of Human Problem-Solving,' *Psychological Review* 65: 151–66.

O'Connor, J. (1969), *Modern Materialism: Readings on Mind-Body Identity*, New York: Harcourt, Brace, and World.

Peacocke, C. (1983), *Sense and Content*, Oxford: Oxford University Press.

Peacocke, C. (1989), 'Perceptual Content,' in J. Almog, J. Perry, and H. Wettstein (eds) (1989), *Themes from Kaplan*, Oxford: Oxford University Press, pp. 297–330.

Peacocke, C. (1992), *A Study of Concepts*, Cambridge: MIT Press.

Place, U. T. (1956), 'Is Consciousness a Brain Process?' *British Journal of Psychology* 47: 44–50.

Posner, M. I. (1963), 'Immediate Memory in Sequential Tasks,' *Psychology Bulletin* 60: 333–49.

Putnam, H. (1975a), 'Brains and Behaviour,' in H. Putnam (1975), *Philosophical Papers*, vol. 2, Cambridge: Cambridge University Press, pp. 325–41.

Putnam, H. (1975b), 'The Nature of Mental States,' in H. Putnam (1975), *Philosophical Papers*, vol. 2, Cambridge: Cambridge University Press, pp. 429–40.

Putnam, H. (1983), *Philosophical Papers*, vol. 3, Cambridge: Cambridge University Press.

Putnam, H. (1988), *Representation and Reality*, Cambridge: MIT Press.

Quine, W. V. O. (1960), *Word and Object*, Cambridge: MIT Press.

Quine, W. V. O. (1966), 'On Mental Entities,' in W. V. O. Quine (1966), *The Ways of Paradox*, New York: Random House, pp. 208–14.

Rey, G. (1992), 'Sensational Sentences,' in M. Davies, and G. Humphries (eds) (1992), *Consciousness: Psychological and Philosophical Essays*, Oxford: Blackwell, pp. 240–57.

Rorty, R. (1965), 'Mind-Body Identity, Privacy, and Categories,' *Review of Metaphysics* 19: 24–54.

Rosenthal, D. (1986), 'Two Concepts of Consciousness,' *Philosophical Studies* 49: 329–59.

Ryle, G. (1949), *The Concept of Mind*, London: Hutchison.

Searle, J. (1980), 'Minds, Brains, and Programs,' *The Behavioural and Brain Sciences* 3: 417–424.

Searle, J. (1983), *Intentionality*, Cambridge: Cambridge University Press.

Searle, J. (1992), *The Rediscovery of Mind*, Cambridge: MIT Press.

Sellars, W. (1963a), *Science, Perception, and Reality*, London: Routledge and Kegan Paul.

Sellars, W. (1963b), 'Some Reflections on Language Games,' in W. Sellars (1963a), *Science, Perception and Reality*, London: Routledge and Kegan Paul, pp. 321–58.

Shoemaker, S. (1982), 'The Inverted Spectrum,' *Journal of Philosophy* 74: 357–81.

Shoemaker, S. (1994), 'Self-Knowledge and "Inner Sense",' *Philosophy and Phenomenological Sense* 54: 249–314.

Shoemaker, S. (1996), *The First-Person Perspective and OtherEssays*, Cambridge: Cambridge University Press.

Shoemaker, S. (2003), 'Functionalism and Qualia', in S. Shoemaker (2003), *Identity, Cause, and Mind*, Oxford: Oxford University Press, pp. 184–205.

Siewart, C. (1998), *The Significance of Consciousness*, Princeton: Princeton University Press.

Smart, J. J. C. (1959),'Sensations and Brain Processes,' *Philosophical Review* 68: 141–56.

Smolensky, P. (1988), 'On the Proper Treatment of Connectionism,' *Journal of Behavioural and Brain Sciences* 11: 1–74.

Sosa, E. (1984), 'Mind-Body Interaction and Supervenient Causation,' *Midwest Studies* 9: 271–82.

Sperling, G. (1960), 'The Information Available in Brief Visual Presentations,' *Psychological Monographs* 24.

Stalnaker, R. (1984), *Inquiry*, Cambridge: MIT Press.

Stalnaker, R. (1989), 'What's in the Head,' *Philosophical Perspectives* 8: 287–316.

Sternberg, S. (1966), 'High-Speed Scanning in Human Memory,' *Science* 153: 652–4.

Stich, S. (1982), 'On the Ascription of Content,' in A. Woodfield (ed.) 1982), *Thought and Object*, London: Oxford University Press, pp. 153–206.

Stich, S. (1983), *From Folk Psychology to Cognitive Science*, Cambridge: MIT Press.

Tye, M. (1990), 'A Representational Theory of Pains and their Phenomenal Character,' in J. Tomberlin (ed.) (1990), *Philosophical Perspectives*, vol. 9, Atascadero: Ridgeview, pp. 223–39.

Tye, M. (1995), *Ten Problems of Consciousness*, Cambridge: MIT Press.

Tymoczko, T. (ed.) (1985), *New Directions in the Philosophy of Mathematics*, Boston: Birkhauser.

White, S. (1982), 'Partial Character and the Language of Thought,' *Pacific Philosophical Quarterly* 63: 347–65.

Wright, C., B. C. Smith, and C. Macdonald (eds), (1998), *Knowing Our Own Minds*.

Philosophy of Mathematics

Jeremy Avigad

1. Introduction

The philosophy of mathematics plays an important role in analytic philosophy, both as a subject of inquiry in its own right, and as an important landmark in the broader philosophical landscape. Mathematical knowledge has long been regarded as a paradigm of human knowledge with truths that are both necessary and certain, so giving an account of mathematical knowledge is an important part of *epistemology*. Mathematical objects like numbers and sets are archetypical examples of abstracta, since we treat such objects in our discourse as though they are independent of time and space; finding a place for such objects in a broader framework of thought is a central task of *ontology*, or *metaphysics*. The rigor and precision of mathematical language depends on the fact that it is based on a limited vocabulary and very structured grammar, and semantic accounts of mathematical discourse often serve as a starting point for the *philosophy of language*. Although mathematical thought has exhibited a strong degree of stability through history, the practice has also evolved over time, and some developments have evoked controversy and debate; clarifying the basic goals of the practice and the methods that are appropriate to it is therefore an important foundational and methodological task, locating the philosophy of mathematics within the broader *philosophy of science*.

In this chapter, I will try to convey a modern philosophical understanding of the subject as it is practiced today. Our contemporary understanding has been shaped by traditional questions and concerns about the nature of mathematics, and Section 2 provides a broad overview of the general array of philosophical positions in place by the turn of the twentieth century. On the other hand, the nineteenth century is generally taken to represent the birth of 'modern' mathematical thought, and many new issues arose with the dramatic conceptual shifts that took place. Sections 3 and 4 summarize some of these developments. Our contemporary philosophical understanding has also been informed by nineteenth- and twentieth-century developments in mathematical logic, which can be viewed as a reflective, mathematical study of the methods of mathematical reasoning itself. Section 5 tries to explain what we have learned from such a study, in philosophical terms. Finally, Sections 6 and 7 try to convey, in broad strokes, some of the central lines of thought in the philosophy of mathematics today.

2. Traditional Questions

Traditionally, the two central questions for the philosophy of mathematics are: What are mathematical objects? How do we (or can we) have knowledge of them? Plato offers the following simple answers: abstract mathematical objects, like triangles and spheres, are *forms*, which have imperfect reflections in this world. Before we are born, our souls have direct interactions with these forms, though we forget most of what we know during the traumatic circumstances of our birth. Recapturing this knowledge is thus a process of recollection, which can be encouraged by the dialectical process. This position is illustrated by Plato's portrayal of Socrates in *Meno*, when Socrates calls over a slave boy and, through a sequence of questions, brings the boy to understand a simple geometric theorem.[1] Socrates leads Meno to the conclusion that since Socrates did not tell the boy the theorem, the boy must have had knowledge of it all along. Although we today may have difficulty with the theory's reliance on otherworldly forms and our soul's prenatal activities, the account does have its advantages: it does justice to the mysterious abstract nature of mathematical objects, and explains why we do not have to appeal to our physical experiences to justify mathematical statements.

In contrast, the Aristotelian account of mathematical knowledge holds that mathematical objects, like triangles and spheres, are *abstractions* from our experiences.[2] That is, from our interactions with various roughly spherical objects, we form the concept of a perfect sphere. Reasoning about spheres in general boils down to reasoning about specific spheres we have encountered, qua their sphericity; that is, we deliberately ignore features like size, weight, and material in the discourse. It is this disciplined behavior that ensures that our conclusions are appropriately general, and even though the spheres we encounter in our experience are not perfect spheres, our conclusions apply insofar as they approximate the latter.

Thus the divide between Plato and Aristotle is an early example of tensions between philosophical theories that give primacy to abstract concepts, and those that give primacy to experience. This has formed the basis for the common distinction between *rationalists* and *empiricists* among the early modern philosophers, the former taking mathematics and 'innate ideas' as the paradigm of knowledge, and the latter basing their accounts of knowledge on the empirical sciences. At times, it can be hard to tell exactly what is at stake. For example, John Locke, as distinctly an empiricist as they come, allows for innate faculties like comparing, compounding, and abstracting, and reflecting on the inner workings of our mind;[3] and he agrees that mathematical knowledge consists of certain knowledge of ideas, although these ideas must ultimately spring from experience.[4] René Descartes, the prototypical rationalist, maintains that mathematics is the paradigm of knowledge, since its truths can be obtained by a clear and unclouded mind reflecting on clear and distinct ideas. At the end of the *Meditations*, he allows that our physical models must have something to do with the world, since God is not a malicious deceiver. But what we have *certain* knowledge of are the mathematical concepts and relationships to each other, in contrast to the approximate knowledge that the world conforms, more or less, to our models.

The distinctions between mathematical and scientific knowledge are expressed in different ways by the early modern philosophers, and such reformulations provide different insights. For example, Gottfried Leibniz distinguished between *necessary* and *contingent* truths: the former, including the truths of mathematics, are true in all possible worlds, and could not be otherwise; the latter, like the facts of scientific discovery, could have been different.[5] Similarly, David Hume distinguished between *relations of ideas* and *matters of fact*. The truths of mathematics are grouped under relations of ideas, 'every affirmation of which is either intuitively or demonstratively certain.' In contrast, any matter of fact could have been otherwise: 'the contrary of every matter of fact is still possible, because it can never imply a contradiction and is conceived by the mind with the same facility and distinctness, as if every so conformable to reality.'[6]

The work of Immanuel Kant went a long way to clarify and defuse some of the differences between rationalist and empiricist stances. For example, Kant helpfully underscored the difference between asserting that a concept arises *from* experience, and asserting that it arises *with* experience.[7] According to Kant, the issue is not whether we are born with a concept of triangle or whether we develop this concept over time. Rather, the relevant fact is that an appropriate *justification* for assertions about triangles need not make reference to experience. Truths that have this character, like the truths of mathematics, Kant called *a priori*. The remaining truths, that is, those we justify by referring to our experiences, he called *a posteriori*.

Kant went on to observe that we can separately distinguish between judgements that depend only on the definition of the concepts involved, and those that don't. In fact, Kant only considered assertions in subject–predicate form; he called a judgement 'A is B' *analytic* when 'the predicate B belongs to the subject A as something that is (covertly) contained in this concept A.'[8] For example, the statement that triangles have three sides relies only on the knowledge of the definition of triangle. This notion of analyticity requires clarification, and we will return to it in Section 4. A judgement that is not analytic he called *synthetic*.

According to Kant, any statement that is analytic is *a priori*; if the truth of a statement rests only on the definition of the concepts involved, then we need not appeal to experience to justify it. Conversely, any statement that is *a posteriori* has to be synthetic. But is there a middle ground, consisting of statements that are *a priori* but synthetic? Kant argued that nontrivial truths of mathematics fall exactly into this category. For example, the justification for the fact that $5 + 7 = 12$ cannot be found in the definition of the concept of '5', or that of '7', or that of '12', or that of '+', or that of '='. But, on the other hand, we don't appeal to experimentation to justify the assertion. Thus, this statement is *a priori* but synthetic.

Given that there are *a priori* synthetic truths, the central question for Kant is to explain how this is possible. Posing the question in this way forms the basis for his transcendental philosophy, which is a form of 'reverse engineering': given that something works, we want to figure out the mechanisms by which it functions. In particular, by reflecting on our mathematical knowledge, Kant aimed to uncover the basic cognitive faculties that made such knowledge possible. Later, followers of Kant faced the challenge of clarifying the line between the analytic and the synthetic, and determining what, concretely, could be classified as *a priori* synthetic.

A common feature of all the views just described is that they take mathematics to deal with abstract objects, whether one takes these to have an independent existence in their own right, or to be abstracted from our experience. An alternative is simply to deny such objects ontological status in the first place, and think of mathematics, instead, as a science governing the use of (relatively concrete) *signs*. The challenge then is to give an account of mathematical knowledge that explains what it is that gives certain manipulations of signs normative force, and also explains the applicability of mathematics to the sciences. Positions that adopt such an approach fall under the rubric of *nominalism*, of which Bishop Berkeley's writings provide an early example.

Though the sketch I have just given is rough, it does provide a sense of the lay of the land. We can take mathematical objects to be independent and abstract, but then we are challenged to account for our knowledge of them; we can take them to be abstractions from experience, but then we have to account for (or deny) the apparent certainty of mathematical truths; or we can take mathematics to be a set of essentially linguistic conventions, in which case we need to explain why their use is worthy of the term 'knowledge.' This vexing trichotomy plagues contemporary thought about mathematics even today.

Thus the philosophy of mathematics lies at a treacherous frontier, where theorizing about the nature of thought, language, and the world must come together. Almost everyone agrees, however, that whatever the nature of mathematical knowledge, mathematical proofs are central to its acquisition. This, at least, poses one useful constraint: any reasonable theory of mathematical knowledge has to square with that fact.

3. Nineteenth-century Developments in Mathematics

Historians of mathematics usually take the nineteenth century to be the birth of the 'modern' style of mathematical thought that is practiced today. Since much of the philosophy of mathematics in the twentieth century was focused on coming to terms with some of the dramatic changes that occurred in the previous century, it will be helpful to survey some of these developments.

One important trend was a gradual increase in abstraction. In particular, modern algebraic concepts began to emerge, and served to unify methods from a number of branches of mathematics. For example, a 'group' is a system of objects with an associative binary operation, an identity element, and inverses. By the middle of the nineteenth century, mathematicians had noticed that a number of important arguments in number theory, geometry, and the theory of equations could be understood as making use of general properties of groups, instances of which were found in these particular domains. So, just as numbers and triangles could be viewed as abstractions from experience, groups could be viewed as abstractions from various number systems and geometric configurations that arose in mathematical practice.

Algebraic reasoning of this sort relies, in part, on a style of reasoning that has come to be called the *axiomatic method*: one characterizes systems, or 'structures,' of interest by their defining properties. Reasoning solely on the basis of these axioms grants the conclusions that one draws full generality, in the sense that any resulting theorems will then hold of any particular system that satisfies the axioms.

Developments in geometry illustrate such an axiomatic point of view. By the middle of the century, it had become clear that one could consistently study systems of points and lines satisfying axioms different from Euclid's. So, instead of viewing geometry as the 'true' science of space, one could take geometry to be the study of properties of various *geometries*, that is, systems of points and lines satisfying various sets of axioms. This view of geometry as nothing more than the study of systems satisfying certain axioms is illustrated by David Hilbert's landmark *Foundations of Geometry*, which begins as follows:

> Definition. Consider three distinct sets of objects. Let the objects of the *first* set be called *points* and be denoted by A, B, C . . . let the objects of the *second* set be called *lines* and be denoted by a, b, c . . . let the objects of the *third* set be called *planes* and be denoted α, β, γ . . . The points, lines, and planes are considered to have certain mutual relations and these relations are denoted by words like '*lie*,' '*between*,' '*congruent*.' The precise and mathematically complete description of these relations follows from the *axioms of geometry*. (Hilbert 1971)

This passage illustrates a modern *structuralist* point of view, in which the objects of mathematical study are taken to be nothing more than elements of structures satisfying various axiomatic requirements.

To support the general study of 'systems' of objects, mathematicians began to develop a language and methods to reason about such systems. Thus, Bernhard Riemann's theory of complex functions, which made use of what we now call Riemann surfaces, led him to the general notion of a *manifold* of points; Richard Dedekind based his development of algebraic number theory on properties of *systems* of objects, and *mappings* between them; and Georg Cantor's work in analysis led him to develop a general theory of infinite *sets*.

These incipient uses of 'set-theoretic' methods came at a cost. At the beginning of the nineteenth century, mathematics was viewed as a science of calculation and construction. For example, existence theorems in Euclid assert that it is possible to construct various geometric objects; in algebra and analysis, one sought algorithms for computing solutions to equations. Now the growing emphasis on abstract characterization of mathematical structures began to draw mathematical practice away from algorithmic concerns. Indeed, thinking about mathematical objects in terms of abstract systems gave rise to the possibility of proving existence statements in the absence of explicit calculations, and such 'conceptual' methods were often *preferred* to explicitly computational ones. One finds, for example, instances of proofs that deliberately suppress algorithmic information in Dedekind's work on algebraic number theory. David Hilbert put such methods to even more striking use in the late 1880s with his famous *Basissatz*, which provided nonconstructive solutions to a broad family of questions of central importance to algebra. What is so striking about Hilbert's work is that he employed the use of mathematical assertions that are computationally false; for example, the fact that in any sequence of polynomials there is an element with minimal degree, even though one may not be able to determine which element it is from an explicit description of the sequence.

More general notions of a *function* or *mapping* arrived hand-in-hand with the more general notions of a *set* (or *system*) of objects. For the eighteenth-century mathematician Leonhard Euler, a 'function' was implicitly assumed to have a certain type of representation (that is, piecewise as a convergent sum of elementary functions). Riemann's work in complex analysis showed that there are other ways of characterizing functions, say, by their algebraic, geometric, or topological properties. Thus a function became viewed as something more abstract, and independent of the various means of description.

The focus on 'arbitrary' sets and mappings (rather than on their means of representation or description) led to a newfound boldness in dealing with infinitary mathematical objects. It is important to note that these new developments were not uniformly welcomed, and there were mathematicians who felt that mathematical practice was in danger of wandering from its proper concerns. These attitudes fed into the 'foundational crisis' of the early twentieth century, and even though such foundational debates have largely subsided, tensions between 'abstract' and 'concrete' views of mathematics remain with us to this day.

4. Nineteenth-century Developments in the Foundations of Mathematics

Work in the foundations of mathematics aims to identify and clarify the subject's fundamental concepts and methods. This task invariably involves presuppositions as to the nature of mathematics, and so foundational work provides a bridge between philosophical reflection and mathematical practice. The nineteenth-century developments we have just discussed, including the cross-fertilization of ideas from different branches of mathematics and the extensions to mathematical terminology and methods, led naturally to reflective and foundational concerns.

Certainly the mathematical developments had bearing on philosophical views. For example, the introduction of infinitary mathematical objects and structures seems to challenge empiricist attempts to account for knowledge in terms of abstractions from experience, since it is not clear how we can have direct experience of the infinite. For another example, recall the Kantian program of accounting for *a priori* synthetic mathematical knowledge in terms of the nature of cognition. In particular, Kant famously (or notoriously) took Euclidean geometry to be a necessary component of our pure intuition of space. But the nineteenth century brought the gradual realization that we can consistently study a range of alternative geometries, and the modern view that mathematicians are free to study any of these systems, leaving the question as to which of these is most appropriate to modeling the physical world to the sciences. Thus the nineteenth century shift towards abstraction seemed to speak against the claim that certain forms of cognition are necessary to mathematical thought.

While raising some new concerns, work in foundations served to allay others. For instance, from its origins in the seventeenth century, mathematicians had been concerned with the foundations of the calculus, with its references to infinitesimal quantities and limiting processes. Berkeley's eighteenth-century critique of calculus, *The Analyst*, laid bare the contradiction inherent in treating infinitesimals as nonzero quantities that are nonetheless smaller than any positive magnitude: 'May we not call them the ghosts of departed quantities?'[10] (Berkeley's goal was not to demean the calculus, but, rather, to buttress the relative rationality of belief in God. In the work, Berkeley mocked apostate scientists 'who strain at a gnat and swallow a camel.')[11] In the nineteenth century, however, work by Bernard Bolzano, Augustin Cauchy, Riemann, Karl Weierstrass, and others showed how one could interpret notions of limit, integral, and derivative in terms of ordinary quantificational statements about the real numbers. This is sometimes referred to today as the *rigorization of analysis*, that is, the reduction of discourse involving infinitesimals to talk of ordinary real numbers.

But what, exactly, is a real number? Towards the end of the nineteenth century, further work (by Weierstrass, Cantor, Dedekind, and others) showed how one could make sense of real numbers in terms of sequences or sets of rational numbers, and it was well known that the rationals could be understood in terms of pairs of natural numbers. But what about the natural numbers? One option is to take these as fundamental, as suggested by Kronecker's oft-quoted remark: 'God created the whole numbers; everything else is the work of man.'[12] Even here, however, some foundational thinkers sought further reduction. For example, Richard Dedekind showed how one could characterize the natural numbers uniquely up to isomorphism (that is, state exactly the properties of a system of objects that make it fit to stand duty as a system of natural numbers); and using his methods for reasoning about systems and mappings, he was able to establish the existence of at least one such system, from the assumption that there exists any infinite set at all.[13]

Dedekind's analysis amounts to a reduction of the natural numbers to an incipient theory of sets and functions. Gottlob Frege aimed for a similar reduction of the natural numbers to an appropriate system of *logic*. Recall that Kant had classified mathematical truths as being *a priori* synthetic. Challenging this, Frege argued that, in fact, the truths of arithmetic should be considered analytic, where now the term 'analytic' was enlarged to include truths that are obtained from definitions of the concepts involved by purely logical reasoning. The claim that substantial portions (or all) of mathematics can be reduced to logic has come to be called *logicism*.

There are two components to any logicist program: identify a system of logic, and show how it can support the relevant mathematics. To be sure, there was no clear and universally accepted definition of 'logic' then, nor is there now. But starting with his *Begriffsschrift* of 1879, Frege began to describe systems of reasoning that, he argued, represent the necessary laws of thought.[14] His achievement was impressive, and his systems include a fairly modern form of higher-order relational and quantificational reasoning. Frege then began to develop the theory of the natural numbers on such a basis.

5. Twentieth-century Developments in Mathematical Logic

Where do we stand? We have considered some of the questions regarding the nature of mathematical objects and our knowledge of them that have, traditionally, been of central concern to the philosophy of mathematics. We have also considered nineteenth-century developments in mathematics that accentuated these issues or cast them in a new light. We have at least hinted at an interplay between philosophical views and methodological issues that had deep and lasting effects on the practice of the subject itself. Finally, we have touched on early foundational and logical developments, representing important attempts to come to terms with these issues.

The study of logic and the foundations of mathematics enjoyed explosive growth after the turn of the twentieth century, and most philosophical theorizing about mathematics since then has been strongly influenced by these developments. The results of this inquiry provide informative clarifications and analyses of notions like proof, truth, and computation, and modern philosophical discussions often rely on these, at least implicitly. Thus, it will be helpful to consider this current logical understanding, before (finally) describing some twentieth-century philosophical views in the next section.

To begin with, developments in the early twentieth century led to the recognition that one can distinguish between two informal notions of 'logical consequence,' based on a corresponding distinction between *syntactic* and *semantic* aspects of mathematical language. Roughly, the syntax of a language consists of the formal grammatical rules that govern the construction of terms and assertions; a semantics is an account of what these syntactic elements mean. The fact that 'Between any two elements, there is another element' is a grammatically correct assertion and is a syntactic one; the fact that this assertion is true when interpreted as a statement about real numbers or points on a line, but false when interpreted as a statement about whole numbers, is a semantic one.

Now we can identify a syntactic notion of logical consequence: an assertion is a deductive consequence of some assumptions if it can be established by a sequence of steps, each representing a permitted inference according to the rules governing the appropriate use of logical connectives, that is, terms like 'and,' 'if . . . then,' 'every,' and 'some.' The early twentieth century saw the identification and analysis of such logical frameworks, in the form of formal axiomatic bases for logical reasoning.

There is also a semantic notion of logical consequence: a statement is a semantic consequence of some hypotheses if, no matter how the nonlogical terms are interpreted, whenever the hypotheses are true under the interpretation, so is the conclusion. For example, the conclusion 'Every X is a Z' is a logical consequence of the assumptions 'Every X is a Y' and 'Every Y is a Z,' since no matter how we interpret X, Y, and Z, if the hypotheses are true, so is the conclusion. Developing a mathematical theory of semantic consequence required not just an analysis of mathematical language, but also a notion of 'true under an interpretation.' Alfred Tarski's theory of 'truth in a model' provides us with just that.

For first-order logic, Kurt Gödel's *completeness theorem* of 1929 shows that these two notions coincide: a statement is a deductive consequence of some hypotheses just in case it is a semantic consequence of these hypotheses. In contrast, second-order logic extends first-order logic with variables ranging over predicates and relations, and it is a consequence of Gödel's *incompleteness theorem* that there is *no* sound, effective deductive system for second-order logic that is complete for the standard semantics, in which variables are taken to range over all predicates on the first-order domain.

(Here, the term 'effective' denotes the reasonable requirement that the axioms and rules be expressed in such a way that there is an algorithmic procedure to determine whether a given text constitutes a valid proof.) Some take this to be an argument against considering second-order (and higher-order) logic to be properly called 'logic.' (See the discussion of this in Section 6.)

With a notion of deductive consequence in hand, one can take a mathematical theory to be the set of deductive logical consequences of a set of axioms describing a particular mathematical domain. The question naturally arises as to where to draw the line between logic and mathematics. For example, recall that Frege aimed to show that the truths of arithmetic could be reduced to logical truths, with the term 'logic' suitably construed. In 1902, however, Bertrand Russell observed that Frege's logical system was inconsistent. Roughly speaking, Russell's paradox is that if one is allowed to form the set S of all sets that are not members of themselves, then S is a member of itself if and only if it isn't, yielding a contradiction. (More precisely, Frege's logical framework allowed one to consider the concept of being the extension of a concept which does not hold of its own extension, but the net effect is the same.) Henri Poincaré, Russell, and others diagnosed the problem as lying in the *impredicativity* of the definitions; for example, Russell's definition of the set S involves a variable ranging over the collection of all sets, of which S itself is a member. Russell responded to the problem by introducing a 'ramified' theory of types, which bars this type of circularity by stratifying the language so that a definition can only quantify over concepts whose definitions are logically prior. Such a system was to form the basis of Russell and Alfred North Whitehead's *Principia Mathematica*, in which portions of mathematics were developed on that basis. The system's ramification, however, made it impossible to handle a number of ordinary mathematical developments, leading Russell to add an additional 'axiom of reducibility.' This addition drew criticism, since it is hard to justify its status as a 'logical' axiom.

Within a few years, Leon Chwistek and Frank Plumpton Ramsey had argued that, on a logicist conception, one could justifiably dispense with Russell's ramification.[15] Indeed, formal axiomatic frameworks for 'simple type theory,' developed by Rudolf Carnap, Kurt Gödel, and Alonzo Church, provide a more workable framework for mathematics while still avoiding the obvious paradoxes. Another axiomatic framework, Zermelo-Fraenkel set theory, was given its modern formulation as a theory based on first-order logic, and was shown to provide a remarkably robust foundation for mathematics.

In 1931, Gödel proved his famous *incompleteness theorems*. The first incompleteness theorem states that no effective deductive system for mathematics strong enough to prove some basic facts about the natural numbers can be complete; in other words, assuming the system is consistent, there will be statements that are neither provable nor refutable in the system. The second incompleteness theorem shows that no such system can prove its own consistency; *a fortiori*, it is not possible to demonstrate the consistency of a formal system using any weaker fragment. The second incompleteness theorem dealt a serious blow to Hilbert's program, which will be discussed in the next section.

The 1930s gave rise to the modern theory of computability. We have already discussed nineteenth-century shifts from algorithmic to set-theoretic reasoning, and the expanded notion of a function that came with it. With the new methods that had been introduced, set-theoretic language and methodology could be brought to bear on the characterization of functions, without a direct computational interpretation. A precise definition of what it means for a function, say, from natural numbers to natural numbers to be *computable* was required, however, before one could give explicit examples of functions that are not computable. This was provided by models of computability given by Alan Turing, Church, Jacques Herbrand, Gödel, and Emile Post. Even though the definitions they provided were, on the surface, quite different, it was soon shown that the definitions agree as to which functions are computable. This, combined with a conceptual analysis of the notion of computability given by Turing, has given weight to the *Church-Turing thesis*, namely, that these definitions in fact capture the informal notion of 'computability.' With this analysis, Turing was able to show that there are specific classes of mathematical problems that do not possess algorithmic solutions. The halting problem – that is, the question as to whether a given algorithm ultimately comes to a final state when presented with a given input – is one such class of problems.

In 1963, Paul Cohen, building on work by Gödel, showed that the 'axiom of choice' and Cantor's 'continuum hypothesis' are independent of the Zermelo-Fraenkel axioms of set theory. In other words, these two fundamental assertions about sets cannot be derived or refuted from the conception of set given by the Zermelo-Fraenkel axioms. These provide two striking and important instances of the first incompleteness theorem.

Thus early twentieth-century research helped clarify mathematical language, the rules of mathematical inference, fundamental mathematical assumptions, and the notion of computability; as well as the limits of formal provability, computability, and definability.

6. Early Twentieth-century Philosophical Views

The advances in mathematical logic just described developed in tandem with inquiry into the nature of mathematics, and we are finally in a position to consider some of the philosophical stances that emerged. Recall that Russell and Whitehead, with the *Principia*, aimed to revive Frege's logicist project. The common view today is that logicism has failed, since the various foundations that have been proposed for mathematics seem to rely on axioms that do not have a purely 'logical' character, like the assertion that there is an infinite set. W. V. O. Quine was further critical of viewing higher-order reasoning itself as properly 'logical' reasoning, arguing that since it is a mistake to admit predicates as logical objects, higher-order logic is really 'set theory in sheep's clothing' (Quine 1970: 66). Thus a general picture emerges in which one views mathematics as consisting of the logical consequences of appropriate mathematical axioms. This has the effect of distinguishing the foundations of mathematics from the foundations of logic; the philosophy of mathematics can then focus on the status of mathematical objects and axioms, consigning the task of accounting for logic and its normative status to a separate office.

In the 1910s, the mathematician L. E. J. Brouwer spearheaded a new movement in mathematics known as *intuitionism*. This movement had both philosophical and methodological components. On the philosophical side, Brouwer gave a somewhat solipsistic account of mathematical knowledge in terms of intuitive constructions; roughly, our assertion that a mathematical statement is true is tantamount to the assertion that we have effected a mental construction that allows us to recognize that this is the case. Basic properties of the natural numbers, say, were to be rooted in our intuitions of time. Logical connectives, however, were also given interpretations in terms of intuitive constructions; for example, an assertion that '*A* or *B*' is true is understood to mean that either we have a construction that enables us to see that *A* is true, or we have a construction that enables us to see that *B* is true (and we know which is the case). Asserting the truth of an implication '*A* implies *B*' amounts to asserting that we are in possession of a construction that transforms sufficient evidence that *A* is true into sufficient evidence that *B* is true. These views have strong implications for the practice of mathematics; for example, on this view, the assertion '*A* or not *A*' is not justified until we know which is the case. Thus Brouwer rejected *tertium non datur*, or the law of the excluded middle, as a generally valid principle of reasoning. This placed serious restrictions on the type of mathematics that one could practice, and, in particular, ruled out the kind of nonconstructive arguments discussed in Section 3. On the other hand, as noted by many logicians over the next two decades, the Brouwerian principles of reasoning could be given a direct computational interpretation. As a result, intuitionistic philosophy was closely allied with a 'constructive,' or algorithmic mathematical orientation.

In light of Russell's paradoxes and similar concerns, some felt a philosophical retrenchment, like Brouwer's, was called for. But although he was sensitive to questions of consistency, Hilbert felt that rejecting modern set-theoretic methods was tantamount to throwing out the baby with the bathwater, and he strongly resisted any restrictions on these newfound mathematical freedoms. In 1922, he launched his program of *Beweistheorie*, or *Proof Theory*, which was to 'settle the question of foundations once and for all.' Hilbert's program involved (1) representing modern mathematical reasoning using formal axiomatic systems, and then (2) proving that these systems are consistent (that is, will never yield a contradiction) using only incontrovertible, 'finitary' methods. This would guarantee, in particular, that every concrete (and, in fact, universal) assertion proved using the new methods is in fact true; thus from one point of view one could interpret references to infinite sets and structures as 'ideal' instruments to facilitate the derivation of finitary, concrete results.

The term 'formalism' is usually associated with the claim that consistency of a formal system alone is sufficient to justify the use of the associated mathematical methods. It is easy to criticize such a view, as did Brouwer: taking the viewpoint to the extreme, mathematics becomes nothing more than a game of manipulating symbols, with nothing to distinguish any one consistent symbol game from another. As a criticism of Hilbert's program, this is partially unfair. Hilbert's program did not commit him to the strong claim that mathematical assertions can have *no* meaning beyond the strict formalist reading above; rather, only the claim that having a finitary guarantee of consistency provides a certain degree of justification. But, of course, we can reasonably expect the philosophy of mathematics to tell us why certain mathematical practices are better than others, and so it is clear that formalism does not tell the whole story.

By the late 1920s, the divisive and often bitter debates over the justification and methodology of mathematics led to what has been called the 'crisis of foundations,' with formalism, intuitionism, and (to a lesser extent) logicism taken to be the central positions. None of these seemed capable of shouldering the burden on its own. Logic in and of itself did not seem sufficient to account for mathematical practice. Appealing to intuition as the final arbiter of mathematical knowledge made it hard to account for the objectivity of mathematical knowledge, and most mathematicians found Brouwer's intuitionistic practice too constraining. Finally, formalism, while offering some insight into the notion of objectivity and rigor, failed to explain how the conventions of mathematics obtain their normative force. Once again, the problem boils down to that of giving a unified account of language, thought, and knowledge of objective mathematical facts.

One might hope to make progress by fitting an account of mathematics into a broader theory of scientific practice. The *logical empiricist* (or *logical positivist*) movement, for example, aimed to divide scientific knowledge into *analytic* and *synthetic* components. Roughly, the analytic component was to consist of those truths whose justification rests on commonly accepted conventions of scientific practice. This notion of analyticity was borrowed from Ludwig Wittgenstein, who used it to characterize logical tautologies as truths that simply reflect the proper use of language.[16] Logical empiricists extended the notion, however, to include mathematics, as well as scientific definitions and conventions. Viewing mathematics as a product of linguistic convention renders it, in a sense, epistemologically empty. Logical empiricists therefore took the nontrivial part of scientific knowledge to be contained in the synthetic component, which consists of assertions whose justification requires some form of appeal to empirical observation.

In his famous attack, 'Two Dogmas of Empiricism,' Quine rejected the possibility of drawing a sharp distinction between the analytic and synthetic components.[17] Instead, he offered a form of empiricism in which the status of any particular claim has to be judged in the context of the entire theory, a position known as *holism*. On this view, mathematics loses much of its privileged status as *a priori*, necessary knowledge. Fundamental mathematical assertions are statements whose truth we assent to and may be very reluctant to give up, but like any other aspect of our scientific theorizing, may ultimately be revised to accommodate experience and theoretical developments in the future.

Quine also rejected any attempts to justify science on 'first principles,' that is, prior metaphysical preconceptions. Instead, he saw the philosopher as working within the framework of contemporary scientific knowledge, engaged in a task of methodological hygiene. That is, the philosopher's task is to survey contemporary science and tidy up the language and conceptual underpinnings. Quine saw this view as a refinement of a *naturalist* philosophy found in nineteenth-century writings of J. S. Mill. Quine's landmark work, *Word and Object*, opens with a quote from a more recent essay by Otto Neurath, in which the philosopher's task is compared to that of a shipbuilder forced to repair a ship at sea, gradually replacing and reshaping old beams rather than starting afresh (Quine 1960).

As far as mathematics is concerned, on Quine's view, we should grant ontological status to those mathematical objects that are needed to make sense of the best scientific theories we have today. As Hilary Putnam colorfully put it, it would be strange to accept the law of universal gravitation, which asserts that the ratio of the force exerted by one object upon another is proportional to the ratio of the product of their masses and the square of the distance between them, without believing in the existence of 'ratios' (Putnam 1971). Thus mathematical ontological claims are justified by, and only by, their *indispensability* to the sciences, modulo some allowances for abstractions that serve to round out the theory and support more general empirical values of economy and simplicity.

7. The Philosophy of Mathematics Today

To the present day, there have been ongoing attempts to adapt and strengthen early twentieth-century attempts to ground mathematical knowledge. For example, the 'Neo-Fregean' program, developed by Crispin Wright and Bob Hale out of a proposal by George Boolos, is a modern form of logicism. First, neo-Fregeans replace the axiom of infinity by a 'number of' operator and a formal axiom, 'Hume's principle.' The latter asserts that for any predicate, S, the notion 'the number of S' has an expected behavior. Next, they show that against the backdrop of second-order logic, Hume's principle suffices to derive the axiom of infinity, and hence a substantial portion of ordinary mathematics. On appeal to linguistic considerations, they argue that Hume's principle (as well as second-order logic) can be considered analytic. The analyticity of the relevant portion of mathematics then follows.

Others have pursued different metaphysical strategies. Philosophers like Hartry Field have presented nominalistic, or 'irrealist,' accounts of mathematical objects, which aim to explain away references to abstract objects via various reinterpretations of mathematical language. Following a suggestion by Putnam, Geoffrey Hellmann has instead tried to account for a portion of mathematical reasoning in terms of an ontology of possible worlds.

A number of philosophers have used logical analyses to help clarify ontological and epistemological stances. For example, William Tait has tried to characterize the notion of finitism implicit in Hilbert's work; Solomon Feferman has clarified the reach of a predicative mathematical ontology, which does not presuppose the totality of all subsets of an infinite set; Wilfried Sieg has clarified the assumptions needed to support the Church-Turing analysis of computability; and Michael Detelfsen has explored the philosophical presuppositions behind Hilbert's program.

The latter half of the twentieth century brought alternative attempts to ground mathematical knowledge in historical terms. Philosophers like Imre Lakatos and Philip Kitcher argued that the appropriate justification for mathematical axioms and methods of proof is that they are the result of a rational historical process of mathematical invention and discovery. This shifts the philosophical burden to the task of developing a theory of rationality. Many are uncomfortable with such an approach, since, for one thing, it relativises mathematical knowledge to particular historical contexts. Furthermore, it seems to make mathematical knowledge *contingent* on haphazard historical developments, since it is conceivable that other 'rational' processes could have brought us to accept different axioms and methods. At issue is not so much the question as to whether this is in fact the case, but, rather, whether the types of philosophical explanation we seek should be cast in terms of such historical contingencies. Some have gone further to suggest that a proper account of mathematical knowledge should take even more into consideration, such as biological, social, political, and institutional factors.

In recent years there have also been efforts to expand, modify, or clarify the Quinean naturalistic framework. Recall that on the Quinean view, the acceptance of basic mathematical assumptions is justified, holistically, by their role in the physical sciences; on that view, parts of mathematics that are not currently required by these sciences are as yet unjustified. Penelope Maddy has recently proposed a variant of this view which she calls *mathematical naturalism*. Once one accepts that mathematics, *as a whole*, is useful to the sciences, she argues, one should evaluate mathematical developments by the internal standards of the community. For example, one may appeal to internal measures of simplicity and generality that may not always line up exactly with broader scientific values, but have proved to be useful for the development of mathematical practice. Thus, in a sense, mathematicians can enjoy a collective bargaining agreement with respect to the broader scientific community.

Attention to the actual practice of mathematics has raised additional philosophical issues. In a foundational essay first published in 1888, Dedekind observed that the question of *what* natural numbers like 2 and 17 are is largely unimportant to mathematics (Dedekind 1888). What is important is that one is dealing with a structure equipped with a starting element, 0, and an injective function, which, given any number, returns its 'successor', so long as the resulting structure satisfies the principle of induction. Furthermore, Dedekind showed that any two structures meeting these criteria are *isomorphic*, so that references to one can be translated to references to the other without any further effects to the theory. This simple observation was revived by Paul Benacerraf in an essay 'What Numbers Could Not Be': Benacerraf tells a parable of two children who seem to have the same understanding of the natural numbers, but are shocked to find, one day, that their set-theoretic definitions of the natural numbers turn out to be different.[18] The point, again, is that the particular choice of definition is irrelevant; what is important is only the structural properties. Such an emphasis on structures has played a central role in twentieth-century mathematics, supported by early algebraic work of Hilbert, Emmy Noether, and others, and the associated body of tools, viewpoints, and methods is usually gathered under the banner of 'structuralism.'

From a foundational point of view, this suggests that one should aim for a characterization of mathematical practice that explains the independence just described. *Category theory* provides just such an account, analyzing mathematical language in terms of talk of structures and mappings between them, without concern for the nature of the particular elements of those structures. Philosophers like Steve

Awodey and Colin McLarty have tried to spell out this philosophical understanding of mathematics. Stewart Shapiro, Michael Resnik, and Charles Parsons have, instead, explored the possibility of using structuralist ideas to fashion a metaphysics for mathematics, in which basic mathematical objects are understood as nothing more than 'places' in structures. There have been ongoing efforts to dissolve the knotty problems that come up when one tries to fill in the details.

Some of the most interesting work in recent years has been the result of a retreat from the 'big' questions of ontology and metaphysics, in favour of analyses of more particular, local features of mathematical practice. Some have tried to make sense of the way we carry out diagrammatic reasoning, which is not well characterized by deductive formalisms. Standard formalizations of geometry do not seem to explain how it is we *understand* an argument that makes reference to diagrams, or why it is that such diagrams can confer a *better* understanding than a purely textual proof. Marcus Giaquinto has therefore tried to find a place for *visualization* in the epistemology of mathematics. Other inquiries have tried to explain features of mathematics that become salient when one considers the subject's history. For example, a recent collection of essays tries to make sense of the historical classification of mathematical arguments as 'analytic' or 'synthetic,' terms that one finds already in the fourth-century writings of Pappus.

Others have tried to make sense of various value judgements that are found in informal mathematical discourse. We have discussed nineteenth-century emphases on 'conceptual' over algorithmic reasoning, and the phrase 'conceptual' is often used today as a term of accolade. Philosophers like Ken Manders and Jamie Tappenden have begun to try to understand these judgements. Aristotle distinguished between scientific demonstrations that show that something is true, and those that explain *why* something is true, and a good deal of work in the philosophy of science aims to provide accounts of scientific explanation. Philosophers like Mark Steiner and Paolo Mancosu have begun to develop theories of mathematical explanation along similar lines. Branches of mathematics that are designed for scientific applications tend to have features that are distinct from their 'purer' cousins; philosophers like Mark Wilson have attempted to understand some of these features.

Such approaches have a number of common features. First, they explore issues that seem to have foundational, epistemological, or methodological interest, but extend beyond the narrow confines of a theory of truth and justification. Second, they support the view that one must pay attention to both modern and historical mathematical practice to get a sense of the issues involved, even if one's ultimate goal is a general theory that is independent of historical terms. Finally, they share a 'bottom up' approach to the philosophy of mathematics, which focuses on specific case studies and more restricted questions, in the hopes that over time a more global and unified theory will emerge. Such approaches do not represent so much a retreat from the traditional questions as the belief that such questions can best be answered in the context of a more robust theory of mathematical understanding.

Notes

1. *Meno*, 82–7. Translation by G. M. A. Grube in Cahn 1999, pp. 9–12.
2. *Metaphysics*, Book M, 1077b-1078b. Translation by Julia Annas (1976), *Aristotle's Metaphysics: M and N*. Oxford: Clarendon Press.
3. *Essay Concerning Human Understanding*, Book II, Chap. XI. Excerpts in Cahn 1999, pp. 600–68.
4. Ibid., Book IV, Chap. IV, para. 6.
5. *Discourse on Metaphysics*, para. 13. Translation by Roger Ariew and Daniel Garber in Cahn 2002, pp. 569–89.
6. *An Enquiry Concerning Human Understanding*, Section IV, Part I. Excerpts in Cahn 2002, pp. 734–802.
7. *Critique of Pure Reason*, B1. Translation by Werner S. Pluhar in Cahn 1999, pp. 878–953.
8. This quote and the views that follow can be found in *Critique of Pure Reason*, B10–B21.
9. For example, *Principles of Human Knowledge*, secs 121–2. These sections are among those excerpted in Ewald 1996, pp. 21–37.
10. Berkeley, George (1734), *The Analyst*, sec. 35. Reprinted in Ewald 1996, pp. 80–1.
11. Ibid, sec. 34.
12. See the footnote on p. 942 of Ewald 1996 for the sources that attribute this quote to Kronecker.
13. Dedekind, R. (1888), *Was sind und was sollen die Zahlen*. Vieweg: Braunschweig. Translation by W. W. Beman in Ewald 1996, pp. 790–833.
14. Frege, G. (1879), 'Begriffschrift, eine der arithmetischen nachgebildete Formelsprache des reinen Denkens,' Halle: Nebert. Translation by Stefan Bauer-Mengelberg in van Heijenoort 1967, pp. 1–82.
15. See Ramsey, F. P. (1925), 'Remarks on the Foundations of Mathematics,' *Proceedings of the London Mathematical Society* 25: 338–84. Reprinted in Ramsey 1931, pp. 1–61.
16. Wittgenstein 1922.
17. Quine, W. V. O. (1951), 'Two Dogmas of Empiricism,' *Philosophical Review* 60: 20–43.
18. Benacerraf, P. (1965), 'What Numbers Could Not Be,' *Philosophical Review* 74: 47–73. Reprinted in Benacerraf and Putnam 1983, pp. 272–94.

References

This survey is not comprehensive, and a number of important topics have been omitted. The References below should help provide a starting point for further inquiry.

Aspray, W., and P. Kitcher (eds) (1988), *History and Philosophy of Modern Mathematics*, Minneapolis: University of Minnesota.
Avigad, J. (forthcoming), 'Mathematical Method and Proof,' to appear in *Synthese*.
Awodey, S. (1996), 'Structure in Mathematics and Logic: A Categorical Perspective.' *Philosophia Mathematica* 4: 209–37.
Beaney, M. (ed.) (1997), *The Frege Reader*, Malden: Blackwell.
Benacerraf, P., and H. Putnam (eds) (1983), *Philosophy of Mathematics: Selected Readings*, 2nd edn, Cambridge: Cambridge University Press.
Burgess, J., and G. Rosen (1997), *A Subject with No Object: Strategies for Nominalistic Interpretation of Mathematics*, Oxford: Oxford University Press.

Cahn, S. M. (2002), *Classics of Western Philosophy*, Sixth edn, Indianapolis: Hackett.

Detlefsen, M. (1986), *Hilbert's Program: An Essay on Mathematical Instrumentalism*, Dordrecht: Kluwer.

Ewald, W. (ed.) (1996), *From Kant to Hilbert: A Source Book in the Foundations of Mathematics*, Oxford: Oxford University Press.

Feferman, S. (1998), *In the Light of Logic*, New York: Oxford University Press.

Giaquinto, M. (2002), *The Search for Certainty: A Philosophical Account of Foundations of Mathematics*, Oxford: Oxford University Press.

Grosholz, E., and H. Breger (eds) (2000), *The Growth of Mathematical Knowledge*, Dordrecht: Kluwer.

Haaparanta, L. (forthcoming), *The History of Modern Logic*, Oxford: Oxford University Press.

Hale, B., and C. Wright (2001), *The Reason's Proper Study: Essays towards a Neo-Fregean Philosophy of Mathematics*, Oxford: Oxford University Press.

Hart, W. D. (ed.) (1997), *The Philosophy of Mathematics*, Oxford: Oxford University Press.

Hellman, G. (1989), *Mathematics without Numbers*, Oxford: Oxford University Press. Maddy, P. (1997), *Naturalism in Mathematics*, Oxford: Oxford University Press.

Hilbert, D. [1899] (1971), *Foundations of Geometry*, trans. L. Unger, La Salle: Open Court.

Jacquette, D. (ed.) (2002), *Philosophy of Mathematics: An Anthology*, Malden: Blackwell.

Kitcher, P. (1984), *The Nature of Mathematical Knowledge*, Oxford: Oxford University Press.

Lakatos, I. (1976), *Proofs and Refutations*, Cambridge: Cambridge University Press.

Mancosu, P. (1998), *From Brouwer to Hilbert: The Debate on the Foundations of Mathematics in the 1920's*, Oxford: Oxford University Press.

Mancosu, P., J. Jorgensen, and S. Pedersen (eds) (2005), *Visualization, Explanation and Reasoning Styles in Mathematics*, Berlin: Springer Verlag.

McClarty, C. (1993), 'Numbers Can Be Just What They Have To,' *Noûs* 47: 487–98.

Otte, M., and M. Panza (eds) (1997), *Analysis and Synthesis in Mathematics: History and Philosophy*, Dordrecht: Kluwer.

Parsons, C. (1990), 'The Structuralist View of Mathematical Objects,' *Synthèse* 84: 303–46.

Putnam, H. (1971), *Philosophy of Logic*, New York: Harper and Row.

Quine, W. V. O. (1951), 'Two Dogmas of Empiricism,' *Philosophical Review* 60: 20–43.

Quine, W. V. O. (1960), *Word and Object*, Cambridge: MIT Press.

Quine, W. V. O. (1970), *The Philosophy of Logic*, 2nd edn, Englewood Cliffs: Prentice-Hall.

Quine. W. V. O. (1995), *From Stimulus to Science*, Cambridge: Harvard University Press.

Ramsey, F. P. (1931), *The Foundations of Mathematics and Other Logical Essays*, ed. by R. B. Braithwaite, London: Dover Publications/Routledge & Kegan Paul.

Resnik, M. (1997), *Mathematics as a Science of Patterns*, Oxford: Oxford University Press.

Russell, B. [1919] (1993), *Introduction to Mathematical Philosophy*, Minneola: Dover Publications.

Schirm, M. (ed.) (2003), *The Philosophy of Mathematics Today*, Oxford: Oxford University Press.

Shapiro, S. (1997), *Philosophy of Mathematics: Structure and Ontology*, New York: Oxford University Press.

Shapiro, S. (2000), *Thinking about Mathematics*, Oxford: Oxford University Press.

Shapiro, S. (ed.) (2005), *The Oxford Handbook of Philosophy of Mathematics and Logic*, Oxford: Oxford University Press.

Sieg, W. (1994), 'Mechanical Procedures and Mathematical Experience,' in A. George (ed.) (1994), *Mathematics and Mind*, Oxford: Oxford University Press.

Steiner, M. (1978), 'Mathematical Explanation,' *Philosophical Studies* 34: 133–51.

Tait, W. (1981), 'Finitism,' *Journal of Philosophy*, 78: 524–46.

Tymoczko, T. (ed.) (1998), *New Directions in the Philosophy of Mathematics: An Anthology*, revd edn, Princeton: Princeton University Press.

van Heijenoort, J. (ed.) (1967), *Frege to Gödel: A Source Book in Mathematical Logic, 1879–1931*, Cambridge: Harvard University Press.

Whitehead, A. N., and B, Russell, [1910–13] (1925–7), *Principia Mathematica*, 3 vols, Cambridge: Cambridge University Press.

Wittgenstein, L. (1922), *Tractatus Logico-Philosophicus*, trans. C. K. Ogden, London: Routledge and Kegan Paul.

Wittgenstein, L. (1983), *Remarks on the Foundations of Mathematics*, revd edn, Cambridge: MIT Press.

Philosophy of Logic

Mathieu Marion

Logic originates with Aristotle and the Megaric-Stoic school in Ancient Greece but, while the logic of terms or syllogistic has acquired many accretions since, there was no real progress until the nineteenth century, when it was replaced by 'modern' or formal logic at the hand of mathematicians such as Boole, Schröder, Frege, and Peano. The developments that this revolution sparked throughout the last century cannot be encompassed in this chapter and only some central threads will be sketched.

Although it has sometimes been described since Frege as the pursuit of truth (Quine 1982: 1), logic is in fact the study of deductively valid inferences, that is, of arguments where the conclusion follows from the premises in such a way that it is impossible that the premises are true while the conclusion is false. In contrast to deductively valid inferences, some inferences are inductively valid if the premises make it likely, to a given degree, that the conclusion is true. Probabilistic induction and systems of inductive logic have been studied extensively in the twentieth century largely as a field of philosophy of science.

Deductive logic is thus concerned with what follows from a given body of propositions, that is, with consequence or entailment. Using the turnstile to express (proof-theoretic) validity, one can symbolise the fact that a conclusion A 'follows from' the body of premises Γ thus:

$$\Gamma \vdash A$$

Such claims are known as 'consecutions' and logic deals with the relation of consecution or consequence. Roughly, a logical system is formed by a formal language (with symbols for variables and constants, including the logical ones, punctuation marks, and rules for well-formed formulas), a consequence relation, and a rule for schematic substitution. It is desirable that one be here in possession of an algorithm that determines for any consecution $\Gamma \vdash A$ in a given language if it is valid or not (decidability). Another such property is 'consistency,' that is the impossibility for any A of a derivation of the contradiction $A \& \neg A$. The reason for this is very simple: if one has both $\neg A$ and A, then in a few steps one can deduce any sentence B, such as 'the moon is made of green cheese'. In other words, one wishes to avoid that $A, \neg A \vdash B$. Indeed, if $A \& \neg A$, then A and, if A, then $A \lor B$. On the other hand, if $A \& \neg A$, then $\neg A$. Now, if one has both $A \lor B$ and $\neg A$, then, by an application of a rule known as the disjunctive syllogism ($A \lor B, \neg A \vdash B$), one has B.

The importance of the conditional 'if A then B' or $A \rightarrow B$ for logic can be seen from a key result, the deduction theorem:

$$\Gamma, A \vdash B \text{ if and only if } \Gamma \vdash A \rightarrow B$$

This theorem states that, if Γ taken together with A entail B, then Γ entails the conditional $A \rightarrow B$ and, conversely, that, if Γ entails $A \rightarrow B$, then one can deduce B from Γ and A. It also indicates that, if the mode of combination of premises (symbolised here by the comma) changes, then the conditional will change. One can thus devise various systems of logic by tinkering with the mode of combination of premises. When properly tailored, logic is thus a powerful tool for the study of reasoning, whether legal or mathematical, defeasible or relevant, about arbitrary objects or involving vague concepts, and so on. So, while 'mathematical logic' is concerned primarily with reasoning in mathematics, a 'philosophical logic' grew in parallel as the study of logical systems (such as the various systems of modal, relevant, or paraconsistent logics) of interest for the study of other forms of reasoning (Gabbay, and Guenthner 2001).

In opposition to 'formal logic' understood as the study of the formal aspects of reasoning, the expression 'philosophical logic' has also been used to designate the study of the notions that are indispensable to reasoning: proposition, reference, predication, identity, existence, truth, necessity, entailment, and so on (Sainsbury 1995). One should, however, turn to the philosophy of language for a study of most of these items. Here, only the last three will be touched upon. While philosophy of mathematics deals with issues concerning the application of 'mathematical' logic to the study of the foundations of mathematics, an early impetus in the development of formal logic, philosophy of logic consists in the examination of systems of logic and the discussion of numerous questions that arise naturally within that context, such as: what is it which is preserved by logical consequence? Typically, a 'realist' will argue that logical consequence preserves truth, while an 'anti-realist' such as Dummett or Brandom will argue that it preserves warrant to assert (Dummett 1991; Brandom 1994). One may ask further about the nature of this preservation: is it in all cases (modal), in virtue of the meaning of the terms involved (analytic), in virtue of the logical structure of the premises and conclusion (formal)? The views will be explained below.

Various types of deductive systems were devised throughout the century (see Sundholm 2001 for details.) A particular system of first-order logic was first developed by Frege in his *Begriffsschrift* (van Heijenoort 1967: 1–82) and refined later by the likes of Russell and Hilbert (Whitehead, and Russell 1927; Hilbert, and Ackermann 1950), which corresponds to what is now known as 'classical' propositional calculus and, with the quantifiers, classical predicate calculus; it is these systems that are usually taught in introductory logic courses. (The expression 'first-order' refers to the fact that the universal and existential quantifiers take as values only individuals and when they also range over functions (classes, properties), one has a 'second-order' logic.)

Frege-style systems were devised in analogy with axiomatic systems in mathematics, their central notion is that of derivability or theoremhood and they usually have a few formulas as axioms, while Modus Ponens is often taken as the only rule of inference:

$$A, A{\rightarrow}B \vdash B$$

It says that if A and $A{\rightarrow}B$ are theorems, so is B. Alternative, 'non-classical' logics, such as many-valued, relevant, and intuitionistic logic were devised almost as early but, because of its role in the foundations of mathematics, only the last was, for most of the century, perceived as a serious challenger. Intuitionistic logic is derived from the constructivist view of existence in mathematics, according to which it is not sufficient to show that $\neg\forall x\neg A(x)$ in order to claim that $\exists x A(x)$. Intuitionists thus reject the (universal) validity of the Law of Excluded Middle, $A(x)\vee\neg A(x)$ as well as that of the principle $\neg\neg A(x){\rightarrow}A(x)$, both valid in classical logic, and a semantic in terms of proofs was first propounded by Heyting in the 1930s (Mancosu 1998: 311–27).

   The analogy with the axiomatic system allowed for the mathematical study of properties of these systems, such as soundness and completeness (see below), but it also hides a number of important phenomena and brought about a number of philosophical problems concerning the status of the axioms; for example, are they analytic or synthetic? Some answers will be given below.

   In the 1930s, Gentzen introduced systems of 'natural deduction' for classical and intuitionistic logic and their associated 'sequent' systems (Gentzen 1969). The idea behind natural deduction systems was to keep close to the 'actual reasoning' of mathematicians, who usually reason in these terms: on the basis of the premise A, suppose that B is true, therefore, since B is true under the hypothesis that A is true, then one may conclude that $A{\rightarrow}B$ independently of any hypothesis, which is thus 'discharged.' The introduction of the implication $A{\rightarrow}B$ is then written (with the discharge of the hypothesis indicated by brackets):

$$[A]$$
$$\cdot$$
$$\cdot$$
$$\cdot$$
$$B$$
$$\overline{\quad\quad\quad}$$
$$A{\rightarrow}B$$

Gentzen presented a system of rules in which such 'introduction' rules are mirrored by 'elimination' rules which show under which conditions the same connective can be eliminated. These systems of 'deduction under assumption' are thus characterized by the absence of axioms and a large number of rules of inference. Natural deduction turns out to be intuitionist (it embodies Heyting semantics) and the system for classical logic is obtained simply by adding to it the following elimination rule for double negation, which is rejected by intuitionists:

$$\frac{\neg\neg A}{A}$$

Following Gentzen, one should note here that introduction rules in his natural deduction systems provide 'definitions' of the logical terms; they are thus an alternative to the definitions in terms of truth tables, and one may speak here of a 'proof-theoretical semantics' (as opposed to the 'model-theoretic semantics' to be introduced shortly). One should also note here that this approach is both analytic, in the sense that it proceeds for the meaning of the terms, and formal, since preservation of truth (or warrant) is in virtue of the structure of the argument.

These systems not only avoid the philosophical problems linked with Frege-style systems (Dummett 1981: 432–5), they turn out to have been more fruitful, after their rediscovery by Prawitz (Prawitz 1965) and the establishment of the Curry-Howard isomorphism (Howard 1980) in the 1960s. The latter specifies a formal isomorphism between intuitionistic natural deduction and simply-typed lambda calculus. This allows one to see formulas as types and proofs in intuitionistic logic as programs (in functional programing) or, conversely, to extract proofs, given the correctness of a program. This result exhibits the intimate nature of the links between (constructive) logic and computer programing. In its wake, numerous programation languages (Automath, ML, NuPrl) and logical systems such as Girard's system F, Reynold's second-order lambda-calculus and Martin-Löf's intuitionistic type theory (Martin-Löf 1984), were devised that completely transformed the logical landscape, a fact which is, alas, largely lost on philosophers. For this new standpoint, Martin-Löf propounded his own anti-realist approach to proof-theoretical semantics (Martin-Löf 1982).

Gentzen also introduced a third type of systems, dealing with 'sequents' (his term for consecutions) of the form $\Gamma \vdash \Delta$ where both the antecedent Γ and the consequent Δ are structures. These structures are sets of formulas linked by punctuation marks that are the equivalent for structures of connectives for formulas. Here, the only punctuation mark is the comma and

$$A_1,..., A_n \vdash B_1,..., B_m$$

reads, taking care not to confuse connectives and punctuation marks:

$$A_1 \& ... \& A_n \rightarrow B_1 \vee ... \vee B_m$$

Along with identity axioms of the form $A \vdash A$, from which all derivations begin, there are 'logical rules' that mirror the introduction and elimination rules of the natural deduction systems; for example, the right-hand rule for implication mirrors the above introduction rule:

$$\frac{\Gamma, A \vdash B, \Delta}{\Gamma \vdash A \rightarrow B, \Delta} \; R\rightarrow$$

And there are 'structural rules' that codify the combination of premises. These rules are thus very important, since any modification of the mode of combination of premises will change the logic. Here, the sole difference between intuitionistic and classical logic is that in the former the consequent is restricted to only one formula, as in $\Gamma \vdash A$, since the presence of more than one formula would allow for the introduction of the Law of Excluded Middle by the back door. Classical logic is thus a multiple-conclusion logic (Shoesmith, and Smiley 1978). One such structural rule is 'Cut' (some of the others will be discussed below):

$$\frac{\Gamma \vdash A, \Delta \qquad \Lambda, A \vdash \Pi}{\Gamma, \Lambda \vdash \Delta, \Pi} \text{ cut}$$

One can see that in this rule the formula A does not appear in the conclusion and a 'cut-elimination' proof that all proofs containing cuts can be eliminated in favour of direct proofs not appealing to foreign elements such as A can thus be seen as a proof of consistency.

Alongside the proof-theoretical notion of consequence, there is also a model-theoretic or 'semantic' notion, first proposed by Tarski (Tarski 1983: 408–20) and usually symbolised:

$$\Gamma \models A$$

It states that A is a consequence of Γ if and only if every interpretation that makes all members of Γ true also makes A true and there is thus no interpretation that makes the premises in Γ true which makes the conclusion A false – in other words there is no counterexample. An interpretation or valuation is a function v, which assigns to each atomic proposition of the language a value, either 1 (true) or 0 (false). Given an interpretation, one can devise, with the following (recursive) clauses, a function that gives to every non-atomic formula a truth value:

$$v(\neg A)=1 \text{ if } v(A)=0, \text{ and 0 otherwise.}$$
$$v(A\&B)=1 \text{ if } v(A)=v(B)=1, \text{ and 0 otherwise.}$$
$$v(A\lor B)=1 \text{ if } v(A)=1 \text{ or } v(B)=1, \text{ and 0 otherwise.}$$
$$v(A\rightarrow B)=1 \text{ if } v(A)=0 \text{ or } v(B)=1, \text{ and 0 otherwise.}$$

These clauses capture the content of the well-known truth-table definitions of the connectives (respectively, negation, conjunction, disjunction, and material implication) first publicized by Wittgenstein in his *Tractatus Logico-Philosophicus*. A proposition A is a 'tautology' if and only if every interpretation makes it true. For a given language L, a structure is a pair $< D, I >$, where D is the domain or universe of discourse and I the interpretation function, such as v, which is sufficient to determine denotations (truth-conditions) for each well-formed formula of the language. (And the truth-table method is an algorithm that determines for any proposition of the classical propositional calculus if it is or is not a tautology.) If the structure renders true all formulas of a given theory T, it is called a model of T.

Two important types of results and a meta-linguistic level (that is from a 'meta-language' that has the language under study as its 'object language') concern the notions of proof- and model-theoretical validity. First, if every proof-theoretically valid inference is model-theoretically valid, then the system is said to be 'sound':

$$\Gamma \vdash A \rightarrow \Gamma \models A$$

Conversely, if every model-theoretically valid inference is proof-theoretically valid, then the proof theory is 'complete':

$$\Gamma \models A \rightarrow \Gamma \vdash A$$

Therefore, when a logical system is both sound and complete, the two notions of validity coincide extensionally (if not in intension). This is the significance of Gödel's first major result on the completeness of classical first-order logic (van Heijenoort 1967: 582–91). The two notions of consequence do not coincide for all systems and it is by no means clear which one is more fundamental. At present, probably a majority of logicians take the model-theoretic notion to be more fundamental (there are technical arguments, for example, by an appeal to the lack of 'compactness' for proof-theoretical consequence). One should note here the parallel with the issue about realism alluded to at the beginning: because of the strong connection between model-theoretical con-sequence and truth, taken in the traditional sense of 'correspondence,' realists who argue that 'logical consequence preserves truth' give precedence to model-theoretical consequence, while anti-realists who argue that it preserves warrant give precedence to proof-theoretical consequence.

In *Philosophy of Logic*, Quine laid out what has been the most influential view on logic in the past century (Quine 1986). According to this very restrictive view, logic is *first-order, classical* predicate logic (with identity), which he described as 'a paragon of clarity, elegance and efficiency' which is free of paradox (Quine 1986: 85). It is first-order since second-order logic is ruled out as 'set theory in sheep's disguise' because one needs sets to interpret second-order quantifiers (Quine 1986: 66). This claim has been rejected, for example by Boolos, who showed how to interpret the latter as 'plural quantifiers' (Boolos 1998: 37–87; Shapiro 1991). Logic is classical and non-classical logics are *eo ipso* banned as 'deviant' (Quine 1986: 66). Here, Quine's reasons are linked with his critique of Carnap's philosophy. According to the latter, the choice of a logic is linked to adoption of a language, logical truths are sentences that would become true automatically given the language adopted and 'there are no morals' in the adoption of a language. This is his 'principle of tolerance':

> *In logic, there are no morals.* Everyone is at liberty to build his own logic, i.e., his own form of language, as he wishes. All that is required of him is that, if he wishes to discuss it, he must state his methods clearly, and give syntactical rules instead of philosophical arguments. (Carnap 2002: sec. 17)

This view of logical truths as 'true by convention' has been deftly criticized by Quine (Quine 1976: 77–106, 107–32) and it is essentially bound up with a notion of analyticity which has also been famously demolished by Quine (Quine 1980: 20–46). But Quine's 'monism' is quite astounding, since taking it at face value implies the rejection of almost all that has been done in the last forty years or so. But, without reverting to Carnap's 'tolerance,' one could adopt a form of 'logical pluralism,' that is the view that there are not one but many relations of logical consequence (Beall, and Restall 2000; Restall 2002). The difference here is that both Carnap and Quine tie logical consequence to the choice of a language, so that to admit of another logical consequence is literally to speak a different language, while pluralists would admit that there is at least more than one consequence relation over one language. Quine's best-known argument against 'deviant' logics is indeed a 'change of language' argument. Considering the arguments for and against the rejection of the Law of Noncontradiction, according to which it is not possible that both A is true and $\neg A$ is true, Quine wrote:

> My view of this dialogue is that neither party knows what he is talking about. They think they are talking about negation, '$\neg$', 'not'; but surely the notation ceased to be recognizable as negation when they took to regarding some conjunction of the form 'p&¬p' as true, and stopped regarding such sentences as implying all others. Here, evidently, is the deviant logician's predicament: when he tries to deny the doctrine he only changes the subject. (Quine 1986: 81)

But this argument is not sufficient to close the door to pluralism, because the disagreement here is not over the reading of '$\neg$' in, for example, $A, \neg A \vdash B$. It is over the consequence relation.

By considering merely Frege-style systems, Quine got into further problems concerning logical truth. Carnap and the logical positivists saw logical truths as analytic but Quine's celebrated arguments against the analytic-synthetic distinction (Quine 1980: 20–46) opened the door to the idea that a revision of the principles of logic could come from scientific theories. Quantum logic is non-classical because it does not respect distribution laws (Dalla Chiara, and Giuntini 2001) and Putnam argued that logic is as empirical as geometry and thus that we live in a non-classical world (Putnam 1969). To this Quine could only reply lamely that a revision in physics would be less disruptive than a revision in our logic (Quine 1986: 100).

To the question 'What is a logical constant?' Quine answered that the logical constants of a language are its grammatical particles, from which complex sentences are built from atomic ones (Quine 1986: Chap. 2). This fits very well for first-order logic but the whole idea verges on circularity, since first-order logic was designed in the first place to adjust grammar to the logical constants. We need some further justification for this particular regimentation of grammar; for Quine, we should look for a language best suited to our scientific theories and most economical for the representation of the truth conditions of their sentences.

But is there a principled way to determine what counts as a logical constant? The skeptical answer according to which there is none, first stated by Bolzano, was shared by Tarski and Quine. Nevertheless, Tarski proposed invariance under arbitrary permutations of the domain of objects as a criterion (Tarski 1986). This line of inquiry is still pursued today, although the results obtained are at times counter-intuitive (Gomez-Torrente 2002). From a proof-theoretical perspective, Kneale proposed that a logical constant is whatever can be given Gentzen-style inference rules (Kneale 1956) but Prior pointed out that this could not do, by giving rules for a new connective called 'tonk,' with which one can infer in two steps from A to any B (Prior 1967). To this, Belnap replied that connectives are never defined *ab initio* like this but always in terms of an 'antecedently given context of deducibility' (Belnap 1967: 133). In sequent calculi, this is given by the structural rules. Belnap gave two conditions for any new definition: uniqueness and conservativity. Uniqueness means simply that two connectives defined by the same rules are the same (meaning is preserved). Conservativity means that a new system obtained from a previous system by the adjunction of a new connective must be a 'conservative extension' of the previous one: the introduction of the new connective should not extend the class of derivations obtained without it. A cut-elimination proof will show that the extension is conservative (Hacking 1979; Kremer 1988). However, the adjunction of the above rule for the elimination of double negation to the system of intuitionistic natural deduction, needed to obtain classical logic, creates a non-conservative extension, as it extends the class of derivations with negation. This fact provides the basis for a powerful critique of classical logic from an anti-realist standpoint by Prawitz and Dummett (Prawitz 1977; Dummett 1991).

Given classical logic as the full structural logic (and, in that restricted sense, the only logic), one may either weaken or supplement it. Dosen postulated the following thesis: 'Two logical systems are alternative if and only if they differ only in their assumptions on structural deductions' (Dosen 1989: 376). This allows for the introduction of non-classical logics (not all of which will be reviewed here): keeping the logical rules invariant, these logics distinguish themselves from classical logic by weakening its structural rules. This is the standpoint of 'substructural logics' (Schroeder-Heister, and Dosen 1993; Restall 2000), which goes along with 'logical pluralism.'

From this point of view, the intuitionistic requisite that sequents can only have one conclusion means revising the rules, and the rule for thinning on the right:

$$\frac{\Gamma \vdash \Delta}{\Gamma \vdash A, \Delta}$$

must be replaced by:

$$\frac{\Gamma \vdash}{\Gamma \vdash A}$$

which corresponds to $A{\rightarrow}(\neg A{\rightarrow}B)$. This is the only difference between classical and intuitionistic logic from a substructural point of view. One interesting phenomenon which is uncovered here is that the fewer the structural rules, the more distinctions: connectives that are equivalent in classical logic are now distinguishable. This is already the case in intuitionistic logic, where $A{\rightarrow}B$ is not equivalent to $\neg(A\&\neg B)$.

As early as 1912, Lewis discussed theorems of classical logic which 'seem suspicious to common sense' (Lewis 1970: 351), also known as the paradoxes of relevance. Examples of these are $A{\rightarrow}(B{\rightarrow}A)$, $A{\rightarrow}(\neg A{\rightarrow}B)$ and $A{\rightarrow}(B\vee\neg B)$; an instance of the latter could be: 'The moon is made of green cheese, therefore, either the Queen likes Corgis or the Queen does not like Corgis.' The culprit seems to be the lack of relevance between the antecedent and the consequent of the material implication. This phenomenon is linked to the rules for thinning, here on the left, with single conclusion:

$$\frac{\Gamma \vdash B}{\Gamma, A \vdash B}$$

Indeed, one can derive $A{\rightarrow}(B{\rightarrow}A)$ as follows:

$$\frac{\dfrac{\dfrac{\dfrac{A \vdash A}{A, B \vdash A}\ \text{Thinning}}{A \vdash B{\rightarrow}A}\ \text{R}{\rightarrow}}{\vdash A{\rightarrow}(B{\rightarrow}A)}}{}\ \text{R}{\rightarrow}$$

So systems of relevant logic were devised to remedy this problem, by rejecting thinning on both sides, while avoiding at the same time intuitionism by keeping to (involutive) classical negation, where one has both $A{\rightarrow}\neg\neg A$ *and* $\neg\neg A{\rightarrow}A$, and the De Morgan laws:

$$\neg(A\vee B) \rightarrow (\neg A\&\neg B)$$
$$\neg(A\&B){\rightarrow}(\neg A\vee\neg B)$$

(Both $\neg\neg A{\rightarrow}A$ and the second law are intuitionistically invalid.) The rather complex cocktails of rules that result from this have been extensively studied, mainly from a Frege-style point of view by Anderson and Belnap (Anderson, and Belnap 1975; Anderson et al. 1992), but Belnap has introduced a fruitful Gentzen-style approach with his 'display logic' (Belnap 1982).

With the rejection of thinning, new connectives can be distinguished: 'fusion' and 'fission.' Fusion has to be distinguished from conjunction: $A\&B$ always implies A but $A.B$, which is equal to $\neg(A{\rightarrow}\neg B)$, may not imply A, because B may be irrelevant. Fusion imitates the comma on the left-hand side of the sequents. Similarly, fission $A+B$, which is equivalent to $\neg A{\rightarrow}B$, resembles disjunction and it imitates the comma on the right-hand side. There are, however, some unappealing properties, such as undecidability, that are linked with the fact that relevant logicians wish to retain distribution of conjunction over disjunction:

$$(C\&(A\vee B)){\rightarrow}(C\&A)\vee(C\&B)$$

which is lacking in absence of thinning. Instead, fusion distributes over disjunction. Relevant logics are also 'paraconsistent' because arguments of the form $A\&\neg A \vdash B$ are not valid.

The rejection of thinning also gives rise to non-monotonic logics (Brewka et al. 1997). These logics are devised to deal with 'defeasible' reasoning. An example of this sort of reasoning happens when John comes out of his house in the morning and notices that A: 'the lawn is wet,' and concludes that C: 'it rained during the night,' but then notices that B: 'the street is dry,' from which he infers that it did not rain: someone has watered the lawn before he got up. In this very common type of reasoning, where the conclusion is potentially defeated by new information, one cannot move from $A \vdash C$ to $A, B \vdash C$; the rule of thinning (or monotonicity) on the left is violated. The resulting logics are useful for the study of reasoning about knowledge and they are also akin to proof methods developed in computer science such as negation-as-failure.

Closely related to but distinct from relevance logics (because they share a rejection of thinning) are the linear logics introduced by Girard (Girard 1987; Troelstra 1992). These logics play a central role in substructural logics and, contrary to relevant logics, they have a clear mathematical rationale (as they are linked, in a more specialized jargon, to 'symmetric monoidal closed categories' in category theory). The key idea here is to take into account the 'physical' cost of deductive moves: if one has \$2 and a pack of chewing-gum costs \$1, then the result of buying a pack of chewing-gum is that one is left with \$1. Thus, in linear logic one cannot get $A \rightarrow B$ from $(A\&A \rightarrow B)$, in other words one rejects both sides of the rule of contraction (here on the left, with single conclusion):

$$\frac{\Gamma, A, A \vdash B}{\Gamma, A \vdash B}$$

As with relevant logics, one distinguishes new connectives, called 'par' for 'fission' and 'times' for 'fusion.' Girard also considered an involutive notion of negation; from these he introduced a form of linear implication. He also introduced modal operators to recover restricted versions of the missing structural rules. Linear logic has generated an intense interest in logic (proof theory) and computer science but so far little attention in philosophy. While Tennant defended intuitionistic relevant logic from an anti-realist standpoint (Tennant 1987), only Dubucs has linked linear logic with a radical form of anti-realism (Dubucs 2002).

Another area where linear logic has philosophical interest is game semantics. In mid-century, Lorenzen introduced the idea of defining logical connectives in terms of rules of a two-persons (the proponent P and the opponent O), non-collaborative game and to define logical truth in terms of the existence of a winning strategy for the proponent. The rules for the connectives are: to attack $A\vee B$, O asks that P selects and defends one of the disjuncts; to attack $A\&B$, O selects either conjuncts and P must defend it; to attack $A \rightarrow B$, O may assert A and then P may either attack A or defend B. With $\neg A$, roles are exchanged, as O has now to defend A. Lorenzen's original intention was to recover intuitionistic provability with his dialogical approach (Felscher 2001). Game semantics was not, however, perceived as a serious rival to the well-established model- and proof-theoretical semantics but the idea was revived by Andreas Blass as a natural semantics for linear logic (Blass 1992) and it has emerged recently as a powerful paradigm in the semantics of programing languages and logical systems (Abramsky 1997), the full philosophical significance of which has yet to be formulated. Girard's 'ludics' and Japaridze's 'computability logic' are among recent developments linked with game semantics.

Among the first 'supplementations' of classical logic were many-valued logics and modal logics. From the substructural point of view, where all sorts of distinction are made that are collapsed in classical logic, the simple two-valued semantics is not rich enough. Many-valued and modal logics can be seen as providing alternative ways to enrich semantics to model behavior in substructural systems: the former consists of an increase in the number of values a sentence might take, the latter of an increase in the number of places at which the sentences are evaluated, while the number of values remains the same.

Many-valued logics, introduced by Lukasiewicz in the 1920s, are similar to classical logic in that they accept truth-functionality but they differ in not restricting the number of truth-values to two. Kleene's proposed a 3–valued logic, where the third value being 'undefined' (Kleene 1938); there are also 4–valued as well as infinite-valued systems. One important offshoot with practical applications to 'soft-computing' is fuzzy logic and one interesting philosophical application of many-valued logics is a solution to the Sorites (heap) paradox: one grain of sand is not a heap and adding one grain of sand to what is not a heap does not turn it into a heap, therefore a single grain of sand can never be turned into a heap. Roughly put, the solution consists here in giving a truth degree to '$n+1$ grains of sand do not make a heap' smaller than that for 'n grains of sand do not make a heap' in such a way that the latter tends to be false as n increases. (On vagueness and the Sorites, see Keefe, and Smith 1997.)

Modal logics arise from the addition to the classical propositional calculus of two new operators, $\Box A$, which means 'It is necessary that A' and $\Diamond A$, equivalent to $\neg \Box \neg A$, which means 'It is possible that A.' The simplest modal logic is the system K resulting from adding to the classical propositional calculus a necessitation rule: if A is a theorem of K, then so is $\Box A$, and the following (distribution) axiom:

$$\Box(A \to B) \to (\Box A \to \Box B)$$

The system M results from adding to K the axiom $\Box A \to A$, while the system S4 results from adding to M the iteration axiom $\Box A \to \Box \Box A$ and S5 from adding instead $\Diamond A \to \Box \Diamond A$. One can also obtain the system B by adding $A \to \Box \Diamond A$ to M and S5 from by adding that axiom to S4. From these, a whole family of systems was built. Kripke gave a semantics to these logics by augmenting the basic structure presented above: not only should there be more than one point at which sentences are evaluated but structured sets were introduced as models (Kripke 1963). An intuitive and well-known interpretation of these is in terms of 'possible worlds.' Instead of one, there is now a family or set W of domains or possible worlds such as w or w', along with an accessibility relation R between them – this pair $< W, R >$ forms what is known as the 'frame' underlying the model – and a valuation v, so that one has now the triplet $< W, R, v >$. The relation R is a relation of relative possibility: wRw' means that w' is possible, relative to w. The function v assigns a truth value to each atomic proposition in each world, so that one writes, for example, $v_w(A)=1$ for 'at world w, proposition A is true.' Although interpretations are now relative to worlds, these play no role in the truth conditions of the usual connectives. However, for the modal operators, one has, for any world w:

$$v_w(\lozenge A)=1 \text{ if for some } w' \in W \text{ such that } wRw', v_{w'}(A)=1; \text{ and } 0 \text{ otherwise}$$
$$v_w(\square A)=1 \text{ if for all } w' \in W \text{ such that } wRw', v_{w'}(A)=1; \text{ and } 0 \text{ otherwise}$$

One can define validity in terms of truth-preservation at all worlds of all interpretations:

$$\Gamma \models A \text{ if and only if for all interpretations } < W, R, v > \text{ and all } w \in W,$$
$$\text{if } v_{w'}(B)=1 \text{ for all } B \in \Gamma, \text{ then } v_{w'}(A)=1$$

This is the modal answer to the problem of the nature of preservation. But Etchemendy has argued instead that the variations of possible worlds are to be understood as 'reinterpretation' of non-logical vocabulary, so that preservation of truth is not necessary truth preservation, but on the basis of the meaning of the logical vocabulary (Etchemendy 1990).

The metaphysical implications of this 'possible world' semantics led to a renewed discussion in the 1970s of a number of topics, from proper names to identity and necessity (Kripke 1980; Schwartz 1977). One alternative is 'situation' semantics (Barwise, and Perry 1983), where 'situations' are merely parts of the world, which make some sentences true or false but leave some undetermined; it has been argued that the logic of 'situations' is not classical but relevant.

Modal logics spawn an amazing array of logical systems, only some of which can only be very briefly reviewed. The modal operators $\square A$ and $\lozenge A$ were reinterpreted by von Wright (von Wright 1951) as, respectively, 'It is obligatory that A' and 'It is permitted that A,' thus giving rise to deontic logics, for the study of legal reasoning, and as 'Agent i knows that A' and 'Agent i believes that A,' thus giving rise to 'epistemic logic' for the study of reasoning with knowledge. Hintikka provided the first (Frege-style) epistemic logic (Hintikka 1962). But this system is monotonic: this property generates the problem of 'logical omniscience,' that is the very unlikely fact that, when an agent knows something, she knows all its logical consequences. Much ink has been spilled trying to solve this problem but epistemic logic has found applications within artificial intelligence (Fagin et al. 1995). Modal logics are also genetically linked with temporal logics (van Benthem 1991) and conditional logics, which were originally devised by Stalnaker to deal with counterfactuals of the form 'If A were to happen, then B would happen'; one major offshoot is Gärdenfors's seminal study of belief revision (Gärdenfors 1988).

Modal logics were also banned by Quine because of the alleged 'intensional' and thus nonscientific nature of the modal operators (Quine 1986: 33–4). This viewpoint is simply without any merit. Developments since the 1970s show that modal languages are about relational structures; to describe these as 'possible worlds' was already restrictive and misleading. There is in fact nothing intrinsically 'modal' about Kripke models and modal logic: under a 'standard translation,' modal logic can be seen as a fragment of classical logic. With the introduction of the 'bisimulation' as the fundamental model-theoretic tool, it can be seen as the bisimulation invariant fragment of first-order logic over models. Alternatively, it can be seen as a non-trivial fragment of second-order logic over frames (Blackburn et al. 2001).

One last set of modifications of the 'supplementing' kind that deserves mention concerns the quantifiers. The standard interpretation of the quantifiers is 'objectual': they are tied to a domain of objects over which they quantify. They can also be interpreted 'substitutionally' when tied instead with a 'substitution class': a universal (an existential) quantification is true if and only if every one (at least one) of its substitution instances is true. Using this, Leblanc devised truth-value semantics (Leblanc 1976), which dispense with models and use only truth-value assignments, and probability semantics, which use probability functions. According to Quine's famous criterion of ontological commitment, 'To be is to be the value of a bound variable' (Quine 1980: 15), one is committed to the existence of the objects that form the domain of quantification of one's theory. 'Free logics' were developed by Leblanc and others in reaction against this, as systems of quantification theory in which at least some singular terms are not denoting (Bencivenga 2001).

Another supplementation concerns 'branching' quantifiers. When we wish to say that for all x there is a y and that for all z there is a w, such that $A(x, y, z, w)$, the usual notation is inappropriate, because we want the choice of y to depend on x and the choice of w to depend on z but in the expression:

$$\forall x \exists y \forall z \exists w \ A(x, y, z, w)$$

the usual conventions for scope make the choice of w depend not only on z but also on x. One could express this appropriately by a second-order formula or by introducing 'branching' quantifiers:

$$(\forall x)(\forall z)(\exists y / \forall z)(\exists w / \forall x) \ A(x, y, z, w)$$

The slash in '$\exists w / \forall x$' means that the choice of w is made independently of that of x. Hintikka has devised an 'independence-friendly' logic that embodies these branching quantifiers, and provided them with a model-theoretical game semantics (Hintikka 1996).

Finally, at the juncture between philosophy of logic and philosophy of language stands the concept of truth, which remains fundamental for the model-theoretical approach and realism, while for the anti-realist approach based on proof-theoretical semantics, it is a 'by-product' of the introduction rules for logical constants. The most important result concerning truth is Tarski's definition (Tarski 1983: 151–278). Tarski provided formal and material adequacy conditions for any definition of truth. One should recall here that the definition of truth for a given *object* language L can only be provided in a *meta*-language M, such that anything that can be said in L can be said (has a copy) in M, while M is also able to talk about sentences of L and their syntax. Moreover, M must contain some set theory, in particular the predicate symbol for 'true,' such as T, which would read 'is a true sentence of L.' Tarski argued that the definition of 'true' should be 'formally correct.' By this he meant that it should be *explicit*, that is of the form:

$$\forall x \ T(x) \text{ if and only if } \varphi(x)$$

with some restrictions, for example, that T does not occur in φ, and so forth. He also argued that the definition should be 'materially adequate' in the sense that the objects satisfying φ should be exactly the sentences that one would intuitively count as being true sentences of L. In other words, one must find a φ such that one can deduce from the axioms of M all sentences of the form:

$$\varphi(s) \text{ if and only if } \psi$$

where s is the name for a sentence of L and ψ the copy of that very sentence in M. This criterion is known as the 'Convention T' or 'T-schema'; the following is a well-known instance:

'Snow is white' is true if and only if snow is white

Tarski went on to show that many formal languages admit of a truth definition that satisfies these conditions. Setting these (and Tarski's own philosophical opinions) aside, one should note that Convention T was used to support both 'correspondence' and 'deflationary' (also known as redundancy, disquotational, or minimalist) conceptions of truth, against traditional rivals such as the coherence or pragmatic conceptions of truth, which have disappeared since from the logical scene. In a nutshell, deflationists claim that Convention T captures all that there is to the concept of truth; other conceptions *add* to it, they are inflationary. For example, a correspondence theory would reformulate the above example thus:

'Snow is white' is true if and only if it corresponds to the fact that the snow is white.

The relation of 'correspondence' and the metaphysical notion of 'fact' do not appear in Convention T. On the other hand, a deflationary account focuses only on the criterion of material adequacy (as embodying all that there is to say about truth) and there is no real attempt at a definition.

One should note further, with Tarski, that, if the language L has enough resources to talk about its own semantics, Convention T leads to the liar paradox, that is the derivation of sentences of the sort, 'What this sentence says is false' (hereafter referred to as 'the Liar'). This is the reason why Tarski believed that his definition could never apply to natural languages. This view was not influential. The two main strategies for dealing with the Liar involve truth-value 'gaps' and 'gluts.' On the one hand, Kripke suggested that the truth predicate T is a partial predicate in the sense that it has 'truth-value gaps' that behave 'truth-functionally,' so that they can be treated as a third truth value or degree. This allows Kripke to use Kleene's 3–valued system and to claim, using a mathematical result about monotonic, increasing, continuous functions having fixed points, that the Liar and related sentences, as fixed points, simply lack a truth value (Kripke 1984).

The other approach derives from paraconsistent logics (Priest 2001). Almost all the logics introduced in this paper possess a relation of logical consequence which is 'explosive' in the sense that:

$$A, \neg A \vdash B$$

In order to block the derivation of B from A and $\neg A$ (see above), paraconsistent logicians must reject some rules (such as the *ex falso*) and the disjunctive syllogism $(A \lor B, \neg A \vdash B)$. The resulting systems are of use for the study of inconsistent but nontrivial scientific theories as well as for the modeling of information processing and belief revision. They also gave rise to a philosophy called 'dialetheism,' which is the view that there are true contradictions (called *dialetheia*); this being a denial of the Law of Noncontradiction (Priest 1987). One of the main planks of dialetheism is the thesis that the Liar is a true contradiction. As opposed to 'gaps,' they are truth-value 'gluts': they are both true and not true. Of course, this is not a position to which a pluralist is committed.

For detailed introductions to the philosophy of logic, see Haack 1978; Engel 1991; and Read 1995.

References

Abramsky, S. (1997), 'Semantics of Interaction: An Introduction to Game Semantics,' in A. M. Pitts, and P. Dybjer (eds) (1997), *Semantics and Logics of Computation*, Cambridge: Cambridge University Press, pp. 1–31.

Anderson, A. R., and N. D. Belnap (1975), *Entailment. The Logic of Relevance and Necessity I*, Princeton: Princeton University Press.

Anderson, A. R., N. D. Belnap, and J. M. Dunn (1992), *Entailment. The Logic of Relevance and Necessity II*, Princeton: Princeton University Press.

Barwise, J., and J. Perry (1983), *Situations and Attitudes*, Cambridge: MIT Press.

Beall, J. C., and G. Restall (2000), 'Logical Pluralism,' *Australasian Journal of Philosophy* 78: pp. 475–93.

Belnap, N. (1967), 'Tonk, Plonk and Plink,' in P. F. Strawson (1967), *Philosophical Logic*, Oxford: Oxford University Press, pp. 132–7.

Belnap, N. (1982), 'Display Logic,' *Journal of Philosophical Logic* 11: 103–16.

Bencivenga, E. (2001), 'Free Logics,' in D. M. Gabbay, and F. Guenthner (eds) (2001), *Handbook of Philosophical Logic*, 2nd edn, vol. 5, Dordrecht: Kluwer, pp. 147–96.

Blackburn, P., and M. de Rijke, and Y. Venema (2001), *Modal Logic*, Cambridge: Cambridge University Press.

Blass, A. (1992), 'A Game Semantics for Linear Logic,' *Annals of Pure and Applied Logic* 56: 183–220.

Boolos, G. (1998), *Logic, Logic, and Logic*, ed. R. Jeffrey, Cambridge: Harvard University Press.

Brandom, R. (1994), *Making it Explicit. Reasoning, Representing and Discursive Commitment*, Cambridge: Harvard University Press.

Brewka, G., J. Dix, and K. Konolige (1997), *Nonmonotonic Reasoning. An Overview*, Stanford: CSLI Publications.

Carnap, R. (2002), *The Logical Syntax of Language*, Lasalle: Open Court.

Dalla Chiara, M.-L., and R. Giuntini (2001), 'Quantum Logics,' in D. M. Gabbay, and F. Guenthner (eds) (2001), *Handbook of Philosophical Logic*, 2nd edn, vol. 6, Dordrecht: Kluwer, pp. 129–228.

Dosen, K. (1989), 'Logical Constants as Punctuation Marks,' *Notre Dame Journal of Formal Logic* 30: 362–81.

Dubucs, J. (2002), 'Feasibility in Logic,' *Synthese* 132: 213–37.

Dummett, M. A. E. (1981), *Frege. Philosophy of Language*, 2nd edn, London: Duckworth.

Dummett, M. A. E. (1991), *The Logical Basis of Metaphysics*, Cambridge: Harvard University Press.

Gentzen, G. (1969), 'Investigations into Logical Deduction,' in M. E. Szabo (ed.) (1969), *The Collected Papers of Gehrard Gentzen*, Amsterdam: North-Holland, pp. 68–131.

Engel, P. (1991), *The Norm of Truth*, Brighton: Harvester.

Etchemendy, J. (1990), *The Concept of Logical Consequence*, Cambridge: Harvard University Press.

Fagin, R., J. Y. Halpern, Y. Moses, and M. Y. Vardi (1995), *Reasoning about Knowledge*, Cambridge: MIT Press.

Felscher, W. (2001), 'Dialogues as a Foundation for Intuitionistic Logic,' in D. M. Gabbay, and Guenthner (eds) (2001), *Handbook of Philosophical Logic*, 2nd edn, vol. 5, Dordrecht: Kluwer, pp. 115–45.

Gabbay, D. M., and F. Guenthner (eds) (2001), *Handbook of Philosophical Logic*, 2nd edn, 11 vols, Dordrecht: Kluwer.

Gärdenfors, P. (1988), *Knowledge in Flux*, Cambridge: MIT Press.

Gentzen, G. (1969), *The Collected Papers of Gerhard Gentzen: Studies in Logic and the Foundations of Mathematics*, ed. M. E. Szabo, Amsterdam: North-Holland.

Girard, J.-Y. (1987), 'Linear Logic,' *Theoretical Computer Science* 50: 1–102.

Gomez-Torrente, M. (2002), 'The Problem of Logical Constants,' *Bulletin of Symbolic Logic* 8: 1–37.

Haack, S. (1978), *Philosophy of Logics*, Cambridge: Cambridge University Press.

Hacking, I. (1979), 'What is Logic?' *Journal of Philosophy* 66: 285–319.

Hilbert, D., and W. Ackermann (1950), *Principles of Mathematical Logic*, New York: Chelsea.

Hintikka, J. (1962), *Knowledge and Belief*, Ithaca: Cornell University Press.

Hintikka, J. (1996), *The Principles of Mathematics Revisited*, Cambridge: Cambridge University Press.

Howard, W. A. (1980), 'The Formula-As-Types Notion of Construction,' in J. P. Seldin, and J. R. Hindley (eds) (1980), *To H. B. Curry: Essays in Combinatory Logic, Lambda Calculus and Formalism*, New York: Academic Press, pp. 479–91.

Keefe, R., and P. Smith (1997), *Vagueness: A Reader*, Cambridge: MIT Press.

Kleene, S. C. (1938), 'On Notation for Ordinal Numbers,' *Journal of Symbolic Logic* 3: 150–5.

Kneale, W. (1956), 'The Province of Logic,' in H. D. Lewis (ed.) (1956), *Contemporary British Philosophy*, third series, London: Allen and Unwin, pp. 235–61.

Kremer, M. (1988), 'Logic and Meaning: The Philosophical Significance of the Sequent Calculus,' *Mind* 97: 50–72.

Kripke, S. (1963), 'Semantic Analysis of Modal Logic I. Normal Propositional Calculi,' *Zeitschrift für mathematische Logik und Grundlagen der Mathematik* 9: 67–96.

Kripke, S. (1980), *Naming and Necessity*, Cambridge: Harvard University Press.

Kripke, S. (1984), 'Outline of a Theory of Truth', in R. L. Martin (ed.) (1984), *Recent Essays on Truth and the Liar Paradox*, Oxford: Oxford University Press, pp. 53–81.

Leblanc, H. (1976), *Truth-Value Semantics*, Amsterdam: North-Holland.

Lewis, C. I. (1970), *Collected Papers of Clarence Irving Lewis*, Stanford: Stanford University Press.

Mancosu, P. (ed.) (1998), *From Brouwer to Hilbert. The Debate about the Foundations of Mathematics in the 1920s*, Oxford: Oxford University Press.

Martin-Löf, P. (1982), 'On the Meanings of the Logical Constants and the Justifications of the Logical Laws,' in C. Bernardi, and P. Pagli (eds) (1982), *Atti degli incontri di logica matematica*, vol. 2, Bologna: CLUEB, pp. 203–81.

Martin-Löf, P. (1984), *Intuitionistic Type Theory*, Naples: Bibliopolis.

Prawitz, D. (1965), *Natural Deduction. A Proof-Theoretical Study*, Stockholm: Almqvist and Wicksell.

Prawitz, D. (1977), 'Meaning and Proofs: On the Conflict between Classical and Intuitionistic Logic,' *Theoria* 43: 1–40.

Priest, G. (1987), *In Contradiction*, Dordrecht: Kluwer.

Priest, G. (2001), 'Paraconsistent Logic,' in D. M. Gabbay, and F. Guenthner (eds) (2001) *Handbook of Philosophical Logic*, 2nd edn, vol. 6, Dordrecht: Kluwer, pp. 287–393.

Prior, A. (1967), 'The Runabout Inference-Ticket,' in P. F. Strawson (ed.) (1967), *Philosophical Logic*, Oxford: Oxford University Press, pp. 129–31.

Putnam, H. (1969), 'Is Logic Empirical?' in R. Cohen et al. (eds) (1969), *Boston Studies in the Philosophy of Science*, vol. 5, Dordrecht: D. Reidel, pp. 216–41.

Quine, W. V. O. (1976), *The Ways of Paradox*, 2nd edn, Cambridge: Harvard University Press.

Quine, W. V. O. (1980), *From a Logical Point of View*, 2nd edn, Cambridge: Harvard University Press.

Quine, W. V. O. (1982), *Methods of Logic*, 4th edn, Cambridge: Harvard University Press.

Quine, W. V. O. (1986), *Philosophy of Logic*, 2nd edn, Cambridge: Harvard University Press.

Read, S. (1995), *Thinking about Logic. An Introduction to the Philosophy of Logic*, Oxford: Oxford University Press.

Restall, G. (2000), *An Introduction to Substructural Logics*, London: Routledge.

Restall, G. (2002), 'Carnap's Tolerance, Meaning, and Logical Pluralism,' *Journal of Philosophy* 99: 426–43.

Sainsbury, M. (1995), 'Philosophical Logic,' in A. C. Grayling (ed.) (1995), *Philosophy. A Guide through the Subject*, Oxford: Oxford University Press, pp. 61–122.

Schroeder-Heister P., and K. Dosen (eds) (1993), *Substructural Logics*, Oxford: Oxford University Press.

Schwartz, S. P. (ed.) (1977), *Naming, Necessity, and Natural Kinds*, Ithaca: Cornell University Press.

Shapiro, S. (1991), *Foundations without Foundationalism. A Case for Second-Order Logic.* Oxford: Oxford University Press.

Shoesmith D., and T. Smiley (1978), *Multiple Conclusion Logic*, Cambridge: Cambridge University Press.

Strawson, P. F. (ed.) (1967), *Philosophical Logic*, Oxford: Oxford University Press.

Sundholm, G. (2001), 'Systems of Deduction,' in D. M. Gabbay, and F. Guenthner (eds) (2001), *Handbook of Philosophical Logic*, 2nd edn, vol. 9, Dordrecht: Kluwer, pp. 165–98.

Tarski, A. (1983), *Logic, Semantics, Metamathematics*, second edition, Indianapolis: Hackett.

Tarski, A. (1986), 'What are Logical Notions?' *History and Philosophy of Logic* 7: 143–54.

Tennant, N. (1987), *Anti-Realism and Logic*, Oxford: Oxford University Press.

Troelstra, A. (1992), *Lectures on Linear Logic*, Stanford: CSLI Publications.

van Benthem, J. (1991), *The Logic of Time*, 2nd edn, Dordrecht: Kluwer.

van Heijenoort, J. (ed.) (1967), *From Frege to Gödel. A Source Book in Mathematical Logic, 1879–1931*, Cambridge: Harvard University Press.

von Wright, G. H. (1951), *An Essay in Modal Logic*, Amsterdam: North-Holland.

Whitehead A. M., and B. Russell (1927), *Principia Mathematica*, 3 vols, Cambridge: Cambridge University Press.

A Century of Transition in the Philosophy of Science

David Castle and Edward Jones-Imhotep

Introduction

Philosophy of science, in the past 100 years, has been propelled forward by the rapid expansion of the natural sciences, and by the coincidental rise of analytic philosophy. Many of the core issues galvanized in the philosophy of science from the 1930s through the 1960s continue to be debated – for example, the nature of causation, the realism/anti-realism controversy in science, and the intricacies of what constitutes scientific explanation.[1] Perhaps less appreciated as a trend in the philosophy of science, however, is the inclusion into the discipline of explanations and theories that have a social or sociological aspect. These issues arose during and after the 1960s, but their impact on the philosophy of science has yet to be fully appreciated.

At the height of positivist theories of science, as described below in Section 1, the conviction shared by scientists and philosophers of science alike was that science is wholly distinct from the social, and should be pursued and explained in terms that are asocial. Section 2 discusses the move away from a totalizing or monolithic conception of the philosophy of science as a kind of 'first philosophy' for science, considers the advent of philosophies of science which are not physics-specific, and the beginnings of the penetration of the social into the philosophy of science via historicism. Historicism focuses on the empirical inadequacy of positivist accounts of scientific practice, and in so doing creates space for social elements to play a role in how science works. Section 3 focuses on how aspects of social life are now openly regarded as important dimensions in the characterisation of science. This progression shows how erstwhile controversial, post-positivist critiques in the philosophy of science have to an extent, despite earlier charges of relativism and worse, become normalized in the philosophy of science. Our conclusion is that these changes represent an obvious expansion of the purview of the philosophy of science: they have generated new and fruitful lines of research, and have made the philosophy of science more socially relevant in the process.

1. Era of Independence

Philosophy at the end of the nineteenth century was dominated by various forms of idealism on both sides of the English Channel. As the influence of Fichte, Schelling and Hegel waned on one side of the Channel, British Idealists such as Wallace, Bradley, and McTaggart were in full force by the end of the century. Speculative philosophy was, however, being overshadowed elsewhere in the academy. The special sciences were flourishing, particularly those sciences which were considered exact science – mathematics, physics and chemistry – because they were expressed in mathematical terms. Science's success began to reflect back into philosophy in the form of a renewed interest in empiricism. At the same time, in the early 1900s, the foundations of philosophical logic, mathematics and physics were being articulated. These intellectual strides forward took place in a period of futurism and scientific and technological progressivism. There was a sense that these endeavors would add up to a profound intellectual step forward for philosophy that would overturn the trappings of speculative philosophy.

Logical positivism, or logical empiricism as it is also known, grew to be among the most important philosophical movements in the late 1920s and early 1930s, and was certainly the most important philosophical movement to address science. It held that if the natural sciences could provide the most basic empirical data in a form that was interpreted in a rational, that is, in this case, explicitly logical framework, the gulf between empiricism and rationalism would be bridged. This doctrine, known as logical atomism, became the cornerstone of a philosophy of science that was based on exact sciences like physics and mathematical logic. Logical positivism's main advocates, the Vienna Circle, had members representing physics, mathematics, and philosophy, and out of this movement came the journal *Erkenntnis* and the *International Encyclopedia of Unified Science* which became the main outlets for this philosophical view.

Logical positivists argued, as did their intellectual predecessor, August Comte (Comte 1975), that there would come a time in civilisation when rational enquiry would supercede the intellectual vestiges of religious belief and metaphysical speculation. Whereas Comte's positivism drove toward the production of a rational social science to improve the human condition, logical positivists argued that scientific rationality was the only intellectually respectable position to adopt. This was supported in part by a principle of verificationism, attributed to Wittgenstein, which claimed that the meaning of a statement is the method of its verification (Hanfling 1981). Verifiable statements were meaningful only if the contents of the statement were traceable to some antecedent, or some potential, sensory perception (Schlick 1979; Carnap 1953). If this turned out to be impossible, the statement was a pseudostatement – and would be considered to be among those statements that ought to be eliminated along with the rest of the pseudostatements that comprise metaphysics (Ayer 1952). Once this conceptual and empirical housekeeping became the norm, the unification of the science could begin via methodological reductionism from the most basic of statements which were verifiable (that is, the irreducibly atomic statements of physics), through to the most complex (that is, chemistry or biology) (Carnap 1938; Oppenheim, and Putnam 1958).

Under these three criteria – the verification principle, the elimination of metaphysics and the unity of science – there is no role for social forces to play in the development and justification of science. In fact, just the opposite was espoused by logical positivists: the reason why social problems arise and why ethics is so indeterminate is because the phenomena are so poorly articulated and do not lend themselves to logical analysis. This position was later reinforced in both forms of hypothetico-deductivism: Popperian falsificationism (Popper 1961) and Hempel's confirmationism (Hempel, and Oppenheim 1953; Hempel 1965). Hypothetico-deductivism argues for a unique philosophical methodology in which empirical claims are grounded in a logical framework; in other words, ordinary speech and non-empirical claims have little or no role to play in the acquisition of truth. Popper championed the idea that science, and philosophy of science along with it, could be demarcated from other forms of inquiry or other types of claim. Like Reichenbach, and his famous distinction between the context of discovery and the context of justification (Reichenbach 1958), Popper eschewed any position that argued that philosophy of science should stray beyond the pursuit of the criteria strictly necessary for the justification of science.

2. The 'Second Wave'

Like so much of early twentieth-century philosophy, logical positivism had been an attempt to escape from the constructivism and relativism of nineteenth-century neo-Kantianism and its suggestions of an inaccessible reality. In the idealism that dominated German universities in the early twentieth century, members of the Vienna Circle had seen an instrument of social and political reaction; and in the logic and epistemology of the sciences, they had seen a way out of its political and intellectual dangers. United in a few central tenets – the verifiability principle, the elimination of metaphysics and the goal of unifying science through inter-theoretic reduction – the logical positivists pursued and promoted a philosophy program that was positively reinforced by the development of science. Their philosophical methodology, with its joint emphasis on empiricism and the logical analysis of language, set the stage for much of the analytic philosophy that followed.

By the late 1950s, battered by attacks from Popper, Hempel, and Quine, and plagued by internal criticisms, logical positivism was largely a spent force. The verifiability principle – once envisioned as the instrument that would destroy metaphysics – had been reduced to a mere methodological recommendation.[2] The reaction against positivism had begun, in a limited way, in the 1930s with Quine's holism, his project for an empirical and descriptive philosophy, his repudiation of a 'first philosophy,' and his notion of the indeterminacy of translation. The impact on the logical positivists' programme was ultimately significant because Quine's naturalism paved the way for methodologies for describing science which weighed the empirical and descriptive above the analytic.

But the full force of the movement came in the 1960s with the work of a number of writers – Thomas Kuhn, Paul Feyerabend, Stephen Toulmin, and Russell Hanson – who challenged the common ground held by positivists and deductivists alike. Rejecting previous accounts of the nature and development of science, and of the ultimate purpose of the philosophy of science, this 'second wave' of historicist philosophy of science carried out nothing short of an upturning of the received view of the scientific enterprise and the branch of philosophy that examined it.

Taken together, the historicists' criticisms attacked four key areas of the positivist program – its mode of philosophical explanation (specifically its tendency towards ahistorical and explicitly normative accounts); its vision of scientific development and the role of scientific theory; its account of scientific method and rationality; and its commitment to the unity of science. It helped spark a crisis in philosophy in the early 1960s that ranged from logic and epistemology to metaphysics and scientific realism; and in doing so it prepared the way for the 'third wave' of philosophical naturalism and the social construction that followed.

Here a brief digression from our main theme of the emerging role of the social in philosophies of science is in order. One of the most significant consequences of critiques of positivism and the advent of post-positivist philosophies of science was the proliferation of 'specialized' philosophies of science. As the demand for intertheoretic reduction of all sciences down to a base in physics waned, it became possible to consider the subject matter and methodology of the special sciences as distinct from physics. Philosophers of science became less confident in J. J. C. Smart's claim in the 1960s that biology would never be a science until it emulated the logical and empirical structure of physics (Smart 1963). This 'physics envy,' as biologist Ernst Mayr described it, properly ended in biology once the modern synthesis of Mendelian genetics and evolutionary theory went molecular after Watson and Crick in 1953. Not long after, with the early work of Marjorie Greene (Greene 1968), David Hull[3] and Michael Ruse (Ruse 1973), philosophy of biology became an important field within the philosophy of science, one which has proliferated ever since. Philosophers of biology, particularly the first generation, sought to bring philosophy and science into close proximity without subsuming one into the other. This led many researchers, such as William Wimsatt and others, to spend extended periods of time in the laboratories of leading biologists like Richard Lewontin, and later paved the way for philosopher-biologist collaborations like those between Robert Brandon and Janos Antonovics (Brandon, and Antonowics 1995). As philosophers of science began to take the biological sciences for what they are, new areas of philosophical investigation such as evolution and development, ethology, ecology, systematics, and so forth, opened up for study. Methodologically speaking, it became relevant to consider whether burgeoning philosophy of biology was wedded to post-Quinean philosophical naturalism, which was titrated to varying extents with historicism (Callebaut 1993a).

Historicism

Despite their profound disagreements over epistemology and the demarcation problem, the positivists and the deductivists had much in common. As Ian Hacking has noted, the two groups shared a core set of beliefs that would be challenged by the historicism of the 1960s. They held that: the sciences in general, and physics in particular, exemplified human rationality; that they were (or ought to be) distinguished from other bodies of knowledge and speculation on methodological grounds; that there was a sharp division between theory and observation; that the growth of knowledge was cumulative; that science had a rigid deductive structure; that scientific terms were precise; and that the sciences were unified. That final unity was, moreover, twofold – a methodological unity, which held that the natural sciences abided by one true method; and a reductionist unity, motivated partly by considerations of elegance, which believed that the distinct scientific disciplines were ultimately part of one general science (Hacking 1983: 3–5).

Methodologically, the groups also shared a vision of the purpose of philosophical investigations. Their aim was to produce what Quine termed a 'first philosophy' – a foundational enterprise intended to be logically and methodologically prior to science and with no empirical content (Callebaut 1993b: 3). The purpose was to uncover the general logical structure of all scientific theories and to lay out the epistemological relations between theory and evidence. By expressing these logical and transhistorical epistemological guidelines – guidelines that any real science ought to follow regardless of discipline and epoch – their philosophy was meant to be timeless, *a priori*, and prescriptive. Their interest was not so much in accounting for actual scientific practice; rather, they sought to articulate, on principled grounds, how an ideally logical scientist ought to think (Giere 1988: 24). They drew support for their view from Reichenbach's formal distinction between, on one hand, the context of justification – dominated by questions of legitimacy, justification, soundness, reason, and logic, questions with which philosophy of science was legitimately concerned; and the context of discovery on the other – the historical details of psychology, culture, and contingency that interested the historian or the sociologist (Hacking 1983: 5–6). History, insofar as it figured at all in their explanations, furnished the schematized illustrations for conclusions arrived at by other means.[4]

In its most sweeping form, then, historicism was a repudiation of a mode of philosophical practice that had dominated the early twentieth century. It sparked an ongoing debate in the mid-1960s over the purpose of philosophy of science. Should it study scientific activity as it happens? Or should its purpose be to reformulate the problems of explanation and confirmation in terms of deductive logic? Should its purpose be description or logical reconstruction?[5] Where Carnap and Popper had put forward seemingly timeless, prescriptive accounts, the historicists aimed to give philosophical accounts of *actual* scientific activity, with varying levels of complexity and richness.

If their predecessors had marginalized history, the historicists made it central to their program. In its most historicist form, the movement treated history as the empirical font for philosophical investigations. Thomas Kuhn's *The Structure of Scientific Revolutions*, arguably the most widely influential book to emerge from twentieth-century philosophy of science, began its critique of positivism and deductivism with a statement about the transformative potential of historical studies: 'History, if viewed as a repository for more than anecdote or chronology, could produce a decisive transformation in the image of science by which we are now possessed.'[6] Conceived while Kuhn was a graduate student in theoretical physics at Harvard, the account built on Russell Hanson's work on conceptual schemes and on the work of the Harvard psychologists, Leo Postman and Jerome Bruner. It was intended as a kinematics of scientific development – a historically rooted, philosophically inflected, empirical *description* of the patterns through which science moved, with little attention to the specific forces behind that movement. Originally published as a monograph in the *International Encyclopedia of Unified Science* – the journal of the logical positivists – the work would later come under criticism for masking its normative aims. But in a discipline dominated by ahistorical accounts, Kuhn's work helped inaugurate a new historicist philosophy of science that brought it much closer to the history of science.[7]

Already in the late 1950s, Russell Hanson had urged an interest in the 'logic of scientific discovery' instead of the 'logic of justification' (Hanson 1958). Kuhn's colleague at Berkeley in the 1960s, Paul Feyerabend, made the same historical and descriptive approach central to his later attacks on the deductivists. A former student of Popper, Feyerabend used historical examples early on to defend traditional deductivist positions, but soon saw the overtly normative program of the logical positivists and the tight deductivism of Popper and his followers as a threat to the success of the actual scientific enterprise.[8] The same impulse would run through the works of Shapere, Toulmin and Laudan. Together, their emphasis would shape not only future philosophical investigations but also the emerging field of the sociology of scientific knowledge.

The historicists argued that the 'received view' of scientific development was deeply flawed. Even as they had disregarded history and disagreed over the precise logical structure of the sciences, philosophers like Carnap and Popper had assumed a logic of scientific development in which a steadily growing and autonomous body of experimental results underwrote theoretical conclusions of varying permanence. The progress of science was linear and cumulative. In place of progress and accretion, the historicists stressed rupture and discontinuity, paradigm shifts and conceptual breaks. In Kuhn's model, for instance, scientific development was a cyclical process – normal science, crisis, revolution, and the return to normal science under a different paradigm. Rather than a steady, cumulative acquisition of knowledge, scientific development was 'a series of peaceful interludes punctuated by intellectually violent revolutions.' In those revolutions, he explained, 'one conceptual world view is replaced by another' (Wade 1977: 144).

Kuhn's emphasis on paradigms and Hanson's conceptual schemes further pointed to the elevated status of scientific theory in the historicist programme. Conceptual schemes had certainly figured in the work of the logical positivists, the post-war work of Philipp Frank and Rudolph Carnap being good examples. But even as conceptual frameworks changed, Frank and Carnap believed that the underlying observations – the empirical basis of the protocol statements so central to the positivist program – remained intact. Observations were theory independent and granted theoretical statements their meaning, so that theory was 'parasitic' on the observation (Feyerabend 1958). Historicism drew no such sharp distinction between theory and experiment. Furthermore, the historicists sought to stand the received view on its head, mounting a devastating critique about the possibility of theory-free observation in the process. Theory, they argued, was primary; observation was subordinate. Writing in the late fifties, Russell Hanson would put it succinctly, claiming that all perception is theory-laden (Hanson 1958: esp. Chap. 1). In a statement that would resonate with the later sociology of science, Feyerabend elaborated the claim: 'Experimental evidence does not consist of facts pure and simple, but of facts analyzed, modeled, and manufactured according to some theory' (Feyerabend 1981: 61). And if the theoretical determined the observational, then ruptures in theory cut deep, running all the way through seemingly transhistorical experimental results. Facts as well as concepts did not carry over from one conceptual scheme to another. They were incommensurable.[9] Although what was meant by incommensurability varied over authors and over time – from Kuhn's early worldview incommensurability to Feyerabend's more limited meaning of incommensurability – the vision of science dominated by theory, plagued by imprecise concepts and language, and developing according to no clear teleology marked a sharp departure from the clean linear narratives of the logical positivists and the Popperians.

The view of cumulative and linear scientific development had been underwritten by the belief in a single true scientific method that distinguished science from other forms of knowledge and belief. The logical positivists had believed that method was rooted in verification; Popper argued that refutation was the key, involving bold conjectures that scientists then did their best to improve by trying to refute them. For the historicists, however, the view of the objective and skeptical scientist did not hold up to the way science was actually done. Rather than the radical skeptics of Popper's philosophy, for instance, scientists on Kuhn's view were naturally conservative, holding on to theories or continuing to work under them even when faced with anomalies or refuting instances, accepting archetypal solutions to certain problems and applying them to current ones. Only after the dominant paradigm could no longer account for a growing mass of anomalies was it seriously challenged, and then usually by young outsiders. Kuhn's analyses focused on the local and the contingent rather than the universal and the abstract. His kinematics of science itself did not threaten rationality. But its rejection of overarching method and its inclusion of metaphysical elements in paradigm choice caused some to interpret the historicist impulse in general as a challenge to rationality in science. Its description of how science had historically progressed did not rule out the possibility that revolution itself was a rational process (Hacking 1983: 9). But it was the dynamics of science it presented – or rather its anti-dynamics – that implicitly threatened the strict rational structure of the positivists and the deductivists. Kuhn likened the conversion of scientists from one paradigm to another as a religious conversion or a Gestalt shift. In doing so, he opened the door to metaphysical considerations in theory choice, which the logical positivists had sought to banish and which Popper had allowed only as a starting point. Kuhn's later work on theory choice played down any epistemological relativism, suggesting that scientists ought to follow a set of more or less universal criteria: accuracy, consistency, breadth of scope, simplicity, fruitfulness for new research (Kuhn 1977: 321–2). But his initial position generated two broad reactions: those who took Kuhn's lead and push it further; and those who argued for a rationality in science despite its complex historical details.

Paul Feyerabend mounted the most energetic attack against scientific method from within the historicist camp. His work was characterized by a rejection of what he saw as the tyranny of method. An early student and follower of Popper, by the late 1960s he had become increasingly dissatisfied with rationalist attempts to articulate or discover rules of scientific method. His views grew out of the Berkeley of the early 1960s, with its increasingly diverse student population, its radical protests, and its general suspicion of overarching formal systems. Like Kuhn, Feyerabend held that the systems of the logical positivists and the Popperians could not do justice to the way science was actually done, and furthermore that rational standards could never recreate the richness and vibrancy of actual science.[10] In *Against Method*, Feyerabend suggested that no exceptionless methodological rules governed the development of science, unless it was the useless injunction that 'anything goes.'[11] If science was not 'irrational,' Feyerabend suggested, it certainly followed no overarching pattern. Instead Feyerabend allowed many rationalities and modes of reason. This 'epistemological anarchism' led him to argue that only a plurality of incompatible theories, all competing against one another, would lead to the advancement of knowledge.

Against Method was originally intended as one half of a larger work to be entitled *For and Against Method*. The argument in favor of the 'rationalist' case – which would defend the existence of clear rules of scientific method for all good science – was supposed to be written by Feyerabend's friend and erstwhile fellow Popperian, Imre Lakatos. Lakatos's unexpected death in February 1974 left Feyerabend to work on the volume alone. The original title nevertheless pointed to the place of rationality and method in Lakatos's philosophy. On Lakatos's view, history was valuable, but mainly in furnishing exemplars for a philosophy of science based on rationality and uniform methodology: 'Guided by this philosophy it ought to be possible to display science as a process which exemplifies its principles and develops in accord with its teachings.' His own philosophy was an attempt to modify Popper's philosophy in light of historicist criticisms like those of Kuhn. While he agreed with Kuhn that theories were not rejected on the basis of a single refutation, he proposed a modified falsificationism that operated at the level of research programs rather than individual instances (Lakatos 1978: 110). For a research programme like Newtonian physics, for example, there was a hard core (what Lakatos also called a 'negative heuristic') made up of the three laws of motion and the law of gravitation. Surrounding that core was a 'protective belt of auxiliary hypotheses' that accommodated anomalies. The protective belt then provided a positive heuristic, indicating how to alter the protective belt or the variants of the research program (Lakatos 1978: 50).

3. Primacy of the Social

Historicism, or post-positivism as some commentators call it, is the source of many critiques of logical positivism and hypothetico-deductivism. Along with the strong program, historicism has had a decisive effect on philosophy on science. Theories of scientific explanation are now expected to respond to historicism, whether to show how they elude claims about the historical or social underpinnings of scientific explanation, or to show how they have accommodated the insights of the different varieties of historicism in the philosophy of science. In this respect, whether one enthusiastically advocates or solemnly rejects historicism, the clear linkage now forged between philosophy of science and sociology of science is indisputable. The 'second wave' has for philosophers of science transformed the possible scope and meaning of theories of scientific explanation to potentially contain social elements (see, for example, McMullin 1983).

Sociology of Science and the Strong Programme

In the 1970s, David Bloor, a philosopher at the University of Edinburgh, launched a critique of the way that previous authors – including Popper, Lakatos, and Laudan – had invoked social factors in the production of scientific knowledge. Referring to their approach as the 'teleological model,' Bloor argued that their explanations tended to divide behavior or belief into two types: rational and irrational, right or wrong, true or false. They then used sociology or psychology to explain the negative side, and logic and epistemology to explain the positive. In his programatic work *Knowledge and Social Imagery* (1976), Bloor laid out a challenge to the teleological model that claimed social factors could be used to explain the content of scientific knowledge, rather than merely its contingent and irrational features. Called the Strong Programme in the Sociology of Scientific Knowledge (SSK), the movement was composed of two schools – the Edinburgh School, led by Bloor and Barry Barnes; and the Bath School, associated with Harry Collins and his student Trevor Pinch.[12]

What united the members of the Strong Programme was a belief that sociological explanations could legitimately lay claim to territory previously claimed by philosophy. Bloor wrote:

> All knowledge, whether it be in the empirical sciences or even in mathematics, should be treated, through and through, as material for investigation . . . There are no limitations which lie in the absolute or transcendent character of scientific knowledge itself, or in the special nature of rationality, validity, truth or objectivity. (Bloor 1991: 3)

They saw their approach as essentially scientific, seeking maximum generality and impartiality while observing four defining tenets: explanations should be (1) causal – they should be concerned with conditions (not merely social) that bring about belief or states of knowledge; (2) impartial with respect to truth and falsity, rationality and irrationality, success and failure – both need explanation; (3) symmetrical – the same types of cause would explain true and false beliefs; and (4) reflexive – patterns of explanation would have to be applicable to sociology itself; otherwise sociology would be a standing refutation of its own theories.[13]

Of the four tenets, the principle of symmetry would prove to be the most philosophically controversial, serving as a target for accusations of epistemological relativism. But the Strong Programme's focus on scientific controversies and on the role of explicitly social factors – political power, dominant interests, and rhetorical strategies – in bringing controversies to a close, further challenged the place of logic and evidence as the ultimate arbiters of scientific disputes. The Bath School's work on experimental replication, for instance, suggested that experiments never furnish the impersonal evidence that allows us to decide between competing claims. For an experimental claim to be sanctioned, it must be replicated. For replication to occur, scientists must agree that the experimental trials have been performed competently. But because experimental work relies on often unarticulated and potentially inarticulable skills – what is often referred to as 'tacit knowledge' – any experimental trial is always in principle vulnerable to claims of incompetence. The only way to verify the competence of the experiment is to know whether the original claim is true or false, which is precisely what the original experiment is designed to decide. Any further experiments are also vulnerable to this 'experimenter's regress,' so that experiments are not the neat algorithmic process that the adherents of the 'teleological model' would have us believe (Hess 1997: 96–7).

Science, Post-Normal Science and the Risk Society

Philosophy of science nevertheless continues to be a discipline distinct from sociology of science. Its methodologies, core questions and organisation in the academy, and in its professional societies are related, but do not significantly overlap with the sociology of science. Philosophy of science is not been absorbed into sociology of science, but it is fair to say that philosophy of science has changed due to its interaction with sociology of science. Philosophers of science have broadened their conception of science, scientific explanation and their conception of their own discipline, which is a different outcome from being imitators of sociology of science. Perhaps the most decisive change resides in the movement from the internalist perspective of theories of scientific explanation espoused by logical positivists to those who articulate theories of science from what might be called an externalist perspective.

Externalist perspectives take the position that science, and what counts as a scientific explanation, can only be understood if the activity of science is considered and described in its broader social context. Integrated into this perspective is the 'second wave' influence under which it is conceivable that citing social forces can partially constitute a theory of explanation about science. The expanded version of this thesis claims that science cannot be understood fully without understanding its internal activities, as well as the intersection and interchange between science and its social context. The study of science and scientific explanation from what can be generically described as a science and society perspective is now a significant component of philosophy of science.

There are five major conceptual shifts in the understanding of the relationship between science and society in the history of the philosophy of science. The first is reflected in positivist theories of science, which hold that science is defined by a methodology of knowledge acquisition and verification, which makes it, among all other intellectual endeavors, the only bona fide arbiter of the truth. Positivists argue that social problems arise due to failures to adopt scientific rationality in non-scientific contexts. Metaphysics and ethics, in which nonverifiable claims allegedly abound, are sources of social problems. This conception about the deficiencies of social existence is challenged indirectly in the second configuration of the relationship between science and society. Social constructivists, following Kuhn, argue that far from being devoid of social elements, historical contingencies always play a role in the development, retention and change of theory in science. On this view, the point of philosophy of science is not to develop an ahistorical account of science, but to understand the historicity of science. The implication is that the social entanglements may trickle down to the level of science. But the reverse, in Kuhn's account in particular, is not really considered because the focus is on the nature of science and change in science. Thus, how science percolates through the social realm and what that might tell us further about science is not the critical issue for Kuhnian social constructivism.

This point of view is reversed in the third juxtaposition of science and society, in which the thesis is that a necessary part of what defines science and what counts as a scientific explanation is a function of its meaning and relevance to a social context. The *locus classicus* of this conception of science is the widely overlooked *Scientific Knowledge and its Social Problems* (Ravetz 1989). In it, Ravetz argues that the Kuhnian project is incomplete unless the realization that theory change in science is fixed to a historical context is balanced with the understanding that the scientific and technological research and development, by virtue of the very activities themselves, always engender social problems that cannot be separated from the research and development process itself. Consequently, science cannot be a monolithic enterprise, anchored by one methodology and with truth as its core objective. Instead, the science-society inter-actions, which make science and technology relevant, but at the same time potentially harmful, to society, change the objectives, methodology, and quality of investigation within the various scientific subspecializations.

From the Strong Programme it had become clear that appraising science with benchmarks of objective truth conditions fell short of the way in which scientists actually evaluate each others' work. Certainly this was true by the time that anthropological studies of bench science by Bruno Latour (Latour 1979) and David Hull's study of the peer review process impact on scientific theory change had been completed (Hull 1988). Ravetz's work had deepened the issue in the early 1970s because in addition to the thesis about the connectivity between science and society, there was also the implication that quality in science could be appraised by the way in which science was practiced and by the impacts that it had on society. This idea appears to be a normative assessment of a fact situation about the practice of science, and to a certain extent that was true of *Scientific Knowledge and its Social Problems*.

In the fourth configuration of science and society, however, what appeared to be a *post facto* normative appraisal of science took on the definitional role originally intended. Funtowicz and Ravetz developed the NUSAP (Numeral; Unit; Spread; Assessment; Pedigree) system for evaluating the quality of science (Funtowicz and Ravetz 1990). This system is an inductive, quasi-formal system for evaluating science quality that incorporates the theoretical and empirical criteria of science with social criteria. Their system is based on the premise that the project of the exact sciences, previously championed by logical positivists and hypothetico-deductivists, is actually an impossible one. They regard much science as being essentially uncertain, prob-abilistic or possibly stochastic given the irreducibly complex systems being investi-gated. Under these conditions, science cannot strive for certainty with assurances it will reach truth just because of its reliance on quantitative methodologies. Instead, the crucial exercise to undertake is to find qualitative measures of science quality, not only to distinguish good from bad science and to learn more about the nature of science by studying its social effects, but also to find ways of appraising science for the sake of regulating science and technology in the public's interest. In this latter respect, the idea that science has a normative dimension in view of its social consequences has culminated in a descriptive methodology and scheme for characterizing science.

This conception of science comes with a practical and political dimension. Since science creates social problems, which cannot be separated from the process of doing science, and are not otherwise eliminable from science, society will constantly face social problems raised by scientific research and technological innovation. The public, which finds itself affected by science, should therefore have a direct say in which science and technology is permitted in society, and how it develops. Science, once subject to the peer review of other scientists, would be open to the appraisal of the public. Unsurprisingly, the 'extended peer-group' of ordinary citizens could be expected to address epistemic and non-epistemic issues alike. The entire process is post-normal science, a term which accounts for the fact that no longer is science simply Kuhnian puzzle solving, and no longer can it be seen as anything but value charged (Funtowicz and Lavetz 1993). In the fifth and final configuration between science and society, this extended peer-group is not restricted to a limited group of democratically engaged individuals. As society finds itself nearing the point of preoccupation with science and technology, it becomes accustomed to the process of considering risks and benefits of post-normal science. At that point the language of scientific risk becomes ordinary discourse in the evaluation of personal and social risk (Beck 1992).

In this final phase of the articulation between science and society, the science-centric modernist program which culminates in logical positivism passes through historicism, post-normal science, and reaches what Beck calls 'reflexive modernization.' At this juncture, the philosophy of science has not swung away from the perennial issues about causation, realism, or the nature of explanation. Philosophy of science has, as this article has attempted to demonstrate, incorporated new insights about the nature of science and the scientific. To some extent these have been launched as post-positivist criticisms of scientism and technocracy, and have stimulated methodological expansion and the proliferation of subspecializations within the philosophy of science. What is less obvious now, and a task for the philosophy of science in the future, is to understand how the historical development of reflexive modernization may have implications for our conception of science and its role in our lives.

Notes

1. For introductions to these subjects, see Toulmin 1960; Hempel 1966; and Kockelmans 1968.
2. Even one of the leaders of British logical positivism, A. J. Ayer, acknowledged in 1959 that metaphysical questions may have philosophical meaning and interest. See Jones and Fogelin 1997: 269–70.
3. For very early philosophy of biology, see Hull 1965, and 1969.
4. Moritz Schlick, for example, held the common positivist conviction that the Michelson-Morley experiment led to Einstein's development of the Special Theory of Relativity. See, for example, Moritz Schlick, *Space and Time in Contemporary Physics* (1917). Einstein himself saw that genetic link as too positivistic. For the debate on the place of the Michelson-Morley experiment in Einstein's development of relativity, see Holton 1988: 279–370.

5. See, for instance, the debate between Ernest Nagel and Stephen Toulmin (1966), *Scientific American* 214 (2) (Feb.), pp. 129–33; and 214 (4) (Apr.), pp. 9–11.

6. Kuhn 1970: 1. In a career that would take him to Harvard, Berkeley, Princeton, and MIT, Kuhn was not trained in philosophy but was aware that his work had philosophical consequences. See Kuhn 2000: 276.

7. Book would be republished by University of Chicago Press, which issued it as a 180–page book in 1962.

8. Feyerabend remarks that the logical positivist Otto Neurath had already put this criticism of Popper some time before. See Feyerabend 1978: 91.

9. In this way, Kuhn's paradigm shifts differed from the theory subsumption of Nagel and others, where a succeeding theory explained new phenomena and made the same accurate predictions as previous ones. See Hacking 1983: 670. Although notionally similar, Kuhn's notion of meaning incommensurability differs from Quine's indeterminacy of translation in important respects. For Quine, the problem is that *many* translations are possible from a given language or theory. For Kuhn, no adequate translation exists, or is even possible. For a later view, see Kuhn 1989: 10. On Feyerabend's discussion of incommensurability across Newtonian and relativisitic gravitation, see Feyerabend 1965.

10. Feyerabend remarks that the logical positivist Otto Neurath had already put this criticism of Popper some time before. See Feyerabend 1978: 91.

11. Feyerabend reportedly began his move towards anarcho-rationalism following a conversation in 1965 with the physicist Carl Von Weizsäcker on the historical origins of quantum theory. This was also the beginning of Feyerabend's stress on actual scientific practice rather than abstract, normative models. See Feyerabend 1978: 117.

12. The two groups differed mainly over the issue of methodological relativism, which treated the social factors as the *cause* of natural phenomena: Collins and the Bath School sanctioned the idea; Bloor found it too Idealist. Methodological relativism is strictly a methodological point, but in treating the social as the cause of the natural, it has metaphysical Idealist implications that the Edinburgh school is not comfortable with. It should be noted that as a methodological point strictly, it has little to say about different philosophical positions.

13. Four tenets define the strong program in sociology of knowledge; they are not new but are an amalgam of strains found in Durkheim, Mannheim, and Znaniecki. See Bloor 1991: 7.

References

Ayer, A. J. (1952), *Language, Truth, and Logic*, New York: Dover Publications.

Beck, U. (1992), *The Risk Society*, New York: Sage Publications.

Bloor, D. [1976] (1991), *Knowledge and Social Imagery*, Chicago: Chicago University Press.

Brandon, R., and J. Antonovics (1995), 'The Coevolution of Organism and Environment,' in R. Brandon (ed.) (1995), *Concepts and Methods in Evolutionary Biology*, Cambridge: Cambridge University Press.

Callebaut, W. (1993a), *Taking the Naturalist Turn, or How Real Philosophy of Science is Done*, Chicago: University of Chicago Press.

Callebaut, W. (1993b), 'Turning Naturalistic: An Introduction,' in W. Callebaut (1993), *Taking the Naturalist Turn, or How Real Philosophy of Science is Done*, Chicago: University of Chicago Press, pp. 1–9.

Carnap, R. (1938), 'Logical Foundations of the Unity of Science,' in O. Neurath, R. Carnap, and C. Morris (eds) (1952), *International Encyclopedia of Unified Science*, Chicago: University of Chicago Press, pp. 42–62

Carnap, R. [1936–37] (1953), 'Testability and Meaning,' in H. Feigl, and H. Brodbeck (eds) (1953), *Readings in the Philosophy of Science*, New York: Appleton-Century-Crofts, pp. 47–92.

Comte, A. [1830–42] (1975), *Cours de philosophie positive*, Paris: Hermann.

Feyerabend, P. (1958), 'An Attempt at a Realistic Interpretation of Experience,' *Proceedings of the Aristotelian Society for the Study of Philosophy* 58: 160–2.

Feyerabend, P. (1965), 'On the "Meaning" of Scientific Terms,' *Journal of Philosophy* 62: 267–71.

Feyerabend, P. (1978), *Science in a Free Society*, London: New Left Books.

Feyerabend, P. (1981), *Realism, Rationalism, and Scientific Method: Philosophical Papers*, vol. 1, Cambridge: Cambridge University Press.

Funtowicz, S. O., and J. R. Ravetz (1990), *Uncertainty and Quality in Science for Policy*, Dordrecht: Kluwer.

Funtowicz, S. O., and J. R. Ravetz (1993), 'Science for the Post-Normal Age,' *Futures* 25: 739–55.

Giere, R. N. (1988), *Explaining Science: A Cognitive Approach*, Chicago: University of Chicago Press.

Greene, M. (1968), *Approaches to a Philosophical Biology*, New York and London: Basic Books.

Hacking, I. (1983), *Representing and Intervening: Introductory Topics in the Philosophy of Natural Science*, Cambridge: Cambridge University Press.

Hanfling, O. (1981), *Essential Readings in Logical Positivism*, Oxford: Blackwell.

Hanson, N. R. (1958), *Patterns of Discovery: An Inquiry into the Conceptual Foundations of Science*, Cambridge: Harvard University Press.

Hempel, C. G. (1966), *Philosophy of Natural Science*, Englewood Cliffs: Prentice Hall.

Hempel, C. G. (1965), *Aspects of Scientific Explanation*, New York: Free Press.

Hempel, C. G., and P. Oppenheim [1948] (1953), 'The Logic of Explanation (secs 1–7),' in H. Feidl, and M. Brodbeck (eds) (1953), *Readings in the Philosophy of Science*, New York: Appleton-Century-Crofts, pp. 319–52.

Hess, D. J. (1997), *Science Studies: An Advance Introduction*, New York: New York University Press.

Holton, G. [1973] (1988), 'Einstein, Michelson, and the Crucial Experiment,' in G. Holton (1988), *Thematic Origins of Scientific Thought*, 2nd edn, Cambridge: Harvard University Press, pp. 279–370.

Hull, D. L. (1965), 'The Effects of Essentialism on Taxonomy: Two Thousand Years of Stasis,' *The British Journal for the Philosophy of Science* 15: 314–26, and 16: 1–18.

Hull, D. L. (1969), 'What Philosophy of Biology Is Not,' *Journal of the History of Biology* 2: 241–68.

Hull, D. L. (1988), *Science as Progress*, Chicago: Chicago University Press.

Jones, W. T., and R. Fogelin (1997), *A History of Western Philosophy: The Twentieth Century to Quine and Derrida*, vol. 5, 3rd edn, New York: Harcourt Brace.

Kockelmans, C. (1968), *Philosophy of Science: The Historical Background*, New York: Free Press.

Kuhn, T. S. [1962] (1970), *The Structure of Scientific Revolutions*, Chicago: University of Chicago Press.

Kuhn, T. S. (1977), 'Objectivity, Value Judgment, and Theory Choice,' in T. S. Kuhn (1977), *The Essential Tension*, Chicago: University of Chicago Press, pp. 356–68.

Kuhn, T. S. (1989), 'Possible Worlds in the History of Science,' in A. Sture (ed.) (1989), *Possible Worlds in Humanities, Arts, and Sciences: Proceedings of the Nobel Symposium 65*, Berlin: de Gruyter, pp. 9–32.

Kuhn, T. S. (2000), *The Road since Structure: Philosophical Essays 1970–1993, with an Autobiographical Interview*, Chicago: University of Chicago Press.

Lakatos, I. (1978), *The Methodology of Scientific Research Programmes: Philosophical Papers*, vol. 1, Cambridge: Cambridge University Press.

Latour, B. (1979), *Laboratory Life: The Social Construction of Scientific Facts*, London: Sage.

McMullin, E. (1983), 'Values in Science,' *Philosophy of Science Association 82* 2: 3–28.

Oppenheim, P., and H. Putnam (1958), 'Unity of Science as Working Hypothesis,' in H. Feigl, M. Scriven, and G. Maxell (eds) (1958). *Minnesota Studies in the Philosophy of Science, Volume II: Concepts, Theories, and the Mind-Body Problem*, Minneapolis: University of Minnesota Press, pp. 3–36.

Popper, K. (1961), *The Logic of Scientific Discovery*, New York: Basic Books.

Ravetz, J. [1972] (1989), *Scientific Knowledge and its Social Problems*, Oxford: Oxford University Press.

Reichenbach, H. (1958), *The Rise of Scientific Philosophy*, Berkeley: University of California Press.

Ruse, M. (1973), *Philosophy of Biology*, London: Hutchinson.

Schlick, M. [1925–36] (1979), 'Meaning and Verification,' in H. L. Mulder, and B. van de Velde-Schlick (eds) (1979), *Philosophical Papers*, vol. 2, Dordrecht: D. Reidel, pp. 456–90.

Smart, J. J. C. (1963), *Philosophy and Scientific Realism*, London: Routledge and Kegan Paul.

Toulmin, S. (1960), *The Philosophy of Science*, New York: Harper.

Wade, N. (1977), 'Thomas Kuhn: Revolutionary Theorist of Science,' *Science, New Series*, 197 4299 (Jul. 8): 144.

Ethics

Jan Narveson

Ethical theory in the twentieth-century Anglo-American philosophical world may be said to have begun with a bang, with the publication of G. E. Moore's *Principia Ethica* (1903), which proclaimed that all forms of ethical naturalism are doomed to fallacy, in the form of what he famously called the 'naturalistic fallacy.' For this purpose, 'naturalism' refers to the view that we can define ethical notions, without loss of meaning, in purely naturalistic terms – terms designating properties or states of affairs whose presence can be confirmed by the methods of empirical science. Soon thereafter, identifying the 'naturalistic fallacy,' or, more rarely, denying that there was such a thing, became a major preoccupation for nearly half of the century. Moore also held that the basic value-predicate – 'good,' as he claimed it was – designates a 'unique nonnatural property.' This position in ethical theory came to be called 'intuitionism.' If he is right about 'good' being the basic predicate in ethics and about its character, then ethics is fundamentally a rather special subject, hard even to relate to all the other matters, both of science and of common sense, in which philosophers have been interested through the years.

Crucial to Moore's argument was a challenge known as the 'Open Question Test.' Suppose that 'good' is synonymous with '*F*,' where '*F*' designates some 'natural' property. Then, says Moore, what is the status of the question 'Is *F* good?' If that is actually a logically open question – things that are *F* being capable of being either good or bad, so far as the meaning of '*F*' is concerned – then the proposed definition must be rejected, since otherwise it would be self-contradictory to say that something was *F* but not good. Moore's argument was widely regarded as a clincher. For if the claim that *F*s are good is really just the claim that *F*s are *F*, it's hard to see how that can be of any ethical interest; yet if the claim really is of ethical interest, then evidently '*F*' and 'good' cannot be synonymous. As it stood in Moore's work, this procedure requires that the inquirer have a pretty firm grasp of what does and what doesn't make sense, and of when something is conceivable and when not – as well as that all these semantic notions are reasonably clear and manageable. Late in the century, all those things were widely denied.

Meanwhile, in the first couple of decades the predominant tendency was to accept both of Moore's major claims: that ethical naturalism is fallacious, and that ethical intuitionism must be the appropriate conceptual remedy. Nevertheless, some intuitionists thought that Moore had the wrong predicates in view: what we really intuit are not truths about what's *intrinsically good*, but rather, say, *duties* (as advocated by W. D. Ross), or perhaps 'oughts' of some more general type. In *Principia Ethica* Moore explicitly held that claims about duty and right were definable: 'right' = 'cause of maximum value.' Ross strongly denies this. He agrees with Moore that the basic ideas of morals are intuited, and even compares them to geometric axioms. But with ethics, there is an interesting twist. For in marked contrast to mathematical axioms, his basic types of moral duties are not, as they stand, simply true universal sentences. Instead they announce what he calls prima facie duties. The idea is that what they identify as, so to say, tentatively duties, are what might turn out to be actual duties, which he in turn calls duties *sans phrase*. The 'prima facie duties' are 'prima facie' in that *insofar* as an act is of the kind identified by the description in question – for example, as the fulfilling of a promise – they are obligatory *unless* doing so would conflict, at the time, with the fulfillment of some other contrary obligation that was in the circumstances more 'stringent.' This extremely important adjustment, as we might call it, to the logic of moral reasoning made it possible to retain the sense that morals is a set of general rules or requirements, and yet to recognize the real complexities of moral life. Of course, it also brought up the question how these rather loose-sounding principles can be 'intuited.' And it means that we apparently have at least three intuitions to be managed in any case of conflict: we intuit each of the two moral prima facie axioms (or more), but then we need also to intuit the relative strengths of the two *in the circumstances*, which we therefore must, of course, understand well enough to see that a problem exists. Ross denied – plausibly – that we could order the list of prima facie principles so as to enable us to decide more or less mechanically which of two conflicting duties was the real thing in the particular case.

Ross claimed, also quite plausibly, to be representing the thought of ordinary people in his system. He develops a list of basic prima facie *duties*, as he calls them – about a half-dozen – which he supposes to be pretty complete. (He lists duties of fidelity, such as to fulfill our commitments, of reparation, of gratitude, of beneficence, of noninjury to others, and of self-improvement.) But he does not claim that it is altogether complete – and this again raises a question about intuitionism: how and why should it be capable of this kind of open-endedness? Further, we need another intuition, of 'relative stringency' or 'weightiness,' if we run into the problem, as we so frequently do, that we have to choose between one duty and another incompatible one.

It does have to be recognized that while perhaps centerfield attention has gone to the intuitionists, all kinds of work was going on, especially in America, that ran very contrary to the 'dominant view'; no simple unqualified generalization about twentieth-century ethics will pass muster. (A major case in point is the work of the American Ralph Barton Perry, developed in his magnum opus, *General Theory of Value* (1926).)

Emotivism

Before long, many philosophers found all this rather hard to swallow. Intuitionism's major challenge came in the 1930s, especially under the influence of logical positivism and its variants. These thinkers continued to accept the idea of the naturalistic fallacy, but they rejected the 'non-naturalism' of the intuitionists. Instead they held that when we say that something is good or bad, right or wrong, we are not in fact making further *statements* about the matters being evaluated at all, over and above the ordinary, fact-laden kinds of reasons we give for those judgements. Rather, they proposed, when we make ethical and other evaluative judgements we are *expressing our attitudes* toward those things – *not* talking *about* those attitudes. We are not, for example, merely stating that we have them; and those attitudes are logically distinguishable, always, from the descriptions of the things toward which they are taken. This general view is known as emotivism. It was initially proposed by A. J. Ayer in the UK, and later expounded more richly by the American Charles Stevenson, notably in his major treatise, *Ethics and Language* (1944). A very important variant, championed notably by the late R. M. Hare of Oxford, has it that what we really do in making judgements is to shift from *description* to *prescription* – hence the view is dubbed 'prescriptivism.' The difference between emotivism and prescriptivism is subtle – to the point where some would hold it to be nonexistent. However, prescriptivism has a clear implication that is less clear in emotivism: Hare held that the sign of assent to a prescription, or imperative, was *action*. If I 'agree' with the command, 'Do X,' then, says Hare, we can expect that I *will* do *x*, given opportunity and capability. Hare argues that assertions of the form '*x* is wrong' entail a prescription, 'Don't do *x*!,' and in fact a prescription addressed to *everyone at large, including the speaker*. If this is so, then we should expect such persons either to avoid doing *x* or else to dissent from the evaluation that *x* is wrong. An interesting subject for discussion throughout the latter twentieth century was whether this implication actually is present in moral claims. We familiarly say of someone who proclaims that a certain kind of conduct is wrong, yet who is caught doing it himself, that he is a 'hypocrite,' and this is regarded as a serious moral criticism. But is it a criticism that applies, as Hare claims, by virtue of the very logic of ethical language? Those inclined to accept the Hare thesis must, somehow, make their peace with apparent counterexamples – with people who agree that what they do is wrong but think nothing of that, or conceivably even regard it as somehow a merit, for instance. The Hare thesis also generated discussion of 'moral weakness.' How much and in what way this diagnosis can help is an interesting question. It is fair to say that the jury is still out on that one. (The implication is notably denied by moral realism, of which more below.)

Both intuitionism and emotivism bring up a major issue: what, if anything, is the connection between the sorts of considerations we tend to think of as *reasons for* ethical judgements, and *those judgements themselves*, if indeed there is a fallacy involved in going from one to the other? How can ethics be in any sense rational or even reasonable, under the circumstances? Broadly speaking, much of ethics in the remainder of the twentieth century has tried to address this question. There have been two main lines of work, along with a further one that deserves more attention than it has received from professional philosophers.

Another kind of 'intuitionism'

One of these lines – by far the dominant one – proceeds from a distinction in the notion of 'intuition' not explicitly recognized by Moore. An intuition in this general sense is a 'hunch' or a *pre-analytic belief*. Almost all of us grow up being taught, and accepting, that murder is wrong, that kindness is a virtue, and some other apophthegms of the kind. These are 'intuitions' in the sense that we don't necessarily know *why* we believe these things or how to analyze those beliefs, and yet we are quite confident in them all the same. The intuitionism of the early twentieth century may be looked on as a sort of metaphysical account of these unanalyzed beliefs: they are unanalyzed because they are indeed, at root, *unanalyzable*, and are so because the properties of good and bad, or whatever the basic ones are claimed to be, are themselves fundamentally 'simple' and as such incapable of further analysis. This we may call official, or metaphysical, intuitionism. But it can be distinguished from the non-metaphysical sense of the term in which we simply leave open the question of what precisely is meant by 'good' or 'right,' and appeal to the judgements in question in epistemic neutrality. Just as we have no hesitation in identifying something as a real material object, though we have little idea what that means or how we can really be justified in believing there are such things, so too we proceed in ethics on the basis of many certainties, or at least strongly held beliefs, even though we can give no account of what they mean or why they are true. According to this approach to ethical theory, then, we simply take our intuitions as they are, without prejudicing the analytical question, but we attempt to render our set of pre-philosophical moral beliefs more systematic, and to make sure that they are consistent with all else that we know. This view, then, can be called methodological intuitionism. The idea was given its canonical and certainly its most influential formulation in the famous work by the American John Rawls, *A Theory of Justice* (1971), where he identifies a procedure called 'reflective equilibrium.' This is the equilibrium, which he supposes we will arrive at in due course, between our most firmly held pre-analytic ethical views and whatever strictly theoretical considerations we find hard to reject; these latter might qualify or even negate some of the earlier beliefs, but cannot, he supposes, justify throwing out the ethical baby with the theoretical bathwater. What emerges is a mix of theory and pre-theoretical belief, the idea being to come up with the best mix possible. In the last decades of the twentieth century, this method has become dominant to the point, some would say, of dogma – critiques of the view are few, far between, and not much attended to in the main.

It is not widely appreciated how *thin* this methodological idea is. Rawls says nothing about the range or type of theories that would be eligible for entering into the 'theory' component of the equilibrium; he says almost nothing about the range of 'intuitions' entering at the nontheory end; and for all he says, the mix *can* range all the way from zero to 100 per cent intuition. This seems to leave us with literally *no* actual guidance. Perhaps the wide acceptance of the idea, then, is due to its being without substance.

To be sure, most writers, including Rawls himself, appear to have supposed that at least *some* of our pre-theoretical moral beliefs will be held so firmly as to be essentially unrejectable – that murder is wrong, for example. But the question now becomes, *why* we should regard this fact of being firmly held as itself constituting some kind of evidential constraint on theory construction. Could our pre-theoretical beliefs *all* be wrong? If not, why not? Perhaps the much-rejected 'metaphysical' version of intuitionism would imply that we *can't* be wrong about such things; but since it is not clear why that would be so, and in any case the idea is universally rejected, a proponent of reflective equilibrium could hardly take such a view. And then there is a further and very troubling point: wielders of this apparatus continually refer to 'our' intuitions. But what does 'our' refer to here? After all, very often the belief in question is by no means universally held. It might even be literally controversial, in the sense that the particular philosophical article at hand appeals to it despite awareness that others simply do not share the intuition in question. What, then, is the writer to say to those who are in the latter position? Alas, we are not told. But surely the role of theory becomes very important in the face of such facts.

Relativism and Egoism

Twentieth-century ethics has not lost sight of one of the major incentives to engage in ethical theory: the challenge of ethical relativism. Most writers on ethics have said at least something about this topic, and many have taken it very seriously. In the main, the tendency has been to regard it, when taken as a strictly moral theory, as basically incoherent. It is especially interesting that writers of emotivist/imperativist leaning have developed the case against it as strongly as others. Charles Stevenson, for instance, in his 'Relativism and Non-Relativism in the Theory of Value' (republished in the collection of his essays, *Facts and Values*) argues that far from entailing relativism, emotivism is basically *incompatible* with it. This constructive move provides an interesting conceptual insight running contrary to many expectations. The problem, simply put, is this: if we say that what is right among the people in group *A* is wrong among those in group *B*, do we mean only that the *A*s *think* it is right and the *B*s think the opposite? Or do we mean, somehow, that they are *both* right? If we do, though, there is the problem that they appear to disagree – after all, I can hardly hold that some action is *both* right, on the whole, and also wrong. If the *B*s agree that the *A*s really ought to do this thing, we must ask why. Perhaps they hold that there is a difference in the circumstances of the two groups which make it appropriate for the one to do the thing and the other to avoid it. But if so, the judgements are not really 'relative,' since both stem from a common principle applicable to all.

Much the same goes for egoism. It is one thing to say that each will do what he thinks best. But it is quite another to say that each *ought* to do whatever he thinks best, no matter what it is, and regardless of everyone else. Moral talk, after all, is used to evaluate the behavior of people generally, not just of oneself. If we say that it is right for someone to do whatever he likes, what would be the point of having the word 'right' in our vocabulary at all? If it does have a point, it must be usable for criticism – for finding that someone has done something wrong, as well as for finding that she has done right. As soon as we take that seriously, however, our talk will soon become quite incoherent if we suppose that each person ought to do whatever is in his or her own interest regardless of others. (Stevenson's discussion of relativism may be compared with a famous earlier analysis of ethical egoism, provided by the Australian Brian Medlin (1955).)

Naturalism Revived

Emotivism and prescriptivism didn't satisfy everyone either, and less so as the century went on. An interesting if much-neglected entry was that of Frances Sparshott, who proposes that 'to say that *x* is good is to say that *x* is such as to satisfy the wants of the person or persons concerned.' His ingenious formula offers many points at which people disagreeing about values may specifically be disagreeing: does *x* really do this? Are these the 'concerned' people, or not? Is getting what you want automatically satisfying, or must it await a sense of satisfaction? Sparshott's formula makes it obvious why those who think something good will also ipso facto favor it, without committing them to puzzling semantic maneuvres.

A different sort of naturalism was pressed for much of the late part of the century by Philippa Foot (Oxford and then UCLA) who seeks to revive talk of virtues and vices, and ultimately to ground those in the nature, biological and otherwise, of humans. The challenge for such a view is to show both that the 'grounding' works, makes sense, and yet retains the normativity central to any evaluative notion. Whether she has succeeded remained controversial at century's end.

The Rise of Applied Ethics

The other large development in ethics in the twentieth century, itself probably a result, in considerable part, of Rawls's idea, is the rise of *applied* ethics – that is, the discussion of concrete moral issues such as euthanasia, specific problems in business or medical ethics, and many more. These came to be pursued in the late twentieth century with a frequency and depth very much exceeding almost anything seen in the first half of the century. During that earlier period, indeed, there was a tendency to hold that philosophy could only properly be concerned with *conceptual analysis* – hands-on ethical problems must be left to others. The idea seemed to be that just as philosophers must leave science to the scientists, so they should leave ethics to the ethicists. One problem with that analogy is that there are no 'ethicists'; there are only all sorts of people, including religious ministers, psychiatrists, counselors, and assorted others, whose jobs get them often enough into ethical problems, but who actually have little training in ethics as such. It was never obvious that such people could be expected to do as well as those who have immersed themselves in the study of ethics for many years.

At any rate, methodological intuitionism, it is thought, erodes the basis for any such division of labor, and reinstates philosophy to an appropriate role as ethical critic on real questions of moral import. The difference between the philosopher and the ordinary person was only that the philosopher was keenly aware of the need for clarity and consistency; but those might, after all, be just the virtues needed for problems that are surrounded by confusion and controversy. The eventual outcome is that we are beginning to see 'philosophical cafes' at which people trained in academic philosophy meet up with ordinary people to try to shed light on their problems, many of which are broadly ethical in nature.

Morality and Society

This brings us to the second trend in ethical analysis. Starting, perhaps, with the work of Baier and some others in the late 1950s, an appreciable number of philosophers have focused on the social aspect of morals, as we may call it, or perhaps the social sense of the word 'moral,' the sense in which morality is a set of socially reinforced general rules and sets of virtues to be promoted. Of course, one familiar view of ethics, generally rejected by most philosophers, is relativism, the view that what is right and wrong simply *is* what the 'mores' or customs of our society calls upon its denizens to do or abstain from. But the philosophers referred to here agree in rejecting unqualified relativism. That general syndrome is, after all, riddled with problems, as we have already seen. The alphas hold that *x* is wrong; the betas hold that it is right. Among fellow alphas or betas, this may be no problem – but what happens when a beta visits alphaland? Does relativism tell him to change his views and go with the alphas ('When in Rome, do as the Romans do'?). Or does it tell him 'To thine own tribe be true' and damn, as it were, the betas's torpedoes? Or what? Relativism appears to be inherently incapable of arriving at a coherent answer to such problems.

However, the theorists we are about to consider do not, as noted, accept relativism. Rather, they ask what might make a social rule *reasonable*, or *rational*. In some areas, for limited purposes, the rule 'Follow the current rule' might turn out to be a good one – but not simply *because* it is the local rule. In their view, the problem of ethics is a problem of *squaring individual values with social norms*, or more precisely, in understanding the latter in terms of the former, which are held to be epistemically prior. And the most general form of their answer has been the revival of an earlier idea, historically advanced mainly in the context of political rather than moral philosophy: that morals is a sort of 'social contract' or 'agreement' among all of us, imposing obligations in light of the interaction of our various interests. Historically, and notably, the main content of this agreement has been to refrain from activities that inflict harm and damage on others, though perhaps also to provide at least certain kinds and amounts of help in some circumstances. Among the most forceful and rigorous of these philosophers has been David Gauthier (1986). The 'contractarian' view had tended previously to be identified with the view of Rawls who characterized his own theoretical construction (1971) as an attempt to bring the original contract view to a new level of sophistication. But Rawls is susceptible to the charge of having injected morality into his characterization of the starting point or 'original position,' whereas the full-blown contractarian project would be to derive *morals* from the *premoral* (nonmoral) interests of persons – and to do so without 'peeking' at the result first in order to force the particular conclusion the theorist hopes to arrive at. In other words, contractarianism is a fully foundationalist view of morals, holding that we can come to understand morals *essentially* on the basis of concepts that do not presuppose morals, as such, at all. So while we may use our pre-philosophical beliefs as working hypotheses, perhaps, we do not attribute to them any basic authority, as is implied by methodological intuitionism. Instead, we find a genuine foundation, a genuine reason why morality should look as it does. Work on the idea of the social contract continues unabated to the present.

Game Theory and Ethics

Contractarian naturalism conceives the rules of morals as subject to rational constraint on the basis of analyses of *interaction* among persons, each reasoning from her own interests, but attentive to the consequences of others' engagement, and especially to that subset of 'consequences' that are rational reactions to our own actions or proposals or *strategies*. Thus the basic tool of moral analysis is 'Game Theory,' in which the actions of different persons are understood as 'strategies' designed to forward their interests, and in which outcomes preferred from both or all points of view are identified as getting the moral nod. Most attention has been devoted to the *Prisoner's Dilemma*, in which there is potential for both conflict and co-operation. One party's premorally best outcome is the other's worst; but if both try to get that outcome, *each* ends up worse off than if she had co-operated. Isolated individuals can do better by successful 'defecting,' then, but collectively they all do better by co-operating; and when the game is repeated indefinitely, the rewards of co-operation increase hugely, while the costs of defection, if chosen, instead multiply. Work on Prisoner's Dilemma and related games has been intense and fruitful. A by-now classic, if controversial, philosophical work in this vein is that of David Gauthier (1986) which proposes an updated version of Thomas Hobbes's Laws of Nature. This calls upon agents to co-operate with co-operators, and to refrain from co-operation with nonco-operators. Such interaction is covered by a more general principle: to refrain from pursuing one's own interests in ways that worsen the situations of those with whom one interacts, unless this is unavoidable to prevent worsening of one's own situation. The contractarian project encourages interface work among philosophy, mathematics, economics, management science, and even evolutionary biology as well as the familiar social sciences. While not identifying himself as 'contractarian,' the work of Peter Danielson (1992) has greatly advanced research in this vein. And indeed, the terminology of 'contract' and 'agreement' is quite misleading, since nothing in the way of an actual contract of any sort is envisaged by these writers. Instead, a logical analysis of the situation simply leads to the conclusion that we ought to aim at the co-operative outcome, which is better for both (or, more precisely, *all*) provided that all go along, and with which there is so much reason for all to go along that there is justified confidence that most will in fact do so. This can also be used, in a more or less evolutionary spirit, to *explain* 'moral intuition' in considerable part. Thus the confident characterization by such writers as Kant and Locke, that the voice of conscience is also the 'voice of reason,' turns out to have credibility – but not in the way they thought.

Moral Realism

Considerable attention has also been devoted in the late twentieth century to a view that came to be known as *moral realism*. According to this, ethical sentences, when true, are so because they reflect reality, even though we cannot specifically define moral terms in naturalistic language. Moral realism, along with the supposedly noncommittal methodological intuitionism, probably owes its origin to developments in epistemology in the mid-century, especially to the work of W. V. O. Quine who criticized sharply the view that all meaningful sentences can be helpfully divided into 'analytic' or 'synthetic' (Quine 1951: 20–43). This is claimed to leave the fabric of human knowledge a complex that defies analysis into sharply distinct 'foundational' (evidential) statements on the one hand and 'theoretical' statements on the other. So the moral realists hold that the structure of morality generally, despite not being decomposable into particular facts, nevertheless is that of a claim about the world, and our place in it, a claim that is true (or false) as a whole despite its irreducibility to old-fashioned 'naturalism.'

But some suspect that moral realism is merely a front for unanalyzed intuitions, and along with that suspect that both theories are guilty of injecting preferred contentious substantive moral views into the discussion under cover of epistemological darkness. (An example is utilitarianism, which seems to be the favored theory of realists.) A major virtue of the contract view, by contrast, is that it appears capable of yielding convincing results at the level of operational moral practice. We can all see that many arrangements in human life are co-operative in just the sense the contractarian emphasizes, and that such arrangements are clearly superior to conflict – and also superior to vague, unexplicated appeals to intuition.

While there is much unclarity about the precise thesis of the Moral Realists, the issue remains much as it was with the emotivists vis-a-vis intuitionists. Is the claim that moral statements *describe* the world as it is? If so, it would seem to be possible to raise the question of whether it should stay that way: do we accept what is depicted as 'moral reality' as it is, or do we try to change it and install a different moral regime? Now, this must either be a live question or not. If it is a live question, then that appears to imply that the thesis of moral realism must be wrong, for the claim that things should be different is surely itself a moral one. If it is held to be a dead question, though, we have to ask why it is. How is the proponent of moral realism to persuade us that we simply can't question the 'reality' he claims to be represented by moral claims? In the absence of some sort of compelling reasons for accepting the moral precepts and principles that the view presumably embodies, it is impossible to claim that no such question can be raised. But if so, moral realism looks to be dead in the water.

Feminism

Late in the twentieth century, though with ample historical antecedent, there arose considerable interest in *feminism*, a view, or perhaps we should say a genre of views, that enters at the level of fundamental moral philosophy in such a way as to raise many questions. Generally speaking, most feminist writers have been concerned to complain of treatment of women at the hands of men, or of male-dominated institutions (as they claim they are), and often to maintain that these abuses continue in one way or another at present. Most agree with some version of at least some such claims, but to do that is not the same as developing a fundamental ethical theory. There the question is just how the gender difference is to make a difference, and what sort of difference it is to make. The main problem here lies in the fact that morals are at least notionally for all people, people in general rather than any subset, however sizable. We think that people of either sex can do evil actions, and also good ones; moreover, the good and evil actions that they can do are familiar and themselves independent of gender: women can murder men, men can murder women, anyone can lie, cheat or steal, anyone can act heroically or abominably, and so on. This enables us to sharpen up the question concerning the aspiring feminist ethicist. She (as it almost always is) might be *addressing* only her fellow women, in which case feminist ethics would be like, say, medical ethics: that is, a code of conduct specifically for women, as medical ethics is a code of conduct specifically for doctors. But while such a project could well be of considerable interest, it is not, as it stands, the sort of project that can do duty for general moral philosophy, since it would leave unanswered the question: 'Yes, and what, meanwhile, are the males supposed to be doing?' Questions of the latter kind are indeed addressed, implicitly or explicitly, by many feminist writers, but there are two different ways to understand answers to them. One way is to take it as simply addressed *by women*: 'This is what we women want you men to do!' But that would hardly qualify as a fundamental moral answer. Why should the viewpoint from which moral principles, to be embraced and followed *by all*, be that of *one* gender rather than the other?

Clearly this is implausible. If any such thing is to be maintained, it would have to be, somehow, on the ground that what spokespersons for women have to say, so to speak, is said from a 'more universal point of view' – analogously to what Marxists have sometimes said about the viewpoint of the 'working class.' Of course in order to make that work, it would then have to be explained just why this allegedly more universal view is indeed more universal, since on the face of it, after all, it is not so but rather the view of one half of humanity. And a claim that women are, for example, inherently more reasonable than men, or more caring, or whatever, would meet with two problems: first, that it is unlikely to be significantly true, and certainly unlikely to be accepted by those to whom it is addressed (males); and second, and more fundamentally, that males, after all, are males – it isn't as though they do, or can be expected to regard that fact as some sort of fault and that they should do something about it in response to that evaluation. Thus the proposed ethics would run the severe risk of being merely sectarian. And any such fault, in a theory purporting to be fundamental moral theory, would be fatal.

That said, it is, of course, quite possible that by general, impartial standards, the behavior of males in general, or specifically in relation to females, has been or still is characteristically less than admirable or even downright unfair or unjust. That is, of course, of considerable interest. But the point is that such criticism presupposes general impartial standards and principles, rather than providing foundations or explanations of them. So the criticisms remain to be established, by reasoning that either ignores such differences as may divide the sexes, or else deduces results concerning what each should do vis-à-vis the other from that more general point of view.

Is Morality Principled?

It remains to say something about a problem that has bedeviled ethical theory since Plato: that of correctly tracking the role of *generalizations* in ethics. At the end of the twentieth century, there came into some prominence the position that ethics doesn't really need principles after all. This view, moral particularism, has been expounded by many writers, among whom the most prominent is Jonathan Dancy. Of course, 'particular' does not quite mean what it sounds, for neither Dancy nor anyone else really thinks that case *x* could be *exactly* like case *y* in *all* other respects, yet *x* be right and *y* wrong. There are two major components to Dancy's theoretical claim. First, there is a thesis that no set of general principles is adequate to supply the moral verdict on a particular case: generalization in ethics always eludes us at this all-important margin. And second, there is an intriguing claim that the same general reason will count one way in one situation, and another in another. How it will count depends on other things – the circumstances. But which circumstances matter, we might ask? A plausible answer, not really denied by these writers, is that what's morally bad or wrong in the way of actions is what tends to *worsen* people's situations, while what's good or right about them is what tends to *better* them. And of course, how a particular feature of action will contribute to this worsening or bettering will indeed depend on circumstances. Where the people we affect are already evil, because what they do or have done does evil to still others, then our 'bettering' their situations is not obviously required, since in so doing we may be helping them to treat others badly. Still, it seems a solid principle in morals that we are to look out for the well-being of those we affect, seeking to make it better rather than worse.

If that is roughly true, we may perhaps have come, if not quite full circle, yet back to a general consonance with some of the moral philosophy of the eighteenth century. Still, the classic writers had little idea how much conceptual water would flow under how many bridges to bring us back there.

References

Binmore, K. [1994] (1998), *Game Theory and the Social Contract*, 2 vols, Cambridge, and London: MIT Press.

Brink, D. O. (1989), *Moral Realism and the Foundations of Ethics*, Cambridge: Cambridge University Press.

Dancy, J. (1993), *Moral Reasons*, Oxford: Blackwell.

Cahn, S. M., and J. G. Haber (1995), *Twentieth Century Ethical Theory*, Englewood Cliffs: Prentice Hall.

Danielson, P. (1992), *Artificial Morality*, London: Routledge.

Foot, P. (1977), *Virtues and Vices*, Oxford: Oxford University Press.

Gauthier, D. (1986), *Morals by Agreement*, New York: Oxford University Press.

Hare, R. M. (1977), *Moral Thinking*, Oxford: Oxford University Press.

LaFollette, H. (ed.) (2000), *The Blackwell Guide to Ethical Theory*, Malden, and Oxford: Blackwell Publishers.

Medlin, B. [1957] (1995), 'Ultimate Principles and Ethical Egoism,' in S. M. Cahn, and J. G. Haber (eds) (1995), *Twentieth-Century Ethical Theory*, Englewood Cliffs: Prentice Hall, pp. 316–21.

Moore, G. E. [1903] (1988), *Principia Ethica*, Amherst: Prometheus Books.

Perry, R. B. (1926), *General Theory of Value*, Cambridge: Harvard University Press.

Quine, W. V. O. (1951), 'Two Dogmas of Empirism,' in *Philosophical Review* 60: 20–43.

Rawls, J. (1971), *A Theory of Justice*, Cambridge: Harvard University Press.

Ross, W. D. [1930] (2002), *The Right and the Good*, Oxford: Oxford University Press.

Sparshott, F. (1958), *An Enquiry into Goodness*, Toronto, and Chicago: University of Toronto Press, and University of Chicago Press.

Stevenson, C. (1960), *Ethics and Language*, Cambridge: Cambridge University Press.

Stevenson, C. (1963), *Facts and Values*, New Haven: Yale University Press.

Sundholm, G. (2001), 'Systems of Deduction,' in *Handbook of Philosophical Logic*, D. M. Gabbay, and F. Guenthner (eds), vol. 2, pp. 1–52.

Political Philosophy

Michael Neumann

Political philosophy plays virtually no role in the early history of analytic philosophy. The most prominent political philosopher after Mill, Thomas Hill Green, had too much of Kant and Rousseau to suit the tastes of the early analytic philosophers. G. E. Moore and C. D. Broad concerned themselves with ethics, not political philosophy. Bertrand Russell went on to write political works, but they had virtually no philosophical stature or influence. But what really blocked the development of an analytic political philosophy was the rise of logical positivism and ordinary language philosophy. These movements manifested not only suspicion but contempt for what were considered the stock abstractions of the political theorists. Collective entities such as the state or the general welfare or the greatest good of all were dismissed as so much nonsense, nonideas born of the misconception that such words must refer to something. Political philosophy was slated either for elimination or for replacement by political science (or the academic field known as 'government'), which stuck to factual issues and discussed norms only as sociological phenomena. Analytic political philosophy, in the sense of normative political theory, was not even a blip on the radar until after 1945.

In the postwar world, it was not philosophical but political motives that got analytic philosophers writing about politics and political theories. The beginning of the Cold War brought with it an urgent sense that intellectuals must speak up for freedom and democracy against the menace of Stalin's Soviet Union. But at this point, analytical philosophers wrote on politics only to warn against any philosophical ambitions in that quarter – a task that A. J. Ayer had found too trivial to undertake in the analytic bible of the time, *Language, Truth and Logic* (1936). The most direct assault was mounted by T. D. Weldon in *The Vocabulary of Politics*, a popular work published in 1953. It ends with a decidedly Ayeresque coda of dismissal:

> The purpose of this [last] Chapter is entirely therapeutic. It is intended to show that when verbal confusions are tidied up most of the questions of traditional political philosophy are not unanswerable. All of them are confused formulations of purely empirical difficulties. This does not mean that these are themselves easy to deal with, but it does mean that writers on political institutions and statesmen, not philosophers, are the proper people to deal with them. (Weldon 1953: 192f.)

Weldon was particularly concerned that writers on politics free themselves of ill-formed questions about freedom, or the legitimacy or morality of the state; it was better simply to speak of attitudes and capacities. Politics was to become a purely empirical discipline.

The most notable excursion of analytic philosophers into politics was far from purely philosophical; it appeared in the unabashedly ideological work of Karl Popper (Popper 1945) and Isaiah Berlin (Berlin 1969). In their desire to refute the political theories they associated with Stalinism and totalitarianism, they could not be as dismissive as Weldon. Their need to confront the doctrines they considered dangerous forced them to seek some common ground on which to do battle. This meant accepting that normative questions and such matters as civil liberties were not, after all, the spawn of mere verbal confusions: it was far more than words that divided democrats from totalitarians. They did not feel that the difference was merely a matter of disagreement about facts or conceptual confusion. Popper spoke of open and closed societies in frankly normative terms; Berlin spoke of the difference between negative liberty – being let alone to do what one likes – and positive liberty, which involved re-forming individuals to pursue their 'real' needs and interests. To affirm one kind of liberty against another was already to tread on ground Weldon had considered metaphysical quicksand.

These unconscious stirrings of political philosophy were not, however, enough to re-ignite the discipline; this would take another decade and different stimuli. While the excursions of philosophers into politics may have been normative, academic work in something like political philosophy remained dutifully empirical. Michael Oakeshott (Oakeshott 1973), one of the most prominent academic thinkers about politics, still worried about whether 'political theory' was an 'empty expression,' and studied the activity of theorizing from quite some distance, as if he did not wish to be contaminated by its dangerously unreliable ties to experience: political theorizing might be an attempt to understand the world, but it was prone to become an exercise in religious or metaphysical ideologizing.

This situation continued into the early 1970s when Brian Barry, writing on 'the state of political theory,' said that 'until fairly recently,' political theory had become, not an investigation of theoretical problems about politics, but a study of 'men who wrote about these problems in the past'. This he attributed to a 'conception of politics . . . as a subject of such broad significance that questions of ends – the criteria of the 'good life' or 'justice' for example – are inextricably bound up with it.' And, he continues, since these questions are regarded as either insoluble or already solved, writers 'happily concur in the conclusion that (to quote Hume) "new discoveries are not to be expected in these matters"' (Barry 1970: 1–2) Barry then says that, surprisingly, there is a revival in political theory of two types: 'One type is axiomatic, economic, mechanical, mathematical; the other is discursive, sociological, organismic, literary' (Barry 1970: 3) The former is meant to be safely formal; the latter to have its foundation in such relentlessly empirical enterprises as the models of Talcott Parsons. There is no sense, reading Barry's survey, that anything like the traditional political theories of Hobbes or Locke could again take center stage. Political theory might touch on what people in fact believed was right under a variety of circumstances, or it might model political behavior as the interactions of rational maximizers. But the notion that either sort of theorizing might produce works of normative advocacy about politics was simply not on Barry's horizon.

Yet the picture was to change fundamentally the very next year, with the publication of John Rawls's *A Theory of Justice* (1971). Rawls' had presented the ideas of this work in *The Philosophical Review* as early as 1958 in 'Justice as Fairness,' but his article was perhaps too sketchy and apparently idiosyncratic to influence the entire character of political philosophy. His book did just that. While others had applied economics to political philosophy before Rawls, they had done so to construct models of political behavior, not to develop political norms such as principles of justice. Rawls relied heavily on work done in decision theory, microeconomics, and utility theory as applied to notions of social welfare. The initial work of economists on social welfare functions gained little attention in normative philosophy, partly because it was of the same fervently empiricist character as logical positivism. Collective welfare was to be a simple function of individual welfare, which in turn involved nonmental revealed preference rather than mysteriously mental utilities. But preference, it was discovered, would not reveal itself so easily. The empirically-minded, behavioral analysis of social choice encountered difficulties with problems such as interpersonal utility compar- isons: attempts at finding refuge in strictly ordinal conceptions of utility were undermined by Arrow's Result[1] – not the only problem for would-be empiricists seeking to reduce economic behavior to mechanical, almost instinctual selfishness. The Prisoner's Dilemma, discovered in 1950 by Melvin Drescher and Merrill Flood and popularized by A. W. Tucker, undermined the notion that there was a straightforward self-interest strategy for economic actors to follow. In this dilemma, two captured criminals find that, if they try to maximize their rational self-interest, they betray one another: it seems better to betray your confederate than to run the risk that he will betray you while you keep silent. This gets them longer sentences than if they had defied their rational self-interest and co-operated by keeping silent. Their self-interest, that is, leads them to do worse, in self-interested terms, than an 'irrationally' trusting, co-operative strategy. This suggests that economic rationality, failing to meet its stated goals, cannot be assumed to provide a basis for decision-making, a result which further undermines the predictive value of decision-theoretic models built on 'economic man.' It was when the behavioral and strongly empiricist models of economic choice began to fray that economics start to provide a powerful incentive to revive political philosophy.

In revival of social contract theory, Rawls provided a catalyst for combining the economists' analyses of behavior with normative political philosophy. As an event that never happened, the social contract was far from popular with earlier, empirically minded analytic philosophers. Rawls, however, conceived it along the lines of an economic model. The actors in the model were still very much like 'economic men' – self-interested individuals out to maximize their utilities. But instead of buying goods and services, they were picking principles of justice. This in itself was not enough to restart normative political philosophy: what principles populations choose is an empirical matter, and political scientists have studied such things in the past. The particular twist in Rawls's model that changed everything was his claim that, if *these* people in *these* circumstances chose a principle, it was the *right* principle, the one we *ought* to follow. This was just the sort of thing that analytic philosophers had scrupulously avoided saying for over half a century. Rawls could say it because his use of economic theory provided an appearance of rigor that rendered this bold move respectable. It represented a complete break with the recent past: Popper and Oakeshott make no appearance in *A Theory of Justice* and Berlin, despite his kindred preoccupation with liberal ideas of liberty, appears only in three footnotes.

Rawls's version of social contract theorizing went as follows. Imagine self-interested individuals in 'the circumstances of justice': not so comfortable as to have no need for justice, nor so desperate that 'every man for himself' was the only strategy. Charge these individuals with the task of choosing principles of justice to regulate the future of their society. But prevent these individuals from too naked a pursuit of self-interest by placing them behind a 'veil of ignorance': they are not to know their social position, their place in history, their personal or ideological prejudices, even their very identities. This is an equalizer, because individuals behind this veil cannot use money or power to rig the choice in their favor: the rich are as blind to their resources as the poor. Rawls called this set of circumstances the 'original position.' The general idea is that, on this level playing field, choices will of necessity be fair to all, because that gives the individuals involved their best chance at an acceptable outcome. These are fair circumstances, and what rational individuals would choose as a principle of justice in such circumstance should bind us as well: it is what we would have chosen were we in their shoes. What is rational for all in fair circumstances is obligatory.

Rawls's conception of a social-contract foundation for principles and his principles themselves were more impressive than the arguments by which he joined the two. The principle for which he is best known was his own invention: the difference principle, which states that departures from equality should be to the greatest benefit of the least advantaged. He argued for it as follows. The parties in the original position fear the terrible outcomes associated with the worst-off social position. They should therefore not play with probabilities, but adopt the conservative 'maximin strategy' which selects whatever alternative gives the most security. It does so by looking at the worst that can happen, and adopting the choice whose worst outcome is best. But, says Rawls, the difference principle is the maximin choice, because the worst outcome is to occupy the worst-off social position, and the difference principles assures that the worst-off position be as good as possible. Others have derived all sorts of principles, including the maximization of utility, from the original position. Perhaps the most telling criticism of Rawls's argument is due to John Harsanyi, who pointed out that to assume the worst is, far from avoiding probabilities, to assign a probability of 1 to the worst outcome (Harsanyi 1977). Rawls never provided a convincing reason for adopting his strategy.

The difference principle has an appeal quite apart from any original position arguments supporting it; it is a radically egalitarian notion of justice. To mitigate its influence, Rawls asserted the 'priority of liberty' over it. Basic political freedoms, he states, normally have priority over the considerations of distributive justice addressed by the difference principle. The priority is reverse only when 'necessary to enhance the quality of civilization so that in due course the equal freedoms can be enjoyed by all.' Whatever the merits of this proposal, Rawls never made a clear case for it, the difference principle therefore gathered the greater share of attention.

Individual freedom was not, however, neglected in the political philosophy that took its cue from Rawls. Now that he had, through models of rational choice borrowed from the economists, legitimated normative political theory, questions of individual rights that had previously been confined to analytic ethics were discussed and, more importantly, defended within an explicitly political context. Many writers, however, did not adopt Rawls's legitimating device of the social contract, or did so more casually than he did. Most prominent among these by far was Robert Nozick. In *Anarchy, State and Utopia* (1974) Nozick, like Rawls, legitimates normative principles by arguing that they would be adopted in an 'original position,' which he calls a 'state of nature.' This, for Nozick, is simply the absence of a government. There are no elaborate suppositions about the circumstances of justice or a veil of ignorance. These are replaced by an account of what would in fact happen, which relies heavily but discretely on Nozick's original area of expertise, decision theory. Nozick recounts how, in such circumstances, the inhabitants of a state of nature would form 'protective associations' which would compete. Eventually one such association would become dominant in a certain area, and that association would count as a minimal state.

Such a state, says Nozick, would be authorized no further than the protection of its members or citizens. This account dovetails with his moral theory of 'side constraints,' which holds that the pursuit of perhaps morally desirable 'end-states' is restricted by certain near-absolute prohibitions against state interference in individual 'entitlements,' including property rights that stem from state-sanctioned acquisitions and state-legitimated transfers. The mix of argument from a state of nature with straightforwardly and partly unsupported assertion is meant to have a pragmatic justification: 'The best reason [for his theory of the state],' says Nozick, 'is the developed theory itself' (Nozick 1974: 3) For an analytic philosophy to make such a claim about reasons he calls 'somewhat abstract and metatheoretical' would have been inconceivable a scant two decades earlier.

Unlike Rawls, Nozick is taken to be either a conservative or a 'libertarian,' with implications more towards conservatism than anarchism. Of his direct arguments for side constraints, the most famous is his 'Wilt Chamberlain' argument, which holds it just for an individual to become rich from the voluntary and legitimate property transfers of others, and unjust to interfere in the outcome of such transfers, even in the name of worthy moral ends. The fans, says Nozick, own their money through legitimate processes of acquisition and transfer. If they make Wilt rich by paying to see him play – another legitimate transfer – then he is entitled to his riches. No dream of 'patterned justice' – of creating the end-state in which property is distributed according to some preconceived model of allocation – can trump the liberties of Wilt and his fans. To impose the pattern would require not only expropriation of legitimately acquired property, but continued and perpetual interference in the entitlements of individuals who want, through voluntary and legitimate transfers, to upset the established pattern. This is a power no state can legitimately acquire.

Nozick's argument generated both heat and light. On the one hand, it provided the first modern analytic treatment of property rights to gain any traction. On the other hand, it failed to repel its numerous critics. Some argued with the underlying premise that a series of legitimate transactions could never produce a (morally) illegitimate outcome: why must transfer always preserve legitimacy? But Nozick's chief problem was that he never quite had the courage of his convictions: he never quite felt confident in imposing the very side constraint on 'patterned justice' he had worked hard to establish. This underconfidence manifested itself in two ways.

First, Nozick from the beginning conceded, albeit in a footnote, that he could not see how to maintain constraints in the face of 'catastrophic moral horror.' Critics quite naturally asked what might fit that description. If property transfers produced a world in which a dozen people starved, was that catastrophic enough? Or would a hundred have to die, or thousands, or millions? Nozick, perhaps too taken with his own theory, wanted to bypass these questions, but when pressed, he simply had no answers.

Second, Nozick had built hesitation into his very theory of property. It contained a 'proviso' whose content was debatable, but which placed restraints on both acquisition and transfer. Nozick felt that the right proviso was a fairly weak one along the lines of Locke's admonition that 'enough, and as good,' be left for others. But there was nothing in his Wilt Chamberlain argument that requires the proviso to be permissive – nothing, in fact, to prevent it from specifying that no transfer or acquisition was allowed if it interfered with the establishment of certain morally desirable distributive patterns. This hesitation proved fatal, because it allowed constant, anti-libertarian interference in acquisition and transfer to get its go-ahead from within the theory of property itself. It must be said that, while the failure of Rawls's inelegant arguments did nothing to undermine the importance of his basic ideas – the difference principle and the social contract model of argumentation – the failure of Nozick's much more impressive arguments left little behind. His influence was perhaps as great as Rawls, but his was a beautiful failure more than a flawed success.

The combined effect of Rawls and Nozick was to open analytic philosophy to the sort of straightforward normative debates that owed very little to logical positivism and ordinary language philosophy but much to the traditional political concerns that Weldon and others had been so sure would be superseded. Analytic philosophy no longer needed the support of economics, a discipline more or less acceptable to logical positivists, because Rawls's and Nozick's use of vaguely economic models prepared the way for wider views of what should count as legitimate political theory. If *a priori* normative reasoning from an economic model was acceptable, the feeling went, it was because it was fruitful: this was always the test of a model. But fruitfulness was a malleable concept, and suggested that reasoning from any set of premises was acceptable if the philosophic community found profit in the result. Since philosophers now did see value in straightforward normative debates over such issues as property rights, a quite traditional sort of political philosophizing had resurrected itself almost unnoticed.

The resurrection affected not only the subject matter but the perspective from which it was approached. There were now philosophers more or less explicitly of the right, left and center. Those who continued to experiment with social contract models tended to be on the right or centre-right. Those clearly on the left tended to write skeptical and critical work, while those on the center or center-left tended to produce work on the border with ethics, defending liberal values in quite general terms.

The reason contractualism became the province of somewhat right-wing thinkers has to do with the sort of foundation it seeks to provide. Rawls adopted the social contract model, not because it was particularly well-suited to his quite egalitarian agenda, but because, on the contrary, he thought it to have weight for those who did not share his point of view. His contractualism aimed to found justice, not on altruism or any other generous sentiment, but on prudential reason among the sort of self-interested individuals familiar to believers in the free market, individualism, and other ideals associated with the (moderate) right. Philosophers to his right took up contractualism for a quite different reason: self-interested individuals might reasonably be expected to reject the very egalitarian ideals Rawls contrived to have them espouse.

To undo the egalitarian bent of Rawls's contractualism, more right-wing thinkers like David Gauthier and Thomas Scanlon rejected the veil of ignorance condition that made it impossible for the contractors to see the particulars of their own situation. Gauthier (1986) did so to bring the contractors into something more like a 'real' bargaining model, one in which the participants bring different assets and powers to the table, and know it. His purpose was not to claim that some actual bargaining session ever did or could be a foundation for justice in society, but to provide a more robust counterfactual argument for the principles selected. For Rawls, one had to suppose individuals very remote from our actual situation, behind a veil of ignorance that could never exist. This raises the question of why what would be chosen in this particular exotic situation, as opposed to some other, should be what necessarily confers legitimacy on the principles selected. In Gauthier's model, however, we are asked to attend only to what rational self-interested members of society would decide if asked to choose principles of distribution. These, Gauthier would say, are people roughly like us in roughly our circumstances. What they would choose confers legitimacy much more straightforwardly than when Rawls's individuals would choose.

Gauthier, having provided himself with a situation very close to what is found in decision theory, stuck closely to the bargaining models in economics. His analysis was much more technical than Rawls's. It suggested that the bargainers would 'split the difference' between the rich and the poor. For Gauthier, this did not mean equal shares, but equal concessions. They would not concede an equal proportion of their assets – why do this? – but an equal proportion of the *gain* they might expect from co-operation. According to Gauthier, this would be reasonable to all, so it should be reasonable to us, and it would preserve both inequalities of wealth and the system of property rights that secured them.

Gauthier's work, though impressive and influential, convinced few. Some criticized the bargaining argument itself: Brian Barry, for instance, wondered why the poor would not use threats to torpedo the whole process and, by intimidation, squeeze more out of the rich. But perhaps the chief weakness of Gauthier's position was his derivation, not of the agreement itself, but of the obligation to uphold it. Gauthier admitted that 'straightforward' maximizers who simply pursued their own advantage would deviate from the agreement whenever circumstances permitted them to do so unpunished. But he suggested that 'constrained maximizers' would not do so: these were individuals who sacrificed their immediate self-interest to the extent that others could be expected to do the same. Constrained maximizers were vulnerable to betrayal by straightforward maximizers who pretended to accept the same constraints. However Gauthier argued that, over time, constrained maximizers would get better at recognizing one another, and would therefore more reliably reap the benefits of mutual co-operation. Some straightforward maximizers, seeing this trend, would become constrained maximizers. The others would become easier to detect and less able to make gains through betrayal of co-operative understandings. Eventually, the constrained element of the population would be dominant, and the co-operative agreement would both hold and prove clearly beneficial. The problem was that Gauthier's argument depended on assuming that the benefits of betrayal were not too much larger than the benefits of co-operation, and he never justified this assumption. For this reason his argument did not command wide acceptance.

Gauthier's was the last prominent work of political philosophy in the twentieth century that offered a technically sophisticated social contract account of justice. Borrowing less from economic and more from analytic ethics, Thomas Scanlon continued Gauthier's anti-welfarist efforts in *What We Owe to Each Other* (1998). Here he distinguished between 'broad' and 'narrow' ethical obligations, the latter resting exclusively on duties to others. His contractualism was of the simplest and most general sort, involving conformity to principles 'that no one could reasonably reject as a basis for informed, unforced general agreement' (Scanlon 1998: 153). Some principles, it turns out, are less reasonably rejectable than others, for example those establishing property rights. This is because other moral problems presuppose them: to ask how much I should give to help others, you must first know how what I have got to be mine. This (Scanlon's model) turns out to yield strong property rights politely infringed by duties of moderate sacrifice to prevent immoderate harms.

Scanlon's work seems to herald an era in which political philosophy divides itself into multiple solitudes. To Scanlon, it is obvious that if one duty logically presupposes another, it should be morally subordinate to the other: if mutual aid presupposes property rights, then it is morally subordinate to those rights. He also takes it as given that what is reasonable for us to accept is what would support a well-functioning community of rational agents; that moral obligations should disrupt the workings of this well-oiled machine is unthinkable. Like Gauthier and Nozick, he is no extremist but a person content with a few assumptions that define his outlook – that they are not shared by all matters little besides his conviction that they ought to be so shared. This general stance is typical, not simply of right-tending political thought, but of contemporary analytic political philosophy in general.

Nozick's notion that a political theory can be judged by its 'fruitfulness' ties into this trend. His approach borrows from the philosophy of science, and indeed from analytic ethics; in both cases it is true that there are widely shared beliefs about what theories are fruitful and what are not. Unfortunately this has never been the case in political theory, which is distinguished precisely by its utter lack of shared assumptions: political theory is perhaps further from a consensus on fruitfulness than any other area of analytic philosophy. This may explain the tendency of political theorists to devise theories that seem fruitful only to their sympathizers, and to mount critiques that are unconvincing to their political opponents.

On the left, this tendency to (quite unwanted) insularity can be seen only in criticism, because no left-wing analytic political philosopher has produced a 'grand theory' of the state or of political norms. Among prominent political philosophers, the most unabashedly left-wing is G. A. Cohen. Cohen makes penetrating criticisms of Nozick and other non-egalitarian philosophers, but shows his awareness of their limitations. For example, he opposes to Nozick's view of things in nature as unowned:

> an alternative view of the original moral relationship between people and things, under which we regard nature as, from the start, collectively owned by everyone. If that different conception of rights over the world is united with the principle of self-ownership, extensive inequality of condition is avoidable. (Cohen 1995: 115)

Cohen is clear that he is simply opposing one set of assumptions to another, and prefers his consequences to Nozick's.

We could hardly be further from Popper's and Berlin's image of the leftist political theorist drunk on grand theories and panaceas to be imposed on others. We are also strikingly far from Nozick's, Rawls's, and Gauthier's attempts to derive models of the state from weak and widely shared assumptions. There is ample communication between different political tendencies at the level of critique, but the assumptions behind the critiques seldom form a common ground from which issues may, even in principle, be resolved. This contrasts even with ethics, where there is at least a larger measure of agreement on what constitutes 'hard cases' and what outcomes are agreed to be morally unacceptable. If utilitarianism, for example, leaves people to starve, that is more universally deplored than if property rights do so.

The most important contributions from the left may occur at the periphery of political philosophy, especially in the work of Jon Elster (Elster 1983), a writer claimed by several disciplines. His critiques aim not at the proposals or even the assumptions of right-wing political theorists, but at the models and formalism underlying those assumptions. The theories of bargaining, of rational behavior and of utility are all subjected to comprehensive critique whose aim is clearly to remove the underpinnings of the sort of right-wing contractualism exemplified by Gauthier. What makes Elster's critique of exceptional value is his ability to develop fundamentally new concepts to demolish his target, the model of self-interested economic man. One well-known instance is his notion of adaptive preference formation, the tendency to rearrange one's choices in response to restrictions on which of them is currently available. Thus he notes that a free citizen might prefer being free to being a prison guard to being a prisoner. An imprisoned citizen, however, might adapt to the loss of his first choice by identifying with and admiring his captors – a known psychological phenomenon. His preference order then becomes being a guard, being a free citizen, and being a prisoner. Elster suggests that this sort of preference formation is not autonomous, and that we must ask, not only whether a course of action satisfies preferences, but also whether these preferences are autonomously formed. Such analysis goes beyond the critique of conventional economic models to contribute an element that might help in replacing them. A. K. Sen (Sen 2002), considered more of an economist than a philosopher, has made similarly fruitful critiques of conventional economic models, suggesting, for instance, that rational choice need not involve a complete ranking of all alternatives available to the agent. These efforts are more enlightening than pitting one set of assumptions against another.

In the modesty of its ambitions, the left is joined by the centre or liberals in current political philosophy. There has been no really major figure in liberal political thought, and certainly nothing like a major system-builder, since Rawls. Probably the most prominent of his successors is Ronald Dworkin (Dworkin 1986), who however comes to the issues from the law and the philosophy of law rather than from within political philosophy. His focus is on the interaction between law and morality, especially in legal decision-making, which he suggests should seek a balance between coherence and social engineering: judges should see that the evolution of the law 'tells the best story' in the sense that it coheres with the previous installments (precedent) but also looks towards a future which may be shaped according to moral principles. His emphasis on the process of establishing rights in society, rather than on the content of rights themselves, is both refreshing and enlightening, but it has its limitations. For one thing, it necessarily makes some sacrifice of universality because Dworkin must devote most of his attention to some legal system or other, and he naturally focuses on the American one. In addition, while process may be central to legal philosophy, it is less so to political philosophy, especially since the processes studied by Dworkin are not those which generate states or fundamental principles, but mechanisms which apply or express principles already adopted.

Dworkin's work has legal foundations of a sort. Other liberal thinkers, who have largely abandoned Rawls's social contract approach, usually produce work whose political character is vestigial. This is partly because they gravitate towards another aspect of Rawls's work, his alleged and self-described 'Kantianism.' Liberal values such as civil liberties and autonomy are defended as demanded by Kantian respect for persons. This value is also invoked to justify, or at least debate, such issues as affirmative action or reverse discrimination. To show that a position derives from or expresses Kantian respect is frequently taken to be a justification of that position. At times it seems almost as if Kant's very name is taken to provide a cachet of ethical legitimacy.

The historical bases of this approach are questionable. Kant respected purely rational or 'noumenal' selves, abstracted from the empirical world. He did not respect empirical selves. Yet the persons liberal theorists want us to respect certainly seem empirical enough. For this reason, perhaps, some writers discard the Kantian trappings of Rawls's liberalism and regard respect for persons or autonomy as foundational concepts in their own right. Democracy, freedom, equality of opportunity, perhaps also various forms or degrees of welfarism, are justified by explanations of how these ideals embody the *über*-ideal of respect, considered the foundation of all morality. Some writers, notably Alan Donegan (Donagan 1977) and Alan Gewirth (Gewirth 1996), attempt to codify this foundation in a principle, some modernized variant of the categorical imperative. This primary rule is understood to be grounded, not in Kantian metaphysics, but in the very conception of what it is to be moral. The ideas of reciprocity implicit in such imperatives in some ways provide a substitute for social contract theory, which normally itself relies heavily on notions of reciprocity to define the rational expectations of the contractors.

These efforts have encountered two sorts of obstacles. First, the age-old problem of defining the precise scope and application of reciprocal respect has not been solved. Do I respect you when I honor mutual agreements? Must I also honor tacit mutual understandings? Does respect go further than this, towards providing you with equal opportunities, or a certain standard of living, or a bundle of rights that protects your identity? How is respect for you to be balanced against respect for others: mightn't the two conflict? Beyond this there is the vexed question of whether, in fact, reciprocity can encompass a willingness to accept outcomes that may be disastrous for both of us. What if I 'respect' you by reserving for myself a right to attack you in defense of my honor, and accord you a corresponding right to respect me? Liberal political philosophers have had more success in linking particular rights to general duties of respect than in defining the nature of those duties themselves.

As well as problems involving the definition of mutual respect, liberal political philosophy has yet to confront modern problems involved in defining freedom: even if freedom is essential to respect and respect is a foundational value, it is still necessary to develop a coherent and normatively robust conception of free individuals. Here critiques from the left, directed more against the notion of economic man than against the notion of freedom itself, have not received sufficient attention. To what extent do societies typically allow for Elster's autonomously formed preferences? If this sort of preference formation is unavailable, does freedom really have overriding moral importance? To what extent is economic freedom a prerequisite for political freedom? At this point, no liberal theory of autonomy has answered these questions.

If the moral theory of freedom is underdetermined, so is its bearing on political institutions. Liberal political theorists do show an awareness that conventional democratic institutions may not provide sufficient scope for individual participation. The result has been an emphasis on 'deliberative' democracy rather than on the mere mechanisms of majority rule. Writers in this area, such as Joshua Cohen (Cohen 1989) have drawn on work outside the mainstream of analytic philosophy, especially Jürgen Habermas's models of 'ideal speech situations.' This work provides a useful link between the highly individualized conventional notions of civil liberties and the collective notion of individuals interacting to determine a common good. However, other collective notions intrude: how are individuals' rights to be balanced against group rights in the deliberative process? Here the normative study of democratic processes ties into an intense debate on multiculturalism, provoked in large part by Charles Taylor's (Taylor, 1992) critique of that doctrine. Once again there is a difficult search for some common ground on which to adjudicate the controversy. So far the tendency has been to fall back on malleable notions of autonomy and respect whose inadequacies have already been noted.

Analytic political philosophy has won one battle it might well have been expected to lose in the 1950s. Its legitimacy is now unquestioned; indeed the very question of its legitimacy is never raised. Its fruitfulness, however, is another matter. The social contract model, revitalized by borrowing from economics, has provided important political theories and generated a great deal of very interesting debate. But as that model begins to lose its appeal, nothing has yet been found to replace it. This has made it difficult for political philosophy to advance beyond a set of dialogues undermined by conflicting or underdeveloped fundamental assumptions.

Note

1. Arrow's Result, very roughly, is an 'impossibility' proof that there is no minimally democratic polling procedure which guarantees a minimally rational derivation of collective choices from individual preferences: any such procedure may try to tell us that society, preferring apples to oranges, also prefers oranges to apples.

References

Arrow, K. [1951] (1963), *Social Choice and Individual Values*, New Haven: Yale University Press.

Barry, B. [1970] (1988), *Sociologists, Economists, and Democracy*, Chicago: University of Chicago Press.

Barry, B. (1989), *Theories of Justice*, Los Angeles: University of California Press.

Berlin, I. (1969), *Four Essays on Liberty*, Oxford: Oxford University Press.

Cohen, J. (1989), 'Deliberation and Democratic Legitimacy,' in A. Hamlin, and P. Pettit (eds) (1989), *The Good Polity: Normative Analysis of the State*, Oxford: Basil Blackwell, pp. 17–34.

Cohen, G. A. (1995), *Self-Ownership, Freedom, and Equality*, Cambridge: Cambridge University Press.

Donagan, A. (1977), *The Theory of Morality*, Chicago: University of Chicago Press.

Dworkin, G. (1988), *The Theory and Practice of Autonomy*, Cambridge: Cambridge University Press.

Dworkin, R. (1986), *Law's Empire*, Cambridge: Belknap Press.

Elster, J. (1983), *Sour Grapes: Studies in the Subversion of Rationality*, Cambridge: Cambridge University Press.

Gauthier, D. (1986), *Morals by Agreement*, Oxford: Clarendon Press.

Gewirth, A. (1996), *The Community of Rights*, Chicago: University of Chicago Press.

Hamlin, A., and P. Pettit (eds) (1989), *The Good Polity: Normative Analysis of the State*, Oxford: Basil Blackwell.

Harsanyi, J. (1977), 'Morality and the Theory of Rational Behaviour,' in A. Sen and B. Williams (eds) (1982), *Utilitarianism and Beyond*, Cambridge: Cambridge University Press, pp. 39–62.

Nozick, R. (1974), *Anarchy, State and Utopia*, New York: Basic Books.

Oakeshott, M. (1973), 'What is Political Theory,' in M. Oakeshott (2004), *What is History and Other Essays*, Thorverton: Imprint Academic, pp. 391–402.

Phelps, E. S. (ed.) (1973), *Economic Justice*, Harmondsworth: Penguin Books.

Popper, K. [1945] (1971), *The Open Society and its Enemies*, 5th revd edn, Princeton: Princeton University Press.

Rawls, J. (1971), *A Theory of Justice*, Cambridge: Belknap Press.

Scanlon T. (1998), *What We Owe to Each Other*, Cambridge: Belknap Press.

Sen, A. K. (2002), *Rationality and Freedom*, Cambridge: Belknap Press.

Sen, A. K. and B. Williams (eds) (1982), *Utilitarianism and Beyond*, Cambridge: Cambridge University Press.

Taylor, Charles (1992), *Multiculturalism and 'The Politics of Recognition.' An Essay by Charles Taylor with Commentary by Amy Gutmann, Steven C. Rockefeller, Michael Walzer, Susan Wolf*, Princeton: Princeton University Press.

Weldon, T. D. (1953), *The Vocabulary of Politics*, London: Penguin Books.

Philosophy of Religion

Charles Taliaferro and Erik S. Christopherson

Analytical philosophers in the twentieth century have produced a rich literature that includes the philosophy of religious language and practice, analyses of divine attributes, arguments for and against the existence of God, and arguments over the significance of religious diversity, religious experience, and religious values. Theists, atheists, agnostics, and adherents to both Christian and nonChristian religions have engaged in a fruitful exchange on these topics with all the hallmarks of analytical philosophy: an emphasis on conceptual clarity, the use of analyses with examples and counter-examples, concentrated arguments about whether concepts of what exists (God, the soul, the afterlife) may be reduced or analyzed in terms of other concepts or eliminated altogether.

A brief recommendation at the outset: for those interested in examining modern philosophy of religion that is prior both to the analytic *and* continental movements, we recommend *Twentieth Century Western Philosophy of Religion* by Eugene Thomas Long. See also Harris 2002, Wainwright 2005 and Taliaferro 2005.

The Meaning of Religious Belief and Practice

At the beginning of the analytic movement, G. E. Moore, Bertrand Russell and other salient figures did not give prominence to religious themes. Russell addressed religion in some of his popular works, such as *Why I Am Not A Christian*, and Moore contributed to the critical evaluation of religious values. Neither of these undertakings, however, was central to the main projects of these philosophers. Religious topics became more mainstream for analytic philosophy after World War II with the emergence of what is variously called positivism, logical positivism or verificationism (in what follows we will refer to this movement as 'positivism'). The positivists were intrigued by the possibility of a theory of meaning that related to the growing field of natural science. Specifically, the positivists wanted a philosophical theory that unified the methodology of natural science with the concepts of truth and, most importantly, meaning. A prominent practitioner and popularizer of the movement, A. J. Ayer, argued that this theory of meaning exposed the meaninglessness of religious belief.

Central to positivism is the concept of empirical observation. Positivism proposes that, in order for a propositional claim to be meaningful, either the claim must concern the formal properties and relations of concepts such as those covered in mathematics, formal logics, and analytic definitions (tautologies), or it must be possible through empirical observation to verify whether the propositional claim is true or false. It is only when these conditions are met, that a statement is a genuine propositional claim. A. J. Ayer and others argued that the claim 'God exists' and other, similar claims ('God is loving, just, and so on') fail this test of meaning. The following is the famous passage in A. J. Ayer's *Language, Truth, and Logic* in which he argues that theism is not merely improbable, but meaningless:

> What is not so generally recognized is that there can be no way of proving that the existence of a god, such as the God of Christianity, is even probable. Yet this also is easily shown. For if the existence of such a god were probable, then the proposition that he existed would be an empirical hypothesis. And in that case it would be possible to deduce from it, and other empirical hypotheses, certain experiential propositions which were not deducible from those other hypotheses alone. But in fact this is not possible. It is sometimes claimed, indeed, that the existence of a certain sort of regularity in nature constitutes sufficient evidence for the existence of a god. But if the sentence 'God exists' entails no more than that certain types of phenomena occur in certain sequences, then to assert the existence of a god will be simply equivalent to asserting that there is the requisite regularity in nature; and no religious man would admit that this was all he intended to assert in asserting the existence of a god. He would say that in talking about God, he was talking about a transcendent being who might be known through certain empirical manifestations, but certainly could not be defined in terms of those manifestations. But in that case the term 'god' is a metaphysical term. And if 'god' is a metaphysical term, then it cannot be even probable that a god exists. For to say that 'god exists' is to make a metaphysical utterance which cannot be either true or false. And by the same criterion, no sentence which purports to describe the nature of a transcendent god can possess any literal significance. (Ayer 1936: 173–4)

Ayer's conclusion works with equal force against any monotheistic religious language in which there are metaphysical claims. The Hindu thesis that 'Atman is Brahman,' for example, is in the same boat as any classical theistic conviction.

After Ayer's *Language, Truth, and Logic*, the most dramatic and well-known positivist case against the meaningfulness of religious language was presented by Antony Flew; in his 'Theology and Falsification,' Flew developed the following parable:

> Once upon a time two explorers came upon a clearing in the jungle. In the clearing were growing many flowers and many weeds. One explorer says, 'Some gardener must tend this plot.' The other disagrees, 'There is no gardener.' So they pitch their tents and set a watch. No gardener is ever seen. 'But perhaps he is an invisible gardener.' So they set up a barbed-wire fence. They electrify it. They patrol it with bloodhounds. (For they remember how H. H. G. Wells' *The Invisible Man* could be both smelt and touched though he could not be seen.) But no shrieks ever suggested that some intruder has received a shock. No movements of the wire ever betray an invisible climber. The bloodhounds never give cry. Yet still the Believer is not

convinced. 'But there is a gardener, invisible, intangible, insensible to electric shocks, a gardener who has no scent and makes no sound, a gardener who comes secretly to look after the garden which he loves.' At last the Skeptic despairs, 'But what remains of your original assertion? Just how does what you call an invisible, intangible, eternally elusive gardener differ from an imaginary gardener or even from no gardener at all?' (Flew 1955: 96)

Flew's critique of theism here is that to the extent that no evidence is allowed to count against it, theism is not a bona fide, meaningful thesis. The claim that there is a God, like the belief that there is an invisible gardener, dies the death of a thousand qualifications.

There are advocates of positivism today (Martin 1990), and arguments against religion that are heavily indebted to positivism (Rundle 2004). Some philosophers seem implicitly to accept the positivist critique and to pursue an alternative analysis of the meaning of religious belief and practice. These philosophers contend that religious claims are not so much claims about what exists (there is a God or Brahman) as they are about ways of living (living a life full of compassion, for example). For a contemporary advocate of this approach, see Howard Wettstein's 'Poetic Imagery and Religious Belief.' But, for the most part, positivism has been challenged on so many fronts that it is no longer the dominant philosophical outlook. Consider five reasons why the prospects of positivism have darkened.

First, science itself posits events and entities that appear to transcend verificationist conditions. Beliefs about the origin of the cosmos, for example, are based on theory, observation, and prediction, but they largely concern matters that cannot be directly or even indirectly observed. We are in a similar position in contemporary physics when assessing whether such entities as quarks or dark energy exist. Positivism seems to thwart rather than support contemporary science.

Second, positivism rules out what appear to be coherent descriptions of genuine possibilities. Ayer wanted to rule out as meaningless the possibility that all our empirical observations could be systematically mistaken. Classic arguments for skepticism ask us whether we can rule out (falsify) the possibility that, for example, we are being deceived by an all powerful demon. If we cannot rule this out, it seems out of place to demand the definite verification of our empirical observations. Skeptical narratives seem to describe meaningful possibilities that we could never conclusively verify or falsify. Ayer himself eventually conceded the meaningfulness of skepticism (Ayer 1940; for a contemporary list of unverifiable but meaningful hypotheses, see van Cleve 1999: 14).

A third problem is whether or not the verifiability principle is itself meaningful according to its own standard. If the verifiability principle is correct, then the principle must be tautological, a matter of formal logics, mathematical (which it is not), or it must be verifiable through empirical observation (but we cannot empirically observe the truth of the principle). Perhaps the best case for the principle is that it satisfactorily describes all propositional claims we reasonably believe to be meaningful and eliminates all of the claims we reasonably believe to be pseudo-claims. But this seems question-begging in light of the second objection which offers apparently intelligible hypotheses that are not covered by the principle. In other words, while we might agree on clear cases of conceptual nonsense (the smile without a face in Alice in Wonderland), such concurrence is not to be found in questions involving metaphysics, religion, and so on.

A fourth problem concerns the very nature of empirical observation. Ayer seemed to be open in principle, to what he called 'mystic intuitions' (Ayer 1936: 180–1). He argued that the mystic's 'intuition' may be considered a vehicle 'to discover truths' so long as these beliefs are then 'verified or confuted' by our empirical observations. But why cannot the mystic's experience itself count as an empirical verification? So long as 'empirical' is understood with sufficient breadth, why exclude *a priori* mystical empirical experiences? Recently a range of philosophers has defended the intelligibility and evidential force of religious experience (see, for example, Alston's *Perceiving God* as a representative work).

Finally, fifth, many philosophers (atheists and theists) have argued that evidence *does* bear on the truth or falsity of 'God exists.' Some take the existence of our cosmos as evidence of God, others construe the evidence of evil to count against God's existence. Unlike the invisible gardener, we can point to features of the universe that make either theism or naturalism or some non-theistic religious belief more reasonable than the alternatives.

One of the lessons of the mid-twentieth century debates over positivism that many philosophers now accept is that propositional claims need to be assessed in light of more comprehensive theories. The intelligibility and reasonability of a specific claim, therefore, needs to be seen not in isolation or in terms of a narrow account of intelligibility, but as part of an overriding theory with interconnected concepts, evidence, and arguments. In a highly influential paper, Carl Hempel made the following claim:

> The idea of cognitive significance, with its suggestion of a sharp distinction between significant and non-significant sentences or systems of such, has lost its promise and fertility . . . and . . . it had better be replaced by certain concepts which admit of differences in degree, such as the formal simplicity of a system; its explanatory and predictive power and its degree of confirmation relative to available evidence. The analysis and theoretical reconstruction of these concepts seem to offer the most promising way of advancing further the clarification of the issues implicit in the idea of cognitive significance. (Hempel 1959: 129)

This verdict has taken hold in philosophy of religion (and in other fields as well). The most prominent works by analytic philosophers that are critical of theism (Sobel, Mackie, Martin) or supportive of theism (Swinburne, Plantinga, Alston, Yandell) are in the form of comprehensive, cumulative arguments. It is rare to see nowadays a case for or against a major religious conviction based on a singular, intentionally narrow line of reasoning such as in Ayer's *Language, Truth, and Logic*.

Divine Attributes and Religious Values

A great deal of analytic philosophy of religion has focused on the critique and elucidation of the concept of God that one finds in classical Judaism, Christianity, and Islam. The central divine attributes include omnipotence, omniscience, goodness or unsurpassable goodness, necessary existence, incorporeality, omnipresence or ubiquity, eternity, and simplicity. Other divine attributes stem from God's activity, for example being the Creator, being worthy of worship, being the Redeemer of the World. Still other features of God differ according to the religion in question: being triune, for example, or being incarnate are specific to Christianity. The philosophical analysis of religious values involve defining the concept of divine commands, the moral implication of revelation claims, the relationship of religious and secular values, and the bearing of religious ethics on different domains such as medicine and the environment.

The literature on divine attributes is enormous. Some of the best work has involved exhibiting how the attributes may be interrelated. This philosophical work is useful in exhibiting the integration or conceptual interdependence of the attributes. (For constructive, comprehensive treatments of theistic divine attributes, see Swinburne, Wicringa, Hughes; for a critique, see Sobel, Martin, Mackie.)

Omnipotence and Goodness: A perennial theme in the philosophy of God involves the scope of omnipotence. Some puzzles arise over whether an omnipotent God can do the metaphysically or logically impossible. Can God make $2 + 2 = 5$ or make a square circle in two dimensional space? These problems are usually dispelled by claiming that omnipotence should not be conceived in terms of a being doing everything, but in terms of a being doing everything possible (coherent, consistently describable). To the extent that it is logically impossible for a square circle to exist, there can be no reasonable expectation that an omnipotent being can create one. Other puzzles having to do with descriptions of events that explicitly exclude omnipotence, seem to be dispensable. So, an omnipotent God cannot bring about something that is not brought about by an omnipotent being. But matters become more serious when we link omnipotence and value.

Many traditional Christian, Jewish, and Islamic philosophers conceive of God as essentially good – God cannot do evil. Does this mean that God is not as powerful as a being that can bring about good and evil? Here is an argument against traditional theism: 1) God is omnipotent; 2) God is essentially good; 3) An essentially good being cannot do evil; 4) An omnipotent being can do evil; 5) Therefore God does not exist. It should be noted, at this point, that there have been philosophers who refuse to accept that God is omnipotent. This is a strategy sometimes defended by process philosophers (followers of A. N. Whitehead; Charles Hartshorne argues against omnipotence in his appropriately titled book *Omnipotence and Other Theological Mistakes*) and personalists (such as Peter Bertocci).

There are many possible replies to the argument stated above, but before getting to them, let us consider the values at stake. If we deny the second premise and hold that part of God's greatness consists in the power to do good or evil, have we enlarged or diminished our understanding of the divine nature? Arguably, we have diminished the concept of God and risked making brute power an attribute worthy of worship. Understanding God's nature as essentially good provides a check on the appeal to authoritative scriptures and informs religious ethics. If, for example, we believe that God's power is absolute, God's will is morally authoritative and, based on 'scriptural revelation,' we also hold that God permits slavery, then we court a highly dangerous ethic. If on the other hand, we believe slavery to be morally impermissible and that, as an essentially good being, God would not permit it, we have grounds for rejecting or reinterpreting 'scriptural revelation.' Similarly, God's essential goodness seems to be an essential feature of much worship in theistic religions. But the worship of God seems best whenever based on the feeling and the expression of awe in view of supreme goodness rather than in view of an all powerful being who does good but is also capable of doing boundless evil.

One of the most promising replies has been to reconceive all of the divine attributes in terms of God's goodness and excellence (Morris 1987). On this view, the philosophical analysis of divine attributes is co-ordinated in terms of *great-making attributes*. Is it a mark of greatness that a being can do boundless evil? Morris and others have argued that this is not the case. This line of reasoning finds precedence in Anselm of Canterbury and Thomas Aquinas, both of whom argued that doing evil (or being able to do it) is a liability and weakness rather than a proper strength. An analysis of omnipotence that is much more in line with the being that God is would be as follows: A being, B, has divine omnipotence = B has maximal power compatible with essential goodness. 'Maximal power' can, in turn, be analyzed in terms of the scope of power, that is, that there can be no essentially good being with a greater scope of power (Taliaferro 1998).

Omniscience and Free Will: If God knows the future, God knows that you will freely do X tomorrow. If God knows X, then X will occur. But if you are truly free to do X tomorrow you must be capable of not doing X tomorrow. Yet, if X will occur tomorrow, it seems that you are *not* actually free to refrain from doing X. Hence, either God does not know the future or you are not free. The puzzle about the compatibility of freedom and foreknowledge is not unique to contemporary philosophy of religion; it was a puzzle that exercised Augustine, Boethius, Ockham, Louis de Molino and many others. But in the analytic context, the analyses of the puzzle have reached extraordinary sophistication. Here are only a few of the replies:

1. It is possible to deny that omniscience includes knowledge of future acts (sometimes referred to as *future free contingents*). This denial sometimes includes the denial that propositions about future free contingents are true or false. Following Aristotle, some contend that it is not now either true or false, that you will freely do X tomorrow. These philosophers then argue that omniscience only concerns what is true and false, and because that does not include future free contingents, the paradox is dissolved. A less severe strategy would be to acknowledge the truth of propositions about future free contingents but claim they are unknowable. One may then claim that omniscience concerns only what is possible to be known, and thus God not knowing the future does not count against God being omniscient.

2. One may deny that free action genuinely involves the possibility of doing otherwise. This is sometimes called the principle of alternative possibilities. Arguably, to act freely simply involves doing what one chooses to do. You may still do what you choose even if you could not do otherwise.

3. One may argue that omniscience of the future is not more puzzling than

knowledge of past free acts. Just as knowledge that agents acted freely in the past does not rob the agents of their freedom, knowledge of the future should not be assumed to undermine free will.

4. Some argue that God not only knows what will occur in the future, but God knows all possible futures. That is, God knows what you would do freely if you were facing some given state of affairs. This is sometimes called middle knowledge.

Clearly, the puzzle regarding God's knowledge and the freedom of the will are linked to another lively debate, the one concerning the relationship of God and time.

God and Time: The majority of philosophers in theistic religious traditions have held that God is not 'temporally extended' – that is, that God does not exist from moment to moment. Time, on the traditional view, is a creation of God. But this position generates a number of paradoxes. Some of the puzzles that arise are a reflection of religious values. If God is not in time, can it be that God is a person? In many traditions, petitionary prayer and religious experience are pivotal. Does it make sense to have an experience of the presence of a being that is outside of time? And if God is outside of time, what is the point of petitionary prayer? For example, why pray for a future event when, from God's eternal viewpoint, the future is already settled? More basically, if God is outside of time, there can be no past, present or future divine action; all God's acts must be fixed eternally so that God atemporally wills that all divine action in the world unfold in time. But if that is true, is God free? After all, if the divine life is fixed in eternity, there is no possibility of God doing otherwise.

There are, of course, replies to these questions. For the best defense of God as nontemporal and eternal see Brian Leftow's *Time and Eternity*; and for the best case that God is temporal, see Nelson Pike's *God and Timelessness*.

Arguments for and against the Existence of God

Some analytic philosophers of religion have made important contributions to arguments against theism by arguing that theism is incoherent (usually taking the form of arguments that the divine attributes are incompatible), that the cosmos is better explained without theism (this may form part of an overall argument for naturalism), and that features of the cosmos (enormous evil, for example) make it unreasonable to accept theism. A negative strategy against the case for theism urges the conclusion that in the absence of strong positive reasons for theism, one should accept atheism or agnosticism. On the other hand, Analytic philosophers have also revived the classical arguments for God's existence and have developed intriguing new ones. Space permits only a brief discussion of these debates.

Some philosophers argue that the experience of the divine is evidence enough that there actually is a divine reality. This argument from religious experience (as it is often called) along with cosmological and design arguments have been probably the most widely discussed and debated in the last century. Moral arguments have also been advanced to the effect that theism offers the best account possible for the objectivity of morality. While this argument has its proponents in the field, it is often considered part of more general design arguments. The same is true for arguments based on the emergence of consciousness: some have argued that theism provides a better account for the emergence of consciousness than naturalism or other nontheistic alternatives.

The ontological argument for God's existence continues to have its friends and foes in the twentieth century. Of all the theistic arguments it is the most perplexing – even maddening. Its line of reasoning begins with the concept of God as that of a supremely great (or perfect or unsurpassably excellent) being. It is then argued that God should have the attribute of necessary existence, that is, that God does not exist contingently. It is, in fact, impossible for God not to exist. It is, however, possible that God exists. The argument for this possibility sometimes takes the form of exhibiting the coherence of divine attributes. The argument then presents the following dilemma: either God exists necessarily or God's existence is impossible. If God's existence is possible, then God's existence is not impossible. Hence God exists necessarily.

Discussions have focused on the grounds for thinking that God's existence is possible, on whether or not 'necessary existence' is intelligible, and on whether or not God is better thought of as being uncaused rather than necessary. For a defense of the argument, see Alvin Plantinga's *The Nature of Necessity*. For a critique see G. Oppy's *Ontological Arguments and Belief in God*. While the majority of analytic philosophers do not accept the argument, the labor that they have expended to its elucidation has been of enormous sophistication, involving modal logic and complex epistemic principles attempting to decide when it is reasonable to believe that some state of affairs (God exists) is possible or impossible.

Cosmological arguments take the form of arguing for a first or ultimate cause of the cosmos. It is argued that the cosmos is contingent; it does not exist due to its own nature or some necessity. The very existence of our world is not something that can be determined merely conceptually but it has to be investigated empirically, because it is contingent. The explanation of any aspect of our contingent cosmos in terms of other contingent beings will either not fully explain the cosmos, or it must include some noncontingent, necessarily existing being. Here is a version of the argument as outlined by Bruce Reichenbach:

1. A contingent being (a being which, if it exists, can not-exist) exists.
2. This contingent being has a cause or explanation of its existence.
3. The cause or explanation of its existence is something other than the contingent being itself.
4. What causes or explains the existence of this contingent being must either be solely other contingent beings or include a non-contingent (necessary) being.
5. Contingent beings alone cannot cause or explain the existence of a contingent being.
6. Therefore, what causes or explains the existence of this contingent being must include a non-contingent (necessary) being.
7. Therefore, a necessary being (a being which, if it exists, cannot not-exist) exists. (Reichenbach 2004: 104)

If successful, the argument does not ipso facto establish theism, but it would give reason to believe that there is a reality with at least some features that are theistic.

The debate over this argument principally regards premise 6. Atheists argue that there is no need to go beyond contingent beings or that going beyond contingent beings makes no sense. Once the natural sciences have accounted for the cosmos, there is no further need for a more ultimate account. On the other hand, the allure of the appeal to a noncontingent cause of the cosmos is well expressed by Philip Quinn:

> Either the regress of explanation terminates in a most fundamental law or it does not. If there is a deepest law, it will be logically contingent, and so the fact that it holds rather than not doing so will be a brute fact. If the regress does not terminate, then for every law in the infinite hierarchy there is a deeper law from which it can be deduced. In this case, however, the whole hierarchy will be logically contingent, and so the question of why it holds rather than some other hierarchy will arise. So if only scientific explanation is allowed, the fact that this particular infinite hierarchy of contingent laws holds will be a brute inexplicable fact. Therefore, on the assumption that scientific laws are logically contingent and are explained by being deduced from other laws, there are bound to be inexplicable brute facts if only scientific explanation is allowed. (Quinn 1993: 607)

Quinn and other theists contend that the best explanation of the cosmos must transcend the contingent world.

A similar conflict emerges in debate over design. In the design argument, it is held that given theism, there is a reason that a contingent cosmos would exist with stable laws of nature, the emergence of life, including conscious life, subject to morality and center of transcendent religious experiences. Given naturalism, however, there is no overriding reason for the existence of such a cosmos. As with the cosmological argument, the opponents of the theist seek to rule out either as nonsense or as unnecessary a being that transcends the cosmos.

How might progress be made in assessing these arguments? The most plausible arguments offered by analytic thinkers (in our opinion) are those that follow Hempel's advice, as stated earlier in this chapter. The arguments are best seen as part of an overall cumulative case for or against the existence of God. Consider, for example, a move in David Hume's *Dialogues concerning Natural Religion* that has often been a reference point for twentieth-century philosophy of religion. Philo, a character in the dialogue said to most resemble Hume, challenges design and cosmological arguments and says:

> But allowing that we were to take the operations of one part of nature upon another for the foundation of our judgement concerning the whole (which never can be admitted), yet why select so minute, so weak, so bounded a principle as the reason and design of animals is found to be upon the planet. What peculiar privilege has this little agitation of the brain which we call thought, that we must thus make it the model of the whole universe? Our particularity in our own favour does indeed prevent it on all occasions, but sound philosophy ought carefully to guard against so natural an illusion. (Hume 1991: 113)

One may, of course, reply that thought is not a mere agitation of the brain. The belief that the mental is distinct from the physical is making a come-back (Hasker, Foster, Swinburne). One may, moreover, argue that ultimate accounts belong to two categories: the intentional and nonintentional. An intentional explanation would permit one to argue that the goodness of the world is a reason why it exists, whereas this option is not available to those adopting a nonintentional framework. Our point is neither to defend nor oppose design and cosmological arguments. We simply point out how one's philosophy of mind and intentionality have a significant impact in the assessment of theistic arguments. If one believes that consciousness does not exist or that it must be physical, an appeal to the divine consciousness will be problematic. On the other hand, a nonreductive account of consciousness opens the door for a more favorable assessment of the theistic case (Taliaferro 1994).

Let us now consider a major case against God's existence. William Rowe formulates his case for atheism as follows:

1. There now exist instances of intense suffering which an omnipotent, omniscient being could have prevented without thereby losing some greater good or permitting some evil equally bad or worse.
2. An omniscient, wholly good being would prevent the occurrence of any intense suffering it could, unless it could not do so without thereby losing some greater good or permitting some evil equally bad or worse.
3. Therefore, there does not exist an omnipotent, omniscient, wholly good being. (Rowe 2003: 364)

Rowe then presents what is now a famous description of suffering:

Suppose in some distant forest lightning strikes a dead tree, resulting in a forest fire. In the fire a fawn is trapped, horribly burned, and lies in terrible agony for several days before death relieves its suffering. So far as we can see, the fawn's intense suffering is pointless. For there does not appear to be any greater good such that the prevention of the fawn's suffering would require either the loss of that good or the occurrence of an evil equally bad or worse. Nor does there seem to be any equally bad or worse evil so connected to the fawn's suffering that it would have had to occur had the fawn's suffering been prevented. Could an omnipotent, omniscient being have prevented the fawn's apparently pointless suffering? (Rowe 2003: 370)

Rowe goes on to contend that this case against theism is not decisive. He thinks it is possible that such evil is essential for a greater good and that if one has independent good reasons to think there is an all good God then the problem of evil would not be persuasive. But if there are no such independent reasons, Rowe holds that atheism is reasonable.

The debate has taken many forms. It has been argued that it is an overall greater good that there exists a cosmos that produces animal and human life. Peter van Inwagen writes:

Only in a universe very much like ours could intelligent life, or even sentient life, develop by the nonmiraculous operation of the laws of nature. And the natural evolution of higher sentient life in a universe like ours essentially involves suffering, or there is every reason to believe it does. This mechanism underlying biological evolution may be just what most biologists seem to suppose – the production of new genes by random mutation and the culling of gene pools by environmental selection pressure – or they may be more subtle. But no one, I believe, would take seriously the idea that conscious animals, animals conscious as a dog is conscious, could evolve naturally without hundreds of millions of years of ancestral suffering. Pain is an indispensable component of evolutionary process after organisms have reached a certain stage of complexity. And, for all we know, the amount of pain that organisms have experienced in the actual world, or some amount morally equivalent to that amount, is necessary for the natural evolution of conscious animals. (van Inwagen 2003: 396)

Van Inwagen further notes that, while it is possible that God could continuously interfere with nature to prevent undue suffering, this would not allow for the world to have significant independence from God. And such independence seems essential if creatures are to possess genuine free will. A world in which God was constantly manifest would not permit persons to act with significant autonomy.

The problem of evil raises concerns related to the existence, nature, and value of freedom; the extent to which some ills are essential for some goods; the magnitude of evil; the existence of an afterlife; and the limitations of our cognition. This last concern is a major focus of some recent analytic philosophy. Imagine we do not know why God allows evil. When does not knowing why become a reason for thinking that there is no reason why God would allow or not prevent the evil? In other words, when does not seeing the point of evil become a reason for thinking evil is pointless? Philosophically interesting work has been done on what is now called 'the hiddenness of God.' There is revived interest in exploring the merits and demerits in Pascal's concept of God's being only partly evident. In the *Pensées*, Pascal contended that our freedom and sense of self would be jeopardized if there was no obscurity in our awareness of God. God's partial concealment allows us room for moral self-awareness and to embody the virtue of seeking God.

Religious Pluralism

Analytical philosophers in the twentieth century have branched out to investigate Hinduism (especially Advaita Vedanta), Confucianism, Buddhism, Taoism, and African religions. There is now an analytic literature defining faith, religion, the sacred, reincarnation, enlightenment, religious duties and experience, in different cultural and different historical contexts. A superb example of constructive work along these lines is the collection *The Meaning of Life in the World Religions* (Martin and Runzo 2001).

To illustrate how the field of philosophy of religion has expanded, consider the Buddhist philosophical themes in light of the three earlier sections of this chapter.

Philosophers have explored the meaning of Buddhist convictions about the self, karma, and reincarnation. To what extent are these claims metaphysical and to what extent do they function principally to define a way of living which does not rest on metaphysics? Interesting work has been done on Buddhist practices of reading and meditating (see Griffiths 1999). While Buddhism is often treated as nontheistic, there are strands in Buddhism that suggest that Buddha or Nirvana constitute a transcendent, God-like reality. But rather than focus on theism, most Buddhist philosophical work has been concentrated on the concept of the self. Buddhist philosophers often advance nonsubstantial concepts of the self, rejecting the idea that the self is a concrete, substantial individual that endures as itself over time. This alternative concept of the self is used in grounding an ethic that is radically altruistic and compassionate. In light of the new, expanded forum for philosophy of religion, there is now a great deal of work on the compatibility of different religious outlooks. Could it be that behind theistic and nontheistic religions there is some core reality that is simply seen from different points of view? It is John Hick who is best known for his effort to see the world religions as different perspectives on the same divine reality:

> Seen in [a] historical context these movements of faith – the Judaic-Christian, the Buddhist, the Hindu, the Muslim – are not essentially rivals. They began at different times and in different places, and each expanded outwards into the surrounding world of primitive natural religion until most of the world was drawn up into one or other of the great revealed faiths. And once this global pattern had become established it has ever since remained fairly stable. It is true that the process of establishment involved claiming their obedience and demanding a new level of righteousness and justice in the life of Israel. Then in Persia the great prophet Zoroaster appeared; China produces Lao-tzu and then the Buddha lived, and Mahavira, the founder of the Jain religion and, probably about the end of this period, the writing of the Bhagavad-Gita; and Greece produced Pythagoras and then, ending this golden age, Socrates and Plato. Then after the gap of some three hundred years came Jesus of Nazareth and the emergence of Christianity; and after another gap the prophet Mohammed and the rise of Islam. The suggestion that we must consider is that these were all moments of divine revelation. (Hick 1989: 136)

While some analytic philosophers of religion embrace Hick's form of religious pluralism, others take more qualified positions. So, for example, some hold that while different religions may be equally well justified (a Buddhist is just as intellectually responsible in accepting a nonsubstantial view of the self as a Christian, Muslim or Jew is in accepting a substantial view of the self), nonetheless it cannot be that incompatible beliefs are all true.

In this chapter, space has limited our coverage to only some of the salient trends in analytic philosophy of religion. While religious pluralism and cross-cultural philosophy of religion are important recent developments, contemporary analytic philosophers have turned to still other areas including feminism, religious dimensions of environmental ethics, the philosophy of religious ritual, and artistic and aesthetic issues as these arise in religious traditions.

References

Adams, M. (2000), *Horrendous Evils and the Goodness of God*, Ithaca: Cornell University Press.

Alston, W. P. (1991), *Perceiving God: The Epistemology of Religious Experience*, Ithaca: Cornell University Press.

Ayer, A. J. (1936), *Language, Truth, and Logic*, London: Victor Gollancz.

Ayer, A. J. (1940), *Foundations of Empirical Knowledge*, London: Macmillan.

Craig, W. (1979), *The Kalam Cosmological Argument*, New York: Barnes and Noble.

Craig, W. (1980), *The Cosmological Argument from Plato to Leibniz*, New York: Barnes and Noble.

Craig, W. L., and Q. Smith (1993), *Theism, Atheism, and Big Bang Cosmology*, Oxford: Clarendon Press.

Eberle, C. J. (2002), *Religious Conviction in Liberal Politics*, Cambridge: Cambridge University Press.

Flew, A. (1955), 'Theology and Falsification,' in A. Flew, and A. MacIntyre (eds) (1955), *New Essays in Philosophical Theology*, London: SCM Press, pp. 96–108

Gellman, J. (1997), *Experience of God and the Rationality of Theistic Belief*, Ithaca: Cornell University Press.

Griffiths, P. J. (1994), *On Being Buddha*, Albany: State University of New York Press.

Griffiths, P. J. (1999), *Religious Reading*, Oxford: Oxford University Press.

Harris, J. F. (2000), *Analytic Philosophy of Religion*, Dordrecht: Kluwer.

Hartshorne, C. (1983), *Omnipotence, and Other Theological Mistakes*, Albany: State University of New York Press.

Hasker, W. (1989), *God, Time, and Knowledge*, Ithaca: Cornell University Press.

Hasker, W. (1999), *The Emergent Self*, Ithaca: Cornell University Press.

Hempel, C. (1959), 'The Empiricist Criterion of Meaning,' in C. Hempel (1959), *Logical Positivism*, Glen Coe: Free Press, 8.

Hick, J. (1989), *An Interpretation of Religion*, New Haven: Yale University Press.

Hughes, G. J. (1995), *The Nature of God*, London: Routledge.

Hume, D. (1991), *Dialogues concerning Natural Religion*, ed. S. Tweyman, London: Routledge.

Kenny, A. (1979), *The God of the Philosophers*, Oxford: Clarendon Press.

Leftow, B. (1991), *Time and Eternity*, Ithaca: Cornell University Press.

Long, E. T. (2001), *Twentieth Century Western Philosophy of Religion*, Dordrecht: Kluwer.

Lucas, J. (1970), *The Freedom of the Will*, Oxford: Clarendon Press.

Mackie, J. (1985), *The Miracle of Theism*, Oxford: Clarendon Press.

Makransky, J. J. (1997), *Buddhahood Embodied*, Albany: State University of New York Press.

Martin, M. (1990), *Atheism*, Philadelphia: Temple University Press.

Martin, N., and J. Runzo (2001), *The Meaning of Life in the World Religions*, Oxford: Oneworld Publications.

Martin, M. (1990), *Atheism: A Philosophical Justification*, Philadelphia: Temple University Press.

Morris, T.V. (1986), *The Logic of God Incarnate*, Ithaca: Cornell University Press.

Morris, T.V. (1987), *Anselmian Explorations*, Notre Dame: University of Notre Dame Press.

Morris, T. V. (ed.) (1987), *The Concept of God*, Oxford: Oxford University Press.

Oppy, G. (1995), *Ontological Arguments and Belief in God*, Cambridge: Cambridge University Press.

Phillips, D. Z. (1991), *From Fantasy to Faith: The Philosophy of Religion and Twentieth-Century Literature*, Basingstoke: Macmillan.

Phillips, D. Z. (1993), *Wittgenstein and Religion*, Basingstoke: Macmillan; and New York: St. Martin's Press.

Phillips, D. Z., and T. Tessin (eds) (1997), *Religion without Transcendence*, Basingstoke: Macmillan.

Phillips, D. Z., and T. Tessin (eds) (2002), *Philosophy of Religion in the 21st Century*, Basingstoke: Palgrave.

Pike, N. (1970), *God and Timelessness*, New York: Schocken Books.

Plantinga, A. (1967), *God and Other Minds*, Ithaca: Cornell University Press.

Plantinga, A. (1974), *The Nature of Necessity*, Oxford: Oxford University Press.

Plantinga, A. (1980), *Does God Have a Nature?*, Milwaukee: Marquette University Press.

Plantinga, A. (2000), *Warranted Christian Belief*, New York, and Oxford: Oxford University Press.

Quinn, P. L. (1993), 'Creation, Conservation, and the Big Bang,' in J. Earman, N. Rescher, G. J. Massey, and A. I. Janis (eds) (1993), *Philosophical Problems of the Internal and External Worlds*. Pittsburgh: University of Pittsburgh Press, pp. 589–612.

Reichenbach, B. (2004), 'Explanation and the Cosmological Argument,' in M. Peterson (ed.) (2004), *Contemporary Debates in Philosophy of Religion*, Oxford: Blackwell, pp. 92–113.

Rowe, W. (2003), 'The Problem of Evil and some Varieties of Atheism,' in C. Taliaferro and P. Griffiths (eds) (2003), *Philosophy of Religion: An Anthology*, Oxford: Clarendon Press, pp. 364–70.

Rundle, B. (2004), *Why There Is Something Rather Than Nothing*, Oxford: Clarendon Press.

Schlesinger, G. (1977), *Religion and Scientific Method*, Dordrecht: Reidel.

Sessions, L. (1994), *The Concept of Faith: A Philosophical Investigation*, Ithaca: Cornell University Press.

Sharma, A. (1990), *A Hindu Perspective on the Philosophy of Religion*, New York: St. Martin's Press.

Sobel, H. (2004), *Logic and Theism*, Cambridge: Cambridge University Press.

Swinburne, R. (1977), *The Coherence of Theism*, Oxford: Clarendon Press.

Swinburne, R. (1979), *The Existence of God*, Oxford: Clarendon Press.

Swinburne, R. (1989), *Responsibility and Atonement*, Oxford: Clarendon Press.

Swinburne, R. (1992), *Revelation: From Metaphor to Analogy*, Oxford: Clarendon Press.

Swinburne, R. (1993), *The Coherence of Theism*, Oxford: Clarendon Press.

Swinburne, R. (1994), *The Christian God*, Oxford: Clarendon Press.

Swinburne, R. (1996), *Is there a God?*, Oxford: Oxford University Press.

Swinburne, R. (1997), *The Evolution of the Soul*, Oxford: Clarendon Press.

Swinburne, R. (1998), *Providence and the Problem of Evil*, Oxford: Oxford University Press.

Taliaferro, C. (1994), *Consciousness and the Mind of God*, Cambridge: Cambridge University Press.

Taliaferro, C. (1998), *Contemporary Philosophy of Religion*, Oxford: Blackwell.

Taliaferro, C. (2001), 'Sensibility and Possibilia: A Defense of Thought Experiments,' *Philosophia Christi* 3(2): 403–2.

Taliaferro, C. (2005), *Evidence and Faith*, New York: Cambridge University Press.

Trigg, R. (1989), *Reality at Risk*, London: Harvester.

van Cleve, J. (1999), *Problems from Kant*, Oxford: Oxford University Press.

van Inwagen, P. (2003), 'The Problem of Evil, of Air, and of Silence,' in C. Taliaferro and P. Griffiths (eds) (2003), *Philosophy of Religion: An Anthology*, Oxford: Clarendon Press, pp. 390–406.

Wainwright, W. (2005), *The Oxford Handbook of Philosophy of Religion*, Oxford: Oxford University Press.

Wainwright, W. (1981), *Mysticism: A Study of its Nature, Cognitive Value, and Moral Implications*, Madison: University of Wisconsin Press.

Wettstein, H. (2002), 'Poetic Imagery and Religious Belief,' in David Shatz (ed.) (2002), *Philosophy and Faith*, Boston: McGraw Hill, pp. 106–14.

Wieringa, E. (1989), *The Nature of God*, Ithaca: Cornell University Press.

Wolterstorff, N. P. (1982), 'God Everlasting,' in S. M. Cahn and D. Shatz (eds) (1982), *Contemporary Philosophy of Religion*, Oxford: Oxford University Press, 77–98.

Wolterstorff, N. P. (2001), *Thomas Reid and the Story of Epistemology*, Cambridge, and New York: Cambridge University Press.

Wykstra, S. (1984), 'The Humean Obstacle to Evidential Arguments from Suffering.' *International Journal for Philosophy of Religion* 16: 73–93.

Yandell, K. (1993), *The Epistemology of Religious Experience*, Cambridge: Cambridge University Press.

Zagzebski, L.T. (1991), *The Dilemma of Freedom and Foreknowledge*, New York: Oxford University Press.

Feminism

Josephine Donovan

The feminist engagement with the analytic tradition in the twentieth century was for the most part a contentious one. Beginning in the early 1970s – when feminist academics began applying propositions formulated in the women's liberation political movement of the late 1960s and early 1970s to their respective intellectual fields, feminist philosophers at first used analytic methodologies and assumptions to examine feminist questions. This was not surprising, given that the dominant philosophical tradition in academic departments at the time was the analytic and that these (mostly women) philosophers had been trained in the analytic tradition. Soon, however – by the mid-1970s – it became clear to many feminist philosophers that the tools and assumptions of the analytic approach were inadequate for feminist purposes. An extensive body of feminist writing emerged in the latter quarter of the century that critiqued the major tenets of the analytic tradition – especially its privileging of the empiricist epistemology of science. Proposals for an alternative feminist epistemology and a feminist philosophy of science dominated feminist philosophical discourse during this period. In the 1990s, however, a few feminist philosophers began to reclaim aspects of the analytic tradition, arguing that it can in fact be used for feminist purposes.

This article will trace the trajectory of this feminist engagement with the analytic tradition, focusing primarily on the epistemological questions that have dominated the debate. In addition, however, there have been significant negotiations between feminist philosophers and the analytic tradition in other fields, notably, aesthetics, ethics, and political philosophy. These too will be treated.

It should be noted at the outset that underlying all feminist critiques of science and the analytic tradition is the patent fact that very few women are scientists or analytic philosophers. Indeed, the history of these fields revealed them to be largely masculine professions. The gendered character of the fields suggested that either (1) overt discrimination was operant – women were simply not hired or promoted because they were women; (2) ideological assumptions and social structures, such as the division of labor, militated against women entering the fields; or (3) there was something about the way science and philosophy were conceived and practiced that was unattractive to women. The latter two positions found theoretical expression in the gynecentric critiques of science, which are detailed below. (A useful survey of the above positions may be found in Nelson 1995.)

In the early 1970s, when academic feminism began to emerge, the dominant philosophical school was the Anglo–Austrian–American analytic tradition, which held that the proper focus of philosophy must be conceptual and linguistic clarification by means of which objective, trans-subjective, indeed universal truths about reality may be established. Much as the scientist proceeds empirically and inductively to evaluate truth claims about a given reality, arriving thereby at a generic truth about the substance in question, so the philosopher by linguistically and conceptually decomposing and logically analyzing linguistic construction can arrive at generic, objective – even *a priori* – truths. Like the scientific, the analytic operation was seen to exist in a social and historical vacuum, and the mind of the analyst was assumed to be disembodied, mechanistic, neutral – unaffected by his or her social, gender, or ethnic location, but functioning as above these contingencies.

The earliest examples of feminist philosophy – such as several articles included in Baker and Elliston 1975, Vetterling-Braggin, et al. 1977, (especially the section 'Sexism in Ordinary Language'), and Gould and Warshofsky 1976 – simply applied analytic techniques to gender issues. For example, in a 1971 article 'A Defense of Abortion,' Judith Jarvis Thomson used the counter-example – an accepted tool of conceptual analysis – to rebut anti-abortion arguments. In 'The Adversary Method,' (1983), however, Janice Moulton critiqued Thomson's article, arguing that it illustrated the limitations of the analytic approach – in particular what she labels its 'Adversary Paradigm' – in providing an adequate defense of abortion ethics. Thomson's narrow linguistic focus neglected to engage with other ethical issues involved in the abortion question, such as considerations about conflicting duties, obligations to self and others, which necessarily impinge upon the abortion decision and cannot be dismissed as logically irrelevant. The socially situated location of the woman's experience is a relevant matter for philosophical reflection and is at least as important to the process of ethical determination as is parsing the logic of anti-abortion arguments. Not all 'philosophical differences,' Moulton argued, 'can be resolved through language' (Moulton 1983: 162).

Moulton's article appeared in the ground-breaking collection *Discovering Reality*, one of the editors of which, Sandra Harding, led the feminist critique of science and the analytic tradition which flourished in the remainder of the century. This critique centered upon several issues. First and foremost was the question of whether analytic methods do yield generic, universal, and/or objective truths about reality; and, second, whether the philosopher who performs rational analytic operations is in fact the neutral, disembodied, autonomous operant assumed in analytic and scientific theory. Feminists questioned, moreover, the paradigmatic status accorded Newtonian physics within the analytic community, noting the insufficiency of its view of nature as objectified and mechanistic when applied to biological and social subjects, which may not operate according to *a priori* laws and principles. Indeed, some claimed, such premises of the scientific method may obscure and distort the truth when recalcitrant matter is forced to conform to predetermined hypotheses.

On the first point, feminists rejected the idea that analytic operations and the alleged objective truths they yield may be separated from their socio-political context. That the analytic process – the search for truth – transcends its historical moment, as well as cultural, class, and gender contexts, was similarly questioned. Indeed, many feminists asserted that presumptions of objectivity and neutrality often mask tacit ideological assumptions, as well as power relations, which influence intellectual outcomes. Moreover, feminists doubted whether the individual philosopher/analyst is capable of divorcing his/her mental operations from enculturated biases. Instead, many feminists claimed, knowledge is always partial and 'embedded' in a particular cultural and historical location.

The feminist critique of analytic/scientific assumptions may be sorted into three positions (adapting Sandra Harding's characterizations in *The Science Question in Feminism*): empiricism, gynecentric theories (which include standpoint theories), and postmodernism. The feminist empiricist approach held that while it was undeniable that existing analytic and scientific practices had not yielded objective truths and indeed often reflected an androcentric bias, this did not mean that the analytic and empiricist methods were at fault; rather it was that they were faultily employed. Thus, if scientists and philosophers would purge themselves of sexist bias and adhere more strictly to genuinely neutral application of analytic/scientific operating principles, the results would be objective and untainted by particularistic distortion. In other words, the feminist empiricist position, later reformulated and revised by analytic feminists, was that the problems were just a matter of bad science or philosophy and that what was needed was a stricter adherence to proper rigorous analysis. As the most obvious biases occurred in the formulation of hypotheses, methods of observation, laboratory procedures, and interpretation of results – all matters of scientific practice, feminist empiricists argued, they were correctable.

The second feminist critique was drawn up by those who argued that analytic and scientific traditions were inherently flawed because they reflected a masculinist way of knowing. These feminists argued for a more gynecentric approach, that is, one that accorded women a distinctive epistemological perspective and an identifiable body of knowledge. An early formulation of this notion came from the neo-Marxist standpoint theorists, but it may also be seen in neo-Freudian feminist theory, such as the idea of *gynesis* articulated by certain French feminists, or in those who rely on 'object relations' psychoanalytic theory. Standpoint theorists drew upon the Marxist tradition, especially that elaborated by Georg Lukács. In *History and Class Consciousness* (1922) Lukács accorded epistemological privilege to the proletariat, arguing that its perspective (or standpoint) was closer to the truth of social and political relations than that of the ruling class. Feminist standpoint theory, as developed by Nancy Hartsock (her first major articulation of the theory, 'The Feminist Standpoint,' appeared in *Discovering Reality*) held that women's oppressed position vis-à-vis men and their historically variant labor experience gave women a privileged epistemological status. As applied to science, feminist standpoint theory rejected the claims that it transcends social and economic factors; rather, like any other institutionalized practice, in the Marxist view, it is a social practice which reflects the class (and gender) it is rooted in. Feminist standpoint theorists therefore argued that science and the analytic tradition were masculinist modes of knowledge and that the truths they yielded were partial, indeed 'perverse.' Certain of the standpoint theorists – notably Hartsock, Hilary Rose, and Dorothy Smith – argued that analytic/scientific modes were partial precisely because of their presumption of disembodiment; they thereby excluded emotional and bodily knowledge, as well as craft-based epistemologies rooted in women's traditional domestic labor. Standpoint theorists argued instead that a feminist epistemology must be seen as grounded in women's traditional activities – all of which were ignored or deemed insignificant and irrelevant by traditional analytic philosophers. Rose (1983) extended the Marxist idea that the divorce between intellectual and manual labor created 'alienated knowledge,' arguing that in addition to the split between the 'brain' and the 'hand,' the 'heart' – women's caring labor – had been left out of the epistemological equation. A more holistic knowledge would incorporate perspectives gleaned from such neglected and suppressed material practices.

Standpoint theory thus abjures the possibility of universal, objective truths, seeing instead all knowledge as politically situated. The basic difficulty therefore with the standpoint approach – as analytic feminists (among others) later pointed out (see below) – is that it risks reducing the determination of truth to a matter of power (Thrasymachus's position in *The Republic* [I.339]), for there is no transcending way of deciding among conflicting partial truths which is the 'truer.' Later feminist critics of science, such as Lorraine Code and Helen Longino, attempted to correct for this difficulty by arguing that truth is not reached by the autonomous rational mind – 'Cartesian man' – operating in isolation (as held in the traditional analytic view) but rather is reached within a 'community of knowers' who nevertheless operate according to agreed-upon objective criteria (here departing from standpoint theory). Code (1991) argued that epistemic justification – the evaluation of truth claims – is done within a 'community of knowers' who share certain values. Code thus injects the question of ethical evaluation into the epistemological frame. Truth and knowledge are arrived at not just through logical and empirical judgements but also through ethical reflections which precede in a sense the formulations of hypotheses and the application of results. In *Science as Social Knowledge*, Helen Longino argued that as knowledge is formed in communities, false propositions are tested and corrected by consultation with others trained in the assumptions and values of the profession. The knowledge gained will not be as irrefutable as an analytic mathematical proposition but it will reflect a relatively truer proposition than otherwise. Scientific truths are therefore not formed in a vacuum, but, on the other hand, they are not entirely contingent and relativistic. Thus, Longino sees science as a social practice that relies on a professionally trained cadre of practitioners who review one another's work and come to a consensus as to the most credible positions on a given problem.

Similarly recognizing the social context of scientific discourse (and following somewhat in the vein of Thomas Kuhn [1970], Evelyn Fox Keller (1985) argued that 'laws' of nature are not established wholly by logical induction but are rather 'metaphors' that scientists come to use to describe what they believe to be reality. Often these metaphors reflect the social and ideological conditioning of a scientist. Moreover, they often remain fixed dogma even when contradictory evidence has been produced. Using her own research as an example (Keller is a mathematical biologist), Keller discovered in the early 1970s that slime mold cells operate without central direction in moving toward the aggregation that precedes the formation of multicellular organisms; however, despite her discovery, the prevailing paradigm remained that of a director or 'pacemaker' cell that organizes the other cells – which Keller suggests shows how ideological background assumptions can favor the adoption of one paradigm over another (Keller 1985: 150–7).

Just as masculinist and other ideological preconceptions may taint the metaphors being used to describe the reality being perceived, so may a masculinist bias infect the way the scientific method is conceived and practiced. Several feminists have critiqued, for example, the Baconian tendency in science to see nature as an *other* that the scientist examines and manipulates in order to arrive at allegedly generic, 'objective' truths. Carolyn Merchant in *The Death of Nature*, a history of science from a feminist point of view, cites as prototypical Francis Bacon's dominative view of nature in his description of the scientific method: 'For you have . . . as it were [to] hound nature in her wanderings, and you will be able when you like to lead and drive her afterward to the same place' (Merchant 1980: 168). The notion of a feminized nature as something to be controlled and coerced into preconceived patterns of appropriate behavior is likely, feminists asserted, to yield inaccurate and distortive knowledge. As Sandra Harding notes:

> It is the scientific subject's voice that speaks only with general and abstract authority; the objects of inquiry 'speak' only in response to what scientists ask them, and they speak in the particular voice of their historically specific conditions and locations. (Harding 1986: 124)

In an earlier article Keller also proposed that traditional analytic/scientific epistemology may reflect a masculine bias in that the male maturation process creates subjects who are inclined toward objectivity and autonomy, because men are required to distinguish their identity from their mothers, thus rejecting all things feminine – a position taken by a number of feminist theorists who rely on the 'object relations' school of psychoanalytic theory, most notably Nancy Chodorow in *The Reproduction of Mothering* (1978). The privileging of these characteristics in scientific and analytic theory may therefore mirror masculine psychological predispositions. There is, Keller proposes, 'a network of interactions between gender development, a belief system which equates objectivity with masculinity, and a set of cultural values which simultaneously elevates what is defined as scientific and what is defined as masculine' (Keller 1983: 199). Susan Bordo similarly argued that Cartesian rationalism reflects a 'masculinization of thought,' a 'flight from the feminine' (Bordo 1987: 439, 441). And in her book *The Man of Reason: 'Male' and 'Female' in Western Philosophy*, Genevieve Lloyd likewise showed how much of Western philosophy, particularly the rationalist tradition, calls for 'transcendence' of realms of experience pejoratively deemed feminine.

Alternative epistemological approaches were proposed by Keller and other feminist theorists in the gynecentric tradition. Instead, for example, of forcing and dominating the reality being examined, scientists should re-envisage the process as more of a conversation, in which the subject matter is allowed to 'speak' dialogically with the inquirer. In 'Feminism and Science', Keller contrasts the attitude of Nobel-prize winning geneticist Barbara McClintock with that of Bacon. McClintock urges that one 'let . . . the material speak to you' and allow it to 'tell you what to do next.' She argues against the idea that scientists should 'impose an answer' upon the material being studied; rather they should respond to it, retaining an empathetic respect for it (cited in Keller 1982: 599). Such a reorientation is likely to yield a less distortive, less 'perverse' knowledge.

The third broad area of the feminist critique of science and the analytic tradition is the postmodernist. Like postmodernism in general, feminists in this camp challenge the idea that any 'grand narratives' or 'totalizing' theories are valid. Rather they contend, following Jean-François Lyotard's *Postmodern Condition* (Engl. trans., 1984), that such metanarratives have been delegitimized in the postmodern era – indeed, that such delegitimization is the hallmark of postmodernism. In her article, 'Postmodernism and Gender Relations,' Jane Flax, one of the leading feminist postmodernists, specifies that postmodernist 'radical doubt' is particularly directed against such central tenets of Enlightenment rationalism as the idea that 'reason and its "science" philosophy . . . can provide an objective, reliable, and universal foundation for knowledge,' that the knowledge gleaned from rational analysis 'will be "True," ' that 'reason exists independently of the self's contingent existence (that is, bodily, historical and social experiences do not affect reason's structure or its capacity to produce atemporal knowledge,' and that science is 'the paradigm for all true knowledge' (Flax 1987: 624–5). Perhaps, Flax further speculates, 'reality can have "a" structure only from the falsely universalizing perspective of the dominant group' (Flax 1987: 634). Perhaps 'such transcendental claims reflect and reify the experience of a few persons – mostly white, Western males' (Flax 1987: 626).

Thus, postmodernist feminists join in the critique of science and the analytic tradition proposed by standpoint theorists in that they question its legitimacy as a reliable means to the truth, suggesting that its claims to objectivity and neutrality are compromised by the political interests of its practitioners. Where the postmodernists part company with standpoint theorists is in their refusal to privilege a women's/feminist standpoint or indeed any other source of knowledge. Donna Haraway, for example, in 'A Manifesto for Cyborgs' – a major document of feminist postmodernism – calls for 'a powerful infidel heteroglossia' (Haraway 1990: 223). The problem with feminism in this vein is the problem endemic in postmodernism generally, that in abjuring the validity of any unitary generic statements it risks dissolving into such radical pluralism that any claims beyond the particular are nullified.

In the 1990s a few feminists began to reclaim aspects of the analytic tradition for feminist use. This new direction was articulated primarily in three publications: Lynn Hankinson Nelson's *Who Knows: From Quine to a Feminist Empiricism*, Louise M. Antony and Charlotte Witt (eds), *A Mind of One's Own: Feminist Essays on Reason and Objectivity*, and a special issue of the journal *Hypatia* on 'Analytic Feminism,' edited by Ann E. Cudd.

In her introduction to the last volume, Cudd notes how analytic feminists are united in their reassertion of the value of such traditional analytic methods as logical and linguistic analysis in order to add 'clarity and precision' to argument. 'Analytic feminist work is [also] characterized by the conviction that there is value in the pursuit of notions of truth, logical consistency, objectivity, rationality, justice, and the good despite the fact that [it] has often been dominated and perverted by androcentrism' (Cudd 1995: 2–3). Analytic feminists thus tend to be negotiating between the critiques proposed by earlier feminists noted above and the assumptions of the analytic tradition. Ideally, like the empiricist feminists, they would purge the analytic approach of its androcentric bias in order to perform its practices in a way consistent with feminist goals.

Lynn Nelson (like Louise Antony, see below) relied on certain of W. V. O. Quine's theories to negotiate between feminist critiques of science and the transparent empiricism of traditional science that sees reality as a neutral entity, unaffected by viewer or context, which is known by sense experience and which can inductively yield generic analytic truths – David Hume's fatal challenge to the latter assumption notwithstanding. Hume had noted in the *Enquiry Concerning Human Understanding* (1748) the unbridgeable disjunction between empirical reality and theory. Scientific 'laws' derived from a repetition of events remain synthetic propositions that lack the certainty of *a priori* truth ('*that the sun will not rise tomorrow* is no less intelligible a proposition, and implies no more contradiction than the affirmation *that it will rise*') (1939: 595).

Quine extended Hume's position, arguing that all statements – even the most purely logical or mathematical – are to some degree synthetic because 'all sentences both organize and share empirical content' (Nelson 1991: 91). Quine also offered a 'naturalized epistemology,' insisting that there can be no 'coherent pretheoretic sensory experience.' We experience the world from birth on through conceptual frames provided to us by our social community. Thus, there can be no 'objective,' extra-theoretic knowledge. We always 'speak from within a community' (Quine, cited in Nelson 1991: 93).

Nelson argues that Quine's views provide an opening for a feminist reappropriation of the analytic tradition. In acknowledging that science is not autonomous and that knowers know through perspectives inculcated by their society, the feminist position (articulated by Code, Longino, and others) would seem to be validated. Where Nelson parted company from Quine, however, was in her emphasis that sense experience is shaped by different 'epistemic communities.' While holding that 'science [is] a social . . . process,' Quine nevertheless assumed 'that in the [scientific] community . . . we will all . . . see the same thing' (Nelson 1991: 184); Nelson argued (in line with gynecentric theory) that perspectives gleaned from different groups may not agree and that alternative perspectives, such as the feminist, may affect and correct 'what it is [considered] *reasonable* to believe' (Nelson 1991: 297). But Nelson also parts company with standpoint theorists and remains closer to the analytic camp in that she holds empirical verification as a valid means to verify knowledge claims.

In her contribution to *A Mind of One's Own*, Louise Antony (1993) also picks up on Quine's 'naturalized epistemology,' noting how it can be used for feminist purposes in that it acknowledges that biases can affect the knower and the analytic process. She rejects the implications, however, of relativist feminists who question whether there are objective truths and whether traditional analytic, allegedly impartial methodologies can reach them. While acknowledging that bias can and does affect the analytic process, Antony notes that if one rejects the possibility of 'impartial' procedures one is reduced to the 'bias paradox,' which is (as noted above) that there is no way of deciding among competing biases. She therefore joins the empiricist feminists in arguing that we can mitigate the effects of biases by analyzing and acknowledging them – which is itself a reprise of analytic methodology.

Elizabeth Anderson extends analytic feminism in her contribution to the 1995 special *Hypatia* issue on 'Analytic Feminism.' Feminist epistemology should not be seen, as standpoint/gynecentric theorists hold, as focusing on a specifically feminine way of knowing; rather it should be considered a branch of 'naturalized, social epistemology that studies the various influences of norms and conceptions of gender . . . on the production of knowledge.' Anderson thus would have feminist epistemology remain within the traditional analytic/empiricist tradition, relying upon 'rationality as a key epistemic ideal and empirical adequacy as a fundamental goal of acceptable theories' (Anderson 1995: 80). Like Antony (as well as earlier critics such as Longino), she believes biases can be corrected through socially interactive criticism within the scientific/philosophical community. Recent analytic feminists have therefore absorbed many of the criticisms made by earlier feminist critics but feel that, as Anderson puts it, 'the core concept of reason, conjoined with . . . empirically supported hypotheses' (Anderson 1995: 51), is the best means we have for arriving at truth.

Feminist theorists in aesthetics have critiqued analytic conceptions of art from much the same theoretical point of view as feminist critics of epistemology. The analytic tradition in art, derived largely from Kant's *Critique of Judgment* (1790), held that the art object was an autonomous entity, a self-referential telos governed by ideal aesthetic laws (*Zweckmässigkeit ohne Zweck*). Moreover, it was divorced from – indeed transcended – 'real world' political and social interests. In many ways, Kant's view of the artist was similar to the classical Newtonian/Baconian view of the scientist as one who organized matter into transcending objective form.

Feminist critics of traditional analytic aesthetics faulted its neglect of the historical and political context of art; its failure to consider that allegedly universal aesthetic criteria may be biased by race, gender, culture, and class; and its assumption of the transcendent autonomy of the art object, ignoring thereby craft-based art that is embedded in local, domestic cultures. They also questioned the implicit analogy of aesthetics to science, wherein fixed, determinable, and universal truths are allegedly established. The feminist critique of these assumptions was first laid out in 'Feminism and Aesthetics,' a special issue of *Hypatia* (1990) edited by Hilde Hein and Carolyn Korsmeyer (later expanded into a book, *Aesthetics in Feminist Perspective*) and 'Feminism and Traditional Aesthetics,' a special issue of *The Journal of Aesthetics and Art Criticism* (1990), edited by Peg Brand and Carolyn Korsmeyer.

In 'Analytic Aesthetics and Feminist Aesthetics: Neither/Nor?', which appeared in the latter journal, Joanne B. Waugh criticizes the analytic tradition's neglect of women and feminist concerns as well as its apolitical/ahistorical perspective. 'Far too often analytic analyses of the "logic of a concept" proceed without recognizing that this "logic" may be the product of historically specific and contingent factors,' and therefore reflect gender and class bias (Waugh 1990: 317). Traditional aesthetics ignores the cultural ideological climates and social practices and institutions that inculcate women with masculine perspectives – what has been famously labeled (by Linda Nochlin in *Women, Art and Power* [1988]) 'the male gaze' (Waugh 1990: 323). Feminists have also questioned, Waugh notes further, the analytic conception of the art object as a 'referential fixity' to which universal 'rational' (Waugh 1990: 319, 320) criteria may be applied.

Like the standpoint theorists, some feminists have proposed an alternative aesthetic grounded in women's knowledges or traditional craft practices. Several French feminists employing a neo-Freudian theory of difference – notably Hélène Cixous and Luce Irigaray – have argued for feminine aesthetic modes and criteria of judgement, a *gynesis*. Others, deriving less from a Freudian perspective than a Marxist, have located a women's aesthetic in women's traditional practices, such as quilt-making, where art is not an autonomous object but rather a 'use-object' located in the everyday world. In her contribution to *Aesthetics in Feminist Perspective*, 'Everyday Use and Moments of Being: Toward a Nondominative Aesthetic,' Josephine Donovan proposes a non-Kantian aesthetic gleaned from Virginia Woolf's *A Room of One's Own* (1929) in which the matter for art is not seen as an *other* to be manipulated and reshaped according to transcendent aesthetic criteria, but rather material with which the artist engages dialogically (as geneticist Barbara McClintock 'listened' to her corn), faithfully recording its 'moments of being' (Donovan 1993: 54).

In another contribution to the same volume, 'Re-enfranchising Art: Feminist Interventions in the Theory of Art,' Estella Lauter similarly rejects 'formalist' aesthetics, arguing for a 'de-objectification' of art (Lauter 1993: 29). Where 'formalism defines art in terms of formal properties, qualities and principles and arranges those elements in a hierarchical order to privilege those least useful to daily life,' a feminist aesthetic sees 'art [as] a continuum of objects, enactments, concepts, and environments' (Lauter 1993: 31). 'The artist is a co-creator of structures in an interactive system which includes both nature and cultures' (Lauter 1993: 32). 'Good art . . . suggest[s] alternative ways of being. Its aesthetic value arises in relationship to moral and cognitive values' (Lauter 1993: 31). In a similar vein Reneé Lorraine outlines 'A Gynecentric Aesthetic' (Lorraine 1993).

In the fields of ethics and moral philosophy feminists have similarly taken issue with analytic Kantian assumptions. The most effective and influential critique was that articulated by Carol Gilligan in her *In A Different Voice: Psychoanalytical Theory and Women's Development*, which was not focused against Kant directly but rather against the Kantian assumptions enunciated by developmental psychologist Lawrence Kohlberg. In his ranking of different kinds of moral reasoning Kohlberg placed a Kantian universalist, rationalist, rights-based, duty-oriented decision-making ethic at the top, considering that those who operated according to it exhibited the 'highest' kind of ethical thinking. Gilligan took issue with Kohlberg, who had found few women reached this level of reflection, which required abstract analysis disconnected from contextual contingencies. Based on her own studies of young women's moral reasoning, she discovered an alternative kind of reasoning, which she argued was just as valid as the Kantian, but one based not on analyzing a moral situation in terms of 'competing rights' but in terms of 'conflicting responsibilities,' requiring 'for its resolution a mode of thinking that is contextual and narrative rather than formal and abstract' (Gilligan 1982: 19). In contrast to the Kantian 'morality of rights,' with 'its emphasis on separation rather than connection [and a] consideration of the individual rather than the relationship as primary,' a 'morality of responsibility' is focused on the 'activity of care' and the needs of the community (Gilligan 1982: 19).

As with other feminist critiques of the analytic tradition, feminist ethicists took issue with the mechanistic, quasi-scientific, disembodied character of Kantian ethics. As Gilligan noted, the analytic approach often seemed like 'a math problem with humans' (Gilligan 1982: 28). Moreover, such universalizing pretenses ignore or repress 'real world' circumstances that may be relevant to the ethical decision. And again, since much of the universalizing had been done by men, it was often androcentric, with women's contingencies ignored or minimized.

Instead, following Gilligan, feminist theorists proposed an alternative, gynecentric approach, which became known as the 'care' tradition in feminist ethics. Major theorists in this tradition include Sara Ruddick, who identified a 'maternal ethic' in her *Maternal Thinking*, one derived from the practice of mothering wherein attentive, preservative care of individuals in context is the dominant ethical mode; and Nel Noddings, who in *Caring* extended care theory, which she characterized as 'a feminine approach,' to the field of moral education.

Seyla Benhabib (1987) summed up the difference between the Kohlberg-Kantian and the Gilligan views as a contrast between a focus on the 'generalized' as opposed to the 'concrete other.' The former view sees the individual as a 'person,' an abstract integer entitled to certain rights and accorded dutiful respect and dignity. The latter view sees the individual as a specific entity with a concrete identity and narrative history to whom one relates emotionally, with care, love, and sympathy. The Kantian universalizing ethic – 'like cases ought to be treated alike' – abstracts from the particular case so as to distort it, leading to what may not in fact be an appropriate ethical response. Moreover, Kant and those in the analytic tradition assumed that everyone was endowed with the same reasoning faculties and therefore would reach the same moral conclusions. 'In Kantian moral theory, moral agents are like geometricians in different rooms, who, reasoning alone for themselves, all arrive at the same solution to a problem' (Benhabib 1987: 167).

In short, care theorists, like feminist critics of the analytical tradition in general, criticized the abstract, universalizing pretenses of Kantian theory, which they saw as eliding the particular circumstances of an ethical event, as well as its contextual and political contingencies. They also faulted its view of individuals as autonomous isolates, neglecting thereby their social relationships. Feminist care theorists attempted to restore such emotional responses as emotion, sympathy, empathy, and compassion to the philosophical debate, revalidating them as relevant ethical and epistemological sources for ethical behavior. Finally, following Gilligan, they urged a narrative, contextually aware form of reasoning, as opposed to the rigid rationalist abstractions of the 'one-size-fits-all' analytic approach, emphasizing instead that we heed the individual particularities of any given case.

In the field of political philosophy, debates within feminism paralleled in many respects the discussions about the analytic tradition in other fields. In political theory the mainstream doctrine criticized by feminists was the Kantian liberal tradition, which emphasized the rights of autonomous individuals and equality of opportunity but which like analytic theory in general tended toward abstract, mechanistic reasoning and the establishment of broad, generic or universal statements that often elided particular 'real world' circumstances, including the power differentials that operate in any society.

As with the analytic tradition in philosophy, feminists at first simply adopted the main tenets of liberal theory, applying its premises to women. From Mary Woll-stonecraft's *Vindication of the Rights of Woman* (1792) through the women's rights campaigns of the nineteenth and twentieth century, liberal feminists saw their cause as a matter of granting basic political rights, such as the right to vote, to women. In the 'second wave,' however, of feminist theory, which developed in the latter quarter of the twentieth century, a voluminous body of literature emerged that critiqued the liberal position. These critiques included gynecentric approaches, such as 'cultural feminism,' which argued that women have a separate cultural tradition that offers new and better ways of organizing and practicing political life, standpoint theory, radical feminism, Freudian feminism, and postmodernism (see Donovan 2000 for a survey of these positions).

By the end of the century a debate – sometimes referred to as the 'rights versus care' or the 'equality versus difference' debate – had been joined between those feminists who adhered to the analytic/liberal tradition and those who were critical of it. In general, the latter criticized its claims of universality, which masked an androcentric bias, ignoring the different social condition of women. Catharine MacKinnon, a prominant feminist legal theorist, argued that while Anglo-American law 'aspired' to the condition of science in being a universal, rational, impartial, neutral discourse, such pretenses masked substantive inequalities in power. 'The problem with neutrality as the definition of principle in constitutional adjudication is that it equates substantive powerlessness with substantive power and calls treating these the same, "equality"' (MacKinnon 1987: 165).

Most feminist critiques of the liberal tradition similarly pointed out its blindnesses, in particular its acceptance of the public/private division, its theoretical elision of the private sphere, and its failure to acknowledge women's physiological, epistemological, social, and historical difference. In her introduction to *Feminist Challenges: Social and Political Theory*, Pateman notes liberal theory provides 'a unitary, undifferentiated framework that assumes there is only one – universal – sex,' thereby 'gloss[ing] over' the existence of 'women *as women*; at best, women can be incorporated [into liberal theory only] as pale reflections of men' (Pateman and Gross 1987: 7–8). Pateman urges the development of an alternative feminist theory which begins from a recognition of difference, from an acceptance 'that individuals are feminine and masculine, that individuality is not a unitary abstraction but . . . embodied and sexually differentiated' (Pateman and Gross 1987: 9).

In a later book, *The Sexual Contract*, Pateman goes to the heart of liberal theory in contending that a tacit 'sexual contract' precedes the so-called social contract by which people consent to being governed. Most Enlightenment liberal theorists, including John Locke, relied on social contract theory – the idea that people agree to government, relinquishing their 'natural' freedom in exchange for protection from the dangers of the natural state and for various civil rights. But:

> women [were] not party to the original contract through which men transform their natural freedom into the security of civil freedom. Women are the subject of the contract. The (sexual) contract is the vehicle through which men transform their natural right over women into the security of civil patriarchal right. (Pateman 1988: 6)

Thus, liberal theory is rooted in a fundamentally unjust social arrangement. Until recently, in fact, marriage contracts and the law of *coverture* guaranteed husbands' control over their wives and the latter's subordination within the domestic sphere.

While acknowledging liberal theory's neglect of the private sphere, Susan Moller Okin attempts, however, in *Justice, Gender, and the Family*, to reform liberal theory from within by extending Kantian liberal John Rawls's theories to cover women in the domestic sphere. In *A Theory of Justice* (1971) Rawls argued that principles of justice may be arrived at through this hypothetical: individuals placed in an 'original position' and operating through a 'veil of ignorance' (that is, not knowing what class, race, sex, nationality, and so on, they are going to be in life) would establish principles that would be fair to all, regardless of the specifics of their situation, because if one could end up as one of the less well-off, one would want to ensure that in this capacity one was treated fairly. In applying Rawls's theory to the family or domestic sphere, Okin argued that the same principles of justice that are stipulated for the public sphere should also govern in the home. In other words, labor such as parenting should be equally shared. Currently, Okin wrote, 'marriage and the family . . . are unjust institutions. They constitute the pivot of a societal system of gender that renders women vulnerable to dependency, exploitation, and abuse (Okin 1989: 135–6). '[W]hat has not been recognized as an equal opportunity problem . . . is the disparity within the family, the fact that its gender structure is itself a major obstacle to equality of opportunity' (Okin 1989: 16).

Feminist critics of the liberal tradition, therefore, join other feminist critics of science and the analytic philosophy in their objection to its claims of universality and neutrality, its abstract acontextual premises, and its focus on autonomous individuals – 'persons' – disregarding their social embeddedness. Underlying the feminist critique overall is an implicit indictment of what are seen as artificial theoretical divisions in the analytic traditions between mind and body, reason and emotions, culture and nature, public and private, justice and care, with the former term in each coupling valorized over the latter.

References

Anderson, E. (1995), 'Feminist Epistemology: An Interpretation and a Defense,' *Hypatia* 10(3): 50–84.

Antony, L. M., and C. Witt (eds) (1993), *A Mind of One's Own: Feminist Essays in Reason and Objectivity*, Boulder: Westview, pp. 185–226.

Antony, L. M. (1993), 'Quine as Feminist: The Radical Import of Naturalized Epistemology,' in L. M. Antony, and C. Witt (eds) (1993), *A Mind of One's Own*, Boulder: Westview, pp. 185–226.

Baker, R., and F. Elliston (eds) (1975), *Feminism and Sex*, Buffalo: Prometheus.

Benhabib, S. (1987), 'The Generalized and the Concrete Other: The Kohlberg-Gilligan Controversy and Moral Theory,' in E. F. Kittay, and D. T. Meyers (eds) (1987), *Women and Moral Theory*, Totowa: Rowman and Littlefield, pp. 154–77.

Bordo, S. (1987), *The Flight to Objectivity: Essays on Cartesianism and Culture*, Albany: State University of New York Press.

Code, L. (1991), *What Can She Know?: Feminist Theory and the Construction of Knowledge*, Ithaca: Cornell University Press.

Cudd, A. E. (ed.) (1995), 'Analytic Feminism: A Brief Introduction,' *Hypatia*, 10(3): 1–6.

Donovan, J. (1993), 'Everyday Use and Moments of Being: Toward a Nondominative Aesthetic,' in H. Hein and C. Korsmeyer (eds) (1993), *Aesthetics in Feminist Perspective*, Bloomington: Indiana University Press, pp. 53–67.

Donovan, J. (2000), *Feminist Theory: The Intellectual Traditions*, 3rd edn, New York: Continuum.

Flax, J. (1987), 'Postmodernism and Gender Relations,' *Signs* 12(4): 621–43.

Gilligan, C. (1982), *In a Different Voice: Psychological Theory and Women's Development*, Cambridge: Harvard University Press.

Gould, C. C., and M. W. Warshofsky (eds) (1976), *Women and Philosophy: Toward a Theory of Liberation*, New York: Putnam's.

Haraway, D. (1990), 'A Manifesto for Cyborgs: Science, Technology, and Socialist Feminism in the 1980s,' in L. J. Nicholson (ed.) (1990), *Feminism/Postmodernism*, New York: Routledge, pp. 190–233.

Harding, S. (1986), *The Science Question in Feminism*, Ithaca: Cornell University Press.

Harding, S., and M. B. Hintikka (eds) (1983), *Discovering Reality: Feminist Perspectives on Epistemology, Metaphysics, Methodologies, and Philosophy of Science*, Dordrecht: D. Reidel.

Hartsock, N. C. M. (1983), 'The Feminist Standpoint: Developing the Ground for a Specifically Feminist Historical Materialism,' in S. Harding and M. B. Hintikka (eds) (1983), *Discovering Reality*, Dordrecht: D. Reidel, pp. 283–310.

Hein, H., and C. Korsmeyer (eds) (1993), *Aesthetics in Feminist Perspective*, Bloomington: Indiana University Press.

Keller, E. F. (1982), 'Feminism and Science,' *Signs* 7(3): 589–602.

Keller, E. F. (1983), 'Gender and Science,' in S. Harding and M. B. Hintikka (eds) (1983), *Discovering Reality*, Dordrecht: D. Reidel, pp. 187–205.

Keller, E. F. (1985), *Reflections on Gender and Science*, New Haven: Yale University Press.

Lauter, E. (1993), 'Re-enfranchising Art: Feminist Interventions in the Theory of Art', in H. Hein and C. Korsmeyer (eds) (1993), *Aesthetics in Feminist Perspective*, Bloomington: Indiana University Press, pp. 21–34.

Lloyd, G. (1984), *The Man of Reason: 'Male' and 'Female' in Western Philosophy*, Minneapolis: University of Minnesota Press.

Longino, H. E. (1990), *Science as Social Knowledge: Values and Objectivity in Scientific Inquiry*, Princeton: Princeton University Press.

Lorraine, R. (1993), 'A Gynecentric Aesthetic,' in H. Hein and C. Korsmeyer (eds) (1993), *Aesthetics in Feminist Perspective*, Bloomington: Indiana University Press, pp. 35–52.

MacKinnon, C. A. (1987), *Feminism Unmodified*, Cambridge: Harvard University Press.

Merchant, C. (1980), *The Death of Nature: Women, Ecology, and the Scientific Revolution*, New York: Harper.

Moulton, J. (1983), 'The Adversary Method,' in S. Harding, and M. B. Hintikka (eds) (1983), *Discovering Reality*, Dordrecht: D. Reidel, pp. 149–64.

Nelson, L. H. (1991), *Who Knows: From Quine to a Feminist Empiricism*, Philadelphia: Temple University Press.

Noddings, N. (1984), *Caring: A Feminine Approach to Ethics and Moral Education*, Berkeley: University of California Press.

Nye, A. (1995), *Philosophy and Feminism: At the Border*, New York: Twayne.

Okin, S. M. (1989), *Justice, Gender, and the Family*, New York: Basic.

Pateman, C., and E. Gross (eds) (1987), *Feminist Challenges: Social and Political Theory*, Boston: Northeastern University Press.

Pateman, C. (1988), *The Sexual Contract*, Stanford: Stanford University Press.

Rose, H. (1983), 'Hand, Brain, and Heart: A Feminist Epistemology for the Natural Sciences,' *Signs* 9(1): 73–90.

Ruddick, S. (1989), *Maternal Thinking: Towards a Politics of Peace*, Boston: Beacon.

Smith, D. E. (1987), *The Everyday World as Problematic: A Feminist Sociology*, Boston: Northeastern University Press.

Thomson, J. J. (1971), 'A Defense of Abortion,' *Philosophy and Public Affairs* 1: 47–66.

Vetterling-Braggin, M., F. Elliston, and J. English (eds) (1977), *Feminism and Philosophy*, Totowa: Littlefield, Adams.

Waugh, J. B. (1990), 'Analytic Aesthetics and Feminist Aesthetics: Neither/Nor?,' *The Journal of Aesthetics and Art Criticism* 48 (4): 317–26.

Aesthetics

Elisabeth Schellekens

The expression 'Analytic Aesthetics,' generally used to refer to Philosophical Aesthetics as pursued in the Anglo-American academic world since the middle of the twentieth century, is best understood in terms of its emphasis on conceptual analysis. The rise of the discipline is clearly related to the widespread championing of cognitive and linguistic causes that distinguishes the broader framework of Analytic Philosophy, and should not in the first instance be thought of as unveiling a hitherto buried treasure of questions and concerns. The novelty of Analytic Aesthetics had rather to do with the approach used to tackle issues about aesthetic value and our experience of it. And whilst this revisionary line certainly did make way for a whole new set of questions about aesthetic experience, the pressure that brought about the change must principally be seen to have been a methodological one.

Perhaps the simplest way to get a grasp on Analytic Aesthetics is to examine the analyses it has made it its business to undertake. These can be seen to fall into six categories, best described in terms of the following questions: 'What is an artwork?' 'What is an aesthetic experience?' 'What are the boundaries of the aesthetic?' 'What is artistic expressiveness?' 'What is it for an artwork to represent something?' and 'Should we opt for realism or anti-realism in Aesthetics?' My aim is to provide the reader not with an overview of the history of Analytic Aesthetics, its authors, their discussions and achievements, but an impression of the progress that *can* be made on aesthetic issues by bringing this method to bear on them. For this reason, I will endeavor to put specific ideas and concerns at the forefront of my investigation, and convey them in relative isolation from particular authors and debates. Not only should this approach chime well with the spirit of the discipline, but it may also allow the reader to follow for herself some of the central arguments of Analytic Aesthetics, regardless of whether these are nowadays considered historical or not.

What is an artwork?

For an Aesthetics conceived as the Philosophy of Art, it is difficult to think of a more pertinent question to pose than 'What is a work of art?' What, in other words, is the nature of the object of our philosophical inquiry, and how can something qualify as such an object? Urged along both by the philosophy of language and the definitive eclipse, in the early twentieth century, of purely mimetic conceptions of art, the question of defining art becomes strongly intertwined with the problem of identifying instances of it. The problem of defining art thus turns into a challenge focused on locating a characteristic displayed by, and only by, artworks.

Definitions along these lines specify necessary conditions which, taken together, are supposed to be sufficient for anything to be a work of art. What could seem more natural than to search for these conditions in the aesthetic character of (certain) artworks, and to define artworks in terms of distinctively aesthetic features or experiences? Nevertheless, and especially if anti-essentialist views about language also have bite in aesthetics, it could be held that art simply cannot be defined in this fashion. One way to proceed if this is indeed the case is to explore the possibility that art should be classified in virtue of the resemblances it holds to other (primarily prior) works of art. However, the attempt to discern any properties common to all and only artworks by some 'family resemblance' method is likely to fail since there is a sense in which everything can be said to resemble everything else in some respect (Weitz 1956).

This problem gains in gravity when we consider what is now broadly called 'conceptual art': since art and nonart can be perceptually indistinguishable (for example, Warhol's *Brillo Boxes*), it must be a nonmanifest relation that makes something an artwork, rather than an observable property (Danto 1981). On this line, artworks acquire intentionality and meaning in virtue of their relations to the historical and social setting constituted by the practices and conventions of art, our artistic heritage, the intentions of artists, and so on – the 'artworld' (Dickie 1974). A refined version of this theory would have it that an artwork is an artefact which has had the status of arthood conferred upon it not by some individual agent's authority, but, instead, by the fact that it has a rightful place within this artworld.

What is emerging here, then, is an analysis of art recursive in form: something is art if it stands in an appropriate relation to previous artworks. The critical relation between a particular work and the body of established works could thus be understood in terms of how the thing is intended to be regarded – that is, regarded in the way that pre-existing works of art are or were appropriately regarded. Alternatively, the defining relation can be cashed out in terms of a shared style, or a kind of narrative (Carroll 1990). In some respects, this approach displays similarities with the one that emphasises the status-conferring role of artistic institutions. For example, it does not locate 'arthood' in an object's intrinsic properties. However, it places the explanatory burden less on contemporary institutions and more on the preceding history of art. Whilst this might avoid a circularity arising from presupposing the meaning of 'art' in the course of defining it in terms of an 'artworld,' artworks for which there seem to be no earlier examples will be highly problematic on this account. And that brings out a more general concern for this or indeed any attempt to explain how something is art by relating it appropriately to a given tradition: such definitions risk charges of incompleteness since a considerable part of the explanation they offer is upheld by an undefined notion of artistic tradition. Put simply, what kind of a definition do we have if one of the definition's necessary elements is ill- or un-defined?

One way of contrasting the approaches sketched above appeals to a distinction between so-called 'functionalist' and 'proceduralist' accounts. The former tends to trace the conditions that need to be met for something to qualify as an artwork to the fulfillment of art's main function, and this is usually understood in terms of providing aesthetic experiences (as in the case of 'aesthetic definitions'). The latter (as with institutional or historicist theories) singles out the application of appropriate procedures. Accordingly, while the main hurdles for functionalists have to do with issues about adequately delimiting the function of art and accounting for particular cases that fail to live up to the aesthetic standards artists intended for them, proceduralist approaches, being principally descriptive, run into difficulties having to do with showing that the relevant procedures are indeed established. All in all, this has led many philosophers working in Analytic Aesthetics to agree on at least two points: first, that art must to some extent be defined in terms of its historical and social context (Levinson 1979; Walton 1970); and second, that art cannot be defined in terms of a set of necessary conditions that are jointly sufficient.

Whilst aesthetic definitions, neo-Wittgensteinian attacks on them, and institutional and historicist theories have all aimed to provide an account of how a thing can qualify as a work of art, there is a neighboring area of investigation which raises very interesting issues of its own. The concern here is this: 'Exactly what *kinds* of things are artworks?' Ontology certainly is a pressing concern for *all* artworks, although it may seem particularly urgent for musical and literary works. Two distinctions seem to buttress much of the debate: first, that between *singular* (for example, Picasso's *Portrait of Dora Maar*) and *multiple* artforms (for example, Mozart's *Don Giovanni*); second, that between *autographic* and *allographic* (that is, nonforgeable) artforms. Generally, literary and musical works are thought of as structures or 'types' of which the copies of the text or score are 'tokens.' No copy of Dostoyevsky's text can be identical with *The Brothers Karamazov*, since no particular copy need survive in order for the work to survive. With music, drama and other multiple works, there are performances to consider as well as copies of the score or text. One development has been to treat musical and literary works as types of a special sort, for instance by incorporating the artist's creative process into the ontology of artworks. In this vein, it could be argued that artworks are *action types*, where the action in question is the complex sequence of steps by which the artist arrives at the manifest object we tend to identify as the artwork (Currie 2004). What attempts such as these highlight is the way in which the creative process an artist engages in when making art must be made central to what it is for a thing to be a work of art.

What is an Aesthetic Experience?

A second set of questions that Analytic Aesthetics has been preoccupied with concerns aesthetic experience: what are its content and distinguishing features? Regardless of whether a satisfactory account of aesthetic experience can provide an answer to the question of what it is for something to be an artwork, a conceptual analysis of the experience at the heart of the discipline is likely to be its most central task. Increasing our understanding of the nature and workings of aesthetic experiences can only be beneficial and clarificatory for every task Analytic Aesthetics may set itself. Yet the outlook underlying this endeavor seems to assume that there is indeed a unified account to be given of aesthetic experiences; that there is such a thing as *the* aesthetic experience. But, as we shall now see, this is actually one of the main points of contention.

A suggestion that ties in neatly with the idea that the objects which afford aesthetic experiences are artworks, as discussed in connection with aesthetic definitions of art, is that the distinguishing feature of such experience is a certain kind of attention. This may be characterised in terms of an experience sharing the unity, intensity, and complexity of the objects onto which it is directed, and its having value in virtue of this (Beardsley 1958). If we are inclined to adopt an account along these lines, however, we must be careful not to confuse an experience of unity, intensity and complexity with the unity, intensity and complexity of an experience. Just because, in more general terms, the object of our experience has a certain property, it doesn't follow that our experience itself has that property (Dickie 1965). The lesson to be learnt here advocates the importance of working with a refined concept of aesthetic experience. And what better way to improve that concept than by making room for the aspect most commonly associated with it, namely pleasure? After all, the pleasure we often gain from looking at a beautiful sculpture or reading a moving poem goes a fair way towards an explanation of our interest in the notion of aesthetic experience.

One way of incorporating pleasure into a theory of aesthetic experience might be to hold that a subject can rightly be said to have an aesthetic experience if her mental activity is united and made pleasurable by being tied to the qualities of the object of aesthetic attention (Beardsley 1969). However, this won't do for all experiences we think of as aesthetic since there seems to be no principled reason to suppose that where such pleasurable responses are indeed aroused, they must be unified. Moreover, there may be aesthetic experiences that arouse none of these pleasurable affects. Rather than taking this to indicate that we should do away with the concept of aesthetic experience as such (Dickie 1974), it might be wise to turn the procedure on its head: instead of using a certain kind of pleasure to qualify aesthetic experience, we could begin by qualifying the conditions under which pleasure can rightly be called 'aesthetic.' In this spirit, we might propound something like the idea that pleasure in an object is aesthetic when it derives from reflection on an object's individual character. To appreciate something aesthetically would then be to attend not only to an object's forms and qualities for its own sake, but also to the way in which all such things emerge from the set of perceptual features that define the object in nonaesthetic terms.

Nonetheless, not all aesthetic experiences seem to be accompanied by pleasure, and so we might not be much nearer a univocal understanding of what a distinctively aesthetic experience consists of. Putting pleasure aside for a moment, is there a unique state of mind, some sort of mental stance that we enter into when we engage in aesthetic contemplation? One avenue that might seem promising centers on the idea that when we appreciate things aesthetically, we do not look at the object for any practical function it may serve, but instead, we assess an object for its aesthetic character alone. Such an 'aesthetic attitude' is usually taken to involve an attention that is contemplative, discerning, and not aiming at anything beyond the object.

Can this attitude help us set aesthetic experiences apart? How do we know that it is not a myth, a philosophical 'phantom'? Perhaps the disinterestedness and distancing alluded to concern only the *motivation* and not the *nature* of the perception. When aesthetic attitude theories describe aesthetic experience in terms of a unique frame of mind in which we take a purely aesthetic interest in a thing or situation, it is often assumed that for each and every time we take such an interest, we look at those things or situations not only in a *unique* fashion, but also in a manner *identical* across cases of aesthetic appreciation. While it is not at all clear that this is indeed the case, a more important and potentially crippling objection arises when we ask how the aesthetic attitude can analyse the aesthetic when it cannot itself be defined independently of that very same notion? If a large part of the raison d'être of the notion is to provide a definition of the distinctively *aesthetic*, and that attitude is cashed out as an attitude focused on taking an *aesthetic* interest in an object, then the very idea of the aesthetic is presupposed by it. There is, in other words, a circularity here that seems to preclude the possibility of the aesthetic attitude helping us make any serious philosophical progress.

Perhaps another more successful strategy might be to appeal to another kind of mental ability, namely our capacity for imaginative thought. The idea is that aesthetic experience is necessarily permeated by the imagination; an object that is not imaginatively conceived in one way or another cannot be an object in which we find aesthetic pleasure. Sadness, for example, is an 'aspect' of the play, and our making the judgement that a play is sad involves imagining that that judgement is entertaining – rather than asserting – the thought that it is sad in the way that people are. Whilst this might be considered an improvement on a notion like the aesthetic attitude in that it avoids positing some rather vague psychological occurrence, it is difficult to consider it distinctive of aesthetic experience.

To the extent that much of the quest for the distinguishing feature of aesthetic experience seems to have been futile, most philosophers working in Analytic Aesthetics today look elsewhere in order to increase our understanding of aesthetic experiences. Rather than searching for a means to define or even circumscribe aesthetic experience, perhaps the most that can be said is that such experiences involve some or all of the following notions: design appreciation, detection of aesthetic properties, and attention to the ways in which the formal, aesthetic, expressive, and intentional properties of the artwork are manufactured (Carroll 2000). While certainly a good deal has been gained by placing the notion of aesthetic experience at the center of our attempts to delimit the concepts of art and the aesthetic, it seems that there remain many unanswered problems. In the lack of further engagement with these, the ambition of discovering some shared quality that runs through aesthetic experiences may fail. This, in turn, raises doubts not only about the possibility that aesthetic experience is able to define art, but also that the project to separate out a realm of the aesthetic is fundamentally misguided.

What are the Boundaries of the Aesthetic?

Uncertainty about the possibility of circumscribing a distinctively aesthetic kind of experience inevitably raises questions on a larger scale about the demarcation of the very domain of aesthetic inquiry. What exactly, one may wonder, delineates the realm of the aesthetic from the nonaesthetic? Where does the aesthetic begin and the nonaesthetic end? (Sibley 1959). With some notable exceptions the main way in which this concern has been discussed in Analytic Aesthetics is in terms of the boundaries of the aesthetic. In particular, this discussion has been pursued in relation to our natural environment and the moral sphere.

In connection with the first of these, the reintroduction of natural objects and environments as foci of aesthetic appreciation has certainly been a distinctive feature of the discipline. Several significant distinctions between the aesthetic experience of art and that of nature have been made (Hepburn 1966). Amongst them, we find the idea that since human beings are both *in* and *part of* nature, we are typically involved with it both in the capacity of actors and spectators. Unlike a painting, a landscape does not control the aesthetic agent's response; natural objects of aesthetic interest are not set apart from their environment – they are 'frameless' – and in that sense may seem to demand a greater creativity on the part of the perceiver.

The question of whether distinctions along these lines should be taken as descriptive or prescriptive, in addition to queries about which kind of aesthetic appreciation is not only logically prior but also philosophically more weighty, admits of no simple answers. On the one hand, we might hold that the experience of nature should be understood in terms of our experience of art; that we only begin to consider nature as an object of aesthetic appreciation once we have learnt how to observe, appreciate, and enjoy works of art. On the other hand, we might defend the view that the appreciator of natural beauty is an active participant in the sense that she is perceptually immersed in the natural world, and that this 'aesthetics of engagement' should be the model for our aesthetic appreciation of art (Berleant 1993).

The resolution of this impasse might have to wait until another issue of contention has been satisfactorily accounted for: exactly *how* should nature be appreciated aesthetically? Either such appreciation consists of appreciating the purely formal qualities of uninterpreted items, which might be precarious: if the natural environment is not 'framed' or delimited in some principled way, our natural environment may not even possess formal qualities because such qualities are largely determined in relation to their frames (environmental formalism). Alternatively, natural environments might best be appreciated through other properties, such as expressive ones (for example, harmony; serenity). On this view, knowledge of nature is required if we are to have meaningful and harmonious experiences, since it provides a setting in which to perceive the salient features of that environment (natural environment model, Carlson 1979). So, just like knowledge of the artist's intention and the history of art provides the background against which aesthetic appreciation and understanding in art is possible, knowledge of ecological systems and relations within particular environments may be necessary or at least beneficial for our aesthetic appreciation of nature. Nonetheless, if natural objects of aesthetic interest are indeed devoid of 'frames,' and the properties we need to engage with are not multiple in kind, it might turn out to be the case that the search for one model of the aesthetic appreciation of nature is a chimerical quest. In any case, it is likely that more will have to be said about exactly what the object of appreciation consists of in nature before anything decisive about the aesthetic appreciation of nature can be established.

The issues surrounding the question of the relation between Aesthetics and the moral sphere are, if anything, more numerous still. How, if at all, do moral commitments influence aesthetic experiences? Is beauty, as Kant held, the symbol of morality? Where does the field of aesthetic inquiry end and that of the moral begin? Focusing on the first of these questions, it soon becomes apparent that a manifold of subtle alternatives present themselves. Perhaps a work's moral character can be said to affect its aesthetic value only if it spoils or promotes a work's aesthetically valuable features (sophisticated aestheticism, Lamarque 1995). Then again, it could be held that a moral defect *may* count as an aesthetic one and a moral virtue *may* constitute an aesthetic one where the emotional responses a work sets out to achieve are withheld or forthcoming *because* of the work's moral character (moderate moralism). On this view, good art need not have moral or cognitive value, and even where a work does have a morally deficient character, this is not always relevant to its value as art (it is appropriate only if it blocks our capacity to be absorbed in the work or react to it). It is not clear, however, whether this view could accommodate the fact that there are works that fail in their aim yet seem aesthetically better as a result (for example, propaganda might fail in a way that renders it aesthetically more valuable). But rather than appealing to whether a work is absorbing and the fact that one *can* react as one is urged to, one could focus on whether one *ought* to react in that way. If so, a third option might take root, which holds that a moral flaw is also an aesthetic one (ethicism). On this approach part of the role of art is to have cognitive value, and where a work prescribes cognitive-affective responses, which are thus tied to the work's value as art, the moral character of a work is always relevant to its value as art.

What is Artistic Expressiveness?

Our fourth set of questions centers around the role of the emotions. Investigations fall roughly into two categories: the first focuses on defining or theorizing about art in terms of its expressive role; the second has the more modest aim of furthering our understanding of the expressive elements of the aesthetic appreciation of art (especially music and fiction). Whilst it seems relatively uncontroversial to assume that emotions figure prominently in our aesthetic experiences, it is less obvious exactly what part they can, or should play in them.

Even if one starts off with the assumption that the principal value of art lies in its ability to express emotion, the question arises of how one should conceive not only the nature of such expression, but also its workings. At first glance, it may seem tempting to assume that any emotion expressed in or by an artwork is that of the artist. But there are many drawbacks to the view that the function of art is simply the 'transmission' of emotions from artist to audience. Most significantly perhaps, it seems to cash out the value of art in purely functional terms, and insofar as something other than art can also transmit the feelings of the maker, art can simply be replaced for something that can fulfill that function equally well. To remedy this weakness, one might be inclined to emphasise the role of the imagination and imaginative experience in artistic expression (Collingwood 1938). One might hold that the making of art is a way for the artist to articulate the exact nature of her emotion. However, if the imaginative treatment of emotion is the main characteristic of art, and the emotion must be that of the artist, there is not only a question about cases where the emotion expressed is not felt by the artist when making the work, but also one about the extent to which this approach can actually remain fundamentally expressivist: if the role of the artist is really that of exploring her own emotions imaginatively, it seems that one of the most central claims of expressivist accounts, namely that the artist's main task is to express her own emotion, falls by the wayside.

What about artistic expression's relation to the artist's state of mind – is it independent or not? Musical and fictional works yet again seem particularly intriguing in this context: how does appreciation of such works give rise to emotional responses, and if so, what exactly is their intentional object? Even if there are good reasons to doubt that artistic expressiveness in general should focus on the imaginative explora- tion of the *artist's* experienced emotion, it might still be possible to explore any of the following views. Perhaps musical expressiveness consists of music's having a sound somehow resembling the behavioral manifestation of an emotion (Kivy 1989)? Alternatively, musical expressiveness might be about metaphorically exemplifying some emotion. Or again, might it consist in the soothing power of the emotions and the way in which an imaginative engagement with music enable the audience to experience emotional responses in a peculiarly satisfying way; or in music's disposition to evoke parallel or related emotions in audiences?

The second case for which artistic expressiveness may seem particularly perplexing is fiction. And perhaps the most puzzling concern of all is the way in which we are to explain our emotional responses to fictional characters or events. The challenge presented by this question – generally referred to as the 'paradox of fiction' – is based on three propositions which simultaneously seem both intuitively correct *and* mutually exclusive: (1) we regularly experience emotions towards characters and situations we know to be purely fictional; (2) having emotions for characters or situations logically presupposes beliefs in the existence of the characters and situations in question; and (3) when we know that a character or situation is fictional we don't believe that they really exist. Attempts to resolve this paradox set out to deny at least one of these three propositions. Denial of (1) tends to be based on one of two views: either that emotional responses to fictions are not instances of emotions as such, but rather of less complex states such as moods; or that emotional responses to fictions cannot, despite appearances, be instances of ordinary emotions, but of 'make-believe' emotions. This suggestion is founded on the theory that crucial to the proper characterization of feelings of this sort is recognition that they occur in the context of games of make-believe that readers of works of fiction play in engaging with those works, using them as props (Walton 1990). On the other hand, we may want to deny (2) on the grounds that the belief conditions for emotional responses should be relaxed. Finally, denying (3), implausible as it may seem, could be made to rest on something like the idea that while caught up in fictions, readers become irrational, responding emotionally to objects that they know do not exist.

One of the most interesting issues raised by attempts to make sense of our emotional responses to fiction concerns the extent to which ordinary beliefs really are necessary for experiences of emotion. In many cases, a particularly vivid imagining seems capable of serving as a substitute (Carroll 1990). Yet if this suggestion is to stick, it will need to provide a satisfactory account of, amongst other things, the distinction between beliefs and imaginings in relation to emotional states. Other issues that stand in need of further development include the kind of mental states accounts of artistic expressiveness take emotions to be; the extent to which there is continuity between artistic and nonartistic expression; and the kind of role emotions can play in our aesthetic education.

What is it for an Artwork to Represent Something?

The relation between a pictorial representation and the thing represented has proved a very hard philosophical nut to crack. For most of the twentieth century, the exploration of this theme has focused on the nature (rather than, say, value) of that relation. While some theories have aimed to pinpoint something unique to pictorial representation, others have emphasized the special kind of duality that our experiences of paintings seem to require. Underlying much of the debate is a point of contention about whether pictorial perception and representation should be understood as continuous with ordinary perception and representation or not.

How do pictures represent? At first sight, the most credible answer to this question might appeal to the notion of resemblance. This would certainly be the basis for an argument from common sense: the shoes in Van Gogh's painting do, or so it seems, simply look like shoes. Of course, the idea of resemblance need not refer exclusively to imitation or copying – in fact, it seems unlikely that painters somehow simply duplicate the appearance of the things they depict (Gombrich 1960). Artists, even those engaged in naturalistic painting, have to learn rules and technical devices and bring their own interpretations to bear on what they depict. But in moving away from the common-sense notion of resemblance, we might wonder why it is necessary to retain the notion at all: it is perfectly possible to combine the idea that knowledge of the history of art and art-making plays an important role in pictorial perception and representation with the claim that representation has little or nothing to do with resemblance. And this option might seem particularly appealing in light of the view that representation cannot amount to resemblance alone since everything resembles everything else in some ways, and resemblance is a reflexive and symmetric relation (that is, I resemble but do not represent myself), while representation is neither.

We might, then, argue that pictorial representation, rather like language, is a system of denotation conventionally established, and that the relation of a painting to the object it represents is mediated by a conventional symbolic system for reference and predication (Goodman 1976). But can accounts whereby there is no significant contrast between depiction and linguistic representation deal with the way, for example, in which the symbolic elements of linguistic systems must be learned one by one? What is special about pictures, as opposed to words, is perhaps what we need to know in order to interpret them: whereas for language, we must know the specific conventions governing the individual word's use, understanding pictures requires a different sort of knowledge which, at least partly, will rely on our ability to recognize the object depicted. On this approach, pictorial representation may be conceived in terms of recognitional capacities, and appeal to facts about ordinary visual processing for support. A representation is, then, pictorial in virtue of making use of the visual recognitional capacities that we already possess for objects familiar to us. Alternatively, we could account for the idea that pictorial representation is to be understood in terms of informational content by emphasising the way in which picture and object furnish similar visual information. This might turn into an aspect-recognition theory of depiction according to which successful pictures embody aspectual information, and this is sufficient to trigger recognition of their objects in suitable perceivers. Recognition of an object in a picture is crucial for representation, but resemblance between the visual experience of a picture and its object depends on such recognition rather than the reverse.

Another slant to pictorial representation focuses on the perceptual experiences we have of such representations. One way of exploring representation from this angle is, as mentioned above, by examining the way in which representational paintings seem to involve a dual awareness, namely an awareness of the represented object on the one hand, and that of the surface of the painting on the other (Wollheim 1980). This 'twofoldness' seems central to our experience of pictorial representation. After all, when we look at a painting, we can simultaneously see *both* the physical object and the scene depicted. This, we may hold, is the key to understanding pictorial representation or depiction: in pictorial experience our awareness of the picture's surface involves the thought of something else, and that thing is just what the picture depicts, that is to say, we 'see in' the picture what is depicted.

While most philosophers working in Analytic Aesthetics have acknowledged the importance of this 'twofoldness,' many see it as the building block upon which a more complete story of the experience of pictorial representation must be built. In accordance with the theory of 'make-believe' appealed to in the context of the paradox of fiction, it might be held that pictures are props in visual games of make-believe, where make-believe is conceived of as an activity of guided imagining (Walton 1990). Confronted with a picture, we may then be prompted to imagine that we are seeing a particular thing or situation by the configuration of marks that constitutes the picture, and we imagine of our seeing those marks that it is a seeing of the object the picture depicts. In other words, a painting depicts an object if it urges us to imagine that our experience of looking at it is a visual experience of the object. Clearly, an account of pictorial representation and the experience of it hinges on whether we do indeed use our imaginative skills in this way, and whether or not the imagining in question involves visualizing.

Realism or Anti-realism in Aesthetics?

The last set of concerns that we will discuss can be grouped together under the umbrella of realism and anti-realism. Despite the fact that the terms are generally used to refer to the metaphysical status of properties, in this context we will also take them to embrace issues relevant to the possibility of objectivity for aesthetic judgements and the correctness or incorrectness of artistic interpretations. To a certain extent, the relatively recent development of viable realist accounts of aesthetic properties and the prospect of plausible theories of correctness for artistic and aesthetic judgements can be seen as indicative of the way in which matters of aesthetics have been taken more seriously as a result of being subjected to the analytic method.

Notwithstanding widespread agreement about the distinctively perceptual character of aesthetic properties, and the likelihood that our experiences of the aesthetic properties of artworks depend on the artistic categories under which they may fall (Walton 1970), there is equally widespread disagreement about the exact nature of that perceptual character. In fact, philosophers haven't even seen eye to eye about what might seem a relatively uncontroversial claim, namely that aesthetic properties need to be experienced first-hand rather than be inferred, an observation from which it follows that the ascription of such properties is at least not invariably rule-governed. On the one hand, we might think that the application of aesthetic concepts is not, or only negatively, governed by sets of nonaesthetic conditions – that is to say, the fact that an aesthetic predicate is true of some object cannot be inferred from any description of the object in nonaesthetic terms. On the other hand, we might hold that some aesthetic concepts *are* condition-governed, and that there is a sense in which we can infer the presence or absence of aesthetic properties in objects from the presence of certain nonaesthetic qualities. Views about the ontology of aesthetic properties cover a wider spectrum of alternatives still, ranging from strong realism to anti-realism via more or less realist theories eager to take the response-dependent character of such properties into account (Levinson 1994). Echoing the debates about the nature of aesthetic experience and the boundaries of the aesthetic, attempts have been made to search for the *one* distinguishing feature of aesthetic properties. That the majority of aesthetic properties have something to do with value, or aesthetic value more precisely, seem undeniable. But how that relation is to be understood is another matter. What cannot be denied is that the class of properties generally grouped together and labeled 'aesthetic' is particularly heterogeneous and diverse.

Analytic Aesthetics' treatment of the role to be played by the artist's intention in the process of interpreting artworks has also been put through stormy weather. Is it simply a fallacy to take the artist's intention into account; or can the intention behind the artwork have something decisive to say about how the artwork is to be understood? Can, in other words, any evidence not presented by the work itself be relevant to the work's meaning? In this mire of questions drawing both on notions of intention and interpretation, it is important to see clearly that the question of whether an artist's intention can be relevant to artistic interpretation is distinct from whether that intention should be allowed to settle which interpretation of the artwork under scrutiny is the best or correct one. Even if there are some exceptions to the rule of thumb that the artist's intention tends to increase our understanding and thus appreciation of artworks, there are still questions to be resolved about whether it is always the case that knowledge of the artist's intention has the 'last word' on which interpretation is the most appropriate or not. If we are inclined to hold that the artist's intention shouldn't simply be eliminated from the interpretative process as a matter of principle, two alternatives present themselves. Either we can argue that the artist's intention is always relevant and always has the final say on which interpretation is correct (actual intentionalisms, Carroll 2000). Or we can defend the view that whilst the artist's intention will more often than not be helpful, what an interpreter should do is to gather all the available information that might be relevant, and construct the best possible interpretation of the artwork out of it. The best possible hypothesis will then always be the correct interpretation of an artwork (Levinson 1996).

Analytic Aesthetics has come a long way from the emotivism, which dominated Anglo-American philosophy at the time of its inception. The relation between aesthetic judgements and emotional responses is no longer conceived in terms of the expression of mental states such as 'Hurrah!' Rather it is seen as a multifaceted and highly complex connection between two distinct kinds of mental event that allow for interactions at different levels. In the process of shedding light on issues such as this relation, it has become apparent that delving deeper into the various elements of our aesthetic psychology and the ways in which they influence each other by no means places the aesthetic further beyond the reach of systematic philosophy. On the contrary; the more philosophers examine the nature and workings of these notions, the more plausible it becomes – as we have seen in relation to aesthetic properties and artistic interpretations – that some kind of objectivity is not beyond its reach. That aesthetic objectivity won't show all the hallmarks of nonaxiological objectivity is almost certainly true, but this is no longer seen as a reason to turn our backs on the possibility of a standard of correctness appropriate for the domain with which it is concerned. The response-dependent character of aesthetic properties, or the disagreements that undeniably do occur about aesthetic value, do not flag the limited applicability of systematic methods of analysis. The result of applying what might be seen as a more 'scientific' method to aesthetic issues has thus been not to diminish but rather to enhance the philosophical credibility of aesthetic concepts and categories.

References

Beardsley, M. (1958), *Aesthetics: Problems in the Philosophy of Criticism*, New York: Harcourt Brace.

Beardsley, M. (1969), 'Aesthetic Experience Regained,' *Journal of Aesthetics and Art Criticism*, 28(1) (Fall): 3–11.

Berleant, A. (1993), *Art and Engagement*, Philadelphia: Temple University Press.

Carlson, A. (1979), 'Appreciation and the Natural Environment,' *Journal of Aesthetics and Art Criticism*, 37: 267–75.

Carroll, N. (1990), *Philosophy of Horror or Paradoxes of the Heart*. London: Routledge.

Carroll, N. (2000), 'Interpretation and Intention: The Debate between Hypothetical and Actual Intentionalism,' *Metaphilosophy*. Special issue on the Philosophy of Interpretation, 31: 75–95.

Collingwood, R. G. (1938), *The Principles of Art*, Oxford: Oxford University Press.

Currie, G. (2004), 'Art Works as Action Types,' in P. Lamarque, and S. H. Olsen (eds) (2004), *Aesthetics and the Philosophy of Art: The Analytical Tradition*, Oxford: Blackwell, pp. 103–22.

Danto, A. C. (1981), *The Transfiguration of the Commonplace*, Cambridge: Harvard University Press.

Dickie, G. (1965), 'Beardsley's Phantom Aesthetic Experience,' *Journal of Philosophy* 62: 129–36.

Dickie, G. (1974), *Art and the Aesthetic: An Institutional Analysis*, Ithaca: Cornell University Press.

Gombrich, E. (1960), *Art and Illusion: A Study in the Psychology of Pictorial Representation*, New York: Pantheon.

Goodman, N. (1976), *Languages of Art*, Indianapolis: Hackett Press.

Hepburn, R. (1966), 'Contemporary Aesthetics and the Neglect of Natural Beauty,' in B. Williams, and A. Montefiore (eds), *British Analytical Philosophy*, London: Routledge, pp. 285–310.

Kivy, P. (1989), *Sound Sentiment*, Philadelphia: Temple University Press.

Lamarque, P. (1995), 'Tragedy and Moral Value,' *Australasian Journal of Philosophy* 73(2)(June): 239–49.

Levinson, J. (1979), 'Defining Art Historically,' *British Journal of Aesthetics*, 19: 232–50.

Levinson, J. (1994), 'Being Realistic about Aesthetic Properties,' *Journal of Aesthetics and Art Criticism*, 52: 351–54.

Levinson, J. (1996), 'Intention and Interpretation in Literature,' in J. Levinson (1996), *The Pleasures of Aesthetics*, Ithaca: Cornell University Press, pp. 175–213.

Sibley, F. (1959), 'Aesthetic Concepts,' *Philosophical Review* 68: 421–68.

Walton, K. (1970), 'Categories of Art,' *Philosophical Review* 79: 334–67.

Walton, K. (1990), *Mimesis as Make-Believe: On the Foundation of the Representational Arts*, Cambridge: Harvard University Press.

Weitz, M. (1956), 'The Role of Theory in Aesthetics,' *Journal of Aesthetics and Art Criticism* 15: 27–35.

Wollheim, R. (1980), *Art and Its Objects*, Cambridge: Cambridge University Press.

Continental Themes in Analytic Philosophy

Taylor Carman

Introduction

For many decades academic philosophy – not only in Europe and English-speaking countries, but throughout much of the world – has regarded itself as divided between two distinct, at times competing, traditions: 'Continental' and 'analytic.' That distinction, however, is problematic in many ways.

To begin with, whereas the term 'analytic' is meant to describe a style or method of inquiry, 'Continental' refers to a large, rather vaguely defined landmass in Europe; contrasting the two seems to involve a category mistake. Of course, neither term can be taken literally: there is no single 'analytical' method in philosophy, just as 'Continental' philosophers can now be found in such places as Britain, Ireland, Australia, New Zealand, and America. 'Continental' has thus come to mean something more than simply the de facto locale of late modern German and French philosophy, yet its metonymic significance remains obscure. What unites so-called Continental philosophers is evidently little more than a cluster of stylistic affinities and a roughly shared sense of relevant intellectual history. Similarly, although analytic philosophy originated in two self-conscious philosophical programs – the logical analysis pioneered by Frege and advanced by Russell and Moore around the turn of the century, and the logical positivism of the Vienna Circle in the 1920s – contemporary work in that tradition is no more systematically unified or coherent than its Continental counterpart. Each is instead a loose bundle centering around a few paradigmatic texts and thinkers, held together by more or less overlapping styles and histories.

One might suppose that the distinction between Continental and analytic extends back into the nineteenth century, but in fact it is much more recent. Analytic philosophy was not actually *called* 'analytic philosophy' until 1936, when Ernst Nagel used the term to describe developments then emerging for the most part (ironically) on the European Continent (Nagel 1936). The label then became widespread only in the 1950s, after the death of Wittgenstein, when it came to refer to traditions thriving primarily in Great Britain and the United States. The real split arguably occurred in the 1920s, however, when Heidegger and Carnap departed, in opposite directions, from the considerably less polarized philosophical climate of the early decades of the century (Friedman 2000). Although the categories 'Continental' and 'analytic' continued to function as a kind of ideological means of professional self-identification, especially in the 1960s and 1970s, actual practice in many areas, and in many countries, has by now dissolved and surpassed the distinction in favor of a more open and pluralistic approach to the subject. The terms still have currency, owing largely to their administrative entrenchment in the organization of academic departments, yet they have arguably outlived their intellectual usefulness. If philosophers continue to draw the distinction, it is because, as Richard Rorty put it some twenty-five years ago, 'The institutional tail is wagging the scientific dog' (Rorty 1982: 217).

It has sometimes been said that analytic philosophers study problems, while Continental philosophers study other philosophers. The distinction is a caricature, but like all good caricatures, it contains a drop of truth. The truth is that, in self-consciously modeling itself on the empirical and deductive sciences, as opposed to more traditional humanistic disciplines, analytic philosophy has tended to neglect both its own history and those thinkers of the nineteenth and twentieth centuries whose work seemed less amenable to formal and systematic treatment, and who have thus subsequently come to be regarded in retrospect as 'Continental' philosophers. European philosophy since Hegel, by contrast, has often moved away from the direct systematic treatment of traditional metaphysical and epistemological problems in favor of phenomenological, hermeneutical, sociopolitical, and methodological issues, together with interpretations and criticisms of past figures in historical context.

To speak of 'Continental themes in analytic philosophy,' then, is to broach two distinct but related issues. First, the title refers to the ways in which twentieth-century Anglo-American philosophy frequently ran parallel to, encountered, opposed, and in some cases appropriated French and German developments of the same period. In what follows I shall concentrate on two such points of contact: the problem of intentionality, and questions pertaining to the historical conditions of knowledge and understanding. The title also alludes to the rediscovery and belated appreciation among English-speaking philosophers of figures once routinely dismissed and excluded from the analytic tradition, whether for substantive or merely stylistic reasons. Obviously, there is no room here to discuss every relevant case. Nevertheless, it is worth noting that in different ways and for different reasons, prominent anglophone philosophers have in recent years shown renewed interest in such traditionally neglected, at times despised, figures as Hegel, Kierkegaard, Nietzsche, Heidegger, Merleau-Ponty, and Foucault.

Problems of Intentionality

During the past fifty years English-speaking philosophers have devoted an enormous amount of attention to *intentionality*, a topic first discussed explicitly by Franz Brentano (1973). Intentionality became the defining theme of phenomenology in the first half of the twentieth century, most prominently in Husserl, Heidegger, Sartre, and Merleau-Ponty. Only by the middle of the century, after the phenomenologists had written their major works, did it become a subject of debate in analytic philosophy of mind and language, as it remains today.

Brentano is often credited with retrieving the word 'intentionality' from medieval philosophy and introducing it into modern discourse with its present meaning, but in fact, as Victor Caston (2003) observes, the term was used to describe psychological attitudes long before the scholastics. As early as the third century BCE, Chrysippus used the Greek word *enteinein* to refer to the extension of the visual cone from the eye to the thing seen, and Saint Augustine reiterated the Stoic theory of vision in Book 11 of *De Trinitate*, where *intentio* means something like thought or attention focused on or aimed at something. This should come as no surprise since, like *tendere*, the verb *intendere* can mean to aim at as well as to extend or stretch. Hence, as Elizabeth Anscombe says, aiming one's mind at (*intendere animum in*) is like aiming one's bow at (*intendere arcum in*) (Anscombe 1981: 4). In Plato's *Theaetetus*, Socrates says that in false judgement, 'like a bad archer, one shoots wide off the mark and misses' (Plato 1973: 194a). There is a powerful analogy, then, between *experiencing* – for example, remembering, perceiving, imagining, or expecting – and literally *aiming* at something, and evidently the analogy seemed no less compelling to ancient and medieval philosophers than it does to us.

The problem of intentionality is twofold. On the one hand, as Brentano observed, an intentional attitude appears to be a relation to something, or as he says, 'direction toward an object' (Brentano 1973: 88). And yet the object need not exist for my attitude to be intentional. But how can a relation obtain in the absence of one of the relata? The first problem therefore has to do with how we can make sense of intentionality at all. What is it, and what is its significance for psychological attitudes such as perception, memory, expectation, and judgement? These are the sorts of problems that inspired the phenomenologists. However, since the sheer fact of intentionality seemed to them to discredit the crude representationalist model of the mind originally associated with Descartes and Locke, they tended to be much less moved by a distinct but related problem, a problem rooted in the early modern rationalist and empiricist traditions and still very much alive in contemporary analytic philosophy. This second problem is not merely conceptual or descriptive, but metaphysical, namely, is intentionality a property of matter? Is the mind a physical or nonphysical thing?

Analytic philosophers have approached these two problems in a variety of ways. Like Husserl and Frege, they have frequently appealed to a conception of meaning or 'sense' (*Sinn*) to distinguish the internal *content* of an intentional state from its external *object* or referent. Such content is what Husserl called the '*noema*' of an attitude, which he defined as a 'generalization of the idea of [linguistic] meaning (*Bedeutung*) to all act-domains' (Husserl 1952: 89, quoted in Føllesdal 1982). This distinction between content and object, or sense and reference, sheds light on the possibility of attitudes about nonexistent objects and failures to recognize identity in the various appearances or modes of presentation of one and the same thing. So, for example, Macbeth can hallucinate a dagger not because the true object of his awareness is a dagger-like idea or representation in his mind, but because his visual experience has no object at all, though its content is '*as if of*' a dagger. Similarly, to use Frege's (1984) example, I can refer to the Morning Star and the Evening Star under those two descriptions without realizing that the objects of my experience are really one and the same thing, namely the planet Venus.

But while it is indeed often possible to distinguish between something like sense and reference in this way, the robust notion of conceptual content common to Frege and Husserl became one of the main targets of criticism for the existential phenomenologists, Heidegger, Sartre, and Merleau-Ponty. Like Fregean senses, Husserlian *noemata* are not concrete or 'real' objects, but 'ideal' intensional (with an *s*) or semantic entities. They are thus strictly speaking not part of the concrete world we inhabit and encounter, but radically distinct from the objects they describe. In *Being and Time*, Heidegger set out to reconceive intentionality as worldly through and through, thus avoiding obscure appeals to extramundane entities such as forms, ideas, representations, concepts, and propositions. Intentional content, he insisted, is inextricably interwoven with our practices, and with the natural and social environments in which we conduct them. Being human is not contingently but essentially *being-in-the-world*. Experience and understanding therefore cannot be carved off, even conceptually, from the external conditions of practical life. Sartre and Merleau-Ponty willingly embraced Heidegger's externalism, without always realizing how far it took them from Husserl, who remained committed to a more traditional Cartesian distinction between mind and world.

Analytic philosophers have been notoriously slow to appreciate Heidegger. In recent decades, however, partly in light of emerging parallels with Dewey and the later Wittgenstein, Heidegger's critique of the lingering traces of Cartesianism in Husserlian phenomenology has enjoyed a much more sympathetic reception. Hubert Dreyfus (1991, 1992), John Haugeland (1992), and Robert Brandom (2002), for example, credit Heidegger with being the first philosopher to recognize that intentionality is grounded not just in thought and consciousness, but in the noncognitive moods, skills, and practices of situated agents. Although no consensus has emerged about the precise implications of Heidegger's existential phenomenology for the philosophy of mind, his way of grounding intentionality in practical life is now acknowledged as a crucial challenge to traditional assumptions concerning the autonomy and self-sufficiency of the mind and subjectivity vis-à-vis the objective world.

Heidegger's account of being-in-the-world is a direct challenge to all sharp conceptual distinctions between mental and physical phenomena. Intentionality, for Heidegger, is not, as Brentano put it, the 'mark of the mental,' but, more primitively, the goal-directedness of practical activity. Thought and consciousness can aim at objects, that is, only because actions can aim at ends. And just as the aboutness of mental states presupposes the purposiveness of behavior, so too intellectual reasoning presupposes ordinary everyday 'know-how,' that is, practical skill or competence, for example knowing how to walk, talk, and eat. Philosophers since Plato have forgotten that reasoning according to general rules or principles rests on a foundation of noncognitive intelligence, and have as a result taken for granted a distorted conception of the mind itself and its relation to the world. The most recent popular manifestation of this sort of confusion is the notion that artificial intelligence could be generated simply by programming machines to manipulate abstract representations according to fully explicit computational algorithms. Dreyfus dealt that research program a fatal blow in his book, *What Computers Still Can't Do* (1992), not by proving that artificial intelligence is impossible in principle, but by showing in concrete detail the overwhelming empirical implausibility of the idea that genuine intelligence is possible in the absence of noncognitive bodily and perceptual skills that have evolved biologically over the course of millions of years.

Dreyfus's arguments against artificial intellgience owe at least as much to Merleau-Ponty as to Heidegger, and there is now growing interest among Anglo-American philosophers in Merleau-Ponty's account in *Phenomenology of Perception* (1962) of the constitutive role of the body and bodily skills in sensory awareness. Specifically, his account of bodily attunement to a perceptual environment, or what he calls '*motor intentionality*,' has found echoes in the work of Gareth Evans (1982) and Christopher Peacocke (1989, 1992), who argue that, in addition to the conceptual content of thought, perceptual experience exhibits a kind of content that is intentionally directed to the world, but *nonconceptual*.

Merleau-Ponty describes perception not as a contingent relation between internal mental states and the external stimuli, but as the body's skillful 'grip' (*prise*) on its physical and social environment. Most philosophers today reject the empiricist notion of brute sensations, or 'sense data,' as symptomatic of a more general failure to appreciate the intentionality of perception. Less widely conceded is the distinction Merleau-Ponty insists on, following Husserl and the Gestalt psychologists, between perception and cognition. The dominant assumption today is that all intentionality is a kind of thinking. What seems mysterious to many is precisely what seemed mysterious to Kant, namely, that two things as heterogeneous as sensation and judgement somehow manage to combine to yield experience of an objective world. Merleau-Ponty avoids that dilemma by denying that sensation and judgement are the only notions available for an account of our awareness of the world. On his view, empiricism and 'intellectualism,' or what is nowadays called *cognitivism*, both offer radically impoverished accounts of intentionality.

In the sixty years since the publication of *Phenomenology of Perception*, intellectualism has made a comeback, both in the cognitive revolution in linguistics and psychology, and in the various forms of linguistic rationalism inspired by Wilfrid Sellars's critique of the 'Myth of the Given' (1963). According to Sellars, our understanding of the contents of our own thoughts and experiences is as linguistically constructed, hence theory-laden, as our understanding of the composition and behavior of physical objects. The mind is not incorrigibly present to itself; rather, we posit 'inner episodes' in psychology just as we posit unobservable particles and forces in physics. For Sellars, '*impressions* are theoretical entities' (Sellars 1963: 192). Moreover, our positing of impressions is inextricably bound up in theory with ascriptions of propositional attitudes, so that 'seeing is a *cognitive* episode which involves the framework of thoughts' (Sellars 1963: 191). Perception is no mere brute confrontation with sensory particulars, but is conceptually and linguistically constituted.

Like Merleau-Ponty, by contrast, Evans and Peacocke maintain that perceptual experience has nonconceptual intentional content. Drawing on Charles Taylor – who was in turn drawing on Merleau-Ponty – Evans first called the attention of analytic philosophers to the nonconceptual sensory content underlying and informing our judgements about the world, for example the content of the information states that allow animals to sense their own bodily position and orientation (Evans 1982: 227, 156; see Taylor 1995). Replying to John McDowell's (1994: 46–65) influential critique of Evans, Peacocke has defended the notion of nonconceptual content on the grounds that concepts are either too crude or too refined to capture the qualities presented to us in perception. For whereas a concept like *red* is too coarse-grained to specify precisely what I see when I see something red, a demonstrative concept such as *this shade of red* imports a notion of *shade* that need not play any role in my sensory experience as such (Peacocke 1989). The inadequacy of concepts in capturing perceived qualities is made even clearer by Sartre's observation, reiterated by Merleau-Ponty, that when Matisse paints a red carpet, he manages to evoke the color not merely as an abstract property, but as a concrete feature of a genuinely tactile object: what he paints is not just red, but 'a woolly red' (Sartre 2004: 190; Merleau-Ponty 1962: 4–5).

Quite apart from the problem of how to understand intentionality, analytic philosophers have also worried, in a way the phenomenologists did not, about whether and how intentional content might be reduced to or identified with physical or functional states of the brain. Such debates are essentially a reiteration of the mind-body problem, but the challenges intentionality is thought to pose to physicalism differ somewhat from those posed by nonintentional phenomena, such as the qualitative character of conscious experience.

In the 1950s Roderick Chisholm revived Brentano's concept of intentionality as the mark of the mental, insisting that intentional idioms, that is, expressions containing verb phrases either directly or obliquely describing psychological attitudes, cannot be reduced to nonintentional language (Chisholm 1957: 11). Quine replied that intentional idioms are indeed irreducible, but inferred from this that intentionality is not strictly speaking part of 'the true and ultimate structure of reality' (Quine 1960: 221). Quine conceded that such idioms are 'practically indispensable,' but his proposal eventually inspired a more radical argument to the effect that intentional notions not only *can* but *should* be eliminated from our language and conceptual scheme. Thus Paul Churchland has argued that ordinary talk about propositional attitudes, or what he calls 'folk psychology,' is no better than alchemy, given 'the explanatory impotence, stagnant history, and systematic isolation of the intentional idioms' from the rest of science (Churchland 1989: 14).

Daniel Dennett (1987) has elaborated this broadly behaviorist line of argument in a view somewhere midway between those of Quine and Churchland. According to Dennett, intentionality is as 'real,' but *only* as real, as any 'pattern' posited by a theory – in this case, psychological theories that rely on intentional idioms in order to explain and predict behavior (Dennett 1998). We ascribe beliefs and desires to organisms, or even nonorganic 'systems,' from a theoretical perspective he calls the 'intentional stance.' For Dennett, then, as for Quine and Churchland, intentionality is not strictly speaking part of the physical structure of reality, but a theoretical construct. Indeed, like Churchland, Dennett believes that intentionality is *real* only to the extent that the intentional language of psychological theory is *useful*, and that it could in principle be eliminated in favor of explanations of behavior referring exclusively to functional features of designed systems, or indeed to underlying physical processes.

John Searle (1992) deplores this skepticism that has emerged from the behaviorist tradition, and his own theory of intentionality instead describes and analyzes the causal and logical relations between our attitudes and the world in a way that has more in common with the phenomenologists. Like Husserl, Searle distinguishes the representational content of an intentional state from the 'psychological mode' or attitude in which it is nested (Searle 1983: 6) and insists that our own conscious experience assures us of the existence of such states and their contents beyond any putative reduction or elimination (Searle 1997: 99). Searle is not a phenomenologist. Unlike his behaviorist and eliminativist opponents, however, he takes the phenomena seriously.

It should come as no surprise that the concept of intentionality has migrated from Continental to analytic philosophy along such a circuitous route. Has progress been made along the way? If so, it lies not in the fact that any one theory of intentionality has prevailed over others, but that almost everyone now at least acknowledges that there *is* such a thing, that the mind is not merely a vessel or container filled with image-like ideas or linguistic representations, whose relation to the world remains enigmatic, but rather an embodied set of capacities directing us toward and orienting us in the external world itself.

Historical Conditions of Understanding

Philosophy has also arguably made some progress, thanks in part to the influence of European thinkers on Anglo-American thought, in its recognition that reason and inquiry are not just contingently but essentially embedded in history and social practice. The recent emphasis on practice in anglophone philosophy is due largely to the later Wittgenstein (1953) and the revival of pragmatism. By contrast, virtually all the major Continental philosophers of the nineteenth and twentieth centuries, and their followers, have taken it for granted that human understanding is not just conditioned, but *constituted* socially and historically. In the view of most post-Hegelian European thinkers, that is, reason and inquiry do not just happen to have a past, but are what they are in virtue of the ways in which they grow out of their histories, which they then recover and appropriate in the form of a tradition. Concepts, as Ian Hacking has said, do not just have histories, they have 'memories' (Hacking 2002: 37).

Analytic philosophy took its first and most important historical turn in the wake of Thomas Kuhn's book, *The Structure of Scientific Revolutions*, which spawned the now widespread interdisciplinary study of the history and philosophy of science. Kuhn argued that the growth of knowledge in the natural sciences cannot be understood as a linear and cumulative approximation to the truth, conceived as a fixed goal of inquiry, but must be seen instead as a discontinuous evolution from one theoretical framework or 'paradigm' to another, whose respective hypotheses, vocabularies, experimental methods, and observational practices resist mutual reduction, translation, and assimilation. Contrary to the objections of some of his critics, Kuhn was not arguing that science is irrational, or that there is no such thing as progress, but that scientific rationality is always in part determined by nonrational conditions of inquiry, such as personal idiosyncrasy and historical accident, and that progress must be measured in terms of open-ended improvements on past practices rather than ultimate arrival at an ideal future state.

Because scientific research programs proceed not piecemeal, but in large bundles of interconnected practical and theoretical commitments, Kuhn maintained that it is impossible to hold individual hypotheses up to the world directly and expect to confirm or disconfirm them in isolated crucial experiments. Tinkering, adjusting, and adding ad hoc hypotheses to save the theory, after all, is always an option. What was revolutionary in Kuhn's account, however, was not its holism. Quine was a holist, too, but his holism was purely semantic and made no reference to actual scientific practice in all its messiness. What was new in Kuhn was the idea that knowledge is essentially embedded in personal biography and social and historical context. What Kuhn was rebelling against was the ahistorical idealization of theory construction and confirmation championed by the logical empiricists, and his work undoubtedly hastened the demise of the positivist program as an account of actual inquiry and the growth of knowledge.

Ironically, Kuhn's argument itself subsequently acquired the status of a kind of paradigm for researchers in the humanities and social sciences, who felt that his account of the normative role of paradigms in the natural sciences, like Wittgenstein's appeal to language games and forms of life and Heidegger's notion of being-in-the-world, shed light generally on the nontheoretical conditions of theory. Consequently, without his having intended or foreseen the association, Kuhn's work coincided broadly with the reemergence of *hermeneutics* in Continental philosophy.

The revival of interest in hermeneutics is due chiefly to Heidegger, but also to Gadamer, whose *Truth and Method* (1989) was published around the same time as Kuhn's book. Heidegger insisted, against Husserl, that philosophical reflection differs fundamentally from scientific inquiry. Whereas Husserl conceived of his own phenomenological project on analogy with morphological description and taxonomic classification in sciences like botany, Heidegger maintained that philosophy is not the cumulative acquisition of knowledge, but always essentially an *interpretive* endeavor. Moreover, observation and description can never be pure and presuppositionless, as Husserl insisted, but instead rest on antecedent situated projections of meaning that can never ultimately be justified or circumvented.

Gadamer adopted and extended Heidegger's account of the projective structure of understanding in what he called his 'philosophical hermeneutics,' which could be said to have done for the humanities and social sciences what Kuhn's account of paradigms and revolutions did for the natural sciences. For both Kuhn and Gadamer, that is, human understanding is historical, contextual, and without ultimate foundations. Inquiry is always embedded in webs of tacit background interpretation, which render discrete beliefs and hypotheses intelligible. Knowledge therefore has no final justification in experience or reason, but proceeds instead in a circular way by elaborating and extending interpretive frameworks into new and unfamiliar domains.

Though their work differed widely in scope and detail, Kuhn and Gadamer together represent a sea change in the way analytic and Continental philosophers have come to regard the structure and growth of human understanding. Richard Rorty (1979) and Charles Taylor (1985) have spelled out this new hermeneutical perspective by arguing that a recognition of the holistic, interpretive character of inquiry has in effect rendered the foundationalism and representationalism of traditional epistemology obsolete.

Gadamerian hermeneutics has also meanwhile found sympathetic echoes in the work of more strictly analytical thinkers such as Donald Davidson (1984) and John McDowell (1994). Gadamer argues that all understanding is historically situated, so that the interpretation of ancient or foreign texts and traditions cannot in principle require that we somehow escape our own perspective, or observe others from some kind of free-floating, disembodied point of view. Understanding others is not a matter of coming to occupy their situation instead of our own, but rather trying initially to take what they do as reasonable, and what they say as true. Only when that effort fails do we then step back to observe them and try to reconstruct their thoughts and experiences objectively: 'It is only when the attempt to accept what is said as true fails that we try to "understand" the text, psychologically or historically, as another's opinion' (Gadamer 1989: 294). In a similar vein, Davidson says of interpretation that:

> the only possibility at the start is to assume general agreement . . . charity is not an option, but a condition of having a workable theory . . . Charity is forced on us; whether we like it or not, if we want to understand others, we must count them right in most matters . . . We make maximum sense of the words and thoughts of others when we interpret in a way that optimizes agreement . . . (Davidson 1984: 196–7)

Along somewhat different lines, McDowell echoes Gadamer's hermeneutical optimism about the possibility of grasping others and the world in conceptual, linguistically expressible terms. In view of what he regards as 'the *conceptual character* (*Begrifflichkeit*) *of all understanding*,' Gadamer insists, 'we must recognize that all understanding is interwoven with concepts and reject any theory that does not accept the intimate unity of word and subject matter (*Sache*)' (Gadamer 1989: 403). Somewhat more dramatically, Gadamer has said, '*Being that can be understood is language*' (Gadamer 1989: 474). McDowell embraces the same sort of optimism in his elaboration of Sellars's critique of the Myth of the Given, drawing likewise on the German idealists who influenced Gadamer. 'It is central to Absolute Idealism to reject the idea that the conceptual realm has an outer boundary,' McDowell observes; rather, 'the conceptual is unbounded; there is nothing outside it' (McDowell 1994: 44).

An even more potent dose of historicism has entered into anglophone philosophy through the works of Michel Foucault (1970, 1979, and 1978). Foucault's impact on contemporary intellectual life exceeds that of virtually any other thinker in the Continental tradition, if only because his most important works were written less than forty years ago and so are still fresh in our collective memory and imagination. His influence extends across a wide spectrum of disciplines in the humanities and social sciences, well beyond the confines of professional philosophy. His emphasis on the concrete power mechanisms that enact and enforce norms of behavior and discourse, moreover, has brought his work to the attention of social and political theorists, while his genealogical treatments of punishment, imprisonment, and sexual desire and identity have transformed cultural and gender studies and even left their mark on political activism, including prison reform and the gay rights movement.

Analytic philosophers have been most impressed by Foucault's claim that a 'historical *a priori*,' or 'episteme' – much like a Kuhnian paradigm – organizes and governs the discursive practices of an entire historical period (Foucault 1970: xxii). So, for example, whereas in the Renaissance things were ordered according to resemblances and analogies, and in the Classical Age of the late seventeenth and eighteenth centuries things manifested their reality by being represented in tables, charts, and objective taxonomies, in modernity things – including, above all, human subjects – come to be defined in more diachronic and functional terms.

What Foucault calls his 'archaeological' study of history is an attempt to describe spontaneously emergent normative structures of discourse without ascribing them to the conscious or unconscious intentions of a transcendental subject. This strategy has the advantage of stressing the contingency of our own conceptual categories, for the very idea of a transcendental subject governing the various domains of knowledge available to it – and in which it, too, occurs as just one more empirical object among others – is not, according to Foucault, a condition of the formation of epistemes in general, but rather an artifact of the modern anthropological conception of man as 'at the same time at the foundation of all positivities and present, in a way that cannot even be termed privileged, in the element of empirical things' (Foucault 1970: 344). Since Kant, modern man has been constituted, in the human sciences but also in Western culture at large, as a paradoxical hybrid, an 'empirico-transcendental doublet' (Foucault 1970: 319). It would be anachronistic and uncritical, Foucault suggests, simply to take for granted that modern picture of ourselves in our account of the various forms of discursive intelligibility governing historical periods other than our own.

Because of its affinity with Kuhn's account of the social conditions of scientific inquiry, Foucault's argument has been especially well received by philosophers of science, for example Ian Hacking (1995, 1999, and 2002), who has drawn connections between the debate over scientific realism and issues concerning the construction of social and psychological kinds. Like Gadamerian hermeneutics, however, Foucault's early 'archaeological' works have invited charges of linguistic idealism. How, after all, do discursive formations as such manage to exercise their authority? What are the mechanisms of power by which they shape and govern their domains?

In subsequent 'genealogical' works such as *Discipline and Punish* and *The History of Sexuality*, Foucault attempted to remedy this problem by turning his attention to the nondiscursive practices that accompany discourse and render it effective, namely those exercises of social power that govern bodily behavior as opposed to mere verbal and symbolic action. According to Foucault, modern discourses and techniques of power have together in effect created new kinds of human beings – delinquents, perverts, homosexuals – by fostering new modes of self-understanding and bodily conduct.

Hacking (2002) has taken up this project, combining it explicitly with post-Kuhnian philosophy of science, in what he calls 'historical ontology.' Hacking has argued elsewhere that it is possible to be a realist about *entities*, while remaining skeptical about the truth of the *theories* describing them, provided we can interact with those entities in concrete ways experimentally. In the case of quarks, for example, he declares, 'So far as I'm concerned, if you can spray them [with positrons or electrons] then they are real' (Hacking 1983: 23). When it comes to 'transient mental illnesses' like Multiple Personality Disorder (Hacking 1995) and heavily theorized social syndromes such as child abuse (Hacking 1999), however, it is impossible to separate the kinds of entities themselves from the practices and theories that, as Hacking puts it, 'make them up' (Hacking 2002: 99–114).

Conclusion

This chapter has been highly selective, perhaps arbitrarily so, but of necessity. The scope and depth of Continental and analytic contributions to philosophy in the twentieth century would make any account of the impact of the former on the latter a truly monumental undertaking. What I have said here, of course, hardly even scratches the surface of the subject. I have tried, nevertheless, at least to gesture in the direction of a few promising points of comparison and analysis. The high profile of themes like intentionality and historicism in analytic philosophy may at times obscure the rich tradition of mutual inspiration among European and Anglo-American thinkers that has in fact made the contemporary debates what they are. Philosophical encounters and retrievals such as these testify to a happy dissolution of the unhappy, polarized state in which professional philosophy found itself in the middle decades of the century. Even greater degrees of openness and innovation await us, though, once philosophers around the world come to see their attempts to understand one another not as a building of bridges between already fatally divided traditions, but rather as enlightened efforts to look beyond the superficial differences and false distinctions that threaten to call attention away from their shared intellectual concerns.

References

Anscombe, G. E. M. [1965] (1981), 'The Intentionality of Sensation: A Grammatical Feature,' in G. E. M. Anscombe (1981), *Collected Philosophical Papers, Vol. 2: Metaphysics and the Philosophy of Mind*, Oxford: Blackwell, pp. 3–20.

Augustine, St. (2002), *On the Trinity: Books 8–15* (ed.) G. B. Matthews, trans. S. McKenna, Cambridge: Cambridge University Press.

Brandom, R. B. (2002), *Tales of the Mighty Dead: Historical Essays in the Metaphysics of Intentionality*, Cambridge: Harvard University Press.

Brentano, F. [1874] (1973), *Psychology from an Empirical Standpoint*, ed. O. Kraus, New York: Humanities Press.

Caston, V. (2003), 'Intentionality in Ancient Greek Philosophy,' in E. Zalta (ed.) (2003), *The Stanford Encyclopedia of Philosophy*, http://plato.stanford.edu/archives/win2003/entries/intentionality-ancient/.

Chisholm, R. M. (1957), *Perceiving: A Philosophical Study*, Ithaca: Cornell University Press.

Churchland, P. M. [1981] (1989), *A Neurocomputational Perspective: The Nature of Mind and the Structure of Science*, Cambridge: MIT Press.

Cohen, G. A. (1978), *Karl Marx's Theory of History: A Defense*, Princeton: Princeton University Press.

Danto, A. (1965), *Nietzsche as Philosopher: An Original Study*, New York: Columbia University Press.

Davidson, D. [1973] (1984), 'Radical Interpretation,' in D. Davidson (1984), *Inquiries into Truth and Interpretation*, Oxford: Oxford University Press, pp. 125–39.

Davidson, D. [1974] (1984), 'On the Very Idea of a Conceptual Scheme,' in D. Davidson (1984), *Inquiries into Truth and Interpretation*, Oxford: Oxford University Press.

Dennett, D. C. (1987), *The Intentional Stance*, Cambridge: MIT Press.

Dennett, D. C. [1991] (1998), 'Real Patterns,' in D. C. Dennett (1998), *Brainchildren: Essays on Designing Minds*, Cambridge: MIT Press, pp. 95–120.

Dreyfus, H. L. (1991), *Being-in-the-World: A Commentary on Heidegger's 'Being and Time,' Division I*, Cambridge: MIT Press.

Dreyfus, H. L. [1972] (1992), *What Computers Still Can't Do: A Critique of Artificial Reason*, Cambridge: MIT Press.

Evans. G. (1982), *Varieties of Reference*, ed. J. McDowell, Oxford: Clarendon Press.

Føllesdal, D. [1969] (1982), 'Husserl's Notion of *Noema*,' in H. L. Dreyfus, and H. Hall (eds) (1982), *Husserl, Intentionality, and Cognitive Science*, Cambridge: MIT Press.

Foucault, M. [1966] (1970), *The Order of Things: An Archaeology of the Human Sciences*, New York: Vintage.

Foucault, M. [1975] (1979), *Discipline and Punish: The Birth of the Prison*, trans. A. Sheridan, New York: Vintage.

Foucault, M. [1976] (1978), *The History of Sexuality, Vol. 1: An Introduction*, trans. R. Hurley, New York: Vintage.

Frege, G. [1892] (1984), 'On Sense and Meaning,' in B. McGuiness (ed.) (1984), *Collected Papers on Mathematics, Logic, and Philosophy*, Oxford: Blackwell, pp. 157–77.

Friedman, M. (2000), *A Parting of the Ways: Carnap, Cassirer, and Heidegger*, Chicago and La Salle: Open Court.

Gadamer, H.-G. [1960] (1989), *Truth and Method*, trans. J. Weinsheimer, and D. G. Marshall, 2nd revd edn, New York: Continuum.

Hacking, I. (1983), *Representing and Intervening*, Cambridge: Cambridge University Press.

Hacking, I. (1995), *Rewriting the Soul: Multiple Personality and the Sciences of Memory*, Princeton: Princeton University Press.

Hacking, I. (1999), *The Social Construction of What?*, Cambridge: Harvard University Press.

Hacking, I. (2002), *Historical Ontology*, Cambridge: Harvard University Press.

Haugeland, J. (1992), 'Dasein's Disclosedness,' in H. L. Dreyfus, and H. Hall (eds) (1992), *Heidegger: A Critical Reader*, Oxford: Blackwell, pp. 27–44.

Hegel, G. W. F. [1807] (1977), *The Phenomenology of Spirit*, trans. A. V. Miller, Oxford: Oxford University Press.

Hegel, G. W. F. [1821] (1991), *Elements of the Philosophy of Right*, ed. A. W. Wood, trans. H. B. Nisbet, Cambridge: Cambridge University Press.

Heidegger, M. [1927] (1962), *Being and Time*, trans. J. Macquarrie and E. Robinson, New York: Harper and Row.

Husserl, E. (1952), *Ideen zu einer reinen Phänomenologie und phänomenologischen Philosophie. Drittes Buch: Die Phänomenologie und die Fundamente der Wissenschaften*, ed. M. Biemel, *Husserliana* V, The Hague: Nijhoff.

Kuhn, T. S. (1962), *The Structure of Scientific Revolutions*, Chicago: University of Chicago Press.

McDowell, J. (1994), *Mind and World*, Cambridge: Harvard University Press.

Merleau-Ponty, M. [1945] (1962), *Phenomenology of Perception*, trans. C. Smith, London: Routledge and Kegan Paul.

Nagel, E. (1936), 'Impressions and Appraisals of Analytic Philosophy in Europe,' *Journal of Philosophy* 33: 5–24, 29–53.

Nehamas, A. (1985), *Nietzsche: Life as Literature*, Cambridge: Harvard University Press.

Peacocke, C. (1989), 'Perceptual Content,' in J. Almog, J. Perry, and H. Wettstein (eds) (1989), *Themes from Kaplan*, New York: Oxford University Press.

Peacocke, C. (1992), *A Study of Concepts*, Cambridge: MIT Press.

Pippin, R. B. (1989), *Hegel's Idealism: The Satisfactions of Self-Consciousness*, Cambridge: Cambridge University Press.

Plato (1973), *Theaetetus*, trans. J. McDowell, Oxford: Clarendon Press.

Quine, W. V. O. (1960), *Word and Object*, Cambridge: MIT Press.

Rorty, R. (1979), *Philosophy and the Mirror of Nature*, Princeton: Princeton University Press.

Rorty, R. (1982), *Consequences of Pragmatism*, Minneapolis: University of Minnesota Press.

Sartre, J.-P. [1940] (2004), *The Imaginary*, trans. J. Webber, London and New York: Routledge.

Searle, J. (1983), *Intentionality: An Essay in the Philosophy of Mind*, Cambridge: Cambridge University Press.

Searle, J. (1992), *The Rediscovery of the Mind*, Cambridge: MIT Press.

Searle, J. (1997), *The Mystery of Consciousness*, New York: New York Review of Books.

Sellars, W. ([1956] 1963), 'Empiricism and the Philosophy of Mind.' in E. Sellars (1963), *Science, Perception and Reality*, New York: Humanities Press, pp. 127–96.

Taylor, C. (1975), *Hegel*, Cambridge: Cambridge University Press.

Taylor, C. [1978–9] (1995), 'The Validity of Transcendental Arguments,' C. Taylor, (1985), *Philosophical Arguments*. Cambridge: Harvard University Press.

Taylor, C. (1985), *Philosophy and the Human Sciences: Philosophical Papers 2*, Cambridge: Cambridge University Press.

Williams, B. (1985), *Ethics and the Limits of Philosophy*, Cambridge: Harvard University Press.

Williams, B. (2002), *Truth and Truthfulness: An Essay in Genealogy*, Princeton: Princeton University Press.

Wittgenstein, L. (1953), *Philosophical Investigations*, 3rd edn, trans. G. E. M. Anscombe, New York: Macmillan.

Twentieth-Century Continental Philosophy

How to recognize Continental European Philosophy

Constantin V. Boundas

In my introduction to the analytic philosophical tendencies in twentieth-century philosophy, I argued that the distinction between analytic and Continental philosophy is unhelpful and that it reflects only a pre-philosophical *doxa* whose origins are found in the national, social, economic, political, and institutional differences of the countries and the type of 'public intellectuals' identified with the one or the other 'school.' Also, in the same introduction, I introduced my view that the obstinacy with which the division has been maintained is due (to agree with Foucault) to the contingent knowledge/power nexus prevalent in different times and spaces (which also includes less refined vested interests and stubborn colonizations of institutional sites). I repeat my claim that 'conceptual analysis' cannot be the proud discovery or exclusive preoccupation of the analysts, given the unrivaled *Begriffgeschichte* (which are far from being only histories) to which German historians of philosophy have accustomed us for a long time, or the intriguing Canguilhem-Bachelard-Foucault archeological investigations of concepts. I could have transcribed the relevant parts of my earlier introduction here, but I trust the reader to want to read these earlier pages without my having to repeat myself. The signs of course, that help in the recognition of Continental European philosophy differ from the signs I offered in the context of analytic tendencies, because the doxic substrate of the former is markedly different from the doxic grounds of the latter. In what follows I offer ten criteria that I consider indicative of the directions followed by Continentals.

1. The Hegelian Legacy. If one puts aside its neo-Kantian beginnings, the twentieth century Continental European philosophy was developed in constant awareness of its proximity to, or distance from, Hegel: the globalizing ambitions of philosophy sustained by the essential ambivalence of what is partial – locus of error and springboard for truth; the indispensability of the negative to the process of becoming-subject of substance; the optimistic anticipation that the desire of another('s) desire will bring about, after the dogged struggle for recognition, the reconciliation of identity and difference; the heart-warming promise that such reconciliation will be concluded on the terms of the subaltern; the (*gauchiste*, existentialist, Maoist) variant that relativizes reconciliations by pluralizing them in the context of perpetual revolution and defeat; the (second half of the century) disenchantment with Hegelian totalities, their being held responsible for almost every major philosophical error and political catastrophe; and the ensuing parricide executed through stealing from father Hegel the fire of the negative and substituting for it the cunning of difference. All of the above helped twentieth-century Continental European philosophy to maintain its conviction that its role in the history and the tribunal of the world mattered; and that it mattered, even when this philosophy was at pains to proclaim that it did not.

2. Transcendentalism. Unlike twentieth-century analytic philosophy where the legacy of classical British empiricism and the occasional formalism create an inhospitable space for transcendentalism, European Continental philosophy, from Husserl down to Deleuze, witnessed the heavy presence of the transcendental. Transcendentalism takes us back to Kant: whether we accept the given for what it is or whether we suspect that a better description of it than the one we have is possible, the transcendental philosophical moment is built around the 'how is the given possible?' question. To be sure, describing transcendentalism in this way shows that the concern that it embodies is older than Kant: the 'saving the phenomena' of Plato can be found along the same trajectory.

Husserl's *epochē*, with its phenomenological and eidetic reductions, are strategies of transcendental philosophy. The operating intentionality of Maurice Merleau-Ponty belongs here. Heidegger's *zukunftiges Erinnerung*, placed in the service of the ontological difference, has no other reason to be. Habermas's 'Interests,' his 'ideal speech situation,' Derrida's 'trace,' Deleuze's 'virtual' – all of them stand for transcendental responses to the question 'how is x possible or actual?'

Given its emphasis on transcendental investigations, Continental European philosophy may appear to be more prone to foundationalism than its analytic counterpart. However, such a conclusion cannot stand in view of Derrida's and Deleuze's repeated appeals to 'unfounding grounds,' the discomforting role of the event and messianic time in Heidegger and Derrida, or the processual nature of the operating intentionality of the phenomenologist. What can plausibly be maintained is that the transcendentalism of European Continental philosophy is more inclined than the analytic philosophical tendencies to distinguish between the 'naive' genetic fallacy and the genealogical or archeological investigations of sense formation, which can be undertaken without ever promising or courting foundations.

3. Language: House of Being and Carceral. The expression 'linguistic turn' is often used in designations of twentieth-century analytic philosophy. But an even more pervasive preoccupation with language is obvious in twentieth-century Continental European trends – except that, here, it is not language as *parole* (discourse) that constitutes the center of attention; it is *langue*, the structure and function of language as such. And language does not become central to philosophical preoccupations because of systematically ambiguous expressions causing philosophical howlers or for the reliability of its ordinary use in pursuing conceptual analysis. For Continental Europeans, for whom language matters because of its unique capacity to reveal and to conceal: for Husserl, for its capacity to reveal or to conceal the originary strata of sense upon which apodeictic descriptions of phenomena can be built; for Heidegger, for its ability to reveal or to conceal the call of Being and be the site of Dasein's authentic response; for Derrida, for the spaces, the absences, and the silences that prevent the full presence of meaning while also rendering it possible in the first place; for Levinas, for the dialectics of the saying and the said, in search of ethics beyond Being and knowledge; finally, for Deleuze, for whom language matters because of the order words (*mots d' ordre*) and passwords (*mots de passe*) that make it a call to conformity and obedience but also a line of flight and transformation. Given these different claims, connoisseurs of the century have come to the conclusion that Continental European philosophical pronouncements about language can be registered in two different columns: on one hand, language is an opening to an outside (originary sense, Being, differance, the past that has never been anyone's present) – positions more often than not associated with hermeneutics; and on the other, language has no outside, it is a prison house, *il n' y a pas d' hors texte*, language has no (subject or) world – positions attributed to the structuralist and poststructuralist trends that invaded European Continental philosophy in the second half of the century. I think that the evidence shows that neither of these trends meant to deprive language of an outside and to turn it into a prison. Their point was that the outside will always be *structured like a language*: the prison was not – even for a moment – language, but rather the ubiquitous structure.

4. Hermeneutics of Suspicion: Demythologizers and Demystifiers. It was Paul Ricoeur who made the opposition between demythologization and demystification central to the philosophical consciousness of the century. The opposition is between a respectful reception of myths and symbols that still wants to be critical of any naive or literal appropriation of them (demythologization) and their unceremonious reduction (read: elimination), undertaken on the grounds that they lack epistemic credentials (demystification). One can sense in this opposition the rivalry between two philosophical traditions, which, without being the creation of the century, nevertheless continued influencing its Continental European philosophical positions: Comtean positivism and hermeneutics. Demythologization and demystification alike belong to what came to be known as hermeneutics of suspicion, the meaning and function of which gains in precision when contrasted with the philosophical program visible, say, in Cartesian philosophy, where the attitude, 'I think, I am, and I am as I take myself to be,' prevails. To this Cartesian programme of 'clear and distinct evidence,' the century counterposed the three thinkers of suspicion, Nietzsche, Marx, and Freud. Behind the evidences and the centrality of consciousness, Nietzsche assigned to the Will to Power the responsibility for the creation of sense and value. Underneath the power of ideas and reason, Marx discovered the causal efficacy of the material (economic) infrastructure of Being and existence. And beyond the illusions of consciousness, Freud revealed the importance of an entire, unconscious theater of shadows. To these three, later on, Spinoza was added, for his naturalization of ethics, and for his resolve to hold the workings and the affects of the body as key to the understanding of the actions and the passions of the mind.

5. Death of God/Death of Man. We think of the nineteenth century as the time that God died at the hands of man. Nietzsche wrote his epitaph, reserving for the murderer his contempt. But – unlike Nietzsche – the murderer wasted a lot of the twentieth century lamenting his deed. One often thinks in this context of the absurd and the rebellion of Albert Camus or Sartre's refusal to live as a lesser God, had God existed, or the continuous railing of the left against the opiate destined for the masses. But one can find even more successful repetitions of the death of God in the resolve of phenomenologists to trace the genesis of sense back to the sanctum of consciousness or in the translation of God-talk according to the needs of existential authenticity. The Christian eschatology kept alive for the sake of Marxist messianicity, the Derridean messianicity without the messiah, and 'the God that passed' of Levinas were mere episodes in the repetition of the death of God, capable of causing existential shivers down our spines, but not able to lift the tombstone of the God who had passed.

During the second half of the century, Continental European philosophy thought that it had found the most efficient way of preventing the Grand Zambie from ever returning: it proclaimed the death of Man. As long as Man is alive, it was argued, God lives on – Feuerbach had not been prudent enough. The theoretical anti-humanisms of Heidegger, Althusser, Foucault, even Derrida and Deleuze – despite their radically different motivations – had this in common: the substitution of a *case vide* responsible for the fabrication of a clearing, a truth-machine, a margin or an outside – a spiritual automaton – that would never be haunted by God again. The farcical return of the religious at the end of the century seems to indicate that gods and men are never wholly and finally buried.

6. The Specter of Marx. The grand narrative of Marxism has throughout the twentieth century been a constant point of reference for Continental philosophers, and Marx, their frequent partner in dialogue. Marxist philosophers abound: Lukacs, Labriola, Gramsci, Althusser, Negri, to name a few. But even philosophers whose research projects were not just Marxist (or not at all Marxist) were unavoidably taken up in the fishnets of what was turning out to be the grand promise of the century – and also its grand disaster: Sartre, Merleau-Ponty, Heidegger, Horkheimer, Adorno, Habermas, Lyotard, Derrida, Deleuze, Badiou. The critical edge of Feuerbach's thesis 11 had been accepted and the Continental philosophers of the century looked like reformed ex-sinners, ready to do anything within their professional competence, provided that they could make up for their former indolence and omissions. In the refined analyses of class-consciousness by Lukacs; the critical theory of society of the Frankfurt School; the anatomy of fascism and of the ambivalent promise of the ideals of the Enlightenment by the same school; the attempt by Merleau-Ponty to explain the Stalinist philosophy of history that made the notorious Moscow trials possible; the bold 'marriage' of existentialism and Marxism proposed by Sartre; the Hegelian Marxism at work in Meszaros's critique of alienation; Althusser's determination of the function of philosophy as class-struggle in the domain of Theory; the efforts of the Praxis Group (again) to give Marxism a human face; the acephalic and acentered post-Marxist unrest of the 1960s, endorsed by Deleuze; as well as in the theory behind the Italian *autonomia* championed by Toni Negri, the century showed its fascination with 'the prophet of justice without mercy who lies, by mistake, in the unbelievers' plot at Highgate Cemetery' (Camus, 1956: 306). It will be difficult to dismiss this impressive rallying behind the Marxist cause as the desire to be engaged in something (anything) other than mere contemplation, by offering one's service to one of the *maîtres-penseurs* of the century. Marxism was one of the constitutive elements of the *doxa* of the century and, therefore, of its consciousness. Given the Hegelian effort inherited by European Continental philosophy to keep alive (even as it was trying to free itself from its grip) the narrative of consciousness becoming self-consciousness, the philosophers of the Continental tradition, in their overwhelming majority, made the choice of letting their reflections ride this becoming and write this narrative. The 'micrology' of the majority of their analytic colleagues, with the Hegelian narrative having been laid to rest in the early century 'revolt against idealism,' and in the context of the Cold War that spread over the second half of the century, made the opposite choice and bracketed the Marxist narrative, when it did not vehemently denounce it.

7. Heterologies. Questions about the meaning, status and function of difference become urgent for philosophers each time that we find we have wandered for a long time in the realm of identity and sameness. Slogans like 'to the things themselves' sooner or later are likely to raise the question as to whether or not there is ever a state of affairs that would permit things *in themselves* to subsist or to be designated *as such*. Considerations of a subject, identical to itself and bearer of changing predicates; search for meaning, capable of not losing its identity in translation; identifications of *epistēmēs* in histories of *long durée* – all such ventures have the tendency to thematize the question of difference. Twentieth-century Continental philosophy witnessed one of the most radical quests for the determination of the different: one that would no longer have the different conceived in the space between two (or more) entities identical to themselves (x is different from y), but, rather, capable of thinking difference as different (or differing) from itself, and therefore no longer absorbable by identity. This philosophical provocation – because this is what it is – was prepared by the realization that Heidegger's ontological difference was not adequately represented by the hackneyed 'Being differs from beings,' but that it required an understanding of Being as an agent in the process of the 'constitution' of beings through differentiation. It was also prepared by the structuralist wave, with its diacritic (differential) determination of the sign; by the realization that the phenomenological account of intersubjectivity required the presence of alterity in the heart of what is supposed to be the same; by the fact that difference enters the phenomenological and hermeneutic constitution of temporal retentions and protentions; and by the fact that the Sartrean 'for itself' and 'for others' had already turned difference into a *causa sui*. Of course, the motivation for getting rid of father Hegel provided the cement for all these fragments to coalesce in the philosophy of difference that characterized French philosophy in the second half of the century. Derrida's differ*a*nce, Deleuze's different/ciation, Levinas's otherwise than being constitute the boldest attempts of the century to theorize heterology without any compromising *lapsi* into identity.

8. Archeology and Genealogy. 'Archeology of knowledge' and 'genealogy of power' are expressions which entered the philosophical vocabulary through the writings of Michel Foucault in the second half of the twentieth century. The epistemological project of the analytic school has spent a lot of effort and time analyzing knowledge claims in terms of beliefs held, and the adequate evidence that is brought to bear on these beliefs. The notion of 'adequate evidence' and the way it relates to the relevant beliefs have proven to be a hard nut to crack. When it comes to the archeology of knowledge, Continental European philosophy may plausibly be taken to grapple with the puzzles generated by the notion of adequate evidence. But to the extent that Continental philosophy has always been more oriented towards whole conceptual schemas, rather than distinct beliefs, the quest for adequate evidence turns quickly into a search for 'modes of visibility' and 'modes of utterability,' which are able to account for what is seen or said in different times and places. It will be too simple to say that these modes give us the grand context for the visible and the sayable, because the modes of visibility and utterability constitute contexts as well as what is seen and said. They are responsible for the production of sense and referent alike, and together they constitute the *epistēmē* of a period. Although the project of the archeology of knowledge has been subjected to charges of relativism, the motivation behind launching it was not the relativization of conceptual frames of reference. Rather, the motivation was the challenge against melioristic and progressivist epistemologies, underwritten by Kantian regulative ideas, Hegelian sublations, or the Husserlian faith in the idea of European rationality. The archeological program tried to escape relativism by endowing the long periods of history that it studied with Rosetta stones: *epistēmēs* are not isolated from one another by gaps and epistemological breaks; they co-exist in various degrees of development and completion, and their co-existence helps us with our questions of transliteration, translation, and mutual impact. Although normally reticent to evaluate the various *epistēmēs*, the research program inquiring into modes of visibility and utterability is not motivated by the search for the strengthening of skeptical intuitions, but rather by the pedagogical desire to think otherwise.

Ultimately, it is to the genealogical project of European Continental philosophy that the analytic tradition (with very few exceptions) will take the strongest exception. Analysis will of course concede that knowledge claims are often being made in contexts of power play; but it will insist that their final validation must arrive at a formulation of the claim made, independently of whatever external to knowledge motivation may have occasioned it. The genealogy of power program of the continental tradition, on the other hand, will insist that shifts, transformations, and struggles of forces and interests are responsible for the co-ordination of forms of visibility and forms of utterability that account for the known. Foucault's 'power/knowledge nexus' means precisely this: since we often speak of what we cannot see and see what we cannot utter, the positivities of the visible and the utterable require another life form: power and the concomitant resistance to power.

9. Nihilism and Superrogation. Continental European philosophy in the twentieth century strikes its *ex post facto* surveyor as a meditation on values and valuing that oscillates endlessly between two extremes: nihilism and superrogation. Dostoevsky's 'if God does not exist, everything is permitted'; the feeling and the concept of the absurd of Camus; the radical contingency and the '*de trop*' of Sartre; even the devaluation of morality in view of a superior ethics by Marxists, Heideggereans and Nietzscheans –

not to mention the devastating wars and revolutions of the century – intensified the lassitude of the 'last man' and the devaluations of all values. The desert of nihilism caused among the philosophers of the century such a revulsion and angst that an incremental or piecemeal solution to the problems that brought nihilism about struck them as totally ineffectual. Those, therefore, who did not succumb to nihilism struck all kinds of superrogatory postures. The decisionism of Sartre, even when placed in the context of the ethical imperative of a freedom for all, is just that. Heidegger's determination of ethics in terms of wanting to have conscience, to be guilty, and to run actively towards our own responsibilities, even when we add the requisite *Sorge* for the sake of the other, leaves such a gap between ethics and morality that the distinction between ethics and meta-ethics of analytic philosophers is nothing compared to it. Levinas's categorical imperative for an asymmetrical ministering to the need of the other, despite his paradoxical reintroduction of symmetry in the name of justice, is an unhelpful hyperbole. Deleuze's becoming worthy of the event, despite the dash of Spinoza's joyful wisdom, remains enigmatic. All these gestures have one thing in common: they outdo each other in their attempt to radicalize the difference between the ethical and the moral, to show that without the hyperbolic demands with which they endow the ethical, the moral would not be possible; but in so doing, they render the 'descending dialectics' from the ethical to the moral forever impossible. This oscillation between nihilist devaluation and the superrogatory demands of the new ethical has been so prominent during the century that voices of moderation (by which I do not mean 'unproblematic'), like Paul Ricoeur's and Jürgen Habermas's, have often been drowned and stifled.

10. The Rhetoric of Continental European Philosophy. I will use as an example here the 'problem of other minds.' The problem of 'other minds' is the name that analytically inclined philosophers give to the conceptual issues arising from the joint assertion that someone else's experiences and mental processes are private to her *and yet* that I am able to gain access to her experience and to her mind. Typically, an analytic philosopher will tackle the problem through a conceptual analysis of 'experience,' 'mental event or property,' 'privacy,' and 'accessibility.' A Continental European philosopher, on the other hand, given the Hegelian legacy that she cannot just forget, will encounter the problem in one of three ways: on her way to theorize the formation and workings of the community (Being with others; Being for others; 'possible worlds'; *partage*); in her attempt to generate the concept of alterity out of the concept of sameness; or through an analysis of how consciousness on its way to becoming self-consciousness is affected by the presence of the other. The result is that the continental philosopher – unlike the analytic colleague – will have the tendency to embed the 'problem of the other' in a wider story about communities, consciousness development, ethics or politics – a tendency that alarms the analytic philosopher, who prefers to move about his business with his usual microscope. A second result, following from the first, is that the wider story of the Continental – unlike the microscopic analysis of her colleague – cannot escape the use of psychological (even when it is called 'transcendental psychological') language: conceptual analysis is possible in terms of 'implies,' 'presupposes' and 'entails' – it may well be the case that our notion of individuals *presupposes* the knowledge of m-predicates and p-predicates, as Strawson argued. But a genealogical account of alterity cannot proceed without the notion of empathy, transference of sense, 'pairing,' or an ontologization of 'shame' and 'pride,' à la Sartre. Similarly, the dissemic character of '*partage*' (dividing/sharing in) may be otiose to a devotee of microscopic analysis, but is very useful to someone who encounters the problem of the other in the context of her attempts to think about a community of those who have nothing in common.

The examples could be multiplied. Their common denominator will be that the unapologetic proximity that Continental European philosophy maintains to culture as a whole; its macroscopic, *long durée*, and genetically constitutive approach to philosophical problems; its refusal to distinguish sharply between philosophical and literary modes of discourse and genres; and the permission, therefore, it gives itself to use the inexhaustible semantic and tropological wealth deposited in natural languages – all this makes for rich, hermeneutically challenging texts, the nightmare of those who prefer uncomplicated ontologies and tidy semantics. I consider the rich text of the best representatives of the Continental tendency to be a virtue. The problem – and it is indeed a problem – is with the less creative epigoni who parrot words depleted of the world-making charge that once upon a time their creators entrusted to the concept that their words designated.

Reference

Camus, A. (1956), *The Rebel: An Essay on Man in Revolt*, New York: Vintage.

The Hegelian Legacy

Bruce Baugh

Hegel's philosophy was renewed and transformed by twentieth-century Continental philosophy. Instead of being a conservative Idealist, Hegel emerged as a revolutionary in thought and politics, a Romantic theorist of the strivings for unity of an alienated and divided self, a thinker who anticipated Freud by attempting to subject the unconscious to rational analysis, and a 'dramatist' of the struggle or *agon* of Being itself. In Merleau-Ponty's oft-cited words:

> All the great philosophical ideas of the past century – the philosophies of Marx and Nietzsche, phenomenology, German existentialism and psychoanalysis – had their beginning in Hegel; it was he who started the attempt to explore the irrational and integrate it into an expanded reason. (Merleau-Ponty 1948: 109; Eng. p. 63)

If other theorists questioned this expansionist reason for its 'totalitarian' tendency (Adorno, Lévinas, Foucault, Derrida), they nonetheless agreed on Hegel's importance. Twentieth-century Marxism, psychoanalysis, existentialism, deconstruction and post-structuralism all bear witness to deep engagement with Hegel's thought.

The beginnings of this new image of Hegel are multiple, but the Italian Benedetto Croce's *What is Living and What is Dead of the Philosophy of Hegel* (1907) set the tone for what was to come. In this work, Croce (1866–1952) accomplished two seemingly incompatible readings of Hegel. On the one hand, Hegel's distinctive achievement is his definition of the philosophical concept as the unity of opposites, or the 'concrete universal,' which preserves the oppositions and distinctions it includes, 'at once difference and unity, discord and concord,' not merely juxtaposed, but contained in a living and organic whole in which one opposite actively becomes its other. Yet whereas development and life may proceed unconsciously, the concept is the rational comprehension of this movement, or the 'ideal form of reality itself.' On the other hand, behind this rationalism stands a Dionysian and 'mad' Hegel. Croce quotes Antonio Rosmini-Serbati, a nineteenth-century anti-Hegelian: 'What reason can be assigned for this alleged desire on the part of Being to negate itself and to not know itself? Why . . . should it make this mad effort to annul itself? For Hegel's system does nothing less than make being go mad, and introduce madness into all things' (Rosmini-Serbati 1883: 371; Eng. p. 28).

Rather than being appalled by this 'Bacchic delirium,' Croce replies that 'Reality seems mad because it is life,' and that Hegel's 'dramatic' and 'tragic' conception of reality encompasses the 'highest wisdom' because it does not deny the reality of the irrational (evil, error, ugliness, passion). What is 'dead' in Hegel is his System, which does violence to the facts through *a priori* constructions that substitute mere formulas for real developments. However, this is an abuse of Hegel's dialectical method, not its core. Marx's historical materialism, similarly, is salvageable as a method of historical interpretation only when it throws off the burden of *a priori* and metaphysical conceptions taken from Hegel, and respects the contingency of facts (Croce 1900).

The connection between Marx and Hegel had been explored in the nineteenth century (Antonio Labriola [1843–1904], Charles Andler [1866–1933]), but received a vital impetus from the Hungarian philosopher Georg Lukács' most influential work, *History and Class Consciousness* (1923). Like Croce, Lukács (1885–1971) separated Hegel's dialectical method from its results in the System and argued that Hegel's method formed the basis of Marx's concrete, historical dialectic. The dialectical method was to be restricted to history and society considered as the products and condition of human action; its aim is to grasp individual facts in relation to the totality of social relations. History is class struggle, the revolutionary process of human liberation carried forward by the proletariat, which becomes conscious of its reification (reduction to the instrumental status of a thing) through revolutionary praxis aiming at negating the conditions that negate its humanity. At the end of history, the subject (universal humanity) recognizes itself in the object it produces (the social world), and so is no longer alienated from itself, its products, or from others. Simultaneously with Lukács, in Germany Karl Korsch (1886–1961) argued in *Marxism and Philosophy* (1923) that Hegelian-Marxism is the theoretical expression of the proletarian revolutionary movement, both of which together comprise 'the concrete totality of the historical process' grasped through a dialectical method in which empirical facts are connected to each other through the 'mediation' of the whole.

The Hegel-Marx connection in the philosophy of praxis was taken up in the 1920s and 1930s in Italy by Antonio Gramsci (1891–1937) and in France by Henri Lefebvre (1901–91), Norbert Guterman (1900–84), and their associates in the 'Philosophies' group of French communist intellectuals. Influenced by both Croce and Labriola, in his *Prison Notebooks* (1971), Gramsci called the philosophy of praxis (or of human action on matter and on social relations) a 'total philosophy,' an 'absolute historicism,' and an 'absolute humanism' that expresses the consciousness not of an existing class, but of that class's collective struggle to achieve a 'total integral civilization' and a 'universal subjectivity' by dissolving society's internal contradictions. This process has a 'logic' of its own superior to contingent facts, which, insofar as they are external to this process, belong to 'chronicle' rather than 'history' proper (see Croce 1921). Lefebvre and Guterman, based on their translations and interpretations of Hegel (1939), Marx (1934) and Lenin (1938), also argue that praxis, as a negation of the given (matter) for the sake of the satisfaction of the subject, is in itself a synthesis of subject (consciousness) and object (nature, existence), and reaches its definitive aim when the division of labor that produces a 'gap' between consciousness and being (alienation) is overcome in a classless society that will realize total and integral humanity. Until that time, the consciousness of the individual is not only divided and alienated (reflecting the division of labor), but also mystified, with no clear self-understanding (Lefebvre and Guterman 1936). The general position of French communist intellectuals of the period, who were aware of Lukács's work (Groethuysen 1923) and of the prominence of alienation in the young Marx's recently published 'Economic and Political Manuscripts of 1844' (1932), was that to be valid, the Hegelian dialectic needed only to be made materialist, such that it dealt with real changes in things and social relations, alienation and praxis, rather than just the interplay of ideas (Baby 1935, Cornu 1934).

This conception of praxis and of history as the overcoming of alienation and the realization of an integral humanity greatly influenced Jean-Paul Sartre (1905–80) in his *Critique of Dialectical Reason* (1960). In this avowedly Marxist work, Sartre held that history was the effort to overcome the negation of human satisfaction resulting from need and scarcity, although he took the unorthodox position that alienation and conflict would always recur because of the recalcitrance of matter to human intentions and the material separation of human subjects. It also inspired Maurice Merleau-Ponty (1908–61), who combined Hegelian-Marxism with his synthesis of Husserlian phenomenology and Gestalt psychology in *Humanism and Terror* (1947), where he argued that just as each present perception prefigured but did not determine the totality of perceptions through which the whole object would be given, so too class struggle prefigured but did not guarantee its future harmonious resolution through the praxis of the proletariat, whose 'historical mission' is to 'realize humanity' 'beyond the alternatives of interior and exterior,' in a classless society where individuals will be the same for themselves as they are for others. Yet in *Adventures of the Dialectic* (1955), Merleau-Ponty argued against the entire Hegelian-Marxist line of thought originating in Lukács, concluding that if the entire truth of history is vested in the proletariat, then there is no dialectic, as dialectic requires opposition, and so neither truth nor history results from a victory that would 'drive ambiguity from history, sum it up and totalize it' (Merleau-Ponty 1973: 221).

A similar shift from optimism to pessimism concerning Hegelian Marxism took place during the historical development of the 'Frankfurt School', the group of thinkers associated with the University of Frankfurt's Institute for Social Research, most prominent among them Max Horkheimer (1895–1971), Theodor W. Adorno (1903–69), and Herbert Marcuse (1898–1979). Like Lukács and Lefebvre, they argued that Hegel's dictum that 'The truth is the Whole' is false so long as the real contradictions of society, which are reproduced in the alienated consciousness of the individual, are not resolved through praxis. The real is *not yet* rational, and will not be until revolutionary praxis has ended domination in all its forms (of others, of nature, of the self).

The question was whether domination could be overcome, and in part this question concerns the dialectic of history itself. If historical development is an indivisible development governed by laws, in which stages follow one another with logical necessity, then this fatalistic determinism rules out human agency, and makes futile 'resistance' or the effort to change the course of history. On the other hand, if 'the realization of freedom and reason requires the free rationality of those who achieve it' (Marcuse 1941: 319), then history at each moment presents an 'untimely' revolutionary possibility (Horkheimer 1982: 106). Consciousness is dominated by economic relations at present, but those relations can be *dominated* by being made means to the gratification of the needs and desires of the whole (Marcuse 1941: 319). Given that consciousness is currently dominated by alienating economic relations, this sounds like picking oneself up by one's own bootstraps. Indeed, the Frankfurt School became more focused on *consciousness* of alienation as an implicit resistance to the status quo, rather than on putative solutions to alienation. When reality is governed by antagonistic relations, Marxism can only be critique, and critique can only be negative: the critique of existing social conditions based on the difference between the rational concept of reality and reality itself (Horkheimer 1982: 108; Adorno 1994: 27–30). The dissatisfaction and feeling of rebellion aroused by recognition of this discrepancy also contain the utopian and revolutionary demand 'that the empirical world be a good and reconciled world, not merely in the Idea, but in the flesh' (Adorno 1994: 30). Critique and revolutionary hope are inseparable, because only in light of the utopian 'whole truth' is the untruth of the present whole revealed (Adorno 1994: 88). In Marcuse, revolutionary hope is also a remembrance of a not entirely forgotten 'archaic past' prior to the reality principle's repression of instinctive drives in the formation of culture and the ego – a past which preserves the promise of the fulfillment of potentialities in a future social organization of the satisfaction of needs (Marcuse 1955, 1978). In Ernst Bloch (1885–1977), a Hegelian Marxist not associated with the Frankfurt School, it is conversely the utopian future, not an archaic past, which leaves traces in the present of unrealized past possibilities striving toward completion, and which relativizes the mere 'factuality' of the present; time is the coexistence on heterogeneous levels of an uncompleted past, a future that announces itself through traces, and a present caught in the tension between anticipation and remembrance (Bloch 1949, 1959, 1967). Dissatisfaction with the present, which resists both resignation and false contentment, can rescue the alienated individual for a genuine individualization not determined by the 'transcendental' and universal exchange relations of the market (Adorno 1969: 501), but only if the empirical subject renounces the domination of what is alien, whether nature, matter, or others (Adorno 1966).

Whether the renunciation of domination can be achieved is moot. In their more pessimistic moods, Horkheimer and Adorno contend that reason itself is the domination and administration of nature and of humans for human use (Adorno and Horkheimer 1944; Horkheimer 1947); in practice, the elimination of what does not conform to reason in society is realized in Fascism's annihilation of non-conformists, Jews, political enemies, asocial persons, and the insane (Horkheimer 1941: 46). For Marcuse, though, reason is both domination (reality principle) and the overcoming of domination in a return from alienation in nonrepressed imaginative play (Marcuse 1955: 113–18, 184–96), although he sometimes expressed the gloomier view that when the needs of individuals are entirely manipulated by the economic-technical organization of capital, neither opposition nor the painful awareness of alienation is possible (Marcuse 1964). In the view of Jürgen Habermas (1929–), who combined the Frankfurt School's 'Critical Theory' with the philosophy of language and hermeneutics, pure communicative action in an 'undistorted speech situation' is a norm implicit in communicative acts themselves insofar as these aim at understanding rather than domination, and can be the basis of a critique of existing social relations which distort or impair communication through coercion (Habermas 1963, 1968, 1979, 1981). Although 'the self-constituting subject of history was and is a fiction,' it can be the future goal of a political practice which produces more democratic and less hierarchical speech communities (Habermas 1981: 398). In that, Habermas restores hope in Hegel's 'rationality of the real' which Adorno and Horkheimer had seemingly abandoned in their total critique of reason. Whether domination and alienation are taken as insuperable, or if they may be overcome in aesthetic enjoyment and play or in noncoercive communication, a Hegelian-Marxist theory of history as alienation and its overcoming can be seen at work in the Frankfurt School's 'critical theory' in all its phases, whatever the misgivings concerning the Lukács reduction of nature to material to be exploited by human praxis.

In twentieth-century French thought, Hegel's influence on conceptions of desire, alienation and satisfaction took forms that sometimes departed quite widely from Marxist materialist dialectics of history, although some of these unorthodox takes on Hegel ended up rejoining Marxist critiques of capitalist society. For the Surrealists such as André Breton (1896–1966), Hegel's dialectic of negation and 'the negation of the negation' was seen as a method for overcoming all the divisions of modern life: between waking and dreaming, subject and object, self and other, ego and id, reason and madness (Breton 1930), and thus as achieving the 'wholeness' or 'totality' sought by the Marxists. From time to time, the Surrealists tried to make common cause with the French Communist Party, but their views concerning labor were quite incompatible. The Surrealists' infinite negation, as the infinite becoming-other of all things and ideas, unchained the negativity of reason from its productive use in labor, in a Bacchanalian revel without repose where the negativity of Reason would destroy Reason itself: this was a truly 'mad' Hegel. Labour or praxis, so prized by the Marxist Hegelians, was seen as a constraint on negativity brought on by the fear of madness, or negativity in its wild state.

This thesis was developed by Alexandre Kojève (1902–68) in his celebrated lectures on Hegel's *Phenomenology* in Paris in the 1930s (Kojève 1947), which Breton attended, as did Georges Bataille (1897–1962), for whom the contrast between work and madness was marked and profound. According to Kojève's analysis of the master-slave dialectic in the *Phenomenology of Spirit*, the slave is the one for whom the fear of death (nothingness) overwhelms the desire for freedom, and the price of this anxiety before nothingness is the work the slave undertakes for the master. Work is by its very nature servitude, the harnessing of negativity to productive ends, and it is a way of fending off the nothingness of death or madness. In a series of works which would greatly influence Michel Foucault (1926–84) and Jacques Derrida (1930–2004), Bataille argues that sovereign negativity, by contrast, would be an 'expenditure without return', negation liberated from the production of objects in work. The result of this negativity would not be absolute knowledge in which Subject and Object are one, as in Hegel, but a non-knowledge (*non-savoir*) in which Subject and Object are both dissolved in infinite negativity (Bataille 1943, 1944, 1945). Foucault takes up the opposition of work and madness in declaring that madness is without works, and that madness is subjected to work when the psychiatric patient is compelled to work on her own subjectivity so that it conforms to an ethical norm issuing from the health authorities, 'the master' (Foucault 1961). For Derrida, 'expenditure without return' serves as a model for deconstruction, in which each term passes into its contrary, but without ever being resolved in a third term or 'synthesis,' such that meaning is endlessly deferred through infinite negation (Derrida 1967a, 1974). In a similar manner, Luce Irigaray (1932–) also uses language to subvert traditional identities and oppositions (man/woman, human/nature) through an open-ended series of becoming-other, but without a speculative synthesis which would sum up and cancel out the difference between terms (Irigaray 1974, 1977). Preserving the difference, and preserving respect for what differs, is at the heart of Irigiray's ethics of difference. More recently, Jean-Luc Nancy (1940–) has opposed Hegel's dialectical *Aufhebung* (which preserves what it cancels in a totalizing synthesis) with the restless negativity that drives the dialectic and 'undoes' all syntheses, and with Bataille proposes a notion of a 'community' of dismantled subjects open to 'the Other' in place of the fusion of subject and object or subject and subject (Nancy 1986, 1997). In this, Nancy is the latest representative of the interpretation of Hegelian negativity as infinite becoming-other which began with the Surrealists.

Kojève's other influential thesis concerned the master–slave relation as a struggle for recognition. Each consciousness desires the Other, and desires the Other's desire, as it desires to be desired for its desire, or for its subjectivity as such, but this results in a struggle in which each tries to subject the Other so that it may enjoy the Other's recognition without reciprocating; the recognized Subject is the Master, the recognizing subject is the Slave. Despite Kojève's own view that the eventual outcome of this dialectic is the state's universal recognition of all Subjects as citizens governed by rational and universal laws, it was the element of conflict in inter-subjective relations which most influenced Merleau-Ponty (Merleau-Ponty 1945, 1947), Sartre (Sartre 1943) and Simone de Beauvoir (1908–86). Sartre, using Hegel's view that consciousness is 'for-itself' only through another as his point of departure, formulates his famous doctrine of the 'gaze' (*le regard*): I experience my being-for-others when another subject looks at me, and renders me an 'object' within a world oriented by the Other's goals and desires, rather than by my own. The gaze comes to me from beyond the world, and is an alienation of my being (self and world) in the Other. I can recover my being only by mastering the Other's subjectivity and making the Other's freedom serve my ends, which requires that I try to objectify the Other through my gaze; attitudes such as desire and love are precisely these attempts to absorb the Other into one's self, while at the same time preserving sufficient distance from the Other so that it is the Other's *free* desire that I possess. Since the Other does the same, conflict is inevitable and perpetual, and since the possession of another freedom that remains free and outside 'the world' is impossible, alienation is inescapable.

In her historic analysis of the oppression of women, de Beauvoir makes use of both Hegel and Sartre to argue that with respect to their social roles and the prevailing ideology, 'Man' is the universal Subject and the master, and Woman is the differing Other and a slave, who is 'free' only to recognize and validate men's projects and values (de Beauvoir 1949). Romantic love, for women, is the attempt to ensnare the subjectivity of a man – whose values the 'woman in love' allows to shape her own tastes, goals, and needs – by 'fascinating' the male gaze, and as in Sartre, this attempted recovery of one's being from the subjectivity of the Other is bound to fail. The dialectic of desire, 'the gaze' and recognition is also at work in the analysis by Jacques Lacan (1901–81) of how the Self is constituted first through identification with its mirror image (imaginary), and then by the subject 'acceding to' the first-person linguistic position ('I') through identifying its subjectivity with that of the 'I' which addresses it, which occurs in the resolution of the Oedipus complex, when the son identifies with and assumes 'the name of the father' (Lacan 1966). For Sartre, de Beauvoir, and Lacan, desire arises from a felt 'lack' in the self, and specifically a lack of wholeness and self-coincidence, and this 'lack' either cannot be fulfilled (Sartre, Lacan), or can fulfilled only through a mutual recognition where each takes the Other's desire and freedom as an end rather than a means (Merleau-Ponty 1945; de Beauvoir 1947, 1949). Pierre Klossowski (1905–2001), who like Lacan and Merleau-Ponty attended Kojève's seminars, also makes use of Kojève's version of the master-slave dialectic in his analysis of the works of the Marquis de Sade (Klossowski 1947), arguing that the libertine (master) who attempts to annihilate the victim (slave) through pain or torture thereby annihilates the subjectivity whose recognition the master seeks. Since as Kojève emphasises, in this dialectic, the 'truth' of the master lies in the slave who grants the master recognition, the libertine thereby destroys his 'being' as master. As in Sartre's analyses of desire and love (and of sadism and masochism), the libertine's victory spells his defeat: the winner loses.

The theme of the lack within the self also derived from an early 'existentialist' reading of Hegel, Jean Wahl's *The Unhappiness of Consciousness in Hegel's Philosophy* (1929). With the publications of Hegel's early writings on religion (Hegel 1907) and Wilhelm Dilthey's study of the young Hegel (Dilthey 1905), Hegel appeared as a Romantic whose philosophy expressed the drive toward wholeness of a divided and contradictory self, closer to Hölderlin and Novalis than to the pedantic expounder of the finished 'System' outlined in the *Encyclopedia* (Hegel 1905). Guided by Hegel's youthful writings, Wahl (1888–1974) sees the 'master-slave' struggle as but the externalization of a deeper struggle within the self between its finite being and its infinite power of negation, which Hegel deals with in the 'Unhappy Consciousness' chapter of the *Phenomenology*, a work that had been relatively neglected until Georg Lasson's new edition of it (Hegel 1921). Hegel's dialectic is not motivated by the speculative desire for knowledge, but by a painful feeling of division and incompletion within the subject; 'absolute knowledge' would be the completion of the self in its 'return' to itself after it has separated itself from itself into various determinate aspects, a synthesis of the multiplicity of determinations and existential unity.

The theme of a self which vainly strives to complete itself would greatly influence Sartre, for whom consciousness attempts to define its being through a future it can never catch up with, and is thus essentially 'unhappy' (Sartre 1943). Although Sartre tended to locate this dialectic within the individual consciousness, for Wahl, the self's journey through division to wholeness is also the history of the universal Spirit. In that respect, Jean Hyppolite (1907–68) is a more faithful follower of Wahl's interpretation, as in his commentary on Hegel's *Phenomenology*, where he makes the 'unhappy consciousness' the driving force of the entire dialectic, both within the individual and within history; the end and goal of the dialectic is a society where individuals recognize themselves in a general culture which is the work of all and each (Hyppolite 1939–41, 1946). Indeed, Hyppolite later resisted the 'humanist' interpretation of Hegel, and placed the dialectic and its contradictions in language, rather than in 'Man' (Hyppolite 1953). In this he anticipated the later anti-humanist thesis of the 'death of Man' in Foucault (1966) and Derrida (1972), although the 'death of Man' had also been advanced by Kojève as the condition of post-historical humanity (humanity after universal mutual recognition had been achieved, which would render human negativity useless and bring history to a close). Derrida also follows Hyppolite in locating the dialectic in language, rather than consciousness, such that the signifier/signified relation takes on the duality and division Wahl had assigned to consciousness, and like the 'unhappy consciousness' subverts its unity through infinite becoming by which every term is negatively related to every other in the 'system of difference' which is language (Derrida 1967b).

Nevertheless, the humanist existentialist reading of Hegel vigorously pursued by Alexandre Koyré (1882–1964) in the 1930s, which relied on the works of Hegel's early Jena period (Hegel 1925, 1932) to argue that the proper locus of the dialectic of being 'which is what it is not and is not what it is' is human existence (Koyré 1961), also had an impact on later philosophies. Koyré argued that Hegel's theory of time, whereby the present is negated by the future which is the goal of action, anticipates Heidegger's thesis in *Being and Time* (Heidegger 1927) of the ontological priority of the future, according to which, argues Koyré, the future is necessarily 'open' in a way that makes the closure of 'the end of history' impossible. At the same time, Benjamin Fondane (1898–1944), like his predecessor in Germany, Franz Rosenzweig (1886–1929), argued that a total reconciliation or fusion of the individual and society or of thought with being was neither possible nor desirable, and would amount in effect to the elimination of any individuals who failed to conform to societal norms, and the reduction of existence to a general category of thought (Rosenzweig 1921; Fondane 1936). This insistence on the openness of history and the resistance to the violence of totalizing synthesis became a major theme in the work of Emmanuel Lévinas (1906–95), whose conception of the Other as 'totally other' was meant to preclude the possibility of the Other being reduced to a category of the Self, including the universal Self of Absolute Spirit, which Hegel had said takes all otherness into itself (Lévinas 1961). In many respects, this position rejoins those of Adorno, Irigaray, and Derrida.

It is important to note that while the French were combining Hegel with the early works of Martin Heidegger (1889–1976) in the 1930s and 1940s, Heidegger was moving away from human existence (*Dasein*) and towards Being, and that this led to a renewed engagement with Hegel's thought. Whereas in *Being and Time* (1927), Hegel had been dealt with rather summarily, the focus being the sections on 'time' in the *Encyclopedia of Philosophical Sciences* (Hegel 1905), Heidegger became increasingly interested in Hegel's *Phenomenology*, in the 1930–1 devoting a seminar dealing with the first two sections of the *Phenomenology* (A. Consciousness, B. Self-Consciousness), including a brief discussion of master and slave and the unhappy consciousness (Heidegger 1980). Heidegger also deals with the 'Introduction' to the *Phenomenology* in a 1942–3 seminar (Heidegger 1950), and gives an account of experience (*Erfahrung*), the process by which consciousness goes beyond itself and negates its claims to truth, resulting in a 'thoroughgoing skepticism' through which consciousness dies and transcends itself into Absolute Spirit, which retrospectively finds its 'truth' in its recollection of the necessity of its errors. Hans-Georg Gadamer (1900–2002) likewise makes Hegel's concept of experience central to his major work, *Truth and Method* (1960), in which the 'truth' of experience lies in a further experience that negates it, not for the individual, but through collective history. However, unlike Hegel, Gadamer holds that experience is an insight into an essential human finitude that is not transcended in some higher knowledge. Rather, at each instant, a new future opens up which has the potential to free us from an illusion that held us captive. History has no end, and infinity does not return into itself in the form of totality. Rather, 'experience' on this interpretation is more akin to what Jean-François Lyotard (1925–98) designates as the feeling of the sublime: the revelation of finitude through the encounter with forces that infinitely surpass and negate the subject (Lyotard 1983, 1991).

As much as Continental thought resists Hegel by trying to preserve difference, the individual or sovereign negativity, it is also indebted to Hegelian conceptions of the dialectic and negation. A total 'break' with Hegel (if one can speak of such) only arises with some forms of Structuralism and with the neo-Nietzscheans of the 1960s, such as Gilles Deleuze (1925–96), Foucault in his 'genealogical' phase (1968–84), and Klossowski's later work (Klossowski 1963, 1969). Deleuze's resistance to Hegel takes the form of a theory of nonnegative difference which leaves the dialectic of negation and the negation of the negation behind; for Deleuze, difference is more fundamental than contradiction or negation, which are but the 'inverted image' of active difference (Deleuze 1962, 1968). For Klossowski, Hegel's theory of history is contested by a Nietzschean idea of eternal return in which what returns does not return into itself, in some stable identity, but doubles and differs from itself. As for Structuralism, we have already seen that Lacan, often classed as 'structuralist,' is greatly indebted to Hegel as interpreted by Kojève and to a lesser degree Sartre. Claude Lévi-Strauss (1908–), who effectively founded 'structuralism' as a general method or school by incorporating the methods of Saussure's structuralist linguistics into anthropology, also had attended Kojève's Hegel seminar, and had an ambiguous relation to Hegel. On the one hand, Lévi-Strauss freely uses terms such as 'mediation' and 'praxis' even in *The Savage Mind* (1962), but in that same work, he argues there is 'a fundamental antipathy between history and systems of classification' (Eng. p. 232) and that the explanatory power of the latter (whether in science or totemism) is greater than the former. History is merely a narrative mode of conveying over time (diachronically) systems of relations that obtain at a given time or independently of time (synchronically), that is, history is a myth. The 'human sciences' then should use synchronic systems of classification like those used in the natural sciences to 'dissolve man' (Eng. p. 247) into his material basis (physical-chemical conditions). This, argued Lévi-Strauss, and not history or dialectics, is the true heritage of Marx's materialism.

This argument had been anticipated by some anti-Hegelian Marxists such as Lucio Colletti (1924–2001) and was taken up by the leading French Marxist of the 1960s, Louis Althusser (1918–90). For Colletti, whereas Hegel's dialectic reduces matter to thought, 'real being' is precisely what exists independently of thought, and is 'extra-logical'. So-called 'Hegelian Marxism,' from Lukács to Sartre and the Frankfurt School, really owes more to irrationalist and anti-scientific 'philosophies of life' (Bergson, Simmel) than to either Marx or Hegel (Colletti 1969). Althusser's Marxism also aims to break with Hegel and to attain 'science.' Like Lévi-Strauss, Althusser argues against any conception of time as linear and homogeneous; rather, different structural levels have different and incommensurable rates of change and scales of measurement. Diachronic dialectical development is an illusion; in Marx's dialectic, there is no point of origin, and no teleological destination, but only structured wholes containing contradictions which displace each other. This is not a narrative of a subject (Spirit, the proletariat) progressing toward emancipation, but 'a process without a subject.' It does not even make sense to speak of 'alienation,' as that term implies a possible return to a unified subject to which the alienated property belongs, when in fact the human subject is itself a decentred structure that has no centre (Althusser 1965, 1972; Althusser et al. 1965). Similar considerations guide Foucault's important essay, 'Nietzsche, Genealogy, History,' (Foucault 1971), which also, like Deleuze, uses Nietzsche's thesis of active masters and reactive slaves to argue that the master-slave relation is not a struggle among equals, and that no mutual recognition of master and slave is possible; history is an 'endlessly repeated play of dominations,' not the progressive liberation of 'Man' or the 'subject' (Foucalt 1971; Eng. p. 85).

Hegel has to be read 'against the grain' (Adorno 1994: 139). All the thinkers discussed in this article attempt to do precisely that. It is in these non-Hegelian interpretations of Hegel that Continental thought has had its most fruitful encounters with the great German Idealist.

References

Adorno, T. W. [1963] (1994), *Hegel: Three Studies*, trans. S. W. Nicholsen (1994), Boston: MIT Press.

Adorno, T. W. (1966), *Negativ Dialektik*, Frankfurt am Main: Suhrkamp; trans. E. B. Ashton (1973), *Negative Dialectics*, New York: Seabury.

Adorno, T. W. (1969), 'Subject and Object,' in A. Arato, and E. Gebhardt (1982) (eds and trans.), *The Essential Frankfurt School Reader*, New York: Continuum, pp. 497–511.

Adorno, T. W., and M. Horkheimer (1944), *Dialektik der Aufklärung*, New York: Institute of Social Research; trans. J. Cumming (1972), *Dialectic of Enlightenment*, New York: Herder and Herder.

Althusser, L. (1965), *Pour Marx*, Paris: F. Maspero; trans. B. Brewster (1969), *For Marx*, London: Allen Lane.

Althusser, L. (1972), *Lenine et la philosophie. Suivi de Marx et Lenine devant Hegel*, Paris: F. Maspero; trans. B. Brewster, *Lenin and Philosophy and Other Essays* (1971), New York: Monthly Review Press.

Althusser, L., et al. (1965), *Lire le capital*, Paris: F. Maspero; trans. B. Brewster (1970), *Reading Capital*, New York: Pantheon Books.

Andler, C. (1897), *Les origines du socialisme d'état en Allemagne*, Paris: F. Alcan.

Andler, C. (1910) *Le manifeste communiste de Karl Marx et F. Engels*, translated with an introduction and commentary by C. Andler, Paris: Cornély.

Arato, A., and E. Gebhardt (ed. and trans.) (1982), *The Essential Frankfurt School Reader*, New York: Continuum.

Baby, J., M. Cohen, G. Friedmann, and R. Maublanc (1935), *A la lumière du Marxisme*, Paris: Éditions Sociales Internationales.

Bataille, G. (1943), *L'expérience intérieure*, Paris: Gallimard; trans. L. A. Boldt (1988), *Inner Experience*, Albany: State University of New York Press.

Bataille, G. (1944), *Le coupable*, Paris: Gallimard; trans. B. Boone (1988), *Guilty*, Venice: Lapis Press.

Bataille, G. (1945), *Sur Nietzsche*, Paris: Gallimard; trans. B. Boone (1992), *On Nietzsche*, New York: Paragon House.

Bloch, E. (1949), *Subjekt-Objekt: Erläuterungen zu Hegel*, Berlin: Aufbau Verlag.

Bloch, E. (1959), *Das Prinzip Hoffnung*, Frankfurt: Suhrkamp; trans. N. Plaice, S. Plaice, and P. Knight (1986), *The Principle of Hope*, Cambridge: MIT Press.

Bloch, E. (1960), *Spuren*, Frankfurt: Suhrkamp.

Bloch, E. (1967), *Tübinger Einleitung in die Philosophie I*, Frankfurt: Suhrkamp; trans. as *Philosophy of the Future* (1970), New York: Herder and Herder.

Breton, André (1930), *Second manifeste du surréalisme*, Paris: Editions Kra. Trans. Richard Seaver and Helen R. Lane (1969), *Manifestoes of Surrealism*, Ann Arbor: University of Michigan Press.

Colletti, L. (1969), *Il Marxismo e Hegel*, Part II, Bari: Laterza; trans. L. Garner (1973), *Marxism and Hegel*, London: New Left Books.

Cornu, A. (1934), *Karl Marx, l'homme et l'œuvre: De l'Hégélienisme au matérialisme historique*, Paris: Alcan.

Croce, B. (1900), *Materialismo storico ed economia marxista*, Palermo; trans. C. M. Meredith (1914), *Historical Materialism and the Economics of Karl Marx*, New York: Macmillan.

Croce, B. (1907), *Ciò che è vivo e ciò che è morte nella filosofia di Hegel*, Bari: Laterza; trans. D. Ainslie (1915), *What is Living and What is Dead of the Philosophy of Hegel*, London: Macmillan and Company.

Croce, B. [1917] (1921), *History – Its Theory and Its Practice*, trans. D. Ainslie, New York: George G. Harrap and Co.

de Beauvoir, S. (1947), *Pour une morale de l'ambiguïté*, Paris: Gallimard; trans. B. Frechtman (1948), *The Ethics of Ambiguity*, New York: Philosophical Library.

de Beauvoir, S. (1949), *Le deuxième sexe*, Paris: Gallimard; trans. H. M. Parshley (1953), *The Second Sex*, New York: Knopf.

Deleuze, G. (1962), *Nietzsche et la philosophie*, Paris: Presses Universitaires de France; trans. H. Tomlinson (1983), *Nietzsche and Philosophy*, London: Athlone Press.

Deleuze, G. (1968), *Différence et répétition*, Paris: Presses Universitaires de France; trans. P. Patton (1994), *Difference and Repetition*, New York: Columbia University Press.

Derrida, J. (1967a), *L'écriture et la différence*, Paris: Seuil; trans. A. Bass (1978), *Writing and Difference*, Chicago: University of Chicago Press.

Derrida, J. (1967b), *De la grammatologie*, Paris: Minuit; trans. G. C. Spivak (1976), *Of Grammatology*, London and Baltimore: Johns Hopkins University Press.

Derrida, J. (1972), *Marges de la philosophie*, Paris: Minuit; trans. A. Bass (1982), *Margins of Philosophy*, Chicago: University of Chicago Press.

Derrida, J. (1974), *Glas*, Paris: Galilée; trans. J. P. Leavey, Jr, and R. Rand (1986), *Glas*, London and Lincoln: University of Nebraska Press.

Dilthey, W. (1905), *Die Jugendgeschichtes Hegels*, Berlin: Verlag der Königl. Akademie der Wissenschaften; 2nd edn (1923), *Gesammelte Schriften* vol. IV, Stuttgart: B. G. Teubner.

Fondane, B. (1936), *La conscience malheureuse*, Paris: Denoël et Steele.

Foucault, M. (1961), *Folie et déraison. Histoire de la folie à l'âge classique*, Paris: Plon; trans. R. Howard (1967), *Madness and Civilization*, London: Tavistock.

Foucault, M. (1966), *Les mots et les choses*, Paris: Gallimard; trans. A. Sheridan (1973), *The Order of Things*, New York: Vintage.

Foucault, M. (1971), 'Nietzsche, la généalogie, l'histoire,' in S. Bachelard et al. (1971), *Hommage à Jean Hyppolite*, Paris: Presses Universitaires de France, in English in P. Rabinow (ed.) (1984), *The Foucault Reader*, New York: Random House.

Gadamer, H.-G. (1960), *Wahrheit und Methode*, Tübingen: J. C. B. Mohr; trans. G. Barden and John Cumming (1975), *Truth and Method*, New York: Seabury.

Gramsci, A. (1971), *Selections from the Prison Notebooks*, ed. and trans. Q. Hoare, London: Lawrence and Wishart.

Groethuysen, B. (1923), 'Les jeunes Hégéliens et les origines du socialisme contemporain en Allemagne,' *Revue philosophique de la France et de l'étranger* 95: 379–402.

Habermas, J. (1963), *Theorie und Praxis; sozialphilosophisches Studien*, Neuwied am Rhein: Luchterhand; trans. J. Viertel (1973), *Theory and Practice*, Boston: Beacon Press.

Habermas, J. (1968), *Erkenntnis und Interesse*, Frankfurt am Main: Suhrkamp; trans. J. J. Shapiro (1972), *Knowledge and Human Interests*, London: Heinemann Educational.

Habermas, J. (1979), *Communication and the Evolution of Society*, trans. T. McCarthy, Boston: Beacon Press.

Habermas, J. (1981), *Theorie des Kommunikativen Handelns*, vol. 1, *Handlungsrationalität und Gesellschaftliche Rationalisierung*, Frankfurt am Main: Suhrkamp; trans. T. McCarthy (1984), *Theory of Communicative Action*, Boston: Beacon Press.

Hegel, G. W. F. (1905), *Encyclopädie der philosophischen Wissenschaften im Grundrisse*, ed. G. Lasson, Leipzig: F. Meiner.

Hegel, G. W. F. (1907), *Theologische Jugendschriften*, ed. H. Nohl, Tübingen: J. C. B. Mohr.

Hegel, G. W. F. (1921), *Phänomenologie des Geistes*, ed. G. Lasson, Leipzig: F. Meiner.

Hegel, G. W. F. (1923), *Wissenschaft der Logik*, ed. G. Lasson, Leipzig: F. Meiner.

Hegel, G. W. F. (1925), *Jenenser Logik, Metaphysik und Naturphilosophie*, *Sämtliche Werke* 18, ed. G. Lasson, Leipzig: F. Meiner.

Hegel, G. W. F. (1932), *Jenenser Realphilosophie*, *Sämtliche Werke* 19–20, ed. J. Hoffmeister, Leipzig: F. Meiner.

Heidegger, M. (1927), *Sein und Zeit*, Halle: Max Niemayer; trans. J. Macquarrie, and E. Robinson (1962), *Being and Time*, New York: Harper and Row.

Heidegger, M. (1950), 'Hegels Begriff der Erfahrung,' in M. Heidegger (1950), *Holzwege*, Frankfurt: Klostermann; trans. (1970) as *Hegel's Concept of Experience*, New York: Harper and Row.

Heidegger, M. (1980), *Hegels Phänomenologie des Geistes*, Frankfurt: Klostermann; trans. P. Emad, and K. Maly, *Hegel's Phenomenology of Spirit*, Bloomington: Indiana University Press.

Horkheimer, M. (1941), 'The End of Reason,' in A. Arato, and E. Gebhardt (eds and trans.) (1982), *The Essential Frankfurt School Reader*, New York: Continuum, pp. 26–48.

Horkheimer, M. (1947), *Eclipse of Reason*, New York: Oxford University Press.

Horkheimer, M. [1940] (1982), 'The Authoritarian State,' in A. Arato, and Eike Gebhardt (eds and trans.) (1982), *The Essential Frankfurt School Reader*, New York: Continuum, pp. 95–117.

Hyppolite, J. (1939–41), *La phénoménologie de l'esprit*, Paris: Éditions Aubier Montaigne.

Hyppolite, J. (1946), *Genèse et structure de la phénoménologie de l'esprit de Hegel*, Paris: Éditions Aubier Montaigne; trans. S. Cherniak, and J. Heckman (1974), *Genesis and Structure of Hegel's Phenomenology of Spirit*, Evanston: Northwestern University Press.

Hyppolite, J. (1953), *Logique et existence*, Paris: Presses Universitaires de France; trans. L. Lawlor, and A. Sen, *Logic and Existence* (1997), Albany: State University of New York Press.

Irigaray, L. (1974), *Speculum de l'autre femme*, Paris: Minuit; trans. G. C. Gill (1985), *Speculum of the Other Woman*, Ithaca: Cornell University Press.

Irigaray, L. (1977), *Ce sexe qui n'en est pas un*, Paris: Minuit; trans. C. Porter with C. Burke (1985), *This Sex Which Is Not One*, Ithaca: Cornell University Press.

Klossowski, P. (1947), *Sade mon prochain*, Paris: Seuil; trans. A. Lingis (1991), *Sade My Neighbour*, Evanston: Northwestern University Press.

Klossowski, P. (1963), *Un si funeste désir*, Paris: Gallimard.

Klossowski, P. (1969), *Nietzsche et le cercle vicieux*, Paris: Mercure de France; trans. D. W. Smith (1997), *Neitzsche and the Vicious Circle*, London: Athlone Press.

Kojève, A. (1947), *Introduction à la lecture de Hegel*, Paris: Gallimard; partial trans. by J. H. Nichols (1980), *Introduction to the Reading of Hegel*, Ithaca: Cornell University Press.

Korsch, K. (1923), *Marxismus und Philosophie*, Leipzig; trans. F. Halliday (1970), *Marxism and Philosophy*, London: New Left Books.

Koyré, A. (1961), *Études d'histoire de la pensée philosophique*, Paris: Gallimard.

Labriola, A. (1897), *Essais sur la conception matérialiste de l'histoire*, Paris; trans. C. H. Kerr (1904), *Essays on the Materialist Conception of History*, Chicago: C. H. Kerr and Co.

Lacan, J. (1966), *Écrits*, Paris: Seuil; trans. A. Sheridan (1977), *Écrits: A Selection*, New York: Norton.

Lefebvre, H. (1939), *Le matérialisme dialectique*, Paris: Gallimard; Eng. trans. J. Sturrock (1969), *Dialectical Materialism*, London: Cape.

Lefebvre, H., and N. Guterman (1934), *Morceaux choisis de Marx*, Paris: Gallimard.

Lefebvre, H., and N. Guterman (1936), *La conscience mystifiée*, Paris: Gallimard.

Lefebvre, H., and N. Guterman (1938), 'Introduction' to V. I. Lenin, *Cahiers sur la dialectique de Hegel*, Paris: Gallimard.

Lefebvre, H., and N. Guterman (1939), *Morceaux choisis de Hegel*, Paris: Gallimard.

Lévi-Strauss, C. (1962), *La pensée sauvage*, Paris: Plon; trans. D. Weightman, and J. Weightman (1966), *The Savage Mind*, London: Weidenfeld and Nicolson.

Lévinas, E. (1961), *Totalité et infini: Essai sur l'extériorité*, The Hague: Martinus Nijhoff; trans. A. Lingis (1969), *Totality and Infinity*, Pittsburgh: Dusquesne University Press.

Lukács, G. (1923), *Geschichte und Klassenbewusstsein*, Berlin; trans. R. Livingstone (1971), *History and Class Consciousness: Studies in Marxist Dialectics*, Boston: MIT Press.

Lyotard, J.-F. (1983), *Le différend*, Paris: Minuit; trans. G. v. d. Abeele (1988), *The Differend: Phrases in Dispute*, Minneapolis: University of Minnesota Press.

Lyotard, J.-F. (1991), *Leçons sur l'analytique du sublime: Kant, critique de la faculté de juger, 23–9*, Paris: Galilée; trans. E. Rottenberg (1994), *Lessons on the Analytic of the Sublime: Kant's Critique of Judgement, [sections] 23–9*, Stanford: Stanford University Press.

Marcuse, H. (1941), *Reason and Revolution: Hegel and the Rise of Social Theory*, New York: Oxford University Press.

Marcuse, H. (1955), *Eros and Civilization: A Philosophical Inquiry into Freud*, Boston: Beacon Press.

Marcuse, H. (1964), *One Dimensional Man: Studies in the Ideology of Advanced Industrial Society*, Boston: Beacon Press.

Marcuse, H. (1978), *The Aesthetic Dimension: Toward a Critique of Marxist Aesthetics*, Boston: Beacon Press.

Marx, K. (1932), *Marx-Engels Gesamtausgabe* Part One, vol. 3, Berlin; trans. M. Milligan (1932), rev'd D. J. Struik, *The Economic and Philosophic Manuscripts of 1844*, New York: International Publishers.

Merleau-Ponty, M. (1945), *Phénoménologie de la perception*, Paris: Gallimard; trans. C. Smith (1962), *Phenomenology of Perception*, London: Routledge and Kegan Paul.

Merleau-Ponty, M. (1947), *Humanisme et terreur, essai sur le probléme Communiste*, Paris: Gallimard; trans. J. O'Neill (1969), *Humanism and Terror*, Boston: Beacon Press.

Merleau-Ponty, M. (1949), Sens et non-sens, Paris: Nagel; trans. H. L. Dreyfus, and P. A. Dreyfus (1964), *Sense and Non-Sense*, Evanston: Northwestern University Press.

Merleau-Ponty, M. [1955] (1973), *Adventures of the Dialectic*, trans. J. Bien, Evanston: Northwestern University Press.

Nancy, J.-L. (1986), *La communauté désoeuvrée*, Paris: Christian Bourgois; trans. P. Connor, L. Garbus, M. Holland, and S. Sawhney (1991), *The Inoperative Community*, Minneapolis: University of Minnesota Press.

Nancy, J.-L. (1997), *Hegel: l'inquiétude du negative*, Paris: Hachette; trans. J. Smith, and S. Miller (2002), *Hegel: The Restlessness of the Negative*, Minneapolis: University of Minnesota Press.

Rosenzweig, F. (1921), *Der Stern der Erlösung*, Frankfurt am Main: J. Kaufmann; trans. W. W. Hallo (1971), *The Star of Redemption*, New York: Holt, Rinehart and Winston.

Rosmini-Serbati, A. (1883), *Saggio storico-critico sulle categorie e la dialecticca*, Turin: Stamperia dell'Unione Tipografico; trans. D. Ainslie (1915), in *What is Living and What is Dead of the Philosophy of Hegel*, London: Macmillan and Company.

Sartre, J.-P. (1943), *L'être et le néant*, Paris: Gallimard; trans. H. Barnes (1992), *Being and Nothingness*, New York: Washington Square Press.

Sartre, J.-P. [1960] (1982), *Critique de la raison dialectique*, Paris: Gallimard, *Critique of Dialectical Reason*, trans. A. S. Smith, London: Verso.

Wahl, J. (1929), *Le malheur de la conscience dans la philosophie de Hegel*, Paris: Rieder.

Phenomenology

Leonard Lawlor

The term 'phenomenology' enters philosophical discourse for the first time in 1764, when J. H. Lambert uses it in his *Neues Organon*. In a 1770 letter to Lambert, Kant defines the term as a 'negative science,' presupposed by metaphysics, in which the principles of sensibility would be determined. The term remains obscure until Hegel's 1807 *Phenomenology of Spirit*. As in Kant, in Hegel too, phenomenology is presupposed by metaphysics but also subordinated to metaphysics; phenomenology is a part of the philosophy of spirit, which itself is a part (along with the philosophy of nature and the logic) of the encyclopedia of philosophical sciences. In 1900, however, Edmund Husserl calls his psychological investigations into logic 'phenomenology' (Husserl 1970: 261–3). As Husserl's thinking matures, he recognizes that phenomenology itself is not restricted to psychology; it is a universal method for philosophizing. For Husserl, phenomenology is not merely presupposed by metaphysics; it is not a part of philosophical sciences; phenomenology is philosophy itself. Despite certain moments of eclipse (by psychoanalysis and structuralism, and analytic philosophy), phenomenology remains, from Husserl's time, the most resilient philosophy of the twentieth century. In fact, at the beginning of the twenty-first century, many 'Continental philosophers' and even many 'analytic philosophers' still consider phenomenology as the central, perhaps the only method of philosophy and even as philosophy itself. Nevertheless, the universalisation of phenomenology that Husserl's thought initiates does not free phenomenology from psychology; Husserl's in particular, but also phenomenology in general remain deeply connected to psychology. Psychology takes on the role of being a propaedeutic for phenomenological philosophy. Therefore, phenomenology's reasoning remains circular: the being of subjectivity (the being of consciousness) given through psychology is also foundational and absolute. Because it is a subjectivism, phenomenology remains within, as Heidegger would say, the forgetfulness of the question of being, within the forgetfulness that has dominated Western metaphysics from its inception. Our question becomes obvious. Is it possible today to find a way out of phenomenology? It seems to me that the only way out of phenomenological subjectivism lies in the transformation of the concept of immanence. Following Deleuze, we must say that immanence must be no longer immanent *to consciousness*, but rather consciousness must be immanent to immanence itself (Deleuze 1968: Chaps 10 and 11).

To answer the question, 'What is phenomenology?, we must recognize the crucial importance of Husserl's idea of the phenomenological reduction. By means of the reduction, phenomenology is defined by a movement that *disentangles*, within the immanence of consciousness, extra-mundane or transcendental experience from mundane or psychological experience. Transcendental experience, transcendental lived-experience (*Erlebnis*), is the experience of self-presence. Yet, at this transcendental level, it is necessary to recognize a moment of nonpresence. The moment of nonpresence transforms the concept of immanence. No longer is immanence immanent *to* consciousness; rather consciousness will be immanent to immanence itself, which is life. Yet, life then will include the nonconscious, difference, blindness, and even death. Although the argumentation for the transformation of immanence starts with Heidegger, it will depend directly upon Derrida's deconstruction of Husserl's phenomenology in his 1967 *La voix et le phénomène*.[1] In *Voice and Phenomenon*, Derrida endeavors to find the exit from phenomenology (VP: 96/86).

1. What is Phenomenology?

The diverse nature and large number of Husserl's published and posthumous writings require that, if we want to define phenomenology, we must locate ourselves in a text that is a 'condensed' expression of Husserl's mature thought. This text is the final draft of the article Husserl wrote in 1927 for the *Encyclopaedia Britannica*.[2] But there is an additional reason to privilege this text. The *Britannica* essay is also, as is well known, the result of a failed collaboration with Heidegger. Thus no other text that Husserl wrote (at least among those he published during his lifetime) manifests not only the boundaries by means of which phenomenology defines itself, but also the way out beyond this frontier. We must start with a summary of this text.

The final 1927 draft of the *Encyclopaedia Britannica* essay aims to introduce phenomenology by means of psychology. Yet, initially, in Part I of the essay, Husserl sets out only to show that *phenomenological* psychology is the foundation for and a reform of *empirical* psychology. 'Modern' psychology, according to Husserl, 'is the science dealing with the psychical in the concrete context of spatio-temporal realities,' dealing with what occurs 'in nature as egoical' (Hua IX: 278/160). So, modern psychology conceives itself as a part of anthropology or zoology, where animals and humans are considered as a part of nature. In order therefore to ground and reform psychology, in order for it to be a science independent of physics (in the broad sense), it is necessary to demonstrate how psychology is different from the physical. Therefore, Husserl focuses on what is peculiar to our experience of the psychical.

In unreflective perception, our gaze focuses on objects out there. By means of reflection, our gaze is able to direct itself towards psychical experience. In other words, by turning our gaze towards the psychical experience, 'we grasp the corresponding subjective lived-experience in which they [that is, the things] become 'conscious' to us, in which in the broadest sense they 'appear' to us' (Hua IX: 279/161). The things in turn are now 'phenomena' and we see that the essential character of lived-experience is to be as 'consciousness of' or 'appearance of.' Following the scholastic tradition, Husserl calls the essential character of lived experiences 'intentionality.' But still, according to Husserl, recognizing that lived-experiences are intentional does not give us a pure field of investigation freed from everything psycho-physical. In order to establish the field, 'A particular method of access is required for the pure phenomenological field: the method of "phenomenological reduction"' (Hua IX: 282/163). Husserl also calls the reduction 'the epochē.' The epochē suspends or disconnects all positing of reality as objective existence, as nature. In other words, in the epochē the phenomenologist inhibits or suspends – 'suspension' is the literal meaning of the word 'epochē' – every accomplishment of objective positing of the world as really existing. The epochē 'puts between parentheses' and therefore 'shuts out, from the phenomenological field, the world as it exists in simple absoluteness for the subject' (Hua IX: 282/163). The world is now relative; the world is given *in* consciousness. Anything that we took as absolute is now replaced by the respective meaning (*Sinn*) of each thing in consciousness (Hua IX: 282/163). Husserl's method of the phenomenological reduction – its importance must not be underestimated and we shall return to it below – is connected to his discovery of intentionality. Neo-Kantianism (such as we find it, for example, in Hans Rickert) had conceived intentionality as a characteristic of *only* the lived-experiences that are directed towards *real* things. This conception implies that there are lived-experiences (such as those of fantasy, memory, or even of mathematics) that are nonintentional. Instead, Husserl's discovery makes intentionality no longer be dependent on reality: for Husserl and for phenomenology in general, *every* lived-experience is a directedness-towards. Lived-experience, in other words, as Husserl says in the *Britannica* essay, consists in a 'relativity' (*Relativität*) (Hua IX: 279/161). If we could locate Husserl's greatest thought, it would be this *relativity*. As in *Ideas I* (in 1913) (Husserl 1962), here in the *Britannica* essay Husserl describes this relativity in terms of *noesis* and *noema*. The purely psychic or reduced field consists in a correlation between noesis (thought) and noema (the object thought about), the *intentio* and the *intentum*. The correlation consists in the relation of the unified meant object (the noema) to the multiplicity of lived experiences (the noesis) but also the multiplicity of lived-experiences, all the specific intentionalities, are centered around an 'I-pole' or 'I-subject' (Hua IX: 283/164).

However, even though the phenomenological reduction has given us the purely psychical, we still have not, according to Husserl, established psychology as a science, as an *a priori* science. The lived-experiences, the correlational intentionalities are *factual* experience. In order to reach the *a priori essences* of the purely psychical, an eidetic reduction is required. The eidetic reduction consists in a free, intuitive variation of the factual psychic experiences, a variation that discloses the *a priori* possible (that is, thinkable) lived-experiences. In other words, the 'theoretical gaze' directs itself to the invariant in the variations, which leads to the eidetically necessary typical form, the *eidos* (Hua IX: 284/165). Thanks to the eidetic reduction, we have the definition of phenomenological psychology: an investigation into the invariant, essential structures of the total sphere of pure lived experience (Hua IX: 285/166). Providing the *a priori* essences (and thus exactness), phenomenological psychology, Husserl says, will be the foundation for empirical psychology. And, although it will not be able to account for everything in psychology (for example, the psycho-physical relation, which would require the *a priori* of the physical), it will be able to account for the strictly psychical.

Now, while, through the investigation into phenomenological psychology, Husserl has been able to ground (through the concept of intentionality) and reform (through the idea of eidetic exactitude) modern empirical psychology, this function is not the sole one for the investigation. The investigation into phenomenological psychology can also function as the preliminary step towards what Husserl calls 'transcendental phenomenology.' According to Husserl – providing here a historical account, which anticipates what we see a few years later in Husserl's so-called *Crisis* texts (Husserl 1954) – the idea of transcendental phenomenology did not grow out of needs peculiar to psychology. The movement we find in British empiricism and in Locke especially towards the subjective was an attempt to solve the transcendental problem that starts with Descartes: 'In Descartes's *Meditations*, the thought that had become the guiding one for "first philosophy" was that, all of "reality" [*Reale*] – and finally the whole world of what exists and is so *for* us [*für uns seiende und so seiende*] – is only as the content of a representation of our own representations [*Vorstellungen*]' (Hua IX: 287/ 167). That Husserl emphasizes 'für uns' is indicative of phenomenology in general and repeats the idea of intentionality being relational. Yet according to Husserl, Descartes's '*mens*' was transcendentally pure, while Locke conceived the mind as the *human* mind. Locke therefore is the founder of psychologism. Psychologism is the position that says that all knowledge and all sense of reality is based on the human mind, which is itself something that exists (*seiende*) or is real. To regain access to the transcendental problem that Descartes initiated, Husserl says that we must overcome every trace of psychologism and yet *at the same time* we must do justice to psychologism's 'transcendentally significant kernel of truth' (Hua IX: 287/168). The source of psychologism's continuous historical power comes from the ambiguity of all concepts of the subjective. Husserl says explicitly that the ambiguity requires 'at once the sharp separation and at the same time the parallel treatment of pure phenomenology psychology . . . and transcendental phenomenology as true transcendental philosophy' (Hua IX: 288/168).

The transcendental problem, according to Husserl, arises from a 'general reversal' of that 'natural attitude,' in which everyday life as a whole as well as the positive sciences operate. Here is Husserl's definition of the natural attitude (which was anticipated in the discussion of the physical): '[T]he world is for us the self-evidently existing universe of realities which are continuously pre-given in question-less presence [*Vorhandenheit*]' (Hua IX: 288/168). In other words, in the natural attitude, the world looks to be given ahead of time, pre-given, in unquestioned presence. When the theoretical interest abandons the natural attitude and *reverses* its gaze to the life of consciousness – 'in which the "world" is for us precisely that, the world which is present [*vorhandene*] *to* us' (Hua IX: 288/168) – we find ourselves in a new cognitive situation. Every sense of the world, both indeterminate and determinate, is now seen as a conscious sense, a sense which is formed in subjective genesis. Even those things that we think exist, self-evidently, in and for themselves without anyone experiencing them are now conscious senses. However, once, according to Husserl, the world in this full 'universality' has been *related* to the subjectivity of consciousness, then its whole mode of being becomes unintelligible and questionable. Therefore, the subjective genesis of the world requires clarification; it has become a problem. The problem is 'how [consciousness], so to speak, manages in its immanence that something which manifests itself can present itself *as* something existent in itself [*als an sich seiend*], and not only as something meant but as something authenticated in concordant experience' (Hua IX: 289/169). This is Husserl's, that is, phenomenology's genuine question: the origin of the world as existing and real in itself. How is it possible that the world gains its sense and validity from the genesis 'in us'? How could we humans be the origin of the world, when we ourselves belong to the world (Hua IX: 289/169)? Nevertheless, we have not yet reached the genuine transcendental problem for Husserl. Another step is necessary. The genuine transcendental or phenomenological problem is not just the origin of this factual world; this problem would be the old medieval cosmological problem. What we must see is that the relativity of consciousness applies not just to the factual world in which we find ourselves, but to every conceivable world as such (Hua IX: 289/169). The genuine transcendental problem is therefore eidetical. And when I imaginatively vary the world relative to us, I also vary the 'us,' thereby transforming ourselves into 'a possible subjectivity.' We must now pursue this question of consciousness in terms of an eidetics (in terms of invariants, a possible subjectivity and a possible world). How could we as a possible subjectivity be the origin of any possible world whatsoever? That question states the transcendental problem.

Now, according to Husserl, it looks so far as though phenomenological psychology is the place to carry out all transcendental elucidation (Hua IX: 290/170). Yet, we must not overlook the fact that psychology is a positive science, a science operating within the natural attitude, in which the simply present world is the thematic ground. What phenomenological psychology wants to explore are the minds and the communities of minds that are actually to be found *in* the world. Husserl says that, even in its eidetic investigation, the mind retains the '*ontological sense* [*Seinsinn*] of *mundane presence* [*weltlich Vorhandenen*]; it is merely related to possible *real* [*reale*] worlds' (Hua IX: 290/170; my emphasis). By no means can psychology be the premises for transcendental philosophy since it does *not* transcend the world as *Vorhandenheit*. Even as an eidetic phenomenologist, the psychologist is transcendentally naive. If, however, according to Husserl, we let the transcendental interest be decisive, instead of the natural-worldly interest, then psychology as a whole becomes what is transcendentally problematic and questionable (Hua IX: 291/170). Yet, 'Like every meaningful question, this transcendental question presupposes a ground of unquestioned being, in which all means of solution must be contained. This ground is here the subjectivity of that kind of conscious life in which a possible world, of whatever kind, is constituted as present [*vorhandene*]' (Hua IX: 291/171). The movement we have here is one that moves from unquestioned presence (in the natural attitude) to making presence questionable, and then from the questionable presence to the unquestioned ground (*Boden*). But Husserl stresses that *we must not confuse* the unquestioned *Boden* with what is transcendentally in question. All positive sciences, including psychology, must be suspended (epochē) as transcendentally naive. We cannot use as our ground or soil one of the things that we are trying to ground; in other words, we cannot use a mundane region (albeit eidetic) to ground all mundane regions. Such a grounding would be circular (Hua IX: 292/171). Therefore, the subjectivity to which the transcendental question recurs can thus really not be the subjectivity with which psychology deals (Hua IX: 292/171).

So, Husserl asks: 'Are "we" then supposed to be dual beings, psychological and human as well as transcendental?' According to Husserl, however, this duality can be clarified. The psychic subjectivity, the 'I' and 'we' of ordinary discourse is experienced in its pure psychic peculiarity through the method of phenomenological-psychological reduction. And this psyche or mind is modified into its eidetic form. Transcendental subjectivity is nothing other, Husserl says, 'than this "I myself" and "we ourselves," but not as found in the natural attitude of the everyday and of the positive sciences; the "I" and the "we" are not perceived as "little pieces of existence [*Bestandstücke*] of the objectively present world before us" ' (Hua IX: 292/172). What Husserl means is that, since we are not little pieces of existence of the objectively present world before us, we must be appearances (*Erscheinungen*) for an intentional life, in which the presence of the world is made (Hua IX: 292/172). 'However,' and this is an important 'however,' 'The . . . I and we present [*vorhandene*] presuppose an . . . I and we, *for* which they [that is, the first I and we] are present, which, however, is not itself present again *in the same sense*' (Hua IX: 292/172). If the 'I' and the 'we' are present, they must be present to something or to someone else: transcendental subjectivity. Because transcendental subjectivity is also present (albeit in a different sense), we have access to it through an intuition or a 'transcendental "inner" experience' (Hua IX: 292–3/173). This experience, according to Husserl, opens up an endless ontological field, which is 'parallel' to the purely psychological one. Continuing on the idea of the two senses of presence, Husserl says:

> My transcendental ego is thus obviously 'different' from the natural ego, but by no means as a second, as one separated from it in the natural sense of the word, just as on the contrary it is by no means bound up with it or intertwined [*verflochtenes*] with it, in the usual sense of these words. (Hua IV: 294/173)

The two subjectivities are therefore different and yet not separate, intertwined and even identical but not in the usual or habitual way of using these words. For Husserl, the 'differentiation' allows us to escape from the circularity of the psychologistic solution to the transcendental problem. It also makes the parallelism of the transcendental and the psychological experiential spheres comprehensible. The parallelism is comprehensible 'as a kind of identity of the complex interpenetration of ontological senses [*Ineinander des Seinsinnes*].' Nevertheless, despite the complexity, the 'ontological ground' (*Seinsboden*) is the transcendental 'we' (transcendental intersubjectivity) from which everything transcendent (that is, 'all real, mundane beings') gets its ontological sense: 'transcendental sense-bestowal' (*Sinngebung*).

Now, according to Husserl, the fact that historically psychologism has not been able to be surmounted rests on deep grounds: 'Its power lies in an essential transcendental *semblance* [*Schein*] which, since undisclosed, had to remain effective' (Hua: IX 295/174). Here we have the word '*Schein*,' with its ambiguity; the term means both a deceptive appearance – Husserl had already anticipated this term when he spoke of the 'I' and the 'we' as 'appearances,' as *Erscheinungen* – a shining through. Psychologism remains compelling because of the duplication of consciousness between psychological and transcendental. The two seem to be the same, seem to be one, the human mind; but they are two and the transcendental, Husserl is implying, shines through the psychological. Because of the '*Schein*,' we can see not only the 'independence' (*Unabhängigkeit*) of transcendental phenomenology from phenomenological pure psychology, but also the propaedeutic usefulness of phenomenological psychology as a means of ascent to transcendental phenomenology (Hua IX: 295/174). Like all positive sciences, phenomenological psychology has the advantage of being accessible. Once phenomenologically pure psychology has become clear, then we must clarify the sense of the transcendental for which the transcendental reduction is required. Thus transcendental phenomenological philosophy should be autonomously established, which would allow us to interpret all transcendental phenomenological doctrine found in natural positivity (for instance, in the natural mind or psyche), and this interpretation would be done by showing the difference between the natural attitude and the transcendental attitude. Moreover, we would be able now to reinterpret transcendental phenomenology as the foundation (*Begründung*) for natural positivity, and not be confused by this movement (which would imply a kind of identity between the two), since we have clarified the difference between the two. As Husserl says, remarkable consequences follow from the meaning of transcendental phenomenology as the foundation.

Transcendental phenomenology realizes the idea of a universal ontology as the systematic unity of all conceivable *a priori* sciences. The ontology, however, would not be based on a dogmatic foundation, but on a foundation given to us by the phenomenological reduction. Phenomenology as the science of all conceivable transcendental phenomena is *eo ipso* the *a priori* science (ontology) of all conceivable beings (*Seienden*). And this ontology is not limited to objective being, objectively existing beings, but rather the full concretion of being in general including subjectivity and even transcendental subjectivity itself. Thus, a phenomenology properly carried through is the truly universal ontology, as opposed to an ontology of positivity. This universal ontology means that every *a priori* is ultimately prescribed in its ontological validity precisely as a transcendental 'achievement.' The subjective method of this achievement is itself made transparent. Thus, for Husserl, there are no paradoxes; no crisis of the foundations can exist. As will become apparent in the *Crisis* texts, the Husserlian concept of crisis is a lack of elucidation of the subjective achievements; in other words, it is objectivism, a mere ontology of the object. All sciences will become branches of 'the one phenomenology as universal eidetic ontology' (Hua IX: 297/176). Even an exact science like mathematics, which is an eidetical science, still requires a subjective grounding. But also the factual sciences (like biology) require phenomenological grounding. In order to have a universal and fully grounded science of empirical fact it is necessary, according to Husserl, that the 'complete universe of the *a priori*' be presented in its relativity to the transcendental subjectivity. Even a universal science of facticity (contingencies, in other words, such as our bodies, history, and community) must have a phenomenological form; Husserl calls this phenomenology of facticity an empirical (rather than transcendental) phenomenology, which would be based on the 'fundament of eidetic phenomenology as the science of any

possible transcendental subjectivity whatsoever' (Hua IX: 298/176). The phenomenological science of facticity is identical with the positive sciences, after they have
been grounded eidetically.

Therefore, according to Husserl, through phenomenology we restore the most
originary concept of philosophy, as universal science based on radical self-justification,
which is alone truly science in the Platonic and Cartesian sense. Phenomenology is
identical with the philosophy that encompasses all genuine knowledge. It consists in
both eidetic phenomenology (universal ontology) as first philosophy, and in second
philosophy, the science of the universe of 'facta' (Hua IX: 299/177). All the traditional
problems of reason, all the traditional philosophical problems have their place in
phenomenology. On the basis of the absolute sources of transcendental experience or
eidetic intuition, these problems obtain their genuine foundation for the first time, and
their possible solution. Phenomenology then recognizes its particular function within a
possible life of humanity at the transcendental level. For Husserl, 'the ultimate and
highest' problem is that of a humanity that lives and moves in truth and genuineness.
Phenomenology brings about the relative resolution of this problem by recognizing
intuitively the absolute norms. Phenomenology is directed teleologically towards the
disclosure of these norms and their conscious practical operation (Hua IX: 299/177).
Phenomenology, in other words, is 'in the service of a universal praxis of reason' (Hua
IX: 299/177). It strives towards the teleological idea of reason in humanity. Or, even
more, phenomenology is the disclosure of the idea and it helps humanity itself
consciously and purposively to direct itself towards the idea (Hua IX: 299/178). But
besides the practical problem being resolved through phenomenology, phenomenology, which proceeds from intuitions to abstractions, also resolves all the old philosophical antitheses. There are half-truths in these oppositions and the positions
themselves are one-sided. So, as Husserl says, '[S]ubjectivism can only be overcome
by the most universal and consistent subjectivism (the transcendental)' (Hua IX: 300/
178). Similarly, relativism can be overcome only through a universal relativism, that of
transcendental phenomenology. This relativity proves itself to be the only possible
sense of absolute being. We find the same solution with empiricism. There must be the
most universal and consistent empiricism, which makes use of a broadened sense of
experience, intuition, eidetic intuition. And yet phenomenology is rationalistic by
overcoming dogmatic rationalism by means of eidetic investigations. Finally, the
tracing back of all being to transcendental subjectivity and its constitutive intentional
functions leaves open no other way of contemplating the world than as teleological.
And yet there is a kernel of truth in naturalism since constitutive intentional functions
originate in what is given passively. Phenomenology, therefore, according to Husserl,
is the pure 'working out' of the methodical intentions which already animated Greek
philosophy from its beginnings. And it continues the great movements of modern
philosophy. But, the way of true science is infinite. So Husserl concludes the
Britannica essay with the teleological infinite idea of philosophy; he says, 'Accordingly,
phenomenology demands that the phenomenologist foreswear the ideal of a philosophic system and yet as a humble worker in community with others, the phenomenologist lives for a *philosophia perennis*' (Hua IX: 301/179).

2. The Transformation of Immanence

As we just saw, the establishment and definition of a purely phenomenological psychology is a 'propaedeutic' for transcendental phenomenology or phenomenological philosophy. The psychological introduction to transcendental phenomenology tells us precisely what is at stake in the entire *Britannica* essay, indeed, in phenomenology as a whole: entanglement (*Verflechtung*). As Husserl says, 'Ultimately, the great difficulty rests on the way that already the self-experience of the psychologist is everywhere intertwined [*verflochten*] with external experience, with that of extra-psychical real things' (Hua IX: 282/325). Phenomenology aims therefore to *disentangle* the psychic from the physical and the psychic from the transcendental. The purpose of the reduction is disentanglement. The disentanglement results in the 'parallelism' between phenomenological psychology and transcendental phenomenology. Yet, in his letter to Husserl concerning the *Britannica* essay – the document that records the failure of their collaboration – Heidegger says, 'We are in agreement on the fact that beings in the sense of what you call "world" cannot be explained in their transcendental constitution by returning to a being of the same mode of being' (Hua IX: 601/ 138). Then he asks, 'What does the absolute ego mean in its difference from the pure psychic? What is the mode of being of this absolute ego – in what sense is it the *same* [*dasselbe*] as the ever factical 'I'; in what sense is it *not* the same?' (Hua IX: 602/139). It is clear that Heidegger thinks that Husserl has not investigated the relativity of *Schein* enough. Or more precisely, Husserl has conceived the relativity of the *Schein* in terms of an 'ambiguity' when he says that the transcendental 'I and we' are 'not itself present again in the same sense' (Hua IX: 292/172). In other words, when Husserl makes the difference between the parallel, he is conceiving the difference as a relation of analogy. Eugen Fink makes the analogical relation explicit in his 1930 draft of the Sixth Cartesian Meditation (Fink 1995: 73, 90–1). After rejecting Aristotle's conception of the 'unity of analogy' of the multiple meanings of being, Fink nevertheless says, '[W]e can press on toward a close determination of the transcendental concept of being only by taking our lead from the analogy relationship' (Fink 1995: 22). The dependence on analogical thinking implies that resemblance unifies the difference between the parallel. The relation that Husserl has in mind is the following: the mundane things are *in* the transcendental or present *to* the transcendental and yet the transcendental resembles them. In other words, the mundane things, which are founded, are *in* the transcendental, the foundation, and yet the foundation is also *in* them (*Ineinander*); while having the things in it, the foundation does not remain therefore in itself; it shines through in them. The presence (*Vorhandenheit*) of the transcendental foundation is 'copied off' the presence (*Vorhandenheit* again) of the mundane things. The copying relation explains why phenomenology remains bound to the presence of subjectivity. Therefore, being bound to the presence of subjectivity, phenomenology betrays its own slogan of 'to the things themselves'; the things themselves have become the subject. Being a form of subjectivism, as the *Encyclopaedia Britannica* essay by Husserl on phenomenology indicates – 'subjectivism can only be overcome by the most universal and consistent subjectivism (the transcendental)' – phenomenology does not escape from the circular reasoning that Husserl himself attributed to psychologism.

Something that is founded, the subject or better the unity of the ego, reappears as the foundation.

In his letter, Heidegger is criticizing Husserl in the same way as he criticized Descartes in *Being and Time*: the being of the subject, the 'sum' of the 'cogito sum,' is left undetermined (Heidegger 1979a: 24; Eng. 1996: 21). In his 1967 *Voice and Phenomenon*, Derrida takes up Heidegger's criticism. Derrida argues that, when Husserl describes absolute subjectivity, he is speaking of an interior monologue, auto-affection as hearing-oneself-speak. According to Derrida, hearing-oneself-speak is 'an absolutely unique kind of auto-affection' (VP: 88/78), because there is no external detour from the hearing to the speaking; in hearing-oneself-speak there is self-proximity. I hear myself speak therefore immediately in the very *moment* that I am speaking. According to Derrida, Husserl's own description of temporalization in his early lectures undermines the idea that I hear myself speak immediately. On the one hand, Husserl describes what he calls the 'living present,' the present that I am experiencing right now, as being perception, and yet Husserl also says that the living present is thick. The living present is thick because it includes phases other than the now, in particular, what Husserl calls 'retention,' the recent past. Yet retention in Husserl has a strange status, since Husserl wants to include it in the present as a kind of perception and at the same time he recognizes that it is different from the present as a kind of nonperception. Derrida calls the nonperception of retention a 'trace' (VP: 73/65); the trace contests Husserl's radical separation, expressed in *Ideas I*, between signs and perception (Husserl 1982 [Eng.]: para. 43). Instead, for Derrida, Husserl's descriptions imply that the living present, by always folding the recent past back into itself, involves a *difference* in the very middle of it (VP: 77/69).[3] In other words, when I speak silently to myself, it must be the case that there is a minuscule hiatus differentiating me into the hearer and into the speaker; there must be *'un écart'* that distances me from myself, without which I would not be a hearer as well as a speaker. Following Heidegger, Derrida says that the *'écart'* in the present does not happen to a subject but produces a subject (VP: 92/82). Derrida also notes that 'moment' or 'instant' translates the German word *'Augenblick,'* which means the blink of the eye. Therefore, we can see here that, for Derrida, the hearing-oneself-speak in fact refers back to perception, to vision, and even to the mirror image (VP: 88/78–9). In the auto-affection of seeing oneself seeing, the eye closes (due to retention), and when the eye closes (blindness), it breaks open the immediacy of temporal auto-affection; the blindness 'spaces': 'the proximity [of hearing-oneself-speak] is broken when, instead of hearing myself speak, I see myself write or gesture' (VP: 90/80). Space or what Derrida calls 'spacing,' *'espacement,'* (VP: 96/86) precedes temporalization. Spacing transforms the concept of immanence in two ways. On the one hand, by desubjectifying life, spacing frees immanence (which is life) from being immanent to consciousness; in turn both subject and object become dependent on immanence; and yet immanence is not a mixture since it includes, always, the minuscule hiatus. On the other hand, by desubjectifying immanence, spacing redefines the lived-experience as a process of dying (finitization). We can determine the 'sum' of the 'cogito sum' only as 'sum moribundus' (VP: 61/54–5) (Heidegger 1979b: 437; Eng. 1985: 316–17).

3. Conclusion: The Thought of the Outside

The relativity that Husserl uncovers is the source of all thinking in twentieth-century European (or Continental) philosophy. We can see the importance of this relativity when Heidegger, in *Being and Time*, defines existence (*Dasein*) as 'the being of the "between" that lies between subject and object' (Heidegger 1979a: 132; Eng. 1996: 21). Yet we can find a way *into* this relativity only through the phenomenological reduction. As Fink says, '[A]ll phenomenology goes through the reduction; a phenomenology that would reject it would be mundane and dogmatic' (Elveton 2000: 73–147). Fink's statement implies that, since contemporary analytic philosophy has nothing like the method of the reduction, since it never makes the presence of the objective world existing in itself as already there and absolute questionable, the use of the term 'phenomenology' in analytic philosophy has only a homonymic relation to the use of the term in Continental philosophy. Indeed, because analytic philosophers do not engage in the reduction, it is possible for them to develop bastard notions such 'objective phenomenology.' We must enter phenomenology through the reduction, which leads us to the presence of the subjective flow of lived-experience. But, since the reduction puts the meaning of existence in general in question, the reduction contains an imperative to conceive the flow of experience as genuinely different, no longer as the presence of consciousness. If we reject this imperative and conceive the flow of experience as consciousness, then we have copied the foundation – as if the foundation were a mirror image – off what is to be founded; we have copied the transcendental off the empirical. Here again Fink's thinking is crucial: at the beginning of the *Sixth Cartesian Meditation*, he argues that phenomenology must be dualist (Fink 1995: 20, 22). Although Fink formulates the dualism by means of analogy, the imperative of the reduction demands a formula not based in resemblance: the founded is *in* the foundation, but the foundation remains *in itself* and is *not* in what it founds. This formula is not one of justification; indeed, it is not one of justice. Rather, the reduction's imperative demands the relativity of injustice.

If we invoke Bergson here to help with the formula, it is because his thinking, like Husserl's, starts from lived-experience. But the Bergsonian duration is not merely subjective or conscious. What Bergson calls the 'turn' of experience in *Matter and Memory* (Bergson 1959: 321; Eng. 1994: 185) – the turn is his version of the phenomenological reduction – consists not in a reduction *to* consciousness but in a reduction *of* consciousness.

With Bergson, we have a reduction of the unity of consciousness ('the transcendence of the ego') to the multiplicity that defines the duration. The duration's multiplicity for Bergson goes as far up as the most spiritual form of memory and as far down as the most inert form of matter. Matter and memory, spirit and inertia, then, form for Bergson a dualism, but one that is itself supported by the duration's multiplicity, which is life itself. Yet, as Bergson himself would say, 'Let us go farther' ('*Allons plus loin*'). In the 'between' of the Bergsonian dualism, there is an extraordinary point at which inertia turns into spirit. This point is the '*écart infime*' that we mentioned above; it is the minuscule hiatus of blindness, of death, of nonpresence, the minuscule hiatus whose nonpresence produces in us only uncertainty and undecidability. The minuscule point is the 'unfold,' in which thinking is possible, indeed demanded, precisely because the point itself cannot be thought. Thinking based in the impossibility of thought turns thinking not into *doxa*, or *Urdoxa* (Deleuze 1995: 137)[4], but into *paradoxa*. Phenomenology then is left behind as thinking becomes no longer the thought of the *cogito*, but the thought of the outside.[5]

Notes

1. Hereafter cited as VP, with reference first to the French, then to the English translation. Throughout, I have modified the English translation and I have rendered the title of this book as *Voice and Phenomenon*.
2. Hereafter cited as Hua IX, with reference first to the German, then to the English translation. Throughout I have modified the English translation.
3. Derrida calls this difference *'différance.'* It is here that we have the entire problem of repetition and memory.
4. When Deleuze mentions *Urdoxa* here, he refers to Merleau-Ponty's *Phenomenology of Perception*. But Merleau-Ponty appropriates this idea from Husserl's *Experience and Judgment*. See Husserl 1973: para. 13.
5. We are taking this phrase from Michel Foucault. See Foucault 2001: Eng. trans. 1997.

References

Bergson, H. (1959), *Oeuvres*, Paris: Presses Universitaires de France; trans. N. M. Paul, and W. S. Palmer (1994), *Matter and Memory*, New York: Zone Books.

Deleuze, G. (1995), *Difference and Repetition*, trans. P. Patton, New York: Columbia University Press.

Derrida, J. [1967] (1983], *La voix et la phenomene*, Paris: Presses Universitaires de France; trans. D. B. Allison (1979), *Speech and Phenomena*, Evanston: Northwestern University Press.

Elveton, R. O. (2003), *The Phenomenolgy of Husserl: Selected Critical Readings*, Seattle: Noesis Press.

Fink, E. (1995), *Sixth Cartesian Meditation: The Idea of a Transcendental Theory of Method, with Textual Notations*, trans. R. Bruzina, Bloomington: Indiana University Press.

Foucault, M. (1994), *The Order of Things: An Archeology of the Human Sciences*, New York: Vintage.

Foucault, M. (2001), 'La pensee de dehors,' in M. Foucault (2001), *Dits et ecrits*, vol. 1, Paris: Gallimard, pp. 546–67; trans. B. Massumi (1997), 'The Thought from Outside,' in J. Mehlman, and B. Massumi (eds and trans.)

Gadamer, H.-G. (1987), *Foucault/Blanchot*, trans. J. Mehlman and B. Massumi, New York: Zone Books, pp. 7–60.

Gadamer, H.-G. (1989), *Truth and Method*, trans. J. Weinsheimer and D. G. Marshall, New York: Crossroad.

Heidegger, M. (1979a), *Sein und Zeit*, Tubingen: Max Niemeyer; trans. J. Stampbaugh (1996), *Being and Time*, Albany: State University of New York Press.

Heidegger, M. (1979b), *Gesamtausgabe II. Ableitung: Vorlesungen 1923–1944. Band. 20. Prolegomena zur Geschichte des Zeitbegriffs*, Frankfurt am Main: Klostermann; trans. T. Kiesal (1985), *The History of the Concept of Time*, Bloomington: Indiana University Press.

Husserl, E. (1954), *Die Krisis der Europaischen Wissenschaften and die transzendentale Phäno-menologie: Eine Einleitung in der phänomenologische Philosophie, Husserliana VI*, ed. W. Biemel, The Hague: Martinus Nijhof; trans. D. Carr (1970), *The Crisis of European Sciences and Transcendental Phenomenology: An Introduction to Phenomenologial Philosophy*, Evanston: Northwestern University Press.

Husserl, E. (1973), *Experience and Judgment*, trans. J. S. Churchill, and K. Ameriks, Evanston: Northwestern University Press.

Husserl, E. (1976a), *Hua IV: Phänomenologische Psychologie*, The Hague: Martinus Nijhoff; Eng. trans. R. E. Palmer (1997), *Edmund Husserl: Psychological and Transcendental Phenom-enology and the Confrontation with Heidegger 1927–1931*, ed. T. Sheehan and R. Palmer, Dordrecht: Kluwer.

Husserl, E. (1976b), *Hua III:1: Ideen zu einer reinen Phänomenologie und phänomenologischen Philosophie: Erstes Buch*, ed. K. Schuhmann, The Hague: Martinus Nijhoff; trans. F. Kersten (1982), *Ideas Pertaining to a Pure Phenomenology and to a Phenomenological Philosophy*, The Hague: Martinus Nijhoff.

Husserl, E. (1999), *The Essential Husserl: Basic Writings in Transcendental Phenomenology*, ed. D. Welton, Bloomington: Indiana University Press.

Lawlor, L. (2002), *Derrida and Husserl: The Basic Problem of Phenomenology*, Bloomington: Indiana University Press.

Merleau-Ponty, M. (2002), *Phenomenology of Perception*, trans. C. Smith, London: Routledge.

Ricoeur, P. (1987), *Husserl: An Analysis of his Phenomenology*, trans. E. G. Ballard, and L. Embree, Evanston: Northwestern University Press.

Sartre, J.-P. (1991), *The Transcendence of the Ego*, trans. F. Williams, and J. Kirkpatrick, New York: Hill and Wang.

Sokolowski, R. (1999), *Introduction to Phenomenology*, New York: Cambridge University Press.

Zahavi, D. (2003), *Husserl's Phenomenology*, Stanford: Stanford University Press.

Hermeneutics

Jean Grondin

Hermeneutics serves to characterize a broad current in contemporary Continental philosophy that deals with the issues of interpretation and stresses the historical and linguistic nature of our world-experience. In contemporary thought, it is mostly associated with the thinking of Hans-Georg Gadamer (1900–2002) and Paul Ricoeur (1913–2005), who situate themselves in the hermeneutic tradition of thinkers such as Wilhelm Dilthey (1833–1911) and Martin Heidegger (1889–1976). All these authors unfolded a distinct *philosophical* understanding of hermeneutics that drew on the more ancient tradition of hermeneutics, which was traditionally understood as an art of interpretation (*ars hermeneutica*, *Auslegungslehre*) that provided rules for the interpretation of sacred texts. Since the philosophical hermeneutics of the twentieth century was to a large extent a radicalization of and reaction to this older conception, it is with it that one must start.

1. Traditional Hermeneutics: The Art of Interpretation of Sacred Texts

Originally, hermeneutics was developed as an auxiliary discipline in the fields that dealt with the interpretation of canonical texts, that is, texts that contain authoritative meaning such as sacred or judicial texts. Hermeneutic rules were especially required when one was confronted with ambiguous passages of Scripture. Some of the most influential treatises in this regard were St Augustine's *De doctrina christiana* and Philipp Melanchton's *Rhetorics* (1519). Since most of these rules had to do with the nature of language, the major thinkers of the hermeneutic tradition, up until the nineteenth century, borrowed their guidelines from the then still very lively tradition of rhetorics, for example the requirement that ambiguous passages should be understood within their context, a rule that later gave rise to the notion of a 'hermeneutical circle' according to which the parts of a text should be comprehended out of the whole in which they stand, such as the whole of a book and its intent, of a literary genre, and of the work and life of an author. Supplying such rules, hermeneutics enjoyed a normative or regulatory function for the interpretation of canonical texts. A specific hermeneutics was developed for the Bible (*hermeneutica sacra*), for law (*hermeneutica juris*), and for classical texts (*hermeneutica profana*).

The German theologian Friedrich Schleiermacher (1768–1834) is a foremost example of this tradition, but also an author who points to a more philosophical and universal understanding of hermeneutics, and in at least two ways: (1) At the beginning of his lectures on hermeneutics, which were published posthumously by his pupil Friedrich Lücke (1791–1855) in 1838, he bemoans that there are many special hermeneutics, but that hermeneutics does not yet exist as a general or universal discipline, that is, as an art (*Kunst, Kunstlehre*) of understanding itself that would establish binding rules for all forms of interpretation; (2) Schleiermacher further laments that hermeneutics has hitherto only consisted of a vague collection of dislocated guidelines. Hermeneutical rules, he urges in *Hermeneutics and Criticism*, should become 'more methodical' (*mehr Methode*). A more rigorous methodology of understanding could enable the interpreter 'to understand the authors as well or even better than they understood themselves,' claims Schleiermacher in a well-known dictum.

2. Dilthey: Hermeneutics as the Methodological Basis of the Human Sciences

Most familiar with the thinking and life of Schleiermacher, of whom he was the biographer, Dilthey devoted his life-work to the challenge of a foundation of the human sciences (*Geisteswissenschaften*). Whereas the exact sciences had already received, in the wake of Immanuel Kant's *Critique of Pure Reason*, a philosophical basis and a methodology guaranteeing the validity of their knowledge, the human sciences still lacked such a foundation. Under the motto of a 'Critique of historical reason,' Dilthey sought a logical, epistemological, and methodological foundation for the human sciences. Without such a foundation, their own scientific legitimacy would remain in jeopardy: is everything in the human sciences merely subjective, historically relative, and, as we tend to say, but with a touch of derision, a mere matter of interpretation? If these areas of our knowledge are to entertain any scientific credibility, Dilthey argued, they need to rest on a sound methodology.

In some of his later texts (most notably in his essay 'The Rise of Hermeneutics,' 1900), Dilthey sought such a methodical basis for the humanities in hermeneutics, the old discipline of text interpretation that could receive renewed actuality in light of this new challenge. His argument was almost syllogistic: all human sciences are sciences of interpretation; the traditional theory of interpretation has been developed under the title of hermeneutics; therefore hermeneutics could serve as the bedrock of all human sciences. It could thus be called upon to fulfill a need that arises out of the emergence of historical conscience and threatens the validity of historical knowledge. Even if it remains largely programmatic in his later texts, the idea that hermeneutics could serve as a universal foundation of the human sciences bestowed upon hermeneutics a philosophical relevance and visibility that it never really enjoyed before Dilthey. Up to this day, important thinkers such as Emilio Betti and E. D. Hirsch look to hermeneutics to deliver a methodical foundation for the truth claim of the humanities, the literary, and the juridical disciplines. According to them, a hermeneutics that would relinquish this task would miss the point of what hermeneutics is all about.

But there was an idea in Dilthey's program that carried the bulk of the hermeneutic tradition in a rather different direction. It is the insight that the understanding developed in the humanities is nothing but the unfolding of a quest of understanding that characterizes human and historical life as such. Life articulates itself, Dilthey says, in manifold forms of expression (*Ausdruck*) that our understanding seeks to penetrate by recreating the inner life-experience (*Erlebnis*) out of which they sprang. Dilthey's far-reaching intuition is that interpretation and understanding are not processes that occur simply in the human sciences but that they are constitutive of our quest for orientation. The notion that historical life is as such hermeneutical, that is, interpretive to the core was only buttressed by Friedrich Nietzsche's (1844–1900) contemporaneous reflections on the interpretive nature of our world-experience. 'There are no facts, only interpretations,' declared Nietzsche in Fragment 481 of *The Will to Power*. This first glimpse of the potential universality of the 'hermeneutic universe' appeared to call into question Dilthey's dream of a methodical foundation of the human sciences, but it raised a new hermeneutic task.

3. Heidegger's Hermeneutics of Existence

Seizing upon this idea that life is intrinsically interpretative, the early Heidegger spoke of a 'hermeneutical intuition' as early as 1919. It was his teacher Edmund Husserl (1859–1938) who had reinstated the urgency and legitimacy of primal 'intuition' in philosophy. But Heidegger revealed himself a reader of Dilthey when he stressed that every intuition is hermeneutical. That meant for him that it is always motivated and replete with anticipations and expectations. Understanding is not first and foremost a cognitive inquiry that the human sciences would methodically refine, it is our primary means of orientation in the world. It is this primary level of 'facticity' that interests Heidegger. Our factual life is involved in this will ('being there': *Dasein*, as he would later put it) by ways of understanding. Relying here on the German expression '*sich auf etwas verstehen*,' which means 'to know one's way about,' 'to be able,' Heidegger puts a new twist on the notion of understanding by viewing it less as an intellectual undertaking than as an ability. It is more akin to a 'know-how,' and it always involves a possibility of myself: the verb form '*sich verstehen*' ('understanding oneself at something') is reflective in German. 'Understanding' is not primarily the reconstruction of the meaning of an expression (as in classical hermeneutics and Dilthey); it always entails the projecting, and self-projecting, of a possibility of my own existence. There is no understanding without projection or anticipations.

We are factually (*faktisch*) thrown into existence as finite beings, in a world that we will never fully master. Chronically insecure about anything, yet tormentingly sure of its mortality, human facticity seeks ways to cope, to make do. This anxiety for our own being is for Heidegger the source and sting of understanding. Overwhelmed by existence and confronted with our mortality, we project ourselves in ways of intelligibility and reason, that help us keep things in check for a while. Every mode of understanding is related to this concernedness of our facticity or our 'being there' (*Dasein*) in this overwhelming world. A momentous shift in the focus of hermeneutics has silently taken place in the work of Heidegger: hermeneutics is less concerned with texts or a certain type of science, as was the case in the entire previous history of hermeneutics, but with existence itself and its quest of understanding.

It is this dramatic notion of hermeneutics and understanding that the early Heidegger first developed in his early lecture course on the 'Hermeneutics of Facticity' (1923), that has only been recently published and plays an important role in contemporary discussions of hermeneutics. The title 'Hermeneutics of Facticity' is to be understood in the two directions of the genitive (subjective and objective). There is, first, a hermeneutics that intrinsically belongs to facticity itself (*genitivus subjectivus*): facticity is hermeneutical because it is: (1) capable of interpretation; (2) desperately in need of it; and (3) always already thrives on some interpretations that are more or less explicit, but that can be spelled out (Heidegger 1999: 11). This leads, secondly, to the more philosophical meaning of the program of a hermeneutics of facticity following the lines of a *genitivus objectivus*: it is precisely with this hermeneutic condition that a hermeneutical theory is concerned. Its intention is, however, by no means merely theoretical. Quite the contrary, it is to contribute to a self-awakening of facticity or *Dasein*: it hopes to 'make it accessible to itself' by 'hunting down the alienation from itself with which it is smitten' (Heidegger 1999: 11).

This rising program was carried over in Heidegger's main work *Being and Time* (1927), but with some slight modifications (Grondin 2003). While it remained obvious that human facticity is forgetful of itself and its interpretive nature, and possibilities, the focus clearly shifted to the question of Being as such. The primary theme of hermeneutics is less the immediate facticity of our Being in this world, than the fact that the presuppositions of the understanding of Being remain hidden in a tradition that needs to be reopened (or 'destroyed,' as Heidegger puts it). Such a hermeneutics still aims at a self-awakening of existence, but it does so by promising to sort out the fundamental structures of our understanding of Being.

These structures, the rest of the work argues, are temporal in nature (hence the title *Being and Time*) and have everything to do with the inauthentic or authentic carrying through of our existence. Heidegger's later philosophy, while relinquishing the notion of hermeneutics as such, nonetheless radicalised this idea by claiming that our understanding of Being is brought about by the event of an overbearing history of Being that commands all our interpretations. Postmodern readings of Heidegger (Michel Foucault, Gianni Vattimo, Richard Rorty, Jacques Derrida) drew relativistic conclusions out of this shift of hermeneutics toward the history of Being. Hence, the tendency, in recent debates, to amalgamate hermeneutics and postmodernism, a tendency that the hermeneutics of Gadamer seems both to encourage and to combat – an apparent inconsistency that we must now try to understand.

4. Gadamer's Hermeneutics of the Event of Understanding

Hans-Georg Gadamer's project is strongly influenced by Heidegger, but in his masterpiece *Truth and Method* (1960), his starting-point is undoubtedly provided by Dilthey's hermeneutical inquiry into the methodology of the human sciences (a notion of hermeneutics Heidegger had dismissed as derivative from the vantage-point of his more radical hermeneutics of existence). While taking anew the dialogue with the human sciences and the open question of their claim to truth, Gadamer calls into question the premise of Dilthey according to which the experience of truth in the

humanities depends on method. In seeking a methodological foundation that alone
could guarantee their scientific or objective status, Dilthey subjected, Gadamer argues,
the humanities to the model of the exact sciences and would thus have forfeited the
specificity of the humanities, where the involvement of the interpreter is constitutive
of the experience of meaning: the texts that we interpret are texts that say something to
us and that are always understood, in some way, out of our questions and 'prejudices.' The
drawing of the interpreter into the 'event' of meaning, as Gadamer likes to put it, can only
be deemed detrimental from the model of objectivity heralded by the natural sciences.
Instead of relying on this methodological notion of objectivity, the human sciences would
do well to understand their contribution to knowledge out of the somewhat forgotten
tradition of humanism and the importance it bestowed upon the notion of *Bildung*
(formation and education). The humanities do not seek to master an object that stands at a
distance (as is the case with the exact sciences), their aim is rather to develop and form the
human spirit. The truth one experiences in the encounter with major texts and history is
one that transforms us, taking us up in the event of meaning itself.

Gadamer finds the most revealing model for this type of understanding in the
experience of art since we are always involved, absorbed, as it were, by the presentation
of an art-work, which Gadamer understands as the revelation of the truth or the
essence of something: a play reveals something about the meaning of existence, just as a
portrait reveals the true essence of someone. Yet it is a truth-experience in which we
partake, in that it can only unfold through a process of interpretation. This notion of
interpretation plays, of course, a crucial role for Gadamer and hermeneutics generally,
but in the case of Gadamer, it is to be understood, first and foremost, out of the arts we
call the 'arts of interpretation' or the 'performative arts': just as a piece of music must
be interpreted by, for example, the violinist (that is, never arbitrarily, but with a leeway
that has to be filled by the virtuosity of interpretation), a drama by the actors or the
ballet by the dancers, a book must be interpreted through the process of reading and a
picture must be contemplated by the eye of the beholder. It is only in this presentation
(*Darstellung* or *Vollzug*) of a meaning to someone, a performance which is always an
interpretation, that meaning comes to be realized. One notices here that 'interpretation' refers both to the interpretation of a work of art by the performers and to the
interpretation of the 'spectators' themselves who attend the performance and cannot
but also 'interpret' the piece.

The difference between the two forms of interpretation is less important for
Gadamer than the fact that the experience of meaning, and the truth experience it
brings out, essentially require the productive implication of the interpreter. The same
holds, according to Gadamer, for the interpretation of a text or a historical event, even
in the scientific context of the human sciences. The point is that interpretation is not
the simple recreation of a meaning that always remains the same and can be
methodically verified, nor, for that matter, the subjective, and potentially relativistic,
bestowing of meaning from the outside upon an objective reality (because the reality to
be understood can only be reached through a renewed attempt of understanding). In
other words: to claim that interpretation is relativistic on the grounds that it implies
the subjectivity of the interpreter is to miss what the humanities and the experience of
meaning are all about.

The objectivistic model of the exact sciences is ill-equipped to do justice to this experience of meaning. Distance, methodical verification, and independence from the observer, Gadamer concludes, are not the sole conditions of knowledge. When we understand, we do not only, nor primarily follow a methodical procedure, we are 'taken up ', as the art experience illustrates, by the meaning that 'seizes' us, as it were. The instrumental sounding idea of procedure is somewhat suspect for Gadamer: understanding is more of an event than a procedure. 'Understanding and Event' is indeed one of the original titles Gadamer thought about for his major work, before settling on 'Truth and Method,' which underlines the very same point: that truth is not only a matter of method and can never be entirely detached from our concerns.

But these concerns come to us from a tradition and a history that are more often than not opaque to consciousness. Every understanding stands in the stream of a *Wirkungsgeschichte* or 'effective history,' in which the horizons of the past and the present coalesce. Understanding thus entails a 'fusion of horizons' between the past and the present, which is at the same time a fusion between the interpreter, with all the history silently at work in his understanding, and his object. This fusion is not to be viewed as an autonomous operation of subjectivity, but as an event of tradition (*Überlieferungsgeschehen*) in the course of which a meaning from the past comes to be applied to the present.

This leads *Truth and Method* to suggest that the best model for the humanities was perhaps offered by the practical disciplines that had been traditionally preoccupied with the questions of interpretation such as juridical and theological hermeneutics, insofar as the meaning that is to be understood in these fields is one that has to be applied to a given situation. In the same way a judge has to apply creatively a text of law to a particular case and a preacher has to apply a text of Scripture to the situation of his congregation, every act of understanding, Gadamer contends, involves an effort of 'application' of what is understood to the present. Gadamer does not mean by this that one first has to understand a meaning of a text or a historical event, and then apply it to a given situation by bestowing new 'relevance' upon it. His idea is rather that every understanding is at its root an application of meaning, where our experience and background are brought to bear. This 'application' is by no means a conscious procedure. It always happens in the course of understanding to the extent that interpretation brings into play the situation and 'prejudices' of the interpreter, which are less 'his' or 'hers' than the ones carved by the effective history in which we all stand.

Gadamer expands on this idea by comparing understanding to a process of translation. 'I understand something' means that I can translate it into my own words, thus applying it to my situation. Any meaning I can relate to is one that is translated into a meaning I can articulate. It is not only important to underline the obvious fact that translation always implies an act of interpretation (a translator is also called in English an interpreter), but even more so to stress that this interpretation is by no means arbitrary: it is bound by the meaning it seeks to render, but it can only do so by translating it into a language where it can speak anew. What occurs in the process of translation is thus a fusion of horizons between the foreign meaning and its interpretation-translation in a new language, horizon, and situation, where the meaning resonates.

Truth and Method draws on this insight to highlight the fundamentally linguistic nature of understanding. Understanding is always an act of developing something into words, and I only understand, Gadamer argues, to the extent that I seek (and find) words to express this understanding. Understanding is not a process that could be separated from its linguistic unfolding: to think, to understand, is to seek words for that which strives to be understood. There is a crucial fusion between the process of interpretation and its linguistic formulation. It is not only the fusion of horizons that interests Gadamer in his hermeneutics of language. His thesis goes indeed even further: not only is the process of interpreting linguistically oriented, what it seeks to understand is also language. Language also determines the object of understanding itself. Any reality I have access to is linguistically couched.

Here, there occurs a fusion between the 'process' of understanding and its 'object' in the sense that no object can be separated from the attempt to understand it. Gadamer's famous phrase to express this fusion between the object and the process of under-standing itself is: 'Being that can be understood is language.' This simple, yet enigmatic dictum can be read in two quite different directions: it can mean, and in the light of Gadamer's unmistakable stress on the historical nature of understanding first seems to mean, that every experience of Being is mediated by language, and thus by a historical and cultural horizon (negatively put: 'There is no experience of Being without a historical understanding or language'). This would seem to draw Gadamer into the 'relativistic camp.'

It is striking to note, however, that Gadamer always resisted this merely relativistic appropriation of his thought. His aim is not primarily to insist on the fact that 'Being' is always appropriated by language or some language. In this understanding, the stress would lay on the instrumental aspect of language that would somehow 'color' Being (by imposing upon it a 'subjective' perspective). Gadamer sees in this an instrumental and very modern understanding of language. This has been overlooked by postmodern readers of Gadamer, but in his dictum 'Being that can be understood is language,' the stress has to be put on Being itself. What Gadamer hopes to say by this is that the effort of understanding is, in a way, ordained to the language of the things themselves. A difficult and unpalatable notion for postmodernism, to be sure, but one that is essential to Gadamer's hermeneutics: language is not only the subjective, say, contingent translation of meaning, it is also the event by which Being itself comes to light. Our language is not only 'our' language, it is also, and more originally, the language of Being itself, the way in which Being presents itself to our understanding. This is why, when one speaks and interprets, one cannot say everything one fancies. One is bound by something like the language of the thing. What is this language? Difficult to say since we can only approach it through *our* language, and the language of tradition, but it is nevertheless the instance that resists too unilateral or too violent readings of this Being. It is this language of Being that I seek to understand, and to the extent that understanding succeeds, a fusion of horizons has happened, a fusion between Being and understanding, an event I do not master, but in which I partake.

5. Gadamer's Critics: Betti, Habermas, Ricoeur, Vattimo, Rorty, and Derrida

The history of hermeneutics after Gadamer can be read as a history of the debates provoked by *Truth and Method* (even though this perspective does not do justice to major figures of the hermeneutical tradition, such as Paul Ricoeur). It can be presented only in a very sketchy manner in what follows.

E. Betti and E. D. Hirsch

Some of the first responses to Gadamer were sparked by the methodological notion of hermeneutics that prevailed in the tradition of Dilthey. After all, it had been the dominant conception of hermeneutics until Gadamer (with the sole, albeit very peculiar, exception of Heidegger's 'hermeneutics of existence,' that had left behind the older hermeneutic tradition, which had been concerned with text interpretation and the human sciences). Gadamer who, in spite of his Heideggerian roots, took his starting-point in Dilthey's inquiry into the truth claim of the humanities, he was often seen, and criticized, out of this tradition. In 1962, Emilio Betti, the Italian jurist who had published a voluminous *General Theory of Interpretation* (in Italian) in 1955, which was intended as a methodical foundation of the humanities in the Dilthey tradition, vigorously criticized Gadamer's seeming rejection of the methodological paradigm. If Gadamer's own 'method' for the humanities consisted in saying that we just have to follow our own prejudices, it had to be condemned as a perversion of the very idea of hermeneutics. Betti, who was followed in this regard by E. D. Hirsch in America, opposed the relativistic idea that interpretation always entails an essential element of application to the present. Surely, texts do acquire different meanings or relevance in the course of their reception, but we have to distinguish the actuality or significance (*Bedeutsamkeit*) thus garnered from the original meaning (*Bedeutung*) of the texts, that is the meaning of the text in the mind of its author (*mens auctoris*), which remains the focus of hermeneutics.

Habermas and the Critique of Ideologies

Coming from the Frankfurt School of social criticism, Jürgen Habermas hailed, for his part, this element of application in understanding, claiming that knowledge is always guided by some interests. This hermeneutical insight, he believed, could help free the social sciences, spearheaded by psychoanalysis and the critique of ideology, from an all too objectivistic understanding of knowledge and science. Hermeneutics teaches us, according to Habermas, that our understanding and practices are always motivated and linguistically articulated. It was Gadamer's too strong insistence on tradition and the role of authority in understanding that Habermas opposed. He faulted it for being 'conservative,' a devastating argument in the climate of the time, to be sure. Habermas's lasting point is that language can also transcend its own limits, following an idea that he discovered in Gadamer, but turned against him: when Gadamer said that our experience of the world was linguistic, he also stressed, for Habermas, that it is 'porous,' that is, susceptible to self-correction, and that it could, to some extent, overcome its own limitations (by seeking better expressions or dissolving its own rigidity) and was thus open to any meaning that could be understood. Habermas and Karl-Otto Apel drew from this self-transcendence of language the important notion of a linguistic or communicative rationality, which is laden with universalistic assumptions that can form the basis of an ethical theory and indeed an open society.

Paul Ricoeur

Ricoeur tried to build a bridge – a most hermeneutical task and virtue in itself – between Habermas and Gadamer, by claiming both authors had stressed different, but complementary elements in the tension that is inherent to understanding: whereas Gadamer underlined the belongingness of the interpreter to his object and his tradition, Habermas took heed of the reflective distance from it. Understanding, viewed as application, does not only have to appropriate naively its subject matter, it can stand at a critical distance from it, a distance that is already given by the fact that the *interpretandum* is an objectified text. This notion of a hermeneutics that seeks to decipher objectivations came mainly from Dilthey, but Ricoeur used it in a productive manner in his decisive confrontations with psychoanalysis (Sigmund Freud) and structuralism (Claude Lévi-Strauss). He linked them to a 'hermeneutics of suspicion,' that is most useful, and indeed essential, he argued, in that it can help us get rid of superstition and false understanding. But such a hermeneutics can only be conducted in the hope of a better and more critical understanding of understanding. A 'hermeneutics of trust' thus remains the ultimate focus of his work: the meaning we seek to understand is one that helps us better understand our world and ourselves. We will return to Ricoeur's hermeneutics below.

Postmodernism (Vattimo and Rorty)

Betti, Hirsch, and Habermas all faulted Gadamer and his hermeneutics for being too 'relativistic' (that is, too reliant on tradition). Postmodernism went, to some degree, in an opposite direction: it welcomed Gadamer's alleged 'relativism' but only believed it did not go far enough. Gadamer would have been incoherent in not acknowledging fully the relativistic consequences of his hermeneutics. To understand this shift in the hermeneutical debates (Gadamer too relativistic for some, not enough for others), it is important to note that authors such as Heidegger (especially the later Heidegger) and Nietzsche play a paramount role for postmodernist thinkers (by comparison, Betti, Hirsch, Habermas, and Ricoeur were all rather hostile to Heidegger and Nietzsche). We think, in this regard, of the Nietzsche who said that there are no facts, only interpretations, or of the Heidegger who claimed that our understanding was framed by the history of Being. The postmodernists lumped this Nietzschean-Heideggerian outlook together with Gadamer's: (1) seeming critique of scientific objectivity; (2) stress on the prejudices of interpretation; and (3) insistence on the linguistic nature of understanding. Stressing these elements, that could only be radicalized from a Nietzschean-Heideggerian backdrop, hermeneutics, they believed, jettisoned the idea of an objective truth. There would be no such thing, given the interpretive and

linguistic nature of our experience. This led Gianni Vattimo to 'nihilistic' consequences (we don't believe in objective truth any more, only in the virtues of tolerance
and charity) and Richard Rorty to a renewed form of pragmatism: some interpretations
are more useful or amenable than others, but none can per se be claimed to be 'closer'
to the Truth. In the name of tolerance and mutual understanding, we have to accept
the plurality of interpretations; it is only the notion that there is only one valid one that
would be harmful.

Derrida's Deconstruction

Derrida can also be seen in the 'postmodern' tradition, since he too depends heavily on
the later Heidegger and Nietzsche, stresses the linguistic nature of our experience, and
also urges a 'deconstructive' attitude toward tradition, and more specifically the
tradition of metaphysics that governs our thinking, an attitude that Paul Ricoeur would
surely, and rightly, classify in the 'hermeneutics of suspicion.' But his deconstruction
does not directly take the path of the pragmatist tradition of Rorty or the nihilism of
Vattimo. Despite the Heideggerian origins of his notion of deconstruction and his pan-
linguisticism, Derrida does not identify himself with the tradition of hermeneutics
either. His 'deconstruction' is indeed distrustful of any form of hermeneutics, and for
an important reason: every understanding, he contends, would involve or hide a form
of 'appropriation' of the other and its otherness. In his discussion with Gadamer in
1981, he challenged Gadamer's rather commonplace assumption that understanding
implies the goodwill to understand the other. What about this will? asked Derrida. Is it
not chained to the will to dominate that is emblematic of our metaphysical and
Western philosophical tradition? Hence Derrida's mistrust of the hermeneutical drive
to understand (and thus perhaps violently absorb) the other and of the hermeneutic
claim to universality. Gadamer was touched by this criticism to the extent that he
claimed that understanding implied some form of application, which can indeed be
read as a form of appropriation. This is perhaps the reason why, in his later writings, he
underlined even more forcefully the open nature of the hermeneutical experience.
'The soul of hermeneutics,' he then said, 'is that the other can be right.'

6. Ricoeur's Hermeneutics of the Historical Self

Paul Ricoeur is besides Gadamer the other major figure of the hermeneutic philosophy
of the twentieth century. Yet his hermeneutic trajectory is quite different and mostly
independent from Gadamer's, since it goes back to his philosophy of the will first
published in 1950, his hermeneutics of religious symbols (1960) and his reading of
Freud that appeared in 1965 (*On Interpretation. An Essay on Freud*, one of his most
famous books). Moreover, his hermeneutic conception is spread out over a wide range
of important books that span more than half a century: after his *Philosophy of the Will*
(vol. 1, 1950; vol. 2: 1960), he wrote on historical understanding (*History and Truth*,
1955), then *The Conflict of Interpretations. Essays on Hermeneutics I* (1969), *The Rule of
Metaphor* (1975), *Time and Narrative* (3 vols, 1983–5), *From Text to Action, Essays on
Hermeneutics II* (1987), *Oneself as Another* (1990), *Memory, History and Forgetfulness*

(2000), and lately *On Recognition* (2004). His incredibly rich hermeneutics thus encompasses the fields of text and biblical interpretation (his starting point), psycho-analysis, linguistic theory and action theory (both mostly understood out of analytic philosophy), ethics, historical consciousness and the phenomenology of time, memory and thankfulness. A breathtaking and impressive path, with many detours (a herme-neutic virtue for Ricoeur) devoted to large-scale historical inquiries, but that makes it at times arduous for some to pinpoint the core of his hermeneutical theory. It is easier to sort out in the case of Gadamer or Heidegger since their conception was for the main part developed in a single work, *Truth and Method* and *Being and Time*, that can be read as coherent hermeneutic projects. It is perhaps for this reason that Ricoeur's hermeneutics, while largely discussed in the vast field of the human sciences, has sparked less momentous *philosophical* debates than was the case with Gadamer's hermeneutics, where the debates with Betti, Habermas, Rorty, Vattimo, and Derrida form an indelible part of his *Wirkungsgeschichte* or legacy. In a way, Ricoeur's hermeneutics has yet to be appreciated to its full and justified merit. This is also why we choose to end this survey with a sketch of his contribution to hermeneutics.

The lack of a totalizing hermeneutic theory is by no means an accident in the case of Ricoeur. In the name of the finitude and the open nature of historical understanding, he steadfastly resists such a 'Hegelian' totalization. Yet we can ask, and have to ask in the scope of this presentation, wherein lies the guiding thread of Ricoeur's herme-neutics? To answer this unavoidable question sparked by such a wide-ranging oeuvre, we can find guidance in some later autobiographical texts that Ricoeur wrote on his own philosophical journey, such as his essay 'On Interpretation,' published in the volume *Philosophy in France Today* (1993) and in the self-presentation he wrote for the Library of Living Philosophers volume on *The Philosophy of Paul Ricoeur* (1995).

In these texts, Ricoeur recalls how his philosophy grew out of the French tradition of 'reflective philosophy,' that was developed, in the footsteps of Ravaisson, Lachelier and Bergson, by authors such as Jean Nabert, Gabriel Marcel and the personalist philosopher Emmanuel Mounier. A reflective outlook means that philosophy has to start with the self-reflection of the ego, in the tradition of Socrates's 'know thyself,' Augustine and Descartes. It was this reflective tradition that later drew Ricoeur to the existentialism of Jaspers and the phenomenology of Husserl, since this tradition also took its starting-point in the thinking ego. Ricoeur's 'hermeneutical turn' (or what he also called his 'graft' of hermeneutics upon phenomenology) came out of the realization, first spelled out in his *Symbolic of Evil* (1960), that the self cannot know itself directly, through some kind of introspection, but only through the detour of the symbols that attempt to make sense of its experience, and more specifically of the experience of evil. The self can only understand itself through the detour of the interpretation of symbols. Dilthey's hermeneutics served here as a model for Ricoeur since it was also devoted to the interpretation of expressions or objectivations and animated by an epistemological quest for objectivity. Ricoeur was fully aware that Heidegger wanted to go beyond Dilthey when he developed a hermeneutics of existence centered on the question of Being. Ricoeur resisted this 'ontologization' of hermeneutics (and the totalization it would entail) and kept the focus instead on the (epistemological, but also existential) challenge that is posed to the self by what he calls the 'conflict of interpretations,' that is, the challenge of concurring views of the self and the act of interpretation itself. As alluded to above, he distinguishes between two distinct approaches of interpretation: a hermeneutics of suspicion, that is suspicious of meaning as it gives itself and that it traces back to a hidden economy (a hermeneutics heralded by Nietzsche, Freud, the critique of ideologies of Marx and their numerous followers), and a hermeneutics of trust that takes meaning as it gives itself and as it guides consciousness. Lessons are to be learned from both, Ricoeur insists: a responsible consciousness must be wary of the false delusions of meaning, but it can only do so in order to understand itself better, even if it has to relinquish the hope of finally finding itself once and for all (hence the unavoidably tragic dimension of human understanding for Ricoeur). This explains why Ricoeur devoted so much attention to the hermeneutical challenge raised by psychoanalysis (Freud), structuralism (Lévi-Strauss) and the objectifying understanding of meaning. They cannot be dismissed out of hand, since they provide consciousness with fundamental insights by warning the *cogito* of the dangers of a merely reflective grasp of its own self. The mirror of reflection is a troubled one and cannot be naively followed. The self that comes out of this hermeneutics of distrust is undoubtedly an injured or 'broken *cogito*,' Ricoeur writes. Yet, it remains a *cogito* that cannot but strive for understanding. But this understanding has to be gained from the objectivations of meaning as it is handed down to us in the grand myths, texts, and narratives of mankind. Through them, the historical and broken self seeks to recognize meaning to its extension in time, while being always aware of its tragic condition. In the last part of *Time and Narrative*, Ricoeur unfolded an impressive hermeneutics of historical consciousness that is reminiscent of Gadamer, but that develops more forcefully than *Truth and Method* a notion of the 'capable human' ('*homme capable*'), which highlights the limited, but nonetheless real possibilities of understanding, action and self-affirmation that the striving self enjoys in spite of its historical condition. This leads to an important ethical bent in Ricoeur's later works: he presented a courageous 'small ethics' in *Oneself as Another* (1990), out of which he later developed a theory of justice (*The Just*, 2000). But when we encompass his philosophical journey as a whole, this was less a shift on his itinerary than a continuation of or a return to his earlier ethical philosophy of the will that has learned decisive lessons from the hermeneutics of distrust. This hermeneutics destroys once and for all the false illusions of a total and transparent knowledge of ourselves, but it does not lead to a form of fatalist resignation. On the contrary, it helps us rediscover the resourcefulness and ethical possibilities of the 'capable self' in light of the evil that threatens it. In retrospect, Ricoeur's complex hermeneutical itinerary appears as a most coherent path with the brightest future.

References

Betti, Emilio [1962] (1980), 'Hermeneutics as the General Methodology of the Geisteswissenschaften,' in J. Bleicher (ed.) (1980), *Contemporary Hermeneutics: Hermeneutics as Method, Philosophy and Critique*, London, and Boston: Routledge and Kegan Paul, pp. 51–94.

Dilthey, W. (1996), *Hermeneutics and the Study of History: Selected Works*, ed. R. A. Makkreel, and F. Rodi, vol. 4, Princeton: Princeton University Press.

Dostal, R. (ed.) (2002), *The Cambridge Companion to Gadamer*, Cambridge: Cambridge University Press.

Gadamer, H.-G. (1976), *Philosophical Hermeneutics*, trans. D. E. Linge, Berkeley, and London: University of California Press.

Gadamer, H.-G. [1960] (1989), *Truth and Method*, trans. J. Weinsheimer, and Donald G. Marschall, New York: Crossroad.

Grondin, J. (1994), *Introduction to Philosophical Hermeneutics*, New Haven: Yale University Press.

Grondin, J. (2003), *Le tournant herméneutique de la phénoménologie*, Paris: Presses Universitaires de France.

Habermas, J. [1967] (1977), 'A Review of Gadamer's Truth and Method,' in F. R. Dallmayr, and T. A. McCarthy (eds) (1977), *Understanding and Social Inquiry*, Notre Dame: University of Notre Dame Press, pp. 181–211.

Habermas, J. (1980), 'The Hermeneutic Claim to Universality', in J. Bleicher (ed.) (1980), *Contemporary Hermeneutics*, London: Routledge and Kegan Paul, pp. 335–63.

Heidegger, M. [1923] (1999), *Ontology – The Hermeneutics of Facticity* [1923], trans. J. v. Buren, Bloomington: Indiana University Press.

Heidegger, M. [1927] (1962), *Being and Time*, trans. J. Macquarrie, and E. Robinson, New York: Harper.

Hirsch, E. D. (1967), *Validity in Interpretation*, New Haven: Yale University Press.

Michelfelder, P., and R. E. Palmer (eds) (1989), *Dialogue and Deconstruction. The Gadamer-Derrida Encounter*, New York: State University of New York Press.

Palmer, R. E. (1969), *Hermeneutics. Interpretation Theory in Schleiermacher, Dilthey, Heidegger, and Gadamer*, Evanston: Northwestern University Press.

Ricoeur, P. [1960] (1970), *Freud and Philosophy: An Essay on Interpretation*, trans. D. Savage, New Haven: Yale University Press.

Ricoeur, Paul [1987] (1991), *From Text to Action. Essays in Hermeneutics*, trans. K. Blamey, and J. B. Thompson, Evanston: Northwestern University Press.

Ricoeur, P. [1983–5] (1984, 1985, 1988), *Time and Narrative*, 3 vols. trans. K. McLaughlin, and D. Pellauer, Chicago: University of Chicago Press.

Rorty, R. (1979), *Philosophy and the Mirror of Nature*, Princeton: Princeton University Press.

Schleiermacher, F. D. E. (1998), *Hermeneutics and Criticism and Other Writings*, ed. A. Bowie, New York: Cambridge University Press.

Vattimo, G. (1997), *Beyond Interpretation: The Meaning of Hermeneutics for Philosophy*, trans. D. Webb, Cambridge: Polity Press.

Existentialism

William L. McBride

The word 'existentialism' became widely used to identify a major movement of twentieth-century thought during the mid-1940s, immediately following the end of World War II. It had, it is true, already been employed by some philosophers: Gabriel Marcel, a committed Christian thinker, had made use of the language of existentialism in the 1920s; the Italian Nicola Abbagnano had elaborated a version of it in his *La struttura dell'esistenza* (1939); and in the form of *Existenzphilosophie*, for which 'existential philosophy' was regarded by many as the most suitable English translation, it had been appropriated by both Martin Heidegger and Karl Jaspers. The latter had acknowledged both the theist, Søren Kierkegaard, and the explorer of the implications of the 'death of God,' Friedrich Nietzsche, as nineteenth-century existentialist ancestors.

Nevertheless, it was primarily in connection with the Parisian left-bank intellectual circle centered around Jean-Paul Sartre that existentialism achieved the status of at once a philosophical position and a popular fad. As magazine articles about it, often wildly distortive as one might expect, proliferated, its supposed adherents were alternately admired as convention-flouting adventurers of the mind (as well as in real life), and denounced as moral degenerates preoccupied with slime and filth. The epithet, *'espèce d'existentialiste'*, came into common usage, and it was not intended as a compliment. Marcel, who had once encouraged Sartre further to develop his ideas after the latter had read a paper at one of the older philosopher's periodic intellectual soirées, came to regard his philosophy as dangerously seductive especially to the younger generation, and as a consequence distanced himself from the 'existentialist' label. And after Sartre, seeking to capitalize on his enormous new prominence but also to correct what he considered particularly egregious misapprehensions, gave a lecture entitled 'Existentialism is a Humanism' to an overflow audience in late 1945 and then agreed, somewhat reluctantly and to his later regret, to have this popularized and greatly simplified version of his thinking published, it was Heidegger's turn to proclaim his distance. The latter's 'Letter on Humanism', originally written in December 1946 (in Heidegger 1977) as a response to a query from his French translator, Jean Beaufret, asking what he thought about Sartre's claims, revealed deep disagreements. Even Albert Camus, who in histories of thought is more often than not treated, with good reason, as an existentialist, and who had ties with Sartre for a decade until a dramatic public quarrel separated them permanently, had already distinguished 'existentialist' from 'absurdist' thinkers in his *The Myth of Sisyphus* (1942), identifying himself as an 'absurdist.'

It is important to take note of these deep differences from the start, in order to avoid any temptation to regard existentialism as a monolithic movement, or 'existentialist' as an univocal label. On the other hand, it would also be a mistake to despair of all efforts to delineate it. Although Heidegger's early philosophy, elaborated at greatest length in his *Being and Time* (1927), obviously anticipated Sartre's more derivative *Being and Nothingness* (1943), it seems more appropriate, from an expository point of view, to concentrate on the latter work and related writings as best capturing existentialist thought at the height of its influence. Heidegger, whose work has undergone a recent re-examination and a certain revival, but one in which the old 'existentialist' label has played a minor role and been rejected as apt for him by many commentators, can then be considered in retrospect, and we can conclude with a brief survey of some elements of what might be called the diaspora of existentialism – a diaspora, that is, of existentialist perspectives and concepts – that was characterized by significantly changed orientations on the parts of Sartre and Heidegger themselves, among others, and that in certain respects lasted late into the twentieth century.

Sartre: *Being and Nothingness*

Shortly before the outbreak of the war, during which he performed military service close to the front lines and was then detained for some months in a German prisoner of war camp after the French government's surrender, Sartre had already published several comparatively short philosophical works making creative use of the phenomenological methodology of Edmund Husserl, and had also become known to the French reading public through his early works of literature, most notably *Nausea* (1938). Sartre had studied Husserlian phenomenology during a fellowship year in Berlin (1933–4), during which he also wrote a long essay critical of what he considered to be Husserl's unfortunate later turn to Idealism, 'The Transcendence of the Ego.' This was published as a regular scholarly contribution to Volume 6 of *Recherches Philosophiques* (1936–7) and as a small book only many years later, but it is important as a first clear expression of Sartre's key idea that the ego is a construct, an always dubitable object of consciousness to which, in a 'magical' way as Sartre puts it, are then attributed certain qualities, states, and actions; whereas consciousness itself is free, spontaneous, and unobjectifiable. The notion of magical incantation also plays a central role in another Sartrean work of roughly the same period, *Outline of a Theory of the Emotions* (1939), where emotions serve an incantatory function. Among Sartre's other philosophical writings of the pre-war era two works on imagination, heavily indebted to Husserl's method, also deserve special mention by way of identifying his early thematic interests, *L'imagination* (1936), and *L'imaginaire* (1940).

It is in *Nausea*, however, that an equally if not even more fundamental intellectual preoccupation of Sartre's is expressed in a more literary form: the problem of contingency. As the autobiographical work of his decades-long companion, Simone de Beauvoir, attests, this old philosophical issue had been a concern of his since his student days; its literary expression required several rewritings over a period of years.

In the climactic scene of *Nausea*, the book's anti-hero, Antoine Roquentin, con-templates a chestnut tree root in a park and experiences a sort of revelation to the effect that it, like everything else in the world, human beings included, is superfluous ('*de trop*'), and is so for eternity. Interwoven through the manuscript are a number of other, related themes that were to come to be associated closely with Sartre's existentialist philosophy – for example, nausea itself, a feeling that is closely connected with anguish; the irrevocable fixedness of the past together with the uncertain character of its meaning; the critique of the hypocrisy of bourgeois moral codes and conventions; the conscious lying to oneself that he was later to denominate 'bad faith'; the importance of creativity, especially artistic creativity; and, above all, human freedom.

During his period of mobilization and then imprisonment, Sartre undertook, among many other readings, a more careful study of *Being and Time* and, while at the same time producing hundreds of pages of notebooks and letters, began work on his own philosophical *magnum opus*. His remarkable intensity as a writer resulted in more than 700 pages being ready for publication while the military occupation of Paris was still in full vigor. Although devoid of overt political or even (with qualifications to be noted later) ethical content and thus successful in not being suppressed by the German censors, *Being and Nothingness* nevertheless constitutes a forceful defense of freedom not only as an ontological ultimate, the basis of human action, but also as a goal. Many of its earliest readers understood its liberatory message, as some of the first postwar scholarly reviews of it demonstrate. These same reviews also prove that, while it evoked considerable hostility particularly from a number of French Catholic intellec-tuals (not only Marcel), *Being and Nothingness* was recognized from the outset as an exceptionally significant, 'breakthrough' work in philosophy

The subtitle of *Being and Nothingness* is 'Essay in Phenomenological Ontology.' This situates it within the phenomenological tradition begun by Husserl, but at the same time signals its claim to go in a direction not pursued, or at least not wholeheartedly pursued, by Husserl himself (because of the latter's methodological injunction to begin by the bracketing of ontological assumptions that he called the *epochē*) – namely, that of elaborating a comprehensive philosophical system, an account of reality; this was the same general direction that had already been taken by Heidegger. Claiming, in this respect like Husserl, to avoid both the Scylla of Idealism and the Charybdis of standard versions of realism, Sartre asserts that there is nothing behind the appearances of things except being-in-itself, massive and undifferentiated. Out of the in-itself there arises a region of being that he calls the 'for-itself,' which is at once consciousness and freedom. But in itself the for-itself is nothing, that is, is entirely insubstantial, lacking substance. Hence, the for-itself must always be found 'in situation' or 'situated,' characterized by what Sartre calls 'facticity.' 'Human reality,' the human being, is a for-itself surrounded by varieties of facticity, beginning with its body, and including its location, its past, its environment, and ultimately its death. In addition, there is yet one other mode of existence that is as fundamental as being-for-itself, namely, being-for-others ('*être-pour-autrui*'). These are the basic notions out of which Sartre constructs his ontology.

Since we are most concerned here with delineating the philosophical tendency and movement known as 'existentialism' rather than the details and problems of Sartre's grand scheme, certain of his major inferences and claims will be of greater interest to us than those details themselves. Of special moment for the later existentialist movement, besides Sartre's constant appeal to freedom, are his reversal of classical philosophical ideas of God and the self, his delineation of bad faith, his focus on the body together with his introduction of considerations of sexuality and gender into philosophical analysis, his linkages with psychoanalysis, and the ethical implications of his philosophy. Sartre had had solid training in the Western philosophical tradition at the elite École Normale Supérieure, and this deeply affected his thinking, which in many ways represents a reversal of that tradition's mainstream from within, as it were. For instance, there is a short section in the introductory chapter of *Being and Nothingness* that is entitled 'The Ontological Proof,' the term traditionally used for Anselm's, Descartes's, and others' argument to the effect that God, as the most perfect Being, must exist. But Sartre's ontological proof purports only to establish the existence of being-in-itself, which is the inert opposite of an active, conscious, all-knowing God. Anything resembling the latter, on the other hand, would for Sartre amount to a conceptually and really impossible coalescence of for-itself and in-itself; the idea of God is thus seen as a self-contradiction. At the same time, Sartre's analysis of human reality as essentially lacking and always striving in vain to fill its lack leads him to assert that the 'fundamental project' of everyone is to be God, and that the utter impossibility of achieving this shows the human being to be an 'unhappy consciousness' – a term that Hegel had used for a certain deeply self-divided type of mentality that he associated with the spirit of the Middle Ages. In a similar way, while Sartre regards Descartes's focus on the *cogito*, 'I think,' as fundamental for philosophical understanding, he totally rejects the central conclusion of Descartes himself that the indubitable reality of the *cogito* proves that I am a mind or soul, that is, a spiritual substance.

Sartre introduces his analysis of 'bad faith' early in *Being and Nothingness* with a view to reinforcing his fundamental insight into the nothingness of consciousness by furnishing examples of ways in which we are constantly surrounded by 'negativities' (*négatités*) – experiences that are especially revelatory of the human condition. One such, made famous by Kierkegaard and later, with due acknowledgement of the latter's contribution, by Heidegger, is anguish (*angoisse, Angst*). Sartre, too, invokes anguish as a revelatory mood, following both of his predecessors in distinguishing anguish, which can open us up to the abyss, from mere fear, which is directed toward particular objects. (In a somewhat strange late-life interview, it should be mentioned in passing, Sartre said that he had written about anguish because it was in vogue at the time, even though he himself had seldom experienced it.) But in *Being and Nothingness* Sartre's initial analyses of vertigo and other types of situations in which we feel anguish and try to flee it or stifle it lead to his even better known discusssion of bad faith, knowingly lying to oneself. The three examples of it that he gives – the woman on a date who knows yet pretends not to know that her companion is trying to seduce her, the café waiter who acts as if his entire identity were bound up with being a perfect waiter while of course realizing that it is not, and the pederast who responds to a friend's accusation by maintaining that, while he may have performed such acts, he is not *essentially* or *by nature* a pederast – are all subject to serious criticisms; but both the theoretical and the practical points that Sartre is using them to make have struck profound chords that have resonated in decades of existentialist literature ever since. Theoretically, Sartre uses the phenomenon of bad faith to reject any and all essentialist views of individuals as well as of 'human nature' as a whole: the human being's fate, he says, is to be what he or she is not and not to be what he or she is. Practically, Sartre uses his analysis as a tool to show the pervasiveness of bad faith in human experience, while holding out, in a tantalizing footnote at the end of the chapter in which he has dealt with it, the possibility of a radically different form of behavior which would be called, using a term already made canonical in Heidegger's work, 'authenticity'; but Sartre then postpones for the time being (and indefinitely, as it would turn out) any direct discussion of this possible mode of conduct.

Sartre's treatments of the body and of sexual and sexually-related behaviors broke new ground for the Western philosophical tradition, especially in relation to his German predecessors. By analyzing at length some of the implications – for such notions as pain and disease, for our relations with others, for our 'hodological' sense of place and space, and so on – of saying that the human being can only exist as embodied, Sartre gave permission, so to speak, to other philosophers to discuss such issues without fearing that they were thereby leaving the field of philosophy. His frank, straightforward phenomenological descriptions of such activities as love, masochism, desire, and sadism, which follow the chapter on the body in *Being and Nothingness*, while they have been criticized severely in many of their details and no doubt helped contribute to the perception by some that existentialism was a philosophy of the gutter, at the same time gave existentialism, and especially the hybrid that came to be known as 'existential phenomenology,' its well-merited reputation as a concrete approach to reality, based in lived experience.

Although Sartre's advocacy, in *Being and Nothingness*, of a type of practice to be known as existential psychoanalysis, combining some of his own most significant concepts and categories with the proposal for a psychoanalysis of *things* that had been advanced by Gaston Bachelard, may not have attracted as many adherents as the Heidegger-inspired method of *Daseinsanalyse* being promulgated at about the same time by the Swiss psychiatrist Ludwig Binswanger, it is quite significant nevertheless. Among other reasons for saying this, it can be argued that Sartre's sharp and carefully articulated disagreements with Freudianism, rooted above all in his suspicion of Freudian determinism, of Freud's quasi-Platonic tripartite scheme of superego, ego, and id, and of the very idea that there could be a compartment of the mind called 'the unconscious,' at least encouraged philosophers, in the existentialist tradition and in traditions that succeeded it, to take Freud and his concerns seriously.

Finally, while containing nothing explicit about the subject of ethics until a promise by its author in the concluding chapter to deal with it at some later time, *Being and Nothingness* is so full of ethical implications as to help give existentialism the image of a primarily action-oriented type of philosophy. In some important respects recalling a central insight of Nietzsche's, Sartre paints a picture of values as being created by human beings and then serving, often enough, as barriers to their freedom. There are obvious ethical redolences in the analysis of bad faith, and in one of the book's briefest sub-sections, entitled 'Freedom and Responsibility,' there is a rather shockingly sweeping assertion to the effect that, since I am 'condemned,' by what it means to be human, to act freely, whatever action I take or refrain from taking is a choice for which I cannot evade responsibility; thus, Sartre says, this war is *my* war as long as I choose not to commit suicide.

The dilemma of how to conduct oneself during wartime is a central part of Sartre's immediate postwar lecture/essay, 'Existentialism Is a Humanism.' The precise case that Sartre analyzes is that of a young Frenchman torn between wanting to leave France to join the Free French forces preparing to combine with the Allies to liberate the country, and staying with his ailing mother to care for her. Sartre's point is that existentialism, while it can offer no definitive resolution of such dilemmas, in a sense takes them more seriously than do traditional, essentialist philosophies because it honestly describes the human condition as one in which, by virtue of our all-pervasive freedom, there are no 'pat' answers. Sartre also tries in this lecture to respond to the charges of Marcel, in whose 'Christian existentialism' (still sometimes so denominated despite Marcel's repudiation of the existentialist label) hope is a central category, and of others that existentialism of the Sartrean variety is a philosophy without hope.

The Parisian Milieu

This theme of ethics was soon to be taken up at much greater length and perhaps more persuasively by Sartre's companion, Simone de Beauvoir, whose *Pour une morale de l'ambiguïté* (1948), misleadingly given the English title, *The Ethics of Ambiguity* (which lacks the intended tentativeness of the original), attempted to delineate an existentialist ethic of the kind that Sartre had only promised. De Beauvoir's work emphasizes an orientation towards a better future in which not only the privileged few, but the entire world's population, will enjoy freedom. While agreeing with Sartre that love can never be the 'union of souls' idealized in fairy tales, she implicitly criticizes his account of it in *Being and Nothingness* for being too negative. She also uses the Heideggerean term '*Mitsein*' (being-with) in a less critical, more accepting way than in Sartre's references to it. In other words, de Beauvoir's effort at an open-ended existentialist ethic had the effect of shifting perspectives from a highly individualistic to a more social one. As we shall see, this was to be the general direction taken by Sartre himself in later years.

De Beauvoir's other greatest philosophical achievement (if we exclude for present purposes her late-life book on old age, *La vieillesse* (1970), which deserves far more critical comment and attention than it has received even several decades after its publication) was *The Second Sex* (1949, in two volumes), which is rightly viewed as the opening knell inspiring the modern feminist movement. Although constantly employing existentialist categories and manifesting an existentialist orientation epitomized in the ringing assertion that opens Volume 2 to the effect that one is not born a woman but rather becomes one, this work was often considered by existentialist philosophers themselves as peripheral to the movement. There are various explanations for this, but probably the best one is the virulent sexism which de Beauvoir's book did so much to expose, but which at the same time was visible in the many expressions of extreme animosity that were directed towards it by some, along with the near-total disregard of it by others. This situation of disregard has now to some extent changed, and *The*

Second Sex is beginning to be seen as one of the 'classics' of existentialism as well as of feminism. Volume 2 in particular, with the sub-title '*Le vécu*,' is filled with brilliant concrete descriptions of the special problems faced by women at various life-stages and in various situations (for example, that of the lesbian, which it was still considered very daring to discuss at the time), all portrayed against a background dialectic of freedom and constraint. All too typically, the philosophically challenged original English translation of *The Second Sex* renders '*le vécu*' as 'woman's life today,' which is banal; but in fact this notion, usually rendered in English as 'lived experience,' is one that Sartre himself claimed to have learned to understand clearly and to employ consistently only after seeing its deployment by de Beauvoir.

However, a long time companion of both of theirs, Maurice Merleau-Ponty, had also already pointed out the centrality of lived experience. He took the origin of this idea to be above all a term developed and stressed by Husserl in his last great work, *The Crisis of the European Sciences and Transcendental Phenomenology* (1936), namely, *die Lebenswelt*, or life-world. While Merleau-Ponty has never been as closely identified with the existentialist movement, at least by most historians, as are Sartre and de Beauvoir, it is useful to regard at least his earlier major nonpolitical works, notably *The Structure of Behavior* (1942) and *The Phenomenology of Perception* (1945), in this context. Steering between the opposite extremes of empiricism and intellectualism, stressing the reality of human freedom while criticizing some of Sartre's more exuberant formulations of it, and making use of a considerable expertise in *Gestalt* as well as other schools of psychology, Merleau-Ponty in these writings offers detailed analyses of the human being as an 'ambiguous' psychophysical entity that are in important respects at least quite compatible with a general existentialist outlook. Unlike his colleagues Sartre and de Beauvoir, however, Merleau-Ponty had no serious literary pretensions beyond his philosophical writing and his editorial work for the leading journal of their milieu, *Les Temps Modernes*, the directorship of which he shared with Sartre until strong political disagreements between them led to his resignation in 1953.

In sharp contrast to Merleau-Ponty, Albert Camus is better known, and was more prolific, as a novelist and playwright than as a philosopher. Although he was highly indebted to his secondary school philosophy teacher in Algeria, Jean Grenier, who, like Camus, later moved to Paris and also came to be identified with existentialist circles, Camus's philosophical background was less extensive than Sartre's or de Beauvoir's. This was to become one of several issues that were aired publicly in his break with Sartre, which was precipitated by an unfavorable review of Camus's *The Rebel* (1951) in *Les Temps Modernes*. In this book Camus distinguishes between the drive to rebellion that has characterized and motivated so many great writers and thinkers, on the one hand, and efforts to bring about political revolution, on the other. For Camus, the latter seems always to issue in disaster, a judgement that he applied to the contemporary Soviet Union. Sartre, together with his associates on the journal's staff, had by that time entered into a period of political activism during which he sought rapprochement with the USSR and criticized French governments for allying themselves too closely with the Cold War stance of the United States government. In responding to Camus's indignant protest against the review, which had been written by a younger colleague, Francis Jeanson, Sartre recalled earlier years in which he had held Camus in the highest regard for the spirit exhibited in *The Myth of Sisyphus*.

In that short work, which Camus had begun by declaring its central problem to be that of suicide (whereas the central problem of *The Rebel* was to be that of murder, especially political murder), he defended an 'absurdist' outlook that accepts the existence of an ineliminable disconnection between the rational pretensions of the human intellect and a nonrational universe. Sisyphus, a figure from Greek mythology, embodies this acceptance as he eternally rolls a large stone up a hill at the command of the gods, only to see it roll back down and require a new round of lifting each time he approaches the summit. Sisyphus, according to Camus, is happy. A similar, highly moralistic outlook reminiscent of Stoicism, combined with an aura of grim adventure, characterizes most of Camus's more purely literary undertakings, of which *The Plague* (1947), in which he imagines the conduct of residents of the Algerian city of Oran if they were to experience an outbreak of the bubonic plague and be quarantined from the outside world, and *The Stranger* (1942) are among the best known. The last ('*The Outsider*' is an alternative, perhaps better, possible translation of the original *L'Étranger*) depicts an ordinary French Algerian settler, Meursault, who is responsible for the unpremeditated killing of an Arab and who, because of his unconventional conduct, finds himself condemned to death by a court. It is a brilliant depiction of Camus's absurdist outlook, as well as a forceful condemnation of capital punishment. The British writer Colin Wilson appropriated *The Outsider* (1982) as the title of a book that attempts to capture the spirit of the existentialist anti-hero in literature.

The Parisian milieu of the existentialists, as they began to proceed in different directions and the movement as such slowly disintegrated, is best captured by Simone de Beauvoir's novel, *The Mandarins* (1956). Although she denied that her fictional characters corresponded exactly to any actual person in this milieu, there are numerous obvious close resemblances. Be this as it may, the atmosphere as it is depicted in this book is one in which political issues and ideologies, especially Marxism and anti-Marxism, and political parties, especially the Communist Party, loom in importance over everything else. One of its central issues is whether the editor of a journal that somewhat resembles *Les Temps Modernes* should publish a new, well authenticated account of the Soviet gulags, about which little had previously been known within this group (*Les Temps Modernes* had done just that). In the process, old alliances and friendships are broken, and lives are destroyed. The story of *The Mandarins* points the way to Sartre's own increasing involvement with Marxism, which eventuated in his sociopolitically-oriented later work, the *Critique of Dialectical Reason*, published in 1960. Camus, who had died in an automobile accident at the beginning of that calendar year, had in his last days been tormented by the war in Algeria, the imminent end of which would put an end to the massive French settlement in this land where he had grown up. Among the stream of exiles from French Algeria were to be found some of the major voices of the next generation of philosophers, most notably Jacques Derrida.

Retrospective and Prospective

By invoking Derrida's name at this point, we are brought to recognize a curious circularity in the evolution of existentialism through the better part of the century. For

Derrida was among the leading advocates of taking certain central ideas of Heidegger's, among others, and moving philosophy in a new direction that came to be identified by the extremely vague name, even vaguer than 'existentialism,' of 'postmodernism.' One important Heideggerean notion, for Derrida's purposes, was what Heidegger had called '*Destruktion*,' which through Derrida and others was transmuted into 'deconstruction.' Although Derrida was to distinguish his deconstructive technique from Heidegger's while still recognizing the latter's importance, both acknowledged the contribution made by Nietzsche to its development.

Heidegger viewed Nietzsche as having gone far, though not quite far enough, along the road to questioning the mainstream history of Western metaphysics, which Heidegger characterized as having effected a concealment of Being. By devising various systematic categories and concepts in order to try to explicate what is ultimate, the great names of Western thought, he claimed, left us a legacy that is focused on particular beings (*Seienden*) instead of Being (*Sein*) itself; or, to use another, parallel Heideggerean distinction, they wrote and thought strictly at the ontic rather than at the ontological level. Nietzsche, he claimed, had been relatively successful in undercutting this entire millennia-old tradition, but unfortunately he had retained at least one metaphysical concept of his own, that of the will to power. Making use, characteristically, of etymology to assist the hermeneutic (interpretative) task which was central to his philosophizing, Heidegger pointed out that the Greek word for truth, *aletheia*, literally means overcoming forgetfulness, or 'unconcealment.' Doing this, he maintained, should be the task of what he at first called 'fundamental ontology.' Later, he decided that this nomenclature had been insufficiently radical, inasmuch as it had still retained the word 'ontology,' even if understood in a special, novel way.

There is, for Heidegger, one unique type of reality that is open to the call of Being, and that is *Dasein* (situated being, being-there), an ordinary German word that Heidegger, also quite characteristically (but in this case imitating Hegel and other predecessors), used in a technical sense. Heidegger's '*Dasein*' refers to 'Man' (in the generic sense of the word), and was translated by Sartre, in texts in *Being and Nothingness* in which he alluded to Heidegger and criticized him, as '*la réalité humaine*,' human reality. (Derrida later criticized Sartre, in turn, for thinking that this was an adequate or accurate translation of what Heidegger intended.) A sizable portion of the text of *Being and Time*, itself truncated in relation to Heidegger's own original conception of it, is devoted to analyzing some of *Dasein*'s most fundamental characteristics and ways of existing. These include: authentic and inauthentic ways – in which the latter involves taking the point of view of the impersonal 'one' (*das man*), as in the expressions, 'one thinks,' 'one says,' and so on; facticity; the privileged mood of dread, or *Angst*, which helps us understand that we are 'held out into nothingness'; the attitude of caring, *Sorge*; the unique importance of our 'being-toward-death'; and the central role of time and historicity in such an analysis.

It is obvious from this list that some key terms from the early Heidegger were appropriated by Sartre and other French existentialists, while some were not. However, the contrasts between Heidegger and Sartre, on fundamental points, are equally if not more numerous. First and foremost is the fact that Sartre's philosophy is unequivocally anthropocentric, whereas Heidegger's, while attributing a very special role to *Dasein*, is centered ultimately on Being. (This is consistent with Heidegger's objection to Sartrean 'humanism.') For Sartre, as contrasted with Heidegger, the future fact of my death is of comparatively minor philosophical importance. Heidegger steadfastly resisted deriving an ethical theory out of his thinking, whereas Sartre promised to develop an ethics at some future time. (In fact, Sartre did compose a large work in ethics that he came to regard as too flawed, too 'idealistic' and insufficiently existentialist in spirit, to publish; it has been published posthumously as *Notebooks for an Ethics*.) In a sense, Sartre's early work is still in the great tradition of philosophical system-builders, even though as we have seen it turns some of the basic ideas of the tradition inside out; whereas Heidegger set out to deconstruct the tradition root and branch, and in his later work, after the so-called 'turning' (*Kehre*) in his thought in the 1930s, proceeded to do so in ever more radical ways. Among other things, the later Heidegger, who had always been more fascinated than Sartre by philosophical issues concerning language, became convinced of the specially revelatory role of poetry, giving pride of place among poets to the nineteenth-century German, Hölderlin. On the other hand, while neither Heidegger nor Sartre was an accomplished poet (Sartre's efforts at writing poetry were, even by his own account, dismal failures), Heidegger's achievements in the world of letters were strictly confined to the domain of philosophy, whereas Sartre's included numerous works of fiction in addition to *Nausea*, some quite successful plays, an elegantly-written autobiographical study of his childhood entitled *Words*, and biographical works as well.

It was also during the 1930s that Heidegger began his flirtation with National Socialism, serving briefly as the first Nazi rector of the University of Freiburg. While scholars disagree as to the extent to which he regarded Nazism, in his interpretation of it, as being compatible with, or even an expression of certain aspects of, his philosophy, there is relatively widespread agreement that this unquestionable involvement (he retained his party membership well into the 1940s) should not be cited in order to interdict all positive evaluations of his contribution to philosophy in general, and to existentialist philosophy in particular. Although, as has already been noted, he insisted that he was not engaged in creating an ethic, and unlike Sartre never promised to write one, interpreters have attempted to derive many quite varied ethical and political implications from his work. There is, for example, the Heidegger who is considered a patron of 'the Greens,' the ecological movement, because of his reverence for nature and his identification of the technological framework, within which we live today, as a mortal threat. And, despite the conservativism of both Heidegger's early background and later political pronouncements, he had considerable respect for the philosophy of Marx because of the latter's emphasis on our historicity.

The later Sartre, however, came to be redefined above all by the philosophy of Marx, although after a period of attempting to marry Marxism with existentialism, with the latter occupying a subordinate, or 'ideological,' role (in *Search for a Method*, 1957), he eventually declared that he no longer considered himself a Marxist, primarily because of the apparent ineliminability of the thesis of determinism from Marxist thought. While never a dominant force in postwar West Germany (nor was it in the United Kingdom or the United States), Marxism exerted a considerable influences over French, Italian, and other West European intellectuals, to say nothing of so-called

'Third World' intellectuals, during that period. Sartre both incarnated and helped guide a cultural shift of emphasis from the sense of individualistic adventure associated with existentialism to the appeal to political commitment (*engagement*) that is also characteristic of Marxism. This sense of commitment found expression especially in his numerous political essays, of which his very strongly-worded support of the Algerian struggle for independence in his Preface to *The Wretched of the Earth* by Frantz Fanon – the Martiniquan-born psychologist who had moved to Algeria and was himself greatly influenced by Sartre – is an outstanding, often-cited example. But the epitomic philosophical embodiment of Sartre's later orientation is the very long yet still incomplete *Critique of Dialectical Reason*, in which *Search for a Method* was incorporated as the preliminary essay.

In this and his still later and longer *The Family Idiot* (1971 and 1972, in three volumes), a study of Gustave Flaubert, Sartre continued to make use of numerous existentialist themes and tropes, though often expressed in new language, and he never renounced his earlier theoretical framework. But the next generation of philosophers was beginning to make itself heard and seemingly to leave existentialism behind. There were, for instance, the quasi-positivist hard-line Marxism of Louis Althusser, the 'archeological' approach to knowledge of Michel Foucault, the deconstructive in-itiative of Derrida, and the exploration of even more novel , 'rhizomatic' modes of philosophizing of Gilles Deleuze, all of whom had already achieved intellectual star status by the end of the 1960s. Existentialism in general, and Sartre in particular, receive little mention in their works, although Deleuze early on acknowledged that Sartre had been '*mon maître*,' and Foucault and especially Derrida eventually expressed an indebtedness to him before their respective deaths. Foucault's strong efforts to depict 'Man' (in the generic sense) as a dubious construct of Western cultures seem at first glance to be extremely anti-Sartrean, as does the postmodernists' severe critique of 'grand narratives,' that is, would-be comprehensive philosophical systems. On the other hand, Sartre had insisted, long before Foucault, on the nothingness that is at the core of human reality; his own early 'system' itself constituted, as we have seen, a reversal and repudiation of the more traditional sorts of Western metaphysical systems; and the anti-essentialism that pervades virtually all postmodern philosophies quite obviously resonates with Sartre's lifelong conviction that 'existence precedes essence.' In short, there are a number of respects in which Sartre as well as other existentialists, whether one applies this label more broadly or more narrowly, demonstrably paved the way for the postmodern turn. But the twentieth century would never again witness a philosophical movement as intensely focused on the situation of the individual human being as was existentialism at its height.

References

de Beauvoir, S. [1949] (1952), *The Second Sex*, trans. H. M. Parshley, New York: Knopf.
de Beauvoir, S. [1956] (1960), *The Mandarins*, trans. L. M. Friedman, New York: Meridian Books.
de Beauvoir, S. [1948] (1976), *The Ethics of Ambiguity*, trans. B. Frechtman, New York: Philosophical Library.

Camus, A. [1942] (1955), *The Myth of Sisyphus, and Other Essays*, trans. J. O'Brien, New York: Knopf.

Camus, A. [1947] (1948), *The Plague*, trans. S. Gilbert, New York: Modern Library.

Camus, A. [1951] (1953), *The Rebel; an Essay on Man in Revolt*, trans. A. Bower, New York: Vintage Books.

Camus, A. [1942] (1946), *The Stranger*, trans. S. Gilbert, New York: Knopf.

Heidegger, M. [1927] (1977), *Basic Writings*, ed. D. F. Krell, New York: Harper & Row.

Heidegger, M. [1927] (1962), *Being and Time*, trans. J. MacQuarrie, and E. Robinson, London: SCM Press.

Heidegger, M. [1936–46] (1979), *Nietzsche*, trans. D. F. Krell, San Francisco: Harper and Row.

Jaspers, K. [1938–71] (1971), *Philosophy of Existence*, trans. R. F. Grabau, Philadelphia: University of Pennsylvania Press.

Marcel, G. (1951), *The Mystery of Being*, trans. G. S. Fraser, and R. Hauge, Chicago: Regnery.

Merleau-Ponty, M. [1945] (1962), *The Phenomenology of Perception*, trans. C. Smith, London: Routledge and Kegan Paul.

Merleau-Ponty, M. [1942] (1963), *The Structure of Behavior*, trans. A. L. Fisher, Boston: Beacon Press.

Sartre, J.-P. [1943] (1992), *Being and Nothingness*, trans. H. Barnes, New York: Washington Square Press.

Sartre, J.-P. [1960] (1976), *Critique of Dialectical Reason*, vol. 1, trans. A. Sheridan-Smith, London: New Left Books.

Sartre, J.-P. [1946] (1947), *Existentialism and Humanism*, trans. P. Mairet, London: Methuen.

Sarte, J.-P. (1957), *The Transcendence of the Ego: An Existentialist Theory of Consciousness*, trans. F. Williams, and R. Kirkpatrick, New York: Noonday.

Sartre, J.-P. [1938] (1964), *Nausea*, trans. L. Alexander, New York: New Directions.

Marxisms

Andrew Wernick

Taking as my point of departure the (re)constitution of a 'Western,' as opposed to Soviet Marxism in the first decades of the twentieth century, my aim in the following remarks is to trace, and reflect upon, some of that tradition's main lines of development. An account of modern Marxism that omits developments to the East, ignores its relation to anti-colonial struggles, and limits itself mainly to Europe, is no doubt ethnocentric. It has the benefit however – beyond sheer convenience – of directing us to examine what has happened to Marxism on its intellectual home ground. Since my concern here is with what pertains to philosophy, I will also leave aside the vast body of concrete analysis/critique with which Marxism has been mainly associated, and that Marx enjoined practical theorizing to focus on Marxist metatheory; that is, on that level of thinking at which its concepts for comprehending and changing the world are themselves reflected and woven together.

It should be said at once that the relation between Marxism, as a revolutionary critique and guide to action, and philosophy, as autonomous reflection on conceptual fundamentals, is contradictory and contentious. There is something anomalous, indeed, about the inclusion of Marxism in this volume. In an ecumenical gathering of trends in European philosophy it is a rambunctious guest at the table. This is not only because of substantive disagreements about the relation of being to consciousness, thought to its object, matter to spirit and so on. It is also a matter of communicative practice. For Marx, the dominant ideas were the ideas of the dominant, the Kantian public stage was an ideological mirage, and in class society the universal was embodied in the partisan. To follow him across the bridge from German philosophy's utopian striving for the absolute to socio-historically grounded transformist politics is to adopt a way of thinking that doubly breaks the rules: first, in its politics-trumps-all disavowal of the autonomy rights of speculative theory; and secondly in its struggle-oriented refusal to engage the community of thought as if in a conversation between universal rational subjects.

The fact, nonetheless, that such thinking can today be treated, without much sense of impropriety, as one conceptual configuration among others, indicates not only the absorbing power of academic discourse. It also indicates that, with the seeming evaporation of socialism as a historical option, Marxism's self-defining link between theory and practice – let alone as incarnated in the praxis of a mass workers' movement, itself conceived as the armature of a tellurian emancipation – has become attenuated to the point where the abstract idea of it risks being all that remains. Which is not to say that, in principle, the 'critico-revolutionary' attitude no longer presents a challenge to (bourgeois) thought; just that, to the extent that the Marx assemblage has broken up, that challenge has become more virtual and dispersed.

But the philosophy/Marxism relation is not only problematic externally, as between incompatible modes or registers of discourse. In all the permutations through which its theory has attempted to grasp the union of theory and practice, Marxism's relation to philosophy has also been contentious for Marxism itself. Whether Marxism is a science (of history, of nature, of science itself) or a 'method' of political and historical analysis (Lukacs 1924); or whether, to the contrary, it is a totalizing historicism, or an ethico-political philosophy of freedom and human self-constitution; and whether, in any case, it amounts to a position *in* philosophy or a position *on* philosophy, are questions that have been long debated. From Marx's 'leaving to the mice' the products of his 'erstwhile philosophical conscience,' to Engels's attempted marriage of positivism and dialectics, to Stalinist 'diamat,' to all the sophisticated shades of position that came from returning to or rejecting Hegel, the history of these debates and of the positions they put in play is – at least on the level of systematics – the history of Marxism itself.

Even a cursory examination of this history makes one thing clear. What is all too simply called 'Marxism' does not have a stable metatheoretical identity. It is a contested site on which a plurality of positions and self-conceptions have struggled to assert themselves as at once correct, and as having a privileged relation to that name.

Running through this plurality have been sharp differences of political orientation, themselves responding to shifts and contradictions in the historical situation. Praxis and dialectic have thematically come to the fore in the context of renewed movement activism and its championing (in the 1920s, and 1960s). A stress on science and determining laws has accompanied centralized political management (the Second and Third Internationals). Bernstein's (1909) revisionist abjuring of Hegel for Kant, which turned socialism into a regulative ideal, drew a line between reform and revolution and helped convert Hegel into a radical figure. With political terms reversed, but still with the ghost of Hegel as battleground, the Althusser controversy of the 1960s and 1970s was indexed to disagreements about vanguardism, the Sino-Soviet split, and the humanist ('all for Man') line of the CPSU and its international allies.

As this last example suggests, however, in which, from the left, Hegelian forms of Marxism were anathematized from across the Rhine (Althusser 1969), the differences between variant Marxisms have not only been political. They have also been articulated with the epistemic differences of a national and even religious kind (the secularized residues of Catholic vs Protestant for example) that traverse post-Enlightenment thought as a whole. Labriola in 1895 had already noted that the international diffusion of Marx and Engels's ideas was leading to versions with distinct German, Polish, Italian, and Russian accents. After 1917, as Marxism's intellectual centre of gravity moved westwards with the spread of the inter-war European crisis, the accents multiplied. This eventuated, finally, not just in distinct national schools, but in a cross-cutting array of Marxisms – from the phenomenological, existentialist, and (post)-structural, to the analytic, Hegelian, empirico-historiographic, and positivist – that replicated, but more vehemently, divisions within the wider philosophical field.

I In play, it should be emphasized, has not only been the passive impress of local intellectual conditions, plus creeping *Kathedersozialismus*. As part of a sustained effort to revitalize Marxism after the collapse of the Second International – with its one-dimensional economism, linear theory of history, and positivistic self-assurance – there came to be an active engagement with 'bourgeois' philosophy and social science, an engagement that marks Western Marxism's entire twentieth-century development. If one side of this was critical and polemical, another was appropriative, driven by the need to address gaps and inadequacies in what had been handed down from the Masters as Marxist theory itself.

One large gap concerned all that made up 'the political and ideological super-structure' – a zone, as Marx (in a preface to the *Communist Manifesto*) put it, at once not amenable to the 'methods of exact science' yet crucial as 'where contradictions come to consciousness and are fought out.' Hence, to supplement political economy (itself always needing to become contemporary with the ever-evolving dynamics of capital), the need on the one hand for a more developed account of the state and the political (a task initially taken forward by Lenin and Gramsci); and, on the other, for better ways than through mechanical base-superstructure models, or reductionist class hermeneutics, to comprehend subjectivity, consciousness, and 'ideology.' The first, with respect to political theory, involved some borrowing, including from other forms of strategic thinking (military, Jacobin, and so on). Given the *sui generis* character of revolutionary politics, however, much needed to be invented. Meeting the second need was more complicated. For the systematic study of the various sites, practices, and discourses relating to subjectivity, consciousness, and ideology was already much advanced. But this advance, under the rubrics of sociology, ethnology, psychology, linguistics, and all the other *Geisteswissenschaften*, had been outside the Marxist orbit and had had a generally culturalist bias. It was here that something like a strategy of critical appropriation presented itself.

The openness with which this strategy was conducted varied across time and tendencies. The CPSU-dominated Third International quickly closed down, for those under its aegis, any truck with the ideological enemy. (This included Freud and Freudism, as Wilhelm Reich found out when he was expelled from the KPD.) In the 1920s and 1930s, among those calling themselves Marxists (or 'historical materialists'), only the independent Frankfurt Institute for Social Research made such a program in any way explicit (Horkheimer 1972). At the same time, Lukacs's integration of Weber on rationalization into his theory of reification (1923), the development of various Freudo-Marxisms outside the Communist Parties, and Gramsci's own absorption of elements from Machiavelli, traditional military theory, and Hegel via Croce, pointed towards what gradually swelled, even within European Communist Parties, into a multi-front engagement. By the last quarter of the twentieth century this had led to direct reflection on the nature of the appropriative exercise, whence Colletti's formulation concerning how to extract from classical bourgeois sociology an under-standing of 'ideological social relations' (Colletti 1969), and Althusser's repositioning of Durkheim's sociology of religion as an account of ideology and 'social reproduction' (Althusser 1971). It had also issued in a polyglot 'cultural Marxism' – as developed for example in Birmingham School cultural studies (Davies 1995) – that had absorbed essential elements not only from psychoanalysis and classical sociology, but also from semiotics, linguistics, language philosophy, and even Nietzsche and the poststructuralists. And all this while grappling with the entry of sex, gender, race, and the globalization of capital into the mix of mediations that a cogent account of the formation and dynamics of consciousness would also have to include.

That Marxism's accretion of determinations could not just be an 'adding on,' as feminist and post-colonial theorists scornfully called it, either of dimensions or of concepts, that it necessitated a correction, even rethinking, not only of whatever was assimilated, but also of what it was assimilated to, is evident. It is also evident that rethinking classical Marxism's map of the socio-historical totality could not but put in question, if only with regard to its causal role, that is, the part of the Marxist apparatus thought to be scientifically secured: political economy. But the implications did not stop there. Efforts to rise to the complexity of the totalities being comprehended could not avoid more general questions about the nature of social being and of being social, the relation of practice to structure, the scope and effectivity of human agency, and the dialectical nature of historical becoming. Nor, indeed, after an encounter with Freud and ethnology, could it avoid having to rethink, with deeper attention to psycho-social mediations, Marxism's master narrative of collective self-production, and the conception of 'human nature' to which it was tied.

Overall, in other words, any operation of critical appropriation could not but go beyond itself to raise fundamental issues of philosophical anthropology and social ontology such as those that eventually surfaced, via Mauss (1990) and Bataille (1985) regarding the gift economy and symbolic exchange, and via Frankfurt regarding technology, and the self-cancellation of enlightenment, as problems in themselves. Nor could such issues be confined to matters of methodology. For they touched on both the foundation and the *ad quem* – 'social humanity or human society' – of the whole emancipatory project.

II In all these ways the moving intellectual front of substantive theory and analysis generated its own questions with respect not only to first-order issues – concerning the nature of advanced capitalism, the dynamics of consciousness, prospects for transformation and son on – but also to second-order ones concerning the totality of theory and practice from whose vantage point substantive analysis proceeded.

But issues of that sort had moved onto twentieth-century Marxism's intellectual agenda in any case. For here, too, there had come to be a felt insufficiency in the classical inheritance. At stake, in trying to address it, was not just the practical benefit of a well-grounded theoretical apparatus in the analysis and understanding of actuality, but also the capacity of historical materialism to secure itself as a position that could be defended and advanced in the arena of thought itself. This was the issue that Labriola himself had raised. A Marxism that did not know how to articulate its own theoretical identity and difference was vulnerable both to frontal attack, and to a more insidious weakening and co-optation.

A natural starting-point for the proper terms in which to present Marxism's conceptualization of itself was in Marx's own thought. But that was just the problem. By abandoning, as a matter of principle, the terrain of philosophy for concrete socio-historical analysis plus active politics, Marx himself had left little clue about how to comprehend the overall logic of what – somewhere between his opting for communism and proletarian revolution in the early 1840s and his co-writing of the *Communist Manifesto* – he had come to think. Nor was this helped by the fact that, until fifty years after his death, most of Marx's early works, and the voluminous body of his notes and unpublished books, were unavailable.

For Engels and the Second International, if the *Communist Manifesto* was the founding political text, the most important theoretically was *Capital*. And here it was Marx's preface to the second edition, with its dictum about setting Hegel's dialectic 'right-side-up,' that provided the initial lead. From the materialist reinversion of Hegel emerged the notion of Marxism, at its core, as the science of a dialectically understood reality. Whence also emerged what, for the Third International as well as the Second, became the orthodox division of Marxism into two compartments: 'historical materialism' (the science of socio-history), and 'dialectical materialism' (the most general principles for understanding nature, including the human, as matter and becoming). But other answers were possible, even within the schema of Marx as corrected/transcended Hegel. These multiplied, moreover, after the founding of the MEGA (Marx-Engels-Gesamtausgabe) archives in Moscow (1927–35), as more of Marx's early and unpublished work came into circulation.

For Labriola, the key text had been the 1845 'Theses on Feuerbach,' that scribbled note in which was deposited, according to Engels (1886), 'the brilliant germ of Marx's whole philosophy.' On this basis, Marxism was better understood as the 'philosophy of praxis' – a formula whose central category encapsulated at once an epistemology (knowing the world through changing it and ourselves), an ontology (human reality as essentially practical), and a political theory whose revolutionary project was inscribed within the developmental dynamics of the class-conflicted world that such a per-spective discloses. Korsch (1923), on the other hand, stressed Marx's critique of Hegel's *Philosophy of Right*, with its formula about philosophy (meaning German Idealist philosophy) abolishing and realizing itself through proletarian revolution. From which angle, contra both Engels and Labriola, there could be no Marxist philosophy as such, except perhaps as the anticipatory thought of philosophy's consummated disappearance. For others, the key to understanding Marx's larger ground-plan lay in what he had done with the master-slave dialectic of the *Phenom-enology of Mind* (Lukacs 1923, Kojève 1947) or – read through the eyes of the young Marx – with the dialectic of becoming embedded in Hegel's *Logic* (Lefebvre 1968).

All of this amounted to rereading Marx via a critical appropriation of German idealist philosophy 'on its active side' (first thesis on Feuerbach). The effect was to dissolve the Engelsian marriage of dialectical reason with a nomothetically conceived science (with its 'laws' of history), together with the schema of historical and dialectical materialism to which it became joined. A further consequence was to bring Marxism's self-questioning with regard to its scientific claims and self-characterization into contact with a wider interrogation of modern science, as exemplified by the Vienna Circle and ordinary language philosophy, and Husserlian phenomenology.

Not surprisingly, the expansion of Marx's published oeuvre led also to battles over the unity, or otherwise, of Marx's own thought. How was its movement to be understood? What was the relationship between the 'early' writings of the 'young' Marx, and the 'later' writings of the 'mature' one? When, to the extent that the question could be rigorously posed, did Marx become 'Marx'? After the publication in 1932 (at the onset of the Stalinist terror) of the *1844 Philosophic and Economic Manuscripts*, these battles sharpened considerably. The field divided between defenders of orthodoxy for whom the later works alone were validly Marxist, those for whom there was a cumulative development, but without any further fundamental break once Marx had made the double move to communism and 'the new materialism' (Korsch's position); and outright opponents of dogmatism and authoritarianism like Lefebvre, Marcuse (1955) and the later Sartre (1976) for whom the early Marx, especially of the *1844 Manuscripts*, provided the key to the whole.

That Marx had to be read against the background of what he had broken from in order to locate and explicate the nature of that same break gave a certain circularity to the exegetical discussion. But it also stimulated a re-examination of Marx's place in his philosophical field: a re-examination that could hardly proceed without reckoning with developments after Marx, as well as before him; and that could not, in any case, confine itself to a few simple questions of influence and difference, considering that its unavoidable point of entry was Marx's critique, both directly and through his criticism of other critics, of a would-be totalizer of the history of philosophy itself.

III Bedevilling the Marx discussion has been the influence of Marxism's vulgarization as a doctrine in relation to the ideological requirements of a movement, and the credal requirements of a party. So when, and how, Marx 'became Marx,' became a highly fraught issue. As the site of a founding gesture, it ramified with organizational politics, and was fought over as the very touchstone of orthodoxy. Marxological issues were important even for those on the outside of the organized Left, bent on rescuing Marx's thought from its deformation at the hands of official doctrine.

That there is something oracular here, even religious, is evident: Marx came to be treated not only as the honored founder of a way of thought (the critique of political economy, socialism coming to scientific self-consciousness) but as the voicing of a revelation, in which what is revealed is the truth of human history. His writings became holy writ, in which the question of which ones were canonical became crucial to establishing the truth-regime proper to correct thinking and practice. But underneath this reverence for Marx the prophet of the Logos of History, we are presented with Marx not only as a dogmatically fought-over authority, but as a real enigma. What *prise de position* underlay the self-certitude with which he conducted all his mature work? Regardless of how it might be epistemologically assessed, was his intuited synthesis coherently formulated? And if not, can it be?

In that context, Althusser's (1969) insistence that Marx's 'coquetting with Hegelian Phrases' covered over what was actually an absence, and that his guiding concepts were active but unthought, and still needed to be produced, seemed like a promising argument. But his helpful attempt to supply Marx with the missing concepts only revealed more of the same problem. For, once we clear away the obfuscation with which Althusser clothed his intervention, we can see that it forged yet another Marx based this time, not on Marx's passage out of Hegel, but on a combination of continuities that could be discerned between Marx and Spinoza (a sin to which Althusser [1976] ultimately confessed) and between Marx and Saint-Simon/Comte (which Althusser, like his critics, passed over in silence). E. P. Thompson's counter-blast, *The Poverty of Theory*, emphasised the necessary rootedeness of materialist theorizing in concrete historiography. Gerry Cohen translated Marx's theory of history into analytic propositions. Henri Lefebvre (1971) had already attacked not just Althusser but the whole structuralist tendency as 'a new Eleatism,' as against the dialectic of becoming that Marx himself had championed. But disjunctive procedures of the kind pursued by all these combatants is not the only way.

It could be, in fact, that the problem posed by Marx is not the absence of a metalanguage but that under the surface are *too many* metalanguages. Lenin noted that scientific socialism had three sources: German philosophy, English (and Scottish) political economy, and French political theory. But these were not just components, to be materialistically corrected, then fitted together. They were epistemically distinct, implicated in a different framework of fundamental categories. The very language about theory and practice in the 'Theses on Feuerbach' and *The German Ideology* conflates the vocabularies of German Idealism (on its 'active side'), British empiricism and Scottish political economy – 'our only premises are the actual individuals in so far as they produce their own mean of life . . .' (Marx and Engels 1845), and French political theory, including its historicisation by Saint-Simon. A curiosity of the Marx debate is that Saint-Simon's idea of a double break from metaphysical philosophy and social metaphysics made its way, via French positivism, into Althusser, just as it had previously made its way, via the Young Hegelians, into Marx. Nor is Marx's mixed genealogy surprising considering that his thought was itself the product of Europe-wide attempts to radicalise and synthesize the totalizations of Enlightenment thinking that intellectually peaked with the French Revolution.

All of which is to suggest that if we are to approach the question of what Marx 'saw' nondoctrinally, without prejudging its truth-value, it would be better to regard what is fundamental in his thought as an assemblage: an assemblage moreover that attempts to integrate and synthesize, not just a multiplicity of first-order languages for comprehending history, society, and politics, but a multiplicity of incompatible second-order ones for comprehending, and intellectually organizing, the results. *Post festum* it may be easier to see this. What actually transpired, however, was a disjunctive multi-plication of Marxisms, which turned fault lines in the original synthesis into conflicting schools, complicating still further a field already divided along other lines.

IV The complexification and self-problematization that Marxism underwent in the course of its European adventures was not a linear process, nor was it driven only from within. It engaged generations with incommensurate experiences, in disparate national contexts, against the backdrop of a capitalism that lurched from crisis to crisis even as it metamorphosed into forms that needed new maps. Most immediately, the course of Marxist theorizing was shaped by the politics in which it was situated – with regard to both the ebbs and flows of the actual class struggle (and more generally of emancipatory movements of the oppressed), and the vicissitudes of the Left. Looming across these was the rise and fall of what came to constitute itself after 1917 as the socialist camp, together with the array of parties and tendencies – Leninist and nonLeninist, orthodox, oppositional, independent, and heretical – that formed and fissured in relation to it.

In a rough and ready way, four phases in the story can be identified. After (1) an initial phase of revitalization linked to resurgent struggle and activism (1900s-1920s), came (2) an intensified turn to philosophy and culture under conditions of defeat and disengagement (1930s-1950s). This was followed, in the context of Cold War tensions, national liberation movements, civil rights struggles, and a diffuse youth radicalization, by (3) a politically re-energized efflorescence of splintering Marxisms (1960s-1980s). With the restoration of order, post-Fordist restructuring and the disintegration of the 'socialist camp,' this was succeeded in turn by (4) a further phase of rethinking (1980s to the present) in which inter alia the boundaries between Marxism, postmarxism and the wider field of critical thought became, perhaps terminally, blurred. The first phase I have already mentioned, and I have skimmed across the two that follow. But before we come to the last, and to the condition of Marxism today, it may be useful to highlight some additional features of these earlier developments.

Worth noting first is that, to an extent never repeated, even in the delirium of 1968, the initial steps towards revitalizing classical Marxism occurred in a context where a socialist transformation across swathes of Europe could plausibly be imagined to be really on the agenda. The militancy and radicalism that stirred before the 1914–18 war foreshadowed the explosion of unrest that followed it. From army and navy mutinies, to civil war in Italy, to a rash of 'red republics' in *Mitteleurop*, spreading rebellion plus crumbling state authority presented the classic outline of a pre-revolutionary situation. To be sure, the fact that the break from capitalism occurred, and only occurred, in backward Russia rather than in advanced Europe was a puzzle that Lenin's formula about imperialism breaking at the weakest link only temporarily resolved. 'Socialism,' it transpired, could not only breed monsters; it could be a statist path through primitive accumulation towards capitalist modernization. Be that as it may, in the turbulent aftermath of the Great War, the October Revolution only reinforced the sense that the historical option of exiting from capitalism was both open and – as in Luxemburg's slogan 'socialism or barbarism' – urgently posed.

The strong interest, then, among those who lived this moment in addressing the conceptual insufficiencies of classical Marxism, did not at all betoken, as it did later, either defeat or flight from active engagement. On the contrary: theorizing was underpinned by the conviction that the present was a period of transition, that the revolutionary project was actual and immanent in the dynamics of contemporary capitalism, and that Marxism (to the extent it could be rescued and refounded on its proper basis) was an indispensable element of the struggle. Leading intellectuals were leading activists. Lukacs was a government minister in Bela Kuhn's brief insurrectionary government in Hungary. Gramsci led the Italian Communist Party till his death in Mussolini's jail.

In this same post-1917 moment, it should be added, the prestige of Lenin's writings was at its height. As too was the attractiveness of the organizational form Lenin had argued for in *What is to be done?* – a form that was appealing to intellectuals in any case, given the indispensable place accorded to 'correct theory' in advancing the workingclass beyond 'trade-union consciousness.' Not all were convinced. Spontaneists like Luxemburg (1906, 1922), Korsch (before joining the KPD in 1929) and the Council Marxists stressed the importance of the grass-roots movement and its own dialectic of consciousness. But the vanguard party had many intellectual partisans, some of whom elaborated it in directions beyond what Lenin could have imagined. Consistent with the utopian themes in *Class and Class Consciousness*, for example, Lukacs's *Lenin* (1970) depicted the organized vanguard, where revolutionary theory and practice fused, as the site for the crystallization of the proletariat's maximal consciousness as the coming-to-be of a universal being. Gramsci's *Modern Prince*, while more concerned with practicalities, pushed the intellectual role of the party, and the reflexivity required of it in the complex conditions of developed capitalism, still further. For him, as the brain of the movement, the prime task was to theorize the socio-historical conscious-ness required of the leadership of a counter-hegemonic popular bloc, engaged, at multiple levels, in a trench warfare type struggle for mental and moral hegemony.

First-stage European Marxism was marked, in sum, both by an activism that took revolutionary transformation as a reality principle, and by a strong element of vanguardism. The latter was manifest, indeed, not only in adhesion to the various 'official' national Communist Parties, but also in the groups and tendencies of the independent and far left, artistic and action-oriented groupuscules. Across the board, then, even on the Surrealism fringe (Breton 1924), there was an inclination towards strategic theorizing in the grand style, mingled with a concern to grasp and account for the epistemological privilege that such a totalizing standpoint presupposed.

V On the surface, the development of European Marxism in its *second* phase (1930s to early 1950s) continued along tracks laid down by the first. There was a continuing preoccupation with Hegel as a propaedeutic for understanding Marx. There was also a deepening attention to consciousness and culture that extended into groundbreaking debates about literature, aesthetics, and modernism. (The richness of Marxist writings on culture and philosophy in this period is striking. Examples include Kojève's lectures on Hegel, Marcuse's *Reason and Revolution*, Benjamin's Arcades project, Lefebvre's *Historical Materialism*, Lukacs's work on literature and aesthetics (Lukacs 1937), and Goldmann's examination of Pascal, Racine, and Kant in the nationally differential epistemic history of early modern thought (Goldmann 1964, 1956).

However, this phase was also marked by the catastrophes of Fascism, National Socialism, and Stalinism, by the forced separation of theory (and critique) from (mass political) practice, and by the formation, where there was freedom for it to form at all, of an independent left intelligentsia more open than party-Marxists to heterodox influences. (The thinkers grouped round Bataille and Callois, preoccupied with the idea of staging a (human) sacrifice, produced from Freud, Nietzsche, Durkheim, and de Sade, a particularly startling concoction.)

The Eurasian descent into totalitarian night had two general effects. First, strategic theorizing began to bifurcate. It gave way, on the one hand, to critique, whether in terms of justice or species-potential, and on the other hand to a kind of descriptive Marxism in which the methods of historical materialism were applied in a growing variety of fields. These ranged from the typology of social formations (Wittfogel 1957) and the 'oriental mode of production', language (Voloshinov 1973), and literature (Lukacs 1937, and many others) to revisionist historiography, including that of classical Greece and Rome (Finley 1973). For some, more dramatically, the social totality that first-wave European Marxists had confidently imagined to be the proper and graspable object of the Marxist method was replaced by an interest in parts and fragments. This even led, in Bataille's 'practical heterology' (Bataille 1985) and Adorno's *Negative Dialectics*, to the abjuring of totalization on principle as that which, through the homogenization implicit in modern production and science, had led the whole thought world astray.

An additional feature of this period was the emergence of the United States as the world-leading exemplar of advanced capitalism. What Britain had been for Europe in the eighteenth and nineteenth centuries America became in the twentieth: not just a dominant power, but the face of its future. This view was tempered by perceptions of American exceptionalism, in which Engels's puzzle concerning the status-conscious *embourgeoisement* of the British workingclass was succeeded by Sombart's (1905) '*Why Is There No Socialism in the United States?*'. But framed by mass production, consumer credit, increasing working-class affluence, and the rise of Hollywood, Tin Pan Alley and Madison Avenue, fascination with America foregrounded, as well, a wholly new set of issues with regard to the integration of (working-class) consciousness. These concerned the impact, increasingly in Europe itself, of consumer culture and commercial mass media. The mass base of fascist movements, not to mention the outpouring of patriotism everywhere in 1914, already pointed to the need for a better grasp of 'the subjective factor.' Disturbing mass-society type parallels could be drawn between 'free' societies, with their conformism and adulation of film stars, and the cults of personality in outrightedly repressive ones. Regardless of how the mediations were analyzed, though, here was a new constellation, presaging a larger shift in the character of capitalism, with respect to the overall relation between 'ideological superstructure' and 'economic base.'

In this politically and cognitively dislocated conjuncture, it is not surprising that European Marxism's 'cultural turn' would deepen, nor that its philosophical ruminations would intensify. After 1945, two tendencies came to the fore. On the one side, aided by the publication of Marx's early writings, there emerged an 'alienation Marxism' that elaborated praxis-philosophy into a teleological or utopian philosophical anthropology, and redefined Marxism as a humanism. *Les Temps Modernes* was a flagship for this tendency. On the other side came an engagement with phenomenology, existentialism, and psychoanalysis. While for some (for example, Sartre, and the 'Budapest School' led by Agnes Heller) this engagement reinforced trends to 'humanize' Marxism, for others (Bataille and his journal *Critique*) it began to raise issues about any 'philosophy of the subject,' a position avidly taken up by proponents of the structuralist paradigm distilled from Durkheimian sociology, Saussurian linguistics, Lévi-Strauss's anthropology, and Freud's analysis of dreams.

Encounters with Husserl, Heidegger, and Nietzsche also deepened the critique of positivism with regard to reification. This extended to a critique of technology as instrumentalization, and began to lead to a (self) critique of Marxism, or at least its 'cold current' (Bloch), as itself implicated in puritanism and instrumental rationality.

(Against this, J. D Bernal's work on the social history of science embodied the more orthodox view that linked socialism to a Baconian view of science and its benefits [Bernal 1939]). Overall, the second phase, with its gathering critique of alienation, technology, and the administered society, brought Marxism into a troubled relation not only with dystopian trends in modernity, but with its own epistemological and historico-anthropological certitudes. From this cauldron emerged concepts like Kojève's *post-histoire*, Bataille's unemployed negativity (Bataille 1985), and Debord's 'spectacle' that led some (notably, later, Baudrillard) to exit from Marxism altogether.

VI The development of European Marxism in its *third* phase, from the 1950s to the 1970s, was sharply paradoxical. In advanced capitalist countries there was a resurgence of radical activism among youth and students (of all classes), that itself condensed the synergistic explosion of contradictions in every sector of the globe. Against this background, the Marxist tradition that had been counted out during the early years of the Cold War acquired a new relevance and was taken over, with brilliant results, by a new generation of militant intellectuals. This theoretical energy led to a resuscitation not only of the mainstream and oppositional labour-oriented Marxisms of the 1920s and 1930s, but also of the minority tendencies of the artistic, libertarian and anarchist Left. Amidst these complex currents a new Left struggled to assert itself against the old one, putting in play all the questions about strategy, capitalist resilience, and Marxism itself, that had agitated a previous generation, as well as a host of other ones about sex and gender, race, and consumer culture, that had scarcely before – let alone under the signs of disalienation, anti-authoritarianism, and *autogestion* – been broached.

Both politically and theoretically, however, the results were fissiparous. The project of refounding the socialist project on updated premises foundered. The old Left – even in nonrevisionist (Maoist or Trotskyist) form – ploughed into a dead-end, with Cambodia a dreadful cautionary tale. Unresolved disputes raged over every aspect of Marxist theory, even over the adequacy of a Marxist standpoint itself. One fundamental issue concerned the contemporary identity, if there was one, of the revolutionary subject. The French general strike of 1968, with its factory occupations and student barricades, kept alive the notion that this subject was still in the workingclass. But the cogency of this response was not self-evident, given both the changed socio-economy of post-industrial capitalism and the actual masses in motion. Other possibilities were therefore advanced: from various forms of third worldism, to the notion that, in contemporary advanced countries, the place of the revolutionary proletariat had been taken by a (potential) coalition of 'new social movements,' autonomously organized with respect to irreducible lines of trans-class oppression related to gender, race/ethnicity and so on.

In this context, too, the metatheoretical contradictions already becoming evident in phase two, blossomed into full-scale paradigm wars. The debates over positivism and history in Germany, and between phenomenology and structuralism in France (Sebag 1964, Lefebvre 1971), seguéed, via the Althusser controversy, into a full-scale debate over Hegelian Marxism and thence over the whole character of Marx's thought. If the epistemological status of Marx's 'science of history' was one side of this, another was the ontology of the social, wherein a subjectless Spinozan and Nietzsche-tinged structuralism was pitted against liberal, existentialist, and Hegelian proponents of a Marxism founded on the notion of the subject's self-emancipation through conscious action. At the same time the ethnographic and phenomenological thematizing of the Other (Lévi-Strauss 1962; Levinas 1969; Sartre 1960; Fanon 1967; and Said 1978) began to lead, via feminist and post-colonial critiques, as well as through the 'turn to language,' to a more general problematization of Western thought including Marxism, as culturally biased, self-privileging, and phallogocentric.

At the centre of these controversies were two main problem constellations: (1) the nature of human subjectivity and the status of the 'subject,' linked to what became, out of praxis philosophy, 'the problem of agency'; and (2) the question of how Marxism, qua historical materialism and praxis philosophy, is (or ought to be) constituted, both as a total thought matrix, and with regard to its ontological, epistemological, and moral-political presuppositions. Problems with regard to the first evidently exacerbated problems with the second. One irony was that the dialectical, revolutionary, and activist response to the anti-subject position, associated in the first half of the twentieth century with laws-of-history forms of Marxism, became associated in the (post)-structuralist reprise not only with the recovery of action-oriented theorizing, including in philosophy (Althusser 1971), but with the most radically 'left' positions. This link is legible in the crypto-Chinois writings of *Tel Quel* and in the 1970s political divigations of Deleuze and Foucault.

VII With the ending of the cold war, the disintegration of the USSR and the onset of the New World Order, the contradictory position that a revived European Marxism had arrived at became stark. The ruse of history had seemingly delivered a capitalism that grew out of the very attempts to abolish it. But capitalism in the age of globalization and flexible accumulation was capitalism nevertheless, and Marxism retained its relevance at least as a source of critical concepts for comprehending the contemporary world, even as the bottom fell out of any serene assumption about the transitional (to socialism) nature of the epoch.

The result was accelerated dispersal. The renewed synthesis at which a revived European Marxism had aimed dissolved back into its elements, leaving a field divided not just, as in the 1920s, between political economy and the study of culture and philosophy, or between 'national' variants, or even (again) between critique and praxis, but with regard to any political, epistemic, and ontological unity that might be conjured at all out of Marxism. In the Anglo world, where Euro-Marxism found a new home (with thinkers like Perry Anderson, Terry Eagleton and Frederic Jameson continuing on a path forged earlier by Raymond Williams), the emblematic journal of the 1960s and 1970s was the *New Left Review*. In the 1980s and 1990s it was *Rethinking Marxism*.

At the same time, Marxisms continued not only to proliferate but to hybridize. The boundaries between schools and paradigms grew porous. With thinkers like Foucault, Habermas, Lyotard, Deleuze, and Guattari, it became hard to say where Marxism ended and something else began. Derrida's deconstructive program was castigated for encouraging the postmodern embrace of irony and play (Best, and Kellner 1997); but it was also a reference point for Althusser, whose eulogy he delivered (Kaplan, and Sprinkler 1993).

Overall, it would seem that the drift, finally, of what in the 1970s and 1980s came to be named European or Western Marxism has been towards a complete loss of definition. Marxism has merged with 'bourgeois' thought on its critical and liberal side. It has adopted the colorations of Western philosophy. It has lost its relation to the working class or any other plausible revolutionary subject. Yet the Marx assemblage has not disappeared without trace from the theoretical scene.

In the first place, even as Marxism was being abandoned as a privileged reference point, three problem areas derived from it have been deposited on the shores of contemporary thought. The first is horizonal. What is the Good which transformist thought presupposes, and aims to realize? Are 'community' and 'justice' – the dominant *leitmotifs* of left-wing values – adequate terms in which to express it? What, in any case, is the meaning and limit of these categories? What do they exclude? To such discussion belong Nancy's interrogations of 'community' and 'freedom' (1991, 1993), Derrida's exploration of futurity and the gift (1992), as well as Habermas (1981) on communicative rationality, Rawls on justice, and Zizek (1989) on 'the sublime object of ideology.' Across all this hovers a further set of issues about how the values of the Left can withstand Zarathustra's laughter. A second set of questions is epistemological. It concerns especially the truth-claims that may be made with respect to the cognitive element in committed thought and action. Amidst endless discussion about how to steer between dogmatism and relativism (Bernstein 1971), discourse theory, with its 'truth effects,' has turned such questions on their head, as too has the decisionist influence of Carl Schmidt. Whence a preoccupation with the figure of the militant and the attempt by Badiou (2001) to restate the asymmetry between Left and Right in terms of an ethics of truth. A third set of issues is ontological, wherein there has been both a renewed interest in the natural substratum (Timpanaro 1976); and efforts to produce a new 'new materialism', without a subject, *telos* or reduction of the many to the one. Marxifying Hegel in the shadow of Aristotle has become yesterday's game. In Deleuze's (1983, 1987, 1988) and Negri's (2000) variant accounts, a dual social ontology of praxis and structure has been replaced with a subjectless energetics of forces and counter-forces that owes much to Nietzsche and more to Spinoza.

Amid these remnants, moreover, something else remains of Marxism that is unassimilable to any pure field of thought. This is its spirit of activism, or to be precise, its spirit of political engagement: an engagement that is at once towards a redemptive and emancipatory horizon ('human society or social humanity'), yet contextually mindful, and immanently entered into the actual conflicts of the world. What is enduringly distinctive about Marxism as a 'position,' in fact, is precisely this: its insistent politicization of thinking. In place of Levinas's 'ethics precedes ontology', the philosophical specter of Marx will continue to propose, at least so long as we remain in a 'state of transition'; 'politics precedes everything.' By which should be understood not politics as moral action, nor politics in its banal electoral-promotional manifestations, but politics as (transformative) action from within and upon the structure of social relations.

But to speak of understanding begs the question. The philosophy of praxis has not only been unhinged by the real movement of history (praxis loses its touchstones in 'the actuality of class struggle,' and in the proletariat as the revolutionary subject): the history of European Marxism has also revealed an incoherence with regard to how to think the generality of that position, linked to unresolved enigmas about the character of Marx's 'break.'

Whence two concluding reflections: first, unpacking what is condensed in Marx needs a form of thinking that avoids becoming short-circuited, so that a metalanguage projected or discerned there has only itself for situating itself with respect to its own thought field. This is a general problem for intellectual historiography, but it is acute for a mode of theorizing that wants to think towards and out of a transcendental space. If we would hang on to the *trans* we must move to the *meta*. What this means is that if Marxism is to be rethought in its fundamentals we would have to think directly about the scissors/paper/stone relation between the three metaparadigms – empiricist, dialectical/idealist, and rationalist/positivist – within which Marxism is inscribed. The relation and difference between the Hegelian and Saint-Simonian (or Comtian) totalizations in particular needs to be pondered, both in their raw state and as corrected from the vantage point of that third position from which, intuitively, Marx proceeded.

The second point is still harder to make in terms of what may still like to recognize itself as a Marxist universe. It is that (albeit in an a/theological sense) Marxism, at its activist core, is indeed theological. It is so not just in its resemblance to a secularized millenarianism, but also, and more precisely, in that the theory-practice complex at its heart is continuous with the general structure of Christian theology, as developed especially in medieval Europe. In its effort to grasp its own elusive rationality, that is to say, Marxist theory has proceeded in line with the ancient injunction of Boethius to 'conjoin if you can faith and reason.' It has done so, however, with a ground-breaking difference. The object of its faith – history's potential orientation to the Good – is immanentized as that which can only be validated as horizon by the experimental transformative praxis that will have actually realized it. What that Good consists of – like any version of the absolute – is neither morally nor politically nor culturally prescribed, but defined only as an open plenitude. To grasp the overall architecture of Marx's thought, then, we may envisage it as transposing the Augustinian and Anselmian espousal of a *fides quaerens intellectum* (a faith seeking to be self-understood), to one of *fides quaerens agendum* (a faith seeking to be actualized). The full meaning of the 11th thesis on Feuerbach is to be found in how such a standpoint substitutes for other-worldly faith the practical imperative to validate the category 'human society or social humanity,' by actually bringing it into being. Marxism, from this angle, is theurgical. Liberation theology approached such a position from the side of Christianity. From an utterly post death-of-God and anti-essentialist position, the recent work of Badiou and Zizek on Saint Paul, and of Agamben (1999) on Benjamin's philosophy of history, has raised related issues. For European Marxism – or at least its postmodern derivatives – the next critically appropriative encounter may well be with theologians.

References

Agamben, G. (1999), *Potentialities: Collected Essays in Philosophy*, ed. and trans. D. Heller-Roazen, Stanford: Stanford University Press.

Althusser, L. [1965] (1969), *For Marx*, trans. B. Brewster, London: Allen Lane; and New York: Pantheon.

Althusser, L. (1971), *Lenin and Philosophy and Other Essays*, trans. G. Brewster, London: New Left Books.

Althusser, L. (1976), *Essays in Self-Criticism*, trans. G. Lock, London: New Left Books.

Anderson, P. (1976), *Considerations on Western Marxism*, London: New Left Books.

Badiou, A. (2001), *Ethics: An Essay on the Understanding of Evil*, trans. P. Hallward, London: Verso.

Badiou, A. [1997] (2003), *St. Paul: The Foundation of Universalism*, trans. R. Brassier, Stanford: Stanford University Press.

Bataille, G. (1985), *Visions of Excess: Selected Writings 1927–1939*, ed. and trans. A. Stoekl, Minneapolis: University of Minnesota Press.

Baudrillard, J. (1975), *The Mirror of Production*, St Louis: Telos Press.

Benjamin, W. (1968), *Illuminations*, New York: Harcourt, Brace & World.

Bernal, J. D. [1939] (1967), *The Social Function of Science*, Cambridge, and London: MIT Press.

Bernstein, E. (1909), *Evolutionary Socialism*, New York: Schocken.

Bernstein, R. (1971), *Praxis and Action: Contemporary Philosophies of Human Activity*, Philadelphia: University of Philadelphia Press.

Best S., and D. Kellner (1997), *The Postmodern Turn*, New York: Guilford Press.

Bloch, E. (1986), *The Principle of Hope*, trans. N. Plaice, S. Plaice, and R. Knight, Cambridge: MIT Press.

Breton, A. [1924] (1997), *The Manifesto of Surrealism*, in P. Waldberg (1997), *Surrealism (World Of Art)*, New York: Thames and Hudson.

Cohen, G. (1978), *Karl Marx's Theory of History: A Defence*, Oxford: Clarendon Press.

Colletti, L. (1969), *Marxism and Hegel*, trans. L. Garner, London: New Left Books.

Davies, I. (1995), *Cultural Studies and Beyond: Fragments of Empire*, London: Routledge.

Deleuze, G. [1962] (1983), *Nietzsche and Philosophy*, trans. H. Tomlinson, London: Athlone Press.

Deleuze, G. [1970] (1988), *Spinoza: Practical Philosophy*, trans. R. Hurley, San Francisco: Harbour Lights.

Deleuze, G., and F. Guattari [1980] (1987), *Capitalism and Schizophrenia: Thousand Plateaus*, trans. B. Massumi, Minneapolis: University of Minnesota Press.

Derrida, J. (1992), *Given Time: 1 Counterfeit Money*, trans. P. Kamuf, Chicago: University of Chicago Press.

Derrida, J. (1993), *Spectres de Marx*, Paris: Galilée.

Derrida, J. (1994), *Specters of Marx*, trans. P. Kamuf, New York: Routledge.

Engels, F. [1886] (1934), *Ludwig Feuerbach and the End of Classical German Philosophy*, trans. F. Engels, New York.

Fanon, F. (1967), *The Wretched of the Earth*, trans. R. Wilcox, Harmondsworth: Penguin.

Finley, M. (1973), *The Ancient Economy*, London: Chatto and Windus.

Gramsci, A. (1957), *The Modern Prince and Other Writings*, trans. L. Marks, London: Lawrence and Wishart.

Gramsci, A. (1971), *Selections from the Prison Notebooks*, ed. Q. Hoare, and G. Nowell-Smith, London: Lawrence and Wishart.

Goldman, L. (1955), *Le Dieu caché. Etude sur la vision tragique dans les Pensées de Pascal at dans le théâtre de Racine*, Paris: Gallimard.

Goldman, L. (1964), *The Hidden God: A Study of Tragic Vision in the Pensées of Pascal and the Tragedies of Racine*, trans. P. Thody, London: Routledge and Kegan Paul; New York: Humanities Press.

Goldmann, L. [1948] (1971), *Immanuel Kant*, London: New Left Books

Goldmann, L. [1964] (1975), *Towards a Sociology of the Novel*, trans. A. Sheridan, London: Tavistock

Habermas, J. (1981), *The Theory of Communicative Action* 2 vols, trans. T. McCarthy, vol. 1, London: Heinemann; vol. 2, Cambridge: Polity.

Hollier, D. (ed.) (1988), *The College de Sociologie 1937–39*, trans. B. Wing, Minneapolis: University of Minnesota Press.

Horkheimer, F. [1968] (1972), *Critical Theory*, trans. M. J. O'Connell et al., New York: Herder and Herder.

Horkheimer, F., and T. Adorno (1973), *Dialectic of Enlightenment*, trans. G. S. Noerr, and E. Jephcot, London: Allen Lane.

Jameson, F. (1971), *Marxism and Form, Twentieth Century Dialectical Theories of Literature*, Princeton NJ and London: Princeton University Press.

Jameson, F. (1991), *Postmodernism, or the Cultural Logic of Late Capitalism*, London: Verso.

Kaplan A., and M. Sprinkler (1993), *The Althusserian Legacy*, London: Verso.

Kojève, A. (1947), *Introduction à la Lecture de Hegel*, Paris: Gallimard.

Korsch, K. [1923] (1970), *Marxism and Philosophy*, trans. F. Halliday, London: New Left Books.

Labriola, A. [1895] (1904), *Essays on the Materialist Philosophy of History*, Chicago: C. H. Kerr.

Lefebvre, H. (1971), *Au délà du structuralisme*, Paris: Anthropos.

Lefebvre, H. [1939] (1968), *Dialectical Materialism*, London: Jonathan Cape.

Lenin, V. (1957), *What Is To Be Done?*, in V. Lenin (1957), *What Is To Be Done? and Other Writings*, London: Dover.

Lévi-Strauss, C. (1962), *The Savage Mind*, Chicago: University of Chicago Press.

Levinas, E. (1969), *Totality and Infinity: An Essay on Exteriority*, Pittsburgh: Duquesne University Press.

Lukacs, G. [1923] (1971), *History and Class Consciousness*, trans. R. Livingsone, London: Merlin.

Lukacs, G. [1924] (1970), *Lenin: A Study of the Unity of his Thought*, trans. N. Jacobs, London: New Left Books.

Lukacs, G. [1937] (1962), *The Historical Novel*, trans. H. Mitchell, and S. Mitchell, London: Merlin.

Luxemburg, R. [1906] (1925), *The Mass Strike, the Political Party, and the Trade Unions*, trans. P. Lavin, Detroit: Marxian Education Society.

Luxemburg, R. [1922] (1961), *The Russian Revolution*, Ann Arbor: University of Michigan Press.

Mandel, E. [1972] (1978), *Late Capitalism*, trans. J. de Bres, London: Verso.

Marcuse, H. [1941] (1955), *Reason and Revolution*, Boston: Beacon Press.

Marx, K. (1978), *The Philosophic and Economic Manuscripts of 1844*, in R. C. Tucker (ed.) (1978), *The Marx-Engels Reader*, New York: Norton.

Marx, K., and F. Engels [1848] (1932), *The Communist Manifesto*, in M. Eastman (ed.) (1948), *Capital, the Communist Manifesto, and Other Writings*, New York: Modern Library.

Marx, K. [1845] (1998), *The German Ideology*, trans. R. Pascal, New York: Prometheus Books.

Mauss, M. (1990), *The Gift: The Form and Reason for Exchange in Archaic Societies*, London: Routledge.

Mitchell, J. (1974), *Psychoanalysis and Feminism*, London: Penguin.

Nancy, J.-L. (1991), *The Inoperative Community*, trans. P. Connor et al., Minneapolis: University of Minnesota Press.

Nancy, J.-L. (1993), *The Experience of Freedom*, trans. B. McDonald, Stanford: Stanford University Press.

Negri, A. (2000), *The Savage Anomaly: The Power of Spinoza's Metaphysics and Politics*, trans. M. Hardt, Minneapolis: University of Minnesota Press.

Poulantzas, N. (1975), *Political Power and Social Classes*, trans. T. O'Hagan, London: New Left Books.

Reich, W. [1945] (1961), *The Sexual Revolution*, London: Vision.

Said, E. (1978), *Orientalism*, London: Routledge and Kegan Paul.

Sartre, J.-P. [1960] (1976), *Critique of Dialectical Reason*, London: New Left Books.

Sebag, L. (1964), *Marxisme et Structuralisme*, Paris: Payot.

Sombart W. [1905] (1976), *Why Is There No Socialism in the United States?*, New York: Sharpe.

Thompson, E. P. (1978), *The Poverty of Theory*, London: Merlin.

Timpanaro, S. (1976), *On Materialism*, London: New Left Books.

Voloshinov, V. N. (1973), *Marxism and the Philosophy of Language*, trans. L. Matejka, and I. R. Titunik, New York and London: Seminar Press.

Williams, R. (1961), *The Long Revolution*, London: Chatto and Windus.

Williams, R. (1980), *Problems in Materialism and Culture: Selected Essays*, London: New Left Books.

Witttfogel, L. (1957), *Oriental Despotism: A Comparative Study of Total Power*, New Haven: Yale University Press.

Žižek, S. (1989), *The Sublime Object of Ideology (Phronesis)*, London: Verso.

Žižek, S. (2002), *Revolution at the Gates: Žižek on Lenin*, London: Verso.

Frankfurt School and Philosophy

Douglas Kellner

The term 'Frankfurt School' refers to the work of members of the *Institut für Sozialforschung* (Institute for Social Research) which was established in Frankfurt, Germany, in 1923 as the first Marxist-oriented research centre affiliated with a major German university. Under its director, Carl Grünberg, the institute's work in the 1920s tended to be empirical, historical, and oriented towards problems of the European working-class movement. (On the Frankfurt School, see the readers edited by Arato and Gebhardt 1978 and Bronner and Kellner 1989, and the critical studies in Jay 1973, Kellner 1989, and Wiggerhaus 1994.)

Under the directorship of Max Horkheimer (1930–72) many talented theorists gathered in the institute, including Erich Fromm, Franz Neumann, Herbert Marcuse, and T. W. Adorno. At that time, the institute sought to develop an interdisciplinary social theory that could serve as an instrument of social transformation. The work of this era was a synthesis of philosophy and social theory, combining sociology, psychology, cultural studies, and political economy. Three of the members of the inner circle of the Frankfurt School were philosophers.

The 1930s: From Fascism to the Critical Theory of Society

The first major institute project in the Horkheimer period was a systematic study of authority – an investigation into individuals who submitted to irrational authority in authoritarian regimes. This culminated in a two-volume work, *Studien über Autorität und Familie* (1936) and a series of studies of fascism. Most members were both Jews and Marxist radicals and were forced to flee Germany after Hitler's ascendancy to power. The majority emigrated to the USA and the institute became affiliated with Columbia University from 1931 until 1949, when it returned to Frankfurt.

Institute theorists challenged traditional academic boundaries between one sphere of social reality and another. For Horkheimer and his colleagues, dividing social reality into specialized spheres of inquiry reproduces the division of labor typical of contemporary modern societies, while intensifying tendencies towards increased professionalization, specialization, and fragmentation. It also mystifies social reality, excludes significant factors from discussion, and abstracts from social conflicts, problems, and complexities, thus occluding fundamental connections within social reality and excluding significant factors from analysis. Within traditional academic disciplines someone analyzing, say, politics or culture in a specialized, 'professional,' manner would abstract from economics in dealing with issues within their specialized discipline. For the Frankfurt School, on the contrary, economics plays a constitutive role in all social processes, so that it would be impossible to discuss politics concretely without discussing economics, just as one cannot adequately discuss economics without considering the role of politics and culture in the workings of the economy.

In particular, institute members subverted the established boundary between philosophy and social theory, and strove – not always successfully – to overcome the division between theory and politics. The intended result was at once a critical philosophy and social theory of the contemporary epoch which attempted constantly to conceptualize and criticize new social conditions, as well as a historical theory which, following Hegel and Marx, sketched the borderlines between various stages of history.

From the mid-1930s, the institute referred to its work as the 'critical theory of society.' For many years, 'critical theory' stood as a code for the institute's Marxism and was distinguished by its attempt to found a radical interdisciplinary social theory rooted in Hegelian-Marxian dialectics, historical materialism, and the critique of political economy and revolution theory. Members argued that Marx's concepts of commodity, money, value, exchange, and fetishism characterize not only the capitalist economy but also social relations under capitalism, where human relations and all forms of life are governed by commodity and exchange relations and values.

In a 1937 article, 'Traditional and Critical Theory,' Horkheimer (Horkheimer 1972) made a seminal contribution to this issue. Max Horkheimer (1894–1972) was born in Stuttgart, Germany, to a wealthy industrialist. After receiving a Ph.D. in philosophy at the University of Frankfurt in 1922 with a dissertation on Kant supervised by Hans Cornelius, Horkheimer joined the Institute for Social Research and became its director in 1930. Horkheimer argued that 'traditional theory' (which included modern philosophy and science since Descartes) tended to be overly abstract, objectivistic, and cut off from social practice. 'Critical theory,' by contrast, was grounded in social theory and (Marxian) political economy, carried out systematic critique of existing society, and allied itself with efforts to produce alternatives to capitalism and bourgeois society (then in its fascist stage in much of Europe). Horkheimer wrote that critical theory's:

> content consists of changing the concepts that thoroughly dominate the economy into their opposites: fair exchange into a deepening of social injustice; a free economy into monopolistic domination; productive labour into the strengthening of relations which inhibit production; the maintenance of society's life into the impoverishment of the people. (Horkheimer 1972: 247)

The goal of critical theory is to transform these social conditions, and provide a theory of 'the historical movement of the period which is now approaching its end' (Horkheimer 1972: 247).

Critical theory produced theoretical analyses of the transformation of competitive capitalism into monopoly capitalism and fascism, and hoped to be part of a historical process through which capitalism would be replaced by socialism. Horkheimer claimed that:

The categories which have arisen under its influence criticize the present. The Marxist categories of class, exploitation, surplus value, profit, impoverishment, and collapse are moments of a conceptual whole whose meaning is to be sought, not in the reproduction of the present society, but in its transformation to a correct society. (Horkheimer 1972: 218)

He saw critical theory, therefore, as motivated by an interest in emancipation and as a philosophy of social practice engaged in 'the struggle for the future.' Critical theory must remain loyal to the 'idea of a future society as the community of free human beings, in so far as such a society is possible, given the present technical means' (Horkheimer 1972: 230).

In a series of studies carried out in the 1930s, the Institute for Social Research developed theories of monopoly capitalism, the new industrial state, the role of technology and giant corporations in monopoly capitalism, the key roles of mass culture and communication in reproducing contemporary societies, and the decline of democracy and of the individual. Drawing on Hegelian dialectics, Marxian theory, Nietzsche, Freud, Max Weber, and other trends of contemporary thought, critical theory articulated theses that were to occupy the centre of social theory for the next several decades. Rarely, if ever, has such a talented group of interdisciplinary intellectuals come together under the auspices of one institute. They managed to keep alive radical philosophy and social theory during a difficult historical era and provided aspects of a neo-Marxian theory of the changed social reality and new historical situation in the transition from competitive capitalism to monopoly capitalism.

During the 1930s, Horkheimer's philosophical essays attempted to validate progressive ideals of reason, democracy and justice, morality, while criticizing assaults on these ideals in the contemporary era and in particular developing critical perspectives on German fascism and its ideology.

Horkheimer's first essay for the Institute, 'A New Concept of Ideology?,' is a critique of Karl Mannheim's widely acclaimed book *Ideology and Utopia*. Horkheimer interpreted Mannheim's work as the latest attempt to incorporate elements of Marx into an idealist philosophy of spirit. He refers to Mannheim's attempt to transform the theory of ideology from an 'armament of a party' into a non-partisan sociological instrument through a 'sociology of knowledge' which would demonstrate the partisan, contextual, and existentially determined nature of all cognition, thought, and theories. The result of this move would be the extension of the concept of ideology and its coming to range over all theories, rather than over those only which are taken to mask ruling class interests.

In opposition to Mannheim, Horkheimer argues that the project of undermining metaphysics was precisely the task of Marx's theory of ideology, and he states his belief that Mannheim vitiates this theory through smuggling metaphysical categories back into it. Throughout the 1930s, Horkheimer and his colleagues attacked the metaphysical assumptions of dominant modes of thought, and consistently applied the Marxian notion of ideology critique to dominant theories in the classical and contemporary philosophical traditions. The philosophical component of the work of the institute included development of a sustained practice of ideology critique involving theoretical confrontation and critique of the dominant ideological trends of the day. Thus 'critique' was initially understood by the institute as a method of attacking the cognitive distortions produced by ideology – later on it would take on further connotations. Various institute members did carry through ideology critiques of idealism, positivism, existentialism, philosophy of life, and the emerging ideology of fascism, as well as of the ideological trends dominant in such disciplines as metaphysics and ethics.

Against all idealist modes of thought, the institute theorists defended materialism. Rejecting both the mechanistic metaphysical materialism already criticized by Marx and Engels in *The Holy Family* (1845) and the current positivistic forms of materialism, Horkheimer and his colleagues defined the objects of materialist theory in terms of material conditions, human needs and social struggles against oppression. Materialism did not signify for the institute a specific metaphysical doctrine but a whole series of ideas and practical attitudes, taking different forms in different contexts.

In 'Materialism and Metaphysics,' (Horkheimer 1972) Horkheimer criticizes metaphysical materialism for attempting to capture the totality of being in a universal philosophical system, making thereby evident his hostility to metaphysical systems, absolutism, and the foundationalist theories that attempt to provide a foundation for knowledge. He then argues that the specific views held by materialists should not be dictated by unchanging metaphysical theses, but rather by the 'tasks which at any given period are to be mastered with the help of the theory.' Criticism, for example, of a religious dogma may, at a particular time and place, play a decisive role, while under other circumstances such criticism may be unimportant (Horkheimer 1972: 20–1).

In the same essay, Horkheimer claims that idealist views generally aim at justification, and are advanced by ruling class ideologues for the sake of the affirmation of dominant class interests; materialist theories, on the other hand, aim at explanation based on material conditions, classes, and specific historical situations (Horkheimer 1972: 22ff.). He rejects metaphysical theses concerning the identity of thought and being – knowledge and the known and argues that there is 'an irreducible tension between concept and being' (Horkheimer 1972: 27) and proposes a post-metaphysical conception of materialism. Concepts are not instruments of absolute knowledge, but rather instruments for achieving certain goals to be constantly developed and modified with experience. He rejects, consequently, the forms of epistemological realism held by many positivistic materialists maintaining that correct thought mirrors or reflects the object of thought. The institute stressed the historical nature of both theories and their subject matter: 'The theoretical activity of humans, like the practical, is not the independent knowledge of a fixed object, but a product of ever-changing reality' (Horkheimer 1972: 29). As historical conditions change, concepts and theories must also change.

Horkheimer also criticizes theories that operate with a subject/object model and distinguish the two rigidly, arguing that:

the subject–object relation is not accurately described by the picture of two fixed realities which are conceptually fully transparent and move towards each other.

Rather, in what we call objective, subjective factors are at work; and in what we call subjective, objective factors are at work. (Horkheimer 1972: 29)

He opts for dialectical materialism, rendering thereby objective conditions constitutive of the subject, and the subject, constitutive of objective (material, historical) conditions. A dialectical process – he writes – is negatively characterized by the fact that it is not to be conceived as the result of individual unchanging factors. To put it positively, its elements continuously change in relation to each other within the process, so that they are not even to be radically distinguished from each other. The development of human character, for example, is conditioned both by the economic situation and by the individual powers of the person in question. 'But both these elements determine each other continuously, so that in that total development neither of them is to be presented as an effective factor without giving the other its role' (Horkheimer 1972: 28).

Horkheimer believes that materialist (that is, Marxist) theories are primarily concerned with human suffering, and with transforming the material conditions responsible for human suffering into conditions likely to generate a more rational society and more humane form of existence. This analysis assumes that 'the wretchedness of our own time is connected with the structure of society; social theory therefore forms the main content of contemporary materialism' (Horkheimer 1972: 24). In particular:

[T]he fundamental historical role of economic relations is characteristic of the materialist position . . . Understanding of the present becomes more idealist, the more it avoids the economic causes of material need and looks to a psychologically naive elaboration of so-called 'basic elements of human existence. (Horkheimer 1972: 25–6)

For the institute, philosophy without empirical scientific research is empty, just as science without philosophy is blind. In the mid-1930s, Horkheimer's unification of science and philosophy involves a dialectical interpenetration and mediation of science and philosophy, without permitting one to dominate the other. He rejects both metaphysics and positivist concepts of science that profess 'the dogma of the invariability of natural laws' (Horkheimer 1972: 36). Dominant positivist theories of science are 'unhistorical,' although 'materialism has in common with positivism that it acknowledges as real only what is given in sense experience, and it has done so since its beginnings' (Horkheimer 1972: 42). Sense experience, however, is mediated through concepts, and both sense perception and cognition are subject to social conditions and historical change. Horkheimer and his colleagues therefore subscribe to a nontranscendental materialist theory of knowledge which acknowledges, with Kant and the idealists, that forms of cognition and theories determine our experience of the external world, while objective material conditions in turn condition forms of thought and knowledge. The results of materialist social theory are thus always provisional, contextual, and subject to revision.

In 'The Latest Attack on Metaphysics' (Horkheimer 1972: 132ff.), Horkheimer articulated his critique of metaphysics and positivistic science, developing at the same time his materialist concept of social theory. Metaphysics was criticized now for its attempts to grasp intuitively the totality of being, with Horkheimer sharply challenging its 'mere opinions, improbable statements, and outright fallacies' (Horkheimer 1972: 134ff.), along with its attempts to provide illusory consolation and compensation (Horkheimer 1972: 137). In contrast, science is presented as 'a body of knowledge which a given society has assembled in its struggle with nature' (Horkheimer 1972: 133). Horkheimer, however, criticizes the (positivist) claim that science provides 'the only possible form of knowledge' (Horkheimer 1972: 136ff.) and defends instead 'critical, dialectical' thought for making connections between the various realms of social reality and for contextualising the 'facts' of science 'as segments of the life process of society' (Horkheimer 1972: 145, 159).

Attacking the fetishism of the isolated and unmediated facts of positivism, 'dialectical thought integrates the empirical constituents into structures of experience which are important not only for the limited purposes served by science, but also for the historical interests with which dialectic thought is connected' (Horkheimer 1972: 162). Dialectical social theory affirms the importance of values, rejects notions of a value-free science, and criticizes society from the standpoint of specific values that the theory considers worthy of defense. Dialectical social theory thus amounts to a synthesis of social theory, morality, and politics.

Herbert Marcuse and Critical Theory

During the 1930s and early 1940s, Herbert Marcuse (1898–1979) was the main philosopher of the group. Born in Berlin of an upper-class German-Jewish family, Marcuse served with the German army in World War I, and then went to Freiburg to pursue studies in philosophy and literature. After receiving his Ph.D. in 1922 with a dissertation on *The German Artist-Novel*, he returned to Berlin and pursued a short career as a bookseller. Returning to Freiburg in 1928, he studied philosophy with Martin Heidegger, one of the most influential thinkers in Germany at the time, and worked out one of the first syntheses of phenomenology, existentialism, and Marxism.

Marcuse argued that official Marxist thought had degenerated into a rigid orthodoxy, and required reference to concrete 'phenomenological' experience in order to be revived. In addition, he criticized Marxism for having neglected questions pertaining to the problem of the individual, and throughout his life tried to maintain a balance between individual liberation and well-being and social transformation. In this context, he was among the first to recognize the importance of the writings of the early Marx for the reconstruction of Marxism, and in 1933 he published a major review of Marx's *Economic and Philosophical Manuscripts of 1844*. Furthermore, his study of *Hegel's Ontology and Theory of Historicity* (1932) contributed to the Hegel renaissance that was then taking place in Europe.

In 1933, Marcuse joined the *Institut für Sozialforschung* in Frankfurt and soon became deeply involved in its interdisciplinary projects. In the process of examining the concepts of essence, happiness, freedom, and, especially, critical reason (the central category of philosophical thought and critique), he provided them with a materialist base, showing how these concepts are relevant to concrete human lives.

The concern with critical reason and the Hegelian and Marxian modalities of dialectical thinking is evident in *Reason and Revolution* (1941) – Marcuse's first major work in English. In this text, he traces the rise of modern social theory through Hegel, Marx, and positivism. Marcuse claims that Hegel instituted a method of rational critique that mobilized the 'power of negative thinking' for the criticism of irrational forms of social life. The close connection between Hegel and Marx and the discussion of the ways in which Marx developed and concretised Hegel's dialectics are the focal points of Marcuse's interpretation that remains to this day one of the most insightful studies of the relation between Hegel and Marx and the origins of modern social theory.

In 1934, Marcuse – a German Jew and also a radical – emigrated to the United States where he lived for the rest of his life. The Institute for Social Research was granted offices and an academic affiliation with Columbia University; Marcuse worked there during the 1930s and early 1940s. His first major work in English, *Reason and Revolution* (1941), traced the genesis of the ideas of Hegel, Marx, and modern social theory; demonstrated the similarities between Hegel and Marx; and introduced English speaking readers to the Hegelian-Marxian tradition of dialectical thinking.

From *Dialectic of Enlightenment* to the Return to Germany

Theodor W. Adorno (1903–69), another important Institute member, was born in Frankfurt, Germany into an upper-class bourgeois family. The son of a German-Jewish father and Italian-Catholic mother, Adorno studied philosophy, psychology, and musicology at the University of Frankfurt where he received his Ph.D. in 1924. He also engaged in professional music training, studying piano and composition with modernist composer Alban Berg. During the 1920s and early 1930s, Adorno edited a musical journal, *Anbruch*, and continued his studies of philosophy. He completed his *Habilitationschrift* on Kierkegaard in 1931 and began teaching at the University of Frankfurt. There, he associated himself with the Institute for Social Research and he worked for it the rest of his life.

Working collaboratively, Adorno and Horkheimer wrote a major text of critical theory, *Dialectic of Enlightenment* (1947; (trans. 1972)). The book sketched out a vision of history from the Greeks to the present that showed how reason and enlightenment turned into their opposites, transforming what promised to be instruments of truth and liberation into tools of domination. Under the pressure of systems of domination, reason becomes instrumental, reducing human beings to things and objects and nature to numbers. While such modes of abstraction enable science and technology to develop apace, they also produce reification and domination, culminating in the concentration camps and the instrumentalization of death. Reason turns instrumental; science and technology creates horrific tools of destruction and death; culture is commodified into articles of a mass-produced culture industry; and democracy ends in fascism, with masses choosing despotic and demagogic rulers. Moreover, individuals are repressing their own bodies and renouncing their own desires allowing themselves to be instruments of alienated labor and war.

In their criticims of enlightenment, scientism, and rationalism, as well as of systems of social domination, Adorno and Horkheimer implicated Marxism inside the 'dialectic of enlightenment' since it too affirmed the primacy of labor, instrumentalized reason in its celebration of 'socialist production,' and participated in the Western domination of nature.

In 'Minima Moralia' and other essays of the period, Adorno continued the studies of the institute concerning the stabilization of capitalism and the integration of the working class as a conservative force in the capitalist system. In this context, Adorno saw only the possibility of individual revolt. Fearing the resurgence of authoritarianism in the United States, he worked together with a group of Berkeley researchers on a ground-breaking collective study of *The Authoritarian Personality* (1950). The project embodied the desire of the institute to merge theoretical construction with empirical research and produced a profile of a disturbing authoritarian potential in the United States.

After World War II, Adorno, Horkheimer and Pollock returned to Frankfurt to re-establish the institute in Germany, while Löwenthal, Marcuse and others remained in the USA. In Germany, Adorno, Horkheimer and their associates were engaged in frequent methodological and substantive debates with other theorists, most notably in 'the positivism dispute,' criticizing empirical and quantitative approaches to social theory and defending their own more speculative and critical brand of thought. During this period, the group around Adorno and Horkheimer became increasingly hostile toward orthodox Marxism and, as a result, they drew the criticism of 'Marxist-Leninists' and 'scientific Marxists' for their alleged surrender of revolutionary and scientific Marxian perspectives.

Horkheimer's *Eclipse of Reason* (1947) represents a popularized version of *Dialectic of Enlightenment* for an English-speaking audience and the *Critique of Instrumental Reason* (1946b) brings together Horkheimer's key essays since the end of World War II. In fact, Horkheimer became increasingly pessimistic and combined Schopenhauer's Stoicism with a quest for the 'totally other,' – a religious desire for transcendence that crept in his materialist philosophy in his later years.

Adorno continued his work in sociology and German culture, but growing increasingly critical of communism and skeptical of Marxism, he focused primarily in cultural criticism and studies of philosophy and aesthetics during his last decade. Deeply shocked by the Holocaust, Adorno's criticism became ever more negative and oppositional: he became increasingly known as a champion of modernist avant-garde art that he saw as the most powerful weapon of liberation. Although he followed Lukacs and other Marxist theorists in his sociological and ideological approach to culture, he broke with standard Marxian normative aesthetics which either championed realist art à la Lukacs, or political modernism à la Brecht. Adorno, by contrast, championed avant-garde modernism, which he believed carried out the most extreme negation possible of existing society and culture.

Adorno's last major published work during his lifetime, *Negative Dialectics* (1966), was deeply philosophical, although many of his essays did not fail to direct themselves toward the political issues of the day and to elaborate the politicization of cultural criticism that he had helped inaugurate in the 1930s.

Many of his students were active in the German student movement in the 1960s;

Adorno, however, was highly critical of the movement and even called in the police during a student occupation of the institute during an anti-war protest. His estrangement from the student movement and the sharp critique that he received from student activists hurt him deeply and he died suddenly of a heart attack in 1969 with his *magnum opus*, *Aesthetic Theory*, still unpublished (it was to be published posthumously, in 1970).

Marcuse's One-Dimensional Man

While Adorno and Horkheimer became increasingly conservative and criticized the student movement of the 1960s, Herbert Marcuse inspired and embraced some of its more radical elements. His *One-Dimensional Man* was one of the most important books of the 1960s. First published in 1964, it was immediately recognized as a significant critical diagnosis of the times and was soon taken up by the emergent New Left as a damning indictment of contemporary Western societies – whether capitalist or communist. Conceived and written in the 1950s and early 1960s, the book reflects the stifling conformity of the era and provides a powerful critique of new modes of domination and social control. Nevertheless, it also expresses the hopes of a radical philosopher that human freedom and happiness are still possible, beyond the prevalent one-dimensional thought and behavior prevalent. Holding on to the vision of liberation articulated in his earlier book *Eros and Civilization*, Marcuse urges that what is must constantly be compared with what could be – the possibility of a freer and happier mode of existence.

One-Dimensional Man contains a theory of 'advanced industrial society' which describes how changes in production, consumption, culture, and thought have produced an advanced state of conformity in which the production of needs and aspirations by the prevailing apparatus integrates individuals into the established societies. Marcuse describes what has become known as the 'technological society' in which technology restructures labor and leisure, influencing life in its entirety, from the organization of labor to the modes of thought and thereby threatens human freedom and individuality in a totally administered society.

Marcuse thought that dialectical philosophy could promote critical thinking and *One-Dimensional Man* is perhaps Marcuse's most sustained attempt to present and develop the categories of the dialectical philosophy developed by Hegel and Marx, while criticizing modes of modern philosophy, including (dominant at the time) analytic philosophy. Dialectical thinking requires, according to Marcuse, the ability to abstract and disengage one's perception and thought from their existing forms. Uncritical thinking draws its beliefs, norms, and values from prevalent thought and social practices, while critical thought seeks alternative modes of thought and behavior, which it then takes as a standpoint for critique. 'Negative thinking' negates existing forms of thought and reality from the standpoint of higher possibilities, and this presupposes the distinction between existence and essence, fact and potentiality, or appearance and reality. Grasping the potentialities for human freedom and happiness would make possible the negation of those conditions that hold individuals in bondage, inhibiting their full development and realization. Dialectical thought therefore posits a different realm of ideas, images, and imagination that serves as a locus of critique and a guide to social transformation. The locus of these potentialities and critical norms is great philosophy and art.

In Marcuse's analysis, the 'one-dimensional man' has lost his individuality, his freedom, and the ability to dissent and to control his own destiny. The private space is being whittled away by a society which shapes aspirations, hopes, fears, and values, and manipulates vital needs. The one-dimensional man does not know his true needs because his needs are administered, superimposed, and heteronomous; Marcuse returns therefore to the stance of a radical individualist who is deeply disturbed by the decline of authentic individuality. He sees one-dimensional society and one-dimensional man as the results of a long historical development that has led to a continual erosion of individuality.

Marcuse is in fact reworking here the Hegelian-Marxian theme of reification and alienation, whereby the subject loses its power of comprehending and transforming subjectivity as it becomes dominated by alien powers and objects. For Marcuse, a human being is distinguished by the features of free and creative subjectivity. Alienated from its powers of being-a-self, one-dimensional man becomes an object of administration and conformity.

Habermas and the Second Generation

It is misleading to think of the critical theorists during the post-war period as members of a monolithic Frankfurt School. Whereas there were both a shared sense of purpose and collective work on interdisciplinary social theory from 1930 to the early 1940s, critical theorists, after the war, frequently diverged, and during the 1950s and 1960s the term 'Frankfurt School' can be applied only to the work of the institute in Germany.

During the 1950s, Jürgen Habermas became known as one of the most distinguished students of Adorno and Horkheimer and took their work in many new directions. He studied the ways that a new public sphere emerged during the time of the Enlightenment, the American and the French revolutions and how it promoted political discussion and debate. His study was placed in the context of the institute's own analysis of the transition from ninenteenth-century liberal market capitalism to the twentieth-century state and monopoly capitalism. His focus on democratization was linked with the emphasis on political participation being the core of democratic society and an essential element in individual self-development. His study *The Structural Transformation of the Public Sphere* was published in 1962 and contrasted various forms of an active, participatory bourgeois public sphere in the heroic era of liberal democracy with the privatized forms of spectator politics in a bureaucratic industrial society in which the media and elites control the public sphere. On this account, big economic and government organizations took over the public sphere, while citizens became content to be primarily consumers of goods, services, political administration, and spectacle.

Generalizing from developments in Britain, France, and Germany in the late 18th and 19th century, Habermas first sketched out a model of what he called the 'bourgeois public sphere' and then analyzed its degeneration in the twentieth century. The function of the bourgeois public sphere, which began appearing around 1700 in Habermas's interpretation, was to mediate between the private concerns of individuals in their familial, economic, and social life; and the demands of social and public life. This involved mediation in the contradiction between *bourgeois* and *citoyen* (terms developed by Hegel and the early Marx), and the overcoming of private interests and opinions for the sake of discovering common interests and consensus. The public sphere consisted of organs of information and political debate such as newspapers and journals, but also institutions of political discussion such as parliaments, political clubs, literary salons, public assemblies, pubs and coffee houses, meeting halls, and other public spaces where socio-political discussion took place. For the first time in history, individuals and groups could shape public opinion, giving direct expression to their needs and interests while influencing political practice. The bourgeois public sphere made it possible to form a realm of public opinion that opposed state power and the powerful interests that were coming to shape bourgeois society. Habermas's notion of public sphere refers to a space of institutions and practices between the private interests of everyday life in civil society and the realm of state power. The public sphere mediates between the domains of the family and the workplace – where private interests prevail – and the state which often exerts arbitrary forms of power and domination.

The public sphere makes possible an open discussion of all issues of general concern, with discursive argumentation employed to ascertain general interests and the public good. It presupposes, therefore, freedom of speech and assembly, free press, and the right freely to participate in political debate and decision-making. After the democratic revolutions, Habermas suggested, the bourgeois public sphere was institutionalized in constitutional orders that guaranteed a wide range of political rights, and established a judicial system meant to mediate claims between various individuals or groups, or between individuals, groups, and the state.

Habermas discerned a process of 'refeudalization' of the public sphere beginning in the late nineteenth century. The transformation occurs when private interests assume direct political functions – as powerful corporations come to control and manipulate the media and the state. Simultaneously, the state begins to play a more fundamental role in the private realm and everyday life, eroding as a result the difference between state and civil society and between the public and private sphere. As the public sphere declines, citizens become consumers, dedicating themselves more to passive consumption and private concerns than to issues of the common good and democratic participation.

While in the bourgeois public sphere, public opinion, on Habermas's analysis, is formed through political debate and consensus, in the debased public sphere of welfare state capitalism, public opinion is administered by political, economic, and media elites. No longer is rational consensus among individuals and groups the norm striving for the articulation of common goods. Rather, it is the struggle among groups to advance their own private interests that characterizes the scene of contemporary politics.

This historical transformation (from liberal public sphere to 'welfare state capitalism and mass democracy') is grounded in Horkheimer and Adorno's analysis of the culture industry in which giant corporations take over the public sphere and transform it from a sphere of rational debate into one of manipulative and passive consumption. In this transformation, 'public opinion' shifts from rational consensus emerging from debate, discussion, and reflection to the manufactured opinion of polls or media experts. 'Publicity loses its critical function in favor of a staged display; even arguments are transmuted into symbols to which again one can not respond by arguing but only by identifying with them' (Habermas 1989: 206). The function of the media has been transformed from facilitating rational discourse and debate inside the public sphere into shaping, constructing, and limiting public discourse to those themes validated and approved by media corporations. Hence, the interconnection between a sphere of public debate and individual participation has been fractured and transmuted into that of a realm of political information and spectacle, in which citizen-consumers ingest and absorb passively entertainment and information. In Habermas's words: 'Inasmuch as the mass media today strip away the literary husks from the kind of bourgeois self-interpretation and utilize them as marketable forms for the public services provided in a culture of consumers, the original meaning is reversed (Habermas 1989: 171).

Habermas offered tentative proposals for the revitalization of the public sphere by setting 'in motion a *critical* process of public communication through the very organizations that mediatize it' (Habermas 1989: 232). He concluded with the suggestion that 'a critical publicity brought to life within intraorganizational public spheres' (Habermas 1989: 232) might lead to democratisation of the major institutions of civil society; the truth of the matter is that he did not provide concrete examples, propose any strategies, or sketch out the features of an oppositional or post-bourgeois public sphere.

Like Horkheimer and Adorno in *Dialectic of Enlightenment*, Habermas had produced an account of how the bourgeois public sphere turned into its opposite. Recognizing that using an earlier form of social organization to criticize its later deformation was rather nostalgic, Habermas called for a renewed democratization of public institutions and spaces at the end of *Structural Transformation* (Habermas 1989: 248ff.), but this was merely a moral exhortation with no discernible institutional basis or social movements to realize the call.

In order to discover a new standpoint for critique, to provide new philosophical foundations for critical theory, and to contribute a new force for democratization, Habermas turned in the 1970s to the realms of language and communication. His argument now was that language itself contains norms enabling the critique of domination and oppression and providing an instrument for the grounding and promotion of democratization. In the capacity to understand the speech of another, to submit to the force of a better argument, and to reach consensus, Habermas locates a rationality inherent in what he came to call 'communicative action' that could generate norms capable of criticizing distortions of communication in processes of domination and manipulation and cultivating a process of rational discursive will-formation. Developing what he called an 'ideal speech situation,' Habermas offers quasi-transcendental grounds for social critique and a model for democratic social communication and interaction.

Habermas in this way tried to establish critical theory on a stronger theoretical foundation and to overcome the impasse that – to his mind – Frankfurt School had become trapped in. Over the past several decades, Habermas has been arguing that language and communication are a central feature of the human lifeworld – one that can resist the systemic imperatives of money and power that undermine communicative structures. This project has both generated a wealth of theoretical discussions and has provided normative bases for social critique and democratization.

References

Adorno, T. W. (1973), *Negative Dialectics*, London: Routledge and Kegan Paul.

Adorno, T. W. [1970] (1984), *Aesthetic Theory*, London, Routledge Kegan Paul.

Arato, A., and E. Gebhardt (eds) (1982), *The Frankfurt School Reader*, New York: Continuum.

Bronner, S., and D. Kellner (eds) (1989), *Politics, Culture and Society: A Critical Theory Reader*, London, and New York: Routledge.

Habermas, J. (1983 and 1987), *Theory of Communicative Action*, 2 vols, Boston: Beacon Press.

Habermas, J. (1989), *Structural Transformation of the Public Sphere*, Cambridge: MIT Press.

Horkheimer, M. (1972), *Critical Theory*, trans. M. J. O'Connell, New York: Herder and Herder.

Horkheimer, M. [1947] (1974a), *Eclipse of Reason*, New York: Seabury.

Horkheimer, M., and T.W. Adorno (1972), *Dialectic of Enlightenment*, New York: Herder and Herder.

Jay, M. (1973), *The Dialectical Imagination*, Boston: Little Brown.

Kellner, D. (1984), *Herbert Marcuse and the Crisis of Marxism*, London, Berkeley: University of California Press.

Kellner, D. (1989), *Critical Theory, Marxism and Modernity*, Baltimore: Johns Hopkins University Press; Cambridge: Polity Press.

Marcuse, H. (1955), *Eros and Civilization*, Boston: Beacon Press.

Marcuse, H. [1941] (1960), *Reason and Revolution*, Boston: Beacon Press.

Marcuse, H. (1964), *One-Dimensional Man*, Boston: Beacon Press.

Wiggershaus, R. (1994), *The Frankfurt School*, Cambridge: Polity Press.

Psychoanalysis

Alenka Zupancic

The focus of this chapter is exclusively on Sigmund Freud's discoveries and theoretical propositions and on Jacques Lacan's 'return to Freud' in his stunning enterprise, in which he cast psychoanalysis on the centre stage of contemporary philosophical debate. The presentation of the theoretical insights of Freud and Lacan follows the thread of two major concepts, that of the unconscious and that of the drive (or sexuality), while trying to indicate the way in which other crucial concepts enter into their scope or follow from them.

From the very beginning, psychoanalysis was surrounded by debates about whether its scope lay more in the realm of natural sciences or of philosophy and cultural sciences. Freud was frequently, and simultaneously, attacked from both sides: some objected to his 'biologism' and 'scientism,' while others attacked his 'cultural relativism' and speculations that went far beyond the clinical circumstances. Regardless of what was (or is) the pertinence of these criticisms in particular conceptual questions, we should never lose sight of the fact that a major dimension of Freud's discovery was precisely the overlapping of the two realms, defined as the physical and the mental. If there is any meaningful general way of describing the object of psychoanalysis, it might be precisely this: the object of psychoanalysis is the zone where the two realms overlap, that is, where the biological or somatic is already mental or cultural and where, at the same time, culture springs from the very impasses of the somatic functions which it tries to resolve (yet, while doing this, it creates new ones). In other words, the overlapping in question is not simply an overlapping of two well-established entities, but an intersection which is generative of both sides that overlap in it. Freud saw very quickly not only to what considerable extent culture and mind were able to affect, even distort and physically change, human bodies, but also, and perhaps more significantly, that there must be something in the human body that makes this possible. And that this something is not a kind of inborn propensity for culture and spirituality, a germ of mind or soul deposited in our bodies, but something much closer to a biological dysfunction, which turns out to be strangely productive. This question will be taken up in more detail à propos the Freudian theory of the drives. As Freud himself put it, '[T]he concept of drive is thus one of those lying on the frontier between the mental and the physical.'[1]

The Unconscious (and related matters)

Freud's discovery of the unconscious was something very precise, and it went against two predominant views on the question. On the one hand, it directly challenged a traditional philosophical view in which 'psychical' (or 'mental') *meant* 'conscious,' so that to speak of 'unconscious psychical processes' amounted to a contradiction in terms. On the other hand, Freud's conceptual suggestion was also very different from the existing psychological notion of the unconscious (shared by certain philosophers), which was used merely to indicate the contrast with the conscious: there are psychical processes going on without our being aware of them. Freud's thesis was much stronger: there exists another, more specific form of the unconscious, which refers to something *inadmissible to consciousness* (Freud 1976: 775). This implies several important things. The unconscious activity, far from being only an activity shut out from consciousness, is also something that actively shuts certain activities from consciousness. Moreover, the unconscious thinks. It does not, however, simply think with its own head, matters are more complicated than that. For Freud was also very reluctant to acknowledge the enthusiastic, rather romantic reception of the unconscious that followed his discoveries. According to this reception, the unconscious was seen as the 'Other', true consciousness, a mastermind behind the scenes, hypostasized as the natural Subject behind the small and somehow artificial subject of consciousness; consciousness was nothing more than a puppet or a superfluous reflected picture of the completed and complex process of the unconscious. Although this perception did a lot to make Freud's theory widely popular, Freud immediately recognized in it a resistance to the real core of his discoveries, a resistance no smaller in its implications than that of the straightforward rejection of the concept of the unconscious. Whereas the latter had a relatively short life, the former continued to haunt psychoanalysis throughout the century. For what, in fact, was the real core of the Freudian discovery? To put it simply: it was not that the unconscious is the true Master behind the scene of our conscious life, and consciousness only its puppet, but something much closer to consciousness being, through the bias of the unconscious, its own (un)willing puppet. There is a certain complicity at work in the opposed fields of consciousness and the unconscious. Or, more precisely, the struggle and tension between the two fields is internal to the unconscious itself and constitutes one of its possible definitions.

Freud first extensively elaborated the concept of the unconscious in his *Interpretation of Dreams*, which combines three major theses: (1) The unconscious is made of *representations*, which are per se in no way different from conscious representations; (2) Unconscious formations are not as irrational and incoherent as they usually strike us – in the case of dreams, by following certain rules of interpretation, we are led from their manifest content to their latent content, which is perfectly coherent; and (3) There is *no fixed key* that would allow us to translate the manifest content into the latent content.

One of Freud's crucial insights was that we should not look for the meaning of representations forming the manifest level of dreams (which is what the 'interpretation of dreams' amounted to before Freud). For these representations contain no deeper, secret meaning. They should be taken quite literally, and they should be taken as bits of an associative chain, the reconstruction of which is the work of analysis and can eventually lead to the coherent narrative of latent thoughts. The linking that forms a certain chain of representations does not take place along the lines of their meaning, but along the lines of two kinds of representative associations. The intensity and meaning of a certain experience can be attached to any element of the situation in which this experience occurred, without there being any meaningful relation between the two. The other kind of association follows the pure resemblance of words or their sounds, as well as condensation of these associative bits, which can lead to the forming of new words. Freud liked to compare dreams to rebuses: in order to 'read' them, we must not look for what every represented figure stands for. Instead, we have to take them at the level of their wording: an image of a horse and an image of a cat playing with a ball of wool, for example, can give us 'horseplay' as the word we are looking for.

If dreams are the 'royal way to the unconscious,' these Freudian observations can be taken as the royal way to one of the crucial aspects of Jacques Lacan's 'return to Freud' and of several of his most famous theoretical propositions, from 'the unconscious is structured like a language,' or 'the subject's unconscious is the other's discourse' (Lacan 2006: 219) to 'a signifier is what represents the subject to another signifier' (Lacan 2006: 694).

It is often thought that Lacan's move in this respect was to supplement the Freudian theory with the findings brought about by structural linguistics (notably by Ferdinand de Saussure and Roman Jakobson). Matters, however, are more complex than that. On one level, Lacan recognized in Freudian observations a stunning anticipation of several central issues that were properly conceptualized, for the first time, by structural linguistics. In this respect, he did indeed consider that due to the absence of any such theory in Freud's time, Freud's observations were given a proper theoretical basis only with the later elaboration of theory of the signifier. On another level, and more importantly, Lacan referred, or returned to the Freudian theory in order to supplement the structural linguistics with something that he considered crucial. The central themes of structural linguistics are the arbitrariness of the sign and the emphasis on differentiality (signifiers only 'make sense,' or produce meaning, as parts of a differential network of places, binary oppositions and so on; the signifying chain is strictly separated from the signified), as well as on the fact that there are no positive entities in language. Lacan concluded that there was an important characteristic of every spoken language that was left out from this account, or was only considered on its margins, as in Saussure's passion for anagrams and popular etymologies. It is not only according to the laws of differentiality that signifiers produce sense, but also according to the two already mentioned mechanisms: sonorous similarities or homonyms and associations that exist in the speaker's memory. Here, we are dealing with something like positive entities, with words functioning strangely similarly to objects. Lacan articulated this in his thesis that the divide separating the signifier from the signified is not an absolute one: in the common use of language it happens quite frequently that the signifier 'falls' into the signified, 'enters it,' and thus 'raises the questions of its place in reality' (Lacan 2006: 417).

In more general terms we could say that signifiers are not simply used to refer to reality, they are part of the same reality they refer to; hence 'there is no such thing as a metalanguage' (Lacan 2006: 737), the Other as the locus of signifiers is constitutively not–all, or 'doesn't exist' (Lacan 2006: 695). These Lacanian formulas are different formulations that follow from his central conceptual move, which could be simply described as follows: Lacan transposed the bar separating the signifier from the signified (S/s) into the bar inherent to the register of the signifier itself. Signifiers are never pure signifiers. They are ridden, from within, by unexpected surpluses that tend to ruin the logic of their pure differentiality. On the one side – the structuralist side that Lacan includes in his theory – they are separated from the signified in the sense that there is no inherent connection leading from the signifier to its meaning. Yet, if this were all, the signifying field would be a consistent system and, as the structuralist motto goes, a structure without subject. Lacan subscribes to this view to the extent to which it convincingly does away with the notion of 'psychological subject,' of intentional subjectivity using the language for its purposes, mastering the field of speech or being its Cause and Source. Yet, he goes a step further. If we focus on the signifying chain, precisely in its independence and autonomy, we are bound to notice that it constantly produces, from itself, quite unexpected effects of meaning, a meaning which is, strictly speaking, a surplus meaning that stains signifiers from within. This surplus meaning is also a carrier of certain quotas of affect or enjoyment, '*jouissance*': Lacan points at the coincidence of the two by writing *jouissance* as *joui-sens*, 'enjoy-meant.' It is precisely through this surplus meaning as enjoyment that signifiers are intrinsically bound to reality to which they refer. Incidentally, this is also the kernel of Lacan's insistence on the truth being not–all: the effect of the signifier cannot be fully reduced back to the signifier as its cause.

Freud was on the track of this with his method of free associations: the more one loosens the imperative of 'wanting to say' (something), the more the language will start to behave like itself very much 'wanting to say' something. And Lacan's move was completely to turn around the common perception of Freud on this point, which was, to put it simply, that there is another, true subject, the subject of the unconscious who is trying to get its voice heard through these peculiar signifying formations. Contrary to this notion, and also against the tide of structuralist dismissal of the notion of subject, he maintained that the subject of the unconscious is the *effect* of the signifiers (Lacan 1979: 207) stumbling upon themselves, producing sense in non-sense. The subject of the unconscious is not some deeply hidden subject that makes its presence known through, say, dreams or the slips of the tongue; it only exists with, and within, these very slips of the tongue. The two Lacanian moves sketched above (the conception of the signifying order as 'barred' from the inside or inherently incon-sistent, and the introduction of the subject on this level) are summed up in his famous definition of the signifying representation: a signifier is what represents the subject for another signifier. On the one hand, the subject is the name for the absent cause that would link one signifier to another in the signifying chain. It is not that the subject fills in this absence of a cause (with its own 'unconscious intentionality'), the subject *is* this very absence. On the other hand, this negative movement, endlessly referring one signifier to another, is stopped from time to time by the short-circuit of the signifier falling into the signified, which expels the subject from the signifying chain, and 'fixes' her (in all meanings of the word) in relation to this particular 'master-signifier' that epitomizes subject's enjoy-meant. For Lacan, the work of analysis ultimately consists in mapping out such master-signifiers, the reason for this being that the fixing of the subject in relation to them is correlative with the 'primal repression,' which, already according to Freud, becomes a sort of attractor and guiding principle of subsequent repressions (Freud 1984: 148). Because of its being a result of the signifier falling into the signified, the master-signifier is different in nature from the rest of the signifying chain. It is not simply a representation, it is a representation bound with enjoyment (*jouissance*), or even more precisely, it is representation *as* enjoyment. This is Lacan's solution of the point that Freud was struggling with, when he came to realize that his early optimistic belief in the sole powers of interpretation (presenting the patients with the right interpretation of their symptoms should bring about the dissolution of the latter) was premature: symptoms persisted beyond their 'being deciphered.' Freud thus started to distinguish between the (repressed) *representation* and the quota of *affect* attached to it, suggesting that their destinies could be very different, and that the destiny of the affect is much more important in the process of repression. With the 'master-signifier' Lacan conceptualizes the point where the two destinies are nevertheless inseparably bound together.

The master-signifier (S_1) is not an unconscious content, it is the principle or the key of its encoding, which can itself not be further decoded. The crucial point is that it is not by finding or possessing this key that the unconscious thoughts can be decoded. Rather the opposite: the unconscious knowledge is put to work in analysis in order to spell out, or 'produce' this key, which is quite meaningless in itself, yet embodies the formula of the subject's relationship to enjoyment.

This point is related to another important aspect of the Freudian conceptualization of the unconscious. What, precisely, is the unconscious? There is no such thing as a direct perception of the unconscious thoughts. Dreams (and other formations of unconscious) are not the place where one can get an unobstructed view in the unconscious, beyond the censorship and repression that otherwise 'hide' them from consciousness. On the contrary, these formations are nothing but the censorship and distortion at work. With years, Freud was more and more emphasizing the fact that the unconscious *is* this very distortion, and not some untarnished content lying beyond these distortions, and contained in the coherent narrative of the latent thoughts reconstructed in the process of analysis. Freud is most clear on this point in his *Introductory Lectures on Psychoanalysis* (1915–17). Starting from the fundamental distinction between the manifest and the latent content, he comes to situate the unconscious not simply in the latent content, but in the very excess of form over content, the excess that *relates* manifest narrative to the latent one (Freud 1973: 261–2).

Something *is added* to the latent thoughts and this surplus, constitutive of a dream, is the unconscious desire. In this perspective the unconscious desire is but this excess of form over content. The unconscious desire is not what is articulated in the latent thoughts, for instance – in the case of Freud's own famous dream of 'Irma's injection' – the wish to be absolved of the responsibility for a patient not getting better. The same applies to some other cases discussed by Freud, wishes related to professional ambitions or aggressive wishes towards our supposedly beloved ones, or 'inappropriate' sexual wishes. All these wishes are not all that unconscious; they are closer to the register of thoughts that we (more or less consciously) *have*, but wouldn't admit to. We could also say that the censorship banning these wishes mostly comes from cultural and social conventions, in the sense that they are banned by the 'interiorized exterior authority/law,' combined with the image of ourselves that we have and would like to keep. However, if this is enough to make us push these disagreeable thoughts away and refuse to face them directly, it is not enough for the repression in the strict sense of the word to take place. Freud makes it very clear that there is a crucial dimension of repression that comes from the inside, which is to say that its causes reside in the intensity of pressure of certain drive impulses. More precisely, repression occurs on account of a short-circuit between a painful quantum of affect and a representation. A representation is thus repressed not for its 'inappropriate' content, but for the intensity of the affect or drive impulse related to it. Freud insists on this point in his 1915 article on 'Repression' (1984).

We recall that the motive and purpose of repression was nothing else than the avoidance of unpleasure. It follows that the vicissitude of the quota of affect belonging to the representative is much more important that the vicissitude of the idea, and this fact is decisive for our assessment of the process of repression (Freud 1984: 153).

It is this degree of displeasure that is 'deemed' inappropriate/inadmissible. Incidentally, this also explains why the progressive liberalization of morals, the shift in the norms and representations of what is culturally acceptable, has not such a significant effect on the levels of repression as it is sometimes believed. There is a very common misperception of psychoanalysis, which could be summed up as follows: sexuality is the central driving force of human nature, which was socially and culturally suppressed for centuries. This suppression resulted in repression (in the Freudian sense of the term), and hence in all kinds of neurotic and psychotic disorders, which were further 'used' for different manipulative purposes, such as stirring up the aggression against this or that designed 'enemy.' In order to stop this process – or so the story goes – we must thus liberate sexuality from this cultural restraint as much as possible.

Freud soon became very well aware that the dialectic of suppression and repression is much more complicated than that. Following his line of thought, Lacan, in his usual radical manner, went as far as to say: 'Even if the memories of familial suppression weren't true, they would have to be invented, and that is certainly done' (Lacan 1990: 30). This is not at all to say that suppression is not real in the sense that it doesn't really take place. What Lacan aims at is that there is a sexual impasse which is not a result of suppression, but which itself 'exudes the fictions that rationalize the impossible within which it originates' (Lacan 1990: 30). Memories of repression are part of just such fictions – not in the sense of being imagined, but in the sense of being used, very much like the day's residues in dreams, to form a narrative that rationalizes, and inscribes into the symbolic, the impossible-real of the sexual impasse. (Contrary to what appears as irrational character of dreams, Freud immediately saw that dreams are in fact the greatest 'rationalisers.') It is here that the Lacanian distinction between the reality and the Real gets its conceptual pertinence. The Real is not the truth of reality, or the reality without distortions, a 'naked reality'; the Real is not beyond the reality – the Real is nothing else but a fundamental, structural impasse to which reality gives this or that form. It is not a realm – Lacan defines it as a 'register.' If we take away the reality, no Real will be left. The fact that reality as we experience it is always-already distorted (in the sense in which the great twentieth-century theme of ideology conceptualized this distortion, or else in the sense in which Lacan proclaimed that all reality is fantasmatic) does not mean that reality is a distortion *of* the Real. The distortions of reality (that is, different narratives that structure our symbolic universe and define the 'roles' that we are expected to assume, starting with 'child,' 'woman,' 'man,' 'mother,' 'father') are different forms built to deal with the impasse of the real that constantly haunts us *from within*. To say that this impasse is structural is to say that it 'ex-sists' as an irreducible surplus element of reality: as its inherent contradiction that may disappear from one place, yet only to reappear in the other.

In *Television*, Lacan thus maintains that 'it is repression that produces suppression. Why couldn't the family, society itself, be creation built from repression? They're nothing less' (Lacan 1990: 28). This might strike the ear as a strange apology for suppression. Suppression is a defense formation, an effect of, or a reaction to the primal repression as *factum* of human nature, which is to say as something structurally and fundamentally unavoidable. And there seems to be only a step from this stance to the reactionary, authoritarian claims, justifying the necessity of suppression, of firm laws and prohibitions that can give us a clearer orientation in our lives. Although there have always been psychoanalysts who actually leaned in this direction, this is absolutely foreign to Lacan's position. In order to see this, we have to bear in mind two things. Firstly, it is not on the basis of abstract speculation that psychoanalysis has come to the conclusion that severe and often 'irrational' social laws and prohibitions are in fact a 'rationalization' of a certain libidinal impasse. On the contrary, this is something to be seen on a daily basis in psychoanalytic work with neurotics. Although it is most evident in obsessional neurosis (the countless 'irrational' prohibitions and rituals that a person invents in order to deal with that impasse), it is also very much present in hysteria (for instance in the form of provoking the Other to firmly 'set a limit,' or as a condition of getting satisfaction from the very impossibility of satisfying a desire). In these cases we can see clearly not only how the unconscious gladly embraces, even grabs certain forms of suppression in order to (re)organize disturbing libidinal pressure, but also how this really *never fully works*: the cure is even more disastrous than the illness. And this is the second crucial point. New forms always need to be added, until this edifice of defense and rationalization becomes itself a major 'irrational' obstacle to any form of 'normal' life.

If psychoanalysis very early discovered a complicity between repression and suppression and saw how various forms of suppression were elaborated to deal with the repressed (and its return, which, as Lacan put it, are one and the same thing), it was not to encourage or justify the suppression, but to warn against the simplistic conviction that the progressive liberalization of laws and prohibitions is *in itself* a guarantee against the discontent in civilization, against the vicious circle that Freud recognized in the relationship between 'culture' (or 'civilization') and 'drives.' To put it simply: the vigor with which culture bends, tames or suppresses the drives, comes from these drives themselves (Freud 1985: 321). This is why dealing with any kind of 'real' suppression involves, as its first and fundamental step, the dealing with repression.

Drives and sexuality

Freudian revolution concerning the field of sexuality is, of course, not unrelated to the themes discussed above. On the one hand, Freud soon came to the idea that there is not only cultural pressure that deters the sexual drive from its full satisfaction, but also something in the very essence of the sexual function (Freud 1985: 295). In 1912, he writes most explicitly: 'It is my belief that, however strange it may sound, we must reckon with the possibility that something in the nature of the sexual drive itself is unfavourable to the realization of complete satisfaction' (Freud 1977: 258). In other words, there is something in human sexuality that never fully adds up. On the other hand, Freud was led to supplement this stance with a further one: there is something in human nature (that is, on the most basic level of the satisfaction of needs) that never adds up without a remainder which divides it from within, and it is within the cracks thus opened up that the sexual takes place. In other words, it is not simply that human sexuality never adds up to form a complete satisfaction, it is also that sexuality is the very name for what does not add up in the coupling of needs and their satisfaction, the name for the surplus satisfaction produced in this coupling. The negative dimension of the sexual drives (their never being fully satisfied), the *lack* they imply, originates in the *surplus* that breaks down the logic of complementarity which could otherwise only be disturbed from without (by exterior obstacles standing in the way of satisfaction).

In his early major work on sexuality, published in 1905 (*Three Essays on the Theory of Sexuality*), Freud already explores the issue in all its complexity. He starts with the discussion of 'sexual aberrations' that were identified as such in the existing corpus of medical knowledge: homosexuality, sodomy, paedophilia, fetishism, voyeurism, sadism, masochism, and so on. In discussing these 'perversions' and the mechanisms involved in them (basically the deviations in respect of the sexual object, which is supposed to be an adult person of the opposite sex, and deviations in respect of the sexual aim – supposedly reproduction) Freud's argument simultaneously moves in two directions. On the one hand, he extensively demonstrates how the 'aberrant' mechanisms involved in these practices are very much present in what is considered as 'normal' or 'natural' sexual behavior. The dividing line between 'natural' and 'unnatural' in this domain is always extremely slippery: insofar as they are well integrated in what is considered to be a 'normal' sexuality, they are not viewed as perversions. They are considered as perverse aberrations only if they become altogether independent of the 'appropriate' sexual object and of the supposed sexual aim, if they become autonomous in their fragmented, partial aims that serve no meaningful purpose. Freud would object, however, to the word 'become' – and this constitutes the second line of his argument. Drives are fragmented, partial, aimless and independent of their object *to start with*. They do not become such due to some ulterior deviation. The deviation of drives is a constitutive deviation. Freud writes that 'the sexual drive is in the first instance independent of its object; nor is its origin likely to be due to its object's attractions' (Freud 1977: 60). This is why 'from the point of view of psychoanalysis the exclusive sexual interest felt by men for women is also a problem that needs elucidating and is not a self-evident fact based upon an attraction that is ultimately of a chemical nature' (Freud 1977: 57).

The discovery of this constitutive and original deviation of drives (which is precisely what distinguishes them from instincts) will gradually lead to one of the major conceptual inventions of psychoanalysis, the concept of the object small *a*, as it was named by Lacan. To put it simply, object *a* will come to name the other (the real) object of the drive as 'independent of its object': object *a* is 'satisfaction as an object' (Miller 1966: 313). And it is also as such that it can function as the *cause* of desire (as different from the need), so that the cause of desire should be distinguished from its object or objective. It is not what the desire 'wants,' but what keeps it going.

But let us look at the origin of this concept in Freud's observations. One of Freud's main examples is thumb-sucking, which he analyzes as a manifestation of infantile sexuality (the existence of which was, for the first time, systematically pointed out by Freud, and was met with strong resistance). In relation to the need for nourishment, to which it attaches itself at the outset, the oral drive pursues an object different from food: it pursues (and aims at repeating) the very sensation of satisfaction produced in the region of the mouth during the act of nutrition. The oral satisfaction, which arises as a by-product of satisfying the need for food, starts to function as autonomous object of the drive; it moves away from its first object and lets itself be led into a series of substitute objects. In other words, the concept of the drive (and of its object) is not simply a concept of the deviation from a natural need, but something that casts a new and surprising light on the nature of the human need as such: in human beings, all satisfaction of a need allows, in principle, for another satisfaction to occur, which tends to become independent and self-perpetuating in pursuing and reproducing itself. There is no natural need that would be absolutely pure, that is, devoid of this surplus element which splits it from within. This split, this interval or void, this original nonconvergence of two different slopes of satisfaction is, for Freud, the very site or ground of human sexuality. This is a crucial point when it comes to understanding Freud and his emphasis on sexuality: 'sexual' is not to be confused with 'genital' (Freud 1977: 96). The 'genital sexual organization' is far from being primordial or 'natural'; it is a result, a product of several stages of development, involving both physiological maturation of reproductive organs and cultural-symbolic parameters. It involves a unification of the originally heterogeneous, dispersed, compound sexual drive: '[S]ince the original disposition is necessarily a complex one, the sexual drive itself must be something put together from various factors' (Freud 1977: 156). This unification bears two major characteristics. First, it is always a forced and artificial unification (it cannot be viewed simply as a natural teleological result of reproductive maturation). And second, it is never really fully achieved or accomplished, which is to say that it never transforms the sexual drive into an organic Unity, with all its components ultimately serving one and the same Purpose. The 'normal', 'healthy' human sexuality is thus a paradoxical artificial naturalization of the originally de-naturalized drives (de-naturalized in the sense of their departing from 'natural' aims of self-preservation and/or the logic of a pure need as unaffected by another, supplementary satisfaction). One could even say that human sexuality is 'sexual' (and not simply 'reproductive') precisely insofar as the unification at stake, the tying of all the drives to one single Purpose, never really works, but allows for different partial drives to continue their circular, self-perpetuating activity.

Freud introduced the concept of libido to refer to the quantum of energy at work in the specific, 'declinational' path of the drives. Libido names the 'energy' involved in the processes of supplementary satisfaction, for instance – to pursue the previous example – thumb-sucking, or consuming food beyond the biological needs of the body, for the sheer pleasure of exciting the mucous membrane. Freud insists on this energy/ excitation being sexual, although 'this sexual excitation is derived not from the so-called sexual parts alone, but from all the bodily organs' (Freud 1977: 139). This point is absolutely crucial, for it allows us to see in what sense Freud actually *discovered* (human) sexuality, and not simply emphasized it or 'reduced' everything to it. It is not that thumb-sucking or gourmandise are sexual against the background of their supposed relationship to the excitation involved in the sexual intercourse; on the contrary, if anything, they are sexual per se, and it is the sexual intercourse which is properly sexual on account of being composed of different partial drives like these (looking, touching, licking, and so on).

It is in relation to this Freudian stance that we can measure the significance of the stakes involved in his break with Carl Gustav Jung, as well as the genuine philosophical implications of Freud's radical conceptual move. Jung adopted the Freudian notion of the libido and, with a seemingly small modification, gave it an entirely different meaning. With Jung, libido becomes a psychical expression of a 'vital energy,' the origin of which is not solely sexual. In this perspective, libido is a general name for psychic energy, which is sexual only in certain segments. Freud immediately saw how to follow this Jungian move would be to 'sacrifice all that we have gained hitherto from psychoanalytic observation' (Freud 1977: 140). With the term 'libido' Freud designates an original and irreducible imbalance of the human nature. Every satisfaction of a need brings with itself the possibility of a supplementary satisfaction, deviating from the object and aim of a given demand while pursuing its own goal, thus constituting a seemingly dysfunctional detour. It is this detour, or the space which it opens up, that constitutes not only the field of the catalogued 'sexual aberrations,' but also the ground, as well as the energy source, for what is generally referred to as human culture in its highest accomplishments. The generative source of culture is sexual in this precise sense of belonging to the supplementary satisfaction that serves no immediate function and satisfies no immediate need. The image of the human nature that follows from these Freudian conceptualizations is that of a split (and conflictual) nature, whereby the 'sexual' refers to this very split. If Freud uses the term 'libido' to refer to a certain field of 'energy,' it is to refer to it as a *surplus* energy, and not to any kind of general energetic level involved in our lives. It cannot designate the whole of energy (as Jung suggested), since it is precisely what makes this whole 'not-whole.' Sexual 'energy' is not an element that has its place within the whole of human life; the central point of Freud's discovery was precisely that there is no 'natural' or pre-established place of human sexuality, that it is constitutively out-of-its-place, fragmented and dispersed, that it exists only in deviations from 'itself' or its supposed natural object, and that sexuality is nothing else but this 'out-of-placeness' of its constitutive satisfaction. In other words, Freud's fundamental move was to desubstantialize sexuality: the sexual is not a substance to be properly described and circumscribed, it is the very impossibility of its own circumscription or delimitation. It can neither be completely separated from biological, organic needs and functions (since it originates within their realm, it starts off by inhabiting them), nor can it be simply reduced to them. The sexual is not a separate domain of human activity or life, and this is why it can inhabit all the domains of human life. What was, and still is, disturbing about the Freudian discovery is not simply the emphasis on sexuality – this kind of resistance, outraged by psychoanalytical 'obsession with indecent matters,' was never the strongest one and was soon marginalized by the progressive liberalism of morals. The even more powerful resistance comes from the liberalism itself, promoting sexuality as a 'natural activity,' as originally balanced and only subsequently thrown out of balance. If anything, such as image of sexuality is bound to bring about the state in which already the smallest shoot of *jouissance* is able to throw us totally out of balance. It completely misses the basic Freudian point which, put in Lacanian terms, could be formulated as follows: the Sexual doesn't exist. There is only the sexual that insists/persists as constitutive imbalance of human nature.

Lacan reflected on this fundamental imbalance with the Freudian notion of the 'death drive,' redefining it as the core of any drive, and thus moving away from the later Freudian hypothesis of the duality of drives (life drives and death drives). Lacan formulated this unification in terms of an internal contradiction of life itself (the 'death drive' being the name of this contradiction), epitomizing it with the following fragment from Heraclitus: 'To the bow (Biós) is given the name of life (Bíos) and its work is death.' Nothing could be further from the Lacanian notion of death drive than the idea that something in us 'wants to die,' and aims at death and destruction. If the death drive can be lethal, it is because, on the contrary, it is altogether indifferent to death. In the human subject, there is something that has for its one and only purpose to go on living and perpetuating itself, regardless of the question of whether it kills the subject or makes her prosper (*jouissance* being one of the principal names for this something). This is why the image that Lacan chooses for the death drive (the myth of lamella) is not an image of destruction, but instead the image of an 'indestructible life' (Lacan 1979: 198). Since this notion of death drive is often at issue in contemporary philosophical debates, and has earned Lacan the reputation of assigning to death the determinant role in human subjectivity (along the lines of the Heideggerian Being-toward-death), we cannot stress this point too much.[2] Lacan's 'death drive' is precisely that on account of which a subject can never be reduced to the horizon of her death, or determined by it. This is not to say, on the other hand, that the death drive saves us from our finitude, but rather that it transposes its configuration. We are not finite simply because we die, we are finite because something that wouldn't die introduces a limit to our life, a limit that divides it from within. Subject is what lives – and dies – on both sides of this limit.

Notes

1. Freud 1977: 83. Translation modified at the point of the Freudian term '*Trieb*' ('instinct' in Strachey's translation): 'drive' has become generally used as more accurate translation.
2. On this controversy see Žižek 2000: 163–7.

References

Althusser, L. (1993), *Écrits sur la psychanalyse. Freud et Lacan*, Paris: STOCK/IMEC.

Baas, B. (1992), *Le désir pur. Parcours philosophiques dans les parages de J. Lacan*, Louvain: Peeters.

Badiou, A. (2005), *Le siècle*, Paris: Seuil.

Copjec, J. (1994), *Read my Desire. Lacan against the Historicists*, Cambridge: MIT Press.

Deguy, M. (1991), *Lacan avec les philosophes*, Paris: Albin Michel.

Deleuze, G. (1967), *Présentation de Sacher-Masoch*, Paris: Minuit.

Dolar, M. (1998), 'Cogito as the Subject of the Unconscious,' in S. Žižek (ed.) (1998), *Cogito and the Unconscious*, Durham, and London: Duke University Press.

Fink, B. (1995), *The Lacanian Subject. Between Language and Jouissance*, Princeton: Princeton University Press.

Freud, S. (1973), *Introductory Lectures on Psychoanalysis*, The Pelican Freud Library, vol. 1, trans. J. Strachey, Harmondsworth: Penguin Books.

Freud, S. (1976), *The Interpretation of Dreams*, The Pelican Freud Library, vol. 4, trans. J. Strachey, Harmondsworth: Penguin Books.

Freud, S. (1977), 'Three Essays on the Theory of Sexuality,' in *On Sexuality*, The Pelican Freud Library, vol 7, trans. J. Strachey, Harmondsworth: Penguin Books, pp. 33–169.

Freud, S. (1984), 'Repression,' in *On Metapsychology*, The Pelican Freud Library, vol 11, trans. J. Strachey, Harmondsworth: Penguin Books, pp. 139–58.

Freud, S. (1985), 'Civilisation and its Discontents,' in *Civilisation, Society and Religion*, The Pelican Freud Library, vol. 12, trans. J. Strachey, Harmondsworth: Penguin Books, pp. 243–340.

Freud, S. (2000), *Studienausgabe I-X*, Frankfurt: Fischer.

Lacan, J. (1966), 'La science et la verité,' in *Écrits*, Paris: Seuil.

Lacan, J. (1979), *The Four Fundamental Concepts of Psychoanalysis*, trans. J. File, Harmondsworth: Penguin Books.

Lacan, J. (1990), *Television*, trans. D. Hollier, R. Krauss, and A. Michelson, London: W. W. Norton and Company.

Lacan, J. (1991a), *Le Séminaire. Livre VIII, Le transfert*, Paris: Seuil.

Lacan, J. (1991b), *Le Séminaire. Livre XVII, L'envers de la psychanalyse*, Paris: Seuil.

Lacan, J. (1992), *The Ethics of Psychoanalysis. The Seminar of Jacques Lacan. Book VII*, trans. D. Porter, London: Routledge.

Lacan, J. (1998), *Le Séminaire. Livre V, Les formations de l'inconscient*, Paris: Seuil.

Lacan, J. (1999), *On Feminine Sexuality. The Limits of Love and Knowledge. The Seminar of Jacques Lacan. Book XX, Encore*, trans. B. Fink, New York, and London: W. W. Norton and Company.

Lacan, J. (2004), *Le Séminaire. Livre X, L'angoisse*, Paris: Seuil.

Lacan, J. (2006), *Écrits*, trans. B. Fink, New York and London: W. W. Norton and Co.

Lear, J. (2005), *Freud, New York and London*: Routledge.

Miller, J.-A. (1996), 'On Perversion,' in Bruce Fink et al. (eds), *Reading Seminars I and II*, Albany: State University of New York Press.

Miller, J.-A. (2000), 'Paradigms of Jouissance,' *Lacanian ink* 17.

Milner, J.-C. (1995), *L'œuvre claire. Lacan, la science, la philosophie*, Paris: Seuil.

Rose, J. (1986), *Sexuality in the Field of Vision*, London: Verso.

Silvestre, M. (1993), *Demain la psychanalyse*, Paris: Seuil.

Wajcman, G. (1998), *L'objet du siècle*, Paris: Verdier.

Žižek, S. (1989), *The Sublime Object of Ideology*, London: Verso.

Žižek, S. (2000), *The Ticklish Subject*, London: Verso.

Structuralism

François Dosse

Broadly speaking, the term 'structure' has functioned as a password for many human sciences and provided them with a unified program. Where does the concept 'structuralism' come from, that caused so much passion and opprobrium? The term initially had an architectural sense deriving from 'structure,' which designated the manner in which an edifice is built. (*Dictionaire de Trévoux*, edition of 1771) During the seventeenth and eighteenth centuries, the meaning of the term 'structure' was modified and enlarged by analogy with living beings: language, for Vaugelas and Bernot, is like the construction that Fontenelle attributes to a man's body. Following this, the term came to describe the way in which the parts of a concrete being are organized in a whole, and thus, it became capable of acquiring several applications (anatomic, psychological, geological, mathematical structures). However, only recently has structural reason appropriated the field of the human sciences, beginning in the nineteenth century with Spencer, Morgan, and Marx. It is, therefore, an enduring phenomenon that, in a complex manner, seeks to tie together the parts of a whole in an abstract sense. 'Structure,' seldom present in Marx (see his preface to the *Critique of Political Economy* [1859]), was consecrated by Durkheim at the end of the nineteenth century in his *Rules of the Sociological Method* (1895). 'Structure' later on (between 1900 and 1926) gave birth to 'structuralism,' which André Lalande's *Vocabulary* qualified as a neologism. At the beginning of the century, psychologists adopted the term 'structuralism' in order to differentiate their practice from the practice of functional psychology.

At any rate, the modern sense of the structuralist program, familiar to contemporary scientists, originated with the evolution of linguistics. Structuralism during the 1950s and the 1960s triumphed to such a spectacular degree that, after 1955, it came to be identified with the entire French intellectual history. During these years, there was no alternative to what was offered as a new outlook on the world and human culture. For at least two decades, structuralism was generating a veritable mass enthusiasm in the ranks of the French intelligentsia, marking a high point of critical thought and giving expression to the emancipatory will of the young social sciences looking for scientific and institutional legitimation.

Then, suddenly, at the beginning of the 1980s, everything collapsed. Most of the French protagonists of this intellectual adventure disappeared, and along with them, a new era hastened to bury their work, giving the impression that an entire period had come to an end. We were spared, therefore, the work of mourning necessary to do justice to one of the most fecund periods of French intellectual history. Was structuralism a miracle or a mirage? If we pause to consider what is left, we see that, apart from some dead ends and the mutilating nature of a few negations based on questions of principle (for example, those of subject and historicity), a great deal of the structuralist lesson has been assimilated – for example, the great insight that communication is never transparent to itself.

The Structuralist Years

Starting from a linguistic center, the term 'structuralism' provoked nothing short of a revolution among the human sciences in the middle of the twentieth century. Michel Foucault was arguing that structuralism 'is not a new method, it is the awakened and restless consciousness of the modern savoir'; Jacques Derrida was defining this approach as an 'adventure of the gaze'; and Roland Barthes was thinking of structuralism as the transition from symbolic to paradigmatic consciousness and the advent of a consciousness of the paradox. We were, therefore, facing a movement of thought, a new relation to the world, considerably larger than a mere methodological binarism, proper to specific fields of investigation. This reading grid, which aspired to becoming a unified picture, privileged the sign at the expense of sense, space at the expense of time, the object at the expense of the subject, relation at the expense of content, and culture to the detriment of nature.

Structuralism functioned as a paradigm – the paradigm of a philosophy of suspicion. Intellectuals saw their task as an unveiling, as an effort to demystify *doxa*, denature and destabilize sense, and search for the expression of bad faith behind what was being said. By postulating the class position – or the libidinal position – of the speaker, the illusion to which all forms of discourse are condemned was denounced. Structuralism came to be inscribed in the filiation of the French epistemological tradition that postulates a suspension – a break between scientific competence and common sense, whereby the latter is consigned to illusion. In the background of this paradigm of suspicion, we find among intellectuals a deep pessimism, a critique of Western modernity, and a search for an alternative in the figures of the child, the madman, and the savage. These figures unmasked the pretensions of the liberating discourse of the Enlightenment, revealing the disciplining of bodies and the grand imprisonment of the social body inside the infernal logic of knowledge and power. Roland Barthes wrote: 'I totally refuse my civilization, to the point of nausea,' and the 'Finale' of Claude Lévi-Strauss's *Homme nu* ends with 'NOTHING' – in capital letters – like in a requiem or the twilight of man. The structuralist paradigm meant to bring about a suspension of sense for the sake of differential thought as the means to fighting eurocentrism and the various forms of Western teleologies.

The second dimension of the structuralist paradigm was the annexing will that it showed, by way of philosophy, towards the three social sciences, on the road to emancipation. All three held in common the valorization of the unconscious as the site of truth: general linguistics which, with Saussure, separated *langue*, as a legitimate object, from *parole*, and relegated the latter to the domain of the non-scientific;

anthropology, which became more interested in the code of the message than the message itself; and psychoanalysis, which saw the unconscious as the effect of language. In their search for becoming legitimate and established, the young social sciences were forced to confront the institutionalization of classical humanities and the tradition and conservatism of the old Sorbonne. Structuralism presented itself as a third discourse, between literature and the exact sciences, seeking the means of institutionalization, and circumventing the mighty Sorbonne through universities at the periphery, publications, the press, and even the venerable institution of the Collège de France, which served as a haven for cutting-edge research. A battle was raging between the ancients and the moderns, during which the thematics of break and rupture would be deployed on several levels. The social sciences, by displaying the efficacy of the scientific method, strove to emancipate themselves, and to sever the umbilical cord that kept them tied to philosophy. In turn, some philosophers, who understood the importance of this work, took up the structuralist program and redefined the function of philosophy as philosophy of the concept. Philosophy recuperated the research in the human sciences, while at the same time deconstructing, from the inside, the classifications in use – what has been called 'effectology.' In this manner, philosophy preserved its central position at the very moment that it noisily proclaimed its own demise. The major role of philosophers in this affair is attributable to their capacity to establish a unitary program during the 1960s, with structuralism, functioning in this respect, as a rallying point.

Another factor accounting for this story is generational. A number of historic events left similar impressions on a generation seriously marked by World War II and by the difficulty of thinking – as Adorno said – after Auschwitz – in other words, of thinking a Western history that had turned to abomination and crimes against humanity, with the same optimism that was present at the beginning of the century. History itself became a source of doubt, of questioning, and ultra-critique. Hell was no longer the others – as Sartre used to say – but I myself. In the context of a society that had reduced the individual to a serial number, there erupted a widespread questioning of the self and its illusory capacity for self-mastery.

The critical distance of suspicion, generated by this loss of hope, increased during the 1950s and the 1960s, at a time when colonized people were casting off the yoke of colonialism and gradually recovering their independence. Many intellectuals perceived this rejection of the Western graft as a confirmation of their critical positions and considered the figure of the 'Other,' as absolute alterity to the West, the manifestation of truth and purity. This exodus from Western history, which allowed some to find in the Bororos or the Nambikwaras an expression of the pure cradle of humanity, was re-enforced by successive revelations of events occurring in places that some had taken to be the embodiment of their hopes – that is, the real Marxism of the communist countries. As a result, 1956 was of the utmost importance to a generation of Marxist intellectuals, who found shelter in a structuralized Marxism – a 'Marxism "in a vacuum"' in Jean-Marie Domenach's expression – that sought to avoid the weight of the disasters of real communism. Several among these intellectuals broke with communist culture, tiptoed away from history, and took refuge in the closure of the text, science, and the evacuation of subject and signified.

Grounding the Scientificity of a Third Discourse

Those hoping for a scientific renewal of the social sciences found in structural linguistics a method and a common language capable of bringing about change. Linguistics emerged as the model for a whole series of sciences in need of formalism. It spread from one point to another, from anthropology and literary criticism to psychoanalysis, and profoundly renewed the mode of philosophical investigation. The sectors most affected by the linguistic virus were those disciplines that existed precariously at the institutional level, those marked by internal contradictions between their aspirations to scientific positivity and their relation to the political – sociology, for example – or, as the case was with literary studies and philosophy, those in the thick of the quarrel between the ancients and the moderns. This conjunction contributed to the weakening of the borders between disciplines and structuralism surged up as a unifying project. This temptation found its best expression in Roland Barthes, who projected a general semiology capable of regrouping all human sciences around the study of the sign.

Modernization and interdisciplinarity went hand in hand in this context; in order for the linguistic sign to penetrate the field of the human sciences, sacrosanct borders had to be breached. The moment when everything is language, the world and all of us become language. The infringement of interdisciplinarity upon the Humboldtian model for a university, in which each discipline maintains its place within strict limits, together with the delegitimation of metanarratives, provoked a genuine infatuation with all sorts of formalisms, for the sake of a knowledge that would be immanent to itself. The key word of the period was 'communication' – a word that generated, together with the homonymous journal, the multidisciplinary euphoria of the times.

Lévi-Strauss was the first, soon after the war, to formulate a unifying programme for the human sciences. Naturally, the constellation that he elaborated gravitated towards the social anthropology he himself represented, which alone was capable of fulfilling this totalizing endeavor. What justified, in Lévi-Strauss's mind, anthropology's special vocation was its position at the intersection of the natural and the human sciences – with no concern, therefore, about anthropology being deemed, in the last analysis, a natural science.

Fresh out of his meeting with Jakobson in the United States during the war, Lévi-Strauss assigned the linguistic model a privileged place within the anthropological endeavor. In his search for constants and his paradigmatic and syntagmatic deconstructions, he took on the teachings of Jakobson's phonology – binary oppositions, differential spaces (*écarts*), and so on. Thanks to the privilege assigned to language and the deciphering of signs, Lévi-Strauss moved anthropology in the direction of culture, without this causing him to abandon his unifying aspirations. With his investigation of the regions of the mind, he also targeted biology. The totality to which Lévi-Strauss aspired saw him take over Marcel Mauss's ambition of developing the 'total social fact,' as he sought to encompass the entire scientific field. In the last analysis, he hoped to turn structural anthropology into the Science of Man, federating the other sciences and turning them into auxiliaries to this pursuit. The outcome was going to be a domain of investigation without borders, fortified with logico-mathematical models and its reference to phonology, encompassing under a single purview societies without history or writing all over the planet.

Anthropology would have access to the unconscious of social practices, and it could retrieve the complex combinatories of rules that preside over all human societies. Understandably, such an ambition represented a major challenge to all those sciences that had Man as their object. Consequently, reactions and challenges to this program emerged within other knowledge domains or in marginal disciplines, still looking for legitimacy, and leaning on this conquering dynamism for support. The excessiveness of the ambition defined here was analogous to the difficulty that anthropology first experienced in its effort to position itself institutionally. Though anthropology by itself did not succeed in decompartmentalizing the human sciences, structuralism, having taken over, became the common paradigm by default, being the school of a series of disciplines laboring along similar lines for the construction of a unified total science.

It was, therefore, in the context of an open crisis that Lacan presented his *Rapport de Rome* in 1953. He undertook to clear an attractive path – a French way to the unconscious – and to win this bet, he embarked on a quest for supports and began looking for foundations – for institutional and theoretical securities. He proposed to give psychoanalysis a new lease on life, and to put an end to the crisis with an aggressive and dynamic strategy of alliances. If Lacan burnt all bridges, he also turned that burning to his advantage, with a better chance of success.

Lacan's new reading of Freud was inscribed inside a Saussurian context, with an emphasis on the synchronic. He fully participated in the structural paradigm, initiating a new reading of Freud that no longer considered the theory of successive stages essential, but rather referred it to an Oedipal base structure. This structure is characterized by its universality, and has become autonomous in relation to the temporal and spatial contingencies, being already there before history. In opposition to Saussure, who privileged *langue*, Lacan privileged *parole* – a displacement made necessary by the demands of therapeutic practice. But *parole* in this case no longer represented the expression of a conscious subject, master of her saying; on the contrary, *parole* was forever cut off from the real, conveying signifiers that only refer to one another. Man existed only in his symbolic function, and he had to be apprehended only through it. Lacan radically rethought the idea of the subject by positing it as a product of language – its effect – giving birth thereby to the famous formula, 'the unconscious is structured like a language.' There is no point in looking for human essence anywhere other than in language. This is what Lacan meant when he said that 'language is an organ'; 'The human being is characterized by the fact that its organs are outside itself.' In his *Roman Discourse*, he opposed the symbolic function that grounds Man's identity to the language of bees, which functions only because its relation to the reality it signifies is fixed. As a result, Lacan found in the Saussurian sign without a referent the quasi-ontological nucleus of the human condition.

This new vision of a decentered and split subject was entirely in keeping with the notion of the subject at work in other structuralist domains of the human sciences during this period. This subject was, in a sense, a fiction, with no existence other than its symbolic dimension through the signifier. The prevalence of the signifier over the signified does not raise the question of the elimination of the signified. What is left are interactions between these different planes, which Lacan attributed to Freud's discovery of the unconscious – something that, in his eyes, would make Freud the first structuralist. The signifier causes the signified to experience a kind of passion. We might say here that Lacan subjected Saussure's concepts to a certain torsion: the notion of a signified sliding under the signifier meant nothing to Saussure; likewise the notion of the unconscious was not in Saussure's work. Lacan appropriated the two central rhetorical figures (metaphor and metonymy) from Jakobson to account for the deployment of discourse, and he assimilated these two procedures to the mechanism of the functioning of the unconscious; the latter, structured like language, is therefore situated in perfect homology vis-à-vis its rules.

A global semiological project: 1964–66

In 1964, a few cracks appeared in the classical apparatus, and structuralism was able to present itself as a program common to many disciplines. Indeed, 1964 was the founding year of the University of Nanterre, which was determined to become a center of modernity for the arts. Around the same time, a special issue of *Communications* dedicated to semiology was published, with Roland Barthes as its editor. In it, Barthes defined 'structuralist activity' as a consciousness of the paradox and a denaturalization of sense. At the same time, Lacan, having been definitely excommunicated from the international association of Freudism, founded the ECF (School of the Freudian Cause/*École de la cause freudienne*) and moved his seminar from Sainte-Anne to the École Normale Supérieure on the Rue d'Ulm – a hub of feverish activity in the humanities, both epistemological and scientistic, favored by Louis Althusser. Althusser not only welcomed Lacan to the Rue d'Ulm but also to Marxism, with his text, 'Freud and Lacan,' which was subscribing to the new directions of psychoanalysis that Lacan had suggested. In Lacan's return to Freud, Althusser saw the repetition of his own endeavor – the return to Marx. The same year, Lévi-Strauss launched his *magnum opus* – his tetralogy on myths, *Mythologies* – with the publication of the *Raw and the Cooked*, which showed that mythic thought is structured like a language.

In the domain of philosophy, a global program was being formulated that transcended the diverse positivities of the social sciences. On the Rue d' Ulm, the high street of structuralism and epicenter of the movement outflanking the resolutely classical Sorbonne, philosophy, under Althusser, with Lacan and Derrida present, became the theory of theoretical practices, the appropriation of the data of the new social sciences, and the subversion of those sciences from the inside. With his return to Marx in the course of seminars beginning in the early 1960s, Althusser reread Marx, finding in his work the advent of Science, made possible by an epistemological break that can be detected in Marx's work around 1845. Of the two Marxs he detected, Althusser retained only the second – the Marx of Science, of structural causality and overdetermination. His reading of Marx became the paradigm for a theoretical anti-humanism, for a 'process without subject or object' – key thematics at work during the 1960s, which maintained that Man is spoken more than he speaks.

The other grand effort to globalize structuralism was initiated by Michel Foucault with the publication of the *Order of Things (Les mots et les choses)*, in 1966, at the apogee of the structuralist movement. Foucault proclaimed the death of philosophy, to be replaced by thought *in actu* – the gift of logic and linguistics. He privileged two particular social sciences – psychoanalysis and ethnology – seeing them as 'anti-sciences' in the sense that they destabilized both history and the subject. Foucault considered humanism our 'middle ages' and saw Man as a transient figure destined to disappear. Once again, the figure of the unconscious of the human sciences exposed the illusory pretension to restore Man to a position of narcissistic mastery – a position that Galileo, Darwin, and Freud had made forever impossible.

Gilles Deleuze, in 1972, defined with precision the structuralist paradigm on the basis of a few common criteria located beyond the diversity of the human sciences. First and foremost in his definition, importance was assigned to the dimension of the symbolic, which intervenes like a third term between the real and the imaginary. Secondly, special attention was given to topological logics of position and localization. The third criterion whereby the structuralist paradigm is recognized is the pertinence of the differential and of the singular extending itself through the construction of a series. Finally, at the center of a structure, we find an 'empty case,' something absent from its place, that permits movement and makes possible multiple displacements – a kind of 'degree zero' as the condition of possibility.

What is left of Structuralism?

A Spinozist attitude towards the reading of texts dominated the structuralist era. The subject was obliterated and re-established upon an abstract universal – an utterance without subject. It was not the truth of the subject that came under question, but rather the conditions of its possibility. Only what was in the text – and nothing else – had to be recovered. However, with the return to sense and the fact that, ever since the mid-1970s, we no longer pay exclusive attention to the instruments of sense, the subject is again finding a central place within the reflective apparatus. Sense is no longer reduced to the sign, nor the author to the scribe; but neither is there a visible movement towards a supreme Subject – a subject enthroned upon its absolute sovereignty. The present configuration does not imply the divinization of man.

The problem today, after the discovery of the unconscious and of historical and social determinations, is to rethink the subject, instead of using the unconscious and the determinations to create dead ends. It is not possible to return to a subject that is transparent to itself – to a noumenal category. Philosophers of humanism – Sartre, for example – had already decided the question by affirming that existence precedes essence. Rather, on the basis of the principle of autonomy, the subject must be rethought and re-articulated. A humanism, grounded on an autonomous subject, allows for alterity and difference, without exacerbating them or rendering them absolute – a position that would necessarily imprison people inside their culture. Such a humanism would attempt to think the status of differences on the basis of identities that constitute the background for their manifestation. It shares the aspirations of the first structuralist generation, personified in Lévi-Strauss, that of retrieving the general from behind the singular, and of deriving the transparency of human existence not from a postulated essence, but rather from the diversity of its irreducible modalities.

The thought of the subject cannot arrest the many and different forms of conditioning – the forms of the subject's subjection in the process of subjectivation. The lessons of Freudianism, revisited by Lacan, prevent us from thinking of the subject as an indivisible unity, transparent to itself; rather, we conceive the subject as a split and opaque reality. In this domain, Lacan's contribution remains fundamental: we can no longer evoke the subject without grounding it, forgetting that it always goes beyond its objects of desire, and that it is fundamentally subjected to the signifier.

Moreover, the subject cannot be thought without reference to the historical context that determines it. The contextual referent, presented in the 1960s as a vulgar and unscientific given, is once again considered as an indispensable horizon. Since the mid-1970s, historicism is no longer condemned as if it were a vice, the way it was during the heyday of structuralism. Remarkably, historicity has returned to prominence in the very discipline that had put its pertinence aside – linguistics and semiotics.

To be sure, this return of the historical point of view cannot be the return of the same historicity that had existed before the structuralist phase. Like the subject, which cannot be the same as it was before, the discoveries of contemporary thought, the historicity under discussion coincides with a crisis in the meaning of history understood as progress. Since the structuralist successes, we can no longer think humanity according to our old schema – the schema of progressive stages through which humanity realizes itself. Structuralist thought has definitively imposed the idea of the equivalence of the members of the human species, for as long as the species has existed. Indeed, this is established to such a degree that we hardly think of it any more. The price that we paid for this insight was the radical break with every notion of historicity. But with the return of historicity, the scope of synchronic modeling has been relativized.

If the media spotlight that structuralism enjoyed in the 1960s continues to diminish (indeed, since 1975, structuralism has been in constant retreat), we should not be led to conclude that the coma has been overcome, and that all we need now is a clean sweep of a mode of thought that has become obsolete. To be sure, major inflections have modified the structural paradigm and shaken it up. Excessive ambitions are no longer stylish and modesty is expected: new alliances are being formed according to the imperatives of a new historical situation and scientific progress.

To the extent that structuralism with the naturalization of its paradigm tries to take on a new life, it has become necessary to historicize it and to distinguish its incontrovertible successes, due to the theoretical effervescence of the structuralist era, from the scientific pretensions and the purely circumstantial of a specific period that is now outmoded. Like the history of an individual, the history of a conquering paradigm follows a temporal course that reaches its highest point before beginning to experience a diminishing yield, as it rediscovers the calm and silence of history. We must not believe that all this agitation has been in vain and the fireworks a mere illusion.

We are the heirs of a particularly fruitful epoch – rich with enduring achievements – that has changed the way we see the world and our reading grids. Its effect has not been of the order of the sensational; rather, it conjures up the digestive and assimilative functions internal to the developmental frameworks of the human sciences. From this perspective, a return to structuralism must avoid what Althusser, following Lenin's advice, anticipated when he said that we must think against the limit. On the contrary, alternating our emphasis between 'only structures,' and 'only the individual,' has had disastrous consequences that miss what is essential, that is, the interaction between the two sides, and fail to recognize the progress made during the previous period. Rendering the previous period fluid and opaque, misunderstanding it deliberately, or relegating it to a space behind a wall of silence, permits us to start again, moving more freely in the opposite direction, but with the same intellectual terrorism that was prevalent during the previous period.

To understand the structuralist phenomenon, we must differentiate between the fascination with, and the promise of unifying the human sciences under a single program; we must differentiate between the methodologies particular to each science that worked to fulfill this promise according to their own object and their specific positions within the global network of universities and research; we must also differentiate between phenomena of disciplinary competition; the fight for positions of leadership; temporary hegemonies; pilot positions; and the tactical alliances that inflamed the conflict between the humanities and the social sciences inside the universities – between modernity and tradition. In this light, structuralism, and the struggles it embodied, can be identified with all French intellectual history during the second half of the twentieth century.

In a diffused but profound way, attentiveness to rigor and the will to take hold of significative assemblages animate contemporary intellectual work – proof of an undeniable assimilation of the structuralist exigency, even by those who feel the need to reject this period altogether and to pronounce its definitive demise.

The structuralist program deconstructed itself in the sense that it was derived, on principle, from a double negation, which inevitably forced structuralists to confront the aporias of the subject and historicity. The result of this – the ontologization of structure – which Ricoeur named 'Kantianism without the transcendental subject' – inevitably led to dead ends. With reason, therefore, Ricoeur cautioned against the excessive dissociation of two levels that should be absolutely complementary: the level of explication, represented by the semiological analysis, and the interpretive level, whereby the subject reappropriates the meaning of the text, giving the text not only sense but also signification. The conjunction of the semiological and the hermeneutic approaches allows for the reappropriation of the diverse components of discourse, which Paul Ricoeur presented as the 'quadrilateral of discourse': (1) the speaker, that is, the singular event of the *prise de parole*; (2) the interlocutor, who causes the dialogical character of discourse to emerge; (3) sense – the theme of discourse that has been the unique and exclusive dimension of structuralism, to the exclusion of all other dimensions; and (4) the reference – that about which we speak. This reappropriation makes possible, not a transparent subject – the master of sense – but an ontology of action grounded in a triangular function, systematized by Ricoeur in his *Oneself as Another*, in a relation between the self (ipseity), the other (alterity) and their institutional background (community). The project is, in this case, to 'remember' the metaphysics of the act, interpersonal ethics, and the problem of the social nexus – a central and urgent task at this moment in the twentieth century, as we experience the 'fallibility' of democracy.

References

Althusser, L., and E. Balibar (1970), *Reading Capital*, trans. B. Brewster, London: New Left Books.

Althusser, L. (1969), *For Marx*, trans. Ben Brewster, London: Penguin.

Barthes, R. (1987), *Criticism and Truth*, trans. K. Pilcher, Minneapolis: University of Minnesota Press.

Barthes, R. (1988), *The Semiotic Challenge*, trans. R. Howard, New York: Hill and Wang.

Barthes, R. (1990), *The Fashion System*, trans. M. Ward, and R. Howard, Berkeley: University of California Press.

Deleuze, G. (2002), 'A quoi reconnaît-on le structuralisme?', in G. Deleuze (2002), *L'île déserte et autres textes*, Paris: Minuit, pp. 238–69.

Derrida, J. (1976), *Of Grammatology*, trans. G. C. Spivak, Baltimore: Johns Hopkins University Press.

Derrida, J. (1978), *Writing and Difference*, trans. A. Bass, Chicago: Chicago University Press.

Derrida J. (1981), *Dissemination*, trans. B. Johnson, Chicago: Chicago University Press.

Dosse, F. (1997), *History of Structuralism*, trans. D. Glassman, 2 vols, Minneapolis: University of Minnesota Press.

Foucault, M. (1976), *Birth of the Clinic*, trans. A. M. S. Smith, London: Tavistock.

Foucault, M. (1974), *The Order of Things: An Archaeology of the Human Sciences*, trans. A. M. S. Smith, London: Tavistock.

Foucault, M. (1972), *The Archaeology of Knowledge*, trans. A. M. S. Smith, New York: Harper Colophon.

Jakobson, R. (1970), *Essais de linguistique générale*, 2 vols, Paris: Le Seuil, coll.

Lacan, J. (1966), *Écrits*, Paris: Le Seuil.

Lévi-Strauss, C. (1969), *The Elementary Structures of Kinship*, trans. J. H. Bell, J. R. von Sturmer, and R. Needham, London: Eyre and Spottiswoode.

Lévi-Strauss, C. (1974), *Tristes Tropiques*, trans. J., and D. Weightman, New York: Atheneum.

Lévi-Strauss, C. (1967), *Structural Anthropology*, trans. C. Jakobson, and B. Grunfest Schoepf, New York: Anchor Books.

Lévi-Strauss, C. (1966), *The Savage Mind*, Chicago: University of Chicago Press.

Lévi-Strauss, C. (1964–71), *Mythologiques*, 4 vols, Paris: Plon.

Saussure F. (1965), *Course in General Linguistics*, Miadenhead: McGraw-Hill.

Wahl, F. (1968), *Qu'est-ce que le structuralisme?*, Paris: Le Seuil.

Discourse about Difference

Calvin O. Schrag

Historical Backgrounds

Discourse about difference, as it plays itself out in the philosophical arena, has been on the table for some time. It is not a philosophical topic of recent date. Questions about the role of discourse about difference extend all the way back to the beginnings of Western philosophy, and there is a substantial literature that testifies of difference as a topic that elicited attention in the Eastern philosophy and religion of more distant times. It would appear to be an issue that resides at the very core of philosophical reflection both past and present.

A mark of the trade of philosophical analysis regarding matters of difference in the Western tradition is to begin with an acknowledgement of Plato's contribution to the inquiry in his dialogue, *The Sophist*. What we learn from this dialogue is how discourse about difference stands in service of solving the perplexing problem of not-being. This was a problem that Plato inherited from Parmenides. Parmenides was of the mind that we do well to stay on the path of *that which is* and dutifully avoid the dead end of *that which is not*. The one path is the way to truth; the other is the slippery slope of opinion. We need, says Parmenides, quite simply to stick with that which is and avoid the entanglements of making claims about that which is not.

The aversion of Parmenides to talking about not-being raised for Plato the unsettling problem of finding a space for negative predications. Given the Parmenidean exclusion of that-which-is-not from meaningful discourse, how is it possible to say that something is not the case? Plato sought to solve this perplexing problem with the help of his alleged discovery of the 'greatest kinds,' or 'superforms,' as they came to be called, which he discusses with a dialectical artistry in *The Sophist*. The list of these greatest kinds of forms, we are told, should include being, sameness, otherness, motion, and rest. With the peculiar conjunctions and disjunctions of these forms in mind, so runs the argument, we will be able to speak meaningfully of that-which-is-not.

Plainly enough, motion is not rest and rest is not motion. This, however, does not entail a denial of either motion or rest. What is required instead is a recognition that each is different from the other. Each combines or blends with the superform of difference, explaining that motion is different from rest and that rest is different from motion. Also, each combines with the superform of sameness. Each remains identical with itself. Motion and rest thus display sameness by virtue of which they exhibit self-identity and they display difference by virtue of their being other than each. As sameness translates into identity, so difference translates into otherness. Motion is other than rest and rest is other than motion, and quite unmistakably we can say of both of them that they *are* – there *is* motion and there *is* rest. So each retains its liaison with the superform of being.

The implications of this dialectical networking of being, sameness, difference, motion, and rest for the status of negative predications is quite decisive. The function of difference as not-being, responsive to that which is other, clearly remains within the problematic of being. It provides the ontological foundation for our knowledge of the entities that make up the furniture of the universe by supplying a matrix of inclusion and exclusion, which guides not only our understanding of the superforms of motion and rest within the constraints of being included and excluded, but also our under-standing of the lesser forms that define the varieties of natural kinds. Forms of natural kinds follow the route of the distinctions between that which combines and that which does not. Octopus readily combines with multi-tentacled but resists combination with feathered. An octopus is not a bald eagle. But in asserting that an octopus is not an eagle, it is not the case that one has nothing at all, a species of negative fact, before one's mind; it is rather that one is referring to a different form. The not-being of this and that, whether octopuses or eagles or whatever, is the basis for meaningful negative predication. And it must be remembered that this not-being as difference retains a combinatory relation to being. Not-being imbues every instance of being and plays itself out in such a manner that it becomes constitutive of that which is. Not-being as difference enters into the very constitution of the dialectical structure of being. Discourse about difference moves about within the determinations of the problematic of being.

Heidegger and the Ontological-Ontic Difference

It is difficult to overestimate the significance of Martin Heidegger's contribution to twentieth-century Continental investigations on the topic of difference. And it is hardly accidental that his book, *Being and Time*, which many scholars still consider to be his defining work, opens with a quotation from Plato's *The Sophist* that brings the question about being into prominence: 'For manifestly you have long been aware of what you mean when you use the expression "*being*". We, however, who used to think we understood it, have now become perplexed' (Heidegger 1962: 1).

We have already observed how in Plato's architectonic of the greatest kinds of forms, difference plays itself out as the not-being of otherness, which itself stays in commerce with the structures of being. In Heidegger's thought difference as a problematic of being makes its reappearance. It does so, however, within the lineaments of an existential hermeneutics that points in the direction of what Heidegger came to call 'the ontological-ontic difference.'

At issue in Heidegger's framing of the ontological-ontic difference is the distinction between Being (*Sein*) and beings (*Seiendes*). Being, according to Heidegger, is to be understood in terms of its infinitive grammatical structure, *modus infinitivus*, of 'to be,' distinguished from the nominative/substantive form that confers entitative status on the assorted particular beings that make up the totality of the cosmos. The type of inquiry that investigates the question about Being is properly characterized as 'ontological'. The inquiry into matters having to do with particular entities, from the lowest to the highest, is defined as 'ontical.' Herein resides the root of Heidegger's ontological-ontic difference.

It is critical for an understanding of the Heideggerian project to recognize that the trajectories of ontological and ontical inquiries unfold by way of a hermeneutical interrogation of the structure of *Dasein*. Now *Dasein*, as somewhat idiosyncratically explicated by Heidegger, is to be properly comprehended as the existent that we ourselves are, a distinctively human mode of being-in-the-world that is ontologically privileged in that it defines a being that is able to comprehend the meaning of Being as it applies to its particular manner of existing in the world. *Dasein* is that being which we ourselves are, not to be confused with the existence of nonhuman objects and things. *Dasein* is a being (*Seiendes*) that is concerned about its Being (*Sein*) and seeks to understand the dynamics of its 'to be' in its everyday preoccupations and concerns. As a being concerned about its Being, seeking to understand itself, *Dasein* is both epistemically and ontologically privileged. It is a hermeneutic of human existence that provides the portal to an understanding of Being.

The description and interpretation of this being which we ourselves are that opens vistas to a primordial understanding of Being is properly named fundamental ontology. The study of beings that are nonhuman existents, (*nichtdaseinmassiges Seienden*), falls within the province of the traditional discipline of metaphysics. And Heidegger is singularly resolute in keeping this distinction between fundamental ontology and metaphysics before us. Metaphysical inquiry in the history of its discipline, he argues, has been woefully unsuccessful in disclosing the meaning of Being as it shows itself (in the originative meaning of 'phenomena' as that which shows itself in its very showing) in the daily preoccupations and concerns of *Dasein*'s being-in-the-world. Indeed, metaphysically rooted ontical inquiry, in its totalizing and tortuous development, has managed to occlude rather than disclose the meaning of Being. The Being of that modality which we ourselves are remains covered up when it is metaphysically construed as an entity simply existing alongside other entities as an instance of finite substance in general. And it is precisely this that sets the requirement for a deconstruction (*Abbau*) of traditional metaphysical scaffolding. The ontological inquiry of fundamental ontology stands at the end of metaphysics as ontical speculation.

This requirement for deconstruction, a building down instead of a building up, an *Abbau* rather than an *Aufbau*, called forth on the grounds of the ontological-ontic difference, is not to be construed as an abandonment of traditional metaphysical inquiries per se. This is not an elimination of metaphysics, similar to the one attempted by the proponents of positivism of yesteryear. Deconstruction sets in place a retrieval of an originative, pre-conceptual understanding of Being that is older than the ensuing metaphysical construction. The principal function of difference, for Heidegger, is to delimit the reach and range of metaphysical inquiry, with its predilections for identity, necessity, universality, and totality. Not only have the protocols of metaphysics occluded the meaning of Being as it pertains to the dynamics of *Dasein*'s world involvements by confining it within the categorical constraints of subject/object and substance/attribute modes of reflection; they have also veritably skewered our grammar in talking about God.

In the development of Western metaphysics, that which is deemed divine, holy, and sacred congealed into a being alongside other beings, allegedly the 'highest' being to be sure, the apex of a vast celestial hierarchy, the *ens causa sui* of all that is, but nonetheless a being caught up within the categorical constraints of ontical inquiry. Such a deity, Heidegger avers, would have little bearing on our concrete religious concerns. This point is made quite explicit in his work, *Identity and Difference*, where he writes:

> The deity enters into philosophy through the perdurance of which we think at first as the approach to the active nature of the difference between Being and beings. The difference constitutes the ground plan in the structure of the essence of metaphysics. The perdurance results in and gives Being as the generative ground. This ground itself needs to be properly accounted for by that for which it accounts, that is, by the causation through the supremely original matter – and that is the cause as *causa sui*. This is the right name for the god of philosophy. Man can neither pray nor sacrifice to this god. Before the *causa sui*, man can neither fall to his knees in awe nor can he play music and dance before this god. (Heidegger 1969: 71–2)

Summarizing Heidegger's understanding and use of difference is an extraordinarily difficult task. It quickly becomes apparent, however, that the play of difference in Heidegger's thought registers its effects across a spectrum moving from an analytic and interpretation of *Dasein* as distinctively human existence to ruminations on the reality of the divine and the holy. What is important to keep in mind is that Heidegger's discourse on difference continues to move within the corridors of the quest for Being. Difference is put in the service of a recovery of the meaning of Being. It remains a species of effect or determination of the truth of Being, as it indeed already was for Plato. What has transpired during the philosophical interregnum from Plato to the postmodern age is the destiny of a deconstruction of ontic signifiers in the pursuit of the issue of Being. Quite clearly, the consequence of a deconstruction of the ontic way to the meaning of Being comprises a quite significant moment in the history of metaphysics, but this does not deflect philosophical interest away from the question about Being as such. And this tie with the Being-problem remains intact even in Heidegger's later reflections when he experiments with an erasure or crossing out of Being – the provocative *kreuzweise Durchstreichung* of which he writes in his short *Seinsfrage* essay of 1956 (Heidegger 1956: 30–5).But even here we note that 'Being' remains written, crossed out to be sure, but still visible, somewhat reminiscent of the Husserlian performance of the *epochē*, whereby the content under investigation is suspended, disconnected, inscribed within brackets. But as Husserl himself made quite clear, this bracketing of the contents of the world of the natural standpoint does not entail an annulment of the contents, which remain within the brackets as that which has been bracketed. Similarly, it would appear that 'Being' in Heidegger's scheme of things continues to be seen and heard after the event of erasure.

Derrida on Difference

The contribution of the left-wing Heideggerian, Jacques Derrida, to advancing inquiry on matters of difference could well be summarized as a shift from the landscape of ontology to the terrain of grammatology. Heidegger's ontological-ontic difference is transposed into a grammatological key. Difference, written as *différance*, juxtaposes the senses of 'to differ' and 'to defer.' The consequence of this juxtaposition of senses is a deconstruction that dissimilates the received semiotic binary of signifier/signified.

In one fell swoop, as it were, the discipline of semiotics, with its theory of the sign as a coupling of signifier with signified content becomes problematized. The content of the signified, within a semiotic field in which signifiers and signifieds are interchangeable and in which difference as deferral remains in play, is destined for perpetual postponement. A distressing undecidability and indeterminacy invades our quest for any presentation and re-presentation of a signified sense and referent. The stability and perdurance of our alleged meanings and referents are undermined by an inescapable fluidity of contents. The content of our presentational immediacy, to say nothing of our sought after *re*-presentational excavations, remains perennially deferred.

Somewhere at the bottom of these vagaries that accompany our efforts at knowledge as presentation/representation is an unspoken commitment to a metaphysics of presence. And such is the case both within a Husserlian quest for essences in his celebrated doctrine of the *Wesenschau* and its representational theory of knowledge, and in an empiricist mindset of representing associated sense data. Derrida is able to credit Heidegger for having been on the right track in his call for an *Abbau*, a deconstruction of the common stock of metaphysical signifiers, but Derrida is of the mind that Heidegger stopped short of utilizing the bountiful resources of his revolutionary project. After having dismantled the ontic/metaphysical supports for doctrines about the being which we are, the being of the world, and the being of God, Heidegger remained optimistic about a possible recovery of a primordial meaning and truth of Being that would proceed by way of an ontological inquiry that is able to deliver the goods pertaining to an originative notion of presence.

Remaining skeptical of such a recovery, such a 'deconstructive retrieve' à la Heidegger, Derrida recommends a more robust deconstruction. This becomes evident in his essay on the topic of 'The Ends of Man' in which he delineates two types and strategies of deconstruction. The one type is defined as 'a deconstruction without changing terrain, by repeating what is implicit in the founding concepts and the original problematic,' while the other type purports 'to change terrain, in a discontinuous and irruptive fashion, by brutally placing oneself outside, and by affirming an absolute break and difference' (Derrida 1982: 135). The former take on deconstruction, that of repeating founding concepts in an original problematic, has very much a Heideggerian ring to it. It tells the story of a deconstructive retrieve that dismantles metaphysics only to enable a return to a more primordial understanding of the meaning and truth of Being. Derrida's second type of deconstruction, with its accent on 'an absolute break and difference,' is more Nietzschean than Heideggerian – and it would be a fair inference that it is also more Derridean. Derrida's spin on the dynamics of *différance* leads him not only beyond a metaphysics of presence but veritably beyond any determination of presence within an original problematic of Being.

The consummatory turn in Derrida's deconstructionist maneuver is that of a deliverance of difference from its subordination to Being. Plainly enough, at this juncture Derrida parts company with Plato's project in *The Sophist*, in which he analyzes difference into a not-being that remains constitutive of that which is. But Derrida also quite clearly distances himself from Heidegger and his effort to locate difference within a scheme of ontological and ontic co-ordinates. Discourse about difference in Derrida's experiment with language forges a species of paradigm shift away from the vocabulary of being, presence, and origins to a grammatological economy of *différance*.

The story of this grammatological liberation begins with a friendly quarrel involving one of Derrida's highly respected mentors, Edmund Husserl, as this story is told in Derrida's *Speech and Phenomena*, a collection of essays that contains the much referenced essay on '*Différance*.' Derrida is intent on showing the failure in Husserl's theory of speech as indication and expression (*Anzeigen* and *Ausdruck)* to disclose the phenomena (Derrida 1973: 17–59). The connection between speech and phenomena is severed due to an intrusion of *différance*. Phenomena as the proper objects of consciousness, which Husserl named the *cogitata*, the objects as meant, remain unceasingly deferred, ever escaping the defining net of expressive claims on the part of the intending act of consciousness, the *cogito*. The task of expression is that of a representation (*Vergegenwartigung*), a repetition or reproduction of a presentation. The burden of representing is somehow to recall a previous content of consciousness. But this representing always founders because of the lack of a trustworthy signifier capable of delivering the signified message.

The root problem in representational theories of knowledge has to do with the search for a fugitive presence. This problem comes to the fore in Husserl's heavy investments in language as expression of meaning in the service of a doctrine of essence as recalled presence. Essence as a structure of meaning is the represented object in the guise of ideality, ripe for an intuition and constitution by a cognitive act. But such a presence of idealized object as a meaning structure forever escapes determination, suffering the fate of being at once different and deferred.

The flip side of this quixotic quest for presence, namely a search for a stable *ego-cogito* as the transcendental seat of consciousness, which Husserl sought to bring to expression in his celebrated transcendental subjective constitution, leads to a similar aporia. As the constituted phenomenological object falls through the net of determinate meaning so does the constituted phenomenological subject. As the object cannot be pinned down because of its multiple and changing perspectives, so the subject is beyond the ken of a representation of stable contents. At most, the subject of consciousness remains a 'tacit *cogito*,' a peculiar unspeakable presence-to-itself, ensconced within an evanescent transcendental field.

The long and short of Derrida's extended discussion of the vagaries in Husserl's theory of representation is that the use of language as indication and expression to provide claims for a presence, either in its presentational immediacy or as a represented content, crumbles under its own weight. Neither the presence of an object as intended nor the presence of a subject as an identity anchor for intentional consciousness can be secured. Appeals to represented objects and represented subjects alike end in failure, caught up in the throes of a circularity of endless deferral. Difference in its posture of *différance* wins the day.

Derrida's critique of Husserl's use of representation as an epistemological foundation needs to be coupled with his radicalization of Heidegger's project of an ontologically based deconstruction that keeps intact the connection between difference and Being as presence. In Derrida the disconnect of the grammar of *différance* with the Being-problematic becomes explicit. We are told that '*différance* (is) "older" than the ontological difference or the truth of Being' (Derrida 1973: 154). At most, Being as presence, as that which is presented in its temporalizing detour, is an 'effect' of *différance* (Derrida 1973: 147). In the beginning was *différance*, but unlike the 'logos' of the ancients that was in the beginning and then took on flesh and dwelt among us, *différance* remains in a beginning that never becomes present and suffers the destiny of an always yet to come.

That Derrida's spin on *différance* should take a messianic turn ought not come as all that much of a surprise. In the conjunction of that which 'differs' and that which 'defers,' distantiality and temporality, alterity and futurity, that which is other and that which is yet to come, it is obvious that *différance* is destined to take on an eschatological posture, heralding a fullness of time that is immemorial in the mode of a futural deferring. This eschatological horizon, which Derrida names '*messianicity* without *messianism*,' provides 'the opening to the future or to the coming of the other as the advent of justice' (Derrida 1988: 17). Messianicity is a landscape without dimensions, a field without stable co-ordinates, opening a vision of how the dynamics of *différance* plays itself out. No longer beholden to the requirements of a presence within the constraints of a problematic of Being, *différance* defines our situationality in a time of promise that has neither a founding *arche* nor a consummatory *telos*.

Levinas on Difference and Transcendence

The principal contribution of Levinas to the topic of difference is that he has radicalized it to the point of absolute otherness. His philosophy is that of a robust and unequivocal transcendence, in which the grammar of difference takes on the lineaments of a hyperbolic alterity that is veritably 'otherwise than being,' exceeding and surpassing the appearance of entities and indeed the presence of Being itself. The reach of difference as transcendence extends to the extremities of thought and discourse and approximates a point of absence.

It soon becomes evident to the reader of Levinas's difficult but provocative writings that he is furrowing a landscape that resides on the fringes of those explored by Heidegger and Derrida. In his move to a hyperbolic alterity in accentuating the otherness of difference, he clearly proceeds beyond the ontological-ontic difference of Heidegger as well as the transposition of difference into a grammatological key by Derrida. Plainly enough, difference as pointing to that which is absolutely and unconditionally other, disrupting the sameness of the presence of that which is, no longer resides within the province of the ontological problematic, nor is it within the constraints of a grammatologically based deconstruction. Other than both beings (*Seiendes*) and Being (*Sein*), and quite beyond the interplay of signifier and signified, a trace rather than a sign, difference as transcendence is situated as a call from that which is otherwise than Being and on the hither side of a semiotic manifold, beyond all temporal horizons, immemorial in its radical transcendence.

The story of Levinas's quite idiosyncratic understanding of difference is a story that moves between and across three of his principal works: *Totality and Infinity*, *Otherwise than Being or Beyond Essence*, and *Of God Who Comes to Mind*. In these works the issue of difference is addressed from related perspectives pertaining to matters of heterogeneity and asymmetry, the saying and the said, and God as illustrative of an ethical transcendence. In *Totality and Infinity* the question of difference is posed against the backdrop of reflections on an infinity that is clearly differentiated from a totality that remains within the categories of ontological construction. The trajectory of analysis lays claim to a metaphysics understood as a probing of a region beyond the confines of totality. Truth to tell, we are here dealing with 'metaphysics' in a distinct and peculiar sense, not to be confused with the Heideggerian take on metaphysics as an ontic analysis of the entities that make up the furniture of the cosmos. It is rather metaphysics as a counter-thrust to the varieties of immanental views of transcendence which have been offered from time to time, including a Husserlian transcendence-within-immanence as well as a Sartrean existential notion of transcendence as the projective posture of the *pour soi*.

Totality and Infinity is a work of notable originality and uncommon erudition, in which the contributions of major twentieth-century philosophers are critically assessed. The volume is appropriately subtitled 'An Essay on Exteriority.' The infinity that is at issue is no mediated infinity, ingressing into the depths of finitude by way of a Hegelian dialectic that purports to deliver a merger of the infinite and the finite in the now of an eternal present. Infinity is at once anterior and exterior to the totality that constitutes and stimulates the economies of terrestrial finitude. In the course of Levinas's explication of the role and relevance of infinity, the vocabularies of exteriority, alterity, heterogeneity, absoluteness, and asymmetry all converge into a grammar of robust and lofty transcendence:

> The alterity, the radical heterogeneity of the other, is possible only if the other as other with respect to a term whose essence is to remain at the point of departure, to serve as *entry* into the relation, to be the same not relatively but absolutely . . . Infinity is characteristic of a transcendent being as transcendent; the infinite is the absolutely other. The transcendent is the sole *ideatum* of which there can be only an idea in us; it is infinitely removed from its idea, that is, exterior, because it is infinite . . . Multiplicity in being, which refuses totalization but takes form as fraternity and discourse, is situated in a 'space' essentially asymmetrical. (Levinas 1969: 36, 49, 216)

These passages from *Totality and Infinity* illustrate the dense interconnectedness of the notions of exteriority, alterity, heterogeneity, asymmetry, and the infinitude of transcendence.

Otherwise than Being or Beyond Essence is Levinas's account of an exit strategy for leading us out of the labyrinth of ontology. The strategy employs the distinction between the said and the saying:

> The birthplace of ontology is in the said. Ontology is stated in the amphibology of being and entities. Fundamental ontology itself, which denounces the confusion between Being and entities, speaks of Being as an identified entity. And the mutation is ambivalent, every nameable identity can turn into a verb. (Levinas 1991: 42–3)

The unnamed referent is quite clearly Heidegger with his investment in the onto-logical-ontic difference for addressing the problem of Being. But this is precisely the problem that needs to be surmounted. And to surmount it one needs to acknowledge 'the pre-ontological weight of language' (Levinas 1991: 43) that informs the distinction between the said and the saying. The said is the locus of identity. It is within the said that meanings are thematized and coagulated. The content of the said is 'fixed in a present.' Saying functions as a deliverance from presence, from the sameness of being as identity:

> The entity that appears *identical* in the light of time *is* its essence in the *already said*. . . But the signification of saying goes beyond the said. It is not ontology that raises up the speaking subject; it is the signifyingness of saying going beyond essence that can justify the exposedness of being, ontology. (Levinas 1991: 37–8)

In tapping the resources of the 'pre-ontological weight of language' as it augers in the direction of a saying that frees one from the sedimented contents of the said, imprisoned within the confines of a fundamental ontology, Levinas is able to under-mine both the projects of Heidegger and Derrida. Heidegger's slant on difference within the play of the ontological-ontic difference, which continues to be beholden to an ontology of Being as presence abridges the intensification of difference as accentuated alterity, absolute otherness, and radical heterogeneity. But Derrida's effort to get a handle on difference as *différance* by way of a grammatological deconstruction of the semiotic play of signifiers and signifieds also falls short of the mark. It is only in a pre-ontological and pre-grammatological saying that the fortunes of difference can be set forth.

It is hardly surprising that Levinas's hermeneutic on difference should in the end take a quite explicit theological turn. Theological interests have always been in the center of Levinas's philosophical concerns, and his unpacking of the pre-ontological weight of language puts him in position to make explicit the ways of the deity via an employment of the grammar of alterity as absolute exteriority and unmitigated otherness. When all the dust has settled we are informed that the alterity of difference, in its hyperbolic modulation, is indeed able to stand in for the deity in its unsurpas-sable otherness. This is made poignantly explicit in his work, *Of God Who Comes to Mind*, when he writes:

God is not simply the 'first other,' or the 'other *par excellence*,' or the 'absolutely other,' but other than the other, other otherwise, and other with an alterity prior to the alterity of the other, prior to the ethical obligation to the other and different from every neighbor, transcendent to the point of absence, to the point of his possible confusion with the agitation of the *there is* [*il y a*]. (Levinas 1998: 69)

Plainly enough, as 'other than the other', transcending the otherness of all others, the difference that features the exceeding and surpassing of the deity is no longer within the province of the ontological–ontic difference of fundamental ontology nor is it within the folds of the markings of grammatological musings. In Levinas's theological turn we are witnesses to a discourse that pushes the signification of difference to its extremities, not only outside the economies of terrestrial beings and events but also beyond and otherwise than the region of Being itself.

References

Derrida, J. (1973), *Speech and Phenomena and Other Essays on Husserl's Theory of Signs*, trans. D. B. Allison, Evanston: Northwestern University Press.

Derrida, J. (1982), *Margins of Philosophy*, trans. A. Bass, Chicago: University of Chicago Press.

Derrida, J. (1988), 'Faith and Knowledge,' J. Derrida, and G. Vattimo (eds), *Religion*, Stanford: Stanford University Press, pp. 1–78.

Heidegger M. (1956), *Zur Seinsfrage*, Frankfurt am Main: Vittorio Klostermann.

Heidegger M. (1962), *Being and Time*, trans. J. Macquarrie, and E. Robinson, New York: Harper and Row.

Heidegger M. (1969), *Identity and Difference*, trans. J. Stambaugh, New York: Harper and Row.

Levinas, E. (1969), *Totality and Infinity: An Essay on Exteriority*, trans. A. Lingis, Pittsburgh: Duquesne University Press.

Levinas, E. (1991), *Otherwise than Being or Beyond Essence*, trans. A. Lingis, Dordrecht: Kluwer.

Levinas, E. (1998), *Of God Who Comes to Mind*, trans. B. Bergo, Stanford: Stanford University Press.

Different/ciations:
The Case of Gilles Deleuze

Constantin V. Boundas

Philosophies of difference, where difference holds its ground without being subordinated to identity, are exceedingly rare. It is not by chance that the fortunes of philosophical heterologies are better served inside process philosophies. Although to be a process philosopher is not a guarantee that one will also be a philosopher of pure difference, movement and the reflection on movement that constitute the raison d'être of the philosophies of process offer a rich soil for the nurture of difference. But a process philosophy, in order to support a purely heterological thought, has to be capable of doing without subjects steering the process or being steered by it, without substantive names designating 'blocks' in motion, and without points of origin or destination invigilating over a predictable trajectory. It seems that Gilles Deleuze's philosophy meets all these requirements and represents, in the wake of Nietzsche, the most consistent difference philosophy of all.

Different/ciating

The mistake in reading Heidegger's 'Being' as if it were a substantive noun is now well recognized. The mistake in reading Deleuze's 'difference' as a noun, on the other hand, is now in the process of being registered. We begin to understand better the sense in which difference is not a concept: concepts are not processes, and 'different/ciation' names a process. The reason for the grapheme, t/c, is that, in Deleuze's ontology, processes are made of two intertwining flows – the one virtual, the other actual – with both flows being real. The virtual is a differentiated and differentiating process whose differentiating dynamism coincides with its differen*c*iated actualization. The product is the process, and the product-process is the realm of solutions and actualizations of problems. Problems are expressions of tendencies and they belong to solutions to the extent that they belong by right to the virtual process that subsists in the product. The plausibility of this point depends on the successful co-ordination of a number of concepts that Deleuze needs in order to build his ontology – force, intensity, tendency, virtuality, and event, and it is to the complex issues stemming from this co-ordination that I am now turning my attention.

Deleuze's ontology is an ontology of forces attempting to correct the mistake we make whenever we think exclusively in terms of things and their qualities: in privileging extension and extended magnitudes, we overlook the intensive genesis of the extended. This is because forces are experienced only in the results they bring about, when the products of forcefields are extended and qualified. The term 'forcefield' is justified here, because, in an ontology of forces, 'force' means relation between forces. Such an ontology amounts to a veritable diacritics of forces in motion: forces are different/ciated – they are what they are only because of the differential relation that they have with other forces. But the differential quantity of forces is called 'intensity' and intensities are the real subjects of processes. Being responsible for the genesis of entities, intensities are virtual yet real events, whose mode of existence is to actualize themselves in states of affairs.

The Deleuzian virtual has generated an endless number of discussions and controversies; but there is nothing mysterious about it. In Deleuze's ontology, the virtual and the actual are two mutually exclusive, yet jointly sufficient, characterizations of the real. Actual/real are states of affairs, that is, bodies and their mixtures or individuals existing in the present. Virtual/real are incorporeal events and singularities in a plane of consistency, belonging to a past that Deleuze qualifies as 'pure,' suggesting thereby that this past has never been present. Virtual is something which, without being or resembling an actual x, has nonetheless the capacity to bring about x, without (in being actualized) ever coming to coincide or to identify itself with, to be depleted or exhausted in the x. The kind of process that we find in Deleuze's ontology is not properly captured in the scheme, actual/real→actual/real; its correct schematization is rather this: virtual/real↔actual/real↔virtual/real.[1] In other words, becoming, instead of being a linear process from one actual to another, should rather be conceived as the movement from an actual state of affairs, through a dynamic field of virtual/real tendencies, to the actualization of this field in a new state of affairs. This schema safeguards the relation of reversibility between the virtual and the actual.

It is best to think of the virtual in terms of tendencies, provided that we remember also to say that tendencies exist in differentiated intensities and subsist in differenciated extended parts. They, rather than the movement of extended elements, guarantee the continuity of intensive transformations. Although they are incited by the differential relations between material forces and are actualized in them, tendencies cannot be reduced to material forces without ruining the continuity and indivisibility of the duration of the process. It is important not to confuse the virtuality of tendencies with Plato's ideational Being: the emphasis that Deleuze places on materiality would by itself be a convincing reminder. The virtual can be apprehended only at the end of a chain reaction starting with sensation, affecting all faculties, and orchestrating their resonance in a kind of discordant harmony. Tendencies are problem-setters, and problems have no final solutions: with every partial solution, the problem transforms itself back again into a tendency. Now, to the extent that tendencies stand for problems on the way to solutions, they provide the actual with sense and intelligibility, without ever resembling it.

This is the reason why the role played by the virtual in processual transformations cannot be overlooked. Indeed, Deleuze often calls the virtual, 'quasi-cause' and 'event-horizon,' as he goes on to distinguish events from states of affairs:

Every event can be said to have a double structure. On the one hand, there is necessarily the present moment of its actualization: the event 'happens' and gets embodied in a state of affairs and in an individual . . . Here the time of the event, its past and future, are evaluated from the perspective of this definitive present and actual embodiment. On the other hand, the event continues to 'live on,' enjoying its own past and future, haunting each present.[2]

Perhaps, now, it is clear why and how Deleuze's ontology is built around a notion of difference that is not contained in the 'than' of the 'x is different from y' – in which case, difference would be relative to identity – but rather around the attempt to capture difference in itself. The centrality that Deleuze attributes to intensity is pivotal here. In order to safeguard the continuity of becoming and to prevent the reduction of temporal sequences to sets of discrete moments, ontology requires the distinction between intensive differences and extended parts. Unlike extended magnitudes whose *partes extra partes* allow themselves to be divided without any corresponding change in their nature (a situation that guarantees the commensurability of their divided parts) intensities cannot be subdivided without corresponding change in their nature. They are, therefore, incommensurable, and their 'distance' from one another makes each one of them a veritable difference in itself. Placed in the context of the two sides of the Deleuzian ontology – the virtual and the actual – intensities catalyze the actualization of the virtual, generating extension, linear, successive time, as well as extended bodies and their qualities. The relation of reversibility between virtual and actual guarantees that intensities will not suffer the fate of negentropic death.

The advantages of these moves, from an ontological point of view, are significant. Becoming, in the name of which Deleuze's entire work is mobilized, cannot be constituted through a juxtaposition of 'immobile cuts.' Participation in immobile cuts has always been responsible for the hieratic and static world of Being. Forces, seized *in actu*, are better candidates for a diagrammatic mapping out of becoming. Of course, the success of these moves depends on the availability of a plausible theory of time and space that will permit the deployment of subject-less processes of a continuum of differentials, with no origin and no end points. No adequate theory of transformation and change can be contemplated as long as it is predicated on a process conceived as a mere sequence of multiple states of affairs. Deleuze's claim that transformation goes from (actual) states of affairs to (virtual) tendencies and back to (actual) states of affairs prevents the time of transformation from collapsing into discrete temporal blocks and from destroying the kind of continuity and mutual imbrications necessary for an adequate characterization of the duration of processes. Without this, processes of continua would be possible only as mathematical formulas, devoid of physical embodiments.

Deleuze articulates the structure of temporality required by his ontology of processes through an ingenious rereading of Bergson's *durée* that permits him to advance the following claims: actual presents are constituted simultaneously as both present and past; in all presents, the entire past is conserved in itself; and there is a past that has never been present as well as a future that will never be present (DR: 70–128). The idea of a past that has never been present (the immemorial past), as well of a future that would never turn into a present, can also be found in the writings of Jacques Derrida and Emmanuel Levinas. The reasons for their postulation vary from one thinker to another, but there is one thing that they all share: any philosophy that puts a premium on the de-actualization of the present, in order to tap the resources of the past or the future, runs the risk of reiifying the past (as in Plato's recollection) and also the future (as in the case of apocalyptic eschatologies). To prevent this reification, the notions of the 'immemorial past' and the 'messianic future' (Deleuze prefers to talk of the pure past and of the eternal repetition of the different) are brought in to safeguard the idea of a process that can be conceived without the dead-weight of tendencies determining it *a tergo* or *ab ende*.

When Is Thinking Possible?

Deleuze's theory of difference has important implications for knowledge claims. It builds on a critique of the image of thought (recognition through representation) that the philosophical tradition has solidified on to a dogma; it ushers in a new understanding of what philosophy is (creation of concepts); it requires a new methodology – that of 'transcendental empiricism'; and it works with a nontraditional understanding of the 'dialectics of truth and error (undecidability between truth and falsehood and 'the power of the false').

Platonism raised re-cognition onto the model of thinking, and grounded the model on postulates that gave it a *de jure* legitimacy which *de facto* it could not have. With these postulates, it vested an image of thought that retained from our cognitive processes few trivial facts illustrating recognition through representation. *Doxa* was mistaken for *epistēmē*. Error was held to be an evil extrinsic to thought, whereas intrinsic to thought malignancies like madness, stupidity and mean-spiritedness were overlooked as inconsequential. This traditional paradigm of thought is not able to think difference, without compromising it. In it, difference turns into an object of recognition and representation, and is subsumed under similitude, opposition, analogy, and identity. An already constituted and familiar world is greeted by an already constituted and familiar subject. An alternative 'model' is needed for thought to become possible, and Deleuze contends that this model will have to jump-start, through 'fundamental encounters' with intensities, our always already reticent and idle thought. It should be the *cogitandum* (*noeteon*) that motivates the construction of a thought model, not the *cogitatum* (*noeton*) – provided that (given the primacy of materiality) the *cogitandum* is reached only after the *sentiendum* and the *memorandum* have prepared us for this task: from that which ought to be sensed, through that which ought to be recalled, to that which ought to be thought – this is what cognition becomes when it is liberated from the constraints of the representative straitjacket.

The gerunds that inspire the cognitive 'ought' are the result of a bold reading and transformation of the Kantian theory of Ideas undertaken in the pages of *Difference and Repetition*. An Idea, for Kant, has no instantiations in the empirical world, yet *it must be thought*. Deleuze retains this imperative when he thinks of the virtual, but he confounds Kantianism with his decision to multiply Ideas by making them the gerunds of all faculties (the *cogitandum*, the *memorandum*, the *loquendum*, the *sentiendum*). Now, Ideas do not obey the Platonic imperative, '*unum nomen unum nominatum.*' They are (differential) structures of singular and ordinary points and intensities, animated by spatio-temporal dynamisms, in the process of actualization. Ideas are virtual and their 'being' is that of problem-setting matrices. This is Deleuze's way of preventing the virtual from being a mere fraudulent and unnecessary duplication of the actual raised to the power of the transcendental: the virtual must not resemble the actual any more than problems resemble or represent their solutions. The tool for this rehabilitation of the transcendental is transcendental empiricism.

Transcendental empiricism – Deleuze's chosen method – attempts to go beyond experience to the conditions that account for things, states of things and their mixtures given to experience. Its object is not what is given immediately but rather the immediate given. But the immediate given is the tendency – in other words, the 'unrepresentable' virtual. The similarity between transcendental empiricism and the Kantian transcendentalism is misleading. For both Kant and Deleuze, the actual with its *de facto* existence, is governed by conditions that exist *de jure*. But the Kantian *de jure* is not like the Deleuzian *in virtu*. What is *de jure* is not characterized by a dynamic thrust toward its own actualization. Moreover, Deleuze's empiricism, unlike the Kantian critique, is capable of providing a genetic (not merely a static) account of the constitution of the actual, because the conditions that it seeks are themselves given in the virtual as the conditions of actual (not possible) experience. Whereas in Kantianism, the sought after conditions are those of possible experience, in the case of Deleuze, the targeted conditions do not exceed the conditioned, and, therefore, the concept they form ends up being identical with its object.

Rather than being indebted to Kant, Deleuzian transcendental empiricism is inspired by Bergson's intuition. Things and states of things are mixtures and as such are subject to qualifications according to the more and the less, that is, according to differences of degree. But these (actual) mixtures are the products of (virtual) tendencies which, unlike mixtures, differ in nature or in kind from each other. Bergsonian intuition then is a method for dividing the mixture according to tendencies, that is, according to real differences. Viewed in this light, Bergson's intuition is identical with Deleuze's transcendental empiricism. In the case of the traditional image of thought, representation, through the mediation of concepts, requires the presence of an identical subject to an identical object. However, the virtuality of the Idea does not require the assistance of an identical subject or an identical object in order to become real. Representation belongs essentially to consciousness and follows the logic of solutions. The Idea, on the contrary, is in Deleuze's expression, 'sub-representative' and is patterned according to the logic of problems and questions. Transcendental empiricism explores the field of this logic.

To be a transcendental empiricist therefore is to hunt for the 'referents' of the gerunds: *sentiendum*→cogitandum. Deleuze, for whom consciousness is the 'opaque blade' in the heart of becoming and therefore subject to intensive reduction, assigns to radical empiricism the responsibility of putting perception inside things, rather than of coaxing eloquently about its ineradicably ambiguous grounding in the 'lived body.' To put perception inside things, to see things as they are, would seem to contradict Deleuze's frequent appropriation of the label 'constructivism' on behalf of his method. But the contradiction evaporates as soon as we understand Deleuze's constructivism to be the history of a redemption. This is how Jacques Rancière expresses this Deleuzian point:

> We must give things the perceptual power that they have already, because they have lost it. And they have lost it, because their phosphorescence and movement have been interrupted by another image – the image of the human brain . . . that confiscated the interval between action and reaction . . . and made itself the center of the world. To put perception inside things is a restitution.[3]

What is redeemed is *aesthesis*. Bergson is at work here too, because for him matter and mind are best reconfigured as a world of images, moving, colliding, being deflected or being arrested. It is the mind that does the arresting, the selecting, and the reacting (after the interpolation of an interval calibrated in a way that permits reactions to 'fit' actions). Prior to the interpolation of the 'opaque blade,' the Bergsonian/Deleuzian *sentiendum* is nothing but the *chaosmos* prior to its being flattened and tamed upon the plane of organization that consciousness constructs.

To this radical empiricism, Deleuze also assigns the responsibility of creating concepts that would be adequate to what ought to be thought and sensed. Being neither reflective (one is perfectly capable of reflecting without philosophy) nor communicative (communication arrives either too early or too late), philosophy is creative of concepts. The concepts that it creates are neither abstract ideas nor universals – they do not name the traditional essence of a thing. They are about the circumstances of the emergence of a thing (the 'how,' the 'when,' the 'where,' the 'particular case.'). A concept, in condensing the conditions of the actualization of an entity, is an assemblage of singularities that must not be confused with individuals. Made up of singularities, the concept is itself a singularity in its internal consistency. Unlike extended magnitudes, concepts cannot be decomposed to their constituent singularities without becoming different concepts – and this is what makes concepts intensities. Although the singularities, that is, the component elements of concepts, are incarnated in actual (sensible, particular) bodies, they are not reducible to the states of affairs of interacting bodies. They are virtual conditions, with no spatio-temporal co-ordinates and, therefore, best thought of as expressing events – virtual and yet real events – in the process of actualization. The task of philosophy is to draw out concepts from states of affairs inasmuch as it extracts the event from them.

The concepts that philosophy creates have a history:

> We say that every concept always has a *history*, even though this history zigzags, though it passes, if need be, through other problems or onto different planes. In any concept there are usually bits or components that come from other concepts, which correspond to other problems and presuppose other planes. This is inevitable because each concept carries out new cut-outs, takes on new contours, and must be reactivated or recut.

This is why to be a Platonist or a Kantian today means to reactivate Plato's or Kant's concepts in the context of our problems. Deleuze quotes approvingly Robbe-Grillet's answer to the question whether or not there is progress in philosophy:

There is of course movement in philosophy, but to try to do philosophy the way Plato did is senseless; not because we know better than Plato, but because Plato cannot be outdone or outsmarted; what he did, he did it for ever. The only choice is between the history of philosophy and Plato-grafts on problems which are no longer his own.[4]

If, as Deleuze proposes, the 'history of philosophy' is best done in stratigraphic time – rather than chronological – that is, in the time of the simultaneous and non-contradictory co-presence of philosophical problems and events, the contradictions of the philosophical propositions that belong to the actual history of philosophy must give way to the 'inclusive disjunctions' of philosophy's own becoming.

The Ethics of the Event

The role of pure difference is not confined to the domains of ontology and epistemology alone. It finds an important place in Deleuze's ethics, which resolves 'to be done with (the) judgement (of God)' and attempts to rid itself of the transcendental *ought*, along with its twin bulwarks of duty and obligation. In its place, a virtue ethic is being recreated, with intensity as its only foundation. In the succinct formulation of François Zourabichvili, '[E]thical difference distinguishes itself absolutely from moral opposition to the extent that it is no longer possible to pass judgment upon existence in general, in the name of transcendental values.' (Zourabichvili 1994: 113) But an ethic of virtue (where 'virtue' is meant in its Greek and Nietzschean sense) could still be typological and essentialist: it could still permit Aristotle in the case of the ambidextrous to muse about the right hand being *phusei* the best. Intensity, on the other hand, disallows showing partiality to the right hand because intensity does not resonate with good and common sense nor is it derived from the habitual insight of the so called *phronimos* and the expert.

An ethics of intensity is defined by Deleuze as life rendering itself worthy of the event. Although the definition reminds us of old Stoic admonitions, a direct appropriation of this formula is bound to lead to misunderstandings, as long as the terrain is not yet prepared by a reduction, which, this time, is intensive. What is reduced now is *my* Self and the *other* Self, on the road to becoming-imperceptible. This is the kind of becoming that carries with it its own pre-personal and pre-subjective intensities – the 'affects,' that is, intensities, modifications, and expressions of our power to be – the *vis existendi* of Spinoza's *conatus* and Deleuze's desire.

Intensity, in other words, in order to be capable of delivering us from the judgement of God, must first free itself from subjectivity, transcendental fields and personological co-ordinates. It must be resituated, away from the typologies of the noetico–noematic complexes of reasons, motives, and deeds, closer to the topological diagrammatic configurations of forces, and counter-forces. It is in *The Logic of Sense* that Deleuze demonstrates that freedom from subjectival and personological transcendental fields requires the reduction of the structure-self and the structure-other – in other words, the decision to commit simultaneously *altrucide* and *suicide*.

I can only summarize the demonstration of this point here. If Sartre, Deleuze claims, is correct in arguing for the contemporaneity of ego and other ego – if both structures are the result of a dialectic of nonegological consciousnesses – the (intensive) reduction of the one will precipitate the reduction of the other. And if, as again Sartre argued, 'being seen by the other is the truth of seeing the other,' it is appropriate to initiate the double murder/suicide through the reduction of the other first. Again, if the other is the structure of the possible (worlds) – as phenomenology tends to maintain – the *sine qua non* of the 'worlding of the world' and of 'lived perception' – and if the possible by not being actual is the source of negativities, it would follow that the reduction of the other/possible will restore to the transcendental field its fullness and affirmation. Once this reduction is complete, the transcendental field will surface as 'otherwise other' (*autre qu'autrui*), and the anthropogenic force – the *vis existendi* or, as Deleuze now calls it, desire – will assert itself as the creative *energeia* of life.

Desire, in Deleuze's work, rather than being a source of phantasms, produces relations and connections that are real in their functions and revolutionary in their rhizomatic multiplicity because the Deleuzian desire is not defined by the intentionality of 'wanting to be or to have'; lacking nothing, it is defined by the expression of its capacity to make connections. It is not assessed according to the extrinsic *telos* of pleasure, since it is desire itself that distributes the intensities of pleasure and attempts to stave off the dissipation of intensities in extension. Desire atrophies inside the dialectic of subject and object: either a fully constituted subject will confront a fully constituted object, in which case desire can only be a relation external to both; or, if desire were to be thought as a relation internal to both subject and object, subject and object alike will have to suffer from a Sartrean hemorrhage of being on their way to being related. It is not strange, therefore, that, under these circumstances, desire is downgraded to the need of the 'have nots.' The way out of this, Deleuze suggests, is to think of desire as *energeia* – not *kinesis*. A process without *telos*, intensity without intention, desire (like Aristotle's pleasure) has its 'specific perfection' in itself, at each moment of its duration.

Conscious of his debt to Spinoza, Deleuze submits that the desire he is describing is not a passive state of being but rather an act, enhanced by joy, facilitating the formation of adequate ideas and striving towards more and 'better encounters' – in other words, desire is the power to annex Being. It is at this point that the 'naturalism' of Deleuze's ethics rings loud and clear: the distinction between good and bad annexations – good and bad encounters – is made, not according to the measuring rod of transcendent norms, but rather on the basis of the ability of the constructed, real encounter to augment the power to be of its *relata*. Experimentation, rather than expertise, is required because 'there are never any criteria other than the tenor of existence, the intensification of life.'[5]

However, the 'tenor of existence' and the 'intensification of life' are capable of grounding an ethic of desire/joy only if they are calibrated according to their alliance with the virtual. What we need is a better understanding of Deleuze's claim that ethics must be an ethics of the event – an 'ethics of the virtual' that would, at the same time, be a 'virtue ethics.' As long as our surrender to the actual has not yet allowed the exploration of the problem-setting virtual, Deleuze's Stoic characterization of ethics as the search for the becoming worthy of the event can easily be mistaken for an invitation to resignation; *amor fati* can in this case be read as the flattest fatalist maxim possible. To prevent this misunderstanding, it is not enough to be reminded, as is frequently done, that the Deleuzian event is not a mere state of affairs. We need also to remember to insert between events and states of affairs the process of 'counter-actualization'; it is this process that reveals the true meaning of 'becoming worthy of the event' – the spinal cord of Deleuze's ethics.

The moment ethics cuts itself loose from the mooring of the infinite obligation and turns itself into a search for ways and means to multiply the powers of existence or to intensify life, the question of the fit between forms of life and affects imposes itself. To put it in a different way, the moment that ethics can no longer be defined in terms of the right habit formation (which is not to say that habit has not its place), the question of counter-memory, which alone can problematize old and new presents, responsible for habits, begins to press. And in order to prevent ethics from being abandoned to the romance of authenticity and bad faith, actual valuations and their standpoints must be accounted for genealogically, and their plane of (virtual) consistency must be constructed.

It follows that a quietist interception of Deleuze's demand that we become worthy of the event is impossible, because Deleuze is not suggesting that we acquiesce without demurring to whatever happens. The ethics of the event is not the ethics of the state of affairs. The event intended in the formula of (Stoic) ethics is virtual and, to the extent that virtual events are still future and always past, the ethics of the event presupposes a will that seeks in states of affairs the eternal truth of the pure, virtual event which is actualized in them. True *amor fati* is not the acceptance of the actual state of affairs but rather the *counter-actualization* of the actual in order for the virtual, pure event to be thought and willed. '[One] wills not exactly what occurs,' writes Deleuze, 'but something *in* that which occurs, something yet to come which would be consistent with what occurs, in accordance with the laws of . . . the Event' (LS: 149). Or again:

> counter-actualization is nothing but the affair of buffoons, if it stands alone and pretends to take the value of *what could have happened.* But to be the mime of *what actually happens*, to double the actualization with a counter-actualization, the identification with a distance, like a true actor or a dancer does, is to give the truth of the event the only chance of not getting confused with its inevitable actualization. (LS: 161)

Consequently, the mime to whom Deleuze entrusts the ethical task is not the hero of the *re*-presentation of the same (the Kantian who 'repeats' a maxim until the categorical imperative acquires the extension of a law of nature). The Deleuzian mime is given the twin obligation to unmask the pretension of the actual to be the only player in the field *and* to re-enact the virtual in its infinite process of differing from itself.

Nietzsche's imperative that Deleuze often makes his own belongs here: *whatever you will, will it in such a way that you also will its eternal return*. If the eternal return were about actual bodies, qualities, and their mixtures, repetition would be the recycling of the Same, and the only ethics possible would then be the morality of resignation. But the eternal return that Deleuze talks about is 'the theory of pure events and their linear condensation on the surface' (LS: 178). Only in their case repetition can be imposed as the task of freedom. Repetition, says Deleuze, is like a festival that repeats that which cannot begin again, not in order to multiply the original by so many festivals, but rather in order to take the first time to the nth power, 'once and for all' and 'for all times' (DR: 300).

In the imperative of the eternal return and in the accompanying invitation that we measure up to the event, we may find, I believe, the elements of an ethics and the means to a delicate negotiation of the relation between obligation and creation, between distance and friendship or sociability, between affect and *phronesis*. What often prevents us from exploring these inclusive disjunctions is that 'ethics' and 'theory of (moral) obligation' have often been taken as synonyms – but we must undo the link between the two. There is something definitely amiss whenever philanthropic avocation is taken to be coextensive with ethics. No one suggests that ethics without morality knows no obligations. What Deleuze suggests is that obligation, in order to be admitted, must be measured, in the first place, by men and women whose souls have already been tried and proven noble in the fire of the eternal return. These men and women are not all that far from Aristotle's *megalopsychoi*. They are the ones worthy of the event, the actors and dancers – the mimes of the counter-actualization.

We are in a position now to draw the elements for a Deleuzian ethics together. The dehumanization and depersonalization of the transcendental field for the sake of singularities and events deconstructs the onto-metaphysical discourse on values, and lifts their subordination to valuers. It clears, therefore, the way for an ethics in which decentered subjects experiment and are experimented upon – encompassing, and also being encompassed – by the *chaosmos* of anorganic life. Here, the self is no longer the master or the servant of the Other; nor is it the Other's equal. But this does not prevent it from freely assuming responsibilities for the sake of a new earth. What Deleuze writes about Tournier's Robinson and his search for a new earth aptly characterizes his own: '[T]he end, that is, Robinson's final goal, is "dehumanization," the coming together of the libido and of the free elements, the discovery of a cosmic energy or a great elemental Health . . .' (LS: 303).

This is what the Deleuzian 'becoming-imperceptible' means, in the last analysis: that 'someone' comes to be where the 'I' used to reign supreme. Becoming-imperceptible would be impossible if the temporality of (*my*) becoming were strictly limited by the metric time and the nested presents of *Chronos*. It is the absolute symmetry of that which never ceases to pass and of that which never arrives – the very definition of *Aion* – which is responsible for the fact that I is another.

It is the depersonalization and dehumanization of the transcendental field that makes the construction of the ethical field necessary through an endless experimentation for the sake of the compossibility of abiding differences, with elements that cannot be expected to resemble the finished product. But this experimentation is never a solitary game. An ethics of becoming worthy of the event must be supplemented with powerful politico-philosophical imperatives and tactics. A life filled as much as possible with active joy, and a life of striving to become worthy of the event may be facilitated or, alternatively, made impossible by the conditions prevailing inside the *polis*.

Deleuze and the Political

The questions of whether or not Deleuze ever succeeded in articulating a philoso-phico-political theory (rather than an ethical attitude and preference); whether or not he was a friend of democracy and of human rights; and whether or not he was capable of moving the discussion past the nostalgia of the veterans of May 1968, have been vigorously debated. From my point of view, Deleuze's reflections on the political are best understood after we come to appreciate the simultaneous presence of two attitudes in his work – subversion and perversion – and the role that difference plays between the two, preventing them from ever freezing in iconic immobility, contaminating the one with the other, and joining them together in the space of an inclusive disjunction.

Before I discuss these attitudes, I think that it is important to understand the source of Deleuze's guarded optimism present in his discussions of the political. In his early work, the fellow traveller (Deleuze would call him an 'intercessor') that becomes the foil for his intuitions is David Hume. Hume assists Deleuze in his claim that the ethico-political project of assembling the multitude inside a livable *polis* does not begin without resources. The ethico-political subject is given only as a task (later on, Deleuze will speak of 'the missing people' being given as a task), but this task is undertaken with the assistance of a natural passion – 'sympathy.' Sympathy – the bonding substance for the constitution of the political subject – naturally belongs to each one of us. But our sympathies are partial, limited, and mutually exclusive. It follows that the constitution of the social space and the limitation of violence requires the extension of our sympathies and their integration through the invention of corrective rules. Deleuze makes no assumptions about subjects prior to the processes of extending and integrating sympathies – assumptions at this point would trap the processes in advance. For him, to be a subject is to invent and experiment – the subject itself is both the process and the unstable result of experimentation and artifice. Without going into the details of this argument, I want to signal the importance, in this context, of the word 'artifice.' The subject is not a substantive foundation of an incorrigible intuition; it is something constructed as the correlate of a 'fiction-of-the-imagination-turned-principle-of-human-nature'; it is the product of a fiction-turned-constitutive. Its precariousness, but also the possibility for its existence, are grounded here.

Equally early in his work, and this time with Spinoza as his intercessor, Deleuze de-emphasizes the will of the individual to annoy and to injure, denouncing instead the passions which have not yet been educated and socialized with the help of adequate ideas. What he deplores is less the universality of violence and more the frailty and vulnerability of man. If the state of nature is unlivable, it is because the individual in it is totally exposed to the threatening chaos of accidental encounters. In nature, bodies encounter other bodies but they are not always compatible with one another. Civil society, on the other hand, is the result of the effort to organize encounters; in other words, the effort to organize the useful and to fend off the detrimental. The greater the numbers of those who come together in one body, the more rights they will have in common. Liberation, that is, freedom from the fortuitousness of external causes and, therefore, the affirmation and increase of one's own *vis existendi* can be promoted by society, under conditions open to experimentation and discovery. Following upon these premises, an explication of modes of existence (forms of life) replaces the appeal to the transcendental 'ought.' It is in these readings of Spinoza's and Hume's ethics that one can locate the source of the optimism that moderates Deleuze's subversive tendencies and ultimately mitigates his perversion.

Now, the presence of subversive tendencies is unmistakable in Deleuze's works (especially in those that he co-authored with Félix Guattari). They tend to cluster around the concepts minority/majority and nomad/sedentary developed in *A Thousand Plateaus* in an attempt to summon those who are in a position to stand against the state's capturing forces. This quest is broader than it initially appears, as it involves minor, transformative forces (of life, politics, thought, artistic creation) capable of escaping the sedentarism and stratification so dear to majorities. 'Nomadic' are called the minority forces – better still, the minor tendencies – which belong to the events of virtual becoming (rather than to the states of affairs of actual history). Nomads, unlike migrants, have territories. And, having portable roots, they reterritorialize upon the line and the trajectory of their deterritorialization. The object of their knowledge is the behavior of the materials they work with and the intensity of forces, rather than the matter and form of hierarchical and hylomorphic sedentary sciences. The singular, rather than the universal essence, is their objective. Deleuze and Guattari hypothesize that nomads (or better, nomadic tendencies), have the ability to ward off the encroaching forces of the sedentaries. In fact, they attribute to them the invention of the 'war machine.' But unlike the state that wages war in order to conserve its integrative power, nomads wage war when their lines of flight are blocked and their deterritorialization prevented.

In this nomadology, one can still find the remnants of the Marxist reading of the state as the 'capturing apparatus' in the hands of the ruling class existing for the sake of that class's interests. Sedentaries (alias the majority or the majoritarians) are the state or the state-apparatus or, rather, the state-form; nomads are the multitudes or the masses or the minorities whose desires do not coincide with the interests of the state. But in a post-Marxist context, the nomads do not want to become the state or to take over the state apparatus, but rather to destroy it or to escape it. Here, Nomad is the one who tries to prevent the social sedimentation of desire from blocking the connective process of the production of desire. Nomadic lines of flight are lines of subversion and transformation of the well-organized and smoothly-functioning institutions of the sedentaries.

Deleuze's subversive tendencies are deployed with the question of fleeing in mind – how best to flee, without being deprived of weapons or of the artifices needed during the journey of deterritorialization. And it is this very question of the best means available for fleeing that leads us to the heart of Deleuze's political 'perversion.'[6] This perversion finds its theoretical support in the discussion of sadism and masochism by Deleuze, and his repudiation of the conventional wisdom that sees in masochism the mere inversion of sadism. The sadist, argues Deleuze, is still steeped in the language of the law; his feat is that, in opposing the deduction of the law from an alleged principle of the good, he chooses to *subvert* the old law ironically by maintaining its form, while, at the same time, he replaces its content with precepts deduced from a 'principle of evil.' *A contrario*, for Deleuze, the masochist chooses to *pervert* the law by submitting to it humorously in order to savor the pleasures that the law prohibits by means of punishments (Deleuze 1989). In the last analysis, Zourabichvili is willing to illustrate Deleuze's perversity with the delicate distinction between '*ne faire rien*'(to do nothing) and '*faire le rien*' (make the nothing) and to conclude that it is the latter that characterizes Deleuze's political posture – a posture that problematizes the field of the possibles, without ever articulating a plan in view of a *telos*. What Deleuze consequently advocates is *ataraxia* which is not to be confused with *apraghia*.

Those, then, who speak of the aristocratic dimension in Deleuze's thought are right, provided that this aristocratic posture is not confused with the hatred for democracy. Despite all the reservations that Deleuze expresses against actual democracies, his opting for a becoming-democratic, conceived as the politics of a universal brotherhood *à venir*, is unmistakable. This universal brotherhood *à venir* is the answer to the political problem colored by the fact that, in the Deleuzian narrative, the people (to whom the political theorist appeals) is missing (*le peuple manque*); 'a new people and a new earth *à venir*' gives Deleuze's political posture 'a purposefulness without purpose' – provided, that is, that the clarion call for a new people and a new earth is not heeded as a teleological anticipation with messianic aspirations. Being not a question of '*les lendemains qui chantent*,' the missing people is both *à venir* and already there.

I spoke of the clarion call for a new people and a new earth; Deleuze speaks of fabulation: the becoming-democratic of the missing people requires the art of fabulation – and fabulation must be distinguished from a mere fiction. Fabulation requires the ability to be receptive to our environment, and the luxury of a 'site,' not too near and not too far from the *demos*. It requires that we permit ourselves to be filled with the affects generated by having seen the intolerable in the present, and a style to speak the possibles that arise as we apprehend the intolerable. It is plausible to assume that the clarion call for the creation of the new people and the new earth will be heard primarily by those who recognize themselves in the fable enunciated by the seer. Deleuze, at any rate, never characterized concretely the people to come or the new earth: he did say that the 'race' that fabulation summons up exists only as an oppressed race, and only in the name of the oppression it suffers. He did claim that there is no race but inferior and minoritarian, and that 'race' is not defined by its purity, but rather by the impurity conferred upon it by a system of domination.

If we now ask for criteria for 'the right' fabulation – the fabulation capable of summoning up the new people and the new earth – we will find Deleuze rather circumspect and guarded with his answers – which does not mean without resources. Fabulation is possible only when imagination is given the task of training sensibility, memory, and understanding – in other words, from the vantage point of a new life praxis moving out of a basis in the arts. This 'moving out' entails the lifting of the Kantian barriers between the cognitive, the practical, and the aesthetic interests, and the fair redistribution of the insights of discordant Reason among all faculties. Aesthetics must free itself from the kind of autonomy that the Kantian narrative imposed on it, and link up with the *aisthesis* of the first *Critique*.

In *Difference and Repetition*, Deleuze did claim that the Idea/problem (the *cogitandum*), in order to be grasped, requires a chain reaction between levels of intensity that must always begin with sensible encounters. Only the violence of the *sentiendum* stands a chance of bringing about the resonance and the compossibility of all Ideas/ problems. In his *Logic of Sensation*, Deleuze decided to reckon with this violence, choosing this time as his laboratory the paintings of Francis Bacon.[7] He showed that the violence of sensation tormenting Bacon's canvases trades off representation for the exploration of a world never before seen, and yet strangely familiar and near. Deleuze pointed out that, in his effort to escape the figurative and representative modes of narration and illustration, as well as the abstractness of pure form, Bacon aimed at the liberation of the figure through iconic isolation and *hysteresis*. Iconic isolation, that is, the neutralization of the background and the enclosure of figures in well-defined spaces, prevents the figure from telling a story or from representing forms external to the canvas. As for '*hysteresis*,' it means subtraction, removal, and extirpation. Even before the painter begins to paint, her canvas and her head are filled with sensations, clichés and probabilities. 'The painter's problem,' writes Deleuze, 'is not how to enter the canvas, since he is already there . . . but rather how to get out of it . . .' (FB: 62). *Hysteresis* situates the problem well, because it takes the form of an intensive reduction. Painting as *hysteresis* is not the filling of an empty surface with the representation of an object. It is imagination aggressively reasserting its rights. Painting, in search of the figural, just like sensation in search of the *sentiendum*, is the operation on an encumbered canvas, a kind of interventionist painting on pre-existing images. It aims at the reversal of the old relation between model and copy – where the reversal sustains the equation, *sentiendum = simulacrum*. In this context, sensation is no longer the response to a form any more than Bacon's painting is a form-giving enterprise. Sensation is intimately related to forces, just as Bacon's painting aims at the capture of forces. And the prize of the artist's subtraction – the figure, beyond representation, narration, and illustration – is the body without organs that subsists underneath the organism – the *bwo* that Deleuze calls 'hysteric body' (FB: 33–8).

Returning for one last time to the question of the 'right' fabulation capable of measuring up to the task of summoning up the missing people, we can now see that fabulation will itself be measured according to the imaging and the imagination of the hysteric body. Although exnominated throughout history, just like the nomads and their opposition to state power have been exnominated, the body without organs (the 'crowned anarchy' of Deleuze and Guattari's texts) has the reality of the *cogitandum*, *memorandum*, and *sentiendum* of every political theory and praxis. Being a virtual reality, it has to be actualized and counter-actualized constantly, in ever different/ciated contexts. Like Althusser's cause, it determines in the last instance the arrangement of the elements of a structure. Like Spinoza's substance, it cannot be conceived without its attributes and modes, as it expresses itself immanently in attributes and modes. And like Lacan's phallus, it is the paradoxical object = *x*, lacking in its place, having an 'identity' that must be grasped in its eternally returning differenciations.

Notes

1. Deleuze 1994: 208–21; hereafter referred to as DR.
2. Deleuze 1990: 151; hereafter referred to as LS.
3. Rancière 2001: 150; hereafter referred to as JR.

4. Deleuze 1998: 23; hereafter referred to as ERB.
5. Gilles Deleuze and Guattari 1994: 74, hereafter referred to as WiPh.
6. I owe the characterization of Deleuze's politics as 'perverse' to François Zourabichvili. See Zourabichvili 1998.
7. See Deleuze 2003, hereafter referred to as FB.

References

Ansell-Pearson, K. (1999), *Germinal Life: The Difference and Repetition of Deleuze*, New York: Routledge.

Badiou, A. (2000), *Deleuze: The Clamor of Being*, trans. L. Burchill, Minneapolis: University of Minnesota Press.

Bergen, V. (2001), *L' Ontologie de Gilles Deleuze*, Paris: L' Harmattan.

Boundas C. (2002), 'An Ontology of Intensities,' *Epoche* 7 1 (Fall): 15–37.

Boundas, C. (2003), 'The Ethics of Counter-Actualization,' *Concepts Hors Série: Gilles Deleuze* 2 (October).

Deleuze, G. (1983), *Nietzsche and Philosophy*, trans. H. Tomlinson, New York: Columbia University Press.

Deleuze, G. (1988), *Bergsonism*, trans. H. Tomlinson and B. Habberjam, New York: Zone Books, esp. Chap. 1.

Deleuze, G. (1989), *Masochism: Coldness and Cruelty*, New York: Zone Books.

Deleuze, G. (1990), *Expressionism in Philosophy: Spinoza*, trans. M. Joughin, New York: Zone Books.

Deleuze, G. (1990), *The Logic of Sense*, trans. M. Poster with C. Stivale, (ed.) C. V. Boundas, New York: Columbia University Press.

Deleuze, G. (1991), *Empiricism and Subjectivity: An Essay on Hume's Theory of Human Nature*, trans. C. V. Boundas, New York: Columbia University Press.

Deleuze, G. (1994), *Difference and Repetition*, trans. Paul Patton, New York: Columbia University Press.

Deleuze, G. (1998), 'Entretiens avec Raymond Bellour and Fraŋois Ewald,' *Le magazine littéraire*: n. 257.

Deleuze, G. (2003), *Francis Bacon: The Logic of Sensation*, trans. D. W. Smith. New York: Continuum.

Deleuze, G., and F. Guattari (1977), *Anti-Oedipus: Capitalism and Schzophrenia*, trans. R. Hurley et al., New York: Viking Press.

Deleuze, G., and F. Guattari (1987), *A Thousand Plateaus: Capitalism and Schizophrenia*, trans. B. Massumi, Minneapolis: University of Minnesota Press.

Deleuze, G., and F. Guattari (1994), *What is Philosophy?* trans. H. Tomlinson, and G. Burchell, New York: Columbia University Press.

May, T. (2005), *Gilles Deleuze: An Introduction*, Cambridge: Cambridge University Press.

Patton, P. (2000), *Deleuze and the Political*, New York: Routledge.

Rancière, J. (2001), 'D' une image à l' autre? Deleuze et les âges du cinema,' in J. Rancière (2001), *La Fable cinématographique*, Paris: Seuil, pp. 145–63.

Simont, J, (1997), *Essai sur la quantité, la qualité, la relation chez Kant, Hegel, Deleuze*. Paris: L' Harmattan.

Zourabichvili, F. (1994), *Une philosophie de l'évènement*, Paris: Presses Universitaires de France.

Zourabichvili, F. (1998), 'Deleuze et le possible (de l' involontarisme en politique),' in E. Alliez (ed.) (1998), *Gilles Deleuze: Une vie philosophique*, Le Plessis-Robinson: Synthelabo, pp. 335–57.

Postmodernism

Charles E. Scott

As I begin this chapter, I confess to having reservations about the term, 'postmodernism.' My reservations have less to do with the philosophical irrelevance of the term that some scholars have alleged, and more with the suffix, *-ism*; the ways of thinking and writing that 'postmodern' names are characterized by departures from thought that is governed by categories and their classifications. This tradition emerged in part as a critique of the ability of categorical thinking to recognize and address appropriately many of the perceptions, processes of thought, experiences, and things that we encounter. This chapter will discuss alternatives to such categorical thinking and will introduce options that arise in postmodern philosophy. It will also discuss options for thinking that arise in postmodern philosophy. These are options the performance of which help to determine postmodern discourses and sensibilities and to show as well that questions concerning thinking and language are primary ones for postmodern philosophy.

'Postmodern' is an appropriate name for this emerging tradition insofar as it designates a group of thinkers who come after philosophers who are grouped together by the word, 'Modern.' The identity of 'postmodern' was shaped largely after World War II, although its lineage reaches far back in Western culture. The word also names, in distinction to other philosophers who have departed from the rationality of 'Modern' thought, those thinkers who work in the influence of Hegel, Nietzsche, Husserl, and Heidegger as well as the influence of Continental readings of Plato, Aristotle, Kant, and many other canonical figures. The vocabulary, signature manners of thinking, and questions that mark this tradition differ considerably from those that identify the movements coming from Hume, Dewey, or Thomas Aquinas, for example. It is not a question of greater or lesser accuracy, or one of better or worse. It is a matter of difference: different lineages, different groups of problems, and different sensibilities characterize these philosophical orientations.

The suffix, *-ism*, suggests a definite property or group of teachings and beliefs that govern a unity of people and their expressions. It suggests adherence to a system or assemblage of principles, an established body of values and assertions that are static enough to encourage strong commitment and institutional establishment. In some conventions of argument one need only address an '*-ism*,' such as determinism, relativism, or, presumably, postmodernism in order to address the defining ideas of a group of philosophers. We shall see that postmodern thinking usually departs from the assumptions and images that make that kind of adherence and address sensible. Different styles of writing and thinking emerge – different disciplines of mentation when compared to both metaphysical and Modern thinking. These disciplines make 'postmodernism' a misleading and highly questionable term. This article discusses some of the strategies of critique and articulation that are recognized as postmodern, notes major departures from previous philosophical assumptions and approaches, and describes a way of departing from 'humanism' that is singularly postmodern. I share a conviction one often encounters in postmodern thinking, namely that the convenience of generalizations, though often helpful in commentary, discourages careful thought and perception. Consequently there is a tension throughout the chapter. This is a tension between a desire to write informatively about some generic characteristics of postmodern thought, and a desire to occasion an opportunity for the reader to engage ways of thinking that put generalization in question. These ways of thinking attempt to address and to make apparent occurrences that do not happen as categories, systems of ideas, representations, agents, or objects. This is a tension often found in postmodern literature and is a symptom of the transition that 'postmodern' names – a transition from powerful images of rational universality to sites that are less grand for engaging with people and things responsibly and intelligently.

In these introductory remarks I have used the words 'Modern,' 'metaphysical' and 'Continental.' Each word could well have its own article. I note in passing that the aspects of Modern philosophy that will play an important role here include a prioritizing of epistemology and the ideas and images of subjectivity, universality, and reason. 'Metaphysical' will be used to refer broadly to thought in the Platonic and Aristotelian traditions. 'Continental' refers to thought that has its origins primarily in Germany and France and that is determined by the formation of phenomenology and departures from it.

Time and Postmodern Critique: Nietzsche

Friedrich Nietzsche had major influence on the formation of postmodern thought. He developed a thought of nonprogressive, nonlinear time that impacted many philosophers, especially those for whom the prevalent optimism of the late nineteenth and early twentieth centuries had lost its persuasive force. As Nietzsche saw it, linear time, as a series of nows, gives the past an exceptional value. Past time is always lost in a present now: now is never a past time. His observation is not that *what* happened in the past thoroughly determines *what* happens now. Rather, past time itself is a temporal determination of finite lives; the past is always accomplished. According to this conception of time, whatever happens is connected to the past as a temporal region that is not alterable. Further, present happening – a 'now' – cannot free itself from the temporal sequence of which the past is a part. 'Now' is temporally determined as not past and not future, and yet past time is absolute in the senses that present time cannot happen without it, and past time cannot be changed. Pastness is already done; whatever is past is finished as it was, engraved by being past, apparently beyond the reach of transformation. When time is conceived in a linear way, anything temporal would seem to have this implacable determination of pastness.

For Nietzsche this force of accomplishment in the linear model of the past precluded entirely the possibility of originating a genuinely new future. One *might* argue that because each now is new, origination happens inevitably with each present occurrence. But Nietzsche, to the contrary, found that in the linear conception present occurrence is shackled by a dead weight of the past, that the past cannot be made anew, and that a new future for humans is inconceivable. People might supplement the past with variations and mutations of what has been but, within the strictures of time viewed in the image of a line, the past persists as the unalterable already done. The past as such is not subject to radical creation.

Motivating this series of observations is Nietzsche's desire to articulate a dimension of time in which a new beginning comes into view. This would not be a moment in a sequence of moments but rather a different kind of originary reality. It would be outside of pastness and beyond temporal determination. It would be a sheer force of beginning anew.

Nietzsche's image for this different reality is not a transcendental entity but rather a wheel that turns eternally. Time is like a slowly turning wheel on which each now returns again and again. The past is in the future as it returns to its presence. The three parts of linear time are now elided into a continuous process without *telos*, justification, or punctuality. The past is saturated with futurity and the future already belongs to the past that is always in a process of alteration.

The introduction of this image and the exceptional force it had in his thought had a high cost for Nietzsche's metaphysical comfort. The happening of time is not grounded in anything timeless. Although meanings, insights, and definitive knowledge abound at any specific moment, no meaning or insight or knowledge, including most particularly those embodied by this image, has authority over the happening of temporal life. The effect of affirming this image, for Nietzsche, was release from the desire for ultimate meaning and purpose. It embodies release from bondage to the past. It carries out – performs – this release in the energy of its affirmation. Although Nietzsche believed that eternal return could be shown to be a fact of nature, the primary impact of the image in his work and as an influence on other philosophers is found in its departure from an ethos that forms around the linear image of time. This departure is performed as Nietzsche's writing and thought are increasingly shaped by recognitions and feelings that fall outside the jurisdiction of linear time. According to Nietzsche this is a shift of consciousness that enables the emergence of values and knowledge that were not previously available and that are salutary for constructive human transformation and creativity.

For Nietzsche, this transformative power is what is most important for human lives. The force of transforming many of the dominant meanings and images in his lineage is the work of the force of life (which he called the 'will to power'). In the context of his departure from the force of the linear image of time, the *conception* of eternal return is itself a living occurrence that is attuned, not to a doctrine about time but to the transformational way time happens. Self-overcoming is one term he used to describe the transformative force of time and the energy of life. Eternal return names an image and concept that require their own transformation. In that sense, the value of 'eternal return' is found in its self-transformational force and not in its representational accuracy: it says in effect that it too will pass away in the emergence of new meanings and images.

I am pointing out some aspects of Nietzsche's thought that have influenced strongly postmodern thought, aspects such as a prioritizing of nonlinear temporality, non-teleological futurity, and new beginnings. Nietzsche found necessary a new style of writing – a voice decisively different from the voices in his philosophical lineage – to articulate and carry out a major shift in philosophical conception and valuation. The purpose of thought for him is found in openings to new images and values. This emphasis on the future and transformation and on the impermanence of authoritative meanings and values embodies a departure from any claim for universal validity. I underscore Nietzsche's observation that argument often is less effective as a force for refutation and construction than are simple departures from weakening values and ideas along with formation of alternative kinds of thought and expression.

A second major critique of conceptions of universality and time that figures prominently in postmodern thought is found in a strategy called genealogy. This approach, that plays significant roles in the work of Heidegger, Foucault, Deleuze, Derrida, and many others, also has one of its inceptual articulations in Nietzsche's work. Rather than attempt to capture the essence of values and truths, Nietzsche investigates, for example, the way the value of good (as opposed to evil) began first in cultures of strength and then transformed in cultures of weakness and resentment. His study of beginnings combined with an emphasis on feeling and attitude, and his tracing the lineages of these beginnings allowed him to give accounts of values, virtues, and ethical dispositions that focused on their historical particularity and conflictual intentions. His is a language that is organized by traceable beginnings, not by affirmation of essences; by conflicts, not harmonies; by irreconcilables, not reconcilia-tion; and by differences, not unifying identities. Subjugation, destructiveness, cruelty, and ambiguity mark the lineages of the West's most lofty affirmations as Nietzsche found them; and not only has the content of this work had significant impact on many postmodern thinkers, its emphases, attunements, rhythms, and manners of departure and affirmation have had a continuing and shaping force in their work.

I am placing emphasis on the forces at play in Nietzsche's thought, on its performative processes, instability, signature departures, and affirmations that form a critique of metaphysical thought and culture as well as of many conceptions of reason that look for universal truths or timeless grounding for beliefs and assertions. Nietzsche's thought moves toward a recognition that history and not *a priori* subjectivity is the site of all affirmations and imperatives, that a sense of timelessness constitutes a sense of ground-lessness, and that thought at its best arises from and participates in a transformation of what has been called human nature. Within a postmodern context Nietzsche's thought and language appear as a beginning for a new lineage, a way of thinking and speaking that departs from some of the more destructive hegemonies and values in Western culture.

Humanism?

Humanism is one of the most forceful and effective conceptions in the Modern period. It has provided the basis and scaffolding for recognition of human identity across racial and cultural barriers and for the values of human dignity and human rights. It figures a theoretical hope for many people in the face of the horror and suffering that humans wreak upon each other. That this conception and its attendant images of humanity have fallen into question in postmodern thought might well give one pause before the appeal of such thought; and many postmodern thinkers might arouse hostile suspicion as they attempt to show in humanism not only a disposition toward colonialization and gender bias but also the seeds of fascism. Humanism, however, often sponsors the unquestioned value of universal truths, universal identity, and universalized teachings. That sponsoring, left unquestioned, does indeed support a politics based on truths that the privileged know and that others need to learn. I think it also inclines toward power relations that, left unchecked, constitute an autocracy of those who have the right morals and politics. If 'fascism' is too strong a word in this context, 'moral and political hierarchies of domination and usually unquestioned doctrines' would be an appropriate phrase.

Postmodern thinkers are in many ways direct inheritors of the humanist tradition. Humanists in varying degrees, beginning in late fourteenth-century Italy, continuing through such thinkers as Thomas Jefferson, Jean-Paul Sartre, and to an important extent Jürgen Habermas, placed emphasis on the central importance of Greek antiquity, political activity, freedom and liberation, tolerance, and human life in the formation of educated intelligence and cultural activity. These emphases occur also in postmodern thought. But postmodern thinkers also rethink and transform basic tenets held by humanists and turn them into different thoughts and values. Humanist conceptions of a fundamental identity or sameness for 'man and nature' and its conception of universe lose their constructive role in most postmodern thought. The image of foundational origins shifts toward that of dispersed beginnings and mutational historical events. The transformation of the humanist tradition is a signature process in postmodern thought and one of the areas where we can see the controversial significance of its work.

By considering Martin Heidegger's and Michel Foucault's departures from a humanistic orientation we can see more clearly what is at stake for many postmodern philosophers when they think in the lineage of the Modern epoch.

Heidegger notes that 'humanism' makes fundamental claims about the lives of everything in the world. In his terminology it constitutes a way of conceiving of being, that is, of the occurrence of whatever is. Within a humanistic orientation, for example, people understand the world as divided between rationality and animality, between enlightened subjectivity and bodies describable in terms of instincts and other natural forces. Reason stands outside of nature and can enjoy in many instances dominion over it, a dominion that at best places nature in the service of human interest and need. Humanism, in other words, leads easily to a view that interprets thinking as an *instrument* to be developed for the purpose of improving human lives and their environments according to true and good moral principles. Thought and language become means for carrying out human interests with the aim of enlightened domination of nature and other, nonhumanistic cultures.

According to Heidegger there is a major alternative to humanistic sensibility. He specifies the alternative in part by a process he calls de-struction, a type of genealogy that takes apart traditional ideas and philosophical systems (de-structures them) and shows both their silent assumptions and questions and their ways of conceiving the eventuation of whatever is. He finds that the *question* of being – a basic, unsettling, and usually unthematized uncertainty about life, its continuation and meaning – is the motivating force in Western metaphysics. For Heidegger the force of this nonconscious question (and not a timeless state of human reason and subjectivity) is the basic motivator for Western thought. He finds that a major portion of our reflective and doctrinal lineage comprises efforts to quiet or hide the profound unrest figured by the question of being. This is not a theoretical question but an anxious uncertainty that composes our lives: the *question* of being, and not an essential identity, defines people's lives. To be 'human,' he says, is to bring to alertness and engage the question of being in all dimensions of human experience. Humanism, in its essentialist and dualistic grounding, thus sponsors an escape from the questionable grounding of human being.

Heidegger calls the alternative to humanistic thought original thinking. 'Original' in this context means beginning with the manifest happening of whatever encounters a person. The region of manifest encounter that Heidegger terms *Dasein*, or being-in-the-world, and not subjectivity, is the site of thinking. His descriptive claim is that original thinking can occur when a person and whatever happens engage each other life to life, as it were, when a person is attuned to the living *manifestness* of the engagement and allows the other to be its noncategorical life, its own disclosure as it happens, its own being. Thinking happens when people find language in this attunement, bespeak it in the way they address what is engaged and the engagement, and intensify the manifestness of what shows itself.

This claim means that thinking is not primarily a subjective event but is rather a way of allowing something to be apparent. Humanistic thought, by contrast, lets things be apparent by means of predetermined and imposed values and concepts. It composes a value judgement as things become apparent. Heidegger addresses the possibility of a pre-judgemental occurrence, fully alert and disciplined in allowing things to be as they are, in all their differences, and in attunement with the indelible questionableness of life and meaning.

Original thinking thus composes a way of being with things, a way of being in the world. It is much more cautious in its assertions and impositions, much more careful in its own questionableness than is customary in humanistic endeavor. It finds destructive insensitivity in doctrinaire assertions, a misattunement to human life in the posited stability of universal essences and values. Heidegger's thought suggests the importance of rethinking our ways of conceiving human value and dignity and also suggests that humanism might well be among the causes of some of the ills it intends to address.

Orders of Representation

The combination in Heidegger's thought of de-struction with its emphasis on careful, textual study of the Western philosophical canon, his unrelenting focus on the finite groundlessness of being, his attention to thought and language, and his alertness to the cultural importance of basic patterns of thought and recognition gave impetus to Foucault's archeological and genealogical accounts of modern discourses. A major difference from Heidegger in Foucault's thought is found in Foucault's focus on social power and his attention to specific institutions, such as prisons, hospitals, and asylums as well as sexuality, insanity, and marriage. In connection with humanism, however, one finds in Foucault's thought profound resonance with Heidegger in addition to significant departure from him.

In contrast to the intentions of 'theoretical' thought and its emphasis on disinterested observation, thinking for Foucault appears as a play of interest and power. It attacks, liberates, conceals, reveals, and enslaves. Thought's life is best described as action – a perilous act, Foucault calls it, because of its ability to coerce, destroy, and oppress as well as to construct, liberate, and generate knowledge. Thinking and speaking, no less for Foucault than for Heidegger, make a decisive difference for everything in a human environment. The ways in which people and things are recognized and identified – as people of power or of submission, for example, or as deviants from accepted norms – are at once ways whereby people and things appear. Recognitions inevitably evaluate things and make them manifest in particular ways. Thought and speech carry forth such identifications, implicit commands are made and broken, future-shaping prescriptions are set forth, dissociation and association occur: the way thinking and speaking happen determines how lives appear and are lived and lost.

For Foucault the *way* in which lives appear is describable in terms of networks of forces. Institutions and broadly accepted practices give rise to people who see and feel in accord with defining networks of control and interest. The ways they live carry out, in Foucault's language, forceful structures of subjection: their subjectivity is in part a function of networks of constructive possibilities and controls. Such subjection might include the structures of reason and knowledge that appear with pretensions to universal validity. Careful genealogical accounts of such knowledge and reasons, however, show forceful, dominating interests at work. They show in many of our culture's unquestioned values and assumptions powerful struggles that carry on in disciplines of knowledge and technical practice as well as in institutions of education, correction, and delivery of health care.

Foucault also showed that disinterested intelligence, as it functioned in seventeenth- and eighteenth-century science and humanistic endeavor, gave dominance to particular kinds of observations and objectification, and to a sense of sovereignty on the part of the observer. Trained observers, regardless of the objects they observed, in this context 'knew' that their judgement was untainted by personal preferences and emotional distortion. Such sovereignty embodies a sense of freedom from control as though the soul ruled the body and the operation of timeless principles of reason ruled particular, individualized interests. This kind of intelligence, according to Foucault, is oblivious to its own desire for power and its service to the limited interests of privileged parts of its society. Foucault finds to the contrary, that such intelligence is subjected to the segments of society that it serves and to an obscure but extremely forceful desire for power. This disinterested, humanistic intelligence is itself far from a free sovereignty. In some of its instances it is subject, for example, to the interests of specific kinds of citizenship and civil authority, or to the class of people who can afford medical care or who can establish and enforce their moral authority in given contexts. It composes a system of practices, values, and knowledge that intends to overcome other systems and the people who live in them.

Foucault's approach to forms of representation is similar to Heidegger's de-structuring approach in the sense that Foucault accounts for and indeed looks for decentering and destabilizing aspects in the structures that hold the authority of representational knowledge in place. In his early work, Foucault names his version of de-structuring 'archeology.' Later, as issues of struggle and power became more valorized in his work, he calls his approach genealogical.

According to Foucault, representational knowledge provides the scaffolding for Modern and hence humanistic rationality. We have seen that in its force of represent-ing it is like a silent 'we.' It imposes schemata of representation on what is experienced and known in disciplined ways. The knowing subject re-presents what is there, and in the process it brings to bear the interests characteristic not only of various kinds of knowledge but also of certain privileged elements of a society or cultural lineage. The order of these schemata of recognition is figured by grids of representation that function according to various typologies and values. These grids also function as interpretations of various kinds of reality (such as things in 'nature,' systems of exchange, or language) and may form a larger unity of knowledge that transcends any of its parts, a supra-unity (an '*episteme*') of guiding images, values, and assumptions.

In the Modern period 'subjectivity' names a major power of organization and unity. The word means a formed agency that provides a universal foundation for human knowledge and experience. With the particularities of individual endeavor comes an active, transcendental capacity for order and will that all people share. It is at once the site and force of representation and the possibility for an integrated, powerful and institutionalized knowledge of the world based on transcendental human truth.

Foucault's detailed, historical accounts of the assumptions, guiding images, and lineage that I have summarized, his uncovering their hidden forms of value and power, and his highlighting the dispersion and dissension that they attempt to eliminate form a kind of knowledge of humanism that is not humanistic. His is an alternative knowledge the lineage for which can be found in the very aspects of marginalization, dispersion, and dissension that modern humanism carries and denies. His is a knowledge that disperses forceful images of unity, contests unquestioned ideological claims, recognizes its own finite and constitutive lineages, and develops a discipline of paying attention to what is suppressed, dominated, and marginalized in projects of representational unification. Foucault makes many claims that attest to representa-tional accuracy, but in most instances the dispersive action of his thought trumps the accuracy of his claims, and he develops a discourse with no pretense to timeless, stabilizing forms, transcendental foundations, or lasting authority. At best and on his own terms, the knowledge he generates and his thoughtful work with it might liberate people from the dominating power of Modern humanism and the institutions that re-enforce it. This liberation takes place as a different way of knowing emerges in his work.

The formation of ways of thinking, knowing, and speaking that provides alternatives to the force of the vast and complex representation of humanism characterizes the work of many postmodern philosophers. One also often finds in their work an emphasis on responsibility (or answerability) in the presence of another's differences. I turn now to this emphasis on difference and responsibility in the context of moving away from a *modern* emphasis on universality, unity, the ideological values of humanism, and toward other questions, other ways of life.

Difference and Responsibility

At the beginning of this discussion I noted a prevailing tension between the purposes of an informative essay like this one is intended to be, and the subject matter of this topic, postmodern philosophy. My notation addresses particularly the awkwardness of attempting to summarize and categorize a way of thinking that puts in question such generalizing conceptualization. The tension increases now as I turn to prioritizing difference over sameness – not prioritizing a category called difference, but prioritizing the happening of differences that appear to withdraw from the kind of presence that categories and other forms of recognition would bestow on them.

Heidegger emphasized the difference between Being and beings, that is, the difference between a particular being and the eventuation, the happening, of its life. The eventuation of lives appears to be the common dimension of all things with all their differences. This difference between Being and beings is not reducible to anything else. It is not a concept or an object or a subject. Traditional images of actuality as a continuing presence seem inappropriate for it. But, according to Heidegger, the difference between beings and Being, that is, between particular things and their happening, appears as a dimension of differencing in all instances of manifestation. To objectify such difference, as I have just done, is to obscure it. Thinking that thinks such difference, not only about it, and language that would speak appropriately of it would need to be decisively different from theories that represent it more or less accurately. The difference between Being and beings is not a matter of accuracy. It composes a phenomenon of difference in the happening of identities and recognitions. When I think and speak in representing ways, I look for present situations that I can re-present conceptually and communicatively and to which I can respond more or less appropriately. I want my thought and language to correspond accurately with their objects, and when I respond responsibly I will expect my actions and concepts to cohere appropriately with the relevant identities.

'Normative presence' describes the object of my responsible conceptualizations and intuitions; I want to be able to establish the correctness of my observations and thoughts by reference to something that is present and whose characteristics are verifiable. Anything that defers such correctness or detours around it would be suspect. Indeed, one of my intentions in this discussion is to report accurately some characteristics of postmodern thinking and to think responsibly about these characteristics in their interrelations and theoretical implications. I would like to make the presence of postmodern thought recognizable. But in that endeavor I also give priority to representational thought and the subjectivity of recognition, and I lose a sense for difference that will not occur as an object of representation. Developing thought and language that are appropriate to such difference, however, is crucial in the lineage of postmodern thought. Hence the difficulty of writing theoretically about nontheoretical thinking.

The occurrence of difference appears to withdraw from objective representation and yet to constitute a dimension in all lives. Nietzsche, for example, attempted to develop a style of thought and writing that made apparent the strange effect and affect of losses of major values and meanings, losses that persist in Western culture. Such losses appear as different from present actualities, as not present but oddly forceful in the absence – loss of the force and meaning of 'God' in previous epochs, for example, or loss of the force and meaning of tragedy in Classical Greek culture.

Foucault accentuated difference from presence in the rupture of continuity in the formation of orders and values that intend unbroken continuity. Addressing loss, rupture, and absence requires a different kind of thinking when compared to most person-centered philosophy in our lineage. How might we think in response to rupture and absence and not turn them into represented presences? Prioritizing difference over sameness in language and conceptualization is a strategic move in that direction. This strategy forecasts a way of thinking that forms and moves in differentiation from representational subjectivity and conceptuality. How such ways of thinking proceed and the way we might interpret them are major issues in postmodern thought.

Gilles Deleuze pays attention to the subordination of difference to resemblance, opposition, and analogy in his accounts of Western philosophy. Rather than this subordination, he wants to think difference itself, to carry out a manner of thought that immediately valorizes difference rather than sameness or similarity. Why? In order to see and hear what previous thought and language have ignored, suppressed, or misperceived, to provide a new opening for thinking, to re-evaluate the effects such suppression has wrought, and to interrupt a guiding sensibility in Western culture. He encounters leading images of identity and sameness that he finds violently constricting even though they seem to enact a good will on the part of the thinker. Deleuze's project is a creative part of the constructive effort of many postmodern philosophers to turn the destructive failures of representational thought into a positive opening for alternatives. Attention to difference provides a portal for this opening as a distinctive logic of temporality, power, and differentiation take shape in his discourse.

When people give priority to sameness and identity they will probably be tacitly predisposed to generalizations, to conceptual and social unities that emphasize a group of connecting likenesses. Orders of resemblance will likely rule recognition and perception as though continuation of such orders does not require repetition of conflicting differences, as though temporal eventuations do not happen as fragmentation, disarray, deviation, and discord. Those who prioritize difference over sameness, such as Nietzsche, Deleuze, Foucault, and Derrida, put in question traditional manners of thought, like those of representational activity and knowledge by means of prepositional coherence. They foresee other kinds of thoughtful expression. Such thought might be freed from the force of often tacit images of subjective control or universal reason. It would point beyond propositional modes of cognition and beyond the limits of Modern epistemologies. With attention to events of radical and nonreducible differences, it would point toward encounters that are not subjugated to representation or conceptual order. It would find ways to address events that are outside of conceptual boundaries, ways that are more like *responses* attuned to the differences than like structures that grasp and hold experiences by formations of enforced similarity.

However postmodern thinkers proceed, they usually find significant motivation in the failures of representational thought and the dominance of recognition when they take account of the range of human awareness. They are attuned particularly to the dangers of prioritizing cognitive subjectivity. Those dangers often appear as requirements to fit into normative 'logics' of good sense, systems of hierarchized identities, and structures of unquestioned assumptions about present, continuing reality. Such dangers often sponsor social and institutional practices that elevate and suppress people according to schemata of likenesses. These schemata are unattuned to the seeming nonactuality of differences that fall outside of the actual, verifiable presence of what is taken to be real and significant.

The emphasis then falls on responding with alertness to what we cannot capture by our representations and our orders of recognition. The works of many postmodern philosophers provide in their performative dimensions various kinds of predisposition to alertness with differences that cannot be incorporated into structures of likeness. *Alterity* is a word that is frequently used for such differences. It names the occurrence of 'what' cannot be recognized as 'what,' such as a person's own living event, the happening of the lives of things, dimensions of beauty and art, mere difference, or the indifference of nature before the values that people affirm most passionately. I believe I can say accurately that a major emphasis in postmodern thought is found in intentions to occasion ways of life that are based on reconsiderations of forgotten or ignored differences from what is often considered in the dominant Western traditions as normal, right, good, and sensible.

To carry out such intentions, postmodern thinkers often work in traditional texts, finding in those texts structures of unacknowledged power, subtle dislocations of meaning, and opposition to the primary claims in those texts. Most postmodern thinkers are, in fact, first and foremost readers of the Western canon who understand their own work to have its beginnings in movements in traditional texts that run counter to the dominant ideas and values that organize those texts. Postmodern thought often retrieves what is obscured in Western thought – differences from the dominant ideas and meanings, for example – differences that Western thought perpetuates almost silently, always marginally. In this context, responsibility with such differences, responsibility to what often seems in our tradition unreal or a mere deviation from good sense, becomes an ethical opportunity. In a postmodern context responsibility is based on the appearance of differences that assume neither a dominant form of autonomy nor a perdurant center of unquestioned authority. It is responsibility without foundations and with a pervasive sense of danger and uncertainty within human communities. Our commonality might well be formed in danger and uncertainty, in the losses that bring us together, and in differences that define our connections.

What Is Not Said

When I understand the present volume as an accompaniment to people's philosophical journey, I think of it less as a guide than as an occasion to further a conversation, or as an aid along the way. 'Postmodernism' is used in so many contexts that its usefulness is extremely limited and, as I said at the beginning, always misleading. By restricting this discussion to observations about conceptualization, representation, humanism, difference and responsibility, I hope to indicate areas of question and problematization that are important in the formation of postmodern thinking. I also hope to indicate an odd failure, should what I report about postmodern thought turn out to be correct: that correctness would keep you on the outside of this stream of thinking. I have not developed a discourse that arises in close engagements with texts or in an attempt to respond to the occurrence of unmasterable differences in the lives of various postmodern ways of thought. I have stayed within the confines of representational thinking, and I have accompanied you as a subject who tells you about postmodern thinking, an irritating subject, I fear, who often confesses failure as he ambles along at an irregular, often untimely gait.

I have this comfort: if you know something of postmodern thinking you will hear the silences in this discussion. You will know the flagrant gaps of reference, you might enjoy the halting attempts at summary (enjoy their differences from postmodern thinking), and, perhaps in a generous moment, you might come across accuracies that you will appreciate in their distance from thinking. This is the truth: postmodern thinking comprises some of the most disciplined, careful, and original philosophical effort in the twentieth century. It is a body of work that, like all thought, requires disciplined, sustained, and careful reading for its understanding. And it is a way of thinking whose ambition is usually to lead to its own overturning, to compose a way of living in its process, and in that way of living to occasion a beginning in which Western senses of identity and order transform, keeping in mind always that it is our certainties, ideals, and unquestioned recognitions that house the greatest dangers in our lives.

References

Blanchot, M. (1995), *The Writing of Disaster*, trans. A. Smock, Lincoln, and London: University of Nebraska Press.

Deleuze, G. (1990), *The Logic of Sense*, (ed.) C. V. Boundas, New York: Columbia University Press.

Deleuze, G. (1994), *Difference and Repetition*, trans. P. Patton, New York: Columbia University Press.

Derrida, J. (1982), *Margins of Philosophy*, trans. A. Bass, Chicago: The University of Chicago Press.

Derrida, J. (1997), *Of Grammatology*, trans. G. C. Spivak, Baltimore, and London: The Johns Hopkins Press.

Foucault, M. (1980), Power/Knowledge, (ed.) G. Colin, New York: Pantheon Books.

Foucault, M. (1994), *The Order of Things*, New York: Vintage Books.

Heidegger, M. (1993), *Basic Writings*, trans. D. F. Krell, San Francisco: Harper San Francisco.

Heidegger, M. (1996), *Being and Time*, trans. J. Stambaugh, Albany: State University of New York Press.

Irigaray, L. (1985), *This Sex Which Is Not One*, trans. C. Porter, Ithaca: Cornell University Press.

Kristeva, J. (1980), *Desire in Language*, (ed.) L. S. Roudiez, New York: Columbia University Press.

Nancy, J.-L. (1993), *The Experience of Freedom*, trans. B. McDonald, Stanford: Stanford University Press.

Nietzsche, F. (1989a), *Beyond Good and Evil*, trans. W. Kaufmann, New York: Random House.

Nietzsche, F. (1989b), *On the Genealogy of Morals and Ecce Homo*, trans. W. Kaufmann, New York: Random House.

Life: An Essay on the Overcoming of Metaphysics

Leonard Lawlor

Life by itself does not constitute a 'twentieth-century philosophy.' But it amounted to a constant theme throughout the twentieth century since European philosophers in particular continuously appropriate and transform the concept of life. So, after the nineteenth-century philosophies of vitalism and *Lebensphilosophie*, two major philosophical movements centering on the concept of life – Bergsonism and Husserlian phenomenology – dominated European philosophy up to the end of the 1920s. However, in 1927, Heidegger published his *Being and Time*. Heidegger himself told us that *Being and Time* was written out of the experience of the 'forgetfulness of being' in Western metaphysics (Heidegger 1993: 232). Being is especially forgotten, according to Heidegger, in the Cartesian conception of being as subjectivity. Since subjectivity always seems to be involved in the conception of life, Heidegger rejects any form of the philosophy of life; Husserl's '*Erlebnis*' (lived-experience) and Bergson's '*durée*' (duration) conceive life by means of an internal flow of experience. In *Being and Time* therefore, Heidegger repeatedly distinguishes the '*Dasein*-analytic,' and 'fundamental ontology,' from any form of biology or philosophy of biology, any form of biologism (Heidegger 1996: 46, 229–31). Making the question of life derivative, Heidegger's thought of *being* dominated European philosophy throughout the middle of the twentieth century. The working notes for *The Visible and the Invisible* that Merleau-Ponty left behind in 1961 not only indicate how much Heidegger's thought of being dominated the middle period, but also these notes anticipate what was about to happen in French thought: the critique of phenomenology (Merleau-Ponty 1968: 183). In their critiques, Derrida, Deleuze, and Foucault, each in his own way, took up once again the concept of life. In his 1968 *Difference and Repetition*, Deleuze talks about 'repetition within a life' (Deleuze 1994: 83). In his 1967 *Voice and Phenomenon*, Derrida speaks of 'the ultra-transcendental concept of life'.[1] Finally, and perhaps most importantly since it shows a shift from Heidegger's ontology, in his 1966 *The Order of Things*, Foucault says that 'there is being only because there is life'.[2] The re-emergence of the question of life during the 1960s resulted in three central texts on this subject at the end of the century: Deleuze's 'Immanence: A Life'; Foucault's 'Life: Experience and Science'; and Derrida's 'The Animal that therefore I Am (More to Follow).' At the end of the century, Derrida reminds us that life is always defined by irritability, spontaneity, auto-affection. Deleuze tells us that 'a life contains only what is virtual'. And finally, Foucault tells us that there are two approaches to the concept of life: lived-experience and the living (*le vécu* and *le vivant*). Yet, it seems that what has initiated the first movements of twenty-first century Continental philosophy is Foucault's diagnosis of the modern regime of power, in his 1976 *The History of Sexuality I*, as *bio-power*.[3] Bio-power is the starting point for Giorgio Agamben's most recent work (Agamben 1998: Part III).

Despite the variety of appropriations and transformations of the concept of life, it is possible to approach life in twentieth-century Continental philosophy not just *genetically* but also *structurally*. Indeed, the chapter that follows is *structural* in its approach to the concept of life; it intends to lay out the structure of a neo-vitalism or what we might call 'life-ism.'[4] The chapter has four sections. First, I will argue that, despite differences, Heidegger's conception of Nietzsche's idea that life is will to power,[5] and Foucault's conception of the modern regime of power as bio-power are similar if not identical conceptions.[6] Both will to power and bio-power are bound up with the Cartesian conception of subjectivity. Coining a term, we can say that 'bio-will to power' is the most current and dangerous form of metaphysics, the form that is the mere reversal of Platonism. It will then turn out that Husserl's phenomenological concept of *Erlebnis* is contemporaneous with bio-will to power. So, second, following the distinction that Foucault has laid out, between lived-experience and the living, I will examine the ambiguity in which phenomenological lived-experience consists. To overcome the Cartesian conception of life as subjectivity, it is necessary to disambiguate this ambiguity. The disambiguation occurs by means of the minuscule but invincible hiatus, the finitude of auto-affection. That a limit is found in life means that death is a teeming presence. Inseparable from 'life-ism' is a kind of 'mortalism.' Our third step, therefore, will determine the living through 'mortalism,' the 'mortalism' that appears in Foucault's two chapters on Xavier Bichat in *The Birth of the Clinic*. The conclusion, the fourth step, will turn to the fact that 'life-ism' follows the line of the inability to preserve and enhance life. Thus it resists the regime of bio-will to power and tries to twist free of metaphysics once and for all.

Life as Will to Power and as Bio-Power (Subjectivism)

It is possible to determine *four similarities* (if not identities) between Heidegger's conception of life as the will to power in Nietzsche (in NW) and Foucault's conception of bio-power (in HS1). The first similarity is the most obvious. Heidegger conceives will to power and Foucault conceives bio-power within the context of the movement of anti-Platonism in the 'modern age' (NW: 218/63; HS1: 155/117). For both Foucault and Heidegger, in the modern age, what was above, the second world of forms or the supersensory, is being pulled down – into life. The collapse of the supersensory into the sensory, into life, is anti-Platonism. The second similarity is that both Heidegger and Foucault understand the transformation from Platonism into anti-Platonism as a transformation in vision. Since God is dead, since the supersensory no longer expends life, the new highest value, for Nietzsche, is 'superabundant life' (NW: 226/70). According to Heidegger, 'In this new highest value there is concealed another *appraisal* of life, i.e. of that wherein lies the determining essence of everything living' (NW: 226/

70, my emphasis). Here, Heidegger is implying that life itself *is* an 'appraising' (NW: 237/81), and this appraising, according to Heidegger, defines life as the will to power in Nietzsche. But to appraise is to value. According to Heidegger, value, in Nietzsche, means 'the point in view [*Augenpunkt*] for a seeing that aims at something' (NW: 227/71). Heidegger immediately connects this seeing (the point at which the eye aims) to representation (*Vorstellung*). This seeing does not just look and let pass; it sees only insofar as it has seen, meaning that, insofar as it has seen, it has brought the object of vision back and has set (*stellen*) it in front of (*vor*) the seeing, has re-presented it and has posited the object of vision as such (NW: 228/71). Values then in Nietzsche according to Heidegger, are things posited by means of a re-presentation; there are no values prior to the positing of them. Values are posited by a 'gaze,' which sets up the point which becomes the 'aim in view.' According to Heidegger, 'Aim, view, field of vision, mean here both the object of vision and the vision, in a sense that is determined from out of Greek thought, but that has undergone the change of idea from *eidos* to *perceptio*' (NW: 228/72). In other words, what is seen must be an object and an object made certain by reckoning and measurement, that is, fixed into what remains as the 'constantly presencing' (NW: 238/83).

Apparently echoing Heidegger or Nietzsche, in *The History of Sexuality I*, Foucault states that bio-power 'distributes the living in the domain of value and utility. Such a power has to qualify, measure, *appraise* [*apprécier*], and hierarchize' (HS1: 189/144; my emphasis). In order to appraise, bio-power needs continuous regulatory and corrective mechanisms, mechanisms which are primarily mechanisms of discipline. Moving back then to his 1974 *Discipline and Punish*, we see that Foucault concludes his discussion of discipline with Bentham's conception of the prison as the Panopticon. Just by means of the literal meaning of this word, we can see that power in Foucault as in Heidegger concerns vision: optics. For Foucault, the Panopticon introduces a *general way* of ordering bodies, surfaces, lights, and gazes so that power operates automatically and without the intervention of a particular individual like a sovereign: Panopticism (SP: 242/207). Appearing in the nineteenth century, Panopticism amounts to a break with antiquity. To speak like Heidegger, we can say that, no longer do we have the idea as *eidos* but rather as *perceptio*. As Foucault says, the spectacle (temples, theaters, and circuses) solved the *ancient* problem of making it possible for a multitude of people to inspect a small number of objects (SP: 252/216). The *modern* problem is the reverse: 'to procure for a small number, or even a single individual, the instantaneous *view* [*vue*] of a great multitude' (SP: 252/216). But, since, in the Panopticon, the prisoners are only ever seen and the guard only ever sees while remaining invisible to the prisoners, Panopticism in fact dissociates the seeing/being seen dyad (SP: 235/201–2). The Panoptic architecture means that the prisoner is only ever 'the object of information' and 'never a subject in communication' (SP: 234/200). Being only ever an object of vision, each prisoner is 'constantly visible' in a state of 'permanent visibility'; the prisoner, in other words, is posited. Therefore, 'from the viewpoint of the guard,' the prisoners are 'a multiplicity that can be numbered and controlled' (SP: 234/201), appraised. Each prisoner is an object made certain – Foucault calls the Panopticon a 'house of certainty' (SP: 236/202), that is, fixed into what remains as the 'constantly presencing.'

The third similarity concerns the aim in view that is posited, the values themselves, in other words, the objective. According to Heidegger, the objective of life as the will to power is the 'preservation and enhancement' of power (NW: 229/72). For Nietzsche, according to Heidegger, preservation and enhancement are the two fundamental and inseparable tendencies of life (NW: 229/73). Life preserves itself in order to grow and enhance itself, in order to enhance its power. But, enhancement is possible only where a 'stable reserve' or a 'standing reserve' (*Bestand*[7]) is already being preserved as secure. The requirement for enhancement of a standing reserve of power means, according to Heidegger, that the will to power in Nietzsche must be distinguished from a mere striving or desire for power based on the feeling of a lack; in this case, one would have willing on one side and power on the other (NW: 233/76). The will to power is not the ordering about of others and it is, according to Heidegger, 'more difficult than obeying' (NW: 234/77). Instead, the will to power in Nietzsche is 'commanding': 'Commanding has its essence in the fact that the master who commands has conscious disposal over the possibilities for effective action' (NW: 234/77). Thus what the will wills it has already; 'it super-enhances itself' (NW: 234/77). The will to power then in Nietzsche, according to Heidegger, is power-enhancement; it commands for itself only power and more power, super-power (NW: 234–5/78).

Like Heidegger, who distinguishes a mere striving for power from the will to power, Foucault in *The History of Sexuality I* distinguishes the juridical power of the sovereign from bio-power. The privileged characteristic of the sovereign's power (going back to ancient times) is the right to decide on life and death (HS1: 178/136). But for Foucault, the sovereign right means that this kind of power is exercised by means of 'exacting' or 'subtracting' the proverbial 'pound of flesh' (HS1: 178–9/136; see also 118/89). Juridical power, therefore, takes away life rather than preserves or enhances life. But also, because juridical power does not enhance life, the effect of juridical power is obedience (HS1: 112/85). In this kind of power, one is constrained and forced to submit; power is taken away and then there is a desire for power based in a feeling of a lack of power. Following Heidegger's formula, we can say that here, with juridical power, will (or desire) and power are on two opposite sides. On the other hand, in Foucault there is bio-power. The mechanisms of bio-power have the function of organizing and optimizing the forces under the control of those mechanisms. In other words, bio-power is a 'power aimed at producing forces, at making them grow, and at ordering them, rather than a power devoted to barring them, to making them compliant, or to destroying them' (HS1: 179/136). Again borrowing a formula from Heidegger, we can say that bio-power consists in positing preservation (the maintenance of the biological existence of a population) and enhancement (optimizing and multiplying life) conditions. The appropriation of this formula lets us see that bio-power is, as Heidegger would say, a 'commanding.' Here in bio-power, there is no desire or will for power. Rather, as Foucault says, what is demanded and what serves 'as an objective is life, understood as the basic need, man's concrete essence, the accomplishment of his virtualities, a plentitude of the possible' (HS1: 191/145). Foucault is saying that modern society does not strive; 'it super-enhances itself.'

The (fourth and final) similarity is that both Heidegger and Foucault conceptually link the modern concept of power to Cartesian subjectivism. For Heidegger, the connection to Descartes occurs by means of value-positing, which must be certain. The certainty then leads to the *ego cogito* as that which presences as fixed and constant the subject as self-consciousness (NW: 238/82–3). Similarly, Foucault claims that 'another way of philosophizing' appears due to the expansion of the role of confession in the Classical Age and then in the Modern age: 'seeking the fundamental relation to the true . . . in the self-examination that yields, through a multitude of fleeting impressions, the fundamental certainties of consciousness' (HS1: 80/59–60). In particular, according to Foucault, Cartesianism appears in the nineteenth century when psychiatry faced the problem of trying to constitute itself as a science, as 'a confessional science'; 'the long discussions concerning the possibility of constituting a science of the subject, the validity of introspection, lived-experience [*vécu*] as evidence, or the presence of consciousness to itself were responses to this problem' (HS1: 86/64). For Foucault therefore, the modern form of Cartesianism that is involved in bio-power is Husserlian phenomenology and the concept of lived-experience. But the same is true for Heidegger, who implies that nihilism ends in phenomenology (NW: 209/54). Phenomenology's unthought and invincible presupposition, Heidegger says, is the un-positing of the supersensible, which in turn *reduces* the difference between the sensible and the supersensible.

Life as Lived-Experience (Immanence)

Expanding on Descartes's idea of methodical doubt, Husserl invents the phenomenological *reduction*. According to the formulas we find in Husserl's *Ideas I* (1913), the phenomenological reduction shuts off the 'natural attitude' judgement about reality; in other words, it shuts off the sense of being as objectivity or as spatio-temporal factual being; it 'puts out of action' the positing of the whole world as it is out there for me. The reduction then leaves behind what cannot be put out of action, the 'residuum of pure consciousness' or pure lived-experience. Husserl defines lived-experience, pure lived-experience, by means of immanent perception in opposition to transcendent perception. In transcendent perception, the object of perception is external to or not unified with the perceiving. However, in immanent perception, 'the perceiving and the perceived form essentially an unmediated unity, that of a single concrete *cogitatio*'[8]. The definition of lived-experience as immanence implies that lived-experience is auto-affection: since the real has been suspended and thus the relation to what is outside of consciousness has been suspended, the one affecting is the same as the one affected. The sameness of auto-affection is why Husserl in *Ideas I* can speak of absolute lived-experience. Yet, despite the sameness, lived-experience in Husserl is complicated. Lived-experience consists in the act of intending which is 'reell,' that is, internal and intentional. There is also the intended meaning called the 'noema'; Husserl states that the noema is 'irreell.' But also, in lived experience there is something that is 'reell,' but which is also 'nonintentional'; this is what Husserl calls 'hyle,' the data of sensation. There are, therefore, in Husserl's concept of lived-experience, several senses of being: the sense of reality (which is reduced); the sense of 'reell,' which is strictly subjective, active, and internal; the sense of 'irreell,' which is not strictly subjective but still internal; and finally the sense of 'reell' but nonintentional, which is internal and passive (Derrida 1967: 243; Eng. 1978: 163). In this regard, Heidegger claims that Husserl fails to ask what the being of the consciousness could be such that it could give rise to all of these senses; in other words, Husserl fails to ask the question of the sense of being as such. Husserl leaves the ontological status of lived-experience in a condition of 'ambiguity.' The senses are mixed together.

For Husserl, the mixture arises because lived-experience is primarily temporal. In lived-experience, I affect myself with an anticipation, which becomes now, and which passes into the past. In other words, there are different phases of time mixed together in lived-experience. Yet, Husserl calls the flux of time 'absolute subjectivity' (Husserl 2000: 429. para. 36; Eng. 1964: 100). No matter what, the phenomenological concept of lived-experience bears the primary (albeit ambiguous) sense of subjectivity. Now, in his 1929 book on Kant, stressing the finitude of knowledge in Kant, Heidegger shows that, for Kant, time is auto-affection (Heidegger 1973: 182, para. 34; Eng. 1990: 129). Heidegger, however, argues that temporal auto-affection, preceding the self, forms the essential structure of subjectivity, which means that temporal auto-affection is either pre-subjective or, better, a-subjective. According to Heidegger, 'Time and the "I think" no longer stand incompatibly and incomparably at odds; they are the ' "same" ' (Heidegger 1990: 131, Eng. trans of Heidegger 1973). Here, Heidegger has transferred the mixture or sameness of temporal phases or senses from subjectivity to being, but he has not made the difference between the phases or senses explicit.

Now, in his 1966 *The Order of Things*, Foucault claims that the interrogation of the mode of being of the *cogito* – Heidegger's question – could be asked only in the Modern epoch, with the appearance of the figure of Man (MC: 323/312). What defines the figure of 'Man' is finitude (MC: 329/318). In the classical epoch (from Descartes to Kant), finitude was conceived in terms of the infinite; there was a metaphysics of the infinite (God). In the modern epoch, however, according to Foucault, finitude is conceived in terms of itself; now we have, as Foucault says 'the end of metaphysics' (MC: 328/317). The modern epoch is indeed the epoch of anti-Platonism. 'Man' is finite insofar as he is subjected to life, language, and work; Man is going to die; he receives the language that he speaks; and he finds himself with needs. But he is also finite insofar as his knowledge of life, labor, and work is itself finite; there is no intellectual intuition for 'Man.' The finitude of the empirical contents is the same as the finitude of the foundational forms. The sameness of finitude means that 'Man' is in the middle of a series of doubles: the foundation and the founded; the empirical and the transcendental; the thought and the unthought; and the return and retreat of the origin. The doubling (as in a mirror image) implies that we can say, according to Foucault, that I am this life since I sense it deep within me, but also I can say that I am not it since it envelops me and grows towards the imminent moment of death (MC: 335/324–5). In 'Man and his doubles' then, we have an auto-affection which is the same (MC: 326/315), but which is also other, which is also hetero-affection. As we saw with the phenomenological concept of lived-experience, the relation – the kind of 'synthesis' that 'Man' represents – is ambiguous (MC: 332/321). Yet Foucault claims that the sameness of the doubles, indicated by the conjunction 'and,' is possible only on the basis of '*un écart infime, mais invincible*,' 'a minuscule, but invisible hiatus' (MC: 351/340). Not only does the '*écart*' differentiate the temporal phases or senses, but also the '*écart*,' according to Foucault, is what in fact makes it possible for the modern epoch to conceive time (MC: 351/340). Here we move away from Heidegger and the entire phenomenological tradition: a profound spatiality – distance – makes time possible.

In *The Order of Things*, however, Foucault provides no argumentation for the claim that a 'profound spatiality' establishes the difference and precedes temporalization. We can find the argumentation in Derrida's 1967 *Voice and Phenomenon*. As we mentioned above, Derrida opens this book by speaking of 'the ultra-transcendental concept of life,' which is auto-affection. Derrida argues that, when Husserl describes lived-experience, even absolute subjectivity, he is speaking of an interior monologue, auto-affection as hearing-oneself-speak. According to Derrida, hearing-oneself-speak is 'an absolutely unique kind of auto-affection' (VP: 88/78), because there is no external detour from the hearing to the speaking; in hearing-oneself-speak there is self-proximity. I hear myself speak, therefore, immediately in the very *moment* that I am speaking. According to Derrida, Husserl's own description of temporalization undermines the idea that I hear myself speak immediately. On the one hand, Husserl describes what he calls the 'living present,' the present that I am experiencing right now, as being perception, and yet Husserl also says that the living present is thick. The living present is thick because it includes phases other than the now, in particular, what Husserl calls 'retention,' the recent past. Yet, retention in Husserl has a strange status since Husserl wants to include it in the present as a kind of perception and at the same time he recognizes that it is different from the present as a kind of nonperception. For Derrida, Husserl's descriptions imply that the living present, by always folding the recent past back into itself, involves a *difference* in the very middle of it (VP: 77/69). In other words, when I silently speak to myself, it must be the case that there is a minuscule hiatus differentiating me into the hearer and the speaker; there must be '*un écart*' that distances me from myself, without which I would not be a hearer as well as a speaker. Following Heidegger, Derrida says that the '*écart*' in the present does not happen to a subject but produces a subject (VP: 92/82). Importantly however, Derrida also notes that 'moment' or 'instant' translates the German word '*Augenblick*,' which means the blink of the eye. Therefore, we can see here that, for Derrida, the hearing-oneself-speak in fact refers back to perception, to vision, and even to the mirror image (VP: 88/78–9). In the auto-affection of seeing oneself seeing, the eye closes (due to retention), and when the eye closes (blindness), it breaks open the immediacy of temporal auto-affection; the blindness 'spaces': 'the proximity [of hearing-oneself-speak] is broken when, instead of hearing myself speak, I see myself write or gesture' (VP: 90/80). As in Foucault, here in Derrida, space or what Derrida calls 'spacing,' '*espacement*,' (VP: 96/86) precedes temporalization. Spacing has a double effect on the concept of lived-experience. On the one hand, by desubjectifying life, spacing frees immanence (life) from being immanent to consciousness; in turn both subject and object become dependent on immanence; and yet immanence is not a mixture since it includes, always, the minuscule hiatus. On the other hand, by desubjectifying life, spacing redefines the living as a process of dying (finitization).

Life as the Living (Mortalism)

As Deleuze says, 'from *The Birth of the Clinic* on [in 1963] Foucault admired [Xavier] Bichat for having invented a new vitalism' (Deleuze 1988: 93; Eng. trans. of Deleuze 1986). Indeed, in *The Birth of the Clinic*, Foucault devotes two chapters to the innovations that Bichat brought about in relation to the concept of life at the threshold between the classical epoch and the modern.[9] According to Foucault, we reach modern biology when the classifiable characteristics of the living come to be 'based upon a principle alien to the domain of the visible' (MC: 239/227). While the classifications involved in classical natural history related visible form to visible form, for example, the visible form of a bird to the visible characteristic of wings, modern biology relates visible form to the functions essential to the living, functions that are themselves buried deeply within the body of the living; the functions form a 'hidden architecture' of the invisible (MC: 242/229). The discontinuity, which consists in a break between a relation of visible to visible and a relation of visible to invisible, brought forth another, a discontinuity in the medical perception. The gaze becomes, as Foucault says, 'the great white eye of death.'[10] Bichat had, of course, become famous during his own time and later, because he had 'opened up a few corpses.' Literally, 'autopsy,' 'auto-opsis,' is a 'seeing with one's own eyes,' not one's own life, but the death of the living. The autopsy is not a lived-experience (NC: 175/170), but rather a dead-experience.

Now Foucault points out that during this period – the Enlightenment – autopsies were possible *immediately* after the moment of death. Consequently, the last stage of the process of the disease, the last stage of 'pathological time,' nearly coincided with the first stage of death, with the first stage of 'cadaveric time' (NC: 143/141). At this very moment, decomposition had only just started. Because the effects of decomposition were nearly suppressed, death became 'a landmark without thickness,' 'the vertical and absolutely thin line that separates but allows the series of symptoms to be related to the series of lesions' (NC: 143/141). Bichat realized that, at the moment of death, one is able to observe the final symptom in the series of symptoms – the final point in the series is still visible – *and*, with the autopsy opening the body, one is also able to observe the series of lesions – a series that, prior to death, had been hidden in the patient's body, invisible. In other words, by means of the immediate autopsy, Bichat was able to look at the 'principle alien to the domain of the visible.' Bichat made what was invisible when alive, visible through the autoposy, through *death*. This is, for Foucault, Bichat's first great innovation: the perception of death allowed Bichat to give a more rigorous and therefore instrumental definition of death (NC:143/141; NC: 149/146). He made the medical gaze pivot away from the elimination of the disease, the cure, and life-preservation, towards death, demanding of death that it give an account of life and disease (NC: 148–9/146).

Because of having done autopsies, Bichat was *also* able to distinguish two different but interrelated series. If one opens up the body at the very moment of death, one is able to see the series of the disease, its progress across tissues; this progress is the 'morbid process.' But, there is also a series of phenomena that announce the coming of death. For instance, muscular flaccidity, as Foucault tells us, would not take place without a disease. But, the flaccidity is not the disease itself; it accompanies any chronic disease. Therefore, the increase in muscular flaccidity 'doubles' the duration of the disease with an evolution that indicates, not the disease, but the proximity of death (NC: 144/141). Foucault calls this kind of process, such as the increasing flaccidity of muscles, 'mortification.' Mortification runs beneath the morbid processes with which it is associated. According to Foucault, however, the signs of mortification are different from symptoms of the disease; symptoms allow one to predict the outcome of the disease towards health or illness. The signs of mortification, however, simply show a process in the course of accomplishment; they are phenomena, as Foucault says, of 'partial or progressive death': 'long after the death of the individual, minuscule, partial deaths continue to dissociate the islets of life that still subsist' (NC: 144–5/142). For Foucault, this idea of a 'moving death' is Bichat's second great innovation in regard to the concept of life. These processes indicate the permeability of life by death. Foucault says: 'Death is therefore multiple, and dispersed in time: it is not the absolute, privileged point at which time stops and moves back; like disease itself, death has a teeming presence' (NC: 144/142). But the idea of partial deaths leads to Bichat's third innovation.

Thanks to the great white eye of death – the autopsy – disease has, Foucault says, 'a mappable land' or 'place' (NC: 151/149). The living is defined by the spacing of disease as a 'great organic vegetation,' with 'a nervure,' with 'its own forms of sprouting, its own way of taking root, and its privileged regions of growth' (NC: 155/152–3). Spatialized in this way, pathological phenomena take on the appearance of living processes. That disease is a living process means that it is inseparable from life; it is no longer an event or nature imported from the exterior of life. Disease is an internal deviation of life (NC: 155/153). But, being an internal deviation of life, disease is also organized according to the model of a living individual; there is, for example, a life of cancer. Both of these consequences – that disease is a living process and that it is a life – for Foucault indicate that disease is now understood as pathological *life* (NC: 156/153). He says: 'From Bichat onwards, the pathological phenomenon was perceived against a background of *life*, thus finding itself linked to the concrete and obligatory forms that life takes in an organic individuality' (NC: 156/153). For Foucault, with the idea that life is the ground of disease, we have Bichat's third innovation, his definition of life as the set of functions that resist death. For Bichat, life 'is not a set of characteristics that are distinguished from the inorganic, but the background against which the opposition between the organism and the non-living may be perceived, situated, and laden with all the positive values of conflict' (NC: 157/154). Life being defined as a conflict with the nonliving means that life, as a process of degeneration, is, at the limit, auto-destruction, and again not preservative (NC: 160–1/157); the degeneration of life always moves towards death. Wear and tear (*l'usure*), Foucault says, 'is the form of degeneration that accompanies life, and throughout its entire duration, defines its confrontation with death' (NC: 161/158). Therefore, for Foucault – this claim is Bichat's third innovation – death is co-extensive with life. The co-extensivity of death with life is why Foucault says that 'vitalism appears against the background of ' "mortalism" ' (NC: 148/145).

But how are we to understand mortalism?[11] Foucault says, '. . . although . . . Bichat plugged the pathological phenomenon into the physiological process and although he makes the pathological phenomenon derive from the physiological process, this deviation, in the hiatus that it constitutes, and which announces the morbid fact, is founded on death. Deviation in life is of the order of life, but of a life that goes towards death' (NC: 158/156). Death, Foucault says here, constitutes '*un écart*,' even '*un écart infime*,' 'a minuscule hiatus' (cf. MC: 351/340). Life, therefore, always contains disease as a potentiality, or better, as a virtuality based on life itself[12]. Foucault stresses that it is not the case that disease is the source of death; rather, death, in life, has always already begun; there is always already a process of mortification in which diseases are virtual. The reversal of what we normally think about the relation between life, disease, and death defines mortalism; mortalism is the virtuality of dying (finitization). The virtuality of dying, however, means that life, or better, 'a life' is always potentially a multiplicity of diseases, which, as we have already seen, are themselves modeled on a living individual, on a life: there is a life of cancer. Multiplicity, being the ground of many lives of diseases, contains virtually singularities (NC: 159/156).

The virtuality of singularities brings us back to the gaze of the autopsy. Bichat's first innovation was the transformation of death into an instrument by means of which the lesions that were invisible during life become visible. Here we have what Foucault calls a 'visible invisible,' in other words, 'an invisible that is potentially visible.' Yet Foucault calls life 'an opaque ground' (NC: 170/166), meaning that this seeing with one's own eyes reaches a limit. Individual diseases exist only because they unfold in the form of individuality (NC: 173/168–9). Therefore, in order to describe a life of a disease, medical experience would have to see all the singularities that support it. To determine the singularity of a disease, we would have to see more qualitatively, more concretely, in a way that is more than individualized; there would have to be a greater refinement of vision; we would be going farther and farther into the gaps between the singular points. Yet, if these singular points that we are approaching are really singular, our eyes would not be able to recognize them with any already acquired general representations; simply, these representations would be general and not singular. These forms would not work and there could be no understanding; there could be no positing. A life would be both sub-representational and informal. Through Bichat, Foucault is able to conceive life as a zone in which there is the constant murmur of conflict, but in which the gaze is uncertain of what it is seeing. Here, in 'Bichat's zone,' we have not a visible invisible, but an invisible visible, a visible that remains obstinately invisible. The autopsy, then, is unable to see clearly in the grayness of this zone and yet it sees more, a strange form of blindness.

Powerlessness and Power

To conclude, let me summarize the structure of life-ism that this chapter has just laid out. Under the pressure of Heidegger's experience of the forgetfulness of being in Western metaphysics, Continental philosophy revolves around the question of overcoming metaphysics. Thus Continental philosophy (understood as a project) always refers itself back to Nietzsche's idea of anti-Platonism. To overcome Platonism, it is necessary to collapse the *division* (as in the divided line) between this world and the second world of forms. The collapse of the difference not only reduces the forms down to life, that is, down to immanence, but it also shifts the level of the concept of life itself. Prior to the nineteenth century, the spontaneity of life is opposed to the determination of machines and this opposition between vitalism and mechanism takes place against the background of the fundamental concept of nature. With the project, however, of the overcoming of Platonism, the concept of life itself becomes the background or ground for all other oppositions. This shift to the level of ground implies that the traditional (pre-nineteenth century) problems associated with the concept of life are pushed to the side, problems such as the unity of life (vegetative versus cognitive), the specificity of life (organic versus inorganic), the opposition between finalism and mechanism, the conceptions of evolution. Instead, replacing being as well, life becomes *ultra-transcendental*. The ultra-transcendental concept of life is auto-affection. What distinguishes the twentieth-century concept of auto-affection from all previous ones is that now auto-affection takes place across a limit, across a difference, across a minuscule but invincible hiatus, across a spacing. Due to the limit, auto-affection is finite; or, since life as auto-affection is fundamental, life is 'originary finitude.' To put this idea another way, below 'life-ism' is 'mortalism' (NC: 148/145). The limit in the middle of auto-affection is death. Yet death is not an absolute limit opposed to life; it is not an end. Rather, death is mobile, a 'teeming presence': life then is 'finitization.'

Finitization means that the power of life rests on a powerlessness. The teeming presence of death means that within the sensing-sensed relation, there is always the nonsensible. If the living is defined by the self-relation, then wherever there is this relation, there must be a gap between the active and passive poles of the relation in order that there might be *two* poles at all. The 'auto' then is always, necessarily out of joint. The necessary being out of joint means that, in auto-affection, understood as seeing-seen, there is always a kind of fundamental blindness; the eye closes (VP: 73/65; see also MC: 337/326). The fundamental blindness, an inability to see, places *powerlessness* right in the very middle of the point of view of *power* understood as preservation-enhancement. There is a fundamental a-perspectivism within the per-spectivism of the 'bio-will to power.' Indeed, life is so finite that it cannot overcome this powerlessness through determination and the will. It seems to me that the argumentation that life as auto-affection is always 'out of joint' amounts to the only way to start to understand Foucault's concept of points of resistance against bio-power (HS1: 126/95–96). As Foucault says: '[T]he forces that resisted [bio-power] relied for support on the very thing [bio-power] invested, that is, on life and man insofar as he is living [*vivant*]' (VS: 190/144). Only where there is blindness, where one (a life) is no longer visible to the general Panopticon, is resistance possible. With blindness, there can be no constant presence; there is always invisibility and thus freedom. In other words, from the points of impossibility (not the plenitude of the possible) comes the possible. Only by *following* the line of this powerlessness will we be able to twist free of the most current and dangerous form of metaphysics, the form that is the *mere* reversal of Platonism. In the regime of bio-will to power, there is 'radical killing' (NW: 263/ 108) and 'wars have never been as bloody' (HS1: 179/136).

Notes

1. Derrida 1967/1973: 14/14. I will use the title, *Voice and Phenomenon*, to refer to this text. Hereafter referred to as VP:, with reference first to the original French, then to the English translation called *Speech and Phenomena*.
2. Foucault 1966: 291; Eng. 1970: 278. Hereafter referred to as MC:, with reference first to the French, then to the English translation. See also Deleuze 1986: 137 n.10; Eng. 1988: 152 n.10. Here Deleuze says that this comment expresses a constant aspect of Foucault's thought.
3. Foucault 1976: esp. pp. 175–211; Eng. 1990: 135–59. Hereafter referred to as HS1, with reference first to the French, then to the English translation.
4. See my '*Verendlichung* (Finitization): The Overcoming of Metaphysics with Life,' in *Philosophy Today* (winter 2004): 390–403
5. The interpretation that I will present is based mainly on Heidegger 1943. Hereafter referred to as NW, with reference first to the original German, then to the English translation
6. The interpretation that I am presenting is based mainly on Foucault 1976; and Foucault 1975. Hereafter cited as SP with reference first to the original French, then to the English translation.
7. 'Bestand' is the word, of course, that Heidegger uses to designate the mode of presencing in modern technology; see Heidegger 2004: 20; Eng. 1977: 17.
8. Husserl 1913; see also Heidegger 1985: 96–7.
9. Xavier Bichat was a French anatomist and biologist (1771–1802). He published four books: *Traité des membranes* (1799); *Recherches physiologiques sur la vie et la mort* (1800); *Anatomie générale appliquée à la médecine* (1801); *Anatomie descriptive* (1801). For a short biographical sketch, see Bichat 1994: 389–91. It is perhaps significant that this biographical sketch speculates that Bichat died from something he contracted after opening up corpses.
10. Foucault 1997: 147; Eng. 1994: 144. Hereafter referred to as NC:, with reference first to the French, then to the English translation.
11. For more on this conception of death, see Deleuze 1968: 148–9; Eng. 1995: 112–3. See also Blanchot 1955.
12. Canguilhem says that life contains a 'superabundance'of solutions to problems that have not yet appeared, a superabundance that can be abused and lead to error. See Canguilhem 1966: 133, 199, and 206; Eng. 1991: 200, 265, and 273.

References

Agamben, G. (1998), *Homo Sacer: Sovereign Power and Bare Life*, trans. D. Heller-Roasen, Stanford: Stanford University Press.
Bichat, X. [1800] (1994), *Recherches physiologiques sur la vie et la mort (premiere partie) et autres textes*, Paris: Flammarion; trans. anon. (1978), *Recherches: Physiological Researches on Life and Death*, Washington, DC: University Publications of America.
Blanchot, M. (1955), 'L'oeuvre et l'espace de la mort,' in M. Blanchot (1955), *L'espace litteraire*, Paris: Gallimard, pp. 99–211; trans. A. Smock (1982), 'The Work and Death's Space,' in *The Space of Literature*, Lincoln: University of Nebraska Press, pp. 101–59.
Canguilhem, G. (1966), *Le normal et le pathologique*, Paris: Presses Universitaires de France; trans. C. R. Fawcett with R. S. Cohen (1991), New York: Zone Books.
Deleuze, G. (1968), *Différence et Repetition*, Paris: Presses Universitaires de France; trans. P. Patton (1994), *Difference and Repetition*, New York: Columbia University Press.

Deleuze, G. (1986), *Foucault*, Paris: Minuit; trans. S. Hand (1988), *Foucault*, Minneapolis: University of Minnesota Press.

Deleuze, G. [1995] (2003), 'Immanence: Une vie,' in G. Deleuze (2003), *Deux regimes de fous*, Paris: Minuit, pp. 359–63; trans. A. Boyman (2001), 'Immanence: A Life,' in *Pure Immanence: Essays on a Life*, New York: Zone Books, pp. 25–33.

Derrida, J. (1967), ' "Genèse et structure" et la phénomènologie,' in J. Derrida (1967), *L'écriture et la différence*, Paris: Seuil, pp. 229–51; trans. A. Bass (1978), ' "Genesis and Structure" and Phenomenology', in *Writing and Difference*, Chicago: University of Chicago Press, pp. 154–68.

Derrida, J. [1967] (1973), *La voix et la phénomène*, Paris: Presses Universitaires de France; trans. D. B. Allison (1973), *Speech and Phenomena*, Evanston: Northwestern University Press.

Derrida, J. [1998] (1999), 'L'animal que donc je suis (à suivre),' in J. Derrida (1999), *L'animal autobiographique, autour de Jacques Derrida*, Paris: Gallimard, pp. 251–302; trans. D. Wills (2002), 'The Animal that therefore I Am (More to Follow),' in *Critical Inquiry* 28 (winter): 369–418.

Foucault, M. (1966), *Les mots et les choses*, Paris: Gallimard; trans. anon. (1970), *The Order of Things*, New York: Random House.

Foucault, M. (1975), *Surveiller et punir*, Paris: Gallimard; trans. A. Sheridan (1995), *Discipline and Punish*, New York: Vintage.

Foucault, M. (1976), *Histoire de la sexualité, la volonté de savoir*, vol. 1, Paris: Gallimard; trans. R. Hurley (1990), *The History of Sexuality: An Introduction*, vol. I, New York: Vintage.

Foucault, M. (1989), *The Birth of the Clinic*, London: Routledge.

Foucault, M. [1984] (1994), 'Vie: Experience et science,' in M. Foucault (1994), *Dits et écrits*, vol. 4, Paris: Gallimard, pp. 763–76; trans. R. Hurley (1998), 'Life: Experience and Science,' in *Essential Works of Michel Foucault: Aesthetics, Method, and Epistemology*, ed. J. D. Faubion, vol. 2, New York: The New Press, pp. 465–78.

Foucault, M. [1963] (1997), *La naissance de la clinique*, Paris: Presses Universitaires de France; trans. A. M. Sheridan (1994), *The Birth of the Clinic*, New York: Vintage.

Heidegger, M. [1929] (1973), *Kant und das Problem der Metaphysik*, 4th edn, Frankfurt am Main: Klostermann; trans. R. Taft (1990), *Kant and the Problem of Metaphysics, Fourth Edition*, Bloomington: Indiana University Press.

Heidegger, M. (1985), *History of the Concept of Time*, trans. T. Kisiel, Bloomington: Indiana University Press.

Heidegger, M. (1996), *Being and Time*, trans. J. Stampbough, Albany: State University of New York Press.

Heidegger, M. [1943] (2003), 'Nietzsche's Wort "Got ist tot," ' in M. Heidegger (2003), *Holzwege*, Frankfurt am Main: Klostermann, pp. 209–67; trans. W. Lovitt (1977), 'Nietzsche's Word "God is Dead" ', in *The Question concerning Technology and Other Essays*, New York: Harper, pp. 53–112.

Heidegger, M. [1953] (2004), 'Die Frage nach der Technik,' in M. Heidegger (2004), *Vortrage und Aufsatze*, Stuttgart: Klett-Cotta, pp. 9–40; trans. W. Lovitt (1977), 'The Question concerning Technology,' in *The Question concerning Technology and Other Essays*, New York: Harper, pp. 3–25.

Husserl, E. [1913] (1982), *Ideas Pertaining to a Pure Phenomenology and to a Phenomenological Philosophy – First Book: General Introduction to a Pure Phenomenology*, trans. F. Kertse, The Hague: Nijhoff.

Husserl, E. [1928] (2000), *Vorlesungen zur Phänomenologie des inneren Zeitbewusstseins*, Tübingen: Niemeyer: trans. J. S. Churchill (1964), *The Phenomenology of Time Consciousness*, The Hague: Nijhof.

Merleau-Ponty, M. (1968), *The Visible and the Invisible*, trans. A. Lingis, Evanston: Northwestern University Press.

Philosophy of Mind

David Morris

The most distinctive feature of philosophy of mind in the Continental tradition is that for the most part there has been no such thing. While the Continental tradition richly contributes to the study of mind, it has not considered the topic a separate department of philosophy. Indeed, the Continental tradition's foremost results challenge typical projects of philosophy of mind.

The reasons for this are three Continental tendencies. First, the tendency is to begin all philosophical study by scrutinizing the philosophizing subject, philosophical method, and the conceptual prejudices of philosophy. Study of what amounts to mind becomes inseparable from ontology, epistemology, and other areas. Second, the tendency is to view mind as inherently embodied or embedded in existential, social, linguistic, perceptual, and other contexts. Consequently, the Continental tradition is not inclined to produce monographs on mind or treat it in isolation, and instead approaches mind within broader studies of being and so on. Third, typical questions of philosophy of mind have originated with a Cartesian or cognitivist problem of how a consciousness that is interior, ineffable, yet transparent to itself, relates to the natural world and other consciousnesses. The Continental tendency is to view this as a false problem. If consciousness is world-embedded, then consciousness is actively involved and manifest in a publicly accessible external world, and is opaque to itself in virtue of its situation. This changes or tempers the problem of other minds and internalist problems about qualia (for example). In general, 'lateral' difficulties about relations between consciousness and the world, or mind and matter, are transposed into 'vertical' difficulties about strata of a mind-world complex (for example, relations between preconceptual awareness and conceptual cognition). This radically reconfigures signature projects of the philosophy of mind.

Since roughly the 1970s, however, philosophers – Continental and analytic – and scientists have been showing how results of Continental philosophy contribute to philosophy of mind and cognitive science. Continental philosophy of mind (CPM) really arises in this 'analytic-scientific-Continental intersection,' which is burgeoning by the minute. This chapter provides a framework for understanding results basic to this intersection, whilst highlighting differences between Continental and analytic-scientific approaches. Brief remarks about Kant and German Idealism help introduce CPM as developing through two major streams of twentieth-century Continental philosophy: phenomenology and existentialism, and philosophies of difference; for reasons mentioned below, the former stream is the focus. More recent work is situated in these streams, and noted in a section about recent developments.

Beginnings in Kant, German Idealism, and Anti-Idealism

Kant's (1724–1804) *Critique of Pure Reason* (1781, 1787) turns the modern *ontological* problem of what mind is and how it connects to the world into a deontological problem about conceptual norms of judgement (cognitive structure) and how we make the world. (Brandom 2002).[1] But Kant's transcendental dialectic proves that the deontological problem is insoluble: reason cannot know all things. This renews skepticism, but (since Kant dismantles modern skepticism as dogmatically prejudiced in first supposing a subject-independent world to be skeptical about) it is a new skepticism: the issue is not whether we can get in touch with the world, but whether subjective, cognitive structures can enable scientific knowledge.

One response to the new skepticism is developed by the neo-Kantian inspired empirical psychology of Ernst Mach (1838–1916) and Hermann Helmholtz (1821–94): naturalize subjective cognitive structure, integrate it into natural science. Another is developed by German Idealism: repair Kant's system by improving its weak point – the deduction of the categories, of cognitive structure. F. W. J. Schelling (1775–1854) does this by studying the transcendental conditions of knowledge in his *System of Transcendental Idealism* (1800), which notably implies that cognitive structure requires an unconscious, and self-organizing bodily activity. In contrast, G. W. F. Hegel (1770–1831) studies the experience of knowing in his *Phenomenology of Spirit* (or, *Mind* [1807]), which remarkably shows that knowing could not be based in faculties 'in the head/subject' (faculties such as sensation, perception or understanding), but must be based in a desiring self's relation to its world. Hegel shows that a rational mind is not merely a natural, brainy thing, it is an inherently social thing, since knowledge depends on ethical, cultural, and moral struggles over rational standards. (Hegel's position influences pragmatism, and more recent work on mind by 'Pittsburgh Hegelians'; see John McDowell [1996] and Robert Brandom [2002].) Kant shows that we make the world, Hegel shows that the *we* is social, and that Kantianism is prejudiced in reducing cognitive structure to faculties 'in the head/subject.' For Friedrich Nietzsche (1844–1900, discussed again below) these results are prejudiced by taking subjectivity as basic; instead, cognitive structure and subjectivity are side-effects of social powers that have nothing like subjectivity or cognition in mind.

These results decisively influence CPM's view that cognitive structure is not (merely) a faculty 'in the head/subject,' but is a kind of norm generated in action/existence responsive to that of which it is a norm. The task is to study cognitive structure as actively/existentially world-embedded, which usually means socially embedded. Phenomenology and existentialism develop this view by showing how cognitive activity or human existence is *endogenously* generative of such structure/norms. Philosophies of difference follow a Nietzschean line in contesting structure/norms and urging the rather different view that they are effects *exogenously* generated in us by material, temporal, or power differences. But for both streams, the naturalizing strategy (inaugurated by empirical psychology) is burdened with an unexamined prejudice, namely phenomenal dualism – the presumption that the phenomenon of mind as we subjectively experience it is nothing like any objective natural phenomenon. On the contrary, if mind is actively responsive in our world, phenomena of mind are as objective as nature. The task is making study of such phenomena rigorous (phenomenology), or 'denormalizing' ourselves so as to detect without prejudice where such phenomena come from in the first place (philosophies of difference).

Phenomenology and Existentialism

Edmund Husserl (1859–1938) founds phenomenology as part of his early efforts to secure foundations for logic and mathematics. His antagonist is psychologism, which naturalizes logic by turning it into a product of psychological faculties. Husserl thinks this outrageous. Are facts of psychology cause for Modus Ponens (MP) counting as a logical rule? Functionalism may try to save psychologism by distinguishing between logical functions and instantiating faculties (faculties do not cause MP's counting as logical, rather faculties count as logical if they instantiate MP). But Husserl permanently challenges functionalism: how do we first of all discern which logical functions are good? And how do we do this without already counting on logical functions?

Husserl's answer lies in his famous reduction. The (transcendental) reduction is an attitude that suspends (in the *epoché*) all assumptions as to what actually exists, and conceptual prejudices about what anything is. It goes back to the phenomenal sphere, letting experience drive formulation of conceptual frameworks. If logic, philosophy, and so on, can be reconstructed within this attitude, we can be sure their foundations are self-evident. But this radical attitude forces us to discard our usual (prejudiced) claims about what subject, object, and so on – even thinking – are. All of these terms need to be reconstituted on transcendental foundations – foundations that cannot be dispensed with as mere prejudice because they are immanent in the flow of experience itself.

At this point Husserl makes discoveries of fundamental interest to CPM. The greatest discovery is intentionality. Examination of cognitive activity in the phenomenal sphere reveals that all consciousness is consciousness *of* something. Whatever presents itself as an act of thinking (noesis) is geared toward an object of thinking (noema); cognitive acts gear into one another about the object to be cognized. For example, in imagining a triangle, we do not first imagine a line segment, repeat thrice, discover relations, and then synthesize this complex as 'triangle.' We imagine segments terminating in triangular vertices, segments already geared toward being parts of a triangle. The significance of intentionality is best brought out by contrast. For Kant, the minimal cognitive acts are judgements, subjective acts structured by the demand that they produce a transcendental object $= X$. Husserl argues that the minimal cognitive act is a noetic-noematic act that cuts across subject and object. Moreover, an object to be cognized (for example, the imagined triangle) is an immanent organizer of cognitive structure. Intentionality rules out the Cartesian concept of mind as a self-contained substance, and the Kantian/modern – and cognitivist – view of objects as final products of already determined structures inside the subject (to link with current themes, cognition has an important feed-forward aspect).

Intentionality's significance is amplified by its link with another great Husserlian discovery, horizons. A triangle's side is imagined as interrelated to other sides of the triangle and to other geometrical entities. If the side did not refer beyond itself in this way, we would lose sense of it as a side. The term 'horizon' designates the circle of objects beyond an object, nevertheless referred to as inherent in that object's sense. Objects on horizons draw our attention and we can focus on them; but each horizonal object has its own further horizons, and so on ad infinitum. Earthly horizons contextualize all our views, but can never themselves be brought into full view; so too with Husserlian horizons.[2]

Cognizing an object, then, is not a matter of producing a final cognitive result (a representation, say), it is an ongoing intentional-horizonal activity in which invariant structures become manifest in a horizonally determined flux of noetic-noematic acts. The sense of objectivity accrues within the invariance of such structures. Crucially, objects are given through a cognitive structure that is pervasively dynamic, open ended and incomplete. Indeed, the phenomenal sphere is transcended from within by dynamic open-endedness. So consciousness can neither fully survey its own cognitive structure nor fully stipulate that structure's formal or material determinations. Husserl thus inaugurates CPM's criticism of the prejudice of presence, the prejudice that cognitive and objective structures are fully given.[3] Instead, these structures manifest themselves only in unfolding tendencies of an experience that we ourselves cannot generate (except perhaps in math or logic). Consequently, Husserl comes to emphasize heavily the temporality of cognition (retentive and protentive ['feed-forward'] aspects of synthesis), and to speak of cognitive structures that are determinately indeterminate (and vice versa).

Analytically based philosophers often confuse phenomenology with introspection, or profess they can see no difference between them. But the stress of phenomenology falls not on an act of 'introspecting' but on forging concepts adequate to experience. For example, our scientific and everyday attitudes lead us to conceive the 'edges' of the visual field on the model of edges of objects seen *in* the visual field. Experience shows this is what Ryle called a category error – field 'edges' demand a new sort of concept. (In fact, so do object edges.) Like horizons, these new concepts scuttle clean cut distinctions between determinacy and indeterminacy, presence and absence, thus contesting foundational commitments of classical science and philosophy. (Indeed, 'introspection' qua supposing a clean cut inside could not be a basis of phenomenological method; it is rather a problematic experience to be described – in harmony with the psychological result that children learn to introspect.)

Briefly, Husserl's importance for CPM is in exposing conceptual prejudices and false problems. If Kant and German Idealism turn an ontological problem of mind and world into a deontological problem of world-constituting cognitive structure, Husserl shows cognitive structure to be inseparable from the temporality of experience and irreducible to something present. For Husserl phenomenological method therefore ends up being a study of the experiential genesis of cognitive structure (in passive syntheses – another great discovery). This Husserlian position fruitfully intersects with recent philosophy of mind and cognitive science, in ways that deepen our point.

For example, Husserl's position implies that cognitivist or computational approaches, which turn cognitive structure into fully present, determinate formal systems, are off-track. Suppose we program a computer to simulate such a system and its 'sensory' inputs. The program can be suspended to be resumed at a later time. When suspended, the 'program's world' goes away, but the program stays the same. But our cognitive structure and world have inherently temporal (and reciprocal) constitutions; you cannot suspend either without changing both (even in the *epochē* something is going on). This (admittedly crude) thought experiment shows we are related to the world in a manner very different from an entity with formal processing faculties. Our consciousness is *in* the world in the sense of having a temporality open to the temporality of the world we know – a point very much deepened by Heidegger.

On the other hand, Husserl anticipates or lends support to enactivist, dynamic, or simulationist views of consciousness, or Dennett's claim that consciousness does not happen in some one spatio-temporal point. In fact, Husserl's study of temporality has inspired recent discussions in neuroscience. Especially important is the work of biologist Francisco J. Varela (1946–2001), whose research in neurobiology and study of Husserlian phenomenology led him (and his followers) to inaugurate 'neurophenomenology'; one of its results is the discovery of neurological correlates of Husserlian retentive and protentive structures. For neurophenomenology, Husserlian temporality fruitfully guides reconception of the brain as not being anything like a (suspendable) computer shifting from one finite (all present) state to another, but rather as a temporally protracted entity shaped by feed-forward and feed-backward processes. Varela's approach has opened new controversies in neurology, especially in Europe where working scientists are more likely to be responsive to philosophical issues. But it is also part of a larger debate about whether phenomenology can be naturalized, integrated into the framework of natural science.

Husserlian phenomenology likely cannot be naturalized. First (by way of analogy): the Husserlian results canvassed so far are transcendental, conceptual claims. Husserlian intentionality (consciousness's constitutive openness to the world) is basic to what consciousness is in the way that Einsteinian simultaneity (which takes time to measure) is basic to what space-time is. Seeking naturalized explanations of either result does not make sense. Doing so mistakes the type of result, confuses transcendental philosophy with phenomenological psychology (see Zahavi 2004), or measurement theory with measuring. Explaining how natural systems realize intentionality or simultaneity does make sense – as a subsequent step. But for Einstein, admitting simultaneity into nature means radically transforming concepts of nature. Similarly with Husserlian intentionality. If intentionality really is natural (not merely epiphenomenal), then likely we have radically to reconceive nature (see Thompson 2004, and below). Naturalizing phenomenology (as usually meant) is like forcing Einsteinian thought experiments about clocks and simultaneity into old Newtonian nature. Instead, naturalizing phenomenology means phenomenologizing nature, in the way that naturalizing relativity means relativizing nature.[4]

Moreover, Husserl's initial suspension of the existence of the external world leaves him with the problem of reconstituting everyday and scientific senses of objectivity. Husserl's solution in his later works turn him to the 'life-world,' that is, to the idea that the phenomenal sphere is not constituted by processes purely immanent to consciousness, but through an intersubjective social-historical world in which we are already embodied. Study of such a life-world is not naturalizable. Logical, mathematical, and scientific norms cannot ultimately be naturalized, for they are idealizations emerging from the life-world. Husserl thus inverts science's claim to priority in explaining human life. And, by highlighting the role of intersubjectivity in human experience – a crucial theme of phenomenology and existentialism – he criticizes the cognitivist prejudice that mind is solely a matter of cognitive structure 'in the head/subject.'

These results are decisively deepened by Martin Heidegger (1889–1976), especially in *Being and Time* (1927). In terms of mind, Heidegger's basic and radical point is that the minimal act of cognition is neither a judgement, nor a noetic-noematic act, nor any cognitive act imagined by classical Western philosophy or science. The basic act of cognition is not a cognitive act at all, it is an 'act' of being. This act of being is what Heidegger calls the being of *Dasein*. Correspondingly, the basic structure of cognition is nothing like a roster of basic judgements (Kantian categories) or even a structure emerging within cognitive process (early Husserl). The basic structure of cognition is the existential structure of *Dasein*. Basically, traditional philosophy conceives being as an object of thinking; Heidegger overturns this cognitivist prejudice and conceives thinking as a kind of being. Explicating this existential reversal in its significance for CPM will take several steps.

Dasein is the term Heidegger appropriates/coins to designate the sort of being that we have. His coinage aims to avoid traditional prejudices, for example, conceiving us as rational animals, in which case the problem of mind is figuring out how part of an animal is an organ of reason. In fact, *Dasein* is nothing like an individual human organism or subject, it is more like the being of Husserl's life-world. Here is one way to formulate it: The being of *Dasein* is the whole world of significances and purposes as an interrelated totality sustained through interpretative activity (both conceptual, pre-conceptual and bodily) together with the equipment, natural objects, and language that make such a totality possible; and this world is intersubjective.

In terms of CPM, this formula has consequences noted in a justly famous passage from *Being and Time* (cf Olafson 1987):

> When Dasein directs itself towards something and grasps it, it does not somehow first get out of an inner sphere in which it has been proximally encapsulated, but its primary kind of Being is such that it is always 'outside' alongside entities which it encounters and which belong to a world already discovered . . . [T]he perceiving of what is known is not a process of returning with one's booty to the 'cabinet' of consciousness after one has gone out and grasped it. (Heidegger 1962: 89)

This attacks the deepest presumptions of Cartesianism, cognitivism, and most traditional philosophy of mind. Thinking and perception are not a matter of dragging offshoots of the outer (say, sensory stimuli) into a special inner 'cabinet' and adding a magic dash of consciousness. We have seen versions of this above, but Heidegger's attack is novel, for it targets an ontological prejudice. For Heidegger, German Idealism and (early) Husserl merely expand subjectivity, whereas Heidegger claims that perceiving and thinking take something ontologically different to being a subject.

To appreciate this, let us observe (with ecological psychology, and so on) that an animal not already attuned to features of its environment would never pay them any mind. A primate hand that did not already reach out for branches as affording purchase would never feel roughness or slipperiness, since perception of such tactile properties depends on specific lateral movement patterns solicited in reaching for purchases (which lateral movements are thus vital to distal reaching, because slippery purchases aren't). Perception does not start with sensory surfaces and culminate in an inner 'cabinet'; the deployment and evolution of sensory surfaces as capable of perception already depends on the animal's whole bodily life being pre-perceptually geared toward vital environmental features.

In this sense the animal is 'always "outside" along entities' that its species (through evolution) has 'discovered' as vital. The animal, we could say, is 'living-in-the-environment.' The hyphenation emphasizes the linkage of these terms in an indivisible complex: the animal's living is inseparable from its environment; what is environment is inseparable from the animal's living (there are no branches-to-grasp in a cow's environment); the animal's way of living in its environment links these terms. The minimal act of animal perceptual cognition is not a cognitive act at all, since perception already depends on and is really and analytically inseparable from the animal's most basic act of being, 'living-in-the-environment.'

But the animal's 'living-in-the-environment' must not be confused with *Dasein*'s being-in-the-world, Heidegger's name for the basic existential structure of *Dasein*. *Dasein* is in a world, not merely an environment. To understand this distinction let us contrast entities in *Dasein*'s world with those in the animal's environment. Consider a stick lying on the ground. We can grasp it as part of a broken tree, as a drumstick, as fuel for fire or philosophical discussion. How we grasp it depends on the purpose we assign it, which meshes with a whole network of entities and purposes (for example, drums and signalling). The purposes we assign coalesce around our being (are we being botanists, musicians or philosophers?) as pursuing one of the purposes open to us. In other words, we take the stick as this or that, interpret it, against an available (yet revisable) background of interrelated things and purposes opened by our sort of being – which includes the being of others referred to by purposes and things (for example, the recipient of the drum signal). The latter means that *Dasein* is always an intersubjective being-with-others, what Heidegger calls *Mitdasein*. The animal too has a background network, but its 'living-in-its-environment' is fixed by its being a member of its species.[5] *Dasein*'s being-in-the-world, in contrast, is a matter of being *Dasein* this or that way in a world thrown open by *Dasein* as *Mitdasein*. (What has just been said explicates our formula for *Dasein*.)

The three terms of *Dasein*'s being-in-the-world (being, world, being-in) are mutually implicated in analogy with the three terms of the animal's 'living-in-the-environment.' And because of this mutual implication, *Dasein* is 'always "outside" along entities,' in analogy with the animal being 'outside' in its environment. We made sense of the latter by realizing that animal perception depends on animal life as pre-perceptually geared toward vital features. In analogy, Heidegger's attack on the cabinet of consciousness amounts to the crucial point that our grasp of the world depends on

Dasein's being pre-perceptually and precognitively oriented toward a meaningful world. But the world is the whole intersubjective network of things, doings, and purposes opened by the being of *Dasein* in general. And so all of that is crucial to perception and cognition. The minimal unit of cognition is not purely cognitive, since cognition is ontologically dependent upon and inseparable from the precognitive act of intersubjective being that first of all orients us to a world to be cognized.

To amplify this existential reversal, consider Heidegger's famous ontological distinction between *Zuhandenheit* (readiness-to-hand, or handiness) and *Vorhandenheit* (presence-at-hand, or objectivity). When taking the stick as handy for this or that, what is at issue is its *Zuhandenheit*. When giving an account of what the stick is in and of itself, as might the natural scientist, what is at issue is its *Vorhandenheit*. The definitive ontological prejudice of classical philosophy and science is the elimination of *Zuhandenheit*, or its reduction to *Vorhandenheit*.[6] On the contrary, Heidegger insists that *Zuhandenheit* is ontologically basic. Scientific knowing is very different from stick-grasping, but both are modalities of our preconceptually orientated being.

The Heideggerian primacy of the *zuhanden* makes a lot of sense. Our scientific and philosophical traditions have usually insisted on two conflicting positions: mind evolves in the world (MEW); the mind reconstructs/represents the world as the scientist comes to understand it (the world as *Vorhandenheit*) (MRV). But science, for example, shows that frogs will tongue-target whatever moves laterally in their visual fields. That is, frogs have not evolved to see objective flies; for frogs, the lateral is the edible; this confuses objective categories, but is an excellent bet for dinner if you eat flies and live in a swamp. Evolution does not conduce objectivity, just whatever it takes to live. In other words, science itself shows if MEW is right, MRV is misguided about animals – even if MRV persists in guiding animal science. MRV is more plausible when applied to our minds – after all, we have evolved into scientists who can know the objective. But Heidegger (in showing *Zuhandenheit* is basic) insists MRV is ontologically misguided about us – even if it persists in guiding philosophy of mind.

Today, though, even roboticists (Rodney Brooks, for example) are beginning to give up on MRV, as are artificial intelligence (AI) researchers. Indeed, older AI paradigms are being abandoned for neural networks and so on partly because the latter do not fall to the Heideggerian criticism – as articulated by Hubert Dreyfus. Dreyfus is an important initiator of CPM-type approaches; his work (Dreyfus 1991, 1992) and that of his school (see Wrathall and Malpas 2000) approach our Heideggerian point through extensive discussion of the role of precognitive coping skills, in ways that speak to working cognitive scientists.

Heidegger's existentialist shift delineates a keystone configuration of CPM's anti-cognitivism. Kant turns ontological problems into deontological problems; with Husserl these become temporal constitutional problems. Heidegger turns us back to an ontological problem, but it is a new problem. The problem of modern philosophy is relations between two different substantial beings (mind and matter). The new problem is relations between different ontological regions of (one) being – relations between *Zuhandenheit* and *Vorhandenheit* in the *Sein* of *Dasein* as *Mitdasein*.

What comes to be the central issue for CPM is this dependency of cognitive experience on a precognitive stratum of being, a stratum with ontological primacy.

Against the ancient view that mind is at one with a divinely driven cosmos, modern philosophy's great discovery is that the very drive of cognitive experience is to claim autonomy from such a primary stratum: modern mind has a kind of self-centeredness; and after Darwin, animality is self-centered too. Without this modern discovery there would be no philosophy of mind or evolutionary theory. CPM's great discovery about mind (and animals) is that this modern self-centeredness is prejudiced and only partially right. What is primary for phenomenology/existentialism is in fact a kind of being (Heidegger), or the life-world and passive syntheses (Husserl), or pre-personal perception as bodily (Merleau-Ponty) – all of which are intersubjective. For philosophies of difference an 'anti-subjective' creative temporality (Bergson), will to power (Nietzsche), or generative matter (Deleuze) is primary. Such discoveries generally resonate with scientific programs, such as ecological psychology, autopoieisis, and dynamic systems theory, that also discover that the self is only partly centered in itself.

Merleau-Ponty (1908–61) deepens this discovery, and because he constantly engages with psychology and biology, brings it into proximity with problems of mind and body. His *Structure of Behaviour* (1942) examines relations between consciousness and nature by studying behavior, because behavior is indissolubly psychical and physical. The crucial result is that soul/mind and body are relative terms. What counts as bodily vs. psychical is inseparable from an organism's behavioral circumstance. A doctor who treats humans by applying a universal disease theory (equally applicable to coral, humans and Jovian gas-bags) is a quack; the method is prejudiced by a phenomenal dualism that fails to grasp that empirically and conceptually diseases are diseases of specific organisms. But Cartesian or computational theories, which would conceive mind (and body) as substances or functions that are universally the same everywhere, are similarly prejudiced by phenomenal dualism, and are empirical and conceptual failures. We need a sort of radical empiricism that does not conceive mind as a universalizable, abstract phenomenon, but rather begins with and describes human mind as a phenomenon embedded in human bodily situations – contra the Cartesian prejudice of thinking our minds are near divine calculators. This also means describing the *body* in terms of mind, contra the Cartesian prejudice that the body is a mere-meat-machine void of mentality, except for a special part (the brain). Merleau-Ponty's criticism of these prejudices is central to a recent primer, *Philosophy of Mind* (Burwood et al. 1999), and is decisive in turning CPM to the mindful body and embodied mind (see Varela et al. 1993).

To develop his radical empiricism, Merleau-Ponty, in the *Phenomenology of Perception* (1945) appropriates and transforms Husserlian phenomenology. Phenomenological study of perception lets Merleau-Ponty identify and richly describe bodily experience as the primary, precognitive stratum of conceptual and perceptual cognition. This stratum – the 'lived body' – cannot be conceived in objectivist, universalist, or subjectivist frameworks, and indeed challenges classical categorial distinctions. Four examples, describing perception in terms of the lived body, will help us here:

1. Modern philosophy, and classical AI and robotics, construe perception as a three-phase activity: gather sensory input, synthesize a perceptual result, act in the perceived environment. Merleau-Ponty argues these phases are inseparable

(which also means that atomic sense data are ill-conceived abstractions). This result anticipates recent emphasis on agency, dynamic self-organization and ecological and prospective relations as crucial to perception. It also blurs subject-object and mind-world distinctions.

2. Objectivist and universalist frameworks must conceive reaching to grasp an object and pointing to the object's location as two different modalities of relating to an objective thing in one and the same objective space. But Merleau-Ponty's analysis of pathological and normal cases argues that reaching and grasping embody relations to two distinct sorts of objects and spaces (pragmatic and abstract). Sean Kelly (2002) shows that recent studies of blind sight bear out Merleau-Ponty's conceptual claim.

3. A perennial problem in classical frameworks is whether color is a subjective qualia or an objective property. Consider a piece of paper in shadow. Is its colour white (as we might subjectively see it) or gray (as the photometer objectively reports it)? Merleau-Ponty argues it is neither. In a masterful article Sean Kelly (2005) writes that what we see 'in a direct bodily manner, [is] *how the light would have to change* for me to see [the paper's] color better' (Kelly 2005: 85). We see a perceptual tension in the scene, and thus see how we would have to move the paper into better light to have it look white; we thereby see grayed white paper. The paper's 'real color' (white) does not directly appear, rather it is inherently apparent in a perceptual tension that is background to the scene. According to Kelly this means that color perception is 'essentially normative' (Kelly 2005: 82). But we would have to note that this is a new sort of norm, for color norms are determinately indeterminate, shifting in ways limited, but never finally resolved, by the tension of the thing, lit environment, and perceiver, as implying a criterion for better or worse seeing.

    Moreover, one cannot abstract these colour norms from lived bodies and their situation – a point amplified by Evan Thompson (1995), who shows that colour emerges through an organism's ecological relation to its environment. Flying bird-bodies, for example, can see navigationally significant differences in sky-colour, colour phenomena different in kind to the thingly surface colours to which grasping human-bodies are tuned.

4. Other analyses show how perception (and cognition) couple with emotional and intersubjective dimensions of the lived body. Emotion is not a hindrance to thinking and perceiving, it is what first grants an orientation to the world – a Heideggerian point deepened by Merleau-Ponty. Similarly, personal habits and a 'pre-personal' tradition (evolutionary bodily legacies, and cultural legacies sedimented in styles of doing, language and technology), are crucial backgrounds of perceiving and thinking – as are ethical orientations (see Gallagher and Marcel 1999). Drawing on Merleau-Ponty and Husserl, phenomenologists have inten-sively studied the lived body as inherently intersubjective and developmental (see Gallagher and Meltzoff 1996; Russon 2003); some link their results with discussion of a recent scientific discovery, 'mirror neurons' (see Thompson and Varela 2001). Ultimately, phenomenology's treatment of intersubjectivity re-configures the problem of other minds, and emphasizes how cognition emerges

not (merely) from brains/faculties 'in the head,' but from the social, a point that Merleau-Ponty develops through study of language and bodily expression.

If anything, Merleau-Ponteian phenomenology is more radically empirical than evolutionary science, simply because it admits concepts driven by what evolution itself has done, concepts refused by science. For science, empiricism means fitting what there is into already fixed scientifically-objective frameworks – shifting paradigms when absolutely required. For phenomenology, empiricism means beginning by first fitting paradigms to what presents itself. But, as Donald Borrett et al. (2000) point out, '[W]e must not confuse the phenomenological fact that the right description of our relation to the world' denies our usual scientific claims, with the fact that this relation 'is physically realized within the brain.' We are back at the question of naturalizing phenomenology. On this head, Merleau-Ponty's claim is not that the brain has no part, but that the minimal unit of naturalization is being-a-brainy-body-in-a-human-intersubjective-world – and that is going to radicalize your concept of the brain. On the other hand, brain science is provocative for phenomenological empiricism.

At this point a grander conceptual issue arises. In his posthumous *The Visible and the Invisible* (1964), Merleau-Ponty avowedly disavows his earlier phenomenology as repeating the classical prejudice of the subject-object division. Correcting this problem, it appears, requires a drastic ontological shift. The real unit of naturalization, the minimal act of cognition, is not this or that being's act of being. The minimal act of cognition is nature's act of being. Needless to say, this requires a concept of nature undreamed of in Western philosophy. Merleau-Ponty's suggestion is a sort of post-Cartesian pre-Socratism in which being isn't one (Parmenides) or becoming (Heraclitus), but 'flesh.' A possible explication (and betrayal) of 'flesh': nature is not space-time-matter/energy unfolding according to laws, nature is moving being organizing.[7] Merleau-Ponty is phenomenologizing nature. This position is today taken by Renaud Barbaras (1999, 2003), Maxine Sheets-Johnstone (1990, 1999) and Evan Thompson (2004), who respectively urge that integrating consciousness with nature means conceiving living desire, animate form or life as basic to nature, a position antagonistic to classical science's concepts (Zahavi 2004).

Philosophies of Difference

Philosophies of difference begin with suspicions about the normativity implied in traditional philosophical concepts – especially concepts of subjectivity. The consequence is further radicalization of subjectivity and nature. The results are so radical that they have not been easily developed for CPM, hence the focus on phenomenology and existentialism. This situation is perhaps changing with recent work on Deleuze.

Henri Bergson's (1859–1941) work, especially *Matter and Memory* (1896) is an important resource for CPM. First, it gives a conceptually innovative account of the brain, not as an organ of representation, but as a center of action, together with an account of the body, habits, and perceptual recognition. Second, his spectacularly novel solution to Cartesian dualism entails an appeal to temporality (*durée*) as creative of novel differences; cognition arises in the rhythmic coupling between mental *durée* and material movement. *Creative Evolution* (1907) is a necessary complement, arguing that the body as site of this coupling evolves in a temporally creative process – which means that nature is drastically reconceived. Bergson's ideas anticipate those of chaos and dynamic systems theory, and other programs that conceive temporal organization and rhythm as basic to cognition. Bergson also informs Deleuze's concept of difference.[8]

Friedrich Nietzsche's core claim, as relevant to CPM, is that the ingredients of cognition (the having of ideas, or of objectivist concepts and practices that let us predict the future and analyze the past) are side effects of human practices, for example, of enforcing promise making and keeping. The cognizing subject is not a basic given, but a side-effect of operations launched against human bodies. Correlatively, for Nietzsche, the body is not a support vehicle for mind, but a site of willful being with its own precognitive imperatives – a significant addition to CPM's focus on the body. Nietzsche seeks to liberate the pre-subjective body from the impress of subjectivity. Conceptually, this requires dismantling purposes that would regulate the body, which ultimately entails reconception of nature as eternal recurrence that generates differences without reason.

Gilles Deleuze (1925–95) combines concepts from Bergson, Nietzsche, and others, including mathematicians and scientists. His philosophy is a transcendental empiricism that links structure and sense not to abstract transcendental foundations, but to what is most empirical: materiality. Deleuze's key concept is the virtual (drawn from Bergson): structure/sense do not arise from an already actual law or pre-programmed possibilities imposing themselves on matter (from we know not where), rather materiality itself has a virtue (a *virtus* or power) generative of new senses. As Manuel Delanda argues in *Intensive Science and Virtual Philosophy* (2002), contemporary science encounters the virtual in chaotic systems that have the power to transition into sharply bifurcated sets of states, without yet having the direction of transition – or even the structure of bifurcation – actually already prescribed in the system. Materiality as virtual generates/expresses radical differences that cannot be assimilated to its previous states, and thus bursts even the sort of determinate indeterminacy discovered by Husserl.

These philosophies of difference all imply that the minimal unit of cognition is an act of nature that precedes the subject. For Bergson, this is creative temporal process; for Nietzsche, a genealogy of willing pre-subjective bodies; for Deleuze, the virtual actualizing/expressing differences. What these philosophies contribute to CPM is a different way of naturalizing mind: naturalizing mind by differentiating nature.

Recent Developments and Further Resources

CPM is growing, with increasingly fruitful conceptual insights. The most important recent development in CPM is the founding of the *Journal for Phenomenology and the Cognitive Sciences* by Shaun Gallagher (USA) and Natalie Depraz (France). This establishes a forum and presence for phenomenological CPM. Gallagher also maintains an important bibliography and list of resources that should be consulted: http://consciousness.arizona.edu/resources/pcs.html (also see the bibliography in Petitot et al. 1999).

A Sartrean philosophy of mind has been developed by Kathleen Wider, Joseph Catalano, and Gregory McCulloch. Other authors of CPM monographs are Dan Zahavi, David Woodruff Smith and Samuel Todes. Phenomenology and Continental philosophy have also impacted recent analytic philosophy of mind, for example, John Haugeland's and Mark Okrent's work on Heidegger; Hilary Putnam's recent work; and the work of Mark Johnson, together with George Lakoff (inspired by Merleau-Ponty and Maxine Sheets-Johnstone).

Notes

1. Brandom is also the source of the theme, developed below, of the 'minimal act of cognition,' On the deontological shift, cf the theme of constitution in Huemer (2004).
2. Cognitive acts also have horizons.
3. On this prejudice, see Russon (2003).
4. See Petitot et al. (1999), Gallagher (1997), and Lutz (2004) for contrary and supporting views. The analogy is not meant to imply that relativity, quantum mechanics, and so on are issues in phenomenologizing nature; the analogy is meant to point out the impact of basic concepts on explanatory frameworks.
5. This is Heidegger's view of animals. Morris (2005) argues that this view needs qualification and is based in a conceptual prejudice.
6. See Brandom (2002).
7. The phrasing (triple gerund, no commas) is deliberately ambiguous as to each word's function (as noun, verb, adverbial); all the options together are what Merleau-Ponty is getting at.
8. Bergson's inspiration of Deleuze motivates positioning him as a difference philosopher. But Bergson's philosophy retrieves subjectivity through *durée*, even if he begins with suspicions about it. So in the end Bergson is not quite a difference philosopher, yet he is not a phenomenologist. He is really just different.

References

Barbaras, R. (1999), *Le désir et la distance: Introduction à une phénoménologie de la perception*, Paris: J. Vrin.

Barbaras, R. (2003), *Vie et intentionalité: Recherches phénoménologiques*, Paris: Vrin.

Borrett, D., S. Kelly, and H. Kwan (2000), 'Phenomenology, Dynamical Neural Networks and Brain Function,' *Philosophical Psychology* 13: 213–28.

Brandom, R. B. (2002), *Tales of the Mighty Dead: Historical Essays in the Metaphysics of Intentionality*, Cambridge: Harvard University Press.

Burwood, S., P. Gilbert, and K. Lennon (1999), *Philosophy of Mind*, Montreal: McGill-Queen's University Press.

Delanda, M. (2002), *Intensive Science and Virtual Philosophy*, London: Continuum.

Dreyfus, H. L. (1991), *Being-in-the-World: A Commentary on Heidegger's Being and Time, Division I*, Cambridge: MIT Press.

Dreyfus, H. L. (1992), *What Computers Still Can't Do: A Critique of Artificial Reason*, Cambridge: MIT Press.

Gallagher, S. (1997), 'Mutual Enlightenment: Recent Phenomenology in Cognitive Science,' *Journal of Consciousness Studies* 4 (3): 195–214.

Gallagher, S., and A. J. Marcel (1999), 'The Self in Contextualized Action', in S. Gallagher and J. Shear (eds) (1999), *Models of the Self*, Thorverton: Imprint Academic, pp. 273–99.

Gallagher, S., and A. Meltzoff (1996), 'The Earliest Sense of Self and Others: Merleau-Ponty and Recent Developmental Studies,' *Philosophical Psychology* 9: 211–33.

Heidegger, M. [1927] (1962), *Being and Time*, New York: Harper and Row.

Huemer, W. (2004), *The Constitution of Consciousness: A Study in Analytic Phenomenology*, London: Routledge.

Kelly, S. D. (2002), 'Merleau-Ponty on the Body,' *Ratio (new series)* 15, 376–91.

Kelly, S. D. (2005), 'Seeing Things in Merleau-Ponty,' in T. Carman and M. B. N. Hansen (eds) (2005), *The Cambridge Companion to Merleau-Ponty*, Cambridge: Cambridge University Press, pp. 74–110.

Lutz, A. (2004), 'Special Issue on Naturalizing Phenomenology', *Phenomenology and the Cognitive Sciences* 3: 325–98.

McDowell, J. (1996), *Mind and World*, Cambridge: Harvard University Press.

Morris, D. (2005), 'Animals and Humans, Thinking and Nature,' *Phenomenology and the Cognitive Sciences* 4: 49–72.

Olafson, F. A. (1987), *Heidegger and the Philosophy of Mind*, New Haven: Yale University Press.

Petitot, J., F. J. Varela, B. Pachoud, and J.-M. Roy (eds) (1999), *Naturalizing Phenomenology: Issues in Contemporary Phenomenology and Cognitive Science*, Stanford: Stanford University Press.

Russon, J. E. (2003), *Human Experience: Philosophy, Neurosis, and the Elements of Everyday Life*, Albany: State University of New York Press.

Sheets-Johnstone, M. (1990), *The Roots of Thinking*, Philadelphia: Temple University Press.

Sheets-Johnstone, M. (1999), *The Primacy of Movement*, Amsterdam: John Benjamins Publishing Company.

Thompson, E. (1995), *Colour Vision: A Study in Cognitive Science and the Philosophy of Perception*, London: Routledge.

Thompson, E. (2004), 'Life and Mind: From Autopoiesis to Neurophenomenology. A Tribute to Francisco Varela,' *Phenomenology and the Cognitive Sciences* 3: 381–98.

Thompson, E., and F. J. Varela (2001), 'Radical Embodiment: Neural Dynamics and Consciousness,' *Trends in Cognitive Sciences* 5 (10): 418–25.

Varela, F. J., E. Thompson, and E. Rosch (1993), *The Embodied Mind: Cognitive Science and Human Experience*, Cambridge: MIT Press.

Wrathall, M., and J. Malpas (eds) (2000), *Heidegger, Coping, and Cognitive Science*, Cambridge: MIT Press.

Zahavi, D. (2004), 'Phenomenology and the Project of Naturalization', *Phenomenology and the Cognitive Sciences* 3: 331–47.

Philosophy of Science

Babette E. Babich

Continental philosophies of science tend to exemplify holistic themes connecting order and contingency, questions and answers, writers and readers, speakers and hearers. Such philosophies of science also tend to feature a fundamental emphasis on the historical and cultural situatedness of discourse as significant; relevance of mutual attunement of speaker and hearer; necessity of pre-linguistic cognition based in human engagement with a common socio-cultural historical world; role of narrative and metaphor as explanatory; sustained emphasis on understanding questioning; truth seen as horizonal, aletheic, or perspectival; and a tolerance for paradoxical and complex forms of expression.

Philosophy of science in the Continental tradition is thus more comprehensive than philosophy of science in the analytic tradition, including (and as analytic philosophy of science does not tend to include) perspectives on the history of science as well as the social and practical dimensions of scientific discovery. Where analytic philosophy is about reducing or, indeed, eliminating the perennial problems of philosophy, Continental philosophy is all about thinking and that will mean, as both Heidegger and Nietzsche emphasize, making such problems more not less problematic. Continental philosophy of science engages not only the world of the scientist (Heelan 1965: 4; see contributions to Babich 2002 as well as Knorr-Cetina 1999) but the scientists themselves: 'I cannot conceive myself,' Merleau-Ponty writes in his *Phenomenology of Perception*, 'as nothing but a bit of the world, a mere object of biological, psychological or sociological investigation' (Merleau-Ponty 1962: viii). For Merleau-Ponty, the scientist-in-the-world is the condition, *sine qua non*, of scientific inquiry. Continuing in this deliberately first-person voice, he writes, 'I cannot shut myself up within the realm of science. All my knowledge of the world, even my scientific knowledge, is gained from my own particular point of view, or from some experience of the world, without which the symbols of science would be meaningless.' (Merleau-Ponty 1962: viii; see too Husserl 1970: 258–261, 295) Like Merleau-Ponty, both Edmund Husserl and Martin Heidegger were deeply responsive to (and Husserl was arguably influential upon [Neumann 1999; Gethmann 1991, 28–77]) then-current developments in natural science. And in the case of Ernst Mach, Pierre Duhem, Gaston Bachelard, Georges Canguilhem, Bernard d'Espagnat, and Patrick A. Heelan, Continental philosophy of science features philosophers trained as scientists just as Edmund Husserl was formally trained as a mathematician and Martin Heidegger was a student of both logic and physics.

Like other areas of Continental philosophy, Continental philosophy of science is not limited to a geographic locality (Prado 2003). But if mainstream philosophy of science is pursued in an analytic tradition that prizes universality and univocity, Continental approaches to the philosophy of science celebrate a plurality of traditions, including post-colonial perspectives, in terms of differing cultures and contexts in the collision between the interests of global capitalism and industrial development understood in terms of scientific management and its technologies and the living earth. Although the original authors of the Frankfurt School addressed the full range of these questions, this techno-scientific focus is less evident in recent critical theory (Honneth 2005; Babich and Cohen 1999a; but see Bohman 1991, as well as Nandy 1988, and Davison 2002.)

It is important to note that although it remains chary of Continental philosophy of science, analytic philosophy of science is changing to accommodate history of science (Anapolitanos 1998: 196–231; Golinski 1998). If Steven Shapin's and Simon Schaffer's *Leviathan and the Air Pump* (1985) illustrates this changing history (an illustration even more radically on offer in Lawrence Principe's *The Aspiring Adept* [1998]), such studies arguably have their high point in A. C. Crombie, *Styles of Scientific Thinking in the European Tradition* (1995), continuing a shift that had begun with Herbert Butterfield's *The Whig Interpretation of History* (1968), and with Pierre Duhem's study of the medieval origins of modern cosmology (1913) – just as historiographical approaches to the physical sciences date back to the nineteenth century (Gregory 1992). Articulations of the history of science vary across cultural-linguistic divides (cf. Crombie 1995; Serres 1995; Böhme 1989). Moreover, as analytic philosophy of science traces its own history (Giere and Richardson 1996), the common origin of both analytic and continental philosophies is plain (Friedmann 2000).

Social studies of science have also been influential. Ludwik Fleck's *The Genesis and Development of a Scientific Fact* (1979) emphasizes the role of superstition and error (as Ernst Mach spoke of error in his *Knowledge and Error* [1976]), as essential to the course of scientific discovery. For Fleck, apart from the error-driven and intrinsically *social* progress of research thought-collectives and thought-styles, the very scientific conceptualization and aetiology of a particular disease entity, namely, the spirochaete in the case of syphilis, could not have come to stand as it historically did (Fleck 1979; Babich 2003a). Thomas Kuhn's *Structure of Scientific Revolutions* is routinely cited as occasioning changes favorable to Continental philosophy of science. But Kuhn's work was dependent upon Continental thought and, as Kuhn himself attests, drew upon the conceptual resources of Fleck's study of the social and historical constitution of scientific facts (Kuhn in Fleck 1979: vi-xi). Following Kuhn, history of science and social studies of science became genuine and imperative concerns, and a review of the role of gender in scientific knowledge calls for further development (Rose 1994; Code 1991; Irigaray 2005).

In the Continental tradition, we may distinguish *critical* (Nietzschean), *phenomenological* (Husserlian), and *hermeneutic phenomenological* (Heideggerian) philosophies of science. Further possibilities with respect to future Continental philosophies of science may be elaborated on the basis of new impulses in the philosophy of nature as well as environmental philosophy in the spirit of the characteristic holism of continental philosophy (Serres 1995) and of newer appropriations of Gilbert Simondon's philosophy of technology (Stiegler 1998). In addition to Michel Foucault whose work has also been signally influential in analytic philosophy of science (notably in the work of Ian Hacking), other influences in analytic philosophy of science may be expected to grow out of other Continental trends in French thought.

Scientism

Contrary to well-disseminated claims that science suffers from a lack of esteem in today's world, Tom Sorrell, at the conclusion of his study of scientism in analytic philosophy, warns that the problem is not to create respect for science but to dissuade people from worshipping it (Sorrell 1991: 177). A consequence of scientism is that any critique of science can be dismissed as anti-science and such a response tends to be a recurrent anxiety for would-be Continental philosophy of science – to the extent that one collection, *Continental Philosophy of Science*, promotes itself as refuting the view that twentieth-century Continental thought is anti-scientific (Gutting 2005).

Nevertheless, scientism is entrenched within Western culture as a whole, as Tzvetan Todorov has analysed it, starting:

> from the hypothesis that the real world is an entirely coherent structure. . . . [and] . . . can be known entirely and without residue by the human mind. The task of acquiring such knowledge is delegated to the requisite praxis, called science. No fragment of the material or spiritual world . . . can ultimately resist the grasp of science. (Todorov 2003: 19–20)

From the scientistic point of view, there will be 'no room for more than one version of scientific truth; errors are many, but the truth is one, and so pluralism becomes irrelevant.' (Todorov 2003: 21) Presupposing the distinction between scientism and science as he does, Todorov is no more anti-science than Husserl (or Heidegger or Nietzsche). Todorov thus echoes Nietzsche's original insight into the parallels between science and religion, and, like Nietzsche, he valorizes the still-unfulfilled promise of the ideal of science: '[W]hereas the general rule in scientific activity is to be as open as possible to criticism, totalitarian societies require blind submission and the silencing of all and any objections – *just as religions do*' (Todorov 2003: 20)

To the degree that Continental philosophy of science is critical of the tendency to attribute a quasi-religious authority to science, it continues the original mandate of the Enlightenment. Inasmuch as it excludes Continental philosophies from its own discourse, consequently inclining to dogmaticism, analytic philosophy of science tends to tend toward scientism. This is hardly an absolute claim. Certain Continental philosophies of science are dogmatically expressed (by Gaston Bachelard for one) and certain analytic philosophies of science are radically open in their articulation (consider Paul Feyerabend's affirmative receptivity) but scientism remains the primary pitfall in our scientific culture.

Critical Philosophy of Science: From Kant to Nietzsche

The exposition of the critical dynamic of questioning is the keystone of Kant's philosophy of science. This is Kant's reflection on the constructive or framing activity that is active questioning. Such questioning supports the possibility of a progressive and secure science of nature. It is the design of the scientific question that ensures its judgement power (*Critique of Pure Reason*: Bxiii). Rather than a science based on observation (inductive regress) which would be no science at all (understanding science in the image of logic and mathematics), Kant is able to resolve the Humean problem of induction in the experimental practice of questioning because the experiment (conceived as a question) both concedes and at the same time exploits the epistemological limits of reason (Bix) and experience (cf. A124–6). Just as mathematics owes its scientific integrity to the axiomatic character of its conceptual groundwork, so physics operates with axioms or defining assumptions on both theoretical and objective levels, that is, in both its fundamental concepts and its experimental processes (B241/A196); A713/B741–A727/B755). Thus analytic philosophy of science and its focus on realism, on probability, and causality in terms of the inductive warrant for claims about the real world (Giere 1996: 341), is to be contrasted with the different orientation of Kantian epistemology which asks for its part – as Continental philosophy of science continues to ask – how is objective scientific knowledge possible?

A recent reading of the role of explanation in Carnap and in Kant emphasizes the importance of both the apodeictic and the hermeneutic in Kant's own understanding of the respective roles of science and philosophy (Boniolo 2003: 297–8). Beyond prototypically analytic readings of Kant's philosophy of science (Buchdahl 1992; Friedman 1992, Pierre Kerszberg's *Critique and Totality* (1997) argues for an interpretation of Kant and science that draws on Heidegger's reading of Kant. Kerszberg's *Kant et la nature* (1999) further articulates the difference between the object of today's natural sciences and the German tradition of *Naturphilosophie* (again, contrast Böhme 1989 and Latour 2004).

Critical philosophies of science pose the question of the possibility of knowledge and truth and thereby reflect upon the possibility and working of scientific inquiry and law. Both Nietzsche and Heidegger shift the focus to the question itself as the constituting constraint of intuition. Thus Nietzsche's philosophy of science radicalizes Kant's critique. An inveterate reader of the natural science of his own day (including Ernst Mach), Nietzsche's critical contributions to a philosophical analysis of science have been the subject of review both by philosophers concerned with science and transcendental philosophy in Kant's sense (most notably Hans Vaihinger) as well as scientists (most notably the chemist Alwin Mittasch) since the start of the twentieth century and this tradition of reflection on Nietzsche and the sciences continues to this day and has recently drawn further readers in this same tradition (see Babich 1994; Babich and Cohen 1999a/1999b, Moore and Brobjer 2004).

Nietzsche would argue, utterly in the spirit of science and its own sense of progressive evolution, that the laws of physics might be regarded as no more than interpretation, a claim offered not only on the basis of the evolving character of scientific thought but in terms of what might now be seen as theoretical underdetermination, in the manner of Quine or, better said, Davidson. Ultimately for Nietzsche, mathematics and logic were humanizations which he did not hesitate to call *fictions*, invented truths imposed for the sake of cognizing a fundamentally nonhuman but exactly real world (compare with Badiou 2003: 165).

Husserl's Phenomenology of Science

Beyond Descartes and bringing his Archimedean spirit down to earth, consciousness, and the body, Husserl proposes a new phenomenological method. By means of the *epoché* or phenomenological reduction, a properly philosophical (and not merely linguistic or scientific) reflection becomes possible for the first time, thereby permitting nothing less than a newly Copernican critique of reason. What we notice in such properly philosophical reflection is an already given engagement of knower and known, which for Husserl circumscribes the *givenness* of things to consciousness. Like Brentano's, Husserl's account of intentionality recovers the scholastic and Aristotelian insight into the ideational essence of mental phenomena: the eidetic heart of consciousness as object to itself. Seeking what is immanent in consciousness itself or as such, the phenomenological *epoché* is the 'necessary operation' or method rendering '*"pure" consciousness accessible to us, and subsequently the whole phenomenological region*' (Husserl 1975: 103). As a remainder, or '*"phenomenological residuum,"*' consciousness is that very 'region of Being which can become the field of phenomenology' (Husserl 1975: 102).

Husserl remained scientifically minded throughout his life, speaking of the phenomenological description of the object (or *noema*) as *noematic analysis*. The phenomenological self-awareness of experience would accordingly be a *noetic analysis* with *noesis* as the corresponding mental activity (see Drummond 1990 and, more generally, Sokolowski 1999). Description, better perhaps, reflective description, then links the method of phenomenology with that of the empirical sciences. Such descriptions correspond to regional ontologies specific to the regionality of intentional concern, be that a physicist's concern with the physical world, a biologist's or an anthropologist's concern with living things or with other human beings or bodily self-presence. Such ontologies include historical and social realms of culture as well as the traditional philosophic concern with the analysis of the human perception or consciousness of space (of Euclidean measure and habitation) and time (past, present, future).

Husserl's most debated (and for some scholars most important contribution [Kockelmans and Kisiel 1970: 33–40, 45–67]) is *The Crisis of European Sciences and Transcendental Phenomenology* (1970). Based on lectures first offered in 1935, Husserl addressed the question of meaning – or meaninglessness – at the heart of any 'rigorous' philosophy, that is, any philosophy worthy of being so named. The extraordinary success of the Enlightenment project of the West in the guise of Galilean science (or what Heidegger called calculative rationality) presupposed, qua rigorous science, the exclusion of 'all valuative positions, all questions of the reason or unreason of their human subject matter and its cultural configurations' (Husserl 1970: 6). This crisis at the heart of scientific reason relegated the normative and evaluative realms of the human dimensions of the life-world to the irrational. The same crisis is manifest in the vulnerability of universal European culture to the fascism, or racism, or consumerism, and so on, characterizing globalization today.

The Galilean distinction between primary and secondary properties privileges the measurable, leading, with Descartes, to the theoretical division of subjective experience (mind) and objective world (body). Only the objective, or measurable, world came to be regarded as the 'real' world whereby the subjective remainder of 'meaning' and 'value,' 'mind' or 'spirit' was reduced, as mere phenomenon, to the domain of the unreal. The scientific worldview excluded 'in principle precisely the questions which human beings, given over in our unhappy times to the most portentous upheavals, find the most burning: questions of the meaning or meaninglessness of the whole of this human existence' (Husserl 1970: 6). For Husserl, as he writes in the 1935 Vienna Lecture, the greatest danger to science is to fail to take up what he calls the 'enigma of all enigmas,' that is, 'the taken-for-grantedness in virtue of which the "world" constantly and prescientifically exists for us, "world" being a title for an infinity of what is taken for granted, what is indispensable for all objective science' (Husserl 1970: 204). The universal natural scientific project presupposes a dualistic vision: 'One causality, simply split into two sectors, encompasses the one world; the sense of rational explanation is everywhere the same, yet in such a way that all explanation of the spirit . . . leads back to the physical' (Husserl 1970: 294). Paradoxically, Husserl argued, the very objectivity of the natural scientific standpoint is grounded in an 'approach that is itself totally lacking in rationality' (Husserl 1970: 295). To the extent that 'the intuitively given surrounding world, this merely subjective realm, is forgotten in scientific investigation, the working subject is himself forgotten; the scientist does not become a subject of investigation' (Husserl 1970: 295). No antipathy to science speaks in this reflection, instead, Husserl's logical claim is that 'no objective science can do justice to the [very] subjectivity which accomplishes science' (Husserl 1970: 295). For Husserl, 'intentional phenomenology has made of the spirit *qua* spirit for the first time a field of systematic experience and has thus brought about a total reorientation of the task of knowledge' (Husserl 1970: 298).

Hermeneutic Phenomenology of Science

Although Martin Heidegger cannot be understood apart from Husserl, the difference between them is likewise key. With Heidegger, we leave the Enlightenment idealization of clarity as the highest expression of philosophic thinking in and through language to meditate or reflect philosophically on the meaning of thought itself and the nature of language as such. For Heidegger, philosophy is no longer a matter of theoretical reflection or scientific analysis but an active questioning. The Heidegger who repeatedly claimed that 'science does not think' (Heidegger 1968; cf. Salanskis 1995 and Babich 2003b) opposes thoughtful and sense-directed reflection (*Besinnung*) to the rational, calculative project of Western technologically articulated and advancing science. The philosophic task of thinking is not that of 'problem solving' as Karl Popper famously defined philosophy but rather, in the attempt to learn thinking (recommended by the later Heidegger in opposition to the technical culture of problem-solving, manufactured knowledge, usable practical wisdom, and so on); 'we must allow ourselves to become involved in questions that seek what no inventions can find' (Heidegger 1968: 8). For Heidegger, in the spirit of Nietzsche's critical philosophy of science, what matters in a philosophical question is 'to keep the question open and that is to say: to make the question problematical' (Heidegger 1968: 159).

Heidegger distinguishes science and philosophy but emphasizes the critical and cognitive priority of philosophy in what is regarded as the philosophy of science. Theoretical competence in science precludes thought on science itself: '[T]he sciences are not in a position at any time to represent themselves to themselves, by means of their theory and to the modes of procedure belonging to theory' (Heidegger 1977: 177; see Husserl 1970: 56–7) Such an observation posits no deficiency in science inasmuch as science is concerned with its object rather than its ground.

For Heidegger the world of modern scientific research technology is the world in which alone the truths of science are articulable: 'Within the complex of machinery that is necessary to physics in order to carry out the smashing of the atom lies the whole of physics' (Heidegger 1977: 127). What is at issue is the *constitution* of the object of scientific investigation, understanding constitution in both the Husserlian phenomenological sense as well as in the mechanically explicit sense of standardized manufacture and institutional technology (compare social studies of science and technology). This delimitation of a specific domain proper to each science is what makes modern science possible in its comprehensiveness and its capacity for novelty. It also means that the most obscure consequences of science, the paradoxes of quantum mechanics, are not matters of mystery as much as they are reflections of the essence of modern science as measurement (Heelan 1989). Whether we are speaking of classical physics or of quantum physics, Heidegger can say that 'nature has in advance to set itself in place for the entrapping securing that science, as theory, accomplishes' (Heidegger 1977: 172–3). This entrapping-securing is measurement or what Heidegger called calculative thinking or machination (Babich 2003b, Glazebrook 2001). But this also means that Heidegger's philosophy of science cannot be conducted apart from concerns that are ordinarily identified with social and political philosophy (Elden 2003).

Hermeneutic Philosophy of Science: Contemporary Expressions

The hermeneutic process at work in science and to which a hermeneutic philosophy of science must attend is a matter of perception and consciousness. Hermeneutics in this sense is not limited to texts alone, rather, the interpretive presuppositions of being- and working-in the life-theoretical world of our scientific understanding are built into the laboratory world of instrumentation and its praxis (as Heidegger and Merleau-Ponty have argued), including conceptual models, narrative schemes and linguistic metaphor. This field is a growing one, as is witnessed by the work of Dimitri Ginev and others. Moreover, the appeal of its legacy beyond the disciplinary borders of philosophy, be it analytic or Continental, can be seen in the work of the late physicist, Martin Eger, who draws on Hans-Georg Gadamer as well as Heidegger, Husserl, and Heelan.

Joseph J. Kockelmans has written extensively on phenomenology and natural science, including existential and hermeneutic phenomenology of science, which Kockelmans approaches from a historical and systematic perspective (Kockelmans 1993). In a philosophically rigorous fashion, Kockelmans (like Glazebrook [2000] from an Aristotelian perspective), defends the ultimately realist perspective of hermeneutic Continental approaches to the philosophy of science and argues these in a manner similar to Merleau-Ponty as propadeutic to the perspectives assumed in analytic philosophy of science. Unlike Heidegger who was clear about the limitations of what he called logistics (which we can plausibly translate as analytic philosophy especially of the scientistic kind), Kockelmans does not see antipathy between the traditions in philosophy but much rather the failure of analytic philosophy to recognize the historical and cognitive offerings of existential and hermeneutic phenomenology in the Continental tradition (Kockelmans 1999). Although Kockelmans's hoped-for recognition may still be some way off, analytic philosophy has recently taken to appropriating the themes and especially the figures of Continental philosophy, not only with respect to Husserl but now Heidegger and Foucault as well as Nietzsche, Deleuze, and Badiou. But just because this turn is conducted on the terms of analytic philosophy, still held to be the only respectable style of doing philosophy, the analytic appropriation of Continental thought has only muddled the stakes without as yet leading to mutual respect and dialogue (Babich 2003b).

Beginning with a Husserlian philosophy of Heisenberg's physics in his *Quantum Mechanics and Objectivity* (1965) and a hermeneutic elaboration of the relevance of Husserl and Merleau-Ponty's phenomenology to spatial perception in the everyday-, the scientific-, and the art-world in *Space-Perception and the Philosophy of Science* (1983), Patrick A. Heelan's approach to the philosophy of science was conditioned by his training in mathematics and science, and his work with scientists such as Erwin Schrödinger, John Wheeler, and Eugene Wigner. Heelan recognizes the important subjective role of 'intentionality' in 'constituting' what is known by using theoretical models to construct/describe empirical data given to observation and measurement, arguing that all inquiry works through what he calls 'cognitive search-engines,' disclosing the perceptual and scientific invariants of group-theoretic transformations of the sensory flux. Heelan's philosophy of science thus integrates a phenomenology of experiment with the theoretical expression of science, holding with Husserl's eidetic project the possibility of approximating the essence of a scientific object through successive profiles. The hermeneutic dimension of such a *horizonal realism* reflects the necessity for considering the historical, social, and disciplinary circumstance of the researcher (Heelan 1998). Theoretical descriptions denominate the experimental profiles that would be perceived under standard laboratory conditions (and thereby the thus-emergent scientific life world) and, following upon a hermeneutic of experimental work, become descriptive of what is eidetically perceived in the laboratory (Heelan 1989). Heelan's perspective thus shares the same focus as analytic readings of experimental science while avoiding the alienation from history (and from the actual and current practice) of science limiting analytic philosophy of science.

Prospects

Whereas the positivists in the person of Auguste Comte (see Allen 2003; Kremer-Marietti 1983; Canguilhelm 1991) and the logical empiricists endorsed the scientistic unity of the sciences, Bachelard maintained the unity of science and poetry, as did Eugene Minkowski (1970) and as we find Badiou arguing today. Indeed, if science is *poiesis*, as *techne*, as Heidegger reminds us, its products or 'phenomeno-technologies' are a kind of poetry. Such a psychoanalytic play of symbols and concepts bears on

Bachelard's poetics of science (Tiles 1984; Babich 1989), eliciting the mythic math-emes of science in the spirit of Paul Veyne's analysis of myth and recurring in newer instaurations in Badiou (2003). As Pierre Duhem retraced the relevance of the poet's voice in his *German Science* (1991) with reference to his Provençal-language encounter with the poet, Frederic Mistral, and as Bernard d'Espagnat has called attention to the significance of Paul Valéry in Bachelard's scientific poetics (d'Espagnat 1990, see also Robinson-Valéry 1983), so Badiou calls upon the poet to speak if only for the sake of setting the French Mallarmé or Celan or even, by way of Ireland, Beckett in place of Heidegger's Hölderlin. As Badiou reads Heidegger's critique of modern technoscience (we recall that Badiou is closer to Irigaray's Lacan rather than to Bernard Stiegler's or even Jacques Ellul's Simondon), he makes the point that, 'if the proposition, commanding the interpretation of the spirit as pragmatic intellect, governs the ravage of the earth, then the only real recourse lies in the poem' (Badiou 2003: 60).

Badiou's arguments are conducted on the terms of an axiomatic systematicity. This is his point of departure as he binds the process of truth to the event in its singularity. For Badiou, 'an event is linked to the notion of the undecidable' (Badiou 2003: 62). In his 'quadratic' illustration (Aeschylean tragedy, Galilean mathematical physics, a life-transforming erotic encounter, the French Revolution), 'a wager has to be made. This is why truth begins with an *axiom of truth*. It begins with a groundless decision – the decision to say that the event has taken place' (Badiou 2003: 62).

Luce Irigaray retraces the same fourfold interplay as a composite in the spirit of her own Lacanian psychoanalytic formation: 'What schiz or what rupture: pure science on one side and politics on another; nature and art on a third or as conditions of possibilities – love on a fourth?' (Irigaray 2005: 284). With Irigaray's symbolic turn, she pays all obeisance to the Lacanian claim that 'discoveries must be expressed in a formal language, a language that makes sense. And that means: expressing oneself in symbols or letters, substitutions for proper names, that refer only to intra-theoretical objects, and therefore never to any real persons or real objects' (Irigaray 2005: 286). Consequently the 'scientist enters into a world of fiction incomprehensible to all who do not participate in it' (Irigaray 2005: 286). Here we recall Badiou's allusion to '*the unnameable* of the situation . . . [Fixing] the limit of the potency of a truth . . . The unnameable is what is excluded from having a proper name' (Badiou 2003: 66).

As W. V. O. Quine had done in the pragmatico-analytic tradition of American philosophy, Badiou draws upon the resources of set theory to return Gödel's legacy to philosophy as a science in the same sense that Kant gives science to philosophy as a possible project. Given Gödel's proof that 'it is impossible to demonstrate, within a mathematical theory, that this very theory is non-contradictory,' Badiou argues that:

> a reasonable ethic of mathematics is to not wish to force this point; to accept that a mathematical truth is never *complete*. But this reasonable thing is difficult to maintain. As can be seen with scientism, or with totalitarianism, there is always a desire for the omnipotence of the True.

Like the more politically-minded sociologist and philosopher, Jean Baudrillard, Badiou does not hesitate to identify this nominative drive as the veritable root of all evil. 'Evil is the will to name *at any price*' (Badiou 2003: 66). For Badiou: Philosophy is prescribed by several conditions that are the types of truth procedures. These types are science (more precisely the matheme), art (more precisely the poem), politics (more precisely, politics in interiority or the politics of emancipation), and love (more precisely, the procedure that makes truth out of the disjunction of sexed positions) (Badiou 2003: 165).

Using fiction, Badiou's Kantian (and Nietzschean) claim is that philosophy seizes truth for the sake of its constructions:

> Fiction of knowing, philosophy imitates the matheme. Fiction of art, it imitates the poem. Intensity of an act, it is like a love without an object, addressed to all such that all may be within the seizure of the existence of truths, it is like a political strategy without the stakes of power. (Badiou 2003: 166)

In Foucault's analyses of power/knowledge, the question is as much the discourse of power and its counter as it is strategy: more Lao Tzu than Machiavelli. Thus Vandana Shiva discusses the 'epistemological violence' that suppresses or discounts local knowledge and experience in favor of totalitarian and reductionist science deployed at massive environmental cost (Shiva 1988; and cf. both Winner 1978 and Davison 2002). Drawing attention to the 'genocidal' consequences of 'the logic of Western science,' Shiv Visvanathan muses on the implicit violence of the 'rational' conception of 'choice' which he illuminated via the nineteenth-century term '*triage*,' combining 'the concepts of rational experiment, the concept of obsolescence, and of vivisection – whereby a society, a subculture, or a species is labelled as obsolete and condemned to death because rational judgment has deemed it incurable' (Visvanathan 1988: 259). This is extended to the elimination of alternate epistemological perspectives: 'the nation state cannot permit ethnicities which serve as competing sites for power and modern science cannot tolerate the legitimacy of folk or ethnic knowledges' (Visvanathan 1988: 279).

To the range of names noted above, we may add Giorgio Agamben, Gunter Anders, Jean Baudrillard, Henri Lefebvre, Bruno Latour, and Jean-François Lyotard, in addition to the variety of readings of Bergson, Deleuze, Foucault hailing from *both* analytic and Continental orientations (see Keith Ansell-Pearson, Constantin Boundas, Manuel Delanda, Val Dusek, Ian Hacking, David Hyder, Dominique Lecourt, Rudi Viskers, and so on), as well as more traditional authors broadly incorporating hermeneutics and phenomenology, such as Ute Guzzoni, Dominique Janicaud, Jean Ladrière, Elisabeth Ströker; and some even argue the case for Jacques Derrida (Friedrich Kittler, Timothy Lenoir, Christopher Norris and Hans-Jörg Rheinberger). These (and, of course, many other) names attest to both the accomplishments and the promise of continental philosophy of science.

References

Allen, B. (2003), 'Carnap Contexts: Comte, Heidegger, Nietzsche,' in C. G. Prado (ed.) (2003), *A House Divided: Comparing Analytic and Continental Philosophy*, Amherst: Humanity Books, pp. 63–103.

Anapolitanos, D., A. Tsinorema, and S. Anapolitanos (eds) (1998), *Philosophy and the Many Faces of Science*, Lanham: Rowman and Littlefield.

Babich, B. (1989), 'Continental Philosophy of Science: Mach, Duhem, and Bachelard,' in R. Kearney (ed.) (1989), *Routledge History of Philosophy: Volume VIII*, London: Routledge, pp. 175–221.

Babich, B. (1994), *Nietzsche's Philosophy of Science: Reflecting Science on the Grounds of Art and Life*, Albany: State University of New York Press.

Babich, B. (2002), *Hermeneutic Philosophy of Science, Van Gogh's Eyes, and God: Essays in Honor of Patrick A. Heelan*, Dordrecht: Kluwer.

Babich, B. E. (2003a), 'From Fleck's *Denkstil* to Kuhn's Paradigm: Conceptual Schemes and Incommensurability,' *International Studies in the Philosophy of Science* 71 (1): 75–92.

Babich, B. (2003b), 'On the Analytic-Continental Divide in Philosophy: Nietzsche's Lying Truth, Heidegger's Speaking Language, and Philosophy,' in C. G. Prado (ed.) *A House Divided*, Amherst: Humanity Books, pp. 63–103.

Babich, B., and R. S. Cohen (eds) (1999a), *Nietzsche, Theories of Knowledge and Critical Theory: Nietzsche and the Sciences I* [*Boston Studies in the Philosophy of Science 203*], Dordrecht: Kluwer.

Babich, B., and R. S. Cohen (eds) (1999b), *Nietzsche, Epistemology and Philosophy of Science: Nietzsche and the Sciences II* [*BSPS 204*], Dordrecht: Kluwer.

Badiou, A. [1992–8] (2003), *Infinite Thought: Truth and the Return of Philosophy*, trans. O. Feltham, and J. Clemens, trans. New York: Continuum.

Bohman, J. (1991), *New Philosophy of Social Science*, Cambridge: MIT Press.

Böhme, G. (1989), *Klassiker der Naturphilosophie. Von den Vorsokratikern bis zur Kopenhagener Schule*, Munich: Beck.

Boniolo, G. (2003), 'Kant's Explication and Carnap's Explication: The *Redde Rationem*,' *International Philosophical Quarterly* 43: 289–98.

Buchdahl, G. (1992), *Kant and the Dynamic of Reason*, London: Blackwell.

Butterfield, H. [1931] (1968), *The Whig Interpretation of History*, Harmondsworth: Penguin.

Canguilhelm, G. [1966] (1991), *The Normal and the Pathological*, Cambridge: MIT Press.

Crombie, A. C. (1995), *Styles of Scientific Thinking in the European Tradition: The History of Argument and Explanation especially in the Mathematical and Biomedical Sciences and Arts*, London: Duckworth.

Code, L. (1991), *What Can She Know? Feminist Theory and the Construction of Knowledge*, Ithaca: Cornell University Press.

Davison, A. (2002), *Technology and the Contested Meanings of Sustainability*, Albany: State University of New York Press.

D'Espagnat, B. (1990), *Penser la science ou les enjeux du savoir*, Paris: Dunod.

Drummond, J. (1990), *Husserlian Intentionality and Non-Foundational Realism*, The Hague: Kluwer.

Duhem, P. [1913] (1959), *Le système du monde: Histoire des doctrines cosmologiques de Platon à Copernic*. Paris: Hermann.

Duhem, P. [1916] (1991), *German Science*, trans. J. Lyon, LaSalle: Open Court.

Elden, S. (2003), 'Taking the Measure of the Beiträge: Heidegger, National Socialism and the Calculation of the Political,' *European Journal of Political Theory* 2(1): 35–56.

Elden, S. (2004), *Understanding Henri Lefebvre: Theory and the Possible*, London: Continuum.

Feist, R. (ed.) (2004), *Husserl and the Sciences*, Toronto: University of Ottawa Press.

Fleck, L. [1935] (1979), *The Genesis and Development of a Scientific Fact*, trans. F. Bradley, and T. J. Trenn, Chicago: University of Chicago Press.

Friedmann, M. (1992), *Kant and the Exact Sciences*, Cambridge: Harvard University Press.

Friedmann, M. (2000), *Parting of the Ways: Carnap, Cassirer, Heidegger*, Chicago: Open Court.

Gethmann, C. F. (1991), 'Phänomenologie, Lebensphilosophie und Konstruktiv Wissenschaftstheorie,' in C. F. Gethmann (ed.), *Lebenswelt und Wissenschaft*, Bonn: Bouvier, pp. 28–77.

Giere, R. N. (1996), 'From *Wissenschaftliche Philosophie* to Philosophy of Science,' in R. N. Giere, and A. W. Richardson (eds) (1996), *Origins of Logical Empiricism*, Minneapolis: University of Minnesota Press, pp. 335–54.

Giere, R. N., and A. W. Richardson (eds) (1996), *Origins of Logical Empiricism*, Minneapolis: University of Minnesota Press.

Ginev, D. (2006), *The Context of Constitution: Beyond the Edge of Epistemological Justification*, Berlin: Springer.

Glazebrook, P. (2000), *Heidegger's Philosophy of Science*, New York: Fordham University Press.

Glazebrook, P. (2001), 'The Role of the *Beiträge* in Heidegger's Critique of Science,' *Philosophy Today* 45(11): 24–32.

Golinski, J. (1998), *Making Natural Knowledge: Constructivism and the History of Science*, Cambridge: Cambridge University Press.

Gregory, F. (1992), *Nature Lost? Natural Science and the German Theological Traditions of the Nineteenth Century*, Cambridge: Harvard University Press.

Gutting, G. (ed.) (2005), *Continental Philosophy of Science* Oxford: Blackwell.

Heelan, P. A. (1998), 'Scope of Hermeneutics in the Philosophy of Natural Science,' *Studies in the History and Philosophy of Science* 29: 273–98.

Heelan, P. A. (1989), 'After Experiment: Research and Reality,' *American Philosophy Quarterly* 26: 297–308.

Heelan, P. A. (1983), *Space-Perception and the Philosophy of Science*, Berkeley: University of California Press.

Heelan, P. A. (1970), 'Complementarity, Context Dependence, and Quantum Logic.' *Foundations of Physics* 1: 95–110.

Heelan, P. A. (1965), *Quantum Mechanics and Objectivity: The Physical Philosophy of Werner Heisenberg*, The Hague: Nijhoff.

Heidegger, M. (1968), *What is Called Thinking?*, trans. F. D. Wieck, and J. G. Gray. New York: Harper and Row.

Heidegger, M. (1977), *The Question Concerning Technology and Other Essays*, trans. W. Lovitt, New York: Harper and Row.

Honneth, A. (2005), 'Bisected Rationality: The Frankfurt School's Critique of Science,' in G. Gutting (ed.) (2005), *Continental Philosophy of Science*, Oxford: Blackwell, pp. 283–93.

Husserl, E. [1954] (1970), *The Crisis of European Sciences and Transcendental Phenomenology*, trans. D. Carr, Evanston: Northwestern University Press.

Husserl, E. (1975), *Ideas*, trans. W. R. B. Gibson, New York: Collier.

Irigaray, L. [1985] (2005), 'In Science, Is the Subject Sexed?' in G. Gutting (ed.) (2005), *Continental Philosophy of Science*, Oxford: Blackwell, pp. 283–92.

Kerszberg, P. (1997), *Critique and Totality*, Albany: State University of New York Press.

Kerszberg, P. (1999), *Kant et la nature*. Paris: Les Belles Lettres.

Knorr-Cetina, K. (1999), *Epistemic Cultures: How the Sciences Make Knowledge*, Cambridge: Harvard University Press.

Kockelmans, J. J. (1999), 'Continental Philosophy of Science,' in R. Popkin (ed.) (1990), *Columbia Encyclopedia of Philosophy*, New York: Columbia University Press, pp. 691–8.

Kockelmans, J. J. (1993), *Ideas for a Hermeneutic Phenomenology of the Natural Sciences*, Dordrecht: Kluwer.

Kockelmans, J. J. (1985), *Heidegger and Science*, Washington, DC: Center for Advanced Research in Phenomenology.

Kockelmans, J. J., and T. J. Kisiel (1970), *Phenomenology and the Natural Sciences*, Evanston: Northwestern University Press.

Kremer-Marietti, A. (1983), *Le concept de science positive*, Paris: Klincksieck.

Kuhn, T. (1979), 'Preface' in L. Fleck (1979), *The Genesis and Development of a Scientific Fact*, trans. F. Bradley, and T. J. Trenn, Chicago: University of Chicago Press, pp. vi–xi.

Latour, B. (2004), *Politics of Nature: How to Bring the Sciences into Democracy*, trans. C. Porter, Cambridge: Harvard University Press.

Mach, E. (1976), *Knowledge and Error: Sketches on the Psychology of Enquiry*, (ed.) B. McGuinness, Dordrecht: Reidel.

Merleau-Ponty, M. [1945] (1962), *Phenomenology of Perception*, trans. C. Smith, London: Routledge and Kegan Paul.

Minkowski, E. (1970), 'Prose and Poetry (Astronomy and Cosmology),' in J. J. Kockelmans, and J. Kisiel (1970), *Phenomenology and the Natural Sciences*. Evanston: Northwestern University Press, pp. 239–247.

Moore, G. M., and T. Brobjer (eds) (2004), *Nietzsche and Science*, Aldershot: Ashgate.

Nandy, A. (ed.) (1988), *Science, Hegemony, and Violence: A Requiem for Modernity*, Oxford: Oxford University Press.

Neumann, G. (1999), *Die phänomenologische Frage nach dem Ursprung der mathematisch-naturwissenschaftlichen Raumauffassung bei Husserl und Heidegger*, Berlin: Duncker and Humblot.

Prado, C. G. (ed.) (2003), *A House Divided: Comparing Analytic and Continental Philosophy*, Amherst: Humanity Books.

Principe, L. (1998), *The Aspiring Adept: Robert Boyle and his Alchemical Quest*, Princeton: Princeton University Press.

Robinson-Valéry, Judith (ed.) (1983), *Functionen des Geistes. Paul Valéry und die Wissenschaften*, Frankfurt am Main: Campus.

Rose, H. (1994), *Love, Power and Knowledge: Towards a Feminist Transformation of the Sciences*, Bloomington: Indiana University Press.

Salanskis, J.-M. [1991] (1995), Die Wissenschaft denkt nicht, *Tekhnema* 2: 60–85.

Salanskis, J.-M. (2003), *Herméneutique et cognition*, Lille: Presses Universitaires du Septentrion.

Serres, M. [1992] (1995), *The Natural Contract*, trans. E. MacArthur, and W. Paulson, Ann Arbor: University of Michigan Press.

Shapin, S., and S. Schaffer (1985), *Leviathan and the Air Pump: Hobbes, Boyle and the Experimental Life*, Princeton: Princeton University Press.

Shiva, V. (1988), 'Reductionist Science as Epistemological Violence,' in A. Nandy (ed.) (1988), *Science, Hegemony, and Violence: A Requiem for Modernity*, Oxford: Oxford University Press, pp. 232–56.

Sokolowski, R. (1999), *Introduction to Phenomenology*, Cambridge: Cambridge University Press.

Sorrell, T. (1991), *Scientism: Philosophy and the Infatuation of Science*, London: Routledge.

Spiekermann, K. (1999), 'Nietzsche and Critical Theory,' in B. Babich, and R. S. Cohen (1999), *Nietzsche, Theories of Knowledge and Critical Theory: Nietzsche and the Sciences I* [*Boston Studies in the Philosophies of Science 203*], Dordrecht: Kluwer, pp. 225–42.

Stiegler, B. [1996] (1998), *Technics and Time*, Stanford: Stanford University Press.

Swindal, J. (1999), 'Nietzsche, Critical Though and a Theory of Knowledge,' in B. Babich, and R. S. Cohen (1999), *Nietzsche, Theories of Knowledge and Critical Theory: Nietzsche and the Sciences I [Boston Studies in the Philosophies of Science 203]*, Dordrecht: Kluwer, pp. 243–52.

Tiles, M. (1984), *Bachelard: Science and Objectivity*, Cambridge: Cambridge University Press, 1984.

Todorov, T. [2000] (2003), *Hope and Memory: Lessons from the Twentieth Century*, Princeton: Princeton University Press.

Visvanathan, S. (1988), 'On the Annals of the Laboratory State,' in A. Nandy, (ed.) (1988), *Science, Hegemony, and Violence: A Requiem for Modernity*, Oxford: Oxford University Press, pp. 257–88.

West, D. (1996), *Introduction to Continental Philosophy*, Cambridge: Polity.

Winner, L. (1978), *Autonomous Technology*, Cambridge: MIT Press.

Ethics

François Raffoul

The development of many ethical theories in the twentieth-century Continental tradition has taken place against the background of Nietzsche's celebrated critique of morality, as well as in response to the Holocaust and the unprecedented horrors of the century. While there have been many noteworthy developments in the areas of feminist ethics, the 'discourse ethics' of Habermas, and the work of the later Foucault, we will focus within the confines of this chapter on Nietzsche, Sartre, Heidegger, Levinas, and Derrida, as representative works in Continental philosophies of ethics.

Nietzsche's attacks on morality have often been described as a nihilistic enterprise of destruction of values leading to the impossibility of ethics. Consequently, Continental philosophies of ethics, which are in their very basis post-Nietzschean reflections, have also been accused of moral relativism and nihilism. However, it could be argued that Nietzsche-inspired critiques are not mere dismissals of ethics, but rather challenges to a certain way of understanding it: Nietzsche targets what he terms 'life-denying' ethical philosophies, which he finds in Christianity and of course Platonism, both of which posit another world beyond this world in their projection of transcendent ideals. His target is the positing of the values, 'good' and 'evil,' as transcendent values lying beyond this world – a movement indicating an implicit rejection and hatred for life in this world (as shown in the presence of guilt and shame as cornerstones of such ethics). The sense of Nietzsche's genealogy of morals lies here: to return to life itself, so as to reveal the material, historical, 'human, all-too human,' origins of ethics and values. Nietzsche calls for a re-evaluation of our ways of evaluating, namely for a life-affirming ethics, known as his philosophy of 'the overman and of joyful wisdom.'

The proper site of ethics, which is Nietzsche's concern, is also at the centre of the phenomenological enterprise, in which ethics is resituated in a phenomenal basis – not in abstract theorizing either of the applied or the theoretical kind. By 'ethics,' we should not indeed understand a mere 'application' of principles to various practical concerns, as if thought could be used as a tool, following consequentialist, utilitarian or instrumental models. In fact, we might argue that the conceptual opposition of 'theoretical' and 'applied' is better suited to the scientific model or perhaps even imported from it. The risk in using such a model is simply to assume or presuppose the very meaning of ethics, which is already considered to be settled through the notion of 'application.' The current and growing development of so-called 'applied ethics' in the curriculum could thus be said to conceal a peculiar and paradoxical blindness regarding the nature of ethics, as well as a neglect of a genuine philosophical questioning concerning the meaning of ethics. It is ethics itself that is in need of a philosophical foundation, even if that would reveal its ultimate groundlessness. The notion of 'application' assumes a ground for ethical precepts: ethics is guaranteed by a theoretical basis. But ethical judgement, as Sartre or Derrida would argue, takes place in an ungrounded way. We cannot secure in advance the norms and the values of the choice of norms and values. The concept of 'applied ethics' is thus self-contradictory, almost an oxymoron.

Jean-Paul Sartre's philosophy of existence, or as he labeled it himself, 'existentialism,' explicitly places itself within the horizon of Nietzsche's questions and challenges to traditional philosophy and theology, and particularly understands itself as a consequence of what Nietzsche called 'the death of God.' Sartre explains that existentialism begins from Nietzsche's claim that God is dead and attempts to draw the consequences of it fully. This recognition reveals the ethical scope of existentialism; for the withdrawal of theological foundations and principles frees existence and makes it responsible for itself, thus revealing its ethical core. This is what the formula 'existence precedes essence' means. Sartre distinguishes between two types of existentialism – the Christian (such as Jaspers's, Gabriel Marcel's and Emmanuel Mounier's), and the atheistic, of which he claims to be the main representative. Atheistic existentialism claims that existence precedes essence because there is no God to provide an essential justification for our existence. Existence before essence or without essence means indeed existence without God and without a theologically founded morality. The death of God has thus an immediate ethical implication. If there is no God to found transcendent values as the basis of our ethical comportment, then the very basis of ethics as traditionally conceived disappears. Sartre would insist that he does not propose a 'secularized' version of a theological foundation through which we would suppress God at the 'least possible expense,' while continuing to appeal to an objective set of values. He rejects any notion of *a priori* values, whether they lie in an atemporal human nature or in the structure of pure reason. There are simply no values or principles inscribed in an intelligible heaven. The existentialist, Sartre insists, draws the consequences of the death of God by stating that if God is dead, then, we are unable to justify our actions by reference to a given human nature. In fact, the existentialist claims that with the disappearance of God, there also disappears all possibility of grounding values in an intelligible heaven. This, however, does not mean that the very possibility of ethics would disappear, for Sartre does not claim that there are no values (this would amount to nihilism); he claims that there are no transcendentally given objective values: values are immanent to existence itself; they are not given *a priori* but must be created and chosen (and once chosen, they are not established once and for all but are to be chosen again and again). Values are not objective, as there is simply no objective realm for Sartre; rather, they express subjective life. It follows that ethics becomes the praxis of our very freedom, and its justification ultimately lies in this praxis. We choose values, and we also choose how we choose them. In that respect, Sartre's ethics takes on its main sense – one of absolute responsibility.

Responsibility constitutes the core of existentialist ethics, insofar as existentialism recognises that human beings invent what they are and the values they live by. Ethics is the heart of human existence ('to be' means to be responsible), ethics and existence become one and consequently ethics is far from being dismissed by Sartre's condemnation of theological thinking. We may even argue that ethics – the absolute responsibility of an essence-less existence – is rendered possible by the death of God. At every moment, without any support, Man needs to invent Man and be responsible for it. To that extent, we are not only absolutely responsible for what we do, but above all for what we are. Ethics is here situated at the heart of existence as absolute responsibility, and is based on the absence of an *a priori* table of values – of an ethical scripture.

Such a responsibility is for Sartre absolute, overwhelming or hyperbolic, excessive or infinite, and universal. It is absolute, because of Sartre's very conception of freedom as absolute, that is, absolutely freed from any determinist principle. Sartre goes so far as to claim that even facticity – that is, the very order of the not chosen, such as birth – is a matter for our responsibility and is in a sense also chosen. Because there is no essence, my responsibility knows no bounds: responsibility is infinite and excessive as there are no 'natural' bounds to restrict it. We are responsible for existence, because there is no foundation for existence – except itself. To be responsible means to be responsible for that very responsibility and for the lack that subtends it. There is therefore a hyperbolic inflation of responsibility, which encounters no limits and becomes infinite and excessive for a finite subject. Sartre claims that there is no event in the world that does not in fact concern me – which is not mine to take on and decide. Responsibility is also universal. Sartre rejects *a priori* given values – values that would impose themselves on all humans. However, he does not embrace a kind of relativism: when I choose a value, I choose a form, a concept or an ideal, a notion or an image of humanity that I project as a value to be embraced by all; I project a universal horizon, or a horizon of universality, to be chosen by others. There is therefore a universal scope of values for Sartre, not because they would be given *a priori*, but because we engage the world in our choices. There is universality, but it is neither given nor objective. Sartre does not believe in a private sphere of subjectivity. We exist in the dimension of the universal, but that universal can only exist as chosen.

In Heidegger's work, the question of ethics is situated in the very event of being and its givenness. If there is an ethics in Heidegger's work, taking into account that Heidegger did not explicitly develop one (although he may have allowed for understanding it anew), we would need to state the following: the ethical can only be approached in Heidegger's work in terms of being and of what he calls 'Dasein' – the human being conceived in its relation to being itself. Traditional accounts of ethics are indeed phenomenologically 'destroyed' or deconstructed in Heidegger's work, in order for a nonmetaphysical, nontheological, more original sense of the ethical to be retrieved. For instance, when Heidegger takes issue with the theme of empathy in *Being and Time*, it is not in order to condemn an ethical motif but rather in order to reveal how much the problematics of empathy remain stuck in Cartesianism and ego-based philosophies. Instead, Heidegger exposes the dimension of 'being-with,' – the originary being-with-others of *Dasein* – rendering moot the question of accessing another mind through empathy. Similarly, when Heidegger takes issue with ethics as a metaphysical discipline in his 'Letter on Humanism,' it is with the intent of uncovering a more originary sense of ethics as 'authentic dwelling' and 'standing-in' the truth of being. Ultimately for Heidegger – as he himself states in the 'Letter on Humanism' – the thinking of being is itself an 'originary ethics' provided that being is not seen as substantial ground but rather as an event that calls for a responsible engagement and praxis.

Heidegger points to this originary dimension (site of his originary ethics) when he takes issue with the model of application. Heidegger often stressed the untimely nature of philosophy and claimed that philosophy is in a certain essential sense useless. Philosophy is not a knowledge that could be acquired nor is it some sort of technical expertise that could be applied and evaluated according to its usefulness. The metaphysical opposition of theory and praxis that has traditionally framed the reflection on ethics is in fact stating that thinking, as theory, is nonpractical – contemplative for example – and that praxis is thoughtless – for example as an application of theory. Both are thought – sold – too short. Further, Heidegger states that his thinking, that is, the thinking that inquires into the truth of being is neither ethics nor ontology. That signifies that ontology and ethics are not different spheres. It also means that ontology is not some sphere of principles that would then be 'applied' to an ontical ethical sphere. That finally means that ontology is ethical and that ethics is ontological. According to Heidegger, asking for philosophy to have a result or a use is a demand of technological thinking, of what he calls in the *Beiträge* 'machination.' Further, is Heidegger's conception of philosophy as untimely, and not for an immediate use, the indication of the impossibility of an ethical philosophy? Heidegger seems to think not, giving us the inkling that the impossibility of application does not necessarily mean the impossibility of ethics.

Heidegger does not propose a system of morality, a series of prescriptive norms or values – he rethinks the site of ethics. An important characteristic of this site is its factical nature. He stresses that no 'values,' no 'ideal norms' float above factical existence. When we consider, for instance, the authenticity/inauthenticity alternative in *Being and Time*, we see that it is a matter of an existence coming into its own, the immanent movement of a radically finite and open existence, and not the 'application' of rules to a previously unethical realm. Existence is ethical through and through and does not need to be 'ethicized' *post facto*. This is doubtless the reason why Heidegger has not written an ethics: because he does not need 'to add' it on to an ontology that would then be conceived as a mere segment of philosophy. In a sense, ethics is ontology itself because being displays an intrinsic ethicality.

Recent publications of Heidegger's early lecture courses have made manifest the development of his thought through an appropriative reading of practical philosophy and its fundamental categories. Courses from that period testify to the influence of practical-ethical categories in the genesis of Heidegger's thought and vocabulary (for instance his appropriative reading of Aristotle's *Nicomachean Ethics*). They show that he understands the structure of Kant's moral law as the mark of the finitude of existence, assigned to the dissymmetry of the law; and that he reinterprets Kant's ethical philosophy in the perspective of an analytic of finitude. Heidegger's ontological appropriation of the motif of freedom in Kant's ethical philosophy, in *On the Essence of*

Human Freedom, must also be noted for the way it reinterprets freedom as the transcendence of *Dasein*. In *Being and Time*, *Dasein* is defined, not in abstract theoretical terms, but as care or concern for its own being, that is, not as the reflexive subject of the modern tradition from Descartes to Husserl, but in a 'practical' sense. In that respect, we could make the claim that all the existentials of *Dasein* should be understood as ontologico-ethical categories. This 'ethical' dimension of the concept of *Dasein* appears early in *Being and Time*, with *Dasein* designating the entity for whom Being is at issue. Being is given in such a way that I have to take it over and be responsible for it. I have being to be as my own because such being is addressed to me as a possible way of being, as a way to be – not as a 'what.' 'Having to be' means that the being that I am is to be taken on. It is this determination of *Dasein* from the outset that defines the self as a responsibility for itself.

Heidegger's characterization of *Dasein*'s authenticity is developed in terms of responsibility. *Dasein*'s authentic being hinges on it being responsible in the sense of responding authentically to the 'call of conscience.' If there is a notion of responsibility in Heidegger's work, it cannot be accountability in the classical sense. Accountability that has defined the traditional concept of responsibility rests upon the notions of agency, free will and subjectivity. A person is accountable as a subject who is the cause of her actions through the freedom of the will. Accountability, as a concept, assumes the position of a subject-cause, an agent or an author who can be displayed as a *subjectum* for her actions. Now Heidegger does not think the human being in terms of the notion 'subject,' does not think freedom in terms of free will, and rejects causality as a category applicable to being. There is therefore no ground in his thought for the concept of accountability; but this does not mean that it does not harbor another thought of responsibility. Indeed, Heidegger explains that *Dasein* – being neither a subject nor an ego – must be thought in terms of responsibility. This is the case in at least three respects: responsibility defines the essence of *Dasein*; it constitutes selfhood; and finally, as it represents its relationship to Being, responsibility constitutes Dasein's very essence.

In *On The Essence of Human Freedom*, Heidegger states that responsibility for ourselves represents the very essence of the human being. Responsibility is therefore not conceptualized as a consequence of a subject 'owning' her actions, but is instead conceived in terms of a response to an event that is also a call – the call of Being. Such a call individuates *Dasein* by constituting its selfhood. Responsibility is not based on subjectness but rather constitutes the self as the called one. Each time, *Dasein* is called to itself. This is why the call is also that which I have to answer. There lies the hidden source and resource of responsibility: to be responsible means, before anything else, to respond – *respondere*. Having to be ourselves is the originary responsibility of *Dasein*. 'Become what you are,' says Heidegger, which is not to be understood ontically, as 'Realize your potential!' but ontologically, that is: what you are, you can only become it, because *Dasein*'s being is to-be. In this 'to-be' resides the ontological sense of responsibility.

In the later works of Heidegger, after *Being and Time*, *Dasein* was referred to more and more as the 'called one' – *der Gerufene* – having to answer for the very openness and givenness of Being by being its 'guardian.' The response does not follow the call but is already given in the call, always already corresponding to the address of Being. In fact, *Dasein* cannot but answer it; it has each time already answered, already said 'yes' to this call of Being; it has always already gained access to itself in such an answer. To be responsible then means to have been struck, always already, by the event of the call. Responsibility refers to that event by which Being '*enowns*' humans. It represents human beings' belonging to Being as well as their essence as humans. Ultimately for Heidegger, ethics cannot be measured in terms of results nor can be reduced to the production of effects on the basis of a theory within the end/means apparatus. Ethics is rather to be conceived in terms of an incalculable finite dwelling of human beings – an authentic inhabiting in the openness of being; it designates the sojourn of humans – that is, of mortals in the finite dimensionality of being. Ethics therefore turns into an ethics of finitude – of finite being.

With Levinas, ethics is situated in the relationship to the other person – in the inter-subjective relation with the other human. This ethical relation is the reverse of violence and dehumanization as it constitutes the acknowledgement of the other's humanity as destitute and vulnerable being. It is also situated in opposition to traditional ontology and the privilege of knowledge in Western philosophy that always reduce the other to a principle of identity or 'the Same.' Levinas aims at reversing the traditional hierarchy that reduces ethics to a branch of ontology and epistemology; he seeks to raise ethics to the level of first philosophy. The ethical experience – however rare it may be – enacts respect for and concern for the other. Faced with the other's vulnerability (ultimately, with the mortality of the other), I am called to care for the other and to attend to the other as other. Ethics understood in this way represents what is truly human in human beings – a new humanism that Levinas calls 'humanism of the other human,' breaking with ego-centered philosophies and opening on to the infinite character of the alterity of the other to whom I am responsible.

Levinas puts the primacy of epistemology and ontology over ethics into question: epistemology and ontology, as they have defined the entirety of Western philosophy from Parmenides to Heidegger, is a thought of the Same – a thought that reduces otherness to the Same by the very power of its theoretical comprehensiveness. For Levinas, theory is a manner of approaching the known being in such a way that its otherness in relation to the knowing being vanishes. In the traditional philosophical correlation between Knowledge and Being, knowledge represents an activity that appropriates and comprehends the alterity of what is known. Consequently, Western philosophy has most often been an epistemology and an ontology, that is to say, a reduction of the Other to the Same. In opposition to the tradition of Western thought, Levinas attempts to go beyond Being and to overcome ontology – to move beyond Being towards the other, beyond ontology towards ethics.

Levinas understands traditional ontology as the knowledge of Being in general. In such a context, beings emerge against a background that exceeds them, as the individual cases against the background of the concept. We must therefore say that, just as individual cases fall under their concept, all beings and relations to beings fall within Being – especially relations to the other. For Levinas, the other entity par excellence is the other person – the other human. Therein lies perhaps his 'un-deconstructed' humanism. Levinas, with the relation and responsibility to the other, seeks to give humanism a new foundation. His conception of humanism is ethical through and through. If the relation to beings takes place within the horizon of Being, then Being as conceptual generality neutralizes the alterity of the other human. It is this dependency or subjection that Levinas vehemently rejects: all entities fall within Being, except for the other human. The other is not one possible case of a relation to entities among others; it escapes the ontological horizon and does not let itself be circumscribed by a thinking of the Same. The comprehension of Being cannot comprehend the relation to the other and cannot dominate the relation with the other. We must in fact invert the hierarchy: it is the ontic encounter with the other that is first – not a neutral ontological/conceptual horizon. The ontic for Levinas precedes the ontological; since he defines ethics as the encounter with an other, it is this relation with the other that commands and precedes the relation with Being. Ethics becomes first philosophy – the ontic encounter with the other precedes any ontological horizon.

On this basis, Levinas undertakes a radical critique of egoistic philosophies. According to him, egoism is present even in Heidegger's 'mineness' (*Jemeinigkeit*) of Dasein. We know how Heidegger establishes that death is only my death and my death alone, that it radically individuates the existent. It would then seem that the others would fade in my authentic assumption of death as only mine. Levinas challenges this egoistic (solipsistic) death and opposes to it a death that would be more primordial – the death of the other. The death of the other is for him the first death. He demands that the I should be concerned for the other before any self-concern – that the death of the other should matter more than my own death, that it should be more authentic than the Heideggerian dying. Levinas opposes to 'solitary mineness' a being-for-the-other that would be more authentic. It is a matter of an alternative between identity, mineness, sameness, and human devotion to the other. It is for the death of the other that I am responsible, to the point of including myself in death. I am responsible for the other insofar as he is mortal. On such premises, Levinas would oppose responsibility for the other to the Heideggerian responsibility for ourselves. We could perhaps object that Heidegger's *Dasein* is essentially *Mit-sein* – being-with. But for Levinas the relation to the other is not a togetherness – a 'communion.' Being-with' reproduces a logic of the same and therefore, for Levinas, the proposition 'with' is unable and inept to express the original relation with the other.

The true relation to the other is not a being-together in a shared world but lies in an encounter with the other face to face; it is the immediacy of a face to face without intermediary. Seeking to open up thought to an experience of alterity that cannot be reduced to the Same, Levinas articulates a different sense of responsibility – a responsibility for the other, nonreciprocal, dissymmetrical, infinite, and nonchosen; an experience of a 'being devoted to the other,' in the guise of a being hostage to the other. All concerns for reciprocity, contracts and agreements with others, are seen by Levinas as (egoistic) calculative thinking. Instead, with responsibility, as he understands it, we are in a relation to the other as other and not a reduction of the other to the same. It is transcendence. Responsibility to the other is opposed to the immanence of the *ego cogito* and permits the exit from ontology and from the rule of the Same; the experience of it gives access to the absolute alterity of the other. Such a responsibility is for Levinas prior to Being and to beings, is not said in the ontological categories. Levinas speaks of responsibility as the essential primary and fundamental structure of subjectivity. Subjectivity is for him to be understood in ethical terms, and not first as an existential basis supplemented by an ethical component. Responsibility is equivalent to an originary passivity before the infinite obligation to the other. I am, Levinas would say, hostage of the other. This being-hostage – this infinite responsibility for the other – testifies, as Derrida shows in his homage to Levinas, *Adieu to Emmanuel Levinas*, to the radical dispossession or expropriation of the subject. The subject is no longer a self-identity, an ego or a self-consciousness – not even an authentic self or *Dasein*: it is an openness to the other; it is a welcome of the other – in the subjective genitive sense (the other's welcome).

Derrida also gives himself the task of problematizing the question of the site and the possibility of ethics in terms of what he calls 'aporetic ethics.' Ethics, for Derrida, is not a system of rules – of moral norms – and to that extent he readily concedes that he does not propose an ethics. What interests him in ethics is instead the aporias of ethics, its limits: not to point to the impossibility of ethics, but on the contrary to reveal such aporias as the possibility of ethics – what he calls the anethical origins of ethics. The aporia is not leading to sterility, but constitutes a limit through which nonetheless something announces itself in an affirmative fashion. Derrida then suggests that a sort of nonpassive endurance or experience of the aporia is the condition of possibility of responsibility and of decision. The aporia he speaks about is not a momentary paralysis in front of an impasse, but the experience of the undecidable through which and only through which a decision can take place. Without such an experience, a decision would be nothing more than the application of a program – not a decision but the application of a rule. Ethical decision is thus based on a not-knowing; Derrida maintains that the moment of decision, and thus the moment of responsibility, supposes a rupture with knowledge, and therefore an opening to the incalculable. When I have to decide, I do not have the knowledge of the norm by which to judge. There lies for Derrida the very opening of ethics: it is when I do not know the right rule that the ethical question arises. This not knowing marks the appearance of the impossible, identified as the anethical origin of ethics.

Responsible decision is thus an openness to the incalculable. If the decision takes place in a leap into the unknown, then alterity is its condition. This is why, for Derrida, we should never say, 'I made a decision': when a decision happens, the subject is not there; it rather awaits itself at the reception of the leap. For a decision to be a decision, it must be made by the other in me. Derrida would then speak of a passive decision, a decision of the other in me. This openness is an exposure to limits that escape the subject's calculability because it is the marker of what is inappropriable for the subject. Derrida stresses that a responsible decision can never be part of a calculable horizon and can never consist in the application of a determinable rule. A leap into the incalculable is necessary for any decision to take place. Deciding without knowing, deciding without being able to calculate all the consequences of the decision, is essential in Derrida's thinking of responsibility. It is a matter of marking an alterity at the heart of responsible decision – an alterity from which the ethical rises. This is what he means by heteronomy, a law that comes from the other, by a responsibility and decision of the other – of the other in me, an other greater and older than I am.

In order to stress the heterogeneity of the responsible decision vis à vis the horizon of calculability of the subject, Derrida stresses what he calls the 'im-possibility' of responsibility. Here 'impossibility' does not refer to that which cannot be but rather to that which happens outside of the conditions of possibility of the egological subject – outside of the horizons of expectation proposed by the subject. The incalculable happens. The impossible is not what cannot be; it marks the excess with respect to the horizon of the conditions of possibility of the subject, it is the limit of subjectivity to which subjectivity is exposed. To the order and power of the 'I can,' Derrida opposes the im-possible, what must remain (in a nonnegative fashion) foreign to the order of my possibilities. The im-possible is that which lies outside the subject, what exceeds it, and yet happens to such a subject, happening to it *as* impossible. Derrida speaks of the absolute weakness and disarmament that allows the incalculable to happen. He speaks of the event of the occasion, chance, the aleatory, which means exposing ourselves to what we cannot appropriate: it is there, before us, without us – there is someone, something, that happens, that happens to us, and that has no need of us to happen (to us). Furthermore, this impossible event – *there is* the impossible – marks the alterity of the event, absolutely – that is, abysmally and infinitely foreign to the 'I can.' Only then ethics would designate an openness to the other, an ethics of the other in the subjective genitive sense.

Derrida's ethical writings on hospitality must be understood in this context. In discussing hospitality as the welcoming of the other, Derrida shows that a conditional hospitality – one that remains regulated by the pre-existing conditions of a welcoming power – is no hospitality. Tolerance, for instance, that is, hospitality up to a point, is not hospitality: the other is there 'welcomed' on the basis of the conditions laid out by the host, that is, regulated by a welcoming power. We must therefore radicalize hospitality to the point of a genuine welcome of the other, in the subjective genitive. The other arrives, in her own terms: whatever happens happens, whoever comes, comes; hospitality registers this arrival. In contrast to conditional hospitality – to hospitality as an exercise of power by the host over the arriving other – Derrida proposes the notion of an unconditional, absolute or pure hospitality: pure and unconditional hospitality, hospitality itself, opens or is in advance open to someone who is neither expected nor invited, to whomever arrives as an absolutely foreign visitor, as a new arrival, nonidentifiable and unforeseeable, in short wholly other. Hospitality, as responsiveness to such arrival of the other, is as well incalculable, im-possible, and absolutely of the other.

Ethics therefore represents, in its aporetic structure, the arrival of the other and the obligation of the welcome. The impossible is the very structure, and possibility, of the alterity of the event, as well as of the responsibility understood as the welcome of (subjective genitive) such an event. Ethics becomes the experience of limits – of what remains inappropriable or 'impossible' for the subject as it registers the arrival of the other. This is why aporia represents the very possibility of a way, as non-way the condition of walking. For Derrida, such an impossibility to find our way is the condition of ethics.

We have seen how Continental philosophy in the twentieth century, far from being oblivious of ethics, instead elaborates anew the very senses of the ethical and re-engages the philosophical basis of ethics by re-evaluating its possibilities and limits. Thus, for example, Sartre finds the origin of ethics in the disappearance of a theological foundation for values; Heidegger rethinks the ethical by way of a critique of the metaphysical tradition of ethics; Levinas finds ethics not in some abstract principles or universal law but in the experience of being exposed to the singularity of the other human in the face to face; and Derrida questions the limits and aporias of ethics, conceiving of these limits as the very possibility of ethical decision. Whether explicitly or implicitly, Continental philosophies allow for a rethinking of ethics as they take issue with traditional models.

References

Derrida, J. (1977), *Adieu to Emmanuel Levinas*, trans. P.-A. Brault, and M. Naas, Stanford: Stanford University Press.

Derrida, J. (1984), *Margins of Philosophy*, trans. A. Bass, Chicago: University of Chicago Press.

Derrida, J. (1994), *Aporias*, trans. T. Dutoit, Stanford: Stanford University Press.

Derrida, J. (1995), *On the Name*, trans. T. Dutoit, Stanford: Stanford University Press.

Derrida, J. (1996), *The Gift of Death*, trans. D. Wills, Chicago: University Of Chicago Press.

Derrida, J. (1997), *Politics of Friendship*, trans. G. Collins, London: Verso.

Derrida, J. (2000), *Of Hospitality. Anee Dufourmantelle Invites Jacques Derrida to Respond*, trans. R. Bowlby, Stanford: Stanford University Press.

Derrida, J. (2001), *On Cosmopolitanism and Forgiveness. Thinking of Action*, New York: Routledge.

Derrida, J. (2001), *A Taste for the Secret*, with M. Ferraris, Cambridge: Polity.

Heidegger, M. (1996), *Being and Time*, trans. J. Stambaugh, Albany: State University of New York Press.

Heidegger, M. (1997), *Basic Writings*, (ed.) D. F. Krell, rev'd edn, New York: Harper and Row.

Heidegger, M. (1999), *Contributions to Philosophy (from Enowning)*, trans. P. Emad, and R. Maly, Bloomington: Indiana University Press.

Heidegger, M. (2003), *Four Seminars*, trans. A. Mitchell, and F. Raffoul, Bloomington: Indiana University Press.

Heidegger, M. (2005a), *Schelling's Treatise: On The Essence of Human Freedom*, trans. J. Stambaugh, London: Continuum.

Heidegger, M. (2005b), *Introduction to Phenomenological Research*, trans. D. O. Dahlstrom, Bloomington: Indiana University Press.

Levinas, E. (1969), *Totality and Infinity: An Essay on Exteriority*, trans. A. Lingis, Pittsburgh: Duquesne University Press.

Levinas, E. (1998), *Otherwise than Being; or Beyond Essence*, trans. A. Lingis, Pittsburgh: Duquesne University Press.

Levinas, E. (2000a), *Entre Nous*, trans. M. B. Smith, and B. Harshav, New York: Columbia University Press.

Levinas, E. (2000b), *Alterity and Transcendence*, trans. M. B. Smith, New York: Columbia University Press.

Levinas, E. (2001a), *Is it Righteous to be?*, trans. J. Robbins, Stanford: Stanford University Press.

Levinas, E. (2001b), *God, Death and Time*, trans. B. Bergo, Stanford: Stanford University Press.

Nietzsche, F. (1966), *Beyond Good and Evil*, trans. W. Kaufman, New York: Random.

Nietzsche, F. (1967), *On the Genealogy of Morals and Ecce Homo*, trans. W. Kaufman, New York: Random.

Nietzsche, F. (1968), *The Will to Power*, trans. W. Kaufman, and R. J. Hollingdale, New York: Vintage.

Nietzsche, F. (1974), *The Gay Science*, trans. W. Kaufman, New York: Random House.

Nietzsche, F. (1990), *The Twilight of the Idols and the Anti-Christ*, trans. R. J. Hollingdale, London: Penguin.

Sartre, J.-P. (1972), *The Philosophy of Jean-Paul Sartre*, (ed.) R. D. Cumming, New York: Vintage.

Sartre, J.-P. (1984), *Existentialism and Human Emotions*, trans. B. Frechtman, London: Citadel Press.

Sartre, J.-P. (1993), *Being and Nothingness: An Essay on Phenomenological Ontology*, trans. H. Barnes, Portland: Washington Square Press.

Sartre, J.-P. (2001), *Basic Writings*, (ed.) S. Preist, London: Routledge.

Political Philosophy

David B. Ingram and John Protevi

Introduction

Political philosophy as usually conceived has two branches. On the one hand, it addresses the concerns of already established political life: the moral justification of political authority, the limits of power in maintaining that authority, the rights and duties of citizens with respect to that power, and other such topics. On the other hand, it also addresses the ontology of political life: the basic concepts of human plurality, living in common in ordered societies, freedom, sovereignty, and the like. Continental political philosophers tend to deal with these topics somewhat differently from their Anglo-American (or analytic) counterparts. By and large, Continental political philosophers are more interested in a critical treatment of the second, ontological, branch, investigating the presuppositions underlying common conceptions of basic terms, and are less concerned with developing and applying principles of justice to already formed societies.

The difference between Continental and Anglo-American political philosophy, however, is deeper than the above contrast suggests and can be summed up accordingly: Continental philosophers believe that the presuppositions underlying basic political terms, and the practices that are said to instantiate them, have tended to focus on identity and should be recast as differential, as emerging from decentered and immanently organized fields or processes. Furthermore, many Continental philosophers believe these presuppositions favoring identity can best be uncovered by engaging the classical philosophical tradition extending from Plato through Nietzsche and Heidegger, though others prefer an analysis of contemporary practice.

The privilege of identity diagnosed by Continental thinkers extends to the very manner of thinking of political philosophers. Whereas many analytic political philosophers rely upon forms of reasoning and argumentation that take for granted the exclusive validity of logic and instrumental calculation in distinguishing unitary and fixed political concepts from one another, deriving subsidiary norms from conceptually more basic principles, and defending the scientific efficiency and consistency of political institutions which are thought to instantiate these basic principles, Continental political philosophers do not. Instead, they hold that such reasoning and argumentation is superficial – taking for granted the inherited privilege of identity which is precisely what needs to be further scrutinized – or, even worse, complicit with a conception of political life that is in some sense oppressive and dehumanizing. In the former instance, analytic reasoning is at best a necessary but insufficient method for clarifying identity-based political concepts and practices, and as such requires supplementation from dialectical, dialogical, or differential forms of synthetic reasoning which show the differential fields from which these concepts and practices emerge. In the latter instance, it is part and parcel of a total way of life – commonly associated with modern technology, science, and rational calculation – that is thought to supplant and subvert authentically human (and political) ways of existing by yoking them to pre-established forms of identity: the people forming a nation-state that controls a territory.

Historical Background: Hegel and Synthetic Reason

Continental political philosophy can be said to go back to Hegel's view (influenced by Kant) that analytic, identity-based reason is inherently self-defeating. Of supreme importance is Hegel's theory (already evident in criticisms developed by eighteenth-century counter-Enlightenment thinkers such as Vico and Rousseau) that the self-defeating nature of analytic reason first comes to the fore at the dawn of the modern age, when reason itself becomes widely disseminated throughout society. Exemplified in Descartes's demand that no belief be accepted as true unless proven to be certain, analytical reason encourages a radical questioning of all social norms and values. As Hegel saw, the kind of critical reflection implicit in reason prevents it from ceasing to question, so that no value or norm can be seen as self-justifying, or for that matter as containing within itself a complete and coherent signification that does not point to some reason or ground outside of it. Critical reason, then, defeats any attempt at arriving at a self-identical ground, dissolving all grounds into a differential field of mutually referring reasons.

Hegel believed that two responses follow from this conclusion, one superficial and false, the other profound and true. The superficial response is skepticism and what Nietzsche would later call nihilism (from the Latin *nihil*, or 'nothing'), the view that all meaning, purpose, and value is reduced to nothing – negated and contradicted by what should be its supporting ground. Difference is here seen as empty, as the nothing that results from negating the positive. Embracing this response, nihilists would urge us to affirm – without reason – the spontaneous creation of values out of nothing. However, what looks like a liberating gesture to the nihilist struck Hegel as anything but. For, if nothing has any rational meaning, purpose, and value, then 'everything is permitted.' To paraphrase Hegel, once values have been reflectively annihilated the only thing that remains absolutely certain (or so it seems) is the merely subjective ego, taken in abstraction from all meaning and higher purpose, save that of self-preservation. From difference conceived as negation springs a new identity, the ego, the subject. When this rational egoism insinuates itself throughout modern society – in the form of unrestrained capitalist greed and competition, bureaucratic 'will to power', and destructive scientific hubris in service to any cause – society itself becomes irrational, and political life, which presupposes mutual self-limitation as much as self-determination, is rendered otiose.

Hegel himself believed that the 'dialectic of enlightenment' (as Adorno and Horkheimer later dubbed it) can be circumvented. Difference need not be merely negative, empty, and nihilistic, but when properly, that is, dialectically conceived, it can be rational. The rational realization that no value, principle, institution, or reason is self-justifying and complete in meaning without supplementation from something that is other than and opposed to it need not issue in a hopeless contradiction or empty difference. Instead, it can lead us to understand the essential complementarity of opposed ideas as these are subsumed within a broader totality (or system) of coherent philosophical thought. Indeed, by showing that no idea (or institution) is complete without its opposing term, dialectical reason 'resolves' the conceptual oppositions created by analytic reason that generate skepticism about the rationality of political life in the first place.

In sum, Hegel thought that the dialectical movement of reason resolves the contradictions (or oppositions) that it itself creates. Ultimately, he thought that reason can do this by establishing a complete system (closed and stable circle) of mutually complementary reasons. (Many contemporary French philosophers believe that here Hegel retains an allegiance to identity beneath his dialectical method, that dialectic merely harnesses difference in service of an identity, albeit a complex one.) However, he believed that philosophical reasoning cannot demonstrate such a system unless the basic categories of reason have not already been fully actualized in concrete reality. In fact, Hegel held that the dialectic of reason is a historical process in which the contradictions implicit in political institutions are gradually worked out. More precisely, he believed that rational enlightenment initially engenders a society in which subjective freedom stands opposed to objective legal constraint. Society here vacillates between the anarchy of revolutionary fervor and unrestrained egoism, on one side, and totalitarian control and assimilation to the state, on the other. This contradiction, he believed, tends toward resolution with the advent of a liberal state that provides for both the general welfare and representation of all citizens – a perfect reconciliation of individual freedom, legal order and the general good.

Continental Philosophy: A Tradition Divided into Two Camps

Contemporary Continental political philosophers can be divided into two general camps: those who believe, with Hegel, that dialectical reason (or in a later development championed by Habermas, 'dialogical' reason) can provide a stable and equitable system of freedom and lawful constraint; and those who do not. At stake in this disagreement is the claim to legitimacy of modern societies themselves, understood as societies that have institutionalized dialectical reason in the form of procedures and activities that underwrite rational dialogue conceived as the very essence of democracy. Two responses are possible here: that of those who uphold dialogue, consensus, and communication as the essence of democracy, but find that our societies fall short of this ideal in demonstrable ways; and that of those who question the identities hidden in dialogue, consensus, and communication and favor still more differential definitions of democracy and justice.

Philosophers of postmodern temperament generally follow Nietzsche (and to a lesser extent, neo-Hegelian materialists, such as Marx) in denying that there is any deep system of dialectical reasoning that can conclusively demonstrate the inherently liberating and equalizing nature of democracy. For them, modern rational society and the political ideas that legitimate it are neither coherent nor emancipating. If anything, modern society threatens to assimilate its atomized subjects into a totalitarian system of efficient production and administration. By contrast, political philosophers of modern temperament believe that modernity and the legacy of European Enlightenment are not only emancipating but are capable – in principle, if not in current practice – of being fully actualized without contradiction.

Corresponding to these two camps of Continental philosophy, which we can tentatively call 'modern' versus 'postmodern,' are two methods of philosophizing: one derived from phenomenology and the other derived from structuralism. The former method begins with the lived experience of persons who more or less consciously understand their political lives, interlinked in dialogue, to be meaningfully structured by rational expectations regarding their own mutual freedom, equality, and orientation to agreement. This method translates Hegel's insights regarding dialectical reason into the register of real dialogue. The identities of individuals no less than the meanings of ideas are thus regarded as reciprocally constituted in a process of intersubjective communication that reconciles self and other. This is the approach taken by two of the most important German political philosophers of the last fifty years: Hannah Arendt and Jürgen Habermas.

The latter method explicitly rejects this approach in favor of what it perceives to be a more objective analysis of structures underlying social, economic, and political practice. These structures, however, are not regarded as fixed and stable, as classical structuralists maintain. Instead they are conceived as embodying historically shifting matrices of power and signification that are irreducibly differential. Each solution to the problem of society, that is, each existing society, is an actualization and hence a selection and limitation of this differential field, which remains in abeyance, as 'virtual' (Deleuze) or as 'to come' (Derrida), and hence defeats any attempt to construe actually existing societies as having fully instantiated a just society. Hence the kind of philosophy using this method is often referred to as 'poststructuralist,' or as the 'philosophy of difference.' This method also translates Hegel's insights regarding the dialectical nature of reason, but without Hegel's belief in the power of dialectic to reconcile opposed terms. A purely negative dialectic of this type (to borrow Adorno's phrase) 'deconstructs' (or dissolves) the stable meaning of ideas no less than the identity of persons, showing their genesis from differential processes in which certain 'constructions' of identity are privileged over others. Indeed, some philosophers of difference are outright materialists, who see that our very 'bodies politic,' both somatic and social, are constructions or congealings of underlying differential processes or material flows. One or the other of these approaches is taken by many prominent contemporary French political philosophers, including among others Jacques Derrida, Michel Foucault, Jean-François Lyotard, Gilles Deleuze, and Alain Badiou.

Arendt and the Phenomenological Tradition

Because poststructuralist and postmodernist varieties of political philosophy arose in reaction to phenomenological antecedents, it is appropriate to begin with them. The first and foremost exponent of phenomenological political philosophy is Hannah Arendt (1906–75). Arendt wrote on such diverse topics as totalitarianism, Zionism and the Jewish Question; the plight of stateless refugees, Adolph Eichmann and the nature of evil; the French and American Revolutions; Kant and the nature of judgement; the crisis of culture in mass society; the decline of the public sphere in the modern world; and above all, the nature of freedom and its relationship to political action. Her most important philosophical work is *The Human Condition* (1958), which reflects the seminal ideas of two of her former mentors: Karl Jaspers, whose philosophy of existence accords a central role to communication, and Martin Heidegger, whose phenomenological method purports to reveal the authentic meaning of human existence.

It is Heidegger's method that is especially pertinent to our present concerns. Heidegger appropriated this method from his mentor, Edmund Husserl, who had argued that our normal way of thinking about the things we experience in the world does not correspond to the way in which we actually experience them. We normally think that the things we experience are objects that stand in no essential relationship to other objects in the world or, for that matter, to the persons who experience them. On the contrary, what we directly experience are not self-standing objects but rather aspects of things, or appearances (phenomena), that flow into one another. Ultimately, the blending together of such aspects into a coherent, meaningful whole depends on the larger context (or horizon) of a world that is likewise experienced as coherent and meaningful. This world, in turn, derives its sense of order from the intentions of persons who perceive and engage it from unique experiential standpoints, which standpoints (or perspectives) likewise refer to one another.

The phenomenological method can be understood as recasting Hegel's point about dialectical reasoning at the level of direct experience: like the relationship between word and text, the meaning that any particular experienced object or event has for us is dependent upon a totality of shared background meanings and relationships, and vice versa. Not surprisingly, phenomenologists also shared Hegel's view about the moral and political implications of regarding experience in this way. 'I' am never alone in the world since my understanding of myself as occupying this utterly singular perspective depends upon the fact that others are with me (and I am with them) in constituting a shared world wherein perspectives first become meaningful. In contrast to the atomistic individualism touted by analytic political philosophy – which sees social relationships as voluntary agreements reached by persons who already possess a definite sense of their particular identities prior to any interrelationship – phenomenology insists that our individuality is inherently social in the way that it is experienced. Here we see a move back from an established identity – the subject – to the differential social field in which subjects are constituted. The natural attitude thus conceals our communal being in the same way that it conceals the con-textuality of the experienced world. But that is not all. The advent of modern analytical reason –

or more precisely, modern science and technology – has exaggerated this attitude to the point where human beings are experienced as mere objects and nothing more. Deprived of their social ground, values are reduced to the utterly singular will to power of individual subjects, who then try to implement them in the most technically efficient manner possible. Other human beings thus appear as obstacles or means within a calculus of instrumental control. In this manner nihilism conspires with political domination and totalitarian social engineering.

Arendt shares Heidegger's concern that the modern age's twin obsessions with science and technology, on one hand, and economic production and consumption, on the other, have concealed and endangered our authentic communal being. Both of them therefore return to a pre-modern political form – the ancient Greek *polis* – for clues in disclosing our communal being in its originality. However, whereas Heidegger thought that our communal ties are grounded in a collective cultural identity that confronts us as a kind of impersonal destiny, whose source resides in the mysterious workings of monumental artistic creativity in response to a 'call' or 'sending' of Being, Arendt believed that they are freely created by citizens engaged in democratic activity who confront one another as equal interlocutors, an insight taken up by post-Marxist French thinkers such as Claude Lefort, Cornelius Castoriadis and Jacques Rancière.

This difference would later take Heidegger and Arendt in opposite political directions. Heidegger's supreme estimation of the revelatory power of the lone thinker/poet/artist to found a new world and new community of being – coupled with his contempt for public opinion and political debate – led him to embrace the notion that a community of people represented a unified will and destiny that could not be represented by divisive parliamentary bodies. His acquiescence to the Nazi's *Führerprinzip* thus reflects the same kind of thinking implicit in the political philosophy of Carl Schmitt, the Nazi's chief philosopher of law. For Heidegger as well as Schmitt, the anarchic fragmentation of modern mass society created a political crisis in which the contrary voices echoing in legislative chambers yielded only 'idle talk' that could never produce the 'resolute decision' needed to recall the German *Volk* back to its proper will and unitary destiny. In Schmitt's philosophy, the general will necessary for legitimating democratic lawmaking (as Rousseau famously put it) could only be realized in the form of a dictatorial will empowered to restore sovereignty during times of supreme states of emergency.

Arendt's entire philosophy, by contrast, can be understood as a sustained argument against assimilating political activity to political sovereignty, conceived as a unified will imposing order from above (however much this order might be equated with some kind of primal will coursing through the subterranean collective consciousness of a people). Heidegger's mistake resided in elevating artistic creativity and its natural and instinctual genius to the supreme form of world-making and community-founding. In Arendt's opinion, however, such creativity is entirely derivative of a more fundamental world-making and community-founding, and seems in any case to reinforce, rather than oppose, the kinds of nihilistic tendencies that Heidegger criticized in Nietzsche. Artistic creation no less than economic production is an instrumental activity that can be undertaken in isolation and can therefore be assimilated to the objectifying will to dominate so characteristic of science and technology.

Arendt believed that the most authentic world-making and community-founding activity is political action understood precisely in the liberal democratic sense that Heidegger found so anarchic and irresolute. In political action a plurality of persons display their unique individuality in spontaneous and unpredictable response to one another and in so doing dialogically create a public space of meaning and value, and therewith a common world of appearance. So-called artistic creativity can serve to 'memorialize' these spoken deeds in permanent narratives and monuments, but it cannot substitute for them. Here again, we see one philosopher (Arendt) providing a differential field (human plurality) that underlies an identity-based action (Heidegger's lone artist grappling with the call of Being). (We are fully aware of the many contributions Heidegger has made to the thinking of difference, as well as the possible differential readings of his political thought, but we will maintain this reading as at least a plausible interpretation of the relation between Arendt and Heidegger.)

Arendt's tripartite distinction between cultural fabrication, economic production (labor), and political action underpins her theory of freedom, understood as a kind of singular eruption (or birth) interrupting the continuity of life. Whereas economic activity is necessitated by biological need and cultural fabrication re-interprets what has already happened, political action itself is characterized by initiating something totally new, unique, and distinctive – the stuff out of which histories are told. It is here – in Arendt's supreme estimation of human *natality* (or the existential need to unfold meaning and appearance out of nothing in response to others) – where we detect Arendt's own deep ambivalence with respect to modernity. The undermining of tradition and authority definitive of radical political rebirths doubtless generates a crisis of nihilism, but it also underscores our responsibility to act, or give ourselves new meaning and value, without relying upon the past or any other external or transcendent authority. This is doubtless why the French and American Revolutions intrigued Arendt so much: here, for the first time, we witness people trying to reconstitute their political identities – indeed, their very freedom – without any other foundation than their own voluntary consent. Some of this radical spontaneity, she believed, still existed in New England town hall meetings and Soviet worker councils. (Arendt's silence concerning the Haitian Revolution, which was by any account more radical than the French and American Revolutions, poses an interesting topic to examine.)

Despite her effusive praise of the American Revolution and its founding fathers, Arendt generally adopted a rather pessimistic and negative assessment of modern mass democracy. In contrast to the French Revolution, the American Revolution did not have to concern itself with the problem of widespread poverty. This enabled it to focus almost exclusively on establishing strong constitutional guarantees of individual freedom. However, this original neglect of the 'social question' did not save the new republic from having to deal with slavery and the race question; nor did it save the republic from its own obsession with commerce and economic progress – an obsession that would later lead to the growth of the social welfare state. For Arendt, the imperative to maintain economic growth invariably comes at the expense of political freedom; indeed, greater citizen participation imposes unpredictable and contradictory demands on government leaders that are viewed by them as severely limiting their capacity scientifically to manage social problems efficiently. Hence, government officials have a powerful incentive to either limit citizen participation to passive voting or manipulate it through propaganda. Either way, active and public deliberation is in some sense violated. But there is further danger in depoliticizing the citizenry. Once citizens are reduced to a passive mass of isolated atoms, nothing remains to resist the totalitarian tendency of the state to dominate all aspects of their lives.

In sum, Arendt's phenomenology of political action retains the existential core of Heidegger's philosophy, which emphasizes the radical contingency of political norms and institutions relative to historically situated human beings, while rejecting its cultural fatalism. However, it is precisely this relativism that seemed most problematic to political philosophers like Leo Strauss and Jürgen Habermas. According to Strauss, the humanism underlying existential political philosophy (including Heidegger's supposedly anti-humanistic variety) is inherently contradictory because it reduces political norms that supposedly condition and limit human political life to the transient practical aims that emerge within that life. In Arendt's case, if the voluntary consent of individuals engaged in democratic debate is the touchstone for determining the legitimacy of norms, then such consent would itself depend upon consent for its own legitimacy, with this latter being entirely uncertain. For Strauss, the political norms that condition political life must be regarded as in some sense transcendent and independent of human consent in precisely the sense understood by the ancients. Plato, for instance, understood that the norms regulating political life are universally valid in a way that essentially resists their practical implementation. As paradoxical as it might seem, such political ideas are not meant to guide reforms or revolutions but to limit them absolutely. True phenomenological political philosophy would thus be purely contemplative in this Platonic sense, and entirely antithetical to the spirit of modern political philosophy inaugurated by Machiavelli.

No doubt Strauss's view of political philosophy is deeply problematic and, in its own way, highly skeptical of liberal democracy. For him, only an elite cadre of philosophers can aspire to the revelation of an eternal natural law that, by its very nature, limits political life from the outside. But is this not just another way of reducing political philosophy to metaphysics, which effectively annihilates political freedom by reducing it to necessity?

Habermas's Discourse Ethics and the Defense of Democracy

Habermas's phenomenological political philosophy attempts to forge a middle path between Arendt's existentialism and Strauss's transcendentalism. Like Arendt, he sees no reason why modern, enlightened political agents would ever voluntarily submit to an authority that transcends their own rational powers of justification. For him, democratic consent that is freely given remains the touchstone for distinguishing violence from legitimately exercised power. However, like Strauss, he holds that existential relativism is self-contradictory and provides no limit on totalitarian excess. Indeed, mass democracy unrestrained by higher law can be tyrannical and even potentially totalitarian. Hence, in contrast to Arendt, he seeks to ground liberal democratic norms in the relatively permanent and universal expectations that are immanent within ordinary speech.

Habermas (1929–) is widely considered to be the most influential contemporary representative of the German school of critical social theory associated with the Frankfurt School. His capacious knowledge – ranging from linguistics, psychology, and social and political science to literature, law, history, theology, and philosophy – is reflected in his prolific publication record, which lists among its many book-length entries such notable tomes as *Knowledge and Human Interests* (1968); *Legitimation Crisis* (1973); *The Theory of Communicative Action: Volumes One and Two* (1985); *The Philosophical Discourse of Modernity* (1985); and *Between Facts and Norms* (1993).

The single most defining feature of Habermas's philosophy over the last forty years has been its reformulation of critical theory. Since the early 1930s, critical theory had been proclaimed as a unique synthesis of Marxian social science, Freudian psycho-analysis, and philosophy that extolled the power of rational enlightenment to free people from false and oppressive ideologies. However, by the 1940s the leading exponents of critical theory – most notably Max Horkheimer, Theodor Adorno, and Herbert Marcuse – had come to doubt the viability of this program. In their opinion, modern capitalism increasingly identifies enlightenment with the analytic reason definitive of science and technology, which uncritically lends itself to social engineer-ing in service to dominant economic and political elites. Under this regime, 'mass democracy' becomes but an instrument of totalitarian manipulation, no different from the illusory freedom of consumers whose choices are all pre-selected and psycholo-gically conditioned by the powers that be. For Marcuse, the only critical response to the 'repressive desublimation' of a system that equates freedom with a consumerism enslaved to oppressive toil, servitude, and self-marketing is a 'great refusal' to participate in the system in any capacity.

Habermas rejects this pessimistic diagnosis and offers a more hopeful understanding of the limits and possibilities of progressive political change within modern liberal democracy. Like Hegel, he believes that the constraining features of modern liberal democracy, such as a market system and administrative bureaucracy, can be under-stood to 'liberate' persons from the need to co-ordinate all aspects of their lives. At the same time, he concedes – up to a point – the concern expressed by his predecessors, that this system of economic and legal necessity can swallow up (or colonize) the public and private spheres of everyday life in which people do democratically co-ordinate their lives.

Unlike his predecessors, then, Habermas extols democracy as an institution capable of realizing the freedom and equality of citizens. Although he defends formal representative democracy as a necessary intermediary between state administration and civil society, he insists that the real locus of democracy resides within civil society itself, or more precisely, in those 'public spheres' where problems are first raised and debated. However, in order to defend this 'informal' type of democracy, he must show that the kind of communication that occurs in everyday debate and discussion embodies a form of rationality that is distinctly dialectical rather than analytical.

Following Arendt's lead, Habermas distinguishes the analytic rationality implicit in work and other forms of instrumental activity from the dialogical rationality implicit in everyday speech and political life, holding that the latter is the more original source of meaning, value, and identity. He goes beyond her, however, in holding that argumentative speech, or discourse, implies certain universal norms of 'ideal speech.' Communicative rationality consists in the concerted effort to reach impartial and unconstrained agreement over contested claims. Agreement is impartial and unconstrained, however, only to the extent that all persons affected by the disputed claim are included in the conversation, and everyone has equal chances to speak, free from internal (ideological) and external pressures. Habermas thus concludes that universal freedom and justice are implicit in the very communicative rationality towards which all communicative interaction aspires.

Together with his colleague Karl-Otto Apel, Habermas has developed a new paradigm of ethical reasoning – what they call 'discourse ethics' – around these presuppositions (which Apel believes are necessary and universal for the very possibility of speech). Discourse ethics designates an approach to ethics that appeals to models of free, equal, undistorted, and inclusive communication as a touchstone for moral deliberation. Its major claim is that moral deliberation is a collective process of reasoning that is best exemplified in democratic forums. In this respect it is quite antithetical to modes of moral deliberation – for example, approaches that appeal directly to the 'inner voice' of moral conscience, reason, natural sentiment, or divine revelation – that take as their point of departure the lone individual who relies for guidance solely on subjective and highly unreliable moral feelings and judgements. Such feelings and judgements no doubt guide our actions, but discourse ethics recommends that they be shaped and transformed in ongoing discussions with others who feel and think differently, for only they provide a critical check on our irrational and otherwise contentious opinions. Even in the moment of decision, when discussion has ceased and they must act, persons should always try to imagine how others – those actually affected by their decisions as well as the 'ideal' community of humanity – would regard their choice. This raises two important qualifications in the application of discourse ethics. First, discourse ethics works best in political forums, in which persons are deliberating together about shared norms of social co-operation. For discourse ethics, only norms that have the general and uncoerced consent of all are truly binding for each taken individually. Second, discourse ethics sharply distinguishes 'sub-rational' discussions whose resolutions are 'constrained' and less binding from those that approximate the conditions of ideal speech.

Some of Habermas's most critical applications of discourse ethics concern the way in which capitalism threatens ethical and political life at its core. In *Legitimation Crisis*, for instance, he argues that the principal contradiction of the welfare state – using public revenue to sustain capitalist growth while simultaneously compensating the victims of such growth – can only be successfully managed by encouraging depoliticized masses oriented toward private consumption to defer uncritically to directives issued by appointed technological-administrative elites. In the *Theory of Communicative Action*, he observes how areas of domestic and public life oriented toward socialization and critical discussion have become increasingly 'colonized' by more instrumental and functional forms of rationality associated with the marketplace and legal bureaucracy. More recently, he has deftly analyzed the tension between neo-liberal policies associated with globalization and the capacity of liberal democracies to control their economic destinies and provide education, health, and welfare services to their citizens.

The (French) Philosophy of Difference: After May 1968

Sartre and Merleau-Ponty: The Constraints of an Existential Politics

In founding the influential journal *Les Temps Modernes* after World War II, Sartre and Merleau-Ponty – along with Beauvoir – were among the pre-eminent political philosophers of their time in France. Both had recently published monumental works in existential phenomenology – *Being and Nothingness* and *Phenomenology of Perception*, respectively – and both now turned to face the challenge of articulating an existential politics. That meant finding a way to counter the tendency of modern bureaucratic states to treat masses of political subjects statistically and hence finding a way to think the singularity of political subjects. For both, the key question was Marxism, especially 'actually existing socialism.'

For Sartre, the theoretical high point of his political philosophy was undoubtedly his *Critique of Dialectical Reason* (1960), but we should not neglect his important championing of Fanon and other Third World revolutionaries. Sartre's *Critique* – as the Kantian echo of the title was meant to imply – was a monumental attempt to envisage the reconciliation of individual freedom and group solidarity. For Sartre, the dispersion and atomization of reified individuals in modern capitalism can only be overcome in revolutionary praxis – which aims at a total reconfiguration of the material conditions that contribute to reification (the 'practico-inert'). If the appeal to 'totalization without totality' reveals Sartre's humanistic double-bind – caught between the determinism ('slime,' as Sartre put it) of objective history and the freedom of the subject – his appeal to social praxis reveals his anti-humanistic anticipation of a poststructural overcoming of 'man' as such. The revolutionary 'group-in-fusion' cannot achieve its end – the overcoming of scarcity and the achievement of freedom – without imposing discipline in the form of 'fraternity terror' and party bureaucracy. This return to 'serial' dispersion amidst domination – aptly summarized by Merleau-Ponty's dictum that 'revolutions are true as movements but false as regimes' – anticipates Foucault's later thinking and, above all, Deleuze's.

Merleau-Ponty deepens his critique of Marxist societies from the time of *Humanism and Terror* (1947) to that of *Adventures of the Dialectic* (1955). The first maintains some hope that Soviet terror might come to acknowledge itself; the second, written after the Korean War, leaves Marxism behind for a modified liberalism which rejects any mechanistic or objectivist philosophy of history. Merleau-Ponty's positive political philosophy seeks to articulate 'political virtue' whereby a leader is neither wholly transcendent nor merely a follower of the will of the people. As always with Merleau-Ponty, it is the middle, where elements cross in a 'chiasm,' which is the key to thought. Leaders must work in an institution that empowers others; they must be part of an open-ended historical project that allows space for democratically articulated discord, a space that must be extended to include all members of society as they put forth rights claims to the community.

Castoriadis and Lefort: Radical Democracy and the Critique of Transcendence

Merleau-Ponty's critique of the Stalinist USSR is picked up by these thinkers, whom we will treat together in this context, notwithstanding important differences in their mature work. Both Castoriadis and Lefort are concerned with articulating a notion of radical democracy by means of a critique of transcendence. They were founders of *Socialisme ou Barbarie*, an influential non-communist left organization journal in the 1950s. In their criticism of the Stalinist USSR, they did not merely see it, as the Trotskyites would have it, as a bureaucratic distortion of a worker's state. Rather, they diagnosed in the USSR an attempt to escape the radically immanent and differential field that is democracy by erecting a transcendent body that would unify the field from its self-present position above and beyond the field. In such a unified field, discord must come from outside, setting up the scapegoating of Jews, revisionists, and so on. In contrast, democracy is precisely the affirmation of discord and difference as the life of politics.

Lyotard and Baudrillard: The Excluded

Both these thinkers focus on what is excluded in capitalist society, in which abstract time is the measure of value for all things, providing universal exchange via the medium of money. For Baudrillard, such equivalence-based exchange excludes symbolic exchange, as exemplified in potlatch practices. The extreme gift destabilizes social relations, destroying equivalence by creating a debt that can never• be made whole. In fact, the one who refuses to up the ante with an even more extreme counter-gift faces social death: shame, ostracism, slavery, exile. In contrast, modern capitalism has us all facing a slow death on the installment plan as we are nibbled away with the presentation of each month's credit card bill and our lives are statistically analyzed and filed away in the mausoleum of the database. But making our equivalence exchange society face societies and practices of inordinate, nonequivalent, symbolic exchange will bring about its death. A death, Baudrillard claims with shocking insouciance, symbolized when the twin towers of the World Trade Center 'imploded,' sucking the suicide planes into their collapse.

Lyotard's diagnosis of capitalism is at once less apocalyptic and less pessimistic in tone than Baudrillard's, since it moves within a series of philosophical frames that depict in various ways the eruption of an ineluctable remainder – the speech acts and oppositional gestures that inevitably inhabit the margins of any dominant economic, political, or cultural paradigm. Lyotard's lifelong fascination with these revolutionary counter-cultural currents can be traced back to his youthful affiliation in the 1950s with the anti-Stalinist, ultra-left movement *Socialisme ou Barbarie*. Yet his political avant-gardism did not reach its mature philosophical stride until the publication of his first major work, *Discours, figure* (1971), which can be understood as a phenomenological defense (in the spirit of Maurice Merleau-Ponty) of the irreducibility of images – here conceived as repositories of wild, polymorphous desires – in the face of the normative straitjackets imposed by the laws of logic and language. Following this critique of Lacanian psychoanalytic structuralism, Lyotard abruptly switched gears and wrote

The Libidinal Economy (1974), which bears the indelible influence of Deleuze's and Guattari's Nietzschean critique of Freud in their masterpiece *Anti-Oedipus* (see below). Proposing a libidinal monism that reduces 'the great ephemeral theater' of all mental, linguistic, and economic structures to wild desire, Lyotard defended the explosive, revolutionary potential of the very polymorphous intensities generated by consumer capitalism itself.

Lyotard's last great works, *The Postmodern Condition* (1979) and *The Differend* (1983), seem to reverse direction once again in their sober investigation of such traditional philosophical themes as truth, knowledge, justice, and the beautiful (and sublime). These works move restlessly between the two antipodal positions staked out by his earlier work: an insistence on quasi-logical incommensurabilities – above all, the irreducibility of modern artistic gestures and all marginal forms of discourse to the established, hegemonic paradigms – and a countervailing insistence on the inevitable impurity and paralogical eruption of spontaneous and oppositional (or contestatory) gestures within any discourse or system, including those of science and capitalism. Although Lyotard hesitates to embrace majoritarian democracy because of its potentially tyrannical and totalitarian abuses, these late works are infused by a certain populist, democratic ardor. By challenging the presumption that political, economic, and cultural systems possess a coherent and self-contained, top–down rationale or logic, they open the way for a more inclusive, more egalitarian, more spontaneous, and more dynamic participation in economic, political, and cultural systems from the 'grass roots.' Although Lyotard insists that expanding popular participation in the circulation of knowledge, public opinion formation, and political power cannot legitimate these systems and their outcomes, he nonetheless allows that it might make them less unjust; indeed he conjectures that it might even bestow upon them a measure of 'legitimation,' if by that term we mean the postmodern disruption of the hegemonic by the singular and novel.

Lyotard's late works focus mainly on the structure of speech in order to establish these political conclusions. *The Postmodern Condition* draws heavily on Wittgenstein's speech act theory, which breaks spoken language down into discrete 'language games,' each of which is governed by its own rules. According to Lyotard, the 'consensus' regarding the rules of the game is always fleeting, since it can – and eventually will – be challenged by an interlocutor. The 'agonal' nature of speech seems to mean that all norms are open to interpretation – at least at the margins – and this postmodern condition affects all language games. Lyotard also draws upon Kant's 'antinomies of reason' to show why the divided (contestatory) nature of everyday speech must replicate itself in the reflexive structure of formal and scientific (theoretical) language games, which aspire to a status of rational completeness and self-foundedness. He here cites Goedel's theorem, which proves that no system of logic can derive axioms in a manner that is simultaneously consistent and determinate; Heisenberg's principle of uncertainty, which proves that the location and direction of subatomic particles is indeterminate with respect to the scientific observer; and Kuhn's theory of scientific revolutions, which shows that rational inquiry guided by theoretical paradigms produces anomalies that cannot be explained by it and that inevitably lead to scientific dissension.

The Postmodern Condition is a frontal attack on all those grand legitimating narratives to which Westerners have had recourse in seeking to reassure themselves of the rational origins and ends of modernity against the contingencies of the utterly parochial, unpredictable, and singular happenings that ultimately shape our 'destinies.' Politically speaking, this philosophy of postmodern contingency and rupture proffers neither utopian hope nor cynical resignation but critical vigilance for the marginalized and an openness toward the unexpected. The common good cannot be realized under postmodern conditions, because these conditions prevent it from being scientifically or (contra Habermas) dialogically adduced. For this reason, positive visions of happiness and justice are potentially totalitarian. The only acceptable alternative is a 'paralogical' form of polity that aims at avoiding the 'greatest harm' by ensuring complete accessibility, openness, and contestation of any consensus. Temporary contracts and computer democracy are the political forms that Lyotard finds most compatible with this negative vision.

The Differend radicalizes this vision further by underscoring the tragic injustice built into any discourse. Extending the political paradigm of language games further, Lyotard argues that, judged by the rules of modern (rational) logic, every discourse involves linking types of phrasal regimes that possess incompatible aims. Here, contradiction issues in suppression: the weaker and dissident voice must be ignored, passed over, or 'silenced.' The result is a linguistic injustice (what Lyotard calls a *differend*) in which the claim of a plaintiff cannot be expressed within any of the officially recognized languages. For instance, taking the discourse of democratic legitimation as a model, Lyotard observes that the prescriptive judgements of judges, elected officials, and petty bureaucrats, which are framed in terms of scientific and technological expertise, will always 'co-opt' the abstract norms of justice embedded in the constitution and statutory law, thereby 'silencing' a potentially critical voice. Something like this, he notes, also happens on a mundane level, as when Holocaust survivors are called upon to bear witness to the factual existence of death camps; when workers are called upon to define their laboring activity as a commodity in the language of the wage contract; and when Native Americans are called upon to treat their ancestral lands as 'private property' in accordance with prevailing legal definitions. The only appropriate response to these differends is to expand the scope of acceptable speech acts within the dominant lingua franca, thereby fashioning a new language, a new discourse. But the incapacity of any language to do justice to the injustices of linguistic life will ultimately require a moral gesture that Kant fully recognized in speaking of the symbolic power of sublime works of art indirectly to represent what is unpresentable.

Derrida: Deconstruction and Aporia

In looking at Derrida's career, many people claim to see a political turn with the 1989 essay 'Force of Law.' So on this reading, the early Derrida is concerned with metaphysics and literature and the later Derrida with politics and ethics. This is misleading. The concerns have always been to reveal the workings of difference in both the metaphysical/literary and political/ethical registers at once, but the way in which that revelation works changes: from deconstruction to aporia.

The early Derrida follows Heidegger in seeing the history of philosophy as the history of texts whose surface allegiance is to presence. This is what they call 'metaphysics.' That is, traditional philosophy tries to ground difference – the world – in a single, self-identical point outside the world: the Good beyond Being for Plato, the Prime Mover of Aristotle, the God of the medieval theologians, and so on. (It should go without saying that this sort of childish shorthand bears no relation to the exemplary rigor of Derrida's own readings.) The reading that reveals such an allegiance to presence is called 'deconstruction.' Its job is to show that the supposedly self-present point outside the world is only a projection, a desire to escape difference. Derrida calls a structure of difference a 'text', so his famous pronouncement in *Of Grammatology* (1967) 'There is nothing outside the text' ('*Il n'y a pas de hors-texte*') simply means 'There's nothing outside the world.' In other words, we cannot make appeals to some transcendent source of meaning: we have to figure it out ourselves down here on earth. This is ontology, though not metaphysics: it describes the structure of being, that identities are constructed from a differential field, but does not ground them in a self-present world-transcendent being. Such an ontological commitment to difference has nothing to do with word–play or with being trapped in language. A text is not simply a book, it is a differential field.

Furthermore, for Derrida philosophical texts in the restricted sense of 'book' are also indices of political structures. We study them to get at the structures, not solely for their own sakes. Another way of saying this is to say we study the way they have been read badly, for Derrida quickly dropped the idea that the orientation to presence is the author's intention. Instead, the orientation to presence becomes one way to read the text, and the demonstration of the role of difference – that is, deconstruction – becomes another reading linked to the first. The political question is: why have the presence-oriented readings of the great books been dominant? What happens when such readings are shown, by deconstruction, to be politically motivated? Here we see that deconstruction is a response to, an affirmation of, political struggles against those systems pledged to presence: the purity of master races, the divine plans that guarantee a land to a people, the march of mankind to the end of history, the civilizing process that will lift up the savages, the development that will help the poor, and so on. Thus Derrida will say, 'Deconstruction is a maximum intensification of a process already under way.' Deconstruction is an academic echo of political struggles against racism, patriarchy, colonialism, capitalism. Or, we should say, since the academy is part of the political machine, deconstruction is directly political from the start: this isn't just academics flattering themselves, because it matters that when racists or patriarchs or colonists or capitalists claim their exploitation follows the word of God or the laws of nature or the science of economics, that we can show how these claims are construc-tions, not divine, natural, or scientific; that they rest on violence and force, not on reason.

So, because after 1989 Derrida began directly addressing justice, friendship, hospitality, cosmopolitanism, forgiveness, rogue states, and the like, it does not mean that he was not always already political. But there is a difference after 1989: Derrida began thematizing his work as revealing 'aporia,' as the call to undergo the 'experience of the impossible.' We will illustrate the thought of aporia with the category of justice;

the 'logic' holds for all Derrida's political concepts addressed after 1989. Justice is impossible: it must both have reference to past judgements and yet not be mere application of precedent; it must be reasoned and yet not be mere calculation; it must take all the time needed to consider all angles and yet it must do justice here and now to the singular case before it. Justice is the impossible: it is undeconstructible (only the possible, that which owes allegiance to presence, can be deconstructed), and it is precisely this impossibility that orients us, forbids us being satisfied with the state of affairs. The focus on aporia holds the future open, shows us the irreducible nature of the 'to come' ('*à venir*' is a play on the French word for 'future,' which is '*avenir*'). Justice has not arrived, even though there are always those who want to tell us not to bother to struggle any more, we already have justice, it has already arrived. But it has not arrived, and we do not simply wait for justice to come, we struggle for it, and only because it never arrives *can* we struggle for it.

Foucault and Deleuze: Micro and Macropolitics

We can approximate the difference between Deleuze's thought and that of Foucault like this: for Foucault, power – the relation of free subjects, action on the action of others – permeates the social field, provoking resistance everywhere; for Deleuze, creative desire is primary, and power relations follow afterwards, trying to rein in experimental 'lines of flight.'

Foucault's most overtly political book is *Discipline and Punish* (1975), where he locates in 'disciplinary practices' the underside of the Enlightenment project that would allow social freedom by promoting the minimal government of liberalism. Here we see an implicit dialogue with Marx. Disciplinary practices are not simply observation – as we might think based on all the attention given to the figure of the Panopticon – but also testing, evaluation, and rehabilitation, which together form practices of 'normalization' conducted in a social field Foucault calls 'micropolitics.' States can now manage a population by comparing individuals to a norm arrived at by statistical analysis of vast numbers of dossiers containing the results of all the tiny observations, tests, evaluations, and rehabilitations. Such a micropolitical field promotes a self-policing that disperses power throughout society in the differential field formed by the relations among doctors and patients, parents and children, teachers and students, bosses and workers, officers and soldiers.

This dispersed and hidden micropolitical power is much more effective than the concentrated and spectacular macropolitical power of the *ancien régime*. It is not that Foucault denies the importance of studying and coming to grips with state power, he simply denies that the state is the sole locus of power. The macropolitics of disciplinary societies is in fact underpinned by the micropolitics of disciplinary practices that form 'docile bodies.' The net result is that discipline allows for collaborative production while making collaborative politics all the more difficult by atomizing citizens, thereby undercutting Marx's hope that socialized production would lead to socialized politics. And with the advent of the micropolitical differential field that underpins the identity of subjects and the state, Foucault claims in the first volume of *The History of Sexuality* (1976), that we find a shift in the historical project of politics: no longer that of the sovereign power of kings, the political project is now one of 'biopolitics.' The project of macropolitics is now the management of the micropolitical field that aims at the fostering of productive life.

At the end of his career, in the last two volumes of his *History of Sexuality* project (1984), Foucault moved to investigating reflexive subject formation practices. Whereas previously he had studied how people are 'made a subject of' a discursive or nondiscursive practice (in the sense of being 'subjected to' such a practice), he now looks at reflexive practices of subject formation, what he calls 'techniques of the self.' Although he looks to the Greeks and Romans for examples of such practices, he is by no means advocating the simple adoption of their practices. Rather, he calls upon us to find ways that would resist our being subjected to dominating practices and would enable us to form networks of subjects engaged not simply in self-fashioning, but also in projects that produce the communal support structures that allow for self-fashioning.

Deleuze's work with his collaborator Guattari also relies upon the distinction of micro and macropolitics, but from the perspective of productive desire rather than that of power. 'Desire' is not subjective for Deleuze and Guattari, as they make clear in *Anti-Oedipus* (1972), their no-holds-barred attack on the tame Marx-Freud synthesis they found ridiculously lacking in the wake of May 1968. Rather, desire is the very force of natural creation. Far from romantics, Deleuze and Guattari insist in their follow-up volume, *A Thousand Plateaus* (1980), that the nonhuman and natural arena of desire doesn't detract from the fact that all desire is 'machined,' that is, arises with the passage of material flows between organs of bodies coupled and decoupled according to either natural or social codes and territories or capitalist 'axiomatics.' To be more precise, all production, 'natural' and 'social' alike, is patterned by processes of coding *and* decoding, reterritorializing and deterritorializing (Deleuze and Guattari consider genetic drift as natural decoding). The differential field that would be the limit of decoding and deterritorializing, in which all flows are free, is named by them the 'Body without Organs' (BwO) or 'socius.' It's important to remember that the insistence on 'machines' shows us that Deleuze and Guattari are no mere flow enthusiasts: purely free flows on the BwO does not yield production but precisely 'anti-production.' The BwO, as purely differential field, is virtual: any actual social machine is a selection from this field which remains to haunt the actual selection as its 'roads not taken.'

Social codes can be either territorial, tying production to the earth, as in 'primitive' hunter-gatherer societies, or deterritorialized in an empire that 'overcodes' the tribal codes and subjects them to agriculture. Instead of production being tied to the earth and codes marked on bodies in the scars and tattoos of initiation rites, imperial production is tied to the body of the despot, who is in turn often directly connected to a sky god. Imperial signification is no longer bodily, but now takes the form of the signifier: that which allows translation between the tribal languages and the imperial language. All this is overturned however, with capitalism, which, Deleuze and Guattari claim, is the realm of decoded and deterritorialized flows which tribal and imperial societies have always tried to conjure. With their analysis of capitalist axiomatics Deleuze and Guattari are also able to indicate the ways in which we have already begun our exit from a purely disciplinary society of the type described by Foucault – an exit of which Foucault himself was perfectly aware. An axiomatic is a set of basic principles that dispenses with exact codings of each transaction in favor of a general guidance. Capitalist axiomatics sets loose a 'schizophrenizing' desire in which we break free of all the old codes: 'Connect any organs you want!' But this 'deterritorializing' desire is immediately reterritorialized onto relations of private property. 'Connect any organs you want, as long as you turn a profit!' In such a situation, the state becomes simply the way in which capitalist relations are protected: contracts enforced, strikes broken, markets enlarged. But having loosed the tiger of desire, states are always reacting, macropolitics always chasing after micropolitical experimentation or 'lines of flight.'

To become more flexible, then, in chasing after and reterritorializing desire or experiment, capitalist society is no longer disciplinary, Deleuze explains in a late essay (Deleuze 1990), but has become a 'control society.' We no longer move from one total institution to the next in a simple line that traces our life trajectory: home, school, army, job, and hospital. Rather, with working while at school and with constant retraining while on the job, with part-time military commitments while at school and at work ('one weekend a month' the US National Guard promised – pre-Iraq, that is), with constant advertising injunctions to try this or that medicine, we are now student, worker, soldier, and patient all at once and all the time. The micropolitical field is all the more dispersed and fine-grained now that it has seeped out of institutions to form 'dividuals,' that is, people whose statistical images captured in multiple databases are simply perspectives dedicated to one aspect of our behavior or the other: automobile driver, camera buff, music fan . . . Of course, an old-fashioned complete dossier can be formed by collating this dispersed data – an individual can be formed again from its 'dividual' dispersion – but this is a latent or virtual potential rarely actualized, although the awareness that it can be so formed does have docilizing effects.

Badiou: Metapolitics and Radical Egalitarianism

Insofar as Alain Badiou's philosophy is the most important ongoing project in contemporary French philosophy, it is fitting that we end with a discussion of his work. Not enough of his work has been translated for him to have a significant presence in the Anglophone world, but this will no doubt change as more of his work appears in translation. For Badiou, mathematics is the science of being qua being. As with many of our French thinkers, here we see a step back from identity to a differential field, or as Badiou would put it, a step back from structure into multiplicity. Being as multiplicity is void or empty, without structure. The event is the disruption of structure: it is revolution, the disruption of the normal state of affairs. The event is composed of all the unnameable immanent triggers of a revolution, plus the name that makes it a 'one': 'the Haitian Revolution.' As such it is the foundation of truth and ethics: subjects are bound to events by their fidelity to the thought or project named by the event. The Haitian revolutionaries become such by their commitment to the cause. In such a commitment, a generic subject is formed; generic, because all people must be able to be subjects to the thought announced in the event. In this way, equality is the principle of politics, which does not seek to justify it or derive it from either empirical investigation or principled argument. (Although their projects differ in many basic areas, Badiou shares his radical egalitarianism with an important French political philosopher space constraints preclude us from discussing here, Jacques Rancière.) Politics, then, as the formation of a generic subject through fidelity to a revolutionary event, is a 'procedure of truth' and hence one of the 'conditions' of philosophy. Philosophy, then, can only be a 'metapolitics' that reflects on the truths produced in political action. Badiou's thought is quite dense and interconnected and a brief résumé of this type cannot do it justice, but the event that occurs through the challenge his thought poses to the 'usual' way of doing French poststructuralist philosophy promises to be among the most important features of the current scene.

References

Agamben, G. [1995] (1998), *Homo Sacer*, Stanford University Press.

Arendt, H. [1958] (1998), *The Human Condition*, Chicago: University of Chicago Press.

Badiou, A. [1998] (2005), *Metapolitics*, trans. J. Baker, London: Verso.

Baudrillard, J. [1976] (1993), *Symbolic Exchange and Death*, trans. I. Hamilton Grant, Thousand Oaks: Sage.

Castoriadis, C. (1998), *The Imaginary Institution of Society*, trans. K. Blamey, Cambridge: MIT Press.

Deleuze, G. (1990), 'Postscript on Control Societies,' in G. Deleuze (1990), *Negotiations*, trans. M. Joughin, New York: Columbia University Press, pp. 177–82.

Deleuze, G., and F. Guattari [1972] (1980), *Anti-Oedipus: Capitalism and Schizophrenia*, trans. R. Hurley, M. Seem, and H. R. Lane, Minneapolis: University of Minnesota Press.

Deleuze, G., and F. Guattari [1972] (1980), *A Thousand Plateaus: Capitalism and Schizophrenia*, trans. B. Massumi, Minneapolis: University of Minnesota Press.

Derrida, J. (1997), *Politics of Friendship*, trans. G. Collins, London: Verso.

Foucault, M. [1975] (1995), *Discipline and Punish*, trans. A. Sheridan, New York: Vintage.

Foucault, M. [1976] (1990), *History of Sexuality*, vol. 1, New York: Vintage.

Habermas, J. [1973] (1975), *Legitimation Crisis*, trans. T. McCarthy, Boston: Beacon Press.

Habermas, J. [1985] (1987), *Theory of Communicative Action*, 2 vols, Boston: Beacon Press.

Hegel, G. W. F. (1991), *Elements of the Philosophy of Right*, trans. H. B. Nisbet, Cambridge: Cambridge University Press.

Heidegger, M. (2000), *Introduction to Metaphysics*, trans. G. Fried, and R. Polt, Cambridge: Yale University Press.

Kant, I. [1970] (1991), *Political Writings*, trans. H. B. Nisbet, Cambridge: Cambridge University Press.

Lefort, C. (1986), *The Political Forms of Modern Society*, trans. J. Thompson, Cambridge: MIT Press.

Lyotard, J.-F. (1971), *Discours, figure*, Paris: Klincksieck.

Lyotard, J.-F. [1979] (1984), *The Postmodern Condition*, trans. G. Bennington, and B. Massumi, Minneapolis: University of Minnesota Press.

Lyotard, J.-F. [1974] (1993), *The Libidinal Economy*, trans. I. H. Grant, Bloomington: Indiana University Press.

Lyotard, J.-F. [1979] (1988), *The Differend*, trans. G. van den Abbele, Minneapolis: University of Minnesota Press.

Marcuse, H. [1964] (1991), *One-Dimensional Man*, Boston: Beacon Press.

Merleau-Ponty, M. [1947] (1990), *Humanism and Terror*, trans. J. O'Neill, Boston: Beacon Press.

Nietzsche, F. (1994), *On the Genealogy of Morality*, trans. K. Ansell-Pearson, Cambridge: Cambridge University Press.

Rancière, J. (1988), *Disagreement: Politics and Philosophy*, Minneapolis: University of Minnesota Press.

Sartre, J.-P. [1960] (2004), *Critique of Dialectical Reason*, trans. A. Sheridan-Smith, London: Verso.

Schmitt, C. [1932] (1996), *The Concept of the Political*, trans. G. Shwab, Chicago: University of Chicago Press.

Strauss, L. [1959] (1988), *What is Political Philosophy?*, Chicago: University of Chicago Press.

Feminist Philosophy

Emilia Angelova

Continental feminist philosophy is a movement of thought unified by the theme of the difference of woman and the difference of the feminine. But it is by no means monolithic in method or content. It begins with Simone de Beauvoir's existentialist feminism in the 1940s. For de Beauvoir, the free transcendence of the 'independent woman' wrests her from linear history and orients her to something more than equal rights for man and woman, something more than egalitarian ideals. With May 1968 a new phase of French feminist theory began, bringing along with it aesthetic experiences, influences from deconstruction, psychoanalysis and literature. The theory of *l'écriture féminine* emerged in this phase, calling for a specifically feminine language for expressing woman's sexual difference. Since the 1980s, a new generation of multicultural feminism has turned to sexual, biological, physiological, and reproductive differences, but also to the question of the symbolic role of woman. This question combines the sexual with the socio-symbolic and the racial, inquiring into the specificity of the feminine and then the specificity of each woman. Race, gender, religion, critique of socialist ideology, utopia and 'philosophies of difference' have become the new topics in the study of woman's desire for affirmation and creativity. The outstanding problem confronting feminism as liberational project in the wake of postmodernism is this: how to make the difference of woman and femininity visible without erasing it or essentializing it – how to make difference appear without sentencing it to disappear.

This chapter focuses on Simone de Beauvoir, Luce Irigaray and Julia Kristeva as figures central to the first two generations of Continental feminism. This leads to discussion of different feminisms in the third generation.

Transcendence and Immanence in de Beauvoir's Existentialist Feminism

De Beauvoir's *The Second Sex* ([1949] 1989) places the question about woman and the feminine on an existentialist ground, a ground brought to view in Sartre's *Being and Nothingness* (1943). To understand de Beauvoir, it is therefore crucial to understand some of Sartre's existentialist tenets – and to understand the difference between their two versions of existentialism.

Sartre's postwar existentialism liberates individual existence from the chains of metaphysical essence. To exist is to precede oneself in a manner that escapes the positive claims of knowledge or self-knowledge. Sartre rethinks Husserlian phenomenology and posits that, while essences can be known, they are neither ontological nor epistemological: they are existentially produced. The production of essence, a being-in-itself, depends upon an existential source, namely, the being of consciousness. Sartre thus places the negating act of consciousness at the very ground of being. The being of consciousness precedes knowledge, yet not as a being-in-itself, but only as act, as being-for-itself. Being-for-itself thus puts its own being into question. But being-for-itself is dependent upon what lies outside it, it depends on something other than itself, a being-in-itself. Consciousness thus presents the self with a nauseating crisis, for I am my authentic possibility only if I am free constantly to put my being and everything else into question. To be is to be free to question tradition, pre-established attitudes, normative values, as well as one's own expectations and projects.

For Sartre, the crisis that looms in this radical questioning is staved off by bad faith, a metastable state or attitude through which consciousness hides from questioning and disowns its being as negating act. De Beauvoir's existentialism places bad faith at the center of the study of woman, but crucially transforms Sartre's conception of bad faith by questioning the origins that Sartre assigns it. In the Sartrean account, being-for-others exposes the self to the judgement of the Other (that is, to shame), which alienates the self from itself and reduces it to an 'object' in the world of the Other. This induces a crisis of consciousness and the flight into bad faith. Instead of committing to being-for-itself, consciousness vacillates between being-for-itself and being-for-others. It thereby opens a negative possibility, a peculiar flight of consciousness from being-for-others and into a lie about itself, a lie that reduces the self to a thing, a being-in-itself. We 'lie' to ourselves, telling ourselves that we are free, at the very same moment that we put freedom aside, and fear it – this freedom without a foundation – as an obstacle to be overcome. Thus for Sartre, in bad faith the self who believes that his essence is a mere 'is,' rather than a project without foundation – a 'to be' – is undoubtedly lying to himself. Yet for de Beauvoir, looking at French society in the 1940s – a bourgeois society in which woman is 'equal but separate' relative to man, subject to a 'trial' in which 'man is judge and party' – the question arises as to the roots of Sartrean bad faith. Woman shares in the general existential tendency of hiding behind her choices. But is this because woman, like man, shares in an existence that is free to choose and free to flee freedom?

De Beauvoir questions whether it is true that women, in their real lives, are free individuals in the manner that Sartre supposes; she questions whether I am, as Sartre says, 'my projects, what I choose and make myself to be.' And she asks what is it to live a life as an individual in the first place. Against Sartre's belief in the free individual, in mastering one's own projects, de Beauvoir insists on a continuity, a sense of commonality, between individuals that overarches and precedes individual embodiment. If bad faith is an existential tool for analyzing what woman is, then it must be modified to reflect this continuity. According to Sartre, in every moment, in every act of my conscious being, I am making myself into what I am out of the radical facticity of my projects. The self that I will be tomorrow is not yet, and I have no choice but to choose to be it, yet in the very act of choosing it, I simultaneously commit my present self (and consequently my past self) to nonbeing, to utter demise, instantaneous death.

But de Beauvoir disagrees. Woman as embodied consciousness cannot be encapsulated in a theory of choice as solipsistic as Sartre's. To develop this point de Beauvoir draws on another of Sartre's categories – the existential situation – but she modifies this category significantly, by taking it to mean a very specific reality, the situation of woman. As she says, 'Woman's body *is* her situation.' For de Beauvoir, the body exceeds biological determination or cultural determination or 'repression' as psychoanalysis wants to claim, or even the group solidarity of a common history of a 'We' (for example, of a proletarian or ethnic community). As 'her situation,' woman's body is 'something other than herself' – it exceeds individual embodiment. The body is 'not a thing but a situation' never identical with itself since women 'have no past, no history, no religion of their own.' The very notion of embodied consciousness is linked with history or rather historicity, not biological organism or psyche. This is where de Beauvoir departs from Sartre: for Sartre, the body is facticity ('I am trapped in my body'), and in choosing what I am to be, I commit the factical body to nonbeing; I transcend it. For de Beauvoir, woman's situation, her body, is what woman *is*, it cannot be transcended in this way; but because the body is not merely facticity or destiny, it can be exceeded in historicity. The body itself is a situation of possible transcendence.

This point links with de Beauvoir's argument that 'woman *is* the Other' – but no longer Sartre's Other. Woman's being-for-others is a 'degradation of existence' into being-in-itself, a transcendence that 'falls back into immanence, stagnation': 'woman is the eternal essence of the feminine,' 'the sex,' 'the womb,' and so on. That woman is the Other means that woman internalizes the gaze – she is never alone, her body is never her own, she looks at herself as the Other looks at her. And so the Other's values are hers – that is, she has no values; her self, being-for-itself, is *nil*. She is defined as Other to man. Yet where Sartre's individual is consumed in face of the Other by a crippling fear, anxiety and the reflexive apprehension that freedom lacks foundation, de Beauvoir no longer speaks of existentialist *angst*. This is because she takes up the relation to the Other through the category of being-with-others, *Mitsein*, which for her is a tool of analysis that undoes the Sartrean being-for-others.

For Sartre, the intersubjective relation, being-for-others, is predicated upon incessant interruptions or nihilations of consciousness, ultimately rooted in the totalizing gaze of the Other. But de Beauvoir speaks in the first place of a historical becoming, 'becoming a woman.' Since woman is not a 'completed reality, but rather a becoming', 'it is in her becoming that she should be compared with man; that is to say, her *possibilities* should be defined' (de Beauvoir 1989: 35). In the first place, woman is not limited to sexuality as something already given, rather in sexuality social and economic factors come into play. This is why for de Beauvoir, 'one is not born, but becomes a woman.' While she argues that woman as Other 'is as primordial as consciousness itself,' this Other is irreducible to oppositional logic, she is a becoming. There is a transcendence possible in her embodiment as situation and this is possible through the relation to the Other. Since there is an overarching continuity of situation, the relation to the Other – *Mitsein* – is not a threat of rupture that seizes upon the body as facticity (as it is for Sartre), but a site of possible transcendence through historicity. Indeed, this sort of transcendence is what de Beauvoir calls for at the end of *The Second Sex*.

De Beauvoir, then, takes up Sartre's existentialist project and turns it against itself and against previous notions of the difference of woman. Woman, as de Beauvoir shows throughout *The Second Sex*, has always been defined as Other – Other to man, Other to the one who is the real thing, the exemplar of self-determination, the subject, humanity itself. But de Beauvoir, by appropriating existentialism, shows that woman is a becoming, her very body and history are a possibility of transcendence that only has to be taken up. The difference of woman cannot be construed biologically, psychoanalytically, or through historical ideologies; as she famously declared, 'anatomy is not destiny' – and neither is anything else. But, against Sartre, she argued that woman is not a pure existence, a freedom that must be opposed to the body as facticity; rather the body is the situation of the becoming of woman as her freedom. That is, de Beauvoir begins to introduce a difference into existence itself, a difference that will give rise to the later feminist thought of sexual difference – even if later feminists criticize de Beauvoir for neglecting this in favor of a transcendence that is often taken to be neuter.

De Beauvoir is an unique figure in feminist philosophy, of importance not just for her philosophy, but for her role in intellectual movements, indeed for her life as inspiration for feminism. So some attention must be paid here to the reception of her work. In the years following de Beauvoir's death in 1986 and the posthumous publication of her letters and notebooks by her adopted daughter Sylvie Le Bon de Beauvoir, her work was revived and reassessed by feminists. Kate and Edward Fullbrook, for example, show that her early novel *She Came to Stay* (1954) may have been of philosophical influence upon Sartre. Murphy and Bergoffen stress her concrete view of situated freedom in *The Ethics of Ambiguity* (1962). In her *Hypparchia's Choice* (1989), Michele Le Doeuff reads Sartre's posthumous *Lettres au Castor* (1990) and criticizes Sartre's efforts to silence de Beauvoir as a philosopher; in de Beauvoir's *Lettres à Sartre* (1991), she traces de Beauvoir's philosophical influences not to Sartre, or Husserl but back to Hegel's *Phenomenology of Spirit*. Rich work is done by Holveck and Vintges on de Beauvoir's phenomenological connection with Husserl; Bergoffen and Kruks explore the connection with Merleau-Ponty and the phenomenology of the incarnate body. Feminists have also addressed the issue of 'assuming one's gender' in de Beauvoir (for example, Klaw's work on *Les Mandarins*). For Margaret Simons, de Beauvoir's contributions as co-editor for *Le Temps Modernes*, together with her political activism and the co-authored book *Djamila Boupacha*, on the 1954–62 Algerian war, give a philosophical foundation for radical feminism. Among criticisms of de Beauvoir, Butler, in her book *Gender Trouble* (1990), while drawing on 'becoming woman,' levels what is now a well-known criticism against an essentialism of 'the second sex' for reducing the social-cultural plane of gender identity to a binary social constructivist view of biological sex.

Irigaray's Sexual Difference

French feminist Luce Irigaray, a linguist, philosopher, and psychoanalyst, continues de Beauvoir's search for the difference of woman, but with Irigaray difference comes to have a new meaning. Her central work, *Speculum of the Other Woman* ([1974] 1994), which provoked her expulsion from the Lacanian school of psychoanalysis, moves entirely beyond the binary oppositions of male and female, man and woman, to focus on sexual difference as such, on the 'sexed body' as being wholly other than gender. *Speculum* is a major text in the post-1968 feminist inquiry in France. Irigaray's second major work, *This Sex Which Is Not One* ([1977] 1985) makes the subversive challenge of the *Speculum* more direct and accessible, questioning classic views of the difference between male and female sex organs and of the experience of erotic pleasure in men and women. This work continues and amplifies a further theme from the *Speculum*, namely, Irigaray's reading of Marx and of the institutionalization of the economic exploitation and subjection of women. Irigaray's recent work continues this more practical side of her feminism by dissecting current linguistic systems and their impact on the marginalization of women, and by calling for an ethics of sexual difference.

Both de Beauvoir and Irigaray criticize the positioning of woman as Other. For de Beauvoir, woman is Other to a consciousness, to a being who 'does' things to 'me' (judges me, nihilates me into an essence, a being-in-itself); the Other is a transcending positivity and a presence in my perceptual field. Irigaray, in contrast, takes up this issue in a Lacanian framework that no longer assumes presence or consciousness. The Other is a signifier, a fiction, a 'fantasy,' an 'enigma' completely dissociated from issues concerning consciousness-based identity. Irigaray, however, criticizes the Lacanian framework for construing woman as Other – as 'lack' ('*manque*') – and in general she takes issue with the Freudian and Lacanian essentialisation of the feminine.

Three categories, the Real, the Imaginary and the Symbolic, are involved in the production of the Lacanian subject. Roughly speaking, in Lacan's development of the Freudian view, the Real is the remainder of our primal relation to others, a lost past that is 'impossible' to experience once the process of socialization, that is, symbolization, is set into motion. The subject needs to stay close to the Real, but suffers the trauma of forced socialization that bars the Real. The Imaginary is whatever the subject is capable of making of this forced choice. The Symbolic is the socio-linguistic realm required to support the reality of normative socialization. Yet the inauguration of the Symbolic depends upon a permanent retranslation of the Imaginary into language, which, for Lacan, reproduces the fantasy of castration anxiety. Lacan understands these categories in terms of Freud's work on infantile sexuality. For Freud, weaning the child off the mother's breast, latency, the transition from pre-genital to a genital organization of the body and the latter's coincidence in time with the activation of the prohibition of incest, are the core around which the family triangle is formed. For Lacan, the incest prohibition marks the subject's entrance into the Symbolic, that is, into language as the place in which society's symbolic reproduction of its laws, norms, and rituals materializes. Because of the incest prohibition that founds the Symbolic, the Symbolic appears as predicated upon the subject's experience of a 'lack' brought about by a power, that is, a phallic law, or the Law-of-the-Father. This law regulates the agent's desire for the Other of sexual difference and simultaneously requires that the 'lack' be mastered via the Symbolic.

Irigaray's objection to this is that the Symbolic, or the Law-of-the-Father, inaugurates the Oedipal body's regulatory desire as desire for exclusive access to the mother's body and thus as prohibited and impossible. The prohibition must be mastered, but it involves a relation to an impossible, fragmented body, a body condemned to hysteria and psychosis because of a lack 'of a valid signifier for her "first" desire and for her sex/organs' (Irigaray 1994: 55). The female body is 'caused,' forced into a mold, by the male desire for the Other. It is a body to be mastered, excized, silenced. For Irigaray, then, Lacanian psychoanalysis has a problematic view of woman as 'lack' and as a body excluded from the Symbolic, from social-cultural structures of universal comprehensibility and accessibility.

Moreover, according to Irigaray, Lacan understands this lack through a biological matrix. On Lacan's view, I (the ego) am never my body, and this is a move away from substantializing the first person singular ('I am'). The body is not 'to be,' it is 'to have.' And it is only the psychoanalytic subject (the id), that has a body. Yet nonetheless the Oedipal body 'has' (a penis) and the female does 'not have' it, it 'lacks' (a penis), it is a body signifying, embodying, 'lack.' In Western metaphysics and culture, woman has been positioned as the 'sexual indifference that underlies the truth of any science, the logic of every discourse,' as the 'dark continent of the unconscious,' and the 'empirical' transcendental condition of the possibility of representation that is itself unrepresentable – and Lacan repeats this positioning.

Central to *Speculum* is Irigaray's uncompromising resistance to Freud and Lacan's psychoanalytic framing of woman as a 'signed object' that at once rejects the phallus and threatens its demise. Psychoanalysis despoils woman of 'all valid, valuable images of her sex/organs, her body' (Irigaray 1994: 55). On the one hand, the male body is that which can be signified positively, that is to say, represented: the alienated Oedipal body raises itself to consciousness since it *can* be represented, reflected in the mirror of the Other. Thanks to its representability, the Oedipal body is elevated to a norm of meaning, it appears as the signifier of the Symbolic. On the other hand, the completion of meaning, the self-identification of the conscious ego, depends upon the totality of representation of the network of signifiers – and Lacan locates the 'last' signifier of the chain in the body of woman. The 'lack' of the phallus upon which the Symbolic is thereby founded means that there is a necessary 'incompleteness' of Truth, meaning, and language, a movement beyond representation and representability, beyond speech. Woman, for Lacan, is thus the imaginary, relegated to hysteria, psychosis, illegibility.

For Irigaray this positioning of woman entirely neglects the sexed difference of woman. The order of the Symbolic reproduces Western patriarchal discourse and condemns woman to unintelligibility; it is responsible for her 'failure' to speak, that is, to retain a position of power in the Symbolic. Effectively, Irigaray objects to patriarchy for sentencing woman to exteriority without the right to interiority, autonomy, or transcendence. In this patriarchal discourse, woman is thought of as *the* negative, the inaccessible aspect of the double articulation of the signifier that cannot itself be represented, 'the blind spot of a symmetry of the science's unknown,' the '(f)rigid' limit of representation, the said, the actual. While not lying entirely outside the Symbolic, woman as limit is yet not entirely inside it either. This structural lack of an inside to/of woman enables the idea of woman as the external limit of the Symbolic. On the other hand, it enables the idea of woman as a 'subliminal' limit that lacks delimitation (because 'polymorphously perverse'), and is, at the same time, capable of setting up a limit of the Symbolic. This double ambiguity in the representation of woman, as lack and absence, and 'unsuccessful repression' ('the horror of this nothing to be seen,' 'the clitoris as a substitute for penis in the little girl') is, in the Lacanian system, productive of discourse. But Irigaray wants to know what it is that suggests that *woman* is the placeholder of this ambiguity.

In answering this question, Irigaray objects to the Lacanian answer that assigns woman the role of limit of the symbolic – of a specular mirror that confirms the self-image of man. In *Speculum* and *This Sex Which Is Not One*, she proposes a reversal from the specular to the tactile, to touching (see, for example, 'When Our Lips Speak Together' in *This Sex*). The ambiguity of woman is not to be found in a prescribed specular order, but in her tangible sexual difference. This difference is amplified by the theme of two-ness: 'She is neither one nor two; she has no 'proper' name, and her sexual organ, which is not *one* organ, is counted as *none*' (Irigaray 1985: 26). Sexual difference is not 'one' but a plurality ('sex organs are more or less everywhere'); it cannot be subsumed under a concept or a phallogocentric order:

> To claim that the feminine can be expressed in the form of a concept is to allow oneself to be caught up again in a system of 'masculine' representations, in which women are trapped in a system of meaning which serves the auto-affection of the masculine subject. (Irigaray 1985: 122–3)

Irigaray seeks the answer about the difference of woman in a pre-Oedipal mother-daughter relationship as a fullness, a fluidity, not as a stage leading up to Oedipal desire. In the Other as lack and specularized image, man seeks to unify 'two' distinct images, the feminine and the maternal. But according to Irigaray, the very category of the maternal is elusive; it escapes this unifying concept. The feminine as mother-daughter, as a two-ness of woman, is a plurality, a fluidity, a red fluidity, a voluminous fluidity, a truly unrepresentable, overflowing difference. Femininity *is* the sexual difference.

With her mimetic style of reading, Irigaray mimics masculine discourse in a discourse of the feminine, thus inscribing the feminine into the canon. In 'mimetizing' the foundational discourse of philosophy, psychoanalysis or science, she inserts a split *in* language, beginning therefore to articulate a sexuate style of discourse that resists rigidity and the conceptual formalizations of referential language. Irigaray's more recent work as a linguist engages her in a study of French and Romantic, and later Romanesque and non-Romanesque languages (for example, Chinese), and the language of women who have mental illnesses (Irigaray 2002). These works demonstrate her commitment to a complete understanding of how language determines the subjectivity of the individual. Indeed, Irigaray's fundamental questioning of the logic of language, which led her in the early 1970s to part ways with Lacanian psychoanalysis, remains determined to develop a 'feminine symbolic' – a language of 'the three genders.' She proposes a reform of current linguistic systems in order to incorporate the existing binary divide between masculine and feminine into a language that would enable a harmonious co-existence of the two separate symbolics, for woman and man.

Irigaray is the author of some of the strongest feminist readings of 'forgotten' sexual difference in works by Nietzsche (1991), Heidegger (1999), Plato, Merleau-Ponty, Descartes, and Hegel. Turning to practice an 'ethics of sexual difference,' she proposes gendered laws for pregnant women and mothers. Chanter (1995) has developed a critique of Irigaray's essentialization of the female body in which she questions the presence of the residual opposites of man and woman. Butler's objection (1990) against the essentialization of the biological female body involves a critique of Irigaray's 'mimetic' or double reading, her (Freudian) essentialism and the prioritization of heterosexual women over lesbian and other-gendered women.

Kristeva's Semiotic Maternal

French feminist Julia Kristeva draws on plural influences, from structural linguistics (from Russian formalism to Saussure, Jakobson and psychoanalysis) to German Idealism (from Kant, Hegel, and Husserl to Heidegger) in order to propose a novel concept of the semiotic (*le sémiotique*) and the semiotization of desire in language and the maternal body. In her *Revolution in Poetic Language* ([1974] 1984) and then in *Desire in Language* ([1977] 1980), Kristeva takes issue, like Irigaray, with Freud, Lacan and the status of the extra-linguistic in the psychoanalytic view of the subject. She introduces a foil for the symbolic subject, which she calls a semiotic subject – a subject as signifying practice, a 'questionable subject-in-process.' Although she does not refer to her writings as feminist, Kristeva has an enormous influence in feminist theory and criticism. Her view of the semiotic *chora* and its linkage with the maternal body and her related view of maternal abjection have a direct impact on feminism. Her specific encounter with feminism is found in 'Women's Time' (Kristeva 2002).

Kristeva's semiotic depends on what she calls *chora* (a term she takes from Plato), a nutritive or semiotic principle 'anterior to naming,' a loose boundary and rupture that gives ordering (rhythm) to meaning yet rejects any imposition of a concept. She situates her work against Hegel for whom the sublation of spirit's past stages its own development, culminating in the totalization of experience, the 'one' absolute concept as a self-consciousness identical with its object. As the principle of semiotization, the Kristevan *chora* enables the positing of the concept as subject, but since it precedes the bifurcations of soma and psyche, nature and culture, matter and representation, and so on, the *chora* rejects the homogeneous unity of the Hegelian concept.

The semiotic principle is nutritive as it relates to the 'maternal body' and the logics of identification and differentiation: the logics of the 'drives' necessary for signification are prefigured or regulated by the maternal body. As a psychoanalyst, Kristeva relies on the psychoanalytic theory that the mother's weaning of the child introduces a crisis, a negativity, at the same time as it also normalizes the child's life. That is, the child's rejection by the mother is followed by rejecting the mother's breast, the 'good' object, and the internalization of rejection, a repudiation of one's own sexuality, the 'bad' object; as the repudiated object is further eroticized, the 'other within,' that is, the mother, is turned into an object of abjection. The very logic of signification depends upon abjecting the mother and this introduces sexual difference at the basis of the subject's access to language, thus engendering a difference at the symbolic level (and of grammar) between the male and the female subject. By introducing the semiotic as a dimension in which the symbolic is prefigured in, and crucially preceded by the psycho-somatic experiences of the subject, Kristeva argues that we are never completely subjects of our own experiences. But Kristeva preserves the case of abjection, which is fundamentally related to the maternal function, as specifically impacting on the subjectivity of woman. While woman, like man, must succumb to the desire for matricide as necessary to becoming subject, she herself must identify as woman and remain a split subject, failing to abject (see 'depressive sexuality' in Kristeva 1989, and 1982).

Giving meaning (semiotization) depends upon the ordering of drives, but the repressed unconscious knows no contradiction. The semiotic *chora* intervenes, stabilizing the arbitrary difference between words, and between words and the extra-linguistic. Language thus arises when the repressed unconscious is endowed with *chora* and the semiotic. And so Kristeva argues that the mother tongue is *no* language, but a 'nonrecoverable syntactic elision,' an unrepresentable (negative) affective speech. Stressing the excess of the 'semiotext' of the subject over the symbolic, Kristeva draws on what she calls 'poetic language.' The creative surplus of artistic meaning that we can find in a poem (Mallarmé), a painting (Bellini), as well as in speech, sound, rhythm, dance, or choreographic movement without determinate structure, is what lends language its reality in the first place. In 'poetic language,' the signifier of the 'I' as subject of the symbolic, brings 'together' in the symbol something 'older' than itself – the semiotic. ('Poetic language would be for its questionable subject-in-process the equivalent of incest' [Kristeva 1980: 136]). Overall, in the semiotic the separation of the psychoanalytic subject from the maternal body is an utter impossibility, and so the maternal body with its internal split becomes the model for all subjective relations. Drawing on the originality of the semiotic, Kristeva's related distinction between genotext (depth-structure) and phenotext (surface-structure), corresponding to semiosis and symbol, give powerful tools for feminist semiotic analysis.

Kristeva valorizes Freud's theory of the drives of the unconscious as discharging and transferring on to, or charging with energy, the representations of the speaking subject, and investing the conscious representation of the 'I' with meaning. But as drives (narcissism, the death drive) operate on the level of matter, they also have no object, only an affective identification with a representation they cannot substantiate – the infant's autoerotic body does not have an object. Ultimately, her way of locating desire 'in' language leads to the controversial claims that 'There is no such thing as Woman. Indeed, she does not exist as with a capital "W"'' (Kristeva 2002: 365). There is no way to define or bring Woman into language because the maternal body is before language. Kristeva here formulates her implicit criticism of the pre-1968 feminism and of de Beauvoir for overlooking sexual difference and rejecting motherhood in the 'independent woman.' She also rejects the post-May 1968 wave of *l'écriture féminine* for glorifying an impossible uniquely feminine language. But she embraces the 'new' upcoming generation of the 1980s for proposing that 'there are as many sexualities as there are individuals.'

Among other critics, Butler targets Kristeva for a residual essentialism that links woman to pregnancy, maternity, heterosexual normativity and for the overall preservation of Freud's Oedipal theory. Taking up Kristeva, Vietnamese filmmaker and feminist Trinh T. Minh-Ha (1989) has developed an influential theory of 'a third world feminism.'

Wittig and Cixous: Sex as Oppression, *l'écriture féminine*

With the political, philosophical and literary work of Monique Wittig, in the early 1970s, feminism enters a new stage of self-definition. Rebelling against the reality of the political situation, Wittig founds the defense of 'women's rights' in a feminist analysis of 'women's oppression.' Heterosexuality is a political regime, 'lesbians are not women' and when the history of class struggle is re-examined from this new and provocative point of view, we have the groundwork of a critique of heterosexuality as a 'political institution.' Against an egalitarian Marxist theory of the division of labor and gender-neutral class consciousness, Wittig's 'lesbian materialism' offers a radically new interpretation of the feminist credo that the personal is political. The usual account of the exploitation of labor, which links it to structures of production that divide the rich from the poor, and owners of the means of production from the disowned workers, leaves out the heterosexual bondage of man and woman. Like Adrienne Rich (and Andrea Dworkin), Wittig argues that since the social contract is made in the 'straight mind,' the real oppression of consciousness is 'sex,' that is, compulsory heterosexuality. Woman as heterosexual is not nature, not anatomy as destiny, she is the 'myth' that de Beauvoir talks about in the first place. Wittig's call for a lesbian materialism is a call for strategic essentialism, a call not to women as a group but to every one of us to step outside of a 'sex-age' that divides between male/female, active/passive, nature/culture, biology/essence, mind/body. The lesbian is not a woman who wants to be a man (as heterosexual normativity would claim) but one who wants to step outside the 'sex-age.' Wittig thus appeals not to a transcendence or body that undoes the Other or established orders – as do de Beauvoir, Irigaray, or Kristeva – but to a route outside of 'sex' as oppressed consciousness. Wittig's literary works, her plays, her work with activist groups have a strong influence on feminist discourse and strategies. Among her critics, Butler detects essentialist sex-gender and erasure of sexual difference in Wittig's overturning of 'sex' as oppression.

Hélène Cixous's *The Newly Born Woman* (1986) – co-authored with Catherine Clément – as well as her manifesto 'The Laugh of the Medusa,' best represent the post May 1968 phase of feminism of 'writing woman,' or feminine writing, *l'écriture féminine*. As a creative feminist alternative to Derrida's deconstruction of the 'text' and writing, *l'écriture féminine* opens up the specificity of the difference of woman's sexuality and the affinity between sexuality and textuality. Writing's question ('Who are I?' '*Qui sont-je?*') inquires into the plurality and poetic creativity of the difference of woman's sexuality – into the aesthetic and symbolic specificity of woman. Apart from being a practical call for women to publish their own work and their experiences, *l'écriture féminine* becomes the inspiration for the unveiling of a nonbiological and a noncultural sexuality or femininity, what Cixous calls controversially a 'bi-sexuality,' referring to a metaphysical tendency, a *jouissance*, of the whole of sexuality. Feminine writing often explores the 'monstrous' and the oppressive images of woman. As a 'writing from the id,' it fashions itself as a dynamism, a speech from the feminine

Imaginary and the 'repressed unconscious' of 'woman's place' in history. Woman's difference is a plurality, a voice, a play, an utopia and an an-archism, a bilingualism. One does not relate directly to one's body but always through language and social structures and at its foundation feminine writing ('in white ink') is a re-appropriation, a revelation. *L'écriture féminine*, then, is not merely a questioning of male/female, nature/culture, biology/ history, rather this writing *is* the 'newly born woman.' Feminist critics (Butler, Kristeva), however, detect a romanticization of woman and writing in Cixous's proposal, but it should be said that in France and in North America the impact of 'writing woman' on feminism has been enormous.

Butler's Performative Gender Theory

In North America, Judith Butler gives the French feminist theory a peculiar twist by turning to a performativity of gender. Her starting point is Foucault's and Nietzsche's genealogical critiques of desire as a performative act that presumes the sovereign subject by way of a unifying structure of discourse. But her theory of gender as masquerade also draws on Levi-Strauss's anthropological structuralism and Lacan, yet turns Lacan against Lacan. 'Sex [is] a performatively enacted signification (and hence not "to be"), one that, released from its naturalized interiority and surface, can occasion the parodic proliferation and subversive play of gendered meanings' (Butler 1990: 33). For Butler, where there is Lacanian psychoanalytic desire, there is already a heteronormative law, a 'repressive hypothesis' at work. Turning to Foucault, she shows that something else, not Desire, Subject, or the Symbolic, but rather a historical discourse of power/knowledge, that is, a sensualization or sexualization of power at the very core of pleasure, is at work where individual sexualities are produced. So the sexualities are always produced as 'types' (rather than acts), for example, *the* homosexual, *the* lesbian, *the* black female, and so on. Both Lacanian feminists (Joan Copjec) and Deleuzian feminists have criticized a residual essentialism in Butler.

Grosz, Braidotti, and Philosophies of Difference

Australian feminist Elizabeth Grosz combines principles of Lacanian psychoanalysis with Merleau-Ponty, Bergson and Deleuze, seeking to integrate the 'lived body' and the 'Body without Organs' into an ontology of multiple differences, a becoming, not 'of' being as an effect, but rather as process. Grosz opens up a new possibility for conceptualizing the female body, through a novel theory of time and space as intensities. Deleuzian feminists, notably Rosi Braidotti (1994) (also Olkowski 1999, Colebrook 2004, Colebrook and Buchanan 2000) pursue a continuity between 'writing woman' and becoming ('becoming-woman' and 'becoming-girl'), by way of a theory of fluidities and inhabituation (re-membering). They ask not what the body 'is,' but rather, what does body mean, how does it work? The problem of totalizing difference does not lie with concepts themselves – for example, the human, the subject, desire, psychoanalytic desire, the female body. The problem is with attaching concepts to being, asking what does this or that being do or want; asking this question invites transcendent concepts that colonize thinking.

Important work in North American feminist deconstruction and Derrida is done by Peggy Kamuf, Peg Birmingham, Nancy Holland, Sarah Kofman and others (see Holland 1997 and Kofman 1985). Post-colonial feminist theory of deconstruction is undertaken by Gayatry Spivak (1988) and others. Also important work in Habermasian and phenomenological feminism is developed by I. M. Young, Drucilla Cornell, Nancy Fraser and Seyla Benhabib.

References

Bartky, S. L. (1990), *Femininity and Domination: Studies in the Phenomenology of Oppression*, New York: Routledge.

de Beauvoir, S. [1949] (1989), *The Second Sex*, New York: Vintage Books.

de Beauvoir, S. (2004), *Philosophical Writings*, Urbana: University of Illinois Press.

Bordo, S. (2004), *Unbearable Weight: Feminism, Western Culture, and the Body*, Berkeley: University of California Press.

Braidotti, R. (1994), *Nomadic Subjects: Embodiment and Sexual Difference in Contemporary Feminist Theory*, New York: Columbia University Press.

Butler, J. (1990), *Gender Trouble*, New York: Routledge.

Chanter, T. (1995), *Ethics of Eros: Irigaray's Re-Writing of the Philosophers*, New York: Routledge.

Cixous, H. and C. Clément (1986), *The Newly Born Woman*, Minneapolis: University of Minnesota Press.

Colebrook, C. (2004), *Gender*, New York: Palgrave Macmillan.

Colebrook, C. and I. Buchanan (2000), *Deleuze and Feminist Theory*, Edinburgh: Edinburgh University Press.

Holland, N. J. (1997), *Feminist Interpretations of Jacques Derrida*, University Park: Pennsylvania State University Press.

Irigaray, L. [1977] (1985), *This Sex Which Is Not One*, Ithaca: Cornell University Press.

Irigaray, L. (1991), *Marine Lover of Friedrich Nietzsche*, New York: Columbia University Press.

Irigaray, L. [1974] (1994), *Speculum of the Other Woman*, Ithaca: Cornell University Press.

Irigaray, L. (1999), *The Forgetting of Air in Martin Heidegger*, Austin: University of Texas Press.

Irigaray, L. (2002), *To Speak is Never Neutral*, New York: Routledge.

Kofman, S. (1985), *The Enigma of Woman: Woman in Freud's Writings*, Ithaca: Cornell University Press.

Kristeva, J. [1977] (1980), *Desire in Language*, New York: Columbia University Press.

Kristeva, J. (1982), *Powers of Horror: An Essay on Abjection*, New York: Columbia University Press.

Kristeva, J. [1974] (1984), *Revolution in Poetic Language*, New York: Columbia University Press

Kristeva, J. (1989), *Black Sun: Depression and Melancholia*, New York: Columbia University Press.

Kristeva, J. (2002), *The Portable Kristeva*, New York: Columbia University Press.

Min-Ha, T. T. (1989), *Woman, Native, Other: Writing Postcoloniality and Feminism*, Bloomington: Indiana University Press.

Olkowski, D. (1999), *Gilles Deleuze and the Ruin of Representation*, Berkeley: University of California Press.

Simons, M. A. (1995), *Feminist Interpretations of Simone de Beauvoir*, University Park: Pennsylvania State University Press.

Simons, M. A. (1999), *Beauvoir and the Second Sex: Feminism, Race, and the Origins of Existentialism*, Lanham: Rowman and Littlefield.

Spivak, G. C. (1988), *In Other Worlds: Essays in Cultural Politics*, New York: Routledge.

Wittig, M. (1986), *The Lesbian Body*, Boston: Beacon Press.

Philosophy of Religion

Merold Westphal

Much of Continental philosophy of religion is reflection on faith (as response to revelation) and reason (as philosophical reflection). Having made the linguistic turn, it intersects with analytic discussion of the problem of religious language, at least if the question is understood as concerning the nature and limits of our God-talk rather than its warrant. Since philosophy often takes the form of phenomenology, the question can be put this way: does reason, so conceived, prescribe the limits within which our God-talk must stay (as in Kant's *Religion Within the Limits of Reason Alone*), or does it describe the limits that it is unable to surpass (as in Kant's *Critique of Pure Reason*), or both? There may be a deeper continuity between 'postmodern' and 'modern' discourses than is often suspected, with German Idealism alive and well throughout the twentieth century.

Heidegger

In the same year in which he published *Being and Time* (1927), Heidegger gave a lecture entitled 'Phenomenology and Theology.' In the former he tells us that phenomenology means 'to let that which shows itself be seen from itself in the very way in which it shows itself from itself,' adding, 'Covered-up-ness is the counter-concept to "phenomenon"' (Heidegger 1962: 58, 60). In the latter he tells us that phenomenology and theology are '*absolutely different*' sciences. Theology is an ontic science, concerned with a particular region of beings, while phenomenology is the ontological science, which shifts our focus from beings to being (Heidegger 1998: 41). Theology is a meta-discourse that presupposes two first-order discourses, those of revelation and of faith. As 'conceptual disclosure and objectification, theology is constituted in thematizing faith and that which is disclosed through faith – that which is "revealed".' Not surprisingly, in relation to *Being and Time*, faith is portrayed not in purely cognitive terms but as 'a way of existence of human Dasein' and as 'an appropriation of revelation.' Faith as rebirth is both the origin and goal of theology (Heidegger 1998: 43–5, 50).

Heidegger says that theology is a 'fully autonomous ontic science,' but he immediately takes that back. He grants that faith does not need philosophy to produce or justify what is given to it through revelation; but for its 'appropriate conceptual interpretation' it requires not only guidance but, as we are told repeatedly, correction from philosophy. This is because all basic concepts belong to a 'primary, self-contained ontological context.' While 'what is revealed in faith can never be founded by way of a rational knowing as exercised by autonomously functioning reason, nevertheless the sense of the Christian occurrence as rebirth is that Dasein's prefaithful, that is, unbelieving existence is sublated [*aufgehoben*] therein.' Thus theological concepts 'are *ontologically* determined by a content that is pre-Christian and that can be grasped purely rationally' (Heidegger 1998: 50–3). This is a Hegelian version of religion within the limits of reason alone. Reason's task is not to separate the kernel from the husk but to guide and correct theology's interpretation of both faith and its content in terms of an autonomous, pre-Christian conceptuality. The only difference is that while Hegel claims that this reinterpretation provides both the appropriate conceptuality and the justification for our God-talk, Heidegger makes only the former claim.

Heidegger's later critique of onto-theology is more consistent with the claim that theology is an autonomous science. He derives this term primarily from Aristotle, whose ontology culminates in a theology. 'Metaphysics thinks beings as beings' (Heidegger 1998: 287). It does not think being qua being either as the revealing event in which beings come to presence or as the light in which they appear. So Aristotle's metaphysics is 'ontology' only as the attempt to think the entire domain of beings as distinct from some particular ontic region. It culminates in the theology of the Unmoved Mover and is thus onto-theology. Thus in the first instance, onto-theology is the theory of the Highest Being who is the key to the meaning of the whole domain of beings (Heidegger 1998: 287). At this point Heidegger's critique is simple. As metaphysics, Western philosophy has been a series of variations on this theme. Instead of recalling being, which is its true task, it forgets being, preoccupied with beings and their relation to some Highest Being or other, of which there have been many versions.

We can deflect this critique in several ways: (1) The theologian can respond, 'Why should the discourse that moves from faith to faith be subjected to philosophy's preoccupation with being? I want to talk about God.' Heidegger is inclined to agree. He directs his critique at the philosophical tradition from Anaximander to Nietzsche (Heidegger 1998: 280) and notes that its origin is Greek and not Christian, and even asks, with reference to 1 Cor. 1: 20, 'Will Christian theology one day resolve to take seriously the word of the apostle and thus also the conception of philosophy as foolishness? (Heidegger 1998: 287–8); (2) The philosopher can respond, 'Why should philosophy take this ontological difference between beings and being seriously? Aren't there other legitimate ways to do philosophy?'; (3) The philosopher-theologian, perhaps Aquinas, can respond, 'I take the question of being seriously. But as you say, being is always the being of some being, and I try to think being by thinking God, the Highest Being. As a result I recognize two radically different modes of being, created and uncreated, a difference more fundamental than the difference between being and beings. Created beings can be grasped in a created light, but Uncreated Being can be grasped only in an uncreated light. So even in revelation God remains beyond our comprehension' (see Marion 2003).

Later on Heidegger renders his concept of the onto-theological constitution of metaphysics at once more concrete and more troublesome. He asks, 'How does the deity enter into philosophy . . .?' His answer: '[T]he deity can come into philosophy only insofar as philosophy, of its own accord and by its own nature, requires and determines that and how the deity enters into it' (Heidegger 1969: 55–6). The gods of metaphysics can remain employed only on its terms and in the service of its project. And what might that project be? To render the whole of reality wholly intelligible to human understanding. By making ourselves the site of ultimate intelligibility, we render the whole of being at our disposal. This is why Heidegger links metaphysics so closely to technology and calls the latter 'the metaphysics of the atomic age' (Heidegger 1969: 52; see also Heidegger 1977: 77, 84, 100).

Heidegger highlights several dimensions of this project. First, it employs abstract, impersonal categories. God is *causa sui* and as such both *causa prima* and *ultima ratio* (Heidegger 1969: 60). Second, in modes of thinking he variously calls objectifying, calculative, or representational, these categories are employed in conjunction with the all-encompassing principle of sufficient reason. Even 'God exists only insofar as the principle of reason holds' (Heidegger 1991: 28). In the light of this principle everything must become intelligible. Third, the sense of mystery, wonder, and awe is lost (Heidegger 1998: 234–8; also Heidegger 1998: 243, 249, 255). We forget that unconcealment is always shadowed by concealment. At this point Heidegger, sounding a lot like Pascal, distinguishes the god of philosophy from the God of the believing soul. 'Man can neither pray nor sacrifice to this god. Before the *causa sui*, man can neither fall to his knees in awe nor can he play music and dance before this god' (Heidegger 1969: 72).

But what about theology? Of whose God does it speak – the philosopher's or the believing soul's? While Heidegger's two paradigms are Aristotle and Hegel and he directs his critique at the tradition that stretches from the Greeks to Nietzsche, he also says 'that the Christian theology, in what it knows and in the way it knows its knowledge, is metaphysics' (Heidegger 1970: 147). But in this claim he misunderstands his own argument. Like many since, he mistakenly assumes that the presence of abstract metaphysical categories is a sure sign of onto-theology. If it were, thinkers like Augustine and Aquinas would stand guilty of this sin. But this analysis fails to note: (1) that such theologies move from faith to faith, arising in faith and having understanding as their *telos* just to the degree that it serves the higher *telos* of faith, hope, and love; (2) that the abstract, impersonal categories they use are teleologically suspended or *aufgehoben* in the personal categories of a God who loves and speaks; and (3) that so far from employing any metaphysical principle to displace mystery with pure intelligibility, they emphatically emphasize the ultimate incomprehensibility of God. They just don't fit Heidegger's profile. But his critique is not without its bite. Onto-theology is the hubris that leads to idolatry by making God a means to our ends. This means that whenever we allow God into our discourses only in the service of our projects, whether they be philosophical, theological, political, or economic, we stand accused by Heidegger's critique of this sin, even if the ontological difference is less important than he thinks.

So what does Heidegger tell us about religious language? Early on, he leaves first order God-talk untouched, but insists that its reflection in theology needs correction by phenomenological reason. The Hegelian implication is that the discourses of the unreflective believing soul and the theologian are conceptually inferior. Later, when philosophy is called thinking rather than phenomenology and is given the task of overcoming metaphysics in its onto-theological constitution, this theme is not entirely lost (Heidegger 1998: 258, 267). But in the critique of onto-theology, Jerusalem is warned to keep its distance from a certain Athenian project, to respect both the autonomy of its own discourses and the mysterious uncanniness of that which exceeds every expression.

Derrida

Though often labeled 'postmodern,' Derrida tells us, 'We cannot and we must not . . . forgo the *Aufklärung*' (Derrida 1992a: 51; also 45, 49) and 'Nothing seems to me less outdated than the classical emancipatory ideal' (Derrida 2002a: 258). He turns out to be a Kantian about religion in terms of the First, Second, and 'Fourth' Critiques. Of his many important writings about religion, I will focus on *The Gift of Death*.

Here, as elsewhere (see, for example, Derrida 2002b and Caputo 1997a: xxvi), he echoes Kant's First Critique which tells us, 'I have therefore found it necessary to deny *knowledge* in order to make room for *faith*.' In dialogue with Patočka, he traces the emergence in Platonism and Christianity of the individual, responsible self from a sense of the sacred mystery described in terms of fusion, the demonic, and the orgiastic (Derrida 1995: 21–2, 35–6). Platonism and Platonized Christianity seek to subordinate responsible decision-making to knowledge. But in its personalism and its sense of the *mysterium tremendum* Christianity also points to a responsible self grounded in a faith 'outside of knowledge' or 'beyond knowledge' (Derrida 1995: 5, 23–6, 37, 53–4). These themes will be crucial when Derrida turns our attention in Chapter 3 to Kierkegaard's *Fear and Trembling* (1843).

Reference to responsibility and decision suggests the primacy of the practical over the theoretical. Like the Kant of the Second Critique, Derrida finds this faith beyond knowledge in the realm of praxis. It essentially involves infinite, unconditional obligation, but with a Levinasian twist. The transcendent as wholly other, as *mysterium tremendum*, is inaccessible to knowledge not simply because my mind is too weak to see it. There is another reason why 'my gaze . . . is no longer the measure of things.' The Christian, or better, monotheistic mystery is that I am seen by God, whom I do not see. In a radical inversion of the intentional relation, I am not the seer but the seen. While I cannot see the one who sees me, I can hear, and the voice I hear is a voice that commands. The heteronomous, asymmetrical character of being seen and spoken to by one I cannot see renders all intentionality, thematization, conceptualization, representation, in short, all knowledge inadequate to this other which is neither object nor essence. The faith that is 'beyond' and 'outside' of knowledge is not merely belief but trusting obedience.

Finally, Derrida is a Kantian in terms of the 'Fourth' Critique. He associates himself with 'a certain *epoché* that consists – rightly or wrongly, for the issue is serious – in thinking religion or making it appear "within the limits of reason alone"' (Derrida 2002b: 47). Reason here, of course, means deconstructive reason, the quasi-Kantian critique that supplants knowledge with faith. As a critique of the metaphysics of presence it denies that meanings, at the semantic level, or facts/events – at the ontic level – are ever fully present to us. This is because of Derrida's Hegelian holism. Meanings, facts, and events are so intimately interconnected with other meanings, facts, and events that for any one to be fully present to us we would have to have the relevant totality in hand. But with Kant (and Heidegger), Derrida denies that we ever achieve the required totality. So it is by faith and not by knowledge that we employ meanings and affirm facts or events, which remain, at least for us, only partially determined and in that sense undecidable. When Derrida insists that deconstructive negation is not negative theology because, unlike Pseudo-Dionysius, it offers neither prayer nor praise to the Holy Trinity (Derrida 1992a), Caputo helpfully highlights its Kantian character by calling it a 'generalized apophatics' (Caputo 1997a: 55–6). Predication is always problematic, not just in relation to God. Thus we walk by faith and not by sight (presence) in relation to shoes, and ships, and sealing wax, and cabbages and kings as well.

But for Derrida 'reason' is not just a deconstructive reading of the First Critique; even more so it is a Levinasian reading of the Second Critique. So religion within the limits of reason alone will mean not only within the limits of merely partial presence but even more so within the limits of a Levinasian responsibility. As with Kant, it will concern the relation of religion to ethics. At one level this distances Derrida from Heidegger, whose *Dasein* is not a responsible self because it is neither seen nor addressed. At another level, Derrida relates religion to ethics as much through Heideggerian as through Levinasian eyes. Heidegger repeats 'on an ontological level Christian themes and texts that have been "de-Christianized"' (Derrida 1995: 23). Similarly, Derrida asks how to think religion that 'would no longer be restricted to a paradigm that was Christian or even Abrahamic?' (Derrida 1995: 53).

The reference to Abraham is doubly significant. First, Derrida rather pointedly asks Patočka whether the experience of being seen by one who remains unseen is uniquely Christian, whether it does not also appear both ' "before" and "after" the Gospels, in Judaism or in Islam' (Derrida 1995: 28; and 2002b: 59–60). In other words, 'religion' here will signify Abrahamic monotheism, and since Derrida does not affirm the God of Abraham (Isaac, and Jacob), religion within the limits of reason alone will turn out to be 'religion without religion.' There is a 'logic' to Christian themes that 'has no need of *the event of a revelation or the revelation of an event.*' This means, as we shall see, more than religion 'without reference to religion as institutional dogma'; it means religion without God. This is a more radical declaration of independence of ethics from religion than we find in Kant.

Derrida tells us there is 'no choice to be made here between a logical deduction [from a concept of responsibility] that is not related to the event, and the reference to a revelatory event. One implies the other' (Derrida 1995: 50). But he regularly treats this issue as undecidable, which calls not for paralysis but for decision; and, without dogmatically denying the event of revelation or the revelation of the event as per Abrahamic faith, he quite clearly chooses as his faith one that involves no faith in the God of Abraham.

Second, the reference to freedom from the Abrahamic points us to a primary site where Derrida will spell this out – the Abraham story as retold by Kierkegaard in *Fear and Trembling*. There Abraham performs a teleological suspension of the ethical in the religious. Now 'teleological suspension' is just another name for Hegel's *Aufhebung*. Something taken to be self-sufficient and autonomous is now seen as subordinate to a *telos* beyond itself that is its proper home. It is recontextualized as part of a whole of which it is not the organizing principle. It is not abolished; but it is relativized.

Derrida recognizes that the ethical here is what Hegel calls *Sittlichkeit*, not the ahistorical, unsituated intuition of eternal moral truth but the laws and customs of an historically particular culture. It is not the abstract universal of Kant's pure practical reason, but the concrete universal of contingent culture. But as universal it supplies norms that apply to everyone (in that culture). In the Abraham story, the religious is the command of God to sacrifice Isaac. Unless this command is a higher norm than the rules of Abraham's society, he is simply a murderer in his willingness to obey it. He can be honored as the father of the faithful only if the ethical is *aufgehoben* in the religious. The laws of the land must be relative, normative only when they conform to the will of God (which is not simply another name for society's practices)[1].

There are two strikingly Levinasian features to Abraham's situation. First, the responsible self is radically individuated. It is the presence of this Other that gives rise to this self, now defined by this responsibility; and none of this derives its meaning from the metaphysical instance/kind relation or the social whole/part relation. Here ethical personalism has the form of ethical nominalism. For just this reason, responsibility cannot be publically justified. It is beyond the logos as discursive reason. Thus Abraham has a secret about which he can only remain silent.

Derrida might easily have dismissed Abraham's predicament as a problem only for Abrahamic monotheists, which he is not. Instead he suggests that this story presents 'the most common and everyday experience of responsibility' (Derrida 1995: 67). In doing so, he appeals to the Levinasian features just mentioned with the slogan, '*tout autre est tout autre*' ('every other is [the] wholly other'). In Patočka's account, Christianity separates itself from Platonism when it grounds responsibility in faith rather than knowledge in terms of the self's relation to the *mysterium tremendum*, the wholly other (*tout autre*) who is the God of Abrahamic monotheism. Derrida's religion without religion, within the limits of reason alone and thus freed from this restriction, replaces God with every human other – the Levinasian widow, orphan, or stranger whose face sees me from a site I cannot see and whose voice commands me with an infinite task.

This is the move that recapitulates Heidegger's 'de-Christianising' of Christian themes. Derrida describes it several ways. We might take the story as a fable whose moral is the relativity of every human law. Or we might think of God as the name of the 'absolute singularity' of 'the absolute other as other and as unique . . .' (Derrida 1995: 66–8). In a somewhat different context, he puts his religion within the limits of reason alone this way:

> We should stop thinking about God as someone, over there, way up there, transcendent . . . Then we might say: 'God is the name of the possibility I have of keeping a secret that is visible from the interior but not from the exterior.' In other words, 'God' signifies 'a structure of conscience . . .' (Derrida 1995: 108)

Derrida notes that along this path 'what I call God exists, (there is) what I call God in me, (it happens that) I call myself God – a phrase that is difficult to distinguish from "God calls me" . . .' (Derrida 1995: 109).

Should we call this simply a reduction of religion to ethics and ask what the point is in still calling it religion at all? Or should we call it a reversal of Kierkegaard, a teleological suspension or *Aufhebung* of religion in the ethical (neither Kantian nor Hegelian, of course, but Levinasian), in which case monotheistic faith would retain a relative but not an absolute validity? This might be hard to sustain, since Derrida treats Abrahamic monotheism and religion without religion more as an either/or than as a mediated both/and. He is careful not to claim that deconstruction determines the choice that is objectively undecidable, and he allows for the possibility that the structure or conceptuality he chooses is historically dependent on (belief in) the event of revelation, but not in such a way that '*we, Aufklärer* of modern times' (Derrida 1992a: 59) cannot free ourselves from this restriction.

Perhaps we can best clarify the matter by recalling the theme of religious language; and perhaps Charles Stevenson's notion of persuasive definition is the tool we need. 'A "persuasive" definition is one which gives a new conceptual meaning to a familiar word without substantially changing its emotive meaning, and which is used with the conscious or unconscious purpose of changing, by this means, the direction of people's interests' (Stevenson 1963: 32). In Derrida's religion, the name 'God' is retained, but only as the name of the structure of conscience, the ethical relation between the uniquely responsible self and the utterly unique human other to whom and for whom that self is responsible. Terminologically, Abrahamic monotheism retains a relative validity, but not substantively. We can only choose between the faith of Abraham and a faith freed of the former's monotheistic substance. Monotheistic religious language can be retained, but only once it has been radically redefined.

Marion

Like Heidegger and Derrida, Jean-Luc Marion seeks to overcome metaphysics. Or rather, he accepts the end of metaphysics as a fait accompli. 'Whether we accept it or not, it dominates us absolutely, as an overwhelming event' (Marion 1997: 283). He understands metaphysics in Heideggerian terms as onto-theology, emphasizing the principle of sufficient reason and the consequent primacy of thinking in terms of grounds and causes. It would be easy to show that he also understands it in Derridean terms as the metaphysics of presence. In either case its aspiration and sometimes claimed accomplishment is total intelligibility. Nietzsche's announcement of the death of God signifies both the end of metaphysics and the death of the God of metaphysics, the Self-Explanatory Explainer employed by metaphysics to achieve that intelligibility.

But this double demise need not be the end of all philosophy and all theology. So far as theology is concerned, the 'God' of metaphysics was an idol in any case (Marion 1997: 284). Good riddance! So far as philosophy is concerned, phenomenology is, or can be, the overcoming of metaphysics that is not numbed by Nietzsche's negations. Marion tells us:

> Phenomenology is present when, and only when, a statement shows us a phenom-
> enon – anything which does not appear, in one way or another, cannot be taken into
> account. To understand is ultimately to see. To speak of something in order to make
> it visible. (Marion 1997: 285)

But, in keeping with Heidegger's definition, phenomenology must not only make
visible; it must let the phenomenon show itself from itself. This means that Husserl's
famous 'principle of principles,' which gives ultimacy to intuitive givenness ('seeing'),
is the paradoxical principle that there is 'no *a priori* (transcendental) principle' but only
'an intuitive *a posteriori*.' In other words, phenomenology 'renounces the transcendental project, to allow an ultimately radical empiricism to unfold . . .' (Marion 1997:
285–6). To the Husserlian slogan, 'To the things themselves,' Marion adds the gloss,
'It is forbidden to forbid! . . . That which shows itself justifies itself by this fact alone'
(Marion 1997: 289).

Such forbidding is just what metaphysics, including transcendental philosophy,
does, with its appeal to *a priori* principles, such as sufficient reason or, in its
transcendental mode, the conditions of possible experience. But Husserl and Heidegger have not lived up to their own phenomenological ideals. They place *a priori*
conditions or restrictions on what can show itself and thereby remain enmeshed in
metaphysics. The structures of the transcendental ego, of which Heidegger's *Dasein*
and its modes of being-in-the-world are an existential/pragmatic variation, become
the conditions of possible experience as fully as the Kantian categories or the principle
of sufficient reason. Corresponding to these structures are the horizons within which
phenomena are compelled to appear, the horizons of objectivity and of being,
respectively. What is needed is a third phenomenology that allows neither the (all
too Cartesian) subject nor its (all too Kantian) horizons to become violations of the
phenomenological rule: it is forbidden to forbid![2]

With all his emphasis on seeing and givenness, Marion might well be asked if
phenomenology isn't a relapse into the metaphysics of presence. His response is quite
direct. For phenomenology, to understand is to see. But at least for his phenomenology, to see is not necessarily to understand. Or, to put it differently, we can see that
what we see exceeds our sight, surpasses our comprehension. While developing the
implications of his general phenomenology for theology and the philosophy of religion,
he develops this point in terms of two central themes: the distinction between idol and
icon and the idea of the saturated phenomenon. Together they provide background for
his affirmation as a theologian of the apophatic traditions (see Marion 1999 and 2001:
paras 13–16).

Idol and icon are not two different objects but two different ways of perceiving. In
the case of the idol, the subject's gaze or intentional aim is prior to its object. By
serving as the measure of its object it makes that object a mirror of itself. Since the
object does not exceed the gaze, the latter need not go beyond it but can stop and rest at
what it sees. With its aim satisfied or fulfilled, whatever was not aimed at or anticipated
disappears without a trace. Concepts and theories become idolatrous when, as in the
case of onto-theology, they purport to mirror the real but actually see in the real only
their own mirror image. The icon, by contrast, points beyond itself for it 'attempts to

render visible the invisible as such.' The intentional aim of the viewer is not the measure of the icon, which is rather its own measure precisely in the abyss of its measureless infinity. It accomplishes this through an inversion of intentionality in which 'the icon opens in a face that gazes at our gazes in order to summon them to its depth' so that 'the gaze of man is lost in the invisible gaze that visibly envisages him.'[3] This notion corresponds to the description of Marion's third way in phenomenology in terms of 'the pure form of the call' and the replacement of 'every *I* or even *Dasein*' by 'the *interloqué*' (Marion 1998: 204). To see in the iconic mode is not to be the condition of possible experience. Just for this reason what is 'seen,' whether sensibly or conceptually, is present as absent. As with Heidegger, unconcealment and concealment are inseparable.

The saturated phenomenon is another model for what comes to presence as absent, to vision as invisible. In relation to a common phenomenon such as a tree or a house, I intend more than is given in intuition. I have never seen it from every possible angle, nor seen every possible cross-section. My intention is only partially fulfilled in intuition. By contrast, the saturated phenomenon gives me more in intuition than I am able to intend. In this way it is the phenomenon par excellence because it is absolute, neither relative to the transcendental, intending I, nor conditioned and restricted by the horizons the I brings with it like a turtle's shell. Thus it is not mastered, controlled, or constituted by the subject, who is rather overwhelmed and bedazzled by what it cannot foresee, anticipate, measure, or even aim at. It is beyond adequation or fulfillment not by shortage but by excess. Only the saturated phenomenon 'appears truly as itself, of itself, and on the basis of itself . . . to the point of giving *itself* as a *self*' (Marion 2002a: 219). To speak of the phenomenon as a self is to emphasize the passivity of the subject upon whom the phenomenon imposes itself. Here we encounter once again that inversion of the gaze, of the act of *Sinngebung* that we found in the icon. Instead of constituting its object, the subject is constituted by it as witness. This is why the subject can be designated as 'the gifted' as well as 'the *interloqué*' (Marion 2002a: Book V). This does not mean that the subject is a wax tablet. It will be active in seeking to interpret the phenomenon. But (1) the meaning it seeks will have been given before any intentional act on its part, and (2) the hermeneutic task will be infinite, forever incomplete.

Marion distinguishes five types of saturated phenomena (Marion 2002a: 228–33). The first is the historical event. It is a particularly good example of the endless hermeneutic just mentioned. There is no complete and final history of, for example, the French Revolution or World War I. The second is the work of art. Marion speaks of the painting in particular, but also gives Kant's notion of the aesthetic idea, which is not so restricted, in this connection. I can never see all that is to be seen, much less grasp it in any concept, but I am fascinated, drawn back to see it again and again. Marion calls this phenomenon 'the idol,' though the meaning of the term has clearly shifted considerably from its earlier use. The third type of saturated phenomenon he calls 'the flesh.' Here he means the identity of sensing and sensed which refers to no object as in feeling, especially painful feelings. When he speaks of agony, suffering, and grief it is clear that 'flesh' is not restricted to the purely physical. The fourth type is called 'the icon.' Here the term signifies the face of the other in the Levinasian sense. It is the paradigm of the inverse intentionality that Marion extends to every saturated phenomenon.

Finally, there is the phenomenon of revelation or epiphany. Marion is thinking in biblical terms of the events which are seen in faith to be acts of divine revelation. They are not merely saturated phenomena, but they combine and unite the essential features of the other four, 'given at once as historic event, idol, flesh, and icon (face)' (Marion 2002a 235). Following Kierkegaard, he calls this fifth type 'paradox.'

In a provocative little book entitled *The Theological Turn of French Phenomenology*,[4] Dominique Janicaud bemoans and berates those, including Levinas, Ricoeur, and Marion, who have introduced theological motifs into phenomenology, thereby confusing phenomenology with theology and betraying its aspirations toward scientific rigor. Marion makes, in effect, a threefold reply. First, by placing no a priori restrictions whatever on givenness, his phenomenology fulfills the original Husserlian ideals of presuppositionless rigor better than either Husserl or Heidegger. Second, while revelation or epiphany is an instance of the saturated phenomenon, it is not the only one. There are numerous purely secular instances as well. The category is not inherently theological. Finally, phenomenology only describes various possibilities of appearance or experience. So far as revelation is concerned, it is only theology, not phenomenology, that affirms in faith the actuality of such an event, appearance, phenomenon. By showing what kind of phenomenon epiphany would be, if there were any authentic revelation, phenomenology does not cross over the line that separates it from theology. It is dogmatic secularism that forgets that 'it is forbidden to forbid.' 'The denunciation, virulent rather than well-argued . . . of a theological hijacking of phenomenology, betrays chiefly . . . a rather positivist drift in the approach of the phenomenological method itself' (Marion 1997: 288).

In summary, all three of our thinkers are agreed that in our God-talk we should eschew onto-theology. This means that we should avoid turning God into an idol by making God a means to our ends, whether they be theoretical or practical. Among other things, this also means that we must never sacrifice the sense of divine mystery to some purported transparency of reason, no matter how we interpret the divine. Another important agreement, but only between Derrida and Marion, is that any phenomenology that rests on the intentional act of the subject must be *aufgehoben* in an inverse intentionality in which we find our gaze gazed upon. This means that we must understand any talk of the *mysterium tremendum* as response to a call or claim and not the articulation of our own *a prioris*.

The most important difference, of course, is that Marion is an Abrahamic mono-theist (in the mode of a Catholic Christian), while Heidegger and Derrida are not. This disagreement underlies two others. Whereas Heidegger thinks that the task of phenomenology is to guide and, more importantly, to correct theology, Marion thinks its task is to articulate the possibility of revelation as a theistic case of a type of phenomenon that is not essentially theological. Finally, whereas Derrida, in seeking to articulate a religion within the limits of reason alone tends to reduce religion to ethics, Marion understands the task of reason as removing all a priori limits so that every phenomenon, including the possible epiphany of the God of Abraham (Isaac and Jacob), can show itself from itself.

Notes

1. In 'Force of Law' Derrida secularizes this notion by arguing that the laws of any people are always relative to a justice that: (1) is not reducible to the laws; and (2) is not presented as the will of God. In 'Derrida as Natural Law Theorist,' *International Philosophical Quarterly*, XXXIV (2) (June, 1994: 247–52), I argue that Derrida incorporates natural law into his deconstructive reason.
2. Marion develops this argument in *Reduction and Givenness*, and in *Being Given*. See especially the summary on pp. 203–5 of the former and secs 1–6 and 19 of the latter. The specific case against Heidegger is argued (Marion 1991: Chap, 2).
3. Marion 1999: 18–22. Levinas is in the background here, as in Derrida's analysis of the *mysterium tremendum* above. In 'Metaphysics', Marion speaks (Marion 1997: 290) of Levinas's 'extraordinary Copernican revolution' in terms of 'contra-intentionality.' The theme of reverse or inverse intentionality pervades *In Excess* (2002).
4. It includes Marion 2000.

References

Caputo, J. D. (1997a), *The Prayers and Tears of Jacques Derrida: Religion without Religion*, Bloomington: Indiana University Press.

Caputo, J. D. (ed.) (1997b), *Deconstruction in a Nutshell*, New York: Fordham University Press.

Derrida, J. (1992a), 'Of an Apocalyptic Tone Newly Adopted in Philosophy,' in H. Coward, and T. Foshay (eds) (1992), *Derrida and Negative Theology*, Albany: State University of New York Press, 25–72.

Derrida, J. (1992b), 'How to Avoid Speaking: Denials,' in H. Coward, and T. Foshay (eds) (1992), *Derrida and Negative Theology*, Albany: State University of New York Press, pp. 73–142.

Derrida, J. (1995), *The Gift of Death*, trans. D. Wills, Chicago: Chicago University Press.

Derrida, J. (2002a), 'Force of Law: The "Mystical Foundation of Authority,"' in G. Anidjas (ed.) (2002), *Acts of Religion*, New York: Routledge, pp. 228–98.

Derrida, J. (2002b), 'Faith and Knowledge: The Two Sources of "Religion" at the Limits of Reason Alone,' in G. Anidjar (ed.) (2002), *Acts of Religion*, New York: Routledge, pp. 40–101.

Heidegger, M. [1927] (1962), *Being and Time*, trans. J. MacQuarrie and E. Robinson, New York: Harper and Row.

Heidegger, M. (1969), *Identity and Difference*, trans. J. Stambaugh, New York: Harper and Row.

Heidegger, M. (1970), *Hegel's Concept of Experience*, trans. K. R. Dove, New York: Harper and Row.

Heidegger, M. (1977), 'The Word of Nietzsche: "God Is Dead,"' in M. Heidegger (1977), *The Question Concerning Technology*. New York: Harper & Row.

Heidegger, M. (1991), *The Principle of Reason*, trans. R. Lilly, Bloomington: Indiana University Press.

Heidegger, M. (1998), 'Phenomenology and Theology,' in W. McNeill (ed.) (1998), *Pathmarks*, New York: Cambridge University Press, pp. 32–63.

Marion, J.-L. (1991), *God Without Being*, trans. T. A. Carlson, Chicago: University of Chicago Press.

Marion, J.-L. (1997), 'Metaphysics and Phenomenology: A Summary for Theologians,' in G. Ward (ed.) (1997), *The Postmodern God: A Theological Reader*, Oxford: Blackwell, pp. 279–317.

Marion, J.-L. (1998), *Reduction and Givenness: Investigations of Husserl, Heidegger, and Phenomenology*, trans. T. A. Carlson, Evanston: Northwestern University Press.

Marion, J.-L. (1999), 'In the Name: How to Avoid Speaking of "Negative Theology" ' in J. D. Caputo and M. J. Scanlon (eds) (1999), *God, the Gift, and Postmodernism*, Bloomington: Indiana University, pp. 20–41.

Marion, J.-L. (2000), 'The Saturated Phenomenon', in D. Janicaud et al. (2000), *Phenomenology and the 'Theological Turn'*, New York: Fordham University Press, pp. 176–216.

Marion, J.-L. (2001), *The Idol and Distance*, trans. T. A. Carlson, New York: Fordham University Press.

Marion, J.-L. (2002a), *Being Given: Toward a Phenomenology of Givenness*, trans. J. L. Kojky, Stanford: Stanford University Press.

Marion, J.-L. (2002b), *In Excess: Studies of Saturated Phenomena*, trans. R. Horner, and V. Bertrand, New York: Fordham University Press.

Marion, J.-L. (2003), 'Thomas Aquinas and Onto-theo-logy,' in M. Kessler, and C. Sheppard (eds) (2003), *Mystics: Presence and Aporia*, Chicago: University of Chicago Press, pp. 38–74.

Stevenson, C. (1963), *Facts and Values: Studies in Ethical Analysis*, New Haven: Yale University Press.

Westphal, M. (2001), 'Derrida as Natural Law Theorist,' in M. Westphal (2001), *Overcoming Onto-Theology*, New York: Fordham University, pp. 219–28.

Aesthetics

Nicholas Davey

Aesthetics: A Twentieth-Century Epiphany

Whitehead described Western philosophy as a footnote to Plato's. As recent philosophical tradition has shown, some footnotes have established texts of their own. Aesthetics is one such footnote. Whereas Plato banished aesthetics to the realm of *doxa*, Continental philosophy stands witness since the late nineteenth century to a renaissance of aesthetic thought. Now, not only has the discipline achieved a philosophical autonomy but aesthetics has come to haunt those philosophies that marginalize the apparent and the subjective. If earlier forms of aesthetics feted order, recent forms of twentieth-century Continental philosophy are attracted to the sublime and its disruptive power. The violence of the twentieth century makes this understandable but the development was not historically contingent. It was the logical outcome of a sequence of potentialities within the concept that specifically relates to the idea of appearance. As Adorno appreciated, the concept of art is inseparable from the notion of something appearing before the senses and the mind's eye. That which appears is the aesthetic object and the experience of such an object is, as Heidegger calls it, an 'event' (*Ereignis*). Experiences of such 'appearances' can, in Gadamer's opinion, force a change in our understanding of art and what it enables us to understand.

Appearance is of the essence in art. Aesthetic appearance catches us unawares. Heraclitus's aphorism concerning the unexpected has an uncanny relevance for modernist aesthetics: 'if one does not expect the unexpected one will not find it out, since it is not to be searched out, and difficult to compass' (Kirk and Raven 1975: 195). As Heidegger asserts, aesthetic appearance *happens*. The inseparability of aesthetics from the concept of appearance goes largely undiscussed in recent compendiums of aesthetics. This is surprising. The relation between aesthetic appearance and subjective pleasure has been much criticized. A *leitmotif* in twentieth-century aesthetics strives to break the association between aesthetic appearance and subjective pleasure. It is an association which has marginalized the 'knowledge' content of art in favor of scientific methodology. Indeed, the connection between traditional 'aesthetics' and the 'philosophy of the subject' is so strong in Heidegger's mind that he hardly mentions aesthetics per se. Yet appearance is indisputably of the essence in his philosophy of art.

This chapter reflects on several of the key transitions that took place in the intellectual history of the concepts of art and appearance during the twentieth century. To grasp how the concepts of appearance and aesthetics are so entwined, two initial co-ordinates are relevant: Kant's aesthetics and Nietzsche's critique of art and appearance. These give rise to the questions: to what extent does the footnote 'aesthetics' betray its parent text? Does twentieth-century aesthetics re-invent neo-Platonic thought? If art can refer to anything more than 'the darkness of the lived moment,' what order of intelligible appearance must it summons? (Bloch 2000: 188, 199). Is it not the case, as Benjamin argues, that art must be 'something more' than appearance in order to allude critically to what is *within* appearance? If, as Adorno and Gadamer argue, it is necessary for artistic appearance to be flecked by the transcendent in order to be more than dumb appearance, does a nod in the direction of neo-Platonic aesthetics become inevitable?

What lies in a word?

'We should never underestimate what a word can tell us' for, as Gadamer observes, a word gives us our first orientation to 'the accomplishment of thought' (the received traditions of meaning) within it.[1] The beginning of the last century betrays four meanings for 'aesthetics.' First: *aisthesis* links aesthetics with the Greek for *sensuous intuition*. Insofar as it is concerned with the representation of how things appear within space and time, Kant's 'transcendental aesthetic' is consistent with ancient usage and fatefully links the notion of appearance with that of sensibility, that is, with the notion that *something* manifests itself to sensibility (Kant 1970: A 19–A 50, B 34–B 73). Second: the notion of an *aesthetic attitude* – a detached, disinterested way of seeing – values seen objects not for their instrumental potential but for their qualities as a 'sensual manifold,' as well-ordered (beautiful) composites or wholes. This notion derives from Baumgarten (1983) who insisted that a contemplation of landscape remains 'aesthetic' so long as it does not pass from the singular particularities of the observed to a reflection of the 'general idea' of landscape. This usage is attached to the notion of 'taste.' Third: Kant's philosophy supplied a dialectical basis for the 'aesthetic' of enormous consequence. Kant rejected Baumgarten's rationalist demarcation of the sensual and the rational (Kant 1970: 66n.) on the grounds that it rendered art unintelligible: '[T]he understanding can intuit nothing, the senses can think nothing.' He proposed a synthesis of great importance for art theory: '[T]houghts without content are empty, intuitions without concepts are blind. It is . . . necessary to make our concepts sensible, that is, to add the object to them in intuition, as to make our intuitions intelligible, that is, to bring them under concepts' (Kant 1970: A 51, B 75). His doctrine of the 'aesthetic idea' demonstrates how aesthetics became the vital converter within a two-way transmission. The doctrine permits the sensuous dimensions of an art object to assume an intelligible content and permits concepts or ideas to acquire a sensible appearance within art objects. Aesthetics demarcates yet binds, combines and yet remains irreducible to the sensuous or the intellectual. Fourth: the word 'aesthetic' is also used in the singular, as a synonym for *Weltanschauung* or perspective. A Marxist 'aesthetic' or, indeed, 'sensibility' structures the perceived world according to its ideological orientation. A work of art may be said to betray a 'socialist' or 'realist' aesthetic (Eagleton 1990: 1–13).These are invariably 'representationalist': they 'show' an uncertain world in a 'certain' way. Thinkers persuaded of a 'materialist aesthetic' also deploy ideology critically. The work of Pierre Bourdieu highlights the social and economic logics which influence the nature of aesthetic appearance (Bourdieu 1984).

These four uses of aesthetic are not mutually exclusive: they indicate that *pace* Benjamin, the aesthetic may be regarded as a 'constellar' term which configures its meaning differently according to where the historical or philosophical interpreter is placed within its cluster. That the 'aesthetic' is associated with such cognate terms as presentation, mimesis and copy gives it a charged meaningfulness that collides with and transforms different philosophical discourses about the real and the apparent. Nietzsche was acutely aware of how different concepts of the real come into conflict in the 'aesthetic.' His critique of the Platonic devaluation of appearance sets the agenda for much twentieth-century aesthetics.

Friedrich Nietzsche and the Question of Appearance

Like Kant's remarks about 'intuitions without concepts,' there is a passage in Nietzsche's *Twilight of the Idols* which though it was not written about aesthetics, has enormous consequences for the discipline. The passage exposes the philosophically enigmatic question about the relationship between art and appearance: 'We have abolished the real world: what world is left? The apparent world perhaps? . . . But no! with the real world we have also abolished the apparent (*scheinbare*) world!'[2] Does this passage retract a previous assertion?

> What is appearance for me now? Certainly not the opposite of some essence: what could I say about essence except to name the attributes of its appearance? Certainly not a dead mask that one could place on an unknown *x* or remove from it! Appearance is for me that which lives and is effective and goes so far in its self-mockery that it makes me feel that this appearance and will-o'the-wisp is a dance of spirits and nothing more . . . (Nietzsche 1976: 1, 54)

If the antithesis between the apparent world and the true world is reduced to the antithesis between 'world' and 'nothing,' Nietzsche's earlier argument about existence in a meaningless flux being possible only because of aesthetic illusion (*Schein*) appears to contradict itself. 'My philosophy is an inverted Platonism: indeed, the further from actual Being it is, the purer, the more beautiful it is. Life in appearance (*Schein*) as goal' (Nietzsche 1978: I, sec. 79). If the distinction between the 'real' and 'apparent world' cannot be justified, the notion of aesthetic appearance is emptied of meaning. This conundrum straddles twentieth-century aesthetics. Nietzsche's response to it is instructive. On the one hand, his metaphysical argument dismantles the ontological division between the so called 'real' world of intelligible being and *this* actual world of appearances. He repudiates the devaluation of *this* 'actual' world as secondary appearance. This rejection of metaphysical reality and the affirmation of actuality as flux raises obvious questions: (1) What is art's objective co-relative?; (2) To what do the representations of art refer?; (3) If there is no justification for the use of the word 'appearance', can there be any validity to Nietzsche's description of art as *Schein*?

The answer to (1) is that concomitant with his earlier remarks in *The Gay Science*, Nietzsche takes 'appearance as reality' (Nietzsche 1976: VII.3.386). The appearances of art *and* reality are of the *same* ontological order. *Both* are processes of bringing-forth, 'eternally self-creating' and 'eternally self-destroying'.[3] Nietzsche proclaims 'the world to be a work of art that gives birth to itself' (WP: sec. 796). This gives rise to another question: if art is *of* this world in that both are processes of bringing-forth, what makes art *art*?

The answer to (2) involves Nietzsche's denial of Being and his assertion that in actuality there are no things, only processes. This undermines the representationalist view of art intrinsic to metaphysical and naturalist realism. Neither are there meta-physical universals that art represents (Schopenhauer), nor a world of things that art can depict. Twentieth-century German art history demonstrates how Nietzsche's ontology of art was predestined to have a profound impact on the development of visual and literary expressionism. That Nietzsche did not fully anticipate this reflects the fact that his aesthetics lacks a crucial conceptual differentiation (central to Gadamer's aesthetics), that is, the distinction between representation (*vorstellen* – what a work depicts, pictures, produces a likeness of) and presentation (*darstellen* – what comes forth through the art work). True, the distinction is implicit in Nietzsche's *semiotics* of art which reads art as sign or rather as a direct expression of distinct evaluative orientations towards existence. Like Heidegger's hermeneutics of facticity, Nietzsche's aesthetic semiotic anticipates twentieth-century forms of *ideological critique*. The worth of art is measured against an essentially inarticulable truth concerning the profoundly disconcerting sublimity of existence. Do art works celebrate existence, allow us to come to terms with it or do they distort and devalue it? As with other ideological approaches to art, this raises the Platonic question of whether art's value is intrinsically *aesthetic* or dependent upon extra-aesthetic values that it supports or inhibits.

The answer to (3) is that Nietzsche's description of art as *Schein* can be justified but not unproblematically. The argument concerns the status of art's objective co-relative or what art is an appearance of. Nietzsche's ontological monism denies both the existence of an intelligible world and a noumenal realm in relation to which our perceptions can be judged 'apparent' (*Erscheinungen*). Such monism undoes the justification for using 'appearance' and yet Nietzsche continues to use it. That he should do so is instructive. As he insists, we live in a world of appearances.

> Appearance itself belongs to reality: it is a form of its being: that is, in a world where there is no being, a certain calculable world of identical cases must first be created through appearance: a tempo at which observation and comparison are possible. (WP: sec. 568)

Actuality is for Nietzsche a world of inter-actions. What is named the apparent world (*die scheinbare Welt*) is in effect a realm of interactive (interpretative) responses:

> Every centre of force adopts a perspective toward the entire remainder . . . The 'apparent world', therefore is reduced to a specific mode of action on the world,

emanating from a centre . . . Other 'entities' act upon us; our adapted apparent world is an adaption and overpowering of their actions. (WP: sec. 569)

Insofar as the world we live in is an ongoing expressive and interpretative response to our interactive world, 'the question is whether there could not be many other ways of creating such an apparent world' (WP: sec. 569). Nietzsche sees such responses as 'artistic' in that they objectify and visualize interactions according to a 'perspective' which arranges, simplifies, and, indeed, falsifies according to the needs of practical instincts: 'everything of which we become conscious is arranged, simplified . . . through and through' (WP: sec. 477). The 'adapted' world in which we live is indeed an apparent world and 'is false, cruel, contradictory, seductive, without meaning' (WP: sec. 853). The correlative of the apparent world is not the true world of being but the actual, inarticulable, realm of Becoming. What then of the claim that art is *Schein*?

Nietzsche offers a brilliant but ironic reworking of Plato's phrase 'an appearance of an appearance.' The constructions of art manifest a refinement of the *artistic* processes already operative within sensibility. In works of art, the character of existence is once more misunderstood and misrepresented. What we find valuable or helpful in the sensuous world of *Scheinbarkeiten* is further idealized within the art work so that art truly becomes the appearance (*Schein*) of an appearance: 'Appearance . . . signifies reality once more, only selected, strengthened, corrected . . .' (TI: 46); 'The compulsion to transform into the perfect is art' (TI: 109). Nietzsche's references to art as *Schein* are dependent upon their relationship to the world they transform: the empiric world of *Scheinbarkeiten*. Insofar as the process of transformation does not take place arbitrarily but according to life-enhancing or life-denying values, Nietzsche asks about the *meaning* of art: 'Is art a consequence of dissatisfaction with reality? Or an expression of gratitude for happiness enjoyed?' (WP: sec. 489)

Nietzsche's aesthetics prompts two critical observations. First: though laudable for its repudiation of the traditional ontological dualism between art and actuality, Nietzsche's aesthetics remain *ideological*. The question of what is good art is not determined by what is intrinsic to art but by whether an art work promotes an affirmative view of existence. Second: regarding the question of aesthetic appearance, Nietzsche does not offer an account of what makes appearance *truly* appearance? He ties appearance to an objective co-relative: the inarticulable flux of actuality in relation to *Scheinbarkeiten*, or the further simplifications of *Scheinbarkeiten* embarked upon by an art work (*Schein*). He positions appearance and its meaning in relation to an inarticulable ontological truth. His aesthetics does not offer an account of the truth of appearance per se. For this reason, he never escapes the Platonism he seeks to invert (WP: sec. 572).

Yet it is precisely this neo-Platonism that underwrites Nietzsche's conception of art. It attributes *Schein* with a negative power. Apollinian art (the art of the fixed image) stands in negative relation to its objective correlative (unintelligible actuality). Such art presents *Schein* for the fixed world of things it presents does not exist. The psychological function of such art would be lost were it not for its threatening objective correlative. It is precisely a consciousness of that correlative that such art seeks to negate. Art throws *another* veil over appearances (Schopenhauer 1969). Apollinian beauty is a palliative for suffering. Nietzsche's view of Dionysian art beautifying the actual world of change still does not escape this neo-Platonic frame-work. Such art seeks to enhance its correlative, that is, the actual world of flux.

In his essay *The Psychology of the Imagination,* Jean Paul Sartre develops Nietzsche's insight into the negating power of imagined appearances *(*Sartre 1978: 207–26*).* The ability of the aesthetic imagination to create alternatives to the contingent world of *Erscheinungen* is indicative of a freedom not just to 'negate' actuality with day-dreams, but to negate such negativity by inspiring different modes of action within actuality. But it is Michel Foucault who is the true heir to the ontological dimension of Nietzsche's aesthetics. He transforms Nietzsche's argument concerning the production of appear-ances as a 'mode of action on the world' into a question of power. It is not an issue of how 'other entities' act on us but of having the power to represent the world according to one's own interests and to have those representations displace and dominate those of others (Foucault 1974). Nietzsche's equation of power and the production of appear-ances evolves into Foucault's aesthetics of the politics of representation.

Theodor Adorno: Appearance as Promise

If Nietzsche's interpretation of *Schein* is on an axis of affirmation and negation, Adorno's is articulated by an axis of hope and disappointment. The problem of neo-Platonism in twentieth-century aesthetics – the question of art's reference and its ability to display nonartistic truths artistically – is explicit in Theodor Adorno's dialectical meditation on *Aesthetic Theory*.[4] He recognizes the world of immediate sensuous experience as a world of appearances, as untransformed, 'unmodified existence' (AT: 160),'ready to be worked on' (AT: 97). Natural appearances are transient. The appearances of art represent duration (AT: 125). Art thus is *Schein* in that what it promises is not real (AT: 118). 'Appearances in the true sense of the word are appearances of an other. Now, works of art become appearances in this sense when they put the accent on the unreality of their being' (AT: 118). An element of their unreality lies in the fact that they are images of duration. 'Art works *qua* images represent duration, whereas as appearances they represent transience. To experience art means to become conscious of its immanent process at the (fertile) moment when it stands still as it were' (AT: 125).

The relationship between aesthetic appearance and actuality is not a simple opposition between what is imagined and what actually the case is. Adorno accepts that artworks flash a message to the effect that 'it is' against a background which says that 'it is not.' He is more sensitive than Nietzsche to the dialectical connotations of the word *Schein.* Aesthetic appearance cannot be the complete antithesis of truth (Plato); for appearance to be mistaken for the truth, it must stand in a plausible relation to the truth. It could not otherwise present itself persuasively as the truth. Appearance must bear some likeness to the truth or else it cannot be judged as apparent, that is, not the whole truth. For Adorno aesthetic appearance does not re-assemble and thereby corrupt an existent truth. It is rather the appearing, the semblance of a truth to come. The aesthetic appearance remains appearance in that it is the semblance of an anticipated truth. Aesthetic appearance indeed remains *appearance* but such appear-ance is not an untruth.

Adorno's account of aesthetic appearance as the semblance of a-truth-to-come indicates that his aesthetic is not one which holds that aesthetic representation represents or imitates an (external) objective correlative. It stands upon the Hegelian notion of art being the coming-into-appearance (*darstellen*) of an anticipated truth or a projected correlative. The argument is inflected with a Marxist stream of thought which suggests that the enigmatic quality of aesthetic appearance can offer a critique of actuality. That aesthetic appearance is always 'more' than it seems shows that how things are presently seen in the world is not how they have to be seen. Adorno insists that 'every art work works against itself' (AT: 154–5). The tension resides between what the artwork pretends – an anticipatory semblance of its positive correlative – and the actuality within which the artwork exists – its negative correlative. A successful composition will have a completeness that defines it as finished. Every artwork pretends that it is complete (AT: 154). Because they possess a coherent meaning, works of art inflate themselves into an in-itself. Meaning is a vehicle of illusion in them. However, Adorno insists that the essence of meaning is not synonymous with illusion alone; it is *more* (AT: 154). The dialectical component within Adorno's reasoning is clear. In relation to their negative correlative, that is, the self-contradictory world of every-day existence which is harassed by repressive self-interest and the blinkered operation of instrumentalist reason, representations of stable meaning appear illusory. However, drawing from Nietzsche's positive account of art, aesthetic appearance transfigures aspects of actuality. Aesthetic illusion is not just illusion: it does not just manifest the mismatch between the coherence of an aesthetic representation and the incoherence of actuality. It anticipates truth, what can be the case. It discloses how hitherto unperceived elements within actuality have the potential for what presently remains unrealized meaning. In relation to their positive correlative, art works are not representations but '*the summoning into appearance of an essence that is otherwise hidden in empirical reality*' (AT: 154). Aesthetic appearance (*Darstellung*) thereby assumes a critical function. By drawing out potential meanings presently hidden in empirical reality, the artwork anticipates what can be but is not yet the case: not *another* (metaphysical) world but aspects of this actual world brought to its presently unrealized truth. Adorno's aesthetics shares the same empirical framework as Nietzsche's: aesthetic appearance draws out what is already in reality, but selected and corrected (TI: 46). There remains, nevertheless, a tragic paradox in Adorno's argument.

Adorno's aesthetics does not view aesthetic appearance as either a negation or a celebration of actuality. Art brings forth an intimation of a promised land of meaning but art cannot actualize that meaning and remain art. Adorno's thought is inflected with the sadness of Walter Benjamin's aesthetics in which art occupies a fragile space between a regression to a mythic nature and elevation to moral dignity. Art offers no more than a vague image or 'semblance' of human unity with the divine. Art anticipates but cannot create such a world (Benjamin 1999: 45–6). For Adorno, art in relationship to its negative correlative is indeed appearance in the derogatory sense: it throws a veil of sense and order over a fractured world. However, the disjuncture between actuality and representation at least exposes art as *art*, as the fabricator of fictions. In relation to its positive correlative, art can only remain art so long as the disjuncture between the presentation and the realization of that truth is maintained.

Art as *Darstellung* can point to such a truth and bring it into appearance but cannot realize that truth. In bringing forth that truth, art can but remain appearance. Adorno concludes that art is indeed an enigma for it 'expresses something while at the same time hiding it' (Adorno 1977: 176). This is a tragic response to Nietzsche's nihilism: art *presents* what could be the case in a world where it is not and presents what is not the case in a world where it should be. The tragedy is that art can only be art if it is held in-between what is and what is not the case. This in-between quality reveals the enigmatic nature of aesthetic appearance as that which shows and hides itself. Appearance has a surplus quality (AT: 116) which permits it to point beyond itself to an as yet non-existent truth for the sake of which appearance exists in the first place (AT: 160). The neo-Platonic element is evident. Such appearance always remains appearance for, insofar as an artwork can only disclose an aspect of an anticipated truth, it discloses that other aspects of that truth remain undisclosed.

Martin Heidegger: The Autonomy of Aesthetic Appearance

If Adorno's interpretation of appearance articulates an axis of hope and disappointment, Heidegger's approach is marked by an emotional comportment towards openness and receptivity. Heidegger's thought initiates another turn in the twentieth-century biography of aesthetic appearance. Appearance is central to the argument of *Being and Time*. Being is conceived as that which *presents* (*darstellen*) itself in time. Being is 'event,' (*Ereignis*), not a subject or agency that shows itself but a process of disclosure. Being's eschatological characteristics are unclear. Temporality hides but partially discloses them. Temporality reveals patterns in how Being shows itself. The character of such disclosures insinuates but never fully reveals the whole to which they belong. The attraction for Heidegger of Heraclitus's aphorism 'nature loves to hide itself' is obvious. Being as that which encompasses us will never be grasped in its entirety. Its full import is withheld and yet what is withheld still upholds human existence. Appearance or rather the process of appearing is no more and no less than the truth of Being.[5]

Heidegger's approach to appearance is driven by an animosity towards metaphysics comparable to Adorno's antipathy towards instrumentalist reasoning. Both thinkers share Nietzsche's contempt for the concept which straitjackets the vitality of living appearance. Heidegger articulates a '*besinnliches Denken*,' a contemplative mode of thinking which will not schematize phenomenological appearances but seeks instead to be open to their disclosures. Aesthetic contemplation does not go beyond appearance but abides within it waiting for another aspect to show itself.

Heidegger uses the notion of *Erscheinung* to reveal the fissures between different modes of appearance. It is what comes forth (*erschliessen*) in the collision between different idioms of appearance. Objects in the world show themselves to us and, for the most part, we take them to be as they appear. This reveals a double-blindness: (1) We tend to be blind to the selective nature of perception that the early Heidegger called the 'hermeneutics of facticity.' What we take to be the world is not a world-in-itself but an interpreted world which we configure according to our mode of being-in-the-world; (2) That mode of being-in-the-world (*Dasein*) tends to disclose itself only when an unexpected experience challenges assumptions about the perceived. Such hermeneutic 'events' bring-forth a 'clearing' in which a pre-interpreted object shows itself in unexpected ways. This uncovers the ordinarily hidden but operative world of assumptions that shape our perceptual expectancies. Heidegger argues that the specific 'work' (task) of the artwork is to create a 'clearing' between what is termed 'earth' and 'world,' two modes of appearing which incite and intensify each other.

Heidegger has an artist's eye for the relational nature of visual qualities. The juxtaposition of stone and sun allows the glowing stone 'to bring out the light of the day' whilst the light of the day brings forth the steadfastness of the stone (OAW: 42). One quality induces the other to show itself more fully. The conflict of appearances allows us 'to get closer to what *is*' (OAW: 43). No hidden essence is involved. One quality of appearance provokes another to become more essentially itself. Like Adorno, Heidegger holds the view that aesthetic appearance has a transcendent element which strives beyond the immediately material. Its 'plus' brings to the mind's eye what Heidegger calls 'world,' that hermeneutic labyrinth of 'paths and relations' which constitute a community's historical self-understanding. It is not just *Dasein* that is invoked but a historical life-world of a community. The artwork does not picture such a world but brings it into appearance. The Platonic devaluation of aesthetic appearance is reversed. Aesthetic appearance is the medium through which a life-world discloses itself and becomes effective because of its appearances. Heidegger's argument emphasizes that aesthetic appearance always points to something more than itself. A life-world that shows itself cannot show itself completely. The reticent aspect of appearance leads Heidegger to a crucial observation concerning the nature of aesthetic appearance: in bringing-forth showing and hiding are simultaneous. The enigma of an artwork lies in the fact that as aesthetic appearance it discloses and conceals its subject matter, brings it forth and yet at the same time demonstrates that there is always more to come forward. Adorno argues in a similar vein. 'Art . . . hides something whilst at the same time showing it' (Adorno 1977: 178). This for Heidegger is the true nature of aesthetic appearance, a disclosure of 'emergence and sheltering.' Art uncovers something of the essence of Being itself: the conflict of revelation and concealment is 'the truth of every being'.[6] Art's 'truth is not constituted simply by its laying bare its meaning but rather by the unfathomable depth of its meaning.' The artwork is a conflict between emergence and sheltering (HW: 107)

The objective correlative of appearance is for Heidegger *appearance* itself . Aesthetic appearance does not invoke another world of ideas as happens in the arguments of Plotinus and Schopenhauer but 'more' appearance albeit that it is not fully disclosed. What an artwork brings to appearance is *another* appearance of an essence that is not independent of how it shows itself but which resides in the continuities of its disclosures and its holdings-back. Heidegger gives an unexpected nuance to the dictum that 'an art work is an appearance of an appearance'. As that which comes forth, Being does not exist apart from how it shows itself but what reveals itself as appearance discloses that not all is revealed.

In Heidegger's phenomenology, aesthetic appearance attains its autonomy. The autonomy of aesthetic appearance resides in its ability to reveal the extent to which it remains concealed within itself. Coming to stand does not indicate a condition of disclosure as opposed to a state of hiddenness but the process whereby an aesthetic object – precisely because it does come partially forward into disclosure – reveals the extent to which it also partly remains undisclosed. The truth of appearance is ontological: it resides within its own nature and its meaning is not correlative to any other order of being:

The closedness and withdrawnness of the work of art is the guarantee of the universal thesis of Heidegger's philosophy, namely, that beings hold themselves back by coming forward into the openness of presence. The standing-in-itself of the work betokens at the same time the standing-in-itself of beings in general. (HW: 108)

In conclusion, 'coming to stand' does not oppose the intelligible dimension of an appearance against its mysterious aspects. Adorno rightly perceives that the task of understanding an artwork must both dissolve and yet preserve its enigmatic quality (AT: 177). For Heidegger, however, it is exactly because certain aspects of a work can be rendered intelligible that the unseen presence of the full mystery of a work can be brought to light. In contrast to Benjamin's notion, the *aura* of the artwork lies in the complexity of its appearances. Its autonomy does not reside in it belonging to a single historical location. That art images can be transmitted beyond their initial cultural location places them in circumstances capable of drawing out unexpected and hitherto withheld configurations of meaning from within them.

A significant aspect of Heidegger's aesthetics is hermeneutical. By bringing a configuration of meaning into an image, an artwork also foregrounds in the viewer's consciousness what normally remains *Hintergrund*, namely, that 'world' of cultural interpretations which is ontologically prior to the emergence of the work. Heidegger's suggestive insight that an artwork discloses our prior involvement in the world is developed in the work of Maurice Merleau-Ponty (Merleau-Ponty 1993). For Merleau-Ponty the body is pre-reflectively entwined in the world. What manifests itself in aesthetic appearance is not the body's perspective of its interactions with its world (Nietzsche) but that world coming into being through its entanglement with the body.

Gadamer: Appearance as effective Being

Heidegger's approach to aesthetic appearance is articulated by an axis of openness and receptivity. Gadamer views aesthetic appearance as instructive, always capable of revealing more of what has been overlooked or forgotten. He is impressed by the ability of aesthetic appearance to question the assumptions governing our visual field. Gadamer's Hegelian emphasis upon the 'negativity of aesthetic experience' – its power to disrupt aesthetic expectancies – is not unlike Barthes' discussion of how the *punctum* of an image (its ability to reveal the unexpected to the viewer) explodes the formal dimensions of its appearance (the *studium*) (Barthes 1980).

Gadamer's writings on aesthetics are extensive. *Truth and Method*, *The Relevance of the Beautiful*, and 'Word and Image' (*Wort und Bilt*), extend Heidegger's stance. The arguments are built around three notions: (1) play: Gadamer resists the argument that aesthetic experience is purely subjective: it is akin to a dramatic event in that what comes-into-play entails a synthesis of the nonsubjective (rules, equipment, players) with the participation of an audience. The argument is not specific enough. (Does not the spontaneity of artistic creation require the breaking of rules?) Yet it establishes that what a viewer participates in is not reducible to subjectivity alone. (2) the festive: this offers a variation on the Kantian theme of aesthetic disinterestedness. We are not indifferent to the outcome of events within a festival. The festival suspends ordinary interests but it permits us to see the everyday differently, to come together as a community in a free and playful way which the individuated nature of social roles does not normally permit. The argument is reminiscent of Heidegger's conception of a hermeneutically revealed *Dasein*: aesthetic appearance has participatory ontological requirements and is capable of bringing a community to another insight into itself; (3) the symbol: here Gadamer applies Heidegger's insight into aesthetic appearance as the simultaneity of the disclosed and the withheld. Whereas a sign is representational, a symbol is presentational. Signs point beyond themselves. Their function is, aesthetically speaking, to negate themselves, to refer to and not to distract from their intended meaning. The symbol, however, makes its meaning manifest. Meaning and symbol do not exist apart. The symbol does not refer to anything other than itself (RB: 32) but the being of the symbol is always fragmentary. The meaning presented is never given completely. Indeed, within aesthetic *appearance* meaning *cannot* be given in its temporal fullness. The symbolic function of art embodies the autonomy of aesthetic appearance: the symbol is the simultaneity of the disclosed and the withheld.

In *Truth and Method*, Gadamer reverses neo-Platonism's ontological devaluation of appearance:

> The world that appears in the play of presentation does not stand like a copy next to the real world, but is that world in the heightened truth of its being . . . In presentation the presence of what is presented reaches its consummation. . . . What we experience in a work of art (likeness) and what invites our attention is how true it is, to what extent one knows and recognises something and oneself . . . The joy of recognition is rather the joy of knowing *more* than is already familiar. In recognition what we know emerges, as if illuminated, from all the contingent and variable circumstances that condition it: It is grasped in its essence. (TM: 137, 114)

What appears in an art work 'is an increase in the being of the original' (TM: 140): it allows what is presented 'to be for the first time what it is' (TM: 143): it 'belongs so closely to what it is related to that it enriches the being of that as if through a new event of being' (TM: 147). How does aesthetic appearance allow its subject matter to 'to become more what it is'? The transformation-into-structure argument and the argument involving likeness are relevant.

Gadamer attributes a positive ontological function to aesthetic appearance. It does not imitate or distort reality (incoherent or unstructured appearance) but has the capacity to *transform reality into its truth*. In unreflective experience, 'reality' (the world of phenomenological appearances) is invariably given 'in a horizon of the future of observed and feared or, at any rate undecided possibilities . . . (in which) . . . lines of meaning scatter in the void' (TM: 112–13). In contrast, everything within artworks seems illusory for they form meaningful wholes in which unlike the undecided possibilities of the everyday, 'no lines of meaning' disperse (TM: 112–13). What in actuality is unfulfilled, art can complete. 'The being of all play (art) is always realisation. . . . The world of the work of art . . . is . . . a wholly transformed world . . . *From this viewpoint 'reality' is defined as what is untransformed, and art as the raising up of this reality into its truth'* (TM: 113; my emphasis). The argument claims that art enables reality to be seen as being more what it is. Aesthetic appearance is not a second version or copy of an original, but a bringing forth an essence. Gadamer argues:

> A work of art belongs so closely to what is related to it that it enriches the being of that as if through a new event of being. To be fixed in a picture, addressed in a poem . . . are not incidental and remote from what the thing is; they are presentations of the essence itself. (TM: 147)

The reference is not to a metaphysical essence. Like Adorno, Gadamer uses 'essence' to refer to what is no more and no less a set of remembered experiential clusters, a conceptual constellation which gathers around and cross-refers to what shows itself as a commonality of theme. After Husserl, Gadamer names this content 'subject matter' (*Sache*). This is what an artwork points to, suggests and addresses. Like the symbol, it is 'always more' than an individual expression of it. An artwork does not address its subject matter in a vacuum: its address is already mediated by how an artist's epoch grasps such a motif. In this sense, a subject matter is already historically effective in that it shapes contemporary approaches towards itself. A subject matter is, then, the sum of its actual and potential appearances. That any appearance of a subject matter points to what is more than itself does not imply that its essence is other than what is given in appearance. Its effective essence is the full range of its past and future appearances: 'appearance becomes being.' No artwork exhausts a subject matter. Since appearances point to other appearances, the totality of a subject matter's past and future appearances is beyond capture. Furthermore, since a subject matter only comes forth in appearance, it shows only an aspect of itself and hides other aspects of itself. This does not imply that an artwork stands in a negative relationship to its subject matter for inasmuch as aesthetic appearance allows a subject matter to come forth in a new way, it adds to its historical effectiveness. The artwork does indeed increase the being of a subject matter.

Philosophical hermeneutics accords aesthetic appearance a positive ontological value. Appearance is what shows itself. Yet what shows itself in art remains 'appearance' for what is revealed is a fiction. Nothing in actuality is whole or complete. Yet this fiction allows us to see reality *as if* it were – as if it were a work of art. Nevertheless, the account of aesthetic appearance as bringing a subject matter to its truth seems at odds with Gadamer's acceptance of the Heideggerian argument that aesthetic appearance is inseparable from the notion of the withheld. But is it? Does not Gadamer's account of the withheld reverse the relationship between art and the real? As the disclosure of the withheld, the artwork reveals the apparent (that is, incomplete) nature of the actual. Art discloses the presence of the withheld within actuality. Does this not transform our perception of subject matters back into their proper reality? Doesn't aesthetic appearance become the medium whereby something emerges as more real, more complete, precisely, because it is shown to remain partly hidden? Does not the reality of a subject matter reside precisely in the hidden depths of its appearances? Does not a subject matter attain a greater resonance when it becomes apparent that 'all is, indeed, not what it seems' and, furthermore, is it not precisely aesthetic appearance which reveals this truth?

In *Truth and Method*, Gadamer occasionally talks of the tyranny of the given and of the dogmatism of the everyday and customary. His notion of the hermeneutic horizon makes him profoundly aware of how meaningful objects given within our perceptual horizons are not always as they appear. The force of the immediately perceived and the power of perceptual expectation blinds us to the fact that such objects are always *more* than they appear, that is, they have complex hermeneutic histories which can provide alternative and different interpretations of their nature. To differing degrees, Heidegger, Gadamer, and Adorno were of the opinion that instrumentalist reasoning promotes a one-dimensional consciousness which encourages the belief that a thing *is* as it appears and is without any 'inner depth of self-sufficiency.' (Lyotard also celebrates what he terms the *differend*, the power of artworks to disrupt the dominant meta-narratives of a community [Lyotard 1993]). Gadamer's and Heidegger's notion of aesthetic appearance frees us from the superficialities of instrumentalist perception and allows us to discern in the given, the presence of the withheld. Art creates in aesthetic appearance a space in which the things it displays can be discerned in the *fullness* of their being, that is, as subject matters whose meaningful allure resides in their holding themselves back whilst they come forward. Derrida would indeed concur with Gadamer that appearance is art's essence. However, the suggestion that an artwork becomes 'more' has nothing to do with that work achieving a definitive authorial or canonic meaning. Deconstructive aesthetics tends to over-emphasize the disruptive power of the aesthetic event in order to dissipate received meaning.[7] It overlooks the centripetal ability of aesthetic appearance to make whole by revealing not a fixed identity but the inseparability of the withheld and the disclosed within a cluster of appearances. In revealing the withheld, art increases the being of the original subject matter (TM: 140), allowing what is presented to 'stand-in-itself' with an inexhaustible self-sufficiency of meaning and to be open to *constant re-interpretation*. Aesthetic appearance is no longer a footnote. Appearance is of art's essence and is also something of being's essence. It reveals why art remains for *all* the philosophers discussed, a profound and enigmatic challenge to reason and interpretation.

Notes

1. Gadamer 1986: 12. This work will be cited in the text as RB.
2. Nietzsche 1968a: 41. This work will be cited in the text as TI.
3. Nietzsche 1968b: sec. 1067. This work will be cited in the text as WP.
4. Adorno 1977. This work will be cited in the text as AT.
5. Heidegger 1975. This work will be cited in the text as OAW.
6. Gadamer 1994: 107. This work will be cited in the text as HW.
7. For Derrida's critique of unity within an artwork, see his *Truth in Painting* (1987).

References

Adorno, T. (1977), *Aesthetic Theory*, London: Routledge.

Barthes, R. (1980), *Camera Lucida*, New York: Hill and Wang.

Benjamin, W. (1999), *Illuminations*, London: Pimlico

Bernstein, J. (1992), *The Fate of Art*, London: Polity.

Bloch, E. (2000), *The Spirit of Utopia*, Stanford: Stanford University Press.

Bourdieu, P. (1984), *Distinction: A Social Critique of the Judgement of Taste*, trans. R. Nice, London: Routledge and Kegan Paul.

Cooper, D. (1992), *A Companion to Aesthetics*, Oxford: Blackwell.

Derrida, J. (1987), *The Truth in Painting*, Chicago: University of Chicago Press.

Eagleton, T. (1990), *The Ideology of the Aesthetic*, Oxford: Blackwell.

Ferris, D. S. (2004), *The Cambridge Companion to Walter Benjamin*, Cambridge: Cambridge University Press.

Foucault, M. (1974), *The Order of Things, An Archaeology of the Human Sciences*, London: Tavistock Publications.

Gadamer H.-G. (1976), *Philosophical Hermeneutics*, (ed.) D. Linge, Berkeley: University of California Press.

Gadamer H.-G. (1986), *The Relevance of the Beautiful*, London: Cambridge University Press.

Gadamer H.-G. (1989), *Truth and Method*, London: Sheed and Ward.

Gadamer H.-G. (1993), 'Wort und Bild' (1992) appears in *Kunst Als Aussage, Gesammelte Werke*, Band 8, Tübingen, J. C. B. Mohr, secs. 373–99.

Gadamer H.-G. (1994), *Heidegger's Ways*, Albany: State University of New York Press.

Heidegger, M. (1962), *Being and Time*, trans. J. Macquarrie, New York: Harper and Row.

Heidegger, M. (1975), 'The Origin of the Art Work,' in A. Hofstadter (ed.) (1975), *Poetry, Language and Thought*, New York: Harper Row, pp. 15–87.

Kelly, M. (ed.) (1998), *Encyclopaedia of Aesthetics*, 3 vols, New York: Oxford University Press.

Kirk, G. S., and J. E. Raven (eds) (1975), *The Presocratic Philosophers*, Cambridge: Cambridge University Press.

Lyotard, J.-F. (1993), *Of the Sublime: Presence in Question*, Albany: State University of New York Press.

Merleau-Ponty, M. (1993), 'Eye and Mind,' in G. A. Johnson (1993), *The Merleau-Ponty Aesthetics Reader*, Evanston: University of New York Press, pp. 121–49.

Murray, C. (2003), *Key Writers on Art, The Twentieth Century*, London: Routledge.

Nietzsche, F. (1968a), *Twilight of the Idols*, trans. R. J. Hollingdale, London: Penguin.

Nietzsche, F. (1968), *The Will to Power*, trans. W. Kaufmann, and R. J. Hollingdale, London: Weidenfeld and Nicolson.

Nietzsche, F. (1976), *The Gay Science*, trans. W. Kaufmann, New York: Vintage.

Nietzsche, F. (1978), *Die Unschuld des Werdens*, Stuttgart: Kroner.

Sartre, J.-P. (1978), *The Psychology of the Imagination*, London: Methuen.

Sartre, J.-P. (1988), *What is Literature and Other Essays*, Cambridge: Harvard University Press.

Schopenhauer, A. (1969), *The World as Will and Representation*, trans. E. F. J. Payne, 2 vols, New York: Dover Books.

Smith P., and C. Wilde (eds) (2002), *A Companion to Art Theory*, Oxford: Blackwell.

Young, J. (1992), *Nietzsche's Philosophy of Art*. Cambridge: Cambridge University Press.

Young, J. (2002), *Heidegger's Philosophy of Art*, Cambridge: Cambridge University Press.

Zuidervaart, L. (1993), *Adorno's Aesthetic Theory*, Cambridge: MIT Press.

Analytic Themes in Continental Philosophy

Todd May

Before I started my graduate work in Continental philosophy at Penn State in the mid-1980s, I took several courses in analytic philosophy at the University of Pittsburgh. I recall a particular evening before class, overhearing one graduate student tell another that she had just read some Foucault and had found him to be interesting, except that he was a terrible writer. I was irritated at the swipe at Foucault's prose, particularly coming from someone enrolled in a program whose mainstay was Wilfrid Sellars. In retrospect, however, the scene takes on a different hue. Rather than seeing it as just another case of an analytic philosopher demeaning a Continental one, it looks to me more to be a case of an analytic philosopher *reading* a Continental one. For all her shortcomings as a literary critic, this student was taking Foucault onto her philosophical itinerary. She was ahead of the game, and, fortunately, the game is beginning to catch up with her.

It was not always like this: analytic philosophers reading Continental ones and vice versa. At the beginning of the twentieth century, there was no distinction between analytic and Continental philosophy. In fact, the two philosophers who are arguably the founders of their respective traditions, Frege and Husserl, were deeply engaged not only with each other's work but also in a common project (if not from a common angle).

Frege read and wrote a review of Husserl's early work *Philosophy of Arithmetic* (Frege 1977). It was not a friendly review. Frege, not known for philosophical generosity in any case, pointedly criticized what he saw as Husserl's 'psychologism,' that is, his alleged attempt to offer a psychological basis for logic. The extent to which this review captures Husserl's position is often debated, but Husserl himself admitted that it had a profound affect on his own thinking about the issue, and the two exchanged letters on some of the issues the book raises.[1] In the end, both Frege and Husserl wound up rejecting all forms of psychologism. Frege's route, however, led him toward a more or less Platonic position with regard to logical entities. By contrast, Husserl's move was toward transcendental subjectivity, one that he was always at pains to distinguish from any form of psychological subjectivity.

If the late 1800s and early 1900s saw no distinction between an 'analytic' and a 'Continental' philosophy, by the time of the formation of the Vienna Circle, a difference in philosophical styles was becoming more marked. By this time, Martin Heidegger was the chief representative of what would soon become Continental philosophy, and Rudolph Carnap among the central protagonists of a more analytic style of philosophy. The latter group, impressed by the accomplishments of science, sought ways to incorporate its strengths into philosophical work. This incorporation could take many forms, but among them we can isolate at least two core tenets. First, we should carefully define and clarify all significant philosophical terms. Second, we should not posit entities that cannot play a meaningful role in our discourse. The second tenet involved complications, since the question of what a meaningful role is remains elusive. But for all who held to the analytic style of philosophy, there had to be some relationship between meaningfulness and empirical experience.

Carnap clarified and illustrated these tenets in his 1932 article 'The Elimination of Metaphysics through Logical Analysis of Language' (Carnap 1959). In this piece, Carnap distinguishes between classical criticisms of metaphysics and more contemporary ones. The earlier criticisms are based on the idea that metaphysics, which Carnap defines as 'the field of the alleged knowledge of the essence of things which transcends the realm of empirically founded, inductive science' (Carnap 1959: 80), is based on the view that metaphysics is false or fabulous. What developments in contemporary logic allow for is a critique from a different angle. The problem with metaphysical claims is not that they are false; rather, it is that they are meaningless.

As an example, Carnap discusses Heidegger's essay 'What is Metaphysics?' with its infamous statement that 'The Nothing nothings.' In this analysis, Carnap finds Heidegger using the word 'nothing' in defiance not only of empirical support, but of any kind of sense whatsoever:

> This sentence . . . is senseless for a twofold reason. I pointed out earlier that the meaningless words of metaphysics usually owe their origin to the fact that a meaningful word is deprived of its meaning through its metaphorical use in metaphysics. But here we must confront one of those rare cases where a new word is introduced which never had a meaning to begin with. (Carnap 1959: 71)

This review is emblematic of the emerging gap between two philosophical approaches, one that focuses on logic, strict definition, a piecemeal approach to philosophical research, and a fondness for science; the other that focuses on building larger philosophical frameworks, a willingness to engage in metaphorical language, a fondness for literature and the arts, and a leeriness of science as a philosophical model. And, although the terms used for these two approaches are Continental and analytic (or Anglo-American), the geographical references are misleading. There have always been analytic style philosophers working on the Continent (although many of them were forced to leave during the Nazi period in Germany) and Continentalists working in the United States and Britain. The division was philosophical rather than geographical.

Over much of the twentieth century, this distinction grew into a chasm. Where Husserl and Frege were engaged by a philosophical frame of reference and where Carnap at least read Heidegger (if, one might argue, not very well), by the middle of the twentieth century the hardened traditions of analytic and Continental philosophy were comfortable to dismiss each other without the benefit of even a cursory reading. Silence reigned.

In some ways it would have been difficult to get a conversation off the ground. On the one hand, given the interest in politics and normative issues in Continental philosophy, there was little analogous work emerging in the analytic tradition. Normative issues were shunted aside as either meaningless or irrelevant. Noncognitivism was the order of the day regarding normative claims: such claims were not of the cognitive order, and therefore not of philosophical concern. The important issues were epistemological, and more specifically scientific.

On the other hand, while there were in the Continental tradition important philosophers of science, for example Gaston Bachelard and Georges Canguilhem, their concerns were outside the mainstream of analytic philosophy of science. It would not be until the emergence of Thomas Kuhn's *The Structure of Scientific Revolutions* as a significant force in philosophy in the 1960s that the issues that concerned Bachelard and Canguilhem – epistemological breaks, for instance, or questions about both the normative and progressive nature of science – would find their way into analytic philosophy. And even then, analytic references to Kuhn's French counterparts went missing, as did Continental references to Kuhn.

The one philosopher that would perhaps have been able to speak across traditions was Ludwig Wittgenstein. Although he had an importantly noncognitivist streak regarding normative matters, he rejected the idea that language was all of one type – of what Jean François Lyotard would later call a single genre. Wittgenstein's claim that language consisted of different *language games* with different types of inferential moves that were irreducible to one another might have intersected with, for example, Maurice Merleau-Ponty's resistance to a purely cognitive view of language, deepening his poetic and at times expressivist view. It was not to be, however, since the period of the 1940s to the 1960s was one of almost complete mutual disregard between the two traditions.

It is difficult to pinpoint when the ice began to break between them, or what caused it to do so. In general, the causes seem to be on the analytic side more than the Continental one. Continentalists did not become noticeably more analytic in orientation, nor did science begin to play a more prominent role in Continental thought. Analytic philosophers, on the other hand, began to widen their areas of concern and loosen their dependence on science, which introduced themes that could be appropriated by Continental thinkers.

We could make a case for Kuhn's pathbreaking work as the key, if still nascent cause of the thaw between the two traditions, because of the damage it did to the primacy of science as a model for philosophical exploration. Alternatively, we might reasonably point to Richard Rorty's *Philosophy and the Mirror of Nature*, which explicitly brings together thinkers such as Quine and Heidegger, and whose 1979 publication was soon followed by many of the philosophical interactions to be discussed below. We might think of Rorty's book, in contrast to Kuhn's, as of the order of a proximate cause.

I would like to suggest another, earlier, and perhaps deeper cause than Rorty's, however: John Rawls's *A Theory of Justice* (1971). This might seem an odd choice, for several reasons: first, Rawls himself refers to no Continental philosophers (although, as we will see, he later became engaged with the thought of Jürgen Habermas); second, because there was no significant thaw between the two traditions until much after the publication of the book; finally, because Rawls continues to be one of the whipping boys of Continental thinkers in the United States. However, my reason for citing the importance of Rawls's book is that it reintroduced into analytic philosophy the normative themes that had never stopped preoccupying Continentalists, and thus paved the way along which later collaborations would travel.

One might say that since this change is from the analytic side rather than the Continental one, it would more likely have paved the way for Continental themes in analytic philosophy than vice versa. However, by opening the door to themes of long standing in Continental thought, the effect of Rawls's book, I believe, was to ease the atmosphere of mutual suspicion. It is *A Theory of Justice* that prepared the way for the reception of *Philosophy and the Mirror of Nature*. And it is no accident, I think, that some of the borrowings that Continentalists make of analytic themes both predate Rorty's book and postdate Rawls's. Moreover, the fact that Rawls has long been a whipping boy among Continentalists is itself significant. He articulates a position that Continentalists can engage, even if it turns out being critical. It is difficult to imagine such engagement with, say A. J. Ayer or W. V. O. Quine.

What, then, are the appropriations that have begun – and, as yet, only begun – to emerge in Continental thought? Before addressing them specifically, let me offer two preliminary remarks. First, what has happened over the last thirty or thirty-five years has been neither a wholesale convergence of the two traditions, nor a systematic borrowing by Continentalists of specific analytic themes. It has been more ad hoc than that. If there is a consistency to the analytic themes that have appeared in Continental thought, it is that most of them have to do with language. This should not be surprising. During much of the twentieth century, the importance of language in philosophical reflection has been highlighted by both traditions. On the analytic side, this importance has issued in a formidable body of working in the 'philosophy of language' as a particular discipline. This body of work has its own set of problems (for example, that of the nature of reference or of the semantics of indexical statements), and various philosophers who think of themselves as philosophers of language offer contributions to solving these problems. On the Continental side the concern with language has more of the character of an ongoing theme than of an integrated body of work, although some philosophers, for instance Derrida, have concerned themselves centrally with language.

The second preliminary remark is this. Not only are the themes of what I have been calling the Continental 'appropriations' of analytic philosophy diverse, the nature of those appropriations has also been diverse. This idea is consistent with the development of Continental, as opposed to analytic, philosophy. Whereas the latter often works, as we have seen with the philosophy of language, by means of more or less integrated sets of problems to which each philosopher contributes, Continental philosophy may be said to work through the development of particular philosophical perspectives. These perspectives are indeed engaged with the thought of their contemporaries – and, more deeply than in much of analytic philosophy, with the history of philosophy generally. However, the perspectives are distinct enough that they do not form an integrated body of work. Habermas and Gadamer have debated about the role of tradition in underpinning reflection, Ricoeur has criticized more purely structuralist approaches to language, Lyotard and Habermas have sparred over the place of modernity in the contemporary world, but it would be pressing a point to say that these thinkers are addressing the same set of problems within a particular tightly woven philosophical framework.

The upshot of this is that Continental 'appropriations' of analytic themes often occur in ways that would be foreign to a more analytic approach to philosophy. For the Continentalists, it is not simply a matter of agreement or disagreement or extension along a similar path. Continental appropriations are as diverse as deconstructive engagement (Derrida), argumentation (Derrida, Ricoeur, Habermas), conceptual appropriation (Lyotard), and dialogue (Habermas and Ricoeur).

Perhaps it would be best to start with Derrida's deconstruction of Austin's concept of performativity in his article 'Signature Event Context,'[2] both because it is one of the earliest intersections (or re-intersections) of Continental with analytic philosophy and because it begins to close the circle on the period of Continental/analytic silence by overturning Carnap's analytic dismissal of Heidegger with a Continental deconstruction of its own. In this essay, Derrida starts by introducing the concept of *iterability*, which is the repeatability of written (and, as it turns out, also spoken) signs as possessing a certain meaningfulness in the absence of both a designated receiver and sender of those signs. If, for instance, the words 'I love you' are found written on a piece of paper by a pedestrian on a city street, the pedestrian will be able to make some sense of those words without knowing either who wrote them or to whom they were written. Put another way, linguistic communication is not reducible to communicative intent.

What does this have to do with Austin? As the original speech-act theorist, Austin saw language not only as a semantic matter but also as a practical one. As the title of his book *How to Do Things with Words* (1962) suggests, language is not simply a matter of saying, it is also a matter of doing. To take a simple example, a justice of the peace who says the words 'I pronounce you man and wife' in a certain context does not only *mean* something; he or she performs a particular act with a variety of legal implications.

In his approach to linguistic performativity, however, Austin distinguishes between what he calls 'successful' performances and unsuccessful ones, and sees the latter as parasitic on the former. An actor who utters the words 'I pronounce you man and wife' on stage does not commit the same act with the same implications as the justice of the peace does. Derrida agrees with this. Where he disagrees is with Austin's view that the actor's performance is importantly parasitic on the justice of the peace's performance. For Austin, it is because a justice of the peace can perform certain kinds of acts with certain words that an actor can mimic that performance. Successful performances are the standard. The possibility of unsuccessful performances is based on the possibility of successful ones.

What this misses, in Derrida's view, is the role of iterability. Derrida asks:

[U]ltimately, isn't it true that what Austin excludes as anomaly, exception, 'non-serious,' (on stage, in a poem, or a soliloquy) is the determined modification of a general citationality – or rather, a general iterability – without which there would not even be a 'successful' performative? (Derrida 1988: 17)

The 'certain meaningfulness' we saw a moment ago that attaches to words is recognizably the same in the performances of both the justice of the peace and the actor. And it is the context in which each performance takes place, interacting with that certain meaningfulness, that gives each the performative character that it has. Therefore, instead of a model – successful performance – and secondary acts that are parasitical upon it, there is a complex interaction between iterability and context in which the contribution of each cannot be strictly delineated or distinguished from the other.

Following the English translation of this paper, there was an exchange between Derrida and the speech act theorist John Searle. Searle argued that Derrida had misunderstood Austin, and Derrida's reply, entitled 'Limited Inc a b c . . .' is a tour de force of Derridean deconstruction. It weaves together philosophical argumentation in defense of his position with a playfulness regarding the authorship of all three pieces, based upon issues raised by the iterability of language. Reading Searle's piece and Derrida's response side by side shows the contrast between Searle's traditionally analytic argumentative style and a Continental style for which the stakes are larger and the kinds of inferential moves that can be made broader. While Searle's reply takes itself to be offering reasons in favor of Austin's position and against Derrida's, Derrida does not take himself to be attacking Austin in the way Searle interprets. Deconstruction is not disagreement. Rather, it is a way of articulating preconceptions informing a work that *both* support and undermine the overt textual operation of that work.

If Derrida's engagement with Austin and Searle is deconstructive, Lyotard's engagement with Wittgenstein, and to a lesser extent Kripke, is more in the way of a traditional conceptual appropriation. It is not surprising to find Lyotard engaging in conceptual appropriation. His earliest extended work, *Discours, Figure* (1971), owes much to Derrida. *Libidinal Economy* (1993) borrows and extends many of Deleuze's concepts. Moreover, with the turn of his thought toward a particular type of postmodernism, the later thought of Wittgenstein forms an appropriate philosophical source.

What captures Lyotard's attention during the period of the late 1970s and the 1980s is the seeming loss of credence in the traditional legitimating narratives that have come down to us from the Enlightenment. Those are the narratives that tell us who we are and that legitimate the course our history has taken, such as narrative of the progressive emancipation of humankind from superstition and ignorance. For Lyotard, as for others, the Holocaust and the experience of Auschwitz give the lie to many of these legitimating narratives. This loss of legitimation is, however, not a bad thing. It loosens the grip of certain kinds of discourse (scientific or cognitive), and allows legitimacy – if a more local legitimacy – to attach to other kinds of discourse (ethical or aesthetic). If these different kinds of discourses, or what Lyotard calls genres, are allowed to flourish, this can help to end certain forms of linguistic and practical domination that have plagued the post-Enlightenment world.

In articulating this position, Lyotard appeals explicitly to Wittgenstein: 'Wittgenstein, taking up the study of language again from scratch, focuses his attention on the fact of different modes of discourse; he calls the various types of utterances he identifies along the way (a few of which I have listed) *language games*' (Lyotard 1984:

10). Language games, as Lyotard sees them, are not self-legitimating but rather are a matter of engagement or participation. The structure of each is that it has its own stakes, its own norms and rules, and its own inferential and practical structure. This is not to say that the stakes, norms, and structures cannot be changed or modified over time. Rather, it is to argue that genres are not reducible one to another, and there is no single genre, whether it be philosophy, or science, or capitalist economics, or Hegelian speculative thought, that is capable of founding or doing justice to them all. In fact, for Lyotard it is in the nature of an injustice to try to reduce or marginalize one genre in favor of another. In his view, 'a critique of political judgment' must, among its conditions:

> be a politics of Ideas in which justice is not placed under a rule of convergence but rather a rule of divergence . . . Every one of us belongs to several minorities, and what is very important, none of them prevails. It is only then that we can say that the society is just' (Lyotard and Thébaud 1985: 95).

In *The Differend* (1988), Lyotard attempts, in a Wittgensteinian vein but in a much more systematic way, to isolate and describe different linguistic genres. In order to articulate the character and pitfalls of the cognitive genre, the genre of claims and arguments and evidence, he appeals to Saul Kripke's concept of the 'rigid designator.' Kripke uses the term 'rigid designator' in rethinking the idea of the reference of proper names. The accepted idea of the reference of such names derived from Gottlob Frege and Bertrand Russell, and has come to be called the theory of definite descriptions. Under this theory, the reference of a name is given by a set of definite descriptions that attach to the name. Rome, for instance, would be 'the capital of Italy' and 'the location of the Piazza Navona,' and so on. What Kripke shows, in *Naming and Necessity* (1972) is that it is possible for all the definite descriptions to be false, but for a name still to designate someone or something. If this is so, then names must be defined not by their definite descriptions but by a causal process of what Kripke calls a 'baptism.' A name is given to an object, and it stays with that object regardless of what true or false things might be said of it using the name.

Lyotard utilizes the theory of rigid designators in order to articulate a level of names that falls between but links the linguistic world of signification and the silent world of ostension. If ostension is limited to pointing and gesturing at the world, and signification works within the inferential structure of an already articulated language, it is the baptisms of naming that bring together the world and signification:

> If the name can act as a linchpin between an ostensive phrase with its deictics and any given phrase with its sense or senses, it is because it is independent of the current showing and deprived of sense even though it has the twin capacity of designating and being signified. (Lyotard 1988: 43)

One of the upshots of this view of the cognitive genre is that the named object can disappear, in which case it becomes lost to the kind of justifications characteristic of the cognitive genre, since the link from signification to ostension is broken. This, Lyotard argues, is how those who wish to deny the Holocaust press their case. Since there are no eyewitnesses (nobody who has been rigidly designated) to the gas chambers, how do we know they did what they were said to have done? One of the lessons of the Holocaust deniers, Lyotard argues, is that the cognitive genre has its limits, and that we must therefore recognize other genres of discourse, such as the ethical.

If Derrida has engaged analytic philosophy through deconstruction, and Lyotard through conceptual appropriation, Paul Ricoeur, in keeping with his philosophical temperament, has engaged the analytic tradition through hermeneutic dialogue. Among the major Continental thinkers, Ricoeur has, at least since 1975, shown the most consistent engagement with analytic themes. His work on narrative critically engages Carl Hempel's covering-law model of explanation (Ricoeur 1984: 111–20), Frege's theory of reference (Ricoeur 1975: 216–29), Nelson Goodman's aesthetics (Ricoeur 1975: 231–39) among others. But his most sustained engagement with analytic themes comes in his late study of personal identity and selfhood, *Oneself as Another* (1992). In that book, Ricoeur develops a concept of the self that seeks to sustain a notion of ethical responsibility without having recourse to discredited theories of a permanent substantial self lying beneath our individual acts.

Ricoeur's general philosophical approach, which he retains in *Oneself as Another*, is to put divergent philosophical positions in dialogue with one another in order to cull the truth from each. In developing the concept of the self, he is sympathetic with recent critiques of substantial concepts of personal identity, but does not want to eliminate it altogether, given that the philosophical costs of such a move, among others, would be to eliminate as well the possibility of ascribing moral responsibility. The strategy, then, is to navigate between two forms of identity, *ipse*-identity and *idem*-identity. He announces at the beginning of the book that 'I shall henceforth take sameness as synonymous with *idem*-identity and shall oppose to it selfhood (*ipseity*), understood as *ipse*-identity' (Ricoeur 1992: 3). The philosophical goal is to see the complex dialectic between these two forms of identity, out of which a concept of personal identity can arise.

Ricoeur opposes Peter Strawson's ontological individuation into particular things (bodies and people) to Donald Davidson's and Derek Parfit's individuation into events, opting for the former rather than the latter. He argues that if events are the primary mode of individuation, with people becoming merely bearers of events, then concepts of personal identity, intention, and ultimately responsibility become lost. The 'Who?' of actions is effaced in favor of the 'Why?' of explanation. As he puts it:

> The dissociation of the 'what?' and the 'who?', resulting in the shift of the problematic of action to the side of an ontology of the anonymous event, was made possible by a coalition in the opposite direction between the question 'what?' and the question 'why?' (Ricoeur 1992: 61)

What is required in order to recover the 'Who?' is an ontological individuation in terms of persons and their bodies (Strawson's approach), and then a conceptualization of those persons in terms not of a substantial unity but rather a unity of a looser nature. That looser nature is to be discovered in a treatment of temporality, which is neglected in most analytic ontology. Basing his considerations on his earlier work on narrative, Ricoeur works out a narrative conception of the self. He points out the difference between personal character, as a permanence that endures through time, and promise-keeping, which implies the retaining of a commitment over changes we undergo through time. Personal identity, then, is based on a narrative unity that brings together elements of the persisting self with those of the changing (but still committed) self:

> [T]he polarity I am going to examine suggests an intervention of narrative identity in the conceptual constitution of personal identity in a manner of a specific mediator between the pole of character, where *idem* and *ipse* tend to coincide, and the pole of self-maintenance, where selfhood frees itself from sameness. (Ricoeur 1992: 118–19)

The constitution of such a narratively based identity meets the challenge of recent thinkers like Parfit, and Continental thinkers inspired by Nietzsche to offer an account of personal identity that allows for change without, like these latter thinkers, jettisoning the concept altogether.

Derrida, Lyotard, and Ricoeur have focused their engagements with analytic philosophy along the register of the philosophy of language. Jürgen Habermas, by contrast, has, among recent major Continental thinkers, been the philosopher with the closest intersection with themes in recent analytic *political* philosophy. Habermas emerged from the Frankfurt School, and was thus influenced by the thought of Max Horkheimer and Theodor Adorno, Marxists who sought to understand the continuing capitalist hegemony over the course of the twentieth century, well past the period when Marx would have predicted a proletarian revolution. While Habermas sympathized with Horkheimer's and Adorno's analyses of the ability of capitalism to co-opt dissent and to blunt critical rationality in favor of a personal calculus of interest, particularly in their magisterial work *Dialectic of Enlightenment* (1972), he worried that their work had painted them into a corner. If capitalism has the ability to undercut all critical reflection, then liberation is doomed in advance. The project, then, as Habermas sees it, is to move beyond critique in order to discover or construct a space of rationality that eludes capitalist co-optation and therefore allows the conception of alternatives to capitalism.

Habermas's work in this area has gone through several phases, but recently has taken on a structure that intersects with the social contract theory revived by John Rawls's *A Theory of Justice*. That structure, which Habermas names 'discourse ethics,' calls for norms to be decided upon solely through rational discussion in which all participants have an equal voice and can agree on as well as discuss any proposed norms. As he puts the point: '[O]nly those norms can claim to be valid that meet (or could meet) with the approval of all concerned in their capacity as participants in a practical discourse' (Habermas 1990: 90). Discourse ethics is a procedural approach to the development of norms of social interaction. Rather than positing specific norms, it posits a procedure from which norms undistorted by the power relations of current society can emerge. The justice of the approach, as with the justice of Rawls's approach, lies in the procedure rather than with any particular norms or principles that derive from it.

There is a deep affinity, it seems to me, between Habermas's discourse ethics and the contractarian approach developed by Thomas Scanlon, which holds that those norms and principles are justified that cannot be reasonably rejected by anyone affected by them.[3] One could see Habermas's and Scanlon's procedures as inversions of each other. While Habermas bases the justification of principles on their actual acceptance or acceptability, Scanlon bases it on their failing to have a reasonable basis for refusal.

However, it is with Rawls that Habermas has put discourse ethics in dialogue, especially in a recent essay, 'Reconciliation through the Public Use of Reason: Remarks on John Rawls' *Political Liberalism*' (Habermas 1995). Here he contrasts the procedure of discourse ethics, which calls for actual conversation among participants in order to arrive at a consensus, with Rawls's more individualistic procedure of imagining what people would countenance in the 'original position,' a situation in which they are stripped of any knowledge of their specific attributes and then required to design principles of the society in which they would want to live based on that ignorance. Although Habermas finds much to admire in Rawls's approach, he is uncomfortable with several aspects of it, among which is the structure of the original position, which seems to move *away* from the social procedure of dialogue and mutual recognition rather than *toward* it:

> Rawls imposes a common perspective on the parties in the original position through informational constraints and thereby neutralizes the multiplicity of particular interpretive practices from the outset. Discourse ethics, by contrast, views the moral point of view as embodied in an intersubjective practice of argumentation which enjoins those involved to an idealizing *enlargement* of their interpretive perspectives. (Habermas 1995: 117)

If, as Habermas claims, the goal of contractarian theory is to arrive at acceptable principles of guidance and governance among diverse parties, then the method must reflect that goal. Rather than placing an anonymous individual behind a veil of ignorance, we must put diverse beings in dialogue with one another in order to clarify and navigate through personal and cultural differences. Otherwise put, the moral recognition of and engagement with diversity must lie in the process of contract formation, not merely in its result.

With Derrida, Lyotard, Ricoeur, and Habermas, much ground has been laid for a more consistent intersection between the Continental and analytic traditions. This intersection does not imply that somehow the 'same things' are happening in one tradition as in the other. In fact, as we have seen, it is often the productive differences between the two that allow for the most interesting dialogue. Nor are the engagements from the Continental side systematic. They are, however, fruitful. Before closing, I would like to point out several other areas in which such fruitful interaction might occur.

The first of these has, in a sense, already begun to take place. It runs through the work of Alain Badiou, who develops an ontological approach based on mathematical set theory. In his major work *L'être et l'évènement* (1988), he utilizes the mathematical work of Georg Cantor and Paul Cohen among others to develop a theory of multi-plicitous Being that lacks any of the unitary quality associated with thinkers like Gilles Deleuze. Although Badiou appeals mostly to the work of mathematicians, one philosopher whose work on set theory is central to his thought is Bertrand Russell. It is Russell's paradox (the set of all sets, which must also include itself) that puts set theory on the path of becoming more purely abstract and self-consistent, thus allowing for a pure multiplicity rather than one based on any empirical notions. Although Badiou has rarely set his work in dialogue with particular contemporary analytic thinkers, he has suggested that it has implications for issues addressed by analytic thinkers. For instance, in a recent article he argues that:

> Where the thinking of Number is concerned, we must abandon not only Frege's approach but also the respective approaches of Peano, Russell and Wittgenstein. The project started by Dedekind and Cantor must be radicalized, exceeded, pushed to the point of its dissolution. (Badiou 2004: 65)

If Badiou's is a program that begins to intersect with the analytic tradition, there are at least two other areas where little intersection has occurred but seems inviting. The first would involve the engagement of hermeneutics, particularly that of Gadamer, with Davidsonian semantics. Gadamer's work, particularly *Truth and Method* (1985) takes seriously Heidegger's claim that interpretation requires a pre-understanding of what is interpreted. We cannot interpret from scratch; all interpretation occurs within a framework of what Gadamer calls 'prejudices' without which interpretation would not get off the ground. This does not mean that interpretation can only discover in a text that which it has already placed there. What interpretation seeks is a 'fusing of horizons' in which the interpreted can at once be incorporated into and expand the framework of the interpreter.

For his part, Donald Davidson views all linguistic communication as a matter of radical interpretation (Davidson 1984). Radical interpretation is a situation in which an interpreter needs to understand another but must start from interpretive scratch, that is, without any understanding of the language of the other. (In cases where the interpreter believes that he or she speaks the same language as the interpreted, it still requires interpretation to assure oneself of *that*.) In order for radical interpretation to occur, we must assume the truth of most of the beliefs of the interpreted in order to make sense of other things the interpreted says and does. For Davidson, truth, meaning, and action form an interpretive whole. The holism of Davidson's semantics is not the same thing as the fusing of horizons of Gadamerian hermeneutics, but there is much room for dialogue here.

Second, there is an opening for work in the intersection of Michel Foucault's discussions of power/knowledge and recent work in the inferentialism of Wilfrid Sellars and Robert Brandom.[4] While the former is political and epistemological and the latter primarily linguistic, there are important convergences in their work. Both take the idea of practices as a central unit of interpretation; both see epistemic commitments as inextricable from those practices; both see those commitments in terms that are nonfoundational and subject to circumstance. While the latter authors articulate the linguistic and epistemic structure of those practices, Foucault concentrates on the political character of their development and intersections. Bringing the two together offers the possibility of a philosophical framework that would address both the epistemic and linguistic issues characteristic of analytic philosophy and the political concerns that have animated Continental thinkers.[5]

Notes

1. For an in-depth discussion of the relationship between Husserl's and Frege's thought, see Mohanty (1982). The appendix to this book includes letters the two philosophers sent to each other detailing their agreements and disagreements.
2. The article first appears in Derrida 1972, although it was delivered as a talk in 1971. The citation below is from the later *Limited Inc* (Derrida 1988), which also includes John Searle's reply and Derrida's reply to Searle.
3. Although this approach appears in many of Scanlon's essays, his full articulation of this position appears in his recent book *What We Owe to Each Other* (1998). Scanlon compares his work briefly with that of Habermas in a couple of footnotes: pp. 393–4, n. 5, and p. 395, n. 18.
4. Sellars's most famous work is his essay, 'Empiricism and the Philosophy of Mind' (1963). Brandom's major philosophical statement is *Making it Explicit* (1994).
5. I have tried to begin this dialogue, especially in *Between Genealogy and Epistemology* (1993), and *Reconsidering Difference* (1997).

References

Ayer, A. J. (1959), *Logical Positivism*, New York: The Free Press.

Badiou, A. (1988), *L'être et l' évènement*, Paris: Éditions du Seuil.

Badiou, A. [1994] (2004), 'The Being of Number,' in R. Brassier, and A. Toscano (eds and trans.) (2004), *Theoretical Writings*, London: Continuum Press.

Brandom, R. (1994), *Making it Explicit*, Cambridge: Harvard University Press.

Carnap, R. [1932] (1959), 'The Elimination of Metaphysics through the Logical Analysis of Language,' in A. J. Ayer (ed.) (1959), *Logical Positivism*, trans. A. Pap, New York: The Free Press, pp. 60–81.

Davidson, D. (1984), *Essays on Truth and Interpretation*, Oxford: Oxford University Press.

Derrida, J. [1972] (1988), 'Signature, Event, Context,' in J. Derrida (1988), *Limited Inc.*, trans. S. Weber and J. Mehlman, Evanston: Northwestern University Press, pp. 1–23.

Frege, G. [1984] (1977) 'Review of Dr. E. Husserl's Philosophy of Arithmetic,' in F. A. Elliston and P. McCormick (eds) (1977), *Husserl: Expositions and Appraisals*, Notre Dame: University of Notre Dame Press, pp. 314–24.

Gadamer, H.-G. [1975] (1985), *Truth and Method*, trans. G. Barden, and J. Cumming, New York: Crossroad.

Habermas, J. [1983] (1990), 'Discourse Ethics: Notes on a Program of Philosophical Justification,' in S. Benhabib, and F. Dallmayr (eds) (1990), *The Communicative Ethics Controversy*, trans. S. W. Nicholsen, and C. Lenhardt, Cambridge: MIT Press, pp. 60–109.

Habermas, J. (1995), 'Reconciliation through the Public Use of Reason: Remarks on John Rawls' *Political Liberalism*,' *Journal of Philosophy*, 92(3) (March): 109–31.

Horkheimer, M., and T. Adorno, [1944] (1972), *Dialectic of Enlightenment*, trans. J. Cumming, New York: Seabury Press.

Kripke, S. (1972), *Naming and Necessity*, Cambridge: Harvard University Press.

Lyotard, J.-F. (1971), *Discours, figure*, Paris: Klincksieck.

Lyotard, J.-F. [1974] (1993), *Libidinal Economy*, trans. I. H. Grant, Bloomington: Indiana University Press.

Lyotard, J.-F. [1979] (1984), *The Postmodern Condition: A Report on Knowledge*, trans. G. Bennington, and B. Massumi, Minneapolis: University of Minnesota Press.

Lyotard, J.-F. [1983] (1988) *The Differend: Phrases in Dispute*, trans. Georges van den Abbeele, Minneapolis: University of Minnesota Press.

Lyotard, J.-F., and J.-L. Thébaud [1979] (1988), *Just Gaming*, trans. W. Godzich, Minneapolis: University of Minnesota Press.

May, T. (1993), *Between Genealogy and Epistemology: Psychology, Politics and Knowledge in the Thought of Michel Foucault*. University Park: Pennsylvania State University Press.

May, T. (1997), *Reconsidering Difference: Nancy, Derrida, Levinas, and Deleuze*, University Park: Pennsylvania State University Press.

Mohanty, J. N. (1982), *Husserl and Frege*, Bloomimgton: Indiana University Press.

Ricoeur, P. [1983] (1984), *Time and Narrative*, vol. 1, trans. K. McLaughlin, and D. Pellauer, Chicago: University of Chicago Press.

Ricoeur, P. [1975] (1977), *The Rule of Metaphor: Multi-Disciplinary Studies of the Creation of Meaning in Language*, trans. R. Czerny, with K. McLaughlin, and J. Costello: University of Toronto Press.

Ricoeur, P. [1977] (1992), *Oneself as Another*, trans. K. Blamey, Chicago: University of Chicago Press.

Scanlon, T. (1998), *What We Owe to Each Other*, Cambridge: Harvard University Press.

Sellars, W. (1963), 'Empiricism and the Philosophy of Mind,' in W. Sellars (1963), *Science, Perception and Reality*, London: Routledge and Kegan Paul.

Non-Western Philosophies in the Twentieth Century

Indian Philosophy

Rohit Dalvi

Tradition and Modernity

At least since Hegel, Indian thought has been excluded from the proper domain of philosophy. Despite the vigorous affirmation by the German Romantics of the value of Sanskrit poetry and literature, and the celebration by philologists like Max Mueller of the cultural and linguistic proximity of Sanskritic civilization to Europe, the European philosophical tradition, with perhaps the exception of Schopenhauer, has rejected the idea of an Indian 'philosophy.' Classical Indian 'philosophy' was not regarded as at par, in terms of rigor and rationality, with the products of European civilization. Indian thinking was devalued as being thoroughly religious in character or as mere existential musings.

Modern Indian philosophy seeks to explicate the 'religiosity' of Indian thinking and to articulate the classical philosophical programs in a modern idiom, adopting a form of discourse and analysis of problems that challenge the presuppositions of any devaluation. Philosophy in twentieth-century India is not restricted to an exegesis of the tradition. In rethinking and offering an exposition of traditional themes and concepts, modern Indian philosophers establish dialogues and comparisons with philosophers ranging from Plato to Kant and Husserl, thus practicing a type of 'comparative' philosophy and creating the space for an inter-illumination of concepts, arguments, and positions. Gradually, European philosophical style, technical vocabulary, and categorial schemes have blended with traditional approaches to produce a 'fusion' philosophy. This hybrid philosophy moves beyond pointing out similarities and contrasts between philosophical traditions. It deploys concepts and arguments across traditions in order better to understand and address genuine philosophical problems.

The Sanskrit term *darsana* is the rubric under which classical India engaged in and understood its philosophical practice. It does not connote a 'love of wisdom' for its own sake, but a vision – an insight into the nature of reality – indispensable for overcoming various forms of suffering. Suffering, it is argued, is a product of a distorted picture of reality and a misunderstanding of its basic principles. Our defective grasp of reality ensnares us in a cycle of birth and death, which is referred to in classical philosophy through the trope of 'bondage.' The task of philosophy, on some interpretations, is to provide a corrective to our distorted picture of reality and free us from this 'bondage.' Despite this mystical sounding concept and all the associations of Indian philosophy with 'spirituality' that would seem to eschew philosophical argument, the classical Indic tradition is deeply invested in rational argumentation brought to bear on philosophical problems. It is nevertheless true that philosophical theorizing and argumentation is seldom an end in itself in the classical Indic context; it is instrumental and often essential, in moving toward liberation (*mukti*, *moksha*).

The *darsanas*, traditionally six in number and each giving rise to a distinct school of philosophy, engage in philosophical speculation – whether as epistemology or meta-physics–arguably with a soteriology in mind. These *darsanas* and their development into systems adopt positions ranging from the naive realism of the Nyaya logicians to the idealism of Vedanta, the doctrines of emptiness in Madhyamika Buddhism, or the relativistic ontology of the Jains. Although certain developments in the Nyaya school of logic and linguistic philosophy seem to be purely intellectual projects, liberation as the goal of philosophical activity is an important theme in the Indic world. In one sense, the modern debates are attempting the reconciliation of the intuitive, liberation-centered approach of the tradition with the perspective according to which rational procedures and norms for evaluating beliefs, that is to say, discursiveness and critical attitude, are integral components of classical philosophy. Is it intuitive awareness or rational inquiry which permits access to reality? Or is it a combination of these that can give us access to reality? What is the place of logical arguments in classical Indian philosophy? What does the 'spirituality' and 'religiosity' of the classical tradition mean? This debate constitutes the lens through which modern Indian philosophy can be viewed.

The philosophical tradition available to the early twentieth-century thinkers in India included not only the canonical scriptures like the Vedas, the more overtly philosophical Upanishads and the Gita, but also the main texts (*sutras*) of the philosophical schools namely Nyaya, Vaisesika, Sankhya, Mimansa, Yoga, and Vedanta as well as the texts of the various schools and sub-schools of the Buddhist and Jain traditions. Besides the founding texts of these schools or lineages (*parampara*), which articulated the basic conceptual framework, a veritable forest of commentaries on these texts, which included lengthy philosophical arguments in the interests of exegesis and debates with opposing schools, was also available. Developments outside the classical Sanskrit milieu, such as the devotional *bhakti* philosophies, enjoyed popular currency.

The classical tradition, although divided into schools which were mutually com-petitive if not antagonistic, shared a methodological framework called the *pramana-sastra* (the discourse of the reliable means of knowledge). Although differing widely in their ontologies and their metaphysical preferences, the classical schools adhered to this methodological framework, which established epistemological standards for assertions about the world. The various classical philosophical schools shared a technical vocabulary and rhetorical style as much as they shared an interest in liberation and related issues.

The Colonial Context

The history of modernity in India is inextricably linked to the transformation of India under British rule. The British colonial apparatus introduced regimes of knowledge that transformed the way in which Indians understood their own philosophical and religious traditions. The traditions were increasingly seen through a Western lens. Whether through the founding of colleges for the study of classical Sanskrit texts, translation programs, the imposition of the English language in education, the introduction of European philosophy and science, or the blatant dismissal of Indian intellectual culture, the colonial program set the stage and provided the context for the development of twentieth-century Indian philosophy. The soteriological concerns of the classical philosophy had been aligned with concerns for social and religious reform since the mid-nineteenth century by liberal reformists like Raja Rammohun Roy, and other figures associated with the Bengal Renaissance. Roy tapped into the Upanishads and the Vedanta tradition to move Hinduism toward what he believed was an implicit monotheism, thus earning from Schopenhauer the epithet 'Brahmin turned Jew.' The nineteenth century witnessed a flurry of intellectual activity which involved rethinking traditional concepts in the light of the encounter with European philosophy ranging from Bacon and Voltaire to Darwin and utilitarianism. Apologetics for Indian intellectual and religious heritage and discussions of social reform proliferated.

Through the nineteenth and early twentieth century, classical philosophical texts were being edited and published by the Asiatic Society, various government agencies, and privately owned presses. The recently founded journal *Pandit* provided a forum for the discussion of classical philosophy. This was complemented by the contributions of European indology, which included the first modern survey of classical Indian philosophy, Max Mueller's *Six Systems of Indian Philosophy* (1899). The colonial context for early twentieth-century Indian philosophy was manifest most importantly in the dominance of English as an academic language. Sanskrit, the language of classical Indian philosophy, which had an aura of the sacral and the arcane, receded from mainstream Indian intellectual life, at least as a medium of exchange and expression. Moreover, philosophy, which had until recently been the domain of *pandits* and *sastris*, that is, the traditional Brahminical scholars and exegetes, became largely the domain of university professors some of whom were traditionally trained scholars (although one of the most influential thinkers of the late nineteenth century, Swami Vivekananda, was not an academic and neither were two important figures of the early twentieth century, Gandhi and Sri Aurobindo). Since the nineteenth century, the classical Indian tradition, especially the Hindu tradition, had been appropriated and deployed in the service of an agenda of social reform. This rethinking of the tradition, outside the hermeneutic constraints of its norms and in the light of the discovery of the European category 'philosophy,' was an impetus for the application of philosophical ideas in the sphere of nationalist politics and religious reform within Hinduism.

The modern philosophical style was a departure from the mould of classical philosophy and indicated that philosophy in India would no longer remain limited to what had hitherto been called 'Indian Philosophy,' but would become syncretistic – not least because it was practiced primarily in English. It was open to European modes of practicing philosophy, as well as adopting a philosophical approach to political and social concerns. However as translations of philosophical texts into English and the influence of English language scholarship proliferated, Ganganath Jha (1871–1941), Professor of Sanskrit and the doyen of translators, warned students of Indian philosophy (in a 1926 presidential address of the recently founded Indian Philosophical Congress) against depending overly on English translations which can not only prove misleading but also distort concepts and arguments, thereby stressing the need to read the texts in the original.

In the twentieth century, philosophy in India has seen an extensive re-interpretation of classical philosophy under the influence of British Neo-Hegelianism – especially in the work of Hiralal Haldar (1865–1942), a self-professed Hegelian. Tradition was re-examined in terms of British analytic philosophy as it started to be influential in Indian universities. This is especially true of the work of Bimal Matilal, P. K. Sen, and Daya Krishna among others. Occasionally, German phenomenology, including Heidegger's, influenced the re-interpretation of traditional texts and arguments as well as original philosophical discussions – most significantly in the work of J. L. Mehta and J. N. Mohanty, in the post-independence milieu.

Modernity for philosophers in India has meant thinking in terms of a horizon of intelligibility which is basically Western. Yet, there is a persistent stance, which contends that philosophy's concern should not be 'to conceive of a philosophical scheme like a toy machine to play with, but to make of it a chariot in which man could ride' (Radhakrishnan and Muirhead 1958: 15).

Nationalism, Reform, and Philosophy

If philosophical ideas are to be judged on the basis of their influence in the world, then Gandhi could easily prove to be the most significant philosopher of twentieth-century India. Although not directly concerned with philosophy as an intellectual or academic pursuit, Gandhi developed political and moral concepts based on core Hindu values and ideas borrowed from Tolstoy, which have transformed India's political and social landscape since. Gandhi, who described himself as a 'humble seeker after truth,' considered liberation, in the traditional sense, as his ultimate goal. Patriotic service was for him a stage in the journey toward liberation, a part of his 'training' for freeing himself 'from the bondage of flesh.' He thought of Hinduism simply as a pursuit of truth by nonviolent means. Such as open view of Hinduism rejected the doctrinal constraints of orthodoxy. This novel approach to Hinduism, Gandhi's concept of nonviolent resistance (*satyagraha*) placed political action within a framework of metaphysical concepts and values. Gandhian values of nonviolence (*ahimsa*) and truth became a cornerstone of the emerging nationalist movement.

As far as philosophy as an academic discipline goes, Swami Vivekananda's (1863–1902) influence cannot be discounted. Vivekananda deployed the classical, especially Vedantic metaphysics and ethical norms, as represented in the Gita and the Upanishads, to articulate a philosophy that concerned itself with modernity in India. The Hindu philosophical-religious tradition was seen as an enabling resource for Indian nationalism and the resurgence of an oppressed Indian civilization, and also as providing the basis for a renewal of Indian or even global 'spirituality.' Vivekananda's international prestige was enough to persuade Harvard to offer him the chair of Oriental philosophy.

The classical nondualistic (*Advaita*) Vedanta system, promoted by Vivekananda, holds that reality is one; differences and the plurality that we experience are nothing more than a product of our mistaken grasp of reality. This philosophical system is based on a monistic interpretation of canonical texts like the Upanishads and the Gita. Under the sway of a 'beginningless' ignorance (*avidya*), we misconstrue the Self and its relation to reality – that which is merely appearance we take to be reality.

Vivekananda energized the nondualism of the Upanishads and presented the formulation of the discipline of action (*karmayoga*) of the Gita in a contemporary idiom. The concept of liberation for Vivekananda became connected to service to others as he sought to bring the 'religiosity' of the Vedanta philosophy into life, that is to say, to make Vedanta 'practical.' After all the 'intellectual gymnastics,' the message of Vedanta is encapsulated in the 'great statements' (*mahavakya*) of the Upanishads, 'That thou art,' which points to the fact that despite appearances the Self is identical with the one Reality (*Brahman*). Liberation is the realization of this identity. The 'practical Vedanta' of Vivekananda moves philosophical insights and spiritual practices away from the arcane disciplines of ancient Indian seers, monks, and yogis. It is a discipline of liberation, which can be adopted by people in their quotidian settings. Nondualistic Vedanta focuses on removing our erroneous conception about ourselves, the world, and plurality by a metaphysics of appearances, and our mistaken apprehension of them as if they were reality. In this monistic philosophy, whose most prolific and significant expositor was the eighth century philosopher Sankara, the themes of oneness, unity and identity become all important as does liberation – the *telos* of philosophy. Vivekananda's 'practical Vedanta' is thus committed to 'concrete moral forms' and 'scientific practical psychology' as its results. The practicality of this version of Vedanta diminishes the importance of concepts like primordial ignorance (*avidya*), power of cosmic illusion (*maya*), undifferentiated being or the absolute (*Brahman*), and the intricate metaphysics of monism and the rejection of difference. This philosophical system, to a large extent because of Vivekananda's prolific and popularly accessible writing and the 'practicality' of his ideas, became the dominant philosophical system and has enjoyed the sympathy of many modern Indian philosophers.

Sri Aurobindo (1872–1950)

Aurobindo Ghose, who began his career as a nationalist struggling against British rule, followed Swami Vivekananda in that his thought represents a rethinking and redeployment of classical Indian philosophy, especially the tradition of the nondualistic interpretation of the Vedas and the Gita. Aurobindo departs from Sankara's interpretation of Vedanta. His system, unlike Sankara's, does not consider the empirical world to be illusory. He 'finds a place for the history of mankind within Advaita and proposes a new kind of yoga adapted not to the goal of an individual's own liberation but to the (collective) goal of elevating mankind to a higher form of consciousness ("supermind")' (Mohanty 2001: 71).

Philosophy for Aurobindo is the search for the truth behind appearances, and religion makes 'the truth dynamic in the soul of man' (Aurobindo 1973: 177). Unlike Vivekananda or Gandhi, who were more interested in the ramifications of their thought for moral, social, and political reform within the context of the nationalist struggle, Aurobindo, especially after his 'retirement' from political life, adopted a more systematic approach. His system, designed to lead one to the Life Divine, remains firmly within the soteriological mode of doing philosophy. For Aurobindo, philosophy that is not invigorated with religiosity is 'barren' in that it can never translate into practice.

The intricate relationship between national aspirations to freedom from British rule and the classical tradition is evident in the role attributed to the tradition in the nationalist struggle and its significance for India and the world. In his address on the occasion of Indian independence, Aurobindo writes:

> For I have always held that India was arising, not to serve her own material interests only . . . and certainly not like others to acquire domination of other peoples, but to live for God and the world as a helper and leader of the whole human race' (Aurobindo 1964: 41).

According to him, India's gift to humanity is the 'spiritual knowledge' that will enable a 'spiritualization of life,' as humanity moves to overcome the divisions of race and ethnicity. Aurobindo reframes the question of liberation in a way reminiscent of Nietzsche. The human being is a 'transitional being' because in Man the potential to acheive a 'divine supermanhood' can be found. Mind – the 'ignorant seeker of truth' – can ascend to a state of consciousness, which is 'supramental.' This state of gnosis is an eternal possession of Truth and is free from the fetters of 'material consciousness.' The *atman* or soul, which Vedantic philosophy makes the centerpiece of its program of spiritual development, Aurobindo understands as a possibility rather than something which is effectively present in human beings. Realizing this possibility does not require mental effort; it is only with the stillness or 'immobility' of the mind that the 'superconscient' Truth can be attained. Awakening to the supermind entails a complete transformation of the human being. Aurobindo believes that the transition to it is the next evolutionary step that will be prompted by the 'intention of inner spirit and the logic of Nature's process.' The danger exists that 'inner luminosity' can become warped, concealed, and distorted by the 'dense outer coating' of the body or of the 'constructed personality.' In keeping with the traditional liberatory program of nondualistic Vedanta, Aurobindo writes:

> Cease inwardly from thought and word, be motionless within you, look upward into the light and outward into the vast cosmic consciousness that is around you. Be more and more one with the brightness and the vastness. Then will truth dawn on you from above and will flow in you from all around. (Aurobindo 1973: 60)

A theory of evolutionary progress is pivotal in Aurobindo's system and is conceived as 'Nature's ascent.' As opposed to the Western idea of evolution, which Aurobindo thinks theorizes a 'process of formation,' his concept of evolution is an 'explanation of our being.' This concept is developed under the assumption that there is 'one original eternal substance of which all things are the forms and one original eternal energy of which all movement of action and consequence is the variation' (Aurobindo 1973: 63).

Like Vivekananda, Aurobindo accepts the monistic premise: evolution which leads to an eventual development beyond the Mind can occur because the 'infinite Spirit' lies hidden – 'involuted' in material nature. In fact Aurobindo describes evolution as 'a growing of the Self in Material nature to the conscious possession of its own spiritual being' (Aurobindo 1973: 72). The evolutionary goal, as he outlines it, is to become 'conscient in the superconscient' allowing our being to be lit by 'another light of knowledge.' The 'field of being' thus 'enlightened' Aurobindo equates with a 'divine birth' – the *telos* toward which all of one's previous births are laborious steps. He writes: 'All this evolution is a growing of the Self in material nature to the conscious possession of its own spiritual being (Aurobindo 1973: 72).

Aurobindo believes that a 'spiritual age' will arise through the agency of individuals and that a new 'self-creation of the Mind' will become evident. These individuals can then lead the masses toward the goal, although the 'following' is likely to be 'very imperfect and confused' (Aurobindo 1973: 188). Difficulties surrounding this advent can be overcome if society is prepared to accept and understand the message of exemplary individuals. The preconditions for this preparedness are shown in the development of the arts and sciences which 'thin the walls between soul and matter.' Religion will have shed the 'weight of dead matter' and revived itself 'in the fountain of the Spirit.' Aurobindo's utopic society will have shed 'external compulsions' because its members will be following the lead of the inner 'divine compulsion.'

In expanding the concept of liberation to a social vision, Aurobindo significantly departs from the individualistic approach to liberation of classical philosophy and of what he calls the 'Olympian egoism' of Goethe and the 'Titanic egoism' of Nietzsche. His own 'Integral *Advaita*,' in its acceptance of an immanent-transcendent Absolute (*Brahman*), is a critique of the nondualism of Sankara, which has dominated modern Indian philosophy.

R. D. Ranade (1886–1957)

Ranade's philosophy also shows the influence of the dominant nondualistic Vedanta school and the writings of the central figure of this tradition, Sankara. The thing that influenced Ranade the most was the fact that a nondualistic philosopher like Sankara, who spent most of his life tackling epistemological and metaphysical issues, could also be the composer of moving devotional songs, that is to say, of an interplay between religiosity and rational argument.

Speaking about his philosophical studies, Ranade writes:

One of the first things I noticed in the course of a few years of my study was that in Philosophic thought the East was East and the West was West. This was not a thing I supposed desirable. The problem of philosophy to me was one and identical all the world over, and there was no distinction of country in the world of thought. (Ranade 1958: 543)

He believes that if Indian philosophers are to follow the advice, 'Indians keep to your philosophy,' they will have to do so only in terms of a 'correlative' study of both philosophical traditions. These correlations take the form of seeing the similarities between Sankara's and Bradley's treatment of the Absolute. The 'numerically pluralistic' but 'qualitatively monistic' system of Ramanuja (1017–1137) has its correlate in the theistic philosophy of James Ward. Ranade believes that correlations in metaphysics, epistemology, logic, and ethics can be profoundly instructive in understanding the universality of philosophical problems and the growth of philosophy itself. These correlations are intended to produce a unity based on the recognition of a single 'Spiritual principle' underlying everything and to fulfill the hope that humanity might come together in a Philosophy of the Spirit.

Ranade also turned his attention to Greek philosophy, especially to Heraclitus, Parmenides, and Aristotle. He is one of the few modern Indian philosophers who cites passages in the Greek original. Offering commentary and criticism on the translations of Burnet and Zeller, he critically engages European scholarly treatments of Greek philosophy. As opposed to the 'materialist' interpretation of Parmenides, Ranade sees in Parmenidean ontology an attack on the concept of the Idea or the Universal and an identification of Thought and Being. Both these concepts had been similarly treated by Sankara for whom reality or the absolute is a unity of being (*sat*), thought (*cit*), and bliss (*ananda*).

Ranade's later work concerns the traditional epistemological problem of Self-realization or self-knowledge as presented in the Upanishads. The Self to be realized is in a sense beyond 'knowledge' in the conventional sense of the term. This self-realization is:

> the unfolding and visualization of the *Atman* within us, rather than the insipid and soulless realization of the various faculties of man – the intellectual, the emotional and the moral – in the sense Bradley and other European moralists have understood the expression. (Ranade 1958: 556)

The problem of self-realization, in the Upanishadic sense, turns on understanding how this self-realization is to be achieved. The argument hinges on a certain intuitive human faculty, in fact a faculty of mystical realization. This theme is treated at length in Ranade's *Indian Mysticism* (1932) – a work replete with references not only to the Indian tradition but to Plotinus, John of the Cross, Theresa of Avila, and other Christian mystics. This faculty, Ranade suggests, underlies all faculties. Mystical experience itself is not something occult or mysterious; it is in fact an 'intuitive' and 'silent' apprehension of God or Reality. Mystical experience acquires its ineffability because of its intuitive character; it falls within the same register as artistic, poetic, or even scientific activity, each of which requires an immediate relation to Reality. Mystical experience points to the fact that the intellect is not sufficient for 'Divine Knowledge'; yet, there is no contradiction between intuition and the intellect. Mystical experience seems to co-opt the intellect or the rational aspect of the human being. Drawing on classical ideas, Ranade discusses a necessary connection between the 'reality of mystical experience' and moral growth. He compares mystical experience without moral development to trying to perform the play *Hamlet* without the Prince of Denmark. Both antinomianism and quietism are not consonant with mystical experience, in fact the virtues go hand in hand with mystical experience (Ranade 1932).

Surendranath Dasgupta (1887–1952)

Dasgupta's most widely read work is his magisterial five volume *History of Indian Philosophy* (1922). Dasgupta, who was active in international philosophical congresses throughout his career, also wrote on the Idealism of Croce and Giovanni Gentile, on German philosophy as well as classical Indian philosophical systems. Philosophy attempts to give a 'systematic explanation of all our experiences in their mutual relatedness' (Dasgupta 1958: 262). Starting with a priori concepts and then deriving (or coercing) all subsequent ideas from them, the way Hegel or Spinoza does, is not the right method for Dasgupta. The classical Indian Vedanta philosophical method, which relies heavily on certain kinds of experiences to justify its concepts, is also denounced by Dasgupta.

Like most philosophers of his generation, Dasgupta undertook a critical self-reflection on Indian tradition. He observes that the study of Indian philosophy in the orthodox as well as the anglicized circles had become merely philological. For Dasgupta, before any productive comparison with European philosophy is possible there needs to be a systematic interpretation of Indian philosophy in the light of the specificity of its history, structures and aim. This task should not remain the province of philologists and specialists in Sanskrit.

The older philosophical interests and tendencies are being dominated, Dasgupta argues, by the modern nationalist concerns and ideals. He laments the loss of a certain cultural milieu not only in India but globally and writes:

We have now . . . a new epoch of culture, progress and ideals in which the entire civilized world is participating. Whether we will or not we are being directed into the whirlpool of our unknown destinies . . . We are thus naturally torn away from the spirit that dominated the philosophy and culture of India. (Dasgupta 1982: 213)

Dasgupta understands that modern Indian philosophy can neither identify with the classical world nor can it identify entirely with the West. With the advent of modernity, the ideals of the Vedic seers and the yogis seem remote, almost anachronistic. Yet, philosophy for Dasgupta is 'the entire epitome of life' or 'a formula for the spiritual existence of man.' This 'spirituality' names a kind of 'harmonious assemblage' of the cognitive, affective, moral, and creative dimensions of human life. Dasgupta remains faithful to the tradition to the extent that he does not see philosophy as primarily consisting of arguments and discussions about reality. Philosophy is also practical in that it aims at addressing our spiritual well-being. In Indian philosophy, Dasgupta finds a strong 'optimism,' which consists in the possibility of achieving a spiritual well-being. This, he believes, is a strength that should not be obscured in any attempt to overcome the old dogmas of the tradition.

Sarvepalli Radhakrishnan (1888–1975)

Radhakrishnan, who was to become a professor at Oxford and President of India, was perhaps the strongest advocate of the interpretation of classical Indian philosophy as pervasively 'spiritual.' This is an attitude which has not only been transmitted to the West but is also prevalent among Indian intellectuals. Radhakrishnan is reflecting his understanding of classical philosophy when he writes that 'philosophy is not a matter of dialectics and intellectual jugglery but a product of life and meditation on it' (Radhakrishnan 1994: 121). From this perspective, a philosophy driven by technical expertise is superficial. He claims to follow the Hindu scriptures in presenting philosophy as an activity which requires a 'sharp intellect and a detached spirit.' Given this attitude, it is no surprise that Radhakrishnan does not hope to find philosophy in the works of mere intellectuals. Philosophy is, in fact, possible only through a rigorous self-discipline: moral and intellectual discipline is a prerequisite for philosophy. Radhakrishnan holds *darsana* to be an insight, 'spiritual perception' or 'intuitive understanding,' in a sense that diminishes the importance of logical proofs and rational inquiry as modes of access to reality. What he calls 'soul sight' is the intuitive mode of access to the real. The concept of the Absolute or the Real in nondualistic Vedanta is one without a second – veiled by language and logical concepts; it is 'a positive but unnamable being.' The real transcends 'our miserable categories' (Radhakrishnan 1996: 43). The Vedantic Absolute in contrast with Hegel's absolute is unapproachable by logical reasoning. Radhakrishnan understands intuitive experience to be 'the crown of intellectual knowledge.' Intuition becomes the mode of access to truth and certainty. This prominence given to direct access to reality, which is 'neither perceptual nor conceptual,' leads us to think that perhaps it is rational discourse which is at the root of philosophy's continued perplexity over its problems. Given Radhakrishnan's position that intuition is a maturation of intellectual or rational thought, it is not surprising that the rational justification procedures – so dear to classical philosophy – are more or less obscured. Radhakrishnan sees the deficiency of the intuitive approach and the prominence of 'intellectuality' as the 'tragedy of our age.'

Radhakrishnan's Vedantic influence in Indian philosophy has been challenged by scholars influenced by the rationality and realism of the Nyaya school. Later in his career, in his 'Reply to Critics,' Radhakrishnan admits that intuition alone is not accepted by the tradition as a sufficient justification in philosophical debates (Radhakrishnan 1952). This is well documented in his *Indian Philosophy* – a work which, like Dasgupta's, rejects the European charge that Indian philosophy is pessimistic. This 'pessimism' or dissatisfaction with what exists is accompanied by a yearning for transcendence and the belief that there is indeed a means to achieve this transcendence.

Radhakrishnan's 'spiritual' interpretation of the tradition can be seen as a reaction to the colonial instrumental reason. He linked instrumental reason, and by implication rational discourse in philosophy, with obscurity. Intuitive awareness and the clarity it produces would be a remedy to the ills of modernity – including the oppressive colonial system.

G. R. Malkani (1892–1977)

The Indian Institute of Philosophy at Amalner, founded in 1916, played a significant role in the history of Indian recent philosophy. It brought together some of the most promising academic philosophers and encouraged interaction between traditional scholars and academic philosophers. The institute was founded to promote its 'official' philosophy – nondualistic Vedanta. A number of philosophers, including G. R. Malkani, Rashvihari Das, K. C. Bhattacharya, and Daya Krishna, were associated with the center at some point in their academic life. In Malkani's work we see the influence of the nondualistic Vedanta: indeed, his work to a large extent is an attempt to systematize the insights of nondualistic Vedanta. Malkani articulates an appreciation for the rational energy of Western thought but is wary of what he calls the 'barrenness of mere rationalism,' insisting in traditional Indian fashion that 'the perception of truth is more important than its rational explanation.' In this vein, he argues that philosophical theories are constructed on the basis of 'personal or spiritual intuitions,' as opposed to being rational constructions. Reason is only of secondary importance in philosophy and its importance lies in its critical, as opposed to its constructive, function. If philosophy, as the ancient Indian seers and sages held, is the knowledge of metaphysical reality, then intuition would be the instrument for seeking it. Reason 'may be a means of elucidation of this intuition. It cannot be a substitute for it' (Malkani 1966: 29).

Although advocating a nondualistic philosophy, Malkani aims at its conclusions independently, rather than through an exposition of the classical texts. Not unlike the classical nondualists, Malkani in his *Philosophy of the Self: A System of Idealism* (1939) seeks the 'ultimate ground of all appearances.' The operative premise here is that disregarding this ground will give us only a partial and 'fragmentary' picture. Although seeking to explicate ultimate reality, Malkani admits that the latter can never become an 'object' of knowledge; it has to be intuited. This ultimate reality for Malkani is the Self, which in essence is pure attributeless being – in other words, the Brahman of the classical nondualistic Vedanta. The logic of nondualism requires the ground of appearance to be sharply distinguished from appearances: to be beyond appearances, that is to say, in no way *apparent*. The task of Malkani's *System* is to give an account of the ontological status of appearances. Malkani writes:

> We now maintain that the intelligent Self is the cause of all things that appear. It is the true substance. The effects are differentiated from it and from one another, not in substance or in real being, but only in name and form. (Malkani 1966: 11)

In the footsteps of classical nondualism, Malkani thinks of the explication of the Self as a kind of 'disentanglement.' The Self remains entangled with other entities (like the mind or the intellect), which are in proximity to it and are 'after the image of the self.' This exercise of 'disentanglement' aims to disclose the Self as 'pure, immutable and eternally resplendent.' It is not simply a matter of accepting claims made in the scriptural texts (the Vedas or the Upanishads) in order to justify the concept of the ground. Neither can the ground be established through *a priori* concepts or somehow deduced from appearances. Malkani grapples with the difficulty of presenting arguments for this ground and thus for the central premise of his system. With the traditional nondualists, he has to admit that the actuality of the ground can only be realized in experience.

Rashvihari Das (1897–1976)

Rashvihari Das, best known in India for his commentaries on Whitehead and *Handbook* to Kant's First Critique, was associated for over two decades with the Indian Institute of Philosophy dominated by Vedantic idealism. This association did not prevent him from inclining toward the naive realism of the Nyaya-Vaisesika school. As he puts it: 'I lived in an idealistic atmosphere, it had tended to harden my inner realism' (Das 1958: 247). In keeping with his realist instinct, Das rejects the notion of philosophy as intuition or a form of mysticism. Philosophy, he argues, is teachable by rational means and is on a par with science and history. Philosophy is not antithetical to science but includes it, although Das admits a distinction between scientific and philosophical knowledge. For Das, philosophy is 'critical reflection.' This concept leads him to argue that it is not the opinions of particular philosophers that are of primary interest. Philosophy is interested in how these conclusions have been arrived at, in other words, philosophy is interested in method and reflective practice.

Das argues that realism itself does not need a philosophical justification; on the contrary, it is the rejection of the seemingly uncontroversial realism that needs justification. Das criticizes the proponents of nondualist Vedanta who regard the object of awareness as an illusion because their position, if true, implies that there is no object as such. Knowledge, in fact, reveals the object to us albeit as mediated by the senses and the mind. The element of distortion leaves room for a healthy skepticism. As Das explains it, the value of skepticism lies not only in freeing our minds of prejudice but in actually uncovering the 'elements of uncertainty, obscurity and vagueness' in what we accept as knowledge. Skepticism is not an ultimate end and has only a moral or educational value. Its value lies in convincing us that holding beliefs entails fallibility. Beliefs have to be open to revision or rejection, if evidence points to the contrary.

Das insists on the distinction between the subjective act of knowing and the known object. Reducing the object to subjective acts is to do away with the category of the object. Understanding idealism as attaching importance and giving priority to subjective acts, and realism as giving priority to objective facts, Das explains his own position as a 'theoretical realism' and a 'practical idealism.' Realism gives epistemic priority to the object, whereas idealism is a product of the determination of 'the will or practical reason' by subjective acts and functions, 'by ideas and ideals.' Das's thought converges with the tradition in the aspiration to escape 'particularity' and 'finitude' and to 'become identified with what is universal, infinite and eternal' in one's concern with the regulative ideals of truth, freedom and love.

J. L. Mehta (1912–88)

Jarava Lal Mehta's thought is a prolonged engagement with the question of the classical Indian tradition's self-understanding, in the face of which, following Husserl, Mehta called the 'Europeanization of the earth and man.' Mehta clearly rejects the Hegelian viewing of the Indian tradition as a mere stage in the development of Spirit, destined to be 'transcended' by Western philosophy in the movement of thought to

Absolute Knowledge. Husserl and Heidegger also stress the 'uniqueness' of philosophy as a Greek-European project and tie it inextricably to the course of Occidental history. Mehta rejects the legitimacy of the categories Occidental and Asiatic as capable of describing two separate realities in the age of technology. Although he rejects the effort to entrench modern Indian philosophers in the Indic traditions, his guiding question concerns traditional philosophical insights. For him, the issue is that of grasping what precisely is lost in the encounter with 'philosophy' – in the European, specifically post-Cartesian sense.

From his point of view, modern Indian philosophy is a denizen of two worlds, the legatee of two traditions. The Western tradition is distant in geographical, cultural, and linguistic terms, but determines the horizon of intelligibility. The Indian tradition is sedimented with 'meanings embodied in the English language' rendering, therefore, access to the tradition in its purity impossible. The aim then is to develop a way of thinking which understands – and here Mehta uses the concept of *verstehen* – both traditions in their 'mutual otherness.' Modern Indian philosophy must explore the tension between its traditional heritage and the essentially 'alien destiny' of the present.

Speaking of his prolonged engagement with Heidegger's thought, Mehta confesses that in Heidegger he finds 'a disclosure of this 'ownmost' essence of the West to non-Western man, calling upon him to go back and retrieve the forgotten foundations of his own spiritual tradition' (Mehta 1992: 29).

But Mehta rejects the Heideggerian *Weltgeschick*, with its implication that, as India appropriates Western technology, it will relate to the essence of technology in the manner the West does. The 'Europeanization of the earth,' which Heidegger explains as the destiny of Being that now envelops the world, is an important notion for Mehta: he understands the Indic traditions as well as philosophy itself to be reflected in this notion. But, for non-Western humanity, the task is to use the resources of Heideggerian philosophy to prevent a recapitulation of the West's relationship to the essence of technology. He writes:

> Listen to the western voice which speaks of the possibility of a turn, a *Wende* in this destiny, if only we are willing to face up to the task of learning to think Truth and Time, Being, World and Man in ways other than those laid out by the Greek founders of this destiny, and wake up at last from this Western dream of which we too have become a part, wake up without forgetting to learn so much that this has yet to teach us. (Mehta 1992: 180)

Thus, Mehta becomes the representative of a hybrid philosophy, approaching issues from within the tradition but allowing this 'within' to be also the place of listening to the call of the Heideggerian moment in European philosophy.

Daya Krishna (1925–)

Unlike Mehta, Daya Krishna is influenced by the analytic tradition. Daya Krishna's philosophical interpretation of the classical Indian tradition goes against the tendency of seeing liberation as a central concern. The position he adopts implies that an undue focus on 'spirituality' is the reason why Indian philosophy has little or no place in the philosophical arena, even in the philosophy curriculum in Indian universities. Liberation is not a concept unique to philosophy; artistic, poetic, and erotic discourses seem to accept *moksha* as a goal. Philosophy is not a mere theoretical clarification of, or prelude to, *moksha*. For Daya Krishna, schools like Nyaya and Vaisesika have 'literally nothing to do with *moksha*' and would be counter-examples to Radhakrishnan's interpretation of the tradition as pervasively liberation-oriented (Krishna 1990: 31). Daya Krishna believes that the modern Indian philosopher and the historian of Indian philosophy have been misled by the *moksha*-centric approach and have thus given priority to something which is one among many factors at work in the classical Indian tradition. With regard to the 'myth' of *moksha*, he writes that 'it is time that the myth is dispelled, and Indian philosophy is treated seriously as philosophy proper' (Krishna 1990: 32).

In dissecting the 'myths' about Indian philosophy, Daya Krishna tries to clarify what the 'spirituality' of Indian philosophy means. If acceptance of 'spiritual reality' entails that only spirit is real and the world of matter is in some sense unreal, then we cannot paint all of Indian philosophy with this brush. Many Indian schools like Nyaya accept a variety of substances as metaphysically real. Besides, even the most spirit-prone of schools, the Vedantists, ascribe a diminished reality to matter and do not dismiss it as utterly unreal. If by spiritual is meant that *moksha* alone motivates philosophy, then Daya Krishna's argument is that the concept of *moksha* is something adopted and articulated by Indian philosophy from Indian culture that sets it up as an individual goal and is far from being Indian philosophy's sole motivating concern. Like philosophy in the West, Indian philosophy is a conceptual analysis and inquiry aiming at a rational understanding of the world.

J. N. Mohanty (1928–)

Analytic philosophy, phenomenology and classical Indian philosophy influence Mohanty and are explicitly addressed in his writings. Mohanty also takes up the question of the status of liberation in classical Indian philosophy and, like Daya Krishna, rejects the notion that Indian philosophy is fundamentally intuitive as opposed to 'intellectual' or 'discursive.' For Mohanty, classical philosophy is an intellectual activity that leads to a kind of 'transformative' knowledge. Implicit in this idea of transformation is the possibility that this knowledge will bring about a radical change in the philosopher's 'mode of being.' Philosophical theory sets and justifies goals like liberation and establishes the path to them. Practice, in the Radhakrishnan-influenced interpretation of classical thought, is the dominant aspect, but for Mohanty practice can only build on theoretical foundations. The myth of Indian philosophy's practicality is systematically rejected by Mohanty. The 'practicality' of Indian philosophy or Indian 'wisdom' and 'spirituality' reflects perhaps what the West has sought in the Indian tradition rather than something which describes the tradition itself.

Mohanty also challenges 'comparative philosophy' as a mode of doing philosophy, especially because of its 'methodological naiveté, an external attitude to each of the traditions being compared which tends to do injustice to both sides' (Mohanty 2001: 60). The fundamental problem with this mode of doing philosophy is that it is not conducive to creativity.

The phenomenology of Mohanty is concerned not with *what* a thing is but, as R. A. Mall explains and emphasizes, 'what we mean when we see, judge, affirm, dream etc., irrespective of the question whether the thing in question is an essence or a fact, exists or does not exist' (Mall 1991: 94). Mohanty's interpretation of Husserl sees him as moving toward phenomenological 'clarification of meanings' as opposed to the early interest in essences. This interest in 'meaning' is the truly descriptive aspect of Husserlian phenomenology. Implicit in this claim is the idea that Husserl's project of a presuppositionless philosophy is not realized solely in the eidetic quest. For Mohanty, it is 'sensible particulars' which will lead us back to a descriptive philosophy without any ontological baggage or 'theoretical prejudices.' Only in this way can the phenomenologist remain entirely within the realm of the given. It is description itself that must become the basis for ontology.

Conclusion

Modern Indian philosophy has, for most of the twentieth century, been attempting to negotiate the meaning of its tradition – its problems and methods – often at the cost of originality. As much as Indian philosophers have tried to participate in Western philosophical discourse, classical philosophy, in a modern idiom, remains a priority. Far from being dead, classical philosophy has been rejuvenated through the work of highly original interpreters. The classical debates about realism and idealism, externalism and internalism, universals and particulars, the nature of perception and knowledge are being revisited and reformulated. As it is hybridized, due to the impact of analytic philosophy, modern Indian philosophy becomes all the more vigorous and moves towards a fusion philosophy that is not content with merely comparing and contrasting concepts and arguments. The stumbling block for philosophy in India, in the foreseeable future, is the active erosion of the humanities in the interests of a globalized techno-culture.

References

Aurobindo, S. (1964), *The Message and Mission of India*, Bombay: Bharatiya Vidya Bhavan.

Aurobindo, S. (1973), *The Essential Aurobindo*, ed. R. A. McDermott, New York: Schocken Books.

Das, R. (1958), 'Pursuit of Truth through Doubt and Belief,' in S. Radhakrishnan, and J. Muirhead (eds) (1958), *Contemporary Indian Philosophy*, London: Allen and Unwin, pp. 231–48.

Dasgupta, S. (1958), 'Philosophy of Dependent Emergence,' in Radhakrishnan, and J. Muirhead (eds) (1958), *Contemporary Indian Philosophy*, London: Allen and Unwin, pp. 251–85.

Dasgupta, S. (1982), *Philosophical Essays*, Delhi: Motilal Banarsidass.

Dubey, S. P. (ed.) (1994), *Facets of Recent Indian Philosophy, Volume 1: Metaphysics of the Spirit*, New Delhi: Indian Council of Philosophical Research.

Dubey, S. P. (ed.) (1996), *Facets of Recent Indian Philosophy, Volume 2: Indian Philosophy and History*, New Delhi: Indian Council of Philosophical Research.

Krishna, D. (1991), *Indian Philosophy: A Counter Perspective*, Delhi: Oxford University Press.

Krishna, D. (ed.) (1991), *The Philosophy of J. N. Mohanty*, New Delhi: Indian Council of Philosophical Research, in association with Munshiram Manoharlal Publishers.

Malkani, G. R. (1966), *Philosophy of the Self: Or, a System of Idealism based upon Advaita Vedanta*, New York: Johnson Reprint Corp.

Mall, R. A. (1991), 'Mohanty as Phenomenologist,' in D. Krishna (ed.) (1991), *The Philosophy of J. N. Mohanty*, New Delhi: Indian Council of Philosophical Research, in association with Munshiram Manoharlal Publishers, pp. 87–120.

Mehta, J. L. (1992), *J. L. Mehta on Heidegger, Hermeneutics, and Indian Tradition*, (ed.) W. J. Jackson, Leiden: E. J. Brill.

Mohanty, J. N. (2001), *Explorations in Philosophy. Essays by J. N. Mohanty*, ed. B. Gupta, New Delhi and New York: Oxford University Press

Radhakrishnan, S. (1952), 'Reply to Critics,' in P. A. Schilpp (ed.) (1952), *The Philosophy of Sarvepalli Radhakrishnan*, New York: Tudor Publishing Co., pp. 787–842.

Radhakrishnan, S., and J. Muirhead (eds) (1958), *Contemporary Indian Philosophy*, London: Allen & Unwin

Radhakrishnan, S. (1994), 'Intuitive Understanding,' in S. P. Dubey (ed.) (1994), *Facets of Recent Indian Philosophy*, vol. 1, New Delhi: Indian Council of Philosophical Research, pp. 120–30.

Radhakrishnan, S. (1996), 'Traditional Philosophy: A Need for Reinterpretation,' in S. P. Dubey (ed.) (1996), *Facets of Recent Indian Philosophy*, vol. 2, New Delhi: Indian Council of Philosophical Research, pp. 148–59.

Ranade, R. D. (1958), 'Evolution of my Thought,' in S. Radhakrishnan, and J. Muirhead (eds) (1958), *Contemporary Indian Philosophy*, London: Allen and Unwin, pp. 539–62.

Schilpp, P. A. (ed.) (1952), *The Philosophy of Sarvepalli Radhakrishnan*: New York: Tudor Publishing Co.

Chinese Philosophy

Roger T. Ames

Mainstream philosophy in the twentieth century has been Anglo-European philosophy. This observation is as true in Tokyo, Seoul, Beijing, Delhi, Nairobi, as it is in Boston London, Paris, and Frankfurt. That is, the indigenous philosophies of East Asia, South Asia, Africa, and indeed America too have been marginalized within their own cultural sites by the dominance of what has been called the Anglo-European analytic and Continental traditions of philosophy. It is within this historical framework that we must distinguish clearly between 'philosophy in China' on the one hand, and 'Chinese philosophy' on the other.

In some academic quarters the important distinction between philosophy in China and the history of Chinese philosophy has been respected by using the foreign term coined in late nineteenth-century Japan by Nishi Amane – 'philosophy' (Ch. *zhexue*, Jap. *tetsugaku*) – to refer to Western philosophy as it has been taught in China, and the vernacular term – 'thought' (*sixiang*) – to refer to the history of Chinese philosophy as the exegetical explication of the Chinese canons of philosophy that continues to be integral to the curricula of departments of both philosophy and literature in China. In fact, to isolate and discuss twentieth-century 'Chinese philosophy' we will need to distinguish yet again between the commentarial history of Chinese philosophy and Chinese philosophy itself. Whereas the Western philosophy curriculum as presented in the Chinese academy has largely been able to ignore its own indigenous tradition, and the commentarial history of Chinese 'thought' has often been taught especially in literature departments without a perceived need to reference Western philosophy, there has been over time a significant cadre of Chinese philosophers who have been shaped in their thinking and writing about their own tradition through a conscious appropriation of the Western canons – particularly German Idealism and Marxist philosophy. It is this subset of original 'comparative' philosophers who have been using Western philosophy as a resource to philosophize about the Chinese tradition itself that will occupy the best part of our discussion of twentieth-century Chinese philosophy in this essay. We will refer to this third category of hybrid Chinese philosophers under the rubric 'New Confucianists' (*xinruxuejia*), a term coined in the mid-1980s to describe a philosophical 'movement' that began in the early twentieth century and that continues today.

Western Learning

A defining characteristic of Chinese philosophy – in particular, Confucian philosophy – from earliest times has been its porousness. When Confucianism emerged in the Han dynasty (206 BCE–220 CE) as a state orthodoxy that continued down into the twentieth century, it was a Confucianism that had absorbed into and fortified itself with many tenets from the competing 'Hundred Schools': Daoism, Mohism, Militarism, School of Names, Legalism, and so on. The influence of Indo-European learning as an invasive species in this philosophical ecology of early China began in the second century CE with the importation of Buddhist philosophy from South Asia. This first wave of Western thought had such a profound influence on the indigenous philosophical narrative that the evolution of both neo-Confucianism and neo-Daoism can only be understood by reference to the response of these home-grown traditions to the powerful, inspirational forces of Buddhist thought. At the same time, East Asian Buddhist philosophy that began as an alien transplant became so thoroughly transformed in its relationship to the indigenous thought systems of Confucianism and Daoism that its later manifestation as Sanlun, Huayan, and Chan (Zen) Buddhist philosophies has a far greater affinity with China's own philosophical soil than with its South Asian roots. It is because of this syncretistic process that a conventional expression dating from pre-modern times frequently invoked to describe the composite narrative of Chinese philosophy has been *sanjiao weiyi* – literally, 'the fusion of the three teachings of Confucianism, Daoism, and Buddhism as one.'

The more recent wave of Western learning (*xixue*) concerning us here constitutes a second sea change in Chinese philosophy that should properly inspire an update and revision of this conventional expression from *sanjiao weiyi* to the more inclusive *sijiao weiyi*, that is, 'the fusion of the *four* teachings of Confucianism, Daoism, Buddhism, *and* Western learning as one.' This second Western incursion began as early as the late sixteenth century with the arrival of Jesuit missionaries who, along with their religious scriptures, were armed with the corpus of classical Western philosophy. With the later arrival of Protestant missionaries, a Western foray into Chinese secular education continued gradually over the centuries, enabled in particular by the translation of large tracts on medicine, astronomy, mathematics, and natural philosophy. The pace of specifically philosophical change accelerated in earnest in the late nineteenth century with the translation and introduction of post-Darwinian Western philosophers – T. H. Huxley and Herbert Spencer in particular – by reformist scholars such as Yan Fu (1853–1921) and Tan Sitong (1865–1898).

For the century and a half that led up to the founding of communist China in 1949, China had been a hapless victim of Western imperialism. Before the ideas of first Charles Darwin and then later Karl Marx arrived in China, they were already spawning revolutionary movements at home that challenged at the most primary level those persistent presuppositions grounding the full spectrum of disciplines within the European academy itself. In China, the popularity of evolutionary ethics like the later appropriation of Marxist socialism, was driven in important measure by practical social concerns of which professional academic philosophy was only a minor part. Still, the resonances that reformist thinkers found between these explicitly revolutionary foreign movements and philosophical sensibilities within their own tradition promised a way of renovating Chinese philosophy to respond effectively to the unrelenting Western aggression that was perceived as threatening the integrity, if not the very survival of Chinese culture. At the end of the day, we will find that what allows contemporary historians of Chinese philosophy to collect a truly disparate range of Chinese thinkers under the category of 'New Confucians' is the shared commitment of these twentieth-century philosophers to rehabilitate and apply their fortified revisions of traditional Chinese philosophy as a tourniquet to control the hemorrhaging of what was a culture reeling from an assault from all sides.

The New Confucians

Given the porousness and synchronicity that has been the persistent signature of the Chinese philosophical tradition over the centuries, twentieth-century Chinese philosophy with all the hybridity it entails should not be construed as a disjunction in kind from its earlier narrative. In fact, this aggregating philosophical amalgam can be seen as a continuing fusion of foreign elements that complement, enrich, and ultimately strengthen its own persisting philosophical sensibilities. It is for this reason that the term 'Confucianism' (*ruxue*) which dates back more than two millennia to proto-Chinese history can continue to be invoked as a name for an ostensibly new and yet still familiar direction in Chinese philosophy.

In reflecting on the question of the continuity and the disjunction of the Chinese philosophical tradition, we might recall the distinguished French sinologist Marcel Granet who claims that 'Chinese wisdom has had no need for the idea of God' (Granet 1934: 478). This characterization of Chinese philosophy has had many iterations albeit in different formulations, by many of our most prominent twentieth-century sinologists, both Chinese and Western alike. Indeed, our best interpreters of Chinese philosophy are explicit in rejecting the idea that Chinese natural cosmology begins from some independent, transcendent principle that entails the metaphysical reality/ appearance distinction and the plethora of dualistic categories arising from such a worldview (Tang 1988a: 100–3; Xiong 1977: 180–91; Zhang 1995: 271–2; Graham 1989: 22; Needham 1956: 290; Sivin 1995: 3; Hansen 1992: 215; Girardot 1983: 64). The philosophical implications of this seemingly off-hand observation are fundamental and pervasive.

For example, in lieu of gods as a separate order of being, within the largely informal and human-centered religiousness of the long Chinese tradition, it is ancestral figures, cultural heroes, and supreme personalities that are elevated and celebrated as objects of popular deference. It is particular historical exemplars rather than abstract principles or ideals that provide the bearings for a continuing community. This need for models to emulate, then, late and soon, has required the philosopher to be a paradigmatic individual – a scout to reconnoiter and recommend a 'way' for the generations to come. The epistemic commitment of such philosophers lies not in 'discovering' the truth about the world, but rather in 'realizing' and perpetuating a viable community.

Another important corollary to the absence of 'God' in Chinese natural cosmology is the need for a different language in thinking about issues as basic as cosmic origins, the source of meaning in the world, and the nature of creativity itself. Darwin's 'dangerous' notion of the 'origins' and mutability of species (*eidos*) – the notion that order in all of its different forms is historicist, particularist, and emergent – has been construed by many to be the death of 'the idea of God' (Dennett 1995: 18–22). If this rejection of a putatively perfect, objective, independent, and unchanging source of order and meaning has constituted a revolution at the very foundations of Western thought, then we might anticipate resonances between post-Darwinian directions in Western philosophy today – particularly our process philosophies – and more traditional yet persistent assumptions within the Chinese natural cosmology.

The Confucian alternative to 'the idea of God' has been a Chinese version of process philosophy in which personal, social, political, and cosmic order is indeed historicist, particularist, and emergent – a cultural ecology defined by virtue of productive correlations among the various elements that are in play within a given historical environment. Most significantly, human beings as the most complex and sophisticated force in the world, must take responsibility as an active and creative partner in the productive unfolding of the epoch in which they are located. It is this correlative sensibility in which the human being and the cosmos are mutually determining – expressed in many different ways and with different terminologies – that continues to be a shared value among the scholars identified as the New Confucians.

Liang Shuming (1893–1988) is often quite properly identified as the first of the New Confucians. In his earliest writings Liang rehearses a kind of 'reverse Hegelian narrative' of the phasal development of philosophy that is then refined and amplified over his long professional career. That is, the first stage in philosophy is its Western phase in which the human will is able to satisfy the basic needs of the human experience by disciplining the environment in which our lives are lived. The second Chinese phase entails a harmonizing of this human will with its natural environment, with all of the joy and satisfaction that such a reconciliation brings with it. The third and final phase is Buddhist philosophy that provides an intuitive negation of the self-other dichotomy, and a true spiritual realization through a regimen of self-cultivation. In many ways, Liang Shuming's own creative philosophizing is an extension of Wang Yangming's (1472–1529) 'philosophy of heart-and-mind' (*xinxue*) that was so thoroughly colored by Yogacara Buddhism's notion of 'consciousness-only' (*weishi*). Like Wang Yangming, Liang Shuming's philosophy is as much religious as philosophical – an existential and aspirational quest for Confucian enlightenment rather than an attempt to establish an expository, systematic account of reality.

Xiong Shili (1885–1968)

There seems to be a consensus among scholars that the most prominent and indeed promising lineage among the New Confucians is that of the teacher and founder of New Confucianism, Xiong Shili, and his two prominent disciples, Mou Zongsan and Tang Junyi. All three of these thinkers quite properly took themselves to be original philosophers in their own right. It is appropriate to begin with Xiong Shili because the greatest foreign influence on the development of his own philosophy was the first wave of Western learning – Buddhist philosophy – with only a passing ripple of the

European canons of philosophy. And probably the source of his own most profound insights into the nature of the human experience was the *Book of Changes* (*Yijing*), the first among the classics generally considered to be the cosmological ground of both Confucian and Daoist philosophical sensibilities.

Unlike the other New Confucians, Xiong Shili was largely self-educated, moving from the Confucian and Daoist canons through a careful reading of the Buddhist tradition. As a young man, he participated enthusiastically in the revolutionary activities that brought about the fall of imperial China and the establishment of the Republic. In the 1920s he began lecturing at Peking University where he made his professional career until his retirement to Shanghai in 1954. With the founding of the Peoples' Republic of China in 1949, most intellectuals either fled the ideologically driven revolution or capitulated to its dogmas. Xiong Shili, however, exhibited enormous courage and integrity in choosing to remain in China while at the same time vocally opposing the doctrinaire Marxist dichotomy between idealism and materialism. While he was tolerated through most of his professional career, he fell foul of the political exuberance of the early years of the Cultural Revolution, and spent the last years of his life as a lonely victim of Red Guard violence and intellectual ostracization.

What made Marxist materialism unpalatable to Xiong Shili was his commitment to the wholeness and processual nature of experience captured in the *Book of Changes* proposition that the world in which we live is ceaselessly procreative (*shengsheng buxi*). It is a nondual world in which mind and matter are two dimensions of the same changing reality, and the creativity of the human heart-and-mind expressed in the process of self-cultivation is necessary to guarantee a creative advance in the world.

One way of focusing Xiong Shili's lasting influence on New Confucianism is to recount briefly his core doctrine of 'the inseparability of forming and functioning' (*tiyong buer*). His basic point is that 'forming' and 'functioning' are an explanatory, nonanalytical vocabulary for describing the dramatic and ceaseless unfolding of our experience. *How* we think, for example, and *what* we think about, are two coterminous aspects of the same continuing process. The dynamic and creative continuity of experience is explained by a common source (*ti*) and the multiplicity and multivalence of experience is explained by the ongoing transformations among things and events (*yong*). There is no ontological disparity between the phenomenal world of experience and its underlying living source. While a knowledge of the manifest world provides us with a kind of habituating, calculative understanding (*liangzhi*) enabling us to discriminate among things and make inferences about them, it is natural under-standing (*xingzhi*) that provides us with the intuitive wisdom to fathom our experience and become fully moral within it. The former knowledge is the science provided most effectively by Western learning; the latter is the philosophical insight promoted most effectively by the indigenous traditions of China.

Given the wholeness of experience that includes both the human mind and the experience of the world, Xiong Shili took the *Book of Changes* natural cosmology to be a model for human self-cultivation. That is, human creativity and the advancement of cosmic meaning are inseparable aspects of the same reality.

Mou Zongsan (1909–95)

Xiong Shili's two most prominent protégés, Mou Zongsan and Tang Junyi, are both associated with the Chinese University of Hong Kong, having fled to Hong Kong from China after the communist revolutionaries came to power in 1949. They continued the Confucian lineage by translating, and in fact transforming the foreign rivals they admired most into a vocabulary consistent with their own premises.

For Mou Zongsan, Kant is the Western philosopher who began to understand the real nature of morality. Indeed, Mou Zongsan is so smitten by Kant that he appeals to his transcendental language to explain what is unique and distinctive about Chinese philosophy. According to Mou Zongsan:

The way of 'Heaven' (*tian*) being high above connotes transcendence. When this way pervades human beings, being immanent in their persons, it becomes their nature. When this happens, the way of Heaven is also made immanent. This being the case, we can use an expression that Kant was fond of using and say that the way of Heaven on the one hand is transcendent, and on the other hand is immanent (transcendent and immanent being opposites). When the way of Heaven is both transcendent and immanent, it can be said to have both religious and moral import: religion stressing the transcendent meaning and morality stressing the immanent. (Mou 1963: 20)

Mou Zongsan makes it clear that whatever might be construed as 'transcendent' in classical Chinese thought is neither independent of the natural world nor theistic. While Kant would claim that the existence of God is a noncausal regulative principle or 'value' lying outside of empirical experience that is a necessary guarantee for highest good, Mou believes the ultimate good to be a real possibility within the world itself. He believes that the infinite heart-and-mind is indeed accessible through the intuition and cultivation of the human heart-and-mind (*xin*), and need not be construed either as some more traditional, personal, and independent divine source, or as some abstract Kantian postulate that is a necessary condition for the possibility of the *summum bonum*. Far from entailing the dualism entailed by Western models of transcendence, classical China's world order, according to Mou, is altogether 'this worldly.'

For Mou Zongsan, the 'transcendence' of the human heart-and-mind is expressed in terms of the ongoing active creation of new values rather than as a simple reiteration and instantiation of what might otherwise be theistically 'given' to the human world. The nature and character of the human being is a creative process that both stimulates and is affected by change. This creativity is expressed as ongoing transformation of the world at the synergistic interface between uniquely human achievements and the boundlessly fertile natural and cultural context in which humanity resides.

In contrasting the Confucian world view with the theologically anchored Western model, Mou places human effort at the center, and dismisses explicitly any association we might make with notions of divine volition. It is the cultivated achievement of wisdom that establishes the congruency between moral conduct and personal happiness. For Mou Zongsan, then, it is the process of becoming fully human that constitutes the substance of Confucian religion, and it is the absence of real constraints to that process that prompts Mou to describe it as 'transcendent.' Since, however, Confucian spiritual sensibilities are human-centered in the manner Mou characterizes, there must be an explicit rejection of any notion of radical 'otherness' or ontological disparity between what he calls the immanent and transcendent or the moral and religious aspects of that process. Mou affirms both the continuity between, and the interdependence of, humanity and what is divine. In one's attainment of Confucian sagehood, there is the traditional correlation between the profoundly religious human being and the way of Heaven.

For a variety of reasons, the disjunction entailed by strict transcendence has dominated Western philosophical speculations. That God should not be contingent upon the world requires that He be disjoined in some way from that world. That Reason has some unsullied realm untouched by the welter of concrete circumstances, disjunction was essential. But for the Chinese, according to both Xiong Shili and his student, Mou Zongsan, there seems no reason, nor any real disposition to accept the consequences of disjunction as these implications have played themselves out in the Western tradition. The evidence for continuity as a preferred value is altogether persuasive in Chinese culture.

Mou Zongsan is concerned that Confucianism not be reduced to an exclusive secular humanism devoid of religious import. In fact, Mou's revisionist interpretation of the neo-Confucian thinkers and his rejection of Zhu Xi (1130–1200) as the orthodox line is an effort to underscore the central importance of the religious dimension in Confucianism. Here again, Mou Zongsan is attempting to promote a 'new Confucianism' fortified by the prestige and rigor of Kant, while at the same time, asserting identifiable assets within the Chinese tradition that can challenge what he takes to be a familiar, misguided appeal to some abstract, external, and scientific universalism, with its own kind of concrete, intuitively available, moral metaphysics.

Tang Junyi (1909–78)

It is Tang Junyi's foremost contribution to world philosophy – his synoptic philosophy of culture – that has led some scholars to associate him explicitly with Hegelian Idealism. Indeed, he does have an uncanny ability to discern and articulate, with truly penetrating acuity, a clear contrast between the presuppositions grounding the metaphysical thinking that has had such prominent play in the Western philosophical narrative, and those persistent cosmological assumptions that continue to shape an always changing Chinese worldview. Hegel in his narrative account of *Geist* in his *Philosophy of History* had pursued just such a project, and in his insights about the relational nature of personal experience he deploys a similar vocabulary. But on closer examination, we see that in the specific range of uncommon assumptions that Tang Junyi argues for as the ground of Chinese cultural uniqueness, he distances himself from German Idealism and the homogenizing closure of Enlightenment teleology and universalism.

Tang Junyi repeatedly insists that any traditional connection that Confucianism might have with the political forms of feudalism, monarchism, and patriarchism with which it has been historically associated are accidental and transient. He takes a holographic, interdependent, and productive relationship between 'part' and 'whole' as *the* distinguishing feature and most crucial contribution of Chinese culture broadly. As the underlying spirit of Chinese culture Tang Junyi endorses:

> the spirit of symbiosis and mutuality of particular and totality. From the perspective of understanding this means an unwillingness to isolate the particular from the totality (this is most evident in the cosmology of the Chinese people), and from the perspective of ties of feeling and affection, it means the commitment of the particular to do its best to realize the totality (this is most evident in the attitude of the Chinese people toward daily life). (Tang 1988b: 8)

We will see that when this mutuality and interdependence of particulars and totality – better, foci and fields, or ecologically situated 'events' and their environments – that grounds Chinese cosmology is translated into the more concrete social and political arena of the human family, it becomes the value of inclusive, consensual, and optimally productive community.

In his characterizations of Chinese natural cosmology, true to his teacher Xiong Shili, Tang Junyi begins by affirming the reality and sufficiency of empirical experience without seeking to go beyond it. He rejects outright the relevance of any notion of substratum, and in so doing, acknowledges the fluidity of the vital energy *qi* in its ceaseless flux and flow. Given the intrinsic nature of relatedness, putative 'things' are in fact a stream of unique, mutually conditioning events, and the web of always shifting relationships that constitutes each 'event' is a novel and unique construal of the totality. Using a more traditional Chinese vocabulary, we can say that the dynamic manifold or totality of these events is *dao* and the unique 'events' themselves are insistently particular foci or *de* that construe the totality from their own particular perspectives.

The processual flow of experience without beginning or end is what Tang Junyi describes as 'the notion of ceaseless procreation': Experience is persistent, historicist, and naturalistic in the sense of having no appeal to any metaphysical or supernatural source. Tang Junyi's corollary to this 'ceaseless procreation' is to reject the relevance of any kind of fatalism or necessity to Confucian cosmology. Experience is the bottomless unfolding of an emergent, contingent world according to the rhythm of its own internal creative processes without any fixed pattern or guiding hand. This feature of Chinese cosmology is described by Tang Junyi with two propositions: 'nothing advances but to return,' and the 'continuity obtains between determinacy and indeterminacy, motion and equilibrium.' Another way Tang Junyi expresses this *creatio in situ* reading of emergent 'particularity' is to invoke as a generic feature of the Chinese processual cosmology: 'the inseparability of the one and the many, of uniqueness and multivalence, of continuity and multiplicity, of integrity and integration.'

Tang Junyi applies this natural cosmology in his extensive work on human nature. He disassociates the conversation among classical Chinese philosophers over the meaning of human nature from the contemporary science of psychology by asserting that in the latter case, there is a desire to treat the human being as an objective phenomenon. For Tang, it is the existential project intuited subjectively that is the fundamental distinguishing characteristic of the Confucian conception of human 'nature.' In fact, it is precisely the indeterminate possibility for creative change that he identifies as the most salient feature of the contextualizing, initial human tendencies. He says that what is 'innate' in the nature of persons is most importantly the propensity for growth, cultivation, and refinement. The important point here is his claim that Confucianism would place an emphasis upon 'second nature' as the primary locus of culture and as the resource for the enculturation of succeeding generations.

Tang Junyi's Confucianism is a pragmatic naturalism directed at achieving the highest integrated cultural, moral, and spiritual growth for the individual-in-community. In appealing to family as the best model for achieving an optimal communal harmony, he affirms rather than challenges his own Confucian tradition. One profound difference between the Western and Chinese philosophical narratives that Tang makes much of is how Chinese culture is grounded in the everyday lives of the people and the natural deference that pervades family living. For him, the meaning and value of family relations is not simply the primary ground of social order – it has cosmological and religious implications as well. Family bonds properly observed are the point of departure for understanding that we each have moral responsibility for an expanding web of relations that reach far beyond our own localized selves, and that it is through these relations that human beings have the power and the responsibility to enchant the cosmos.

Other New Confucians

In relating the development of Chinese philosophy in this past century, we cannot neglect three other figures who belong largely to the more traditional exegetical stream of Confucian philosophy: Feng Youlan (1889–1990), Qian Mu (1895–1991), and Xu Fuguan (1904–82).

Feng Youlan's two-volume *History of Chinese Philosophy*, although now dated, has been the standard work on this subject since its first appearance in translation in 1953. Although Feng considered himself to be a philosopher first and an historian of Chinese philosophy second, his own speculative revision of a kind of neo-Confucianism that takes advantage of a Western sense of system and logical rigor is, when referenced at all, usually regarded as an unsuccessful attempt to 'modernize' Chinese philosophy by overwriting it with Western assumptions. After his 'materialist' period, his more important contribution lies in his nuanced and sophisticated clarification of the vocabulary of Chinese philosophy by treating its language as dynamic and developmental – a living organism that will ultimately overcome any rationalization imposed upon it.

Qian Mu was the model Confucian scholar stepping out of history – a living encyclopedia of traditional learning who in his person contributed a sense of ground and horizon through a stormy night in Chinese culture. In emphasizing the historical, contextual, and practical commitment of Chinese philosophy, Qian Mu developed a historiography that contrasted palpably with the analytic, dialectical, logocentric sensibilities he associated with Western philosophy. By demonstrating the organic unity and integrity of Zhu Xi's neo-Confucian philosophy against Western-inspired dualistic and idealistic readings, Qian Mu provided a philosophical touchstone for the more creative adventures in New Confucianism.

Xu Fuguan from his early years committed himself to a military and political career, and became a scholar and public intellectual only after his own sense of personal failure in having made no practical difference in the world finally overwhelmed him. Even so, far from abandoning his ambition to reform and modernize China, he simply assumed an alternative strategy for doing so. Xu Fuguan never claimed to be a philosopher, and his most widely acclaimed talent was his sense of the historical context in which the intellectual drama was staged. Probably his most influential work has been his history of the notion of human nature in the Confucian tradition. Although a vocal critic of the transcendentalism and rationalism he took as his sometimes simplistic characterization of Western culture, he sought to muster a historically-informed understanding of Confucian values as a complement to the science and democracy that could be profitably appropriated from Western learning. He died a frustrated yet unconquered advocate of a Confucian democracy that has, in our own historical moment, become an increasingly real possibility for modern China.

The Transformation of Marxism

The first players in our story of twentieth-century Chinese philosophy are the Marxists who, in having appropriated a Western heresy, constitute one more strong current in the syncretic evolution of Chinese philosophy. That is, for several generations in the mid-twentieth century an increasingly sinosized variation on Marxist-Leninism submerged the last vestiges of old Confucianism and smothered the first tremblings of a Western-inspired liberalism to become a new cultural orthodoxy. While this Marxism-Maoism has in the last few decades largely subsided, it has still made its contribution to contemporary Chinese philosophy, and provides yet another example of how 'Confucian' syncretism has indeed transformed the Prussian Kant into the Chinaman of Konigsberg.

First, there is Mao Zedong (1893–1976) himself. Although from early in his career with his commitment to Leninism, his own philosophical contribution is couched in a familiar Marxist idiom, the question often raised is whether Maoism is a sinification of Marxism or a Marxification of traditional Chinese philosophy. As Mao Zedong gains more confidence in his propagandist role as a self-confessed Marxist thinker, he increasingly particularizes and historicizes Marxist theory with the concrete conditions of the Chinese experience, challenging those teleological and deterministic elements of Marxism by emphasizing the potency of the particular and communal moral will in shaping history. Much careful study has been made of how his most philosophical work, 'On Contradictions' was revised after first appearing in 1937 and then revised for the *Selected Works* of 1952 (Knight 1992; Tian 2005). The claim is that in the mature Mao Zedong, Marxist dialectics had become Chinese dialectics with its roots firmly planted in the correlative *tongbian* or *yinyang* thinking of the *Book of Changes* in which there is a distinctive 'continuity through change' between opposites. Simply put, Mao reads a familiar and persistent Chinese cosmology into Marxist dialectical materialism.

The Kantian scholar, Li Zehou, has been one of contemporary China's most prominent social critics. Woei Lien Chong demonstrates specifically how Li Zehou's commentary on Kant is an integral and foundational element in his rejection of Maoist voluntarism – the idea that the power of the human will can accomplish all things. Mao's voluntarism is not new, but emerges out of and is consistent with the traditional Confucian position that human realization lies with the transformative powers of the unmediated moral will. For Li Zehou, unbridled confidence in the moral will – a belief that in Maoist China translated into practice as ideologically driven mass mobilization campaigns – has been responsible for China's contemporary crises, from Western colonialization down to the Great Leap Forward and the Cultural Revolution (Chong 1996).

The argument, simply put, is that Chinese philosophers from classical times have recognized a continuity between human beings and their natural environments captured in the phrase: 'the continuity between human experience and the divine' (*tianren heyi*). The nature of this continuity, however, has often been misunderstood to the detriment of the natural sciences. Instead of being a continuity between subject and object, respecting both the ability of the collective human community to transform its environment productively, *as well as* acknowledging the resistance of the natural world to this human transformation, it has been dominated by the belief that the moral subject holds absolute transformative powers over an infinitely malleable natural world. It has become a kind of raw subjectivism which discounts the need for collective human efforts in science and technology to 'humanize' nature and establish a productive relationship between subject and object, a relationship that Li Zehou takes to be a precondition for human freedom.

Where does Kant come in? Li Zehou sees Kant as confronting a problem similar to contemporary Chinese intellectuals. For Marxist China, how can 'deterministic' scientific progress and its political expression, totalitarian socialism, be reconciled with human freedom? And for Kant's world, how can mechanistic Newtonian science, Church dogma, and Leibnizian rationalism be reconciled with Rousseauesque humanism? Kant's epistemic move is to claim that the forms and categories of science do not exist independently of the human being, but constitute an *active* structure of the human mind. This *a priori* structure of the mind acts to synthesize our experiences and to construct our world of scientific understanding. Hence, scientific understanding, far from contradicting the possibility of human freedom, is an expression of it. Li Zehou appropriates this notion of 'categories' of human understanding from Kant, but attempts to 'sinocize' this structure by historicizing and particularizing it. How so? First, China *contra* the passive Marxian 'mirror' conception of mind, has traditionally embraced a resolutely active notion of heart-mind (*xin*), as expressed in the performative, 'ontological' force of knowledge. Li Zehou extends this assumption by offering a theory of 'sedimentation' – the form of the human cultural psychology (*wenhua xinli jiegou*) – that is synchronic, diachronic, and evolutionary. The 'structure' of human understanding – Li Zehou actually prefers the more processional translation 'formation' for *jiegou* – is not an *a priori* given, but is dynamic – a function of shared human experience that is historically and culturally specific. As human beings have trans-formed their various environments, the transformed environments have shaped their categories of understanding.

Sedimentation is the accumulation of a contingent social memory through which each individual human being is socialized and enculturated. As Woei Lien Chong observes, it begins at the level of the human species through the designing and making of tools:

> The process of the 'humanization of nature' (*ziran de renhua*) works in two ways: Human beings humanize external nature in the sense of making it a fit place for them to live in, and at the same time, by this very activity, they humanize their own physical and mental constitution by becoming increasingly de-animalized and adapted to life in organized society. (Chong 1996: 150)

The argument moves from the human being as a species to specific cultural sites and experiences when Li Zehou insists that Chinese scholars must look to their own traditional resources in shaping a vision for China's future. Chong summarizes her conversations with Li Zehou in the following terms:

> When it comes to cultural regeneration, in Li's view, the Chinese should go back to their own heritage rather than start from premises derived from Western world-views, such as Christianity, liberalism, and Freudianism . . . These Western premises, Li holds, cannot take root in the collective Chinese consciousness, which is based on entirely different foundations. (Chong 1996: 141)

Jane Cauvel summarizes not two, but three dimensions of sedimentation in her examination of Li Zehou's philosophy of art:

> [W]e each have 'species sedimentation' (forms common to all human beings), 'cultural sedimentation,' (ways of thinking and feeling common to our culture), and 'individual sedimentation,' (those ways of looking at the world accumulated from our own individual life experiences). (Cauvel 1999: 158)

Li Zehou with his theory of sedimentation, like Kant, is able to reconcile causal science and human freedom, but in a way that, from the Chinese perspective, resists Kantian metaphysics of the mind. What begins early in Li's career as Kantian commentary becomes a turn in Chinese philosophy consistent with underlying premises of the Confucian tradition, releasing the dragon and imbuing it with new energy to continue, undeterred. The Kantian categories, far from providing a basis for discovering universal claims, become a dynamic process for formulating and respect-ing cultural differences. A signal of Li Zehou's continuing commitment to the aestheticism of the Confucian tradition is his belief that the highest form of cultural sedimentation is expressed as art.

On the Edge of the Twenty-first Century

As Chinese philosophy crosses into the new century, on its horizon lies the stirrings of an important new relationship between the antinomian and processual tradition of American pragmatism, and these new directions in Confucianism. What are the resonances between a Deweyan pragmatism and Confucianism that might make a dialogue between them illuminating?

We might begin from the relational and radically contextualized 'focus-field' Confucian notion of person. While good China scholars certainly disagree, there is minimal dispute with respect to the symbiotic relationship that obtains among the radial spheres of personal, communal, political, and cosmic cultivation, the process of self-cultivation through ritualized living, the centrality of communication and the attunement of language, the inseparability of the cognitive and affective dimensions of experience, an understanding of the heart-and-mind (or 'thinking and feeling') as a disposition to act rather than a 'state of mind' or a framework of ideas and beliefs, the construal of knowing as an epistemology of caring – of trust rather than truth, the prevalence of correlative (rather than dualistic) thinking, the mutual shaping of reform and function (*tiyong*), the pursuit of self-realizing as authentication in practice, the familial nature of all relationships, the centrality of family and filial deference, the high value of inclusive harmony, the priority of ritual propriety to rule or law, the role of exemplary modeling, the didactic function of sage as virtuosic communicator, the expression of sagacity as focusing and enchanting the familiar affairs of the day, a recognition of a continuity between humanity and the numinous, and so on.

There is much in this processive model of human 'becoming' as a communal 'doing and undergoing' that sounds like Dewey. One virtue of pursuing a comparison between Dewey and Confucianism is that until now, much of the recent discussion of Chinese philosophy both within China and without tends to take place within the framework and categories of the Western philosophical tradition. Dewey's attempt to reconstruct philosophy largely abandons the technical vocabulary of professional philosophy in favour of ordinary language, although an ordinary language that is often used in rather extraordinary and unfamiliar ways.

Chinese philosophy will continue to evolve out of those relationships that it takes to be most important and productive in shaping the new social order. And given that China is undergoing the greatest revolution in Chinese history in our own times, syncretic Chinese philosophy will be influenced by events that might as yet remain unclear, but events that are certain to precipitate a dramatic transformation in Chinese ways of living and thinking.

References

All translations from Chinese into English are by R. T. Ames

Alitto, G. S., (1979), *The Last Confucian: Liang Shu-ming and the Chinese Dilemma of Modernity*, Berkeley: University of California Press.

Cauvel, J. (1999), 'The Transformative Power of Art: Li Zehou's Aesthetic Theory,' *Philosophy East and West* 49(2): 150–73.

Cheng C., and N. Bunnin (eds) (2002), *Contemporary Chinese Philosophy*, Oxford: Blackwell.

Chong, W. L. (1996), 'Mankind and Nature in Chinese Thought: Li Zehou on the Traditional Roots of Maoist Voluntarism,' *China Information* 11 (2–3) (autumn/winter): 138–75.

Cua, A. S. (ed.) (2003), *Encyclopedia of Chinese Philosophy*, New York: Routledge.

Dennett, D. C. (1995), *Darwin's Dangerous Idea: Evolution and the Meanings of Life*, New York: Simon and Shuster.

Dizrlik, A. (1995), 'Confucius in the Borderlands: Global Capitalism and the Reinvention of Confucianism,' *Boundary 2* 22(3): 229–73.

Girardot, N. J. (1983), *Myth and Meaning in Early Taoism: The Theme of Chaos (Hun-tun)*, Berkeley: University of California Press.

Graham, A. C. (1989), *Disputers of the Tao*, La Salle: Open Court.

Graham, A. C. (1991), 'Reflections and Replies,' in H. Rosemont, Jr. (ed.) (1991), *Chinese Texts and Philosophical Contexts: Essays Dedicated to Angus C. Graham*, La Salle: Open Court, pp. 267–322.

Granet, M. C. (1934), *La pensée chinoise*, Paris: Albin Michel.

Hansen, C. (1992), *A Daoist Theory of Chinese Thought*, Oxford: Oxford University Press.

Knight, N. (ed.) (1992), 'The Philosophical Thought of Mao Zedong: Studies from China, 1981–1989,' *Chinese Studies in Philosophy* 23 (3–4), pp. 3–56.

Levenson, J. (1968), *Confucian China and its Modern Fate: A Trilogy*, Berkeley: University of California Press.

Levenson, J. (1959), 'The Suggestiveness of Vestiges: Confucianism and Monarchy at the Last,' *Confucianism in Action*, pp. 244–67.

Makeham, J. (ed.) (2003), *New Confucianism: A Critical Examination*, New York: Palgrave Macmillan.

Mou Z. (1963), *Zhongguo zhesue de tezhi* (*The Unique Character of Chinese Philosophy*), Taipei: Xuesheng shuju.

Needham, J. (1956), *Science and Civilisation*, vol. 2, Cambridge: Cambridge University Press.

Sivin, N. (1995), *Medicine, Philosophy and Religion in Ancient China: Researches and Reflections*, Aldershot: Variorum.

Tang J. (1988a), 'Zhongguo zhexuezhong ziranyuzhouguan zhi tezhi (The Distinctive Features of Natural Cosmology in Chinese Philosophy),' in J. Tang (1998), *Zhongxi zhexue sixiang zhi bijiao lunwenji* (*Collected Essays on the Comparison between Chinese and Western Philosophical Thought*), Taipei: Xuesheng shuju.

Tang J. (1988b), *Complete Works*, vol. 11 Taipei: Xuesheng shuju.

Tian C. (2005), *Chinese Dialectics: From Yijing to Marxism*, Lanham: Lexington Books.

Tu W. (1992), 'Intellectual Effervescence in China,' *Daedalus* 121 (2) (Spring): 250–92.

Wolf, M. (1994), 'Beyond the Patrilineal Self: Constructing Gender in China,' in R. T. Ames, T. P. Kasulis, and W. Dissanayake (eds) (1994), *Self as Person in in Asian Theory and Practice*, Albany: State University of New York Press, pp. 251–69.

Xiong, S. (1977), *Mingxinpian*, Taipei: Xuesheng shuju.

Zhang D. (1995), *Zhishi yu wenhua: Zhang Dongsun wenhua lunzhu jiyao*, (ed.) Y. Zhang, Beijing: Zhongguo guangbo dianshi chubanshe.

Japanese Philosophy

Robert E. Carter

It may be that the most striking and penetrating cross-cultural philosophical exploration of the twentieth century originated in Japan. Nishida Kitaro (1870–1945) and the 'Kyoto School' had as their focal purpose the establishing of a dialogue of quality between traditional Eastern ways of thinking and the long established philosophical traditions of the West. Japan had isolated itself from nearly all possible external influences for two and a half centuries, and it was the American captain, William Perry, who forcibly opened Japan to the outside world once more in 1854. It was not a change that was entered into willingly, but after a relatively brief, but intense period of national soul-searching, Japan threw itself into the task of modernizing a culture that had not kept pace with scientific and technological developments. Philosophically, the Japanese knew little of what the West had been thinking, but here, too, they threw themselves into a process of discovery which would very quickly bring Japanese philosophers into the mainstream of Western philosophizing, while maintaining their own distinctive heritage and history. James Heisig aptly describes the situation in which Japanese academics found themselves:

> To say that philosophy is new to Japan – just over a century old – does not mean that it enjoyed a normal infancy. It was denied the natural aging process that produced Western philosophy as we know it. Fully twenty-three centuries earlier, the Greeks on the coast of Asia Minor, pressured by the advance of surrounding civilizations, had sought to break free of the confines of a mythical world-view and describe the world and its origins in natural, realistic terms . . . The Japanese, in contrast, entered the world of modern philosophy standing on the shoulders of post-Kantian preoccupation with epistemology, scientific methodology, and the overcoming of metaphysics. Despite the remarkable advances that the study of philosophy made in Japan's institutions of higher learning, and the more remarkable fact that it took them only one generation to produce their first original philosopher in the person of Nishida Kitaro, they did not inherit the problem of where to locate literal truth and where the symbolic, or of how to deal with the progressive triumph of reason over myth and science over religion . . . One might say that in Japanese Buddhism – especially in the Zen form with which Nishida was most familiar – there is a spontaneous sense that, in matters of the heart, literalness is pathological. It was the very failure to be moved by one of the major

motive forces of received philosophical tradition that laid the ground for his own fresh and original contribution. (Heisig 1990)

It is not that the Japanese knew nothing at all of scientific, technological, and intellectual developments occurring in various parts of the West. The so-called 'Christian century' of Japan (1549–1614) began with the arrival of Christian missionaries. The Jesuits brought with them works in economics, philosophy, and, of course, theology. After the expulsion of the missionaries, while there was little contact with the outside world, the Japanese did permit a sort of outpost of Western, mostly Dutch traders to remain in the port of Deshima, in present-day Nagasaki. Shogun Yoshimune's edict of 1720 permitted limited freedom to translate books dealing with Dutch science. Other works were smuggled into Japan on trading ships from Holland and China, and some of these were philosophical. Piovesana confirms the considerable influence of these 'illegal' books when he writes that Takano Choie was able to write a book entitled 'Casual Record of Things Seen and Heard,' which included a brief history of philosophy from Thales to Kant, together with a critique of Aristotle's take on science (Piovesana 1969:4). There are further instances of direct Western influence on Japanese thinking throughout the eighteenth and nineteenth centuries, but not in anything like an open and permissive environment. Takano himself was imprisoned for advocating the opening of Japan to the West, escaped, and eventually committed ritual suicide to avoid capture, electing instead the honor of dying by his own sword.

The Meiji Restoration (1868–1912)

It was not until the opening of Japan in 1854 that Japanese officials became fully alert to the changes which loomed on the world-horizon, and of the need to bring Japan into the modern world by means of 'Western learning.' What the leaders hoped for is amply evident in the slogan, 'Western techniques, Eastern morality.' In other words, the Japanese hoped that they could adopt Western knowledge, without taking in as well Western cultural values. Sixty-eight of the brightest young men were dispatched to the West between 1862 and 1867, assigned to bring back expertise in economics, political science, commerce, law, science, technology, and in other disciplines, including philosophy. It will come as no surprise, however, that philosophy as a discipline was not a high priority for those officials at 'The Center for Western Studies,' whose job it was to dispatch and monitor those going abroad.

Nishi Amane was sent to Leyden in 1862. He was to study law and political science, which he did, but he chose to study philosophy as well. Nishi was attracted to both the positivism of Comte and Mill, and the idealism of Kant and Hegel. Nearly a decade after his return, Nishi gave lectures to the Emperor Meiji on the history of Western philosophy. More significantly, it was Nishi, who is sometimes referred to as the 'father of Japanese Western philosophy,' who coined the term still used to refer to Western philosophy: *tetsugaku*, or 'the science of questing wisdom.' He also prepared 'A Dictionary of Philosophical Terms,' which still remains the basis for rendering Western philosophical terms and concepts into Japanese.

While all of this was happening, philosophers from the West made the long journey to Japan to teach philosophy, amongst other subjects: James Summer in 1875; Professor Syle in 1877 came to teach logic; Edward S. Morse, a Darwinist, came in 1877, and subsequently persuaded Ernest F. Fellonosa, of Harvard, to replace him in 1879. Fellonosa remained in Japan until 1890, teaching the history of Western philosophy. His influence was considerable, and his academic specialties included the study of Oriental art.

While it is evident that Western philosophy was an influence in Japanese philosophy and culture as early as the sixteenth century, it was with this re-opening of Japan to the world in the mid-nineteenth century that Western influences became a clear focus for the Japanese. Scholars in Japan were first impressed by positivism, which then gave way, after a surprisingly short period of ascendency, to German Idealism. While the reasons for this philosophic sea-change are no doubt many and complex, a major reason is likely to be that German Idealism provided a robust metaphysics, which the Buddhist influence in Japan had long since encouraged. Positivism was more ethically oriented, and was an attempt to move away from what it considered to be the 'excesses' of previous metaphysical speculation. All the while, the Japanese were searching for clear signs of what they were becoming, or ought to become, in the cauldron of rapid change and confusion. They sought 'expertise for themselves in everything the West was pressing on them. "Catch up, overtake!" went the slogan directed at the cooperation of the populace at large' (Heisig 2001: 10). However, while the goal was to catch up, it was the fervent hope and expectation that Japanese cultural ways and values could be maintained by adapting, rather than adopting, foreign ideas, as had been done so many times in the past history of Japanese openness to foreign ideas, at least until Japan closed itself off from outside influence. Watsuji Tetsuro (see below) argues that isolationism was a tragedy for Japan, and a deviation from Japan's traditional openness to foreign ideas.

Nishida Kitaro (1870–1945)

Out of this confusing and agitated milieu, a thinker appeared on the scene who, for the first time, attempted to give voice to much of Japan's historical ways of philosophizing, using the tools and insights provided by Western philosophers. Nishitani Keiji, Nishida's student and eventual successor at the University of Kyoto, writes that in Nishida, 'the spirit of the East and the spirit of the West are joined together' (Nishitani 1991: 52). Nishida burst on the scene with a work which captured the imagination of scholars, and even a wider audience, from its first appearance in 1911. When he began writing *An Inquiry Into the Good*, he was a high school teacher. Having attended the University of Tokyo as a 'special' student, he studied mathematics and philosophy. By 1909, he was teaching German at Peer's College, in Tokyo, and in 1910 he was appointed to Kyoto University. It was here that the so-called 'Kyoto School' was born, largely as a result of Nishida's unique way of philosophizing.

Nishida's thought blended the influences of China, Japan, and India, with that of Western thinkers from Plato and Aristotle, to Augustine, Nicholas of Cusa, Meister Eckhart and Jacob Boehme, to Descartes, Kant, Hegel, Bergson, and William James. It was from James that Nishida took the term 'pure experience,' the pivotal notion of his

Inquiry. Himself a student of Zen Buddhism, Nishida found in James's approach an appeal to the immediacy of experience which served as an expression of the heart of Zen awareness. Nishida's starting-point was intended to explicate the commonality to be found at the roots of both science and technology, and the humanities and religion. Pure experience refers to that state of awareness which is preconceptual, prior to all judgement and to the attachment of meaning. Nishida begins the *Inquiry* by claiming that:

> to experience means to know facts just as they are, to know in accordance with facts by relinquishing one's own fabrications. What we usually refer to as experience is adulterated with some sort of thought, so by 'pure' I am referring to the state of experience just as it is without the least addition of deliberative discrimination. (Nishida 1990: 3)

What is given in this primal immediacy is a reality which is unified, yet which constantly changes: a unity in flux. The continual play of the unfolding of this reality can be discerned by human consciousness alone, and in this sense, it is we humans who are the points of self-consciousness of reality. Thomas Henry Huxley taught that human beings are evolution become conscious of itself, and Nishida taught that we constitute God's self-consciousness, but he cautions that he does not have in mind a 'God as something like a great human who stands outside the universe and controls it. This notion of God is extremely infantile' (Nishida 1990: 80).

Most scholars would agree that Zen Buddhism is the seminal background to Nishida's thinking. Both Zen and James share the attempt to return to immediate experience as the ground of their respective philosophies. Nishida claims that pure experience offers us 'facts just as they are,' directly, and unmediated by our conceptual grid of understanding, our evaluative judgement, or our various contexts of meaning-granting. Additionally, pure experience is a state of immediate awareness prior to the distinction between subject and object: '[W]hen one directly experiences one's own state of consciousness, there is not yet a subject or an object, and knowing and its object are completely unified' (Nishida 1990: 3–4). Such experiences are also prior to the distinction of the various conscious abilities, that is, knowing, feeling, and willing. From this originary experience, Nishida charts a view of reality that is, in the broadest sense, religious. To see facts just as they are is to see things by 'becoming' them; it is to empty the self-centered ego and 'to become one at that primal point in which there is neither self nor others' (Nishida 1958: 362). Furthermore, beneath our ego-self we discover the absolute, that same primal awareness which is the outside within. The point of Zen practice is to remove our conceptual, abstract glasses in order to see things as they are, without the processing lenses of the dualistic mind.

Part of Nishida's uniqueness is his demand that we return from reasoning about experience to pure experience itself. He maintains that there is another layer of experiential awareness beneath the everyday phenomena of which Kant and Husserl speak, and it is directly apprehended. In this sense, the noumenal is available to us.

However, neither pure experience nor the deep self can be objectified, or spoken of directly. It is a *basho* – an emptiness – a nothingness in which the knower and the known, the subject and the object are not yet distinguished. It is the move beyond these that leads to Nishida's sense of the religious: '[O]ur true self is the very study of the universe. To know the true self is not only to be joined to the good of humanity in general, but also to melt into the stuff of the universe and to blend in with the divine will' (Nishida 1990: 145). To grasp the same unifying activity of experience both within ourselves, and outside of ourselves, is enlightenment. But our language, concepts, and theories simply cannot deal with that undivided experience which is prior to all thing-ification and, hence, is no-thing. It is a direct awareness of our oneness with all that is.

Nishida continued to improve on his initial formulation, first exploring conscious-ness itself, and then, in 1927, introducing what one commentator called 'a more powerful metaphysical base' through his concept of the *topos* or *basho* of nothingness (Dilworth 1978: 252). His approach was to develop a concrete logic – a systematic approach to knowledge-as-action ('action intuition') – in the everyday world of social and historical encounter, and this took him beyond a focus on self-consciousness, to the dialectical world of action. The term 'action intuition' serves as epistemological notice that seeing, intuiting, perceiving, and sensing are not to be conceived of in purely intellectual terms, trapping us within our philosophical heads with no internal guarantees that the way we see the world is actually the way it is. In our everyday lives we encounter and engage the world in a mutuality of being affected by it, and affecting it directly ourselves through our actions. We are changed in the very process of acting to bring about change. Yet even though this more powerful metaphysics is a new departure, it is also a different way of explaining the meaning of enlightenment (*jikaku*, or self-awakening), as pure experience and as a spontaneous way of acting. Like the martial artist, after lengthy preparation, if we are lucky, we can act without acting, moving in a spontaneous and effortless manner to block blows and counter-attack. In our ordinary lives, we can similarly learn to act without acting, without calculation, and without emotional confusion. Intuition and action, seeing and doing spring forth at the same time. There is no time for thinking, even for an instant. This is to encounter the deep or true self, which lurks beneath the ego in everyone, but which only a few disciplined souls actually encounter. It is a selfless-self, a no-self, a no-thing.

Nishida's later philosophy was concerned with applying his insights to the ordinary person engaged in the day-to-day activities of ordinary life. As Nishitani observed, action intuition is 'nothing other than all our ordinary thinking and acting.' In this sense, it is even referred to as an 'eschatological ordinariness' (Nishitani 1991: 181). The path of the masters leads to a way of being where distinctions give way to a direct immersion into the very flow of being and becoming, and then into the primal creativity of sheer distinctionless nothingness. Ultimately, each of us can learn to live in this 'now' of momentary presentness, whose background is a reality which is without distinction. Every thing and everyone is lined with nothingness which, like the lining of a fine garment remains invisible, but which yet is now evidently present because of the 'hang' of everything. The world looks incredibly different to one who is able to see the interconnectedness of all things, and the emptiness of all things in their depths. Nevertheless, absolute nothingness, the nothingness that dissolves substance-thinking, must not be clung to as nothingness. It must not be taken as a kind of substance but must itself be emptied, just as pure experience must be emptied leaving only the flow which we experience in being-time. Nothingness is emptying as a process, revealing the incredible divinity of every moment and every thing in the world. It is the Zen world where mountains are mountains, and red blossoms are simply red blossoms, in their suchness, never before apprehended with such beauty, such force, and, like the cherry blossoms of spring, are gone, emptied, each and every moment. And each of us is the place, the *basho* of awareness where each thing persists for its moment, renewed and reborn in each and every subsequent instant. Such awareness is an awareness of impermanence as the only reality, and it is a reality of such incredible richness that it is expressible only in the flash of insight of a *haiku* (seventeen-syllable poem) or in the sound of a soaked bamboo water conduit as it hits with a 'thwark' sound in the silence – the emptiness of a landscape garden. It is to be immersed in the immediacy of the present, and only that. It is experiences such as these that we take back into the ordinary world, and the world is now transformed, as a result.

Tanabe Hajime (1885–1962)

In 1919, Tanabe, with the support of Nishida as departmental chair, was appointed an assistant professor at Kyoto University. For some years Tanabe's wish had been to study in Germany, and Nishida supported his idea. In 1922 Tanabe received a grant from Japan's Ministry of Education to study in Berlin. For a year, he worked with Alois Riehl, a neo-Kantian. Riehl sent him on to study with Rickert in Heidelberg, but Tanabe chose Freiburg instead, where Husserl was located. Heisig reports that in 1923:

> he was invited to Husserl's home to address a small gathering. Although the impression he left is reported to have been favorable, Husserl seems to have taken over in midstream and left the young Japanese philosopher, already fumbling with the German language, to one side. Husserl made clear his hopes that Tanabe would be a bridge for the phenomenological movement to the east. Tanabe would have none of it. (Heisig 2001: 108)

Finding little of interest in Husserl's approach, he journeyed to Marburg where Martin Heidegger was already creating a stir. Tanabe's philosophic aims were much more in accord with Heidegger's, and they became friends. Heidegger acted as a private tutor in German philosophy for Tanabe.

Tanabe returned to Japan in 1924, eager to begin lecturing on the material which he had amassed while in Germany, but instead, Nishida asked him to lecture on Kant. Subsequently, he lectured on Fichte, Schelling, and Hegel. It was Hegel's philosophy that caught his full attention, and he devoted two years to the *Encyclopedia* followed by thirteen years spent on the *Phenomenology of Spirit* (Heisig 2001: 108). He soon became an advocate of the dialectic, which occupies a central place in his own, later, original philosophy. In 1927 Nishida retired, and Tanabe was given his chair. In 1930, in response to *Nishida's System of the Self-awareness of the Universal*, Tanabe published a critical essay of that work, 'Looking Up to Nishida's Teachings.' Nishida was angered by this criticism, calling it 'heartless,' and the relational break that occurred never healed. Friends were now enemies, and their ideas grew increasingly further apart. Sad as this relational rupture was, it no doubt was the major cause of the coming into existence of the Kyoto School. The disagreement became a lively debate about key issues, fostering further debate on many fronts as others joined sides. This mix of exploration and heated dialogue placed Kyoto philosophy at the center of academic study in philosophy in Japan. In 1957, Heidegger recommended Tanabe for an honorary doctorate from the University of Freiburg, which was awarded in absentia because of his age and worsening health.

Both mathematics and philosophy had appealed to the young Tanabe, and his interest in science led to his first book, *The Natural Sciences Today*, in which he both praised the achievements of science, and critiqued it because of its unwillingness to include issues of value, such as subjectivity and freedom. This exclusive emphasis on objective knowledge would make it impossible for science to grasp the importance of pure experience and religion.

Tanabe continued to write on science and mathematics, but his interest in human relationships as mediated by other relationships began to take center stage. His central guides along this developing pathway were Kierkegaard and Shinran. The focus was on absolute nothingness, which he began to see as a central source of disagreement with Nishida's approach. The loss of the subject/object distinction in Nishida's sense of nothingness, was, for Tanabe, a loss of the sense of history, as well. The dialectic of history as continual change from what is, to its negation by what will be, is in itself meaningless, he concluded, unless it is guided in some way by divine providence. But he could not bring himself to accept God as Christians believed in him, and so he returned to the Buddhist notion of nothingness. And rather than being aloof as a transcendent God would be, or beyond the subject/object distinction as with Nishida, nothingness for Tanabe was immanent in each and every thing.

Reasonably, we might well argue that this was similar to Nishida's understanding of nothingness, which also was immanent in all things. Not a few authors have argued that Tanabe really misunderstood, or misread Nishida, and that his own philosophy was not all that different from Nishida's. I would concur with this assessment, but that does not take away from Tanabe's originality in other respects. In particular, in the 1930s he proposed his logic of species, and after the war, his 'metanoetics.'

Instead of Nishida's logic of place, or *topos*, Tanabe contributed a 'logic of species.' Piovesana suggests that 'Tanabe's opposition to Nishida was in general due to the excessively "contemplative" nature of Nishida's thought. To state it more concretely, though negatively, Tanabe was of the opinion that Nishida's thought was not social-minded enough' (Piovesana 1969: 149). While the logic of species established Tanabe as a philosopher, it also set him on a path that eventually others condemned, for his seeming support of Japanese nationalism, and his right-wing apology for the state. Adapting Hegel's tripartite dialectic, Tanabe emphasized the species as the mediator between the individual and the universal: as individuals we come to be who we are because of the group to which we belong, and the group, in turn, is influenced by the individuals who make it up. We come to understand the fact that we are part of the human race through the mediation of the species, that is, the society or culture created by our particular race. The universal does not directly inform the individual, but rather the individual is informed in his or her nature via its membership in a species or culture. Tanabe was convinced that philosophers had forgotten the logical importance of the particular, or species, as the mediator between the universal, or type, and the individual.

The problem was that Tanabe tended to exaggerate the homogeneity of Japanese society as representative of the species. Under the genus, there should be many cultural instances or species, each readily distinguishable from the others, yet all of them falling under the universal as humankind. Also, the universal began to change in connotation from a barren universal, to absolute nothingness, to the state as the best instance, to this point in history, to that of the genus materialized. The state now took on something of the flavor of an absolute, which seemingly opened the door to a totalitarian understanding.

Eventually, Tanabe abandoned this approach precisely because it left open the kind of excess of interpretation which World War II made all too evident. He underwent a radical conversion, and the religious aspect of his philosophy took center stage as he critiqued not only his own philosophy, but all philosophy, because it did not allow the guidance of a transcendent power. In his most important work, *Philosophy as Metanoetics*, he speaks of repentance, both for his excesses during the war, and in general, as a new approach to philosophizing. As the war was coming to its tragic close, Tanabe struggled to answer his own questions about truth as opposed to expediency, and in a state of exhaustion and despair, he concluded that he was no longer fit to be a philosopher. Then came his breakthrough:

> At that moment something astonishing happened. In the midst of my distress I let go and surrendered myself humbly to my own inability. I was suddenly brought to new insight! My penitent confession – *metanoesis* – unexpectedly threw me back on my own interiority and away from things external. (Tanabe 1986: 1)

In this flash of insight he discovered his own powerlessness, lack of freedom to bring about the desired changes, and in particular, the limits of reason itself. Abandoning faith in the power of reason, performing an existential self-surrender, he gave up 'self-power' (*jiriki*), and professed his faith in 'other-power' (*tariki*). As did Kierkegaard before him, he abandoned reason's power and accepted the power of faith, without guarantee, for grace would befall one out of the mystery and incomprehensibility of nothingness.

The ultimate irrationality of reality – of species – requires that reason will fail to supply the answers needed. Kant's critique of reason is not radical enough. Kant ends with critical insight of the highest order, but what is needed is not criticism, but an awakening. In the very acts of repentance, confession and faith, the old ego undergoes a death and resurrection. The ephemeral ego is annihilated, and the transformation of the self is to nothingness. The absolute to which one now appeals, is not a thing, but a power of transformation. As with Shinran, and Pure Land Buddhism, it is enough to call upon the name of Amida Buddha, humbly admitting one's failures and inabilities, and requesting the assistance of divine grace. Repentance itself is already an act of absolute nothingness due to its radical humility. It is a conversion and, hopefully, the gift of transformation. Repentance (*Zange*) is the mediator between the individual, and absolute nothingness.

Watsuji Tetsuro (1889–1960)

There is disagreement about whether Watsuji should be considered a member of the Kyoto School. In the first place, the major portion of his academic career was spent at Tokyo University, and in the second, rather than concerning himself with metaphysics or religion, his focus was on ethics. Nevertheless, he, too, dealt with such issues as nothingness, and dialectical contradiction. Undecided as to whether to study literature or philosophy, his early influence was the famous novelist and early advocate of Western values, especially individualism, Natsume Sôseki. In 1925, Nishida offered him a position at Kyoto University, where his chief responsibility was the courses on ethics.

In 1927, he was awarded a three-year scholarship to pursue further studies in Germany. In fact, he spent only fourteen months in Europe, forced to return to Japan in 1928 because of the death of his father. His reflections on that sojourn in Europe, where he did some traveling, resulted in a book, *Climate and Culture* [Fûdo (1961)], in which he critiques Heidegger for his emphasis on temporality at the expense of spatiality.

Although appointed professor at Kyoto University in 1931, when offered a professorship at Tokyo University in 1934, he enthusiastically accepted, and continued to teach there until his retirement in 1949. His publication record is enormous, with twenty-seven volumes of his collected works, ranging from studies of ancient Japanese and Chinese culture, primitive Christianity, primitive Buddhism, Japanese art and architecture, a critique of Homer, several works on ethics, to a study of the tragedy of Japan and World War II as a direct result of its earlier decision to isolate itself from the rest of the world.

In *Climate and Culture*, Watsuji argues that 'climate' should be taken to mean more than weather patterns, temperature and humidity; it should also include soils, oceans, and other water masses, flora and fauna, and the resultant human styles of living such as food choices, clothing, housing, natural and artificial heating and cooling, the resultant artifacts which describe a people, as well as its architecture. The list is exhaustive, and includes much of what might ordinarily be gathered under the word 'culture,' except that it includes weather, topography, and other geological conditions, as well. Watsuji calls to our attention the many ways in which our environment, taken in its broad sense, shapes who we are from birth to death. Heidegger's emphasis was on time and the individual, and too little on space and the social dimensions of human beings. When we add to our sense of climate the social environment of family, community, society at large, lifestyle, and even the technological apparatus that supports community survival and interaction, then we begin to glimpse what Watsuji had in mind by 'climate,' and how there exists a mutuality of influence from human to environment, and environment to human being which allows for the continued development and change of both. Climate is the whole interconnected network of influences that together create an entire people's attitudes and values.

Even before plunging into his study of the contrasts of European, Middle Eastern, and Far Eastern cultures, which he classed as meadow, desert, and monsoon cultures, Watsuji had regained focal interest in Japanese thought and culture. As with Soseki, who abandoned his earlier interest in Western culture and returned to the values of his own cultural tradition, at about the same time Watsuji left behind his earlier identification with individualism, and sought to understand the depths of the Japanese cultural tradition instead. As part of cultural climate, the past inevitably operates still in the present of every Japanese. It is this still operative value-cluster that Watsuji attempts to make explicit, and conscious. Heidegger's mistake, as Watsuji sees it, is to deal with human existence on the level of individual consciousness alone, in isolative reflection, whereas if we recognize the 'dual character' of human beings as existing both in time and space – as both individuals and as social being – 'then it is immediately clear that space must be regarded as linked with time' (Watsuji 1961: 9). We objectivize human life in climate. And it is climate that is the ever present background to what becomes the foreground focus for Watsuji, the study of Japanese ethics in theory and practice. There are many who would still claim that his work in ethics remains the definitive study of Japanese ethics.

Ethics

Ethics is the study of the ways in which men and women, adults and children, rulers and those ruled, have come to deal with each other in their specific climatic conditions. Ethics is the pattern of proper and effective social interaction. Watsuji's objection to individualistic ethics, which he associates with virtually all Western thinkers to some degree, is that it loses touch with the vast network of interconnections that serves to make us human. Unlike Hobbes, Nishida argues that we necessarily come into the world always already linked to various social groups or contexts: we are never just individuals. His analysis of the term '*ningen*,' which means human being or person, is that it has a threefold meaning: human being as individual, as a member of various social groups, and as the 'betweenness' between us which can serve either as a barrier, or as a possibility for friendship or intimacy. Using a logical form of expression similar to Nishida's self-contradictory identity, Watsuji maintains that we are individuals, and yet we are not just individuals, for we are also social beings; and we are social beings, but we are not just social beings, for we are also individuals. Ideally, the Japanese are not collectivists, but individualists and collectivists, and while the extreme of collectivism over individualism is always possible, it is no more or less possible than it is for Western democracies to be individualistic at the expense of any significant sense of community responsibility.

We expresses our individuality by negating the social group or by rebelling against various social expectations or requirements. To be an individual demands that we negate the supremacy of the group. On the other hand, to envision ourselves as members of a group is to negate our individuality. He adds to this what he terms a 'double negation.' That is, we break from the authority of a group or a tradition by affirming our independence from it. But the second negation occurs when we become a truly ethical human being by negating our individual separateness and joining with others. It is necessary to forget the self in order truly to become a member of a tradition – but only in the sense of becoming selfless. To be truly human is not the asserting of our individuality, but an annihilation of self-centeredness such that we are now identified with others in a nondualistic merging of self and others. Benevolence or compassion results from this selfless identification. This is our authentic 'home ground,' and it rekindles our awareness of our true and original nature, a kind of pure experience of the self. This home ground he calls 'nothingness,' which is a common theme for all members of the Kyoto School.

To be fully human is to live robustly in the midst of our communities, at the crossroads of various relational interconnections. We enter the world already within a network of relationships and obligations. Each of us is a nexus of pathways and roads, and our betweenness is already etched by the natural and cultural climate that we inherit and live our lives within. The Japanese live their lives within this relational network. It is crucial that we learn how to navigate these relational waters successfully, appropriately, and with relative ease and assurance. The study of these relational navigational patterns is the study of ethics. Ethics is concerned with the ways in which we, as individuals, respect, preserve, and persevere in the vast complexity of inter-connections which etch themselves upon us as individuals, thereby forming our natures as social selves. The Japanese word for ethics is *rinri*, which describes the system of relations guiding human relationships. Between each of us there is betweenness, or an empty space, a place of relational potential. Nevertheless, every encounter is already etched with the cultural traditions of genuine encounter; ideally, positive expectation, good will, open-heartedness, trustworthiness, cheerfulness, sincerity, fellow-feeling, and availability.

The State

Watsuji's theory of the state, and his vocal support of the imperial system, garnered considerable criticism after World War II. He argues that the culmination of the double negation is the restoration of an absolute totality. It is a surrender to totality, moving us beyond the myriad specific groups to the one total and absolute whole. It would seem that this ultimate wholeness would have been the home ground of nothingness, but Watsuji argues that it is the state that takes on the authority of totality. It is the highest and best social structure thus far.

There is no doubt that Watsuji's position could easily be interpreted as a totalitarian state ethics. Perhaps the fault lies not in his analysis per se, but in his all too sanguine collapsing of the descriptive and the prescriptive. Still in his studies of ethics he argues that no one nation has chartered the correct political and cultural path, and that the diversity of each is to be both encouraged and respected. He advocates unity in diversity, and rejects the idea that any nation has the right culturally to assimilate or dominate another. Each nation is shaped by its particular geography, climate, culture, and history, and the resultant diversity is both to be protected and appreciated. The notion of a universal state is, therefore, but an unwanted and dangerous delusion. We must know and cherish our own traditions, but we must not extol them as superior out of our ignorance of other ways and cultural traditions. Nationalism must not express itself at the expense of internationalism, and internationalism must not establish itself at the expense of nationalism.

Nishitani Keiji (1900–90)

Nishitani Keiji studied under Nishida at Kyoto University, and his graduate thesis was on Schelling. He taught at Otani and Kyoto Universities. In 1937 he, too, was sent to Europe by the Ministry of Education to study under Henri Bergson. Bergson was ill, however, and so instead, Nishitani went to Freiburg University to study with Heidegger.

The three philosophers discussed thus far were more or less of the same generation. Nishitani was a student and disciple of Nishida, and so belonged to the next generation. His work, however, is probably better known in the West than that of any of the founding three. His best known work is *Religion and Nothingness*, published first in Japanese in 1961, and in English in 1982. An ardent follower of Nishida's philosophy, Nishitani's genius was to show how Nishida's approach was a telling response to the existential concerns of such thinkers as Nietzsche and Heidegger. It was Nietzsche's work that served as a sexton which led Nishitani into the most difficult areas of contemporary concern. Chief amongst these was nihilism. Nietzsche's bold pronouncement that the old values were moribund carried with it the seeking of a way to remake Western culture by overcoming the old with a new sense of vigor and purpose in a Godless world. Nishitani greatly admired Nietzsche's insights, and in his *The Self-Overcoming of Nihilism*, he praises Nietzsche amply, but suggests that he did not go far enough – that he did not escape the nihilism which he had identified. The abyss, which Nietzsche revealed, included concern about death, together with a recognition of the impermanence of all that is. Nishitani labels this the 'standpoint of nihility.' All that is, is as though nothing, but this nothing, or nothingness, is only a relative nothingness, and not the absolute nothingness about which Nishitani writes. While Nietzsche offers the perpetual overcoming of the *Übermensch*, each overcoming is transient and a step closer to death. The abyss remains as the groundlessness of whatever we choose.

Nishitani accepts the reality of the abyss as revealed by Nietzsche, yet argues that this standpoint remains an egoic one. What is needed is a standpoint which transcends the ego, one which he terms the 'standpoint of emptiness,' or *sunyata*. Rather than imposing values and standards on things, things now appear in their 'suchness.' By letting go of the ego and self-centeredness, a self that is not a self emerges. Nishitani writes: 'In the Existenz of non-ego, non-ego does not mean simply that self is not ego. It has also to mean at the same time that non-ego is the self' (Nishitani 1982: 251). Only then can the standpoint of *sunyata* arise, in which the self and other are apprehended nondualistically. Using Buber's language, Nishitani contends that the other, including things, becomes a 'thou,' rather than an object (or 'it'), and the distance between observer and observed altogether collapses, leaving only the oneness of immediacy, yet retaining all distinctions and details. Here lies the basis for ethics and community: I am the other, and the other is me. Everyone and everything now appears just as they are, in their suchness. All things are now grasped from the inside, rather than merely 'objectively,' observed from the outside. We enter into the mode of being of a thing; we let the thing speak itself, for the self emptied of itself opens to emcompass all things. This is the standpoint of *sunyata*, of absolute nothingness.

Yet nothingness or emptiness must not be thought of as a thing. It is not some far off reality such as God is often imagined as being, but is to be found directly 'underfoot,' and is identical with each and every thing that exists. Just as I am the other, and the other is me, so nothingness is everything, and everything is nothing, no-thing. Looking at things with enlightened eyes, everything is now 'lined' with absolute nothingness (Nishida 1973:133). Using Nishida's language, like a finely tailored garment, we do not see, or look for the lining itself, but can discern the workmanship in the 'hang' of the garment. The lining is not actually seen, yet in another sense it is seen. So it is with nothingness: the standpoint of *sunyata* allows us to see that everything is a manifestation of nothingness, yet nothingness can only be detected in things. There is no nothingness alone, for, after all, it is empty. The realization that all is empty is 'the realization of nihilism in its authentic sense of absolute nothingness,' and 'is an awareness of all phenomena in the world as basically void, situated as they are in indefinitely factorable networks of causation' (Dilworth et al. 1998: 376).

Philosophy in Japan

While the twentieth-century focus must be on the Kyoto School as the most significant development in and contribution to Japanese philosophy, others were doing quality work as well: Kuki Shûzô (1888–1941), phenomenologist and aesthetician; Miki Kiyoshi (1897–1945), student first of Nishida, and then, while in Europe, of Heinrich Rickert, Karl Mannheim, Eugen Herringel, and Martin Heidegger (humanist, Heideggerian, and Marxist, and a prolific writer on a wide range of philosophic and social issues); Tosaka Jun (1900–45), Marxist thinker and activist, and critic of Nishida; Hisamatsu Shin'ichi (1889–1980), influential Zen Buddhist philosopher and popularizer; Ueda Shizuteru (1926–), student of Nishitani, one of Nishida's most outstanding interpreters, and an interpreter of the work of Meister Eckhart; Yuasa Yasuo (1925–2005), student of Watsuji, and major contributor to mind-body studies; and Abe Masao (1915–), philosopher of religion, and major contributor to the Buddhist-Christian dialogue and D. T. Suzuki (1870–1966) who almost single-handedly introduced Zen Buddhist philosophy to the West.

There is a remarkable irony in all of this, however, for while the Kyoto School, because of strong interest, is having an increasing role to play in the West, for the most part only Western philosophy is taught in Japan. Even at Kyoto University, during most of the twentieth century, Japanese philosophy was not taught to any great extent; and at most other Japanese universities, there were no courses at all on the Kyoto School. Recently, the Institute for the Study of Japanese Philosophy was established at Kyoto University, and is presently thriving with major research under way by both faculty and eager graduate students. Still, such interest is the exception rather than the rule in present-day Japan.

References

Abe, M. (1985), *Zen and Western Thought*, ed. W. R. LaFleur, Honolulu: University of Hawai'i Press.

Carter, R. E. (1997), *The Nothingness Beyond God: An Introduction to the Philosophy of Nishida Kitaro*, 2nd edn, St Paul: Paragon House.

Carter, R. E. (2004), 'Watsuji Tetsuro,' *Stanford Encyclopedia of Philosophy* http://plato.stanford.edu.

Dilworth, D. A. (1978), 'The Concrete World of Action in Nishida's Later Thought,' in N. Yoshihiro and T. Hirotaka (eds) (1978), *Analecta Husserliana*, vol. 8, Dordrecht: Reidel, pp. 249–70.

Dilworth, D. A., V. H. Viglielmo, with Agustin Jacinto (eds) (1998), *Sourcebook for Modern Japanese Philosophy*, Westport: Greenwood Press.

Dumoulin, H. (1992), *Zen Buddhism in the 20th Century*, trans. J. S. O'Leary, New York: Weatherhill.

Heisig, J. W. (1990), 'The Religious Philosophy of the Kyoto School – An Overview,' *Japanese Journal of Religious Studies* 17 (1): 55–6.

Heisig, J. W. (2001), *Philosophers of Nothingness*, Honolulu: University of Hawai'i Press.

Heisig, J. W. and J. C. Maraldo (eds) (1994), *Rude Awakenings: Zen, the Kyoto School, & the Question of Nationalism*, Honolulu: University of Hawai'i Press.

Kasulis, T. P. (1982), 'The Kyoto School and the West: Review and Evaluation,' *Eastern Buddhist* 15 (2): 125–44.

Nakamura, H. (1967), *A History of the Development of Japanese Thought: From 592 to 1868*, 2 vols, Tokyo: Kokusai Bunka Shinkokai [The Society for International Cultural Relations].

Nishida, K. (1958), 'The Problem of Japanese Culture,' in W. T. deBary et al. (eds) (1958), *Sources of Japanese Tradition*, vol. 2, New York: Columbia University Press, pp. 350–65

Nishida, K. (1973), *Intelligibility and the Philosophy of Nothingness: Three Philosophical Essays*, trans. R. Schinzinger, Westport: Greenwood Press.

Nishida, K. (1987), *Last Writings: Nothingness and the Religious Worldview*, trans. D. A. Dilworth, Honolulu: University of Hawai'i Press.

Nishida, K. (1990), *An Inquiry into the Good*, trans. A. Masao, and C. Ives, New Haven and London: Yale University Press.

Nishitani, K. (1982), *Religion and Nothingness*, Nanzan Studies in Religion and Culture, trans. J. V. Bragt, Berkeley: University of California Press.

Nishitani, K. (1990), *The Self-Overcoming of Nihilism*, trans. G. Parkes with S. Aihara, Albany: State University of New York Press.

Nishitani, K. (1991), *Nishida Kitaro*, Nanzan Studies in Religion and Culture, trans. Y. Seisaku and, J. W. Heisig, Berkeley: University of California Press.

Piovesana, G. K., and S. J. (1969), *Contemporary Japanese Philosophical Thought*, Asian Philosophical Studies 4, New York: St. John's University Press.

Tanabe, H. (1986), *Philosophy as Metanoetics*, Nanzan Studies in Religion and Culture, trans. T. Yoshinori, Berkeley: University of California Press.

Watsuji, T. (1961), *Climate and Culture: A Philosophical Study*, trans. G. Bownas, Tokyo: The Hokuseido Press; Ministry of Education.

Watsuji, T. (1996), *Watsuji Tetsuro's Rinrigaku: Ethics in Japan*, trans. Y. Seisaku and R. E. Carter, Albany: State University of New York Press.

Yusa, M. (2002), *Zen and Philosophy: An Intellectual Biography of Nishida Kitaro*, Honolulu: University of Hawai'i Press.

African Philosophy

Bruce B. Janz

African philosophy's development in the twentieth century is both relatively recent, traceable to some seminal texts, and ancient, drawing on cultural forms that stretch back in time and space. This seeming contradiction can be understood if we realize that philosophy itself is ambiguous. It designates on one hand a set of reflective practices rooted in culture and reason, which rigorously and critically explicate a life-world, and on the other a discipline in the university, with a set of codes, standards, recognized practitioners, and customs. More than almost any other site of philosophy, African philosophy has struggled with the similarities and differences between these two senses of philosophy. For some, there can be no philosophy without the disciplinary structures, which makes African philosophy recent and derivative. For others, there can be no disciplinary structure without critical engagement in a life-world, which means that African philosophy may well exist in traditional Africa, and indeed may form the basis or model for philosophy in the rest of the world.

African philosophy is not so much an area or topic within philosophy as it is a set of culturally original questions about the full range of philosophical issues. It deals with metaphysics, epistemology, axiology, and methodology, as well as with the problems and opportunities of intercultural philosophizing, and does so in ways that cover the gamut of the analytic/Continental divide in Western philosophy. The best we can hope to do here is to hit some high points, and direct the reader to more complete introductions for further information.

The central concern in African philosophy in the twentieth century, often to the frustration of its practitioners, is over its existence and nature. Historically, it is clear that the academic study of philosophy has its roots in various colonial versions of philosophy, and yet many African philosophers argue that African philosophy is not limited or reducible to that history, but can be found in indigenous places. Questions about African philosophy's existence by non-Africans have often amounted to an implicit dismissal of Africa, as those questions come with the presumption that there is no philosophy in Africa, and the onus is on those who claim there is to prove it. Taken most charitably, these seemingly dismissive questions may be understood as the perennial impulse of philosophy anywhere – the move back to sources, roots, beginnings, or the things themselves. In other words, we might take the requirement for the investigation into the possibility and identity of African philosophy as an implied insult or challenge to be answered or ignored, or as an opportunity to exercise a fundamental philosophical impulse, which is self-critically to examine the foundations or starting-points of truth, meaning, existence, and value. While the challenge is often present, many African philosophers have chosen the philosophically creative path.

More so than other philosophical traditions, African philosophy struggles with a central tension within its very name. On the one hand, philosophy has tended to contemplate universals, regarding them either as the foundation or beginning point of thought or as the goal of thought, and seeing them as a nonnegotiable requirement of philosophy (of course, some philosophers in the twentieth century have been suspicious of universals); on the other, the term 'African' designates a particularity (albeit a problematic, possibly constructed or imposed category). The problem is not as easily dealt with as in 'British philosophy' or 'Chinese philosophy', where there is a history of textuality that allows the philosopher to refer to a historically specific set of ideas and issues that have been part of a conversation over time. African philosophy has comparatively few texts before the middle of the twentieth century, and fewer sustained conversations among those texts. British philosophy tends not to reflect philosophically on the question of what it means to be British, while African philosophy does tend to reflect philosophically on the question of what it means to be African. So, a great deal of African philosophy in the twentieth century has focused on addressing metaphilosophical questions.

This tension has governed some of the important questions that African philosophy has grappled with over the century. Is there something both uniquely African and fundamentally philosophical within African culture or tradition? If there is, what is it? If there really is a tension here, can it (or should it) be resolved? Is it by finally privileging one or the other side of the tension, for example, by arguing that African philosophy fundamentally resides in some universal feature such as reason, or conversely that reason itself is always fundamentally particular and located, related to race, culture, history or politics?

There is another significant tension. We might distinguish between African philosophy as a spatial or a platial activity. African philosophy is spatial when it thinks of itself as analogous to a country on a map, and sets out to reclaim intellectual territory that was appropriated in the eighteenth, nineteenth, and twentieth centuries by European thinkers (indeed, Ngugi wa Thiong'o suggests this metaphor in the title of his well-known book, *Decolonizing the Mind*). It defines its borders, establishes citizenry, and defends the 'country' against invaders. African philosophy is 'platial' when it focuses on phenomenological analysis, that is, when it explicates the meaning of an African life-world for Africans. A platial understanding works out what it means to live in a country (that is, what it means to connect practice and thought in an African context). To the extent that we fight the defensive battle imposed or implied by European thought as it dismisses African philosophy as legitimate, we are engaging in spatial thought. While these battles may be necessary, what makes African philosophy a vital and urgent pursuit for many people is not the spatial response to an external challenge, but rather the explication of meaningful lived experience.

This essay will be more platial than spatial, although I do not wish to suggest that the spatial project is illegitimate. African philosophy, I will assume, is fundamentally defined and unified not by its geography, nor by the identity of its practitioners, its concepts or claims, or its history, but rather by its questions, and more particularly, by working out adequate questions. It is not that these other things are unimportant to the African philosopher, but that none of them provide a positive basis for creative work in African philosophy. African philosophy in the twentieth century has not tended to cluster in schools, apart from those which trace their heritage back to the forms of philosophy brought by colonial powers or inculcated by the graduate schools of particular African philosophers. All these other ways of defining African philosophy are finally contingent on the kinds of questions that have mattered to those for whom African existence matters. The circularity of this statement points to the fact that African identity is being worked out at the same time as is the content of African philosophy, and in relation to it (not only to it, of course, but reflective and philosophical thought is certainly one way of establishing and exploring what it means to be African). I take this circularity to be hermeneutical, and at the core, not only of African philosophy, but of all philosophy. The key, then, is in the recurring questions. I will outline some of the key questions that have currency in the field, recognizing that in each case, what makes African philosophy vibrant is the contesting of these questions.

Where is Africa?

The question 'Where is Africa?' is not simply a request for geographical location. Africa has existed in the desire and imagination of the world, both African and non-African, for hundreds of years. A common response to those who wish to discuss African philosophy is that there is no one Africa, but many, made up of various interlacing and conflicting groups such as tribes, nations, countries, and linguistic groups. How could there be an African philosophy? And yet, despite this skepticism toward the usefulness of 'African' as a category, it persists.

There are reasons for this persistence. Africa since the Enlightenment had been regarded as a place incapable of philosophy. In the *Philosophy of History*, Hegel used Africa as the foil against which all reason could be contrasted. It was not the Akan or the Kikuyu in particular that were regarded as incapable of reason, but all (sub-Saharan) Africans. To be unified in rejection in this manner meant that it made sense to see a common resistance to this theorized and pervasive racism. To the extent that Africa continues to be seen as a unified and coherent category by the rest of the world, if only in rejection, it continues to make sense to resist the reductionist move which would locate philosophy primarily in ethnic groupings. V. Y. Mudimbe (Mudimbe 1988) has articulated this by arguing that Africa has been a construction of Europe, in the sense that Europe needed its 'other' on which to project its fears and aspirations, and Kwame Anthony Appiah has also taken up the question of the meaning of Africa, specifically in terms of race (Appiah 1992).

'Where is Africa?' is also a question of boundaries. Hegel called North Africa 'European Africa,' and for some today, northern Africa has more in common culturally and intellectually with the Mid-East than with the rest of Africa. Where, intellectually, does Africa end and the rest of the world start? What is the intellectual relationship between Africa and its various diasporas? Is there such a thing as a 'pure' culture in Africa, which allows us to identify truly African concepts or cultural artifacts and can possibly ground and guarantee a truly African philosophy? 'Where is Africa?' requires us to also ask 'What is Africa?'

To ask where Africa is, is also to ask where it is in the development of disciplinary knowledge. For many, African philosophy is necessarily rooted in the traditional belief systems of African ethnic and linguistic groups. This means that anthropology, not philosophy, has been the first source of African philosophy (even among indigenous scholars), as it articulates and analyzes local thought. But it also means that Africa has tended to be the object of analysis, the site for the application of Western methods of social scientific analysis. Also, Africa has been the focal point for a variety of interdisciplinary studies which draw at least in part on philosophy. These include Black Studies, African-American Studies, Afrocentrism, Cultural Theory, Postcolonial Studies, and Race Theory. For some, African philosophy has included African spirituality, religion, cultural tradition, and activism, while for others, African philosophy is only philosophy if it is modeled closely on European forms of disciplinary methodology. Locating African philosophy in the disciplinary and interdisciplinary matrix can be difficult, but the pursuit of a pure disciplinary definition of African philosophy that fails to recognize linkages, debts, dynamic movement, and the history of discipline development is too restrictive. This, though, does not mean that just anything can be called African philosophy.

If we have asked the question 'Where is Africa?', and have answered that not only in geographical but also intellectual terms, one of the results is to try to map the territory. Henry Odera Oruka, for instance, mapped the 'trends' of African philosophy. These were not exactly schools of philosophy – they were not that organized (Oruka does have another list of schools, less well known, which partially overlap with his trends). They were, rather, answers to the question of particularity ('African') and universality ('philosophy') which had found currency. Initially there were four:

1. **Ethnophilosophy**: This approach to philosophy regarded the collective traditional wisdom or the generally held ontological assumptions and worldview of African ethnic groups or tribes as having the status of philosophy.

2. **Sage Philosophy**: This is Oruka's own substantive contribution. Through interviews, he identifies the 'philosophical sages' within a culture, those who are more than repositories of cultural wisdom (these he calls 'folk sages'), and bring a critical edge to that wisdom.

3. **Nationalistic/Ideological Philosophy**: Oruka recognizes that political figures such as Senghor, Nkrumah, Nyerere, and others dealt with philosophical issues even as they engaged in emancipatory projects and nation-building.

4. **Professional Philosophy**: This category includes those trained in Western techniques or in Western universities. Thus, it is a category that describes the identity of a group of philosophers, rather than a specific style of philosophy, most explicitly

working on European traditions – occasionally with little attention to the particularity of Africa itself.

Toward the end of his life, Oruka added two more trends:

5. Literary/Artistic Philosophy: Literary figures such as Ngugi wa Thiongo, Wole Soyinka, Chinua Achebe, Okot p'Bitek, and Taban lo Liyong all reflect on philosophical issues within essays, as well as fictional works.

6. Hermeneutic Philosophy: This was the analysis of African languages for the sake of finding philosophical content. The work of Barry Hallen and J. O. Sodipo, as well as the work of Kwame Gyekye, would fit here. The term 'hermeneutic' has been used by a number of other philosophers (Okere 1983; Serequeberhan 1994) to mean something closer to the contemporary European sense – the philosophy of interpretation, in an African context.

Other taxonomies of African philosophy were also advanced. Smet and Nkombe suggest four categories: 'Ideological philosophy,' or the reaction to theories and prejudices which, in the past, supported the slave trade and later justified colonization; 'traditional philosophy,' or the reaction to the myth of the 'primitive mentality' of Africans which, through hermeneutical restoration, speaks of asserting the existence, solidity, and coherence of traditional African philosophies; 'critical philosophy,' or the reaction to and questions about theses or projects of the two preceding trends; and 'synthetic philosophy,' or the assumption of preceding trends and the orientation of the data collected toward a hermeneutical, functional philosophy or a search for new problematics. V. Y. Mudimbe distinguishes between African philosophy in the broad and the narrow sense. Defined broadly, ethnophilosophy and ideological-philosophical thought addresses African social life in the past and the present, respectively. Defined narrowly, Mudimbe sees four stages of development in African philosophy, beginning with those who reflect on the possibility of African philosophy and ending with those who engage in philosophical hermeneutics (Mudimbe 1983).

These taxonomies, and others, give direction to a developing field, while also become contested sites. They inevitably prioritize some activities over others, and in some cases suggest a historical or conceptual development (sometimes culminating in the thinker's own approach to African philosophy).

Who is African?

A perennial concern in African philosophy has been the nature of African personhood and identity. Is being African in some way unique, qualitatively different from other ways of being human, or is one human first and African (or some other particularization) second? What is African identity – who counts as African, and what does being African entail? Is race a necessary and central feature of Africanity, or is it contingent and incidental? Who can speak for Africa? And finally, can African philosophy theorize other identity categories, such as feminism?

Many philosophers trace the beginning of African philosophy in the twentieth century to the publication of Father Placide Tempels's book *La Philosophie Bantu* in

1945. In fact, Tempels was reacting to the prevailing belief about Africans, argued in earlier works by anthropologists such as Lucien Levi-Bruhl, and by his own Catholic church, that Africans were incapable of rational thought, and hence were less than human. Tempels responded by arguing that there was a coherent and interesting philosophy among the Bantu (more specifically, the tribes of the inner Congo, where he worked). His work was heralded by many early on, and inspired other works of African philosophy, such as that by the Rwandan Alexis Kagame. It did not take long, though, for African scholars to recognize the political naivety of Tempels's work, and its tendency to reify a static view of culture which did not reflect African experience.

But while Tempels's work may be seen as the starting point for the academic study of African philosophy, questions of African identity began long before his work. Leopold Sedar Senghor and others championed negritude, for instance, or the idea that African identity was different but equal to that of Europeans, and consisted in emotional rather than abstract reason.

And there were other proposals on African identity after Tempels as well. For instance, many thinkers followed Tempels in emphasizing the irreducibly communal nature of individual African existence. This often goes by the name *Ubuntu* (*Muntu* = 'a human being', *Ntu* = 'human'), and has been described by, among others, Jahnheinz Jahn (Jahn 1961) (and championed in other terms by John Mbiti). Others (for example, Kwame Gyekye [Gyekye 1995]) have focused on the composition of the person and the relationships between parts such as mind, soul, and body. But the question of personhood has also taken a more existential form. Some writers have asked what it means to exist as African (Mbembe 2001), and whether that means to exist fundamentally culturally, racially, or otherwise, rather than focusing on the composition of the self and its relation to community.

Beyond these metaphysical and existential approaches, though, the social construction of identity has also received some attention, although less within Africa than in the African diaspora. The role of culture in the formation of identity is certainly critical, and the most discussed version of identity construction. Race has received some attention (Appiah 1992; Eze 1997), although less than in African-American philosophy. Feminist approaches, while they exist in twentieth-century African philosophy, have not yet received the attention they have in other traditions (such as African-American and Asian philosophy). And, for many sub-Saharan African philosophers (unlike post-colonial theorists, for instance), the category of 'African' has remained relatively pure, that is, it has not been seen as a hybrid, shifting, or provisional category with other identity markers such as other ethnicities. This suggests that 'African' as a category stands in tension, as a particularized identity category, but one which as yet is relatively unwilling to take other possible particularizations seriously.

Where does African philosophy come from? To what extent must African philosophy engage traditional thought and culture to be truly African?

The perennial issue of the origin and foundation of African philosophy takes several forms. First, it is a question about sources. Are there texts, and what counts as a text?

Do cultural forms such as proverbs, songs, tales, and other forms of oral tradition count as philosophy in themselves, or are they merely the potential objects of philosophical analysis? Does the wisdom of sages count as philosophy, or is that wisdom at best merely the object of philosophical analysis? Is African philosophy African because it draws on tradition in some way? To take another line of inquiry, if we think of African philosophy as a discipline, where does disciplinarity come from, and what is its justification? Is African philosophy really a form of anthropology? Does it have more in common with literature, religion, or politics than with Western philosophy?

The first question is best framed in one of the most fundamental controversies in African philosophy, which is over ethnophilosophy. Originally a term coined by Paulin Hountondji (Hountondji 1983), it referred to philosophy that was basically the shared wisdom of a people. Hountondji used the term dismissively, to distinguish his own approach to philosophy from that of Marcel Griaule, Placide Tempels, Alexis Kagame, John Mbiti and others who located philosophy within traditional communal wisdom. He held that African philosophy was still a future (or at least a recent) project, and would develop in tandem with and based on scientific advancement.

There were many reactions to this position. First, some people simply continued to believe that African philosophy was the anonymously held and uncritical world-views of communities, along with their description and analysis. Second, others (Hallen and Sodipo 1997) used Quinean linguistic philosophy and phenomenology to argue that there was philosophical content in the shared worldviews of traditional Africans, and that it was accessible by closely analyzing language. Third, some attempted to locate specific philosophical beliefs or statements in traditional African culture, in folk tales, proverbs, dilemma tales, and so forth (for instance, Kwami Gyekye, Gerald Wanjohi). Fourth, writers such as Claude Sumner argued that the textual history was deeper than it seemed, and that there were in fact philosophical texts in traditional Africa. Fifth, some [Karp and Masolo 2000]) suggested hybrid or more sophisticated approaches that drew on the cultural insight of ethnophilosophy while giving it a more rigorous form. Sixth, others (for example, Odera Oruka) argued that there was an intermediate position between ethnophilosophy and academic philosophy. There was philosophy in traditional Africa that was not simply folk wisdom (located in the sages), but it often required the mediation of a trained philosopher to bring it to the surface. And, seventh and finally, there was a group of people who agreed with Hountondji, and therefore downplayed folk wisdom. Philosophy, for them, was rigorous textual and explicitly critical analysis, and traditional worldviews in Africa were no different than Western folk tales, and no more philosophical.

Some of the responses to Hountondji were extended and elaborate. The most notable of these was Henry Odera Oruka's sage philosophy project in Kenya (although it should be noted that Oruka's work was much more than just a response to Hountondji). Oruka originally wanted to demonstrate that philosophy existed in traditional Africa, and as such wanted to address both Western thought, which made no place for African philosophy, and Hountondji who tended to downplay traditional forms as philosophy. Oruka interviewed sages from traditional groups, and divided them into two groups – folk sages, who embodied community wisdom, and philosophical sages, who held a critical stance toward that wisdom. Oruka argued that the fact that he could find philosophical sages meant that both the West and Hountondji were incorrect, that in fact philosophy existed in traditional Africa.

This controversy leads us into the second question, which concerns the relationship of African philosophy to the disciplines. For many people, for instance, African philosophy is simply the study of systems of knowledge and belief, and as such is ethnography. These traditional systems were studied by anthropologists and ethnographers of various sorts before philosophers began addressing them. However, the history of anthropology in Africa during the twentieth century has been mixed. Earlier in the century, writers such as Lucien Levi-Bruhl attempted to identify the 'primitive' or 'savage' mind and place it in relation to more developed European thought. It was a vestige of nineteenth-century scientific racism, but it persisted in the work of some early anthropologists.

Beyond the longstanding ties to ethnography, African philosophy has one of the most porous boundaries with other disciplines of any philosophical tradition. Philosophers who draw from other disciplines such as politics, art, religious studies, linguistics and history seem to be the rule rather than the exception. These ties to disciplines that focus more on material culture and practices suggest that African philosophy requires the resources of culture itself (traditional or otherwise) in order for it to be 'African' philosophy. Even something as abstract as logic may be rooted in culture, and yet nevertheless have philosophical implications. The key, as I have already suggested, is not in the objects of investigation, but in the questions asked about those objects.

How can and does Africa relate to the West, to other philosophical, cultural, scientific and religious traditions, to colonizing countries, to its diaspora?

African philosophy seems inevitably to be a philosophy of cross-cultural conversation and encounter. At the most basic level, the conversation is between different ethnic, linguistic, cultural, and religious traditions within the continent. There is, secondly, the sustained conversation between African philosophy and European philosophy, a conversation that for some time has been rather one-sided. Thirdly, there is the conversation, or encounter, that occurred between African cultures and other cultures. Fourthly, there is the conversation that resulted from the history of slavery and emigration, that is, the conversations between African philosophy and the philosophies of the various African diasporas.

The term 'conversation' seems odd in this context. Can the history of slavery and exploitation really be thought of as a conversation? The term seems far too mild, and too liable to suggest an equal exchange. I use the term 'conversation,' though, to cover all meaningful exchange, ranging from mutually equitable and beneficial to brutal and even genocidal. The term is not meant to diminish or obscure the extreme pain and injustice that some encounters have caused, but rather to suggest that even in the most extreme circumstances, modes of existence are made manifest for all parties involved. Even if those modes are not on our own terms, a version of a life-world is made available. Even genocide requires a 'response,' a term of conversation. This is one of the central insights of Achille Mbembe's *On the Postcolony* (Mbembe 2001).

The fact of colonialism in Africa has meant that the major intellectual engagement of African philosophy has been with various strands of European philosophy. Many find this regrettable, wishing that there could be a richer conversation with other world traditions, but that has yet to develop. Even among African philosophers, little work has been done on intercultural dialogue apart from those with Western thought (to be fair, other world traditions of philosophy have not particularly sought out African philosophy for conversation either). Nevertheless, European forms of philosophy have often been replicated in Africa, and it is not uncommon to see the styles of philosophy dominant in colonial powers mirrored in the former colonies. This is also true for religious philosophy, particularly Catholic versions of African philosophy.

The question of the basis for cultural communication, specifically the issue of whether there are cultural universals, has been a live one in African circles. Kwasi Wiredu (Wiredu 1996) argues that such universals must exist since cross-cultural communication exists, and he roots their existence in the biological similarities of all humans. But the question of cross-cultural relationship can be taken historically rather than synchronically. Chiekh Anta Diop argues that if we carefully trace lines of influence in ancient Greek thought, we find African sources. This line of thought was anticipated in a better known, though less rigorous manner by American George James, and further developed by Henry Olela and Martin Bernal. While Wiredu strives to establish epistemological similarity, Diop and others strive to establish an epistemological debt.

Is reason culturally specific? How are reason and language related?

One of the more extended debates in this area was sparked by the work of Peter Winch and Robin Horton. Winch (Winch 1964) takes the position that reason is inextricably linked to language and culture, and therefore (following Wittgenstein) it is possible to consider separate systems to be rational yet incommensurable. Others, including Horton (Horton 1967), argue that there is only one reality, and so there can be only one rationality as well. Societies that do not use the modern Western scientific method are 'closed' societies because they cannot imagine alternatives to their views of the world, and also because there is no real distinction between words and reality. Words are not reality in the modern society, and Horton argues that this allows the words to take on explanatory rather than magical characteristics. Kwasi Wiredu and D. A. Masolo agree with Horton's commitment to the universality of reason, although both would argue that it is a mistake to compare Western science and traditional African thought.

Although words might not be reality, language itself has been a central concern in African philosophy. This has followed both 'the linguistic turn' in twentieth-century analytic philosophy, and the focus on language in Continental philosophy, and has been an attempt to identify some unique feature of African life that is both truly African and truly philosophical. As has already been mentioned, some attempt to locate African philosophy in artifacts of language such as tales, proverbs, riddles, and so forth. Others look more deeply into language to find philosophical content. This goes back to Alexis Kagame's analysis of Kinyarwanda, and was done in a more sophisticated manner in Hallen and Sodipo's work on Yoruba.

What is fundamental reality, in an African context?

Questions of the nature of reality in an African context can be wide-ranging, mythological, and cosmological, and they can also be detailed, specific, and analytic. An example of the first is Marcel Graiule's work with the Dogon elder Ogotemmêli (Graiule 1965). For thirty-three days in 1933, Ogotemmêli described an intricate, orderly stratified system of thought to Graiule. Each level of social and metaphysical existence mirrors and integrates the other levels in a logically rigorous manner. Graiule's work flouts the anthropological convention of participant observation to give voice to what he sees as the philosophical core of Dogon thought (a core which, it should be said, bears as strong a resemblance to contemporary French thought such as that of Bergson as it does to traditional wisdom).

But many philosophers are suspicious of such grand systems, regarding them as insufficiently critical and too prone to influence by outside researchers. Some thinkers have focused more on specific metaphysical beliefs that they argue are either unique to Africa or original to Africa. For example John Mbiti has outlined an African concept of time that differs from Western versions of time. Mbiti argues that in Africa, there is a deep conception of the past (*zamani*) and the present (*sasa*), but little idea about the future. People immediately exist in *sasa*, while they draw on *zamani*, which has its own structure and overlaps with *sasa*. The overlap allows society to regard the living, the recently dead, and the distant ancestors in a kind of continuum. Western time, Mbiti argues, is more abstract. As with other attempts to find a unique feature of African existence, Mbiti's approach to time has been criticized as simply another version of Levy-Bruhl's notion of the primitive.

Others have tried to think about the place that belief in witches, spirits, or departed ancestors might hold in philosophy. While some such as Kwasi Wiredu reject these beliefs as superstition, others argue that philosophy must take into account this important feature of traditional African life, and not simply reject it out of hand. Boniface Abanuka, for instance (Abanuka 1994), argues that ancestors form a central part of an African life by forming the basis for morality and providing the means for asking questions about ultimate reality. Fundamental reality, then, is a question of hermeneutics rather than metaphysics, as he focuses not on whether ancestors are metaphysical entities but rather on what they mean within African existence.

The question of witches, spirits, and ancestors raises an important question in African thought: is there anything substantive that can be said to be commonly held within African philosophy? Do African philosophers, for example, tend to accept or reject the existence of spirits, or the existence of God? Is there any common starting point? In fact, African philosophy tends to define itself less by commonly held beliefs or metaphysical commitments, and more by the question of how philosophical inquiry might be rooted in African cultural experience and production. It is not that African philosophers tend to hold to a belief in witchcraft, for instance, but rather that witchcraft continues to hold significance for many within African culture, and therefore becomes an interesting object of philosophical inquiry. It is a live aspect of culture, and therefore a live question.

How can (and how should) political, social and ethical life be imagined in Africa?

A central concern in African political philosophy has to do with whether there is an indigenous and unique form of political organization, particularly ones that are both emancipatory and democratic. Various thinkers, most of them heavily engaged in politics, have proposed political systems that are rooted in strong forms of communalism. Kwame Nkrumah of Ghana, for instance, proposes 'Consciencism,' which is a way of understanding the influence of the West and of Islam through the lens of traditional African experience, and later argues for a pan-African political and economic alliance as a means of enhancing common interests rooted in historical commonalities. Julius Nyerere of Tanzania speaks of *Ujamaa*, or 'familyhood,' a form of socialism rooted in African traditional culture. In different ways, both of these are attempts to draw a link between the communalism of traditional Africa and larger scale political entities. Kwasi Wiredu, as well, argues that consensus government is a form native to Africa, and is rooted in the close relationship between individual and community. Many of these versions of government are rooted in the oft repeated communalist phrase 'I am because we are.'

A second issue related to political organization has to do with the question of how the fact of Africa's colonization and marginalization should be addressed. Some thinkers (for example, Amilcar Cabral) attempt to theorize modern nationhood in Africa with a view to the realities of African culture. Some, such as Frantz Fanon, Albert Memmi and Tsenay Serequeberhan, have produced volumes on the effects of and responses to colonialism. Fanon in particular makes a case for the necessity of violence to overcome the psychological brutality of colonialism (Fanon 1967).

Various writers have worked in ethics, and not surprisingly the question of the relationship between the individual and the community has been central to much of that work. Most would be classified as applied ethics rather than ethical theory or meta-ethics, as most ethical work in African philosophy has either tried to explicate or schematize specific ethical codes and structures, or applied traditional ethical insights to contemporary problems such as corruption in society. This is one place (along with African theories of personhood) where a great deal has been done to explicate local beliefs in order to uncover fine distinctions that could contribute to the larger ethical vocabulary.

What is the relationship between thought and practice in Africa? Can and should African philosophy be practical?

A final question that has received a great deal of attention by various African thinkers in the twentieth century has been whether African philosophy is unique because of its attention to African issues or problems. Various thinkers have suggested that the point of African philosophy is to delve into traditional forms of life for solutions to contemporary problems such as issues of governance, political and social organization, and ethics. Some (for example, Kwame Gyekye) have seen in traditional Africa a response to very specific issues such as corruption in government and society. Others, like Odera Oruka, have argued for unique approaches in traditional knowledge to the environment. Still others have seen in African society strong models for conflict resolution, social maturity, and the expression of individual or minority voices within traditional ruling structures. Some argue that the real goal of African philosophy must be to address African problems, although even here a minority demurs, seeing philosophy as the disinterested analysis of ideas whose pragmatic concerns are irrelevant.

The relationship between thought and practice has another side as well. Some have argued, for instance, that there is no such thing as African art because the traditional objects that we might consider to be art do not meet the Kantian requirement that the objects serve only an aesthetic imperative. In other words, something is only art if it has a kind of purity to it, and is considered in itself, rather than in its cultural or social context. On this criterion, a decorated stool or mask is not truly art because it has a function, either in the economy or in ritual.

Many African philosophers have resisted this reduction, arguing that the abstract Kantian definition of art is really a cultural definition. But the significance of this example, I would argue, extends past the aesthetic, and is in the end a central feature of African philosophy. African philosophers continually want to argue and assume that ideas and their places (whether those places be sources, contexts, or applications) cannot be separated. It matters where ideas come from, who holds them, what cultural context they developed in, and it matters for philosophy, not simply for anthropology or sociology of knowledge.

Looking Forward to the Twenty-first Century

This list of questions is not designed to be exhaustive. It merely gives an idea of some of the major currents of thought in African philosophy in the twentieth century. I have argued that a great deal of effort has been expended in solidifying African philosophy's place in the philosophical world, and that this impulse, while important, does not exhaust the creative possibilities for African philosophy. In the coming decades, we can expect African philosophy to mature, by which I mean that it will find new conversations (other than primarily with Western philosophy); it will find ways of including groups that are currently under-represented (particularly women); it will further develop conversations among scholars themselves, rather than focusing on interpreting traditional culture or applying Western modes of thought to African issues; and it will include 'platial' rather than only 'spatial' philosophy in the sense I have described. African philosophy stands as both an important critical and reflective moment in world philosophy, and a contribution to the world of philosophy by working out how, in the words of Derrida, philosophy can honour its 'debts and duties.'

References

The entries that are starred are particularly useful as introductions.

Abanuka, B. (1994), *A New Essay on African Philosophy*, Nsukka: Spiritan Publications.

Appiah, K. A. (1992), *In My Father's House: Africa in the Philosophy of Culture*, Oxford: Oxford University Press.

*Bell, R. (2002), *Understanding African Philosophy*, London: Routledge.

*Coetzee P. H., and A. P. J. Roux (eds) (2003), *The African Philosophy Reader*, 2nd edn, London: Routledge.

Eze, E. (1997), *Race and the Enlightenment: A Reader*, Oxford: Blackwell Publishers.

*Eze, E. (1998), *African Philosophy: An Anthology*, Oxford: Blackwell Publishers.

Fanon, F. (1967), *The Wretched of the Earth*, trans. C. Farrington, New York: Grove Press.

Graiule, M. (1965), *Conversations with Ogotemmêli*, London: Oxford University Press for the International African Institute.

Gyekye, K. (1995), *An Essay on African Philosophical Thought*, Philadelphia: Temple University Press.

*Hallen, B. (2002), *A Short History of African Philosophy*, Bloomington: Indiana University Press.

Hallen, B., and J. O. Sodipo (1997), *Knowledge, Belief and Witchcraft: Analytic Experiments in African Philosophy*, Palo Alto: Stanford University Press.

Horton, R. (1967), 'African Traditional Religion and Western Science,' *Africa* 37, (1 and 2): 50–71, 155–87.

Hountondji, P. (1983), *African Philosophy: Myth and Reality*, Bloomington: Indiana University Press.

Jahn, J. (1961), *Muntu: African Culture and the Western World*, New York: Grove Press.

Karp, I. and D. A. Masolo (eds) (2000), *African Philosophy as Cultural Inquiry*, Bloomington: Indiana University Press.

*Masolo, D. A. (1994), *African Philosophy in Search of Identity*, Bloomington: Indiana University Press.

Mbembe, A. (2001), *On the Postcolony*, Berkeley: University of California Press.

Mudimbe, V. Y. (1983), 'African Philosophy as an Ideological Practice: The Case of French-Speaking Africa', in *African Studies Review* 26 (3–4) (Sept./Dec.): 133–54.

Mudimbe, V. Y. (1988), *The Invention of Africa: Gnosis, Philosophy and the Order of Knowledge (African Systems of Thought)*, Bloomington: Indiana University Press.

Mudimbe, V. Y. (1994), *The Idea of Africa*, Bloomington: Indiana University Press.

Okere, T. (1983), *African Philosophy: A Historico-Hermeneutical Investigation of the Conditions of its Possibility*, Lanham: University Press of America.

Serequeberhan, T. (1994), *The Hermeneutics of African Philosophy: Horizon and Discourse*, New York: Routledge.

Tempels, P. (1945), *La Philosophie bantoue*, Elizabethville: Lovania.

Winch, P. (1964), 'Understanding a Primitive Society,' *American Philosophical Quarterly* 1: 307–24.

Wiredu, K. (1996), *Cultural Universals and Particulars: An African Perspective*. Bloomington: Indiana University Press.

*Wiredu, K., W. E. Abraham, A. Irele, and I. A. Menkiti (eds) (2003), *Companion to African Philosophy (Blackwell Companions to Philosophy)*, Oxford: Blackwell Publishers.

Contributors

Roger T. Ames is Professor of Philosophy at the University of Hawai'i. He was the Director of the Center for Chinese Studies from 1991 to 2000 and has been the editor of *Philosophy East and West* since 1987 and *China Review International* since its launch in 1993. He is co-director of the Asian Studies Development Program, a partnership between the East-West Center and the University of Hawai'i. His teaching and research interests focus on comparative philosophy, the philosophy of culture, pragmatism and process philosophy, and classical Confucian and Daoist philosophy. His publications include *Daodejing: Making this Life Significant: A Philosophical Translation* (with David Hall) (2003); *Focusing the Familiar: A Translation and Philosophical Interpretation of the Zhongyong* (with David Hall) (2001); *The Analects of Confucius: A Philosophical Translation* (with H. Rosemount) (1999); *The Democracy of the Dead* (with David Hall) (1998); *Thinking from the Han: Self, Truth, and Transcendence in Chinese and Western Culture* (with David Hall) (1997); *Self and Deception: A Cross Cultural Philosophical Inquiry* (ed. with W. Dissanayake) (1996); *Sun-Tzu: The Art of Warfare* (1993); *Nature in Asian Traditions of Thought: Essays in Environmental Philosophy* (ed. with J. Baird Callicott) (1989); and *Thinking through Confucius* (with David L. Hall) (1987).

Emilia Angelova is Assistant Professor of Philosophy at Trent University, Canada. She was Assistant Professor of Philosophy at Sofia University in Bulgaria, where she published on Wittgenstein and Gadamer, and translated texts from Heidegger and Schelling into Bulgarian. Her doctoral work at the University of Toronto was on Heidegger and Kant. Her current research interests are in Kant and twentieth-century Continental philosophy (Heidegger and Lacan) and feminism.

Leslie Armour, with a Ph.D. from London and a B.A. from the University of British Columbia, works in metaphysics and its epistemological relations, the theory of the history of philosophy, and moral, social, and economic philosophy and their relations to culture and religion. He is a Research Professor of Philosophy at the Dominican University College, Ottawa, the editor of the *International Journal of Social Economics*, a member of the editorial boards of *Laval Philosophique et Théologique* and a fellow of the Royal Society of Canada. His publications include *The Rational and the Real* (1962); *The Concept of Truth* (1969); *Logic and Reality* (1972); *The Conceptualization of* *the Inner Life* (with E. T. Bartlett III) (1980); *The Faces of Reason: Philosophy in English Canada, 1850–1950* (with Elizabeth Trott) (1981); and *Infini-Rien, Pascal's Wager and the Human Paradox* (1993).

Jeremy Avigad is Associate Professor of Philosophy at Carnegie Mellon University. His research interests include mathematical logic, proof theory, automated reasoning, and the history and philosophy of mathematics.

Babette E. Babich is Professor of Philosophy at Fordham University in New York City and Adjunct Research Professor of Philosophy at Georgetown University, Washington, DC. She is author of *Words in Blood, Like Flowers: Philosophy and Poetry, Music and Eros in Hölderlin, Nietzsche, and Heidegger* (2006); and *Nietzsche's Philosophy of Science: Reflecting Science on the Ground of Art and Life* (1994, translated into Italian 1996). A three-time Fulbright Scholar and Nietzsche-Fellow (Weimar), she is founder and executive editor of *New Nietzsche Studies* and contributing editor to *Habermas, Nietzsche, and Critical Theory* (2004); *Hermeneutic Philosophy of Science, Van Gogh's Eyes, and God* (2002); *Theories of Knowledge, Critical Theory, and the Sciences* (1999), *Nietzsche, Epistemology, and the Philosophy of Science* (1999); and *From Phenomenology to Thought, Errancy, and Desire* (1996).

Bruce Baugh is Professor of Philosophy at Thompson Rivers University (Kamloops, BC, Canada). Most recent publications: *French Hegel: From Surrealism to Postmodernism* (2003); 'Sartre, Derrida and Commitment: The Case of Algeria,' *Sartre Studies International* 9 (2003); 'The Influence of German Thought,' in C. J. Murray (ed.), *Encyclopedia of Modern French Thought* (2004); 'Temps, Durée et Mort chez Spinoza,' *Philosophiques* 29 (2002).

Constantin V. Boundas is Professor Emeritus of Philosophy at Trent University, and a member of the Trent Center for the Study of Theory, Politics and Culture. His publications include *The Deleuze Reader* (1993); with Dorothea Olkowski, *The Theater of Philosophy: Critical Essays on Gilles Deleuze* (1994); and *Deleuze and Philosophy* (2006). He organized four international conferences on Gilles Deleuze at Trent University in 1992, 1996, 1999, and 2004, and was the guest editor of five special journal issues on Deleuze's work: *Journal of the British Society for Phenomenology* (Jan. 1993); *Man and World* (July 1996); *Angelaki* (Aug. 2000); *Angelaki* (Aug. 2001); and *Symposium* (spring 2006). His translations include (with Mark Lester and Charles Stivale) Gilles Deleuze's *The Logic of Sense* (1990), and Gilles Deleuze's *Empiricism and Subjectivity: An Essay in Human Nature* (1991).

Tyler Burge is Distinguished Professor of Philosophy at the University of California, Los Angeles. He is a member of the American Academy of Arts and Sciences, of the Institute International de Philosophie, and a Corresponding Fellow of the British Academy. He is a past president of the American Philosophical Association, Pacific Division. He has written in philosophy of mind, philosophy of psychology, philosophy of language and logic, epistemology, and the history of philosophy. There are two anthologies of essays on his work, with substantial replies: *Reflections and Replies: Essays on the Philosophy of Tyler Burge* (ed. Hahn and Ramberg) (2003); and *Meaning, Basic Self-Knowledge, and Mind* (ed. Frapolli and Romero) (2003). The first of several projected volumes of his essays is *Truth, Thought, Reason: Essays on Frege* (2005).

Taylor Carman is Associate Professor of Philosophy at Barnard College, Columbia University. He is the author of *Heidegger's Analytic: Interpretation, Discourse, and Authenticity in 'Being and Time'* (2003); and co-editor of *The Cambridge Companion to Merleau-Ponty* (2004). He is currently writing a book on Merleau-Ponty.

Robert E. Carter is Professor Emeritus in the Philosophy Department of Trent University in Ontario. He has long been interested in the writings of Nishida and in a synthesis of Eastern and Western ideas. He is author/editor of several books including *Dimensions of Moral Education* (1984); *God, the Self and Nothingness: Reflections Eastern and Western* (1990); *Nothingness beyond God: An Introduction to the Philosophy of Nishida Kitaro* (1998); and *Encounters with Enlightenment: A Study of Japanese Ethics* (2001).

David Castle is Canada Research Chair in Science and Society at the University of Ottawa. His research addresses the interaction between science and technology innovation and society, particularly the ethical and legal issues posed by new biotechnology. Castle's publications include *Genetically Modified Foods: Debating Biotechnology, Science, Society and the Supermarket: Opportunities and Challenges for Nutrigenomics* (2002); and *Aquaculture, Innovation and Social Transformation* (2006). He has also published in *Postgraduate Medical Journal, Biology and Philosophy, Dialectica, American Journal of Bioethics, Trends in Biotechnology* and *Public Affairs Quarterly*.

Erik S. Christopherson studied at St Olaf College and Oxford University. He is a member of the British Society for the Philosophy of Religion. Apart from the philosophy of religion, his research interests include metaphysics, epistemology and philosophical logic.

Rohit Dalvi, who has a Ph.D. from the University of Hawaii at Manoa, is Assistant Professor in the Department of Philosophy at Brock University in Ontario, with special interest in Indian philosophy and contemporary French philosophy.

Nicholas Davey was educated at the Universities of York, Sussex and Tübingen. He has lectured at the City University, London (1976–9), at the University of Manchester (1989–90), the University of Wales Institute Cardiff Institute (1981–96), and is presently Professor of Philosophy and Dean of Humanities at the University of Dundee. His principal teaching and research interests are in aesthetics and hermeneutics. He has published widely in the field of Continental philosophy, aesthetics, and hermeneutic theory. His book *Unquiet Understanding, Gadamer and Philosophical Hermeneutics*, was published in 2006. He is currently working on a study of Gadamer's aesthetics.

Josephine Donovan, who has a Ph.D. in Comparative Literature from the University of Wisconsin, is Professor Emerita at the University of Maine. Her fields of specialization include animal defense theory, feminist criticism and theory, American women's literature, and early modern women's literature. She is the author of seven books and the editor of four, including *Women and the Rise of the Novel* (1999); *Feminist Theory: The Intellectual Traditions* (1985); *Uncle Tom's Cabin: Evil, Affliction and Redemptive Love* (1991); *After the Fall: The Demeter-Persephone Myth in Cather, Wharton, and Glasgow* (1989); *New England Local Color Literature* (1998); and *Sarah Orne Joewett* (2002).

François Dosse is a historian, research associate in the Centre d'histoire culturelle des sociétés contemporaines of the Université de Saint-Quentin en Yvelines and in the Institut d'histoire du temps present. He is a member of the editorial board of *EspacesTemps*. His publications include *L'histoire en miettes* (1987); *Histoire du structuralisme, Le champ du signe*, Tome 1 (1991); *Le chant du cygne*, Tome 2 (1992); *L'Instant éclaté*, entretiens avec Pierre Chaunu (1994); *L'empire du sens, l'humanisation des sciences humaines* (1995); *Paul Ricoeur, les sens d'une vie* (1997); *L'histoire* (1999); and *Michel de Certeau, le marcheur blessé* (2002).

John Greco has a Ph.D. from Brown University, and is Leonard and Elizabeth Eslick Chair in Philosophy at St Louis University. He has authored and edited five books: *The Oxford Handbook of Skepticism* (forthcoming); *Rationality and the Good* (co-edited with Mark Timmons and Alfred Mele) (forthcoming); *Sosa and his Critics* (2004); *Putting Skeptics in their Place: The Nature of Skeptical Arguments and their Role in Philosophical Inquiry* (2000); and *The Blackwell Guide to Epistemology* (co-edited with Ernest Sosa) (1999). He has published widely in the area of epistemology.

Jean Grondin is Professor of Philosophy at the Université de Montréal. His books include: *Kant et le problème de la philosophie: l'a priori* (1989); *Introduction to Philosophical Hermeneutics* (1994); *Sources of Hermeneutics* (1995); *The Philosophy of Gadamer* (2002); *Hans-Georg Gadamer. A Biography*, (2003); *Du sens de la vie* (2003); and *Introduction à la métaphysique* (2004).

Robert Hanna is Professor of Philosophy at the University of Colorado at Boulder, and works on Kant, the philosophy of mind, and ethics. He is the author of four books: *Kant and the Foundations of Analytic Philosophy* (2001); *Rationality and Logic* (2006); *Kant, Science and Human Nature* (2006); and *Embodied Minds in Action* (with Michelle Maiese) (forthcoming). His current project is a study of the links between the nonconceptual content of perceptual cognition, embodiment, rationality, and free agency.

Bernard Hodgson is Professor of Philosophy at Trent University. He received his B.A. (philosophy and economics) from the University of Toronto and his Ph.D. (philosophy) from the University of Western Ontario. Dr Hodgson has been a visiting fellow with the Department of History and Philosophy of Science and St Edmund's

College at the University of Cambridge, and, recently, has been the author of *Economics as Moral Science* (2001), the editor of *The Invisible Hand and the Common Good* (2004); and also editor for philosophical foundations of the *Journal of Business Ethics*.

David B. Ingram is Professor of Philosophy at Loyola University in Chicago. He is the author of six books, including *Rights, Democracy, and Fulfillment in the Era of Identity Politics: Principled Compromises in a Compromised World* (2004); *Critical Theory and Philosophy* (1990); and *Habermas and the Dialectic of Reason* (1987). He has edited two books: *The Political: Readings in Continental Philosophy* (2002); and *Critical Theory: The Essential Readings* (1991); and published several essays on political philosophy.

Bruce B. Janz is Associate Professor of Humanities at the University of Central Florida. His areas of work include African philosophy, contemporary European philosophy, and the concepts of place and space. He has published in *Philosophy Today*, *Philosophia Africana*, *Janus Head*, *Studies in Religion*, *City and Community*, and elsewhere. He has recently completed a book titled *Philosophy as if Place Mattered: Hermeneutics and Contemporary African Philosophy*.

Edward Jones-Imhotep is Assistant Professor of Science and Technology Studies at York University in Canada. He received his Ph.D. in the History of Science from Harvard University in 2001, and held a SSHRC postdoctoral fellowship, a visiting research fellowship at the University of Toronto, and a cross-appointment to the departments of History and Philosophy at the University of Guelph before joining York. Although interests span the history and philosophy of modern science and technology, his most recent research project, entitled 'Reliable Humans, Trustworthy Machines,' focuses on the history and philosophy of electronic reliability during the Cold War.

Kelly Dean Jolley is Alumni Professor and Chair of Philosophy at Auburn University. He works in the theory of judgement, the history of twentieth-century philosophy, metaphilosophy, and aesthetics.

Douglas Kellner is George Kneller Chair in the Philosophy of Education at UCLA and is author of many books on social theory, politics, history, and culture, including *Herbert Marcuse and the Crisis of Marxism* (1984) and *Critical Theory, Marxism, and Modernity* (1989). His work in cultural studies includes *Media Culture* (1995) and *Media Spectacle* (2003). He has published a trilogy of books on postmodern theory with Steve Best, a trilogy of books on the Bush administration, including *Grand Theft 2000* (2001), and *From 9/11 to Terror War: Dangers of the Bush Legacy* (2003); and his latest book *Media Spectacle and the Crisis of Democracy* (2005).

Leonard Lawlor is Faudree-Hardin University Professor of Philosophy at the University of Memphis. He is the author of four books: *Derrida and Husserl: The*

Basic Problem of Phenomenology (2002); *Thinking through French Philosophy: The Being of the Question* (2003); *The Challenge of Bergsonism: Phenomenology, Ontology, Ethics* (2003); and *Imagination and Chance: The Difference between the Thought of Ricoeur and Derrida* (1992). He is one of the co-editors of *Chiasmi International: Trilingual Studies concerning the Thought of Merleau-Ponty*; and has translated Merleau-Ponty and Hyppolite into English. He has written dozens of articles on Derrida, Foucault, Deleuze, Bergson, Merleau-Ponty, Ricoeur, and Gadamer. A new book is forthcoming with Fordham University Press, *Un écart infime, A Miniscule Hiatus: Essays Contributing to a New Concept of Life*. He is in the process of writing a new book on Derrida.

Peter Loptson holds an M.A. and and a Ph.D. from the University of Pittsburgh. He is Professor of Philosophy at the University of Guelph. His interests include metaphysics, early modern philosophy and philosophical logic. His current research projects include papers on modality and also on skepticism in the history of philosophy. He is completing at a book-length study of the competing claims of naturalist and exceptionalist accounts of rational agency, and a biography of Hume, co-authored with a historian of the Scottish Enlightenment. His publications include *Reality: Fundamental Topics in Metaphysics* (2001); *Theories of Human Nature* (3rd edn 2001); and 'Locke, Reid, and Personal Identity,' *The Philosophical Forum* (2004).

Mathieu Marion has a Ph.D. from the University of Oxford. After post-doctoral fellowships in St. Andrews, Boston, and Montreal, he taught philosophy at the University of Ottawa from 1994 to 2003 and he has since held the Canada Research Chair in the Philosophy of Logic and Mathematics at the Université du Québec à Montréal. He specializes in the philosophy of Wittgenstein and the history of analytic philosophy, as well as in philosophy of logic and of mathematics. He is the author of *Wittgenstein, Finitism, and the Foundations of Mathematics* (1998); of *Ludwig Wittgenstein. Une introduction au Tractatus logico-philosophicus* (2004); and of numerous essays. He has co-edited with R. S. Cohen the *Québec Studies in the Philosophy of Science* (1995), 2 volumes; with A. Voizard, *Frege. Logique et philosophie* (1997); and with P. Engel, a French translation of the collected papers of F. P. Ramsey, *Logique, Philosophie et Probabilités* (2003).

Todd May is Professor of Philosophy at Clemson University. He is the author of six books of philosophy, most recently *The Philosophy of Foucault* (2006). His area of research is in recent French philosophy, especially the thought of Michel Foucault and Gilles Deleuze. Recently, he has begun to develop the politics of equality found in the thought of Jacques Rancière.

William L. McBride is Arthur G. Hansen Distinguished Professor of Philosophy at Purdue University and the current General Secretary of the International Federation of Philosophical Societies (FISP). He is past President of the North American Society for Social Philosophy and was the co-founder and first director of the North American Sartre Society. Among his extensive publications are *Sartre's Political Theory* (1991) and an 8-volume edited collection of secondary literature entitled *Sartre and Existentialism* (1997).

Douglas McDermid, who has an M.A. and a Ph.D. from Brown University, is currently Assistant Professor of Philosophy at Trent University. He is the author of *The Varieties of Pragmatism* (2006); and of numerous journal articles dealing with topics in epistemology, metaphysics, and the history of philosophy.

David Morris is Associate Professor of Philosophy at Trent University. His recent work focuses on the phenomenology of mind, body, and nature. He is the author of *The Sense of Space* (2004).

Jan Narveson was educated at the University of Chicago (B.A. in political science, 1955, and in philosophy, 1956), and earned a Ph.D. at Harvard (1961) with a year at Oxford (1959–60) on a traveling fellowship. He taught at the University of New Hampshire from 1961 to 1963, and since then has been at the University of Waterloo. He is also an officer of the Order of Canada. He is or has been on the editorial boards of many journals, such as *Ethics, Social Philosophy and Policy, Journal of Social Philosophy, International Journal of Applied Philosophy, Philosophy Research Archives, The Journal of Value Inquiry, The Canadian Journal of Philosophy, Dialogue,* and *Public Affairs Quarterly*. His publications include *Morality and Utility* (1967); *Moral Issues* (ed.) (1983); *The Libertarian Idea*; *Moral Matters* (1993); (2nd edn, with changes, 1999); *Political Correctness – For and Against* (with Marilyn Friedman) (1995); *For and Against the State* (co-edited with John T. Sanders) (1996); and *Respecting Persons in Theory and Practice* (2002).

Michael Neumann has a B.A. in English and history from Columbia University and a Ph.D. in philosophy from the University of Toronto. His interests include ethics, political philosophy, philosophy of logic, and metaphysics. His publications include articles on utilitarianism, behavioral rationality, and the rule of law. He is the author of two books, *What's Left?* (1988); and *The Rule of Law: Politicizing Ethics* (2002).

John Protevi is Associate Professor of French Studies at Louisiana State University in Baton Rouge. He received an M.A. in philosophy from Pennsylvania State University, where he studied with Joseph Kockelmans and Alphonso Lingis, among others. He received a Ph.D. in philosophy from Loyola University of Chicago in 1990, with a dissertation under the direction of John Sallis. He is the author of *Time and Exteriority: Aristotle, Heidegger, Derrida* (1994); *Political Physics: Deleuze, Derrida and the Body Politic* (2001); and co-author (with Mark Bonta) of *Deleuze and Geophilosophy: A Guide and Glossary* (2004). In addition, he is co-editor (with Paul Patton) of *Between Deleuze and Derrida* (2003); and editor of the *Edinburgh Dictionary of Continental Philosophy* (2005).

François Raffoul is Associate Professor of Philosophy at Louisiana State University. He is the author of *Heidegger and the Subject* (1999); *A chaque fois mien* (2004), and has edited and co-edited several volumes on contemporary Continental philosophy, including *Disseminating Lacan* (1996); *Heidegger and Practical Philosophy* (2002); and *Rethinking Facticity* (forthcoming). He has co-translated numerous works of French philosophers into English, such as Jean-Luc Nancy, Philippe Lacoue-Labarthe, and Françoise Dastur, as well as Heidegger's last seminars, *Four Seminars* (2004). He is currently preparing a book on a phenomenology of ethics, tentatively entitled *The Origins of Responsibility*.

Nicholas Rescher is University Professor of Philosophy at the University of Pittsburgh where he is also Chairman of the Center for Philosophy of Science. He has served as President of the American Philosophical Association, of the American Catholic Philosophy Association, of the American G. W. Leibniz Society, and of the C. S. Peirce Society and the American Metaphysical Society. An honorary member of Corpus Christi College, Oxford, he has been elected to membership in the Academia Europaea, the Institut International de Philosophie, and several other learned academies. Author of some hundred books ranging over many areas of philosophy, over a dozen of them translated from English into other languages, he is the recipient of six honorary degrees from universities on three continents and was awarded the Alexander von Humboldt Prize for Humanistic Scholarship in 1984.

Elisabeth Schellekens is a post-doctoral research fellow at the University of Manchester and a visiting lecturer at King's College, London. Her main areas of interest include meta-aesthetics, meta-ethics, Kant's aesthetic theory, and the fact/value distinction. She is currently working on a research project about aesthetic psychology, the main theme of her Ph.D. thesis. She has published on aesthetic perception, the cognitive value of art, and Humean subjectivism, and is currently preparing two volumes – *Aesthetics and Morality*, and *Who's Afraid of Conceptual Art?* (with Peter Goldie). In addition, she is the reviews editor of *The British Journal of Aesthetics*.

Charles E. Scott is Distinguished Professor of Philosophy and Director of the Vanderbilt University Center for Ethics at Vanderbilt University. His most recent books include *The Time of Memory* (1999); *The Lives of Things* (2002); and he is now completing the book, *Living with Indifference*.

Calvin O. Schrag is George Ade Distinguished Professor of Philosophy Emeritus at Purdue University. He is the author of many books including *Existence and Freedom* (1970); *Experience and Being* (1969); *Resources of Rationality* (1992); *The Self after Postmodernity* (1997), and *God as Otherwise than Being* (2002).

Charles Taliaferro, Professor of Philosophy at St Olaf College, is the author of *Consciousness and the Mind of God* (1994); *Contemporary Philosophy of Religion* (1998); and *Evidence and Faith; Philosophy and Religion since the Seventeenth Century* (2005). He is the co-editor of *A Companion to Philosophy of Religion* (1998).

Andrew Wernick is Chair of the Cultural Studies Program at Trent University. He is also a regular visiting professor in cultural studies and sociology at Ivan Franko National University, Lviv, and a life member of Clare Hall, Cambridge. A social theorist, cultural critic, intellectual historian, and sometime musician, his writings include *Promotional Culture: Advertising, Ideology and Symbolic Expression* (1991); *Shadow of Spririt: Religion and Postmodernism* (co-edited with Philippa Berry) (1993); *Images of Aging* (co-edited with Mike Featherstone) (1994); and *Auguste Comte and the Religion of Humanity: The Post Theistic Project of French Social Theory* (2001).

Merold Westphal is Distinguished Professor of Philosophy at Fordham University. He has been President of the Hegel Society of America and of the Søren Kierkegaard Society, and as Executive Co-Director of the Society for Phenomenology and Existential Philosophy. He has served on the National Board of the American Philosophical Association, and on the Executive Committee of its Eastern Division. In addition to two books on Hegel and two on Kierkegaard, he is the author of *God, Guilt, and Death: An Existential Phenomenology of Religion* (1948); *Suspicion and Faith: The Religious Uses of Modern Atheism* (1999); *Overcoming Onto-Theology: Toward a Postmodern Christian Faith* (2001); and *Transcendence and Self-Transcendence: On God and Soul* (2004). He is the editor of the Indiana Series in the philosophy of religion, published by Indiana University Press.

Alenka Zupancic is a researcher at the Institute of Philosophy, Scientific Research Center of the Slovene Academy of Sciences and Arts, Ljubljana. She is the author of *Ethics of the Real: Kant, Lacan* (2000); *Das Reale einer Illusion* (2001); *Esthétique du désir, éthique de la jouissance* (2001); and *The Shortest Shadow: Nietzsche's Philosophy of the Two* (2003).

Chronology

The following chronology is highly selective. It lists philosophical texts and the dates they were published, which, in the opinion of the editor, formed the philosophical traditions of the twentieth century. It also lists a few texts which, without receiving universal attention, nonetheless influenced significantly the adventure of ideas in the countries and languages in which they appeared. Finally, in an equally selective manner, it registers the years of the demise of philosophers who played a central role in the philosophical dialogue of the century.

1900　　　　　　　Sigmund Freud, *Psychopathology of Every Day Life*
　　　　　　　　　Lloyd C. Morgan, *Animal Behaviour*
　　　　　　　　　Georg Simmel, *Philosophie des Geldes*
　　　　　　　　　Vladimir Solovyev, *Tri razgonova o voine, progresse I kontse
　　　　　　　　　　　vserminoi istorii* (*Three Conversations on War, Progress, and
　　　　　　　　　　　the God of History*)
　　　　　　　　　Georges Sorel, *Réflexions sur la violence*
　　　　　　　　　Friedrich Nietzsche dies
　　　　　　　　　Henry Sidwick dies
　　1899–1901　　Josiah Royce, *The World and the Individual*, 2 vols
　　1900–1　　　Edmund Husserl, *Logische Untersuchungen*
　　1901　　　　Giuseppe Peano, *Formulaire de mathématiques*, vol 3
　　1901–2　　　William James, *The Varieties of Religious Experience*
　　1902　　　　Benedetto Croce, *Estetica come scienza dell' expressione e
　　　　　　　　　　linguistica generale*
　　　　　　　　　Theodor Lipps, *Vom Füllen, Wollen und Denken*
　　　　　　　　　Paul Natorp, *Platons Ideenlehre*
　　　　　　　　　Otto Neurath, 'Protokollsätzsche'
　　　　　　　　　Jules Henri Poincaré, *La Science et l' hypothèse*
　　1903　　　　George Edward Moore, 'The Refutation of Idealism'
　　　　　　　　　George Edward Moore, *Principia Ethica*
　　　　　　　　　George Santayana, *Reason and Art*
　　　　　　　　　Ferdinand C. S. Schiller, *Humanism: Philosophical Essays*
　　　　　　　　　Herbert Spencer dies
　　1904　　　　Anatoli Lunacharski, *K Voprova ob otsenske* (*On the Question
　　　　　　　　　　of Valuation*)

1904 *contd* Alexius Meinong, "Über Gegenstandstheorie."

Max Weber, *Der protestantische Ethic und der 'Geist' das Kapitalismus*

1904–06 Alexander A. Bogdanov, *Empiriomonism: Stati po Filosofi*

1905 Louis Couturat, *Les principes des mathématiques*

Sigmund Freud, *Three Essays on the Theory of Sexuality*

Betrand Russell, 'On Denoting'

Heinrich Rickert, *Die Probleme der Geschichtsphilosophie*

1905–06 George Santayana, *The Life of Reason or the Phases of Human Progress.* 5 vols

1905–08 Giuseppe Peano, *Formulario mathematico* vol. 5

1905–14 Raimundo de Farias Brito, *Ensaios sobre la Filosofia do Espírito*, 3 vols

1906 Pierre M. M. Duhem, *La théorie physique*

Ernst Mach, *Die Analyse der Empfindungen*

1906–8 Edward A. Westermarck, *The Origins and Development of the Moral Ideas*

1907 Henri Bergson, *L' évolution créatrice*

Antonio Labriola, *Socialism and Philosophy*

William James, *Pragmatism* .

1908 Friedrich Nietzsche, *Ecce Homo*

Jules Henri Poincaré, *Science et méthode*

Josiah Royce, *The Philosophy of Loyalty*

Georges Sorel, *Reflexions sur la violence*

1908–26 Alois Riehl, *Der philosophische Kritizismus*, 3 vols

1909 Ludwig Boltzmann, *Wissenschaftliche Abhandlungen*

Émile Boutroux, *Science et religion dans la philosophie contemporaine*

William James, *A Pluralistic Universe*

Vladimir I. Lenin, *Materialism i Empirio- Kritizism*

Julius Schultz, *Die Maschinentheorie des Lebens*

Jakob J. Uexkull, *Umwelt und Innenweld der Tiere*

1910 Lucien Lévy-Bruhl, *Les fonctions mentales dans les sociétés inférieure*

Vladimir A. Bazarn, *Na Dua Fronta*

Wilhelm Dilthey, *Der Aufbau der geschichtlichen Welt in den Geisteswissenschaften*

Charles Péguy, *Mystère de la charité de Jeanne d' Arc*

Bertrand Russell and Alfred North Whitehead, *Principia Mathematica*

Hans Vaihinger, *Die Philosophie des Als Ob*

William James dies

1911 Nishida Kitaro, *A Study of Good* (*Japanese*)

Wilhelm Dilthey dies

1912	Émile Durkheim, *Les formes élémentaires de la vie religieuse*
	Hans A. E. Driesch, *Ordnungslehre*
	Peter Kropotkin, *Modern Science and Anarchism* (Eng. trans of Russian text publ. 1901)
	Bertrand Russell and Alfred North Whitehead, *Principia Mathematica*
	Max Scheler, *Über Ressentiment und moralisches Werturteil*
	Henri Poincaré dies
1913	Edmund Husserl, *Ideen zu reiner Phänomenologie*
	Giovanni Papini, *Pragmatism*
	Adolf Phalén, *Beitrag zur Klärung des Begriffs des inneren Erfährung*
	Max Scheler, *Zur Phänomenologie und Theorie der Sympathie-gefühle und von Liebe und Hass*
	Miguel de Unamuno y Jugo, *Del sentimento trágico de la vida en los hombres y en los pueblos*
	Ferdinand de Saussure dies
1913–17	Pierre Duhem, *Le système du monde*
1914	Francis H. Bradley, *Essays on Truth and Reality*
	Pavel Florensky, *Stolp I utver-zhdenie istiny* (*The Pillar and Ground of Truth*)
	Gustav G. Shpet, *Stolp I utverzhdenie istiny Javleniye i Smyel* (*Appearance and Sense*)
	Louis Couturat dies
	Charles S. Peirce dies
1915	Wilhelm Windelband dies
1916	Giovanni Gentile, *Teoria generale della spirito come atto puro*
	Roy Wood Sellars, *Critical Realism*
	Ferdinand de Saussure, *Cours de linguistique générale*
	Josiah Royce dies
	Ernst Mach dies
	Pierre Duhem dies
1917	Franz Brentano dies
1918	Ernst Bloch, *Vom Geist der Utopie*
	Bertrand Russell, *The Philosophy of Logical Atomism*
	Moritz Schlick, *Allgemeine Erkenntnislehre*
	Oswald Spengler, *Der Untergang des Abendlandes*
	Carlos Vaz Ferreira, *Sobre la proprided de la tierra*
	Georg Cantor dies
	Hermann Cohen dies
	Georg Simmel dies
1919	Antonio Caso, *La existencía como economia, como desinterés y como caridad*

1919 *contd*   Gottlob Frege, *Der Gedanke*
Bertrand Russell, 'Descriptions'
John Watson, *Psychology from the Standpoint of a Behaviourist*

1920   Alfred Adler, *Praxis und Theorie der Individualpsychologie*
Charlie D. Broad, *Five Types of Ethical Theory*
John Dewey, *Reconstruction in Philosophy*
Sigmund Freud, *Beyond the Pleasure Principle*
Moritz Schlick, *Raum und Zeit in der gegendwärtigen Physik*
Alexius Meinong dies
Max Weber dies

1921   Carl G. Jung, *Psychological Types*
Franz Rosenzweig, *Der Stern der Erlösung*
Edward Sapir, *Language*
Ludwig Wittgenstein, *Tractatus Logico-Philosophicus*
Émile Boutroux dies

1920–1   Max Weber, *Gesammelte Aufsätze zur Religionsoziologie*
1921–7   John McT. E. McTaggart, *The Nature of Existence*
1922   Léon Brunschvicg, *L' expérience humaine et la causalité physique*
Karl Kautsky, *Die Materialistische Geschichte-auffassung*
Alejandro Korn, *La liberdad creadora*
Lucien Lévy-Bruhl, *La mentalité primitive*
Max Planck, *The Origin and Development of the Quantum Theory*
Carl Schmitt, *Political Theology*
Rabidranath Tagore, *Creative Unity*
Ernst Troeltsch, *Der Historismus und seine Probleme*

1923   Martin Buber, *Ich und Du*
Alejandro Deustua, *Estética General*
Sigmund Freud, *The Ego and the Id*
Georg Lukács, *Geschichte und Klassenbewusstsein*
José Ortega y Gasset, *El tema de nuestro tempo*
Ernst Troeltsch dies

1924   Nikolai Berdyaev, *Smysl Istorii* (*The Meaning of History*)
André Breton, *Premier Manifeste du surréalisme*
Robin G. Collingwood, *Speculum Mentis*
Karl Mannheim, 'Historismus'
Jean Piaget, *Le jugement et le raisonnement chez l' enfant*
Francis H. Bradley dies
Paul Natorp dies

1923–9   Ernst Cassirer, *Philosophie der Symbolischen Formen*, 3 vols.
1925   Rudolf Carnap, *Der logische Aufbau der Welt*
Tanabe Hajime, *A Study in the Philosophy of Mathematics* (Japanese)

1925 *contd* George Edward Moore, 'A Defense of Common Sense'
              John McD. E. McTaggart dies
              Gottlob Frege dies
1926   Abram M. Deborin, *Filosofia i Marksizm*
              Nicolai Hartmann, *Ethik.*
              Ralph B. Perry, *General Theory of Value*
              Sarvepalli Radhkrishnan, *The Hindu View of Life*
              Alfred Tarski, *Logic, Semantics, Metamathematics*
1927   Léon Brunschvicg, *Le progrès de la conscience dans la
                  philosophie occidentale*
              Martin Heidegger, *Sein und Zeit*
              Gabriel Marcel, *Journal métaphysique*
              Ivan P.Pavlov *Conditional Reflexes*
              Giuseppe Rensi, *Il materialismo critico*
              George Santayana, *The Realm of Being* 4 vols.
              Carl Schmitt, *The Concept of the Political*
1927–33   Carl Schmitt, *Der Begriff des Potitischen*
1928   Harald Høffding, *Les conceptions de la vie*
              Hans Raichenbach, *Philosophie des Raum-Zeit Lehre*
              Max Scheler dies
1928–69   *Schriften zur wissenschaftliches Weltauffassung* (Vienna Circle)
1929   John Dewey, *The Quest for Certainty*
              Wolfgang Köhler, *Gestalt Psychology*
              Tadeusz Kotarbinski, *Elementi Teorii Poznania, Logiki
                  Formalnej I Metodologii Nauk* (*Elements of Theory of
                  Knowledge, Formal Logic, and Scientific Methodology*)
              Clarence I. Lewis, *Mind and the World Order*
              Jan Lukasiewicz, *Elementi logiki mathematycznej*
              Alfred North Whitchead, *Process and Reality*

1930   Sigmund Freud, *Civilization and its Discontents*
              José Ortega y Gasset, *La Rebelion de las Masas*
              Alejandro Korn, *Axiología*
              Arthur O. Lovejoy, *The Revolt against Dualism*
              David W. Ross, *The Right and the Good*
              Ludwig Wittgenstein, *Philosophical Investigations*
1931   Carlos Astrada, *Hegel y el presente*
              Nikolai Berdyaev, *O Naznanachenie Chelovyeka* (*The Destiny
                  of Man*)
              Kurt Gödel, 'Über formal unentscheiber Satze der *Principia
                  Mathematica* und verwandter System I'
              Edmund Husserl, *Kartesianische Meditationonen*
              Roman Ingarden, *Das literarische Kunstwerke*
              Karl Jaspers, *Die geistige Situation des Zeit*
              Jørgen Jørgensen, *A Treatise of Formal Logic, I–III*

1931 *contd*   Frank P. Ramsey, *The Foundations of Mathematics*
George F. Stout, *Mind and Matter*
José Vasconcelos, *Pessimismo alegre*
Zeitschrift für Sozialforschung

1931–35   Charles S. Pierce, Collected Papers, vols 1–6
Georg H. Mead dies

1932   Henri Bergson, *Les deux sources de la morale et de la
religion*
Eugen Fink, *Sixth Cartesian Meditation*
Miki Kiyoshi, *Philosophy of History* (Japanese)
Moritz Schlick, *The Future of Philosophy*
Rabidranath Tagore, *The Religion of Man*
Giuseppe Peano dies

1933   Gaston Bachelard, *La dialectique de la durée*
Gaston Bachelard, *Le nouvel esprit scientifique*
Georges Bataille, 'The Notion of Expenditure'
Vladimir Jankélévitch, *La mauvaise conscience*
André Malraux, *La condition humaine*
Émile Meyerson, *Réel et déterminisme dans la physique
Quantique*
Wilhelm Reich, *Die Massenpsychologie des Faschismus*
Alfred North Whitehead, *Adventures of Ideas*

1934   Gaston Bachelard, *Essai d' une philosophie du nouvel esprit
scientifique*
Rudolf Carnap, *Logische Syntax der Sprache*
Watsuji Tetsuro, *Climate and Culture* (Japanese)
George H. Mead, *Mind, Self and Society from the Standpoint
of a Social Behaviorist*
Karl Popper, *Logik der Forschung*
Walter T. Stace, 'The Refutation of Realism'

1936   Alfred Jules Ayer, *Language, Truth and Logic*
Walter Benjamin, 'The Work of Art in the Age of Mechanical
Production'
Alonzo Church, 'An Unresolvable Problem of Elemental
Number Theory'
Edmund Husserl, *Die Krisis der europäischen Wissenschaften
und die transzendetale Phänomenologie*
Arthur O. Lovejoy, *The Great Chain of Being*
Jacques Maritain, *Humanisme intégral*
Friedrich Meinecke, *Die Entstehung des Historismus*
Enrique G. Molina, *De lo espiritual en la vída humana*
Emmanuel Mounier, *Manifeste au service des personnalismes*
Arne Naess, *Erkenntnis und wissenschaftliches Verhalten*
Miguel de Unamuno dies
Heinrich Ricker dies

1937   Max Horkheimer, 'Traditional and Critical Theory'
André Malraux, *L'espoir*
Mao Zedung, 'On Contradictions'
Jean-Paul Sartre, *La transcendance de l' ego*
Walter T. Stace, *The Concept of Morals*
Antonio Gramsci dies

1938   Nicholas O. Lossky, *Chuvstvennaya, Intellektulnaya i Misticheskaya Intuitsiya* (*Sensory, Intellectual, and Mystical Intuition*)
Hans Reichenbach, *Experience and Prediction*
Moritz Schlick, *Gesammelte Aufsatze*
Carlos Vaz Ferreira, *Fermentario*
Edmund Husserl dies

1938–69   *International Encyclopedia of Unified Science* (under the auspices of logical positivists)

1939   Miki Kiyoshi, *The Logic of the Power of the Imagination* (Japanese)
Sigmund Freud dies

1940   Gaston Bachelard, *La philosophie du non*
Nishitani Keiji, *The Philosophy of Fundamental Selfhood* (Japanese)
Bertrand Russell, *An Inquiry into Meaning and Truth*
Walter Benjamin dies

1941   Robin G. Collingwood, *An Essay on Metaphysics*
Charles Hartshorne, *Man's Vision of God*
Ingemar Hedenius, *Rätt och Moral*
Max Horkheimer and Theodor Adorno, *The Dialectic of Enlightenment*
Henri Bergson dies

1942   Albert Camus, *Le mythe de Sisyphe*
Jean Cavaillès, *Sur la logique et la théorie de la science*

1943   Martin Heidegger, *Vom Wesen des Wahrheit*
Konrad Marc-Wogau, *Die Theorie der Sinnendaten*
Alfred Rosenberg, *Der Mythus des Zwanzigsten Jahrhunderts*
Jean-Paul Sartre, *L'Etre et néant*
Simone Weil, *L' enracinement*
Xavier Zubiri, *Naturaleza, historia, Dios*
Robin Collingwood dies

1944   Ernst Cassirer, *An Essay on Man*
Eino Kaila, *Über den physikalischen Realitätsbegriff*
Clarence I. Lewis, *An Analysis of Knowledge and Valuation*
Otto Neurath, *Foundation of the Social Sciences*
Karl R. Popper, *The Open Society and its Enemies*

1944 *contd*   Charles L. Stevenson, *Ethics and Language*
                 Léon Brunschvicg dies
                 Giovanni Gentile dies
                 Jean Cavaillès dies
                 George F. Stout dies
1945   Robin George Collingwood, *The Idea of History*
                 Alexandre Kojève, *Introduction to the Reading of Hegel*
                 Maurice Merleau-Ponty, *Phénomenologie de la perception*
                 Ernst Cassirer dies
                 Nishida Kitaro dies
1946   Jean Hyppolite, *Genèse et structure de la phénoménologie de
                    l'esprit de Hegel*
                 Tanabe Hajime, *Philosophy as Metanoesis* (Japanese)
1946–50   Nicola Abbagnano, *Storia della filosofia*, 3 vols
1947   Antonio Gramsci, *Lettere dal carcere*
                 Karl Jaspers, *Von der Wahrheit*
                 Franz E. E. Spranger, *Gibt es ein Kultur pathologie?*
                 Alfred North Whitehead dies
1948   Carlos Astrada, *Mito Gaucho*
                 Simone de Beauvoir, *Pour une morale de l' ambuiguité*
                 André Lalande *La raison et les norms*
                 Willard Van Orman Quine, 'On What There Is'
                 Georges Bataille, *La part maudite*
1949   Simone de Beauvoir, *Le deuxième Sexe*
                 E. M. Cioran, *A Short History of Decay*
                 Martin Heidegger, *Brief über den Humanismus*
                 Gilbert Ryle, *The Concept of Mind*
                 Maurice Blondel dies
1949–66   *Socialism ou Barbarie* (Trotskyite Group in France)

1950   Maurice Blondel, *L'action*, rev. ed.
                 Georges Canguilhem, *Le normal et le pathologique*
                 Samuel Ramos, *Filosofía de la vida artistica*
                 Paul Ricoeur, *Le volontaire et l' involontaire*
                 Stephen Toulmin, *An Examination of the Place of Reason in
                    Ethics*
                 A. M. Turing, 'Computing Machinery and Intelligence'
                 Nikolai Hartmann dies
1951   Curt J. Ducasse, *Nature, Mind and Death*
                 Willard Van Orman Quine, 'Two Dogmas of Empiricism'
                 Georg H. Von Wright, *A Treatise on Induction and Probability*
                 Ludwig Wittgenstein dies
1952   Franz Brentano, *Grundlegung und Aufbau der Ethik*
                 Francesco Romero, *Teoria del hombre*

1952 *contd*   Paul Tillich, *The Courage to Be*
                Watsuji Tetsuro, *History of Japanese Ethical Thought*
                    (Japanese)
                George Santayana dies
                John Dewey dies
                Benedetto Croce dies
1953   Axel Hägerström, *Inquiries into the Nature of Law and Morals*
                Richard M. Hare, *Language of Morals*
                Leo Strauss, *Natural Law and History*
                Ludwig Wittgenstein, *Philosophical Investigations*
                Hans Reichenbach dies
1954   Nelson Goodman, *Fact, Fiction, and Forecast*
                Gilbert Ryle, *Dilemmas*
1954–9   Ernst Bloch, *Das Prinzip Hoffnung*, 3 vols
1955   Anthony Flew, 'Theology and Falsification'
                Herbert Marcuse, *Eros and Civilization*
                Pierre Teilhard de Chardin, *Le phénomène humain*
                Albert Einstein dies
                Josè Ortega y Gasset dies
1956   Hans Reichenbach, *The Direction of Time*
                Alfred Tarski, *Logic, Semantics, Metamathematics*
1957   Gaston Bachelard, *La Poétique de l'espace*
                Roland Barthes, *Mythologies*
                David Bohm, *Causality and Chance in Modern Physics*
                Albert Camus, *L'étranger*
                Roderick M. Chisholm, *Perceiving*
                Noam Chomsky, *Syntactic Structures*
                Martin Heidegger, *Gelassenheit*
                Charles S. Peirce, *Collected Papers*, vols 7 and 8
                Karl R. Popper, *The Poverty of Historicism*
                Erwin Schrödinger, *Science, Theory, and Man*
                Ludwig Wittgenstein dies
1958   Kurt Baier, *The Moral Point of View*
                Monroe Beardsley, *Aesthetics: Problems in the Philosophy of
                    Criticism*
                John Rawls, *Justice as Fairness*
                Gilbert Simondon, *Du mode de l' existence des objets
                    techniques*
                George E. Moore dies
1958–61   Henri Lefebvre, *Critique de la vie quotidienne*, 2 vols
1959   Stuart Hampshire, *Thought and Action*
                Peter Strawson, *Individuals*

1960 Hans-Georg Gadamer, *Wahrheit und Methode*
Wilfrid Sellars, *Philosophy and the Scientific Image of Man*
Ernest Nagel, *The Structure of Science*
Jean-Paul Sartre, *Critique de la raison dialectique*
Willard Van Orman Quine, *Word and Object*
Tel Quel begins its publication
Albert Camus dies

1961 Frantz Fanon, *The Wretched of the Earth*
Michel Foucault, *Madness and Civilization*
Herbert L. A. Hart, *The Concept of Law*
Emmanuel Levinas, *Totalité et infini*
Maurice Merleau-Ponty dies
Carl Jung dies
Watsuji Tetsuro dies

1962 John L. Austin, *How to Do Things with Words*
Ludwig Binswanger, *Grundformen und Erkenntnis menschlichen Daseins*
Max Black, *Models and Metaphors*
Thomas Kuhn, *The Structure of Scientific Revolutions*
Michael Oakeshott, *Rationalism in Politics*
Wilfrid Sellars, 'Time and the World Order'
Claude Lévi-Strauss, *La pensée sauvage*
Georges Bataille dies
Gaston Bachelard dies
John L. Austin dies
Tanabe Hajime dies

1963 Michel Foucault, *Naissance de la clinique*
Adolf Grünbaum, *Philosophical Problems of Space and Time*
Richard M. Hare, *Freedom and Reason*
Herbert L. A. Hart, *Law, Liberty and Morality*
Norman Malcolm, *Knowledge and Certainty*
Mou Zongsan, *The Unique Character of Chinese Philosophy* (Chinese)
Enzo Paci, *Funzione delle Scienze e Significato dell' Uomo*
Karl R. Popper, *Conjectures and Refutations*
Hatano Seiichi, *Time and Eternity* (Japanese)
John J. C. Smart, *Philosophy of Scientific Realism*
Georg H. Von Wright, *The Varieties of Goodness*

1964 Emilio Betti, *Teoria generale della Interpretazione*
Emile M. Cioran, *The Fall into Time*
Étienne H. Gilson, *The Spirit of Thomism*
Jacques Lacan, *Le séminaire, tome 11: Les quatre concepts fondamentaux de la psychanalyse*
Gilbert Simondon, *L' individu et sa genèse physico-biologique*

1964 *contd*   John Wisdom, *Philosophy and Psycho-Analysis*
                 Clarence I. Lewis dies
1965   Louis Althusser, *Pour Marx*
                 Mikhail Bakhtin, *Rabelais and his World*
                 Carl G. Hempel, *Aspects of Scientific Explanation*
                 Paul Ricoeur, *Freud and Philosophy:An Essay on Interpretation*
                 Paul Tillich dies
1966   Theodor Adorno, *Negativ Dialektik*
                 Michel Foucault, *Les mots et les choses*
                 Carl G. Hempel, *Philosophy of Natural Science*
                 Hans Jonas, *The Phenomenon of Life*
                 Jacques Lacan, *Écrits*
1967   Donald Davidson, 'Truth and Meaning'
                 Guy Debord, *La societé du spectacle*
                 Jacques Derrida, *La voix et le phénomène*
                 Jacques Derrida, *De la grammatologie*
                 Jacques Derrida, *L' écriture et la différence*
                 Jürgen Habermas, *Knowledge and Human Interests*
                 Alvin Plantiga, *God and Other Minds*
1968   Jean Baudrillard, *Le système des objets*
                 Gilles Deleuze, *Différence et répétition*
                 Nelson Goodman, *Languages of Art*
                 Paul Grice, 'Utterer's Meaning, Sentence-Meaning, and
                    Word-Meaning'
                 Jürgen Habermas, *Erkenntnis und Interesse*
                 Vladimir Jankélévitch, *Traité des vertus*
                 Jan Patoçka, Télo spotécenstvi, janyk, svis (*Body, Community,
                    Language, World*)
                 Jean Hyppolite dies
                 Alexandre Kojève dies
                 Xiang Shili dies
1969   Louis Althusser, *Lenin et la philosophie*
                 Maurice Blanchot, *L'entretien infini*
                 Isaiah Berlin, *Four Essays on Liberty*
                 Stanley Cavell, *Must We Mean What We Say?*
                 Donald Davidson, 'True to the Facts'
                 John R. Searle, *Speech Acts*
                 Karl Jaspers dies
                 Theodor Adorno dies
1969–80   Michel Serres, *Hermès I–V*

1970   Theodor Adorno, *Ästhetische Theorie*
                 Jean Piaget, *Genetic Epistemology*
                 Roman Ingarden dies
                 Bertrand Russell dies

1971	Jean-François Lyotard, *Discours, figure*
	Judith Jarvis Thomson, 'A Defense of Abortion'
	Charlie Broad dies
	Georg Lukács dies
	Rudolf Carnap dies
	Groupe d' informations sur le prisons (RIP) founded in France
1972	Jean Baudrillard, *Pour une critique de l' économie politique du signe*
	Pierre Bourdieu, *Esquisse d' une théorie de la pratique*
	Gilles Deleuze and Félix Guattari, *L'anti-Oedipe*
	René Gerard, *La violence et le sacré*
	Félix Guattari, *Psychanalyse et transversalité*
	Frederic Jameson, *The Prison House of Language*
	Sarah Kofman, *Nietzsche et la métaphore*
1973	Jürgen Habermas, *Legitimation Crisis*
	Eric D. Hirsch *Validity in the Interpretation*
	John J. C. Smart and Bernard Williams, *Utilitarianism, For and Against*
	Gabriel Marcel dies
	Jacques Maritain dies
	Max Horkheimer dies
	Leo Strauss dies
1974	Pierre Clastres, *La société contre l' état*
	Donald Davidson, 'On the Very Idea of a Conceptual Scheme'
	Luce Irigaray, *Speculum, de l' autre femme*
	Julia Kristeva, *La révolution du langage poétique*
	Emmanuel Levinas, *Autrement qu' être ou au-delà de l'essence*
1975	Mikhail Bakhtin, *The Dialogic Imagination*
	Cornelius Castoriades, *L' institution imaginaire de la société*
	Hélène Cixous, *The Newly Born Woman*
	Paul Ricoeur, *La métataphore vive*
	John Sallis, *Being and Logos*
	Hannah Arendt dies
	Mikail Bakhtin dies
1976	Umberto Eco, *A Theory of Semiotics*
	Michel Foucault, *Histoire de la sexualité. La volonté de savoir*
	Martin Heidegger dies
	Gilbert Ryle dies
	Mao Zedung dies
1977	Ronald Dworkin, *Taking Rights Seriously*
	Luce Irigaray, *Ce sexe qui n'est pas un*
	Paul Virilio, *Vitesse et politique*
	Xiaon Shili, *On the Enlightened Heart and Mind* (Chinese)
	Ernst Bloch dies

1978   Hannah Arendt, *The Life of Mind*
        Michael Dummett, *Truth and Other Essays*
        Jean-François Lyotard, *The Postmodern Condition*
        Edward Said, *Orientalism*
        Tang Junji dies
1979   Karl-Otto Apel, *Die Erklären-Verstehen-Kontroverse in Transzendental Prgmatischer Sicht*
        Richard Rorty, *Philosophy and the Mirror of Nature*
        Herbert Marcuse dies

1980   Maurice Blanchot, *L'Écriture du désastre*
        Gilles Deleuze and Félix Guattari, *Milles Plateaux*
        Michele Le Doeuff, *L' imaginaire philosophique*
        Saul Kripke, *Naming and Necessity*
        Julia Kristeva, *Pouvoirs de l' horreur*
        Francisco Varela and H. Maturana, *Autopoiesis and Cognition*
        Richard Wolheim, *Art and Its Objects*
        Jean-Paul Sartre dies
        Roland Barthes dies
        Jean Piaget dies
1981   Fredric Jameson, *The Political Unconscious*
        Hilary Putnam, *Reason, Truth and History*
        Jacques Lacan dies
1982   Hannah Arendt, *Lectures on Kant's Political Philosophy*
        Carol Gilligan, *In a Different Voice*
        Jürgen Habermas, *Theorie des Kommunikative Handelns*, vol. 1
        Richard Rorty, *Consequences of Pragmatism*
1983   Jean-Luc Nancy, *La communauté désoeuvrée*
        John R. Searle, *Intentionality*
        Alfred Tarski dies
1983–5 Paul Ricoeur, *Temps et récits*
1984   Donald Davidson, *Inquiries into Truth and Interpretation*
        Luce Irigaray, *Ethique de la différence sexuelle*
        Fredric Jameson, 'Postmodenism, or, the Cultural Logic of Late Capitalism'
        Evelyn Fox Keller, *Reflections on Gender and Science*
        Jean François Lyotard, *Le différend*
        Robert Nozick, *Anarchy, State, and Utopia*
        Michel Foucault dies
1985   Jürgen Habermas, *The Philosophical Discourse of Modernity*
        Donna Haraway, 'A Cyborg Manifesto'
        John Llewelyn, *Beyond Metaphysics?*
        Bernard Williams, *Ethics and the Limits of Philosophy*
        Ernst Nagel dies

1986   Jacques Bouveresse, 'Le mythe de l'intériorité'
Sandra Harding, *The Science Question in Feminism*
Thomas Nagel, *The View from Nowhere*
Martha Nussbaum, *The Fragility of Goodness*
Monique Wittig, *Le corps lesbien*
Simone de Beauvoir dies
Gayatri C. Spivak, *In Other Worlds: Essays in Cultural Politics*

1988   Alain Badiou, *L' Être et l' événement*
Hélène Cixous, *La jeune née*
Ronald Dworkin, *The Theory and Practice of Autonomy*
Philippe Lacoue-Labarthe, *La fiction du politique*
Alasdair MacIntyre, *After Virtue*
Carole Pateman, *The Sexual Contract*
Ilya Prigogine and Isabelle Stengers, *Entre le temps et l'éternité*
Hilary Putnam, *Representation and Reality*
Tang Junji, *The Distinctive Features of Natural Cosmology in Chinese Philosophy* (Chinese)

1989   Jaakko Hintikka, *The Logic of Epistemology and the Epistemology of Logic*
Michele Le Doeuff, *L'étude et le rouet*
Alphonso Lingis, *Deathbound Subjectivity*
Michel Serres, *Éléments d' histoire des sciences*
Charles Taylor, *Sources of the Self*
Slavoj Žižek, *The Sublime Object of Ideology*
Alfred J. Ayer dies
Gilbert Simondon dies
Wilfrid Sellars dies

1990   Giorgio Agamben, *Communita che viene*
Judith Butler, *Gender Trouble*
Michel Henri, *Phénoménologie matérielle*
Hilary Putnam, *Realism with a Human Face*
Frank P. Ramsey, *Philosophical Papers*
Norman Malcolm dies
Louis Althusser dies
Nishitani Keiji dies

1991   Jacques Derrida, *Donner la mort*
Dominique Janicaud, *Le tournant théologique de la phénoménologie française*
Fredric Jameson. *Postmodernism*
Teresa de Lauretis, 'Queer Theory, Lesbian and Gay Studies'
Nicholas Resher, *Human Knowledge in Idealistic Perspective*
Wilfrid Sellars, *Science, Perception and Reality*
Charles Taylor, *The Ethics of Authenticity*
Francisco J. Varela, Evan Thompson and Eleanor Rosch, *The Embodied Mind*

1992   Kwame Anthony Appiah, *In My Father's House; Africa in the Philosophy of Culture*
          Maurice de Gandillac, *Genèses de la modernité*
          Slavoj Žižek, *Enjoy your Symptom*
          Herbert Hart dies
          Félix Guattari dies
1993   Michael Dummett, *Origins of Analytical Philosophy*
          Joseph J. Kockelmans, *Ideas for a Hermeneutic Phenomenology of the Natural Science*
          Bruno Latour, *We Have Never Been Modern*
1994   Jacques Derrida, *Politiques de l' amitié*
          John McDowell, *Mind and World*
          Kwari Mudimbe, *The Idea of Africa*
          Karl Popper dies
          Guy Debord dies
1995   Giorgio Agamben, *Homo Sacer*
          Éric Alliez, *De l' impossibilité de la phénoménologie*
          Kwame Gyekye, *An Essay on Africal Philosophical Thought*
          Alonzo Church dies
          Gilles Deleuze dies
          Emmanuel Levinas dies
          Mou Zongsan dies
1996   Karl-Otto Apel, *The Response of Discourse Ethics*
          Kwari Wiredo, *Cultural Universals and Particulars: An African Perspective*
          Georges Canguilhem dies
1997   Alain Badiou, *Saint Paul, la fondation de l' universalisme*
          Jean-Luc Marion, *Etant donné*
          Carl Hempel dies
          Cornelius Castoriades dies
1998   Alain Badiou, *Metapolitics*
          Hélène Cixous, *Neutre*
          Patrick A. Heelan, 'Scope of Hermeneutics in the Philosophy of Natural Science'
          Michele Le Doeuff, *Le sexe du savoir*
          Jean-François Lyotard dies
1999   Giorgio Agamben, *Potentialities*
          Edward Casey, *The Fate of Place*
          Jaakko Hintikka, *Inquiry as Inquiry: A Logic of Scientific Discourse*
          Bruno Latour, *Pandora's Hope*
          Gayatri C. Spivak, *A Critique of Post-Colonial Reason*

Index